The Düsseldorf Art Academy
Making History since 1945

KUNSTAKADEMIE DÜSSELDORF (ED.)

The Düsseldorf Art Academy Making History since 1945

DEUTSCHER KUNSTVERLAG

CONTENTS

FOREWORD

Anthony Cragg

In 1762 Lambert Krahe founded a private drawing school in Düsseldorf which became the Electoral Painter, Sculptor, and Architecture Academy in 1773 and ultimately, through a decree issued by Friedrich Wilhelm III of Prussia, the Royal Art Academy at Düsseldorf in 1819.

With a history that goes back more than 250 years, the Düsseldorf Art Academy has always exerted a seminal influence on the art and cultural life of its immediate Rhenish surroundings and has been influential at a national and international level. By the Second World War, the Düsseldorf Art Academy looked back on an impressive history. Its renown was based on the many internationally famous artists from the Düsseldorf Art Academy who had worked in Düsseldorf between 1819 and 1918. Even after 1945, however, the Düsseldorf Art Academy has retained its attraction for artists from all fields and of all persuasions because of its location and its liberal cultural tradition.

The Düsseldorf Art Academy. Making History since 1945 is the first book to have been published on the history of the Academy since the Festschrift *Zweihundert Jahre Kunstakademie Düsseldorf* [Two Hundred Years of the Düsseldorf Art Academy], which was published to commemorate the Academy bicentenary in 1973.The present publication encompasses an art historical development that is virtually unparalleled. An introductory section discusses the founding of the Art Academy and its development until 1933 as well as the events that shaped the years from 1933 to 1945. An informative study of the Academy as a state institution and community of artists is followed by a systematic description of training in the various departments and workshops. The last part of the book is devoted to the collecting and exhibition activities engaged in by the Düsseldorf Art Academy. Here the yearly Academy Tours of student work as well as the exhibitions that have been curated in recent years by Professor Dr Siegfried Gohr for the Academy Gallery are discussed. The essays are lavishly illustrated with numerous photographs from archives and collections, some of them published here for the first time. Several picture sections present the work of the artists who have taught at the Art Academy as professors since 1945.

The Düsseldorf Art Academy is an extraordinary place for artistic debate that is conducted in the freedom prized and protected by all artists. The discourse is often enlivened by contradictory opinions and ideas that are advocated with passion and vehemence, actually something that should go without saying considering that what is at stake are often entirely different aesthetic stances and ideals. Hence great importance has been attached in this book to reporting on this historical representation without bias and allowing for a wide variety of viewpoints and statements. The Joseph Beuys controversy, for instance, has been placed in a wider context and thus put into perspective as only one of many chapters in the history of the Düsseldorf Art Academy.

The Düsseldorf Art Academy. Making History since 1945 describes an era of art history in which our Academy has brought forth an unusually large number of artists who are renowned worldwide as well as groundbreaking developments in the arts.

Publication of this book has been made possible with the support of the Society of Friends and Sponsors of the Art Academy e. V., Netjets Europe GmbH, and the Swiss Red Cross. Finally, I should like to thank Thomas A. Lange, Nationalbank Essen, for his unstinting support. We are grateful indeed to all of them for their help in seeing that this book, which is so important for the Art Academy, is published.

My grateful thanks go to all my colleagues in the art-related Arts and Humanities Department, who have met regularly in a working group for some time now, for many productive discussions, help, and suggestions, and to Professor Dr Peter M. Lynen for his unswerving commitment to this project. I am especially indebted to all my colleagues and the authors from outside the Academy for contributing to it. Heartfelt thanks to Tanja Wessolowski, who has coordinated this project at the Academy, also to Rudolf Winterstein and Eva Maurer of Deutscher Kunstverlag, to Jane Slominsky Smith for her superb translations, and to reader Wendy Brouwer. We are grateful to all archives and galleries who have so willingly supported us in our research. In this connection, I should like to single out Brigitte Blockhaus, head of our library, and Miriam Müller from our own archives, for special mention. To my former colleagues Ernst Althoff, Konrad Klapheck, Peter Kleemann, Markus Lüpertz, Klaus Rinke, Rissa, Erich Reusch, and Oswald Wiener for sharing their memories and their reports on their years at the Academy, as well as Siegfried Gohr, who has thrown his support behind this project from the outset and has tirelessly driven it forward, I should like to express my sincere gratitude and thank them from the heart in my name and in the names of all other colleagues.

THE HISTORY AND DEVELOPMENT OF THE ACADEMY FROM ITS BEGINNINGS TO THE PRESENT DAY

THE HISTORY OF THE DÜSSELDORF ART ACADEMY UP TO 1933*

Johannes Myssok

LAMBERT KRAHE AND THE FOUNDING OF THE ART ACADEMY

Like so many other European academies in the eighteenth century, the Düsseldorf Art Academy was founded as an institute for training artists in the capital of a principality.[1] Thus it profited, on the one hand, from developments in Mannheim, the main residency of Karl Theodor, the Elector Palatine, but, on the other hand, it was often affected by the shadows those developments cast. As elsewhere, too, drawing was intended to be the focus of artist training at the Düsseldorf Academy,[2] which is why the founding of the Academy must be seen as premised on and built around the acquisition of an extensive collection of drawings in Rome by the founding director, Lambert Krahe (Fig. 1). The drawings were eventually bought for the Academy in 1778 by the Bergish States of the Realm so that they might be used as a model teaching collection along with the celebrated collection of paintings amassed by the Elector Palatine.[3]

Krahe began his teaching career in 1762, starting a private drawing school from which the Academy would grow in the early 1770s, instituted as documented by a rescript issued on 3 March 1773 by the Elector Palatine.[4] Although its charter had been drafted in 1774, it was not ratified until 1777, in an act which finally completed the formal founding of the Academy and enabled it to fulfil its function.[5]

From its inception the Art Academy was intended as an institution for training not only painters but also architects and sculptors. However, it only succeeded in attaining mediocre ranking among German academies – even though some artists who would later be important studied in Düsseldorf.[6]

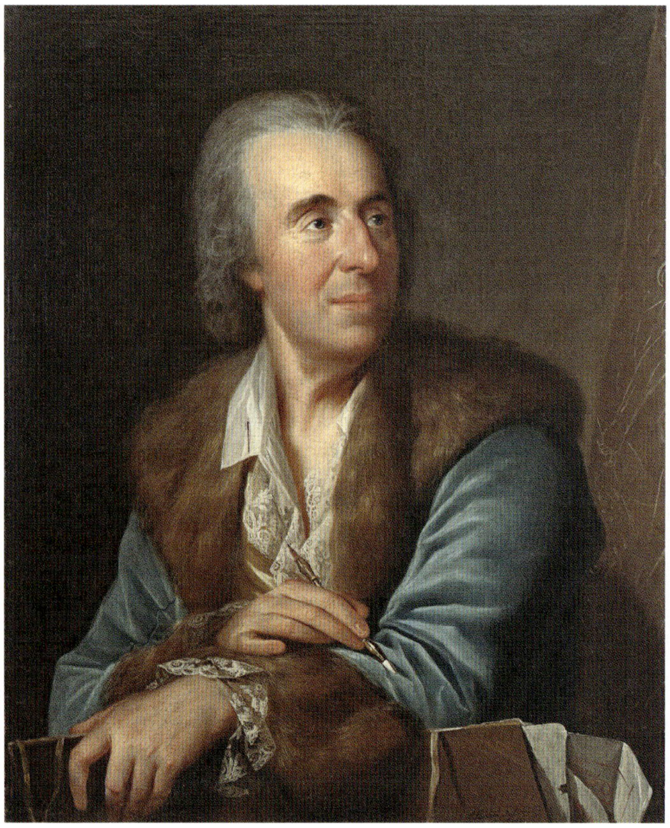

Fig. 1: Erik Pauelsen, portrait of Lambert Krahe, director of the Academy, 1781, oil on canvas, 76 × 63 cm, Düsseldorf Art Academy

THE ACADEMY UNDER JOHANN PETER LANGER (1790–1806)

On Krahe's death in 1790, Johann Peter Langer succeeded him as the new director of the Academy. Although its student body included such future luminaries as Peter Cornelius, the Academy under Langer was in a state of noticeable decline, which reached its nadir when the Electoral paintings collection was 'rescued' in 1805 by being moved to Munich – allegedly to safeguard it during the ongoing battles between Prussia and France. From then on Düsseldorf lacked an element crucial to both artist training and public art appreciation.[7] Intervention by Joachim Murat, however, ensured that the collection of drawings remained in Düsseldorf.[8] Langer followed the paintings collection to Munich only a year later to become director of the new art academy there.[9] His departure marked the end of the old Academy, which, although it had survived French occupation, had lingered on as a mere shadow of its former self.

A FRESH START UNDER PETER CORNELIUS (1819)

After the close of the Napoleonic era and the integration of what would be the Rhine Province in the Kingdom of Prussia, the decision was taken to promote the cultural institutions there and to found a new university in the West. As a result, Bonn advanced to the status of university town, and the Academy was to be re-established in Düsseldorf.[10] The necessary negotiations were conducted in Berlin by Barthold Georg Niebuhr, who had made the acquaintance of Peter Cornelius in Rome in 1816 and was so enthusiastic about him that he promptly recommended to the Ministry that the painter be appointed director of the institution.[11]

While the negotiations dragged on, Cornelius was commissioned by the crown prince of Bavaria to decorate the Glyptothek in Munich with a cycle of frescoes.[12] The conflict of interest was not resolved until 1819, when a bilateral agreement was concluded: Cornelius was appointed to the Academy post on condition that he would teach his pupils in Düsseldorf during the winter and would work on the cartoons for the frescoes, which he would realise in Munich with the help of his students, the following summer.[13] Before taking up his appointment as Academy director in June 1820, Cornelius collaborated with Carl Josef Ignaz Mosler, on drawing up a 'Plan for the Art School for Düsseldorf' that outlined the 'programme' of the new Academy.[14]

The model for training artists that Cornelius developed in the spirit of the Nazarene School of painters in Rome provided for a three-tiered course of studies, which in the two lower classes – the elementary level and the preliminary course – still largely matched traditional ideas of artist training based on using plaster copies of statues as models and copying the Old Masters. What broke new ground, on the other hand, was the conception underpinning the actual art school, in which advanced pupils were supposed to produce works in close collaboration with their masters.[15] Although that system was, somewhat anachronistically, based on the medieval workshop as the ideal of working and training in art, the emphasis nonetheless lay on artistic freedom and the intention of encouraging students to become inventive on their own as soon as possible, a novel, forward-looking element of the programme designed by Cornelius. The entire curriculum aimed at reviving history painting on a monumental scale and, more specifically even, fresco painting with political content on nationalist lines. However, Cornelius realised very little of his agenda in the brief time span between 1821 and 1824 that he spent in Düsseldorf as Academy director before leaving for good for Munich in May 1824 to succeed Langer as head of the Academy there.[16]

WILHELM VON SCHADOW AND THE FOUNDING OF THE DÜSSELDORF SCHOOL OF PAINTING: THE NEW TEACHING MODEL AND ITS CONSEQUENCES

The first candidate seriously considered as a successor to Cornelius was Julius Schnorr von Carolsfeld, yet the Ministry decided against him because it was expected that he would persist in upholding the curricular focus on monumental fresco painting. Wilhelm von Schadow was appointed to the post in his stead in 1826. Like Cornelius a member of the Nazarene School of painters in Rome, Schadow had made a name for himself in Berlin as an easel painter and gifted portraitist.[17] In Berlin, Schadow had managed to run a private training studio of his own so he was able to apply the administrative experience he had gained there to the post in Düsseldorf, where he based his ideas of a training curriculum for artists on it.[18] With the important pupils of his who moved with him to the Rhine, Schadow also founded the nucleus of what from then on became known as the Düsseldorf School of Painting. The influence of that community of artists would spread far beyond the Academy, earning it an international reputation.[19]

Like the programme implemented by Cornelius, the study model laid out in the 1831 charter provided for a three-tiered system of instruction,[20] beginning with a preliminary course, going on to a preparatory course, and finishing with a master class. The latter was the new and revolutionary aspect of Schadow's programme because its purpose was to foster the student in his own studio within the Academy, side by side with artists who had already completed their studies.[21] The aim, however, was not – like that of Cornelius's third tier – for such recent graduates to collaborate on large-scale projects the master had in hand to promote the development of artistic maturity. To the contrary, Schadow's master class was to emphasise the individuality and independence of pupils who were already acknowledged masters in their own right. The two models – both that advocated by Cornelius and the Schadow proposal – were ultimately informed by the new and originally even anti-academic idea that some parts of the training undergone by artists could not be taught but had to include hands-on practical experience, which might be best acquired under the close supervision of the director or another experienced artist. Hence the course of training envisaged by Schadow focused chiefly, alongside an increase in modular

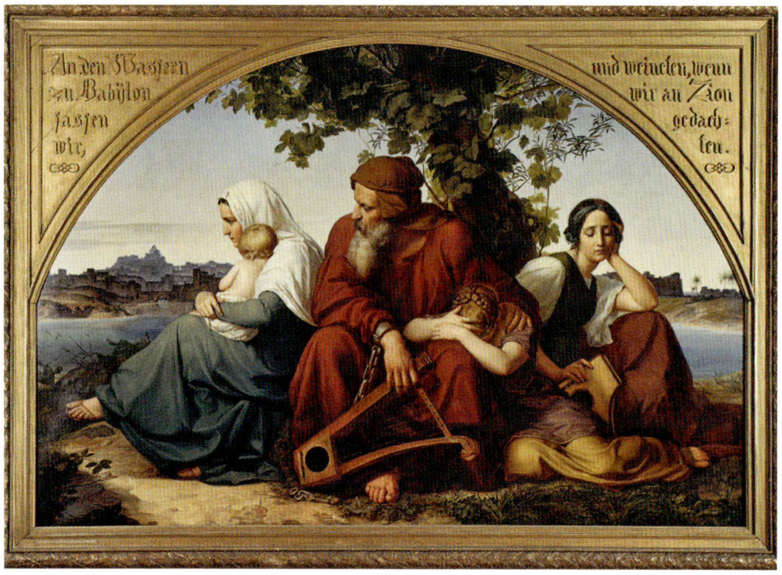

Fig. 2: Eduard Bendemann, Die trauernden Juden im Exil *[The Mourning Jews in Exile], 1832, oil on canvas, 183 × 280 cm, Wallraf-Richartz-Museum & Fondation Corboud, Cologne*

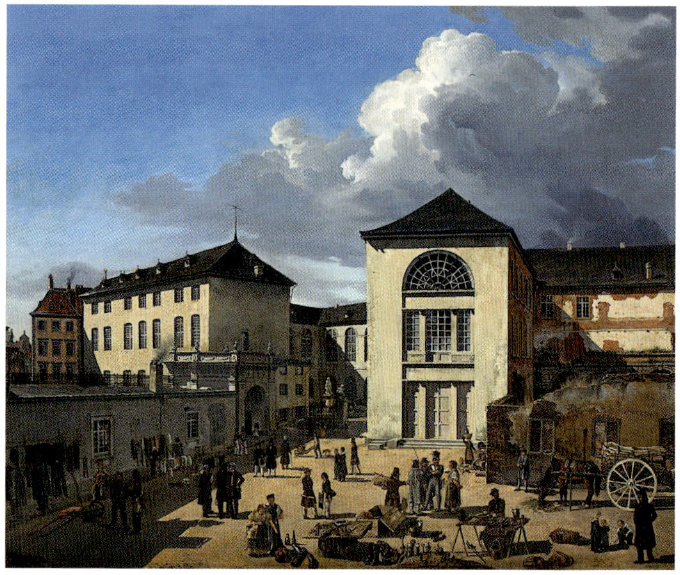

Fig. 3: Andreas Achenbach, Der Akademiehof (Die alte Akademie in Düsseldorf) *[The Academy Courtyard (The Old Academy in Düsseldorf)], 1831, oil on canvas, 65 × 81.2 cm, Stiftung Museum Kunstpalast, Düsseldorf*

classes, on colour, which, as a subjective element, was deliberately accepted as unteachable by schematic methods.[22]

However, Schadow's success as Academy director was not only due to this forward-looking education concept with its focus on the master class that was soon to be internationally acknowledged as groundbreaking. It also rested to a great extent on its creator's far-sighted linkage of the Academy with the contemporary art scene. Viewed under that aspect, the founding of the Art Association of the Rhineland and Westphalia in 1829 with Schadow as its first director was certainly the most important step towards not only guaranteeing sales of works by members of the Academy – both instructors and pupils – over the long term but also providing a reliable agency for procuring public commissions from the Prussian state according to an established quota linked to Academy production.[23] Furthermore, of major importance for the 'poetic' (history) painting represented by Schadow and his pupils (Fig. 2) was forging links with the men of letters and musicians in the city. Just as it attracted many artists, the Academy acted as a magnet on increasingly large numbers of writers and musicians, with both eventually forming a cultural circle with its members.[24] Occupying the rooms of the former paintings gallery wing in the Electoral palace (Fig. 3), the Academy became the focal point of a wide variety of activities undertaken by Schadow in Düsseldorf, which included not only private parties at his own house and artist fêtes but also semi-official engagements with the Komponierverein [Composer Society]. All those activities consolidated the communal spirit of the school and concomitantly integrated more facets of artist training from a non-academic context.[25]

Finally, the Malkasten [Paint Box] Association, founded in 1848 as an overarching arts federation, provided the Academy and its members with a further outreach opportunity for putting down roots in the city. Membership of the Malkasten was not, however, restricted to artists associated with the Academy. It also functioned as the mouthpiece for the freelance artists who had settled in the city and were becoming increasingly vocal in their opposition to Schadow.[26]

In its beginnings under Wilhelm von Schadow, the Academy stood with him and pupils of his, including Eduard Bendemann, Carl Friedrich Lessing, and Theodor Hildebrandt, for a romanticising style of painting, which caused a sensation with history paintings, some of which resembled genre pictures in conception (Fig. 4).[27] However, students at the Academy considerably widened the range of both subject matter and stylistic orientation, following the international trends prevailing in the first half of the nineteenth century. Perhaps the most important 'new' trend, and one that was also officially approved, was landscape painting, which was added to the curriculum of the Academy in 1839 when Johann Wilhelm Schirmer was appointed to teach there.[28] Although Peter Cornelius had still had reservations about splitting painting into different genres or courses of study, during Schadow's tenure the Academy did go so far as to include landscape painting, which was particularly popular with the public at large and collectors. It represented another internationally acclaimed focus of study at the Düsseldorf Academy until Schirmer departed in 1854 to take up an appointment at the Karlsruhe Academy.[29] Schirmer and his pupils are associated with a rejection of ideal landscape painting in the academic tradition and a reorientation towards real landscape as observed in the immediate vicinity of the Academy. Schirmer himself, on the other hand, never took the return to reality seriously enough to regard the innovative sketches in oils he did while painting outdoors as autonomous works of art – the step with which French painting of the time was already smoothing the way to Modernism.

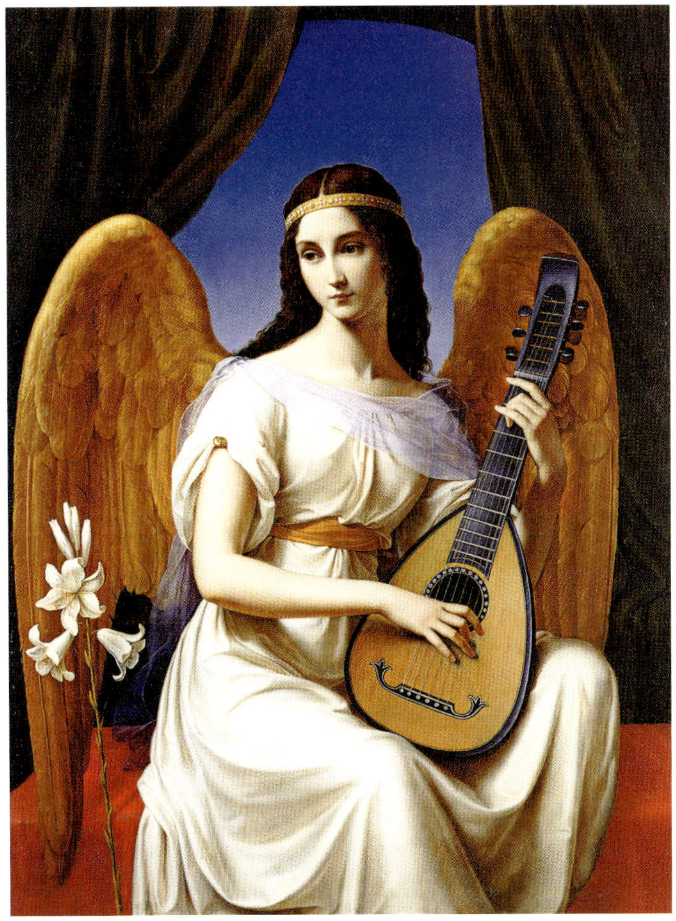

Fig. 4: Friedrich Wilhelm von Schadow, Mignon, *1828, oil on canvas, 118 × 92 cm, Museum der bildenden Künste, Leipzig*

From the beginning, relations between the 'Easterners' – the artists who had followed Schadow from Berlin – and those from the new Prussian provinces of Westphalia and the Rhineland had been fraught. The 1830s saw things come to a head with the departure of a number of artists.[30] The tension was heightened by the ever more dogmatic attitude taken by Schadow since travelling in Italy in 1839/40. The upshot was that in his tenure the Academy became increasingly unreceptive to innovation despite, or perhaps because of, the great success it enjoyed.[31] The trend towards landscape painting was matched by an at least equally strong bias in favour of the new genre painting which was developing in and around the Academy and increasingly threatened the dominance of history painting upheld by Schadow and his pupils.[32] Unsurprisingly, the director refused, despite the popularity of landscape painting with the public, to include genre painting in the Academy curriculum – this would not change until 1874 with the appointment of Wilhelm Sohn as teacher of the newly established genre class.

In view of the political developments in the years leading up to the March Revolution of 1848, the form of history painting advocated in Düsseldorf soon proved to be behind the times: its attitudinising poetic introspection seemed anachronistic in a political climate seething with revolutionary patriotism.[33] Opposition to Schadow, which formed mainly around the Malkasten Association, ultimately led him to resign his posts in 1859 after he had suffered a stroke.[34]

EDUARD BENDEMANN'S DIRECTORSHIP (1859–1867)

In this difficult situation and against the background of a looming loss of prestige for the Academy, Eduard Bendemann, who had been a pupil of Schadow's in Berlin and was his son-in-law, was appointed director of the institution in 1859.[35] Originally, Carl Friedrich Lessing had been the preferred candidate but he went to Karlsruhe and so Bendemann was chosen.[36] Great hopes were linked with his appointment. He had been headhunted from the Dresden Academy to bring him back to the Rhine. Taking both the artistic and the staff situation at the Academy into consideration, he was believed capable of overcoming the schism between the Rhinelanders and the 'Easterners', which was in part also due to differences in religious affiliation.[37]

From the art side, he was expected to rescue what Schadow had accomplished in his tenure but at the same time to set the Academy on a new, forward-looking course. He had proved with his frescoes in the Dresden palace that he not only mastered religious monumental painting in the Schadow manner but could also represent the patriotic monumental art becoming popular at the time of his appointment.[38] Ultimately, however, Bendemann turned out to be merely a preserver of the Schadow system; hence in his tenure the Academy again failed to experience the renewal it so urgently needed – although he did take some important steps towards reacting to changes taking place in the art world by appointing Oswald Achenbach to succeed Hans Fredrik Gude as head of the landscape class and trying to secure the genre painter Wilhelm Sohn for the Academy.[39]

The most important innovation in Bendemann's tenure was the foundation of the sculpture class, which had been repeatedly challenged by the Berlin Academy as sculpture was already taught there. A sculpture class had always existed in name only alongside the actual architecture class at the Düsseldorf Academy,[40] but since its inception the Academy had in fact only presented itself as an academy for painters.

This was the state of affairs even though Wilhelm von Schadow's father had been a sculptor himself and director of

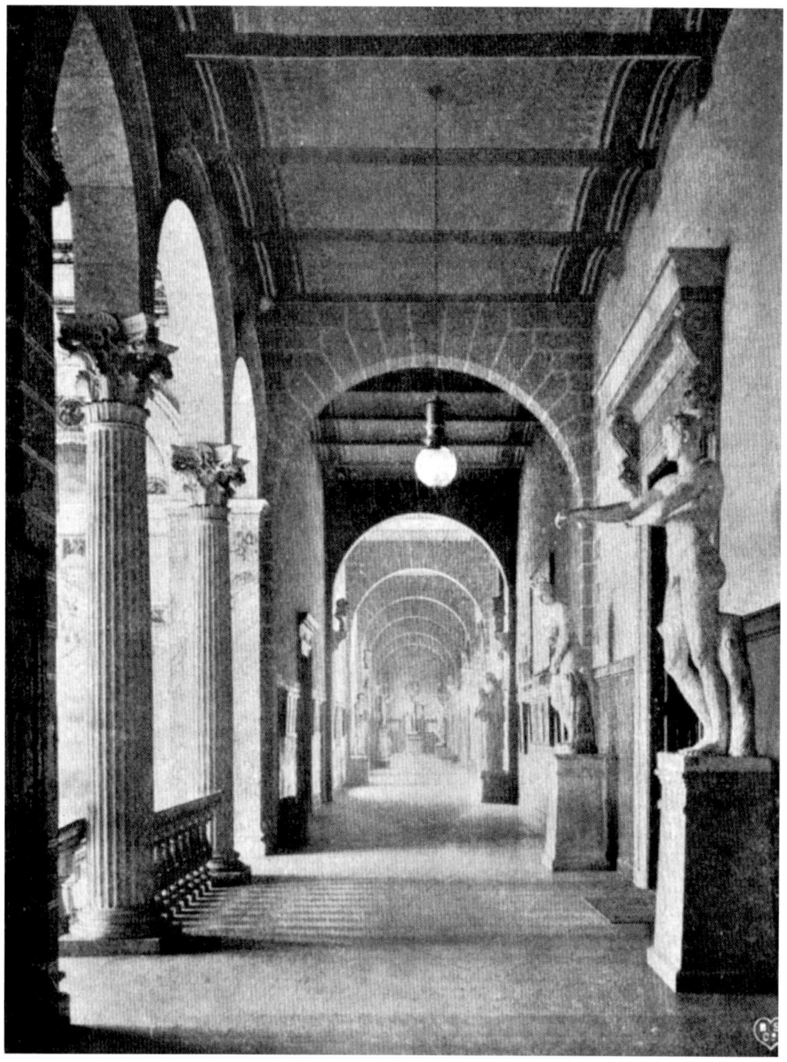

Fig. 5: The hall on the second floor of the Düsseldorf Art Academy. On the right the entrance to the Great Hall, flanked by two plaster casts of antique sculptures, before 1930

the Berlin Academy. The situation would not change in essentials until August Wittig, a pupil of Christian Daniel Rauch's, was appointed to teach sculpture in 1862. Even so, the number of pupils Wittig had and the influence he exerted remained slight compared to the status enjoyed by the painters.[41] The great innovation introduced by Wittig was an extensive collection of plaster casts (Fig. 5), which, along with the collection of second casts of antique sculpture taken over in Krahe's day from the Mannheim Antikensaal, also made modern-age works available for teaching purposes.[42]

THE DIFFICULT TRANSITIONAL YEARS: DEGER AS DIRECTOR – WISLICENUS – GIESE – ALTGELT – LOTZ (1867–1895)

The Düsseldorf Academy had reached its nadir by the time Bendemann, worn down by sheer exhaustion, retired in 1867 for health reasons.[43] Although several individual candidates were discussed as successors to Bendemann, the Academy on the Rhine, like its counterpart in Berlin, ended up being managed by a board of governors, to whom the leading artists on the staff were accountable.[44] This change in the administrative structure exposed the lack of direction and weakness crippling an Academy caught up in a situation that saw it increasingly dependent on the vagaries of public taste and the art market. There had been attempts to react to the prevailing circumstances. Hermann Wislicenus, a pupil of Bendemann's from Dresden and a history painter focusing on political content with a nationalist bias, was appointed to a teaching post in 1868 in response to the trend towards nationalist content and to displace the religious history painting in the manner of the Nazarene School traditionally espoused in Düsseldorf, which at that time was still being taught in Ernst Deger's class.[45]

After Lessing again rejected an overture made to him to sound out his willingness to become director, Wislicenus was at first made executive director of the Academy, but, significantly, not art director. The next step saw the post of executive director go to a man who was not even an artist, Councillor Johann Hermann Altgelt.[46] The students at the Academy had such serious misgivings about the appointment of a layman that protests marred the 1869 festivities celebrating the 50th anniversary of the founding of the Academy.[47] Reacting to the pressure increasingly put upon him, Altgelt resigned on 13 July 1870.[48] In the face of numerous attempts made to reform the Academy from within, Wislicenus and others remained directors until 1879, when it was finally decided to hand over the administration to a triumvirate of alternating directors.[49] By 1882, however, this solution, too, was viewed as unsatisfactory and calls for the reintroduction of a single director could no longer be overheard, although they were not answered with action until Peter Janssen was appointed sole director in 1894.[50]

Nor did this protracted unfortunate phase at the Academy end with these administrative upheavals. During the night of 19 March 1872, the Düsseldorf Palace, much of which now housed the Academy, was gutted by fire. The circumstances surrounding the conflagration were never entirely clarified.[51] With only a few exceptions, the studios containing the works of the artist professors and their pupils were destroyed. The collection and the library were all that remained unharmed.[52] Even before the fire, some professors had maintained private studios in the city, a practice which the other professors were now forced to emulate until the money needed for a new building might be raised.[53] Designed by Hermann Riffart, the new Academy building, under construction from 1875 until 1879 at the Sicherheitshafen, was not fully operational until it was officially inaugurated in 1896 (Fig. 6).[54]

It was at this difficult juncture that a class for genre painting was finally established in 1874. Taught by Wilhelm Sohn, it was very successful. Genre painting, however, had only shortly before led to a decline in the reputation of Düsseldorf painting. Hence the belated establishment of a class in genre painting at a time when demand for monumental patriotic art was rife must have seemed downright anachronistic. The years following the foundation of the Empire saw an upturn at the Düsseldorf Academy and not just because Wilhelm Sohn was appointed to teach there. A rise in student enrolment led to increasingly cramped conditions at the Academy. As in Berlin and abroad, proposals for the founding of a complementary decorative arts school were mooted in Düsseldorf to take over the elementary training of Academy students in the drawing class and, on the other hand, to house both the applied arts and architecture. It was finally inaugurated in 1883.[55]

PETER JANSSEN'S DIRECTORSHIP (1895–1908)

With the appointment of Peter Janssen, the Art Academy finally had a sole director again, who introduced the new teaching concept of working from the live model.[56] With Janssen at the helm, the curriculum continued to focus on monumental painting; state commissions for paintings of this kind also meant that it was publicly subsidised.[57] The Great Hall (Fig. 7) in the new Academy building, which was decorated by Janssen with murals and ceiling paintings, was inaugurated on 30 October 1896.[58] Stylistically, however, little had changed, and the idealistic tendency with its model naturalism espoused by Schadow was fiercely defended against the encroachment of more modern stylistic trends, such as Munich Naturalism and early Impressionism. Martial and military painting was added as a new field of specialisation in Düsseldorf, although prevailing new trends tentatively showed up, as in the past, in landscape and genre painting.[59] Since even the Düsseldorf Academy could not completely close itself off from the more recent, Naturalist approaches in artist education, studios for open-air and animal

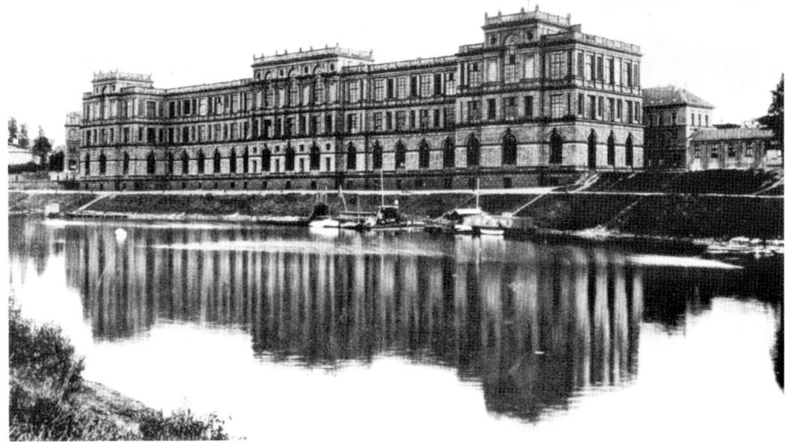

Fig. 6: The new Academy building at the Sicherheitshafen

painting along the lines pioneered in Munich were established in 1898 and 1900 respectively.[60]

Although it had departments of architecture and sculpture, the Art Academy had remained essentially a painting academy. Now, however, it had to face growing competition from the Decorative Arts School affiliated to it, which had quickly consolidated and since 1903 had boasted Peter Behrens as director.[61] That was where Wilhelm Lehmbruck, later one of the most important Academy alumni, had begun his studies, although he switched in 1901 to the sculpture class taught by Karl Janssen, the brother of the Academy director. Like his brother, Karl Janssen was an exponent of a conservative, neo-Baroque style.[62]

THE ACADEMY UNDER FRIEDRICH ROEBER (1908–1924)

On the death of Peter Janssen, yet another history painter became director of the Academy in the person of Fritz Roeber, who had studied under Bendemann and had been in charge of a class at the Academy since 1893.[63] Unsurprisingly, training at the Academy in the Wilhelmine era still retained the focus on monumental painting, which was further reinforced by the founding of a class for ecclesiastical art and a workshop for mosaic and glass painting in 1909.[64] Following in the footsteps of Schadow in the early years of his tenure, Roeber worked on closely meshing activities at the Academy with the cultural life of the city – for example, by hosting an exhibition of Christian art the year the class in that field was established.[65] Under Roeber, a new Art Academy building was even planned on the Stockum Rhine embankment because the building which had just been inaugurated was said to be bedevilled with inadequate space and poor lighting. In Stockum there would also be

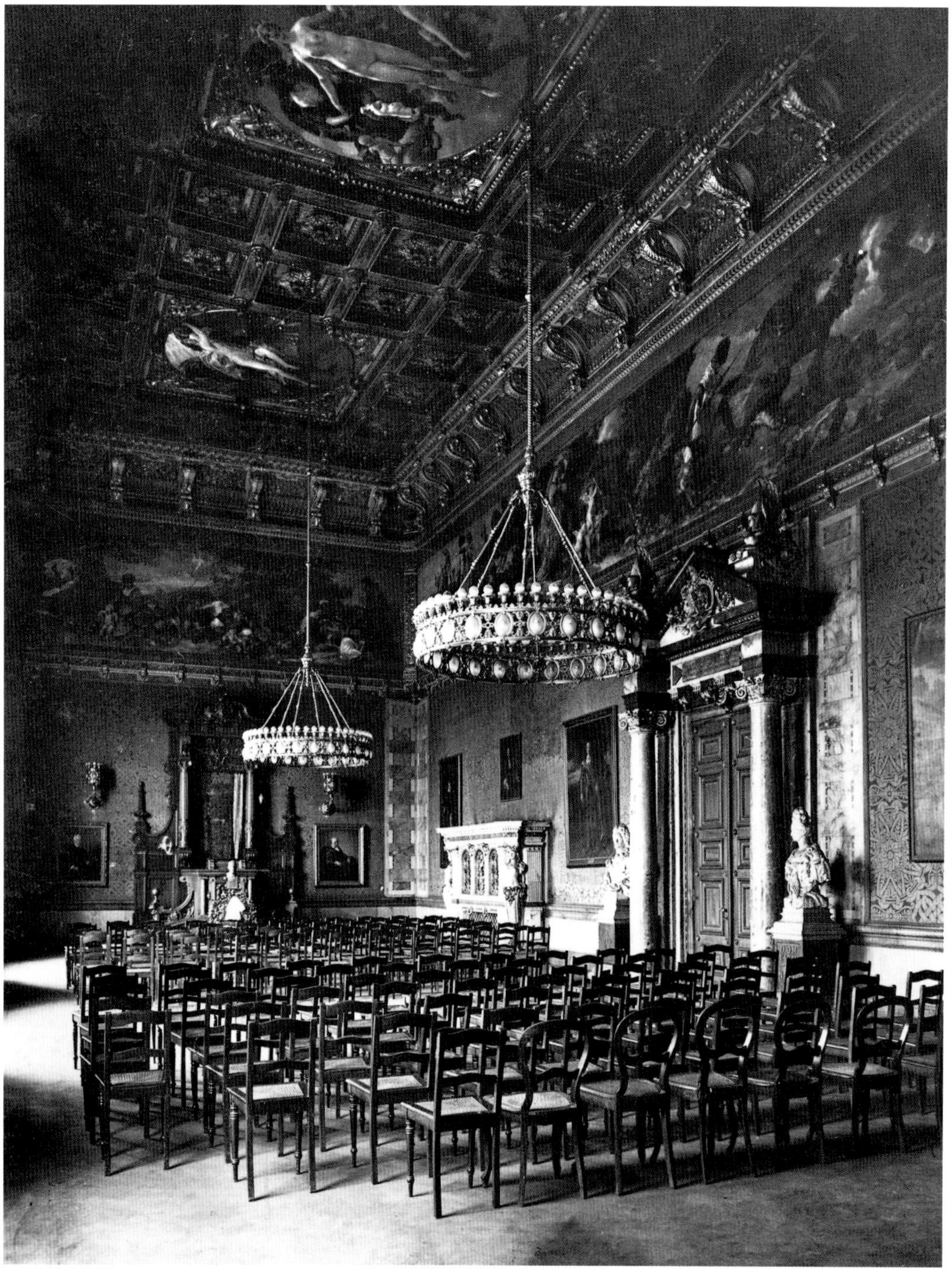

Fig. 7: The Great Hall, c. 1900

more space for pavilions and gardens where animals could be kept. Work began on the new structure, a project which was doomed to remain incomplete because it was not finished before war broke out in 1914. Only the main wing was finally built in 1919 after plans by Karl Wach (Fig. 8).[66]

Long before that, however, the Academy had failed to keep up with ongoing trends and movements in art. As it had at other academies, the antagonism between modern art and academic training or academies as an institution came to a head while Roeber was director of the Düsseldorf Academy.[67] New developments in art in the city itself were supported by exhibitions mounted by the Sonderbund and the Flechtheim Gallery to organise independent artists who were exponents of early Modernism in the Rhineland. Roeber by contrast made a point of stepping up his campaign against the Modernism of the kind vigorously promoted until 1907 by Peter Behrens from the Decorative Arts School and subsequently by his successor, Wilhelm Kreis. Roeber won out in the long run: the Decorative Arts School was disbanded in 1919 and part of it – the Architecture Department – was incorporated in the Art Academy.[68]

Modernism had no place at the Academy until 1921, when at first Heinrich Nauen and then Jan Thorn-Prikker were made professors there; it was not long before Otto Dix was in the master class taught by Nauen. Despite such isolated breakthroughs, trends in the Rhineland art scene continued to be set outside the Academy, by groups such as the vociferously anti-academic artists union the Young Rhineland.

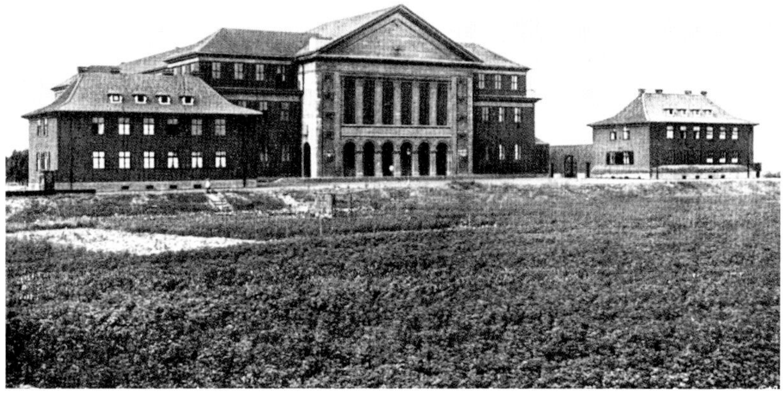

Fig. 8: The new Academy building in Stockum, 1924

WALTER KAESBACH AND REFORM AT THE ACADEMY UNDER THE MODERNIST BANNER (1924–1933)

The end of Fritz Roeber's tenure definitively put paid to a long tradition in painting at the Düsseldorf Academy. The appointment of Walter Kaesbach to succeed him represented a deliberate break with the past underpinned by a decision for fundamental change.[69] Through his museum career – first under Hugo von Tschudi and Ludwig Justi in Berlin, then as director of the Anger Museum in Erfurt – Kaesbach, an art historian, had earned a reputation as one of the most zealous promoters of Modernism in Germany. His friends and network of supporters included important artists and gallerists both in the Rhineland and Berlin.[70] In the face of opposition from a large part of the upper echelon of Academy teaching staff, Heinrich Nauen pushed through the appointment of his friend Kaesbach with the backing of the Ministry.[71]

In the few years he was head of the Academy, Kaesbach carried out a consistent course of reform. The agenda he pursued derived from both Wilhelm Waetzoldt in Berlin and teaching concepts developed at the Bauhaus. At the Düsseldorf Academy all art genres were to be subsumed under the overarching aim of interrelating art and architecture along Bauhaus lines.[72] Implementing the full programme required departments such as urban planning and landscape gardening to be enlarged, and that in turn led – accompanied by a limit on student admissions – to an expansion of the entire education process.[73] The syllabus was restructured to include a probationary-period class, two years at lower level, followed by higher level instruction and ultimately the master class.[74] Admission to the Academy was rendered more difficult by more stringent entrance examinations, and the probationary-period class was made tougher to prevent the emergence of an 'artist proletariat'.[75]

Incorporated in the Academy curriculum since 1921, the seminar for drawing teachers was upgraded to a department for training art teachers for state secondary schools. In no time at all a successful class in theatre design and another in painting techniques had been added.[76]

Kaesbach wanted to bridge the gap between the Academy and artists at large and thus reposition the institution at the centre of a vibrant art scene. To that end, he had the Great Hall modernised as soon as he took office and promoted opening up the Academy to the public by hosting events.[77] Further approaches taken by Kaesbach to modernising the Academy included having two halls emptied so works by students could be exhibited in them; in January 1932 he took the unprecedented step of opening the Academy studios to the public for a week – the *Rundgang* [Academy Tour] was born.[78]

One of his major innovations was the groundbreaking decision taken that same year to move the Academy Collection to the City Art Museum where it was to remain on permanent loan, a previously unthinkable option but one which opened the Academy to the public as he had envisaged.[79]

He also succeeded in gradually changing the orientation of the Academy by judicious teaching appointments.[80] In 1926 he hired Heinrich Campendonk to teach at the Academy and, finally, in 1931, he lured Paul Klee away from the Bauhaus in Dessau.[81] Ewald Mataré and Oskar Moll came from Berlin in 1932 to join the staff.[82] In Düsseldorf, however, a ground swell of fierce opposition to Kaesbach had long since arisen. Informed by nationalist thinking, it was again fomented by the Malkasten Association. Everything Kaesbach did was vocally condemned: his conduct in office, his reforms, his appointment policy, and his promotion of Expressionist art.[83]

'In March 1933 the swastika banner was raised above the Academy building. Kaesbach was forced to leave the Academy within one hour and was forbidden to enter it ever again.'[84] It was only a matter of weeks, often days, before most of the progressive-minded artist teachers followed him, dismissed from their posts by the National Socialists or pressured to resign voluntarily.[85]

NOTES

* My sincere thanks to Heinrich Theissing for reading the manuscript and for his advice which helped to clarify some basic historical and epistemological issues.

1 For the establishment of art academies in the eighteenth century, see the still essential discussion in Nikolaus Pevsner, *Die Geschichte der Kunstakademien*, Munich 1986, pp. 143–185.

2 Thus already Heinz Peters, 'Wilhelm Lambert Krahe und die Gründung der Kunstakademie Düsseldorf', in: Eduard Trier (ed.), with Paul Böhringer, M. T. Engels, Graf Wend von Kalnein, and Heinrich Theissing, *Zweihundert Jahre Kunstakademie Düsseldorf*, Düsseldorf 1973, pp. 1–30, here: p. 26; the information that follows without annotation has been taken – unless otherwise indicated – from Dietrich Bieber, 'Aus der Chronik der Kunstakademie. Personen und Ereignisse', in: Trier, pp. 215–221.

3 Richard Klapheck, *Die Kunstsammlungen der Staatlichen Kunstakademie zu Düsseldorf*, Düsseldorf 1928, p. 7; Ekkehard Mai, *Die Deutschen Kunstakademien im 19. Jahrhundert. Künstlerausbildung zwischen Tradition und Avantgarde*, Cologne and elsewhere 2010, p. 109. Most recently on the collection, Sonja Brink, 'Eine Künstlersammlung für Künstler', in: Kunibert Bering (ed.), *Lambert Krahe (1712–1790), Maler – Sammler – Akademiegründer. Ergebnisse des Symposions zum 300. Geburtstag des Gründers der Kunstakademie Düsseldorf, 8.–10. November 2012*, Oberhausen 2013, pp. 17–27, and Sonja Brink, '"Non tanto per piacere [...] quanto per istruzione [...]". Lambert Krahes Kunstsammlung – eine Künstlersammlung für Künstler', in: Sonja Brink and Beat Wismer (eds.), *Akademie. Sammlung. Krahe. Eine Künstlersammlung für Künstler*, exhib. cat. Düsseldorf, Berlin/Munich 2013, pp. 13–37.

4 Peters (see n. 2), pp. 14f.; also Mai (see n. 3), p. 107.

5 Peters (see n. 2), pp. 18f.; Mai (see n. 3), p. 107.

6 Thus already Friedrich Schaarschmidt, *Zur Geschichte der Düsseldorfer Kunst, insbesondere im 19. Jahrhundert*, Düsseldorf 1902, p. 23; after all Johann Heinrich Lips and Friedrich Bury studied in Düsseldorf, see Mai (see n. 3), pp. 107f.

7 Rudolf Wiegmann, *Die Königliche Kunst-Akademie zu Düsseldorf. Ihre Geschichte, Einrichtung und Wirksamkeit und die Düsseldorfer Künstler*, Düsseldorf 1856, p. 4; Mai (see n. 3), p. 109; for Cornelius's beginnings in Düsseldorf, see Frank Büttner, 'Peter Cornelius in Düsseldorf', in: Wend von Kalnein (ed.), *Die Düsseldorfer Malerschule*, exhib. cat. Düsseldorf/Darmstadt, Mainz 1979, pp. 48–55.

8 Klaus Müller, 'Unter pfalz-neuburgischer und pfalz-bayerischer Herrschaft (1614–1806)', in: Hugo Weidenhaupt (ed.), *Von der Residenzstadt zur Beamtenstadt (1614–1900)*, Düsseldorf 1988, p. 50. Vol. 2 of *Düsseldorf. Geschichte von den Ursprüngen bis ins 20. Jahrhundert*.

9 Wiegmann (see n. 7), p. 4.

10 For the process as a whole, Mai (see n. 3), pp. 109f.

11 Pevsner (see n. 1), pp. 206–208; Mai (see n. 3), pp. 111f.

12 Frank Büttner, *Peter Cornelius. Fresken und Freskenprojekte*, Vols. 1–2, Wiesbaden 1980–1999, Vol. 1, pp. 130–134.

13 Büttner (see n. 7), p. 53, and Büttner (see n. 12), Vol. 1, pp. 130–134.

14 In Büttner (see n. 12), Vol. 1, pp. 230–234. Also see Mai (see n. 3), pp. 112–114.

15 Büttner (see n. 7), pp. 53f.; Mai (see n. 3), pp. 113f.

16 Büttner (see n. 12), Vol. 1, p. 133, and Vol. 2, pp. 21f.; Ekkehard Mai, 'Schadows Erfolgsmodell. Die Düsseldorfer Kunstakademie im Vergleich', in: Bettina Baumgärtel (ed.), *Die Düsseldorfer Malerschule und ihre internationale Ausstrahlung 1819–1918*, exhib. cat. Düsseldorf, Vols. 1–2, Petersberg 2011, Vol. 1, p. 52.

17 For the circumstances, see Mai (see n. 3), pp. 121f. and Mai (see n. 16), p. 53; on Schadow, see Helmut Börsch-Supan, 'Das Frühwerk Wilhelm von Schadows und die berlinischen Voraussetzungen der Düsseldorfer Schule', in: Kalnein (see n. 7), pp. 56–67; Barbara Camilla Tucholski, *Friedrich Wilhelm von Schadow 1789–1862. Künstlerische Konzeption und poetische Malerei* [Univ. Diss. Bonn 1980], Bonn 1984; Cordula A. Grewe, *Wilhelm Schadow (1788–1862). Monographie und Catalogue raisonné* [Univ. Diss. Freiburg 1998].

18 Pevsner (see n. 1), pp. 212–214; Mai (see n. 16), pp. 53f.

19 Ekkehard Mai, 'Die Düsseldorfer Malerschule und die Malerei des 19. Jahrhunderts', in: Kalnein (see n. 7), pp. 19–40; most recent Bettina Baumgärtel, 'Die Düsseldorfer Malerschule und ihre internationale Ausstrahlung', in: Baumgärtel (see n. 16), Vol. 1, pp. 24–49; Mai (see n. 16), p. 54.

20 Already developed in Wilhelm von Schadow, 'Meine Gedanken über eine folgerichtige Ausbildung des Malers', *Berliner Kunstblatt* 1, 1828, pp. 264–273; also in Athanasius Raczyński, *Düsseldorf und das Rheinland*, Berlin 1836, pp. 319–330. Vol. 1 of *Geschichte der neueren deutschen Kunst*, translated from French by Friedrich Heinrich von der Hagen; now in: Baumgärtel (see n. 16), Vol. 1, pp. 379–385. Also Pevsner (see n. 1), pp. 214f.; Mai (see n. 3), pp. 123f.

21 Similarly Mai (see n. 3), p. 124.

22 Raczyński (see n. 20), Vol. 1, pp. 321–327; Johannes Myssok, 'Farbe bei den ersten Direktoren der Düsseldorfer Kunstakademie', *Jahreshefte der Kunstakademie Düsseldorf* [gone to press].

23 See Birgit Biedermann, *Bürgerliches Mäzenatentum im 19. Jahrhundert. Die Förderung öffentlicher Kunstwerke durch den Kunstverein für die Rheinlande und Westfalen*, Petersberg 2001; Thomas Schmitz, *Die deutschen Kunstvereine im 19. und frühen 20. Jahrhundert. Ein Beitrag zur Kultur-, Konsum und Sozialgeschichte der bildenden Kunst im bürgerlichen Zeitalter* [Univ. Diss. Düsseldorf 1997], Neuried 2001; Walter Grasskamp, 'Kunst – Kommerz – Konsum – Kommunikation. Der Kunstverein für die Rheinlande und Westfalen im Kontext', in: *175 Jahre Kunstverein für die Rheinlande und Westfalen*, Düsseldorf 2004, pp. 22–35; Mai (see n. 3), pp. 124–126; Benedikt Mauer, 'Die Malerschule zuhause: örtliche Kunstvereine und die Stadt Düsseldorf als Auftraggeber', in: Baumgärtel (see n. 16), Vol. 1, pp. 304–311.

24 Jochen Hörisch, 'Ut Poesis Pictura. Korrespondenzen zwischen der Düsseldorfer Malerschule und der romantischen Dichtung', in: Kalnein (see n. 7), pp. 41–47; now Gabriele Ewenz, '"... dass der Künstler selbst ein Dichter sei": das Verhältnis von Poesie und Malerei in der Düsseldorfer Malerschule', in: Baumgärtel (see n. 16), Vol. 1, pp. 262–271; Mai (see n. 16), p. 54.

25 Mai (see n. 3), pp. 124–132.

26 Kurt Loup, 'Kunstakademie und freie Künstlerschaft', in: Trier (see n. 2), pp. 173–184, especially pp. 179–181; Sabine Schroyen, *Quellen zur Geschichte des Künstlervereins Malkasten: ein Zentrum bürgerlicher Kunst und Kultur in Düsseldorf seit 1848*, Bonn 1992; Wolfgang Hütt, *Die Düsseldorfer Malerschule 1819–1869*, Leipzig 1995, pp. 195–198; finally Sabine Schroyen, '"A true brotherhood seems to reign among them": der Künstlerverein Malkasten und seine internationalen Mitglieder', in: Baumgärtel (see n. 16), Vol. 1, pp. 272–279.

27 Mai (see n. 19); now Hans Körner, *'Unsichtbare Malerei': Reflexion und Sentimentalität in Bildern der Düsseldorfer Malerschule*, Düsseldorf 2011.

28 See Pevsner (see n. 1), pp. 226f.; Mai (see n. 3), p. 128; Rudolf Theilmann, 'Schirmer und die Düsseldorfer Landschaftsmalerei', in: Kalnein (see n. 16), pp. 130–144; Rudolf Theilmann, 'Der Landschaftsmaler und Akademiedirektor Johann Wilhelm Schirmer', in: Marcell Perse (ed.), *Natur im Blick. Die Landschaften des Johann Wilhelm Schirmer (Jülich 1807–Karlsruhe 1863)*, exhib. cat. Jülich 2001, pp. 54–115, here: pp. 54–83; Bettina Baumgärtel, 'Naturstudie und landschaftliche Komposition. Johann Wilhelm Schirmers Anfänge in Düsseldorf und der "Landschaftliche Komponierverein"', in: *Johann Wilhelm Schirmer in seiner Zeit. Landschaft im 19. Jahrhundert zwischen Wirklichkeit und Ideal*, exhib. cat. Karlsruhe/Aachen, Heidelberg 2002, pp. 17–23; Marcell Perse (ed.), *Johann Wilhelm Schirmer. Vom Rheinland in die Welt*, Vol. 1, exhib. cat. Neuss and other places, Petersberg 2010, here particularly the essay by Ekkehard Mai, '"... denn Schirmer war ein großer Mann" (Hans Thoma 1863): Positionen deutscher Landschaftsmalerei im 19. Jahrhundert', Vol. 1, pp. 12–31.

29 For the echo abroad, see the references listed in the previous note and especially Susanne Richter, 'Bilder auf Reisen: Schirmer und Amerika', in: Perse (see n. 28), Vol. 1, pp. 260–279.

30 See Mai (see n. 3), p. 129; Mai (see n. 16), p. 55.

31 Also see Mai (see p. 3), pp. 129–132, pp. 200f.

32 Ute Ricke-Immel, 'Die Düsseldorfer Genremalerei', in: Kalnein (see n. 7), pp. 149–164; Mai (see n. 3), pp. 130f.

33 See Hanna Gagel, 'Die Düsseldorfer Malerschule in der politischen Situation des Vormärz und 1848', in: Kalnein (see n. 7), pp. 68–85; Mai (see n. 3), pp. 131f.

34 Wulf Aschenborn, *Eduard Bendemann (1811–1889). Das Direktorat an der Düsseldorfer Kunstakademie 1859–1867* [Univ. Diss. Cologne 1998], Cologne 1998, pp. 41f.; Mai (see n. 3), p. 201.

35 Aschenborn (see n. 34), especially pp. 58–63; Mai (see n. 3), p. 202.

36 Aschenborn (see n. 34), pp. 52–56.

37 Ibid., pp. 57f.

38 Ibid., pp. 58f.

39 For Bendemann's appointments, see ibid., pp. 121–123, pp. 147–150; Mai (see n. 3), pp. 202f.

40 The first studio for sculpture was founded in 1854 by Julius Bayerle, who was a pupil of Wilhelm von Schadow's. See Peter Bloch, 'Der Düsseldorfer Bildhauer Julius Bayerle', in: *Festschrift Heinz Ladendorf*, Cologne/Vienna 1970, pp. 115–117; Peter Bloch, 'Der Bildhauer August Wittig', in: Trier (see n. 2), pp. 121–126, here: p. 124; for sculpture in Düsseldorf at the Academy and in its circle, see now Michael Puls, '"... und einer modellierte": Skulptur im Kreis der Düsseldorfer Malerschule', in: Baumgärtel (see n. 16), Vol. 1, pp. 328–339.

41 Wittig did not, however, take up his professorship until two years afterwards, in 1864. For Wittig and his appointment to Düsseldorf, Trier (see n. 2), pp. 124f.; Aschenborn (see n. 34), pp. 118–121, pp. 127f.; Mai (see n. 3), p. 202.

42 His 'Museum für Abgüsse antiker und anderer hervorragender Skulpturwerke' [museum for casts of ancient sculpture and other outstanding works of sculpture] was housed on the ground floor of the archive wing; this is discussed in *Zeitschrift für bildende Kunst* 6, 1871, Suppl. No. 18, p. 148; also see Trier (see n. 2), p. 124.

43 Aschenborn (see n. 34), pp. 136–143, pp. 150–153.

44 Ibid., pp. 154–159; Mai (see n. 3), p. 203.

45 Aschenborn (see n. 34), pp. 156–158; Mai (see n. 3), p. 203.

46 Aschenborn (see n. 34), p. 158; Mai (see n. 3), p. 203.

47 Also on this, see the essay by Eduard Trier, 'Die Düsseldorfer Kunstakademie in der permanenten Reform', in: Trier (see n. 2), pp. 203–212, here: p. 206, and Aschenborn (see n. 34), pp. 163–167.

48 Mai (see n. 3), p. 204.

49 Siegfried Gehrecke, *Hermann Wislicenus 1825–1899*, Göttingen 1987, p. 36; Mai (see n. 3), p. 204.

50 Mai (see n. 3), p. 204.

51 Karl Woermann, *Zur Geschichte der Düsseldorfer Kunstakademie. Abriss ihres letzten Jahrzehnts und Denkschrift zur Einweihung des Neubaus*, Düsseldorf 1880, pp. 9–13; Mai (see n. 3), p. 300.

52 Woermann (see n. 51), p. 22.

53 Ibid., pp. 13f.

54 For the back story, ibid., pp. 23–25. For the building, see Eva Brües, 'Das Akademiegebäude', in: Trier (see n. 2), pp. 127–138.

55 Mai (see n. 3), pp. 245–277, p. 301.

56 Before being appointed sole director of the Art Academy, he had, however, already been a member of the previous board of governors. Dietrich Bieber and Ekkehard Mai, 'Gebhardt und Janssen. Religiöse und Monumentalmalerei im späten 19. Jahrhundert', in: Kalnein (see n. 7), pp. 165–185, on Janssen in particular: pp. 176–184.

57 See Mai (see n. 3), pp. 299f.

58 Janssen had begun his paintings in 1886 – long before he was appointed director – and had already finished them by 1894. They showed scenes and allegories that were intended to illustrate for first-year students the areas of representation and the art media and techniques as exemplified by an artist's life. See also Dietrich Bieber, 'Die Wand- und Deckenbilder Peter Janssens in der alten Aula der Kunstakademie', in: Trier (see n. 2), pp. 139–146; Brües (see n. 54), p. 134. The other decoration and furnishings of the room, which was supposed to recall a Venetian Renaissance banquet hall, was the work of Adolf Schill; see Anna Klapheck, 'Die "goldnen" zwanziger Jahre. Die Akademie zwischen den beiden Kriegen', in: Trier (see n. 2), pp. 147–160, here: p. 147.

59 Mai (see n. 3), p. 302.

60 Brües (see n. 54), p. 134; Mai (see n. 3), p. 371.

61 Alan Windsor, *Peter Behrens. Architekt und Designer*, translated from English by Kyra Stromberg, Stuttgart 1985, pp. 57–87; Gisela Moeller, *Peter Behrens in Düsseldorf. Die Jahre von 1903–1907* [Bonn Univ. Diss. 1987], Weinheim 1991, pp. 153–155 on the situation in Düsseldorf; for the rivalry between the Academy and the Decorative Arts School under Behrens, also see Mai (see n. 3), pp. 371–373.

62 For Lehmbruck's beginnings, see Dietrich Schubert, *Die Kunst Lehmbrucks*, 2nd edn, Worms 1990, pp. 75–153; Frauke Mankartz, 'Wilhelm Lehmbruck. Lebensstationen', in: Martina Rudloff and Dietrich Schubert (eds.), *Wilhelm Lehmbruck*, exhib. cat. Bremen 2000, pp. 29–37; Dietrich Schubert, *Wilhelm Lehmbruck. Catalogue raisonné der Skulpturen, 1898–1919*, Worms 2001, pp. 11–22.

63 Friedrich Schaarschmidt, *Fritz Roeber, Kunst für Alle* 9, Munich 1900/01, pp. 201–207.

64 Mai (see n. 3), p. 371.

65 Even before his tenure began, he had been the main founder of the Industrial and Applied Arts exhibition in 1902 and had had the idea of having the Golzheimer Insel area as its location; see ibid., p. 371.

66 Klapheck (see n. 58), p. 150.

67 Also see ibid., pp. 150f.; Mai (see n. 3), p. 373.

68 Dawn Leach, 'Ausdifferenzierung und Kontinuität in der Künstlerausbildung an der Kunstakademie Düsseldorf', in: Wolfgang Ruppert and Christian Fuhrmeister (eds.), *Zwischen Deutscher Kunst und internationaler Modernität. Formen der Künstlerausbildung 1918 bis 1968*, Weimar 2007, pp. 147–167, here: pp. 147f.; Mai (see n. 3), p. 373; still Roeber, too, had espoused the new workshop idea – admittedly from a different angle – and planned to integrate the arts under the aegis of architecture; see Klapheck (see n. 58), pp. 148f.

69 He was appointed by Becker, the Prussian Minister of Culture; for the circumstances, see Klapheck (see n. 58), pp. 151f., and Christoph Bauer, 'Akademiereform und innere Immigration. Walter Kaesbach in Düsseldorf und in Hemmenhofen 1924–1945', in: Christoph Bauer and Barbara Stark (eds.), *Walter Kaesbach. Mentor der Moderne*, exhib. cat. Singen/Konstanz, Lengwil am Bodensee 2008, pp. 27–47, here: p. 27.

70 For that period of his activity, see Anna Klapheck, *Walter Kaesbach und die zwanziger Jahre an der Düsseldorfer Kunstakademie*, Düsseldorf 1961, pp. 8–10; Andreas Gabelmann, 'Im Brennpunkt der Moderne. Walter Kaesbach und die Expressionisten', in: Bauer and Stark (see n. 69), pp. 9–25.

71 In this sense Bauer (see n. 69), p. 28.

72 Ibid., p. 27.

73 Leach (see n. 68), p. 148; Bauer (see n. 69), p. 28.

74 For the syllabus, see Richard Klapheck, 'Die Staatliche Kunsthochschule in Preussen', in: Walter Kaesbach (ed.), *Die Kunsthochschule von heute*, Düsseldorf 1932, pp. 3–11. Also Bauer (see n. 69), p. 27.

75 Thus Kaesbach in a 1932 press conference, quoted in Klapheck (see n. 58), p. 152.

76 Ibid., p. 152; Leach (see n. 68), p. 148; Bauer (see n. 69), pp. 27f.

77 For the drastic removal of the Wilhelmine decoration, which was only thirty years old at the time, by Janssen und Schill and the extremely reductive redesign under Kaesbach, see Klapheck (see n. 58), p. 147. The work was done by Clemens Holzmeister, an Austrian architect who taught at the Academy from 1928 to 1930. It consisted in removing all the decoration from the side walls and replacing it with a simple gold-coloured wall, which explains why the room was called the 'golden Aula'. Crucial for the impact made by the room were also the stringently geometric glass windows created for the purpose by Heinrich Campendonk: Klapheck (see n. 58), p. 148, p. 155; for Campendonk's glass windows: Mathias T. Engels, *Campendonk als Glasmaler*, Krefeld 1966, pp. 10f., p. 81, cat. no. 2.

78 Bauer (see n. 69), p. 28.

79 The collection was handed over to the Städtische Kunstsammlungen in 1932 as a permanent loan; see Wend von Kalnein, 'Die Kunstakademie im Spiegel der Städtischen Kunstsammlungen', in: Trier (see n. 2), pp. 167–172; Bauer (see n. 69), p. 28.

80 For Kaesbach's appointment, see Klapheck (see n. 58), p. 152; Bauer (see n. 69), pp. 28f.

81 See Klapheck (see n. 58), p. 156; Bauer (see n. 69), p. 29.

82 Klapheck (see n. 58), pp. 158f.

83 Bauer (see n. 69), p. 33.

84 Klapheck (see n. 58), p. 160 – from Anna Klapheck's memoirs: 'Kaesbach was at first "put on leave of absence" on 29 March 1933, then officially forced to retire on 6 April; he was forbidden to enter the Academy'; see Bauer (see n. 69), pp. 33f.

85 Bauer (see n. 69), pp. 33f.

THE ACADEMY DURING THE NATIONAL SOCIALIST ERA, 1933–1945

Kunibert Bering

'CASTING DOWN ART IDOLS'

Kopf eines Märtyrers [Head of a Martyr] was the title Paul Klee gave to the picture with which he reacted in 1933 to his dismissal from the Düsseldorf Art Academy due to pressure exerted by the National Socialists after Hitler had come to power: a human face congealed to a mask, the eyes half shut, the teeth apparently knocked out – a broken man (Fig. 1).[1] The original gold borders of the frame, however, elevate the representation to the devotional sphere, like the image of a saint. Along with *Von der Liste gestrichen* [Struck from the List], an abstract composition with a black X over the colour surfaces which he also painted that year, *Kopf eines Märtyrers* signalises the painter's fate and the extinction of painting – a portent of the destruction of modern art to follow under National Socialism (Fig. 2). Klee bade farewell to his Düsseldorf students with the chilling words, 'Gentlemen, it stinks worryingly of corpses in Europe.'[2]

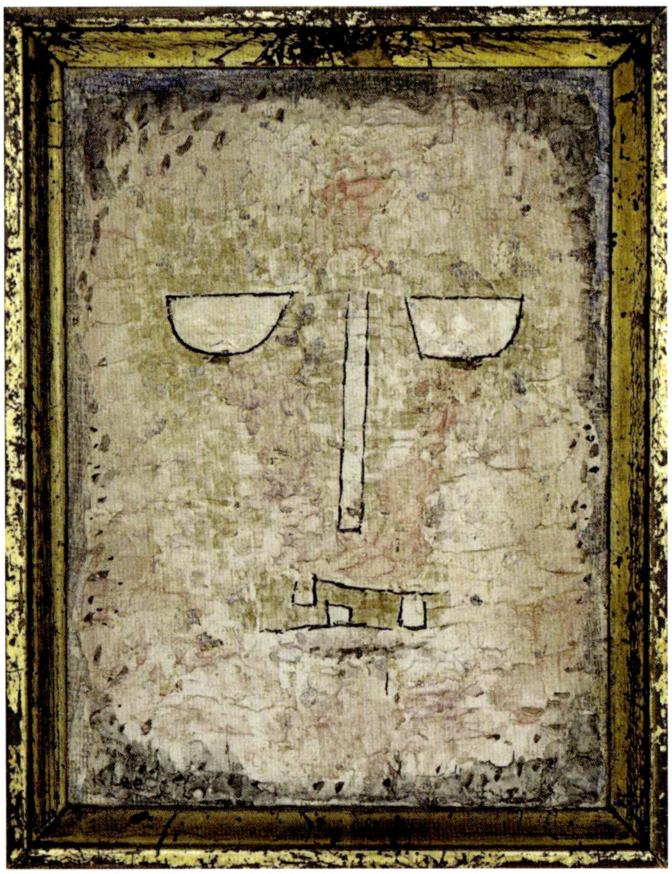

Fig. 1: Paul Klee, Kopf eines Märtyrers *[Head of a Martyr], 1933, watercolour on plaster ground on gauze, original gold borders, 26 × 20.5 cm, Zentrum Paul Klee, Bern*

In an article entitled 'Kunstgötzen stürzen' [Casting Down Art Idols], which he wrote for the magazine *Deutsche Kultur-Wacht* soon after the National Socialists came to power, Robert Scholz stirred up hatred against Klee, calling him 'one of the most obvious examples of the complete spiritual and intellectual degeneration of the individualist cultural era'.[3] Klee's dismissal was part of a radical 'cleansing' of the Academy during the consolidation phase of the Third Reich, when the venerable and highly esteemed institution was transformed into a hotbed of activity and training for artists affiliated with the NS regime. In the following, an attempt will be made to trace the structures of the Düsseldorf Art Academy during the National Socialist era. It will be shown that the NS regime was not a 'glitch' in German history, as is demonstrated, on the one hand, by the events surrounding the appointment of Walter Kaesbach as director of the Academy in 1924. On the other hand, the problematic new beginnings of 1945 show that there never was a 'zero hour'.

PRELUDE 1924: WALTER KAESBACH IS APPOINTED DIRECTOR OF THE DÜSSELDORF ART ACADEMY

The controversy surrounding the appointment of a successor to Fritz Roeber, who had died in May 1924, seems to prefigure the events of 1933: an ominous conflict broke out between professors who espoused the tradition-conscious Wilhelmine nationalist ideals and artists with leanings towards 'Modernism' – a clash that would be blown up to monumental proportions under the NS regime.[4]

In the person of Walter Kaesbach (1879–1961) an art historian and museum expert became director of the Academy. After taking his doctorate in 1905 under Georg Dehio, Kaesbach had been employed at the National Gallery in Berlin.[5] During the First World War he saw to it that artist friends of his, including Max Beckmann, Erich Heckel, Anton Kerschbaumer, Heinrich Nauen, and Otto Herbig, served as medical orderlies. As director of the Erfurt City Museum, Kaesbach

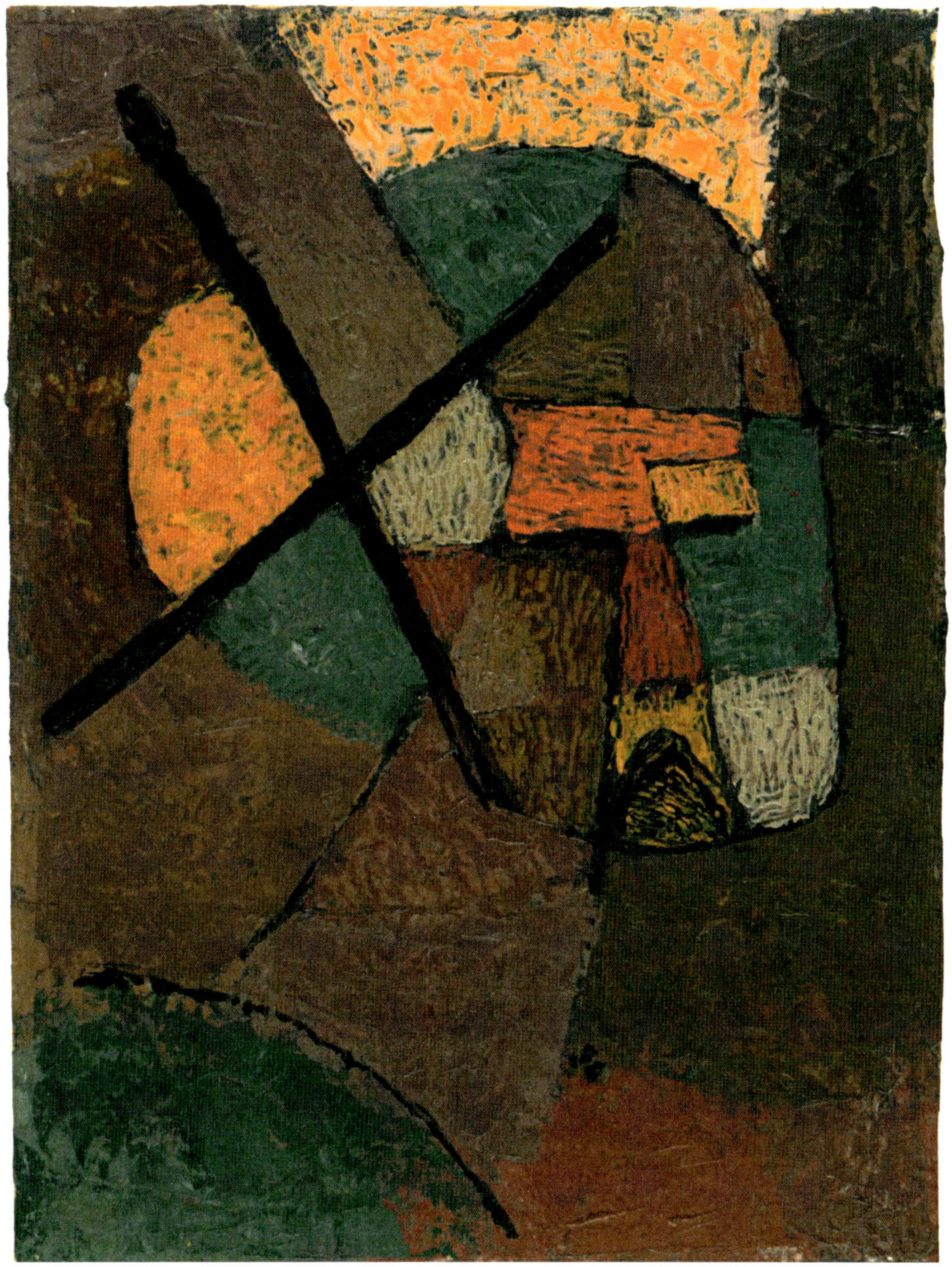

Fig. 2: Paul Klee, Von der Liste gestrichen *[Struck from the List], 1933, oil on paper, 31.5 × 24 cm, Zentrum Paul Klee, Bern*

enthusiastically promoted Expressionist painters and organised exhibitions featuring the work of Wassily Kandinsky, Lyonel Feininger, Erich Heckel, Paul Klee, Karl Schmidt-Rottluff, Otto Mueller, and Max Pechstein. Kaesbach forged close ties with collectors, notably also Jewish patrons of the arts, and with Wilhelm Waetzoldt, later general director of the State Museums in Berlin. From 1920 until 1927 Waetzoldt had been assistant head of the Ministry of Culture, where his responsibilities had included overseeing the Prussian art schools. In that capacity, Waetzoldt had refused to approve the appointment of the painter August Deusser, who had been put forward by the professors at the Düsseldorf Art Academy to succeed Roeber as director.[6] Waetzoldt threw his weight behind the appointment of Kaesbach instead of Deusser, who had been a professor for history painting since 1917. The appointment of Heinrich Nauen, Werner Heuser, Heinrich Campendonk, Paul Klee, Alexander Zschokke, and Ewald Mataré to teach at the Academy clearly attests to a decisive shift towards Modernism, the turnaround Kaesbach had intended (Fig. 3).[7]

In a submission made by Hans Kohlschein, who had been at the Academy since 1921 and was discharged by Kaesbach in 1927, the events of 1924 are described with the intent of denunciation. Kohlschein had become fairly well known in 1902 for a painting entitled *Schlesische Landwehr bei Waterloo* [The Silesian Militia at Waterloo] and later as a war painter. The submission with which Kohlschein sought reinstatement

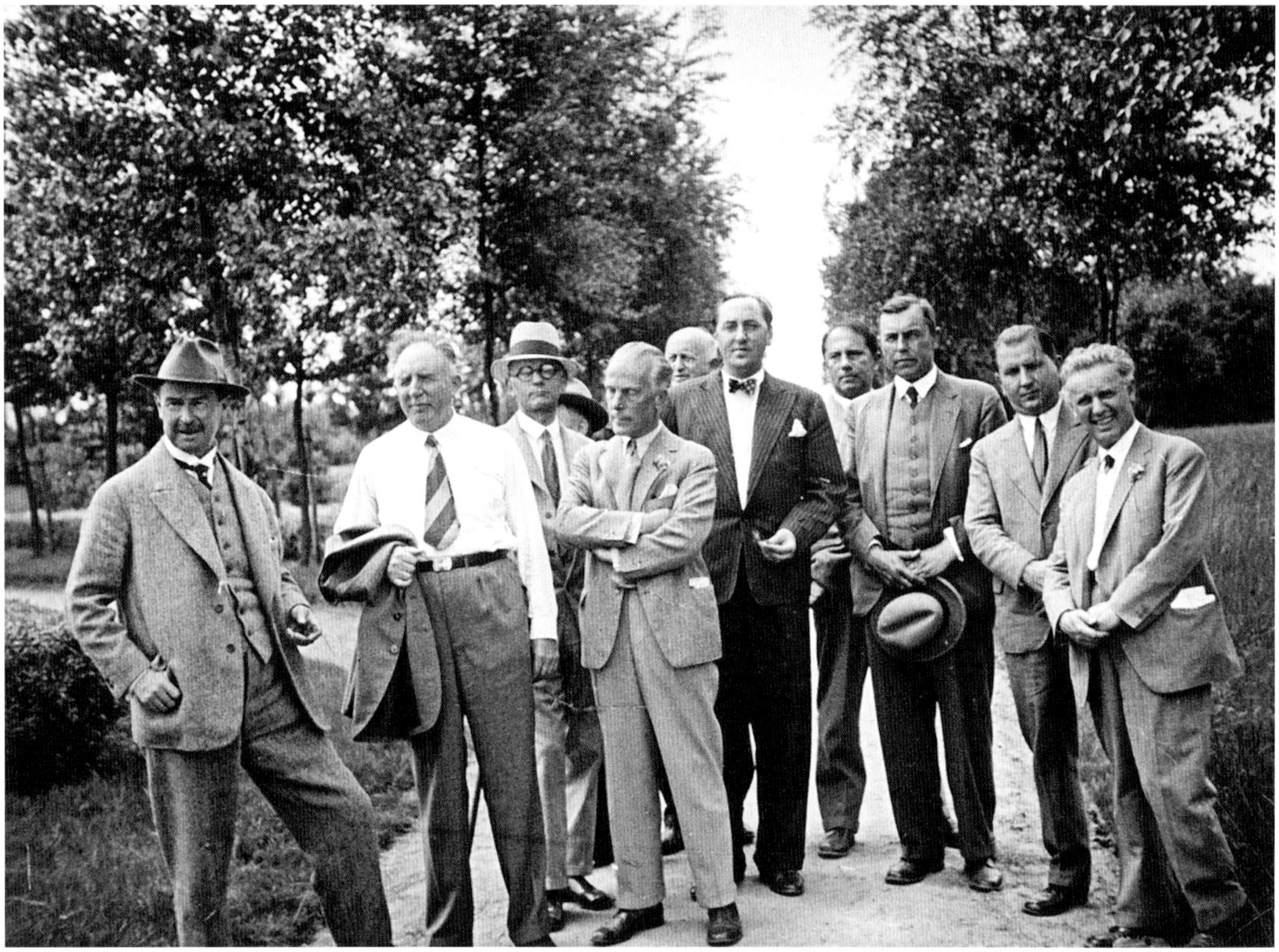

Fig. 3: The Düsseldorf Art Academy teaching staff on Fürstenberg in Xanten, 1928; from left to right: Professors Franz Kiederich, Ernst Albrecht, Wilhelm Schmurr, Walter Kaesbach, Walter von Wecus (left, behind him unknown), Ernst Aufseeser, Heinrich Campendonk, Julius Paul Junghanns, and Wilhelm Herberholz

at the Academy in 1933 describes the appointment of Kaesbach as a hush-hush affair staged during a holiday break at the Academy, in which 'secretly and unbeknownst to the others [professors], former teachers from the municipal Decorative Arts School who had been taken over by the Art Academy travelled to Erfurt [...]. They set out and brought Dr Kaesbach [...] to Düsseldorf as head of the Art Academy.'[8] What matters here is the emphasis on the link between Kaesbach and Waetzoldt, allegedly a Marxist, who ran a 'display window' at the Berlin National Gallery for a 'distorted image of German art' and exhibited with Alfred Flechtheim, the art dealer, who was particularly singled out for defamation and who had sold 'French rubbish' even before the First World War.

The text refers to a submission made to the relevant ministry in 1926, in which Kohlschein and eight other professors stated that they had been unable to work under Kaesbach as director. On the whole, in those conflicts dating back to the 1920s, issues had already emerged which, after Hitler came to power, would culminate in slanderous accusations directed at a 'Kaesbach system': collaboration with Waetzoldt and Flechtheim. Moreover, Kohlschein's petition of 1 April 1933 accuses Kaesbach of 'crimes against the young generation of German art' and closes with the words, 'An end must be made to pinchbeck art ["fake art"]; the left-wing art programme must be dismantled at once [...]. Only thus can German art once again attain its old renown.'[9]

The 'Purge' in 1933 The Düsseldorf Academy in Step with the NS Regime

Dismissals in 1933

'Clean sweep at the Düsseldorf Art Academy. Crimes committed by the Kaesbach system!' roared a headline in the *Volksparole* of 15 March 1933, thus paving the way for a 'purge' at the Academy with propaganda. The article in the paper accused Kaesbach 'of subverting art, of Bolshevism, and of Separatism' and imputed to him 'the spirit of the November

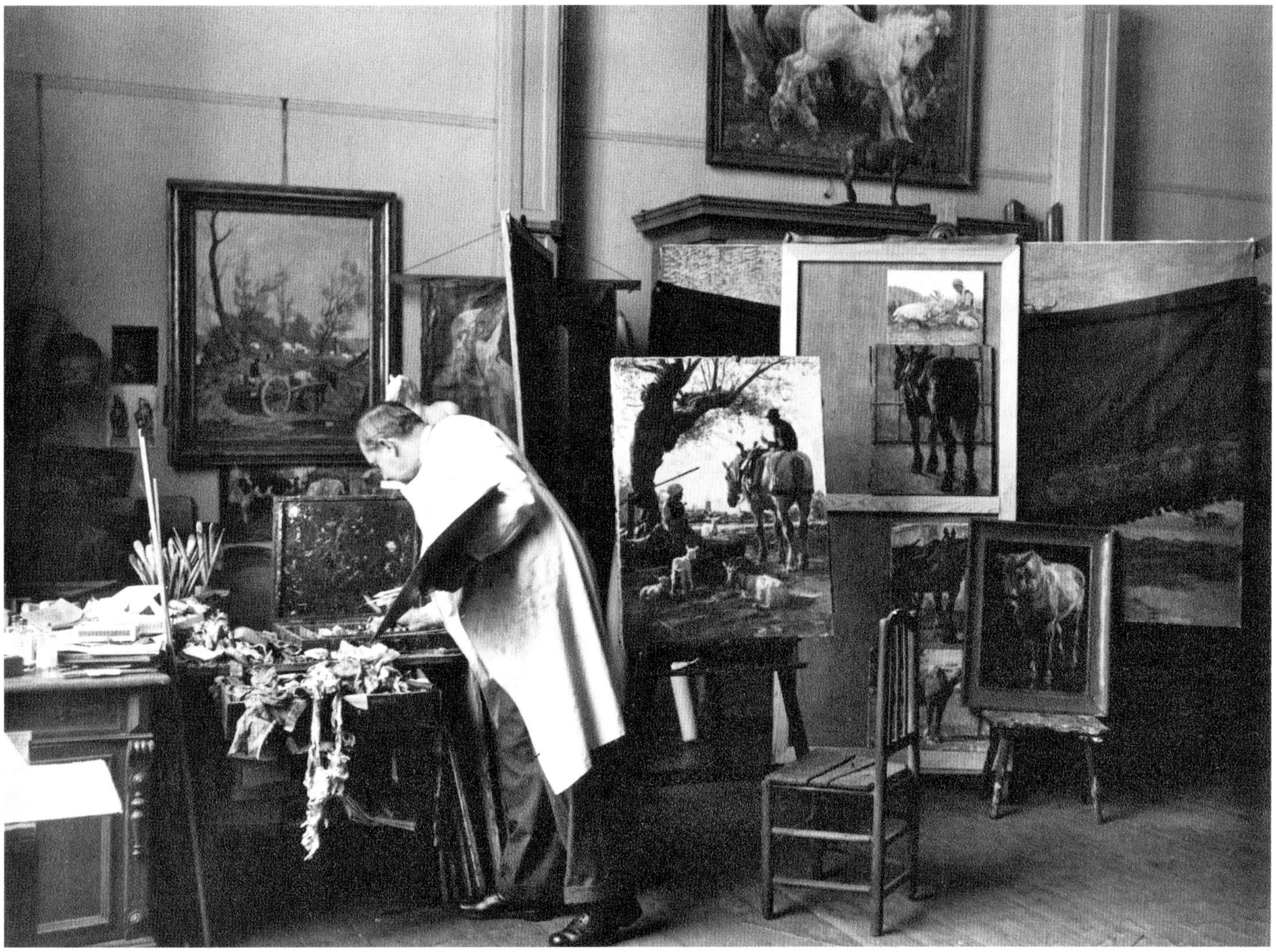

Fig. 4: Julius Paul Junghanns working in his studio at the Düsseldorf Art Academy

criminals'; it spoke of the 'Kaesbach system' and favouritism shown towards Jews and Communists in the appointment of teaching staff. The goal was clearly set out:

'The Third Reich has dawned and in Berlin and everywhere in the Reich cultural stalls are also being mucked out. Now it is high time to settle accounts with Kaesbach, too, and to put a man in his place who will once again make our Düsseldorf Art Academy what it once [...] was: a German art academy, imbued with the German spirit and capable of making genuine German artists out of its disciples, who are so eager to learn.'[10]

It was not long before decisive steps were taken: two weeks after that article in the *Volksparole* a directive was issued on 29 March 1933 by Dr Bernhard Rust, Minister for Science, Art, and Popular Education in Berlin 'to put Kaesbach immediately on leave of absence and to authorise Professor Junghan[n]s as a temporary replacement'.[11]

Thus an outspoken opponent of Kaesbach's[12] was placed in charge of 'purging' the Art Academy in the critical months, a man who proved a willing tool of the National Socialists. A native of Vienna, Julius Paul Junghanns (1876–1958) had, after studying under the Munich animal painter Heinrich von Zügel, been appointed in 1904 to head the class at the Düsseldorf Academy for animal and outdoor painting (Fig. 4). An exponent of 1920s Realism, Junghanns advanced with blood-and-soil motifs he developed out of that style to the status of a leading National Socialist painter.[13]

His role in restructuring the Art Academy can be used as a case study that sheds light on the collaboration between organs of the state and members of the NSDAP. On 31 March 1933 Ludwig Siekmeyer, a former student at the Art Academy, turned up as a member of the National Socialist district leadership – 'Specialist Group for Fine Art, Theatre, and Music for Handling Urgent Issues'[14] – to demand documents from the Academy and the Social Welfare Fund pertaining to the Society of Friends and Promoters as well as the health insurance and the student refectory, all of which Junghanns willingly handed over.

By April 1933 the findings of the NSDAP District Leadership Committee of Inquiry on the dismissal of Academy teachers had been submitted and Junghanns acknowledged them without reservation, reporting them to the district president on 6 April.[15] The upshot was that the Academy was to dismiss the following professors and lecturers: Albrecht, Aufseeser, Budde, Clarenbach, Engelhardt, Grosche, Heuser, Holzmeister, Huber, Klee, Nauen, Rappaport, Simons, Soeder, Thomas, and Zschokke. The reasons given for the desired dismissals are particularly enlightening. Ernst Aufseeser and Paul Klee[16] were found unsuitable because they were of Jewish descent, and Ernst Albrecht was regarded as a Marxist; close links with Walter Kaesbach and Alfred Flechtheim led to Heinrich Nauen's dismissal and being of Swiss origin to Alexander Zschokke's (although he was allowed to remain until 1937). Werner Heuser (not dismissed until 1937) and Maximilian Clarenbach fell victim to 'doubts about their character'. Hans Soeder was classified as unimportant, while the rest were essentially made redundant to save money.

The painter Jankel Adler (1895–1945) was a teacher at the Art Academy and a member of the group of artists who called themselves the Young Rhineland. As a Jew of Polish descent, he had left Düsseldorf for Paris soon after the National Socialists came to power. Another who was served notice was Oskar Moll, who had been director of the Breslau Academy of Arts and Crafts from 1925 until 1932. After it closed down, he became an instructor at the Düsseldorf Art Academy on the basis of emergency regulations but was dismissed immediately when the National Socialists took over the government – the paramount reason was apparently his abstract painting, for which he would later be proscribed as 'degenerate'.

Two further members of the Academy teaching staff who were dismissed in 1933 on the basis of the report of 6 April were Heinrich Campendonk, who had been head of the class for glass and mural painting since 1926, and the sculptor Ewald Mataré, who was hired in 1932,[17] both of them exponents of stances that positioned them close to Expressionism. A flood of denunciations accompanied the slanderous accusations and dismissals, reinforced by unsuccessful attempts made by some artists whom Kaesbach had not appointed to be admitted to the Academy teaching staff.[18]

The art historian Richard Klapheck (1883–1939) was one of the professors dismissed during those months. Klapheck had been a formally appointed teacher at the Academy since mid-1918 and the following year was appointed professor, also assuming the functions of librarian and conservator of the Academy art collections.[19] The Prussian Ministry of Science used the notorious Law for the Reinstitution of Professionals in the Civil Service to justify Klapheck's dismissal on 19 January 1934,[20] but it was evidently preceded by denunciations which forced Klapheck to leave the Academy. The housekeeper of an acquaintance had reported on remarks allegedly made by Klapheck at an evening engagement. On the occasion of that denunciation, allegations of deficiencies in Klapheck's professional conduct made some ten years previously were again tabled.[21]

Appointments 1933/34

The many dismissals were balanced by appointments that would break new ground in reflecting the alignment of the Art Academy with the NS regime and at the same time clearly show how powerful the influence exerted by Berlin really was.[22] Heinrich Reifferscheid (1872–1945) came to the Academy on 1 July 1933.[23] Although Reifferscheid had also been a member of the Berlin Secession since 1898 and had participated in group shows with Lovis Corinth, Max Liebermann, and Max Slevogt, he nonetheless remained true to his original predilection for romantic motifs, as shown, for instance, in his correspondence with Hans Thoma; the NS regime could, therefore, definitely co-opt Reifferscheid's landscape studies.

The appointment of Walter Maria Kersting (1892–1970) followed on 1 October 1933.[24] While employed as a professor at the Cologne Werkschulen (1927–1932), Kersting had designed a radio cabinet which the 1933 Berlin Radio Exhibition presented as a *Volksempfänger* ['people's receiver'] – by 1939 more than twelve million radios of that type would be produced. The appointment of Kersting to the Academy already clearly indicated the political intention of making over the Düsseldorf Academy into an art institute on National Socialist lines.

On 1 October 1933 Franz Radziwill (1895–1983)[25] was appointed to succeed Paul Klee at the Academy. Radziwill's attitude to National Socialism seems quite ambivalent. Two factors seem to have been of paramount importance for the appointment: he joined the Party on 1 May 1933 but also had ties with the Commissioner for the Prussian Ministry of Culture, Bernhard Rust. Radziwill's interests in art, especially his study of Caspar David Friedrich and Dutch painting of the sixteenth to the eighteenth centuries, added to his attractiveness. Moreover, the appointment of Radziwill to the Academy post shows – as is also shown in the case of the painter Werner Peiner – that the late 1920s movement known as Magic Realism definitely resonated with those now in power.[26] In October 1933 Radziwill represented the Art Academy at the Day of German Art in Munich. However, only two years later he was dismissed from the Academy on the grounds that he was 'unfit to teach'.[27] The fact is that art students in Hamburg had found some works dating back to Radziwill's early Expressionist phase, three of which were shown at the exhibition *Entartete Kunst* [Degenerate Art]. In addition, he was subjected to several bans on showing work publicly and they were still valid even after he had been rehabilitated in 1936 by the Reich Ministry for Folk Enlightenment and Propaganda. This state of affairs induced him to step up his commitment to the NS regime: Radziwill worked as an NSDAP functionary in Dangast, where his zeal in denunciation attracted attention. On 15 October 1933 the Art Academy appointed Richard Schwarzkopf[28] (1893–1963), who had been a member of the Young Rhineland since 1919, to teach applied graphic art; he was a man who made a substantial contribution to glorifying the NS regime with woodcuts bearing such lurid titles as *Totentanz der SA* [SA Dance of Death] (1936)[29] and *Deutsche Passion* [German Passion] (1937). Appointed on 1 November 1933 to teach monumental painting, Leo Sebastian Humer (1896–1965)[30] had originally also been close to New Objectivity and had first attracted public notice in 1931 as a fresco painter in the Mariahilfkirche in Bregenz. By May 1934 Humer was showing a large fresco in the Hall of Honour for those who fell in the First World War. For the SA, the SS, and the Hitler Youth he executed vast murals under the aegis of the exhibition *Der Kampf der NSDAP* [The Struggle of the NSDAP] in Düsseldorf (Fig. 5).[31] In 1936 he painted large murals in the NS educational centre Ordensburg Krössinsee, which, however, were overpainted because they were criticised for exaggerated stylisation.

In the person of Edwin Scharff (1887–1955)[32] a sculptor came in November 1933 to the Art Academy whose monumental works were sensational at the time: for the entrance to the Düsseldorf Nordpark, planned since 1936 as part of the *Reichsausstellung Schaffendes Volk* [Reich Exhibition of Productive Folk], he created two *Rossebändiger* [Horse Tamers],

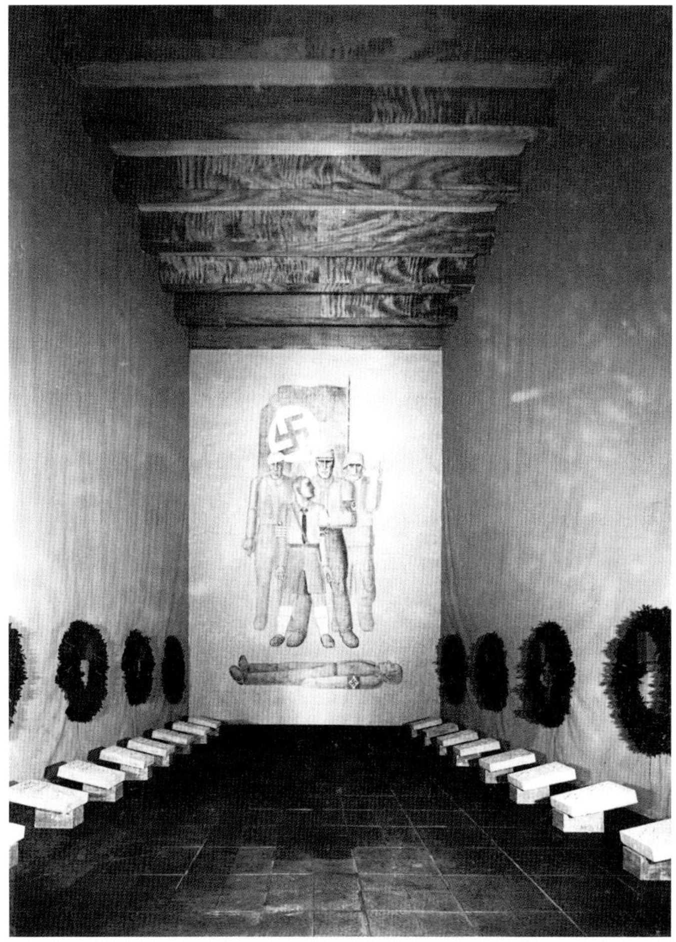

Fig. 5: Leo Sebastian Humer, fresco in the Hall of Honour for those who fell in the First World War from the SA, SS, and Hitler Youth in the exhibition Der Kampf der NSDAP *[The Struggle of the NSDAP], Düsseldorf, 1934*

which caused a scandal, however, because they had not been finished by the time the exhibition opened. When photographs of the *Rossebändiger* were shown at the Munich exhibition *Entartete Kunst* (possibly by mistake), Scharff was forced to leave the Academy in 1938.

The appointments to the Academy made in 1933 and 1934 showed no deviation from the path trodden since Hitler had come to power: in the appointment of Werner Peiner (1897–1984)[33] in 1933 or early in 1934[34] as professor for monumental painting, the Academy took a further step towards meeting NS aesthetic standards. Peiner had tried to give up the post by summer 1934 because of fierce disagreements with Peter Grund (1892–1966), the then Academy director, but the Prussian Ministry for Culture refused to accept his resignation. As a student at the Düsseldorf Art Academy, Peiner had studied history painting with Fritz Roeber and battle painting with Wilhelm Döringer, head of the drawing class. Paul Gerhardt, a restorer who was later employed at the Hermann Göring Meisterschule in Kronenburg, taught Peiner techniques used by the German Old Masters, to whom Peiner felt especially close, despite sporadic forays into New Objectivity.[35] In 1927 Peiner began to create his works on a grand scale, notably tapestries,

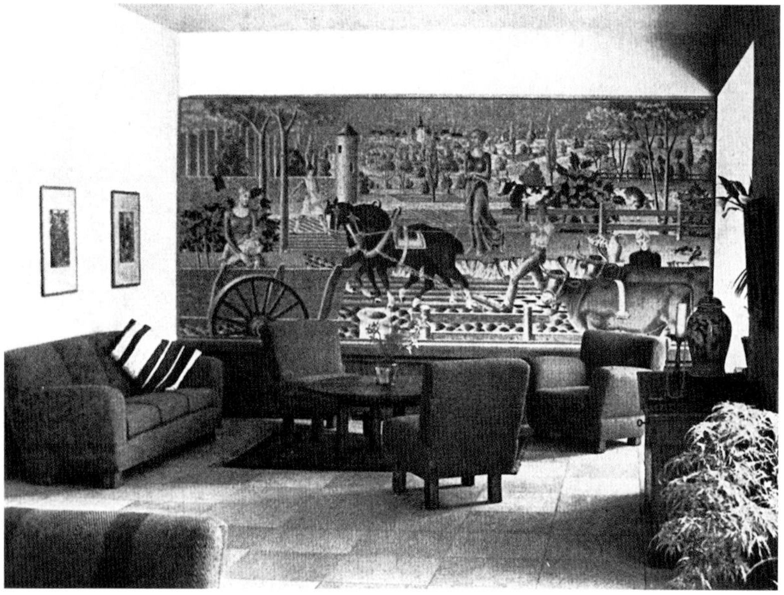

Fig. 6: Werner Peiner, Die drei Lebensalter *[The Three Ages of Man], 1930, tapestry in the home of Walter Kruspig, Hamburg*

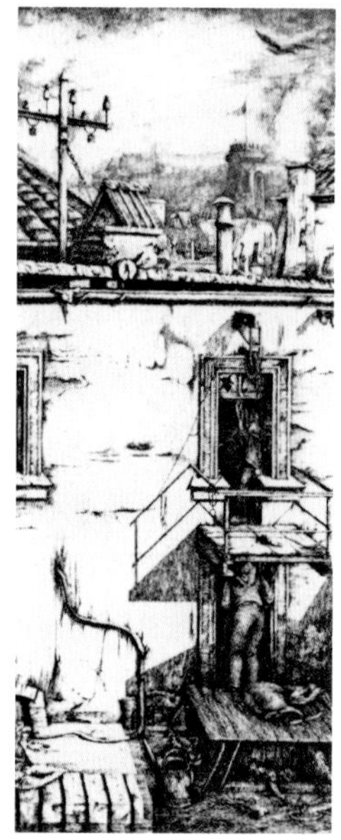

Fig. 7: Otto Coester, Gegenüber/Blick aus dem Atelierfenster *[Opposite/View from the Studio Window], 1935, etching, 30.8 x 13.8 cm*

in a studio in the New Academy in Düsseldorf-Stockum. There he was already collaborating with Emil Gustav Fahrenkamp (1885–1966), who would later become director of the Academy. Peiner designed mosaics as well as murals and tapestries for Fahrenkamp's buildings (Fig. 6).[36]

His 1933 representation of a peasant ploughing his furrow in *Deutsche Erde* [German Soil], which was later 'owned by the Führer', marked Peiner's complete conversion to the *völkisch* blood-and-soil ideology. Thus his career as an artist seamlessly linked the cultural legacy of the Wilhelmine era with propaganda painting in the National Socialist mould.

In 1943 Peiner penned 'Die Malerei und ihre Aufgabe' [Painting and its Mission], a treatise in which he laid out a blueprint for a cult of genius as the term was understood in National Socialist parlance, and attempted to reconcile the Aryan ethnic community as advocated in NS propaganda and the outsider status of the 'genius' by rewarding the loner with a 'leadership role' in the state.[37]

Joining forces with his colleague Julius Paul Junghanns, Peiner had begun by May 1934 to move painting to Kronenburg in the Eifel area at least part of the time.[38] In subsequent years a countryside academy took shape there. Initially a branch of the Düsseldorf Art Academy, it grew in 1937 into the Hermann Göring Meisterschule, with Peiner as its director.

The year 1934 saw the Academy continue to move into alignment with the NS regime, shown, for example, in the hiring of Dr Friedrich E. Haag, a human geneticist who was a member of the SA, as a non-tenured professor 'for the field of race studies' (he was at the Academy from May 1934 until 1940).[39]

Martin Paatz, a painter appointed to teach in January 1934, devoted himself to depicting Lower Rhenish landscapes with a thematic focus on motifs, such as *Pflügender Bauer* [Peasant Ploughing].[40] Other appointments made were those of Otto Coester (professor from 1939) for etching (Fig. 7), Dr Schneider for dramatic theory, the sculptor Josef Sommer for wood carving, and Dr Ing. Döll to teach urban planning.[41]

Appointments made in 1933 and 1934 clearly indicated the integration of the Art Academy in the propaganda machine run by Bernhard Rust. Although this trend was obviously underpinned by the appointment of the architect Peter Grund as director of the Academy on 18 October 1933, that appointment also marked the end of it (for the time being). The letter confirms Grund's 'Chair for architecture [...] and [adds that he is to be] at the same time [entrusted with assuming] temporarily the function of [acting] director of the institution. [...] The appointment is made on condition that you and your spouse are of Aryan descent.'[42]

Over the long history of the Art Academy, painters – with the exception of the art historian Walter Kaesbach – were always named as directors of the institution. In the National Socialist era, on the other hand, things clearly changed, a trend that began with the appointment of Peter Grund and continued in 1937 with the appointment of Emil Gustav Fahrenkamp, another architect, to succeed him. Fahrenkamp was particularly representative of the monumental architecture approved by the state under National Socialism (Fig. 8). The appointment of Grund had in essentials met the requirements of the regime for restructuring the Art Academy as a submission dated 17 May 1933 made by the acting director Junghanns to the Ministry in Berlin had already stated. It was concerned with a change in the Academy charter regarding the choice of directors: 'It goes without saying that the teaching staff of the Düsseldorf State Art Academy must consist of men of a decidedly nationalist

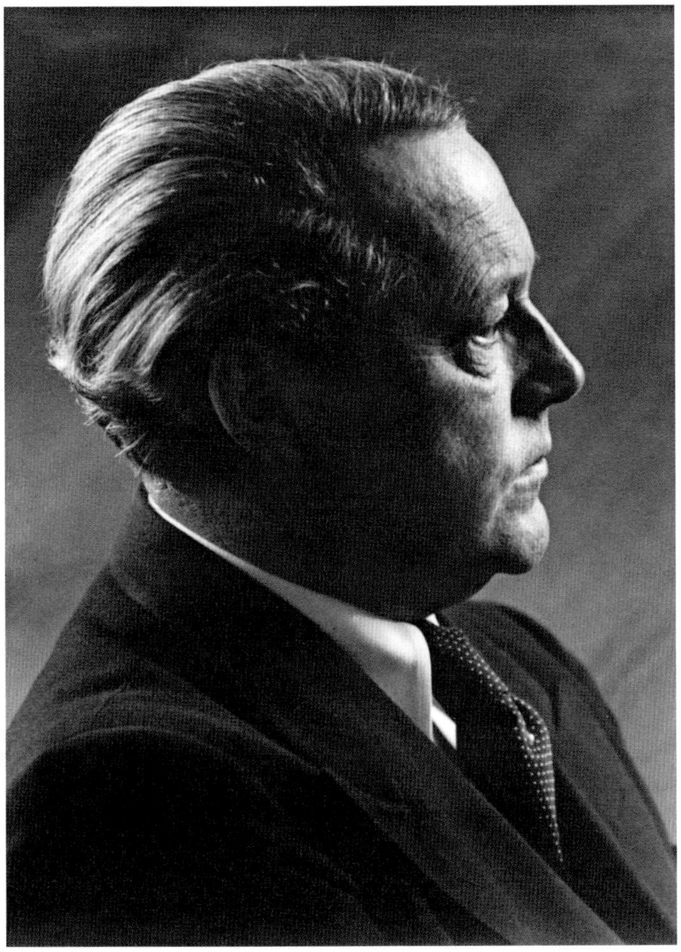

Fig. 8: Portrait of Emil Gustav Fahrenkamp, 1919

persuasion with positive affirmation of the new state and firm resolution to regain an ethnic affinity to a still greater degree than the Düsseldorf Academy was renowned for decades ago.'[43]

Peter Grund's effective commitment became important not only regarding Academy concerns but also for reshaping Düsseldorf in conformity with the National Socialist ideology. It made it possible to interlink the position of Academy director with public service positions such as that of acting regional office director for the Rhineland of the Reich Chamber for Fine Arts, to which Grund was appointed on 18 December 1933.[44] By 5 May 1934 Grund was in a position to open the *Gemeinschaftsausstellung Deutscher Künstler* [Group Show of German Artists], a joint exhibition with *Der Kampf der NSDAP*. Alfred Rosenberg was present.[45] In an article published in the *Volksparole* of 11 April 1934, Grund expatiated on his ideology, describing as his aims 'returning to *Volkstum* [ethnicity] and *Bodenverbundenheit* [closeness to the soil], reforging the broken links to the homeland art tradition, cleanliness in the creation of art and a nationalist cast of mind, subordinating oneself to a collective way of thinking'.[46] For all that, disagreements with the NSDAP about issues of cultural policy led to Grund's dismissal in 1937.

STANCES ADOPTED BY THE DÜSSELDORF ART ACADEMY DURING THE NS ERA

At the very latest the appointment of Emil Gustav Fahrenkamp (1885–1966), an architect, as director in 1937 clearly showed that the Düsseldorf Art Academy was supposed to focus heavily on showy architecture representative of the state, while the Hermann Göring Meisterschule, founded that year in Kronenburg, was to devote itself to monumental painting. Fahrenkamp's activities in particular mirror the continuity of the official Wilhelmine attitude to art in the NS era and how easily that stance accommodated the NS ideology: in 1901 Fahrenkamp had started to work for the Carl Sieben architectural practice in Aachen without having trained as an architect, and in 1909 he transferred as 'head worker' to Wilhelm Kreis's private studio.[47]

In 1911 Fahrenkamp became an instructor at the Düsseldorf Decorative Arts School and, when it was disbanded in 1919, was appointed to a professorship at the Art Academy along with Wilhelm Kreis.

As the years went by, Fahrenkamp became a leading exponent of New Building, as exemplified by his Michel Department Store in Wuppertal, which was built in 1929/30.[48] Between 1930 and 1932 Fahrenkamp realised another important Modernist building, the Shell-Haus [Shell House] in Berlin. After the National Socialists came to power, Fahrenkamp aligned himself with their notions of neo-Classical monumental architecture as represented by the Bayer Atrium in Wuppertal, a sports hall he built in 1937 (in Simonsstraße, now a car dealership).[49] In collaboration with Norbert Demmel, an architect and SS leader, Fahrenkamp built the German Red Cross headquarters in Potsdam, where he replaced a planned pillared portico with a jutting portal supporting a 'Führer balcony' modelled on Albert Speer's stand at the Zeppelinfeld in Nuremberg.

The German House at the 1939 hydraulic engineering trade fair in Liège was built after plans submitted by Fahrenkamp (Figs. 9, 10), a structure typical of National Socialist architecture with a monumental pillared entrance; the national emblem – an eagle with the Swastika in its claws – was the work of Josef (Sepp) Mages, who was appointed to a post at the Academy in 1938.[50]

Fahrenkamp also designed the building that housed the Meisterschule in Kronenburg[51] and participated in a competition to design the North-South Axis in Berlin in 1938.[52]

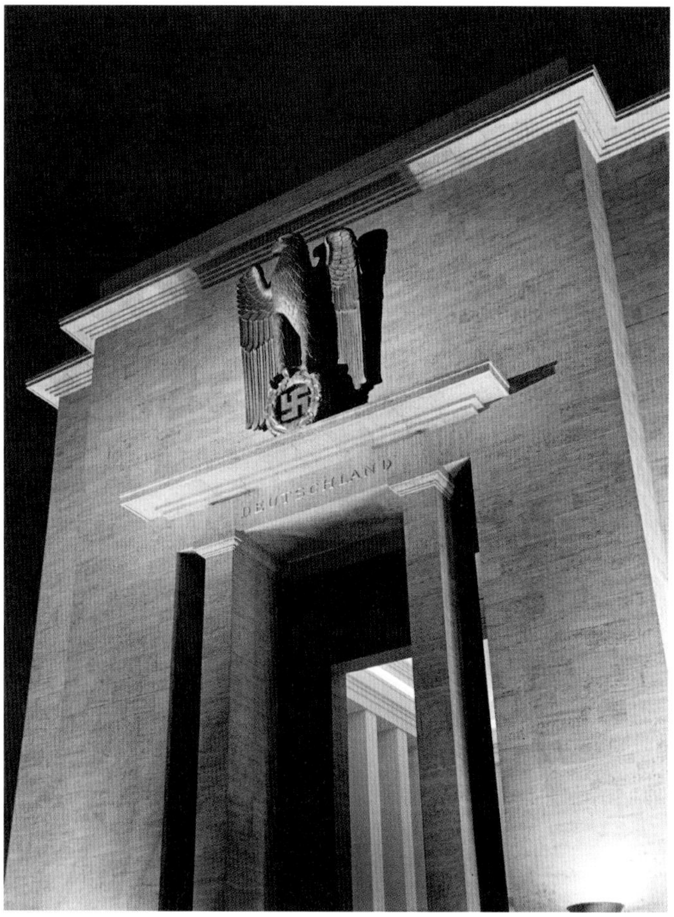

Fig. 9: Emil Gustav Fahrenkamp, the German House, entrance, hydrological engineering trade fair, Liège, 1939, national emblem by Josef (Sepp) Mages

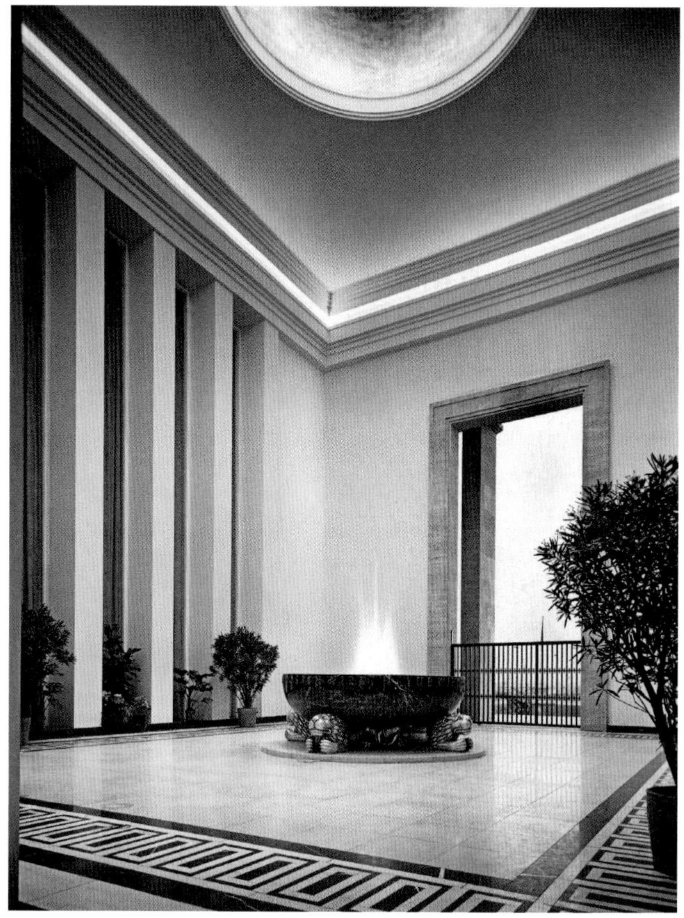

Fig. 10: Emil Gustav Fahrenkamp, the German House, interior, hydrological engineering trade fair, Liège, 1939

In a speech he gave on 29 April 1939 to open the Academy summer term, Fahrenkamp waxed eloquent on architecture and ideology:

'As they have been in politics, all essentially alien elements and influences have been entirely eliminated. The decay of form, which had in part had catastrophic effects, has yielded to a healthy striving for a uniform style. Whereas architecture once believed it could dispense with the other arts, nowadays it has again assumed leadership as the mother of all arts and with a clear conscience makes use of its sister arts [...]. The exhaustive deployment of the fine arts as a whole is essential for the great building projects envisaged by the Third Reich. The arts [...] have also once again become servants to our ethnic community and servants to the new polity in an excellent way. [...] Heading an art school is today more than ever a service to the state [...]; the great task is given to us through the new life in the greater Germany of Adolf Hitler.'[53]

A few activities engaged in by members of the Art Academy during those years illustrate the extent to which those guiding principles of Fahrenkamp's, which must also be interpreted as an academic agenda, were brought closer to realisation. Buildings designed by Rudolf Krüger, a professor of architecture at the Academy from 1939 until 1944, included the Adolf Hitler School in Landstuhl and the Regional Leaders School in Annweiler.[54] Karl Pfeiffer, also an architect, taught at the Academy from 1939 until 1945. The Reich authorities put him in charge of urban planning projects for new towns near Wilhelmshaven and Kiel.[55] Artists working at the Academy were kept busy with commissions for designing memorial sites and monuments in numerous cities and towns for fallen soldiers and SA and SS men who had been killed.

The painters at the Düsseldorf Art Academy were also caught up in glorifying the NS regime. Junghanns showed work regularly at the House of German Art in Munich – some of his paintings were bought by Adolf Hitler and Joseph Goebbels.[56] Hans Schmitz-Wiedenbrück (1907–1944, appointed in 1939) was another Academy painter who expressed his unquestioning allegiance to the regime in 1939 with motifs such as *Bauern im Gewitter* [Peasants in a Thunderstorm] and *Arbeiter, Bauern und Soldaten* [Workers, Peasants, and Soldiers].[57] Leo Sebastian Humer produced works such as *Handgranatenwerfer* [Throwing Hand Grenades], *Ernte* [Harvest], and *Vesper* [Evening Prayer], also in 1939.[58] Similarly, Werner Peiner was listed in 1937 as a member of the Prussian Academy of the Arts, three years later as a Prussian councillor of state, and finally from 1944 as an 'irreplaceable artist'.[59] The paintings

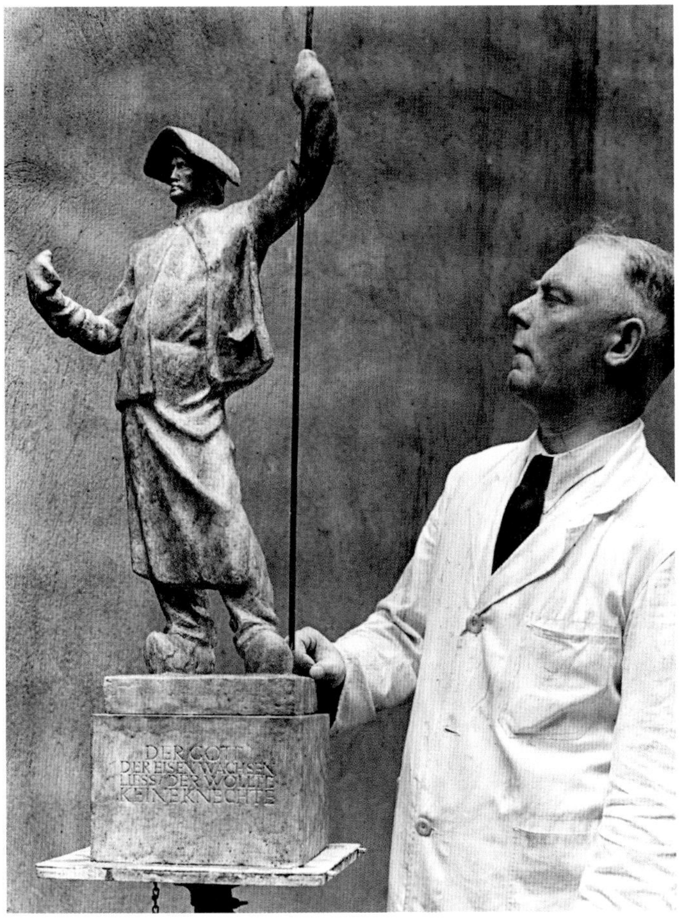

Fig. 11: Joseph Enseling with the model for the sculpture Der Eisenhüttenmann *[Man from the Ironworks], 1940*

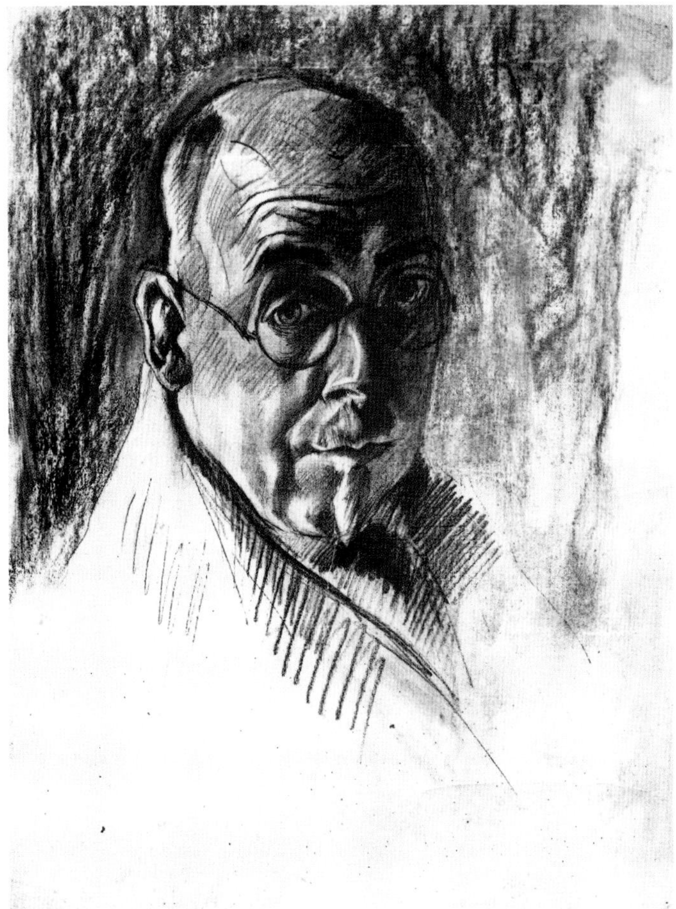

Fig. 12: Heinrich Nauen, self-portrait, c. *1927, black chalk, 61.1 × 45.2 cm, Kunstmuseum Bonn*

done by Heinrich von Richthofen (1889–1986, appointed to the Academy in 1938), who had earned a reputation for portraits and markedly veristic landscapes, fitted in perfectly with what had by then become the established Art Academy concept.

In 1938 Joseph (Sepp) Mages and Joseph Enseling were appointed to teach sculpture (Fig. 11). Mages had even studied with Richard Riemerschmid in Munich. He designed *[Sports]Kameraden* [Comrades (in Sports)], a sculptural group in travertine, for the 1936 Berlin Olympia Park. Designed to be viewed from a distance, it depicts two heroic male figures, which still stand south of the Maifeld sports green. By the latter years of the NS era, the archaising style represented here by Mages, which emulates the military monuments erected after the First World War, was no longer important.[60]

Mages had stood out with bronze statuary such as *Große Stehende* [Large Standing Figures], a sculpture he produced in 1932 that differs stylistically from the sculpture Mages did in 1925 for the Baedeker House in Essen, which is reminiscent of Ernst Barlach, and instead is more in the classical mould. This style also informed the works Enseling produced in the 1930s, such as his 1935 bronze statue of *Säerin* [Woman Sowing] on the grounds of the Margarethenhöhe estate in Essen. A stance which in this work had come to represent a world view, and, moreover, one also represented by Kolbe, it was definitely reconcilable with the aesthetic espoused by the NS regime and so Enseling was appointed in 1938 to teach at the Düsseldorf Art Academy.[61]

Heinrich Nauen, who had studied at the Art Academy in 1898 and had been made a professor of painting there in 1921, managed to keep his post until 1937 (Fig. 12). His painting revealed the influence of Van Gogh and the Expressionists – that led in 1937 to his works being shown at the *Entartete Kunst* exhibition and, in 1939, to his dismissal, allegedly 'at his own request'.[62] Paul Bindel, professor of painting at the Art Academy since 1920, held a lavish retrospective of his works on the occasion of the 1936 Olympic Games in Berlin.[63]

THE ART ACADEMY AND 1930S CULTURAL LIFE IN DÜSSELDORF

The *Düsseldorfer Nachrichten* of 20 March 1934 reported on a forthcoming 'restructuring of the Düsseldorf exhibition scene',[64] to be carried out jointly by the city and the Art Academy. Two exhibitions demonstrate how closely cultural life was brought into line with the NS regime: from May to July 1934 the Kunstpalast in the Ehrenhof hosted the propaganda spectacular *Der Kampf der NSDAP*, which included work by

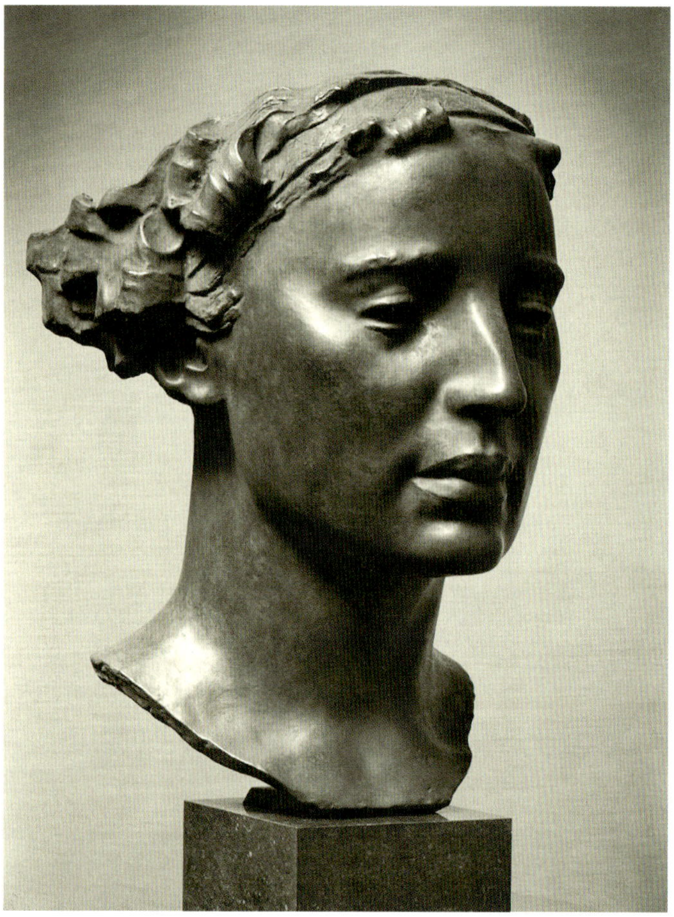

Fig. 13: Hans Rompel, Kopf eines jungen Mädchens *[Head of a Young Girl], 1940, bronze*

Academy artists. It ran at the same time as the *Gemeinschaftsausstellung Deutscher Künstler*, curated by Peter Grund, then director of the Academy.[65]

With the full thrust of its agenda aimed at modern art, *Meister und Schüler* [Masters and Pupils] opened at the Academy on 12 January 1936, an exhibition which – as the *Volksparole* wrote – was committed to the idea of the medieval stonemasons' guild and communal work as opposed to 'overdone artistic individuality'.[66] In January 1937 the Kunstverein [Art Association] mounted the retrospective *Julius Paul Junghanns*, thus showcasing a leading exponent of the art that was now trendsetting, an artist who masterfully demonstrated a seamless continuity devoid of 'modern' influences between the painting of the Wilhelmine era and the art of the NS period.[67]

The National Socialist propaganda also appropriated Peter von Cornelius, who had been director of the Academy in 1819 after it had been refounded. In the *Jahresbericht der Staatlichen Kunstakademie Düsseldorf 1937/38* [Annual Report of the Düsseldorf Art Academy 1937/38], it says Cornelius had been 'the driving force behind rebuilding the Academy on the basis of the creative development of strongly artistic personalities with the aim of laying the groundwork for a national art'.[68] In 23 September 1933 there had been a Cornelius memorial exhibition at the Art Academy,[69] which was followed up in 1936 by the endowment of a Cornelius Prize by the Academy. Each year thereafter the Art Academy would always reveal the name of the prizewinner on 26 May, the anniversary of the court martial of Albert Leo Schlageter, the leader of the voluntary paramilitary Freikorps and his execution by the French occupying forces on the Golzheimer Heath, a man revered as a 'martyr' by the NS regime and the city of Düsseldorf in particular. The prize, which had been sponsored by the city since 1939, continued to be awarded until 1943 (and after the endowment was renewed, from 1948 until 1967).[70]

Thus the Art Academy became closely linked with the growing trend towards advertising Düsseldorf as the 'Schlageter city' – as early as May 1933 there had been a number of events commemorating the leader of the Freikorps: a memorial exhibition at the Historical Museum and the unveiling of a bust of Schlageter at the District Court as well as festivals hosted on several occasions by various National Socialist associations and fireworks displays, called Schlageter Fire, set off by the Hitler Youth.[71] In Düsseldorf director Peter Grund took a particularly active part in designing Schlageter memorial sites.

In 1936 Grund built a house of his own in the Düsseldorf Schlageter estate. Two years later he redesigned the Schlageter Grove.[72] Those urbanistic measures taken in Düsseldorf-Golzheim were all directly associated with planning for the exhibition *Schaffendes Volk* [Productive Folk] – mounted in the area which is now the Nordpark – one of the largest grandstanding events to have been put on by the NS regime. Peter Grund curated it until he was replaced in 1937 by Fahrenkamp in this function as in all others.[73] In his capacity as NSDAP Consultant for Urban Planning (1935–1937) Peter Grund was actively involved in projects for restructuring Düsseldorf: modelled on Berlin, a court garden radiating out from coordinate axes with numerous buildings on a grand scale, including a town hall and the Schlageter Hall on the Rhine embankment, was to be built at the centre of the city.[74] Grund's contribution to those plans was designing an opera house.

The festivities celebrating Hitler's fiftieth birthday took place in Düsseldorf with the Art Academy weighing in heavily, notably with a torchlight procession in the garden of the Malkasten [Paint Box] Association and speeches by Fahrenkamp and Schwarzkopf.[75] On that occasion, the Art Academy presented Hitler with the bronze cast of *Kopf eines jungen Mädchens* [Head of a Young Girl], a work by Hans Rompel, an Academy student (Fig. 13).[76]

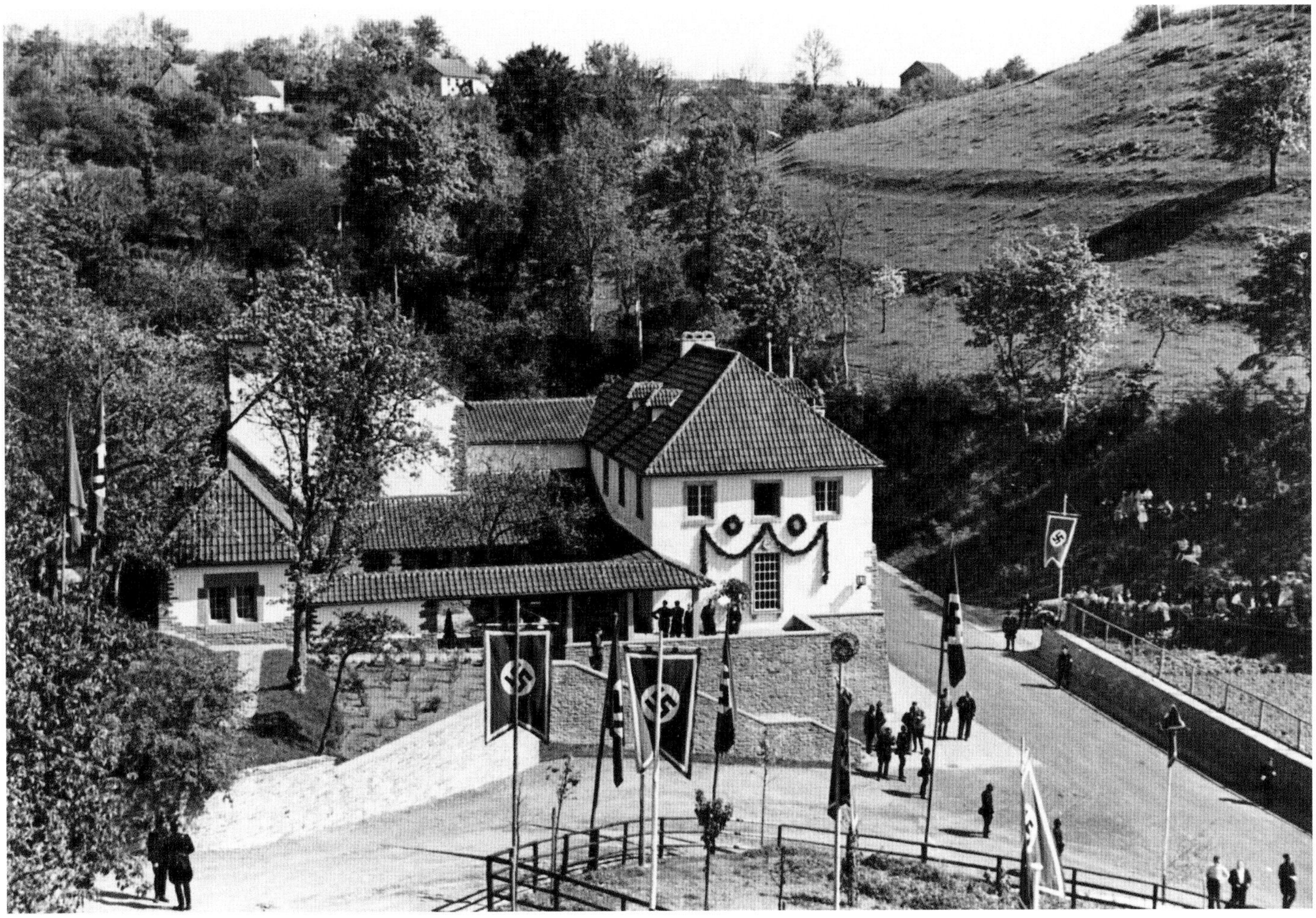

Fig. 14: Hermann Göring Meisterschule in Kronenburg, the day it was inaugurated, 9 June 1938

THE HERMANN GÖRING MEISTERSCHULE AT KRONENBURG IN THE EIFEL

Werner Peiner had lived in Kronenburg since the early 1930s. In the nineteenth century the village had attracted painters, including Johann Wilhelm Schirmer (1807–1863) and Carl Friedrich Lessing (1808–1880). Emil Fahrenkamp bought a farmstead there, which he decorated and furnished in the 'Old German style'.[77] After preparing for the move in 1934, Peiner – along with his colleague Julius Paul Junghanns – transferred their class to Kronenburg the following year.

Walter Kruspig, director general of Deutsche Shell AG, for whom Fahrenkamp had designed a pioneering building in Berlin, was the crucial connection for arranging a meeting with Hermann Göring. In his capacity as premier of Prussia, Göring instigated the founding of a Country Academy in Kronenburg, which grew into the Herman Göring Meisterschule in 1937[78] (Figs. 14, 15). Although the Country Academy was still associated with the Düsseldorf Art Academy for a one-year probationary period, the two institutions were beginning to go their separate ways by spring 1936 with instructions from Göring to the Reich Ministry for Science, Education, and Popular Education to detach Peiner's class from the Art Academy.[79]

The autonomy of the Kronenburg institution was based on a decree issued by Göring in connection with the binding Intellectual Charter of the Hermann Göring Meisterschule for Painting, which prescribed a strict hierarchy borrowed from the workshop concept with apprentice, journeyman, master-class pupil, and master grades. A 'political certificate of clearance' and the oath of allegiance to Führer and Reich were admission requirements.[80]

The scope of artist training offered at the Hermann Göring Meisterschule was enlarged by the work of Hans Zieher in the field of miniature painting and, from 1937, by courses given by Joseph Zimmermann, an art historian. So-called community evenings for art history studies focused on subjects related to fifteenth- and sixteenth-century Dutch and German painting, and medieval manuscript illustration – with guest lectures given by Alfred Stange, a Bonn art historian – as well as Gothic architecture.[81]

In 1938 the Meisterschule studios began to work on numerous highly important state commissions, such as a tapestry cycle depicting 'fateful German battles' for Hitler's new Reich Chancellery, allegories of the 'female virtues' for the Munich Führer building, and tapestries depicting 'pageants of the planets' for Carinhall, Göring's residence.[82]

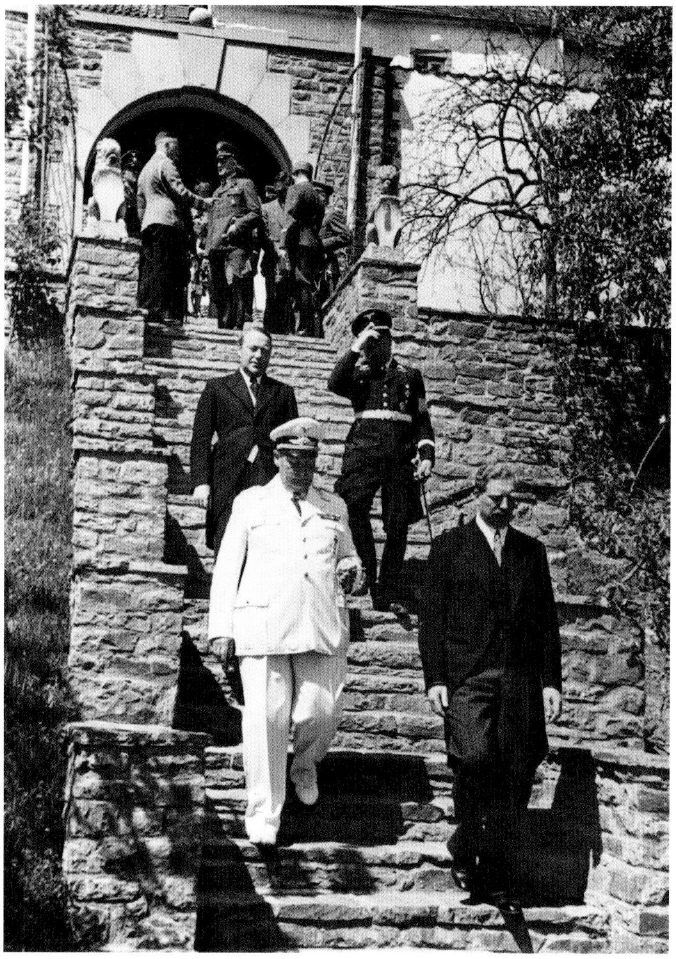

Fig. 15: The inauguration of the Hermann Göring Meisterschule in Kronenburg, 9 June 1938. Descending the stairs: Emil Fahrenkamp, Hermann Göring, and Werner Peiner

In 1943 Albert Speer initiated the founding of a tapestry factory in Wriezen on the Oder (north-east of Berlin), where tapestries designed by Werner Peiner for the buildings of Germania, the projected future Reich capital, were to be woven.[83]

After 1945 most graduates of the Hermann Göring Meisterschule remained in art-related professions, receiving commissions mainly for murals, glass windows, or mosaics. Worth mentioning in this connection is Willi Sitte, a painter who studied for only one year (1940) in Kronenburg yet succeeded in continuing to use the monumental style he was taught there to great effect – especially for commissions he received in the GDR.[84] In the Federal Republic Heinz Hindorf, another former student at the Meisterschule, was showered with offers in the field of ecclesiastical glass painting.[85]

THE ART ACADEMY IN THE SECOND WORLD WAR

A photograph in the Düsseldorf Municipal Archives shows students clad in Wehrmacht uniforms drawing a fighter pilot at the Academy (Fig. 16). The following explanatory text accompanies the picture: 'Men in grey uniforms have been given special leave in order to complete their diploma work in painting, sculpture, or architecture. After passing their examinations, they return to the Front. With the seriousness that is integral to being an artist, here they are working on the artistic representation of a fighter pilot' (Fig. 17).[86]

A patriotic exhortation spoken in the era of the Wars of Liberation by Peter von Cornelius, who refounded the Academy, was used during the Second World War as morale-boosting slogans: 'Onwards, then, you noble German heroic youth, a new virile race! [...] We shall fight a joyous battle, and a victorious banner waves before us. Does it matter if we fall? Beneath palm trees one breathes one's last breath exulting in freedom.'[87]

Both students and teaching staff from the Academy took active part in the war. As highlighted by a document dated 5 February 1943, Bindel, Felbecker, Isenmann, Humer, Klonk, Schwarzkopf, Spindler, and Vahle all served with the Wehrmacht.[88] Wilhelm Schmurr travelled to Belgium and France in May 1942 'for the purpose of cultural services to the Wehrmacht'.[89] When Clarenbach tried in spring 1944 to be transferred for health reasons attested in a doctor's report to work with a student group in Altastenberg in the Sauerland, Finger, the senior government official responsible, at first rejected his petition. The reason for the rejection given in the report sent to the district president on 9 May 1944 (as curator of the State Art Academy) was characteristic: 'The necessity of strongly upholding morale as a defensive front against the enemy terror from the air' and the avoidance of 'appear[ing] to seek to dodge the terror from the air'.[90]

A roll of the dead in the annual Academy reports for the years 1941 to 1944 lists twenty-six members of the Academy as fallen or killed in air raids.[91]

A British air raid damaged the Academy buildings on 1 August 1942; the east tract was gutted by another air raid on 12 June 1943. Heavy strafing on 23 April 1944 caused a lot more damage.[92] Artillery fire set the Art Academy building on fire on 14 and 21 March 1945 (Fig. 18). The bridge over the Rhine was blown up on 3 March 1945 following artillery shelling, leaving the Academy building on the front line – it was used as barracks for soldiers and as a weapons and munitions depot. Fahrenkamp had the Academy administrative office moved to Haan on 7 March.

After the Air Defence had set up a machine-gun battery on the roof, the Academy building was heavily bombed with

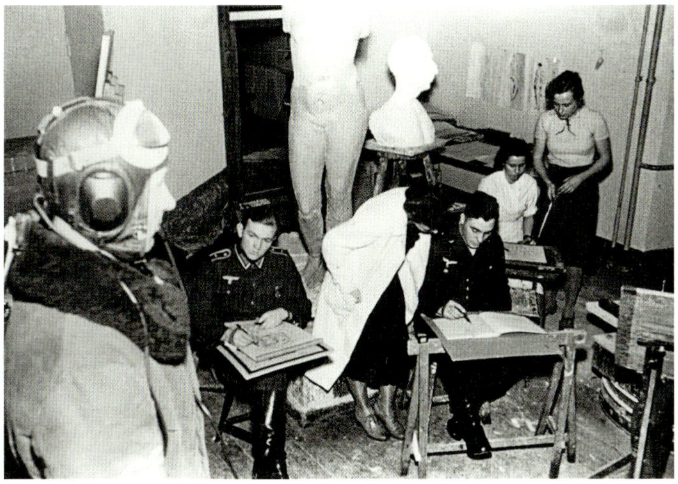

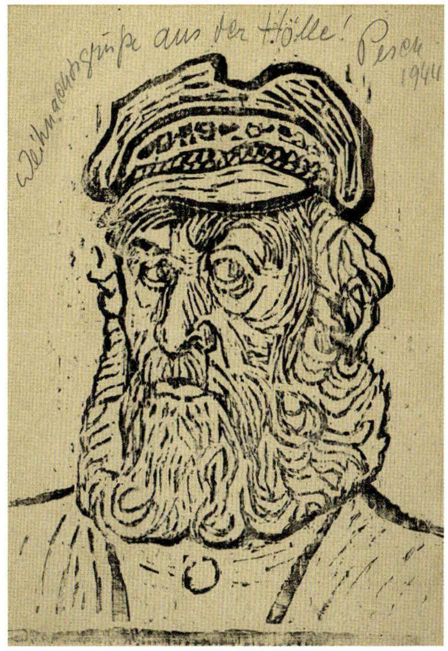

Fig. 16: Students at the Düsseldorf Art Academy on leave, April 1940

Fig. 17: Otto Pankok, Weihnachtsgrüße aus der Hölle! *[Christmas Greetings from Hell!], 1944, woodcut, 32.1 × 22.7 cm, Stadtmuseum Düsseldorf*

incendiary grenades on 14 March. Even though the fire that broke out caused particularly severe damage to the central tract, the caretaker and the stoker managed to prevent further damage. With great effort, personnel managed to safeguard the records and parts of the library. By that time none of the professors seems to have been living in the city.[93]

Nonetheless, what was happening did not keep Academy artists from continuing to work on the lines approved by the NS regime. To take just one example, Paul Bindel painted *Alte Kriegsandenken* [Old War Souvenirs] – a drum, tobacco pipe, and plume of feathers in the Prussian manner – which trivialised war when one considers the horrors of that time.[94] Junghanns carried on with his usual serial motifs, painting pictures such as *Frühlingsabend* [Spring Evening] and *Sich kratzende Kuh* [Cow Scratching Itself], both exhibited in 1944.[95]

DENAZIFICATION AND NEW BEGINNINGS

On 17 April 1945 American troops entered Düsseldorf after encountering no local resistance – the Second World War had ended for Düsseldorf and a crucial phase of restructuring began for the Art Academy. Fahrenkamp requested the governor of the North Rhine provinces for a discharge.[96] Three decisive developments in parallel shaped the new beginnings of the Art Academy in the months that followed: reconstruction, the struggle to determine the future course the Academy was to take, and the denazification process.

A specialist committee for reconstruction headed by Fahrenkamp and Monerjan, an architect in charge of the building site, coordinated the measures to be taken. Subsequent years saw what were known as construction troops hard at work: before taking up their studies, students spent an entire term removing rubble and helping with the reconstruction work. Deployments of this kind were kept up until the Currency Reform in 1948, which provided the first funding for hiring construction workers.[97]

Following the example of Cologne, Bonn, and Göttingen Universities, a consultative council was formed at the request of the Academy teaching staff, in this case a so-called triumvirate, composed of Professors Joseph (Sepp) Mages, Franz Kiederich, and Walter von Wecus, with Otto Coester and Werner Heuser as 'surrogate members'. The provincial governor was asked by the consultative council to reinstate Ewald Mataré so that he could become director of the Academy.[98]

According to entries in his diary, Mataré envisaged the restructuring of the Art Academy as a 'revolution' – the general outline of those ideas, particularly with regard to opening up the Academy admissions policy, would resurface two decades later in his pupil Joseph Beuys. To eliminate the possibility of adherents of the NS regime being present in the student body, Mataré proposed admitting students as young as fourteen years old. Mataré made a point of objecting to professors tainted by National Socialism staying on at the Academy and advocated dismissing the entire staff. That suggestion, however, met with fierce opposition from the professors.[99] At a session held on 28 November 1945, Mataré's proposals were rejected as 'impracticable' by the consultative council because they represented 'destroying the venerable institution that is the Academy'.[100] In rejecting Mataré's plans, the district governor also applied the Royal Academy charter of 24 November 1831 because it prescribed that changes to the orientation of the Academy had to be approved by the curator.[101]

Early in January 1946 the consultative council unanimously proposed Werner Heuser, who had been teaching at the Academy again since 1945, as director. Remaining in office until 1949, Heuser was instrumental in overseeing the new beginnings of the Art Academy.[102] The replacement of Mataré and

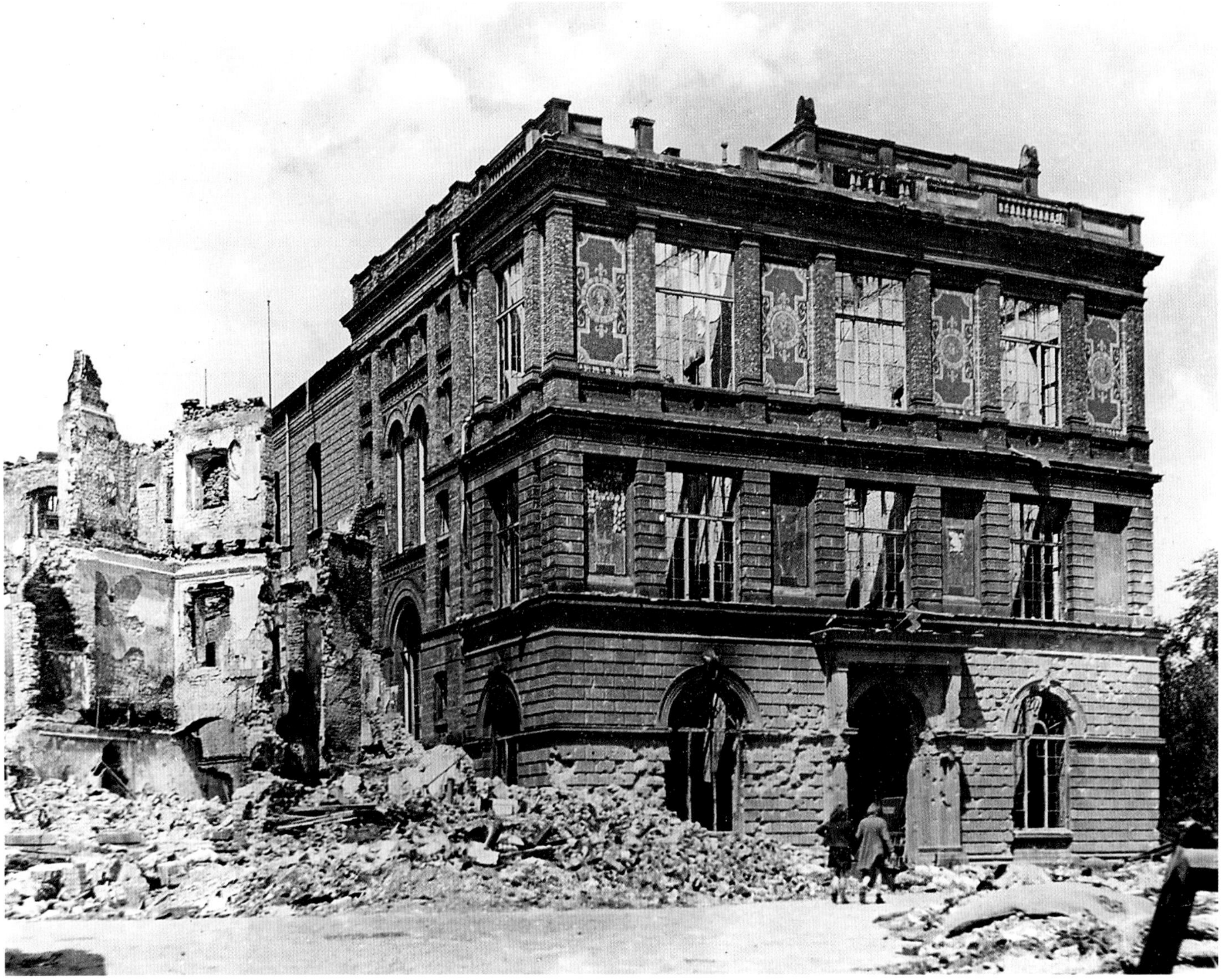

Fig. 18: The condition of the Düsseldorf Art Academy in 1946

the appointment of Heuser were evidently the legal prerequisites for teaching to begin again at the Academy on 23 January 1946 and for the institution to be reinaugurated on 31 January 1946.[103]

Although the questionnaire which had been part of the denazification process mandated by the Potsdam Conference had been evaluated by 22 October 1945, negotiations lasted until 19 December of that year.[104] A so-called A-list contained the names of professors who were no longer acceptable: Clarenbach, Junghanns, Schwarzkopf, and Humer as well as the glass painter Erhardt Klonk and the sculptor Hermann Isenmann.[105] The names on the B-list were those of professors who, according to the commission, should remain at the Academy. Even though almost all of them had been classified as Party members, no activity, or only very little activity, for the NSDAP on their part was certified. The Commission even attested to an apolitical stance in the case of Joseph Enseling although his membership of the Party and his activity as a 'supporting member of the SS' are mentioned.[106] A denazification committee was not instituted at the Academy until May 1946, when it was authorised by Lieutenant Colonel Walker, a member of the military government. Professors Heuser, Coester, and Mataré as well as two members of the district denazification commission sat on the Academy committee.[107]

In 1948 the class taught by Otto Pankok, a painter who had been appointed the previous year, stood out in particular for rebelling against the professors with a National Socialist past who still remained at the Academy. In this revolt against the reverberations of the National Socialist past lie crucial forces for good that would lead the Art Academy to an unencumbered future.

NOTES

1 Back in 1932 Klee painted *Maske mit drei Zähnen* [Mask with Three Teeth] (watercolour on oil varnish ground on paper on cardboard, 50 × 35 cm, UK private collection, catalogue of works no. 5911), which, however, shows the eyes wide open.
2 Carola Giedion-Welcker, *Paul Klee*, Stuttgart 1954, p. 45.
3 Robert Scholz, 'Kunstgötzen stürzen', in: *Deutsche Kultur-Wacht*, H. 10, Berlin 1933, p. 5.
4 For the 1920s at the Düsseldorf Art Academy, see Anna Klapheck, 'Die "goldnen" zwanziger Jahre. Die Akademie zwischen den beiden Kriegen', in: Eduard Trier (ed.), *Zweihundert Jahre Kunstakademie Düsseldorf*, Düsseldorf 1973, pp. 147–160.
5 Christoph Bauer and Barbara Stark (eds.), *Walter Kaesbach. Mentor der Moderne*, exhib. cat. Singen/Konstanz, Lengwil am Bodensee 2008.
6 August Deusser (1870–1942) began as a traditionally minded history and military painter but took up some ideas from Max Liebermann's outdoor painting and was a co-founder of the Sonderbund in 1909. See Klara Drenker-Nagels (ed.), *August Deusser. Leben und Werk*, Cologne 1995, pp. 11–61.
7 Klapheck (see n. 4).
8 Landesarchiv NRW Abteilung [Dept] Rheinland – BR 1012 No. 2, Bl. [fol.] 229.
9 Landesarchiv NRW Abteilung [Dept] Rheinland – BR 1012 No. 2, Bl. [fol.] 232.
10 Landesarchiv NRW Abteilung [Dept] Rheinland – BR 1012 No. 2, Bl. [fol.] 236.
11 Ibid., Bl. [fol.] 237; followed two days later, on 31 March 1933, by the official statement made by the chief of the Düsseldorf police. His report did not, however, suffice to clear Kaesbach of suspicion: 'Nothing has been ascertained to confirm the accusations made against the former director [of the Art Academy], Dr Kaesbach, concerning political activity of a Bolshevist or separatist tendency.' The above-mentioned submission of 21 March 1933 made by Kohlschein was addressed to both the district president and Minister Rust: ibid., Bl. [fol.] 227.
12 In August 1932 Junghanns had made two submissions to the district government because of serious disagreements with Kaesbach: Landesarchiv NRW Abteilung [Dept] Rheinland – BR 1021 No. 39.
13 Reinhard Müller-Mehlis, *Die Kunst im Dritten Reich*, 2nd edn, Munich 1977, p. 182; for the honours, see Reinhard Merker, *Die bildenden Künste im Nationalsozialismus*, Cologne 1983, p. 306.
14 Two letters written by Junghanns to the district president: Landesarchiv NRW Abteilung [Dept] Rheinland – BR 1021 No. 39, Bl. [fols.] 217f.; Junghanns reported the return of the documents on 3 April 1933: Landesarchiv NRW Abteilung [Dept] Rheinland – BR 1021 No. 39, Bl. [fol.] 222; Ludwig Siekmeyer worked as an art teacher at the Ernst Kalkuhl Gymnasium [higher secondary school] after the war and taught the young Jörg Immendorff: http://www.ernst-kalkuhl-internat.de/55.html (last retrieved 14 September 2015). In 1963 Siekmeyer persuaded Immendorff's parents to send their son to the Düsseldorf Art Academy after he had passed the Mittlere Reife [equivalent to GCSE examinations].
15 Landesarchiv NRW Abteilung [Dept] Rheinland – BR 1021 No. 39, Bl. [fols.] 240–243; see Werner Alberg, in: Stadtmuseum Düsseldorf (ed.), *Düsseldorfer Kunstszene 1933–1945*, exhib. cat. Düsseldorf 1987, pp. 37–145, here: pp. 37–41.
16 Landesarchiv NRW [Dept] Abteilung Rheinland – BR 1021 No. 39, Bl. [fol.] 242: Klee 'is regarded as a Jew and impossible and superfluous'.
17 Mataré's probationary period ended on 1 October 1933: Landesarchiv NRW Abteilung [Dept] Rheinland – BR 1021 No. 39, Bl. [fol.] 370.
18 Alberg (see n. 15), p. 39 refers to the (for the most part unpublished) writings of the painter Carl Lauterbach.
19 Landesarchiv NRW Abteilung [Dept] Rheinland – LA 55854 I Bl. [fols.] 1, 28; previously since 1910 supply teacher at the Düsseldorf Decorative Arts School: ibid., Bl. [fol.] 68.
20 Ibid., Bl. [fols.] 70/71; see Bl. [fol.] 34 dated 16 April 1934 with the change in the justification now according to § 6 [simplification of administration] instead of § 4 [previous political activity as the reason for dismissal].
21 Landesarchiv NRW Abteilung [Dept] Rheinland – LA 55854 I Bl. [fols.] 35–39; Ludwig Siekmeyer also had a hand in this denunciation: Landesarchiv NRW Abteilung [Dept] Rheinland – LA 55854 II Bl. [fol.] 12; in subsequent years Klapheck tried in vain to be reinstated.
22 Bernhard Rust should be particularly mentioned in this connection. A partisan of Hitler's of many years' standing, Rust was commissioner for the Prussian Ministry of Culture in 1933/34 and from 1934 Reich minster for Science, Education, and Popular Education. Acting in that capacity, he applied the Law for the Reinstitution of Professionals in the Civil Service with such stringency that about a thousand professors were dismissed and numerous other instructors at institutions of tertiary education were forced to emigrate.
23 He worked at the Art Academy until 1937: *Jahresbericht der Staatlichen Kunstakademie Düsseldorf 1937/38*, Düsseldorf [1939], p. 22.
24 Ibid., p. 22; Walter M. Kersting left the Academy in 1944 for political and personal reasons. Christopher Oestereich, *'Gute Form' im Wiederaufbau. Zur Geschichte der Produktgestaltung in Westdeutschland*, Berlin 2000, p. 206; Wiltrud Baum, Hermann Schäfer, and Heinz G. Pfaender, *Walter Maria Kersting. Architekt, Formgestalter, Ingenieur, Grafiker*. From his estate, n.p., n.d. [Darmstadt 1974].
25 *Jahresbericht 1937/38* (see n. 23), p. 23.
26 Müller-Mehlis (see n. 13), p. 45.
27 Dawn Leach, 'Ausdifferenzierung und Kontinuität in der Künstlerausbildung an der Kunstakademie Düsseldorf', in: Wolfgang Ruppert and Christian Fuhrmeister (eds.), *Zwischen Deutscher Kunst und internationaler Modernität. Formen der Künstlerausbildung 1918 bis 1968*, Weimar 2007, pp. 147–167, here: p. 148 with reference to the personnel file.
28 *Jahresbericht 1937/38* (see n. 23), p. 23.
29 Alberg (see n. 15), Figs. 46 a–f, pp. 62–67.
30 Joined the Party in 1932; *Jahresbericht 1937/38* (see n. 23), p. 23.
31 Alberg (see n. 15), p. 17.
32 *Jahresbericht 1937/38* (see n. 23), p. 23; since 1923 Scharff had been a professor at the then Fine Arts Institute Berlin. The NSDAP defamed him as a 'Bolshevist' and a 'degenerate artist' (Scharff's 'explanatory statement' in October 1945: Landesarchiv NRW Abteilung [Dept] Rheinland – LA 55848 Bl. [fol.] 228). He was given leave of absence for that reason in April 1933 and transferred to Düsseldorf that autumn. In spring 1937 a denunciation was submitted to the NSDAP because Scharff's mother-in-law was of 'non-Aryan' descent; the following year he was excluded from the Party. In 1939 Scharff was forced to retire and was forbidden to work: Landesarchiv NRW Abteilung [Dept] Rheinland – LA 55848 Bl. [fols.] 230, 346; see Ernst Klee, *Das Kulturlexikon zum Dritten Reich. Wer war was vor und nach 1945?*, Frankfurt am Main 2007, p. 515.
33 Anja Hesse, *Malerei im Nationalsozialismus. Der Maler Werner Peiner (1897–1984)*, Hildesheim 1995; Dieter Pesch and Martin Pesch, *Kunst im Dritten Reich. Werner Peiner. Verführer oder Verführter*, Munich 2012.
34 Dietrich Bieber, 'Aus der Chronik der Kunstakademie. Personen und Ereignisse', in: Trier (see n. 4), p. 216; in contrast to Nikola Doll, *Mäzenatentum und Kunstförderung im Nationalsozialismus. Werner Peiner und Hermann Göring*, Weimar 2009, p. 36.
35 Hesse (see n. 33), p. 22; Doll (see n. 34), pp. 36f.
36 Doll (see n. 34), p. 36.
37 Ibid., pp. 30f.
38 Summarised ibid., pp. 38f.
39 *Jahresbericht 1937/38* (see n. 23), p. 23; see Heidrun Kaupen-Haas and Christian Saller (eds.), *Wissenschaftlicher Rassismus. Analysen einer Kontinuität in den Human- und Geisteswissenschaften*, Frankfurt am Main 1999, pp. 12–64; here: p. 37, n. 87 with reference to the personnel files in the Berlin Document Center, and Uwe Hossfeld, *Geschichte der biologischen Anthropologie in Deutschland*, Stuttgart 2005, p. 213. Vol. 2 of *Wissenschaftskultur um 1900*.
40 *Jahresbericht 1937/38* (see n. 23), p. 23.
41 Ibid., p. 23.
42 Landesarchiv NRW Abteilung [Dept] Rheinland – BR 1021 No. 39, Bl. [fol.] 351.
43 Ibid., Bl. [fols.] 367f.
44 Peter Grund had had some considerable success at regional level as an architect in Dortmund since 1923.
45 Alberg (see n. 15), p. 17, pp. 47f.
46 *Volksparole* of 11 April 1934, cited in Alberg (see n. 15), p. 50.

47 Hermann J. Mahlberg and Hella Nußbaum (eds.), *Der Aufbruch um 1900 und die Moderne in der Architektur des Wuppertales. Abendrot einer Epoche*, Wuppertal 2008, pp. 294–304.
48 The building is modelled on Erich Mendelsohn's Schocken Department Store in Chemnitz (1927). Fenestration is found on all sides to articulate the façade of the Wuppertal building, which evokes an impression of dynamic Modernism with its convexity and rounded-off corners.
49 Monumentalisation of his style is in the offing in his design for the Haus Rechen Hotel (1927–1929) in Bochum, when Fahrenkamp switched to angular architectural forms linked with a pillar portico.
50 *Jahresbericht der Staatlichen Kunstakademie Düsseldorf 1939*, Düsseldorf [1940], frontispiece; Bieber (see n. 34), p. 216.
51 Doll (see n. 34), pp. 65–70.
52 *Jahresbericht 1939* (see n. 50), p. 57.
53 Ibid., p. 17, p. 24.
54 Ibid., p. 58, Fig. 6.
55 Ibid., p. 58; *Jahresbericht der Staatlichen Kunstakademie Düsseldorf 1940*, Düsseldorf [1941], p. 47; for his 'work as an urban planner', see ibid., p. 38.
56 *Jahresbericht 1937/38* (see n. 23), pp. 60f., p. 63, and *Jahresbericht 1940* (n. 55), p. 51. For art auctions held in the years 1930 to 1945, see 'GDK Research. Bildbasierte Forschungsplattform zu den großen deutschen Kunstausstellungen 1937–1944 in Munich': http://www.gdk-research.de (last retrieved 14 September 2015).
57 *Jahresbericht 1939* (see n. 50), p. 26, Fig. 7; Berthold Hinz, *Die Malerei im deutschen Faschismus*, Frankfurt am Main 1974, Fig. 130.
58 *Jahresbericht 1939* (see n. 50), p. 60.
59 Doll (see n. 34), p. 26.
60 Mages taught at the Düsseldorf Academy until 1961. In 1948 Günter Grass began to study under Mages, but disagreements with Mages soon caused Grass to switch to Otto Pankok to continue his studies. In his novel *Die Blechtrommel* [The Tin Drum], Grass modelled the figure of Professor Maruhn on Josef (Sepp) Mages.
61 Enseling remained at the Academy after 1945. Joseph Beuys began his studies in Enseling's class in 1946; most recently: Christine Demele, 'Einleitung' [Introduction], in: Ulrich Müller (ed.), *Joseph Beuys Parallelprozesse*, exhib. cat. Düsseldorf 2010, p. 16.
62 Stadtmuseum Düsseldorf (see n. 15), p. 27; Klara Drenker-Nagels (ed.), *Heinrich Nauen. Monographie und Werkverzeichnis*, Cologne 2001.
63 Alberg (see n. 15), p. 68.
64 Cited in Alberg (see n. 15), p. 47.
65 Ibid., pp. 47f.
66 Ibid., p. 61.
67 Stadtmuseum Düsseldorf (see n. 15), p. 23.
68 *Jahresbericht 1937/38* (see n. 23), p. 11.
69 Stadtmuseum Düsseldorf (see n. 15), p. 15.
70 Alberg (see n. 15), p. 68.
71 Stadtmuseum Düsseldorf (see n. 15), pp. 13f.
72 Alberg (see n. 15), p. 152.
73 Stadtmuseum Düsseldorf (see n. 15), pp. 24f.
74 Hugo Weidenhaupt, *Kleine Geschichte der Stadt Düsseldorf*, 5th edn, Düsseldorf 1972, pp. 190f.; Alberg (see n. 15), p. 87.
75 *Jahresbericht 1939* (see n. 50), p. 40; for Fahrenkamp's address, see pp. 13–16.
76 Ibid., p. 9, Fig. 2; see Figs. 13, 16; Stadtmuseum Düsseldorf (see n. 15), p. 27. Hans Rompel, by profession an artist blacksmith, studied at the Art Academy from 1933 until 1939.
77 References in Doll (see n. 34), p. 34.
78 Ibid., pp. 41–47, pp. 65–80, pp. 303f.
79 Ibid., pp. 39–41.
80 Ibid., pp. 50f.
81 Ibid., p. 43, pp. 48f.
82 Ibid., p. 44.
83 Ibid., p. 47.
84 Ibid., p. 107.
85 Ingrid Westerhoff, *Heinz Hindorf. Das grafische Werk und die Gemälde*, Michelstadt 2000.
86 Alberg (see n. 15), p. 109.
87 *Jahresbericht der Staatlichen Kunstakademie Düsseldorf 1941–1944*, Düsseldorf [1945], p. 20.
88 Landesarchiv NRW Abteilung [Dept] Rheinland – BR 2195–2.
89 Ibid., report of 20 May 1942.
90 Bundesarchiv Koblenz BArch R/4901/12248, fol. 34.
91 *Jahresbericht 1941–1944* (see n. 87), p. 5.
92 Ibid., p. 17. The attack on 12 June 1943 destroyed important Art Academy records (Landesarchiv NRW Abteilung [Dept] Rheinland – BR 2195–2 – 'Bericht an das Reichsministerium' [Report to the Reich Ministry] of 17 July 1943).
93 'Bericht an das Reichsministerium für Wissenschaft, Erziehung und Volksbildung' [Report to the Reich Ministry for Science, Education, and Popular Education] of 22 March 1945 (Bundesarchiv Koblenz BArch R 4901/12251).
94 Alberg (see n. 15), p. 123, Fig. 128.
95 Ibid., p. 141, Figs. 144f.
96 Ministerialarchiv im Landesarchiv NRW Abteilung [Dept] Rheinland – NW 60 No. 179, Bl. [fol.] 38. Here a file note is also referred to, according to which the military government had already approved the resumption of teaching by 21 September 1945.
97 A conversation with Günter H. Blecks on 16 February 2011: see pp. 175–177 in the present volume.
98 Ministerialarchiv im Landesarchiv NWR Abteilung [Dept] Rheinland – NW 60 No. 179, Bl. [fol.] 38.
99 Thus Mataré in his diary: references in Leach (see n. 27), p. 149.
100 Ministerialarchiv im Landesarchiv NRW Abteilung [Dept] Rheinland – NW 60 No. 179, Bl. [fol.] 14.
101 Leach (see n. 27), p. 156.
102 Ministerialarchiv im Landesarchiv NRW Abteilung [Dept] Rheinland – NW 60 No. 179, Bl. [fol.] 8.
103 Ministerialarchiv im Landesarchiv NRW Abteilung [Dept] Rheinland – NW 60 No. 178, Bl. [fol.] 1; *Jahresbericht der Staatlichen Kunstakademie Düsseldorf 1945–1947*, Düsseldorf [1948], pp. 7f., pp. 9–12; for events and trends after 1945, also see the essay by Guido Reuter in the present volume, pp. 132–155.
104 Ministerialarchiv im Landesarchiv NWR Abteilung [Dept] Rheinland – NW 60 No. 178, Bl. [fol.] 2.
105 Hermann Isenmann did, however, return for summer term of 1949 and remained head of the workshop for making plaster moulds until May 1975.
106 Enseling remained at the Art Academy until 1952; he was Joseph Beuys's first teacher.
107 Ministerialarchiv im Landesarchiv NRW Abteilung [Dept] Rheinland – NW 60 No. 177, Bl. [fol.] 3 of 6 May 1946.

THE DÜSSELDORF ART ACADEMY AS A STATE INSTITUTION AND ARTIST COMMUNITY. AMBITION AND REALITY FROM 1945 TO THE PRESENT DAY

Peter M. Lynen

THE ART ACADEMY AS A MODEL FOR SUCCESS AND PRODUCTIVE CONTRASTS THROUGH THE YEARS

The Düsseldorf Art Academy has been a state institution since time immemorial.[1] Founded in 1773 by Karl Theodor, the Elector Palatine, as a 'kurfürstlich-pfälzische Accademie der Mahler-, Bildhauer- und Baukunst' [Electoral-Palatinate Academy for the Arts of Painting, Sculpture, and Architecture], it was reinstituted as a royal art academy in 1819 by King Friedrich Wilhelm III of Prussia. After the First World War it continued to function as a state art academy run by the Free State (Republic) of Prussia.[2] Even after the Second World War it was still publicly administered, by the then new federal state[3] of North Rhine-Westphalia. It has always been the public purse which has invariably and seamlessly – of course under widely varying systems of government – not only financed the Art Academy but also shaped it in the organisational sense and has informed essential – also legally defined – relations between members of the Academy within its walls and with the outside world. This is the factor common to the Düsseldorf Art Academy and other renowned art academies and conservatories in both Germany and Austria, all of which represent a discrete group within the public tertiary education sector of those countries.[4] Privately funded – that is, commercially orientated – cultural organisations that are 'free of the state' and engaged in scholarship, teaching, and study are also occasionally encountered. Either privately funded or organised in the 'third sector' between the state and the market, they, too, are called art academies or art (institute) universities. However, neither as competitors of their state-run sisters nor as art-related institutions have they hitherto succeeded in attaining comparable importance in terms of seniority,[5] quantity,[6] or quality.[7] In Germany (and Austria) we are still far from a dual education system based on the parity of state and private art institutes – as is the case in the cultural sector with television and radio with both public and private broadcasters.[8] Most German art academies and art universities are corporations under public law nowadays and are at the same time institutions maintained by the federal state in which they are located.

A glance at the CVs of men and women who have been successful artists both domestically and internationally since 1945 (and this also holds for earlier periods) reveals that they have increasingly tended to be graduates of an art institute, with self-taught artists becoming more and more the exception. Building up a career in art is not premised on certificates attesting to formal training and diplomas, yet distinguished artists are essentially the product of art institutes, and this is widespread. As the present book so compellingly demonstrates, there is a tradition that former students later return to their alma mater to teach there as professors, succeeded in the third generation by their students, resulting in a multigenerational concatenation of teacher-pupil relationships.[9] The 'system' is self-sustaining in that teaching staff at art institutes return to the art institutes after 'long-term' success in the 'art world' and forge ties with the younger generation to their mutual benefit. Not only is this success premised on teaching and study but it also directly affects art production and creativity. In this process the state-run art institutes are at once important training centres and major cultural enterprises. Hence they should also be viewed as hubs for the production of art and dedicated to the aim of making an impact with and through art. Priority is given less to academic observations 'on' art than to a 'hands-on' approach to shaping art, to making works of art as well as directly fostering artists as personalities. The Düsseldorf Art Academy ranks high on this scale.

There have been many expressions of criticism, numerous changes and problems that have emerged over nearly two and a half centuries. The focus in the following will be on the period beginning in 1945. Despite all these issues, it is safe to say that the state-controlled constitution of the Düsseldorf Art Academy is a 'successful model' because it is the foundation on which the long life of the Academy and the artistic impulses and substantial cultural impact discussed in this book are based and is the guarantor of them. The state has provided security, above all financial security, and has governed with a light hand that has, for the most part, allowed artistic developments to follow their own course and usually (with short-lived exceptions) to obey laws of their own making. The public, both in-house and at large, has not always been sufficiently aware that this is so for the reason that individual issues and problems (even individual mistakes) that usually arise sporadically and situationally as well as anecdotal and subjective ways of looking at things have been prioritised in evaluations over that continuously guaranteeing basis under public law and the warranties linked with it. Criticism of a conservative 'academism' opposing modern trends has cropped up, albeit only sporadically, aimed at specific persons and related to specific, definable time spans. Such criticism is, however, untenable if intended to address a fundamental principle underpinning the Art Academy over the long term. This is particularly true of the period after 1945, a time span during which scope was made within the Academy to encompass creative diversity in artistic freedom. This approach has meant that the Academy is anything but an 'ivory tower' isolated from society. Nor have the Academy and its members persisted in pursuing utilitarian aims or rigid dogmatism. Art purely for its own sake has always been a core value of the Düsseldorf Art Academy. In this respect, the art content of this institution which was close to the state after 1945 has always also been 'at a far remove from the state' since there have been no shaping prescriptions on the part of the state of a programmatic, stylistic, or content-related kind worthy of mention that would have to be taken into consideration.[10] This paradox and its resolution into individual problems and events will be discussed in more depth in the following. On the whole, it can be confirmed that the Düsseldorf Art Academy has, in the time span to be discussed here, always been a receptive art forum and at the same time a vital transmitter and receiver of cultural stimuli both internally and externally. The links maintained by the Academy with contemporary and international developments in art have always been intensive and reciprocal. Indications that this is indeed the case are art awards, participation in international exhibitions such as the Venice Biennale and documenta in Kassel, numerous solo and group shows of work by artists at the Academy – both instructors and learners – and the acclaim they have garnered both nationally and internationally in the art scene and in the history and theory of art. Evaluation along such lines, however, requires pointing out that the 'state institution and artist community' antinomy signalised at the beginning in the title of this essay is a typological duality that is systemic in any state institution of higher learning. After all, the Academy *qua* institution has a corporative and normatively constituted core, which does, admittedly, guarantee specific rights to its members but equally obliges them to collaborate in defined relationships. Artists, on the other hand, are individuals who define and indeed must find their own, distinctive personal stances – stances which over the course of an individual life are intrinsically inalterable yet flexible in the face of situational change – in the charged field of vocation and profession. That is neither easy to accomplish nor free of conflicts because what is at stake is a virtually incalculable amalgamation of many – very different – artists and a few scholars (spanning several generations) whose interests do not always coincide. An institution supported by the state, which must make do with the individual member under pre-existing and in part prescribed conditions, is bound to encounter difficulties in communication, rejection that may go as far as open rebellion, contradictions, minority opinions, and divergent aims both in general and specific to individual issues. The sections of this essay to follow will underpin that assertion with numerous examples. 'We are past masters at subversion'[11] is a message that representatives of both the state and the Academy quite often hear (or experience first-hand), especially when they come up with new, politically based 'control mechanisms' (nowadays under the auspices of the New Public Management model). Moreover, related issues constantly re-emerge in different guises so they cannot be regarded as having been 'dealt with once and for all'. This is so because the institution continues to exist but its members change constantly and different people reconfigure the same old issues. A consensus once reached or states of knowledge attained collectively cannot, therefore, claim to remain inalterable. In this connection, organisational normative bracketing and boundaries are constantly being formed and reformed under the auspices of state administration, academic self-administration, and freedoms granted to the individual in terms of decision-making.[12] The 'art academy' *qua* institution and its members have not only found ready-made parameters. They have also been able to shape and change them. In the following, the question will be addressed of how the state and society specifically have confronted the Düsseldorf Art Academy and its members over nearly seventy years of that dichotomy. When one considers that force field, the way the Art Academy has functioned has been anything but 'dull'. This is equally true of the decades since 1945 although the Academy has enjoyed quite stable external conditions during this period, unlike those established previously over nearly two centuries in which the Academy was caught up in large-scale wars, social upheavals, and drastic systemic changes.

VARYING CULTURAL AND INSTITUTIONAL POLICY PHASES SINCE 1945

Before specific details and events within the Düsseldorf Art Academy can be studied in depth, three different cultural and institutional policy phases must be distinguished because they have also been of proximate and contingent relevance for this particular institution.[13]

After 1945 priority was given to establishing the Federal Republic of Germany premised on the constitutional Basic Law governing the reconstruction of the body politic. That state of affairs also concerned art and culture, which, rather than being subject to overarching state control through ideologically informed governance, were to be promoted on a regional and even local basis. As far as culture being within the remit of the state was concerned, the terms 'public service' and 'the common good' were the order of the day. This affected not only the provision of vital goods and infrastructure measures but also all cultural assets accessible to the public. 'Man lives not by bread alone' was the public perception; hence the 1950s would be memorable not only as the era of the German 'economic miracle' and the concomitant 'wave of gourmandise' but equally as a period of consolidation and differentiation of state-run organisations as well as agendas specific to art and to culture in general.

A second phase evolved from the late 1960s and continued on into the 1980s. Related to specific situations, it was shaped by the cultural revolution of 1968 and was captured in slogans such as 'Culture for all'[14] and 'Catastrophe in education'.[15] The thrust behind this second phase was essentially twofold: first to enhance and widen the cultural opportunities offered – including those in education, science, art, and culture – both by the state itself and in the private sector, the latter being made possible by the dissolution of state monopolies and the authorisation of private competitors. Second came democratisation, which was a misnomer in as much as the focus was on sharing or participation by citizens who enjoyed fundamental rights rather than on making changes to the principle of democracy by means of the legitimation chain from people via parliament and government to the state administration. In retrospect, what has remained above and beyond the hustle and bustle of daily events at any given time is indeed impressive: the state has substantially enlarged its resources in education, science, art, and culture on several levels – federal, state, and communal. New 'jobs' (full-time permanent employment), entire institutions, and promotional instruments as well as cultural policies were created or enlarged in scope. On the other hand, even at the beginning of this phase a wide-ranging juridification and the detailed formation of new administrative structures set in, processes that became ever more clearly evident, in the course of which the intermeshing of self-administration and state administration was redefined. Thus the traditional and charismatic legitimation yielded to the rational-legal and normative kind. This trend also affected art and art-related institutions, hence the Düsseldorf Art Academy directly.

From the mid-1980s until the first decade of the new millennium, the state approached the limits of its potential for designing and supplementing on all levels. In this third phase, culture was viewed as not only valuable but also costly, whereby a 'too' soon crept into thinking and the public coffers were written off as 'empty'. The call for autonomy and self-administration, in particular in the arts and humanities, however, refused to die down. Instead it became a *ceterum censeo* effort to shape cultural policies. Cultural institutions and their representatives, including the artists themselves, asserted emphatically and with well-reasoned arguments that the state had to 'let go' and allow more strongly decentralised possibilities of self-administration and self-organisation. This trend in turn led to the aforementioned New Public Management models. Thus principles, including foreign ones (for example, from the English-speaking countries and the United States in particular) derived from business management, entered German cultural administration.

Currently we are on the threshold of a fourth phase. Here, too, there was a triggering factor – in this case, the banking and financial crisis. On the one hand, this has increased pressure on the public purse and competition for assignment to the various tasks that need to be performed and creating priorities has become even more obvious and harsh. On the other hand, the cultural side (art, culture, education, and science) has taken this state of affairs as a pretext for confidently pointing out that this is primarily a failure of economic systems rather than a crisis in the sponsoring of culture by the state.[16] In the third phase of cultural policy since 1945, the public side definitely learnt and profited from the private economy. Now what is called for is more cultivation of the economy instead

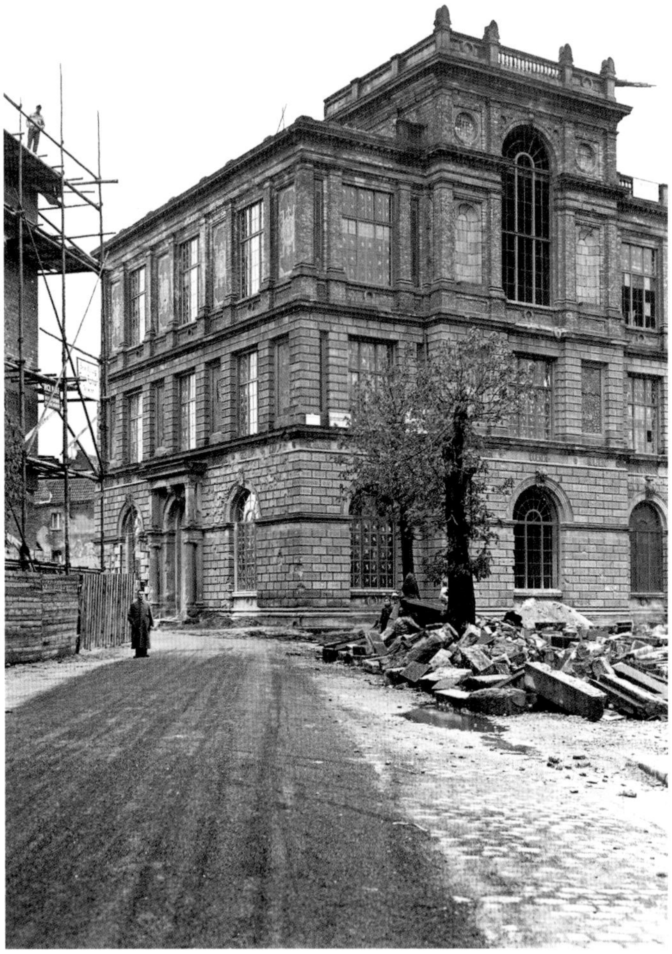

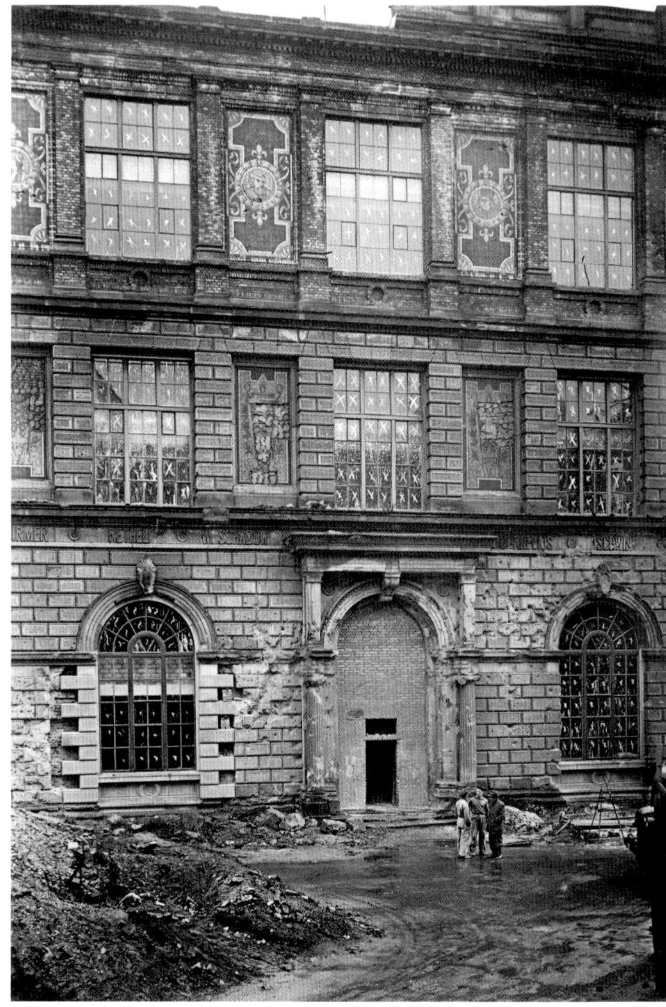

Figs. 1, 2: The partly destroyed Academy building, 1950

of even more economising in the cultural sector. The autonomy of art and science should be championed instead of a capitalist or state-controlled planned economy. Institutions such as the Düsseldorf Art Academy could show the way here. To do so requires healthy self-awareness, a quality that the Academy, with its more than two hundred years of history and its representatives and members who are renowned as artists, is certainly not lacking.

THE ART ACADEMY IN THE RECONSTRUCTION PHASE

As Düsseldorf lay in ruins in 1945, the Art Academy building was not without bomb damage and the consequences of heavy shelling. Most of the damage was not sustained until March of that year. The corridor of the upper floor and the Great Hall were open to the sky (Figs. 1, 2). Nor had the teaching staff and student body survived without suffering physical and mental, not to mention intellectual-moral, harm. Many of them returned as soldiers or from internment as prisoners of war. To match the above-outlined spirit of 'reconstruction', however, everyone was willing and able to knuckle down to work:

'An ethnic entity that has lost its integrity, a ravaged country, destroyed cities, disappointed people, need and hopelessness have been the godfathers of the new beginnings at the State Art Academy in Düsseldorf, and its christening present is a tangled knot of oppressive circumstances and conditions that is not easy to untangle and whose kinks would not be successfully resolved by cutting. The only positive aspect has been the hopeful will to live in spite of everything!'[17]

Those are the first words of the foreword written by Werner Heuser, at that time director of the Academy, in the still impressive *Jahresbericht der Staatlichen Kunstakademie Düsseldorf 1945–1947* [Annual Report of the Düsseldorf Art Academy 1945–1947]. The quote and the entire report with addresses, essays, and chronicles not only perfectly reflects the general trends outlined above but also shows how energetic and forward-looking the Academy and its representatives and members were from the outset in devoting themselves to the task at hand. Here Lyonel Feininger's assertion that art is a necessity rather than a luxury has gained a workaday and practical dimension.

For all practical purposes, the Academy had actually opened its doors by the latter half of 1945 although the official reinauguration did not take place until 31 January 1946. 'In September 1945 the first students returned and made themselves available for clearing rubble and reconstruction work.'[18] On the one hand, the building was again in the service of art; on the other, even the artists were servicing the building. Opening again made it possible for 'concluding the 1945/46 winter term according to plan even though there were still some insufficiencies in many areas'.[19] A statement like that must induce astonishment and shame in our spoilt times, in which even the locking of a lecture hall by accident can lead to rebellious protests.

The year 1945 also saw the first post-war change in directors at the Art Academy. After his dismissal in the National Socialist era, Ewald Mataré had returned to the Academy once the war ended, and not only as a professor. As an important artist and a person without political taint, he was appointed curator of the Academy by the then governor of the North Rhine Province and at the same time – at the suggestion of the Düsseldorf district president and with the approval of the Education Division of the military government – made executive director of the State Düsseldorf Art Academy on a revocable basis. Mataré made demands – for instance, that fourteen-year-olds should be admitted by the Art Academy to ensure that the student body would be as young as possible. That was just as unlikely to be acceptable then as it would still be nowadays – even despite the prevailing tendency to openness and the legality of student matriculation before the age of majority, exemplified by precocious students or pre-colleges at conservatories. The curator for his part invoked the 1831 Düsseldorf Prussian Art Academy regulations, of which more will be said later about their continuity. The reason given for the rejection of Mataré's proposal – one that is still understandable today – was that such demands were in conflict with the 'character of the Art Academy as an institution of higher learning in art'.[20] That ended Mataré's stint as director and the constitutional reforms he had proposed. A professor at the Art Academy until 1957, he had been enormously influential, and Joseph Beuys and Erwin Heerich were among the distinguished pupils he had taught. Drawing on Ewald Mataré's diaries, however, leads one to the inevitable conclusion that the conflict probably had further-reaching implications.[21] In the diaries, Mataré expresses his disappointment at the negotiations in autumn and winter 1945 and describes his ideas of reform entailing changes to the programme and the teaching staff in the context of a fresh beginning unencumbered by the past.

Tasks on that scale were left to his successor, Werner Heuser (director 1946–1949), named and quoted above, and the teaching staff of the early post-war years. As it had done in the past, the range of subjects taught included painting, sculpture, fine arts and applied graphics, art teaching at state schools, architecture, state design, and art history. The Academy teaching staff consisted in 1947[22] of Fritz Becker (architect), Theo Champion (painter), Otto Coester (etcher), Joseph Enseling (sculptor), Wilhelm Herberholz (painter), Werner Heuser (painter), Heinrich Kamps (painter, teaching art at state schools), Walter Köngeter (architect), Joseph (Sepp) Mages (sculptor), Ewald Mataré (sculptor), Otto Pankok (printmaker), Jakob Heinrich Schmidt (art historian), Wilhelm Schmurr (painter), Hans Schwippert (architect), and Walter von Wecus (stage designer). Three of those artists would succeed Heuser as directors, namely Heinrich Kamps (1949–1954), Heinrich Schmidt (1954–1956 as deputy director), and Hans Schwippert (1956–1966).

Enumerations of the above kind are instructive in two respects: first, the teaching staff were even then broad ranging and well selected in terms of subjects taught and finding the best instructors for teaching them. The reputation of some staff members (notably Mataré, Pankok, and Schwippert) has remained to the present day considerably more than local. Second, there was willingness to practise self-administration and to assume tasks – including directorial functions – within the Academy. Leading an artist's life did not preclude viewing oneself as a responsible member of the Academy as an institution. To that generation, being a member of the Academy undoubtedly also meant placing oneself at the service of the institution rather than focusing exclusively on one's own career in art and one's teaching duties as a professor.

The Academy was neither legally nor organisationally autonomous. Even after the era of military governance and the founding of the state of North Rhine-Westphalia in 1946, the Academy did not possess legal responsibility (in this it resembled a school). It fell within the jurisdiction of the premier of the state as curator and intermediary authority and of the state government, specifically of the Ministry of Culture, later (under different names) of the Science Ministry responsible for all institutions of higher learning in the state as the top-tier state authority. The federal state was in particular responsible for 'personnel appointment and management', which means that all those employed by institutions of tertiary education in the state were either civil servants or employees (this also applied to some workers) of the state; hence their contracts, depending on their status, were drawn up and appointments were made and/or had to be authorised by the premier of the state or the minister responsible. The federal state, in our case North Rhine-Westphalia, was also responsible for financing in the sense that it kept the books, which means that the Academy budget was meticulously allocated (in individual entitlements), and funding was distributed 'from above' but managed 'in-house'. Nor did the Academy have a charter of its own dealing with academic matters (here mainly teaching, study, self-administration) – for all the actual scope permitted in artistic matters, even in teaching. The above-mentioned Regulations of 24 November 1831 for the Royal Art Academy at Düsseldorf (Reglement vom 24. November 1831 für die Königliche Kunst-Akademie zu Düsseldorf)[23] continued to serve as its charter. It had definitively shaped the idea of the Academy as an institute of higher learning in the arts and for artists into a viable manifesto although it is indissolubly part of nineteenth-century thinking.[24] This set of rules was in force until 1976 (more on this later). In fact, it was not replaced until the two Art Institute Laws were enacted in 1987 and 2008. For many years it was viewed as a practicable basis not only for the Academy as an institution but also for structuring instruction and study around the class principle and the master-pupil relationship.

Nonetheless, constructive thinking on how the challenges of the present were to be met had gone on within the Academy even immediately after the war. In January 1949 the general assembly of professors at the State Düsseldorf Art Academy convened to issue a statement on 'securing the given high expenses of the institution under the terms of [the means provided by] the existing constitution' and a declaration on 'the fundamental charter'. The author and the undersigned[25] started with the insight that the concerns and expenses of the state were a serious and difficult matter. They had no illusions about the institution being able to represent an extralegal space. Hence they realised the importance of distinguishing 'directorial or curatorial functions in the administrative sector' from issues related to the 'artistic, specialist, and intellectual direction of the institution'. In this connection, they recommended a clear-cut separation of powers and functions in the sense of distinct functional division of powers. Moreover, by 1949, far-sighted ideas and structures had been outlined which today must be viewed as important pillars of the legal framework governing art institutes in the tertiary education sphere. However, at the time it was proposed, the plan was not taken up. This is equally true of the other – and there were others – organisational restructuring plans mooted in the 1950s[26] until the upheavals of the mid-1960s put paid to organisational stability at the Academy.

Two aspects must be borne in mind in any consideration of the subjects and courses, courses of study, and curricular content as well as lecture and teaching formats at the Academy:[27] on the one hand, the Academy became increasingly receptive to domestic and international trends in contemporary art, an aspect that is revealed most notably in the appointment of distinguished teaching staff commensurate with the importance of the Academy to art. The following painters had been appointed by the mid-1960s: Joseph Fassbender, Rupprecht Geiger, Bruno Goller, Karl Otto Götz, Gerhard Hoehme, Georg Meistermann, and Robert Pudlich (later, for instance, also Peter Brüning in 1969). In sculpture the professors appointed were Joseph Beuys, Karl Bobek, Norbert Kricke, Beate Schiff, Manfred Sieler, and Zoltán Székessy; in commercial and art graphics Walter Breker and Rolf Sackenheim; in stage design Teo Otto; and in architecture Hans Hollein, Karl Thomas Robaschik, Rudolf Schwarz, and Karl Wimmenauer. A cursory glance at the roll of winners of the Great Art Prize of the State of North Rhine-Westphalia for the years 1953 to 1965 shows that without exception the recipients of that prize taught at the Düsseldorf Art Academy. And the above list is in part repeated (Goller, Fassbender, Kricke, Mataré, Meistermann, Schwarz, Schwippert, and Székessy as award winners).[28] Even then the Academy as an art institute was a beacon whose light shone far beyond Düsseldorf. It would only grow stronger with the passage of time (Fig. 3).

On the other hand, the curriculum continued to be based on the three traditional courses of study: fine art, training as an art teacher at state schools, and architecture. Instruction continued to take place in classes taught by artists. The important hands-on practical instruction and realisation in art workshops was accompanied by the teaching of art history and art theory – which promotes understanding and knowledge. The theoretical side was also consolidated by the appointment of distinguished scholars such as Anna Klapheck (art history) and Walter Warnach (philosophy). The individual subjects or fields (painting, sculpture, the graphic arts, and so forth) were not regarded then – nor are they today – as discrete courses of study or disciplines that can be kept separate. Instead, they are the focus of specialisation in any given artist's work. That means, work in the graphic arts or sculpture was also done in painting classes. This practice was followed by both instructors and students. Not only was the possibility of interdisciplinary approaches never ruled out; they were, in fact, the natural option.[29] An artist cannot be reduced to a single medium, material, or technique, a fact of which many were aware even then although this would later become even more obvious (in the 1970s, for instance).

There were no formal final examinations and certificates in the fine arts course, nor were there any prescribed examinations and set curricula. From the administrative standpoint, this was still largely a 'pre-constitutional' era based on common law (and the legal fiction of the special legal relationship), traditional forms of practice, and the charismatic rule of the art teacher. Successful applicants for a place at the Academy – who had passed the admissions examinations (giving proof of artistic aptitude), found a teacher, and pursued their studies for eight to ten terms while producing artworks during that time – left the Academy with testimonials to the effect that their studies 'were regarded' as having been completed. Having been a member of a master class associated with the name of the artist-professor who had taught it was an additional honour that might help to smooth the path to professional recognition.

Even then the course of study preparing for teaching art at state schools was more formally structured. The first state examinations (that is, examinations that were not set by the Academy) marked the end of study. Members of the Academy examined the candidates, but the regulations governing the examinations (the law governing the training of teachers and the examination regulations) were enacted by the state. Candidates were required to take courses in art history and education. The obligatory second teaching subject was taken at a university. Candidates for these examinations attended separate classes and there was talk of a 'specialist department for teaching candidates'.[30] All this meant that the Academy student body was in

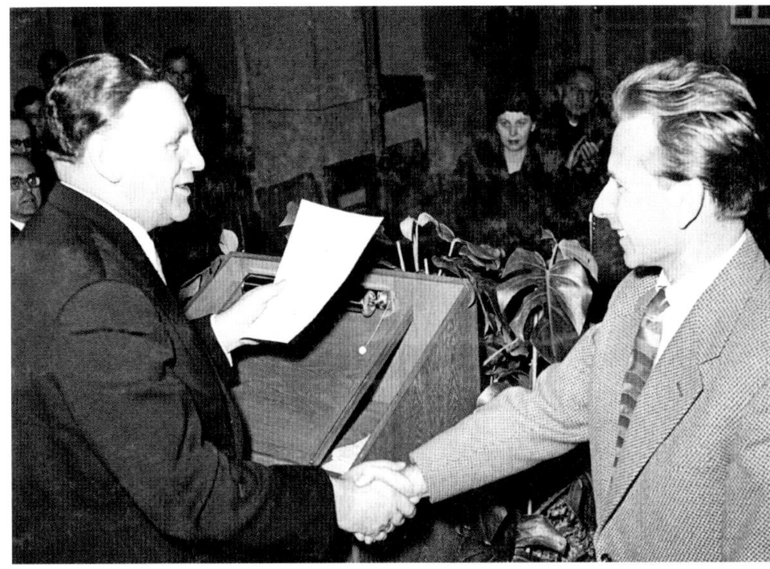

Fig. 3: Lord Mayor Josef Gockeln awarding Gerhard Hoehme the first City of Düsseldorf Promotional Prize, 1954

fact split into two groups. At that time the 'art teaching candidates' represented the larger group, a state of affairs that led to mutual recriminations, prejudices, and conflicts.[31]

In architecture a middle course was followed between fine art and art for teaching candidates. Here, too, studies were quite informal, were about art, and above all featured the pupil-teacher relationship in the teaching of architecture: 'The Art Academy teaches architecture in master studios.'[32] In this connection, the Academy could quote as a precedent that architecture had always been viewed as the art of building there since the Academy was founded in the eighteenth century and had always been taught through the master-pupil relationship rather than in the lecture hall. Since skills in construction and technique were required for admission, talented architectural draughtsmen, for instance, might be awarded a place. The term 'architect' – unlike the word 'artist' – represents a registered professional designation. Qualifying for and subsequently practising the profession of architect are normatively regulated. Most importantly, membership of a professional organisation and professional listing are the prerequisites for practising the profession on a self-employed basis with the right to draw up plans. For all these reasons, it was necessary to link training with professional life, so final examinations had to be set. Passing them attested to the graduate's 'fitness for registration in the designated professional organisation'.

The applied arts were fringe fields but some possibilities for studying them were available, mainly in the graphic arts. Otherwise the workshops, too, were used for the purpose of producing art. The Academy was essentially – as it had been in the past and would be later – an institute of higher learning dedicated to the arts and artists, not a school for the applied arts and design (the applied arts and design remained the prerogative of vocational art schools and later polytechnics although

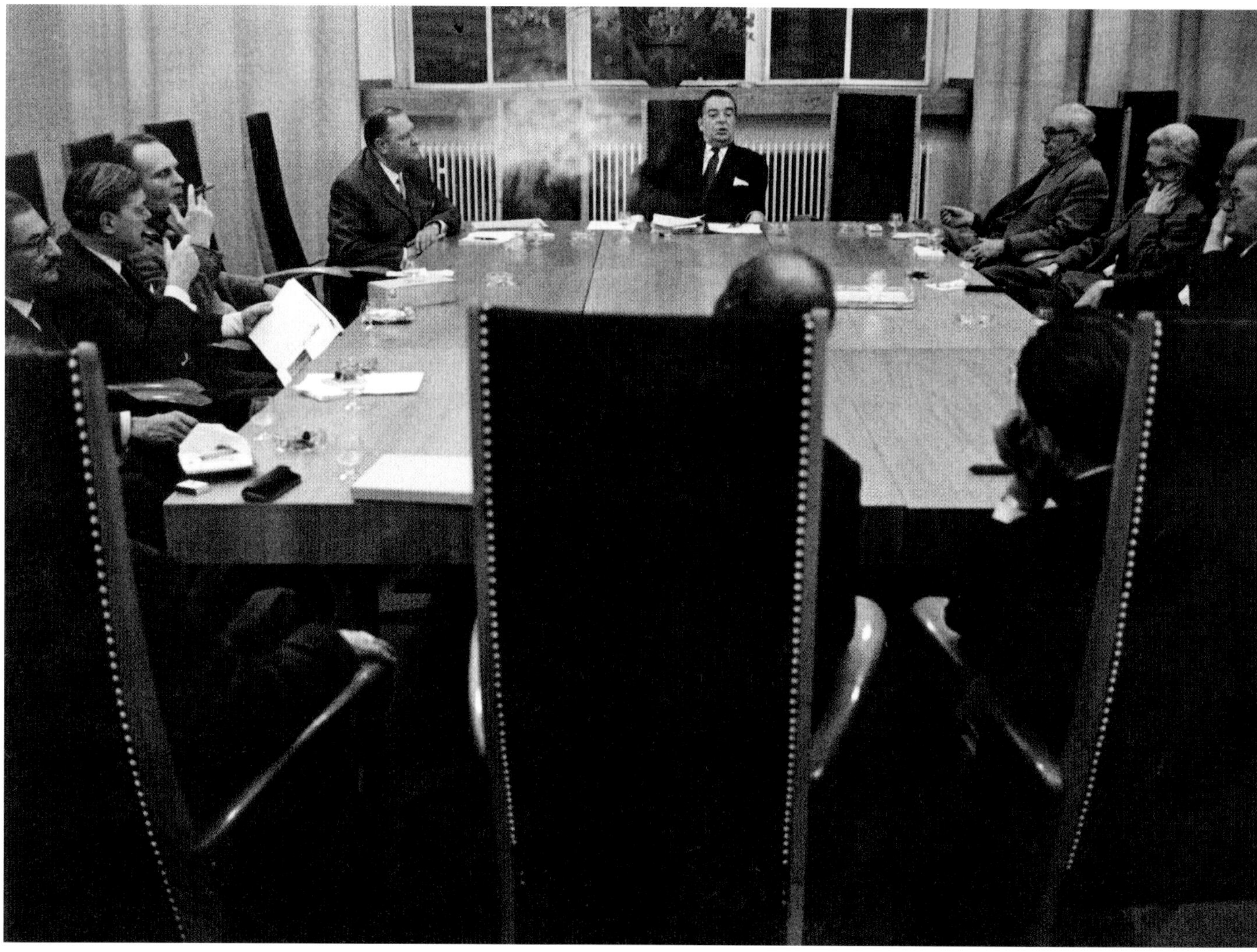

Fig. 4: The professors' conference; at the centre Hans Schwippert, c.1960

there have occasionally been attempts at incorporating them in broad-based vocational universities).

Für die Kunst leben. Bilder aus der Staatlichen Kunstakademie zu Düsseldorf (1960), a book edited by Schwippert,[33] is 'not about achievements but about people'. It shows Academy students and teachers going about their work. The heady atmosphere of concentration is apparent, with photographs of the teaching staff in conference – all wearing suits and most of them smoking heavily (Fig. 4) – and views of the (now legendary) Carnival festivities figuring just as prominently as a shot of children outside peering curiously through a window into the mysterious world of the Academy.

An address given by Schwippert on 24 November 1965 at the matriculation ceremony may be regarded as marking the end of this period and the transition to the next.[34] Admonitory in tenor, the gist of the speech is that 'the revolutionary era has come to an end, also at the behest of the powers that be because it, too, will inevitably end again in terrorisms that ultimately terrify those who actuate them.'[35]

THE 'CULTURE FOR ALL' PHASE AT THE ACADEMY

The spirit of optimism that reigned in the late 1960s and early 1970s, along with its culture revolution side and phenomena that were at variance with the above warnings voiced by Schwippert, existed within the walls of the Düsseldorf Art Academy in a particularly crass form with distinctive features. Although it is closely linked with the name of Professor Joseph Beuys, his followers, and his legendary claim that everyone was an artist, it would not be fair to reduce the events and views to this one person and his entourage. Similar upheavals took place at other institutions of higher learning both at home and abroad. This essay is not the place for enumerating all the goings-on and evaluating them.[36] However, some light should be shed on the general trends of that era as touched on above with the Düsseldorf Art Academy serving as a case study. Institutional, structural, and personnel- and content-related issues made for a volatile mix.

The extrinsic reason for renewed and intensified debate about the constitution in force at the Academy since 1965 was

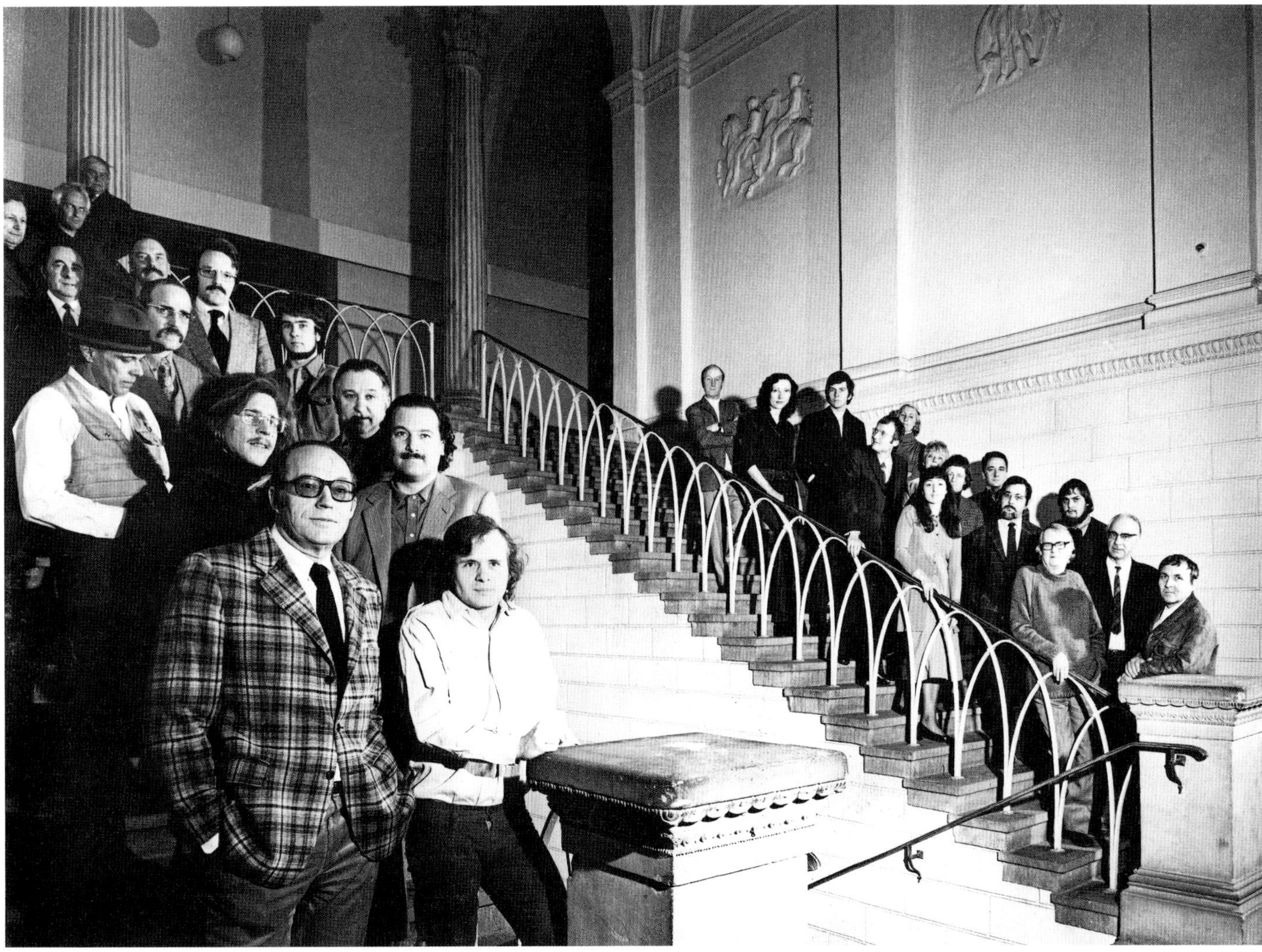

Fig. 5: The professorial staff in the Academy stairwell, c. 1973

personnel related: the search for a successor to Hans Schwippert as director. Once again – and not for the last time – this issue gave rise to a query as to whether the Academy should be given a constitution 'that provided for a rectorate' or should continue to be headed by a director (Fig. 5). In February 1965 the assembled professors drew up a resolution which the director passed on via the district president *qua* curator to the minister for education. The wording of the resolution was as follows:

'The teaching staff of the institute regrets there is not yet a new constitution for the State Art Academy in Düsseldorf. Their concerns about a meaningful successor to the present director are most closely related to that issue. The staff have specific thoughts and wishes in this matter. They are working on proposals for a constitution. The staff would be grateful if a discussion with the minister or his representatives could take place.'[37]

A conference did take place as requested in summer 1965. At the meeting a representative of the Ministry of Culture put forward a proposal for a constitution and explained it. A plan for a constitution that had been worked out by the Academy professors existed at the time of the conference.[38] But that was not all: the ongoing discussion was summarised by Eduard Trier, then provisional director and later fully accredited head of the Academy (1966–1972), in a memorandum dated September 1967 that did not, however, represent an uncontested proposal. The following were the salient points of that constitutional model:

- Autonomy for the Art Academy and equal ranking with the universities
- Educating the artistic person, hence promoting the arts as the main business [of the Academy]
- Subdivision into general goals (aims) and specific, department-related tasks; division accordingly into departments within the framework of an integrative Academy. The departments were to be:
  1. Fine Art
  2. Art Education (i.e. training art teachers for state schools)

Entwurf

Die Akademie ist keine Ausbildungsanstalt.

Sie ist ein Ort lebendiger Auseinandersetzung zwischen Lehrern und Schülern, ohne einen bestimmten Studiengang und ohne ein bestimmtes Studienziel.

Daher muß die Akademie jede Form eines vorkonzipierten Studienganges ablehnen.

Dies schliesst nicht aus, dass in bestehenden anderen Abteilungen ein festgelegter Studiengang mit einem bestimmten Ausbildungsziel möglich ist.

Die Berufung der Lehrer erfolgt auf Grund der Wirksamkeit ihrer freikünstlerischen Arbeit in der Welt, die auch hier im Hause erhalten, gefördert und geschützt werden muss, denn Wert und Wirkung der Akademie sind abhängig von dieser freien künstlerischen Tätigkeit.

Der Schüler betritt die Akademie nur mit dem Nachweis seiner Begabung. Über diese entscheidet sein jeweils zukünftiger Lehrer. Ebenfalls über die Dauer des Studiums.

Die freie Abteilung ist der Kern der Akademie. Infolgedessen sollte dieser nicht durch Ausdehnungstendenzen anderer Abteilungen eingeengt werden. Der Erfindung, dem Experiment und der Forschung des freien Künstlers (Lehrer und Schüler!) sollte z.B. räumlich und bei Berufungen mehr entsprochen werden als dem Ausbildungsgang des Kunsterziehers.

Für den zeitgemäßen Ausbau der freien Abteilung sind folgende zusätzliche Lehrstühle erforderlich:

1. ein zweiter Lehrstuhl für Kunstgeschichte
2. ein Kunstsoziologe
3. ein Psychologe (Wahrnehmungspsychologie)

gez.: Professor Beuys

Protokoll vom 18.7.1966 der freien Abteilung

332

10 Durchschläge

Verteiler:

Götz
Hoehme
Sackenheim
Kricke
Sieler
Beuys
Geiger
Macketanz
Fassbender
Direktor Dr. Trier

Verwaltungsakten der Kunstakademie Düsseldorf

333

Fig. 6: Minutes of the Fine Art Department of 18 July 1966, printed in the first volume of Jahreshefte der Kunstakademie Düsseldorf

3. Architecture
4. Applied Art
5. Arts and Humanities

- The right to academic self-administration, with the following legal entities: director, deputy director, professorial staff, student representation

A particularly moot point had been structuring the departments; this applied to both 'whether' and 'how'. Nor were the individual competences, jurisdiction, and obligations of the self-administrating legal entities clarified. A notable counter-proposal was the one put forward in January 1967 by Gerhard Hoehme in a memorandum of that date. Among the points he made in it was a demand that the departments be disbanded. He emphasised the view that the Academy was a place where teachers and students might meet rather than an institution for training. In this Hoehme was ahead of his time because principles of that kind not only won out later but today are structurally integrated and even anchored in law (more on this in the following). The question of the extent to which organisational and content-related differences between the courses of study offered to aspiring art teachers and practitioners of fine art should be taken into consideration also played an important role. A memorandum written by Karl Otto Götz late in 1966 is particularly relevant in this connection. The Academy administrative archives also contain a protocol from the Fine Art Department written in Joseph Beuys's hand and dated 18 July 1966,[39] which reflects the consensus reached among the fine arts professors at the time (Fig. 6). In short, the inference can be drawn that, in this phase of deliberations on reform, discussions within the Academy were conducted both with commitment and relevance. The starting points of the deliberations were, on the one hand, the continuity of the Academy (Cornelius, Schadow, and the 1831 charter were pointedly referred to) and, on the other, the consequences of the realisation that art was 'unteachable' and the 'old Academy was dead'.

Discussions about a new version of the proposals began very soon after the memorandum of September 1967 (conference resolution of 8 July 1968). The debates were carried out while the student rebellion was raging. The discussions heated up. Results in the form of viable resolutions receded further and further into the distance and the members of the Academy

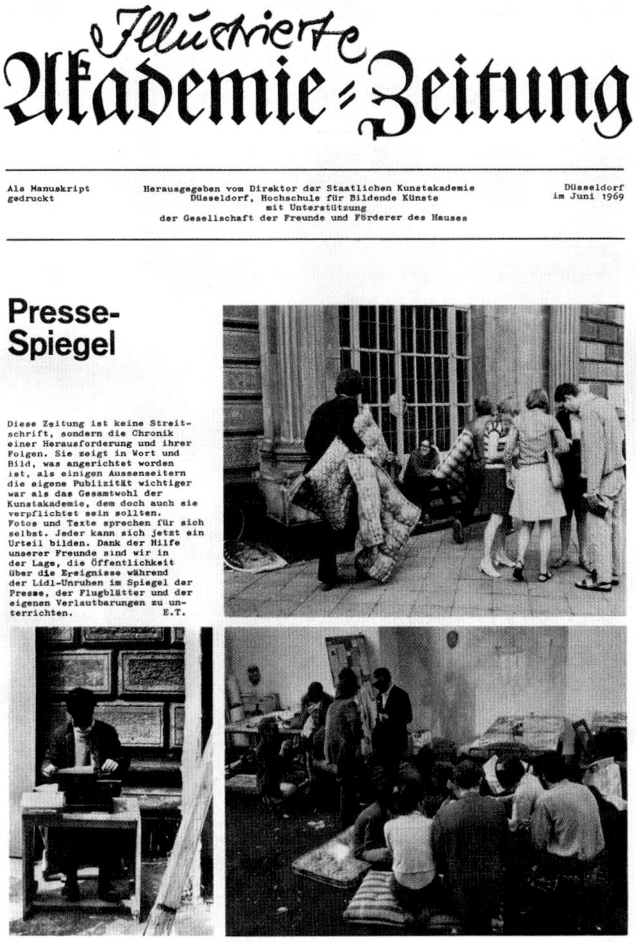

Illustrierte
Akademie-Zeitung

Als Manuskript gedruckt

Herausgegeben vom Direktor der Staatlichen Kunstakademie Düsseldorf, Hochschule für Bildende Künste mit Unterstützung der Gesellschaft der Freunde und Förderer des Hauses

Düsseldorf im Juni 1969

Presse-Spiegel

Diese Zeitung ist keine Streitschrift, sondern die Chronik einer Herausforderung und ihrer Folgen. Sie zeigt in Wort und Bild, was angerichtet worden ist, als einigen Aussenseitern die eigene Publizität wichtiger war als das Gesamtwohl der Kunstakademie, dem doch auch sie verpflichtet sein sollten. Fotos und Texte sprechen für sich selbst. Jeder kann sich jetzt ein Urteil bilden. Dank der Hilfe unserer Freunde sind wir in der Lage, die Öffentlichkeit über die Ereignisse während der Lidl-Unruhen im Spiegel der Presse, der Flugblätter und der eigenen Verlautbarungen zu unterrichten. E.T.

Fig. 7: Akademie-Zeitung *newspaper, 1969*

split into status groups (professors, artistic and other employees, and students) as well as factions shaped by content and political bias. The founding of the German Student Party by Beuys and others is an event symptomatic of this context. Political trends breached the Academy walls (Figs. 7–10), and the professors did not present a united front. The gulf deepened between the Beuys faction on the one side and the directorial staff represented by Trier and distinguished professors such as Hoehme, Götz, and Bobek, who were later joined by Kricke, on the other. It was never simply a dispute between an institute of higher learning and the state authorities as has occasionally been suggested. To the contrary, it was a case of profound disagreement on several levels, not least within the Academy itself. On the basis of resolutions enacted in April 1968 and November 1972, the assembly of professors reconstituted itself as something more like a general assembly by admitting representatives of other status groups, notably students. Here the aforementioned universal trend towards 'more democracy' (rather, more participation or sharing) bore fruit. Thinking along those lines has asserted itself in university politics as well as university law and the combined university concept and it has persisted in essentials to the present day (senate, department councils, and other higher academic bodies). Hence it has been in principle for the most part constructive. Nonetheless, it is clear to everyone today with a knowledge of organisations and how they arrive at productive outcomes that, when it comes down to specifics, a giant unstructured and politically radicalised gathering like the general assembly could not by any stretch of the imagination be able to come up with viable results in terms of functional management of an institution of higher learning. Minutes from meetings of the time do not record results so much as they reflect numerous verbal reports and debates; in the process much remained visionary but blurry, above all controversial.

Further, a student parliament was created to replace the previous student representation by class. The parliament corresponded in fundamentals with university structures and has continued to exist to the present day in principle according to the current higher education laws enacted by the constituted student body (student parliament and the General Students' Committee).

Late in1968 Beuys was asked in writing by Academy director Trier to submit a written exposé of his ideas for the future of the Academy so that this representation might also be incorporated in future negotiations with the Ministry of Education. The director's letter remained for some time unanswered so Trier was resigned to being forced 'to assume' that 'he [Beuys] has chosen to eschew committing to writing his conception of what the future of the Academy might be.'[40] However, there is a later text – dated May 1970 – on the subject with Beuys's writing covering one side of a page in the Art Academy administration archives. Its core statement runs: 'The Academy is an institution for society. Its mission consists in permeating all areas of experience with the concept of art (science concept).'[41] The other sentences are essentially also on the same plane of abstraction (Fig. 11).

The dispute about the modalities for admitting students to the Academy, which ultimately led to Beuys's dismissal, shows how closely linked the constitution controversy was with content-related issues.[42] Allegations – made due to lack of knowledge or blurring of the problem yet nonetheless fallacious – equating the limitations on admissions and a *numerus clausus* policy have persisted to the present day. The truth of the matter is that the Academy admissions policy consisted in ascertaining

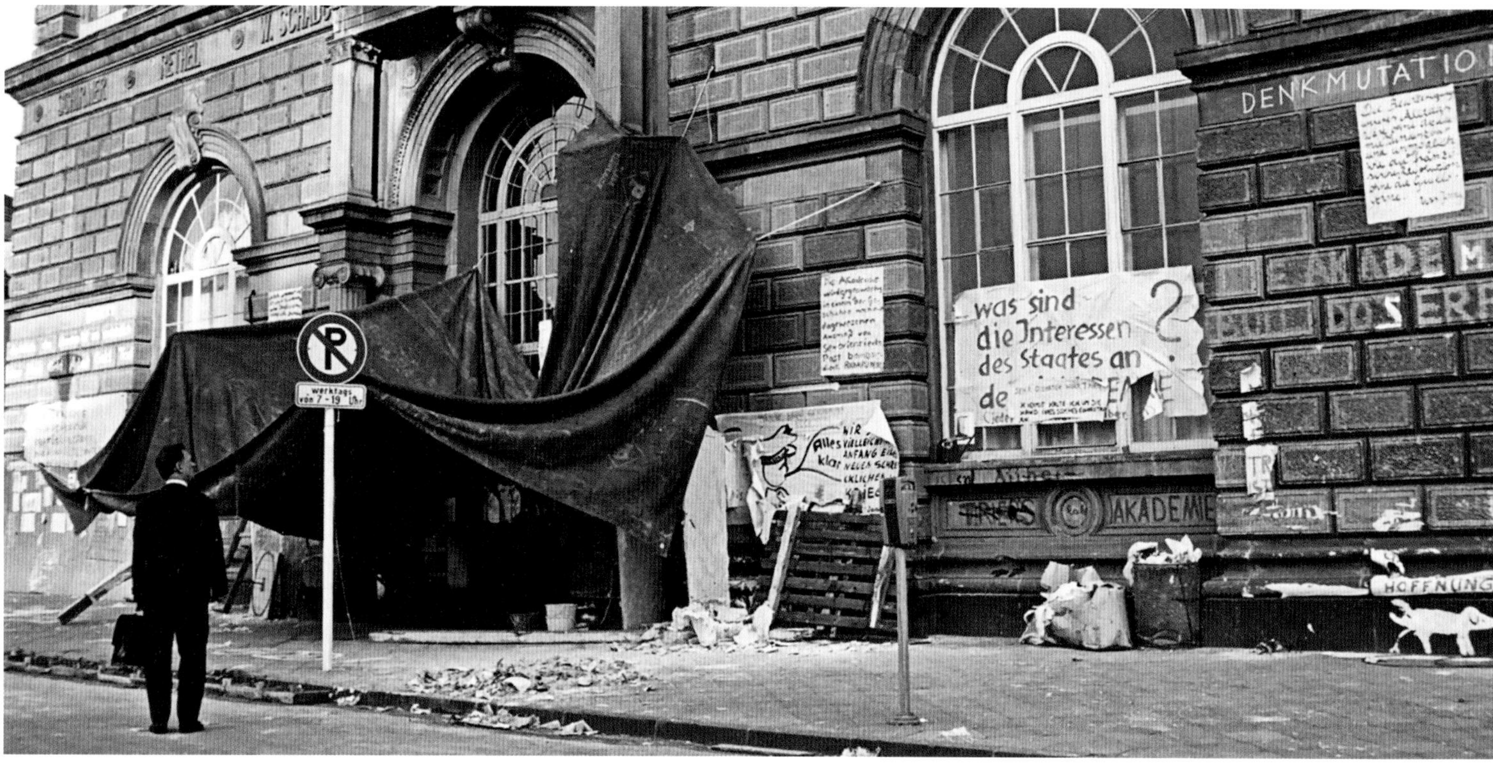

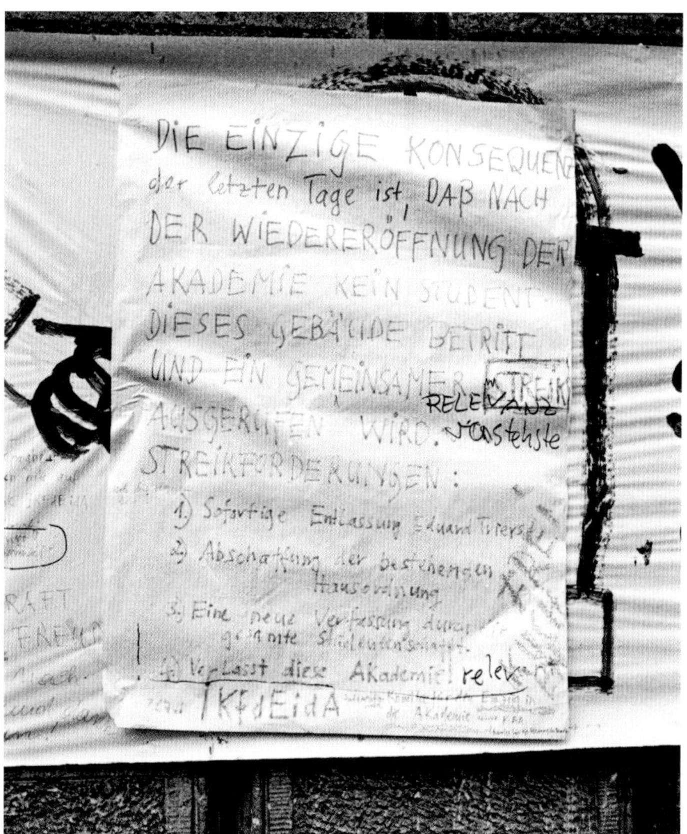

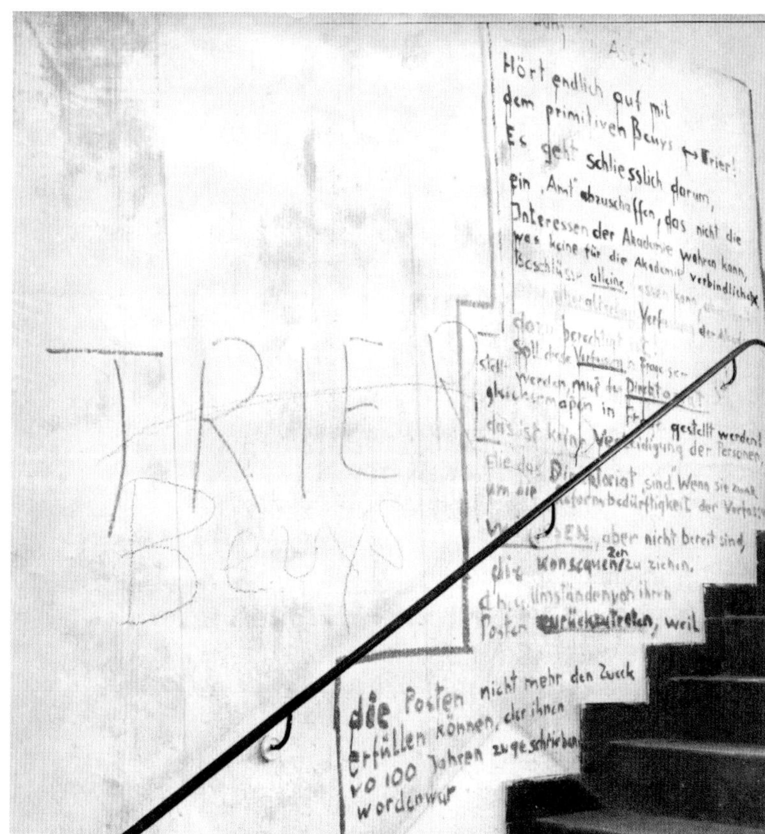

Fig. 8: The entrance to the Academy, 1969

Fig. 9: A poster on the Academy façade with demands made by strikers, 1969

Fig. 10: The Art Academy stairwell, 1969

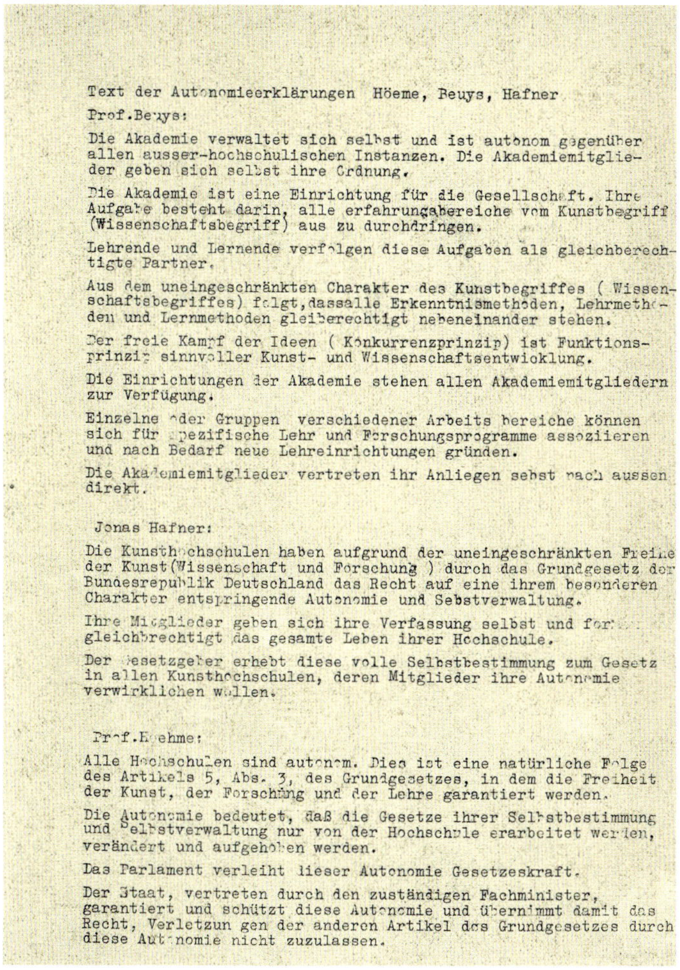

Text der Autonomieerklärungen Höeme, Beuys, Hafner

Prof.Beuys:

Die Akademie verwaltet sich selbst und ist autonom gegenüber allen ausser-hochschulischen Instanzen. Die Akademiemitglieder geben sich selbst ihre Ordnung.

Die Akademie ist eine Einrichtung für die Gesellschaft. Ihre Aufgabe besteht darin, alle erfahrungsbereiche vom Kunstbegriff (Wissenschaftsbegriff) aus zu durchdringen.

Lehrende und Lernende verfolgen diese Aufgaben als gleichberechtigte Partner.

Aus dem uneingeschränkten Charakter des Kunstbegriffes (Wissenschaftsbegriffes) folgt,dassalle Erkenntnismethoden, Lehrmethoden und Lernmethoden gleiberechtigt nebeneinander stehen.

Der freie Kampf der Ideen (Konkurrenzprinzip) ist Funktionsprinzip sinnvoller Kunst- und Wissenschaftsentwicklung.

Die Einrichtungen der Akademie stehen allen Akademiemitgliedern zur Verfügung.

Einzelne oder Gruppen verschiedener Arbeits bereiche können sich für spezifische Lehr und Forschungsprogramme assoziieren und nach Bedarf neue Lehreinrichtungen gründen.

Die Akademiemitglieder vertreten ihr Anliegen sebst nach aussen direkt.

Jonas Hafner:

Die Kunsthochschulen haben aufgrund der uneingeschränkten Freihe der Kunst(Wissenschaft und Forschung) durch das Grundgesetz der Bundesrepublik Deutschland das Recht auf eine ihrem besonderen Charakter entspringende Autonomie und Sebstverwaltung.

Ihre Mitglieder geben sich ihre Verfassung selbst und for... gleichbrechtigt das gesamte Leben ihrer Hochschule.

Der Gesetzgeber erhebt diese volle Selbstbestimmung zum Gesetz in allen Kunsthochschulen, deren Mitglieder ihre Autonomie verwirklichen wollen.

Prof.Hoehme:

Alle Hochschulen sind autonom. Dies ist eine natürliche Folge des Artikels 5, Abs. 3, des Grundgesetzes, in dem die Freiheit der Kunst, der Forschung und der Lehre garantiert werden.

Die Autonomie bedeutet, daß die Gesetze ihrer Selbstbestimmung und Selbstverwaltung nur von der Hochschule erarbeitet werden, verändert und aufgehoben werden.

Das Parlament verleiht dieser Autonomie Gesetzeskraft.

Der Staat, vertreten durch den zuständigen Fachminister, garantiert und schützt diese Autonomie und übernimmt damit das Recht, Verletzun gen der anderen Artikel des Grundgesetzes durch diese Autonomie nicht zuzulassen.

Fig. 11: The text by Joseph Beuys on the future of the Academy, May 1970

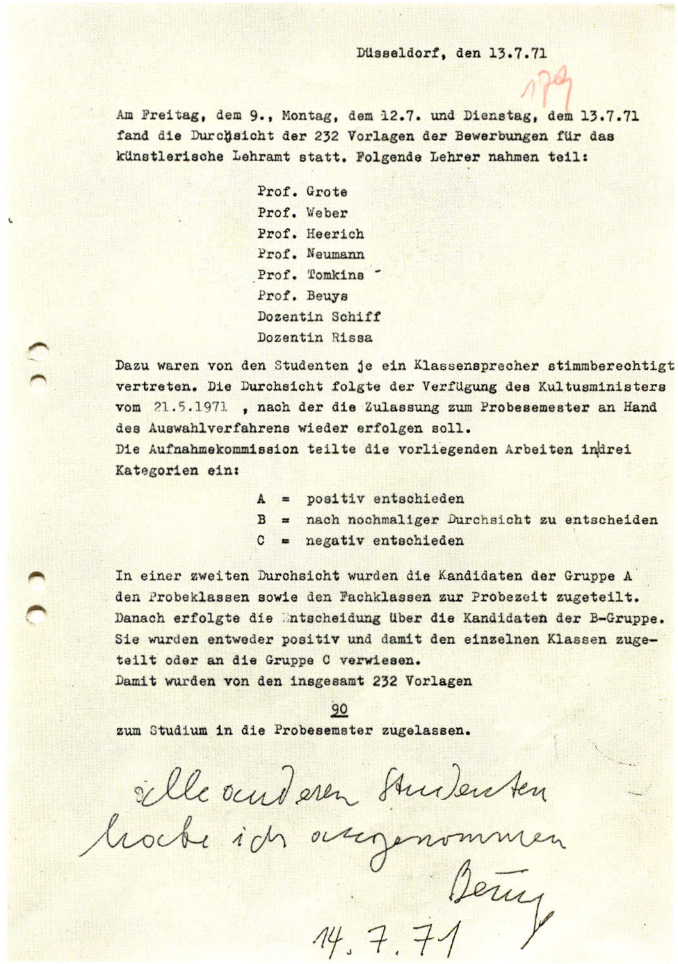

Düsseldorf, den 13.7.71

179

Am Freitag, dem 9., Montag, dem 12.7. und Dienstag, dem 13.7.71 fand die Durchsicht der 232 Vorlagen der Bewerbungen für das künstlerische Lehramt statt. Folgende Lehrer nahmen teil:

Prof. Grote
Prof. Weber
Prof. Heerich
Prof. Neumann
Prof. Tomkins
Prof. Beuys
Dozentin Schiff
Dozentin Rissa

Dazu waren von den Studenten je ein Klassensprecher stimmberechtigt vertreten. Die Durchsicht folgte der Verfügung des Kultusministers vom 21.5.1971 , nach der die Zulassung zum Probesemester an Hand des Auswahlverfahrens wieder erfolgen soll.
Die Aufnahmekommission teilte die vorliegenden Arbeiten in drei Kategorien ein:

A = positiv entschieden
B = nach nochmaliger Durchsicht zu entscheiden
C = negativ entschieden

In einer zweiten Durchsicht wurden die Kandidaten der Gruppe A den Probeklassen sowie den Fachklassen zur Probezeit zugeteilt. Danach erfolgte die Entscheidung über die Kandidaten der B-Gruppe. Sie wurden entweder positiv und damit den einzelnen Klassen zugeteilt oder an die Gruppe C verwiesen.
Damit wurden von den insgesamt 232 Vorlagen

90

zum Studium in die Probesemster zugelassen.

Alle anderen Studenten habe ich aufgenommen
Beuys
14.7.71

Fig. 12: Minutes of the assessment of applicants' portfolios of 13 July 1871, with an addition in Joseph Beuys's handwriting

whether an applicant for a place possessed the necessary artistic talent specific to his or her chosen course of study (in the legal sense, therefore, an objective limitation on admissions, which is not influenced by individual applicants) rather than a policy of prescribing a specific number of students to be admitted. The Academy admissions policy entailed selecting those who seemed suitable for studying there rather than taking an arbitrary number of applicants, so admissions officers could be – and were – flexible. For a century before the period discussed here and afterwards, consensus had reigned that, while examinations set by Academy staff as well as general school leaving certificates (qualifying for university entrance) might be necessary for ascertaining intellectual aptitude, those criteria did not, on the other hand, suffice to meet admissions requirements for studying art. Beuys was – as we know – of a different opinion. The bone of contention at that time was, first, how the admissions procedure should be carried out and what its content and consequences should be. Now there is a legal framework that has been supplemented by a set of Academy regulations as a charter, which the Academy has given itself as a matter for self-administration. At that time, however, there were no normative principles of that kind – just internally proceeding on precedent as in common law and externally following ordinances issued by the Ministry – and the Academy professors disagreed on which procedures and standards were to be applied.

A glance at the minutes from assessing applicant portfolios at the Art Academy of 13 July 1971 provides exemplary insight into the problem.[43] There were 232 applications for places to study art education for state schools alone. Professors (and instructors) Joseph Beuys, Günter Grote, Erwin Heerich, Ellen Neumann, Rissa, Beate Schiff, André Thomkins, and Gert Weber, and speakers for each class with a vote each representing the students, were the Academy committee responsible for choosing ninety applicants (a higher quota than the one used nowadays) in two staggered portfolio reviews from that pool to be admitted to the probationary terms. In his distinctive but highly legible handwriting, Beuys added to the minutes: 'I accepted all the other students. Beuys, 14 July '71' (Fig. 12). Thus Beuys had essentially reduced to absurdity the entire proceedings that had been undergone and in which he had participated. The class structure with its personal master-pupil relationships and collective work leading to individual artistic outcomes was also subverted.

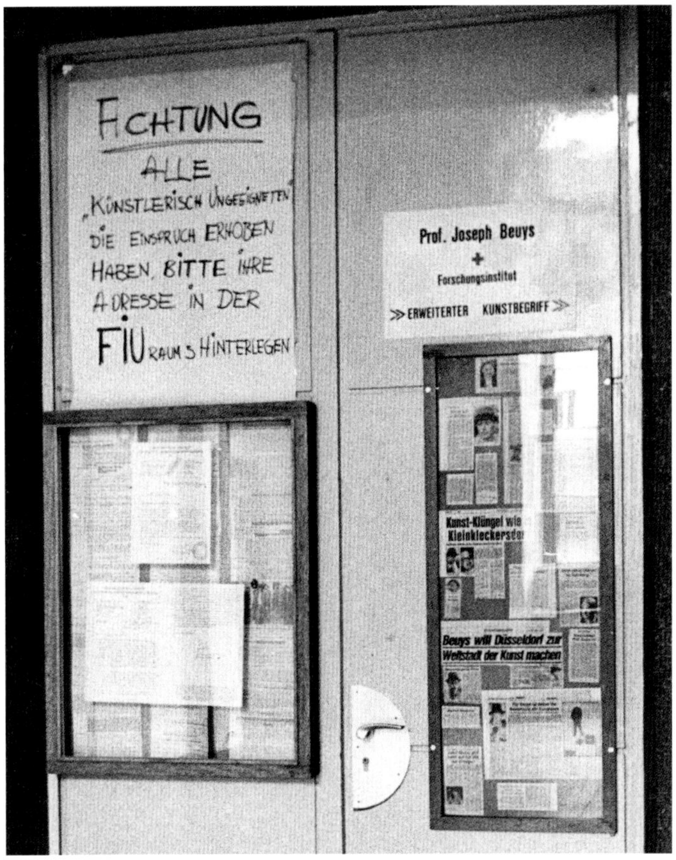

Fig. 13: The door to Joseph Beuys's classroom, early/mid-80s

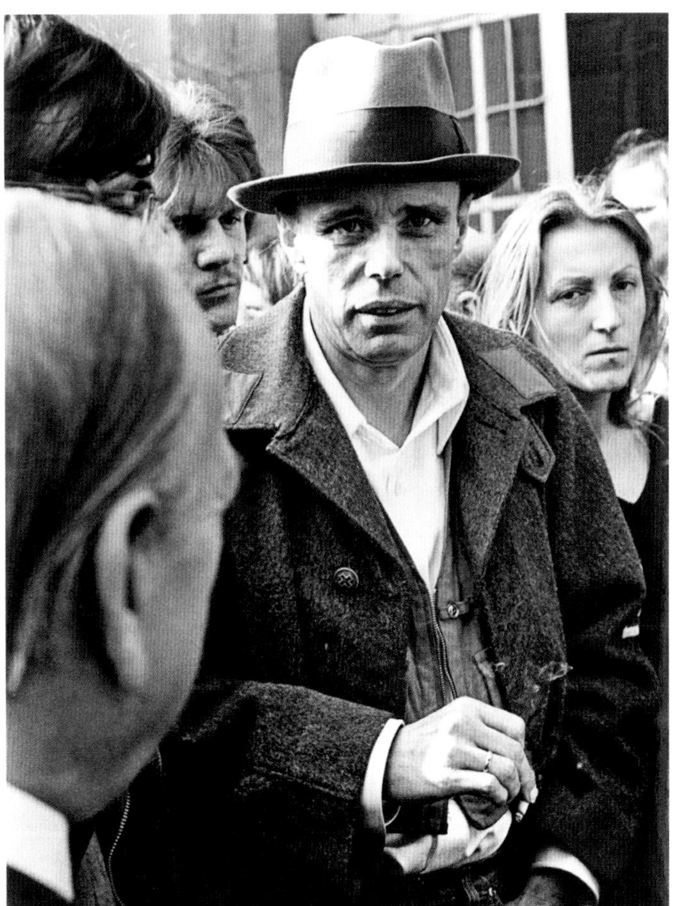

Fig. 14: Joseph Beuys after dismissal, 1972

Behaviour like that could not elicit a consensual response (consistent application of the pronouncement 'Everyone is an artist' along such lines has never attained majority opinion status in the Academy or anywhere else in the art world for that matter). Indeed it led to the final break the following year when Beuys, accompanied by '54 of the rejected applicants and an indeterminate number of other persons' occupied the student secretariat of the Art Academy from 11 to 12 October 1972 – that is, for a workday and an entire night – to force the matriculation of those rejected applicants (Fig. 13).[44] The affair culminated in a police operation and led to the summary dismissal of Beuys by Johannes Rau, then Minister of Science in North Rhine-Westphalia (Fig. 14). It is interesting to note in this connection that the subsequent labour tribunal proceedings found that, although Beuys's aims and arguments were not legally objectionable in view of the discussion process and the unclarified legal situation respecting admissions modalities, the means he employed were not commensurate with the end desired.[45] Even at that time, free expression of opinion and free discussion were not prohibited by law.

Although Beuys had been forced to resign, the hearing ended with his being conceded a studio within the Academy by way of compensation.[46] That studio became the headquarters of his Free International University (FIU), which had nothing at all to do with the Academy *qua* institution, and the situation quietened down over the years. For a while the admissions tests continued to be a flashpoint eliciting protests and disruptions, but work in art both within the Academy and outside it gradually resumed its usual tenor. Symptomatic of that time were exhibitions and publications such as *Letztes Mal hast du doch gesagt daß du keine Kunst machst 21.–28. März 1976 Museum Wiesbaden, die Rinke-Klasse Kunstakademie Düsseldorf* [But Last Time you Said you Didn't Do Art, 21–28 March 1976 at Museum Wiesbaden, the Rinke Class at the Düsseldorf Art Academy]. The interrelationship of politics and art again tended to focus on aesthetic content and forms of expression in art as exemplified, for instance, by Jörg Immendorff's life and work. As a student of the Lidl Academy and instigator of the concomitant mayhem, Immendorff had caused the Düsseldorf Art Academy to close for several days. Some three decades later, however, after a distinguished career as an artist, Immendorff was again at the Academy as a professor teaching a class of artists (after holding a similar post at the Frankfurt Städelschule) with a markedly stringent artistic regimen and participating as a matter of course in the admissions tests as a professor and examiner (now with an average admissions quota of approximately 1:10).

Within the context of the constitutional debate, a further point should be touched on, which, although it posed such a great threat to the very existence of the Academy as an institution, has continued to attract far less public attention than the aforementioned upheavals: the autonomy of the Academy, which was called into question on the grounds of the (long since refuted) hypothesis that the Academy might acquire university status only by being affiliated with a university. That issue – at the time loaded with political dynamite – was decidedly to the fore while the debate about vocational universities and the establishment of new ones raged in North Rhine-Westphalia in 1971. At that time the Academy was unable to reach a consensus due to the events described above. Since there was no overriding agreement, the Academy sent a declaration to the Ministry late in 1971[47] which 'revealed opinions split three ways to result in the following different stances:

I. A temporising attitude ...
II. Acceptance of not including art institutes in the law governing the development of vocational universities
III. A demand that art institutes should be incorporated in the law governing the development of vocational universities'

The Academy can thank its lucky stars that the state of North Rhine-Westphalia did not exploit its weakness at the time (although perhaps an Academy in the state it was then in would not have been welcomed in a combined university) and that it was left to enjoy its solitary status. Nonetheless, an institutional measure was taken in 1971 (not by the state legislative but by the executive, the state government) and very rapidly implemented: founding the Münster Institute for Art Teachers of the Düsseldorf State Art Academy (now the Münster Art Academy; more on this to follow). The close affiliation of this new institution with the Düsseldorf Art Academy was expressed both institutionally and personnel-wise. From the legal angle, it was a non-autonomous division of the Düsseldorf Academy, which, however, gave the new institute 'free rein' and granted it ample scope in creative matters. As for personnel, there was strong continuity between the new institute and the parent institution in as much as the young inaugural professors were drawn from the pool of Academy graduates with distinction and appointed after fast-track appointment proceedings. As the name indicated, the purpose of the new institute was to train artists who planned to teach at state schools as civil servants, thus relieving some of the admissions pressure on the Düsseldorf Academy. And it did, particularly since the first generation of professors in Münster felt committed from the outset to fine art as well, based studying on the artist-taught class principle, and took over the Düsseldorf Art Academy model, filling it with their own art content.

By then it was again time for a change in directors in Düsseldorf. Eduard Trier, an art historian who had had to bear the entire brunt of the events described above and endure many unjust – including *ad hominem* – attacks and whose tenure as director had been anything but fun and games, moved to Bonn University as a professor. His successor in Düsseldorf was Norbert Kricke, a sculptor whose work had been acclaimed in the art world. A professor at the Academy for years, Norbert Kricke became director in 1972 and remained in the post until 1981. He encountered a combination of fortunate circumstances in that he was able to link his own creative powers as an artist and his knowledge of the art world and its actors with the favourable conditions established in the 'art for all' phase and the need of the state of North Rhine-Westphalia to consolidate the position of the Düsseldorf Art Academy in the context of an expanding tertiary education sector. The state of North Rhine-Westphalia, the Science Ministry, and its representatives were also happy to have found in Kricke a person who was determined to lead the Art Academy into calmer waters. Whenever Kricke wanted a new post to be created or had to assert himself for a person he wanted to have appointed (or to prevent an appointment he did not want), he was supported. Radical cost-cutting fell to his successors and the smooth and efficient functioning of the Art Academy undeniably had priority.

The impressive roll of teaching staff by the end of Kricke's tenure in 1981 – and beyond – was as follows:[48]

Ernst Althoff (architecture), Bernhard Becher (photography), Walter Biemel (philosophy), Günter Blecks (teaching art and art education), Karl Bobek (sculpture), Daniel Buren (a visiting professor who would return to the Academy for several years when Markus Lüpertz was rector), Edgar Callahan (interdisciplinary project development), Tony Cragg (at that time instructor in the orientation programme, he was appointed to a chair in sculpture during Lüpertz's tenure as rector and ultimately became rector himself), Siegfried Cremer (painting techniques), Rolf Crummenauer (painting, formerly free-hand drawing), Eugen Gomringer (aesthetics), Rissa (painting), Gotthard Graubner (painting), Erwin Heerich (sculpture), Dr Liesel-Lotte Herkenrath (education), Gerhard Hoehme (painting), Dr Walter Jürgen Hofmann (art history), Alfonso Hüppi (painting), Irmin Kamp (sculpture), Ernst Kasper (architecture), Luise Kimme (orientation programme), Konrad Klapheck (painting), Karl Kneidl (stage design), Tünn Konerding (font, book design), Norbert Kricke (sculpture), Dieter Krieg (painting), Christian Megert (integration of fine art and architecture), Ellen Neumann (painting), Nam June Paik (video), Erich Reusch (integration of fine art and architecture), Gerhard Richter (painting), Klaus Rinke (sculpture), Rolf Sackenheim (graphic arts), Beate Schiff (sculpture), Fritz Schwegler (painting, later sculpture), Dr Werner Spies (art history), James Stirling (architecture), Dr Heinrich Theissing (art history), Dr Hans Peter Thurn (sociology), and Günther Uecker (sculpture).

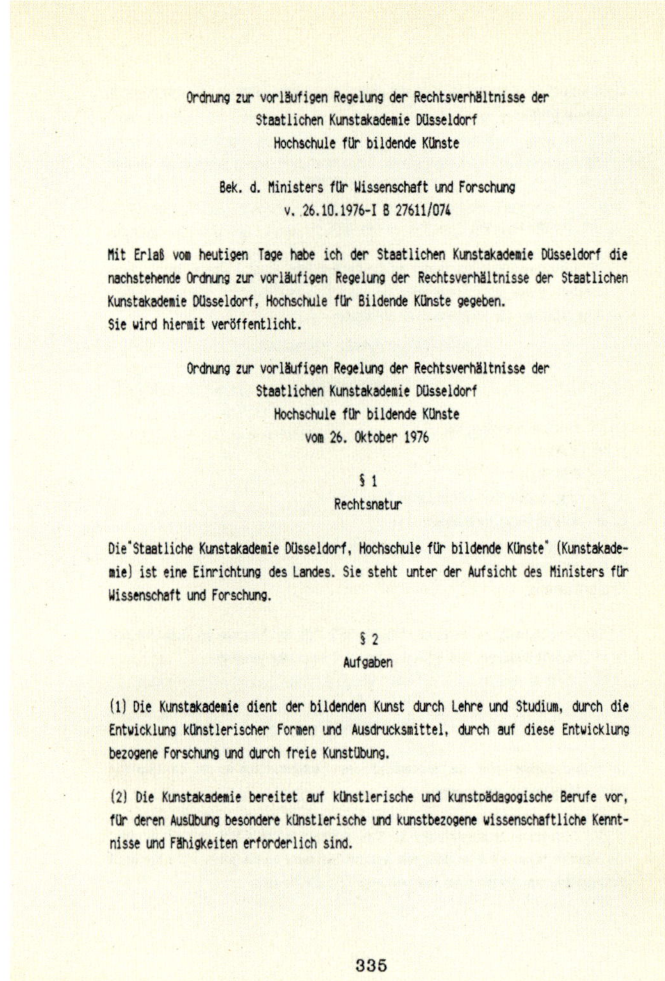
Ordnung zur vorläufigen Regelung der Rechtsverhältnisse der
Staatlichen Kunstakademie Düsseldorf
Hochschule für bildende Künste

Bek. d. Ministers für Wissenschaft und Forschung
v. 26.10.1976-I B 27611/074

Mit Erlaß vom heutigen Tage habe ich der Staatlichen Kunstakademie Düsseldorf die nachstehende Ordnung zur vorläufigen Regelung der Rechtsverhältnisse der Staatlichen Kunstakademie Düsseldorf, Hochschule für Bildende Künste gegeben.
Sie wird hiermit veröffentlicht.

Ordnung zur vorläufigen Regelung der Rechtsverhältnisse der
Staatlichen Kunstakademie Düsseldorf
Hochschule für bildende Künste
vom 26. Oktober 1976

§ 1
Rechtsnatur

Die "Staatliche Kunstakademie Düsseldorf, Hochschule für bildende Künste" (Kunstakademie) ist eine Einrichtung des Landes. Sie steht unter der Aufsicht des Ministers für Wissenschaft und Forschung.

§ 2
Aufgaben

(1) Die Kunstakademie dient der bildenden Kunst durch Lehre und Studium, durch die Entwicklung künstlerischer Formen und Ausdrucksmittel, durch auf diese Entwicklung bezogene Forschung und durch freie Kunstübung.

(2) Die Kunstakademie bereitet auf künstlerische und kunstpädagogische Berufe vor, für deren Ausübung besondere künstlerische und kunstbezogene wissenschaftliche Kenntnisse und Fähigkeiten erforderlich sind.

335

Not only were personnel added but space and material resources were enlarged and consolidated, a practice that was continued in the subsequent tenures of Irmin Kamp and Markus Lüpertz. Kricke's tenure is particularly notable for the temporary annexe for the orientation programme (the two probationary terms) on the grounds in front of the Academy building and some rented premises in the city centre for some of the classes taught by artists (Becher, Kneidl, Richter, and Uecker). Thus the Düsseldorf Art Academy added personnel and space to become all the more important to art.

The state government implemented a constitutional reform of the executive, which for the time being put an administratively decreed end to all debates within the Academy and the statutes of 1831: the provisional regime of 1976 (Figs. 15, 16).[49] Parts of the 1970 North Rhine-Westphalian Higher Education Law (Hochschulgesetz) were taken over and, without any legal basis, were linked by the Science Ministry by decree with tried and tested fundamental rules typical of the Academy and previous traditions. The move was motivated by the experiences of the past few years. This hybrid constitution (concentrated in a handful of provisions) must be viewed as a viable – despite quite considerable inconsistencies[50] – temporary expedient for the decade to come while the debate about a new, first law governing the state art institutes was postponed for a time. It was taken up again in the early 1980s (more on this later). Until 1987 the Academy continued to be an institution without autonomy and corporative status and without a charter of its own. University status had yet to be attained both legally and officially but, for all intents and practical purposes, it was already in the offing.

Despite such stopgap measures and all the concomitant personal disagreements and despite the fact that distrust and marginalisation persisted within the Academy even then and were not least associated with Kricke's combative personality, the Düsseldorf Art Academy was not only considerably consolidated and for the most part pacified by the end of his tenure. It was also manifestly a large art institute of international standing and worldwide importance and, as such, was making a huge impact on art. The Academy was particularly committed to fine art, apart from the course of study in teaching at state schools, a bias which was not without controversy.

Kricke chose Irmin Kamp, a sculptor – who had been transitional deputy director, a practice known under earlier directors – as his successor as director of the Academy

(3) Die Kunstakademie arbeitet bei der Wahrnehmung ihrer Aufgaben mit anderen Hochschulen zusammen.

§ 3

Sitz und Gliederung

(1) Die Kunstakademie hat ihren Sitz in Düsseldorf.

(2) Die Kunstakademie gliedert sich in die Fachbereiche Kunst I (Freie Kunst), Kunst II (Kunsterziehung) und Kunstbezogene Wissenschaften in Düsseldorf. Die Kunstakademie hat eine Abteilung für Kunsterziehung in Münster.

§ 4

Hochschulangehörige

(1) der Hochschule gehören an:
1. der Direktor
2. die Hochschullehrer
3. die künstlerisch-technischen Lehrkräfte
4. der leitende Verwaltungsbeamte
5. die Mitarbeiter
6. die Lehrbeauftragten
7. die Studenten.

(2) Die Hochschulangehörigen wirken bei der Erfüllung der Aufgaben der Kunstakademie in der Freiheit zusammen, die Artikel 5 Abs. 3 Grundgesetz verbürgt.

§ 5

Hochschullehrer

(1) Hochschullehrer sind die hauptamtlich oder hauptberuflich an der Kunstakademie tätigen Professoren und Dozenten.

(2) Die Professoren nehmen Aufgaben der Kunstakademie in ihrem Fach selbständig wahr. Die Dozenten nehmen künstlerische oder wissenschaftliche Lehraufgaben sowie die damit zusammenhängenden Aufgaben der Kunstakademie selbständig wahr.

336

(3) Die Hochschullehrer sind im Rahmen der für ihr Dienstverhältnis geltenden Regelungen verpflichtet, Lehrveranstaltungen ihrer Fächer in den an der Kunstakademie angebotenen Studiengängen abzuhalten und die von den zuständigen Gremien der Kunstakademie zur Sicherstellung des Lehrangebots gefaßten Beschlüsse zu verwirklichen.

(4) Die Hochschullehrer werden auf Vorschlag der Kunstakademie vom Minister für Wissenschaft und Forschung berufen. Stellen für Hochschullehrer sind unter Angabe des Aufgabenbereiches der Anforderungen die an die Bewerber gestellt werden, der Art der Stelle und des Zeitpunkts der Besetzung öffentlich auszuschreiben.

§ 6

Künstlerisch-technische Lehrkräfte

Den künstlerisch-technischen Lehrkräften obliegt die Vermittlung künstlerisch-technischer Fertigkeiten und Kenntnisse. In diesem Tätigkeitsbereich unterstützen sie die Hochschullehrer bei deren Aufgaben und ergänzen das Lehrangebot.

§ 7

Mitarbeiter

Mitarbeiter sind die an der Kunstakademie tätigen Beamten, Angestellten und Arbeiter, die keine Lehrtätigkeit wahrnehmen.

§ 8

Studenten

(1) Studenten werden durch Einschreibung für einen der Studiengänge in die Kunstakademie aufgenommen. Die Voraussetzungen der Einschreibung, ihre Rücknahme sowie die Zulassung von Zweit- und Gasthörern werden in einer Einschreibungsordnung geregelt, die der Minister für Wissenschaft und Forschung erläßt.

(2) Das aktive und passive Wahlrecht zu den Gremien haben nur die eingeschriebenen Studenten. Wählbar sind nur Studenten, die das Probestudium erfolgreich absolviert haben.

337

Figs. 15, 16: An extract from the provisional charter of the State Düsseldorf Art Academy of 26 October 1976

(1982–1987). Irmin Kamp viewed herself, on the one hand, as clearly in the tradition of her immediate predecessor, whom she highly esteemed. On the other, the constitutional debate and the question of structuring the executive of the Academy arose again (Fig. 17). Before she was officially confirmed as director, Walter Biemel, a philosopher and deputy director, functioned as an interim executive director. Moreover, confirmation of her tenure was dogged by the question of whether the post might better be filled by someone from the external – from the Academy standpoint – culture industry (perhaps from the museum sector). Here presidential models featuring 'external managers' as directors in the tertiary education sector spring to mind. Later they would be introduced at quite a few other (art) institutes of higher education, but they never gained acceptance at the Düsseldorf Academy. An external management model would not have been permissible under the aforementioned set of provisional regulations; if an external manager had been chosen, previous appointment to a chair in the Fine Art Department (Art I) would have been a non-negotiable requirement. An appointment of this kind was indeed mooted – with specific external candidates in mind – despite the contradiction in terms that the candidates were not artists, but nothing came of it. Nevertheless, a fixed-term chair for art and public relations was later established (while Irmin Kamp was still director) and Kaspar König was appointed to it for the time span then envisaged (now there is another fixed-term chair in the art-related arts and humanities to which Robert Fleck has been appointed).

The 1976 provisional set of regulations abolished the general assembly. The senate, which had been instituted in Kricke's tenure and was composed of representatives of all groups, a large majority of them professors, served as the governing board of the Academy, which was subdivided into three departments: Fine Art (or Art I), Art Education (or Art II), and art-related Arts and Humanities (see par. 3, sub. 2, Provisional Regulations [vorläufige Ordnung]). Both in the senate and the departmental councils there were a number of urgent appointment-related issues, with priority given to resolving the issue of in-house appointments. Loaded with personal concerns and heated debates in the senate, this was such a contentious issue because at one time newly appointed external professors, no matter how highly qualified they were, had to serve first as employees or civil servants in a lower pay bracket and later – when vacancies opened up higher on the scale – were promoted

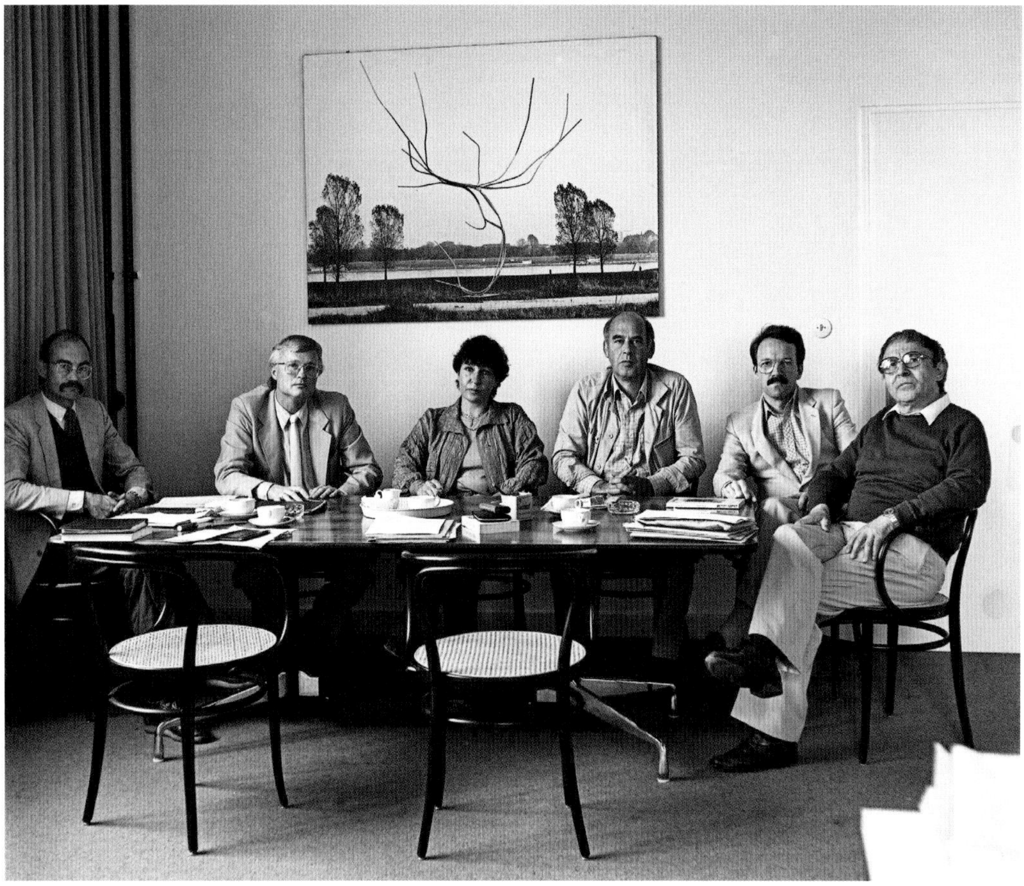

Fig. 17: Irmin Kamp and the rectorate team, 1982; from left to right: Peter M. Lynen, Heinrich Theissing, Irmin Kamp, Christian Megert, Hans Peter Thurn, Erwin Heerich

for all intents and purposes in-house. At the latest when the C-scale system was adopted for paying civil servants and appointment procedures approached those established for universities, such mechanisms that were decried as being 'more suitable for schools' became untenable, and justified and binding limits to the number of 'in-house appointments' were made mandatory (and are still in force). They apply above all when in-house chairs have become vacant. By law, vacancies for professors must be publicly advertised.[51]

The Academy could by then act on those lines only in a few, conclusively justified, exceptional cases but certainly not as a rule so it had to dash staff members' hopes of promotion – no matter how subjectively understandable their expectations might have been.

The change succeeded and the following external staff were appointed in Irmin Kamp's tenure: Michael Buthe (painting), Jan Dibbets (painting), Franz Eggenschwiler (graphic art), Dr Paul Good (philosophy), Kaspar König (art and public relations), Markus Lüpertz (painting), Walter Nikkels (design, book design), Laurids Ortner (architecture), David Rabinowitch (sculpture), and Ulrich Rückriem (sculpture). The concept informing appointments to the Academy, which was committed to both diversity and quality and was not at all like the training provided by schools or restricted in content, again proved its worth, and appointments led to a strengthening of the staff on the whole. The class principle not only survived but came out of the restructuring stronger than before, premised on the provisions that every art professor should bear the responsibility for art content, forms of teaching, and presentations mounted by his/her classes, and teachers might also codetermine with their students the aims and eventual outcomes themselves. One of the reasons for the positive impact made by the new regimen was that both the Academy as a whole with its Tours (yearly exhibitions that look back on a long tradition at the Academy and are participated in by each of the classes taught by artists although they all present at the same time) and the individual classes have increasingly sought public recognition both within the Academy and outside it with specific projects and one-man shows and, in so doing, have earned acclaim and attracted attention far beyond the Academy itself. Kamp, among whose priorities promotion and presentation of students ranked particularly high, supported activities of that kind. The Tours are recorded in synoptic illustrated volumes,[52] and the importance of some individual classes and class projects still resonates today in a wide range of publications.[53] With the Academy participating, the state of North Rhine-Westphalia later presented the seven art academies and conservatories with student work and projects in several exhibitions – backed by the Ministry of Science. A series of exhibitions entitled *Kunst Studenten stellen aus* [Art Students Show their Work] was launched across the Federal Republic.

Apart from those – traditional yet each launched with modern flair – forms of practising and presenting art, there were projects which, since that time, have been called 'arts development projects'. By now the term has been incorporated in the Higher Education Law and its usage is preferred to 'art research'.[54] The Academy was certainly receptive to such projects, which occasionally also received financial backing from the state of North Rhine-Westphalia and were singled out for recognition by it. The wide variety of noteworthy and varied projects carried out by the Academy with such backing include the interdisciplinary project managed by Irmin Kamp herself, *Gezielte Umgebungsbeeinflussung mit künstlerischen Mitteln* [Targeting One's Surroundings with Artistic Means]; Gerhard Hoehme's, *l'Etna – Mythos und Wirklichkeit* [L'Etna – Myth and Reality], an arts development project featuring a cycle of pictures in large formats (and an explanatory catalogue) and shown in the Great Hall at the Academy; Gerhard Richter's series of pictures dealing with 18 October 1977 (the Baader-Meinhof cycle), for which he was given leave from his teaching commitments in the framework of sabbatical terms for research; and, Günther Uecker's many projects with his classes, specifically those related to scientific issues.[55] Although 'arts development projects' is a fuzzy concept,[56] the artists themselves are definitely in a position to breathe life into the term. In this respect, Beuys, with his interdisciplinary approaches, ideas, and projects that blurred the boundaries between art and science, could certainly be regarded as a harbinger of things to come.

At that time, architecture at the Academy was in dire need of reform as a course of study because, on the one hand, undergraduate studies in architecture leading to a degree at an art institute could not meet the requirements of the profession as practised and, on the other, numerous architecture courses (competing with the Academy and leading to university diplomas) offered at universities, technical universities, and polytechnics, which had been expanding rapidly since the 1970s – when the general conditions provided by the state were conducive to growth – were no longer sustainable. With the participation of the architecture professors as the driving force behind it, the Academy directorate designed a post-graduate course in architecture and the Ministry of Science approved it. This post-graduate course was still based on the idea of architecture as the art of building and on the principle of classes taught by experts in the field. The requirement for admission to the Academy architecture course was now, however, a completed architecture degree (diploma) from a (technical) university or a polytechnic. In addition, it went without saying that an applicant's aptitude for art still had to be assessed by an Academy committee. Quite a number of Academy publications[57] are instructive on which artistic and planning tasks were to be intensively worked on. Incidentally, the Academy architecture classes also participated in the general Academy Tours.

Complex negotiations with the city of Düsseldorf and the state of North Rhine-Westphalia conducted by Irmin Kamp and Peter M. Lynen provided the initial foundations for an architectural and spatial restructuring of the Academy, which were then actually implemented by the directorate that succeeded them. After several alternatives had been investigated and rejected (including having the Düsseldorf Art Academy take over the buildings of what had once been the Education Institute [polytechnic] in Neuss – it would have provided many square metres of floor space but was unsuitably far from the main building), the city of Düsseldorf transferred, under the terms of inheritance law, the building formerly occupied by the municipal pawnbrokers in the street Reuterkaserne (at that time still occupied by municipal offices, which were subsequently moved to a new technical administration building) to the state of North Rhine-Westphalia on behalf of the Düsseldorf Art Academy. Thus the Academy finally succeeded in obtaining a second large building in its immediate vicinity (now the Rheinflügel [Rhine Tract]), a property at which both Schwippert and Beuys – independently of each other – had already cast covetous glances (Figs. 18, 19).

Since that time the Düsseldorf Art Academy has possessed its own, enclosed little campus in the heart of the city.[58] What the Academy was required to do in exchange was to give up the properties it had rented at the time and the provisional container structure for the Orientation Department – the latter was demolished. But that, too, furthered the campus idea. Moreover, considerable renovation and redesigning of the new second building had to be undertaken but the city of Düsseldorf did not share the costs. Instead the Academy had to apply for federal and state government financing under the provisions of the Law for the Support of Building Higher Education Institutions (Hochschulbauförderungsgesetz). At the same time, an elaborate overhaul of the main building (together with the Academy directorate and administration as well as the state civil engineering administration) began that would take many years. Most of the work was undertaken during Lüpertz's tenure and

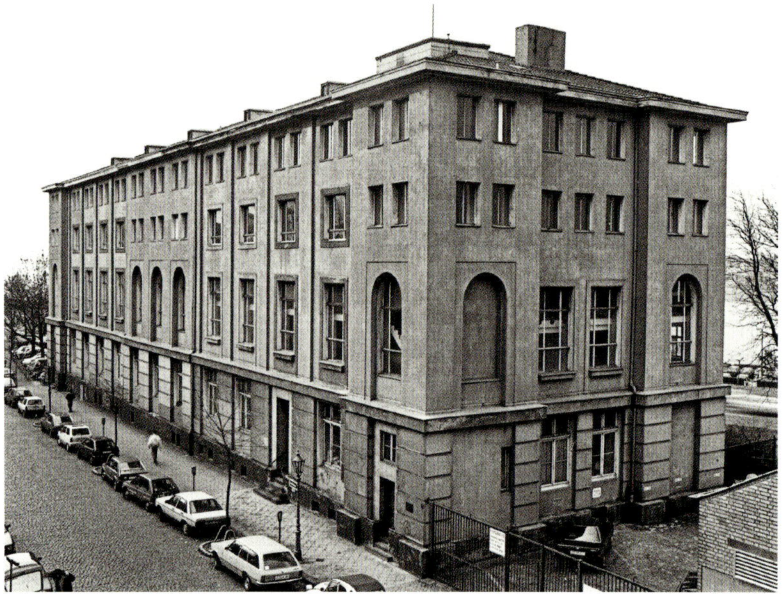

Fig. 18: The former municipal pawnbrokers before it was converted for Academy use, 1987

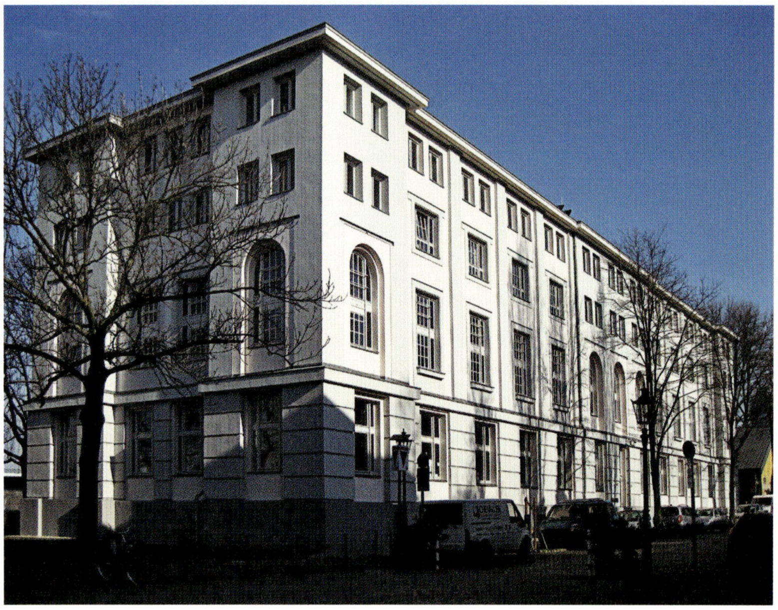

Fig. 19: The Rhine Tract of the Düsseldorf Art Academy, 2013

was finished while he was still director. Important aims in restoring and preserving the building as a listed structure included strengthening the building to meet the requirements of use as an art academy and modernising it. On the whole, this combination was very successful, especially since the initial overhaul budget was never exceeded. Under the terms of the provisional constitution of 1976, the district president was no longer curator of the Academy. Nonetheless, functions of that kind were at first actually assumed by an intermediate authority (notably in the personnel administration sector). Since that was not a viable long-term option, personnel records and areas of functional competence were transferred to the Academy and its administration in the 1980s. Another step had thus been taken towards autonomy – also in what had hitherto been known to be matters for the state – and towards a university-style administration. This circumstance coincided with thinking on reform in the tertiary education sector, whereby the legislature of the state of North Rhine-Westphalia at that time had to execute the Framing Law for Higher Education (Hochschulrahmengesetz) enacted by the federal government. This hearing, accompanied by numerous debates and policy briefs within the Academy and outside it, took up nearly a decade (and Irmin Kamp's entire tenure) until the first Art Institute Law (Kunsthochschulgesetz) of the State of North Rhine-Westphalia finally went into force in November 1987. The framework of the law-making procedure also concerned the number and structure of the art academies and conservatories in the state of North Rhine-Westphalia. The upshot was that their number was increased from four to seven, including the departments of the art academy in Münster and the Robert-Schumann-Hochschule in Düsseldorf that became independent as well as the new Academy of Media Arts that was founded in Cologne. Integrating the Art and Design Departments at Cologne Polytechnic in the Düsseldorf Art Academy had previously been mooted. The Art Academy, however, rejected that proposal so decisively and with such well-reasoned arguments – with reference to orientation and areas of specialisation – that it was never implemented.

Like her predecessor's tenure as director, that of Irmin Kamp and her executive team was not without conflicts, internecine squabbles, and external controversies. Yet for all that, it led on the whole to a further consolidation of the Academy and emphasised its continuity *qua* institution with internationally acclaimed aesthetic and academic standards.

THE ART ACADEMY IN THE ERA OF NEW PUBLIC MANAGEMENT

Before the new Art Institute Law came into force, the painter Markus Lüpertz, who had been a professor at the Düsseldorf Art Academy since 1986 – before coming to Düsseldorf he had been at the Karlsruhe Academy – was appointed director of the Düsseldorf Academy (still under the terms of the provisional constitution) in 1987 before the first rector was elected. Only a year later, the election was held and Lüpertz was confirmed as rector for a tenure of four years. Lüpertz was re-elected four more times plus an extra year until 2008. Tony

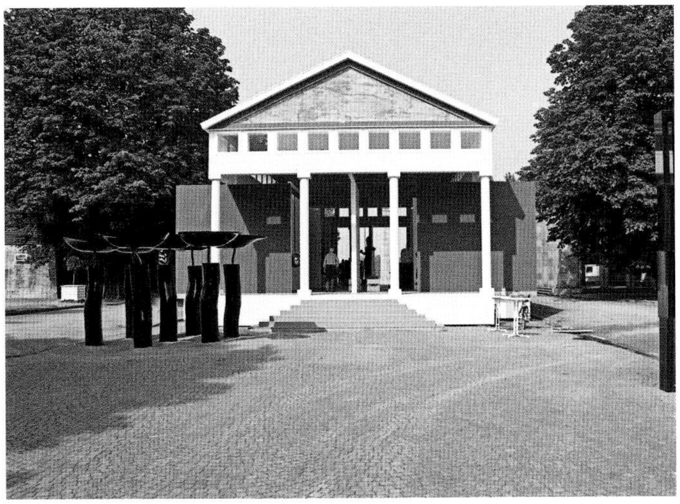

Fig. 20: The Sculpture Pavilion, Quadriennale 2006, Düsseldorf

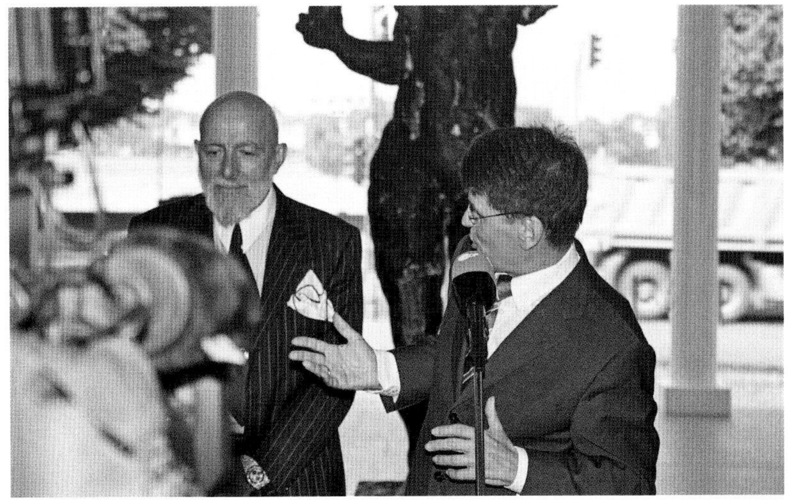

Fig. 21: Inaugurating the Sculpture Pavilion, Quadriennale 2006, Markus Lüpertz and Joachim Erwin, Lord Mayor of Düsseldorf

Cragg was elected as the next rector in 2009. Lüpertz's tenure – he was elected six times altogether by the Academy members in the senate, with a large majority of the votes cast, in fact usually unanimously – lasted twenty-two years in total, considerably surpassing those of all predecessors since 1945.

The early part of this period saw the new Art Institute Law implemented. It finally granted the Academy university-equivalent status as a corporation under public law with legally guaranteed self-administration rights including the right to draw up a charter (all this in addition to the continuance of its legal status as a state institution).[59] The Academy lost no time in enacting its first basic law of its own as well as voting regulations, thus laying the groundwork for the first election to the rectorate. Since then the Academy executive has consisted in a rectorate, which comprises a rector as its head, two prorectors, and a chancellor. The first prorector was Walter J. Hofmann (until then a professor and sporadically dean of the art-related Arts and Humanities Department), who remained in office throughout Lüpertz's tenure. The second prorector was the painter Rissa, succeeded by the sculptor Tony Cragg. Throughout the rectorates until 2008, Peter M. Lynen, a lawyer (already a top-tier administration civil servant with a total of twenty-six years of service at the Academy), was chancellor.

Implementation of the 1987 Art Institute Law not only wrought changes in the executive structure. It also restructured the departments. Departments I (Fine Art) and II (Art Education) were merged into a single Art Department. The second department was, as it had been, Art Theory and Art History. All artists who were professors (including the architects) were members of the Art Department. This arrangement not only entailed organisational subdivision but also put paid satisfactorily to the invidious distinction between 'fine art' and 'training for teaching art at state schools' and ultimately guaranteed the equality of all teachers and students. Students of both courses (fine art and training as art teachers) were permitted to study in all classes, and all artists who were professors were obliged to devote themselves to both groups. Since then, the difference between those two student groups has tended to be noticed only by chance in the practical teaching situation in the artists' classes.

As for syllabus design in the artist-taught classes, the rectorate, including the rector personally, guaranteed that no professor would be subjected to teaching a prescribed curriculum and all would be allowed enormous freedom in their choice of teaching methods. It was up to the individual teachers whether they worked with individual students on correcting them (and their work) or in discussion gatherings and other forms of group teaching with several or all students being taught at once, and how those students were influenced or interacted with each other, or whether the subject matter was handled more in a hands-on artistic manner or subjects were discussed that went beyond the matter at hand, and how strongly the professors deployed their own work and their personalities as artists as role models, or, on the other hand, were reticent and eschewed transmitting their own forms of expression. As a result, a wide variety of personal viewpoints and 'class styles' existed at the Academy, as had indeed been intended. There was no standard, let alone 'prescribed', conception of what art had to be. The public could gain some insight into this internal freedom and creative power, especially through the Academy Tours, but this has not always been understood and has even led to criticism, groundless though it might be. Academy exhibitions are more than mere instruments for public-relations work; they serve directly as the practice of art and enhance its outreach efficacy. Similarly, there have also been exhibitions of work by professors teaching at the Academy, and special contributions by the Academy – for instance, under the auspices of the first Düsseldorf Quadriennale in 2006 in a pavilion designed by Lüpertz and filled with sculpture by Academy members on the premises at the Ehrenhof in front of the Kunstpalast Museum (Figs. 20, 21).[60]

The later Art Institute Law of 2008 reflects this wide range – as practised for a long time by the Düsseldorf Art Academy – both making it the norm and guaranteeing it: 'In the art subjects, art teaching and art study in artist-taught classes can be concentrated according to the principles of group and individual teaching as well as of what is project-related in the creative encounter between instructors and students (class principle)' (par. 50, sub. 2, clause 1, Art Institute Law North Rhine-Westphalia. Here in the expression 'in the creative encounter' the unwieldy legal language yields to 'narrative' norms that are capable of descriptively laying out the alternatives on offer.[61]

The autonomy of the Academy – granted by law and in fact almost achieved by the time the law was enacted – was expressed overall in matters relating to both academic affairs and public concerns. The Academy was given a seal of its own (design: Markus Lüpertz) and proudly faced the public under the name Düsseldorf Art Academy (without using the term 'state', which is also not usual in the names of German universities) with its legal entities and dignitaries, for instance, at conferences for rectors and chancellors or within the framework of statements and hearings in the cultural and academic sectors.

In addition, another new, specialised institution was created: the Academy Gallery on Burgplatz with an art collection of its own that was soon enlarged. Within the Academy (as a collection of teaching aids and the basis for artistic and art historical observation) and outside it (with museum functions) it documented the influence of Academy teachers. This institution derived from an idea advanced by Lüpertz on his own initiative and when it was established given strong external support by the city of Düsseldorf (especially by the then Lord Mayor Joachim Erwin) and the government of the state of North Rhine-Westphalia (notably by Minister Michael Vesper). Within the Academy, the campaign for the gallery was led by Siegfried Gohr, an art historian, so the project could soon be successfully realised because it had met from the outset with broad-ranging acceptance from the professors (even former ones) and employees (artists, scholars, and members of the Academy administration headed by the chancellor as well as many voluntary helpers) and was sustained and fostered by the enormous commitment shown by all those who had been involved with it. By now the collection is quite large and there have been quite a few exhibitions, which are also documented in catalogues. The misunderstanding, or rather, prejudice, that the Academy wanted to use the gallery to further the commercial interests of its artists has long since been discredited.

Before the New Collection could be built up, the status of the 'old' collection, which is indissolubly linked with the founding of the Art Academy and its founders, the Elector Karl Theodor and Lambert Krahe, had to be secured. To that end, permanent-loan contracts had existed with the Art Museum and the city of Düsseldorf since 1932. Those contracts would have been automatically renewed for another fifty years from 1992 had the Art Academy rectorate not terminated the last contract that year. This was done to attain better terms because the Academy and its rectorate still felt responsible for that exceptional collection and were anxious to consolidate curating and high visibility. The new contract, which represents a cooperation agreement – now chiefly with the Kunstpalast Museum – and enumerates formal undertakings (including provisions on personnel) to which the museum and its principal were to commit themselves, does not expire until 2022. Then a review will be called for to determine once again what measures for curating, presenting, and publishing the collection would be commensurate within the cooperation framework between the Academy and the Museum.

Two waves of reform – large and basically affecting all tertiary education institutions at university level – coincided with the tenure of this rectorate: the diploma debate in the 1970s and 1980s with specific provisions from the Düsseldorf Art Academy in accordance with the first Art Institute Law of 1987, and the Bologna Process higher education reforms of the late twentieth and early twenty-first centuries with specific provisions from the second Art Institute Law of 2008.

Under the terms of the 1987 Art Institute Law, all courses of study offered had to provide graduates with a certificate attesting to successful completion of a course of studies. In principle there was little to object to in this because confirmation that a course of study has been successfully completed is an essential feature of all institutions of higher learning. In the fine arts course, on the other hand, there had been the tradition described above of leaving the Academy without having had to sit final examinations. Master-class status was never a formal qualification attesting to successful completion of study – attainable by all students – even though it has in practice been viewed as such on occasion. Quite to the contrary, it represents an honour awarded on an individual basis.[62] The Academy and its representatives, however, displayed considerable reservations about awarding diplomas and the necessarily concomitant introduction of curricular regulations, and they also presented good reasons for their attitude. In this respect the law has permitted – wisely, as it has turned out – three options: it has also made possible a legally equivalent alternative tertiary education qualification in addition to the diploma and master's degree 'with the authorisation of the Minister for Science and Research'.[63]

Here the Academy entered the fray to demand a tertiary education qualification of its own in the form of a self-created *Akademiebrief* [Academy certificate]. The final examination for this qualification consisted of a presentation of the student candidate's work with a *viva voce* in the form of a discussion in which the candidate's class teacher and one professor each from the Fine Art and art-related Arts and Humanities Departments. Previously achieved freedom of choice in designing one's personal curriculum within the framework of the class principle continued to be guaranteed. In this connection there was agreement within the Academy (and between academics and artists) that attending a small canon of academic coursework should be mandatory and proof of attendance should be required for admission to the final examination. Both the course of study and the qualification were soon officially approved.[64] Thus the Düsseldorf Academy found a solution which the Münster Academy – now an independent institution of higher learning in its own right – took over, making North Rhine-Westphalia with its two art academies the envy of other federal German states.

The model continued to exist without further ado, impressively so, for some two decades until it was once again called into question, this time in the context of the Bologna Process discussion and the staggered implementation of courses of study leading to bachelor's and master's degrees. The Academy rectorate again succeeded in getting what it wanted, in this case being permitted to keep the *Akademiebrief* as the sole qualification it offered (whereas the *Akademiebrief* used to be the equivalent of a diploma, now it is equal to a master's degree). Moreover, the 2008 Higher Education Law contains provisions that confirm this qualification and expressly guarantee it in exemption clauses.[65] Thus the Academy's independent thinking withstood a second time political reform efforts that were intended to be across the board. The aim of teaching and studying art as 'developing artist personalities' was written expressly into the law (par. 50, sub. 1, clause 1, Art Institute Law) so that priority was not merely given to the utilitarian aspect of professional training. Hence study reform was not simply 'imposed on' the Academy from outside but was designed by it to suit its needs. The 'Bologna wall', which had seemed unbreachable to so many, did, after all, have doors in it that could be opened.

Similar reforms – for the most part on the Academy's own responsibility – also again affected architecture (as the art of building) at the Academy. The post-graduate course that until then had been intended to follow a diploma from elsewhere could no longer remain in this form after the Bologna Process reform. Nonetheless, the Bologna specifications turned out to be useful for the Academy in the case of architecture because the new bachelor's degrees from other types of institutions of higher learning (universities, technical universities, polytechnics) could be defined as the admission requirement for the immediately following post-graduate course at the Academy. In addition, the test to determine artistic aptitude and suitability for the course applied to, in this case architecture, continued to be required by the Academy as the *sine qua non* for admission to study. The requirements for Academy qualification in architecture, based as it was on architecture as art and the master-pupil relationship, were met and could continue in use. The Academy qualification in architecture is equivalent to a master's degree. These improvements to the course of study – once again with the aim of compliance with the professional regulation governing registering graduates in the 'role of architects' and Europe-wide recognition of qualifications – have been taken up and upheld in Tony Cragg's tenure.

The results of more than forty professorial appointments (including several jobs management posts) proceedings were particularly remarkable during Lüpertz's tenure as rector. The number would have been exceeded by quite a few appointments if the employment of non-professorial teaching staff had been included but this is not the place to go into that issue. The following professors were appointed at that time: Siegfried Anzinger (painting), Dr Kunibert Bering (teaching art), Dr Johannes Bilstein (theory and practice of education), Herbert Brandl (painting), Reinhold Braun (painting, jobs management), Daniel Buren (painting, jobs management), Tony Cragg (sculpture, reappointed after working at Universität der Künste, Berlin), Richard Deacon (sculpture), Peter Doig (painting), Max Dudler (architecture), Udo Dziersk (orientation), Helmut

Federle (painting), Vadim Glowna (film, jobs management), Dr Siegfried Gohr (art history), Martin Gostner (sculpture), Durs Grünbein (poetics, aesthetics), Thomas Grünfeld (sculpture), Georg Herold (sculpture), Dr Friedrich Wolfgang Heubach (education, psychology), Nan Hoover (video), Jörg Immendorff (painting), Magdalena Jetelová (sculpture), Hubert Kiecol (integrating fine art and architecture, sculpture), Josef Paul Kleihues (architecture), Jannis Kounellis (sculpture), Rita McBride (sculpture), Gerhard Merz (painting), Dr Johannes Myssok (art history), Albert Oehlen (painting), A. R. Penck (painting), Karl-Heinz Petzinka (architecture), Tal R (graphic art, painting), Dr Guido Reuter (art history), Thomas Ruff (photography), Axel Schultes (architecture), Andreas Schulze (painting), Dr Ludger Schwarte (philosophy), Rosemarie Trockel (sculpture), Oswald Mathias Ungers (architecture), Didier Vermeiren (sculpture), Jeff Wall (photography), Oswald Wiener (poetics, aesthetics), Christopher Williams (photography), and Elia Zenghelis (architecture). In addition, the Centre for International Art Management (CIAM) was founded in 2005 as a collective undertaking with the Düsseldorf Art Academy, the Robert-Schumann-Hochschule in Düsseldorf, the Academy of Media Arts in Cologne, and the Hochschule für Musik und Tanz [University of Music and Dance], also in Cologne.

The above appointments meant that all fields of art including architecture and art-related arts and humanities subjects were essentially covered. Once again the arts focused on the 'diversity and quality' principle. There was no question of limiting appointments to specific groups of forms of expression in art or of pandering to personal preferences, let alone countenancing the formation of schools.

The professors' conference had not existed for decades. Nor was it mentioned in the official, authorised catalogue of governing bodies. Nonetheless, Lüpertz reinstated it as an informal assembly before senate sessions to provide the teaching staff with an opportunity for exchanging information and expressing opinions. The actual instruments and governing boards that dealt with self-administration and employee co-management and co-determination (the senate, the department councils, and committees as well as employee councils and the student body organisations) were also used extensively but only as much as necessary so that no one might have grounds for thinking that employees were excessively caught up in self-administration work or that their involvement in it was too time-consuming.

During the early years of the rectorate (the late 1980s), a new space allocation programme was drawn up by the rectorate and the administration. Covering the main building and the Rheinflügel, it envisaged a more systematic and fairer use of space than in the past and specifically assigned study areas to the two buildings. Although it was only natural that not everyone could be a winner, the allocation process proceeded for the most part calmly and in a spirit of cordial cooperation. Apart from the rectorate and the state civil engineering administration, the Academy's Architecture Department, notably Ernst Kasper and his practice, played a paramount role in working on important design issues related to building restoration and refurbishment – specifically of the Rheinflügel and later the Academy Gallery. In the course of redesigning the Great Hall, the Academy and civil engineering administration successfully collaborated on restoring the fenestration, designed by former Academy professor Heinrich Campendonk, from the old state parliament building and making it once again accessible to the public.

The competences and flexible approaches to budget and personnel issues (chiefly through the implementation of lump-sum budgets and delegation of decisions affecting personnel to the relevant organisational and functional units of the Academy) granted to the Academy and its administration enabled the Academy not only to perform its tasks but also to undertake the aforementioned enlargements and redesigning projects without having to report much in the way of additions to personnel and financing. This arrangement also had a positive effect on the technical and material appointments within the building and the artistic and academic facilities (such as the workshops and the library) because the Academy administration financially supported not only many measures on its own responsibility but also those put forward by the building administration, thus making quite a number of both types of projects possible in the first place. The same holds for public-relations undertakings. The inauguration events associated with the Academy Tours were enhanced by impressive collaborative projects, in which, for instance, professors and students from the neighbouring Robert-Schumann-Hochschule took an active part.

In the last years of Lüpertz's tenure, legislation was again on the Academy policy agenda. Through collaborative efforts (also jointly with other art academies and conservatories and

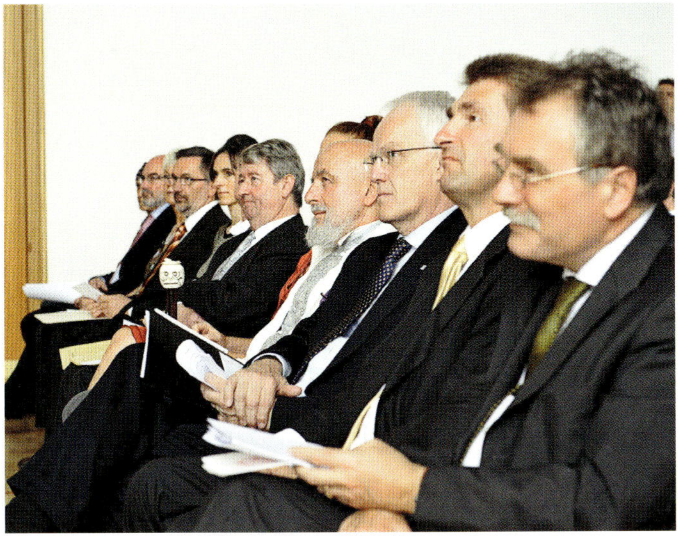

Fig. 22: The farewell party for Markus Lüpertz on 1 July 2009, in the Great Hall at the Düsseldorf Art Academy; from left to right: Peter M. Lynen, Klaus Heinrich, Tatjana Valsang, Siegfried Gohr, Markus Lüpertz, Jürgen Rüttgers, Andreas Pinkwart, and Hans-Heinrich Grosse-Brockhoff

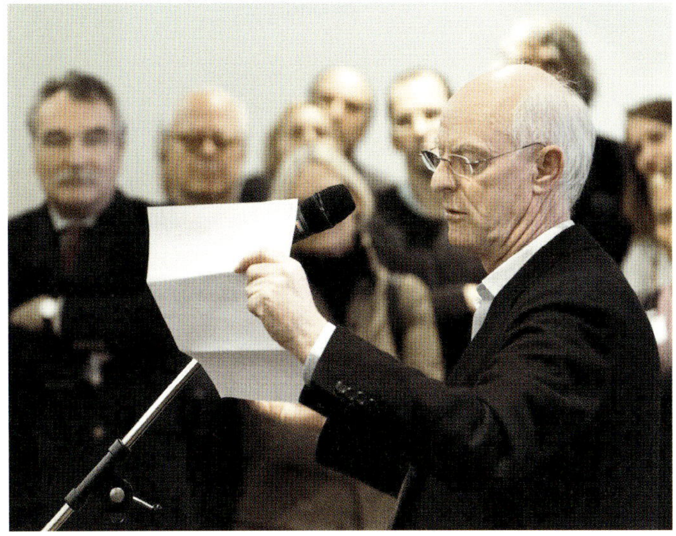

Fig. 23: Anthony Cragg giving the inaugural speech at the preview of the exhibition Die Bildhauer *[The Sculptors] in K20 on 18 February 2013*

their representatives) during two legislative periods, another higher education act specific to institutions like the Academy was – after a brief interval – enacted (the state government of North Rhine-Westphalia and the Science Ministry were at first opposed to it). The new law not only guarantees the autonomy of art academies and conservatories but also takes into consideration to a greater degree than in the past (and in laws of this kind enacted in other German federal states) the features specific to this type of institution of higher education. A development that had begun in the late 1940s now came triumphantly to fruition, which, one hopes, will be in force for a long time to come and will be able to withstand the regulation mania hitherto shown by parliaments and governments in the sectors of academic and higher education law.

As for the change in rectors that took place in 2009, it is safe to say that the Academy – on the whole, high-ranking in art and sophisticated as it is – was handed over in accordance with the legal framework as a consolidated and pacified institution, materially speaking, in very good condition, a model for other institutions of higher learning and other federal states as far as both its buildings and its finances were concerned (Figs. 22, 23). This does not mean, of course, that new rectorates may not have to devote themselves to important and difficult tasks and problems both at present and in the future.

THE ART ACADEMY AT PRESENT AND IN THE IMMEDIATE FUTURE

Since 2009 the new rectorate has consisted of the sculptor Anthony Cragg as rector, and Dr Siegfried Gohr, an art historian, and Georg Herold, a sculptor, as prorectors as well as Dietrich Koska, a lawyer, as chancellor.

Once again, there were appointments proceedings from the outset, and they have further strengthened the professorial staff both artistically and academically. The following were appointed: Tomma Abts (painting), Dr Robert Fleck (art and public relations), Katharina Fritsch (sculptor), Dr Peter Gansen (junior professor for education), Katharina Grosse (painting), Andreas Gursky (fine art), Eberhard Havekost (painting), Gereon Krebber (orientation), Dr Oliver Marchart (sociology), Lucy McKenzie (painting), Marcel Odenbach (film and video), Jórunn Ragnarsdóttir (architecture), Johannes Schütz (stage design), and Nathalie de Vries (architecture).

This – also impressive – roll of over ten appointments covering a span of four years again proves that since 1945 the Academy has never ceased to link diversity and quality, that it has remained a magnet for proven artistic talent from Germany and abroad, and at the same time that its charismatic appeal for the domestic and international art world is undimmed. Moreover, the range of artistic and academic disciplines and institutions offered at the academy has not only continued to exist but has been diversified too.

Two consequences of the Bologna Reform process remain to be influenced by the Academy and its rectorate at present and in the near future: reforming the course of study leading to qualification to teach art at state schools and the question of how a third tier (actually a second one at the Academy) to follow the *Akademiebrief* as a qualification in art might be designed and the younger generation of artists more effectively and more specifically fostered.

Respecting reform of the art-teaching course, what is at stake at present is harmonising the qualifications, examinations, and the curriculum as well as the accreditation process, or the necessary recognition by the state with such special features of the Academy as studio study, the class principle, and the master-pupil relationship. For those aims the Academy has fought hard, notably during the tenures of Kamp and Lüpertz (for instance, through the efforts of Erwin Heerich and many others), and has come closer to attaining the goal that graduates of that course should also be viewed as artists (and not just as art teachers) so that they can be effective and receive the recognition they deserve. The Cragg rectorate has championed this approach, also by joining forces with the Münster Art Academy, which has been traditionally committed to the courses leading to teaching qualifications.

The second question relates to the circumstance that, at universities and in academic courses in general, the possible third university-level examination generally leads to a doctorate following bachelor's and master's degrees. With respect to academic courses of study, the Academy has no problem with that because it has possessed the right to grant doctorates in the academic subjects taught there since the first Art Institute Law in 1987 (and, since 2008, also has the right to grant postdoctoral degrees). In the art courses, on the other hand, things are considerably more complicated. There a doctorate or a doctoral degree has also been mooted[66] but was supposed to be out of bounds for the Academy. This is where the art-related initiative launched by the Cragg rectorate and the rector, who is, of course, an artist himself, to create and run studios supervised by the Academy and members of it (in particular the professors) for exceptional art graduates comes into play. Related to the issue of promoting a younger generation of artists with adequate instruments and programmes, the proposal links up with earlier forms of teaching and working and the traditional master-class studio praxis. In view of the fact that some issues are still under discussion and that realising the proposal is fraught with difficulties, it is only to be hoped for the Academy that this way will successfully lead to another facility at the Düsseldorf Academy, that the third tier will be suited to the essence of art and the Academy, and that the younger generation of artists will be helped with commensurate means.

From these last remarks it becomes apparent that the rectorate from 2013 and the Academy as a whole will not be free of challenges and important problems to solve. That this is so is exemplified by the apparatus provided by the agreement on objectives resulting from the 2008 Art Institute Law and already processed by the Cragg rectorate[67] and the quality standards agreement (in collaboration with the Ministry), discussions with the new Art Institute Council of the State of North Rhine-Westphalia, and by the recent revision of the Academy Basic Charter. The last-named undertakings have led to an enlargement of the Academy senate to ensure greater participation by members of the Academy. They have taken up discussions that have cropped up again and again at the Academy.

CONCLUDING REMARKS

'The Art Academy is a corridor. We all go through it, some of us more quickly; others linger somewhat longer. What remains is the house. It survives all of us.' Thus, or in a similar vein (by word of mouth), Markus Lüpertz when he first became rector. Lüpertz himself, the author of this, and many colleagues, both men and women, remained 'somewhat longer': two to four decades. Of those who did remain longer, the following – in addition to those mentioned in previous chapters of this book but with no claims to completeness – shall be named as representative of all: Gotthard Graubner, Konrad Klapheck, Christian Megert, Rolf Sackenheim, Fritz Schwegler, and Erich Reusch (artists) and Johannes Bilstein, Heinrich Theissing, and Hans Peter Thurn (academics). Still the content of the sentences quoted above aptly describes those people in particular, those who moulded the Academy for rather long periods of time and held important positions (deans, deputy directors). Life is breathed into the Academy by its members and they bequeath lasting impressions both at the Academy and in the world of art, science, and culture. Still the institution has outlasted them. May it have the staying power to do so for centuries to come.

The continued existence of the Academy as a successful house for art, for artists, and art-related arts and humanities can, however, be secured only so long as people can be found who associate their own aims and tasks as artists, academics, and administrators with those of the Art Academy as an institution, people who 'love the house', know, respect, and show enough consideration for each other, enter on vital communications processes, and view the Academy *qua* institution in principle as a community of teachers and learners. If, on the other hand, the Academy is regarded merely as a workplace or training establishment, as a sideline, or, in fact, simply as a business or as a state institution for which others (are supposed to) provide, it will wither away. Further, it is so much more than a mere forum for proclaiming personal views or asserting political or private interests. Provided the principle that first-class people appoint their equals has been sufficiently honoured, the Academy has always succeeded in turning round the occasional wrong personnel choice and mistake, things that can happen anywhere at any time. There has always been the danger of internal and external mismanagement and it can happen again. The Academy should accept advice and prescriptions in such matters only after careful consideration. Above all, it should keep in mind the skills and responsibilities it possesses and can procure. The past nearly seventy years of Academy history have shown that the Academy is not immune to risk, but, 'at the end of the day', it has invariably succeeded in mastering the challenge.

NOTES

1 For more on this, see Peter M. Lynen, 'Stetigkeit und Wandel. Zur Verfassungsgeschichte der Kunstakademie Düsseldorf', *Jahreshefte der Kunstakademie Düsseldorf*, Vol. 1, Düsseldorf 1988, pp. 257–353. The present text is in part based on the above article.

2 The reign of injustice during the Third Reich, which was not merely centralistic but also ideologically informed, will be left out here; see on this the essay by Kunibert Bering in the present volume, pp. 20–36.

3 Before the creation of the Federal Republic of Germany and the federal state of North Rhine-Westphalia in the North Rhine Province under British military governance.

4 For more on this, see Friedhelm Hufen, *Die Freiheit der Kunst in staatlichen Institutionen, dargestellt am Beispiel der Kunst- und Musikhochschulen*, Baden-Baden 1982; Peter M. Lynen, 'Das Recht der Kunsthochschulen', in: Kay Hailbronner and Max-Emanuel Geis (eds.), *Hochschulrecht im Bund und Ländern*, loose-leaf collection, 18. Lfg. [18th instalment], August 1997; Peter M. Lynen, 'Kommentar zum Kunsthochschulgesetz NRW', in: Dieter Leuze and Volker Epping (eds.), *Hochschulgesetze NRW*, commentary, loose-leaf collection, 5.-9, Ergänzungslieferung [supplementary instalment], Bielefeld 2010. There are about fifty state art academies and conservatories in Germany, whereby roughly half are art institutes for fine art.

5 On the history of art academies and the continuity of individual institutions, see especially Nikolaus Pevsner, *Die Geschichte der Kunstakademien*, Munich 1986.

6 Here a growing trend towards so-called 'fine' art (institutes) can be observed in recent decades.

7 This means, above all, the impact made on art and culture by members of the art institutes.

8 A further indication that this is so is that the private art institutes are striving for state accreditation (in North Rhine-Westphalia in compliance with pars. 70f. Art Institute Law) and, when they are successful in attaining the desired accreditation status, also use it as a marketing tool. On the requirements for, and consequences of, state accreditation, see Lynen (see n. 4), pars. 70f. State monopolies still exist where the granting of academic degrees and titles are concerned, which, however, are not of such importance as they are in the sciences, arts, and humanities.

9 Mataré–Beuys–Immendorff exemplifies this tradition although we shall have to wait and see whether this chain will continue.

10 This is what distinguishes a democratic state of law shaped by the Basic Law from totalitarian and autocratic systems.

11 The statement was coined by Markus Lüpertz, formerly rector of the Art Academy.

12 In this connection, the phenomenon that at least in recent decades each law-giving session of the state legislature has had tertiary education reform in its sights, which has also affected the Düsseldorf Art Academy, should be pointed out. 'Organisational calm' is out of the question and the Academy or its representatives have constantly had to act as effective lobbyists.

13 For more on this, see Peter M. Lynen, 'Zeit für eine neue Kulturpolitik?' in: *Nordrhein-Westfälische Akademie der Wissenschaften und der Künste. Klasse für Künste. Vortrag [Lecture] K 21*, Düsseldorf 2010; Peter M. Lynen, *Kunstrecht 2. Schwerpunkte des Kunstgewährleistungsrechts*, Wiesbaden 2013, pp. 56f.

14 See Hilmar Hoffmann, *Kultur für alle. Perspektiven und Modelle*, Frankfurt am Main, 1979.

15 Under the heading 'Die deutsche Bildungskatastrophe' [The German Education Catastrophe], Georg Picht sparked off a heated and momentous debate, at first in a series of four articles (31 January–21 February 1964) in the weekly *Christ und Welt* (subsequently also published as a book: Georg Picht, *Die deutsche Bildungskatastrophe. Analyse und Dokumentation*, Freiburg im Breisgau 1964).

16 Publications such as Dieter Haselbach et al., *Der Kulturinfarkt. Von Allem zu viel und überall das Gleiche. Eine Polemik über Kulturpolitik, Kulturstaat, Kultursubventionen*, Munich 2012, have been counterproductive; on this, see Peter M. Lynen, http://kupoge.wordpress.com/2012/05/08 (last retrieved 14 September 2015). The authors of the above book would like to 'reallocate' public financing in favour of art institutes, but this is neither realistic nor does it remove art institutes from such a line of reasoning for planned economic control.

17 *Jahresbericht der Staatlichen Kunstakademie Düsseldorf 1945–1947*, Düsseldorf [1948], p. 3.

18 Ibid., p. 21.

19 Ibid., p. 22.

20 Report of the district governor of 13 December 1945 to the Oberpräsidenten [highest civilian official] of the North Rhine Province, Art Academy administrative records.

21 See Hanna Mataré and Franz Müller (eds.), *Ewald Mataré, Tagebücher* [Diaries], Cologne 1973, especially the entries made for 29 September 1945 (pp. 200f.) and 15 December of that year (pp. 204–208); Wolfgang Horn, *Kulturpolitik in Düsseldorf. Situation und Neubeginn nach 1945*, Opladen 1981, provides, on pp. 82–85, a comprehensive description of the proceedings and reasons for ending Mataré's tenure as director and, on p. 86, gives another model for reform (dividing the Academy into two faculties) in the post-war period, which was not carried out.

22 *Jahresbericht 1945–1947* (see n. 17), p. 101.

23 Printed in *Jahreshefte der Kunstakademie Düsseldorf* (see n. 1), pp. 317–331; the hand-written original is in the archives of the Düsseldorf Art Academy, Archiv No. 5.

24 For more detail on these regulations, see Lynen (see n. 1), pp. 262–279; also see Eduard Trier, 'Die Kunstakademie in der permanenten Reform', in: Eduard Trier (ed.), *Zweihundert Jahre Kunstakademie Düsseldorf*, Düsseldorf 1973, pp. 203–212.

25 The paper was written by Köngeter, Schwippert, and von Wecus and signed by the entire professorial conference (Bindel, Champion, Coester, Enseling, Herberholz, Heuser, Kamps, Köngeter, Mages, Mataré, Pankok, Schmidt, Schwippert, and von Wecus); for this and for the citations, also in the following, see the conference minutes of 27 January 1949 in the Art Academy administrative records.

26 More extensively Lynen (see n. 1), pp. 282–290.

27 A brochure issued by the Art Academy in 1956 repeats the courses for study enumerated above as the art of building, sculpture, painting, the graphic arts, stage design, and art education and refers to supplementary lectures and tutorials in anatomy, perspective and linear drawing, dramaturgy, art history, philosophy, education, and materials science. This brochure also emphasises the resources available through such facilities as the library, the Institute for Painting Techniques, the Plaster Mould-Making Institute, the foundry, the printers, and the collection of teaching resources. Further, the admission requirements and aptitude in art as well as a suitable educational foundation as prerequisites are pointed out.

28 See Trier (see n. 24), p. 217.

29 Heinrich Kamps (ed.), *Jahrbuch der Staatlichen Kunstakademie Düsseldorf 1948–1950*, Düsseldorf 1951; cloth-bound and elaborately produced (with lavish illustrations), it not only illustrates the views of the time but also shows what had been achieved by then.

30 Heinrich Kamps and Paul Bindel, 'Klassen für das Künstlerische Lehramt', in: ibid., pp. 11–16

31 Later sections will return to this.

32 Thus Schwippert in his essay 'Zur baukünstlerischen Erziehung an der Staatlichen Kunstakademie', *Jahrbuch 1948–1950* (see n. 29), p. 59.

33 *Für die Kunst leben. Bilder aus der Staatlichen Kunstakademie zu Düsseldorf*, photographs by Siegfried Kühl, Düsseldorf n.d. [1960], without a colophon but with a list of the staff at the time.

34 Published in the leaflet 'Nachrichten, Bilder, Berichte, Staatliche Kunstakademie Düsseldorf', n.p. 1966.

35 Ibid., on p. 3 of the leaflet.

36 There are many details and documents related to the impact made by Beuys as a professor at the Academy in Susanne Anna (ed.), *Joseph Beuys, Düsseldorf*, exhib. cat. Düsseldorf, Ostfildern 2008; on Düsseldorf there is a book illustrating a collection of photographs by Renate Buschmann, *Zeitsprung. Rebellisches Düsseldorf 1966–1972*, photographs by Jörg Boström, Bielefeld 2007.

37 Düsseldorf Art Academy conference minutes.

38 Düsseldorf Art Academy administrative records.

39 Printed in Lynen (see n. 1), pp. 332f.

40 Düsseldorf Art Academy administrative records.

41 Printed in Lynen (see n. 1) p. 334.

42 Discussed in more depth by Peter M. Lynen, 'Das ambivalente Verhältnis des Künstlers zum Recht. Am Beispiel Joseph Beuys', in: Bettina Paust et al. (eds.), *Aufbauen – Zerstören. Phänomene und Prozesse der Kunst*, Oberhausen 2007, pp. 43–56. Vol. 1 of *Moyländer Diskurse zu Kunst und Wissenschaft.*

43 Landesarchiv NRW, [Dept] Abteilung Rheinland, Düsseldorf, NW 678 No. 82, p. 179.

44 With more evidence in Lynen (see n. 42), pp. 47f.

45 Ibid., p. 53.

46 The text for comparison is in Anna (see n. 36), p. 167.

47 See the statements made on the design for a Vocational University Developmental Law (Gesamthochschulentwicklungsgesetz), *Schriftenreihe des Ministers für Wissenschaft und Forschung des Landes Nordrhein-Westfalen*, Vol. 2, 1972, p. 158; the statement was written by Professors Crummenauer (I) and Dr Warnach (II) and a student, Stein (III).

48 See *Who's Who der Staatlichen Kunstakademie Düsseldorf, Hochschule für Bildende Künste*, Düsseldorf 1980.

49 More precisely on this Lynen (see n. 1), pp. 291–293; printed constitution pp. 335–353.

50 The Academy continued to be headed by a director but only professors from the Fine Art Department were permitted to hold this position, and the head of the administration (top-tier civil servant) – under the lawyer Peter M. Lynen, appointed in 1982 at the beginning of Irmin Kamp's tenure as director and with her support – had in principle the same range of tasks as university administrations and the chancellors at universities in compliance with the Higher Education Law of 1970: ('[…] conducts the business of the administration of the institute of higher learning and is accountable to the director or rector or president of the institute of higher learning. He is in charge of the budget.'). Cf. par. 27, the provisional regulations with par. 39, Higher Education Law 1970. Thus the office of director was close to that of a rector and the overall directorate of the Academy resembled the rectorate constitution (with a chancellor) typical of North Rhine-Westphalia, albeit retaining the old terminology, with traditional prior understandings, and excluding part of the body of professors from eligibility for being elected director and without formally giving the Academy corporation status with the guarantee of self-administration. That could not remain free of conflicts, although self-administration instruments and boards were conceded in practice and despite the provision par. 5, sub. 2, clause 1 of the provisional charter ('Professors assume Art Academy duties in their subject on their own responsibility'), and indeed even led to protests, for instance from Academy professors teaching academic subjects, which also led to a – albeit unsuccessful – constitutional complaint against the provisional charter. On this, with more evidence, Lynen (see n. 1) pp. 291–293.

51 For the legal problem, see Hubert Detmer, 'Die sogenannte Hausberufung', in: Michael Hartmer and Hubert Detmer (eds.), *Hochschulrecht. Ein Handbuch für die Praxis*, 2nd edn, Heidelberg 2011, pp. 146f., recital nos. 105–108.

52 Rektorat der Kunstakademie Düsseldorf (ed.), *Erika Kiffl, Fotos. Rundgänge, 1979–1989*, exhib. cat. Düsseldorf 1990; Rektorat der Kunstakademie Düsseldorf (ed.), *Spazierraum Kunstakademie. Fünfundzwanzigmal Rundgang, 1982–2006*, with photographs by Hubertus Neuerburg, Düsseldorf 2006.

53 Each of the following representative summaries stands as an example of many others: Katrin Berger (ed.), *Im Studium bei Erwin Heerich 1961–1987*, Cologne 2001; Kunstmuseum Düsseldorf im Ehrenhof (ed.), *Saldo. 23 Jahre Rinke Klasse*, exhib. cat. Düsseldorf 1997; Kunsthalle Düsseldorf (ed.), *Klasse Kamp 1974–2006*, exhib. cat. Düsseldorf 2006; Aedes Galerie für Architektur und Raum (ed.), *Kunstakademie Düsseldorf Architekturklasse James Stirling*, exhib. cat. Berlin 1987.

54 On the current debate in more depth, Lynen (see n. 4), par. 59, recital no. 3, with more back-up evidence.

55 See Günther Uecker and Hans Geigenmüller (eds.), *Littenheid. Eine Studie. Littenheider Schriften I*, St. Gallen 1980, as well as Günther Uecker (ed.), *Künstler und Wissenschaftler. Eine Studie*, Düsseldorf 1987. Uecker (like many other professors, for instance Alfonso Hüppi) also undertook extensive study trips with his students, and those trips resulted in publications: see *Made in Mauritius. Ein Projekt der Uecker-Klasse*, Düsseldorf 1995. That made his teaching and his class particularly influential.

56 See today par. 61, sub. 2, Art Institute Law 2008 with commentary by Lynen (see n. 4).

57 See Staatliche Kunstakademie Düsseldorf (ed.), *Studienarbeiten aus der Abteilung Baukunst 1959*, Düsseldorf 1959; Staatliche Kunstakademie Düsseldorf, *Studienarbeiten aus den Architekturklassen*, Düsseldorf 1979; Kunstakademie Düsseldorf, *Architektur Kunstakademie Düsseldorf, 1977–1992*, Düsseldorf 1993; Kunstakademie Düsseldorf, *Dudler Ortner Petzinka Schultes. Baukunst an der Kunstakademie Düsseldorf*, exhib. cat. Düsseldorf 2002.

58 Many ideas for enlarging the Academy buildings tabled before and after those measures, which were largely put forward by Academy architecture professors and their classes (for instance Kasper, Kleihues, Ortner, Stirling, Ungers, and Wimmenauer), never came to fruition (they are likely to be advocated by architecture professors today as well) but were overtaken by reality (for the time being at least).

59 In German university law one speaks of a 'dual nature' or 'Janus-headed' status.

60 See 'Pavillon der Bildhauerei', in: *Quadriennale 06*, exhib. cat. Düsseldorf 2007.

61 On narrative norms in art-related law, see Peter M. Lynen (invoking Jayme) in *Kunstrecht 1, Grundlagen des Kunstrechts*, Wiesbaden 2013, pp. 51–53.

62 See Peter M. Lynen, 'Von Meisterschülern und Diplomkünstlern. Akademische Grade und Titel an Kunsthochschulen und der "Akademiebrief" der Kunstakademie Düsseldorf', *Jahreshefte der Kunstakademie Düsseldorf*, Vol. 3, Düsseldorf 1990/91, pp. 297–317.

63 Par. 42, sub. 1, Art Institute Law 1987.

64 Thus the general regulations for conducting diploma examinations at the Academy were rendered obsolete. Further, attempts to split up the overarching subject of art into individual disciplines failed to achieve their aims.

65 See pars. 50f., especially par. 52, sub. 4, clause 2, Art Institute Law 2008, which expressly exempts the field of fine art from the requirement to switch the previous courses of study to the bachelor-master's system, with commentaries by Peter M. Lynen (see n. 4).

66 See Peter M. Lynen, 'Die Verleihung des Dr. art. and Dr. mus. Ein Bärendienst für Kunst und Wissenschaft', *Forschung & Lehre*, March 2011, pp. 218–221.

67 See the interim report of 31 December 2011 on the agreements as to aims and achievement requirements concluded between the North Rhine-Westphalian Ministry for Innovation, Science, and Research and the Düsseldorf Art Academy.

MY TIME AT THE ART ACADEMY 1974–2004

Klaus Rinke

KEEP ON MAKING ART AS A PROMISE (VOW) – THE ART ACADEMY IS NOT AN ARTIST GRAVEYARD!

Norbert Kricke wanted to have Gerry Schum teach a film class. Gerry launched our films and his at the Academy. His television gallery was, after all, in Ratinger Straße right next to the En de Retematäng pub, a stone's throw from the Academy. Kricke thought that a film-maker having a gallery was a good recommendation for an art professorship. But the film class around Ole John, which was recruited from former students from the Beuys class, Maoists, DKP members, adherents of state monopoly capitalism, wanted to establish a film academy of their own at the Academy. They blocked Gerry Schum because there were clandestine meetings with Johannes Rau for realising it. Gerhard Hoehme was also vehemently opposed to the sort of art Gerry presented in his films and video tapes. Schum took his rabid rejection by the Academy very seriously; he fell into a depression. Even though he looked so 'tough', he was very sensitive.

Norbert Kricke contacted me after Beuys was thrown out and forbidden to teach by Johannes Rau. Early in 1974 he rang me up to ask whether he might come round. Yes, certainly! He came, went through my live-in studio at Fürstenwall 163. David Rabinowitch was living with me for two months at that time because of the exhibition at the Cologne Kunsthalle. A lot of drawings were leant against the wall in my studio. Kricke said nothing, just gave a thumbs up or thumbs down – without saying a word. I wanted nothing more than to kick him out.

The old wartime generation looked down on us, but they secretly admired us. 'Uh, Rinke, wouldn't you like to do a class at the Academy?' Caught off guard, I thought to myself, why not. 'But I don't want to take Beuys's place.' 'No, you won't have to. Just rent a big room for yourself outside the Academy; then you can show the aspiring art teachers what teaching is!!!'

I WAS VOTED IN BUT FIRST ONLY FOR THREE YEARS ON PROBATION!!!

All summer long I kept looking at buildings in rear courtyards and factories until I finally got the upper floor at Karl-Anton-Straße, which was rented by the state of North Rhine-Westphalia. In the Old Town, in Uel, students of Beuys's threatened to beat me up if I went there. As for me, a working-class lad from the Ruhr, I liked nothing better than clear stances that clashed. So then I went to the Orientation Department and picked out my first generation of students.

THE OLDER PROFESSORS DIDN'T KNOW HOW TO HANDLE THE POLITICALLY HIGHLY ACTIVE '68 GENERATION

In October 1972 I had tried to explain my work at a show in Tübingen and had already publicly engaged in aggressive debate with students of Ernst Bloch's. They gave me the title of 'Late Capitalist Ego-Trip Artist'. I was so proud of that title. My reply, my line of reasoning, was, 'I have no need to make my excuses to God the Father nor must I read Karl Marx's *Das Kapital* or imbibe Mao's "little red book". I have my own, very personal vision of the world; I stand by it, that's my intrinsic motivation.' So I was armed for those debates. Being on a quest for 'relevance' – that was the buzzword of the day.

On the day of my investiture, a general assembly was convened. The Great Hall was packed to the rafters. In the last row sat Kricke, who sent me on stage alone to debate with the students. A baptism by fire! When I'm put under pressure, I have a nasty tongue. After some time, a vote was passed to forbid me to speak. Somebody else was put in to lead the discussion, but he never let me speak again.

I could only laugh at the accusations. But, with Taurus as my star sign, I have a lot of patience before I go on the offensive; however, when I do, I really get going. I never forget an injury.

A few weeks later there was another meeting, this time in the assembly room, which was packed with teachers and students. The debates lasted for hours. We broke up late in the afternoon after ending our meeting without any satisfactory outcomes. Those interminable speeches – they just went on and on. In those days general assemblies were constantly being convened to debate the issue of our political future. Once we wanted to open the door to get out. To our surprise, we were all walled in; bricks had been placed and cemented to cover the door. We held out, laughed ourselves sick, managed to reach the caretaker by telephone, and he called the fire brigade, who freed us with hammers and chisels. We used to be at the Academy every day then, because if we hadn't been, there was an ever present danger that the AStA [General Students' Committee] representatives with their left-wing bias would take over the Academy.

HATE AND DEBATES

Whenever there was a question of having the media at the Academy, it was my responsibility to deal with it. A chair of photography was being discussed. But who was to fill it? I suggested Hilla and Bernd Becher. Everyone objected: 'But there are two of them and there's only one chair to fill!' My answer was: 'Just wait and see; only one of them will come.' Bernd Becher came. Uecker came a year later. We rented two floors down in Karl-Anton-Straße. The Uecker class was below the Rinke class; the Becher class was in the house next door.

The Becher students were often at my class reunions. Axel Hütte, Thomas Ruff, Thomas Struth were, after all, friends with my students. Because I also photographed, I was always assigned to Becher at admissions examinations. So I also did my bit to ensure that Becher got just the students he wanted. He loathed subjective photography or the photography master class. Everything had to be documentary. He preferred a good draughtsman to a master photographer.

The film class – the big issue. I was always having to sit through films that had a left-wing bias. The film-makers received special financing from the Ministry. A left-wing film was endowed with 54,000 DM just to shoot some scenes in Königsallee, ladies in mink coats, or the swans on the Schwanenspiegel lake. I was getting more and more fed up with such trivial stuff.

In those days I was invited to attend the Oberhausen Short Film Days with Ursula Wevers, whom we had in the meantime made lecturer for a video workshop. In the discussions about a film academy at the Academy, I publicly argued that film is an art, just as sculpture and painting are, so why would we need a designated film academy at the Academy: simply join our art classes. I was treated as an idiot and an arsehole. But Cornelia Schlingmann and Kay Uwe Kaul pointedly came up on the stage in front of all those people in the room and asked to be in my class. I had no paper with me. 'Has anyone got a biro and a piece of paper?' I wrote down 'Cornelia Schlingmann and Kay Uwe Kaul are as of now in my sculpture class.' Even today there are film-makers who would like nothing better than to string me up.

A year later Cornelia Schlingmann was awarded the Federal Film Prize for a film she had shot in a brothel in Aachen. She worked there as a barmaid and gained the trust of the ladies.

In 1977/78 I was invited to Australia and returned home from there that spring. Rolf Sackenheim, the deputy rector, had just walked out on Kricke, who was left there without a deputy. I was in the rector's office to report back from my exhibition tour. He was isolated, left all alone without a deputy director. He immediately put me down for the job: 'You must become my deputy.' 'Who, me??? No, no ...' I wouldn't have dreamt of that. 'Holding office ... impossible on top of my class, no, no ...' Kricke: 'I'd like to pick my heir, to have the right person in position after me.' So I was supposed to take over the Academy after Kricke as the heir to the throne? I thought things over; then I said yes. The upshot was that I was given a post in the C4 pay bracket. Kricke and I were of one heart and mind, loved and hated by the others. The 'new Academy' was slowly taking shape.

One day Kricke and I were sitting together in the late afternoon, mulling over how the Art Academy might be improved. Since I was always going to New York, I knew Nam June Paik. He didn't have much money and earned a living by serving as a guide for art lovers doing the rounds of the art scene, galleries, and studios in SoHo. I knew he was strapped for cash.

Kricke: 'Who should we hire?' I said: 'Nam June Paik.' 'All right, we'll ring him up in New York,' which we did. The telephone rang. 'Kricke speaking, Düsseldorf. Hey, Nam June in New York, who do you think is sitting next to me? Rinke, the one with the hair. Uh, Rinke thinks you should start a class for video performance at the Academy. Yes, right away!' He accepted straight off: 'Then I'll finally have money coming in regularly every month.' He came (Fig. 1). The first performance was with Janice Guy, a student of mine with a beautiful body. She lay naked on our Steinway grand, and while playing the piano, he had her big toe in his mouth. A new era dawned.

A new sculptor was wanted. Tony Cragg was a very successful instructor in the O[rientation] Department with Luise Kimme. I contacted him because he was living in Wuppertal. Living in Haan – I was close friends with Stella and Gustav

Adolf Baum, who were almost like family – I had close connections to Wuppertal-Vohwinkel. Tony was reluctant. 'Oh, no, I don't know.' What was he afraid of? Was it fear of failure? 'Go on, Tony, apply; I'll get you in.' He became a professor.

A chair of painting became vacant; artists from abroad were always wanted. In those days I was often invited to eat in Düsseldorf, often by Heinz Althöfer, head of the Restoration Centre. Konrad Klapheck was also there. Whenever I ran into him, we always had interesting and intelligent conversations. He was a unique artist with his machine surrealism – man, bizarre, but a unique type as an artist.

Why look so far afield when there were also brilliant painters just a stone's throw away. Who then? Yes, Konrad Klapheck. After all the Klaphecks were an Academy dynasty: Father Klapheck was rector at one time before the war. Mutter Anna, a professor of art history, wrote very good articles on art in the *Rheinische Post*. She was already over ninety years old, a phenomenon. I suggested him. Horror of horrors, everybody at the Academy was against him. I pleaded his case before the senate and the appointments committee. There weren't just friends; there were also a couple of enemies. Klapheck was then elected by a majority of a single vote. Konrad Adenauer was also only voted Chancellor by a single vote; it must have been his own.

In summer 1978 I'm sitting in the Viennese Succession with Joseph Beuys. Since both of us always made our installations at exhibitions, we had been there together for several days building them up. It was about noon. The caretaker: 'Rinke, Professor Rinke, telephone!' 'Telephone? Who's calling, then?' 'The Ministry in Düsseldorf.' I went through the big exhibition room, passing Beuys on the way. 'Well, what do they want of you?' 'I don't know.' Reimut Jochimsen, the new science minister, was on the phone. 'Er, Klaus, I have something awful to tell you ...' 'What is it?' 'Kricke has had a heart attack.' 'Nooo!!!' 'Klaus, you'll have to do the Academy now.' 'Man, do I have to?' 'Yes, you're deputy head. Now you're acting rector.' My God, what had I let myself in for! I hung up and went back, passing Beuys. 'Well, what did they want?' 'Er, Kricke has had a heart attack. I have to be head of the Academy now.' 'Well, good luck with it!' said Beuys with an ironic undertone. We kept on working on our installations. The exhibition opened a day later. Dieter Rot, totally drunk, trashed the Beuys work and even tried to knock over my *Expansions-Doppelnadel* [Expanding

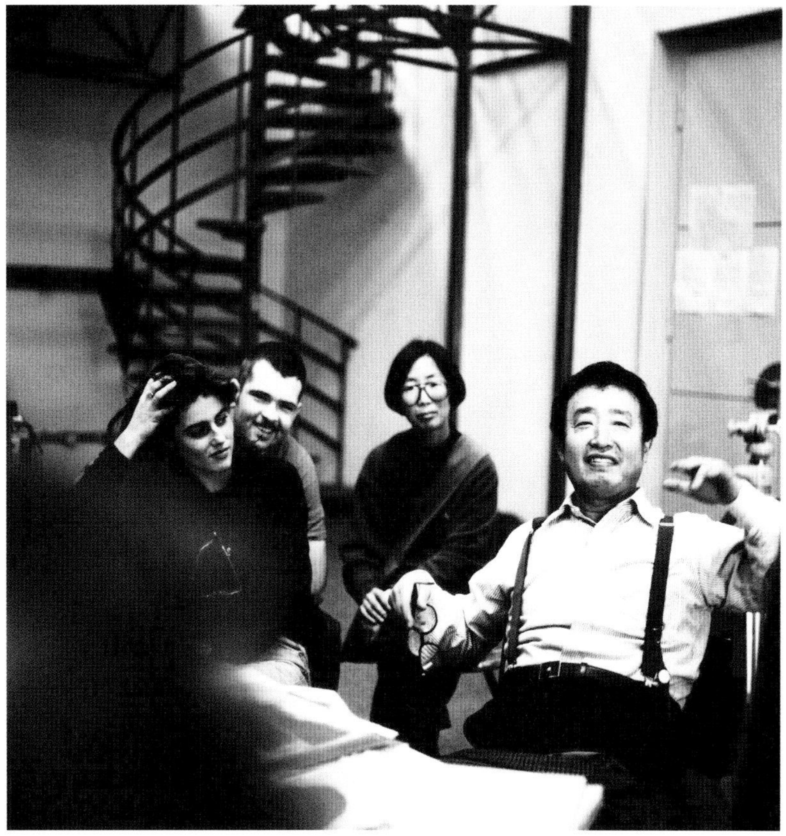

Fig. 1: Nam June Paik in his class at the Düsseldorf Art Academy on 11 October 1988

Double Pin]. I said I'd hit him if he did. He took me seriously and left it. The next day, in the hotel, he was sober and apologised. Beuys didn't get upset. He probably understood psychologically Dieter Rot and his attack. Everything was happening at once then: *Allemagne aujourd'hui*, the exhibition at the Musée d'Art Moderne in Paris, plus the rectorate ...

Beuys and I drove with Didi Geyer in the Opel and stayed at the Hotel La Louisiane. I spoke French, he didn't. Beuys had had his show at the Guggenheim Museum before we went. Didi Geyer hired several of my students to assemble his works. So I assume he knew a lot about me.

We were together all day every day. I had to interpret. The press conference took place. The journalists asked questions. Beuys the artist, the Green politician, was the centre of attention. I interpreted. One journalist asked Beuys: 'Monsieur Beuys, are you the Richard Wagner of fine art'?' I answered for Beuys: 'Beuys is Beuys, not Richard Wagner.' Another journalist's reply to that was: 'But you, Rinke, you're Siegfried the hero.'

Every evening Beuys would come over and ask: 'Hey, Klaus, where're we going to eat?' I: 'Where do you want to go?' The first day we went to an Algerian in the Latin Quarter. From then on he only wanted to go there, and we ate couscous, mouton, poulet, merguez washed down with Algerian red wine, Mascara, dark red, almost black. The dado of the restaurant was painted orange, and above painted turquoise, high gloss.

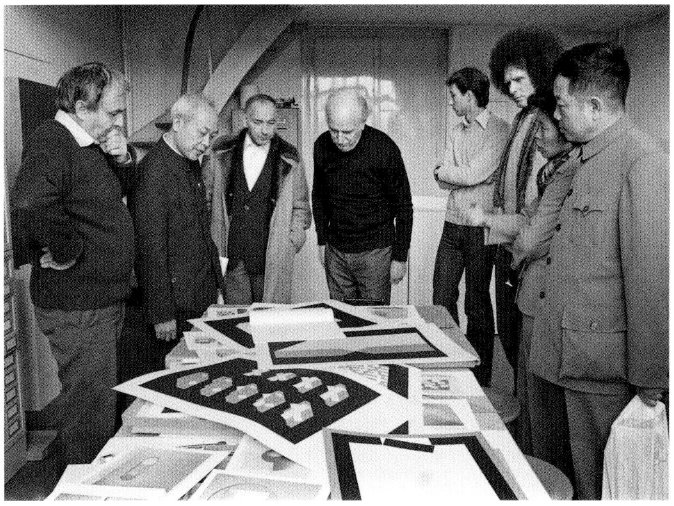

Fig. 2: Guiding a Chinese delegation through the Düsseldorf Art Academy, 1979. Left: Erwin Heerich; centre: Eugen Gomringer and Walter Biemel; right: Klaus Rinke

House painting, that's something French painters do extraordinarily well.

It was a small restaurant, perhaps eight or nine wooden tables, natural-coloured paper tablecloths, not bleached, and sawdust on the floor; the Arabs threw everything they didn't eat, bones and scraps, on the floor, which was sometimes swept clean. We often talked about the Academy there. I was firmly established as acting rector (Fig. 2). I had the idea of reinstating Beuys as a teacher with his expanded art concept. But he didn't believe it would happen: 'You won't be able to pull that off!' 'Joseph, I think I can!' I envisaged the Rinke–Beuys–Beuys–Rinke concept as a conglomerate, without a rectorate, with a round table, and the students could be involved. Then new chairs for extra-artistic media and disciplines. Because painters, sculptors, photographers, film-makers, and art historians have to get smarter. It might have become the best and most interesting art institute in the world. But it was my friends who opposed it; the Ministry was all for it.

When the Staatsgalerie organised a show of my drawings, *Rinke, Hand-Zeichner* [Rinke, Draughtsman], in 1981, I wanted to know who would be giving the opening address. I said to Ulrike Gauss: 'It would be best to have an artist who's a good draughtsman.' 'Well, who's a good draughtsman?' I thought about it a bit and said: 'Er, Beuys, or can you think of anyone else?' Ulrike Gauss spoke with Beuys on the telephone behind my back: 'Rinke has a solo show of his drawings here. Would you open the exhibition?' Beuys: 'Rinke and I haven't got a thing in common except for a couple of tubes. All right, he should come up here right away.'

Reinhard Mucha and Jürgen Drescher continued hanging my drawings while I took the next train to Düsseldorf. When I got to Drakeplatz, Beuys let me in. 'Come in, do you want some coffee?' 'Yes.' He went to the hob and put some water on to boil. I started talking immediately, which he didn't want to do: first coffee, then talk. 'First things first: first the drawing and the opening, then point 2, the Art Academy.' He brought the coffee. 'Do you take milk?' He poured milk into my coffee. I said 'Stop!' 'Do you want sugar?' 'Yes, one lump!' He put the sugar into my coffee and even stirred it in. Not a word was said. He went for some paper (white), DIN A4, a pile for me and a pile for him. He gave me a pencil. Then we both started to draw. After we had been drawing for some time, Beuys said: 'Klaus, when you do something, it's always something; there's nothing to interpret there. I don't finish things; others have to do that. Everything must be open and stay open.' We left everything else until he would be in Stuttgart. I promised him that I would set up a stage for our dialogue.

Beuys arrived in Stuttgart. We had agreed on what we would say in front of the audience. It was general election time; his constituency for the Greens was the Ruhr. So his theme was 'Society as drawing'. And mine was 'The beginnings of human sign giving' because I was in Australia every year and was intensively involved with the Australian Aborigines and their pictures and stories. All those encounters brought Beuys and me together, both as friends and as artists. After all, we were both also at the Alfred Schmela Gallery. Schmela often used to invite us with his other artists, Graubner and Uecker, to eat mussels at Muschelhaus Reusch: 'Klaus, have you got some time this evening? Are you in the mood? We're going out to eat this evening, to Muschelhaus Reusch. I'm inviting all my artists.' The Schmelas as a family with their children, Ulrike and Franzi; Gotthard Graubner with his girlfriend; Beuys with his wife, Eva, daughter, Jessyka, and his son, Wenzel; I with my partner, Monika Baumgartl; Elliot Bouchard with his wife, Dorothee, Jürgen Harten's sister. The mood was good because Schmela could be really fun and witty. That made for ambience, and the word went round in the Old Town that Schmela had reserved the whole back of the restaurant at Muschelhaus Reusch.

When it came to Schmela's birthday, his sixtieth I think, Kricke and I were deep in consultation – 'What should we give Schmela?' – in the rector's office about what we could give Schmela as a present at the birthday celebration in the Mutter-Ey-Straße gallery, such as honorary membership of the Art Academy. Many in the senate were for it but others were opposed: Why a gallerist? I said: 'He's contributed a lot more to art in Düsseldorf than many artists have.' When his honorary membership certificate was handed to him, Schmela had tears in his eyes.

The following points were always associated with Kricke:

Good art professors put even better ones in vacant chairs.
Bad art professors put worse ones in vacant chairs.
That is the end for any art school, total provincialism. The Academy is not an artist graveyard!
A promise to always keep on making art!

I was in Stuttgart again, installing my new drawing show at Max Hetzler, when a call came from Kricke: 'Get up to Düsseldorf straight away!' I said: 'Not until the show has opened!' After that I went back. By the time I arrived in Düsseldorf, a lot of negative things were brewing. A vote of no confidence initiated by Kricke as he lay on his sickbed against Klaus Rinke. Erwin Heerich to me: 'Klaus, do you think you can keep Beuys under control?' 'Don't want to', was my answer.

As executive rector I had to conduct the vote of no confidence against myself. It was like the Heinrich von Kleist play *Der zerbrochene Krug* [The Broken Jug]. Kricke had stirred them all up against me just because I had sided with Beuys: 'Do the Academy on your own. Why with him?'

I didn't want to do the Academy all on my own without friends like Günther Uecker and Gerhard Richter, my neighbours at Fürstenwall. So not without Beuys, who was at the height of his fame, the best-known German artist abroad. What a school we could have made. I was still young and strong, Beuys with his past and his aims for art; he was a real artist and a man with social demands. What a time with such opportunities!

After the vote of no confidence, I threw in the towel. Kricke was actually quite unsure of himself; inside, he was weak and mistrustful. The Ministry obliged me to keep on as rector until a new rector could be elected. Beuys then said to me in a very friendly way: 'Well, Klaus, I told you that from the beginning. You won't succeed in recalibrating the colleagues. But: the main thing was we thought together.' I added later 'laughed'. Ha, ha ...

The Kricke story ended very sadly. I prefer to keep the details private. But he was a good artist – a sculptor. He was broken by his ambition and his resentments against other arts – too bad! After the no confidence vote affair I went to the United States for a while in 1982 and set up a studio in Venice Beach, California, where I still work today.

Irmin Kamp as head of department became provisional rector; I believe she was also elected later. After her came Markus Lüpertz with his 'painters' Academy'.

During my tenure as deputy rector, two big Carnival parties took place at the Academy at the end of winter term, when the *Rundgang* [Academy Tour] was going on: the Boiler Room Balls. Uecker and I were put in charge. For the first party I invited a circus director; he needed money for his animals on the Dutch border. I had already invited him to Brückenstraße on New Year's Eve, with two camels. We had only one Near Eastern record and a barrel-organ, waltz music. It was the Academy's turn at Carnival. Kricke said: 'I'll only come if you pick me up with elephants.' We'll see! I rang up the circus director and he came with two elephants and four camels in a livestock trailer. The elephants were attached to the main entrance by tie rings. Elephants are sensitive and timid; later they refused to get back into their trailer. All the students could ride through the Academy corridors on the camels. That was fun and a huge success!

The second party was a music festival. Karl-Heinrich Müller, president of the Gesellschaft von Freunden und Förderern [Society of Friends and Sponsors], was determined to have a different band in each class. He gave us the money; I paid in cash from my pocket: reggae bands from London, a big band from Amsterdam, an African band from Zaire came from Paris, the Gerresheim gypsy band Rigoletto Winterstein, the Padlt Noidlt Academy jazz band, Turkish musicians from Recklinghausen. The Academy had become sound. Jango Edwards, the only rock clown from Detroit and a former performance artist, came from Amsterdam, waiving fees. The party was attended by 6,000 people.

The next year I wanted to have a summer fete with a circus tent on the Rhine Meadows in Oberkassel. Bolo Mayweg, who was then the senior case officer for the property, was willing to let us have the Rhine Meadows for a week in summer because no one wanted to take the responsibility again for hosting so many people in the Academy. I stayed with the caretaker until six o'clock in the morning checking for fire flashpoints; all the fire extinguishers were empty, everything was white, a window had been pushed out and lay in the courtyard, the radiators had been torn from the wall because people had stood on them. The caretaker: 'The Great Hall doesn't have the capacity for so many people!' They were packed in like sardines. The floor held – thank God! It took Minister Reimut Jochimsen half an hour to get out of the Academy. Before the fete I was presented with a contract to sign that meant I had to assume the full responsibility. The state is not insured in such cases! But it was so much fun. I was in my element!

After the fete came the vote of no confidence, and after my departure as acting rector, Walter Biemel, a philosopher and Martin Heidegger's assistant, was appointed to the post. They wanted to be absolutely sure that there would be no more parties at the Academy.

In 1989 the Wall came down. I said to Uecker in Leipzig: 'Now the Rhineland will be provincial again.'

Those are just a few details of that period at the Academy, which was very political at that time. All of us contributed to making Düsseldorf the art centre that it still is today.

MARKUS LÜPERTZ ON HIS TIME AT THE DÜSSELDORF ACADEMY

A conversation with Siegfried Gohr in Düsseldorf on 6 June 2013

Siegfried Gohr: When did you come to the Art Academy and what circumstances led to your being elected rector?
Markus Lüpertz: I was a professor in Karlsruhe for fourteen years, and in those days, changing institutes at least once was the thing to do. Following the siren call of the grass being greener on the other side showcased one's own values. Offers came in from Berlin and Düsseldorf at the same time. I still had a bone to pick with Berlin because I had once been rejected in a final round of voting there, which I really took offence at. Now I started off by conducting negotiations with both sides and opted for the city on the Rhine for Gotthard Graubner's sake because he had recommended me there. Besides, this Academy had a stronger attraction for me and represented a greater challenge. And it was most certainly the more interesting school with a worldwide reputation. Berlin was nothing but a disaster area then as far as its academy was concerned, and the city has still not recovered from that.

S. G.: So that was in the mid-1980s?
M. L.: Yes.

S. G.: That means you hadn't been in Düsseldorf very long before you were elected rector?
M. L.: That went very quickly. After only one term I was elected rector. One of the reasons was that the teaching staff were split into entrenched factions. The prevailing disagreement between the administration and the rectorate was irreconcilable. The sessions were marked by heated disputes, and there was no authority to mediate. Irmin Kamp, as serious and deserving as she was, was overtaxed by the situation and did not want to go on with it. Someone from outside had to fix things, someone who stood above the feuds and animosities that blocked everything. A fresh breeze had to blow from a new rectorate.

S. G.: Were there several candidates or were you the only one?
M. L.: I was the sole candidate and remained so during my entire stint at the Academy.

S. G.: Did Graubner have any ambition to become rector himself?
M. L.: No – when he brought me to Düsseldorf, he already had the ulterior motive of making me rector. He was indeed discussed as a candidate but did not enjoy universal popularity. Consistent and straightforward as he is, he had made up his mind: 'I can only do that if everyone is for it.' And then it was up to him to say: 'Elect Lüpertz rector!'

S. G.: Did you find a rectorate team already in place?
M. L.: Yes. Peter Lynen and Walter Hofmann. But those disastrous incompatibilities dominated the rectorate. Lynen didn't get on with Irmin Kamp, and that gave rise to considerable tensions. The competences hadn't been correctly allocated. I studied the thing briefly and asked myself, what do I want? How do I set about it? What can I change here? The art was there. The great artists were there. Fundamentally, there was no need to change anything on that plane. Perhaps the tone, the mood. Yes, the atmosphere at the Academy had to change. At first the differences of opinion persisted because Norbert Kricke had appointed professors all too arbitrarily and very much on his own authority. There were resentments among the artists and this disagreeable mood had to be cleared up. In this situation, I invited Walter Hofmann and Peter Lynen to have a talk with me and soon realised that they were great people, open-minded and willing to rejig the Academy along the lines I envisaged and to commit themselves to that unstintingly. My intention consisted solely in letting this wonderful Academy again breathe the atmosphere of art. An 'artists' hang-out' was to be created in which one could get in touch with where one was going and with the great traditions. Considering what great artists we have had and have now at the Academy, there should be no doubt about the singularity in the world of this exceptional institution. Everything centred on calming it down inside and formulating its recovered vitality as an institution for the world outside.

S. G.: Which specific measures did you take?
M. L.: I revived the artist as a creative authority and carried my point about him as a teacher. From then on the artist has been regarded as an unfettered institution. He stood in the foreground, and every single artist on the staff acted fully in the open as a representative of his stance. Then, and only then, come the students, and not the other way round. On arrival I found the sticky residue of the protest actions from the student rebellion in which the Academy was still mired. At a far remove from art, attempts were being made to functionalise the Academy in events that were political nonsense. I was able to

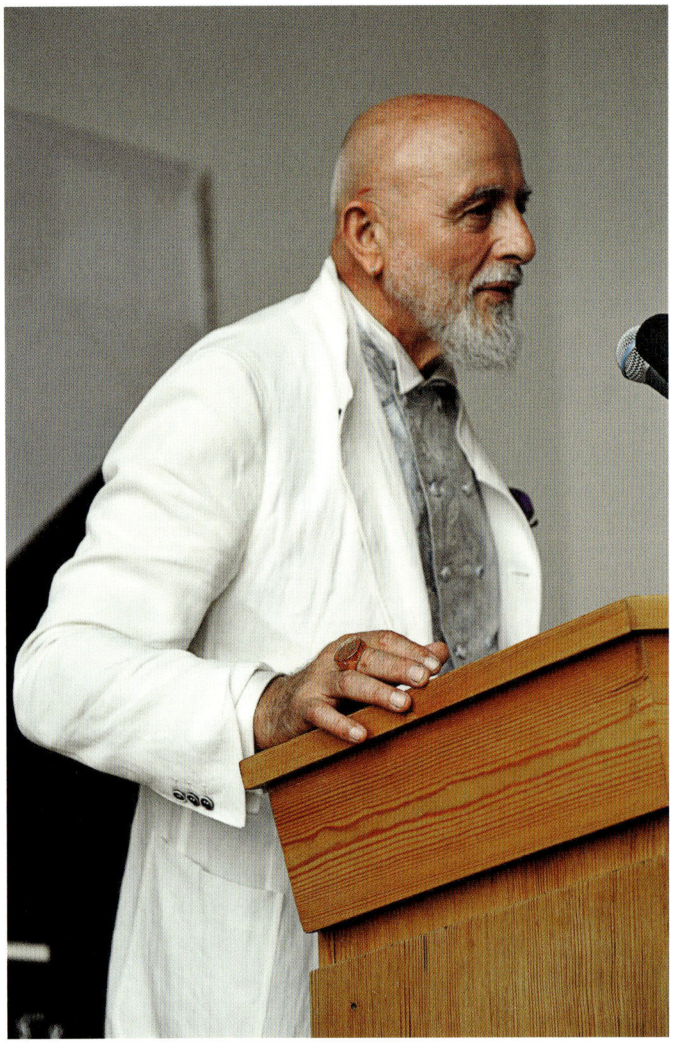

Markus Lüpertz giving his farewell address in the Great Hall at the Düsseldorf Art Academy on 1 July 2009

banish all that, one thing at a time and relatively easily. After all, the excitement had long since evaporated. The freedoms – long since won – were by then being lived as a matter of course. Active politicisation had given way by then to vapid grandstanding that amounted to masturbation. That had nothing at all to do with art. And I was chiefly concerned with art being made at the 'hang-out'. Those studying art should not behave like students but act like pupils. My chief concern was redefining the relationship between pupil and master.

At first not an easy undertaking because restructuring was the magic word in those days. Attempts were going on to make over the Academy into a presidentially managed institution. That meant headhunting someone from outside and instating them – usually administrative types. The alternative to me at the time would have been Kasper König. But that would have meant the downfall of the Academy. Not because of Kasper König, but just the very thought of not having an institution of this kind headed by an artist. I am firmly convinced that the Academy must always be headed by an artist so that it retains the special status of being an Academy. So I also prevented the name 'Academy' being dropped. It was supposed to be designated a 'Higher Institution of the Arts', or, as the silly term in Berlin is, 'University of the Arts'. The Academy is something different. Being a professor at the Academy means, as I see it, being a master with the authorisation to teach. That would be the appropriate title. I was concerned with breathing life into this master-pupil relationship. Even in the earliest sessions I found sympathetic ears among the other professors. They had not dared talk about art in front of the students for a long time. The protest movement left traces here, too; no one dared lay hands on the master-pupil relationship. It was simply not discussed. They were all caught up in the throes of a superficial tolerance, a sort of live and let live. Under my tutelage, they quickly caught on that it's important to take responsibility for the spirit of the Academy.

I never introduced compulsory attendance. I never monitored a colleague, which the state did request I should do, but I absolutely refused to because an artist is free in how he teaches. But this institution was so attractive in my era that everyone came of their own accord.

S. G.: On the question of appointments policy, was there a specific ideal wish list on your part, limitations?

M. L.: No. That is often insinuated. Of course, the one in charge has influence. It would be silly to say otherwise. I have always stood up for my idea of painting and sculpture and even today keep trying to realise it and put it across. That's the reason why I was elected. Everyone who voted for me knew that I cared about painting and sculpture. That is the point. And it was a painters' and sculptors' academy that I took over; at least it claimed to be. I pushed this aspect hard in long conversations and heated debates. Realisation always happened with the inclusion of all those in the community of masters. I didn't leave such things up to the senate. There were no secret deals behind closed doors. Everything was discussed and thrashed out in endless debates. With appointments especially, it quite often took a long time to reach a decision and to find a common denominator. Let me give you an egregious example of this: I wanted Förg. There were professors who wanted Förg, others rejected him. So things went back and forth. And when Förg was as good as appointed, protest broke out that had to be taken seriously and was supported by more than a few of the teaching staff. In that situation, I refrained from appointing him because I didn't want to bring anyone into the Academy who would be met with reservations by half of their future colleagues. At that time I convened them all and said: 'Look here, I refuse to bring any man into this house under such conditions. A broad consensus has to exist.' The possibility can never be eliminated that one or two are opposed. But the spirit of the Academy, represented by the community of masters, must be behind a new appointee. I always tried to take individual wishes and ideas into consideration, which is very important. The teachers should feel comfortable in the house because an Academy only exists through the masters and the lively exchange of ideas among them. I went to the Academy solely to cultivate an exchange of ideas in the society of other artists, and the Academy offered me a forum for getting to know all sorts of artists, of whatever persuasion or tendency. That, to me, was the actual benefit I had from my time as rector and also as professor.

S. G.: How was your teaching structured – that is, your work in class?

M. L.: With me, the focus was always on the beginning of the week. Mornings were given over to administrative work. What I shied away from and what wasn't in my nature was taken over by Walter Hofmann, who had a fine nose for, and knowledge of, all the dodges and machinations of the Ministry and could counter them with great skill. He was supported with unstinting commitment by Peter Lynen, who covered the legal side and gave us great backing. We were, in my eyes, all three on an equal footing. Boss – there was none of that with us. Of course, I was *primus inter pares*, but that only applied to representing the Academy and defining the idea informing it as an institution. That was my portfolio and I exhausted its full potential. It takes some learning to administer an institution as it should be administered. As an artist, one is dependent on administrative personnel who, infected with art, champion it with enthusiasm. Colleagues of that kind keep open the space creative artists need. I was usually fortunate in having people who – knowing they were on an equal footing with me – all pulled together. No one behaved like a subordinate; everybody was autonomous. Everyone among the colleagues was the equal of everyone else, and everybody acted on his or her own responsibility. That is the only way an Academy can remain powerful, alive, and expressive.

At noon I would go into class. My pupils were supervised during the week by Friedrich Dickgießer, my assistant. I would look at what had been done and then go into detail with the pupils' work and their development. All pupils had to attend life drawing, had to take courses in painting techniques, and had to educate themselves in art theory and art history. But what I found so disappointing about the young people all those years was their lack of knowledge. Most of them didn't begin to educate themselves until they were under instruction, when they came to the Academy. In my eyes they were illiterate in speech and in writing and possessed no knowledge worth mentioning. They had to make up for it. I told them what books were to be read and what artists were to be studied.

Actually, art cannot be learnt. But the boundaries can be defined; knowledge, education, and the craft can be conveyed. I always felt responsible for the *esprit* of art. The noblest task consists in drawing pupils into the atmosphere of art and enabling them to draw breath freely there. There is a dire need for breathing exercises because nowadays students are flat-chested and have to be given coaching in the relevant courses. I really kept after them about that. And, as I said, drawing from the nude, the means and techniques of painting, a thorough grounding in anatomy, and the craft of the graphic arts belong to the irremissible musts. And painting was done in the class with these basic skills. That had to be placed in the context of my work and the works of artists I recommended. After all, study only becomes productive through comparison, and a framework can be demarcated within which the pupil can move in the beginning. All these beginnings and all these examples that are taught to pupils are merely the entrée to a first building. Even while still at the Academy or immediately afterwards, pupils should break away from it with all their might. Not by forgetting or even repudiating the basic skills that have been acquired but by freeing themselves from within in order to build houses of their own. The best pupil is one who consigns his master to oblivion, says Friedrich Nietzsche aptly in a passage somewhere. The method is interchangeable. The Academy represents for me the royal road to art but is not the only one as it turns out. There are certainly other ways, the way of the dilettante, the self-taught, and others. However, the academy opens up the finest and a communal way of the creative. Living in this exceptional community within the bourgeois world means to me living as a bohemian.

Important academies exert a societal influence, have an impact on the city as a community on site. I always tried to keep close contact with the Lord Mayor of Düsseldorf in order to realise specific things and make them possible. In awareness of the importance of the Academy for the city, the head of the municipal administration should assume responsibility for it as an institution. I also pushed that through in Karlsruhe, and that included festivities and all sorts of events, such as readings and crazy music gigs. Everything happened so that the citizens could perceive and see the artists as part of the urban image. This is always being completely neglected and goes hand in hand with the universal brutalisation in aesthetic matters. In my youth, art students were immediately recognisable: their appearance in respect of clothing and bearing was, in fact, exemplary. But nowadays they all look like secondary school pupils. They aren't artists. They're just trendy.

S. G.: The founding of the Academy Gallery happened in your time. Perhaps we might go into that.
M. L.: The Academy is defined by the contributions made by the artists, by the works they bequeath to the world. What happens with the legacies of important Academy professors? From the standpoint of the Academy, ought they simply to be left in the hands of amateurish widows, sons, and daughters without our doing anything about it? As I see it, that would be nothing less than negligent. And I think, with the agreement of the family concerned, the Academy should be prepared to act as voluntary legatee to treat the works as they should be treated and ensure their authors are not forgotten.

Another thought I had was to give the artists teaching at the Academy a forum in which to present themselves to the public, the city, the Academy pupils. Even if they happen not to be mainstream at the moment and their works are not shown much. Those are, essentially, the tasks of the Academy Gallery. At that time I saw in London that the Royal Academy has a gallery of its own, and my mind kept buzzing with the idea. Of course, I also insisted – something that is gradually being watered down now – that no pupils' work be shown. The Academy Gallery was intended solely as a forum for masters. I could, however, get what I wanted only as long as I had any influence. That it is becoming more and more socialised is the wrong way to go. It should actually remain Olympian. The special character of this gallery is being a Hall of Olympus. Anyone who abandons that misses out on the idea behind founding it [the Academy Gallery].

S. G.: How did it happen to be this building?
M. L.: We had been given the municipal pawnbrokers' building by the city and we desperately needed its rooms for the academic department and for supervising the probationary terms. I originally envisaged designing the municipal pawnbrokers' building as a museum area. An attractive space that, however, turned out to be too small. The ministry responsible for the Academy showed itself to be not very helpful at this stage, so I turned to Erwin, who was then in office as Lord Mayor and was very well disposed towards the Academy and was later designated its first honorary senator. But even Erwin gave us the cold shoulder at first. Still he warmed up to the project more and more and more until he caught fire and gave top priority to the Academy Gallery. The decision to place rooms at our disposal within the Town Hall complex directly on Burgplatz – a historic spot because this is where the celebrated Electoral paintings gallery used to be – was more than serendipitous. Right after that the Ministry gave us the go-ahead for financing the conversion. But at some point the state abandoned its financial commitment.

Then I went to Erwin, and he – a go-getter if ever there was one – didn't hesitate about accommodating the state with credit so that we could set up the museum. The Lord Mayor, who died far too young, cannot be praised enough for that. It was exceptionally far-sighted to act as he did, and he took the right decision. Today the Academy Gallery presents itself as a high-profile advertisement by the Academy in the city for the city.

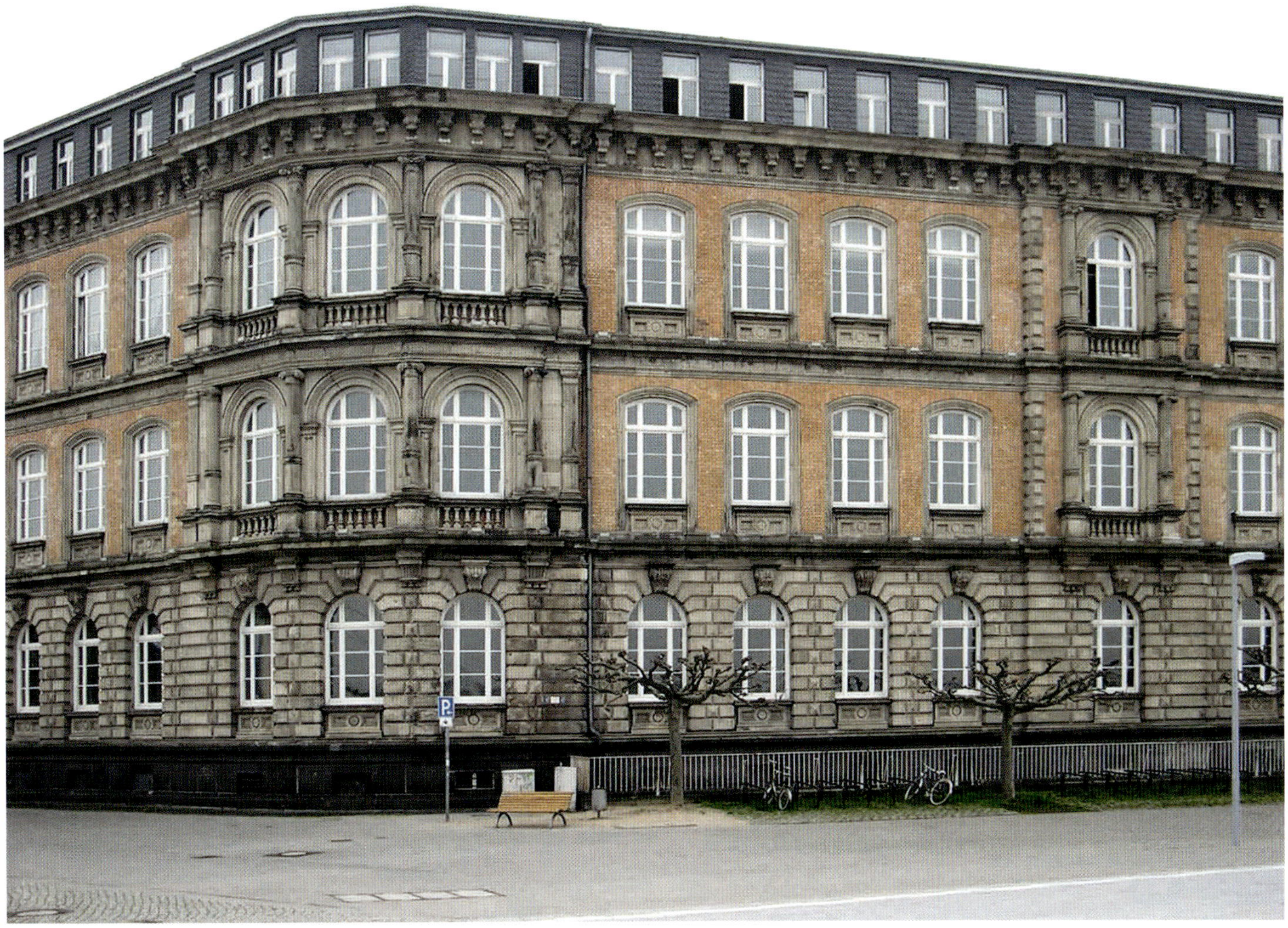

View of the building in which the Academy Gallery is located on the mezzanine floor.

STUDYING AT THE ACADEMY SINCE 1945

ACADEMICS AND ACADEMIC COURSES AT THE ART ACADEMY SINCE 1945

Hans Peter Thurn

NEW BEGINNINGS

'Work with us to rebuild the Düsseldorf Art Academy': thus the appeal directed at the public in May 1948 by Werner Heuser, the then director of the Academy. In an eight-page folder he and Josef Wilden, head of the Gesellschaft von Freunden und Förderern [Society of Friends and Sponsors], called for financial support in reconstructing the ruined building and its facilities.[1] The ravages of war were contrasted in photographs with the former beauty of the institution inside and out. Help was sorely needed because however hard students and teachers, the administration, residents of Düsseldorf, representatives of the British occupational forces, and local politicians might labour away at removing the rubble, there would be a great deal to do for years to come to repair the damage sustained and to restore conditions conducive to nurturing art. Not only was the aim in the years of reawakening to restore the celebrated institution both spatially and organisationally; after defeat, modernisation within art and, in association with this process, a fresh start in the arts and humanities seemed no less important. Lectures and seminars had indeed again been held in the winter term 1945/46, but the subject matter taught covered historically safe territory for the time being. Ancient Greece, the Middle Ages and the Renaissance, and Rembrandt and Michelangelo were the focus of interest.

As meritorious as such endeavours to restart regular academic teaching might sound, it was nonetheless impossible to ignore the fact that late nineteenth- and early twentieth-century art, which had been proscribed under the National Socialist regime, had to be intellectually addressed. This was done mainly in individual lectures that accompanied the regular study programme: from 1946 onwards lectures of that kind were devoted to Expressionism or painters such as Hans von Marées, Pierre-Auguste Renoir, Edgar Degas, and Lovis Corinth. This agenda was anything but uncontroversial since in the post-war era heated debate raged about so-called modern art and abstract art in particular. Only recently, in 1948, the year the Art Academy called out for help, the art historian Hans Sedlmayr had published *Verlust der Mitte*, a book which unleased vicious clashes throughout West Germany.[2] Should Sedlmayr's accusation that the exponents of Modernism refused 'to abandon the belief' that they might inaugurate 'a Thousand Year Reich of abstract art, Bauhaus architecture, and atonal music' be allowed to remain uncontested?[3]

How much innovative drive did the intellectual and artistic renewal need? How much added restoration could it stand? The first 'Darmstädter Gespräch' [Darmstadt Colloquy] in 1950 on 'Man's image in our time' sparked off a dispute characteristic of that era, which culminated in Sedlmayr demonstratively boycotting a lecture by the painter Willi Baumeister and the non-appearance of another critic of Modernism, Wilhelm Hausenstein, who had been expected to attend. The year before, Hausenstein had attacked Expressionists, Cubists, and Futurists as destructive and nihilistic.[4] Not long afterwards Karl Scheffler blamed what he thought of as 'substanceless art' for the 'disintegration' that in fact the National Socialists, who condemned modernity in any form, had brought about.[5]

In this volatile climate of discontent, it was not at all easy for old avant-gardists and young experimenters to make themselves heard, let alone respected. Even those who were on their side, the open-minded critics and hands-on mediators, only gradually succeeded in providing a thriving art industry. In 1946, on the occasion of the inaugural ceremonies in the Great Hall marking the reopening of the Art Academy, even the – otherwise helpful – representative of the military authorities, Lieutenant Colonel Walker, had no qualms about expressing his scepticism about 'modern art', openly admitting that he 'belonged to the school of those who believe that a painting should have a certain degree of discernible similarity with the object reproduced'.[6]

Despite such reservations, Walker made a plea for tolerance, diversity, and change from the intellectual, aesthetic, and artistic standpoint. At the same time, he lavished praise on the academic who had shouldered the greatest burden in reviving the Art Academy: Professor Dr Jakob Heinrich Schmidt, also known as simply Heinrich Schmidt (Fig. 1). Dr Sträter, the new district governor, expressed his respect for the art historian even more pointedly:

'In the last year of the terrible war, one man rendered such outstanding service in saving the art owned by the Düsseldorf administrative district that I consider myself under an obligation to make a point of singling him out for mention. This was Heinrich Schmidt, executive professor and teacher of art history at the Düsseldorf State Art Academy, to whom I express the particular thanks of the curator today and in this distinguished circle of participants. Looking back on the untiring work done

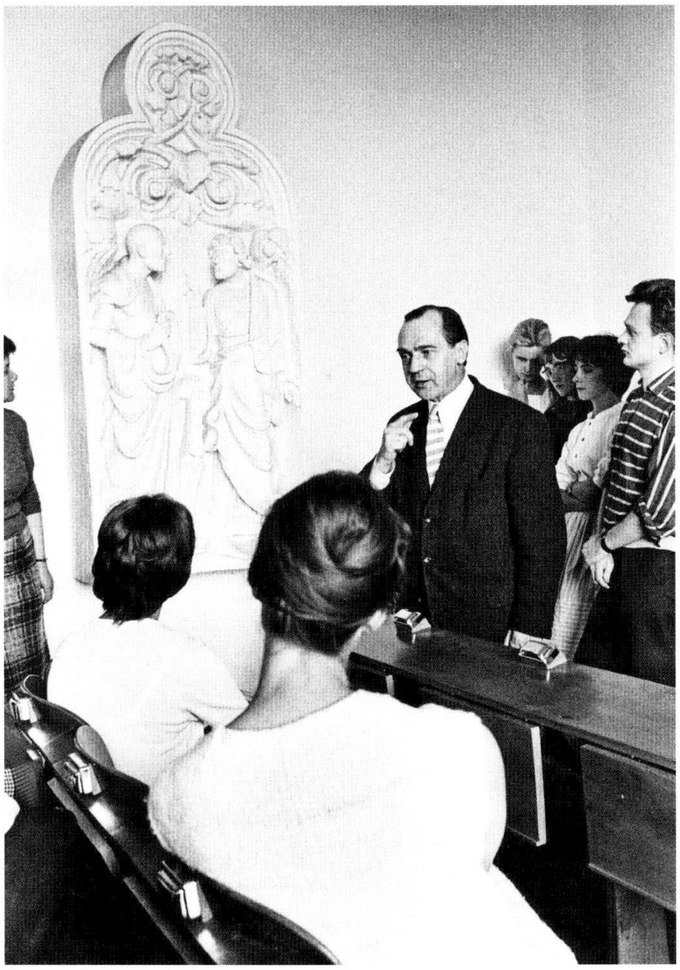

Fig. 1: Jakob Heinrich Schmidt with students, 1960

under the harshest of conditions by Professor Schmidt to save and preserve many artworks in the administrative district and his unremitting labours in reconstructing the Academy building makes me dare to hope that in future, too, there will be men who dedicate their acts and their skills to art and art education enthusiastically and selflessly.'[7]

The man thus honoured had taught at the Art Academy since 1935 and was at the same time its head librarian. He served as deputy director until 1954 and until 1956 as acting director of the Institute, which he left in 1962 on reaching retirement age. His academic specialisation was, apart from the Renaissance and Rembrandt, nineteenth-century German painting and the centres of Rhenish art; in several studies he examined the turbulent history of the Art Academy, to which he felt most deeply attached. Anyone who encountered him there experienced a teacher and scholar who was committed to his subject yet personally reticent. 'He was a fatherly friend to his pupils,'[8] wrote Anna Klapheck of her colleague in an obituary. Even in the earliest post-war days, despite financial constraints and poor public transport connections, he would undertake excursions with his students. Over the years the radius of such trips was gradually extended from the immediate environs to more distant destinations. The sheer range of his interests was also revealed in the fact that he, on the one hand, supervised an 'exhibition of drawings and portraits by former members of the Academy' in 1953,[9] and, on the other, frequently addressed himself to the study of antique Oriental silks, on which he not only published individual essays but also a handbook in 1958.[10]

The art history courses offered were supplemented by lessons in Christian iconography, which were first taught by Alexander Pottgießer, a prelate, and after him by Leonhard Küppers, a university Catholic priest and writer on theology, until the late 1960s. However, for quite some time an increasing number of artists and students at the Academy had argued for reorientating that programme to include more on the recent modern art as well as current trends in art. As early as 1952 Anna Klapheck was entrusted with that task. Her husband, Richard, had been dismissed from his chair of art history by the National Socialists in 1934. The appointment of the new instructor soon turned out to be a fortunate choice because no one knew anywhere near as much as she did about the Rhineland art scene and its context. Long before, in December 1946, she had given a talk for Academy students on 'Paula Modersohn and the beginnings of modern art in Germany'. From then on she emerged as a tireless contributor, versed in both art and literature, to the culture pages of the Düsseldorf press, as the author of widely read books, and in the building in Eiskellerstraße, at first as an instructor and ultimately as a professor. Like her texts, Anna Klapheck's lectures and seminars were based in large part on direct experience because she loved enriching her writings with her personal recollections and spicing her teaching with anecdotes (Fig. 2). She felt justified in doing so because she had closely observed the new departures in art during the 1920s and early 1930s at her husband's side as well as the reorientation of the Art Academy under the innovative director Walter Kaesbach. She had also made the acquaintance of, and occasionally also become friends with, artists such as Heinrich Campendonk and Heinrich Nauen, Paul Klee, Oskar Moll, and Ewald Mataré. Thus developments in twentieth-century art became living history for her and she wanted to share it with others. This attitude lent whatever she said and wrote the inimitable vividness that made her so popular with both her students and the public at large. That is attested even today by her monographs on Bruno Goller and Jankel Adler, her multiply published report on Johanna Ey, her studies on Mataré,

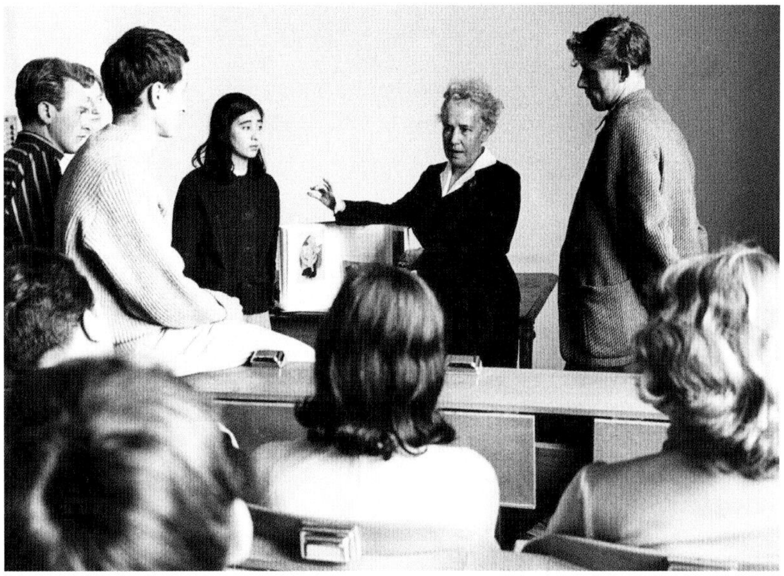

Fig. 2: Anna Klapheck with students, 1960

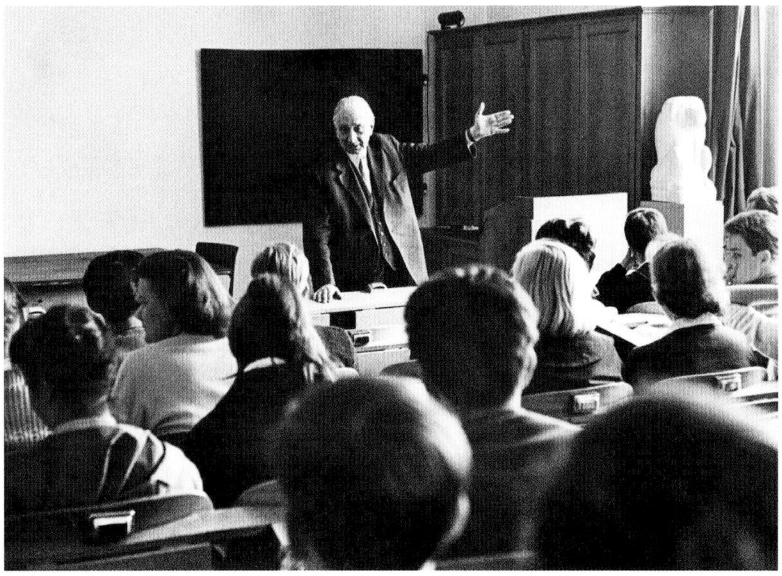

Fig. 3: Philosophy with Peter Mennicken, 1960

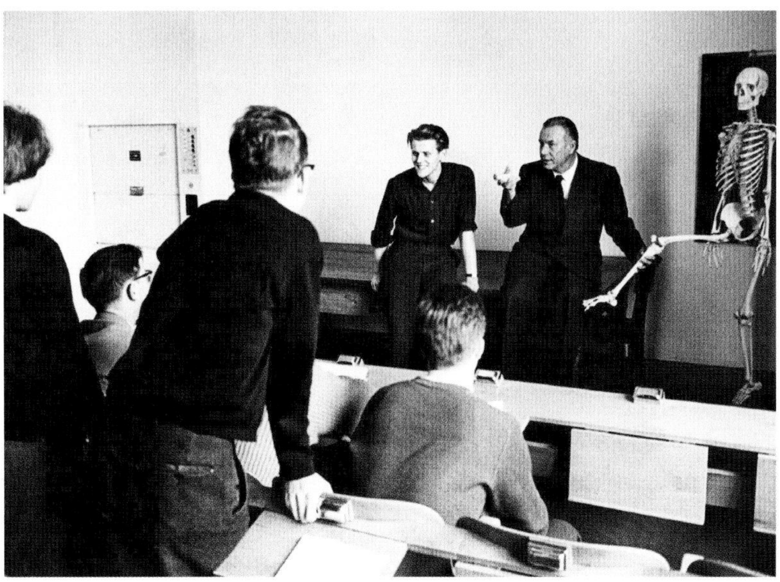

Fig. 4: Anatomy with Kurt Herzog, 1960

and the instructive and entertaining sketches in which she commented on the post-war world of pictures 'on their way from stopgaps to the art of affluence'.[11] Her attachment to the Art Academy, where she taught until the mid-1960s, is expressed in a knowledgeable description shot through with personal reminiscences of the way taken by the institution from the era of the conservative director Fritz Roeber via the reformer Walter Kaesbach to the sinister period after 1933.[12]

Its refreshingly contemporary style also attracted fine arts students to Anna Klapheck's lectures and classes. The upshot was that she occasionally had to share the teaching load with Heinrich Schmidt, a colleague who tended to look backwards rather than forwards and whose students were mainly aspiring art teachers. During the 1950s, thoughts on enlarging the range of the academic curriculum taught at the Academy to include other subjects to accompany instruction in art history surfaced only occasionally. Peter Mennicken, who held a chair in Aachen, had been available as a lecturer in philosophy since 1949; Kurt Herzog, a university professor of medicine, was another external lecturer at the Academy. He lectured on 'topographic anatomy and the theory of movement' (Figs. 3, 4). Budget constraints at first left no room for curricular extravagance. In the reconstruction phase, budgeting for additional personnel had to take second place to building expenses; the restoration of classrooms, seminar rooms, and lecture theatres; procurement of tools, facilities, and materials needed for working in art; and refurbishing the student cafeteria and the library. Hence teacher candidates aspiring to permanent employment at state higher secondary and secondary modern schools were instructed in education and teaching methods by instructors paid on an hourly basis and by experienced state school teachers on secondment to help out at the Academy. The Academy knew how to improvise and make do with temporary solutions.

Besides, the amount of theory that was to be taught along with art remained pretty much undefined during those years and this issue needed further clarification. How much knowledge of history and how much systematic reflection on what they were doing and on what was going on around them should be expected of young painters, exponents of the graphic arts, and sculptors? And how much of that should be administered by compulsory attendance at courses? Which subjects should the Academy tolerate alongside art history, which had been taught since the era of Lambert Krahe? In this respect

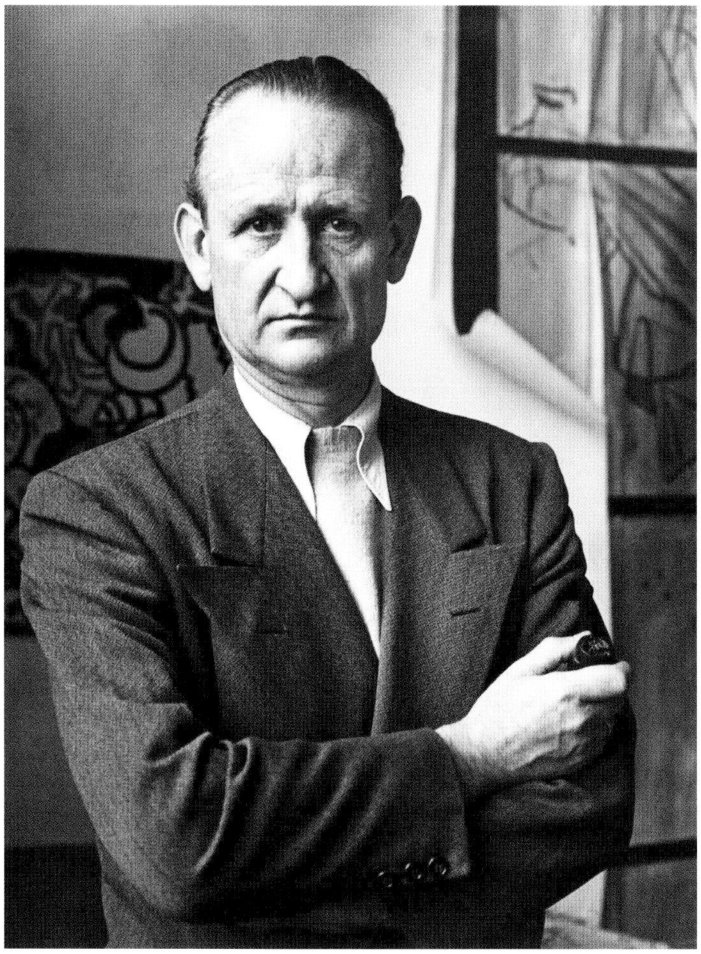

Fig. 5: Heinrich Kamps, director, 1949–1954

Kaesbach's reforms had accomplished little since they had aimed at practical instruction given by recognised exponents of modern art and the establishment of new workshops suited to contemporary art as well as the technical improvement of existing ones. Even the manifesto *Die Kunsthochschule* [The Art Academy], written by Lothar von Kunowski and published by the Academy in 1929 with Kaesbach's support, tended to be reticent – quite negative, in fact – about academic participation in drawing up a curriculum for the Academy, warning as it did against burdening the fine and applied arts, architecture, and even education – in brief, everything that had to do with art, with 'excess educational baggage', and too much 'brain culture'. It even invoked a menacing 'beast of burden laden too heavily with unnecessary knowledge'.[13] Heinrich Kamps (Fig. 5), a former graduate of the seminar for teachers of drawing, who was once taught outside the Academy and then in it by Kunowski, who was both a painter and a writer, had been a professor and head of the Art Education Department at the Academy since 1949. He could never altogether rid himself of such reservations despite some timid attempts at expanding the curriculum during his tenure. The prevailing practical bias still kept the arts and humanities canon at bay instead of seeking harmonious cooperation.

HEADY TURBULENCE

During the 1960s, however, things changed. *Die Unruhe wächst* [Unrest is Growing] was the title Gerhard Hoehme gave in 1963 to a painting of his in which he seismographically envisaged the events of the coming decade. Hoehme, who had only been appointed to his post three years previously, Karl Otto Götz, Joseph Beuys, Karl Bobek, and colleagues of theirs represented a new generation of teachers to take up posts at the Academy. More than their predecessors, they sought a dialogue in parallel with and through their work as artists. At the suggestion of Hans Schwippert, who had been director of the Academy since 1956, painters, practitioners of the graphic arts, and sculptors regularly gave addresses at the matriculation ceremony marking the beginning of each term and ventured on subjects that went beyond the scope of their work in art. To cite some examples: Georg Meistermann talked about 'The artist and society', Gert Weber talked about 'Art education at schools', and Karl Otto Götz about 'The visual arts and communication'. Public statements like those took into consideration the increasing need for an exchange of ideas within the Academy and beyond its confines. There was no lack of attention paid to them. At that time student numbers were surging; concomitantly the debates grew livelier and often louder. After the defensive political slogans of the Adenauer era, which intolerantly counselled 'No experiments!', had worn thin, people at the Art Academy were no different from others elsewhere in wanting to 'risk more democracy!' This campaign was boosted by disputes and panel discussions, debates in classes and in corridors, after lectures, and during seminars (Fig. 6). Demanding enlightenment, young and old turned against the concerted cover-up of the compromised German past. Protest flared up against contemporary trends that were ominous because they were warmongering. At some political events, the space available was too cramped and the venues were full to bursting.

The arts were stirred up inside the Academy as they were outside it, and with them humanities, too. Almost everything seemed 'urgently in need of commentary and explanation' on the lines of the then fashionable Arnold Gehlen catchphrase;[14] the answers to many questions promised new ways of looking at things and new methods. Could the loss of the monopoly on the image that the arts had suffered since the inven-

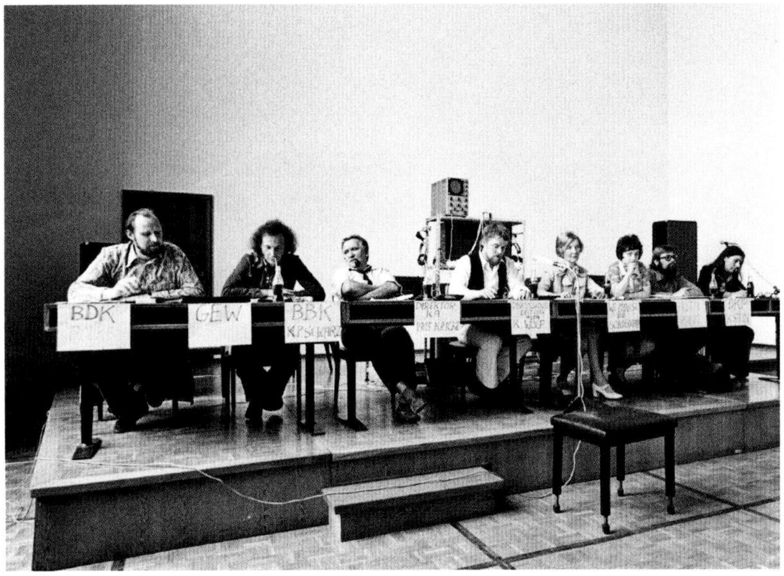

Fig. 6: Panel discussion with Norbert Kricke in the Great Hall at the Düsseldorf Art Academy, 1973

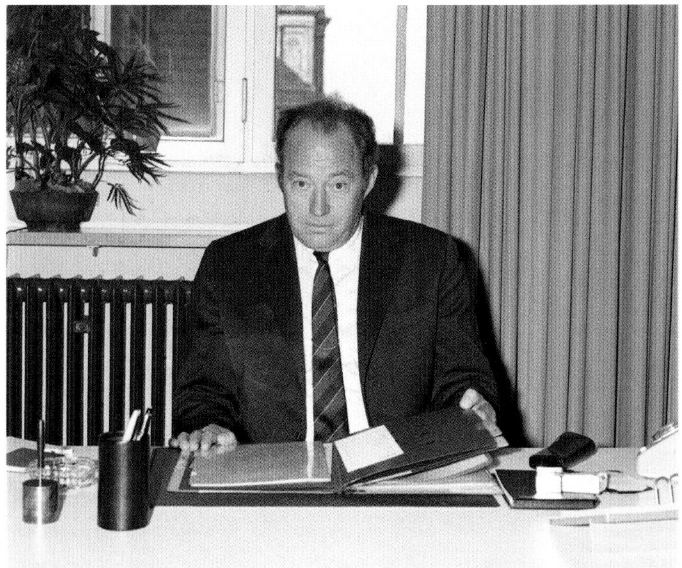

Fig. 7: Eduard Trier, director 1966–1972

tion of the camera, the film camera, the television camera, and the video recorder be adequately grasped with the interpretation techniques applied by the traditional arts and humanities? Weren't new disciplines called for? The sceptical view of 'The Work of Art in the Age of Mechanical Reproducibility' – thus the title of the celebrated essay by Walter Benjamin – lent the Critical Theory of the Frankfurt School new popularity, forcing the products of the culture industry and art for the masses that were expanding in the affluent society under the magnifying glass of a 'consumer aesthetic' that was yet to be formulated although analytically tested in classes taught by art historians, philosophers, and educationalists with reference to Benjamin, Theodor W. Adorno, and Siegfried Kracauer. At the same time Aby Warburg's iconology made more precise perception of the dissolution of visual boundaries, of parallel phenomena in 'higher' and 'applied' art. 'Interdisciplinarity' and 'cooperation' were the demands made of the established arts and humanities, which were met in collective interdisciplinary seminars, by restructuring courses of study and examinations. All those approaches resonated with a desire for more 'communication'. It was no coincidence that a magazine of that name was launched by students from the film class, including Susanne Ebert and Peter Holtfreter. Within the context of lively debate about reform, the first issue of *Kommunikation* was devoted to the question of the sense, purpose, and teachability of visual communication that was still not being sufficiently addressed in Germany and was bothering artists as well as academics. Even though Joseph Beuys dismissed out of hand anything of the sort in an interview, instead plumping for his 'expanded conception of art',[15] some of his colleagues turned out to be more open-minded. As early as 1963 Karl Otto Götz had made a case in his matriculation address for approaching communications and information theory without prejudice and accused the all too stringent demarcation between university and academy disciplines of being responsible for the failure to address the issue. 'Communication between man and visual art', he emphasised, was an event too complex to be dealt with fairly and analytically within the confines of narrow-minded compartmentalisation.[16] The triumphal entry of the 'new visual media' – film, photography, and video – not long afterwards into the Art Academy proved Götz and Rissa, the co-author of his manifesto,[17] right and also compelled the arts and humanities already there to explore the art character of such additions to the curriculum.

Eduard Trier, who was appointed to the chair of art history in 1964 to succeed Heinrich Schmidt and Anna Klapheck, was the ideal answer to the prevailing wish for a colleague and teacher who was at once committed to art, open to the arts and humanities, and cosmopolitan in outlook. Trier was not a denizen of the ivory tower. He stepped up to the lectern at the Art Academy as a polyglot intellectual who had collected the broadest possible range of experiences through manifold activities. He had earned a reputation as a critic and curator, organiser of exhibitions and a member of art juries, an author, a publisher of series, and a speaker that brought him international acclaim far beyond the borders of Germany. His personal preference was sculpture, but he wrote and spoke with equal assurance on painting and architecture, photography and film, and urban planning and developments in cultural policy. For all his contemporary bias, he never neglected the historical perspectives in which everything that happens in art is rooted. Nor was he above occasionally leavening the seriousness of his arguments with cryptic anecdotes and whimsical jokes. Thus he succeeded in extracting the light side from the heaviest of materials while reporting and commentating and taught his auditors and readers something while entertaining them because his chief concern – as he emphasised in a conversation he had with Wilfried Dörstel in 1990 – was always to win people over to art, to 'demonstrate possibilities for understanding', to reveal 'how one might approach artworks'.[18]

Working at the Art Academy made it possible for Eduard Trier (Fig. 7) to convey his wide-ranging insights into current scenes and his encyclopaedic knowledge of history to young artists, future art teachers, and aspiring academics in the arts and humanities. That is why, apart from his historical survey lectures, he also regularly tabled for discussion 'problems of contemporary art' in seminars and classes. His view was that a harmonious relationship might be aspired to at an institute that was orientated towards the practical side of art between two dimensions, between analysis of the past and observation of the present. In a matriculation address, 'On evaluating contemporary art or the joys and sorrows of an exhibition-maker', which Trier gave in 1964, he confessed that he felt 'brotherly bonds with all artists' and wanted to work as a 'possible mediator between art and the public' – he should not, nor did he wish to, neglect or even forget his duties as an art historian because that was what he primarily saw himself as being.[19]

Eduard Trier also acted as a poised communicator, one who preferred conciliating to polarising, in the office of Academy director. Since he saw the Academy as an institution 'in permanent reform', he personally sought to preserve the legacy and also smooth the way to introducing viable innovations.[20] In line with the academic 'tradition of the questioning self',[21] he promoted internal debates on desired changes, opened up a new representation forum to the extant work areas in the form of folders labelled 'News, Pictures, Reports', and dedicated himself energetically to solving the problem of cramped space in view of surging enrolment numbers. After times marred by crisis and repeated attempts at pragmatic integration, he finally had some successes to report by the early 1970s. They also benefited the arts and humanities by including a 'lectureship in sociology, several staff appointments in art theory, visiting professorships in both art and academic subjects, notably the teaching of art', and, finally, last but not least, 'modernising the library and slide collection'.[22] Yet by the time those reforms took hold, Eduard Trier had left the Art Academy, to the regret of many (and not just academic) colleagues.

The chair of philosophy that had finally been established after protracted debate and its occupant, Walter Warnach (Fig. 8), turned out to be mainstays of the Academy in this turbulent era. The Cologne thinker and poet was in many ways predestined for that office.[23] Partial to the arts, he had trained as a teacher but also distinguished himself as a man of letters, a translator, and a publisher. His intellectual interests had led him professionally to France on several occasions before he settled in the Rhine area as a reader for a publisher. He had wrested his first major work from the incisive experience of war: in *Die Welt des Schmerzes* [World of Pain] the themes emerged in the early 1950s with which Warnach would continue to engage,[24] that the incomprehensible reality of a world so difficult to designate should plunge man into an existence that brings

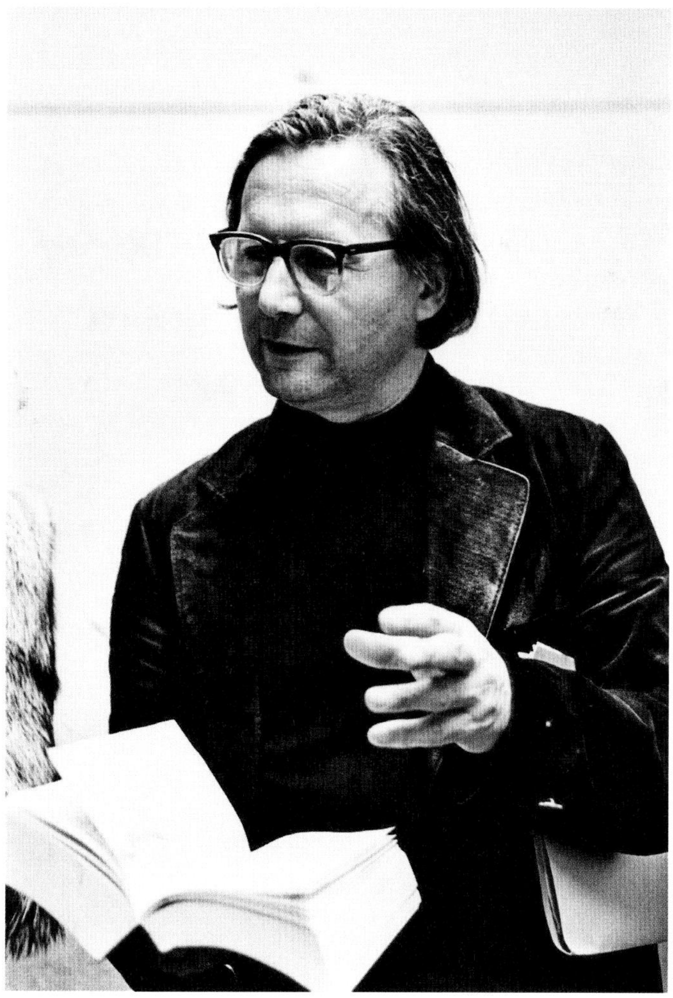

Fig. 8: Walter Warnach, 1972

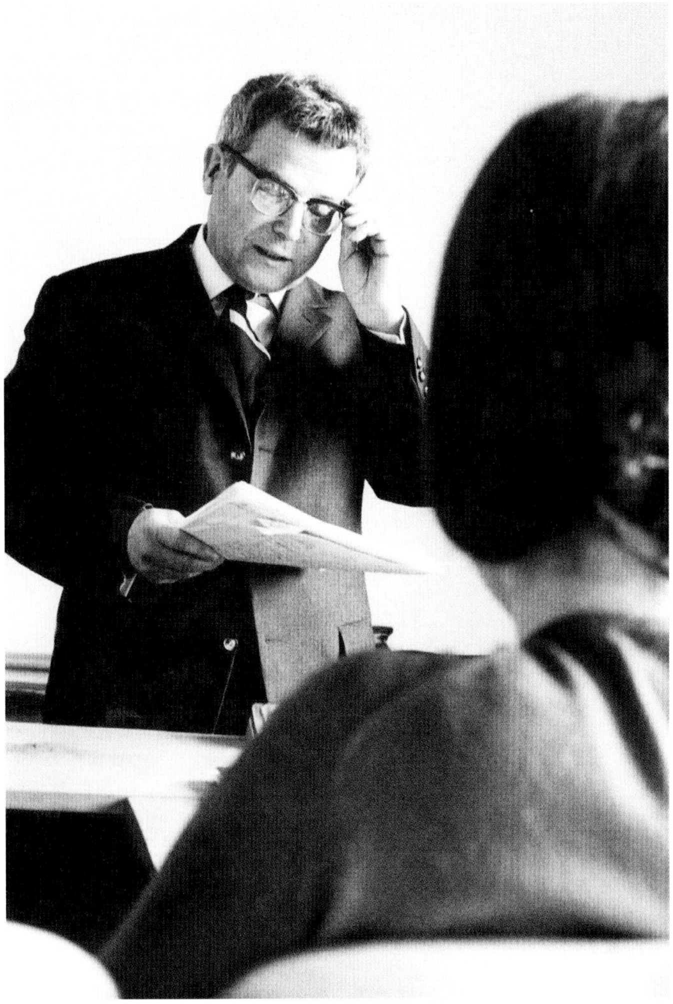

Fig. 9: Alfred Mundhenk, teaching, 1960

him almost intolerable suffering, that demands shocking sacrifice of him in the midst of joyful experiences. This dilemma, which he had experienced in his own life, was bound to challenge a man who was both a devout Christian and a sceptical philosopher. Warnach subordinated his search for answers to the questions thus arising to the metaphor of the labyrinth; he saw man as wandering about lost in a labyrinth and his thinking, like his own, searching for ways out of it. With Werner von Trott zu Solz, Heinrich Böll, and HAP Grieshaber he edited a periodical of that title[25] and had his complete works published in the early 1980s.[26] Warnach appeared throughout both reticent and clearly unambiguous in his line of reasoning. He sought the exchange of ideas and cultivated relationships both with Catholics who were critical of the Church and controversial intellectuals such as Carl Schmitt.[27] He attracted and held the attention of a growing public because he was tolerant yet unequivocally insisted on his constantly further developing concept nurtured on piety and reflectiveness (and also in an ongoing dialogue with his brother, the eminent theologian Viktor Warnach[28]) of a 'we science' and 'complicity', ensuring him respect from friend and foe alike even in the most controversial debates.[29] Heinrich Böll spoke for many when he confessed, 'I personally owe Warnach more than he knows and more than I could express here.'[30]

In line with his approach to philosophy, Warnach appeared in the role of colleague and teacher at the Art Academy as a gentle proponent of enlightenment who was always willing to talk. Art, he never tired of emphasising, was supposed to address itself to man, had to be 'art of and for man', should not neglect its 'freedom', should strive for 'autonomy', and should not, therefore, even within the Academy *qua* institution, venture too far into the clutches of the nanny state because, by its very nature, it tended all too easily to be domineering.[31] Insofar as philosophy followed the same principle, it was, admittedly, a 'risky business', like any work on attaining a state of consciousness, yet in that, it proclaimed its affinity with the artistic.[32] It goes almost without saying that Warnach's solidarity with Joseph Beuys, who had been shown the door in 1972, grew out of that conviction. Like Beuys, Warnach regarded art as 'a form of self-actualisation', which any person might strive for in his own way and should do so, as 'the activity engaged in by man to which he commits his entire being'.[33] Warnach did not follow Beuys's demagoguery and plebiscitary politics in all their ramifications yet in their basic socio-anthropological thrust, the philosopher and the artist were in agreement.

Alfred Mundhenk was another who participated in the discussion of the expanded art concept and an evolving idea of art (Fig. 9). He had taken the chair of education in 1966 and from then on advocated an anthropologically grounded view of the tasks confronting art teachers. An experienced school master, Mundhenk based his line of reasoning less on theoretical considerations than on practical insights. He voted with Rudolf Arnheim for 'visualised thinking' both in the classroom and in all contemplation of art and designed a 'methodology of sensitivity training', which was beneficial not only to the study of pictures, drawings, and works of sculpture but also to the shaping of man's behaviour and his life design as a whole.[34] 'Art teaching', orientated towards those goals and wide-ranging, should not be done according to the rules of traditional 'art education', should not 'retreat into the preserve traditionally allocated to art' or, by following the recipe for the now fashionable 'visual communication', train its sights solely on dealing with the mass media;[35] on the contrary, in cooperation with related disciplines it should contribute to a cosmopolitan, polysensory holistic personal development.

CONSOLIDATION

Insofar as he developed a concept for an 'integral art didactic', Günter Blecks represented his discipline from a similar angle. After studying both at the Art Academy and at Cologne and Münster Universities, he had gained experience in teaching at higher state secondary schools, at the Krefeld Werkkunstschule, and at the studio for art education at Bonn University before accepting an appointment to teach at the Art Academy as an instructor. From the mid-1960s he developed methodology, which was then still a fringe subject, into a fully fledged art didactic in its own right. In 1975 he was appointed to a chair in that subject. From then on he consolidated his discipline by championing reform of outdated curricula and examination structures, advocating an interdisciplinary programme that could accommodate rapidly changing life conditions. In all this Blecks was inspired by his commitment to spreading the thinking of the philosophical anthropologist Jean Gebser,[36] seeking to translate to the teaching of art the latter's vision of a necessary change in the spatial and temporal constitution of human consciousness structures. Out of this approach grew the paradigm of an 'integral art education', which took into consideration the jettisoning of traditional views on space and time discussed in many arts and sciences in the twentieth century and saw itself confirmed in this through the development of modern art towards aperspectivity, sensory multidimensionality, and polysemy as well as culture on the whole towards Postmodernism. The change in expression that had already taken place in contemporary art was regarded by Gebser, and with him Günter Blecks, as confirmation of the possibility of a comprehensive turnaround in the human world view as well as its being fertilised on the aesthetic-receptive and creative-active planes.

Thinking of that kind struck a chord with an era that was increasingly prone to self-doubt. The negative consequences of the technological and industrial lifeworld made necessary the revision of traditional interpretation patterns and formulation of arts and science standpoints to address problems adequately. Just as the conception of space expanded in the cosmonaut years, earthly time and, with it, how it was shown in art experienced increasing interpretative pressure. The temporality of existence could no longer be viewed in one dimension.[37] One learnt that existence was contingent on many temporal structures, that, for instance, cherished notions of linear 'progress' in man's activities could not really be trusted,[38] that the arts, on the other hand, had since time immemorial expressed more or less openly the disturbances that were now increasingly coming to the fore. This realisation led Heinrich Theissing (Fig. 10), who had held the chair of art history since the 1970s as Eduard Trier's successor, to devote himself to focusing on the representation of time in artworks alongside his usual workload. His numerous individual studies culminated in an examination of *Die Zeit im Bild* [Time in the Image], which since then has belonged to the canon of art historical writings.[39] In parallel with this research into temporality in art and his exploration of the grotesque in the visual arts, Theissing also continued to address the question of the historicity of all creativity and understanding, therefore also of his academic discipline and his teaching. In his lectures he strove, as he emphasised in setting out his agenda, to 'take on reality by means of historical materials in the medium of seeing'.[40] After all, only he who was cognisant of the historical contingency of all visual culture might attain self-knowledge and a free view of what his presence in the here and now was premised on, which alone might open up to him a vista of things to come. Dealing with

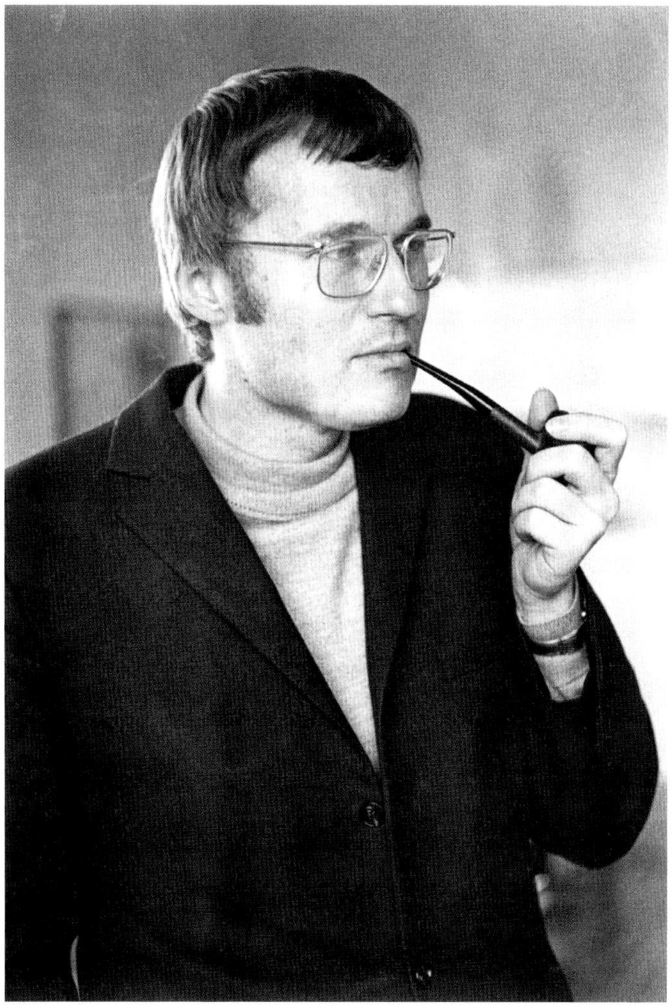

Fig. 10: Heinrich Theissing, 1972

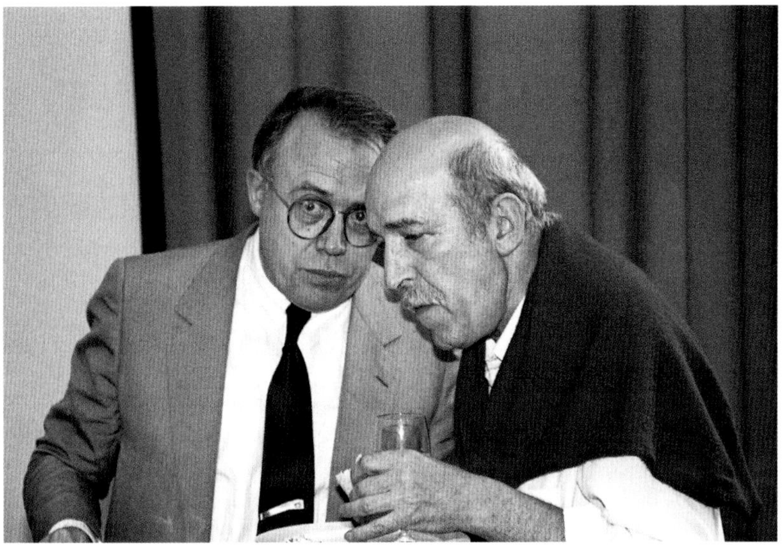

Fig. 11: Walter Jürgen Hofmann talking with Ernst Kasper, 1990

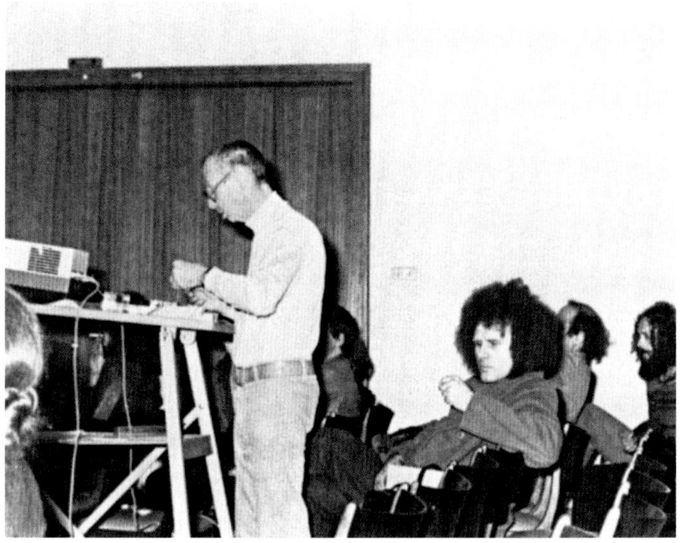

Fig. 12: A lecture by John Anthony Thwaites; on the right Klaus Rinke, 1972

artworks of whatever era was suitable for leading one onto this path. 'Only he who has history' might 'have a future at all'. In view of that realisation, 'art and history', artist and art historian 'were sitting in the same swaying boat' of a life's journey from the past through the present towards a 'futurum' that was uncertain yet ineluctable.[41]

Like Heinrich Theissing, his colleague, the art historian Walter Jürgen Hofmann (Fig. 11), also rendered great service to the Art Academy, as its deputy director of long years' standing. He came to Düsseldorf from Erlangen-Nuremberg. His academic specialisations were the art of the early modern age and the Baroque, but he was also versed in European architectural history with a particular interest in old and modern architecture. During his twenty years as prorector, he earned a reputation as a committed champion of academic interests, carefully stabilised the inner workings of the Academy, and, through many an initiative, contributed to its reputation. In the *Jahreshefte* [Annual Notebooks] he created a mouthpiece for both artistic and academic colleagues that was published on a regular basis. By reworking the contracts, he and the chancellor, Peter M. Lynen, secured a permanent home at the Academy for the collections amassed by Lambert Krahe, which had been housed in the Kunstmuseum der Stadt Düsseldorf. The idea mooted by Markus Lüpertz when he was rector of founding an 'Academy Gallery' within the Academy to link up with a forgotten tradition found an eloquent and energetic advocate in the person of Walter Jürgen Hofmann. Moreover, during those years, stopgap structures were often replaced with better ones. Whereas so many academics had had to teach in decrepit pavilions fringing the north façade of the main Academy building, only minimal office space was available to some of them. However, better classrooms and offices and more acceptable working conditions were arranged for them, and the library was better housed during the rectorates of Irmin Kamp and Heinrich Theissing and of Hofmann and Lüpertz in the renovated and refurbished former municipal pawnbrokers on the street Reuterkaserne. A solution to the pressing problem of a lack of space, a situation to which Eduard Trier had already drawn attention and which Norbert Kricke as Academy director had done his best to remedy by conducting negotiations with the city of Düsseldorf, had finally been found.

Chief among Kricke's concerns, which were seconded by students and colleagues, was promoting a stronger focus in academic teaching on contemporary art. A distinguished art critic, John Anthony Thwaites (Fig. 12),[42] was accordingly hired to teach. In line with his previous activity, he devoted himself as a teacher primarily to the analysis of current phenomena in art and to personally counselling students. His helpful visits to classrooms and studios, walks through exhibitions with students and teaching staff, and his congenial personality laced with sceptical expertise ensured that Thwaites was universally acclaimed and popular. To everyone's regret, he retired after only a few years on grounds of age.

Still Kricke did not want to leave any stone unturned in the search for a more contemporary focus. One day he encountered a young connoisseur of art on the Côte d'Azur who seemed suitable for the position that Kricke had upgraded to a chair in twentieth-century art: Werner Spies. In his memoirs, Spies described why taking on the task appealed to him and how he approached it.[43] While living in Paris, he had mediated between German and French culture. Spies had been a much sought-after newspaper correspondent, a translator, curator, and author. He had always found the company of distinguished painters, draughtsmen, sculptors, photographers, and their aspirants to initiation in the arts fascinating in an ambience steeped in art. With them he engaged in regular exchanges of ideas in colloquies, visits to exhibitions, and studio conversations alongside his lectures and seminars (Fig. 13). His widely disseminated culture-page articles, his presence in the media, and the spectacular exhibitions that Spies inspired and organised in Germany and abroad continued to lure interested people into the Art Academy lecture hall who had no desire to dedicate themselves to specialised study or whose student days in art history were long past. Werner Spies treated such visiting students – the numbers of which had been continually rising since the mid-1980s not only in his lectures but also in those of the other art historians and some philosophers teaching at the Academy – as he did his students and colleagues, with unwavering kindness and eloquence. In all this he enjoyed, as he later confessed, not just 'having something to tell about the distinguished people he met and his impressions of them'.[44] He also took note of and gratefully accepted the inspiration thus encountered, which lifted him out of his daily routine and confronted him with the surprising attitudes and the practices of a new, more mobile media age: 'Students' work showed how promptly and alertly they reacted to everything they had learnt about somewhere.'[45] When he retired from teaching after twenty-seven years, Werner Spies could look back on a career that had enriched both himself and his public because it had opened all their eyes to and raised their consciousness of the diversity of modern ways of viewing the world and the concomitant phenomena in art.

The question of the interrelationship between art and everyday reality also informed the context of Walter Biemel's (Fig. 14) thinking. Appointed in 1976 to the chair of philosophy, he had gone from Bucharest via Freiburg, Liège, and Cologne to Aachen. On the way he had become familiar with the phenomenology of both Edmund Husserl and Martin Heidegger and matured into a polyglot man of letters, whose monographs on Sartre and Heidegger were published in large editions, opening up to many readers a first approach to those thinkers.[46] For all his dedication to phenomenology, Biemel did not forget his fondness for literature, music (which he practised himself as a violin player), and the aesthetics of the visual arts. When he was offered the chance to move to Düsseldorf, what attracted him – as he wrote in a biographical preface to his *Collected Works* – was 'the task itself, especially also the direct contact with the artists'.[47] During his seven years at the Art Academy, he moved through its hemispheres, open-minded as always, made contact with established personalities and newcomers, gave addresses to open exhibitions, wrote catalogue texts, was deputy director for two years, and made some new friends.[48] The number of philosophical analyses of contemporary art he wrote – first

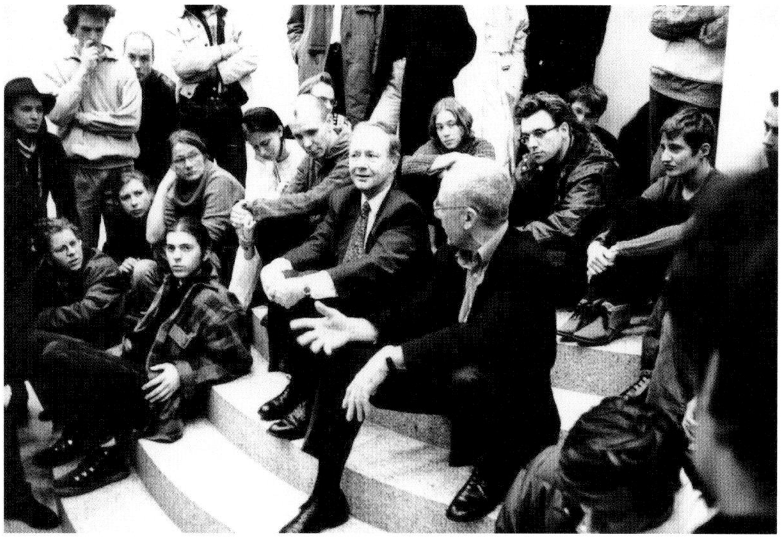

Fig. 13: Werner Spies and students talking with Gerhard Richter while visiting a Richter retrospective mounted at the Art and Exhibition Hall in Bonn, 1994

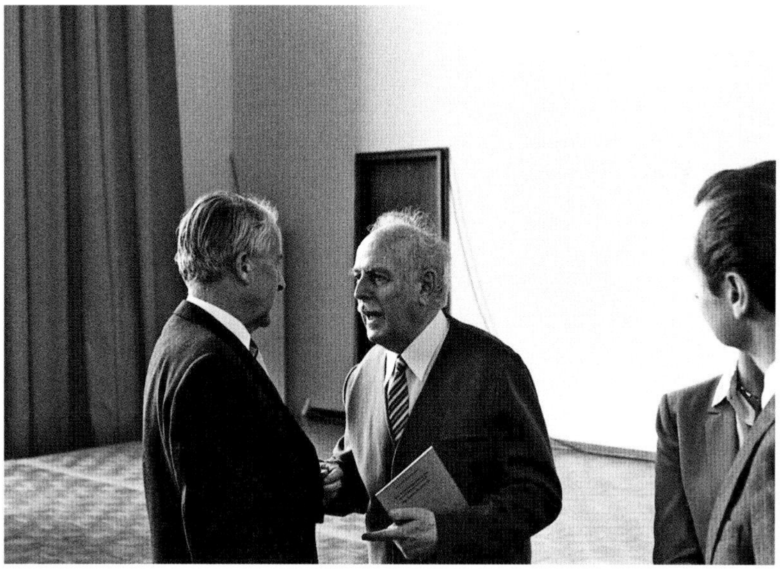

Fig. 14: Walter Biemel saying farewell to the Art Academy, 1983

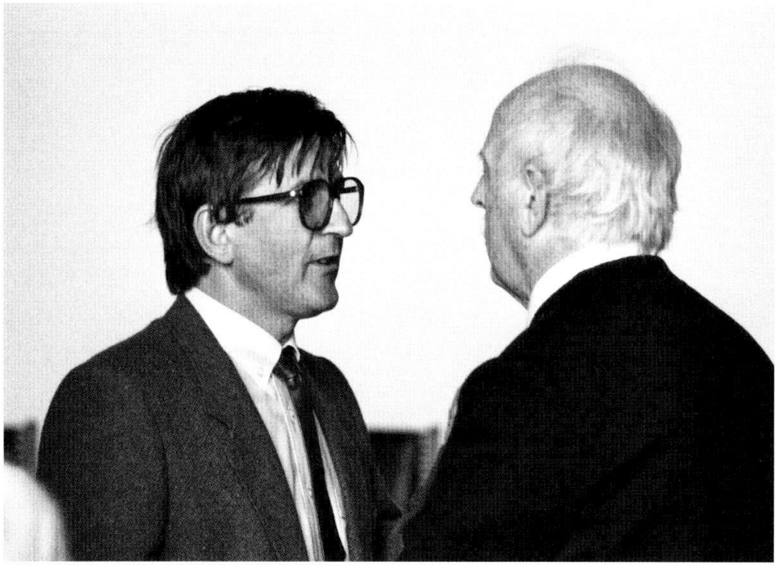

Fig. 15: Paul Good talking with his predecessor, Walter Biemel, 1983

published in book form in 1968 – continued to grow apace.[49] In them, as he later summarised it in a second collection of essays, was to 'be made visible how the interplay of art and philosophy evolves, how, as in art, an interpretation of the world takes place that we need in order to be able to understand the condition of our historical existence'.[50]

Walter Biemel was succeeded by the Swiss philosopher Paul Good, who taught at the Art Academy until 2008 (Fig. 15). Good had followed up studies in theology with philosophical schooling in Munich, Paris, and St. Gallen. After completing his postdoctorate, he spent some time researching at the University of California, Berkeley. He captivated audiences in Düsseldorf by passionately bringing to life for them the ongoing French philosophy debates conducted by the likes of Gilles Deleuze, Jacques Derrida, et al. Not only did Paul Good teach introductions to the thinking of Maurice Merleau-Ponty and Max Scheler,[51] he also distinguished himself by publishing a great many studies focused on the enigmatic character, the incomprehensibility, the sheer inconceivability, of contemporary art.[52]

His thoughts constantly recurred to the problem of speech, the fraught relationship between a statement couched in words and visual illustration, which he felt might best be conveyed through metaphor and poetry. Good argued for his standpoint with rhetorical verve. He had no qualms about resorting to pointed criticism whenever the congenial atmosphere of life at the Academy seemed threatened. In Albrecht Fabri, a Cologne art lover, essayist, and coiner of aphorisms, Good found a kindred spirit with whom he enjoyed conversing and whose writings he edited.[53]

An ambiguously mischievous polemicist and irenicist who was not fond of being reduced to monosemy, Paul Good also conducted his philosophical activities as 'la pensée de la différence', as 'thinking in terms of diversity rather than unity, of idiosyncrasy rather than mentality, of intensities rather than extensions, of becoming rather than being', as reflection under the aegis of the 'new (ancient) god Hermes', to whom he caused a stimulating nature, culture, and art memorial place to be established in the Hombroich Island Museum in Neuss, which he also wrote about.[54]

By the mid-1970s, the steady increase in the number of aspirants to qualify as art teachers at state higher secondary schools made it seem opportune to lend the subject of general education a more academic character. This came about in 1974 through the appointment of Liesel-Lotte Herkenrath (Fig. 16). After studying protestant theology and German language and literature, she added sociology and psychoanalysis to her CV before taking a doctorate in education. *Wege zum Menschen* [Ways to Man] was a periodical which she co-edited and the tenor of which informed all her endeavours. The Art Academy offered her the chance of linking her inclination to pastoral psychology with accompanying a young generation of artists in a climate that was – as she wrote shortly before taking up her teaching post in Düsseldorf – refreshingly free of 'very specific feelings of alienation and fears that are in general inherent in the tertiary education scene'.[55] She also viewed this appraisal as a commitment to upholding the liberal spirit of the Academy and to promote it there through reforms wherever she deemed them appropriate. To that end she became involved as an adviser in the constitutional debates at the Academy, successfully advocating the placement of Academy professors on an equal footing with their colleagues at universities, the upgrading of anthropological subjects, the employment of student assistants, and the introduction of sabbatical terms for research in both art and scholarship.[56] Through all this, Liesel-Lotte Herkenrath's sense of humour rarely left her: as a Protestant, her comment on her occasional journeys homewards in the company of Walter Warnach, a Catholic, was that this in a way anticipated ecumenism; further, as staunch natives of Cologne, they had agreed to eschew reciprocal attempts at conversion. By the time she was forced by ill health to resign prematurely from her chair in 1988, the Art Academy, and especially its scholars, were very much in her debt.

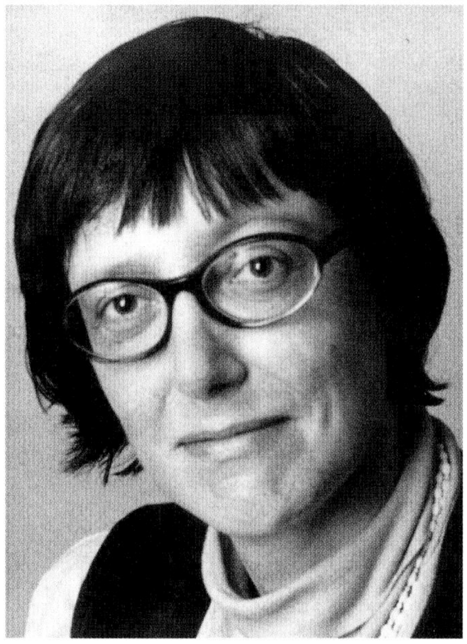

Fig. 16: Liesel-Lotte Herkenrath, 1980s

Friedrich Wolfram Heubach lent the subject Liesel-Lotte Herkenrath had taught an even stronger psychological bias (Fig. 17). He was, so to speak, predestined on biographical grounds to teach and research at the Art Academy because he had been an observer of what was going on around it during his schooldays in Düsseldorf. First, however, he went to Cologne to study, where he encountered in the person of Wilhelm Salber a university teacher who devoted himself to the interrelationship of artistic creativity and constitutional psychology. While still a student Heubach spent six years publishing the periodical that would make him known in the 'scene': *interfunktionen*. In it he provided artists from almost all fields as well as numerous authors with a journalistic forum in which they could confront the tastes in prevailing art with their own products and views. It soon established itself as the widely acclaimed mouthpiece for Fluxus and Lidl, Happenings and Actions, Environments and Land Art, in fact for almost everything that looked like an aesthetic protest – however, the editor shut down *interfunktionen* after only ten issues because he was interested in dynamic rough edges rather than static slickness.[57] Heubach's further career took him in a consistent trajectory via the Cologne Werkschulen and the University of Fine Arts Hamburg to the Düsseldorf Art Academy. There he infiltrated education as a discipline with psychological dynamite that captivated his students all the more because he kept them from treading intellectual beaten tracks that would all too soon be standardised, memorably confronting them with the question of whether they really wanted to be or to become artists and, if so, why, thus inculcating in them the wary alertness and the critical flexibility they needed for their creative work. Heubach felt that the cult of the genius, monarchical tendencies, waffling, and glib verdicts were an impertinence and as such to be condemned, and encountered them both in conversation and in his writings with clarifications that quite often achieved the status of trenchant insights.[58]

At the same time Johannes Bilstein was giving the education debates a stronger anthropological bias (Fig. 18). Before coming to the Art Academy in 1980, he had studied education, finishing with state examinations and a doctorate; he then gained experience variously as a university assistant, a teacher at higher secondary school level, and in adult education. His work in Düsseldorf benefited hugely from the knowledge and skills he had thus acquired. He was supported in tasks related to school internships by Günter Becker, an instructor. In his theoretical teaching and research, Bilstein championed the incorporation of the 'cultural turn', which during those years saw the humanities and social sciences turn aside from the societal contingencies and constellations of human life and instead focus more intensively on the cultural imprinting resulting from them. Close to art as he was, he made this shift productive by addressing the questions arising from metaphorological analysis of the artwork to the modalities of linguistic imagery in the expression of both the individual self and intersubjective communication. With this analytical approach he gained for his own studies in education and training a productive alignment with the semasiological perspectives that had been opened up in Germany notably by Hans Blumenberg and in France by Paul Ricœur.[59] The many studies on this he published under the collective title *Gesprochene Bilder* [Spoken Images] were incorporated in his postdoctoral thesis. They earned Bilstein a

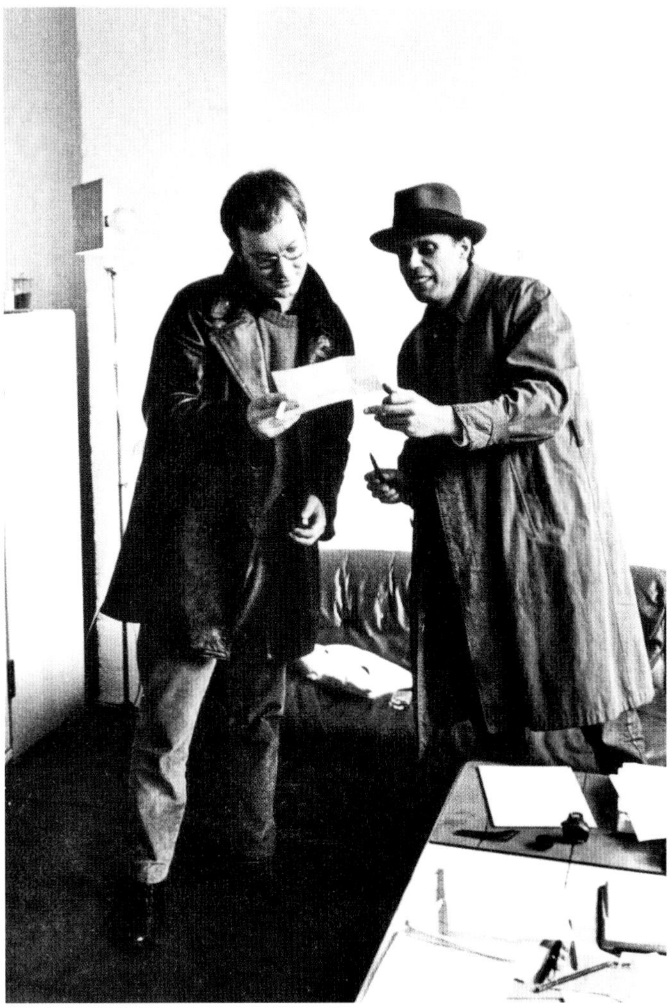

Fig. 17: Friedrich Wolfram Heubach and Joseph Beuys, 1972

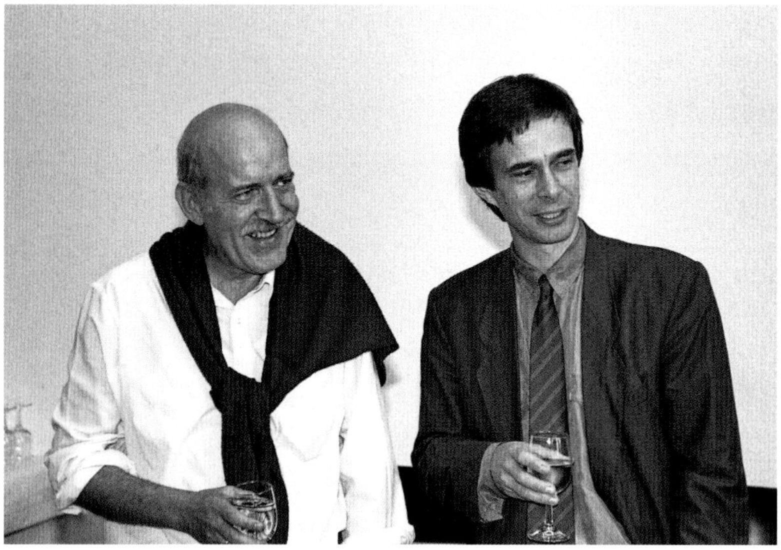

Fig. 18: Ernst Kasper and Johannes Bilstein, 1990

reputation as an original thinker, one who – as Micha Brumlik emphasised – has indefatigably 'investigated the aesthetic determinants of the intellect'.[60]

He has been a speaker who is much in demand at congresses, conferences, and symposia, some of which he inspired in turn and successfully organised.[61] As a writer he has contributed substantially to collections of essays and brought out many as a general editor. Under the aegis of the Deutsche Gesellschaft für Erziehungswissenschaft [German Education Studies Society], he became chairman of the Committee for Anthropology in Education and a member of the General Education Studies division. He has demonstrated his commitment to the concerns of his subject and of those his subject targets in foundations, on advisory boards, and on councils. Much in demand as the writer of expert reports, he was the academic counsel for the city of Düsseldorf's Artists to the Schools project for many years. It goes without saying that he has always done his best to include the Art Academy in these activities. That this is so is attested by the 'Moyländer Diskurse zu Kunst und Wissenschaft' [Moyland Discourses on Art and the Humanities], of which he is a co-founder, dealing with art collecting or the rituals on which the Art Academy has collaborated every two years with the Museum Schloss Moyland and the Centre for International Art Management (CIAM), and his regular participation in the lectures series that have been given since 2009, in which scholars from outside the Academy are invited to take part. Moreover, Johannes Bilstein has continued to investigate the issue – with a view to both secondary and tertiary education – 'of whether art can teach anything at all, and what that might be, and especially: what is the good of what one learns from it?' And he has answered the 'question about teaching art' in turn with a metaphorical reference to 'sluices, rafts, rag rugs' as paradigms that are helpful for teaching, which have been inherent in art since time immemorial and, therefore, could – in fact, should – also be guidelines for 'the art of teaching'.[62]

THE PRESENT

From the 1970s onwards more and more tasks have devolved upon the arts and humanities at the Art Academy. Study and examination regulations were once again revised. The implementation of the *Akademiebrief* [Academy certificate] for fine arts graduates also made it compulsory for them to attend academic courses. As a result, freely elected student representatives of the various academic disciplines have sat in on the *viva voce* finals from then on. Similarly, a student representative has participated in the final examinations leading to a postgraduate degree in architecture. In tandem with institutional restructuring, theoretical subjects have been pooled under the heading of 'art-related academic courses'. This new department has in turn been authorised to award doctoral and postdoctoral degrees. It can now give its courses in rooms with technical equipment that is constantly being upgraded to the newest standards. A mediatheque permitting the use of digital image storing and retrieval has replaced the old slide library. Finally, the Art Academy has not been able to avoid bringing its degree courses in line with the bachelor and master's model proposed by the Bologna Process for European degree standardisation.

The last mentioned changes have also affected the course on teaching methods, which is in part also responsible for the training of future art teachers at state schools. Kunibert Bering (Fig. 19), who has been in charge of teaching this subject since 1998, has dedicated himself knowledgeably to the tasks associated with it. He was superlatively prepared for it because he brought to the chair of teaching methods the double qualification of being an experienced teacher and an erudite art historian.[63] In parallel with teaching at a higher secondary school, he had made a name for himself as a university lecturer and had taught at various institutions of higher learning and research institutes in Germany and abroad. As he has done throughout his career, he refuses to be satisfied at the Art Academy with sticking to what is well known and tried and tested but aims at revising the approach by sensitively investigating new possibilities. Joachim Littke has for many years been in charge of the teaching practice accompanying regular coursework.

Bering is committed to plurality in thought and deed. Unsurprisingly, he has initiated many improvements that have contributed to enhancing the reputation of the Art Academy: they include special research groups[64] and *Artificium*, a

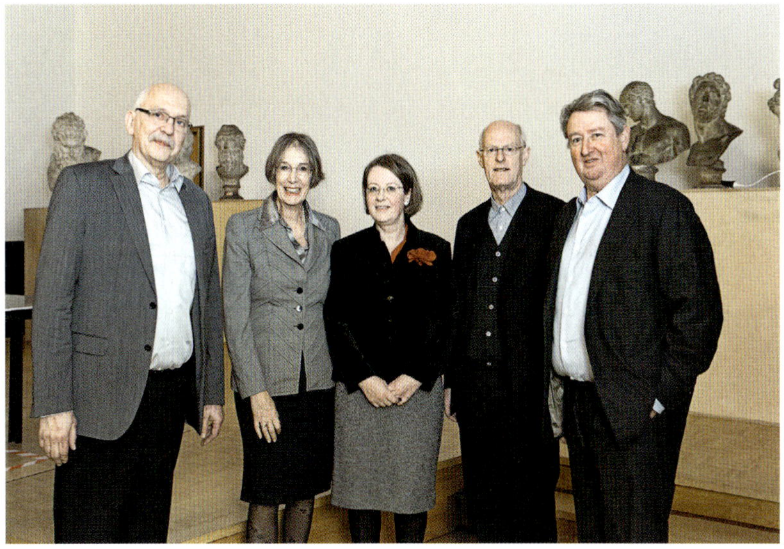

Fig. 19: From left to right: Kunibert Bering, Steffi Roettgen, Sonja Brink, Anthony Cragg, and Siegfried Gohr at the 'Lambert Krahe' symposium, 8 November 2012

steadily growing book series, as well as *Impulse. Kunstdidaktik* [Impulse. Art Didactic], a biannual periodical which he co-edits with Rolf Niehoff.[65] Keen educationalist that he is, Bering always sees to it that young talent also has a say in these work groups and departmental publications. The same holds for the big events he has hosted at the Art Academy, at which colleagues take stock and estimate future prospects of Bering's subject for an interested public – for instance, in April 2000 at 'Perspektiven einer Didaktik der Bildenden Künste' [Perspectives on Teaching Visual Arts], a symposium with papers that were published in *Jahreshefte der Kunstakademie Düsseldorf* [Annual Notebooks of the Düsseldorf Art Academy],[66] and in October 2009 at the Bundeskongress der Kunstpädagogik [Federal Congress of Art Teaching]; the talks given at it fill a massive documentary volume.[67] Finally, when Kunibert Bering suggested commemorating Lambert Krahe on the occasion of his 300th birthday with several days of lectures in autumn 2012, he thus handsomely paid off a long-standing debt owed to the founder of the Academy, who was an untiring art collector, a painter in the Rococo style, an astute man of business, and a promoter of young colleagues.[68]

Bering's art teaching concept centres on key notions such as 'visual experience', 'orientation', and 'competence'. As he has written in a manifesto, active art teaching should aim 'at cultural competence in developing identity, in the capability of coping in sophisticated contexts'.[69] Priority must be given to schooling perception, visual education, if those aims are to be achieved. The task of contemporary art teaching is to promote the necessary 'orientation in visual cultures' of diverse origins.[70] Further, art teaching should no longer be restricted to the school as the place for acquiring that skill but should be widened in scope to include areas of life outside school.[71] Only a broad-based 'aesthetic education' of that kind might, by raising visual intelligence, promote both competent visual reception and pictorial design that is informed by history in three ways: by the history on which it is premised, in line with the living present, and with a view to the future.

Alongside his theoretical writings, Siegfried Gohr has shown a hands-on approach to addressing the issue thus raised of teaching art in a way adequate to addressing aspirations that are at once profound and contemporary. When, on the departure of Werner Spies, a new occupant had to be found for the chair of art history focusing on the twentieth century, the range of Siegfried Gohr's experience and professional activities made him the ideal successor, so he was appointed to it in 2004. After studying and taking a doctorate, he became director of the Kunsthalle in Cologne and subsequently of the Museum Ludwig. Then he was appointed professor of art history and theory as well as media history at the Karlsruhe University of Art and Design. He had stood out both in Germany and abroad as an organiser of monographic and themed exhibitions of a quality that have made him much sought after as a curator of modern and contemporary art. Viewing himself as both a promoter of contemporary trends and a preserver of established tradition, he has remained true to his profession as an art historian and equally devoted to the self-appointed task of accompanying and counselling artists on their way through the jungle of museums, galleries, and publicity. He has been untiring in his efforts to help them by writing informative catalogue texts, giving expert talks at exhibitions, conducting public dialogues with artists, and working on retrospectives that include compendious multi-volume work catalogues. This diversity of roles coupled with innovative curiosity has ensured that he is in demand as an art mediator both at the Düsseldorf Academy and elsewhere.

Gohr considers it absolutely necessary, indeed appropriate, not only to confront the institutions in which and for which he works with questions that are not always accommodating but also to encounter established artist cultures critically as he has always done despite the companionship he has enjoyed with them. He knows that the most enduring quality of both life in general and in creating art, even more so in the art industry, is constant fluctuation – in a word, change. He understands this and manages the Academy Gallery – Die Neue Sammlung der Kunstakademie Düsseldorf [The New Collection of the Düsseldorf Art Academy] – of which he is director, accordingly. Proposed while Markus Lüpertz was rector and inaugurated in 2005 (Fig. 20), this institution continues activities of earlier eras, Academy directors, and art historians that had been disrupted. Lambert Krahe was in charge of the Electoral collection and also cooperated with external exhibition spaces. Professor Carl Joseph Ignaz Mosler was a co-founder of the Kunst-Verein für die Rheinlande und Westphalen [Rhineland and Westphalian Art Association] and wrote that it was intended both for show purposes and to serve commercial ends.[72] Walter Kaesbach saw to it that presentation rooms were provided in the Academy building. In Heinrich Schmidt's day the Kunstverein was temporarily housed in a partly bombed-out building in Eiskellerstraße. The present-day Academy Gallery seeks, on the one hand, to link up with such undertakings but, on the other, to deal with them in a new spirit. Its mission is, as Siegfried Gohr has written, to 'achieve a balance between creativity and preservation'. The Academy Gallery must not be a lifeless, passive magazine but rather a useful resource for those interested in art of any age and persuasion, an 'image store' that is always there and can be activated in multiple ways.[73] What it provides should vividly contribute to ensuring that the art character of artworks is preserved in the mediocre visual overload of the present day and that it continues to be recognised and appreciated as such. With his commitment to this institute, as an art historical scholar, as a teacher and mediator, Siegfried Gohr sets an example of that mediating energy without which, he feels, no academy can be 'abreast of art' in the dynamic sense of the word and, therefore, continue to exist in future.[74]

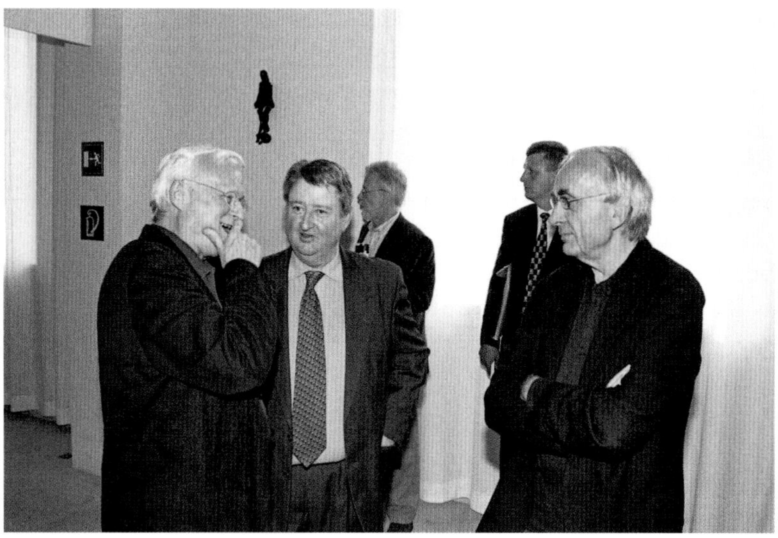

Fig. 20: Heinrich Theissing and Siegfried Gohr in conversation with Walter Nikkels at the opening of the Ewald Mataré *exhibition at the Academy Gallery, 2005*

Caught up in an 'iconic turn', the scholarly debate since the 1980s has focused intensively on the unique character and intrinsic value of artistic endeavour in the visual arts and at the same time confronted the conclusions drawn from that debate with the nugatory usances prevailing in the pictorial media. An interdisciplinary approach to a hermeneutics of visual theory has traced the both materially and immaterially constituted idiom specific to artistic productions, their inherent logic, and the emergence of meaning in them. Knowledge gained in the context of those debates also informs the studies written by Guido Reuter, who has held the chair of early modern and modern art history since 2008. While still a student and while teaching for several years at the Art Historical Seminar at Düsseldorf University, he continued to expand his research interests heuristically and thematically, epoch by epoch. Reuter's study entitled 'Statue und Zeitlichkeit 1400–1800' [Statue and Temporality 1400–1800] demonstrates what a 'descriptive-phenomenological' method can achieve if it incorporates the widest possible variety of sources while at the same time remaining aware of the tension 'between artistic production and theoretical-conceptual reception'.[75] The study also marks two invariants about which his analyses continue to revolve: temporal contingencies and forms of expression in artworks, and sculptural diversity from the early modern age to the present day. He has found his way to the Academy not least because of his constant interest in art from the years since 1945 and the present, which is attested by a growing number of enlightening catalogue essays. Although they showcase his individual achievement, he is equally concerned with promoting collective projects among colleagues, which he has initiated and organised in the form of international conferences and symposia, devoted *inter alia* to 'The studio in contemporary art',[76] 'Abstract Expressionism and Informel', and 'The plinth in nineteenth- and twentieth-century sculpture'. Guido Reuter has cemented the long overdue collaboration in teaching and research between the academic department at the Academy and the Art Historical Institute at Düsseldorf University on a contractual basis. The stimulating talks he has contributed to the regular lecture series for an audience that includes not only students but also residents of the city has, moreover, resonated with the public to enhance the reputation of the Art Academy (Fig. 21).[77]

Johannes Myssok has been professor of modern art at the Academy since 2009 (Fig. 22). He, too, has written studies based on the question – already mooted by Walter Warnach – posed by visual hermeneutics concerning the relationship of the conceptuality provided by art to the actuality of life, hence the extent to which a work that represents a reality *sui generis* and co-exists with lived reality in a state of tension emerges from the influence exerted by the artist. He has demonstrated this approach in an exemplary study of artist portraits in the sixteenth century.[78] It makes clear that the multiply fragmented, disparate constitution that man inhabits psycho-physically, in body and soul, corporeally and intellectually, as a multi-active and polyvalent being, is transformed aesthetically, only to recur in artworks as meaningfully emergent, that those works do not, therefore, engage in mimesis but rather invention and can only be commensurately understood in view of the latter. As a result, Myssok's analytical approach is a dual one, based on both art semantics and the human constitution without an anthropology to interrelate them via a superficial striving for harmony. His approach interprets a picture, a sculpture, a drawing as a complex enigmatic construct that in one way or another refers to the dubiousness of human situative perception, interpretation of the self, or self-representation and thus at the same time recalls a possible otherness with respect to any given realities. Myssok, a multiple award-winning art historian, has seen confirmed again and again on his scholarly path from the Italian Renaissance through the nineteenth century and on into the present that artists themselves, as the creators of such enigmatic configurations, are also exposed to the contradictory tension between the search for identity and the experience of alterity. Apart from his publications, he conveys his insights in the concentration of the lecture hall and also on site when he is on excursions in an invariably subtle rapprochement with the artworks. Moreover, he contributes those insights, for instance, into temporal aspects of artistic and mundane visualisation, into the changes in the shaping of sculptural plinths, or into change in sculpture in recent decades, at conferences and lecture series hosted together with colleagues.

The philosopher Ludger Schwarte – who has been teaching in Düsseldorf since 2009 – takes into account the necessary openness of scholarly debates in view of the polysemy and ambiguity of artworks by advocating an 'experimental aesthetic'. That was the title he gave to the congress that he organised at the Academy in autumn 2011 under the aegis of the Deutsche Gesellschaft für Ästhetik [German Society for Aesthetics].[79]

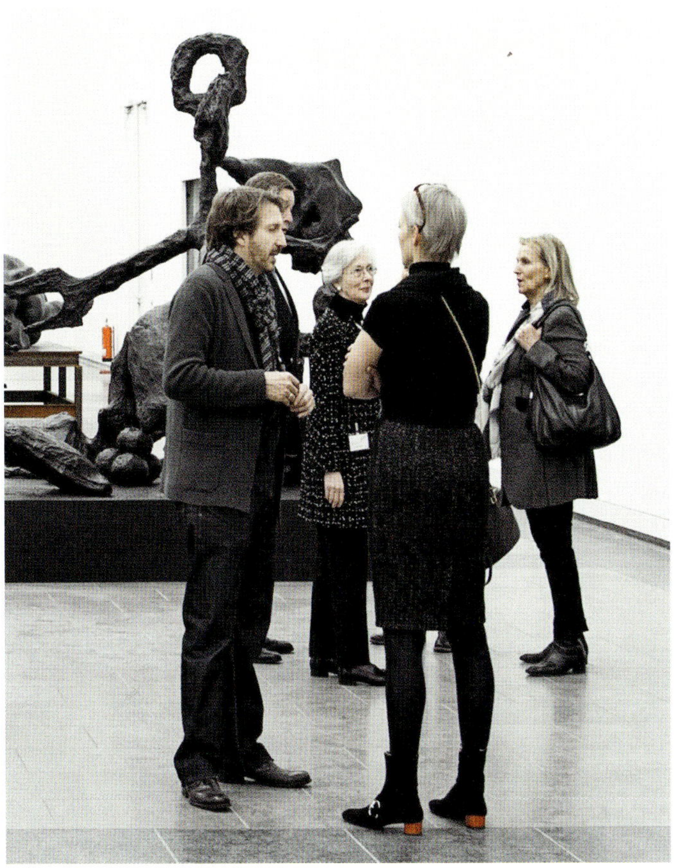

Fig. 21: Guido Reuter in conversation at the opening of Die Bildhauer *[The Sculptors], an exhibition at K20, on 18 February 2013*

His own thinking gropes 'along the boundaries of meaning', avoids static assessments, traces the processuality of cultural creations. Accordingly, he regards an artwork as 'performative potential', which the viewer must approach without mental prefigurations because, after all, pictures are 'demiurgic'. Anyone dealing with them – be it productively, be it receptively – enters 'into a world as it could be'.[80] Elements of the aesthetics of eighteenth-century Enlightenment as well as inspiration from contemporary French philosophy, which Schwarte became acquainted with while still a student and subsequently on visiting professorships in Paris, live on in this conception – which also includes architecture and theatre – that contrasts accessible reality with configurable possibilities. At the Art Academy he delves deeper into them in dialogue with students at his 'studio for free thinking'. He also tabled for discussion the inherent question of the temporality of cultural and artistic acts in the lecture series he organised in 2010/11 with Johannes Myssok on aspects of 'Visualisation'. The findings were subsequently published in a volume of essays.[81] In addition, Ludger Schwarte devotes his philosophical attention

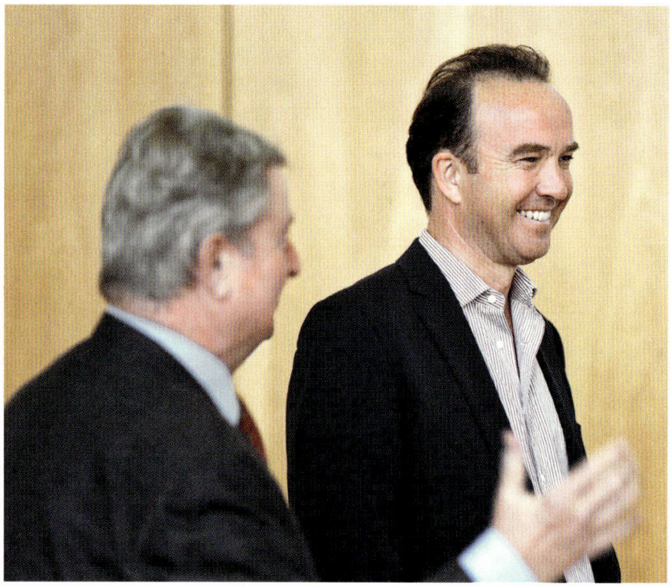

Fig. 22: Siegfried Gohr and Johannes Myssok, the Great Hall at the Art Academy, 15 September 2011

to the political implications of what goes on in the civilisation process and also of aesthetic events. That was the subject of a conference at the Art Academy in 2010 on 'Demonstrations of power'. Since transferring to Düsseldorf from the Zurich University of the Arts, he has been investigating it for some years under the heading of 'The Violence of representation'.

Insofar as the present contents itself with temporary cultural solutions due to loss of tradition, the weakening of conventions, and a powerful drive for innovation, it also subjects the arts to increasing uncertainty about their worth and need for mediation. To reach its addressees and achieve the effect desired, artworks and their creators need strategic aids. Art mediators must be schooled in the techniques of aesthetic, intellectual, expositional, and commercial distribution in the bewildering jungle of institutions and means of mass communication. Oliver Marchart, a political theorist and media studies specialist, and Robert Fleck, an exhibition curator and writer on art, have been devoting themselves to those tasks at the Academy since 2012. Both are internationally educated and active. Their areas of interest include the trend towards globalisation that has also affected art and the art industry and was examined in public lectures in 2012/13 under the heading 'WELT BILDER' [Global Images].[82] Since 2005 the professional requirements of art mediation today have been both studied and taught at the CIAM, founded by Peter M. Lynen, who is its director (Fig. 23). Established at the Cologne Hochschule für Musik und Tanz, this institute lives on and functions through cooperation with affiliated institutions, not least with the Düsseldorf Art Academy. CIAM offers a two-year course in art management leading to a master's degree and is also open to graduates of the Art Academy. In addition, it hosts conferences and congresses on subjects in the border areas of art, economics, politics, and law. For several years it has co-hosted the 'Moyländer Diskurse zu Kunst und Wissenschaft' and in 2010 invited experts from many countries to a global forum on educational and commercial problems associated with mediating culture and art.[83] The regular curriculum is designed by representatives of specialist disciplines from the Art Academy in tandem with external theorists and practitioners of those disciplines. The director of the institute regularly publishes information on ongoing and additional events in Cologne and Düsseldorf, on projects and findings in an annual report. In the meantime Peter M. Lynen has published a three-volume standard work on the juridical aspects of art management containing the findings of his own research and consultation practice.[84]

The Cologne-Düsseldorf Centre that links institutes of higher learning, wrote Lynen as the prelude to his initiative – for which he had amassed a wealth of experience as chancellor of the Art Academy for many years – sees itself as being 'in the service of art'.[85] That is what all scholars have thought who have worked in Eiskellerstraße over the generations from the difficult new beginnings of the post-war era through phases of academic turbulence and years of consolidation down to the present. In research and teaching, as well as through the commitment they have shown on Art Academy committees, it has always been their aim to contribute to the good of and the understanding of art and to the prosperity of the Art Academy, of its artists, students, and teaching colleagues. Their common purpose over the long term is to resourcefully continue what has been hitherto accomplished and attained.

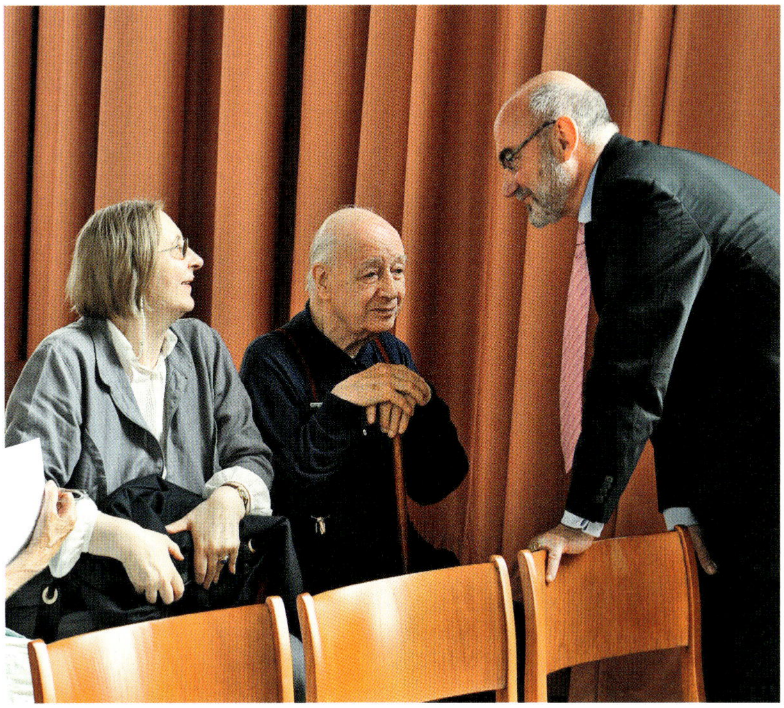

Fig. 23: Peter M. Lynen in conversation with Rissa and Karl Otto Götz, on the occasion of Markus Lüpertz's departure from the Art Academy on 1 July 2009

NOTES

1 Folder 'Düsseldorf, im Mai 1948'; undersigned: 'Der Akademiedirektor [Academy director], gez. Prof. Werner Heuser' and 'Der Vorsitzende [chairman], gez. Prof. Dr. Josef Wilden'.
2 Hans Sedlmayr, *Verlust der Mitte. Die bildende Kunst des 19. und 20. Jahrhunderts als Symptom und Symbol der Zeit*, Salzburg 1948. Published in English as *Art in Crisis. The Lost Center*, London 1957.
3 Hans Sedlmayr, 'Über die Gefahren der modernen Kunst', in: Hans Gerhard Evers (ed.), *Darmstädter Gespräch 1950. Das Menschenbild in unserer Zeit*, Darmstadt n.d., pp. 48–62; here: p. 60.
4 Wilhelm Hausenstein, *Was bedeutet die moderne Kunst? Ein Wort der Besinnung*, Leutstetten nr Munich 1949, p. 19, p. 24, p. 29.
5 Karl Scheffler, *Kunst ohne Stoff*, Überlingen am Bodensee 1950, p. 38, p. 39, p. 43.
6 Lt Colonel H. J. Walker, 'Ansprache zur Wiedereröffnung der Staatlichen Kunstakademie am 31. Januar 1946' [Address given at the reinauguration of the State Art Academy on 31 January 1946], in: *Jahresbericht der Staatlichen Kunstakademie Düsseldorf 1945–1947*, Düsseldorf [1948], p. 15.
7 Regierungspräsident Dr Eduard Sträter, 'Ansprache zur Wiedereröffnung der Staatlichen Kunstakademie am 31. Januar 1946', in: *Jahresbericht 1945–1947* (see n. 6), pp. 19f.
8 Anna Klapheck, 'Lehrer und Gelehrter. Zum Tode von J. Heinrich Schmidt', *Rheinische Post*, 23 February 1974.
9 Jakob Heinrich Schmidt (ed.), *Von Gabriel Grupello bis Paul Klee, von Lambert Krahe bis Theo Champion*, exhib. cat. Düsseldorf 1953.
10 Jakob Heinrich Schmidt, *Alte Seidenstoffe. Ein Handbuch für Sammler und Liebhaber*, Braunschweig 1958. Vol. 10 of *Bibliothek für Kunst- und Antiquitätenfreunde*.
11 Anna Klapheck, *Vom Notbehelf zur Wohlstandskunst. Kunst im Rheinland der Nachkriegszeit*, Cologne 1979.
12 First published as an Art Academy Sonderdruck [off-print]: Anna Klapheck, *Walter Kaesbach und die zwanziger Jahre an der Düsseldorfer Kunstakademie*, Düsseldorf 1961, and republished in a considerably enlarged version: Anna Klapheck, 'Die "goldnen" zwanziger Jahre. Die Akademie zwischen den beiden Kriegen', in: Eduard Trier (ed.), *Zweihundert Jahre Kunstakademie Düsseldorf*, Düsseldorf 1973, pp. 147–160.
13 Lothar von Kunowski, *Die Kunsthochschule. Einführung in Lehrgang und Ziele*, Düsseldorf 1929, p. 17, p. 77, p. 102. Nonetheless Kunowski did at least approve of the 'artistic teaching staff linking' their practical work, 'with psychological, philosophical, art historical studies' (p. 102).
14 See Arnold Gehlen, *Zeit-Bilder. Zur Soziologie und Ästhetik der modernen Malerei*, Frankfurt am Main/Bonn 1960, especially pp. 162–169.
15 See Peter Holtfreter, Susanne Ebert, Manfred König, and Eberhardt Schweigert (eds.), 'Interview mit Joseph Beuys', *Kommunikation* 1, Düsseldorf 1973, n.p.
16 Karl Otto Götz, *Bildende Kunst und Kommunikation. Ansprache zur Immatrikulationsfeier am 12. November 1963*, Düsseldorf 1965, p. 5, p. 26.
17 Karl Otto Götz and Karin Götz [= Rissa], *Probleme der Bildästhetik. Eine Einführung in die Grundlagen des anschaulichen Denkens*, Düsseldorf 1972.
18 Eduard Trier, *Jetzt ist die Katze aus dem Sack. Kritiken und Kommentare. Eine Auswahl*, ed. Wilfried Dörstel as Vol. 5 of *Sediment trouvé*, im Zentralarchiv des Internationalen Kunsthandels e. V., Bonn/Cologne 2000, p. 27.
19 Eduard Trier, *Über die Bewertung zeitgenössischer Kunst oder Freuden und Leiden eines Ausstellungsmachers. Ansprache zur Immatrikulationsfeier am 4. Dezember 1964*, Düsseldorf 1965, p. 5, p. 6, p. 10.
20 Eduard Trier, 'Die Düsseldorfer Kunstakademie in der permanenten Reform', in: Trier (see n. 12), pp. 203–212.
21 Ibid., p. 210.
22 Ibid., p. 212, n. 62.
23 For his lyrical work, which is for the most part yet to be discovered, see Walter Warnach, *Der Morgen. Weltliche Sequenz zu Ehren der heiligen Büßerin Maria Magdalena von der Sainte-Baume*, Pfullingen 1954.
24 Walter Warnach, *Die Welt des Schmerzes*, Pfullingen n.d. [1952].
25 Werner von Trott zu Solz with Walter Warnach, Heinrich Böll, and HAP Grieshaber, *labyrinth*, 1960–1962; for the historical circumstances of this undertaking, see Wolfgang Matthias Schwiedrzik, *Konservativ und rebellisch. Die Zeitschrift 'labyrinth'. Gespräche mit Heinrich Böll und Walter Warnach*, Neckargemünd 2000.
26 Walter Warnach, *Wege im Labyrinth. Schriften zur Zeit*, ed. Karl-Dieter Ulke, Pfullingen 1982.
27 See, on this and also on Warnach's *Complete Works*, Christoph Lange, *Mysterium Wirklichkeit. Walter Warnach und der politische Manierismus Carl Schmitts*, Munich 2003.
28 Viktor Warnach, *Agape. Die Liebe als Grundmotiv der neutestamentlichen Theologie*, Düsseldorf 1951.
29 In revolving around key concepts such as desire, determination, and overarching consciousness, Warnach's thinking shows striking parallels, despite difference in all other respects, to that of the French psychoanalyst Jacques Lacan (who, like Warnach, came from a Catholic family and, again like Warnach, had a brother who entered a monastery).
30 Heinrich Böll, 'Vorwort' [Foreword], in: Warnach (see n. 26), pp. 9–16; here: p. 14. At the same time Böll emphasised that his novel 'Ansichten eines Clowns', published in 1963, was 'a sequel to "labyrinth"' (p. 12).
31 See Walter Warnach, 'Rückblick auf ein Hohes Haus', in: Hilde Hofmeister and Klaus Ulrich Düsselberg (eds.), *Eiskellerstraße 1. Fotografien aus der Kunstakademie Düsseldorf von Rolf Sackenheim*, Krefeld 1979, n.p.
32 Walter Warnach, *Vom Bewusstsein in der Kunst. Vortrag zur Immatrikulationsfeier der Staatlichen Kunstakademie Düsseldorf am 15. November 1961*, Düsseldorf 1962, p. 5.
33 Walter Warnach, 'Die Philosophie der Wir-Wissenschaft und die soziale Plastik. Interview von Stephan von Wiese mit Walter Warnach, Februar 1987', in: Stephan von Wiese (ed.), *Brennpunkt Düsseldorf. Joseph Beuys. Die Akademie. Der allgemeine Aufbruch. 1962–1987*, exhib. cat. Düsseldorf 1987, pp. 86–89; here: p. 89. This attempt to integrate art and philosophy was supported by Jonas Hafner, who had studied under Beuys and Warnach and after taking his doctorate in the early 1970s was an instructor at the Art Academy.
34 Alfred Mundhenk, *Der bildnerische Unterricht und das System unserer Schulbildung*, Düsseldorf 1972, especially p. 32.
35 Ibid., p. 36, p. 39.
36 See Jean Gebser, *Ursprung und Gegenwart*, 2 vols., Munich 1949 and 1953, and Jean Gebser, *Verfall und Teilhabe*, Salzburg 1974. Günter Blecks championed Gebser's ideas in the organisational sense by co-founding the International Jean Gebser Society and serving on its board of directors.
37 Hence the academic discussion of the time problem increased: Rudolf Wendorff, *Zeit und Kultur. Geschichte des Zeitbewusstseins in Europa*, Wiesbaden 1980; Norbert Elias, *Über die Zeit. Arbeiten zur Wissenssoziologie II*, Frankfurt am

Main 1984; Günter Dux, *Die Zeit in der Geschichte. Ihre Entwicklungslogik vom Mythos zur Weltzeit*, Frankfurt am Main 1989.

38 Characteristic of the debates of the day: Rudolf W. Meyer (ed.), *Das Problem des Fortschrittes – heute*, Darmstadt 1969; Karl Löwith, 'Das Verhängnis des Fortschritts' (1963), in: id., *Weltgeschichte und Heilsgeschehen. Zur Kritik der Geschichtsphilosophie. Sämtliche Schriften 2*, Stuttgart 1983, pp. 392–410, with reference to art p. 395; Ernst H. Gombrich, *Kunst und Fortschritt. Wirkung und Wandlung einer Idee*, Cologne 1978.

39 Heinrich Theissing, *Die Zeit im Bild*, Darmstadt 1987.

40 Heinrich Theissing, 'Kunstgeschichte an der Kunstakademie' (from a lecture given in the summer term of 1973), in: Norbert Kricke and Rolf Sackenheim (eds.), *Akademie heute. Eine Dokumentation über die Kunstakademie Düsseldorf 1975*, Düsseldorf 1975, n.p.

41 Heinrich Theissing, 'Brief an einen Maler im Jahre 1984', in: Erwin Heerich and Rolf Sackenheim (eds.), *Übungen, Experimente, Impulse III. Arbeiten der Kunstakademie Düsseldorf 1985*, Düsseldorf/Münsterschwarzach 1985, n.p.

42 For Thwaites's thinking on art, his activities, and publications, see Beate Eickhoff, *John Anthony Thwaites und die Kunstkritik der fünfziger Jahre*, Weimar 2004.

43 Werner Spies, *Mein Glück. Erinnerungen*, Munich 2012, especially pp. 538–543.

44 Ibid., p. 542.

45 Ibid., p. 566.

46 Walter Biemel, *Jean-Paul Sartre in Selbstzeugnissen und Bilddokumenten*, Reinbek bei Hamburg 1964; Walter Biemel, *Martin Heidegger in Selbstzeugnissen und Bilddokumenten*, Reinbek bei Hamburg 1973.

47 Walter Biemel, 'Rückblick an Stelle eines Vorworts', in: id., *Schriften zur Philosophie*, Stuttgart-Bad Cannstatt 1996, pp. 7–10; here: p. 9. Vol. 1 of *Gesammelte Schriften*.

48 That is also attested by a book dedicated to the philosopher on the occasion of his retirement from the Art Academy and published with its support: Petra Jaeger and Rolf Lüthe (eds.), *Distanz und Nähe. Reflexionen und Analysen zur Kunst der Gegenwart* (with drawings by Norbert Kricke, Günther Uecker, Erwin Heerich, Konrad Klapheck, Gerhard Hoehme, and Rolf Sackenheim, all artists teaching at the Academy), Würzburg 1983.

49 Walter Biemel, *Philosophische Analysen zur Kunst der Gegenwart*, The Hague 1968.

50 Biemel (see n. 47), pp. 9f. The second volume of this collection of essays is another collection of important writings on art by the author.

51 Paul Good, *Maurice Merleau-Ponty. Eine Einführung*, Düsseldorf 1998; Paul Good, *Max Scheler. Eine Einführung*, Düsseldorf 1998.

52 See Paul Good, *Die Unbezüglichkeit der Kunst*, Munich 1998.

53 Albrecht Fabri, *Divertimenti. Ausgewählte Texte aus fünf Jahrzehnten*, ed. Paul Good, Düsseldorf/Bonn 1996; also see Paul Good, 'Das Rätsel. Ein philosophisches Streitgespräch mit Albrecht Fabri', in: Good (see n. 52), pp. 135–158.

54 Paul Good, *Hermes oder die Philosophie der Insel Hombroich/Hermes or the Philosophy of the Island Hombroich*, Neuss 1987; here: pp. 38f.

55 Liesel-Lotte Herkenrath, 'Der Aufbau der Wahrnehmung. Pädagogik an der Kunstakademie', in: Kricke and Sackenheim (see n. 40), n.p.

56 These achievements were honoured as they deserved to be by Walter Jürgen Hofmann, 'Abschied für Liesel-Lotte Herkenrath-Püschel', *Jahreshefte der Kunstakademie Düsseldorf*, Vol. 1, Düsseldorf 1988, pp. 147–152.

57 See the retrospective by Friedrich W. Heubach, 'interfunktionen, 1968–1975', in: Gloria Moure (ed.), *behind the facts. interfunktionen 1968–1975*, exhib. cat. Barcelona/Porto/Kassel, Barcelona 2004, pp. 46–59. The book provides a survey of the artists in various fields who were published in *interfunktionen*.

58 For instance, when he put in their place the advocates of 'art in public spaces' as 'rhapsodes of a new niceness' and exposed 'public art' as the 'triumph of a cheer-leader aesthetic' or as 'the sentimental art of conviction'; see Friedrich Wolfram Heubach, 'Kunst im öffentlichen Raum oder Ein Gemeinplatz und sein Elend', in: Heike Behrend et al. (eds.), *Geist, Bild und Narr. Zu einer Ethnologie kultureller Konversionen. Festschrift für Fritz Kramer*, Berlin/Vienna 2001, pp. 269–275; here: p. 269, p. 274; as a further example of the style in which he caustically exposed such attitudinising to ridicule, see Friederich Wolfram Heubach, 'Was der Soldat im Manne, ist in der Frau die Mutter', in: Johannes Bilstein, Eckart Liebau, and Matthias Winzen (eds.), *Mutter Kind Vater. Bilder aus Kunst und Wissenschaft*, Cologne 2000, pp. 41–44.

59 See Hans Blumenberg, *Paradigmen zu einer Metaphorologie*, Bonn 1960 (Frankfurt am Main 2009); Paul Ricœur, *Die lebendige Metapher*, Munich 1986.

60 Thus Brumlik in introductory remarks in a book dedicated by colleagues and friends to Johannes Bilstein on the occasion of his sixtieth birthday: Micha Brumlik, 'Geist der Bildung. Bildung des Geistes', in: Eckart Liebau (ed.), *Lebensbilder. Streifzüge in Kunst und Pädagogik*, Oberhausen 2009, pp. 1–23; here: p. 11; from the wealth of studies mentioned here, see, for instance, Johannes Bilstein, 'Bilder für die Gestaltung des Menschen', *Neue Sammlung. Vierteljahres-Zeitschrift für Erziehung und Gesellschaft* 32, No. 1, Seelze-Velber 1992, pp. 110–133; Johannes Bilstein, 'Zur Metaphorik des Generationenverhältnisses', in: Eckart Liebau and Christoph Wulf (eds.), *Generation. Versuche über eine pädagogisch-anthropologische Grundbedingung*, Weinheim 1996, pp. 157–189; Johannes Bilstein, 'Zur metaphorischen Potenz der Kunst', in: id. (ed.), *Die Künste als Metaphern*, Oberhausen 2011, pp. 13–41.

61 They included series of events like those mentioned in note 58 addressed to 'Mutter Kind Vater', the conferences organised jointly with Matthias Winzen: 'Big Nothing. Die jenseitigen Ebenbilder des Menschen' (2001), 'Ich bin mein Auto' (2001), 'Das Tier in mir. Die animalischen Ebenbilder des Menschen' (2002), and the trilogy 'Multiple Räume. Seele, Park, Film' (2003–2005), all of which were accompanied by exhibitions and documented in catalogues.

62 Johannes Bilstein, 'Fortifikationen', *Jahreshefte der Kunstakademie Düsseldorf*, Vol. 5.1, Düsseldorf 2002, pp. 173–208; here: p. 175, p. 189, p. 196.

63 See Kunibert Bering, *Die Ära Konstantins. Kulturelle Kontexte – historische Dimensionen. Eine Synopse*, Oberhausen 2012.

64 For instance the research group Kunstdidaktik with Kunibert Bering, Rolf Niehoff, Karina Pauls, Stefan Hölscher, Julia Gerber, Nadja Nafe; see Kunibert Bering, Stefan Hölscher, and Rolf Niehoff (eds.), *Nach der Bilderflut. Ästhetisches Handeln von Jugendlichen*, Oberhausen 2012.

65 See Kunibert Bering (ed.), *Artificium. Schriften zu Kunst und Kunstvermittlung*, Oberhausen since 1998; Kunibert Bering and Rolf Niehoff (eds.), *Impulse. Kunstdidaktik*, Oberhausen since 2007.

66 Kunibert Bering (ed.), *Perspektiven einer Didaktik der Bildenden Künste. Jahreshefte der Kunstakademie Düsseldorf*, Vols. 5.1 and 5.2, Düsseldorf 2002.

67 Kunibert Bering, Clemens Höxter, and Rolf Niehoff (eds.), *Orientierung. Kunstpädagogik. Bundeskongress der Kunstpädagogik, 22–25 October 2009*, Oberhausen 2010.

68 As the outcome of that conference see Kunibert Bering (ed.), *Lambert Krahe 1712–1790. Maler* – Sammler – *Akademiegründer*, Oberhausen 2013.

69 Kunibert Bering, 'Visuelle Kompetenz', in: Kunibert Bering and Rolf Niehoff (eds.), *Bilder. Eine Herausforderung für die Bildung*, Oberhausen 2005, pp. 47–56; here: p. 50.

70 Kunibert Bering, 'Kunstpädagogik und Bildkultur', in: Bering, Höxter, and Niehoff (see n. 67), pp. 283–294; here: p. 285.

71 Thus Bering in the foreword, *Jahreshefte der Kunstakademie Düsseldorf* (see n. 66), p. 14.

72 Carl Joseph Ignaz Mosler, 'Andeutungen über den Zweck des Kunst-Vereins für die Rheinlande und Westphalen (1829)', reprinted in Karl-Heinz Hering (ed.), *5 x 30 Düsseldorfer Kunstszene aus fünf Generationen. 150 Jahre Kunstverein für die Rheinlande und Westfalen 1829–1979*, Düsseldorf 1979, n.p.

73 Siegfried Gohr, 'Bildspeicher. Zur Akademie-Galerie "Die Neue Sammlung" der Kunstakademie Düsseldorf', in: Kunibert Bering and Rolf Niehoff (eds.), *Bildkompetenz(en). Beiträge des Kunstunterrichts zur Bildung*, Oberhausen 2009, pp. 215–218; here: pp. 215f.

74 See Siegfried Gohr, 'Die Kunstakademie Düsseldorf während der letzten Jahrzehnte', in: *Kunstgegenwärtig. Erinnerungen an die Gegenwart*, accompanying booklet for Quadriennale 2010, Düsseldorf 2010, pp. 13–16.

75 Guido Reuter, *Statue und Zeitlichkeit, 1400–1800*, Petersberg 2012; here: p. 8.

76 The fruits of these cooperative events are published regularly; see, for instance, Guido Reuter and Martin Schieder (eds.), *Inside/Outside. Das Atelier in der zeitgenössischen Kunst*, Petersberg 2012; Johannes Myssok and Guido Reuter (eds.), *Der Sockel in der Skulptur des 19. und 20. Jahrhunderts*, Cologne and elsewhere 2013.

77 See, for instance, Johannes Bilstein and Guido Reuter (eds.), *Auge und Hand*, Oberhausen 2011.

78 Johannes Myssok, 'La man che ubbidisce all'intelletto. Auge und Hand in Künstlerbildnissen des 16. Jahrhunderts', in: Bilstein and Reuter (see n. 77), pp. 101–116.

79 A selection of the contributions to that congress was published in *Zeitschrift für Ästhetik und allgemeine Kunstwissenschaft* 57, No. 2, *Schwerpunktthema: Experimentelle Ästhetik*, Hamburg 2012.

80 The philosopher outlined this performative analysis with examples during a lecture from a series given at the Art Academy: Ludger Schwarte, 'Taktisches Sehen. Auge und Hand in der Bildtheorie', in: Bilstein and Reuter (see n. 77), pp. 211–228; here: p. 219, p. 223, p. 226.

81 Johannes Myssok and Ludger Schwarte (eds.), *Zeitstrukturen. Techniken der Vergegenwärtigung in Wissenschaft und Kunst*, Berlin 2013.

82 See Kunibert Bering and Robert Fleck (eds.), *WeltBilder. Kunst und Globalisierung*, Oberhausen 2013.

83 See Peter M. Lynen et al. (eds.), *International Arts Management Concepts. Higher Education for the Market?*, Cologne 2011.

84 Peter M. Lynen, *Kunstrecht 1. Grundlagen des Kunstrechts*; *Kunstrecht 2. Schwerpunkte des Kunstgewährleistungsrechts*; *Kunstrecht 3. Schwerpunkte des Kunstwirtschaftsrechts*, Wiesbaden 2013.

85 Peter M. Lynen (ed.), 'Vorwort' [Foreword], in: *CIAM. Das erste Jahr, 2005/06*. Cologne/Düsseldorf 2006, p. 7.

HANS PETER THURN AS A MEMBER OF THE DÜSSELDORF ART ACADEMY

Peter M. Lynen

A major scholar who for more than four decades shaped the essence and content of the Düsseldorf Art Academy as a teacher and researcher as well as a person in important self-administrative functions and one who has exerted an enormous influence on the scholarly and artistic development of a great many members of the institution is missing in the impressive descriptive account contributed by Hans Peter Thurn: the man himself. This omission underscores his own reticence and modesty, but a supplementary contribution by a colleague is nonetheless called for.

Hans Peter Thurn was born in Krefeld in 1943 and studied sociology, philosophy, literature, and art history at Heidelberg, Frankfurt am Main, and Cologne Universities, taking his doctorate in 1970. He was a pupil and friend of the sociologist René König, whose vast learning, significant scholarship, and obvious commitment made him a role model for Thurn and influenced his own attitude – in particular to the arts and humanities. Thurn was a young man when he came to the Academy as a lecturer (1970), and he lost no time in building up sociology as a subject with a focus on the sociology of art, which he represented as a professor from 1983 to 2011. Not only did he know this institution and its members well – over several generations – but he also revealed intense commitment where the affairs of the Academy were concerned. He did so specifically in his administrative capacity as dean and deputy dean of the Department for Art-Related Subjects, positions which he held several times and for several years. Even now co-operation between artists and academics and mutual understanding between the two groups are a major concern of his, and he is well aware of both the difficulties involved and the importance of good relations.

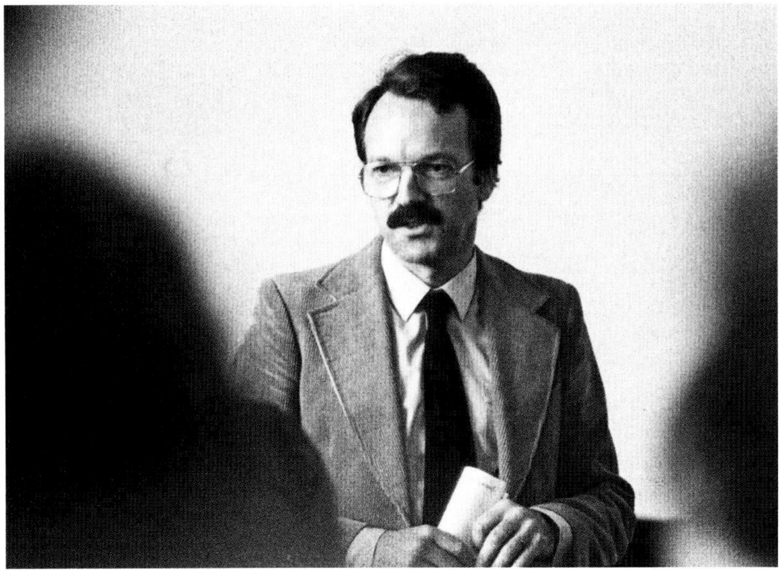

Hans Peter Thurn at a beginning-of-term ceremony, 1982

Thurn's scholarly work is not merely substantial but represents the epicentre of art sociology in recent decades. His approach is both empirical and descriptive, analytical and targeted, giving impressive evidence of the range of his learning, which goes far beyond scholarship and methodology focused purely on sociology in the narrower academic sense. The extensive body of monographic and other works of his can be briefly surveyed here from his first great writings on the sociology of art (1973) and culture (1976) through illuminating insights into people in everyday situations (1980), to the artist in society (1985), via man caught up in the dilemma of his possibilities as the founder of culture and destroyer of the world (1990), the art dealer (1994), the power of images and social entitlements (1997), the vernissage (1999), cultural dilemmas (2001), and the sociology of colour (2007). In his capacity as editor of books and organiser of lecture series, symposia, and other academic congresses, he has united a profound understanding of his subject and a wide-ranging knowledge with the capability of arriving both correctly and rapidly at substantial findings that can be built on. His work editing the writings of René König is particularly noteworthy in this connection.

Apart from the diverse and profound content of his works, the language in which they are written should be pointed out. Thurn has no use for German sociological jargon studded with deterrent arrays of foreign words that are difficult to understand and even unnecessary but are so often deployed to command respect. Thurn, who is, on the one hand, intellectually sophisticated and gets straight to the point with the terminology needed, succeeds, on the other, in an extraordinarily vivid, understandable, and illustrative manner, in forging vigorous and effective communicative relationships between his readers and the objects of his observations. This approach also informed both his teaching and his other activities at the Art Academy in every way. As for artists, he has made many contributions to smoothing their way to the public and helping them plan this. His retirement in 2011 has done nothing to change that, nor has it kept him from continuing his scholarly work.

TRAINING ART TEACHERS AT THE ART ACADEMY FROM 1945 TO THE PRESENT

Kunibert Bering and Johannes Bilstein

The history of training art teachers at the Düsseldorf Art Academy begins in 1921 with the incorporation of the existing state drawing teachers' seminary at the Düsseldorf Decorative Arts School in the Academy. Not only drawing teachers but also scholars – such as the art historian Otto Förster – were carried over with it.[1] A separate department for training art teachers for state schools was established (1921–1932, Lothar von Kunowski), which was expanded between 1924 and 1933.

Students sitting the first state exams for aspiring art teachers at state schools in the winter term 1946/47 marked a fresh start after the end of the National Socialist regime and the ravages of war. In 1949/50 the city of Düsseldorf inaugurated an applied arts teachers' seminary that viewed itself as being in the tradition of the Deutscher Werkbund and also enabled Art Academy students preparing to be art teachers to train as applied arts teachers.[2] In 1963 Ellen Neumann, a lecturer on a temporary contract, was appointed professor, charged specifically with training teachers for lower secondary schools. From then on teachers for higher secondary schools and – for a while – lower secondary schools trained at the Academy. After passing the first state examinations at the Art Academy, they could transfer to schools for their practical teacher training. Candidates for training as art teachers were admitted to the Art Academy on the basis of a portfolio and a three-day admissions examination made up of design-related problems. Once admitted, students had to take two foundation or probationary terms, which were supervised by Karl Bobek and later by Beate Schiff (Fig. 1), before they could transfer into the art classes – which until 1987 were organised as a separate department under the heading of 'Art Education' or 'Art II'. Those classes were taught by professors who did their best to convey diverse conceptions of how studying art for teaching might be approached: Heinrich Kamps, Paul Bindel, Kurt Arnscheidt, Günter Grote, Gert Weber (Figs. 2–4). Rolf Crummenauer's (Fig. 5) long years of intensive teaching experience proved particularly effective. Both fine arts students and candidates for teaching at state schools worked in his classes, which were usually large.

Taking a second – academic – subject so as to be able to teach it was mandatory for all students planning to teach art; they usually met this requirement by taking their second subject at Düsseldorf University. After that regulation was rescinded in 2003, art could be studied as a subject to be taught at schools without the need to study a second subject because art as such was declared a 'shortage' subject with too few candidates available to teach it. That led to increased concentration on their art studies by students planning to teach art and, moreover, to the possibility of their being able to complete the entire academic part of their studies at the Düsseldorf Art Academy.

In addition to such specialised academic courses, students had to have a Philosophikum certificate – that is, proof of having successfully sat an examination in philosophy and education tailored to the needs of the teaching profession – until the late 1970s.[3] The Philosophikum was then replaced by a more broad-based course in education studies, which was bolstered

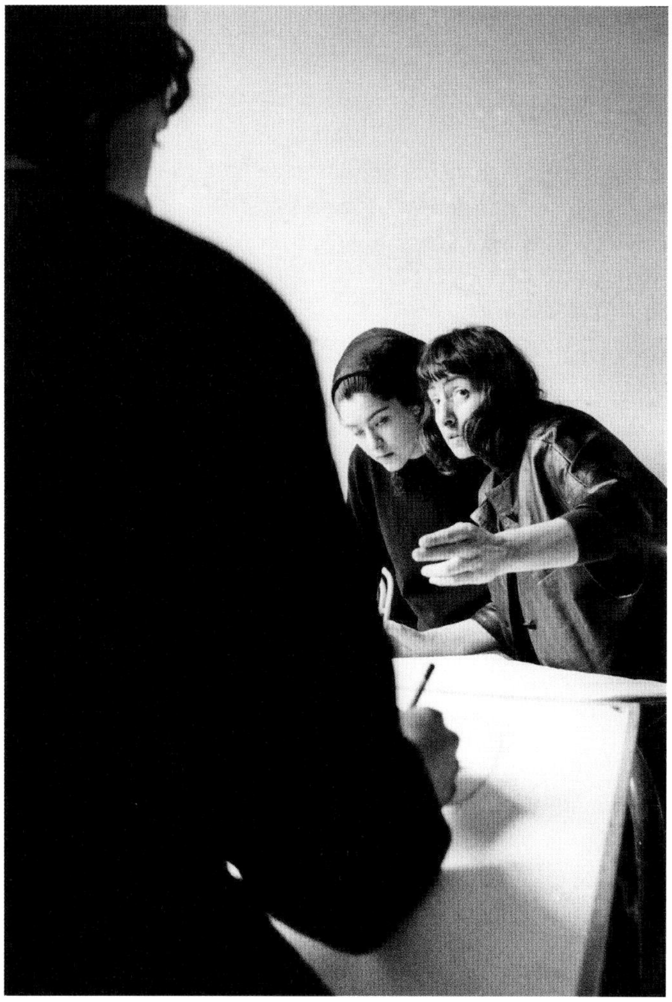

Fig. 1: Beate Schiff with art teacher trainees, 1960

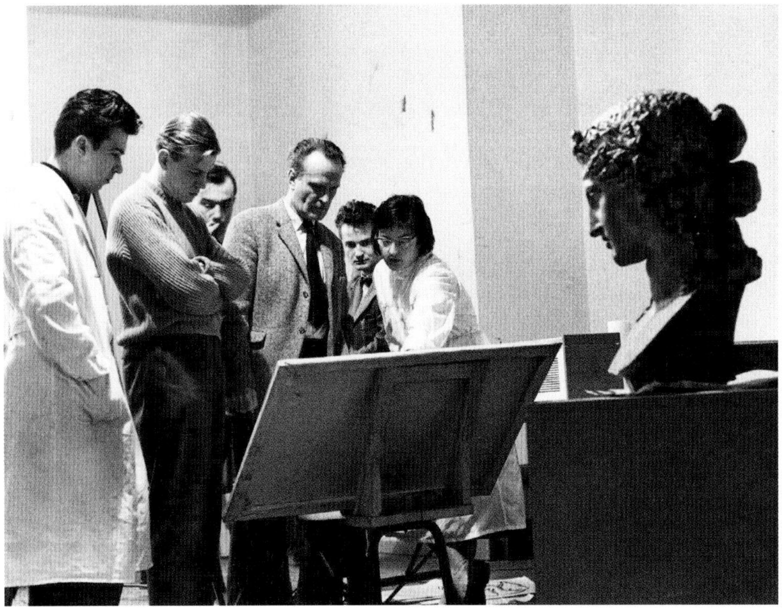

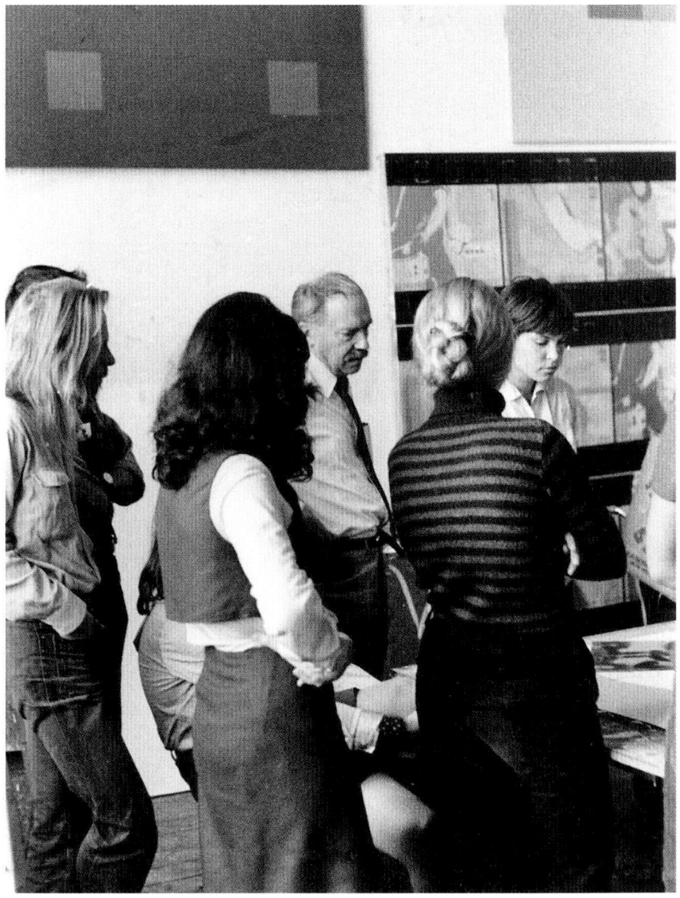

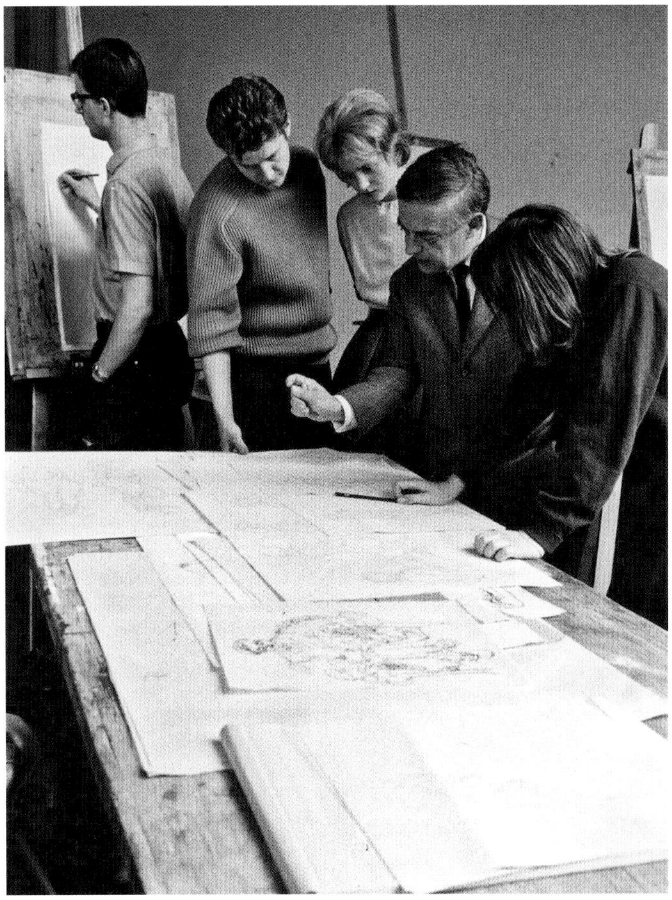

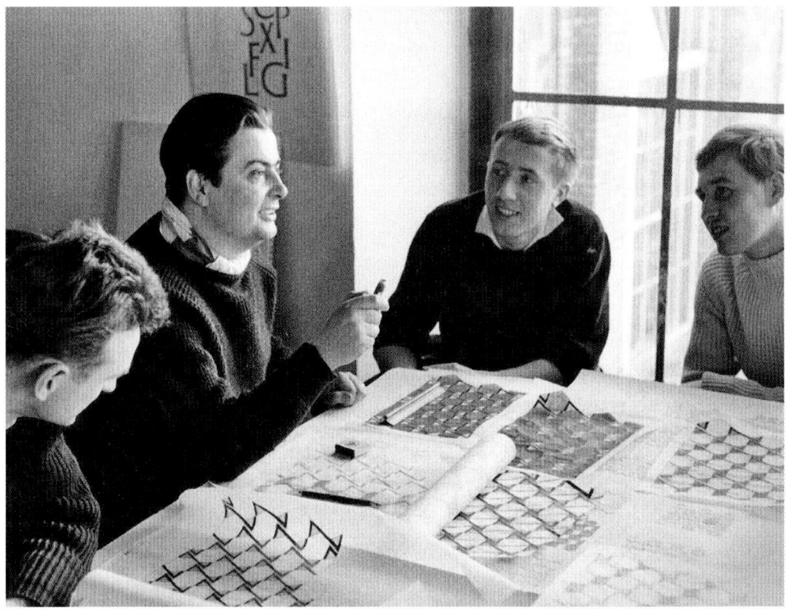

Fig. 2: Kurt Arnscheidt with art teacher trainees, 1960

Fig. 3: Günter Grote with art teacher trainees, 1960

Fig. 4: Gert Weber with art teacher trainees, 1960

Fig. 5: Rolf Crummenauer with art teacher trainees, 1960

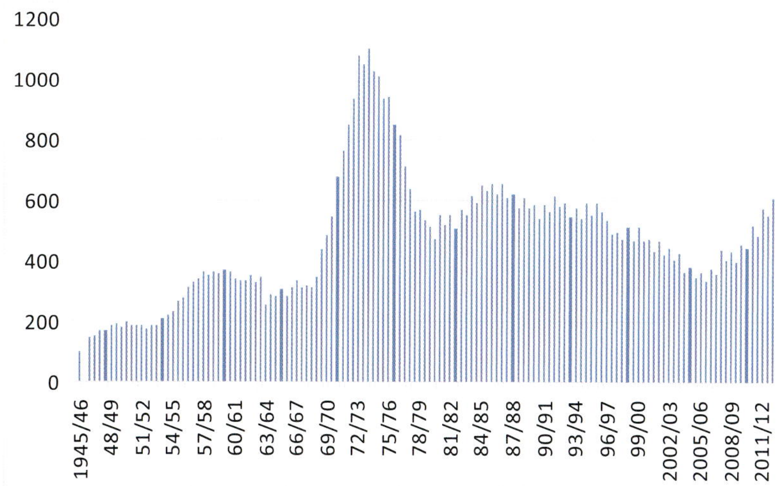

Fig. 6: Table showing growth in the number of students at the Düsseldorf Art Academy from 1915 to 2012

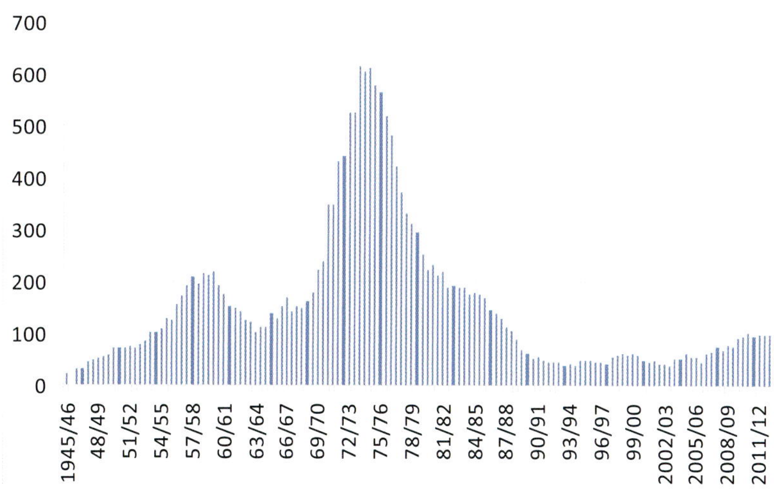

Fig. 7: Table showing the percentage of students training to be art teachers at the Düsseldorf Art Academy from 1945 to 2012

by considerably more theoretical and empirical education-related content. The implementation of those courses at the Art Academy was accompanied by the introduction of requirements in more disciplines under the heading of 'Art-Related Subjects': lessons and lectures in education as well as philosophy and sociology now provided proof of academic achievement for the Education Studies Department as well.

In any case, the appointment of Günter Blecks as professor of the principles of teaching fine arts (1964) and Alfred Mundhenk to a chair in education (1966) marked important steps towards further developing teacher training and putting education and teaching methodology on a more professional basis at the Düsseldorf Art Academy. These chairs were also retained even after their first occupants had left. Kunibert Bering (from 1998) and in education studies Liesel-Lotte Herkenrath (1974–1988), Friedrich Wolfram Heubach (1992–2010), and Johannes Bilstein (since 2008) made their own distinctive contributions to further developing the fields of teaching methodology and education studies respectively.

As for the student side, matriculation numbers have fluctuated considerably, particularly in respect of the ratio of fine arts students to candidates for teaching art at state schools, and those fluctuations are definitely interesting – both in absolute numbers as well as the percentage of teacher candidates in the Art Academy student body (Figs. 6, 7). On the one hand, the fluctuations evidently indicate a reaction to changing needs – more teachers were needed after the war – and, on the other, they reflect dramatic shifts in the Academy's self-image and self-concept – especially in the context of the movements and debates centred on Joseph Beuys. Training teaching candidates at the Art Academy began with twenty-five young men and women in 1946, who represented roughly twenty-five per cent of the student body at the time. This percentage rose steadily until 1959/60, when the number of teaching candidates reached about 220, which then represented about sixty per cent of the student body. The percentage dropped for a time until 1963, only to reach an all-time high in 1975 – in parallel with the growth in overall matriculation numbers at the Academy. By the summer term 1975, 580 students of a student body of 940 were matriculated in the art teaching course. That makes sixty-two per cent – definitely a solid majority.

After that the percentage of teaching candidates declined consistently and without interruption until by the winter term 1991/92 just seven per cent of a student body of 618 had matriculated as teaching candidates: a total of only 46 students. This figure increased to about twenty per cent and has remained there until the present day. To summarise the development: viewed from the angle of student numbers, for many years the Düsseldorf Art Academy was notable for having a preponderance of teaching candidates in its student body until 1975, when the percentage of those students began to decline steadily.

As for development in the content of the art teaching course at the Düsseldorf Art Academy, the curriculum has always been shaped by both external changes – especially of a political or administrative nature – and shifts in focus within the Academy itself. Since the very beginning, the course for training art teachers has been restricted at the Academy to candidates for

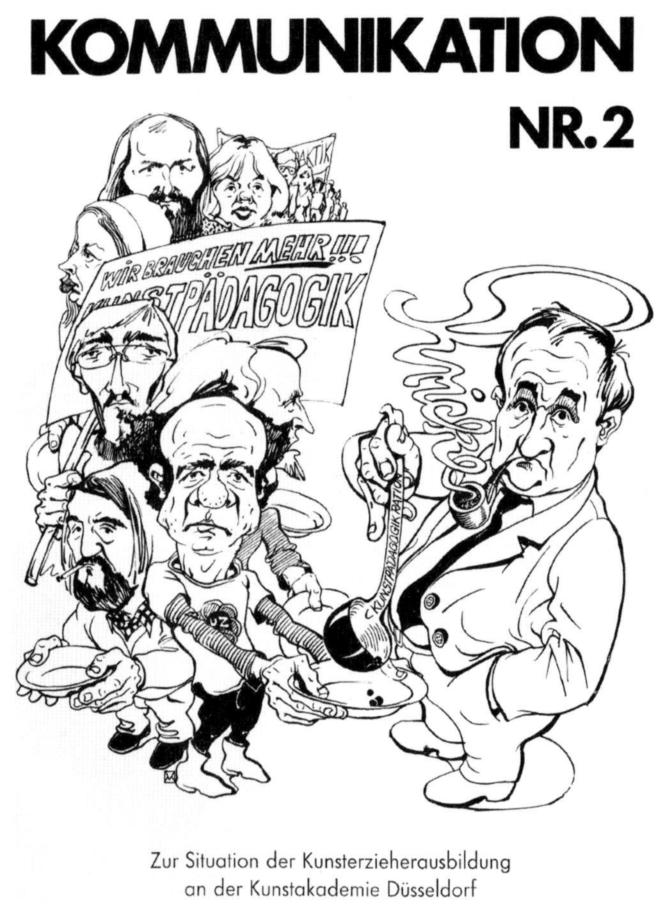

Fig. 8: A caricature of Manfred Vogel on the cover of the second issue of Kommunikation, *the student newspaper, 1974*

lower and upper secondary schools: primary school art teachers are not educated here.

Since 2012 the course for art teachers at the Art Academy has also had to switch to a modularised structure under the aegis of the so-called Bologna Process, which has replaced the course leading to a first state examination with one geared to a master's degree preceded by a mandatory bachelor's.

The course for art teachers in the state system has always been the subject of heated debate and controversy at the Art Academy, not least, in fact, primarily, because with this course of study, regulations and systemic constraints intrude in the Academy that are foreign to the spirit of fine arts study: a detailed syllabus, an extensive curriculum of required subjects, and so forth. These discussions have not, of course, concentrated solely on the course load burdening students in terms both of study time and quantity of material to be mastered but also on where the emphasis should lie in a meaningful curriculum for candidates aspiring to teach art at state schools. In the early 1970s particularly, an at times highly vocal debate raged about how the Academy might imagine a good art teacher at higher secondary school level, for instance, and what the Academy in turn should provide in the way of training for such teachers (Fig. 8). One person who showed particular commitment in this context was Karl Bobek, who had been a professor for sculpture at the Academy since 1963. On 25 March 1971 he submitted an 'Initiative Draft for Restructuring Art Education' and did this in the framework of the debates on reforming art teaching which were hosted by the Krefeld circle of the Krefeld Kunstverein [Art Association]. Those debates were so popular and attracted so much attention that even the organisers were dumbfounded.

Bobek's proposal discernibly relates, on the one hand, in many points to the Düsseldorf Academy although it went further with an overarching aim that in any case might be applied to the entire federal state of North Rhine-Westphalia. Bobek began this rather detailed plan with scathing criticism of school art classes as they were at the time and called for all-day school and more autonomy for individual schools. Ultimately, he went on to design an academic curriculum that in his opinion could structure the training offered at the Art Academy and that – also presented with highly sophisticated graphics – provided professional training for both practitioners of the fine arts (artists) and art teachers or art theorists and historians. On the practical side (Fig. 9, diagram a) Bobek's efforts to include new art forms and new requirements relating to the core of 'fine arts teaching' are obvious. On the theoretical side (Fig. 10, diagram b) he designed a curriculum organised around the primary disciplines art theory, sociology, education, and psychology, which is recognisably shaped by prevailing trends in the social sciences (group dynamics, information aesthetics, social psychology) and was obviously intended to ensure that art teacher training at the Art Academy kept up with the ongoing discussion. At the same time, however, Bobek was clear about the desirability of retaining the special conditions of Academy study: the system of classes taught by artists, the good balance between the art and academic sides of the curriculum. Reforming the examination system was important to Bobek. He wanted former students to remain members of the Academy after they had finished their studies: 'During teaching practice students are regarded as on leave from the Academy. But they shall have the right of continuing to attend individual courses to round off their education and to follow up possible inspiration they may have experienced while doing teaching practice in schools with targeted studies. Study at the Academy and the teaching practice internship will end at the same time with a state examination.'[4]

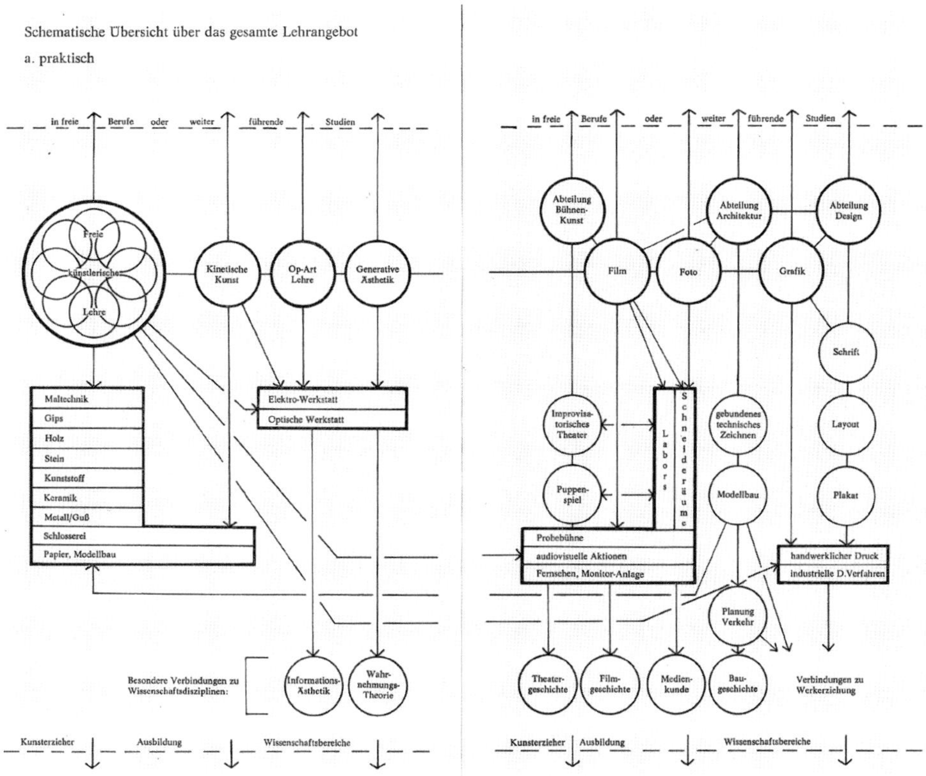

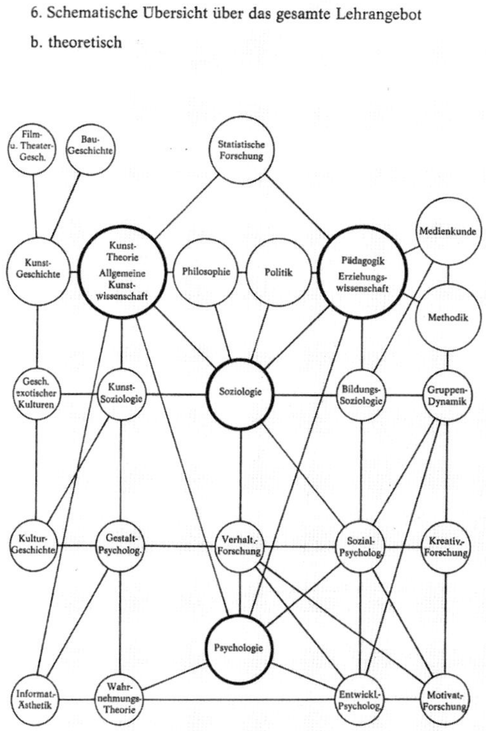

Figs. 9, 10: Karl Bobek, diagram showing the full range of courses taught, a) practical, b) theoretical, 1971

The debates that ensued once the above proposal was tabled – and in particular Bobek's direct alignment with the guiding principle of maturity – have also been documented. He advocated strict adherence to individual creativity to counter the prevailing utilitarian bias. 'I have an idea of society, namely, the idea of it as a taut and diversified organism into which the productivity specific to the individual is integrated. The person who becomes mature will first of all become mature towards themself.'[5]

This initiative remained in one respect unsuccessful: studying for teaching at state schools developed along other lines in North Rhine-Westphalia as it did elsewhere. Still the proposal does document the commitment and acute awareness of the problem of teacher education that existed even among the artists at the Academy in the 1970s.

NOTES

1 Eduard Trier (ed.), *Zweihundert Jahre Kunstakademie Düsseldorf*, Düsseldorf 1973, p. 220; see Historisches Archiv der Stadt Köln, Best. 1232 [City of Cologne Historical Archives, clause 1232].

2 Trier (see n. 1), p. 220; see Ulrike Scheffler-Rother, *Das Städtische Werkseminar in Düsseldorf. Künstlerisches und handwerkliches Gestalten im Spannungsfeld zwischen Pädagogik und konkreten Anwendungsbezügen*, Düsseldorf 2006.

3 Jörn Schützenmeister, *Professionalisierung und Polyvalenz in der Lehrerausbildung*, Marburg 2002, especially pp. 145–235 on the development of teacher training 1960–1970.

4 Hans Joachim Albrecht and Klaus Ulrich Düsselberg (eds.), *Krefelder Kreis, Tonbandprotokolle und Konzepte. Initiativen zur Veränderung der Kunsterziehung*, Krefeld 1971, p. 148.

5 Albrecht and Düsselberg (see n. 4), p. 154.

ERICH REUSCH ON TEACHER TRAINING AT THE ART ACADEMY

A conversation with Siegfried Gohr in Neuenrade on 9 October 2012

Siegfried Gohr: What induced you to come to the Academy and when was that?
Erich Reusch: 1973. I was interested in living and working in an artistic community. In that artistic community one made contact with artists as human beings that led to closer acquaintance.

S. G.: Had you ever taught before?
E. R.: No.

S. G.: Which artists were your contacts there?
E. R.: My first contact with an artist there was with Norbert Kricke, whom I knew for years. Kricke was a pupil of the sculptor Richard Scheibe in Berlin, as I was later myself. Kricke went to Düsseldorf. I got to know him in Düsseldorf, and we soon became friends. We had very fierce clashes but practised very close friendship. The themes varied, even when we travelled together – to Tenerife, for instance – but the discourses were always very exciting. Kricke had an assurance and generosity that no one else had. He was very inspired, even when we went to motor races together. He was always amusing and had lots of experiences. I got on very well with him. The last years were overshadowed by his illness. We had less contact with each other during the last two years of his life.

S. G.: Was he already rector then?
E. R.: He had just become rector and then had me brought to the Academy. I was pleased to take up that appointment and not just for materialistic reasons. It was the contact with other artists that interested me, as I've just said.

S. G.: Who were those other artists?
E. R.: During that time at the Academy I actually had good contacts with everybody. Those weren't friendships that went deeper. I had a good relationship with Erwin Heerich, with Günther Uecker, and other artists who taught there. I didn't have any substantial problems with people.

S. G.: What was it like with the students? How did they get into your class? Did you pick them out?
E. R.: Kricke took over the Academy after Joseph Beuys had left and a great many people were studying at this Academy who were not suited for art as a profession. As you know, Beuys took in lots of students and deluded them into thinking that they, too, could become professional artists. 'Every person is an artist' is a pronouncement that leaves a lot up for grabs. However, only a very few people are suited. But Beuys induced many to want to be professional artists. Those students suffered burnout after two or three terms because they had no visual issues that went further than that. He took students whose aptitude could not be expanded. Of course he also had very good and successful students. Having lots of students is advertising, of course. Even Raphael, who would stroll through Rome with a retinue of three hundred pupils, was aware of that. There were students at the Academy who didn't progress, who would then go into another class – for instance, to [Wolf-Jürgen] Seeßelberg, who had a short-term teaching contract. I was asked to take over his course and went into the classroom upstairs. I opened the door and right in the doorway stood a life-size picture of a working woman with a Communist Red flag. That was a blatant provocation. I asked, 'Who painted this picture?' A student spoke up, who, as I later learnt, was the Leninist-Marxist member designate of the state legislature. I said to her: 'You painted that? What you've done here is insulting to the Party. You can't show such a lousy Red flag. That's an insult to the very idea! Take a look at the Delacroix painting *Die Freiheit führt das Volk* [Liberty Leading the People]. The red of the banner in that picture is brilliantly painted. Downstairs in this building there's a class in painting techniques. There you can acquire the technical skills that will lead to better painting. In this case here, underpainting in glazes of egg-white tempera might be called for.' In any case, the scandal I had expected was defused.

Should I go on to describe the development of that student? The student stayed with me. She was studying to be an art teacher at state schools. She painted in the manner of Communist propaganda pictures. The Russian Itinerants movement also served her as a model. Highly narrative art concerned with social issues. She was evidently uninterested in visual problems. She sat her exams later and passed the theoretical exam with very high marks. But what she herself painted was agitprop devoid of aesthetic qualities. With the courses on offer here it isn't possible to develop artistic sensitivity in young people. That was that and she failed. We didn't want an attitude like hers to be passed on to pupils.

Finally I was approached by Beuys, who was of the opinion the student had been treated unfairly. I asked him, 'Do you want your children to experience classroom teaching of that kind or would you rather not?' To which he replied: 'I don't want that either!'

S. G.: And the other students in the class? Roughly how many were there?
E. R.: There were about eighteen of them. Perhaps even twenty-two at times. The last year, when I stopped teaching, there were fewer. Of course there were colleagues who promoted group dynamics in their classes.

S. G.: Holding hands!
E. R.: I held the view that a student had to have learnt by then that their future activity can only be determined by them and their individual decision.

S. G.: You've already touched on Beuys and Kricke. Then the student with extreme views. That would seem to suggest how controversies about political and non-political art might turn out or how political art can or cannot be. Beuys was no longer there?
E. R.: Beuys was no longer there. He would drop by occasionally.

S. G.: How would you judge Kricke's achievements as rector?
E. R.: Kricke was very capable. He was a superb pianist, for instance. He spoke with authority. He was eloquent. He could govern. He could also have held high political office. He was well read. He had global contacts. Siegfried Giedeon was a friend of his; Martin Gropius was a friend of his. Gropius came to Düsseldorf once and visited him. Kricke rang me up and said, 'Gropius is coming here tomorrow. We'll spend the whole day with him and take him to the airport in the evening. We'll all have a great time.' Gropius came, and we spent a day with him. He was, you know, also a friend of Richard Scheibe's, and we went sightseeing with him in the city, talked about projects in architecture. That was the human side of Kricke, which could be very much to the fore.

S. G.: How did he rule at home? There are all sorts of stories. That he could be very harsh and very domineering. How did you experience that?
E. R.: I experienced that, too. I was witness to how a student, a girl from Gelsenkirchen, sought him out and said, 'There really is no art in Gelsenkirchen!' Now Kricke had done those famous works there with Yves Klein, and so he gave the student a good dressing-down as an ignoramus – not just because he was personally annoyed or because he felt insulted but simply on principle. After she had left the room in a state of shock, Kricke said, 'That was a hard but necessary blow, but now we must help her to get on to her feet again. How can we help her?'

S. G.: And with his colleagues? Was there a lot of discussion? Were orders given?
E. R.: There was discussion. A 'kitchen cabinet' was occasionally in operation behind the scenes. Things were discussed in advance with certain teachers. Rolf Sackenheim as deputy director was staunchly aligned with us. That didn't go down well with some colleagues. Gerhard Hoehme, to take one example, was not so much on our side. I personally got on all right with Hoehme. Hoehme had a somewhat more conciliatory stance. We sought the toughest solutions. Not against other people but the toughest solutions in respect of things and against ourselves. That included working intensively on art and having to accept criticism without feeling personally insulted. Also that seemingly bizarre intentions were also followed up and realised.

S. G.: What were the standards?
E. R.: For instance, the work of important past and present artists. Also going to important exhibitions.

S. G.: How large was the catchment area of the exhibitions you went to?
E. R.: The bus was acquired while Kricke was in office. We looked at exhibitions and also went to museums here and there. The North Rhine-Westphalia Collection was still in Schloss Jägerhof then. One day we went to the Collection with students. A girl, a fifth-term student perhaps, studying to be an art teacher, was asked, 'Who is that picture over there in the opposite corner by?' The student said, 'I dunno.' It was a picture by Piet Mondrian. Then I went over to the picture with the student. She stood in front of it, still clueless, and asked, 'What is that picture actually supposed to mean?' After I had recovered somewhat from the question, I took her over to the window and pointed out a house with a modernist rectangular façade diagonally across from us and told her, 'Mondrian is

one of the guiding lights of our generation of artists. By now he has reached even third-class architecture.' In the classroom we spoke about it in more depth.

You might experience astonishing things on other occasions too. Once we went to Amsterdam and went to exhibitions there. A Karel Appel retrospective was on at the Stedelijk Museum. Afterwards we went to the Vincent van Gogh Museum nearby. An outstanding exhibition was running there that also enlarged my own ideas of Van Gogh. This exhibition in this particular hanging and with this particular selection of works was especially impressive. One of the students, however, had his doubts about it. Trying to clarify matters, I asked him, 'So what do you think of the exhibition?' Then, in front of the picture of a street in a small town, he said he had no relationship to that picture. But it would be different if a Siemens switchboard control box were visible over there by the side of the street. A peculiar association to say the least. He hadn't in the slightest grasped the scope of the aesthetic message emanating from the picture. This student, however, later worked seriously hard. Recently I saw one of his works in a south German museum.

S. G.: What was the relationship between the students planning to teach art at state schools and the fine arts students at that time actually like? Wasn't there frequent friction?
E. R.: The teaching contingent was always being cut down to size by Kricke. But not in a way that hurt and with wry humour. For example, he once said before a senate session, 'Our art teaching colleagues will have to stand during the session. We'll sit down.'

S. G.: So there was a hierarchy?
E. R.: That might be putting it too crassly. With Kricke there were certain differences. He usually masked them with humour.

S. G.: And so that also caused resentment?
E. R.: Kricke's personality was such that resentment had a low boiling point.

S. G.: That's been entirely defused nowadays, that subject, because the percentage of students studying to be art teachers was once much higher whereas now they make up only twenty per cent and so conflicts of that kind don't amount to anything.
E. R.: I think it was forty per cent in my day, but I don't really remember the exact figure. Kricke would occasionally say to prospective art teachers, 'After all, you're an artist who's out for security.' He even personally attacked Erwin Heerich like that. Nevertheless the contacts were friendly.

S. G.: Who instituted the orientation courses?
E. R.: Kricke instituted the orientation courses.

S. G.: Were there any clashes about that?
E. R.: Can't remember any. It was viewed as a sensible decision.

S. G.: I've heard from other sources that there definitely were heated discussions about whether it should be done or not?
E. R.: Not that I know of. I haven't seen any problems at all; quite to the contrary, we welcomed it. Luise Kimme did it first and was very popular with the students. Then came Tony Cragg, who soon took over a sculpture class.

Laying the groundwork in the orientation courses called for heavy investment. Later on we also had difficulties with students who were often handicapped by coming from a background with culture-vulture parents. Creativity calls for freedom that does not tolerate fixed ideas. Trying to eliminate those predispositions was often heavy going. Often enough, it didn't work out anyway.

S. G.: How were the classes allocated?
E. R.: Everyone took what he wanted.

S. G.: Was there even an orientation-course exam?
E. R.: There were exams. That's another story. At the beginning there was what was known as the portfolio conference. That portfolio conference generally took up two days.

S. G.: Can you still remember how many applicants there were?
E. R.: Yes, the maximum number of portfolios submitted was some 720. Review of them later always took place on the Rhine Embankment, in the governmental building, because there wasn't enough room for it at the Academy. The Ministry – this happened every year – would tell us to admit as many students as possible. That meant several hundred. We, on the other hand, were of the opinion only twenty-five to thirty should be

admitted. The lowest number of admissions we had was forty-two from an applicant pool of about 680.

In my capacity of deputy director I was promptly summoned to the Ministry, to Frau Sonderkamp. She said to me then, 'But we've always said as many students as possible should be admitted.' I said to her, 'Do you want to produce welfare cases or artists who may have a future ahead of them?' In any case, the Ministry was first and foremost concerned with keeping the young people off the streets.

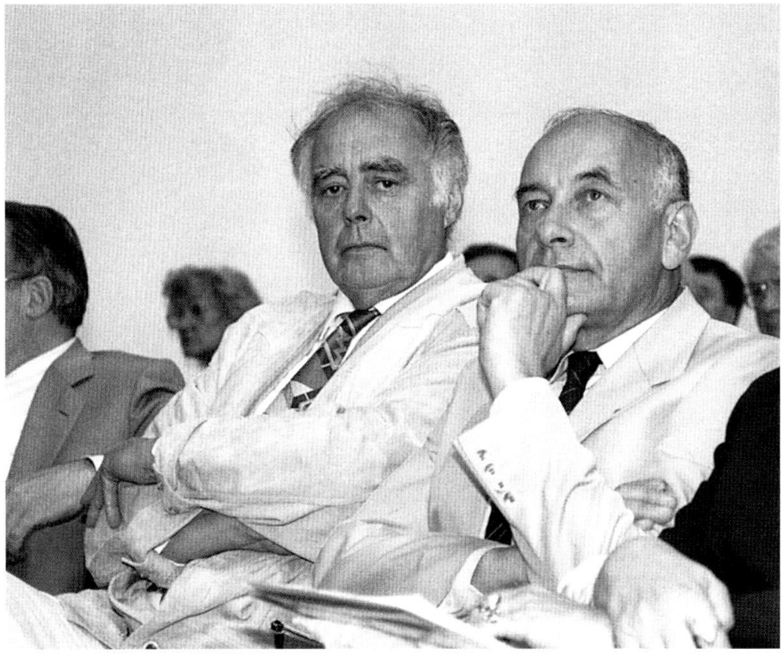

Saying goodbye to Erich Reusch and Eugen Gomringer in the Great Hall of the Academy, 1990

S. G.: The Ministry has more subtle methods nowadays.
E. R.: Kricke had gone by then, and our new director, Markus Lüpertz, had introduced himself to Frau Sonderkamp. She said to me, 'That's a great guy; you'll have to make him director!'

Now to return to the Ministry. A directive was issued that the film class be built up to such an extent that it would be possible to make feature films. Which of course would have completely overtaxed the available facilities. I ventured to say, 'That's definitely possible. To create the right conditions in respect of technology and personnel, we would perhaps need four million for new rooms, for materials, for equipment, and for suitable specialist personnel. That would include teachers for choreography, direction, cutting, and other subjects that would have to be taught. The running costs incurred annually would of course have to be added to the cost of instituting it.' So that entailed considerable sums. However the Ministry was of the opinion that expansion could be practicable with the personnel at hand for making films that would attract attention to the political activities of the federal state. Certainly, relations [between the Academy and the Ministry] varied from Minister of Science to Minister of Science. They were particularly good with [Johannes] Rau as Minister; talks with him were subject-related but leavened with humorous anecdotes. He sympathised with the Academy and promoted it benevolently and in the context of its historical development.

NOTES ON JOSEPH BEUYS AS A TEACHER AT THE DÜSSELDORF ART ACADEMY AND THE BEUYS CLASS 1961–1972*

Johannes Stüttgen

From the 1960s and on into the 1970s the Düsseldorf Art Academy was caught up in turbulence that shook it to its foundations and has left a permanent mark on it. One man from the circle of professors, who also assumed an outsider stance in teaching, rose to worldwide acclaim as an artist at that time: Joseph Beuys had mounted a campaign for a concept of art that was ultimately impossible to reconcile with the prevailing idea of art, including avant-garde movements (with Düsseldorf as a bastion of such tendencies). The Düsseldorf Academy, where Beuys himself had studied sculpture after the war with Joseph Enseling and Ewald Mataré, was Beuys's chief theatre of operations for more than a decade – to be precise, until 11 October 1972 (Fig. 1). It was the setting for consolidating his conception of 'sculpture' with its specific manifestation as Action Art – and within it the core function: his teaching and the emergence of his class as an Action model *sui generis*. However, the Academy was not just the scene and birthplace of this new concept of art as inaugurated by Joseph Beuys but – as events overtook it soon appeared – also the object of his Action. That turned everything upside down. The Academy, by definition a state approved and authorised place and warranty for the freedom of art, now became its object, which had to be liberated, to be emancipated from the tutelage of the nanny state and made autonomous in accordance with the values of art. That entailed ultimately nothing less than transforming society as a whole into the object of art. A systemic leap – but what mattered here – one rooted in art itself. Consequently, thus Beuys, what an art academy was all about! Precisely that – namely, the legitimation of this Action agenda in art itself, in its own conception and nothing else, not in an ideology or personal preference – was what made it dynamite. It struck at the very heart of the Art Academy because it was launched from within.

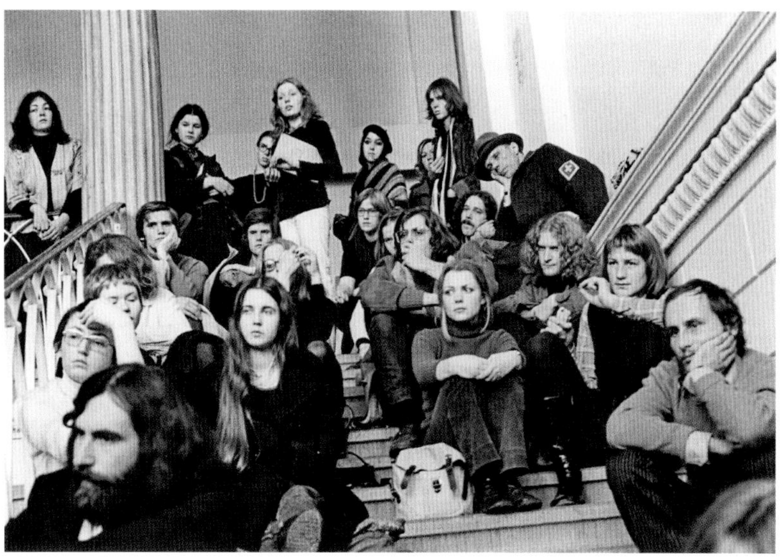

Fig. 1: Students at a discussion in the Art Academy stairwell; centre right: Joseph Beuys, 1972

The political system must have sniffed out this explosive logic with its energy potential linked to Beuys's own person and seen it as aimed at itself long before his fellow artists at the Academy, who had protected their colleague in mutual agreement against the massive broadsides fired at him by politicians and the Ministry during his early years as a teacher there as someone who had already raised quite a stir in public with such spectacular Action performances in the context of Fluxus and Antikunst, as authorised by director Hans Schwippert (later: Eduard Trier). What was at stake was the freedom of art, the freedom of all of them and of the Academy – grassroots policy, which at that juncture was not yet being made specifically by Beuys alone but was also applied to him. The basic principle was valid – that was the consensus – unconditionally. Hence Beuys was the exemplary case. Exemplary for art. That would become his trademark – in the Academy and beyond the Academy. At that time there was not yet any talk of the Academy as being autonomous as an Action agenda on the lines of an 'expanded concept of art'. It, the freedom of the Academy, had been regarded since the new beginnings after the war as real, as a given. However, just so that no misunderstandings might arise about that, the state had long since taken precautions: the remark placed by Joseph Beuys at the end of *Lebenslauf Werklauf* [Life Course Work Course] at the *festival of new art* mounted by Aachen Technical University on 20 July 1964 cost its author his civil servant status, thus securing for the state the possibility of dismissing him at any time: 'Beuys recommends raising the Berlin Wall by 5 cm (better proportions!)'.[1]

The students in his class realised from the beginning, and were the first to do so, that Joseph Beuys indeed had incomparably more crucial things in mind with art than the everyday operations of the Academy that were in name certainly not unambitious yet so well oiled that they ran without friction always in the same groove. With Beuys any distinction between teacher and artist was completely unthinkable, and even the status of artist was redefined in the light of his take on it. What Joseph Beuys had presented as theory back in 1964, at the latest since 1966 under the aegis of the public 'serial talks', surfaced here with immediate effect: art, that seemed in his hands to cover literally everything, him directly as a person, his public persona, every measure, everything with which he was concerned, especially also his students' work. Art, that was not simply a subject as he taught it, a subject to be taught, or the designation of a field of activity thus defined but rather an entitlement. Nothing was excepted from that entitlement. Just as a wolf flaunts his lupine nature with every movement, Beuys conveyed the presence and application of a CONCEPT that, without having to be named (and perhaps a name for it could not be found all that quickly), made sense immediately, was a hit. No one could elude that idiosyncratic conceptual presence. Beuys spent every day from morning to evening at the Academy, in his class, and accompanied his students' work with his unbelievable instinct for nosing out what was wanted deep down and what was supposed to be wanted. His corrections were merciless, feared, extremely fruitful, and always liberating, however rigorous and painful they might be. Very early on Beuys had exerted a magnetic attraction as a teacher. The troop of students assembled about him, often enough students who would not have allowed anyone else to be viewed as their teacher, soon enjoyed exceptional status within the Academy as a class. It was said that if art was taking place anywhere at all, then it was there. Art and anti-art. Beuys in 1964: 'Art comprises art and anti-art.'[2] This was a teacher who had something of a rogue about him; he conveyed to his students the impression of a mission that went far beyond the bounds of what was being done here at the Academy at that time, as if he still had something else up his sleeve. The question of whether Beuys's own art was something that could be exhibited sorted itself out for all intents and purposes, at least in his early years as a teacher. In the period before the great 1967 autumn exhibition in Mönchengladbach (by then Beuys had already taught at the Academy for six years), there were some people in his class who hadn't the foggiest notion that any artwork had been produced by their teacher. They might indeed have known about the Actions, certainly the 1964 Aachen Action mentioned above, which had done the rounds in the press, but they experienced it, so to speak, as a natural extension of his work at the Academy. With Beuys everything was Action and everything was teaching. *Stuhl mit Fett* [Fat Chair], now one of his most famous workpieces (Block Beuys, Hessisches Landesmuseum Darmstadt, shown on p. 202), first appeared in 1964 at a winter *Rundgang* [Academy Tour], the mandatory annual exhibition of Academy students' work. It was the very first exhibit contributed by a teacher to those Tours and, as such, was an Action object. And what an Action object it was. Joseph Beuys had hung it up above the door frame of the entrance to his classroom, Room 20.

Beuys stood for art in his own person – that went beyond the normal, even the avant-gardist, definition of an artist – and his teaching was part of that. Here was someone going at everything in a way unlike anything that had been known, more precisely, with quicker wits, more directly, always hitting the nail on the head, causing trouble, attracting attention. The point was art – measure, access, Action. No definition. At first there was no talk at all of an 'expanded concept of art', but at some point there was. However, it was obvious that what was being conveyed there, what was emerging, beggared conceptual description (that is, also: subverted the system). That had nothing in the slightest to do with politics. Politics didn't come into play until the German Student Party was founded on the meadow in front of the Düsseldorf Academy in June 1967, albeit as its self-appointed opposition ('anti-party'/'meta-party') and, typically, 'in parallel with' the first large museum exhibition in Mönchengladbach, mentioned above. At that show Beuys made public in one go his entire body of works, which until then had only been known to a small circle of insiders (still left out to be meted out in portions later on was the vast body of drawings). Both events, seemingly two worlds completely apart, in reality belonged together. The exhibition was an instant hit but the founding of the party (three months earlier) less so, except at the Academy itself. Beuys juxtaposed the two in *Lebenslauf Werklauf* (see above). The expanded version of that life and works chronicle for the 1967 Mönchengladbach exhibition catalogue closes with the entry: 'Düsseldorf 21 June Beuys founds the German Student Party'.[3] A subsequent addition in 1969 immediately following the above entry runs: '1967 Mönchengladbach (Johannes Cladders) Parallel process 1'.[4] In the same catalogue (cardboard box, contents: two fan-folded picture albums / a double folder + a piece of felt stamped BRAUNKREUZ [BROWN CROSS]), Johannes Cladders, director of the museum, noted, 'Asked about his founding a party, he [Beuys] was of the opinion that not regarding it as a work of art would mean misunderstanding it. It was to be regarded as just as much a work of art as his teaching at the Academy or any other activity he developed.' 'Here', as Cladders closes his remarks, 'we find ourselves at a point comparable to that at which Malevich painted a white cross on a white ground almost five decades ago and thus pushed the boundaries of painting as far as they could go.'[5]

With reference to the concept of art and the historical context of the time, the launch in 1967 of that double pack, founding a party and showing his work, represented a quantum leap, a charge, as it were, shot from behind over the heads and the level of awareness of his contemporaries into the future. Heralded in *Lebenslauf Werklauf* in 1966: 'Beuys The Difference between Picture Head and Moving Head'.[6] In 1967 Joseph Beuys stepped onto the world stage not only as an artist but also within the Düsseldorf Art Academy as the initiator and protagonist of an Action agenda that had the Academy itself in its sights. Synchronously with the student protests flaring up in western Europe and the United States, the Beuys class established regular public 'serial talks' as they were called, in which the role of art was tabled for discussion with a view to the overall social situation in East and West, questioning the system, indeed the concepts of art, freedom, the state, democracy, and above all the status of the Art Academy as a state institution. Joseph Beuys, a professor himself, admittedly, but soon to be at the head of a doughty squad of students, who also made up the AStA [General Students' Committee] in 1968, proclaimed the idea of self-administration – that is, freedom as a design principle directly derived from a concept of art contrasting with the Marxist-orientated class-struggle line that would soon prevail. The axiomatic self-administered, 'autonomous' – that is, denationalised – Academy met with vehement opposition, not only from the Marxist student cadres, who championed a strong state, albeit not the existing bourgeois state, but also from the overwhelming majority of professors (in fact all of them except for the philosopher Walter Warnach). Whereas the Marxist students belittled freedom in art as a petty bourgeois relic of a bygone age, the professors could simply not grasp Beuys's postulate of freedom, which they believed to have long since been fulfilled in the prevailing status quo. They would let no one, they protested to Beuys and his followers, tell them how to set about their work. Art and the Art Academy, they were convinced, were free, nothing more so! That freedom, thus Joseph Beuys, arguing for the other side, was a playground of privilege for a handful of 'artists', a field of fools defined by the state (that was not even permitted to give itself a legal form of its own, a constitution!), immured from all other human life and fields of endeavour. Art, as Beuys conceived of it, quintessentially as a principle of form and design, had a bearing on all human endeavour and not least on the form of society as a whole in that freedom was the ultimate determinant – art also questioned the system. According to that definition, 'every person was an artist' (Beuys), and an art academy was the place where that concept was to be activated in everyone. It followed, therefore, that anyone who wanted to must have access to that study of art.

Thus Action centred on questioning the system but not in the manner of Marxist ideology. With the German Student Party in charge, specific points were laid out that outlined the process of demanding autonomy: students were to have a voice and the right to vote at the Conference, the top-tier decision-making body at the Art Academy; students were to have a say in appointments policy; and, finally, the admissions modalities were to be revised. In the legendary year 1968, which 'in parallel' with the political activities also represented a high point in the history of the Beuys class where art was concerned – 'political' and 'artistic' are still defined in the conventional sense of the terms here – the students actually pushed through their right to have a seat and a vote at the Conference, which from then on was known as the General Conference. But things came to a head in autumn that year. Ten of a total of twenty-two professors published an open letter in which, it was claimed, among other things, that 'the internal and external order' of the Academy was threatened by an 'evil spectre which essentially comes from the circle of ideas and the influence of Herr Joseph Beuys. Hubristic political amateurishness, addiction to ideological domination, demagogical conduct, and – consequently – intolerance, defamation, and lack of consideration for colleagues aim at disbanding present orders, meddle disruptively in artistic and educational areas, and debase humane values in a deliberately offensive manner.'[7] From then on no amount of oil poured on them could smooth the troubled waters. The disputes roiled on and would persist for four more years. The North Rhine-Westphalian Science Ministry was lying in wait for him, for the time being without any legal basis for action. Beuys was too clever to provide them with an excuse! He continued to invoke in his defence art and otherwise valid resolutions passed in Conference. Right to the end.

In said autumn 1968 a remarkable article by Georg Jappe on Beuys as an Academy teacher was printed in the *Frankfurter Allgemeine Zeitung* under the headline 'Joseph Beuys Must Go. Should He?' It runs:

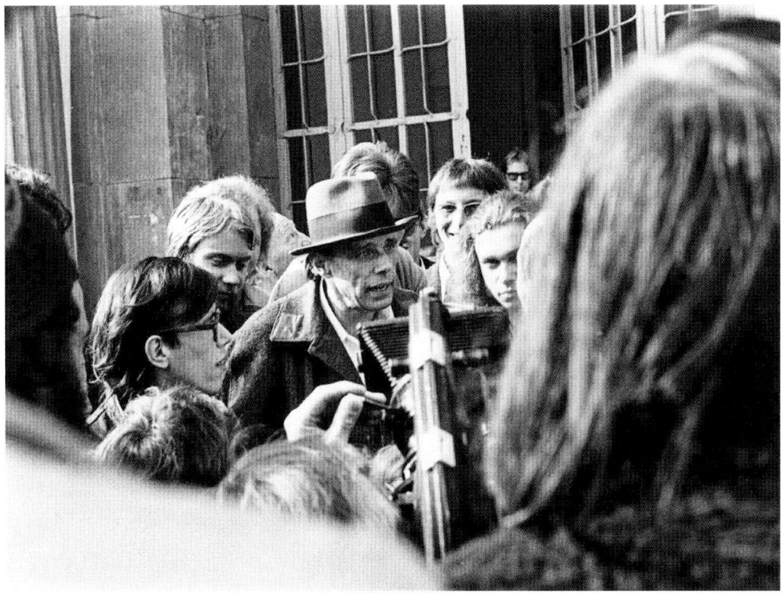

Fig. 2: Joseph Beuys after dismissal, 1972

'Beuys is no [Rudi] Dutschke. He is not even an agitator. There are sporadic discussions and symposia in his class in which composers and writers and not just sculptors sit. Beuys is a distinguished educationalist and a very charismatic one. He defines his role as follows: "Everyone must lead to anthropological knowledge through his subject. That includes all of life, even politics. If a pupil should one day be better at bringing up her children, that would mean more to me than having trained a great artist. One can no longer proceed from the old academic concept of training great artists; that remains lucky coincidence. Where one can, however, set something in motion is the idea that art and knowledge gained from art can form an element that flows back into life." Thus informing life with a union of psychic and intellectual knowledge has much more to do with Novalis than with blatant political agitation. Whatever one's views on this brouhaha, it all boils down to the big question: Can federal German society afford Beuys as a teacher or not?'[8]

It remains for me to add that an exceptionally large number of men and women who have gone on to be very successful artists even in conventional fields of art have come from Joseph Beuys's circle as a teacher and above all from his class. This just as a marginal note.

A collision was ineluctable. Towards the close of 1969, after the Düsseldorf Art Academy had been shut down in May for ten days by order of the Minister of Culture because of an Action by Jörg Immendorff, a pupil of Beuys's, in which Beuys himself had had a hand, and the internecine strife was hardening to the point of futility, Joseph Beuys opened the final round, which led to his being summarily dismissed in October 1972 (Fig. 2). Viewing the admission procedures as no longer justifiable, he and the student representatives to the General Conference had fought, ultimately in vain, for abolishing admission on the basis of portfolio acceptance and for freely admitting all applicants for at least two probationary terms. Without going into the factual arguments (which no one seriously questioned), this petition, which had been submitted repeatedly, was rejected time and again by Beuys's fellow professors on the grounds of shortage of space and teaching personnel. What was in the end accepted was a petition subsequently submitted for debate by Beuys for permission to be granted to every teacher to admit any applicant he wanted to his class on his own responsibility. With that Joseph Beuys, who was concerned with publicly demonstrating the right of everyone to study and who from then on would admit all students rejected by other professors to his class, had opened the floodgates. The unequivocal subtext: the Art Academy is defined by art and the civil right enjoyed by all to training and study. The state as the judicial body of society must accordingly supply the means, space, and money needed and otherwise keep out of all questions concerning design and process! Whatever one might think of the case, the fact was the amount of energy that Joseph Beuys cast into the scale pan more than matched that expended by the system. On 7 April 1978 he won the lawsuit he had brought in the Federal Labour Court against the state of North Rhine-Westphalia after his summary dismissal. Beuys's dismissal, *ex post facto* notice of which the Ministry had for its part sent in due time as a 'precautionary measure', ended on 23 November 1878 with a compromise: Joseph Beuys agreed to withdraw his suit, was permitted to keep using his then studio, Room 3, at the Düsseldorf Art Academy until the end of his sixty-fifth year and to keep the title of professor. He then proceeded to convert Room 3 into the headquarters of the Free International University (FIU), which he had founded in 1972 (with me as managing director). Equipping it with a *Fettecke* [Fat Corner], he called Room 3 a 'denationalised zone in the midst of a nationalised institute'. After Beuys died in 1986 the *Fettecke* was destroyed by Academy personnel. Traces of it can still be visited in Room 3 (now Room 002).

However, what had a bearing on the dramatic months of that period of winter 1968/69, which, as I see it, represented the artistic acme of the Beuys class, is to be found in the following notes in Joseph Beuys, 'Lebenslauf Werklauf': 'Christmas 1968: Intersection of the trajectory of PICTURE HEAD with the trajectory of MOVING HEAD in the universe (Space) Parallel process – 1969 Düsseldorf Schmela Gallery REAR SECTION III; 12.2.69 Apparition of MOVING HEAD above the Düsseldorf Art Academy; Beuys pleads guilty to the snowfall of 15 to 20 February'.[9]

* General editor's note

Johannes Stüttgen has here described the situation at the Düsseldorf Art Academy in the 1960s and 1970s from his personal standpoint, which in details is not shared by the general editor. Stüttgen was a close friend and former student of Joseph Beuys's at the Düsseldorf Art Academy. He is the author of the following publications:

Der Ganze Riemen. Der Auftritt von Joseph Beuys als Lehrer. Die Chronologie der Ereignisse an der Staatlichen Kunstakademie Düsseldorf, 1966–1972, Cologne 2008.

Fettecke. Die Geschichte der Fettecke von Joseph Beuys in Raum 3, Staatl. Kunstakademie Düsseldorf und der Prozeß J. Stüttgen gegen das Land NRW, Düsseldorf 1989.

Der Keilrahmen des Imi Knoebel, 1968/89, Bonn/Cologne 1991.

NOTES

1 Joseph Beuys, 'Lebenslauf Werklauf', in: *Joseph Beuys. Werke aus der Sammlung Karl Ströher*, exhib. cat. Basel 1969, pp. 4–7; here: p. 5.
2 'Krawall in Aachen. Interview with Joseph Beuys', *Kunstmagazin für moderne Malerei, Grafik, Plastik*, Issue 4, Mainz 1964, pp. 95–97.
3 Beuys (see n. 1), p. 6.
4 Ibid., p. 6.
5 Johannes Cladders, *Beuys – und das weiße Kreuz von Malewitsch*, exhib. cat. Mönchengladbach 1967, n.p.
6 Beuys (see n. 1), p. 6.
7 A hectographed information sheet by Karl Bobek, Gert Weber, Kurt Arnscheidt, Thomas Robaschik, and Gerhard Hoehme, 'An alle Lehrkräfte, Klassensprecher und den Allg. Studentenausschuss vom 12.11.1968' [To all teachers, class speakers, and the General Students Committee of 12 November 1968], Landesarchiv NRW, [Dept] Abteilung Rheinland, NW 681_696.
8 *Frankfurter Allgemeine Zeitung*, 24 September 1968.
9 Beuys (see n. 1), p. 6.

THE ORIENTATION DEPARTMENT AT THE ART ACADEMY

Anthony Cragg

THE PROBATIONARY CLASS 1945–1973

Today's Orientation Department at the Düsseldorf Art Academy – known as the Probationary Class until 1973 – was implemented when the Düsseldorf Art Academy reopened after the Second World War. From then on there were two probationary terms for beginners in the Fine Art, Art Education, and Architecture Departments before they could take up regular studies in an art class. Before that time the usual practice had been to allow professors in most cases to choose between the students they wanted to have in their classes and those they did not. To be admitted to the Academy, applicants had to hand in a portfolio containing from twenty to thirty works – drawings and works in colour. The works would then be assessed by all fine arts and art education professors in conference.

At that time it was usual for some art professors to have had contact with some applicants to the Academy even before the admissions conference so that they could take their favourites into their classes during the portfolio review without having to fear objections from other colleagues. Applicants who had not had contact to professors but had applied to the Art Academy directly from their schools or from a crafts trade were either accepted or rejected through this process by a simple majority of votes cast by all professors. The additional admission requirement for applicants who wished to study art education was they had to have the school leaving certificate qualifying them for university entrance on admission.

In tune with the zeitgeist, those professors' meetings were usually informal. It was not unusual for them to smoke cigars and drink cognac at sessions. Since Hans Schwippert believed freedom was essential for artistic creativity, professors were encouraged during his tenure as director to feel as free and independent as possible.

In 1960 the Düsseldorf Art Academy student body consisted of 337 students divided up into nineteen classes. The painter Rissa reports that when she entered the Academy in 1959, there were 150 applicants for places, of whom fifteen – that is, ten per cent – were admitted.[1] What is so interesting about the ratio of applicants to admissions is the fact that, although there has never been any official ruling or guideline from the Ministry, the ratio has remained virtually constant.

As a student, Rissa took her two probationary terms with Holger Runge, a teacher on a short-term contract at the Academy. After Runge was dismissed, Hans Schwippert required the most recently appointed art professors, including Karl Otto Götz, Gerhard Hoehme, and Rupprecht Geiger, to teach two probationary terms each.

In 1969 a second Probationary Class was established because far more applicants had been admitted to study that year. After finishing her studies, Rissa was asked by Gert Weber in 1969 to come to the Academy to teach beginning students. She taught some of the beginners from October 1969 until 1971 as an assistant and as a lecturer until 1975, when she was appointed professor with a class of her own at the Academy, which she taught until 2007.

JOSEPH BEUYS'S INFLUENCE ON THE DEVELOPMENT OF THE ORIENTATION DEPARTMENT

Joseph Beuys and his rejection of the admissions criteria applied until he challenged them played an important role in the transformation of the Probationary Class into today's Orientation Department. Beuys had been a student at the Düsseldorf Art Academy from 1945 until 1954. During that time he had enjoyed the relative comfort of sharing a studio with Erwin Heerich while he was in Ewald Mataré's master class whereas the students who had him as a professor from 1961 on were taught as a very large class. Beuys was always close to students: while an Academy student he had been a member of the first body of student representatives (AStA: the General Students' Committee).[2] As a professor he continued to champion the students' right to have a say in Academy affairs, supporting the 1968/69 student movement and participating actively in the 1969 Lidl Academy (Fig. 1).

By the time Beuys was dismissed from his post in 1972, the number of students in his class had risen so sharply that eventually there were 480 enrolled in his class, including 182 new students,[3] but the Ministry intervened before the class could begin work. This development was discussed at endless senate sessions and conferences. The only way of testing applicants' aptitude for art was still the portfolio conference, at which more students now had to be rejected due to the overall increase in applications. Beuys criticised this approach: 'I have always been against portfolio assessment. Only the influx of students wasn't so huge. The art teacher training contingent

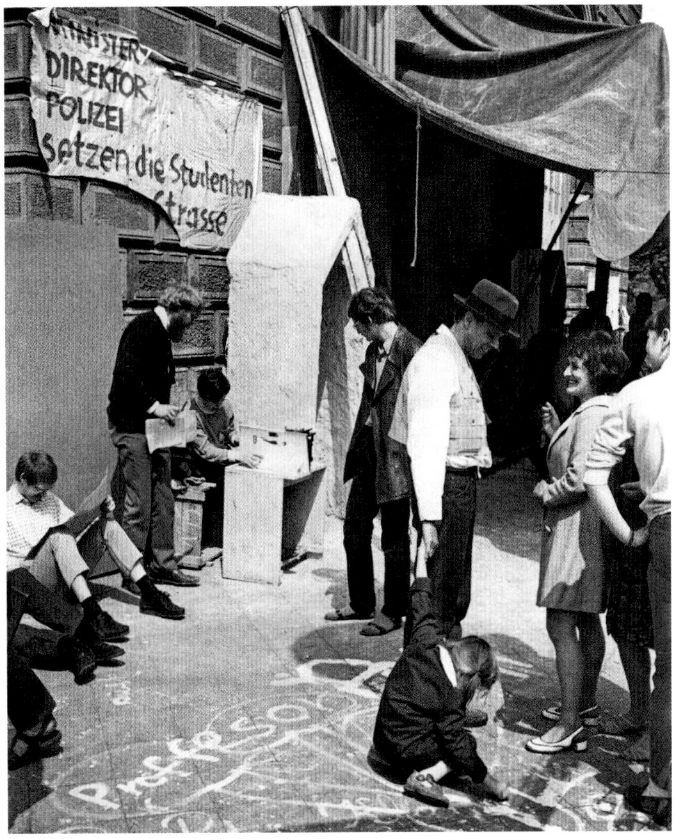

Fig. 1: Joseph Beuys in front of the Düsseldorf Art Academy, which had closed because of the Lidl Academy controversy; in the background Wachturm *[Watchtower] (destroyed), a work by Inge Mahn, 1969*

sorted things out. Only twelve out of a hundred applicants were taken. Then there weren't enough art teachers; from 1965 on they could also study in the fine arts classes and increasingly did so. Departmentalised thinking ceased to be.'[4]

Beuys was of the opinion that there were no criteria suitable for selecting applicants and described his problem with admissions as follows: 'In 1969 it became urgently apparent that portfolio review was not an adequate procedure for assessing aptitude. At first I stood alone in this with Dieter Roth: I'll take anyone who wants to come here. Their ability will be checked in two probationary terms, in difficult cases in three.'[5]

Beuys was even permitted by an Academy conference resolution of 31 January 1972 to take rejected applicants into his class.[6] At that time, however, there was no idea of the consequences that decision would have. Beuys's class now became so large that normal teaching could not take place. Still he defended having a class of 330 pupils with the argument that only half at most of his students were present on a daily basis and that they were not there the entire day but only came for talks and to seek his advice on corrections. By then one-on-one conversations were no longer possible, even if the professor was always present.[7] Beuys's idea of art, the intensive colloquies, correction sessions, and group discussions that made his teaching distinctive as well as his political commitment were not only in tune with the zeitgeist but were simply revolutionary by any standards compared to the education previously practised at the Art Academy. All this and his Performances aimed at specific targets – also in public spaces – in no time at all made Beuys into a cult figure, with whose plumes the Academy also wanted to adorn itself.

The pull Beuys exerted on students was not, however, always viewed positively by his colleagues. Some supported Beuys in his ventures, but others utterly rejected him and his public persona. Thus the Academy split into two camps, and Beuys the man and artist was the cause of the professorial schism.

The steadily increasing number of students placed increasing pressure on the Academy directorate because of course they wanted to accept all talented applicants, although they now feared for the reputation of the venerable institution, which seemed endangered by the presence of so many mediocre talents (notably in the Beuys class) who felt called to study art. In addition, the Science Ministry increased its pressure on the Academy directorate because it, too, wanted to curb the dramatic rise in student numbers and restore order to the admissions procedure. After all, there simply was not enough space at the Academy to accommodate the four hundred students who had ultimately joined Beuys's class.

The situation escalated in 1972 when Beuys occupied the student secretariat in an attempt to back up with deeds his announcement that he would admit to his class anyone who wanted to study art. Already turning into a forum for discussion, the Academy was conceding less and less space to classic studies in painting and sculpture. As a result, the admissions procedure and the need for a probationary year were also among the pivotal points of contention during these well-documented and highly explosive events. At this historic juncture, when social reform and redefining student rights were the order of the day, the freedom and power professors possessed over the admissions procedure were subjected to critical scrutiny and called into question.

In the end, the state government of North Rhine-Westphalia and Johannes Rau, then Minister for Science, won the day. Evidently alarmed at the apparent freedom and autonomy enjoyed by the Düsseldorf Art Academy and worried that students who automatically qualified as art teachers might demand places at state schools, they not only put an end to

Joseph Beuys's classroom teaching but also demanded numerous changes at the Academy, which were codified in the 1976 Framing Law for Higher Education (Hochschulrahmengesetz) enacted several years after Beuys's dismissal from the Academy. This law governed admissions and examination procedures. Since attempts were also made to apply it to many other aspects of Academy regulations, it can, at least in part, be viewed as the direct outcome of Beuys's Performances.

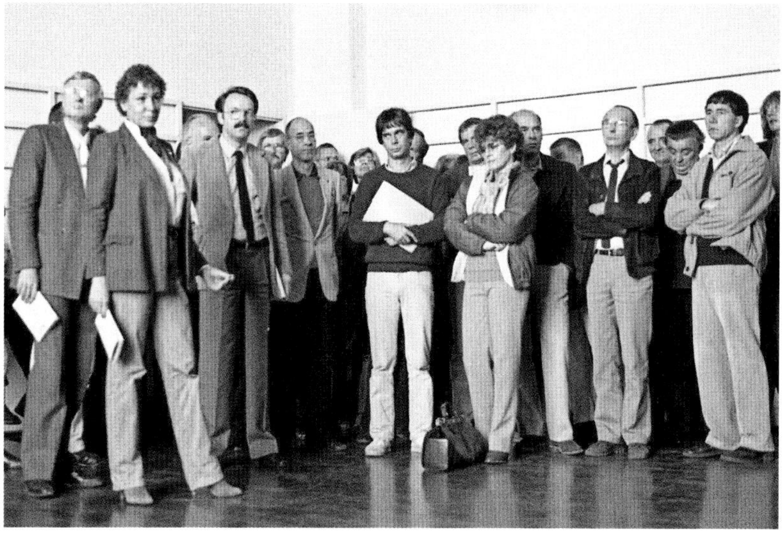

Fig. 2: The assembled professors welcoming students in the Academy conference room at the beginning of term; from left to right: Heinrich Theissing, Irmin Kamp, Hans Peter Thurn, Konrad Klapheck, Johannes Bilstein, Petra Jaeger, Christian Megert, Siegfried Cremer, Fritz Schwegler, 1982

THE ORIENTATION DEPARTMENT IS ESTABLISHED UNDER NORBERT KRICKE

When the sculptor Norbert Kricke succeeded Eduard Trier as director of the Academy in 1972, he was not just caught up in the roiling Beuys controversy. While trying to reform the Düsseldorf Art Academy on the basis of a new charter, he also had to stand his ground against the opposition of professors such as Karl Bobek and Edgar Georg Callahan. Kricke's proposal to put all beginner students into an orientation class for their first two terms on a probationary basis and have them supervised by specially qualified teachers was passed with a large majority at a staff conference on 29 January 1973.[8] At that conference Kricke explained '[...] the purpose of this class, into which all newly admitted applicants are to be placed who have not already found a teacher through a previous conversation with one. Draughtsmen and sculptors with good basic crafts skills should as far as possible be in charge of this class.'[9]
Even today the purpose of this class is that 'students who have been admitted via the (application) "portfolio conference" for two terms [...] [should] not be integrated in the existing classes from the start but should be able to find their bearings in all directions: in the classes and about the Academy teachers, in the workshops and about the academic courses offered here.'[10]

Proposals for a head of the orientation class were made at the same conference session: after a 'work presentation' a sizeable majority came out in favour of Peter Nettesheim.[11] More candidates introduced themselves at the conference a week later, and Fritz Schwegler was elected second supervisor.[12] On 3 April 1973 Norbert Kricke's motion to make Schwegler head supervisor was accepted. So Schwegler took over the orientation class at the start of the summer term (Fig. 2). Peter Nettesheim was designated – over the short term until 30 September 1973 – second lecturer.[13] In addition, the painters Peter Kleemann and Lambert Wintersberger as well as Marianne Roetzel, a sculptor, were elected lecturers to the class on 3 July 1973 by an overwhelming majority (Fig. 3).[14] With all that taken care of, the Orientation Department was implemented in the academic year 1973/74 with 120 students.[15]

How high the hopes invested in this innovation were is shown in the foreword Norbert Kricke wrote to the Festschrift commemorating the bicentenary of the founding of the Düsseldorf Art Academy:

'A real fresh start is the Orientation Department, which every student must go through. Working in this area will make clear to him what he really wants. He will discover his inclinations, pursue them, and thus go a way towards finding himself. Fascination as the kindling point of the artistic imagination awaits him here. If he doesn't find it, he'll see early enough that he is not suited to that way. Seeking and finding and again seeking is to be the guiding principle of this new Academy, which is in fact nothing other than a broad-based orientation field.'[16]

Peter Kleemann recollects those years:

'Rooms for independent work were at their [first-term students'] disposal in a makeshift annexe. Weekly conferences with the O-Department teachers were planned for, plus brief introductions to elementary art techniques and communal activities. The students' work was to be exhibited at the end of each term and discussed collectively, whereby after the second term a senate committee had to decide along with the O-Department teachers on which students should be permitted to continue studying.'[17]

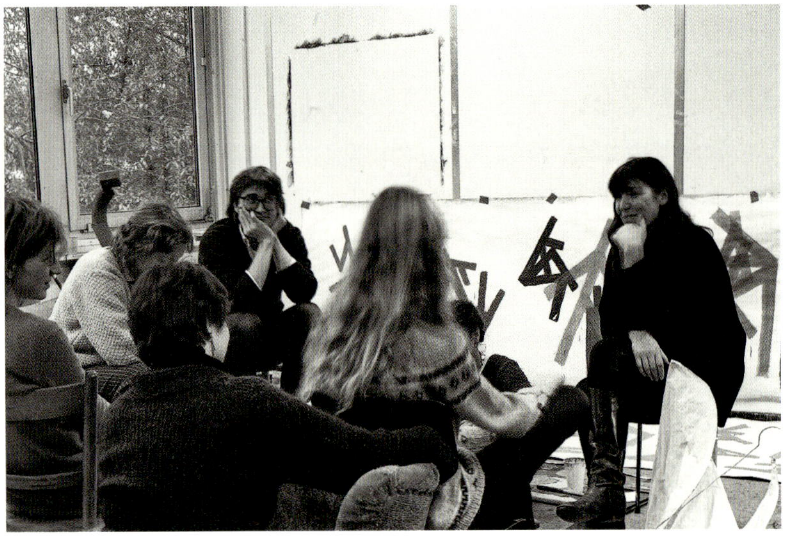

Fig. 3: Ulla Hahn (right) with students in the Düsseldorf Art Academy Orientation Department, n.d.

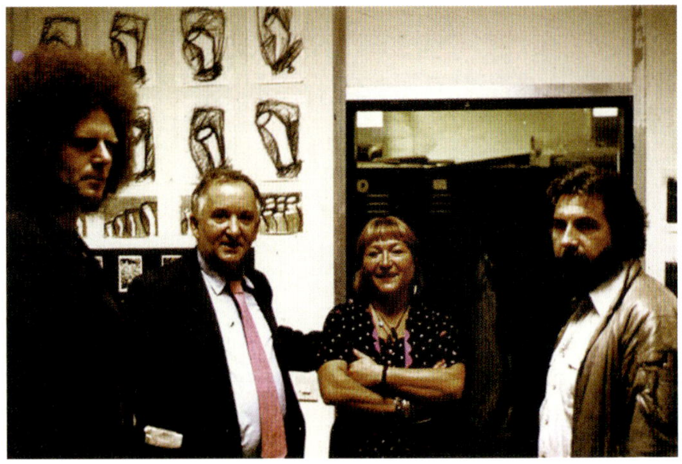

Fig. 4: From left to right: Klaus Rinke, Norbert Kricke, Luise Kimme, and Gotthard Graubner, c.1977

In 1975 it was decided to extend Fritz Schwegler's contract as a lecturer in the Orientation Department, and that year the decision was taken to appoint him to a professorship for painting in the Art Education Department.[18]

Moreover, a professorship was established for the Orientation Department, probably to raise its profile and to counter internal attempts at promoting in-house candidates to head it.[19] On 20 October 1975 an application was made to appoint the sculptor Luise Kimme, who had studied at Saint Martin's School of Art in London with Irmin Kamp, head of the Orientation Department.[20] Kimme took up the post on 1 April 1976 and, although it had been initially limited to three years, she held it until she retired in 2002 (Fig. 4).[21]

She was supported by Peter Kleemann, who had been a lecturer with a short-term contract in the Orientation Department since 1973. He, too, would stay on there to teach – later as a tenured lecturer – until he retired in 2002. Kleemann reports on working in the Orientation Department:

'In 1978 Kimme wrote in a report on the Orientation Department: in England and the United States, Foundation Courses look as follows: teaching form and colour, sticking strictly to working on prescribed subject areas; the upshot is a fettered, independent way of working. This is true of the first two terms. After that the first Academy year begins, structured to correspond to the teaching we do in the O-Department. On my travels giving lectures I have noticed that both students and teachers were very impressed by the high level and the independence of students in our O-Department.'[22]

From the outset the Orientation Department was intended as preparatory to studying in a class taught by an artist. Offering courses for students or guiding them in any particular direction as artists was for the most part eschewed. The chief aim of the Orientation Department was to provide students with a framework within which they had the possibility of finding out which subjects interested them personally as well as their own forms of expression. Apart from critique sessions and colloquies, most supervision of students was on an individual, one-on-one basis. Even drawing from the nude – regarded by some as an indispensable part of any study of art but by others as completely unnecessary and outmoded – had always been part of the courses on offer although it had never been made a compulsory part of the curriculum. To give priority to the aesthetic and hands-on art side, academic subjects were even omitted at first.

Based on the view that only artists could teach art, equal treatment of students aspiring to teach art at state schools and fine arts students was another important principle informing the Orientation Department. What was new, however, was that there were examinations after the Orientation phase. This was met with vehement student resistance: the professors – among them Irmin Kamp, Gerhard Richter, and Norbert Kricke – were put under such pressure at the first examination that onlookers had to be excluded before it could take place.

Ultimately, however, just a handful of students were threatened with exclusion from the Academy, and even they were granted eight days' time to obtain the endorsement of a professor, which would ensure the continuance of their studies. The only students to be categorically rejected were those who had not exhibited any work at all. The Kimme-Kleemann team – whose attitudes differed radically in some respects – took care of the Orientation Department for decades, their open-mindedness and liberal approaches providing several generations of young artists with a good start. Luise Kimme, an energetic person full of zest for life, had a positive effect on all students who came into contact with her whereas Peter Kleemann was a rather introverted and thoughtful teacher, who devoted most of his time to intensively and methodically mentoring the painters in the orientation class. The teaching offered in the Orientation Department was constantly enriched and varied by the presence of new tenured and non-tenured lecturers. The main reason for the regular change in non-tenured lecturers was the higher education law, which required that a third teaching contract extension had to be followed by tenure, which would not have been in the interests of the Academy.

The artists who taught for a while at least in the Orientation Department also included, in addition to the above mentioned, Lothar Baumgarten (1986/87), Jürgen Drescher (1993–1995), Isa Genzken (1976–1978), Bernd Koberling (1978/79), Bernd Minnich (1981–1983), Inge Mahn (1981–1983), Bernard Lüthi (1979/80), and Wilhelm Mundt (1989/90).

In 1978 Norbert Kricke offered me a short-term contract, which surprised me – as I was a completely unknown outsider – but I was glad to accept. After my contract had been renewed twice, my status became tenured. During the years I worked in the Orientation Department, I noticed how important the right start to studying art is and how necessary it is to stop understandable gaps in one's education as well as promoting the emergence of forms of expression in art without, however, intervening in the actual individual artistic decision-making process, guiding it, or disrupting it.

When the Orientation Department was instituted in 1973, pavilions comprising a surface area of some 1,000 square metres and connected with the main building were erected on the Academy lawn at Fritz Roeber Straße.[23] Both the Film and Video Department, which was founded at the same time as the Orientation Department and was first headed by Ursula Wevers and later by Nam June Paik, followed by Nan Hoover, and a seminar room for art history were also housed in the same temporary annexe.

While they were in the Orientation Department, students were always encouraged to take part in academic events. Attendance was especially high at the seminars on contemporary art given by Dr Ulrich Krempel and Kasper König. For this purpose 'interviews' were also arranged with representatives of this subject area. Events of that kind gave students in the Orientation Department insight into the teaching that went on in the various academic departments at the Academy, such as education, sociology, and art history. Professors who stood out here were Johannes Bilstein and Hans Peter Thurn, as well as

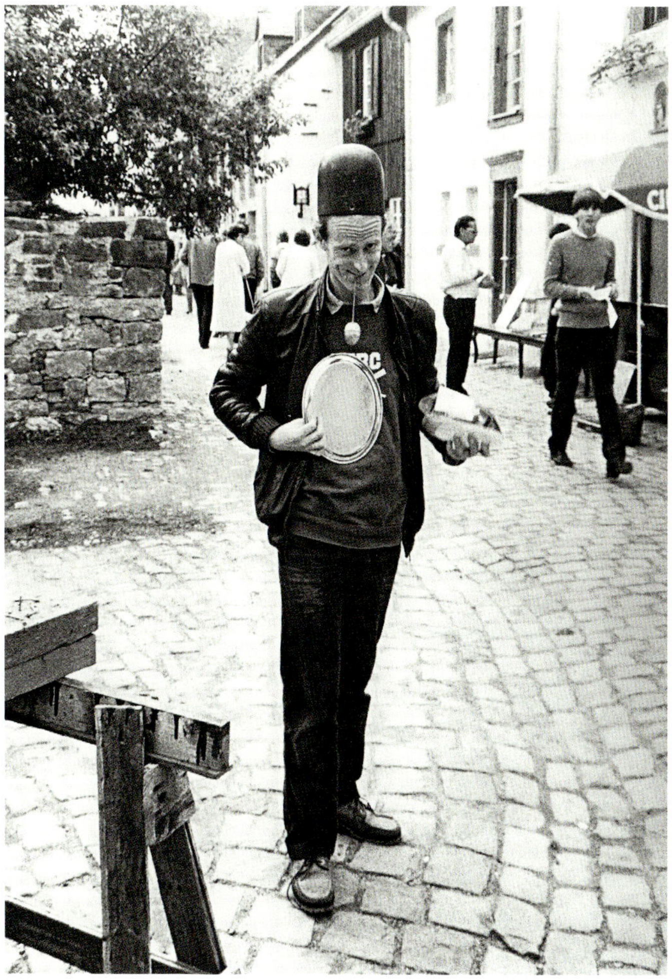

Fig. 5: Anthony Cragg with a flea-market find during a trip to Kronenburg for students from the Orientation Department, 1982

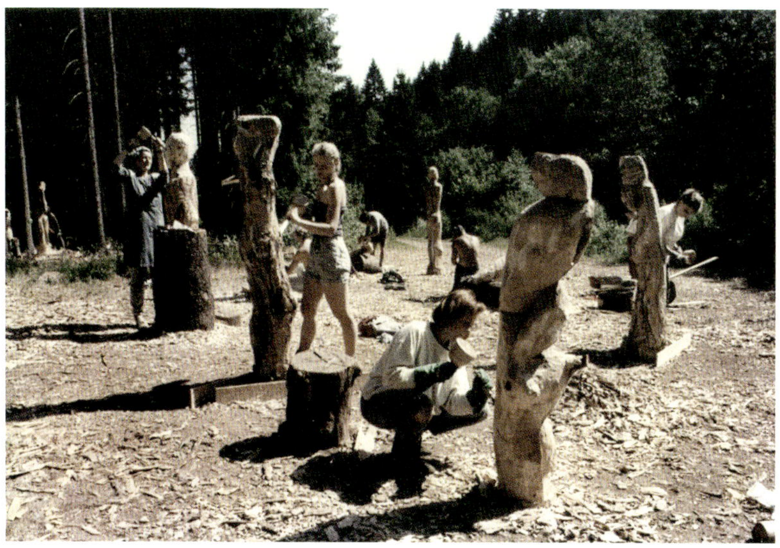

Fig. 6: Students from the Orientation Department in Kronenburg, c.1985

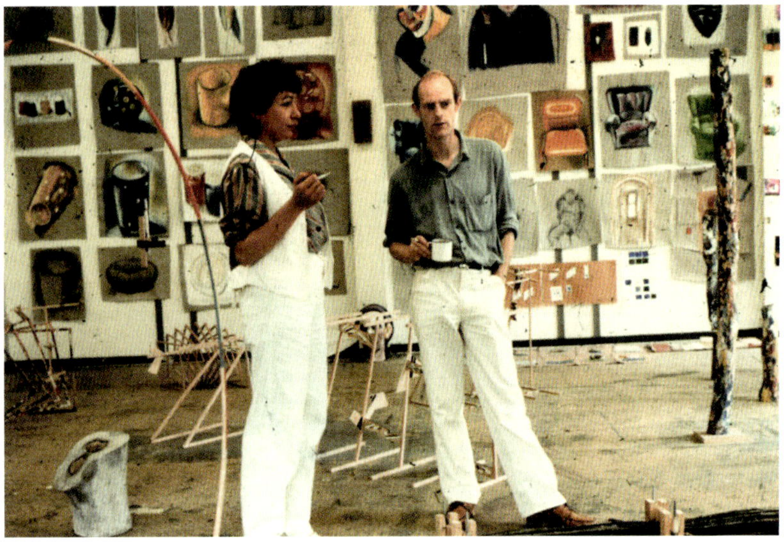

Fig. 7: Irmin Kamp and Anthony Cragg in the rooms of the Orientation Department, c.1983

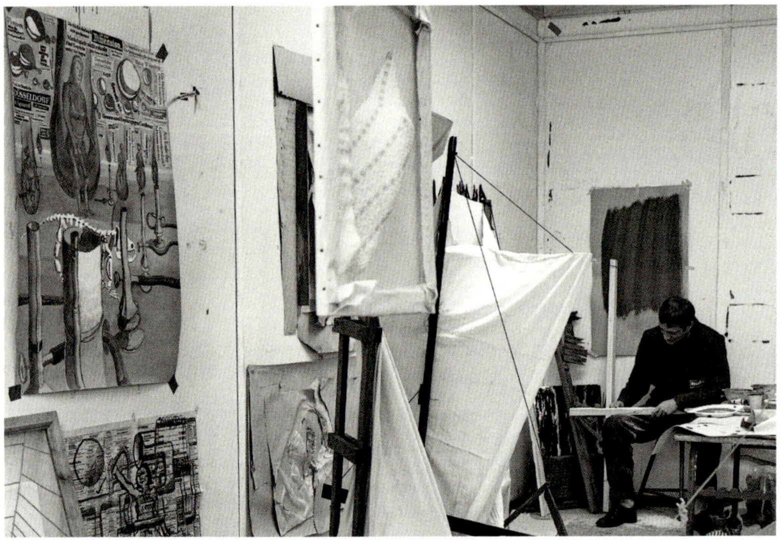

Fig. 8: A student in the Orientation Department, mid-1980s

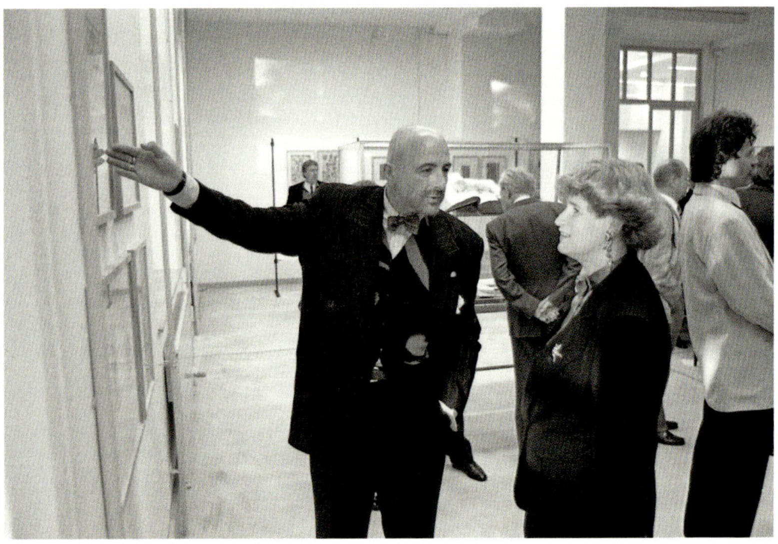

Fig. 9: Markus Lüpertz guiding Minister Anke Brunn through the opening exhibition in the basement of the Rhine Tract, 1989

Walter Jürgen Hofmann, who was willing to let himself in for very open discussions in his 'School of Seeing'.[24]

Since 1977 students in the Orientation Department have been offered the chance to spend two weeks at the former branch of the Art Academy in Kronenburg in the Eifel region (Figs. 5, 6).[25] This practice has become a customary end-of-term excursion and represents a high point of the Orientation Department, with new approaches to work often being discovered at it just before final examinations. The contacts and friendships made during the time spent in the Orientation Department are often of great importance for a student's further Academy career and later life.

Originally planned as a 'five-year stopgap solution',[26] the pavilions continued in use until 1989 because the extension of the Academy to incorporate the municipal pawnbroker's building was constantly delayed (Figs. 7, 8). Since 1989 the Orientation Department has been housed on the ground floor of this adjacent structure, now the Rheinflügel [Rhine Tract] of the Academy (Fig. 9).

After Professor Kimme left in 2002, Udo Dziersk, a painter who had been a student of Markus Lüpertz's, was made a professor and charged with heading the Orientation Department. He has in the meantime succeeded in building up a rigorously structured course in which the relatively brief time spent in it is put to the best use possible. Moreover, writing a paper has been a mandatory part of the Orientation Department examination since the winter term of 2011/12. Finally, and very importantly, the Orientation Department courses have been an important module of the bachelor's and master's course of studies, which has replaced the state examinations for students training to teach art at state schools.

Most recently, highly committed young men and women teaching on short-term contracts in the Orientation Department have included Franziska von Hasselbach (2003–2005), Lin-May Saeed (2009/10), Felix Schramm (2011–2013), Max Schulze (2007–2009), Elke Nebel (2009–2011), and Rosilene Ludovico (2011–2013).

In 2012 the number of teachers on short-term contracts was increased from four to five under the auspices of the Higher Education Pact to improve the study content. Oliver Helbig was the first to be given a short-term contract for photography in the Orientation Department. In addition, Gereon Krebber was made its second professor.

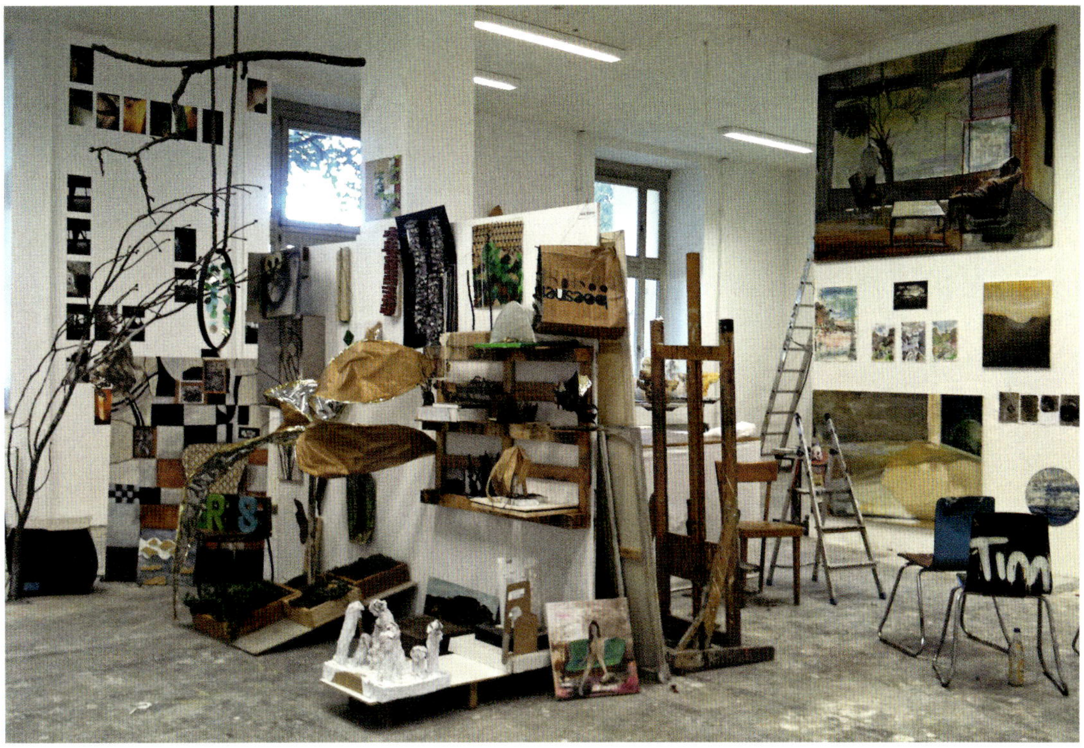

Fig. 10: An exhibition in the Orientation Department, July 2013

Since it was first established, the Orientation Department has constantly been subjected to criticism for all sorts of reasons. Now it is such an important part of the courses taught at the Academy that no one can imagine studying art without it (Fig. 10).

If the training offered by an academy is to be judged on the basis of how many successful artists it has produced, the Düsseldorf Art Academy can be (more than) proud of the results it has achieved since implementing the Orientation Department.

NOTES

1 Letter from Rissa to the author of 5 October 2013.
2 Susanne Anna (ed.), *Joseph Beuys, Düsseldorf*, exhib. cat. Düsseldorf, Ostfildern 2008, p. 27.
3 Johannes Stüttgen, *Der ganze Riemen. Der Auftritt von Joseph Beuys als Lehrer. Die Chronologie der Ereignisse an der Staatlichen Kunstakademie Düsseldorf 1966–1972*, Cologne 2008, p. 908.
4 Georg Jappe, 'Nicht einige wenige sind berufen, sondern alle. Interview mit Joseph Beuys über ästhetische Erziehung', *Kunstnachrichten*, Issue 9, No. 6, February 1973, n.p.
5 Anna (see n. 2), p. 103. Further events are well documented there.
6 Jappe (see n. 4).
7 Ibid.
8 Session on 9 February 1973, 'Konferenzakten der Kunstakademie Düsseldorf', in: *Chronik der Kunstakademie*, year 1973, Düsseldorf Art Academy archives.
9 Session on 2 February 1973, in: ibid.
10 Letter from Peter Kleemann to the author dated 3 September 2013.
11 Session on 2 February 1973 (see n. 9).
12 Session on 9 February 1973 (see n. 8).
13 Session on 1 April 1973, in: *Chronik der Kunstakademie*, year 1973, Düsseldorf Art Academy archives.
14 Session on 3 July 1973, in: ibid.
15 Kleemann, (see n. 10).
16 Norbert Kricke, 'Die neue Akademie', in: Eduard Trier (ed.), *Zweihundert Jahre Kunstakademie Düsseldorf*, Düsseldorf 1973, p. XIII.
17 Kleemann (see n. 10).
18 *Chronik der Kunstakademie Düsseldorf*, year 1975, Düsseldorf Art Academy archives.
19 Ibid.
20 Ibid.
21 Ibid.
22 Kleemann (see n. 10).
23 Minutes of 1 April 1973 (see n. 13); also see Helga Meister, 'Studienanfänger in den Garten "verbannt" – Die Orientierungsstufe wird weiter ausgebaut', *Düsseldorfer Nachrichten*, 18 August 1973.
24 Kleemann (see n. 10).
25 Since 1962 the house, which has been changed into an educational establishment of the state of North Rhine-Westphalia, had been used for Art Academy probationary classes yet it was not until 1977 that these trips were regularly scheduled. Luise Kimme also regularly schooled participants in wood sculpture in her own studio there.
26 Ibid. and Meister (see n. 23).

TEACHING AND ART – OR WHAT IS TEACHABLE?

Markus Lüpertz: Apocrypha

1. ART IS NOT TEACHABLE

An old Bauhaus thesis: The only thing that is teachable is the craft – understanding and practising. Craft at a high level of skill is merely an intensification or a lofty precondition for coming closer to art. On the basis of that thesis the Bauhaus cultivated design and fashion, practised taste, in order to sensitise the era for great art.

Art is not teachable. But teaching can influence the environment to allow art to happen. Teaching art means violating it. Trying to track it down means laying traps for it. Killing it, eviscerating it, and selling it to fools and soldiers at picturesque market stalls.

Then art dies as an earthly toy and remains childless.

Let us abandon the attempt to approach art more closely by teaching. Instead, let us prepare an atmosphere or landscape for it, in which cymbals and shawms replace breathing. Look at meadows with grass that never turns brown, with flowers that never fade. And every billowing and blowing sounds like a song, and rippling laughter accompanies rivers. Let us be astonished that shade despite all that light is only lush green moss and knows nothing of darkness and menace.

Let us prepare a broad tent in which everything is bathed in light and red glows, yellow burns, and blue is as translucent as the wings of the angels dancing with us.

2. CONVEY ATMOSPHERE

What is teachable about art then? Most certainly being an artist. Wearing a costume helps and makes this particular vocation visible. One begins by moving one's bed or one sleeps on the floor for a while. One drinks one's coffee black, splays out one's little finger while drinking it, and has one's hair cut or has it tumbling in loose locks over one's forehead. Wears an open collar like an artist and keeps the tailors busy making bespoke skin-tight velvet coats. Cultivates a glance that takes it all in and attracts attention by making erratic gestures (as if to shoo away midges).

3. BEING AN ARTIST

Being an artist means engaging with the bourgeois environment. The artist is the artist of the bourgeoisie. Not of art. Because the citizen as one's contemporary is merely the vehicle or rather the host (of art) but is unaware of being necessary.
And the artist makes him – the unaware citizen – eternal. For he has an established place in the choir of the tides and is a witness and step to Olympus in the eternal song of art.

4. EVERYDAY AESTHETICS

One can teach, for instance, and learn. An exerting of influence. Influence on the responsibility that the artist has for these times. When the artist tortures his surroundings with genius and restlessness, he places innovations as traps in front of door and bed and shows these times their permanent inadequacy. That is why the artist demands detail, venerates the poetry of beauty, views himself as an ongoing aesthetic monitor, knows nothing of slackening powers and ageing, and forces his contemporaries to think about things and ask questions if they want to understand him (the artist).

5. BEING AN ARTIST MEANS BEING A CLUBMAN THROUGH AND THROUGH

Teaching and learning means the necessity of togetherness.

For being an artist is an entertaining evening event in which artists juggle with their problems, allow themselves to be spewed with fire, and make balls dance on their fingers and the tips of their toes. Conversations are witty tirades full of casual solutions, and levity of presentation is what makes the seriousness of great art visible. Then, at a late hour, their mouths overflowing, they – the artists – sing choral odes to genius and the eternal good fortune of being a master who has fallen from the skies.

6. BELONGING TO THE CASTE

Belonging must be earned by attitude, demeanour, bearing, and aura. He who lives noble values belongs, is careless – that means, flippant, squanders his work and his knowledge, keeps back no thoughts, and is ready to have everyone share in his exceptionalism.

He who has no fear of the achievements of his fellow colleagues belongs. An artist, therefore, who is rewarded with the achievement of all and in the time is duty bound only to the work and to accomplishing his own contribution.

7. ACCEPTANCE OF A TEMPORARY HIERARCHY

One can also teach and learn that there is always the first in a given time. Our guild needs the stars also as a justification for claims of quality and guidelines.

Accepting the hierarchy of one's time is certainly not a problem. (Of course one is obliged to try constantly to influence this ranking.) For the 'best' is only the 'best' of his time, yet he still achieves a great work. For the future he is a value guide and a guideline of the largest dimension possible.

And time is fleeting and nothing lasts in it.

Nor, therefore, any judgement. We do better to establish ourselves in an eternity whose duration must exceed a single day. Let us settle the morning and prevent the day from ending.

8. EDUCATION IS QUESTIONABLE, IN MY OPINION NECESSARY

Education is a matter of controversy in fine art. For the genius needs nothing. For genius is responsible for all failure and need not know anything. However, everything is accessible to the genius, hence also education.

In addition, education adorns genius, is a gracefully curving gold band which holds in place the fine, wavy hair of the exalted head and now and then distracts from a wanton yellow flash from the depths of the eyes. Education enables genius to seduce delicate souls who are repelled by the power of his great art and prefer to venerate his knowledge and essence.

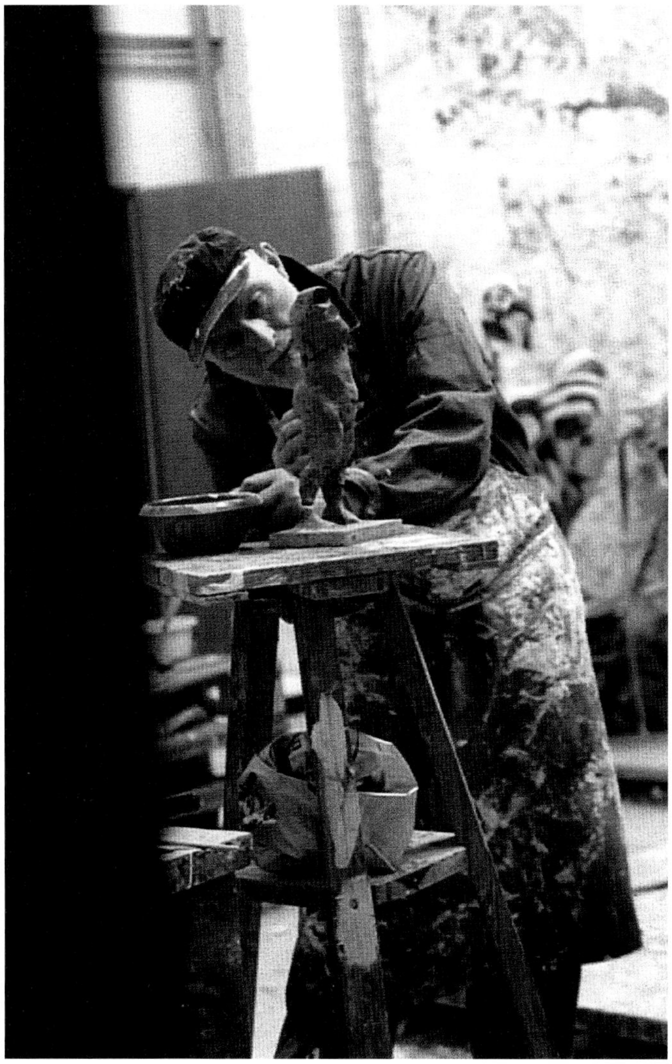

Markus Lüpertz in his studio, 2005

9. COMMUNICATION OR REFLECTING ON HIS INTENTIONS

For the artist there are only questions, no answers.

The next question is always an answer and warranty for his next work. The artist always presents his work to the public as a question. And only very rarely does the viewer succeed in answering – but the artist never does. The artist asks the birds in the tree. The wind about its journey. Asks the mute fish, then asks the question himself, which, however, threatens with answers and drives the artist away.

10. A LESSON: LEARN TO CONVERSE WITHOUT TIRING OF CONVERSATION!

Speaking is the artist's most joyous, his keenest, pleasure. Chatting about overturned pots of paint, treading on tubes of oils and squashing them, and cursing about dried-up brushes are buried crocks of gold over which arches a colourful bow of cheerful scraps of words.

11. IDOL

Gods need art and art needs gods.

The idol is a standard for measuring quality.

For quality can only be ascertained through comparison. And we must, therefore, compare ourselves with the best; we decide who the best are. And that again and again. We must force ourselves to deluge the idol with our best skill and knowledge. To give as our tribute to the idol a loftiness such that it is never attainable. A loftiness that we can only surpass in our most divine moments. But ultimately do not want because attaining perfection would be the end of creating, for perfection is death.

The Tower of Babel was unnecessary, for if you want to meet God, dig a pit.

12. EFFUSIVE CHARACTER

Being effusive distinguishes the artist from all enthusiasts. For being effusive does not mean giving up one's own identity. But being enthusiastic does.

Being effusive is a crucial aspiration of one's own possibilities and ideas. I am effusive about the inspirational works of friends and companions. In the firm belief that the possibility of the impossible is a mission and a vocation for all of us in our time. Being effusive is an entirely real concept and a wing the angels have lent us.

13. SENSE OF MISSION

The artist must preach. He is always out and about on a mission. To conquer inertia and oblivion, foes that house in the trenches and in the nooks and crannies of blasé souls.

The artist who uses the word as a broom to clean streets and wields a hammer to break milky panes that stare blind and opaque is in a necessary rage and inspirited by his mission and vocation. For art is the sole wrath that rages in the here and now and is right.

14. CLAIM TO ETERNITY

Art, painting, is of divine origin.

Painting is after all the content of seeing and makes what is seen real. Man cannot extinguish that light. Yet growing blind by degrees dims the spirit of perception. In our idea of eternity, painting is a warranty for seeing, and this seeing is given to us by God as a gift every day anew. Every opening of an eye is proof of the necessity of pictures. And painting illustrates light. Day is the piece of paper on which clear thoughts and understanding are captured in the most beautiful script.

First light – which dispels a dream – the always renewed birth of colour. For colour, light's most beautiful child, knows nothing of the boards nailed askew that deny light and promise night; the morning has died or drowned in the last sunset.

Yet the angels assure us that eternity is light and, reflected by thousands of crystals, dyes the rainbow.

15. IS ART THE OPPOSITE OF BEING DEAD?

Art is more eternal than death.

Death is an end, but art lasts and tells the artists – because it lives longer than its creator – beautiful fairy tales and amusing anecdotes about eternity – a rather plump, serious-minded female – eternally busy killing time, unloved.

And the Grim Reaper is too emaciated for her liking; she doesn't want to kiss him. He's more interested in us humans and spoils love, makes flowers fade, and sees to it that a kiss does not keep for ever. And Death hates art as he hates everything divine that has been given to man. He only clutches the flesh but he cannot get his hands on the God within us.

The artist sees Death as his opposite number, observes decay and ceasing to be. Notes the swish of the scythe. And lives parting and loss and is always one step ahead of Death.

For the victor is always the demiurge who uses the genius of the world to create what is eternal. For we live in pictures, and time remains an episode, does not travel with us to Arcadia. Does not hear the eternal rustling of a painted tree. Time knows nothing of eternally taking fright when a nymph hastens away from a faun. Time is at best a stomach ache or lovelornness, merely a wind, a light breeze. In front of pictures Death can only be amazed at the diversity and imagination which painters have dedicated to his importance and his power.

Death is only in the terrors of the living; Death is his comrade and liberates him. That, too, can be taught and learnt.

THE DEVELOPMENT OF THE ART WORKSHOPS SINCE 1945

Lothar Krüll

'Workshops? Pardon me, what do you mean by workshops?' Nor were there any, confirms Sonja Mataré, daughter of the acting director of the Düsseldorf Art Academy in 1945 and 1946. 'And my father didn't need much for his students except perhaps a couple of woodcarving knives. He had them whittle wooden spoons, model pottery pots; for the first three or four terms they did no work of their own.'[1]

Ewald Mataré found the journey by boat – the bridges had been destroyed in the war – to Düsseldorf to the Academy from Büderich too time-consuming. So without further ado he arranged for rooms for some students nearby. Beuys lived on the Meerbusch side anyway so his students worked together with their professor in his studio.[2]

While Mataré practised the classic teacher and pupil communal studio, he envisaged for academy training 'teaching entirely based on drawing; not until two years of thorough drawing study had been completed would there be workshop study in wood or stone and for painters a painting class. [...] At the end, that is, after four years of drawing and workshop study, would come the transition to a master class, where students can work independently.'[3]

All that was available until well into the 1950s for that workshop study he wanted were a foundry, a plaster-mould-making workshop, a weaving workshop, and a workshop for lithography.

After the workshop idea had increasingly gained influence at German academies early in the twentieth century,[4] by the 1930s there was already a typography workshop (J. Spindler), a plaster-mould-making workshop (1937 E. Meyer, *c.*1940 H. Isenmann), a bronze foundry (K. Mühl, *c.*1940, no other name known), and a weaving workshop (Miss M. Jahns). It should be noted here that the existence of a division for painting techniques was a given at a painting academy like the one in Düsseldorf. It was, however, dressed up with a chair and a professor,[5] hence was not classified as a workshop.[6] In about 1946, even after the Academy building had sustained such severe damage, the workshop for lithography (P. Marliani), the plaster-mould-making workshop (E. Meyer), and the weaving workshop (Miss M. Jahns) were in operation; in 1948,[7] on the other hand, only the lithography workshop (P. Marliani) and the bronze foundry (P. Lindner) were left. Director Kamps reported in the *Jahrbuch der Staatlichen Kunstakademie Düsseldorf 1948–1950* [Düsseldorf Art Academy Yearbook 1948–1950] that Hermann Isenmann had returned on 1 June 1949 to repair the plaster cast collection, first in Room 11, then in Room 25. Isenmann would also 'as formerly, teach an introductory course for students in plaster mould-making as well as the crafts techniques used in stone and wood carving. Thus another gap has been closed in the curriculum. The small gas-fired muffle furnace in the plaster-mould-maker's workshop has been set up following the completion of restoration work on it. It is in operation.'[8]

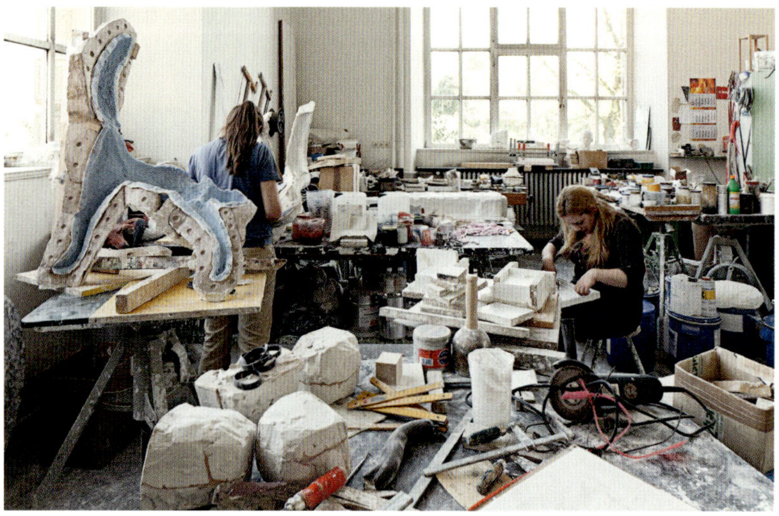

Fig. 1: The plaster-mould-making workshop, Düsseldorf Art Academy, 2013

The Academy admission requirements reveal how important good crafts skills still were for prospective students as late as the 1940s: for aspiring painters and graphic artists 'crafts training as a decoration painter or preliminary schooling attested to by successful attendance at a German Crafts Guild master school' and for sculptors 'crafts training in stone, wood, or metalworking' were required. Only candidates for admission to the stage design course got off lightly with 'proof of particular aptitude' as the only practical admissions requirement.[9] A shift in priorities can be observed soon afterwards, and workshops reverted to secondary importance in the teaching of artistic and technical skills. Evidently the desirability of admitting students who had been less 'spoilt' by so much crafts training was beginning to override earlier requirements.

Mataré even wanted to admit fourteen-year-olds as students 'in order to ensure a well-rounded education as early as possible',[10] a proposal, which, however, was rejected. The upshot was that by the 1950s the only practical requirement for admission to the Academy was 'proof of crafts skills'.[11]

From 1956 on, the following practical training resources were listed in the course calendar under the heading 'Workshops and Institutes': a printing workshop headed by Willi Sibbel, a master typesetter, a plaster-mould-making workshop under Hermann Isenmann, a bronze foundry under P. Lindner, and the Institute for Painting Techniques under Alfred Eckhardt – for some time supported by Dr Jakob Koch, a chemist.[12] In 1977 Siegfried Cremer was appointed to a chair of painting techniques, assisted by Theodor Ramrath as a permanently employed technician. Kirsten Lampert has been professor of painting techniques since 1998.

Hermann Isenmann, who had been in charge of plaster-mould-making since 1949, resided in the old studio building on the west side of the Academy, which sustained damage during the war. Kurt Räder, formerly a lecturer of sculpture in stone and plastics, reports that Isenmann took on the teaching appointment on condition he would be able to use the tools and studio for his freelance work as well. The studio had a raised floor to facilitate the delivery by horse-drawn wagons of models, plaster figures, and moulds. Isenmann executed work for Düsseldorf sculptors as well as Academy professors. Räder, in his capacity as a trained sculptor in stone, executed works for fellow professors Zoltán Székessy and Josef (Sepp) Mages.[13] When Isenmann retired, Franz Küsters became head of the plaster-mould-making workshop in 1976, who was succeeded in 2003 by Bernhard Kucken.

As Kurt Räder tells it, Hans Schwippert, director of the Academy, summoned him to his office in the early 1960s: Schwippert proposed to expand the Academy workshop facilities on Bauhaus lines.[14] A bronze foundry, a plaster-mould-making facility, and workshops for printing and painting techniques were already in operation. However, no appointments for teaching wood and stone sculpture were forthcoming (Figs. 1–3). To advance the expansion of the individual disciplines despite the lack of teachers, Schwippert succeeded in hiring Wilhelm Hable from Professor Székessy's master class as an assistant to Székessy in wood sculpture, and Kurt Räder as assistant to Manfred Sieler, professor of sculpture in stone. Claus Rudolf

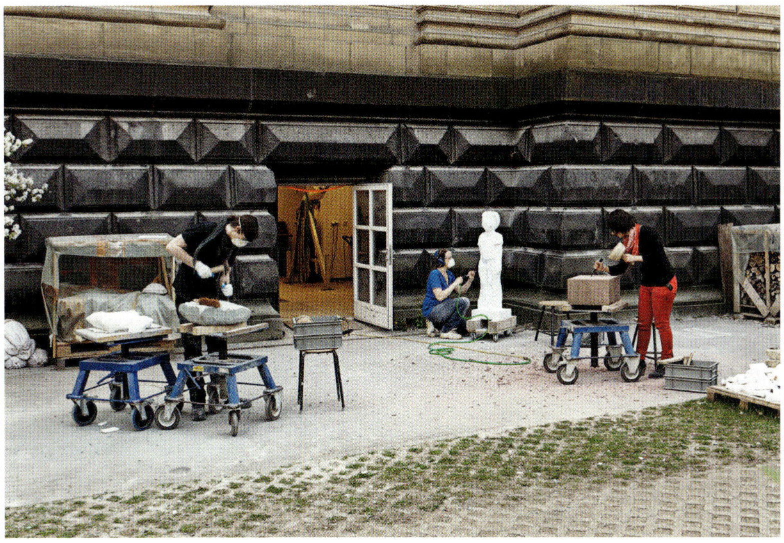

Fig. 2: The stone-sculpture workshop, Düsseldorf Art Academy, 2013

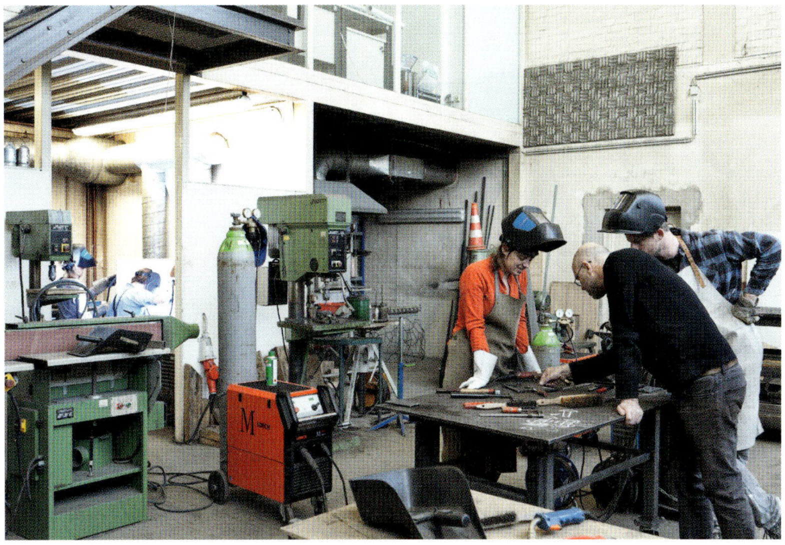

Fig. 3: The metal-sculpture workshop, Düsseldorf Art Academy, 2013

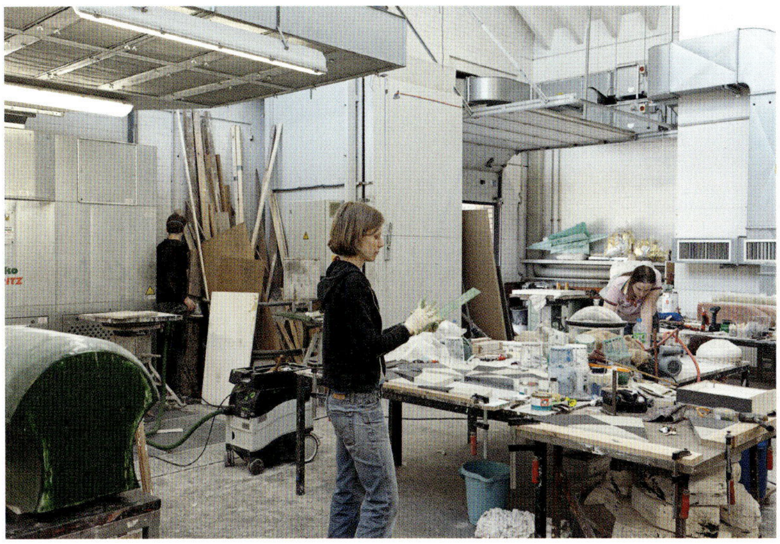

Fig. 4: The plastics workshop, Düsseldorf Art Academy, 2013

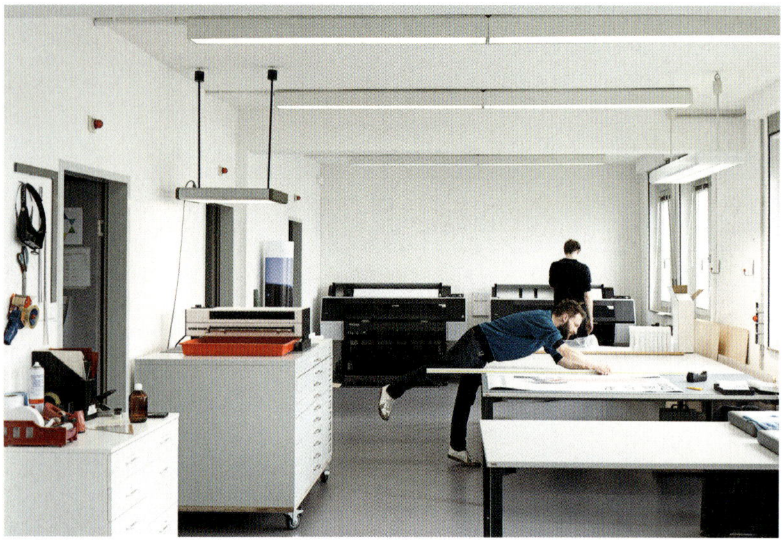

Fig. 5: The photo workshop, Düsseldorf Art Academy, 2013

Barthelmess, a sculptor and grand master of the Potters' Guild, joined the Art Academy on a contract to teach ceramics.

Räder moved into the studio building, which had been built for the purpose by Rudolf Schwarz in 1956 and was known as the Steinhaus [Stone House]. There Räder was head of stone sculpture from 1962 on. He began to experiment with plastics there, at first with moulded plastic. Later he attended courses in Duroplast and thermosetting plastic in Aachen. Hence he was able to annexe an institute for plastics to the stone-sculpture building and head it as well. From 1974 on he was supported by Monika Staiger. The workshop was finally split in 1977. Rolf Jörres took over the stone sculpture side. His successor, Gunnar Krabbe, added to the technical facilities in the workshop so that it could also offer working in composite stone and poured concrete. After Staiger and Räder left, the plastics workshop has been headed by Andreas Bee and Lothar Krüll since 1993 (Fig. 4).

Another split took place in the workshop for bronze founding and metalworking. Hein Lemmen, who headed it, offered the entire range of subjects and techniques related to metalworking until 1974, when Richard Tesch, a master industrial metalworker, came to work there as a technician employed by the technical service before becoming head of the metal-sculpture workshop in 1975. Gerd-Werner Theil also came that year. He had solved technical problems Professor Norbert Kricke had with his steel sculpture and was now wanted in the workshops. Since, however, there were not enough permanent posts, Theil was hired in 1976 as a stoker at the Academy. By 1984 he was able to take over a post as technician. After Tesch left in 1984, Kricke's former assistant for metal sculpture, Dirk Gottfriedt, became head of the workshop, which moved into Kricke's old classroom in the Steinhaus. In 1995 Gerd-Werner Theil also became a teacher for specialised tasks. Axel Kreiser succeeded Gottfriedt in 2011. Herbert Willems, assistant to Professor Anthony Cragg, succeeded Theil in the winter term of 2013.

Hiving off the metal sculpture section left the bronze foundry with still very little space and limited technical facilities. After Hein Lemmen left, Raimund Kittl, who ran a foundry of his own in Düsseldorf harbour, offered to teach Academy students in his own workshop, and in 1977 he became head of the Academy foundry. Working on site and off campus proved viable in practice, so Karl-Heinz Schmäke, Kittl's successor, who also runs a foundry in Düsseldorf, continued to teach students off campus. Agata Kowalska has been head of the Academy foundry since 2012. However, since the technical facilities no longer meet today's standards and students' requirements, founding is still done off campus after the casting moulds have been prepared.

The tried-and-tested way to the workshop via an assistantship was continued under directors Eduard Trier and Norbert Kricke. Mladen Lipecki, for instance, started out as an assistant and went on to a workshop for photography open to all students: it was left to the photographer Hilla Becher, already rigorously trained in her profession, to set up a small darkroom with a photo lab in her class with the permission of her professor, Walter Breker, where she could also instruct other students in techniques.[15] Lipecki, who had freelanced for several professors since 1960, later took over the task of organising and building up a photo lab as an assistant. Since 1990 Babette Bangemann has been head of the photo workshop. She has kept up with the rapid pace of technical developments by introducing digital photography and digital processing of photographs (Fig. 5, 6).

Similarly, assistantships in the stage design class have led to a stage design workshop, which, however, has remained the sole prerogative of this class. Over the decades, this workshop was accompanied by a succession of teachers on limited contracts and assistants, until Ruth Groß became head of it in 1991.

In 1968 an attempt was made to devote Academy facilities to more modern and interdisciplinary fields. To that end, the stage design class merged with the film class in 1969 and was renamed 'Theatre and Film' – although the two were to remain independent departments.[16] Wolf-Jürgen Seeßelberg was given a limited (until 1973) teaching contract, and two years later Ole John Povlsen, a Dane, became artistic director of the department. Discussions with far-reaching implications followed in 1973, questioning the value of a film class with workshop function. Negative remarks were made in the senate about the orientation of the film class towards documentary film-making: the training was too one-sided and deficient from both the technical and the aesthetic angles. Only a single vote stood in the way of abolishing the film class. Director Kricke asked for a vote on changing the class into a workshop, which, however, ended in a draw.[17] A new film department was supposed to build up the subject of media education for television, radio, and other communications media whereas the stage design class was reduced in size in 1975 and became independent again under Professor Karl Kneidl. Finally, in 1976, Ole John, head of the film class, was dismissed without notice.[18] In July 1976 Hugo Sartorius, who had until then been a driver for the Academy, advanced to employee status as a technician in the Film Department. A year later, Ursula Schum-Wevers became temporary head of the Film and Video Department. In 1977 the senate resolved to use the class as a facility for the entire Academy. Finally Nam June Paik was appointed in 1979 to a chair for video and film. When Schum-Wevers left the Academy in 1986 to become a professor at Wuppertal University, Hubertus Neuerburg temporarily served as professor for film and took up a lectureship in film documentation.[19] In 1987 Nan Hoover, an American, was appointed to the Academy as a professor of video and film. Hubertus Neuerburg and Heinz Getrost became joint heads of this department in 1990, assisted by a succession of lecturers on short-term contracts, including Axel Klepsch. From 2000 until 2009 Vadim Glowna deputised until the chair in this department was again occupied. Neuerburg left in 2007, and Marcel Odenbach has been professor for film and video since 2010. Now the focus of the department is on the fields of video and computer, hence more immediately related to the concerns of practitioners of the fine arts because it provides direct access to pictorial design – unlike film, which requires detailed planning in advance.

Towards the close of the 1990s, the student body began to voice a desire for the establishment of a computer workshop, which Rector Lüpertz dismissed out of hand. However, since he could not avoid being swept along by the tempestuous pace of developments in the electronic media, a chair for experimental sculpture was established, which, among other things, was also intended to make the use of computers possible. All the while the advance of the computer into the workshops, notably photography, video, and film as well as printing, has been inexorable. By now the establishment of a dedicated computer workshop seems just a matter of time. As early as 1988 Günther Uecker was making a point of asserting, 'Academies should make use of all technical, all engineering inventions, [...] even though that means an enormous increase in expenses.'[20] If 'the other world of highly developed civilisation continues to expand and if we do not enter into it, then that omission can develop into a strong re-barbarisation phenomenon, which in turn can become dangerous for all human beings.'[21]

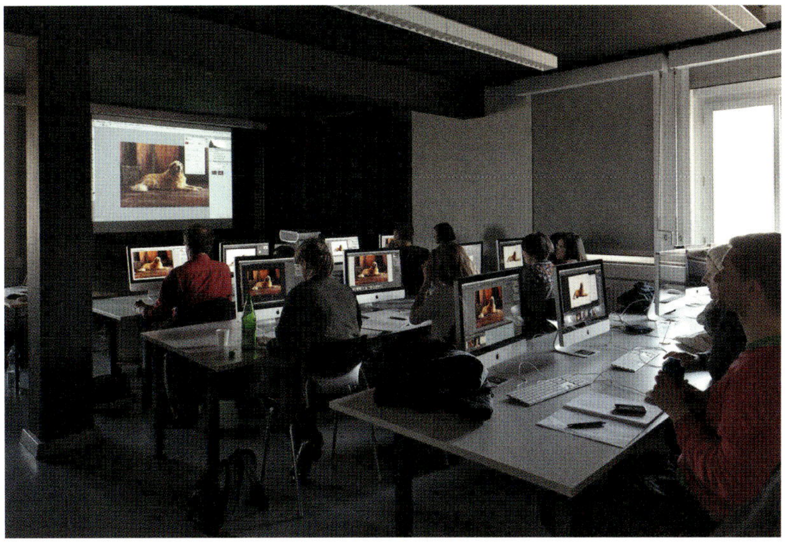

Fig. 6: The Photoshop workshop, Düsseldorf Art Academy, 2013

In 1972 director Eduard Trier described the status quo attained up to that point in an informal series of Academy publications, and laid down guidelines that have continued to be valid in that form to the present day. In an era of rapid change in ideas of what art is or should be, there would be consequences for the Academy workshops. Art is constantly discovering new materials and techniques, a development which should be met with the enlargement of the workshops in respect of technical facilities and personnel. In addition, lack of space was a further problem, considering the rise in student numbers. Trier did concede that better artistic results might not be attained with new appliances and technical aids, but he did not want to see the Academy inferior in this respect to polytechnics and vocational schools in this field. Another goal that remained was supporting the overburdened teachers through the employment of more teaching staff and technicians. The addition of more teaching positions and the implementation of basic schooling would create more scope for supervising students on a one-to-one basis and for teachers to try out new materials and working methods. Consequently, the main aims of supervising students in the workshops were to be:

- The first conversation establishing contact between pupil and teacher should concentrate on the student's formal area of art through suggestion, instruction, and correction.
- Students should have close contact with their working materials and the properties of those materials.
- Students' artistic ideas should be realised independently in a way that is commensurate with the work.
- After leaving, students should be able to explain their projects so clearly to their technician partners by means of drawings or models that they can be technically carried out.[22]

Despite Trier's efforts to upgrade 'underprivileged' teachers – some of whom were working on the basis of limited contracts – to the status of university teachers, he only partly succeeded. The prevailing economic and political situation allowed only for lectureships that had already been filled to be converted into posts for 'teachers for special tasks'.[23]

'Art cannot be taught,' wrote Director Norbert Kricke in a Festschrift, *Zweihundert Jahre Kunstakademie Düsseldorf* [Two Hundred Years of the Düsseldorf Art Academy], in 1973.[24] 'The artistic and technical workshops accessible to all, as well as the academic working groups, represent the area of what can be taught. Here is where what actually can be taught and learnt lies. [...] The teachable area forms the core of the Academy.'[25] From then on that would be the guideline that drove the establishment and enlargement of workshops.

The workshops have to the present day always been much in use. In the Printing Department, silkscreen printing was assigned to Gunter Lorenz. In 1974 he was supported by Rainer Komers, who was teaching on a short-term contract. Hans Möller became head of the workshop in 1975, later reinforced by Christoph Eckhardt, who taught the artistic and technical side, and Helmut Pawlitza, a technician. By 1978 printing technology and silkscreen printing had been reunited in a single workshop. Eckhardt was succeeded by Anton Grech in 1996 and Möller later by Geza Ziga. Currently the printing workshop is headed by Markus Löhrwald.

In the woodcarving workshop Wilhelm Hable was supported in 1975 by Hermann Hertel, a technician. Hertel enlarged the design possibilities open to classical wood sculpture to include machine-powered technical and construction work with wood and working materials made from wood. In 1980 Hertel was made co-director of the workshop along with Hable. When Hable left in 1988, Gerhard Moritzen succeeded him. Berthold Langnickel in turn succeeded Hertel in 1996.

Claus-Andreas Barthelmess was given a short-term contract for teaching ceramics in 1970, thus following in his late father's footsteps. In 1980 Barthelmess submitted a request for a ceramics class of his own and a chair to accompany it. This petition was rejected by the senate.[26] In 1982 Rose-Marie Nöcker replaced Barthelmess. To emphasise the distance to pottery-making, the workshop was renamed 'Clay/Terracotta'. Finally Claudia Schmacke took over the workshop, which had again been renamed, this time as 'Workshop, Modelling', in 1993.

Drawing from the nude, which had been offered as required in the classes or the Orientation Department longer than anyone could remember by artists who taught, appeared to be losing ground in the 1980s. Taught only a few hours a week by teachers on short-term contracts taking turns, drawing from the nude had by then dwindled to a fringe phenomenon. Interest in it would not be not rekindled until the mid-1990s. By 1999, however, it had once again become a permanent institution in the form of a workshop headed by Arnim Tölke, who had been in Markus Lüpertz's master class.

Crafts training as an admissions requirement as it had been in the 1940s and 1950s is no longer a condition for studying art at the Düsseldorf Art Academy. The heads of the workshops have only rarely been craftsmen rather than practitioners of the fine arts and most of them have been graduates of the Düsseldorf Academy. Students can as needed and at any time make use of the technical facilities provided by the workshops under the daily supervision of the workshop teachers concerned. Choosing materials and the techniques for working them are not crafts options where art projects are concerned. They are artistic decisions that are subject to ongoing reflection in consultation, in discourse, and during execution. That is how art happens. In the workshops.

NOTES

1 Conversation of the author with Sonja Mataré in spring 2013.
2 Ibid.
3 Sonja Mataré and Sabine Maja Schilling (eds.), *Ewald Mataré, Tagebücher* [Diaries] *1915–1965*, Cologne 1997, p. 325.
4 Anna Klapheck, 'Die "goldnen" zwanziger Jahre. Die Akademie zwischen den beiden Kriegen', in: Eduard Trier (ed.), *Zweihundert Jahre Kunstakademie Düsseldorf*, Düsseldorf 1973, p. 148.
5 It was held until 1950 by Wilhelm Herberholz, who had taken charge of restoring the façade mosaics while the Academy was being rebuilt; see Heinrich Kamps (ed.), *Jahrbuch der Staatlichen Kunstakademie Düsseldorf 1948–1950*, Düsseldorf 1951, p. 135.
6 Staatliche Kunstakademie Düsseldorf, Hochschule für bildende Künste [Studienhinweise (pointers for students)], n.d. [*c.*1940].
7 More precise dates are, unfortunately, not possible due to poor documentation.
8 *Jahrbuch 1948–1950* (see n. 5), p. 136.
9 Staatliche Kunstakademie Düsseldorf (see n. 6).
10 Mataré and Schilling (see n. 3), p. 331.
11 Staatliche Kunstakademie Düsseldorf, Hochschule für bildende Künste [Studienhinweise], n.d. [*c.*1950].
12 Staatliche Kunstakademie Düsseldorf, Hochschule für bildende Künste [Studienhinweise], 1956.
13 Conversation of the author with Kurt Räder in spring 2013.
14 Ibid.
15 Information provided by Hilla Becher.
16 Dawn Leach, 'Ausdifferenzierung und Kontinuität in der Künstlerausbildung an der Kunstakademie Düsseldorf', in: Wolfgang Ruppert and Christian Fuhrmeister (eds.), *Zwischen Deutscher Kunst und internationaler Modernität. Formen der Künstlerausbildung 1918 bis 1968*, Weimar 2007, pp. 147–167; here: p. 159. For the changes and events in the stage design class as well as the film/video class, also see the essays by Michael Matzigkeit, Maren Polte, and Klaus Rinke in the present volume, pp. 348–373, pp. 310–347, and pp. 65–70.
17 See *Chronik der Kunstakademie Düsseldorf*, year 1973, Düsseldorf Art Academy archives.
18 Ibid., years 1975 and 1976.
19 Ibid., year 1986.
20 Günther Uecker, 'Ist Kunst lehrbar', *Jahreshefte der Kunstakademie Düsseldorf*, Vol. 1, Düsseldorf 1988, pp. 162–179; here: p. 165.
21 Ibid.
22 Eduard Trier (ed.), *Nachrichten, Bilder, Berichte, Staatliche Kunstakademie Düsseldorf, Hochschule für bildende Künste* 9, Düsseldorf 1972.
23 Conversation of the author with Kurt Räder in spring 2013.
24 Norbert Kricke, 'Die neue Akademie', in: Trier (see n. 4), p. XIII.
25 Ibid.
26 See *Chronik der Kunstakademie Düsseldorf*, year 1980, Düsseldorf Art Academy archives.

FINE ART AT THE ACADEMY FROM 1945 TO THE PRESENT

TRAINING IN ART DURING THE RECONSTRUCTION YEARS

Guido Reuter

'THE CURRENT SITUATION REQUIRES MUCH MORE TALENT FOR IMPROVISING IN A WAY ADAPTED TO THE CIRCUMSTANCES.'

The Düsseldorf Art Academy building, in which teaching and learning had kept on as usual until 1944 even though it had sustained air raid damage in 1942/43 and 1944, was ravaged by phosphorus grenades during the nights of 14 and 21 March 1945. The incendiary grenades had set fire to the building, which caused all roofs in the east tract to collapse. Hard work put in by the remaining Academy personnel made it possible to contain the fire to the original flashpoint and to extinguish it in the west wing so that the ceilings there were preserved even though the roof had been completely destroyed.[1]

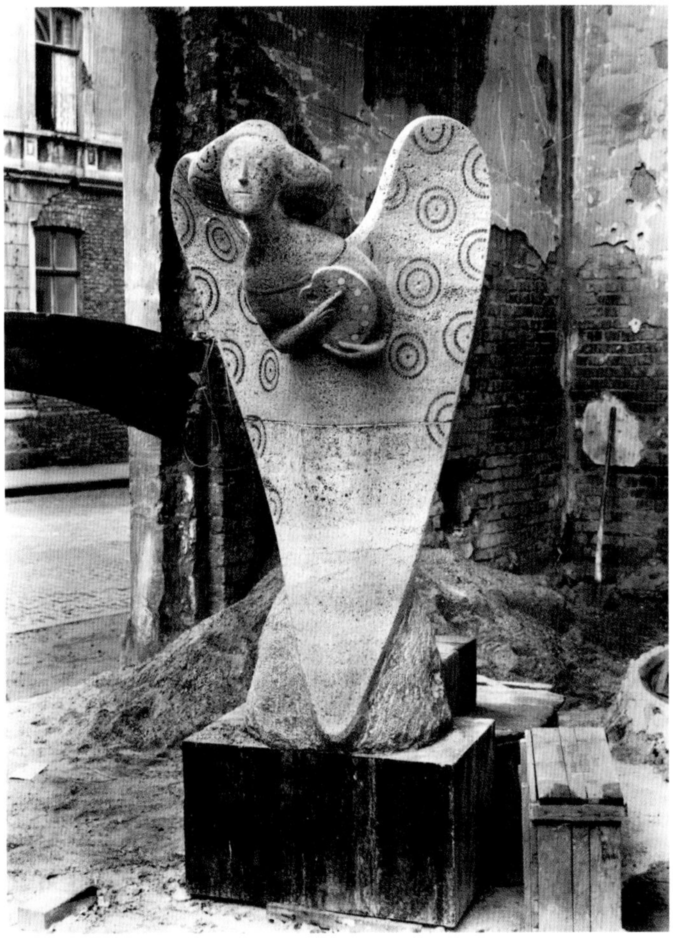

Fig. 1: Sculpture by Ewald Mataré for the Stefan Lochner Fountain in Cologne, c. 1953, in the severely damaged sculpture studio that was demolished in 1957

September 1945 saw the return to the Art Academy of its first students, who joined forces with the Academy technical personnel to start on clearing the rubble and rebuilding.[2] By the beginning of the 1945/46 winter term, their combined efforts had succeeded in making some rooms sufficiently usable that the students could begin to work in them.[3]

While the makeshift repair work was at its height in September 1945, the Art Academy teaching staff had unanimously proposed the sculptor Ewald Mataré, who had returned to his old domain a few weeks before, as acting director. The artist had first been appointed by Walter Kaesbach in 1932 to a post at the Düsseldorf Academy but had been dismissed only seven months later in 1933 by the National Socialists without giving reasons for the measure. Like so many sculptors of his generation – Georg Kolbe and Ernesto de Fiori may be cited in this connection – Mataré had begun his career in art as a painter. After studying for several years in Berlin with Lovis Corinth and Arthur Kampf, the history painter, and others, Mataré switched from painting to printmaking and sculpture in the 1920s. The main themes of his work came to be animals and religious figures. The artist's works of sculpture, although abstract, are informed by a summarising stylisation of the natural model that is far from naturalistic (Fig. 1). After 1945 the sculptor devoted himself more to architectural sculpture, often involving his pupils in the process of making it, a practice he would continue until he left the Art Academy in 1957.

Although Ewald Mataré had been appointed acting director of the Academy in October 1945, his plans for restructuring the curriculum and syllabus and restoring the Academy building failed to meet with support and approval from the district president and the British military authorities. Resistance to his ideas also soon mounted among his colleagues at the Art Academy.[4] Mataré's plans allowed for shutting down the Academy in order to restore the building to such an extent that students would not have to work in the handful of provisional studios available. Moreover, at first only pupils who had studied at the Academy before or during the war were to be readmitted in order to continue working for the time being with the remaining teachers.[5] Mataré did not want to admit new students until both space for them became available and new professors had replaced the old teaching staff.[6] His diary entry for

29 September 1945 contains the illuminating remark, 'I don't have much use for the professors who are there now, and my preference would be to have them all disappear; some of them have earned quite good money in the Nazi era so that removing them would not mean hardship.'[7]

In addition, the sculptor had developed concrete plans for the curriculum: students should already be admitted at fourteen years of age 'to attain an all-round education as early as possible'.[8] As Mataré saw it, beginning to train in art at a more advanced age did not ensure the scope and intensity that would enable students to receive a thorough education in art that ultimately would leave them capable of developing their own artistic ideas. Mataré's proposed curriculum envisaged giving students a thorough grounding in drawing in the first two years as well as instruction in script and 'viewing art'.[9] Further, the proposal allowed for classes in German, religion, and biology.[10] The first two years would be followed by a 'workshop course of study in wood and stone' and, for painters, time spent in a painting class.[11] 'I could get on with just a few classes at little expense, and that seemed to me the most important thing at the time.'[12] The four years of instruction in drawing and working in workshops were to be followed by working freely in a master class.[13] Mataré's proposed curriculum, and especially his idea that students should be admitted at the age of fourteen, met with no sympathy from the politicians who would be responsible for authorising and implementing it and the British military authorities.[14] When the sculptor persisted in refusing to open the doors of the Art Academy by 3 December 1945, the date set by the British authorities, because he did not want to be held accountable for the condition of the studios and for the lack of suitable teaching personnel,[15] external pressure was brought to bear on him to such an extent that he saw no future prospects for himself in the office of acting director. Mataré was designated director of the Art Academy on 15 October 1945, but before the year ended, he submitted his resignation.[16]

NEW AND OLD COLLEAGUES

Werner Heuser

Like Ewald Mataré, the painter Werner Heuser was appointed by the British military authorities to a post as professor at the Academy after the war ended (Fig. 2). Heuser had had links with the Düsseldorf Art Academy since 1900, when he began studying there with Eduard von Gebhardt. After spending years studying in Dresden with Carl Bantzer, followed by a seven-year stay in Rome, where his close friends included the painter Karl Hofer and the sculptor Hermann Haller, he went on to Paris, the South of France, Berlin, Rome, and Kiev before settling in Düsseldorf in 1919. Walter Kaesbach made Heuser head of a drawing and composition class at the Düsseldorf Art

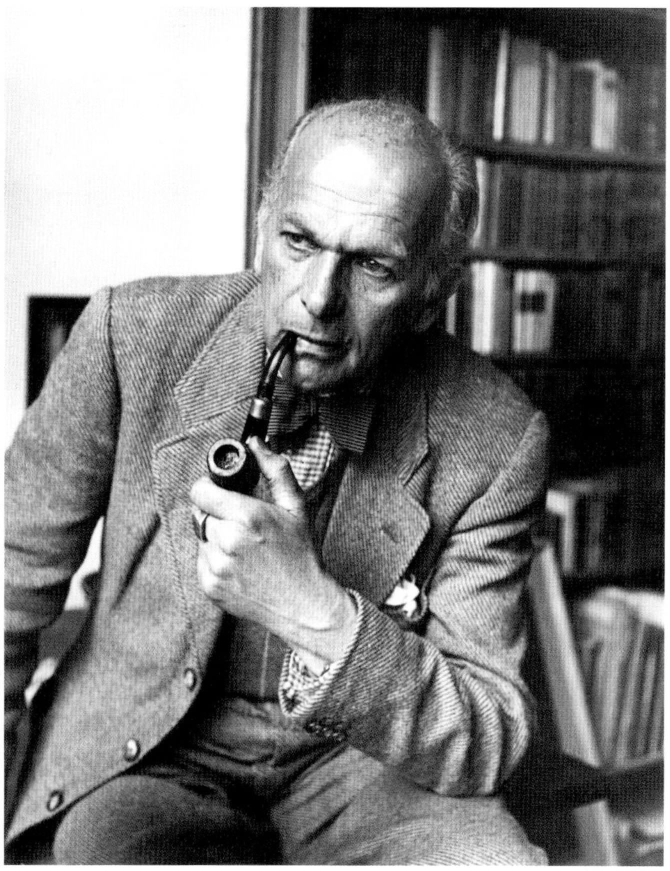

Fig. 2: Werner Heuser, director 1946–1949

Academy in 1926. By 1938, proscribed as a 'degenerate Expressionist', Heuser was dismissed from his Academy post by the National Socialists. From 1938 until 1945 Heuser continued to work secretly on his pictures on the other side of the Rhine in Meerbusch, where he lived with his sculptor colleague Mataré and had a studio until he was once again summoned to the Academy, this time by the British. Gerd Vielhaber wrote about Werner Heuser a year after the artist's death in the catalogue to the 1965 commemorative retrospective mounted by the Art Association for the Rhinelands and Westphalia:

'The problem for him as a painter, but also for him as an educationalist and professor venerated by his pupils, was always the human being, preserving the dignity of the human individual in real life and even more urgently so in his spiritual existence. [...] His temperament as a composer flared up, uninfluenced by the manifold, often fashionable, changing stylistic developments, in the figurative and in its magic backgrounds. He was fascinated by the tragi-comical, the witchlike and spectral, the clownish grotesque, the menace of demons.'[17]

In the early reconstruction years at the Düsseldorf Art Academy, Heuser taught with Wilhelm Schmurr in the drawing class.[18] In addition, he was head of a painting class. His far-sighted thoughts on education are conveyed in the various texts he wrote after succeeding Mataré as acting director of the Art Academy.[19]

Heinrich Kamps

Along with Ewald Mataré and Werner Heuser, Heinrich Kamps was appointed on 1 March 1946 to swell the ranks of the remaining staff and was entrusted with instituting the course of studies leading to civil service employment teaching art at state schools (Fig. 3). A painter, glass painter, and mosaicist, Heinrich Kamps had studied at the Decorative Arts Schools in Krefeld and Hamburg before the First World War. Declared unfit for military service in 1916 on the basis of an injury sustained while he was on active duty, Kamps subsequently spent the years from 1917 to 1919 attending a seminar for drawing teachers in Düsseldorf taught by Lothar von Kunowski.[20] After freelancing as an artist for two years, he was appointed to teach

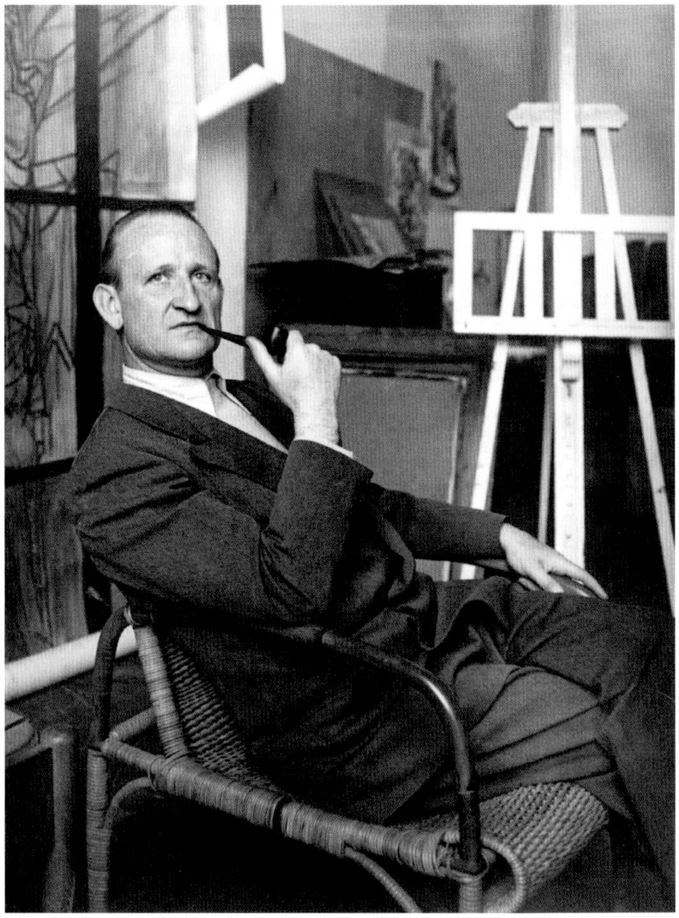

Fig. 3: Heinrich Kamps, director 1949–1954

drawing at the Rethelgymnasium [Rethel Grammar School] in Düsseldorf in 1921. In the 1920s he exhibited work as a painter at a number of group shows organised by Düsseldorf artists and became a member of the Junges Rheinland [Young Rhineland] artists' association. In 1926 Walter Kaesbach appointed Heinrich Kamps senior lecturer for training prospective state school art teachers at the Düsseldorf Art Academy. After almost four years at this institution, Kamps was appointed director of the State Art School in Berlin-Schöneberg late in 1929.[21] The artist fell victim to the radical political change that took place in 1933 and was dismissed from his post as director. Nonetheless he was given a post as professor of art, glass, and mosaics at the Vereinigte Staatsschulen für Freie und Angewandte Kunst [United State Schools for Fine and Applied Art] in Berlin-Charlottenburg, where he was able to work 'relatively undisturbed' until 1937.[22] Since Kamps refused to become an NSDAP party member in 1937, the Ministry for Science, Art, and Folk Education, which was responsible for his employment, summarily forced him to retire on a pension. After Kamps's Berlin studio was destroyed in air raids in 1943, he moved with his family, first to Kevelaer on the Lower Rhine and in 1944 to Olpe in the Sauerland. After the war he again placed himself at the disposal of what was then North Rhineland for rebuilding institutions where art teachers trained.[23] In 1946 he was appointed to the Düsseldorf Art Academy to build up the course for training prospective state school art teachers, since Paul Bindel, who had been in charge of that department since 1930, was still interned as a prisoner of war. Until summer term 1948 – Bindel did not return from internment camp until the beginning of that year – Kamps was responsible on his own for training the aspiring art teachers in art and organising their course of study. In addition, he headed a class in glass and mosaics at first, because there was a shortage of qualified teachers at the Academy.[24] His diverse oeuvre comprises paintings on canvas, drawings, watercolours, mosaics, verre églomisé pictures, murals, and glass windows[25] and is distinguished by numerous changes in style, with a noticeable tendency on the part of the artist to incorporate current styles productively in his own works. Kamps's approach to teaching was informed by a strong moral and ethical tenor. In 1947 he had this to say on his views about art teaching at state schools: 'Art, crafts, and education are the foundations on which the work of the art school must rest. They are, basically, united in spirit, for crafts, art, and education only grow on the soil of pure spirit; human shortcomings are the reason for imperfection in respect of craftsmanship, art, and teaching.'[26]

The artist did not view the Academy as primarily a hotbed for fostering the talents of exceptionally gifted individuals but saw it rather as a place where the broad mass of students could be given a thorough grounding in art skills. Kamps elucidated his views in a 1950 manifesto entitled *Akademie heute* [Academy Today], which he wrote while in office as the third acting director of the post-war Düsseldorf Art Academy.[27]

Ideological and practical grounds had been the main reasons for appointing Mataré, Heuser, and Kamps to the Düsseldorf Art Academy again in 1945/46: all three artists had been dismissed from their posts by the National Socialists and had been domiciled near Düsseldorf after the war and were working as artists there.

When teaching began again in summer term 1946, the following professors, who had remained at the Academy after the war, became the colleagues of the reappointed artists: the painters Wilhelm Herberholz, Wilhelm Schmurr, and Paul Bindel, the sculptors Joseph Enseling and Josef 'Sepp' Mages, and Otto Coester representing the graphic arts. Werner von Wecus taught the stage design class.

Wilhelm Herberholz

Very little is known about Wilhelm Herberholz's life and work, and what is known is full of gaps. He began training as an artist at the age of twelve at the Applied Arts School in Kassel (Fig. 4).[28] From 1896 until 1899 he studied at the Kassel Art Academy, where his teachers included Hermann Knackfuss, a painter, illustrator, and writer on art who had trained at the Düsseldorf Art Academy. From 1899 until 1910 Herberholz continued to study at the Düsseldorf Art Academy with the painters Peter Janssen, Eduard von Gebhardt, Willy

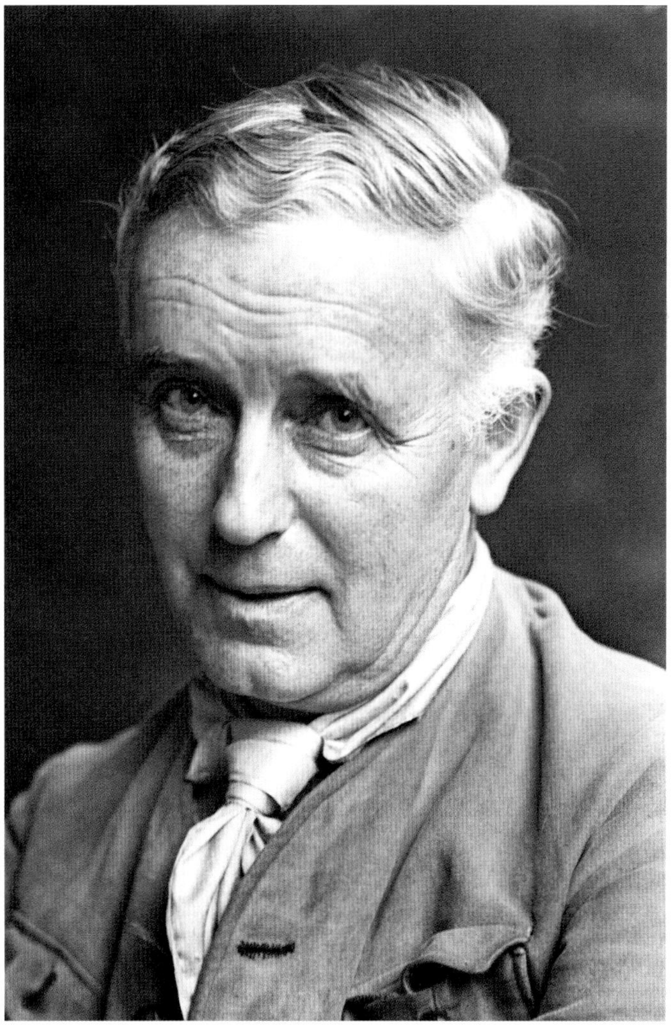

Fig. 4: The painter Wilhelm Herberholz, date unknown

Spatz, Eduard Claus-Meyer, and Carl Ernst Forberg, a painter, copper engraver, and etcher. Like his later colleague, Wilhelm Schmurr, Herberholz finished his studies in the master class taught by Eduard Claus-Meyer. Both a painter and printmaker, Herberholz taught at the Düsseldorf Art Academy from 1922 until 1950 as a professor for painting techniques and the graphic arts. Before returning in 1945 to his old workplace, he spent some time in Gestapo internment, beginning in 1938.[29] Together with his colleague, the printmaker Otto Coester, Herberholz was kept busy in the post-war years mainly establishing workshops for painting and graphics techniques.[30] In the first Art Academy annual report after teaching had begun again in the winter term of 1945/46, the artist remarks with evident pride in his article on the workshops that, despite the lack of space and some shortages of materials, students could once again be instructed in mural painting techniques, such as *fresco buono*, *secco*, *sgrafitto*, and *stuccolustro*, as well as techniques of easel painting in various media, such as 'oil painting, tempera painting, mixed media, watercolour, and painting in pastels'.[31]

Otto Coester

Otto Coester, who teamed up with Wilhelm Herberholz to build new workshops for painting techniques and the graphic arts, had first come to the Düsseldorf Art Academy in 1934 as a lecturer in graphic arts before being appointed to a chair in that field in 1938. After studying at the Applied Art School in Barmen (in the class for interior decoration and the metal workshop) in the early 1920s and at the ceramics workshop at the Staatlichen Bauhausschule [State Bauhaus School] in Weimar in Dornburg late in the decade, he turned to etching as a self-taught practitioner. From 1933 onwards he worked exclusively in the graphic arts although he had attracted notice while still a student in the 1920s with works in metal as church appointments.[32] The first inventory catalogue of the Düsseldorf Academy Gallery notes on Coester's development as an artist:

'At first under the sway of Picasso, Coester became preoccupied with Hieronymus Bosch in 1927, later with Marc Chagall, and, from the mid-1930s on, was inspired by Caspar David Friedrich, whose Romantic style influenced Coester's pictorial idiom. Apart from landscape, portrayals of architecture were one of his favourite motifs, which are reminiscent of Piranesi engravings or the works of the French etcher Charles Méryon. In the mid-1950s his etchings were changed by the "zeitgeist". The influence of stylistic movements of that period is undeniable.'[33]

In a newspaper article devoted to the artist written in 1959, Anna Klapheck stated that he had enjoyed a very good reputation among his students (Fig. 5):

'Coester's will to educate goes far beyond art education; he is concerned with education of the whole person in the widest

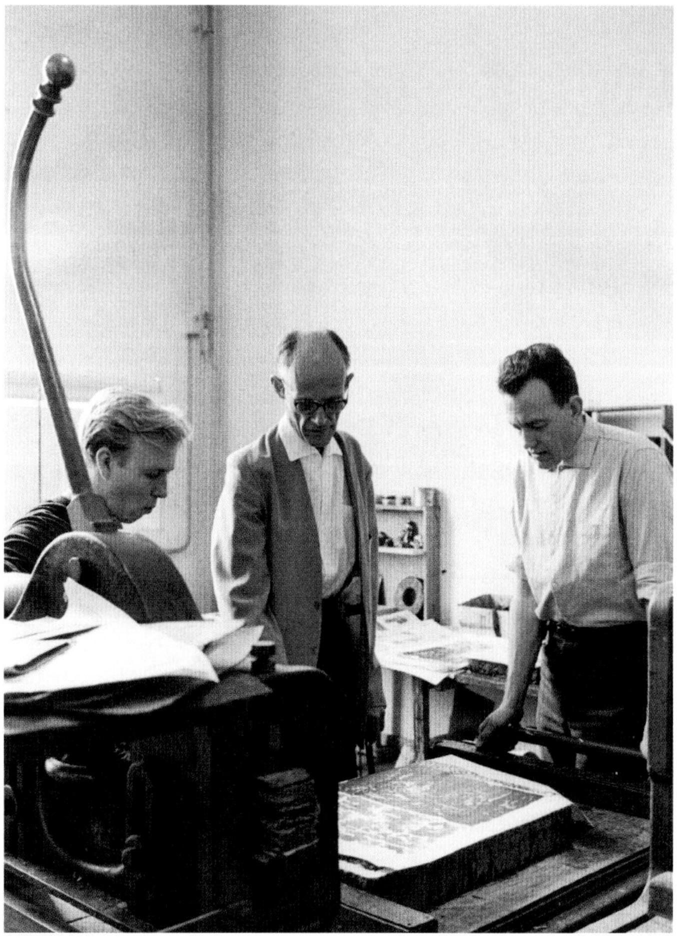

Fig. 5: The printmaker Otto Coester with students in the printing workshop at the Düsseldorf Art Academy, 1960

sense, as Goethe meant it. Coester is always "there", always ready for questions. He tends to the most minor details, such as fair distribution of materials and the places where the students work, but above all he wants the class to fuse into a unit. An ethical trait informs his teaching. No wonder his pupils idolise him.'[34]

Pupils from the painting classes always also worked in Coester's graphic arts class alongside his own students. For the former, however, admission to the printmaking class was linked to the requirement that the visiting student stayed for two terms because Coester made a point of teaching in a stringently systematic way. 'Coester's teaching follows a plan and is based on being extremely disciplined.'[35] The memorable recollections of his pupils indicate that the artist was concerned in his teaching with far more than merely conveying how to attain craftsmanship and technical precision. As Coester himself said in 1950, working with students was directed above all at their 'intellectus'.[36] In winter term 1946/47, for instance, Coester started a Monday evening literary gathering.[37] Students read and discussed with their professor numerous literary, philosophical, religious, and art historical texts.[38] However, Coester did not assume the role of interpreter in the discussions. Instead he tactfully presented the students and their contributions.[39] It has also come down to us through the pupils of the Coester class that the artist would spend much of the day in his own studio, separate from the rooms in which the students worked, so they did not see him, although his authority as an artist was such that they sensed it 'through the wall'. This telling image has left its stamp on publications dealing with Coester.[40] Although the artist-teacher also sought to converse directly with his pupils, he tended to communicate with the students mainly by letter or handing them books from his studio which were supposed to support them intellectually in their work.[41] The intellectual curiosity in Coester's class was accompanied by great open-mindedness about art. The printmaker is known to have supported the wide-ranging interests of his students at all times, an attitude that ensured the most diverse approaches imaginable in the class.[42] In the 1950s Coester was in charge not only of the graphic arts class but also of the preliminary course for prospective art teachers at state schools.[43] It was due to his unstinting commitment to serving the interests of the Art Academy that the Graphic Arts Department had the most sophisticated and most modern printing facilities of all institutes of higher learning in the Federal Republic, an attraction that was a magnet to pupils from across the world.[44]

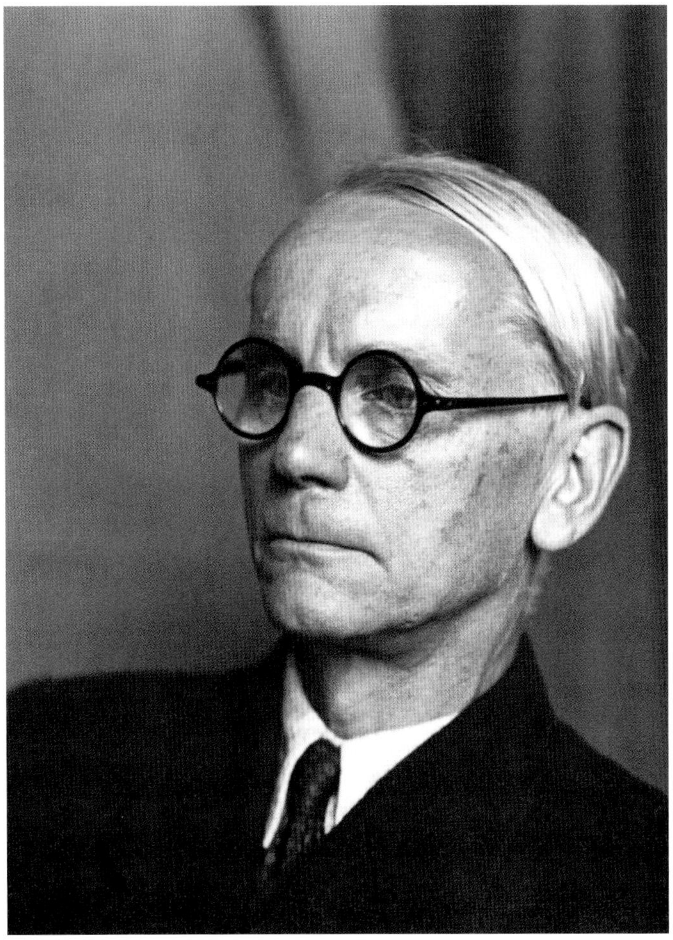

Fig. 6: The painter Wilhelm Schmurr, date unknown

Wilhelm Schmurr

The painter Wilhelm Schmurr (Fig. 6) was another of the artist-professors after 1945 but left in 1947 for reasons of age. He had studied painting at the Academy from 1894 until 1904 with Peter Janssen, Arthur Kampf, Eduard von Gebhardt, and Eduard Claus-Meyer, finishing his studies in the master class taught by Claus-Meyer.

Schmurr spent his adult life as a member of numerous artist societies, including the Rhenish Secession and the West German Künstlerbund [Association of Artists]. From 1927 until 1947 Schmurr was a senior lecturer in painting at the Düsseldorf Art Academy.[45] Schmurr's oeuvre comprised still lifes, portraits, and landscapes as well as paintings with devotional content. His pictures are stylistically an idiosyncratic fusion of realistic tendencies with Symbolist overtones and a conception of figure and colour occasionally reminiscent of Henri Rousseau. From 1946 until he left the Academy in 1947, Schmurr taught alongside Werner Heuser in the drawing class.[46]

Moreover, he supervised a class in 'portrait, nude, landscape, and still life' – matching his own diverse oeuvre.[47]

Paul Bindel

Little is known of Paul Bindel's life and work. A painter and draughtsman, he was appointed to teach at the Düsseldorf Art Academy by Walter Kaesbach in 1930. Before 1914 Bindel had studied at the Düsseldorf Decorative Arts School and after 1918 continued his studies at the Düsseldorf seminary for drawing teachers.[48] Anna Klapheck knew enough about him to report in 1959 that the painter had played a leading part in the Junges Rheinland in the 1920s and that visitors to the Düsseldorf Kunsthalle queued up in front of his painting *Die Kappesschaberin* [Woman Scraping Cabbages].[49] 'Rhenish Late Impressionism, which has grown somewhat flaccid, has gained elasticity and freshness through Bindel.'[50] After the Second World War the artist did not return to Düsseldorf from internment as a prisoner of war in Russia until 1948. His painting – 'mainly watercolours of flowers – [...] subsequently became more cheerful and blooming than ever before, gratefully affirmative of the new world that had been given to him as a gift'.[51]

The works of Bindel's that have survived are chiefly those from the period after 1948. His early work was almost all lost during the war years.[52] The Academy Gallery at the Düsseldorf Art Academy owns some drawings and works in ink on paper, among which some landscapes of his attest to Bindel's fine feeling for light and shade and represent a distillation of a multi-faceted impression of nature.[53]

Drawing not only played an important role in Bindel's oeuvre. It was also a mainstay of the artist's teaching – as it was in the overarching concept of art training at the Düsseldorf Art Academy in the 1940s and 1950s (Fig. 7). Bindel expressed his thoughts on this to Anna Klapheck in 1959: 'We cannot put freedom at the beginning; there's a sort of basic schooling that forms the skeleton of the rest of the training course – that is, from what pedagogues of old experienced, drawing.'[54] However, drawing classes taught by Bindel did not start immediately with life drawing from the model or even with still life but instead featured learning how to represent small, nondescript objects.

Bindel is fond of talking about the 'little world of Nature' – that is, wood, stones, or parts of plants, such as a stalk or a seed pod. These things must be properly investigated by feel; that should happen entirely without haste, wholly in a contemplative way. Gradually one rises to the richer forms, only much later to the nude and landscape, colour and free invention.[55]

An article on the Düsseldorf Art Academy shows that Paul Bindel could demonstrate a high degree of consistency towards his students where what was at stake was correctly understanding this 'little world of Nature' and getting it onto paper with a pencil. Here it says about his class: 'Professor Paul Bindel is relentlessly open-minded. He brings students to Nature. He does not allow them to draw false landscapes. He tells them that a

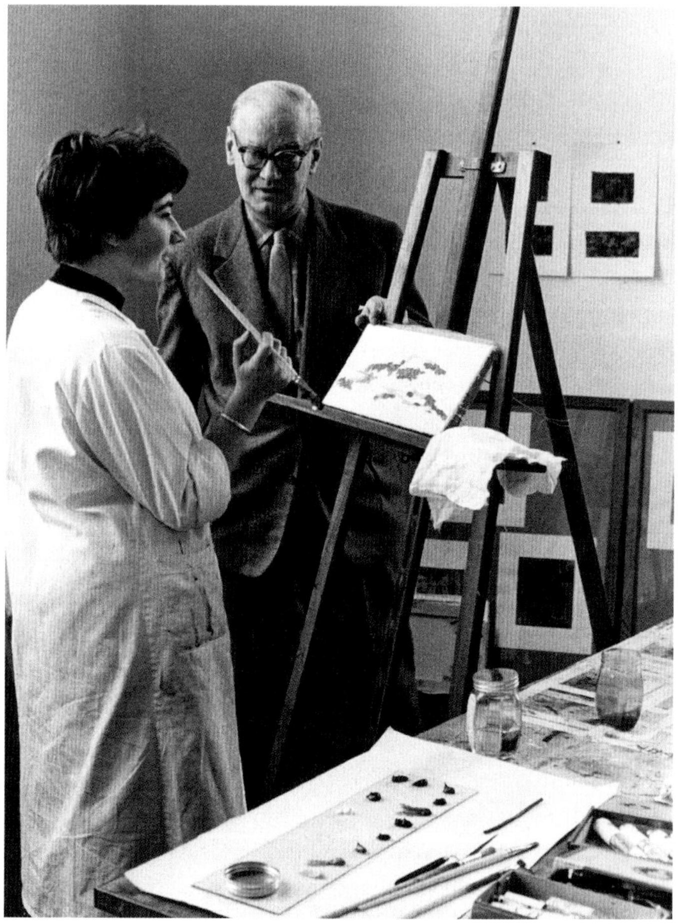

Fig. 7: The painter Paul Bindel with a student, 1960

stone they step on, for instance, is Nature. And that stone or a humble daisy is drawn, if need be, for an entire term.'[56]

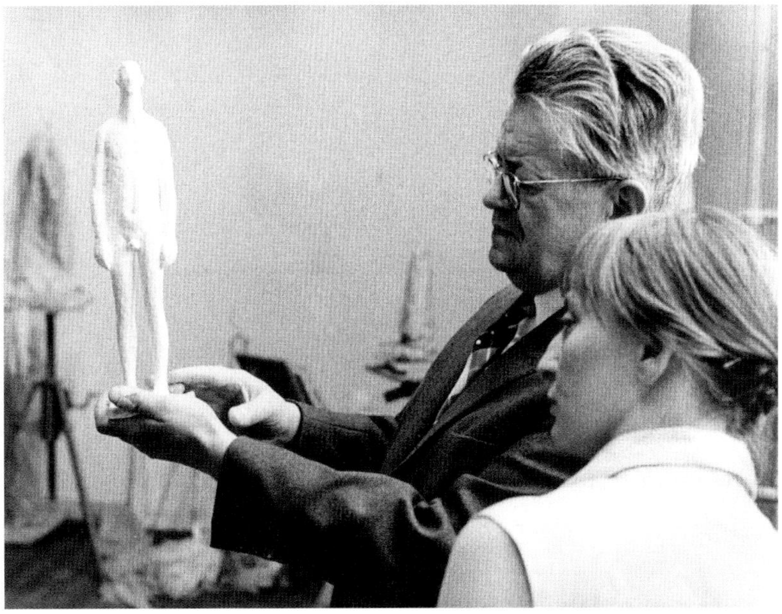

Fig. 8: The sculptor Sepp Mages with a student, 1960

Josef Mages

Josef 'Sepp' Mages, Joseph Enseling, and Ewald Mataré were three very different sculptors, all of whom taught at the Düsseldorf Art Academy during the late 1940s and early 1950s.[57] Mages and Enseling had both been appointed to teach at the Academy in 1938. So little is known about Sepp Mages's life and work that a picture of this artist can only be sketched in rough outlines.[58] The artist had his first experience of sculpture in his father's stonemason's workshop. He began studying at the Kaiserslautern Decorative Arts School but transferred to the Royal Decorative Arts School in Munich, where he studied with Richard Riemerschmid and Joseph Wackerle from 1913 until 1920. Sharing a workshop with Wackerle enabled Mages to carry out commissions for decorative architectural sculpture on a large scale with his teacher.[59] In the 1920s the young sculptor realised some public commissions in and near Kaiserslautern, including a fountain featuring playfully grotesque majolica figures for the Kaiserslautern municipal exhibition grounds, which was later classified as 'degenerate' by the National Socialists and demolished.[60]

Irrespective of the sign of official disapproval that was to come, Mages was commissioned to create the monumental group of sculptures *[Sports] Kameraden* [Comrades (in Sport)], which was set up in 1936 on the grounds of the former Reich sports field (now the Olympia Park) in Berlin.[61] The commission is likely to have been wangled for the sculptor by his teacher as Wackerle had a good reputation at the time and was also working on sculpture for the grounds. In 1938 Mages was also appointed to teach at the Düsseldorf Art Academy, just one of many examples of the heterogeneous way politicians responsible for art and cultural policy dealt with them in the fascist era. Even then the sculptor focused on mortuary sculpture as a major source of commissions. Later on in his career, Mages specialised in developing standard forms for tombstones in granite. The artist developed some forty reproducible types distinguished by bold simplicity in shape and script.[62]

'In them he reverts to the simplest of basic forms – the square, the rectangle, the triangle – is most economical in his use of decoration and of clear, obvious symbols.'[63] In 1959 Anna Klapheck also reported that the sculptor had made more than a hundred tombstones over a lifetime and continued to create numerous commemorative monuments and a great deal of decorative architectural sculpture.[64] Mages himself had discussed his concerns as an artist in a 1947 newspaper article: 'All my works of sculpture bear the features of what is decidedly architectural sculpture. I make the basic motifs present in the architectural framework continue to reverberate in it and give it a tectonic character.'[65] When one considers the extant works of the sculptor's, one is not surprised that there was no place in Mages's class for 'avant-gardist experiments' and that his teaching was representative of 'the traditional element' at the Academy.[66] The sculptor primarily supported craftsmanly skills in his pupils. Studying from the model represented the basis but pupils should 'definitely not "model" nudes from the model; they should develop a "poetic image" of Nature and correct their inner idea on the model', thus the sculptor's standpoint (Fig. 8).[67] To that end, 'the earliest exercises were done in small, often in the smallest, formats from a single "pose", sometimes 8 to 10 such trials in a row in Mages's classes.'[68] This practice would reveal 'the direction towards which an individual pupil tended'.[69] In the 1951 *Jahrbuch der Staatlichen Kunstakademie Düsseldorf* [Düsseldorf Art Academy Yearbook] Sepp Mages himself explains that what made his class in architectural sculpture so special was that he not only had to convey to the students the essence of sculpture as such but also had to school their perception of the specific conditions that 'accrue to sculpture from a given architectural context',[70] and, moreover:

'In parallel with the structural givens, planning and carrying out a work play an important role. Overall situation and

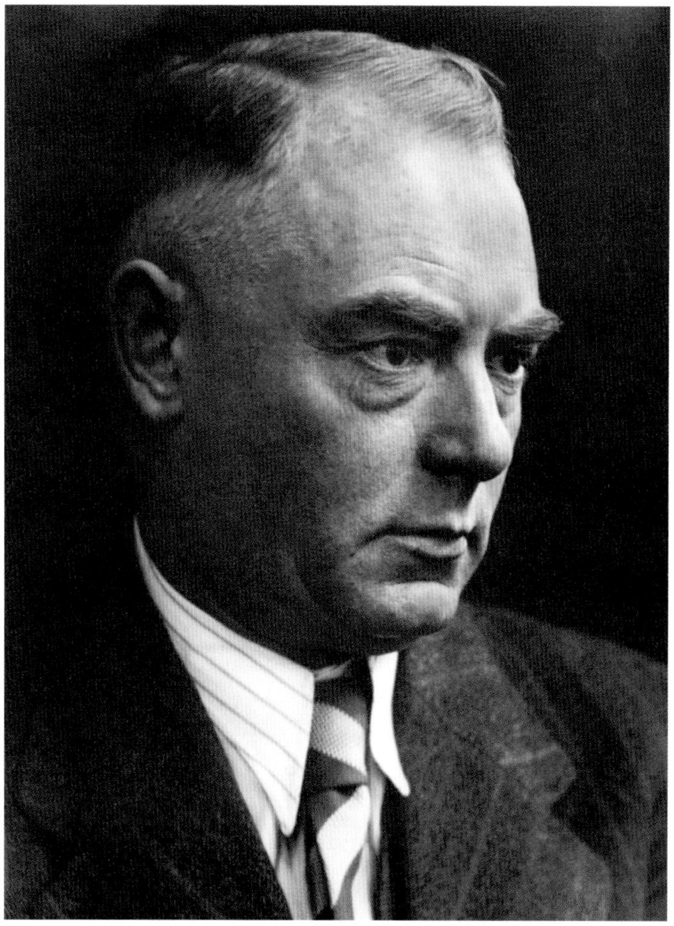

Fig. 9: The sculptor Joseph Enseling, date unknown

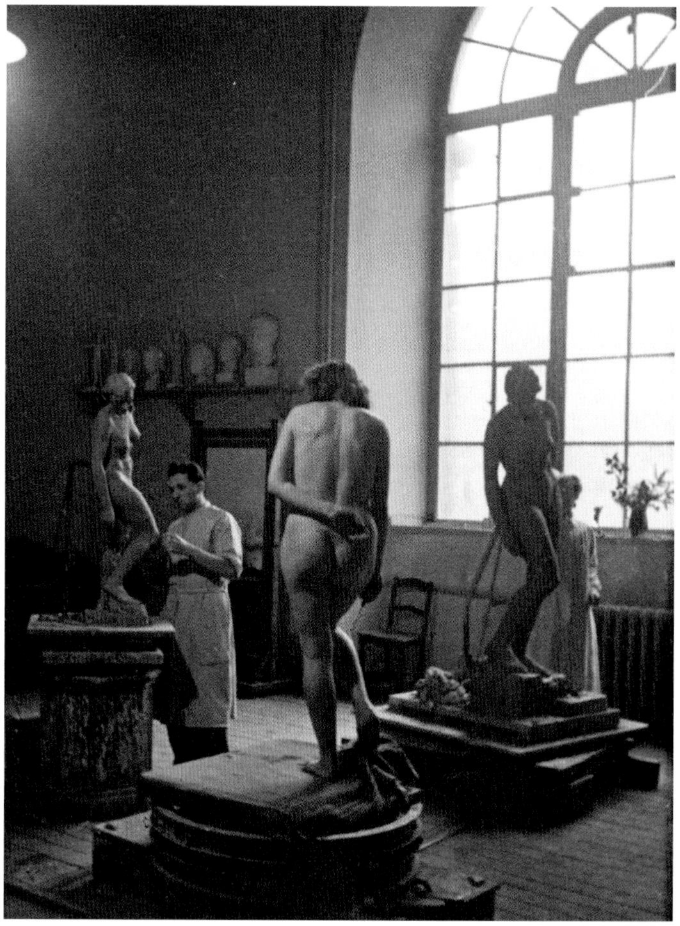

Fig. 10: The sculpture class taught by Joseph Enseling, 1950s

material result in the foundation; this is where the artistic conception of the sculptural work begins. [...] Whether it is a question of a figurative sculpture, decoration, or writing, everything must develop out of the overarching structure; this is where the chords that were struck there must continue to resonate.'[71]

The effect of that approach on students' work was that not just small exercises, such as making an inscribed plaque or a floor vase, were in principle realised in relation to a given or assumed architectural context, but even 'life studies from the model were carried out largely with a view to the purpose for which they would later be used'.[72] The sculptor seems to have been quite successful with his training methods because many of his pupils had commissions for architectural sculpture soon after their time at the Academy.[73]

Joseph Enseling

Sepp Mages's fellow sculptor, Joseph Enseling, was also appointed to a post at the Academy in 1938. He had studied with the sculptor Rudolf Bosselt from 1905 until 1910 at the Düsseldorf Decorative Arts School and had attended lectures in architecture given by Wilhelm Kreis and Peter Behrens. From 1910 until 1912 Enseling studied in Paris at the private Académie Colarossi. During that time he was intensively preoccupied with the work of Aristide Maillol, with whom he was personally well acquainted.[74] In 1913 Enseling began to teach a class in sculpture at the Applied Arts School in Essen and from 1928 at the Folkwang School for Design. Along with Will Lammert and Elisabeth von Treskow, Enseling belonged to the Margarethenhöhe circle of artists in Essen. In the 1920s the sculptor produced architectural sculpture, mainly in the Ruhr area, on the Baedeker House in Essen, to take one example. Portrait sculpture also played a major role in Enseling's oeuvre. In 1938 the artist was appointed to teach at the Düsseldorf Art Academy on the recommendation of the architect Emil Fahrenkamp. Since Enseling intended to leave the Folkwang School as soon as possible because the new head appointed by the National Socialists wanted to force the sculptor to give up his studio, the chance to teach in Düsseldorf came at just the right time.[75] Enseling would teach at the Art Academy until 1952 (Figs. 9, 10). Peter Bloch has remarked on the artist's style:

'His works reveal simplicity and immediacy. They eschew hollow pathos, loquacity, and mannerisms. They also eschew all formal experiments, do not act but rather react to the general stylistic development of the time. The world of work, which is illustrated in the medium of human figures, is made to speak earnestly, not without pride in what has been accomplished, as those who gave the commissions must have wanted to have it represented, but always also with an awareness of the limits of human endeavour.'[76]

The eulogy given by Hans Schwippert in 1957 indicates that the sculptor enjoyed a good reputation among the pupils at the Academy and his colleagues there. In it, the architect, who had been a friend of the deceased and at the time director of the Düsseldorf Art Academy, singled out for praise both the 'humanity and reticence devoid of bathos' of the 'figurative sculpture' created by Enseling and his 'memorials to the working man' as well as his 'mastery' of 'portraiture and sculpted likenesses'.[77] Enseling himself wrote about his aims in teaching at the Academy in the 1951 *Jahrbuch der Staatlichen Kunstakademie Düsseldorf*: 'I lead my pupils to the wellspring of all art – Nature. Through understanding its forms comes the inner liberation to the flight of one's own imagination. When one is confronted with a task, what has been learnt from Nature is the basis for independent creativity. We strive for the simple, uncomplicated, and wholesome expression of sculptural design.'[78]

It would probably be wrong to recognise a dying echo of the fascist notion of art in the last statement of the sculptor's on the collective striving for a 'wholesome' expression of cultural design. To the contrary, the choice of words makes clear that Enseling came from a generation of sculptors who even before 1933 saw abstraction of the human figure as dealing with sculptural form in a destructive way – that view was widely held by many sculptors who worked figuratively. The works by his pupils reproduced after Enseling's text in the *Jahrbuch* quoted above show that, in his class, moderate stylisation of the natural impression represented the upper limit of simplification; hence the pupils' figurative work recalls works of the 1920s and 1930s rather than the figurative style of the late 1940s and 1950s.[79]

Ewald Mataré

Just as Ewald Mataré's art was markedly different in style from that of his two colleagues Mages and Enseling, his teaching method also diverged from theirs, although giving a thorough grounding in craftsmanly skills must have been the common denominator of training in all three classes. In a 1957 publication on Mataré as a teacher at the Düsseldorf Art Academy, Anna Klapheck gives a rundown in memorably systematic form of how study was structured in the sculptor's class:

'In the beginning is writing. A pupil must incise several letters in the surface in a sort of monogram and carve them from a wooden ground. That is supposed to awaken a feeling for scale and order. The second assignment is to carve a wooden spoon of any size but one that is well suited to scooping. The spoon is

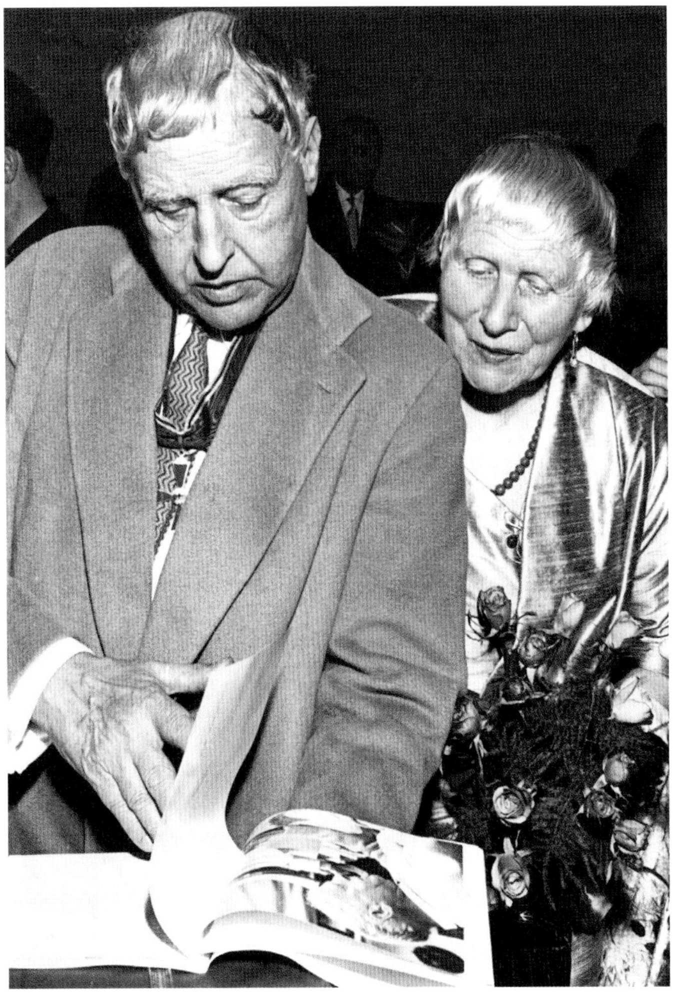

Fig. 11: Ewald Mataré and his wife, Hanna, on the occasion of the Grand Cross being awarded to Mataré on his seventieth birthday at the Düsseldorf Art Academy on 25 February 1957

"beautiful" if it fulfils all the functions required of it. With the third assignment, forming a pot in clay – the primary sculptural form, the ideal of all sculpture in the round – is to be recognised. The pot, the interpenetration of several spheres, must be thoroughly sensed as a mathematical configuration with nothing arbitrary about it and every part related to the whole in an exact ratio. Adorning this pot with decoration represents a further step. The decoration discloses how the pot is structured; form and decoration interact. The class does not begin to deal with the "object" until after those preliminary exercises and first of all in its relationship to the surface = relief, and only then as sculpture in the round. The invention of the motif is not what matters; Mataré is fond of having an old woodcut translated into relief, where the figure must be fully clear and entirely there, and the way to sculpture in the round is not open until this stage has been dealt with. However, given the brevity of the time spent training, this path, says Mataré, has not yet been taken the whole way by any pupil. However, he probably has managed to involve many pupils in practical collaboration on his own commissions while they were still in training, and it is the real assignment that provides the possibility of making clear to pupils what is the wrong way and what is the right way of setting about craftsmanship.'[80]

As an Academy teacher in Düsseldorf, Ewald Mataré exerted a strong influence on the generation of sculptors who began training in art after 1945 (Fig. 11). As Eduard Trier observed, Mataré led his pupils towards decorative applied sculpture. But the older pupils from his master class – Joseph Beuys, Erwin Heerich, or Günter Haese might be named as representative – clearly exemplify how far some had distanced themselves from Mataré as a role model.[81]

THE DÜSSELDORF ART ACADEMY REOPENS ON 31 JANUARY 1946

After Ewald Mataré had announced in December 1945 that he was retiring as acting director, Werner Heuser was appointed to succeed him on 12 January 1946. The official start into the future in Eiskellerstraße on 31 January 1946 with Heuser as the new acting director was made under exceptionally makeshift conditions because the British military authorities had insisted on fresh beginnings at the Düsseldorf Art Academy as soon as possible in order to set a further example in the cultural sector in the North Rhine Province. The Art Academy was the last of what were then five tertiary education institutions in the North Rhine Province to open again early in the first year after the war (Fig. 12).

Since the Great Hall of the Academy had been completely destroyed early in 1946 and the building was in a ruinous state, the reinauguration ceremony took place in the auditorium of the Luisengymnasium, a higher secondary grammar school nearby.[82] Numerous guests as well as students and professors were present. Among the guests welcomed by Werner Heuser, the new Academy director, were representatives of the British military authorities and distinguished figures from public life in the North Rhine Province and the city of Düsseldorf. Further, Rhineland artists were represented by many of their number at the reinauguration ceremony.[83]

In the addresses given on the occasion of the reinauguration of the Academy, the speakers – Robert Lehr, former Lord Mayor of Düsseldorf, who had been designated new head of the provincial government by the British; Eduard Sträter, who had been appointed district governor by the British occupation forces of the city of Düsseldorf; Werner Heuser, Academy director; and Lieutenant Colonel Henry J. Walker representing the military government – concentrated on underscoring the grand tradition of the Düsseldorf Art Academy. The memorable emphasis placed on the important history of the institution is sure to have been linked by all speakers with a hope that the years from 1933 to 1945 had not damaged the Art Academy permanently so that it might – for all the problems at the time – soon again be a beacon of culture for post-war Germany.[84] Walker and Heuser also called for a rebirth of artistic open-mindedness comparable to the attitude that had prevailed at the Art Academy before 1933, which had, among other things, expressed itself in assimilating influences from Western neighbours.[85] Further, all intellectual dogmatism was to be eschewed.[86] Heuser went on to emphasise in his address that, apart from the goal of promoting as much diversity as possible in aesthetic ideation, a pivotal task for the professors would be teaching the basics of design in art.[87]

A glance at the 1946 Academy syllabus reveals that teaching the basics of art techniques indeed took up an important part of the curriculum.[88] The training of aspiring painters, sculptors, and practitioners of the graphic arts was divided in the post-war years into a preliminary stage comprising two terms, which might only be skipped by 'applicants with sufficient previous training', who were immediately assigned to a class on the basis of the work they had done. Teaching in the preliminary stage provided for 'training in the elementary subjects'. That training in the basics consisted of freehand drawing from nature, practising drawing and painting techniques, linear drawing, writing script, fonts, and typography as well as an introduction to the techniques used in lithography and woodcut. For painters, the preliminary stage was followed by two terms in a drawing class. The drawing class syllabus included live drawing from the model, simple exercises in composition as preparation for dealing with space in art, and etching. After that, prospective painters would spend six terms in a painting class. The formal goals set out for the painting class included composition in paintings. From the third term on, groups were given assignments in decoration jointly with the architects, and tutorials in mosaic- and glass-painting were implemented. At that time, moreover, students had to decide on the course their specialist training would take. That means a decision was taken on the basis of samples of student work on whether they should specialise in figurative painting, landscape, portraiture, or the applied arts.

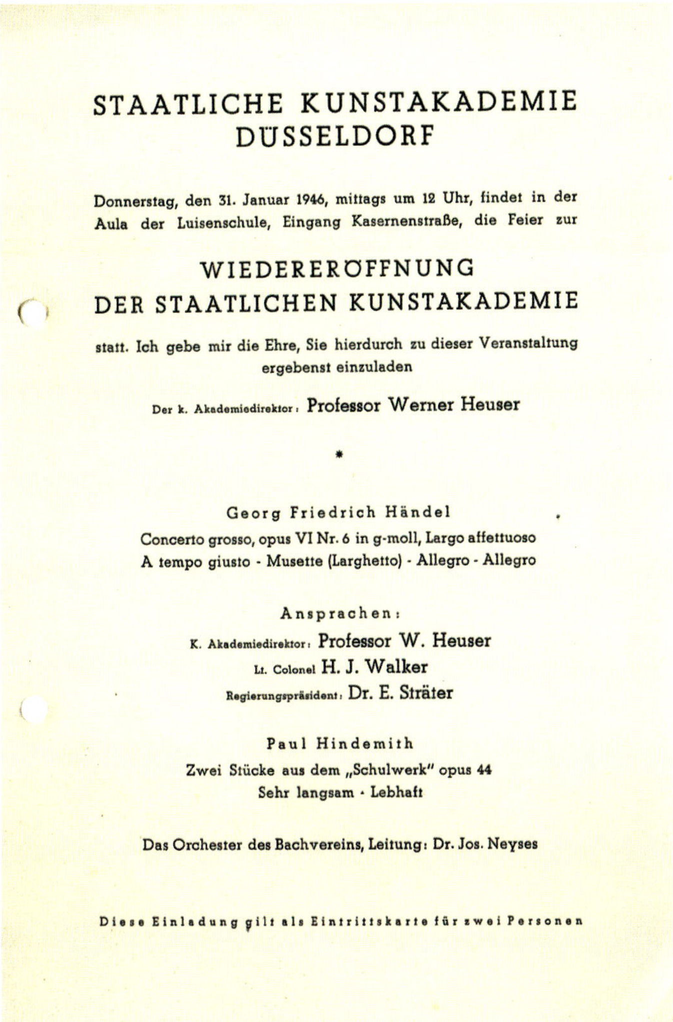

STAATLICHE KUNSTAKADEMIE
DÜSSELDORF

Donnerstag, den 31. Januar 1946, mittags um 12 Uhr, findet in der Aula der Luisenschule, Eingang Kasernenstraße, die Feier zur

WIEDERERÖFFNUNG
DER STAATLICHEN KUNSTAKADEMIE

statt. Ich gebe mir die Ehre, Sie hierdurch zu dieser Veranstaltung ergebenst einzuladen

Der k. Akademiedirektor: Professor Werner Heuser

*

Georg Friedrich Händel
Concerto grosso, opus VI Nr. 6 in g-moll, Largo affettuoso
A tempo giusto · Musette (Larghetto) · Allegro · Allegro

Ansprachen:
K. Akademiedirektor: Professor W. Heuser
Lt. Colonel H. J. Walker
Regierungspräsident: Dr. E. Sträter

Paul Hindemith
Zwei Stücke aus dem „Schulwerk" opus 44
Sehr langsam · Lebhaft

Das Orchester des Bachvereins, Leitung: Dr. Jos. Neyses

Diese Einladung gilt als Eintrittskarte für zwei Personen

Fig. 12: Invitation to the reinauguration of the State Düsseldorf Art Academy on 31 January 1946

The syllabus for sculptors, also based on study over six terms, provided for training in modelling, wood carving, and working in stone and metal. Like the course of study for painters, the course for sculptors also included doing assignments together with the architects from the third semester on.

A comparison of the syllabus for 1946 and 1948 with that of 1937 reveals that the resumption of teaching in 1946 was not linked with plans for restructuring the course of study in any way. To the contrary, the comparison highlights a seamless continuity in the basic structure of the various courses of study. To take one example, in 1937 painters had to spend four terms in the drawing class whereas from 1946 until 1948 they only had to complete two terms in it. After the war, however, the time they had to spend in the painting class was lengthened by two terms. The prescribed accompanying courses in subjects such as art history and anatomy were compulsory for all. The only accompanying course to be struck from the syllabus after 1945 was race studies. The fact that the first number of the Art Academy's annual report to be issued after the Second World War ended with a reprint of the Regulations of 24 November 1831 for the Royal Art Academy at Düsseldorf (Reglement vom 24. November 1831 für die Königliche Kunst-Akademie zu Düsseldorf)[89] makes it all the clearer that upholding the traditions of the venerable institution, steeped in history as it was – not least as a place for acquiring thorough training in the tools of the trade – had priority over any attempts at entirely overhauling the curriculum.

As Werner Heuser saw it and had emphasised in the address he gave at the reinauguration of the Art Academy, the chief duty of the professors lay not only in giving a thorough grounding in the praxis of art. The newly appointed acting director saw an important mission for his colleagues, the professors, and their students in helping to rebuild the Rhine Province. In this connection Heuser pointed out that the Art Academy was planning, among other things, a specialist class in restoration.[90] The *Jahresbericht der Staatlichen Kunstakademie Düsseldorf 1945–1947* [Annual Report of the Düsseldorf Art Academy 1945–1947] reveals that this specialist class was soon instituted and, as the Department for Restoration was attached to the also reorganised Painting Techniques Department.[91] In an essay on art academies in North Rhine-Westphalia, Ekkehard Mai remarked on Heuser's special areas of interest as Academy director in the reconstruction era after 1945: 'Heuser's intentions – in agreement with the military government and moderately modern artists – were mainly directed at reviving basic craftsmanship in the arts by mastering techniques and materials. So, apart from the fine arts, interest tended to be paid to applied art and the installation of workshops alongside re-establishing an architecture department – sparking off a resurgence of the old debate: "Academy or workshops?"'[92]

Heuser's ongoing interest in building up workshops for crafts was based in part on the idea that artists should place their craftsmanly skills at the service of the reconstruction effort as he had expressed it in his inaugural address. On the other hand, his commitment to practical skills was rooted in his awareness of the economic difficulties facing artists in the postwar era. Expressing his thoughts on this connection, he said in 1947:

'What lies ahead is likely to be the assignment of new tasks to the formation of artists and the inability to grant as much scope to free design as it was able to claim in the past. Our economic situation will hardly be able to grant the concerns of the muses particularly fortunate living conditions, but the demands of securing the basic needs of life will create a field of activity for talented persons who, in the fields of spatial art and the crafts, are able after thorough schooling to act in a way that is both exemplary and useful. Hence, considering what is needed, attaching applied arts workshops to state art academies – but certainly not decorative arts schools – is a step to be welcomed so that a rewarding and viable way to achievement and goals may be opened up to many. Practitioners of fine art will be in the minority, and they must – possibly exposed to all the vicissitudes of lack of recognition, a life of misery and squalor – accept a difficult destiny and thus be ready to provide proof of importance that transcends time without being driven mad by their creative powers.'[93]

While he was in office, Heuser devoted his energies in particular to the goal of 'ensuring in connection with a strong architecture department the establishment of workshops for the most important applied arts fields' to be in readiness 'for the manifold tasks of reconstruction'.[94] To realise those goals, architects Hans Schwippert and Walter Köngeter were appointed to the Art Academy.[95] Moreover, establishing a department for architecture and applied arts required the old master classes, which had once been housed under the roof in the attic. Since, however, reinstating those classes was still unthinkable while reconstruction was going on and the Academy building was being restored, an agreement was reached with the Cologne Werkkunstschule, headed by August Hoff, to house them there temporarily.[96] Debate raged publicly on the 'academy or workshops?' issue – as touched on above in the quotation from Ekkehard Mai. Whereas *Die Welt* of 15 February 1947 reported objectively on the planned changes to the Academy, some of which had already been carried out, notably the projected Applied Arts Department,[97] the planned fusion of the Art Academy and the Decorative Arts School was scathingly criticised in an essay printed in *Freiheit* on 29 July 1947.[98] The dissolution of the celebrated Düsseldorf Decorative Arts School in 1919 and the integration of its Architecture Department in the Art Academy had brought no gains, it was asserted. For that reason the author called for a clear division between the Art Academy and its workshops and attacked the planned 'inflation' of the former. Groundbreaking developments could only emerge from the two fields – fine and applied art – if the areas were kept separate with clearly distinctive contours, which would not be possible if they were both under the same roof.[99]

Heinrich Kamps, who succeeded Werner Heuser as acting director in the summer term of 1949 since Heuser had to retire from the Art Academy at sixty-eight, stuck to his predecessor's course. Kamps felt the Academy had an obligation to its students, who, as he saw it – in this resembling his predecessor – consisted in conveying to the majority of graduates a basis in art and crafts which would enable them to earn a livelihood:

'Today's Academy must not make the basic educational mistake of yesterday's Academy. It focused on the extraordinary genius instead of on the average while still training countless many lesser talents in drawing and painting alone, of which only a very few became real architects or painters. The mass of those so onesidedly trained academicians full of false hopes were exposed to social squalor and were not in a position to be able to make themselves useful in the working life of the people. The reunion of the work world with the creative artist has yet to take place. This does not mean that the Academy should embark straight off on a utilitarian curriculum.'[100]

Kamps viewed practising art as 'an activity of practical ordering, no matter whether an artisan or an artist were concerned'.[101] For that reason, thus the painter, the chief task in teaching should consist in making students familiar with 'the means' and 'tools'.[102]

During Kamps's tenure, plans for realising workshops were carried out to the extent that by 1953 the Art Academy had studios for commercial graphics, monumental painting, glass painting, and tapestry weaving.

STRUCTURING AND EXPANDING THE FINE ARTS COURSE IN THE LATE 1940s

Apart from the particular interest in the applied arts and the installation of workshops, the Fine Arts and Art Teaching Departments were, it goes without saying, in the sights of those responsible for them at the Düsseldorf Art Academy. The persisting problem of space in the severely damaged building was directly related to any curricular considerations. Ewald Mataré had decided to teach his sculpture students from 1946 until 1949 in his own studio in Meerbusch-Büderich because the rooms available were both makeshift and cramped. For all the other artist-professors and their students, classroom work at the Academy during those years entailed having to be organised in the most cramped quarters under difficult conditions.

Reconstruction began in 1946 with three rooms. By late 1947, thirty-five of the original eighty rooms in the Academy building and the roof over the west tract had been restored. The Academy had even housed the Art Association for the Rhinelands and Westphalia until the summer term of 1946, when it found new quarters in the city, leaving the rooms it had occupied free for teaching. The library was moved from its temporary home in the cellar so that the refectory could start cooking and serving food again in the winter term of 1947/48. Students had had to take their meals at the Malkasten [Paint Box] Association from 1946 until the Academy cafeteria reopened. At the Malkasten, they had had to stand guard in shifts to prevent the small supply of provisions available to them there from landing on the black market.[103]

The east tract of the Academy was still in ruins. That section was separated by walls in all the corridors from the restored part of the building so that work could begin on removing the rubble. In a newspaper article on the Art Academy from the summer of 1947, it was said about the state of the building and the teaching taking place within it:

'The sun and the moon alternate in shining down into the Great Hall of the Art Academy, and the frescoes in the gutted, roofless hall have been blurred to unrecognisability by rain and wind. Draughts moan in the wide corridors, and through some doors one looks down into bottomless depths. The consequences of war have not, however, hindered teaching. One hundred and fifty Academy pupils work together with their professors in a few restored rooms that are walled off from the corridors by partitions knocked together from rough planks [...]. A mixture of ruin and new build – that is the Art Academy on the Rhine today.'[104]

The majority of those who studied art in Düsseldorf in the post-war years were between twenty-five and thirty-two years old.[105] Many of the male students were also marked by the experience of serving in the armed forces and being interned as prisoners of war. In addition, all students had been influenced by the NS regime's official notions of art. Moreover, the number of students from socially deprived backgrounds was very high.[106] In 1947 Werner Heuser wrote in a 1947 newspaper article about the difficulties and particular tasks confronting professors who taught: the first step would be making the 'intellectual soil fertile in the students by carefully loosening it and with sympathetic understanding cleansing it of all the ravages of the era just past'.[107] Unlike earlier times, Heuser goes on to say, the contemporary idea of art was still too strongly informed by the influence of the previous National Socialist era:

'The youth of today, who in the era of National Socialism were without contacts to interests in art outside Germany and with vision impaired, suddenly find themselves lashed by a bewildering welter of artistic choices; on the one hand, willing to receive and to give – although still without discernment – on the other, they have been rendered distrustful of all new revelations by the bankruptcy of previous truths. Hence they swing back and forth – seeking firm ground to stand on – between belief and scepticism, between inclination and resistance, young yet at the same time unyouthful.'[108]

In addition, Heuser went on to add, material needs exerted at the time an equally strong influence on how art-related issues might develop. Hence the task confronting professors was to 'liberate productive forces from the constraints of being buried intellectually and disarranged' and to 'switch off the inhibitions that of necessity through the vicissitudes of these times negatively affect body and mind and paralyse both through their influence'.[109]

No details are known of how the professors succeeded in influencing students in their classes to distract them from the manifold hardships of the post-war years and the Currency Reform era and focus their minds on art. What is known, however, is that students were encouraged by the Academy to participate in the restoration of numerous public artworks and were paid to do so. Commissions for restoration work evidently went not just to the special restoration class but to all students interested in doing their share.[110] Moreover, by 1950, for the first time since the war, the Düsseldorf Art Academy once again had more than twenty-five master studios, a facility that enabled particularly gifted students to have a studio of their own free of charge for a specified time.

However, the factor that was of the greatest importance for inculcating ideals, craftsmanship, and universally humane qualities in students was the appointment of new professors. Although the lack of space at the Art Academy was a situation that could only be altered with time, two architects, Hans Schwippert and Walter Köngeter, as well as Theo Champion, a painter, and Otto Pankok, a draughtsman, printmaker, and sculptor, were appointed to teach there, beginning in the winter term of 1947/48.

New Appointments Made During Werner Heuser's Tenure 1946–1949

Theo Champion

The appointment of Theo Champion (Fig. 13) to the Düsseldorf Art Academy at the start of winter term 1947/48 was linked with the wish that the artist would lead the venerable tradition of landscape painting there into the present and set new priorities in teaching. 'In the grand array of landscape painters who have worked at the Academy since Johann Wilhelm Schirmer, Carl Friedrich Lessing, Hans Fredrik Gude, Oswald Achenbach, Eugen Dücker, and Max Clarenbach, Champion will transfigure this art anew and provides the best guarantee of good supervision of the coming generation.'[111]

Like most of his colleagues, the artist had studied at the Düsseldorf Academy. Beginning his study of painting there with Eduard von Gebhardt in 1906 and 1907, he transferred to the Weimar Art Academy, where he was in the classes taught by the landscape painter Theo Hagen until 1909 and then studied under Ludwig von Hofmann, a painter close to Symbolism and Jugendstil/Art Nouveau, and the painter Sascha Schneider. Born in Oberkassel, Theo Champion returned to Düsseldorf after travels for study and military service in the First World War, remaining domiciled there for the rest of his life. On his return, he began to paint mainly in the environs of Düsseldorf and in the Lower Rhine area. Like the oeuvres of so many Rhenish artists of the day, Champion's work is, stylistically speaking, inhomogeneous. His paintings reveal a kaleidoscope of influences ranging from Van Gogh, the Fauves, Impressionism, Expressionism, and even the Düsseldorf landscape painters of the late nineteenth and early twentieth centuries. In 1950 the artist remarked on working with his pupils: 'I try to make my pupils aware of the inner content of a picture; they should attach little importance to externals, the manner; more important is what a picture expresses spiritually and intellectually, the artist's inner stance.'[112] Although the artist had not done much drawing himself, he had his students practise drawing techniques by sketching from nature, as is shown by works of theirs featured in the 1951 *Jahrbuch der Staatlichen Kunstakademie Düsseldorf.*[113] Appointed to teach at the age of sixty, Champion was only granted the space of a few years in which to transmit his knowledge to students because he died in 1952 at the age of sixty-five.

The appointment of Theo Champion in 1947 exemplifies the circumstance that the main interest in Düsseldorf – as in many other places in Germany – was in restoring continuity, linking up with art as it had been before 1933, and not in trying something new. Taking a look at the average age of the professors teaching at the Düsseldorf Art Academy from 1946 until well into the 1950s, one is struck by the fact that all of them were born between the late 1870s and the early years of the twentieth century. Hence the teachers at the Academy in the post-war era already looked back on long careers with oeuvres that had been chiefly shaped by late nineteenth-century and early twentieth-century developments in art. As idiosyncratic as the individual stance might be, the basic aesthetic tenor was that of a moderate Modernism, which also came into play in the appointment of Otto Pankok, who, like Champion, came to teach at the Art Academy at the beginning of the winter term of 1947/48.

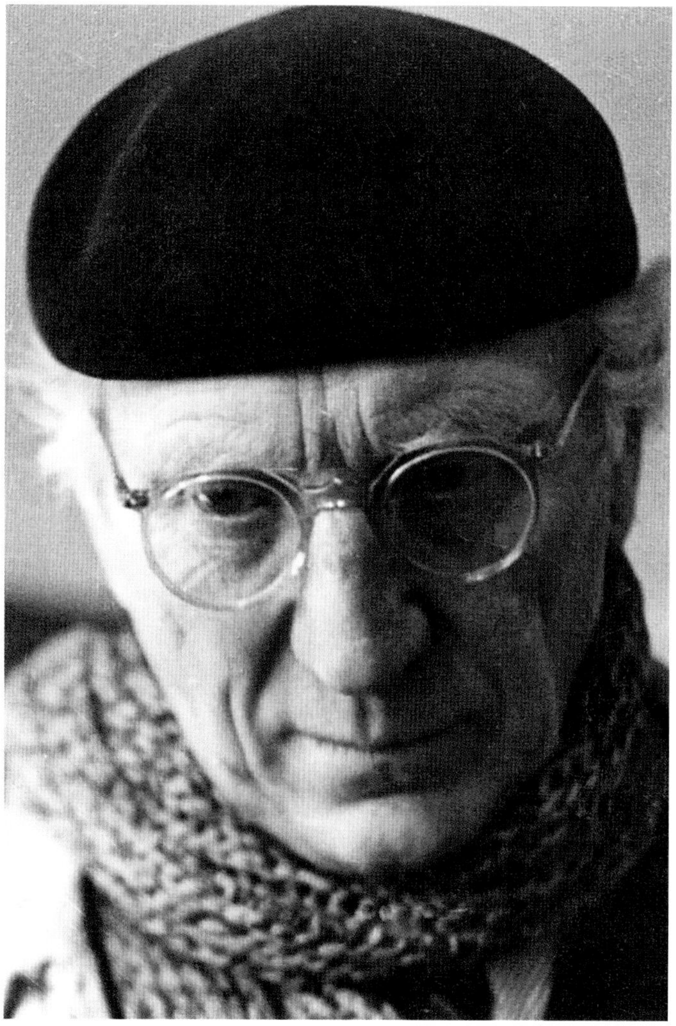

Fig. 13: The painter Theo Champion, date unknown

Otto Pankok

According to the *Jahresbericht der Staatlichen Kunstakademie 1945–1947*, great hopes were linked with the appointment of Otto Pankok: as the 'supervisor of the drawing class and monumental composition', he was tasked with imparting to his students a profound understanding of drawing as an elementary foundation for art.[114] In addition, Pankok, who had displayed political and social commitment all his life, was presented as the epitome of the morally and ethically conscientious artist whose unimpeachable character could be expected to exert a positive influence on students and their work (Fig. 14).

The great political and social commitment and profound interest in humanity and Nature that informed the expressive style of the draughtsman, painter, printmaker, and sculptor was also expressed in the way he treated his students. In 1948, for instance, Pankok talked eloquently in a *Westdeutsche Rundschau* article about how education at an academy should look: 'Drawing will once again become the distillation of an artist's thinking [...]. However, the assured development of the artistic imagination will stand above everything and the aesthetic conscience, which in this case comprises the entire conscience, to which the artist [Pankok] has always remained uniquely true.'[115]

Unlike his colleagues, all of whom had spent several years studying at applied arts schools and/or art academies, Pankok had fled the Art Academies in Düsseldorf and Weimar after brief stays at them in his youth – he had spent six weeks in class in Düsseldorf in 1912/13 and seven months in Weimar. After military service and travels, the artist, who was born in Mülheim on the Ruhr, settled in Düsseldorf in 1920, becoming, among other things, a member of the Junges Rheinland. He maintained close ties of friendship with both Gerd Wollheim and Otto Dix. Between 1935 and the end of the Second World War, Pankok and his family moved many times, fleeing persecution by the National Socialists and the ravages of war. In 1946 the artist and his family returned to Düsseldorf because the house where he had lived, which had been destroyed in the war, had been rebuilt. A year later he was appointed to teach at the Art Academy.

'It is high time that the academies ditch the barrack-room manner – that is, masses of pupils are not drilled like companies of soldiers doing rifle drill [the tedious repetition of specific

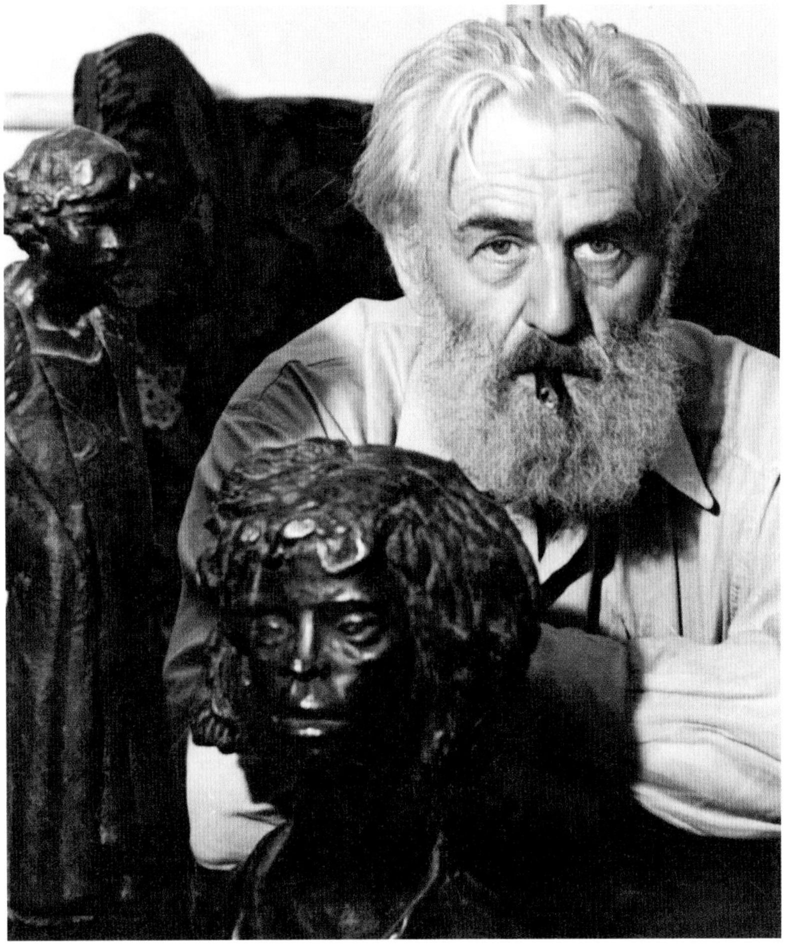

Fig. 14: Otto Pankok with bronze sculptures Hilda, Hände auf dem Rücken *[Hilda, Hands behind her Back] (left) and* Gaisa II, *Düsseldorf,* c. *1948*

handholds]. [...] This constant spying on and examining their thoughts and deeds, this Nazidom must be swept from the academies! I want to help the young people find a way to pictures that grow entirely out of their own personalities. A feeling for the freedom and beauty of life must be awakened. Making students mindlessly slave away for years in congested classrooms in front of a dull commonplace model not only ruins their eyes but also destroys any desire to work, and nothing beautiful, free, and new has ever been created in this world without desire and love. Art is always a risky venture, an adventure which takes courage to commit oneself to.'[116]

Pankok's personality was such that students thronged his classes. Although he had taken over a drawing class, he also instructed his pupils in painting, sculpture, and the graphic arts. On the occasion of the artist's sixtieth birthday in 1953, Anna Klapheck reported on his class in a newspaper article about him:

'He [Pankok] tends to let beginners and advanced pupils work together. He is even less likely to divide up by subject. The fields of art must interact. Many a student also moves over to sculpture. So there is equal enthusiasm for painting, carving in wood, or drawing on stone in the "Pankok drawing class". [...] The method behind his teaching consists in, thus Pankok, "letting everyone develop from what is in him, eliciting the utmost from him".'[117]

The freedom individuals enjoyed in Pankok's class did, however, turn out to have its limits, where representation of the human figure or Nature was abandoned for experiments in form. In an essay entitled 'Unser Glaube an das Leben' [Our Belief in Life], published in *Jahrbuch der Staatlichen Kunstakademie* in 1951, the artist expressed deep-rooted misgivings about the experiments in painting conducted by American colleagues whose work was increasingly attracting attention in America and Europe at that time – and certainly also among Art Academy students. Pankok, humanitarian to the core, called the products of the 'New York industrialists stillborn arrangements of circles and squares' and decried abstract painting in general as 'a lapse into play, shying away from truth in a domain out of control'.[118] In the series of texts published in the Düsseldorf Art Academy's yearbook, Pankok's article represented the sole reflection of the heated debate about abstract art conducted in Germany at the time by the art historian Walter Sedlmayr, the painter Willi Baumeister, and the philosopher Theodor W. Adorno, among others.[119] Pankok, however, did not bother to engage in nuanced debate. His terse response to the pivotal discussion of the day led Walter Romain to conclude that 'the Academy – at least as far as the teaching staff are concerned – is little moved by, let alone excited about, the vehement discussions on theory taking place elsewhere. The reconstruction years have been quiet ones at the Düsseldorf Academy with respect to the great aesthetic issues of the time.'[120]

ADDING TO ART STUDIES WITH HEINRICH KAMPS AS DIRECTOR 1949–1954

After the west tract of the Düsseldorf Art Academy had been fully restored by 1948, construction work began on the top floor in spring 1949. Work also commenced on the east tract in autumn that year. Gradually but steadily the Art Academy building, much of which had been destroyed in the Second World War, began to look like its old self, and by 1953 it was being enlarged and modernised to meet the needs of a new era.[121] For all the progress made in rebuilding during the late 1940s and early 1950s, classwork could not be carried out to the full extent because there was still a shortage of studio rooms.

Heinrich Kamps, who had succeeded Werner Heuser as acting director in summer term 1949, shared his thoughts on the task entrusted to him in view of the current situation: 'I definitely do not view my appointment as an administrative task that fulfils an established agenda. To the contrary, the current situation calls for a lively talent for improvisation adapted to the prevailing conditions, which will be able to deal with both the organisational and the artistic tasks facing the Academy.'[122]

The newly appointed director very soon had to deal with criticism voiced by the public that the Art Academy had too few painter-professors so that it could not regain its former reputation as an academy for painters.[123] Despite the lack of space, painters Bruno Goller and Ferdinand Macketanz as well as the sculptor Zoltán Székessy were engaged to teach at the Art Academy during Heinrich Kamps's tenure, which was cut off prematurely in 1954 when he died after a series of heart attacks.

Bruno Goller

After Werner Heuser had retired from teaching for reasons of age at the close of the winter term of 1948/49, Bruno Goller, a painter living in Düsseldorf, was given a short-term contract to teach a drawing class. Goller would not be appointed professor until 1953 – after the death of Theo Champion the year before. Goller, who had never attended an art academy, trained in art from 1919 until 1921 in the Düsseldorf studio of the landscape painter Julius Jungheim. In the 1920s Goller belonged to the art dealer Mutter Ey's circle and was a member of the Junges Rheinland and the Rhenish Secession as well as other groups. His admission to the select circle of artists teaching at the Art Academy in the late 1940s should be viewed as an indication that Heinrich Kamps continued the appointment policies of his predecessor, Werner Heuser, in associating as many individualists as possible with the Academy rather than insisting on representatives of a particular art movement to ensure that the Art Academy after years of fascist art doctrine would present internally and externally as broad a range in art as possible.

Goller's painting – his flat, almost colourless, pictures resembling intarsia, in which many motifs from the artist's immediate surroundings were translated into a pictorial universe reminiscent of Surrealism and Magic Realism yet always distinctly his own – and his quiet, concentrated approach in the classroom situation contributed to his rapidly becoming very popular with the students as a teacher at the Art Academy (Fig. 15).[124] 'He's gollering' became a byword among students although the painter himself is likely to have been most anxious that his students should not copy his works but should form their own styles.[125] According to Anna Klapheck, Goller personified the 'no movement no agenda' policy adhered to at the Düsseldorf Art Academy in the 1940s and 1950s. Instead, the individual pupil with his own personal abilities was always the focus of his teaching, and Goller, as a distinguished artist, was always responsible for the content of what he taught.[126]

From 1949 until 1958 Goller, like many of his colleagues, was entrusted with the dual task of being in charge of teaching beginners in a drawing class and supervising a painting class of his own. Between 1959 and 1964, when he left the Academy, the painter was relieved of the obligation to supervise a drawing class so that he could concentrate entirely on teaching his painting class.[127]

Ferdinand Macketanz

In 1950 Heinrich Kamps enlarged the teaching staff at the Düsseldorf Art Academy to include Ferdinand Macketanz, a painter who would not be appointed to a tenured professorship until seven years later. Macketanz taught at the Academy until 1968 (Fig. 16). In admitting Macketanz to the staff, Kamps may have gone some way towards mollifying those critics who felt that there were too few painters at the Academy then – after all, this was an artist who had trained in the glorious era of the Kaesbach directorate. Macketanz, whose life and work have yet to be thoroughly studied, had moved in his youth with his parents to Düsseldorf. Before 1933 he was in the master class taught by Heinrich Campendonk at the Düsseldorf Art Academy. Walter Kaesbach, who was director of the Düsseldorf Art Academy from 1924 until 1933, helped Macketanz during the

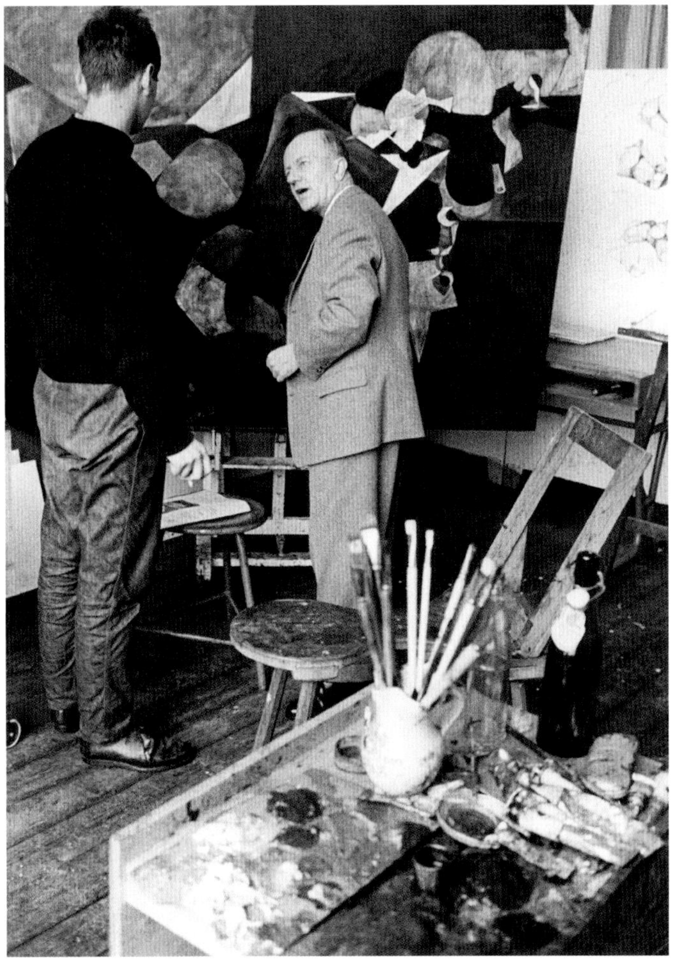

Fig. 15: The painter Bruno Goller with a student from his class, 1960

National Socialist regime to move to Lake Constance, where he belonged to the group of artists known as the Höri circle.[128] Macketanz's oeuvre comprises mainly portraits but also includes landscapes and still lifes. In 1960 the artist told Anna Klapheck that the starting point for his portraits was always the sitter but that after a certain point he no longer needed the sitter to be present since his thoughts from then on were directed solely at 'bringing everything together'.[129] The Düsseldorf art historian remarked on Macketanz's style:

'Things in the real sense, even though he is a "representational" painter, are not particularly important to him; instead every form has its own function in the picture as a whole. A colour without form is unthinkable to him; the individual colour, too, makes no sense to him either. A picture only develops in the interrelationship of colours to each other; one colour "makes" another just as light and shade, cold and warm, round and angular depend on each other. A feeling for form and picture structure is the legacy of classicism.'[130]

According to Klapheck, as a teacher, Macketanz was always anxious not to impose a system on his pupils or stereotype them. Macketanz viewed students' time at the Academy as 'a sort of "chilling period", [...] which aided inner growth before the realities and hardships of everyday living caught up with them'.[131]

Zoltán Székessy

After the sculptor Joseph Enseling reached retirement age and left the Art Academy in 1952, he was succeeded by Zoltán Székessy, a Hungarian (Fig. 17). Székessy had studied at the Free Art School in Budapest from 1921 to 1922. The young student wanted to follow that year up with studies in Paris but the French immigration authorities refused him a permit to stay so he went to Düsseldorf. There he studied until 1924 'in Wilhelm Döringer's "head" class, where you worked hard at live drawing from the model'.[132] Galloping inflation forced Székessy to return to Hungary, where he served an apprenticeship as a wood carver in Budapest. In 1926 he returned to Düsseldorf and studied at the Art Academy until 1927 with Richard Langer, who held a chair in architectural and ornamental sculpture. Székessy subsequently studied with Gerhard Marcks at the Burg Giebichenstein Applied Arts School and Munich Art Academy with Bernhard Bleeker. In 1929 Székessy returned to Düsseldorf and settled there. Anna Klapheck discussed Zoltán Székessy's work in 1959:

'The last time we saw a selection of his work was at the Art Association in 1951. Portraits and bronzes in small formats, intended for private spaces, formed the nucleus of his work at that time. As intellectual as it is, his art has never lost its link with Nature. His portraits are fully accountable to the sitter yet are both individual and universal; they represent "gaze" rather than "eye", dormant form rather than mutable life. In the reconstruction years Székessy was increasingly in demand for applied arts commissions, also in ecclesiastical space, which often called for larger than life-size formats. His assured mastery of all materials and techniques, even mosaic and glass, for instance, has stood him in good stead. Rarely does he have recourse to assistants; he works even large figures on his own right through to the end.'[133]

Should one go even further back to the work Székessy produced in the 1920s and 1930s, which already reveals a noticeable

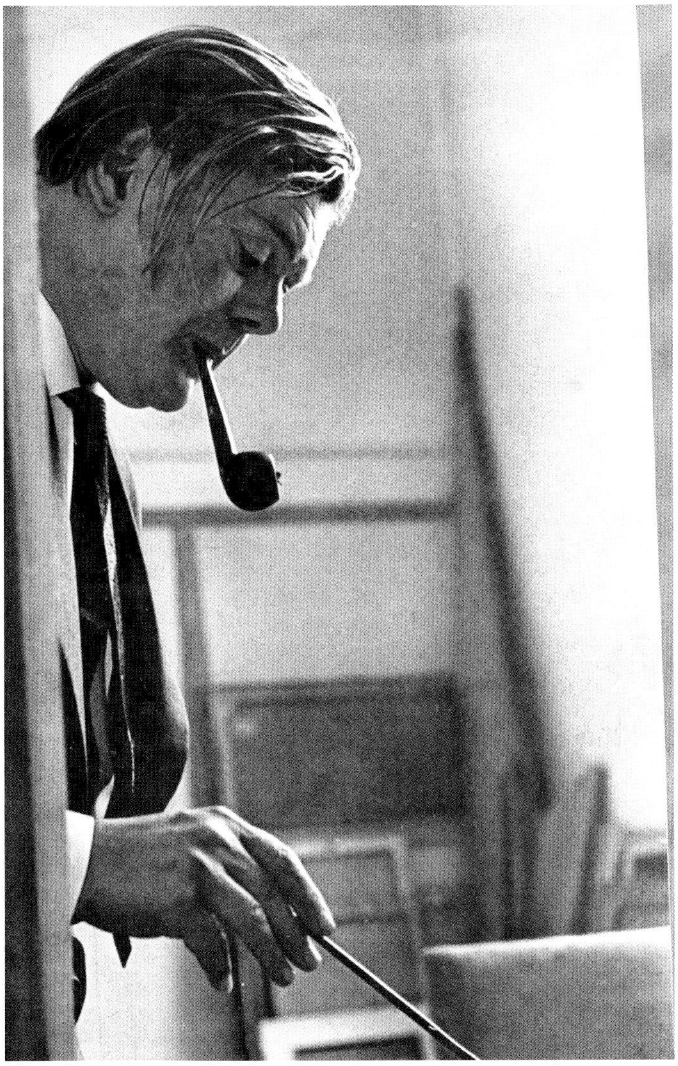

Fig. 16: The painter Ferdinand Macketanz, 1960

stylistic resemblance to later works of his, the utter lack of bathos and severity and the predominance of a simple, really naive naturalness are the distinguishing features, unusually so for the time, of works that were often in small formats.

Texts on Székessy as a teacher at the Düsseldorf Art Academy suggest that the sculptor tried to give his students the greatest possible scope for developing their individual approaches to art, a practise that quite obviously set him apart from both his predecessor, Enseling, and his colleagues at the time, Mages and Mataré.[134] The idea of having students imitate his own works was repugnant to him, thus Anna Klapheck.[135] Franz Josef Kampmann reported on how the sculptor taught in his classes:

'His training centres on the study of Nature. He leads his pupils to design from the object rather than from the visual or technical means. In that way observation is rendered more acute and perception deepened. [...] Form is to be attained from experiencing the object and the possibilities of the material rather than imposing it on the object. The inexhaustible bounty of natural forms demands different expression in each instance, and the pupil remains receptive to new experiences of form and new formal languages.'[136]

A 'rainbow class' was the consequence of Székessy's teaching method.[137]

APPOINTMENTS FROM THE MID- TO THE LATE 1950s: BETWEEN TRADITIONALISM AND INNOVATION

Robert Pudlich

The death of Heinrich Kamps led not only to the appointment of the long-established art historian Jakob Heinrich Schmidt as director of the Düsseldorf Art Academy for a brief transitional interval – in 1956 Hans Schwippert was appointed to the post and remained in office for ten years until he left the Academy – but also to Kamps's chair in painting and his position as supervisor to prospective art teachers being left vacant. In 1955 the next occupant of the chair was appointed: the Düsseldorf painter, draughtsman, and set designer Robert Pudlich, who taught at the Art Academy until he died in 1962 (Fig. 18). The subjects Pudlich had studied at Cologne University included art history and mathematics. From 1925 until 1927 he had trained on the side and then full-time with Lothar von Kunowski at the Düsseldorf Art Academy, taking the state examinations conferring 'senior drawing teacher' status. Pudlich, however, chose not to become a teacher after finishing his studies. Instead he became a freelance artist. As a young man in the 1920s, the painter frequented Mutter Ey's circle and belonged to both the Rhenish Secession and the Deutscher Künstlerbund. Pudlich's work reveals numerous influences: Pablo Picasso, Karl Hofer, Max Beckmann, Paul Cézanne – the names of many other artists could be added to the list. The even-handed approach to incorporating sources of inspiration in his own work evidently also informed the artist's treatment of his students. He told Anna Klapheck in 1959 that he was schooling prospective art teachers in aesthetic discipline and precise workmanship. Moreover, he said he allowed both 'representational' and 'non-representational' experiments in his class because he always took the distinctive personality of the individual into consideration.[138]

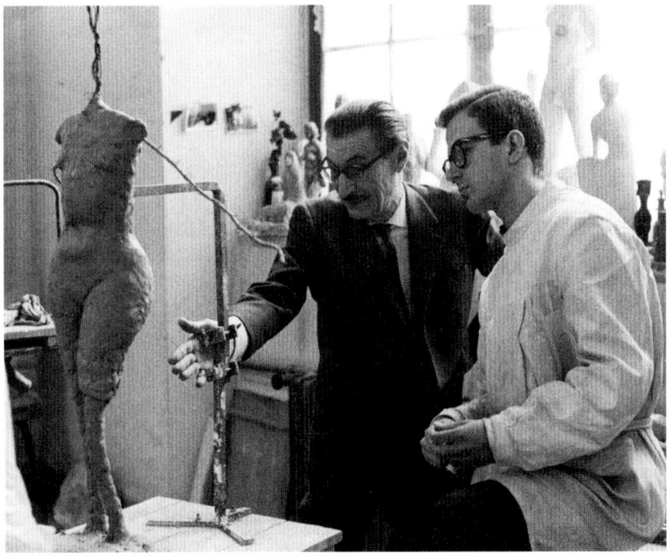

Fig. 17: The sculptor Zoltán Székessy with a student from his class, 1960

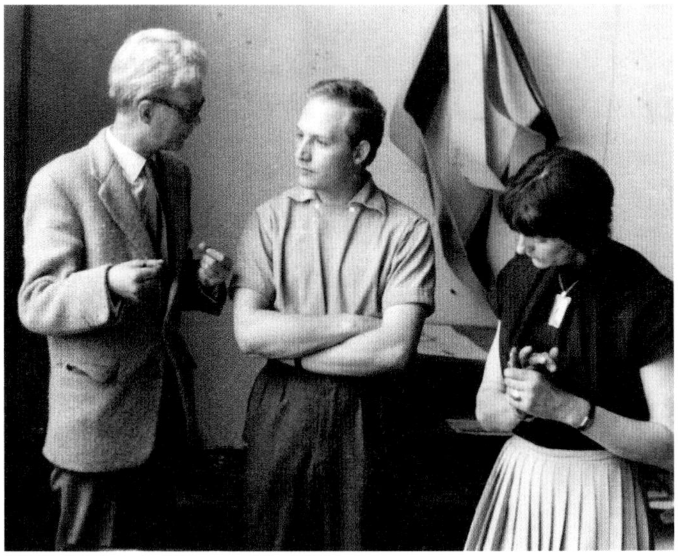

Fig. 18: Robert Pudlich, painter, draughtsman, and stage designer, teaching students, 1957

Georg Meistermann

Georg Meistermann was appointed to teach at the Düsseldorf Art Academy in 1955 along with Robert Pudlich. Meistermann had a class in 'fine art and monumental painting' until 1960 – the year that he transferred to the Karlsruhe Art Academy. Appointing this artist, who at the time was enjoying considerable success, particularly as a glass painter, definitely represented the first great step taken by the Art Academy in a new direction. By the time he was appointed, Meistermann's style had developed into abstraction from figurative beginnings. Even in his early paintings the young artist had simplified objects and reduced them to essentials. He had received the crucial encouragement to do so while studying with Heinrich Nauen and Ewald Mataré at the Düsseldorf Art Academy from 1928 until 1933. After the Second World War Meistermann became a leading light in the development of abstract painting in Germany. While he was at the Düsseldorf Art Academy, the artist, who had first attracted attention as a glass painter in 1938, made a series of glass windows, always also including his students in the process. Since his studio at the Düsseldorf Art Academy was not always large enough for window designs – some of them monumental in scale – to be realised, Meistermann frequently moved with his students to the Academy Great Hall.

The teaching Meistermann did in his class was informed by strict discipline but also allowed for great freedom. A former pupil and friend of Ewald Mataré's, Meistermann had developed the plans for a new Academy curriculum together with Mataré in 1945, but it did not meet with a positive response from the politicians who would have been responsible for implementing it. Young students probably had to go through systematically structured courses and even draw from plaster casts.[139] The more they advanced, the more freedom his students were given. Meistermann even encouraged older students to take part in competitions.[140] He also saw to it that his students received commissions.[141]

LOOKING AHEAD TO THE LATE 1950s

During the latter half of the 1950s the Düsseldorf Art Academy, with the architect Hans Schwippert as director, developed into the best place for training in art in Germany.[142] Student numbers had risen by then to over 350. Alongside Georg Meistermann, who had been appointed in 1955, two painters, Joseph Fassbender and Karl Otto Götz, joined the staff, in 1958 and 1959, respectively, to represent the vanguard of the abstract artists who would soon follow. Manfred Sieler, at the time just thirty-one years old, was appointed in 1958 to succeed Ewald Mataré although Joseph Beuys had been designated to take over Mataré's class (Fig. 19). Sieler, however, who had been a pupil of Karl Hartung's at the Berlin Art Academy, was, like his predecessor Mataré and his colleagues Mages and Székessy, an exponent of figurative art. Although the Düsseldorf Art Academy was moving slowly but surely towards alignment with contemporary trends in art, it would still take six years until the appointment of Norbert Kricke in 1964 finally opened the Academy gates to abstract sculpture.

NOTES

1 *Jahresbericht der Staatlichen Kunstakademie Düsseldorf 1945–1947*, Düsseldorf [1948], p. 21. I should like to express my appreciation to Brigitte Blockhaus, Miriam Müller, Tanja Wessolowski, and Matthias Leeck for their energetic support in researching for this text.

2 Even after the Art Academy officially reopened on 31 January 1946, students continued to be drafted for what was known as 'holiday work deployment', which entailed clearing away rubble and rebuilding.

3 *Jahresbericht 1945–1947* (see n. 1), p. 21.

4 On this see Sonja Mataré and Sabine Maja Schilling (eds.), *Ewald Mataré, Tagebücher* [Diaries] *1915–1965*, Cologne 1997, p. 331. For Mataré's plans and his failure to realise them, also see Ekkehard Mai, 'Kunst lehren, mit der Kunst leben. Kunsthochschulen in NRW – Umrisse', in: Karl Ruhrberg (ed.), *Zeitzeichen. Stationen Bildender Kunst in Nordrhein-Westfalen*, exhib. cat. Bonn/Leipzig/Duisburg, Cologne 1989, pp. 191–203; here: p. 191; Volker Rattemeyer, 'Kunstakademien. Ihre Bedeutung für die Kunstentwicklung in der Bundesrepublik im Beispiel von Karlsruhe und Düsseldorf', in: Dieter Honisch (ed.), *1945–1985. Kunst in der Bundesrepublik Deutschland*, exhib. cat. Berlin 1985, pp. 646–654; here: p. 649.

5 Mataré and Schilling (see n. 4), p. 325.

6 Ibid., p. 331.

7 Ibid.

8 Ibid.

9 Ibid.

10 More detailed glimpses than Mataré's diary are provided by his plans for curriculum change, which have survived on typed pages printed in Roland Meyer-Petzold, *Ewald Matarés Kunst der Lehre. Ihre Wirkungsgeschichte an der Kunstakademie Düsseldorf aus der Sicht der Schüler*, Weinheim 1989, pp. 254–260.

11 Mataré and Schilling (see n. 4), p. 331.

12 Ibid.

13 Ibid.

14 Ibid.

15 Ibid.

16 Ibid., p. 330. However, Mataré decided against giving up his professorship because of the difficult economic situation at the time: ibid., p. 331.

17 Gerd Vielhaber, 'Werner Heuser', in: Kunstverein für die Rheinlande und Westfalen Düsseldorf (ed.), *Werner Heuser*, exhib. cat. Düsseldorf 1965, n.p.

18 *Jahresbericht 1945–1947* (see n. 1), p. 24.

19 More on this on pp. 141f. in this essay.

20 On this see Beatrice Thön, *Heinrich Kamps, 1896–1954. Monographie mit Werkverzeichnis* [Monograph with Catalogue of Works], Pfinztal 1992, p. 12.

21 Thon (see n. 20), p. 39.

22 Ibid., p. 57.

23 Ibid., p. 84.

24 Ibid.

25 On this see 'Werkkatalog' [Catalogue of Works], in: ibid., pp. 109–188.

26 Heinrich Kamps, 'Staatliche Kunstakademie Düsseldorf', 1947, article in the Düsseldorf Art Academy archives (without further citation of references and sources).

27 More on this on pp. 148f. in this essay.

28 All biographical data on Wilhelm Herberholz have come from the Düsseldorf Art Academy archives.

29 Hans Vollmer, 'Wilhelm Herberholz', in: Hans Vollmer (ed.), *Allgemeines Lexikon der bildenden Künstler des 20. Jahrhunderts*, Vol. 2, Leipzig 1955, unrevised reprint, Leipzig 1999, p. 425 verso. Here is the reference to Gestapo incarceration with date '1938ff.'.

30 *Jahresbericht 1945–1947* (see n. 1), p. 27.

31 Ibid., p. 34.

32 Vanessa Sondermann, 'Otto Coester', in: Siegfried Gohr (ed.), *Akademie-Galerie 2005–2009. Die Neue Sammlung*, Düsseldorf 2009, p. 28.

33 Sondermann (see n. 32).

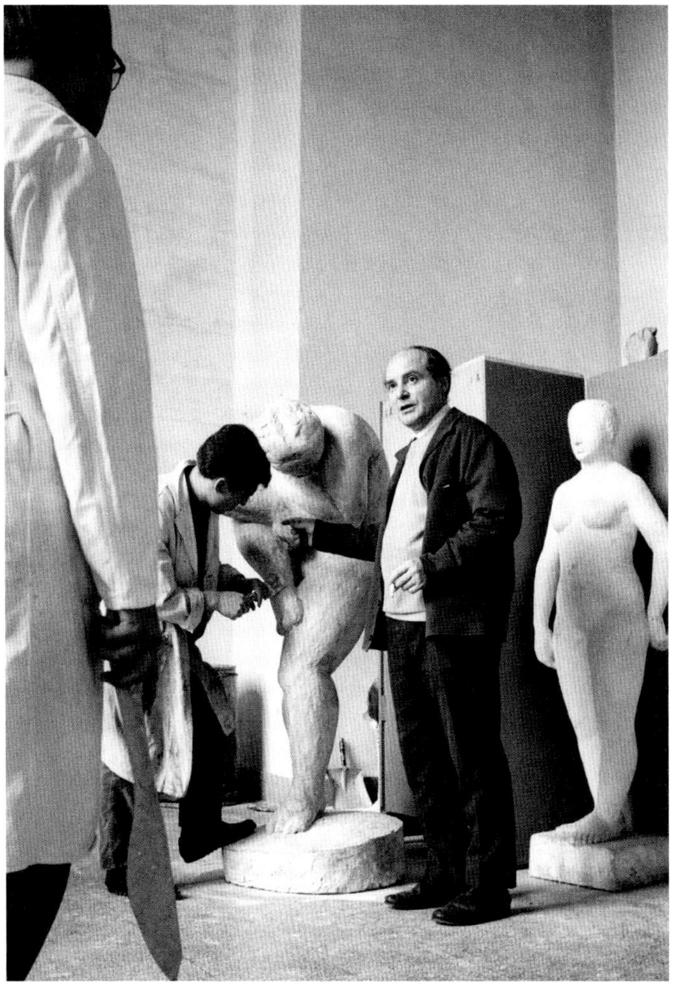

Fig. 19: The sculptor Manfred Sieler with students from his class, 1960

34 Anna Klapheck, 'Lehrer an der Kunstakademie. Porträts der Professoren (VI): Otto Coester', *Rheinische Post*, 4 April 1959.

35 Klapheck (see n. 34).

36 'Otto Coester. Lehrer und Schüler' (1950), in: Hans and Franz Joseph van der Grinten, *Otto Coester. Ein Liber Amicorum zum 3. April 1982*, Nimwegen 1982, p. 7.

37 Hans Georg Lenzen, 'Der Montagabend', in: Van der Grinten (see n. 36), pp. 8–11; here: p. 8.

38 Lenzen (see n. 37).

39 Ibid.

40 Imgard Zept, 'Otto Coester als Künstler-Lehrer', in: Clemens-Sels Museum (ed.), *Otto Coester zum 85. Geburtstag. Druckgrafik der Jahre 1929 bis 1961*, exhib. cat. Neuss 1987, pp. 5–9; here: p. 8.

41 Zept (see n. 40).

42 Ibid., p. 6.

43 Ibid., p. 8.

44 Ibid.

45 Since Schmurr was not a civil servant when he left the Academy, he was not entitled to a state pension. In a letter he wrote in 1947 he begs the Minister of Culture for a compassionate pension. For this, see Vera Bachmann and Bernd Ernsting, *Alles Große ist still und ernst. Der Maler Wilhelm Schmurr*, Cologne 2009, pp. 291f. Vol. 18 of *LETTER Schriften*.

46 *Jahresbericht 1945–1947* (see n. 1), p. 24.

47 In the brochure for students published by the Düsseldorf Art Academy in 1946 on the guidelines of the institution and the structure of the architecture, painting and fine arts graphics, commercial graphics, sculpture, stage design, and teaching art at state schools courses, Schmurr's name is accompanied by various generic terms, which implies that he taught a class in those fields.

48 All biographical data on Paul Bindel have come from the Düsseldorf Art Academy archives.

49 Anna Klapheck, 'Lehrer an der Kunstakademie. Porträts der Professoren (IV): Paul Bindel', *Rheinische Post*, 21 March 1959. The author does not know

whether the picture is still in existence or whether, like so many of Bindel's works, was lost in the war.

50 Klapheck (see n. 49).

51 Ibid.

52 Vanessa Sondermann, 'Paul Bindel', in: Gohr (see n. 32), p. 16.

53 Ibid., pp. 17–19.

54 Klapheck (see n. 49).

55 Ibid.

56 Wernher Witthaus, 'Vom Aufbau der Staatlichen Kunstakademie. Die elementare Grundlage ist der Zeichenunterricht – Architektur-Schüler modellierten neue Aufstockung'. Newspaper cutting of 7 May 1950 in the Düsseldorf Art Academy archives (without further citation of references and sources).

57 Enseling left the Art Academy when he reached retirement age in 1952. He was succeeded by Zoltán Székessy, also a figurative sculptor, albeit an exponent of an entirely different style. More on this on pp. 150f. in this essay.

58 This has also been noted by Josephine Gabler in her brief biography of Mages: http://www.bildhauerei-in-berlin.de/_html/_katalog/kuenstler-2330-Sepp%20Mages.html (last retrieved 14 September 2015).

59 Anna Klapheck, 'Lehrer an der Kunstakademie. Porträts der Professoren (VII): Sepp Mages', *Rheinische Post*, 6 May 1959.

60 See Gabler (see n. 58).

61 On this, see Hermann Leber, *Rodin – Breker – Hrdlicka. Die Entstehung der faschistischen Bildsprache und ihre Überwindung. Untersuchung zu Entstehungsprozess, politischer Bedeutung und Beurteilbarkeit des Kunstwerks*, Hildesheim/Zurich/New York 1998, p. 24 and Fig. 22 on p. 210.

62 On this, see Sepp Mages, *Granitmale*, Munich 1962.

63 Klapheck (see n. 59).

64 Ibid.

65 Mages (see n. 62).

66 Klapheck (see n. 59).

67 Ibid.

68 Ibid.

69 Ibid.

70 Sepp Mages, 'Zur Architekturplastik', in: Heinrich Kamps (ed.), *Jahrbuch der Staatlichen Kunstakademie Düsseldorf 1948–1950*, Düsseldorf 1951, p. 47.

71 Mages (see n. 70).

72 Ibid.

73 On this see Klapheck (see n. 59).

74 Stadtmuseum Düsseldorf (ed.), *Joseph Enseling. Skulpturen*, exhib. cat. Düsseldorf 1986, p. 112.

75 Peter Bloch, 'Der Bildhauer Joseph Enseling', in: ibid., p. 28.

76 Ibid., p. 29.

77 Hans Schwippert, 'Grabrede für Joseph Enseling', *Der Malkasten. Blätter des Kunstvereins Malkasten*, No. 3, March 1957, pp. 5–7; here: p. 7.

78 Joseph Enseling, in: *Jahrbuch 1948–1950* (see n. 70), p. 43.

79 Illustrations of pupils' work in ibid., pp. 43–46.

80 Anna Klapheck, *Staatliche Kunstakademie Düsseldorf: Ewald Mataré als Lehrer*, Düsseldorf 1957, n.p.

81 Eduard Trier, 'Sieben magere Jahre? Zur Situation der westdeutschen Plastik', in: Klaus Honnef and Hans M. Schmidt (eds.), *Aus den Trümmern. Kunst und Kultur im Rheinland und Westfalen 1945–1952. Neubeginn und Kontinuität*, exhib. cat. Bonn/Düsseldorf/Bochum, Cologne 1985, pp. 367–370; here: p. 368.

82 In 1945/46 thirty-eight performances by the Düsseldorf Schauspielhaus [Theatre] were put on in the auditorium of that higher secondary school, which had been spared the ravages of war because the theatre had already been completely destroyed in air raids in 1943.

83 The information comes from a 1946 newspaper article entitled 'Wiedereröffnung der Staatlichen Kunstakademie Düsseldorf' in the Düsseldorf Art Academy archives (without further citation of references and sources).

84 The Düsseldorf Art Academy and the Munich Art Academy were the only functioning art academies in the Federal Republic during the first post-war years. A desire for continuity and the seamless resumption of tradition were expressed in 1947 in the first post-war annual report, which also printed the entire Regulations of 24 November 1831 for the Royal Art Academy at Düsseldorf (Reglement vom 24. November 1831 für die Königliche Kunst-Akademie zu Düsseldorf). On this, see *Jahresbericht 1945–1947* (see n. 1), pp. 87–94.

85 On this, see the speeches printed in ibid., especially p. 11, p. 16.

86 Ibid.

87 Ibid., pp. 11–12.

88 The curriculum is part of a brochure representing a combination of course descriptions and curriculum: *Staatliche Kunstakademie Düsseldorf*, n.d., pp. 6f. The date 1946 has been handwritten on the brochure, which, if the professors listed in it are anything to go by, does seem correct. Comparable course description brochures for the years 1937, 1948, 1956, 1957, 1959, and 1960 are in the Düsseldorf Art Academy archives.

89 See *Jahresbericht 1945–1947* (see n. 1), pp. 87–94.

90 Ibid., p. 12.

91 Ibid., p. 33.

92 Mai (see n. 4), p. 192.

93 The statements made by Heuser have been taken from a 1947 newspaper or magazine article entitled 'Staatliche Kunstakademie Düsseldorf', Düsseldorf Art Academy archives (without further citation of references and sources).

94 *Jahresbericht 1945–1947* (see n. 1), p. 30.

95 Köngeter was first made a non-tenured professor in 1947 and was given tenured status in 1954.

96 At first, however, it was candidates for teaching art at state schools who underwent training as crafts teachers at the Cologne Werkschulen as called for in the study description of training as 'Zeichenlehrer an höheren Schulen' [drawing teachers at higher secondary schools]. On this, see *Jahresbericht 1945–1947* (see n. 1), p. 30.

97 'Kunstakademie auf neuen Wegen. Meister des Handwerks als Lehrer der Kunst', *Die Welt*, 15 February 1947.

98 'Kunstakademie – Schule für angewandte Kunst. Betrachtungen zum geplanten Ausbau der Düsseldorfer Kunstakademie', *Freiheit*, 29 July 1947.

99 Ibid.

100 Heinrich Kamps, 'Kunstakademie heute', in: *Jahrbuch 1948–1950* (see n. 70), pp. 9–10.

101 Ibid.

102 Ibid.

103 'Die Arbeit an der Kunstakademie. Einhundertfünfzig Schüler bevölkern das bereits zu einem Drittel wiederhergestellte Gebäude', newspaper article of 2 July 1947 in the Düsseldorf Art Academy archives (without further citation of references and sources).

104 Quoted ibid.

105 Karl Poerschke, 'Die Kunst lebt ewig. Düsseldorfer Kunstakademie baute auf Trümmern wieder auf', *Benjamin*, Issue 2, No. 20, 1946, n.p. In 1947, according to the article in *Die Welt*, there were thirty women students and twelve non-German students in a student body comprising approx. 130 to 150 (the figures vary depending on the source); see 'Kunstakademie auf neuen Wegen' (see n. 97).

106 See on this, Andreas Berg, 'Ateliers sind Herzkammern des Musentempels. Seine Kunst muß jeder beweisen – Ein Besuch in der Düsseldorfer Kunstakademie', *Düsseldorfer Nachrichten*, 7 January 1950.

107 Heuser (see n. 93).

108 Ibid.

109 Ibid.

110 'Erziehung zur Kunst. Die Ausbildungsmethode der Staatlichen Kunstakademie Düsseldorf', *Dreigroschenblatt*, 1 April 1949; further, there is a 1949 newspaper article in the Düsseldorf Art Academy archives entitled 'Menschen unserer Stadt. Kunststudenten' (without further citation of references and sources), which is also informative on giving commissions to students.

111 *Jahresbericht 1945–1947* (see n. 1), p. 28.

112 Theo Champion, quoted by Inge Zacher, 'Theo Champion – sein Leben und seine künstlerische Entwicklung', in: Stadtmuseum Düsseldorf and Museum Haus Koekkoek Kleve (eds.), *Theo Champion 1887–1952. Gemälde und Graphik*, exhib. cat. Düsseldorf/Kleve, Kleve 1987, pp. 7–21; here: p. 17.

113 *Jahrbuch 1948–1950* (see n. 70), Figs. 78–82.

114 *Jahresbericht 1945–1947* (see n. 1), p. 29.

115 Ibid.

116 Otto Pankok, quoted in 'Sie Malen Wieder. Düsseldorfer Atelier-Gespräche und Künstler-Porträts von Fabian', *Westdeutsche Rundschau*, 15 May 1948.
117 Anna Klapheck, 'Blick auf Otto Pankok. Zum 60. Geburtstag am 6. Juni', *Rheinische Post*, 6 June 1953.
118 Otto Pankok, 'Unserer Glaube an das Leben', in: *Jahrbuch 1948–1950* (see n. 70), pp. 25–28; here: p. 26.
119 On this see Timo Skrandies, 'Verlust der Mitte?', in: Hans Körner (ed.), *'Flächenland'. Die abstrakte Malerei im frühen Nachkriegsdeutschland und in der jungen Bundesrepublik*, Tübingen/Basel 1996, pp. 20–51.
120 Walter Romain, '"Nicht beim Alten bleiben!" Die Düsseldorfer Kunstakademie in den Jahren nach dem Krieg', in: Honnef and Schmidt (see n. 81), pp. 419–421; here: p. 421.
121 On this, see the essay by Agatha Buslei-Wuppermann in the present volume, pp. 398–408.
122 Heinrich Kamps, quoted by Thön (see n. 20), p. 85.
123 'Direktor Kamps sagt: "Wir sind optimistisch". Die Düsseldorfer Kunstakademie beginnt das Semester – Pläne und Wirklichkeit', in: 'Echo der Landeshauptstadt', 1949, article in the Düsseldorf Academy archives (without further citation of references and sources).
124 For Goller as a teacher at the Art Academy, see Anna Klapheck, *Bruno Goller*, Recklinghausen 1958, pp. 6f. Vol. 10 of *Monographien der rheinisch-westfälischen Kunst der Gegenwart*; Anna Klapheck, 'Lehrer an der Kunstakademie. Porträts der Professoren (V): Bruno Goller', *Rheinische Post*, 10 April 1959; Volker Kahmen, *Bruno Goller*, Bonn 1981, pp. 24f.
125 Klapheck 1958 (see n. 124), p. 6.
126 Klapheck 1959 (see n. 124).
127 Kahmen (see n. 124), p. 24.
128 Friendship with Kaesbach enabled a number of painters, most of them Expressionists, to evade the National Socialists by living safely on the Höri Peninsula on Lake Constance from 1933 to 1945. Otto Dix and Erich Heckel were two of the most famous artists to have belonged to the Höri circle of painters.
129 Anna Klapheck, 'Lehrer an der Kunstakademie. Porträts der Professoren (XIV): Ferdinand Macketanz', *Rheinische Post*, 23 January 1960.
130 Klapheck (see n. 129).
131 Ibid.
132 Anna Klapheck, 'Lehrer an der Kunstakademie. Porträts der Professoren (II): Zoltán Székessy', *Rheinische Post*, 7 March 1959.
133 Klapheck (see n. 132).
134 On this see Franz Josef Kampmann, *Zoltán Székessy als Lehrer*, ed. Staatliche Kunstakademie Düsseldorf, Hochschule für Bildende Künste, Düsseldorf 1962, n.p.
135 Klapheck (see n. 132).
136 Kampmann (see n. 134).
137 Ibid.
138 Anna Klapheck, 'Lehrer an der Kunstakademie. Porträts der Professoren (XII): Robert Pudlich', *Rheinische Post*, 16 October 1959.
139 Anna Klapheck, 'Lehrer an der Kunstakademie. Porträts der Professoren (III): Georg Meistermann', *Rheinische Post*, 13 March 1959.
140 Klapheck (see n. 139).
141 Ibid.
142 On this also see Mai (see n. 4).

SELECTED WORKS BY ACADEMY PROFESSORS 1945 TO 1960

Zoltán Székessy
Joseph Enseling
Otto Pankok
Theo Champion
Otto Coester
Werner Heuser
Robert Pudlich
Wilhelm Schmurr
Heinrich Kamps
Ferdinand Macketanz
Paul Bindel
Ewald Mataré
Bruno Goller
Georg Meistermann
Rolf Crummenauer
Günter Grote
Walter Köngeter
Ernst Althoff
Rudolf Schwarz

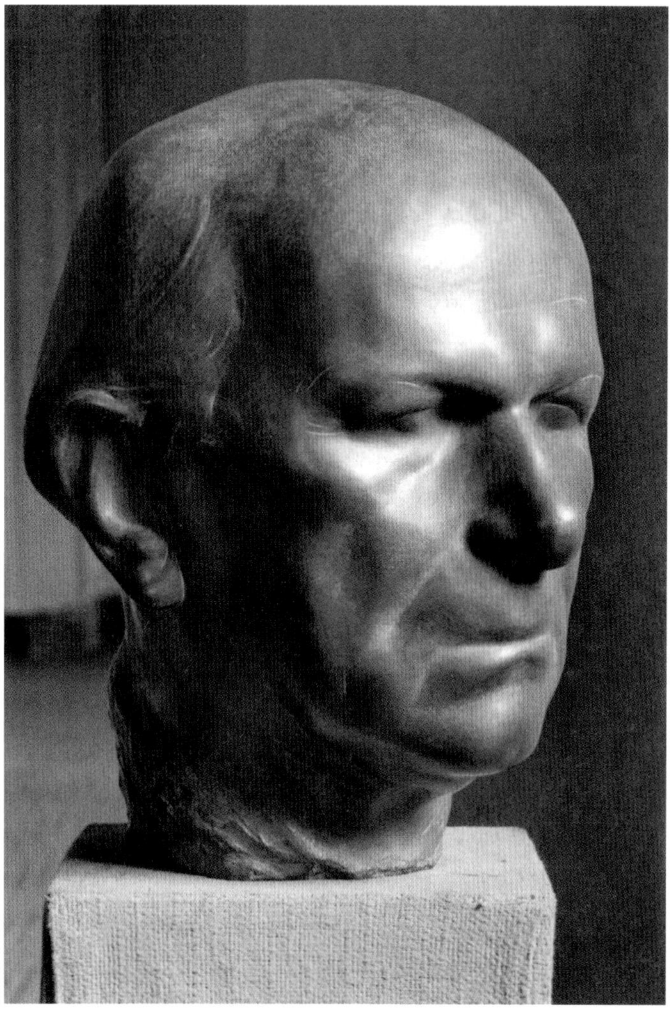

Zoltán Székessy, bust of Werner Heuser, 1949, bronze, life-size

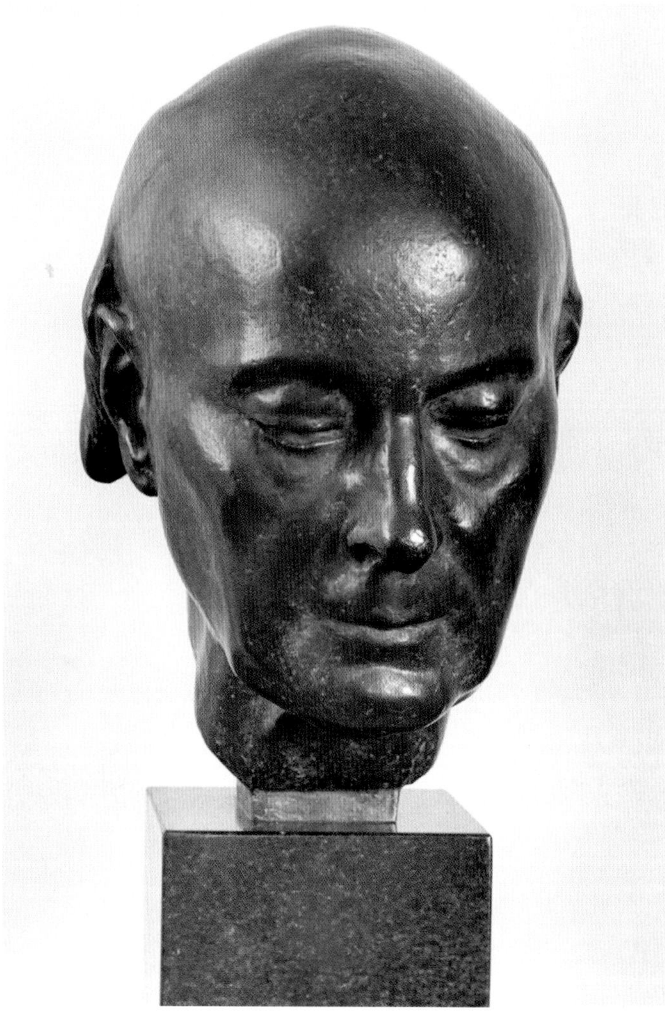

Joseph Enseling, bust of the writer Herbert Eulenberg, 1946, bronze, 35 cm high, Museum Kunstpalast Düsseldorf, on permanent loan from the Stadtmuseum Düsseldorf

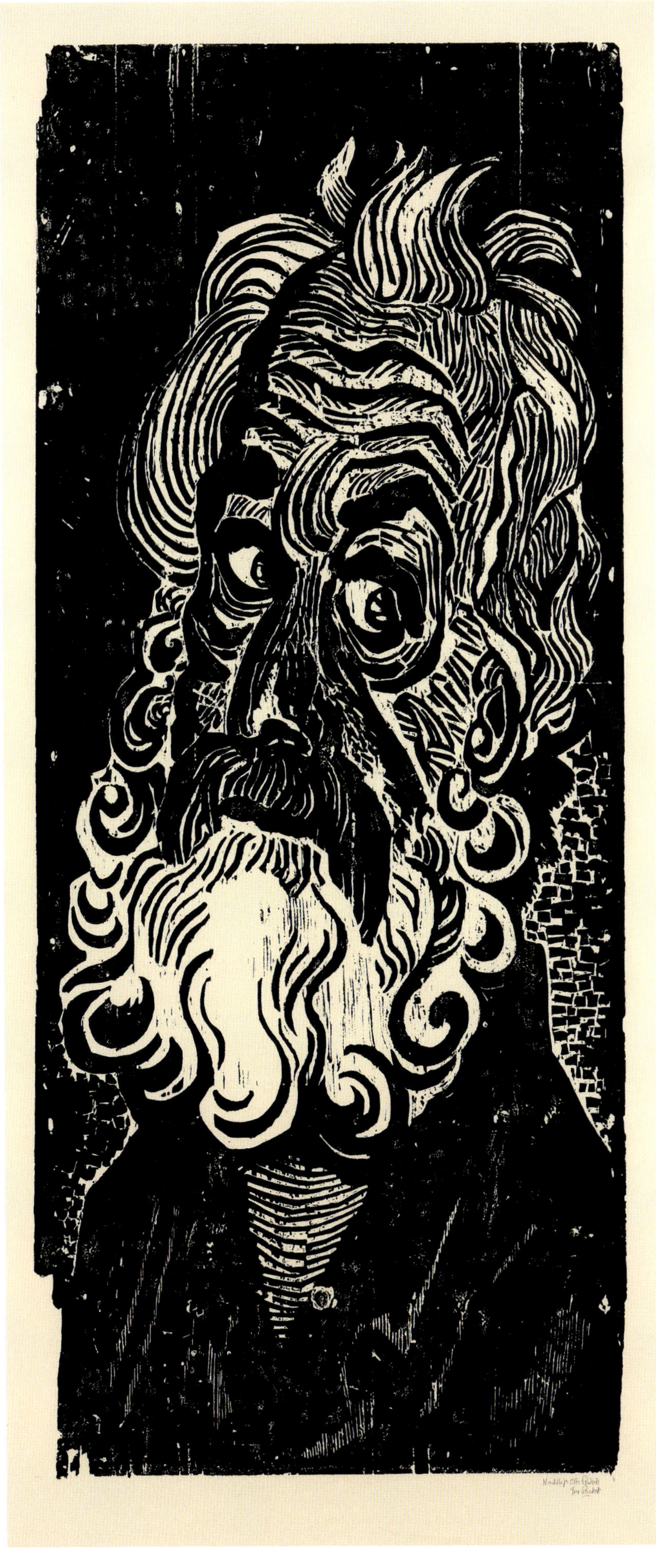

Otto Pankok, self-portrait, 1958, woodcut, 182 × 78 cm, Akademie-Galerie – Die Neue Sammlung, Düsseldorf

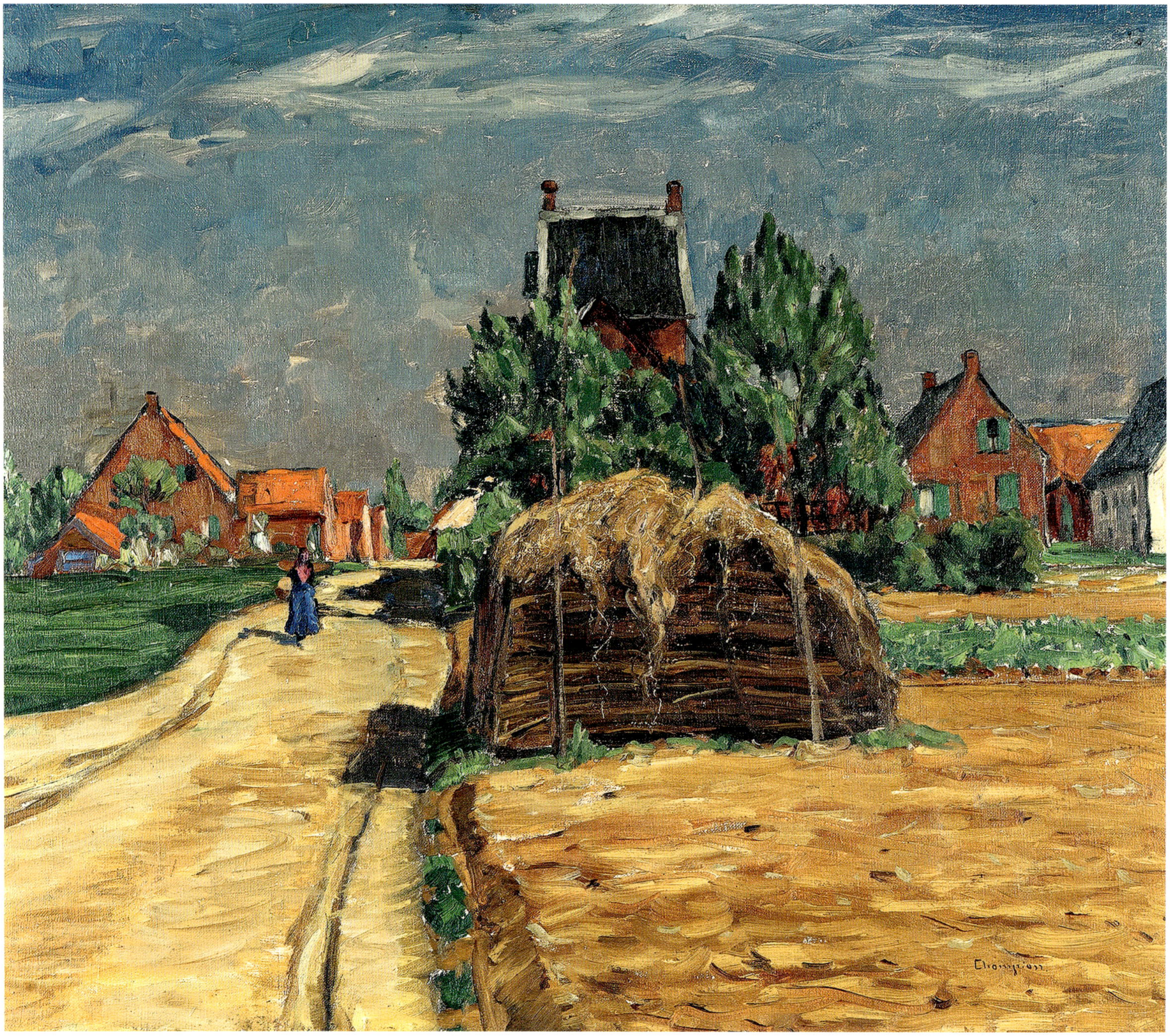

Theo Champion, Dorfstraße mit Heuschober *[Village Street with Haystack], after 1920, oil on canvas, 80 × 90 cm, Akademie-Galerie – Die Neue Sammlung, Düsseldorf*

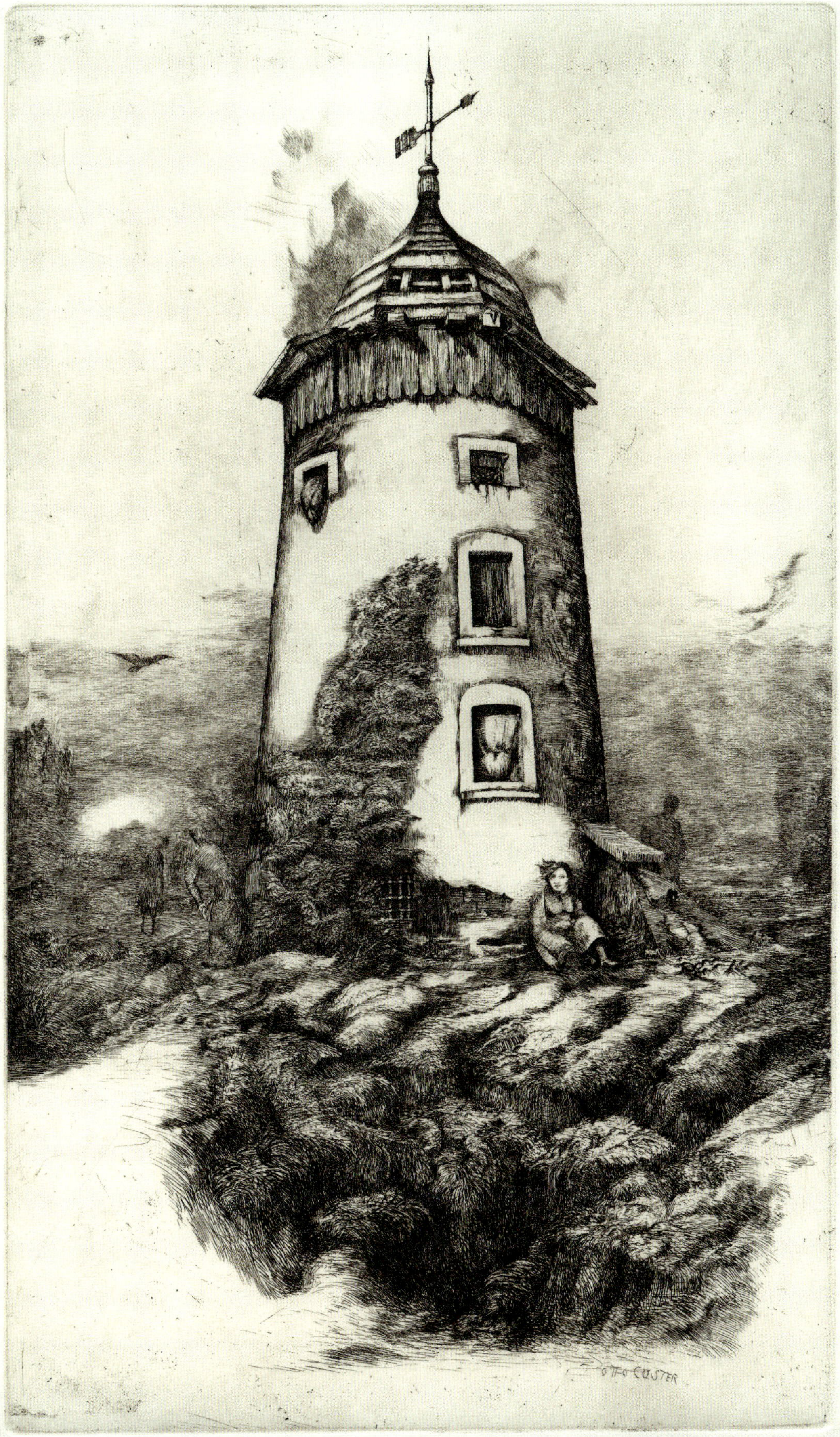

Otto Coester, Turm bei Moritzburg *[Tower near Moritzburg], 1939, etching, 29.8 × 17.7 cm, Akademie-Galerie – Die Neue Sammlung, Düsseldorf*

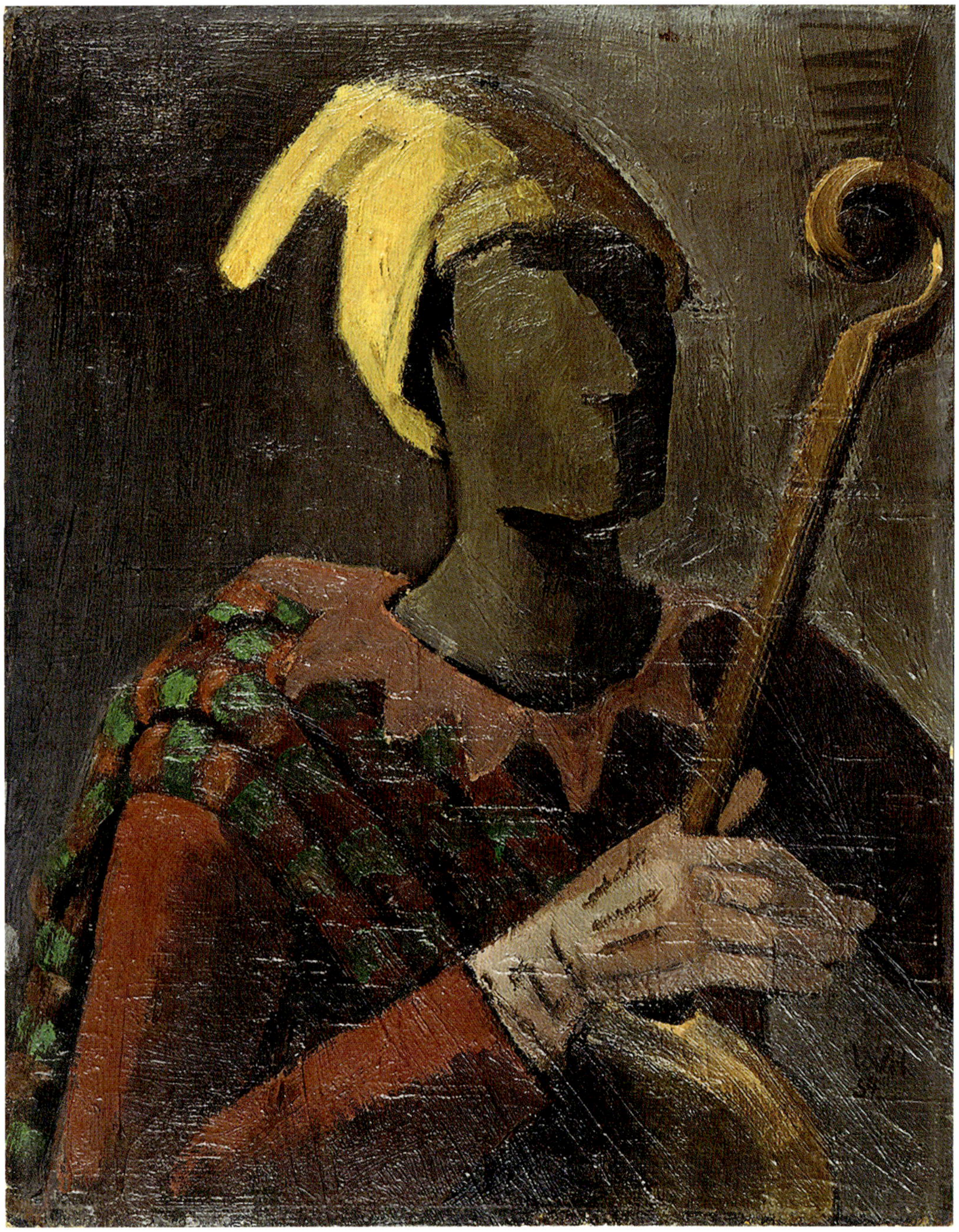

Werner Heuser, Clown, *1954, oil on thick cardboard, 49.5 × 39.8 cm, Dr Gerhard Schneider, Olpe*

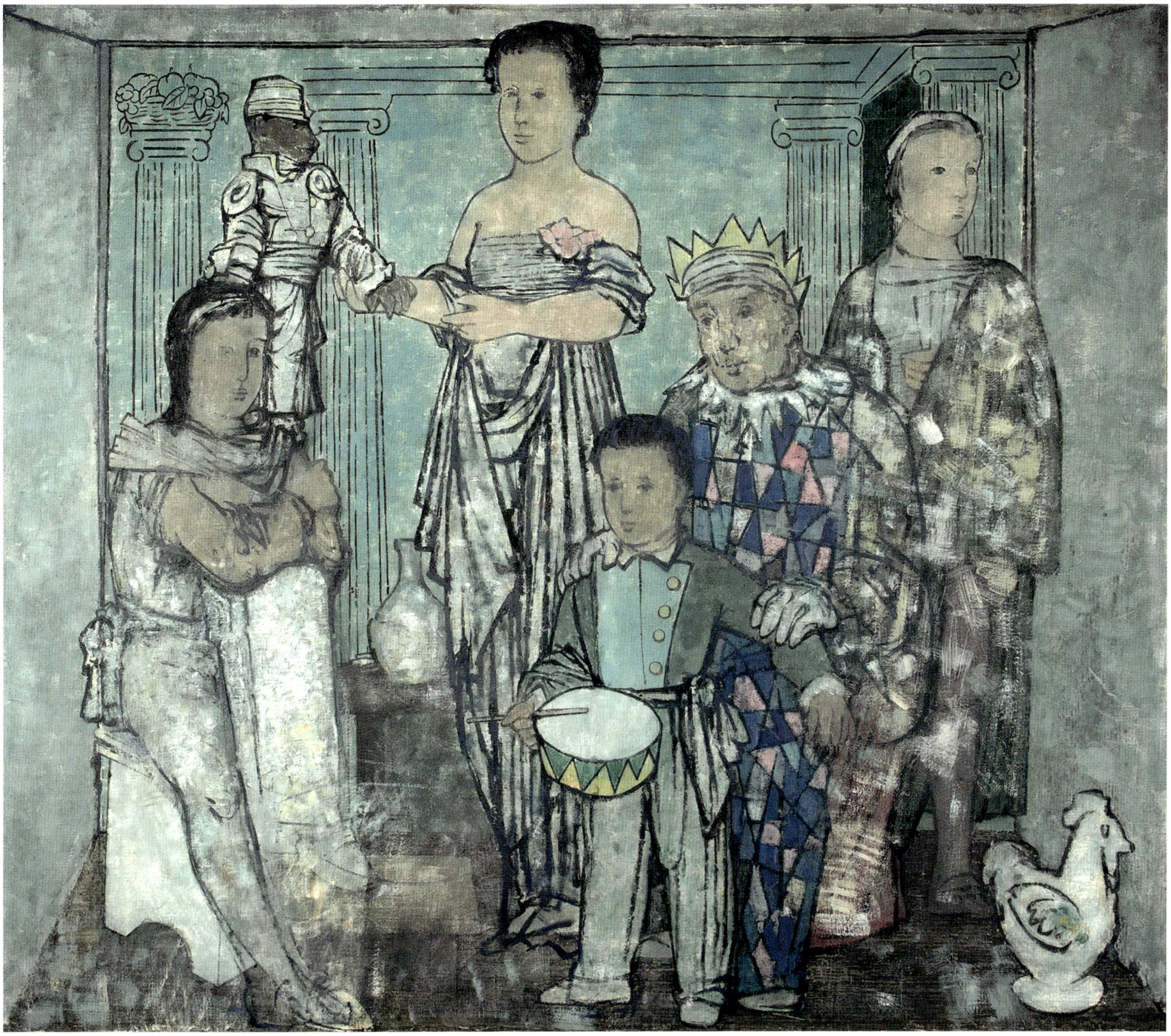

Robert Pudlich, Artisten II *[Performers II]*, c.*1955, 102 × 119 cm, privately owned*

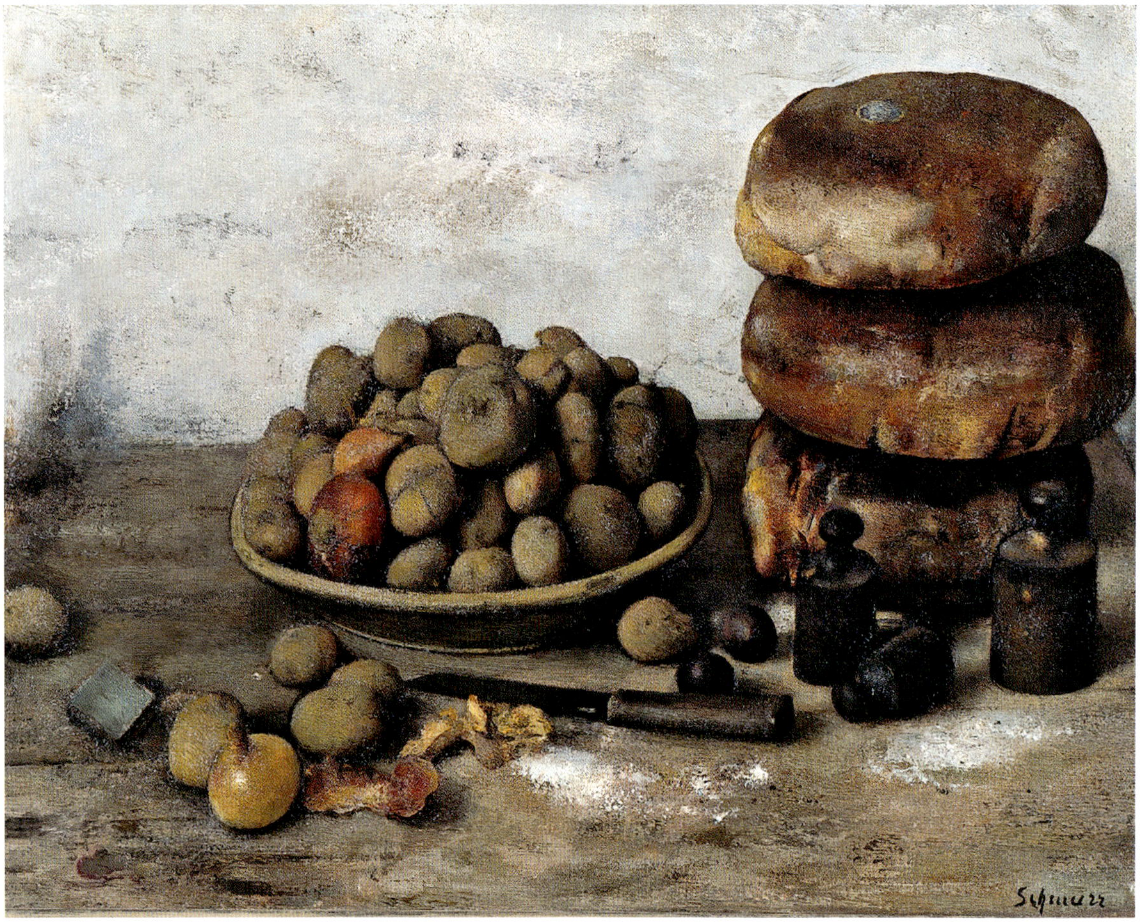

Wilhelm Schmurr, Brotstillleben *[Still Life with Bread], 1941, oil on canvas, 60 × 80 cm, courtesy of Galerie an der Börse, Wilhelm Körs, Düsseldorf*

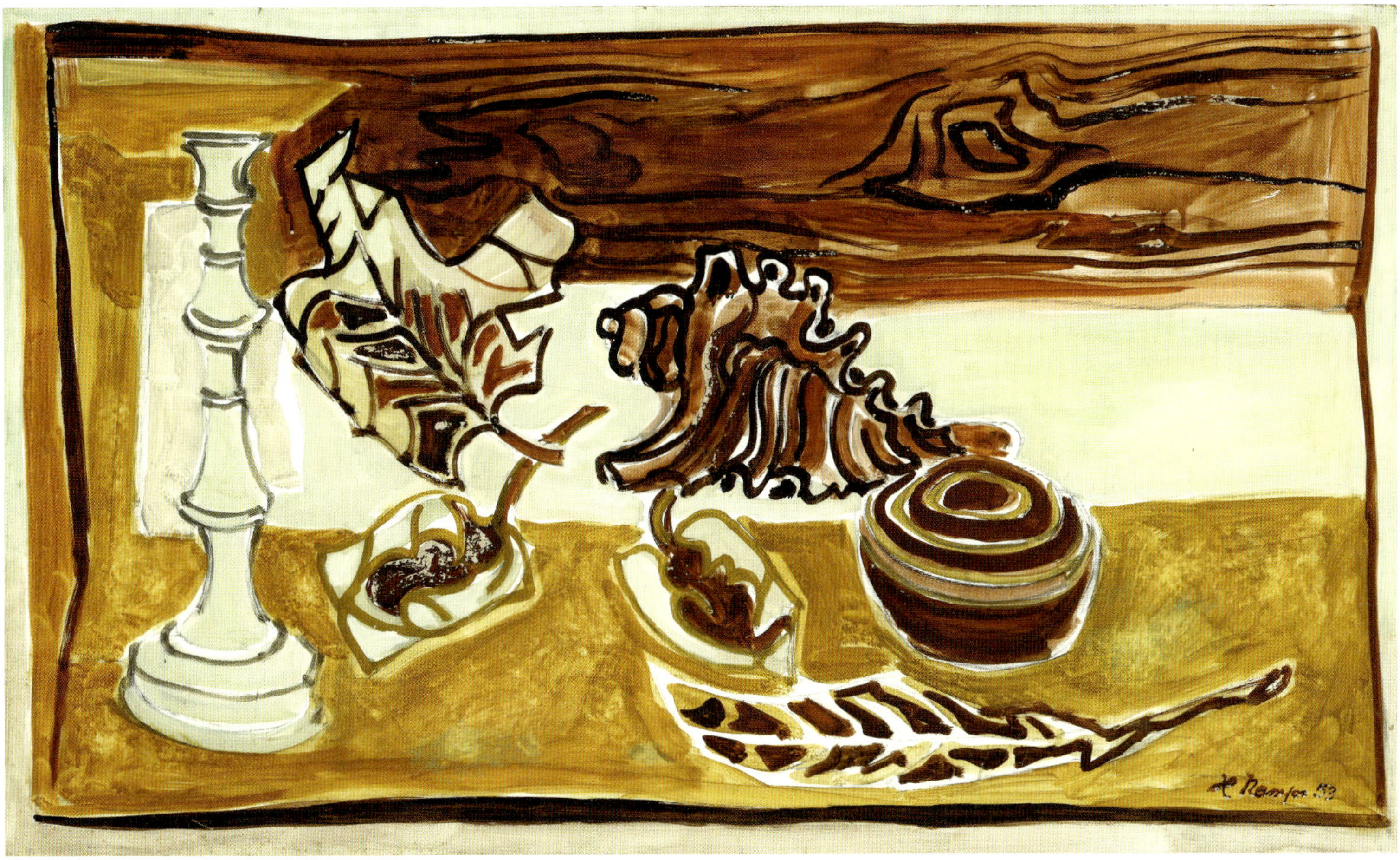

Heinrich Kamps, Stillleben mit weißer Kerze *[Still Life with White Candle], 1953, mixed media on hardboard, 70 × 120 cm, Akademie-Galerie – Die Neue Sammlung, Düsseldorf*

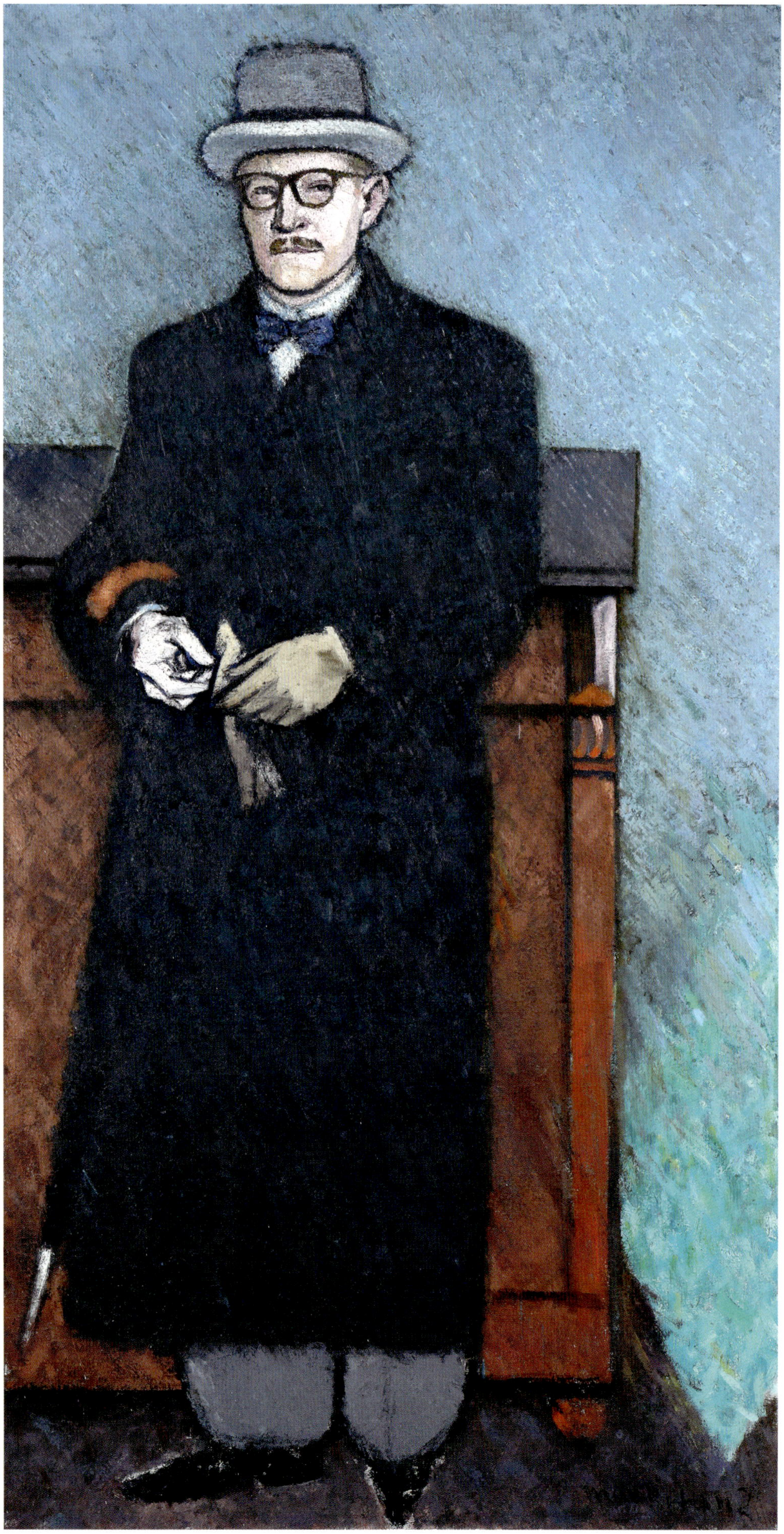

Ferdinand Macketanz, Der letzte Bohemien von Düsseldorf *[Düsseldorf's Last Bohemian], 1959, oil on canvas, 182 × 100 cm, Akademie-Galerie – Die Neue Sammlung, Düsseldorf*

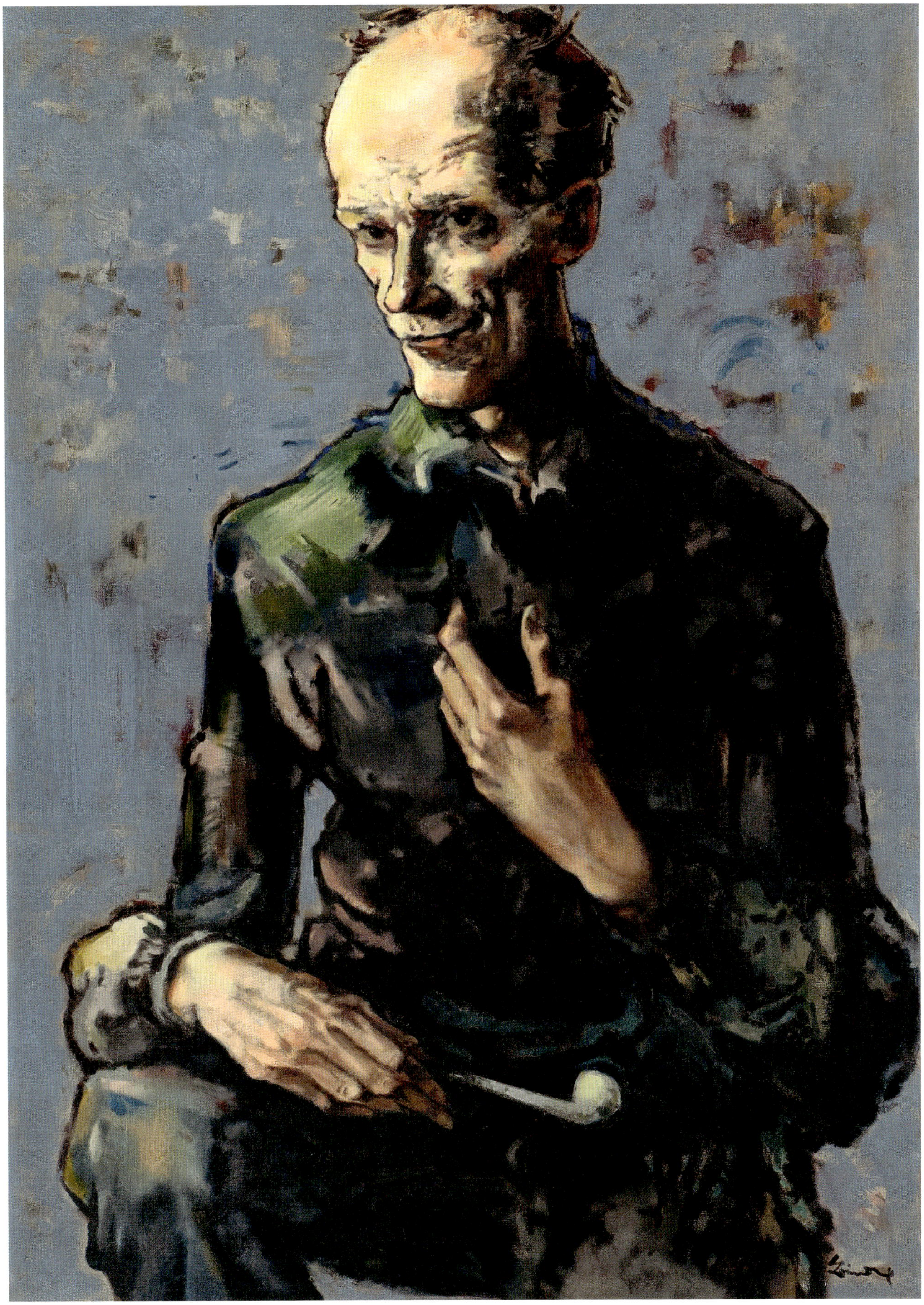

Paul Bindel, portrait of Otto Coester, c. 1959, oil on canvas, 111 × 80.5 cm, Düsseldorf Art Academy

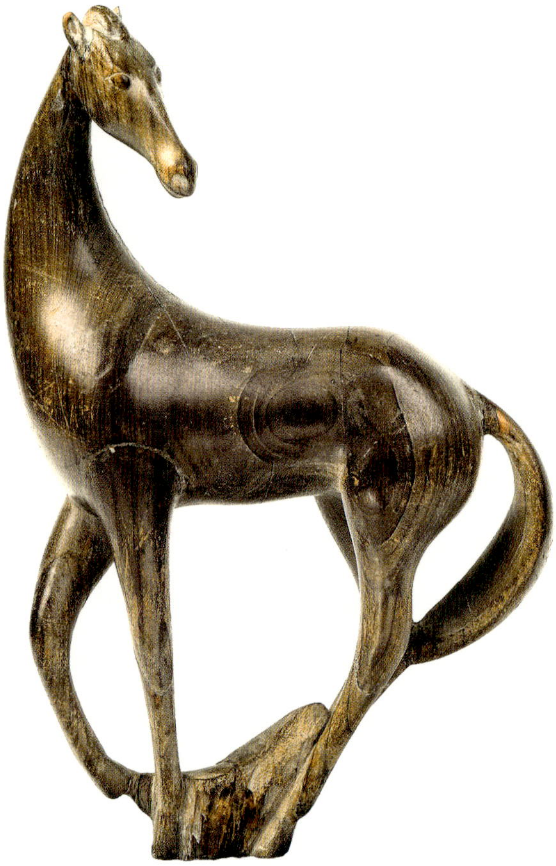

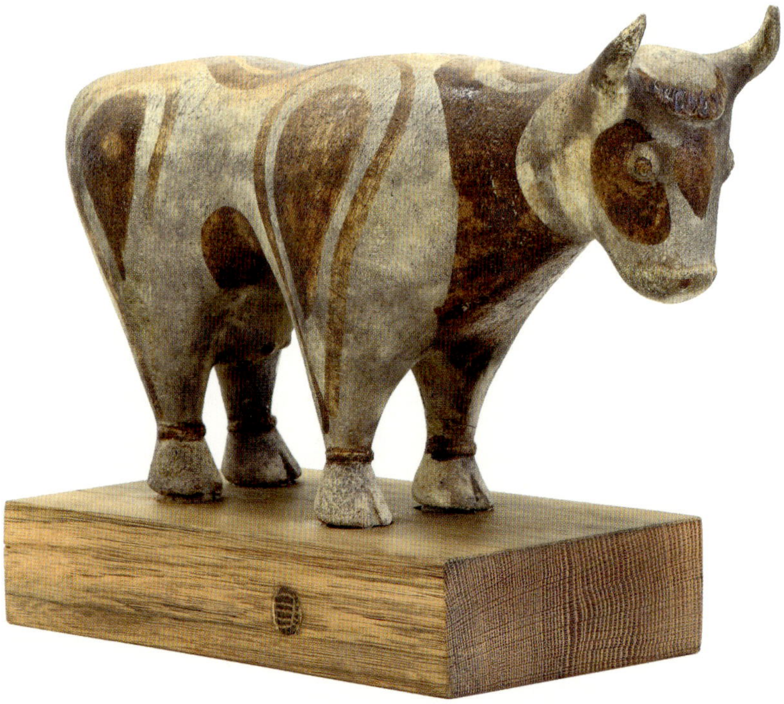

Ewald Mataré, Tänzelndes (Chinesisches) Pferd *[Curvetting (Chinese) Horse], 1943, cedar, 21 × 15 cm, Museum Kurhaus Kleve – Ewald Mataré Collection, Kleve*

Ewald Mataré, Stehende Kuh, Große Terrakotta Kuh *[Cow, Standing, Large Terracotta Cow], 1939, terracotta painted with brown ferrous oxides, 22 × 40 cm, private collection*

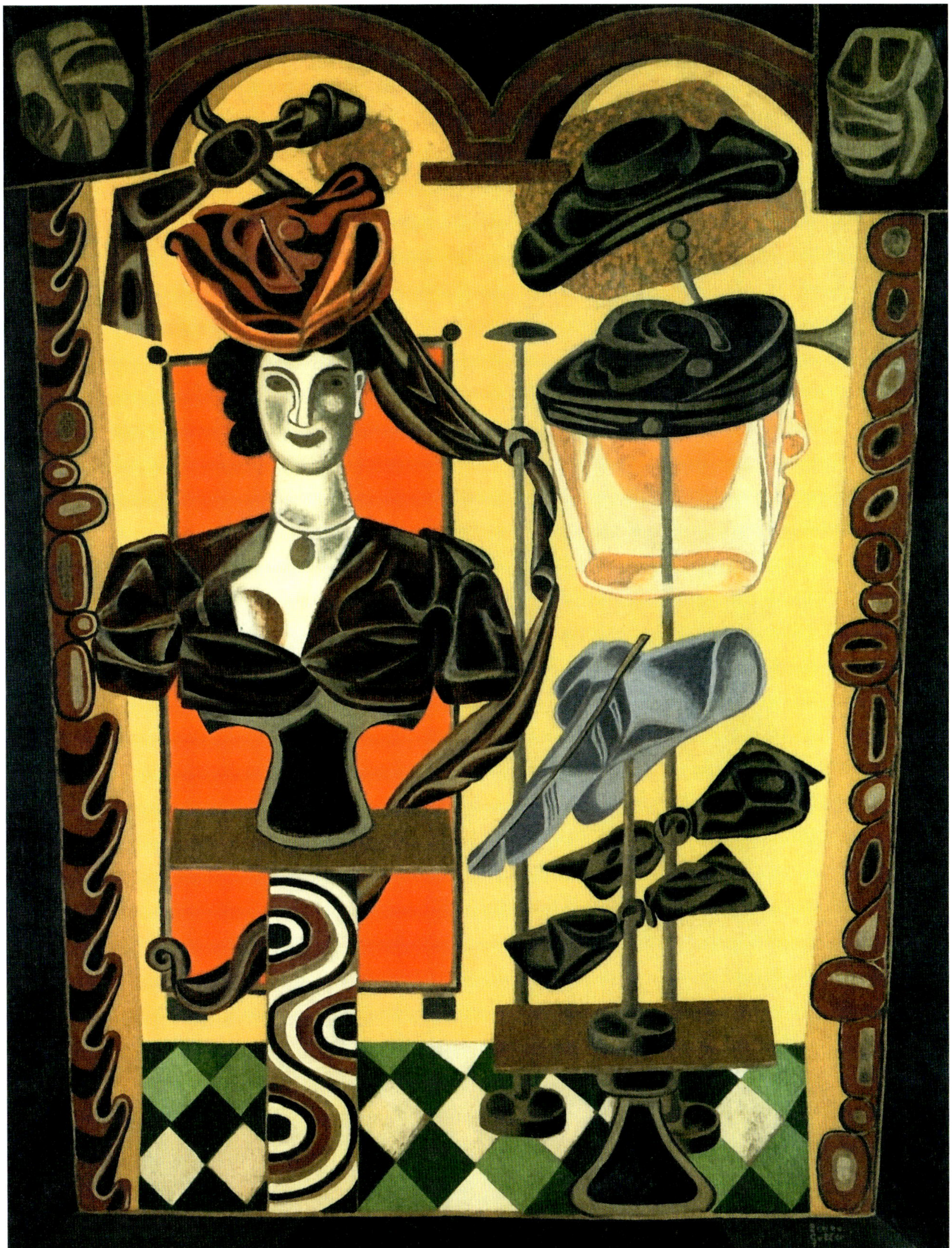

Bruno Goller, Großes Schaufenster *[Large Shop Window], 1953, oil on canvas, 150 × 115 cm, Kunstsammlung Nordrhein-Westfalen, Düsseldorf*

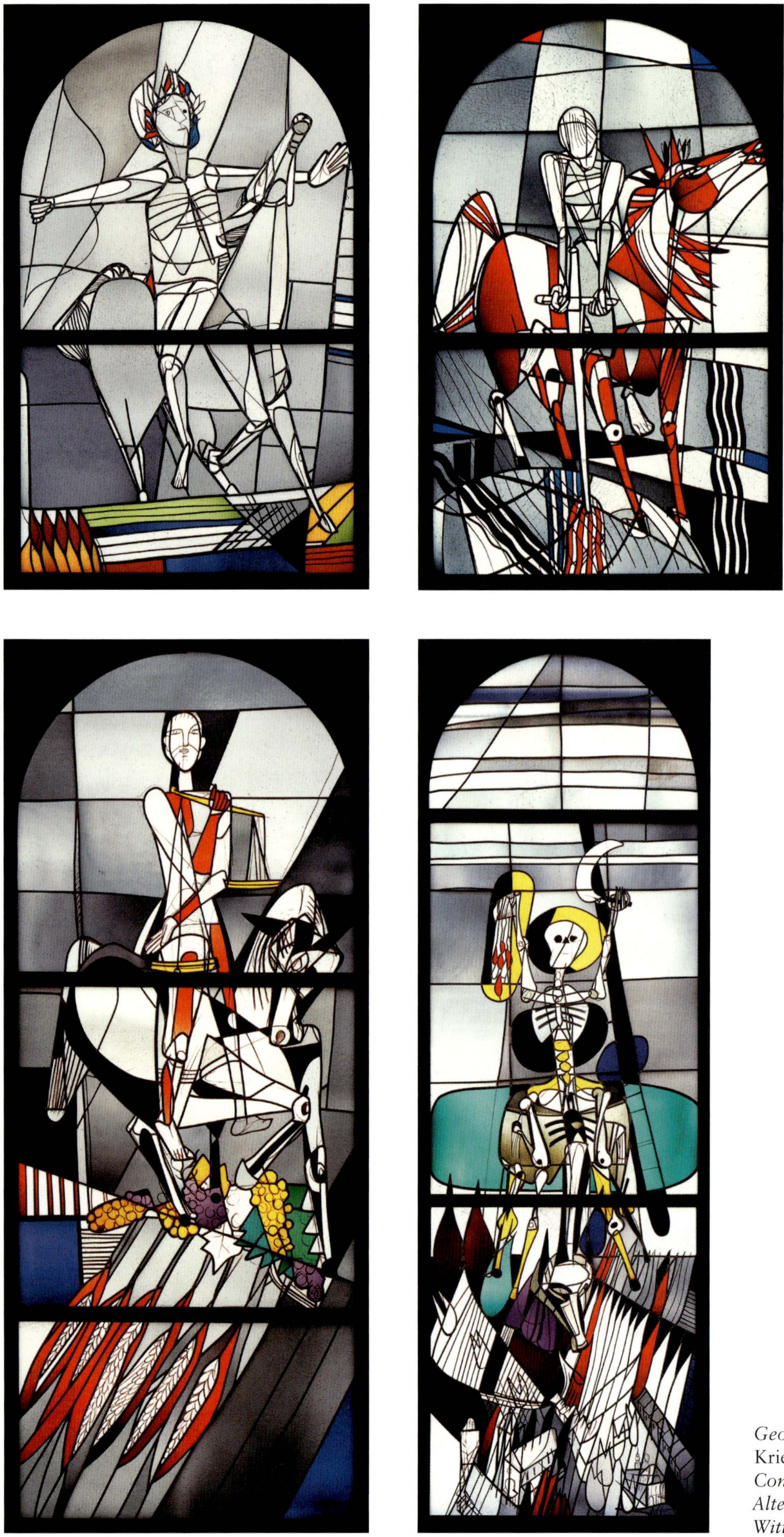

Georg Meistermann, Apokalyptische Reiter: Sieger, Krieg, Hunger, Tod *[Four Horsemen of the Apocalypse: Conqueror, War, Famine, Death], 1954, glass window, Altes Rathaus – Städtische Galerie für moderne Kunst, Wittlich*

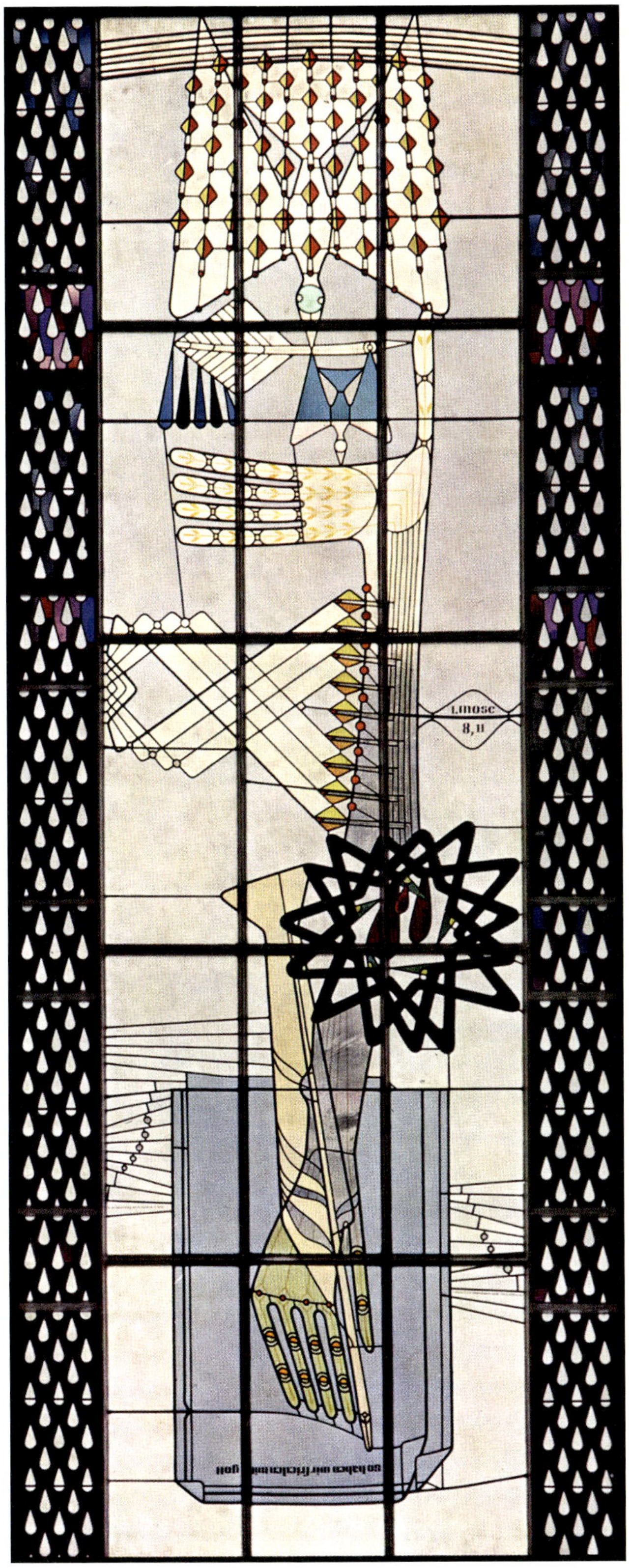

Rolf Crummenauer, Der Bund Gottes mit dem Menschen in seinem Wort *[God's Covenant with Man in His Word], 1957, chancel window, 585 × 240 cm, Martin Luther Kirche, Gleuel/Frechen*

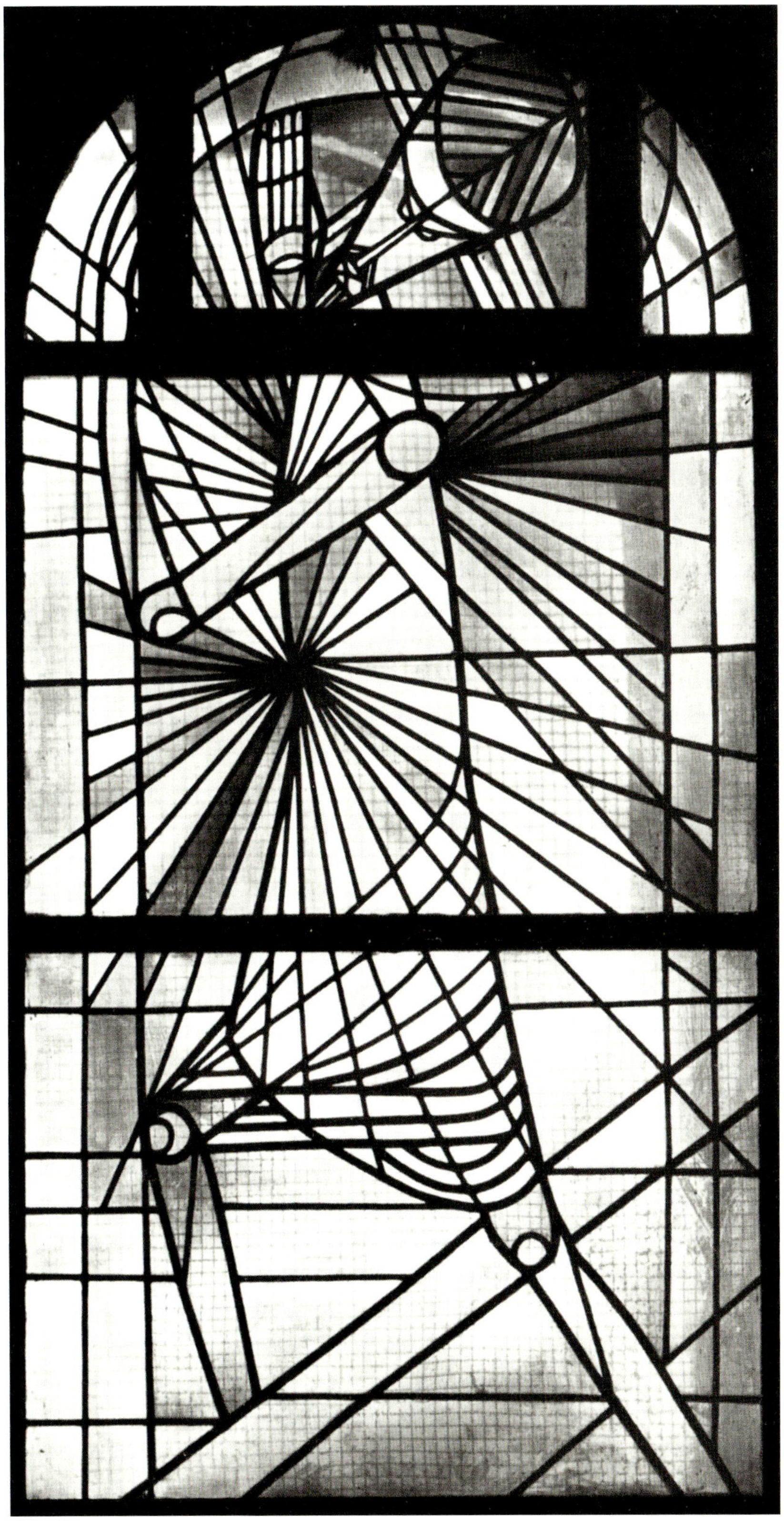

Günter Grote, Der auferstandene Christus *[Christ Arisen], 1956, chancel window, 200 × 100 cm, St. Jakobus Kirche, Homberg*

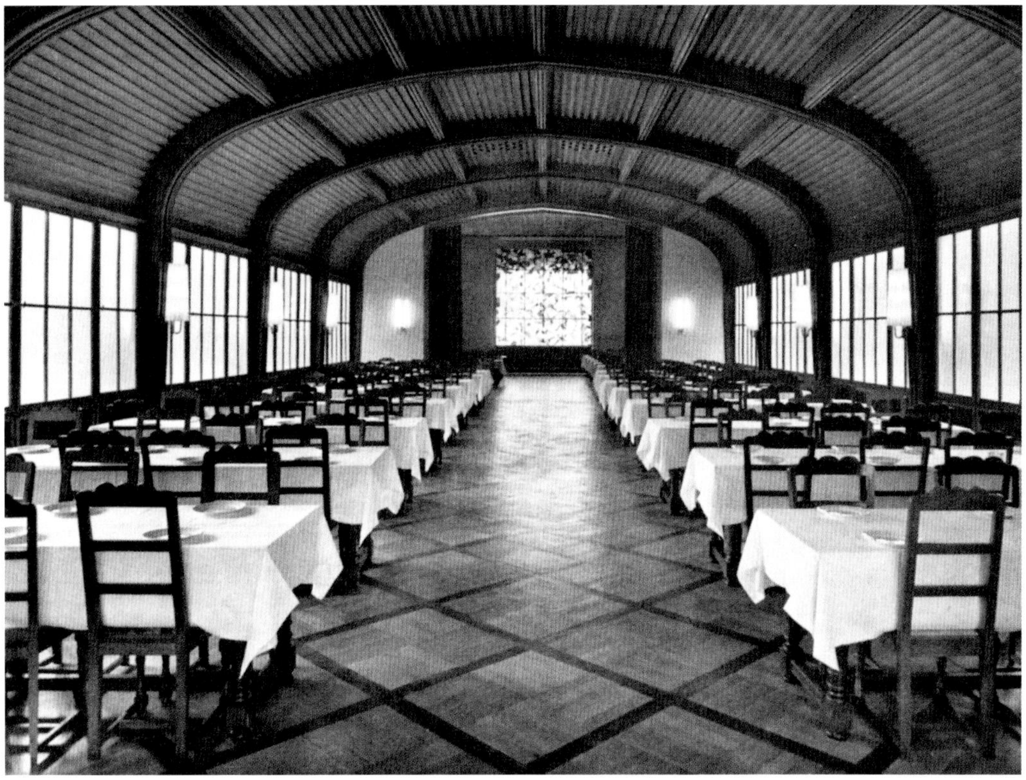

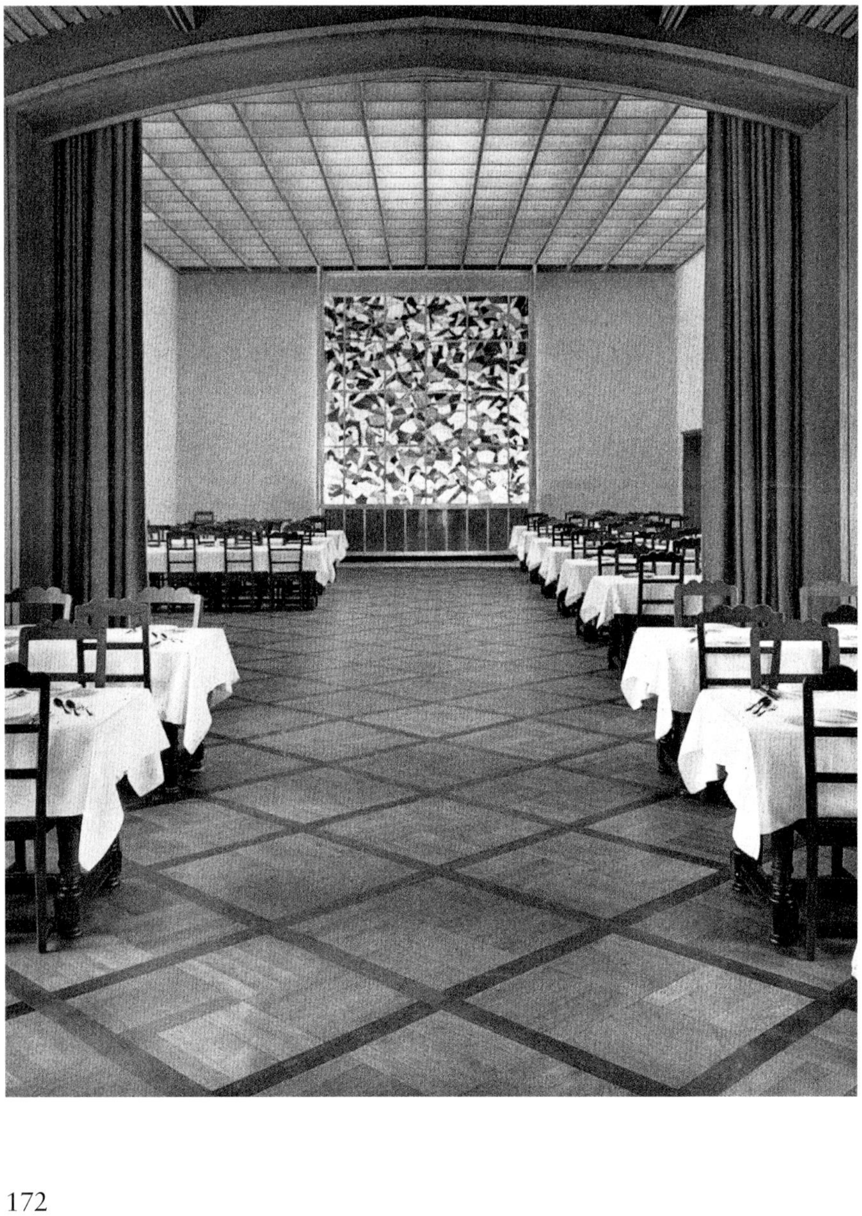

Walter Köngeter, Gothic Hall, Henkel Works refectory in Düsseldorf, c. *1950; in the background windows by Heinrich Kamps*

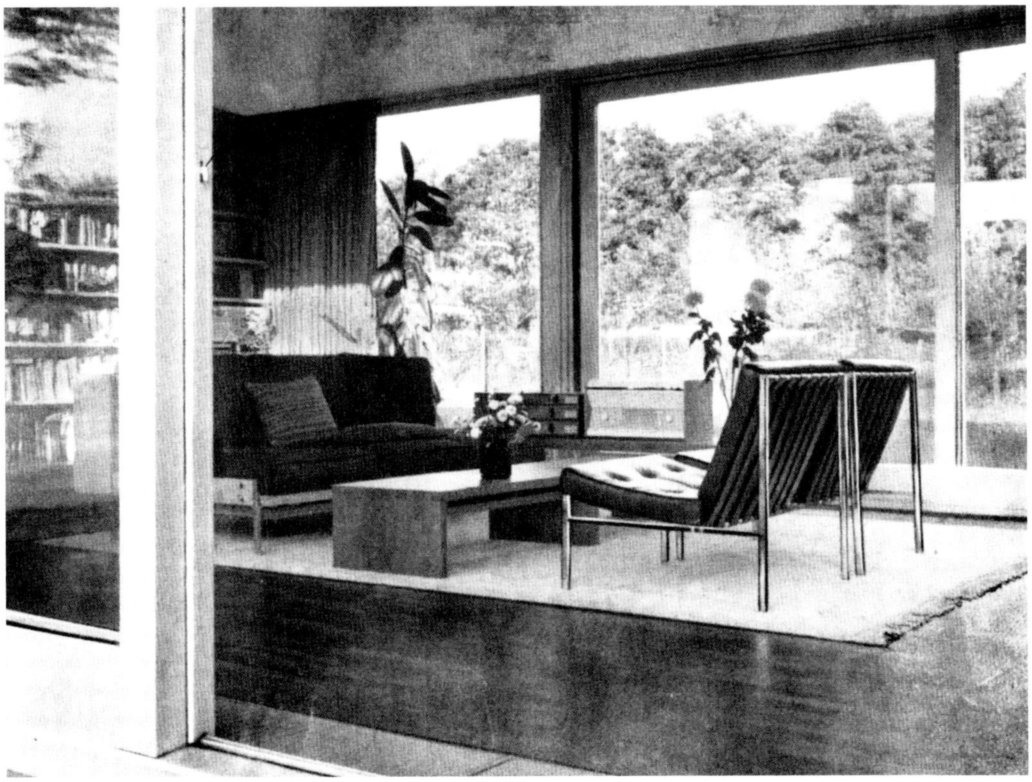

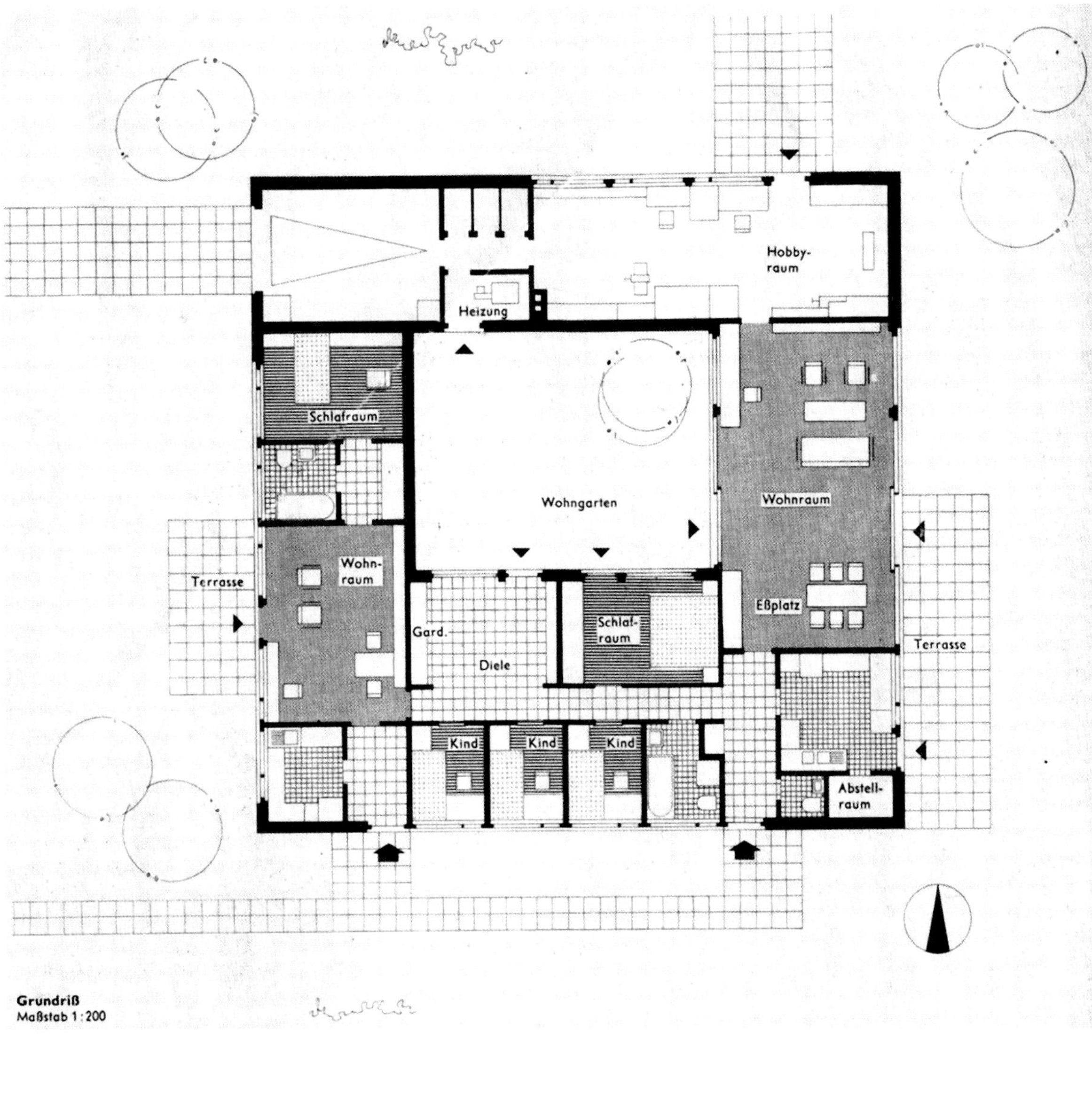

Ernst Althoff, ground plan and interior of the atrium house in Osterrath, 1965

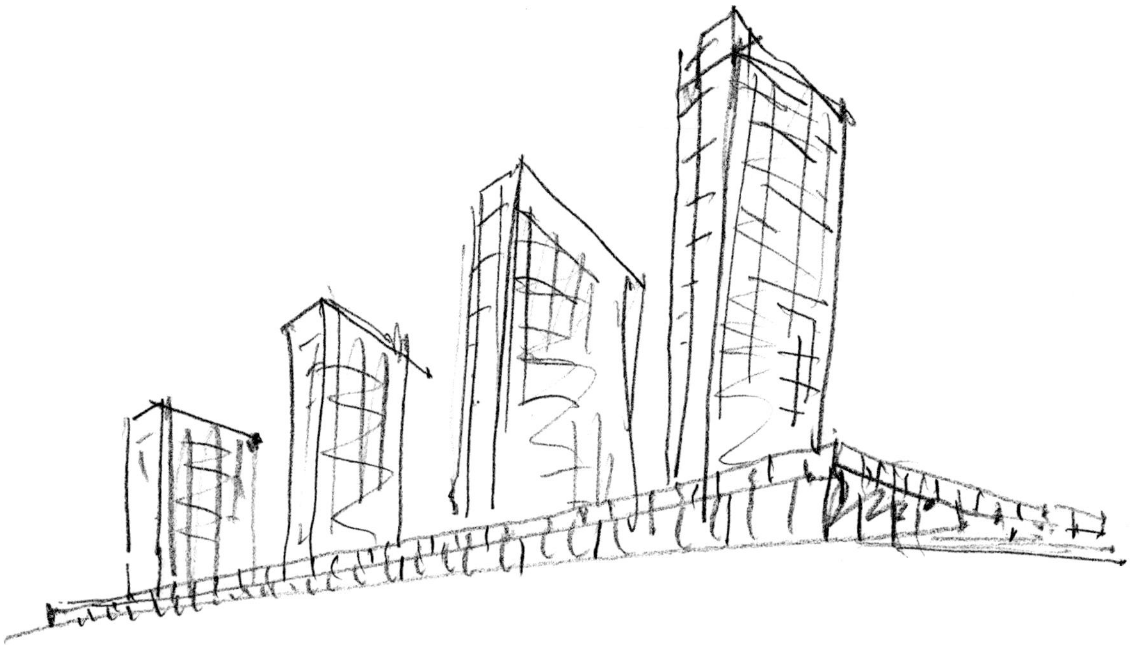

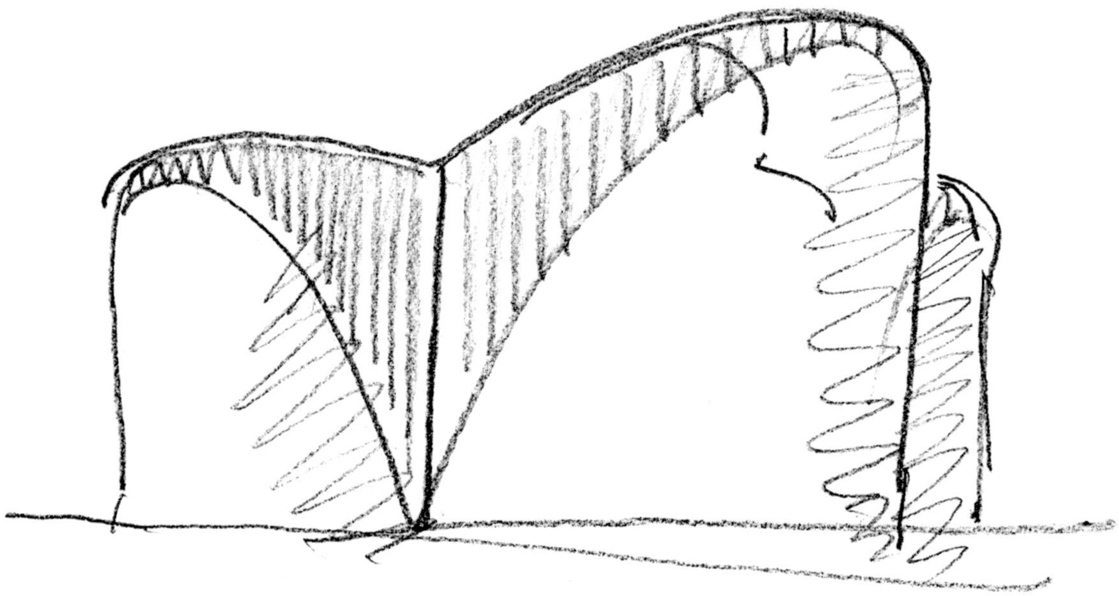

Rudolf Schwarz, plans of Marl Town Hall, 1957, pencil on paper, never built

Rudolf Schwarz, plans of St Mary Queen, Saarbrücken, 1954–61, pencil on paper, built in a different form

GÜNTER H. BLECKS ON THE EARLY YEARS AT THE ART ACADEMY AFTER THE SECOND WORLD WAR

A conversation with Kunibert Bering and Vanessa Sondermann in Düsseldorf on 16 February 2011

Günter H. Blecks: Due to the particular situation during the Third Reich and after the war, I was able to sit my university admittance qualifying exams at the tender age of seventeen and did something considered impossible at the time: being admitted to the Academy by eighteen. When I made my first attempt at introducing myself at the Academy to the then head of training art teachers, Professor Heinrich Kamps, he asked me, after I had shown him my drawings, how old I was, and I said, 'I'm about to turn sixteen.' At that he almost blew his top and intoned, 'We've people here who are thirty-six years old. Those are fathers of families. We have to take care of them first. At sixteen, you've still got plenty of time before it's your turn.' But then it came about anyway: when I had just turned eighteen, I was admitted and at that time – we're talking about the post-war era – you had to work for a term in what was called the 'construction squad' before taking up your studies.

Vanessa Sondermann: Can you clarify that? What is the 'construction squad'?
G. B.: Yes. During the last days of the Second World War, the Düsseldorf Old Town was bombarded from Oberkassel. On that occasion the Academy caught fire from the shooting and the back part was gutted; that means, there were empty doorframes – it was incredibly dangerous – and holes where there had once been wooden ceilings, which had been burnt out.
Half the Academy was unusable. Everything that went on in the Academy in the beginning only took place in the front half. To give you one example: lectures were only given in the room which is now the passage through to the refectory. So you can imagine when the students had eaten their midday meal and were dozy from digesting it, there they were sitting in a dark room – the passageway isn't all that easy to light – and you were sitting there cramped for space. That also made it hard to stay awake, and Professor Schmidt, who was the art historian then, had the habit of saying from time to time (raises his voice), 'AND IF YOU LIKE'. Then the heads would nod back up – he had woken up the students – and then he could keep on talking. And when a quotation from Dante came, followed by a German translation of it, you knew that it would soon be over and the lecture was coming to an end. And when there were no lectures there, it was the work room for the students who were doing 'script'. There were students who specialised in 'script', and they used to work there.
They had to see to it that the second half of the Academy could somehow be made usable. To do that they had to start from the bottom. Now there were students who were supposed to start on their studies; they had to go on the job with the construction workers. For example, I worked on one of the mezzanine ceilings in the studios. That was 1948, and then came the famous day of the Currency Reform, and Monday morning we all went expectantly to the Academy; the construction foreman was standing there, and he said, 'You can go home. There'll be workmen again starting today.'

V. S.: That means before that students were drafted to do hands-on work rebuilding the Academy. That was the condition for being allowed to study?
G. B.: Yes, that's the way it was. That was the 'construction squad'.

V. S.: You came to the Academy in 1948. Can you explain the goals with which you arrived at the Academy? Who were the teachers you were with and with whom did you have contact? We'd also be interested in knowing which students you had contact with at that time.
G. B.: In 1948 I was the only first-term male student in the teacher training section. That is how low the admissions figures were, and there was a girl student who began then besides me but she had already studied at the School of Applied Arts in Kassel for a term. So there were just the two of us who began then. The class we went to was taught by Professor Heinrich Kamps, who had been head of the Art Education Department at the University of Fine Art in Berlin until 1933 – that is, until he was dismissed by the Nazis. That will soon become an important point about post-war history. He had been in Weimar for his training as a drawing teacher, at the Applied Arts School headed by Henry Van der Velde, and he was, as Professor Schmidt said in his eulogy for Professor Kamps, 'shaped by Jugendstil', and he worked a lot with the method we used to call 'graphic structuring' – meaning that what is sometimes called texturing. That same term Professor Paul Bindel returned to the Academy. He had been a colleague of Kamps's[1] and had collaborated with Kamps in 1924 or 1925 on the exhibition *Das schöpferische Kind* [The Creative Child][2] and then with Ernst Röttger, who later worked in Kassel. Now here comes a situation typical of the post-war era: Professor Kamps had been

fired by the Nazis. That was a really dramatic scene because his favourite pupil in Berlin had captured him in a lift, one which could be secured, so he could be arrested. Paul Klee is said to have gone through something similar, being betrayed by his favourite pupil. Bindel had just been promoted from drawing teacher to higher secondary school civil servant status. Bindel then became something like an inspector general for the Rhinelands and had to examine teachers on the job to ascertain whether they could be granted senior civil servant status on the basis of what they had achieved at their schools. A lot of money and social status depended on that. He became a professor at the Academy before the war and during the war was a captain in a cavalry company.

V. S.: What company was that? When did Bindel return to the Academy? Which class? When was Bindel at the Academy after 1933?

G. B.: He managed to make himself very unpopular in no time at all in the class he fetched up in after the war. What he did, with no reason for doing so, was to put a picture from the Wars of Liberation in the class, a drum with black-and-white triangles or drum loops, with the regalia of a Prussian lancer on it, topped by a helmet. The picture was painted in the true Old Master manner. But when we found the picture, a classmate had put a label on it: 'Dusty kit to be decommissioned at once!' The picture disappeared then but Bindel knew he'd been sussed out. So he did meet with resistance. Whenever he came into the classroom, it was like being in the barrack yard.

V. S.: That's getting closer to what we'd like to have more light shed on. We know that Ewald Mataré resigned from the post of acting director partly because there were still old boy networks in the Academy then and he also found fault with the fact that there were still teachers on the staff who had been active in the Third Reich. We know something similar from K. O. Götz, who said that even fourteen years after the collapse of the Third Reich there were still professors at the Academy who had also taught during the Nazi era. Which professors might Mataré and Götz have meant by that?

G. B.: What I know most about is the Bindel-Kamps combination. That is something that, looking back, is really surprising, that old friends went such different ways during the Third Reich. One was dismissed from his post by the Nazis; the other got on well under them. After the war they were together again at the Academy, and the one who had been booted out by the Nazis was naturally, as you might expect, more highly esteemed and, like Kamps, was also given the post of director. And what is still surprising to me today is that those people who didn't collaborate with the Nazis have accepted and protected old friends who were on the other side during the Third Reich. I remember a very typical case, which may also really be useful for the history of the Academy. In our class there was a student named Günther Forst. He was a very intelligent, very gifted student, extremely witty and with no qualms about calling a spade a spade. Forst got on particularly well with Otto Coester. Then came the art exam in 1952, and Günther Forst said before the exam: 'I refuse to be examined by an old Nazi.' That was giving advance notice. And at that time there was a separate section for art teaching candidates. Otto Coester also belonged to it, and the art historian of course. The exam looked like this: there were practical examinations. Forst went into the examinations and handed in work that was the exact opposite of what he was capable of doing, as everyone in the 'KL' [the department for prospective art teachers at state schools] was well aware. His work was somewhat reminiscent of Egon Schiele. Here, however, he drew a nude that didn't come close to fitting into the surface area, and the professors who had to judge that knew the chap could actually do that properly. [...] So Forst failed the exam. That meant Kamps had ruthlessly sacrificed Günther Forst to please his friend Bindel, and so when it came to the 'I refuse to be examined by a Nazi!' showdown, the old boy network won. That is definitely a clear answer to your question, isn't it?

Kunibert Bering: Yes, it certainly is. And also what you were saying about how people got together again after the interruption during the Nazi era.

G. B.: There was another story that's important. One of the first directors was Werner Heuser. Mataré didn't want any Nazis as students and said, 'I'd prefer to take fourteen-year-olds'. Werner Heuser had also been against the Nazis in the Third Reich and had also suffered for it, but after the war, and as director, he had been assigned a painter who was a friend of his[3] as his assistant. But it wasn't long before 'U-Boote westwärts' [Submarines westward!] appeared on the ground-floor notice board next to one of the assistant's pictures.

V. S.: Bindel then retired in 1959. That same year K. O. Götz came to the Academy. He was one of the young professors who were appointed at the time to teach painting. But he, too, says that there were still professors then who had taught under the Nazis. Now, we have just heard about Paul Bindel. So who can that have been?
G. B.: Perhaps Enseling. But I'm not sure about that.

V. S.: That was Joseph Beuys's first teacher until he switched to Ewald Mataré. Perhaps you might still tell us something about the situation within the teaching staff. Mataré and Kamps were the ones who were booted out by the Nazis before the war and were brought back to the Academy for the new beginning and the new reformation of the Institute, and then Bindel returned from prison camp in 1954, I believe. How did those two factions, who were, after all, polar opposites, get on? Could you as a student observe that?
G. B.: The classes were in fact very isolated so you didn't catch much of what was going on in the neighbouring classes. The year I was with Otto Coester and doing etchings I was also making etchings from nude studies, and since I was in a class without a model, I moved from one class to another. I went to Bruno Goller's class, for example.

V. S.: Last week we had the Rundgang *[Academy Tour] of the Academy with more than 40,000 visitors. Was the* Rundgang *already an institution in the post-war era?*
G. B.: Yes, works were presented but that was more of an internal tour. But there was the *Jahrbuch*. If you take the 1951 issue, you'll find three drawings of mine in it. There's an odd story about that. One day I went to the Academy. There was Klapheck standing at the gate with his bicycle and he said, 'Herr Blecks, I didn't even know you could draw so well. I've seen the early drawings in the *Jahrbuch*. Keep it up.' Some time later I ran into him again and said, 'I'm actually drawing again,' and he said, 'Yes, drawing makes you happy.'

NOTES

1 In Berlin.
2 Karl Röttger (ed.), *Das schöpferische Kind, Ausstellung und Vortragsreihe* [exhibition and lecture series], Düsseldorf, October 1924. Programme. Contains *Das Kind als Gestalter* [The Child as Designer], Düsseldorf 1924. 24 pages (with 8 black-and-white plates in the middle section). A series of lectures, given jointly with the Academy courses, the Deutschkundliches Institut, the Philologists' Association, and members of the teaching staff from a working committee. Exhibition in the rooms of the Düsseldorf Musterschau [trade fair] (from 5 October 1924).
3 Richard Schreiber (1904–1963).

THE ARTS BETWEEN 1960 AND 1985

Siegfried Gohr

How can developments in the arts at the Düsseldorf Academy be divided up into historical periods? Does an institution like this move in parallel with history in general? Is its rhythm predetermined by the course taken by the arts in a specific historical period? What role do academy directors play in this? Can the appointment of a particular director be regarded in itself as a nod to a historical situation? Or does tenure instead depend on fortuitous power blocs? These are just a few of the questions that arise when the structures that inform the inner life of an academy are examined. When, however, the prevailing circumstances are under scrutiny, the diversity of a configuration that defies simple division into historical periods not only because of its sheer size but also because of the biographical asynchronicity of those involved with it soon becomes apparent. The realisation soon dawns that diversity is in itself one of the strengths of a great academy. After all, areas of tension charged with what already exists and what is new have always been, and are constantly being, generated, created by distinguished individuals whose personalities differ widely and whose conceptions of what their academy should be have always been far from unanimous.

A fact that cannot be overlooked in the choice of teaching staff at an academy is that in any given generation only a limited number of outstanding artists will want to be attached to one. Here individual capabilities and preferences must be taken into account. However, the decision to teach or not to teach also depends on the historical circumstances. Understandably, therefore, some artists leapt at the chance to teach after the Second World War, considering that museums seemed to be in terminal decline and the art market had yet to develop. Many artists soon received public commissions, chiefly from the churches, the state, or big business. Of course those commissions were for monuments and memorials that were intended to recall and commemorate events of the very recent past and thus make a first contribution to overcoming the recent historical catastrophe. Moreover, there was a great need for restoring or adding to important cultural monuments, and that ensured many artists a livelihood. In the years just after the war, Ewald Mataré had a large share in such projects, so had Gerhard Marcks, Ludwig Gies, Hans Wimmer, Fritz Koenig, and many others. At that time a number of professors taught in Düsseldorf who were still strongly rooted in the pre-war environment. After such leading exponents of the avant-garde as Paul Klee, Heinrich Campendonk, and Alexander Zschokke had been dismissed, that milieu tended to be rather conventional in character. Mataré was the only one to have presented a fundamentally new concept for the post-war Academy which would have restructured the curriculum, but it was rejected by the authorities responsible in the English cultural administration. Incidentally, a number of professors were appointed specifically for training art teachers for employment at state schools, which at that time attracted many students who wanted to become state school teachers. With a few exceptions, the Academy teaching staff, unlike the teachers appointed before 1933 by the then director, Walter Kaesbach, were anything but abreast of the times.

That first post-war phase ended by 1960 for, concomitantly with the consolidation of West German society in the first decade of the Federal Republic, the economic upturn had begun in 1949 that would later be called the 'economic miracle'. Social diversification and economic success were paralleled by a phase of new developments in art. Germany and other Western countries put the immediate post-war years behind them in the arts, too. The climate of the art market, however, did not begin to improve until the latter half of the 1960s – for instance, with the 1967 launch of Kölner Kunstmarkt [Cologne Artmarket]. A good share of the reparations financing during the early post-war years and even later went to artists proscribed as 'degenerate' during the Nazi era, had emigrated, or been forced to work clandestinely.

In addition, teaching appointments made before and after 1960 reveal that an academy tends to entrust an artist with a professorship only after his achievements have been consolidated and their significance and scope have become apparent. No wonder that a number of exponents of post-war abstraction, including Karl Otto Götz, Joseph Fassbender, Gerhard Hoehme, and Gert Weberg, did not hold Academy chairs until then (Figs. 1–4). Beneath the surface of that Abstract-Gestural environment, however, subliminal ideas and urges were already stirring that would soon lead to new figuration and representationalism. The students of the above-mentioned abstract painters were either gradually abandoning their teachers as stylistic models or occasionally even losing no time in doing so. Karin Martin, whose *nom d'artiste* was Rissa, studied in the class taught by Karl Otto Götz. She experimented with various styles before establishing in 1965 a pictorial idiom

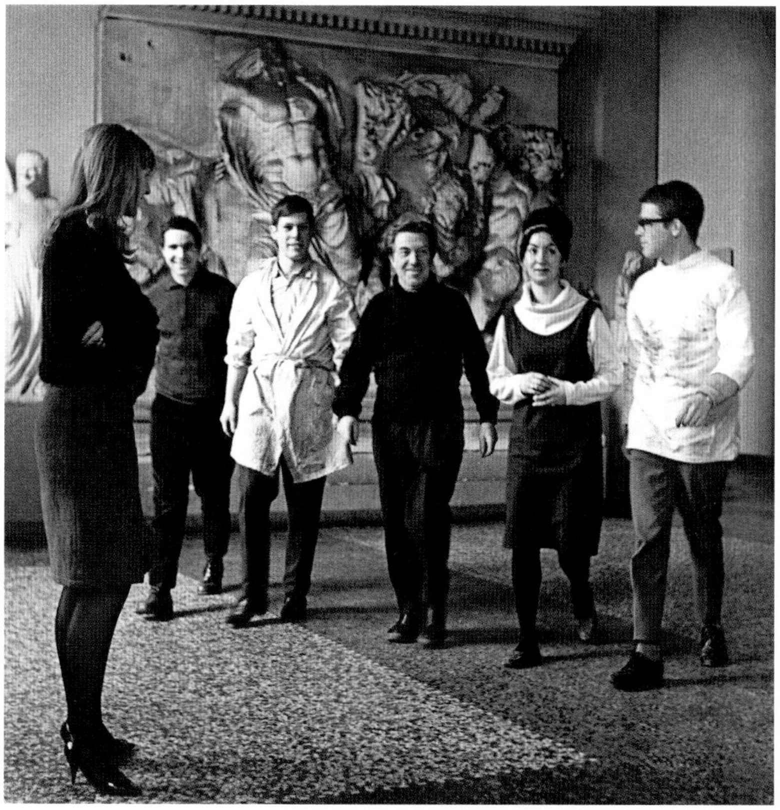

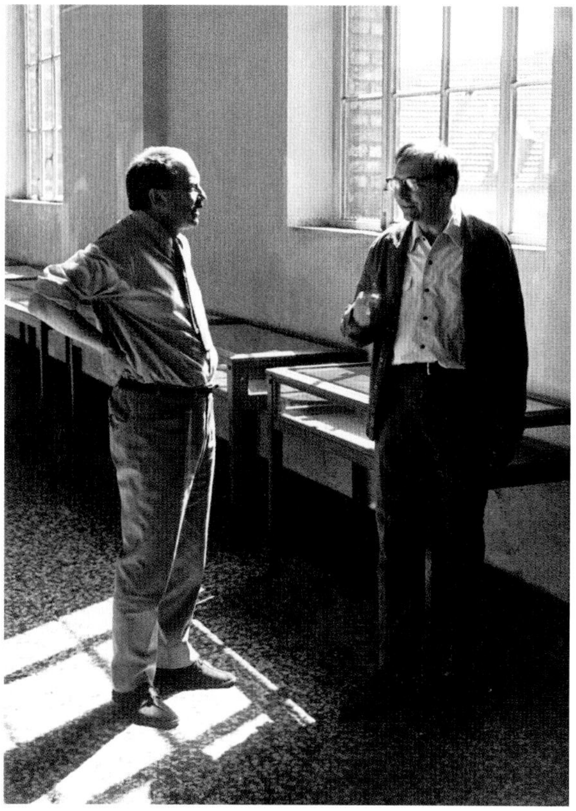

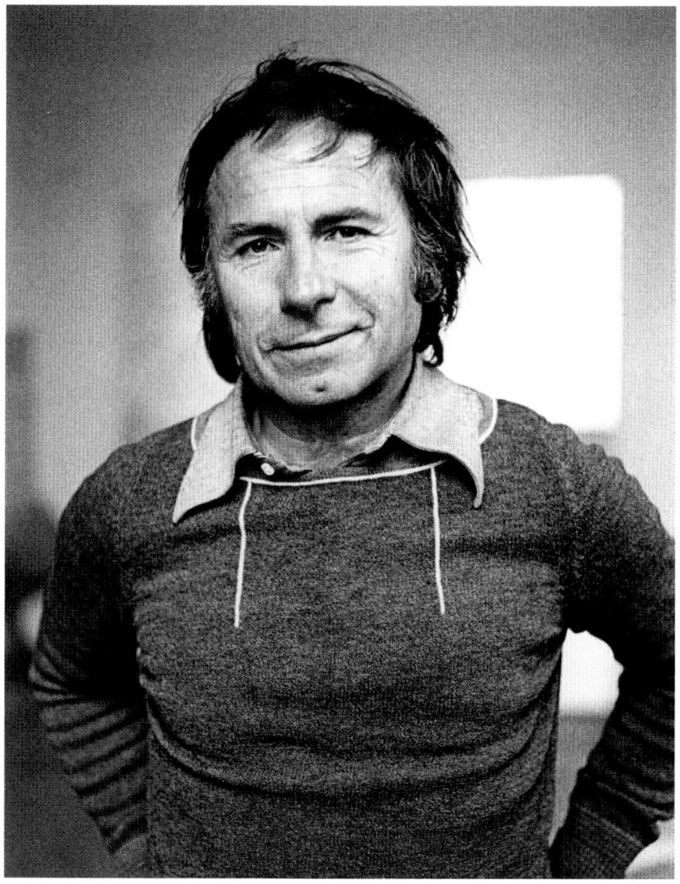

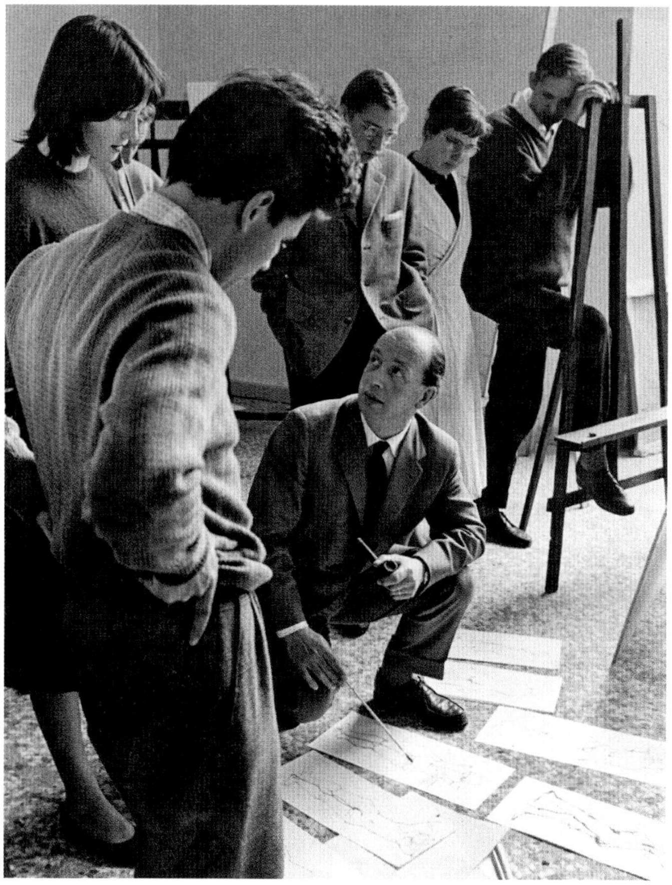

Fig. 1: Joseph Fassbender with students, 1959

Fig. 2: Gerhard Hoehme, 1972

Fig. 3: Gert Weberg and Karl Bobek in conversation, c. 1970

Fig. 4: Karl Otto Götz with students, 1960

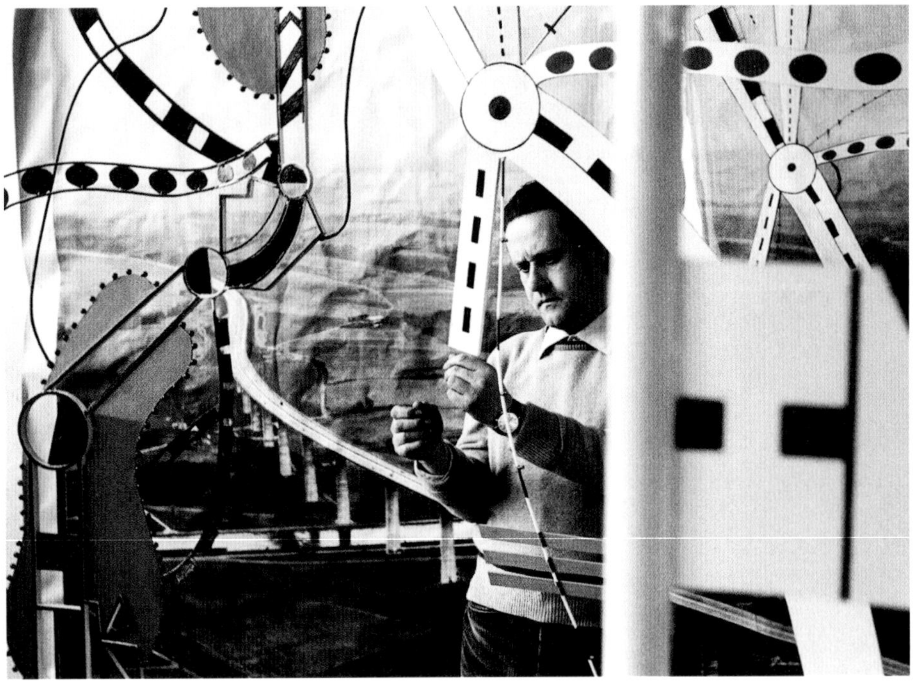

Fig. 5: Peter Brüning, studio in Ratingen, 1967; in the background, the still unfinished picture Superland mit Ruhrtalbrücke *[Superland with Ruhr Valley Bridge], in front of it the sculpture* Straßenmühle *[Street Mill]*

of her own using objects and human figures in narrative contexts which showed no affinities with Götz's work (she married him in 1965). In the 1950s Peter Brüning, who had studied with Willi Baumeister, was a leading exponent of Informel in Germany (Fig. 5). Brüning had begun to incorporate symbols from modern traffic scapes in his compositions by 1964, and it was not long before he was producing painted objects such as the *Autobahndenkmal* [Motorway Monument] by a Wuppertal motorway access road.

Sigmar Polke started studying at the Academy in 1961, at first with Götz and later in the master class taught by Gerhard Hoehme. Polke then went on to address the iconography of everyday living. He often attended Joseph Beuys's class, where he made contact with younger students whose work he knew and discussed. Although he would later go to Hamburg as an instructor, Polke never broke off contact with Düsseldorf. Gerhard Richter had a different relationship with Informel; he used a Gestural approach in some of his early works but only in respect of technique was it related to the previous generation because he combined it with motifs taken from photos. Later, in a new phase of cool abstraction after the overpaintings of the 1970s, Richter would thoroughly rethink non-geometric abstraction. As in previous trends his take on abstraction is also non-representational, but in Richter abstraction flaunts its full potential range despite obvious inconsistencies. Whereas the painting process is driven in Informel by a subjective energy, Richter behaves as if conducting an experiment in abstract arrangement. Nonetheless, his abstract language is unthinkable without the predecessors Richter was personally able to observe during his studies at the Düsseldorf Academy.

Konrad Klapheck and Joseph Beuys exemplify how in the early 1960s the forces driving artistic expression might be drawn not only from fellow students but also from teachers who had worked out their ideas on art in the interwar years, specifically from Bruno Goller and Ewald Mataré (Fig. 6). Here the asynchronicity principle proved its true worth. Goller had been shaped by the poetic manifestation of *pittura metafisica* and a moderate New Objectivity whereas Mataré had found his way to a concentrated formal language heavy on signs after a brief Expressionist phase as a member of the November Group. Before painting his first typewriter in 1955, Klapheck had flirted with the methodology of Gestural painting. Beuys was shaped, on the one hand, by Mataré's sculptural precision but, on the other, was influenced very early on by Dadaist thinking of the kind informing Kurt Schwitters's work and, most notably, Marcel Duchamp's. Back in 1958 there had been a Dada exhibition at the Düsseldorf Kunstverein [Art Association] featuring the most important Duchamp ready-mades. A return to artistic thinking from the era of the First World War and its aftermath was in the air – a belated reaction to the Second World War with a ten-year delay.

In Düsseldorf there were events and encounters that were not directly linked to the Academy. Apart from institutional activities, it was primarily two galleries that provided important sources of information – that is, Jean-Pierre Wilhelm and his Galerie 22 and Alfred Schmela. The ZERO Group formed in 1957 and Yves Klein was in contact with it. Links to Paris were forged, especially to Nouveau Réalisme and the critic Pierre Restany.

During the 1960s international contacts widened significantly in scope. This was due, for one thing, to the Fluxus movement, which had spread throughout the Western art scene and as far away as Japan, and to the far-flung network of contacts in both Europe and America made by Norbert Kricke, who utilised them productively in his work at the Academy. Although Beuys cannot be regarded as an adherent of Fluxus in

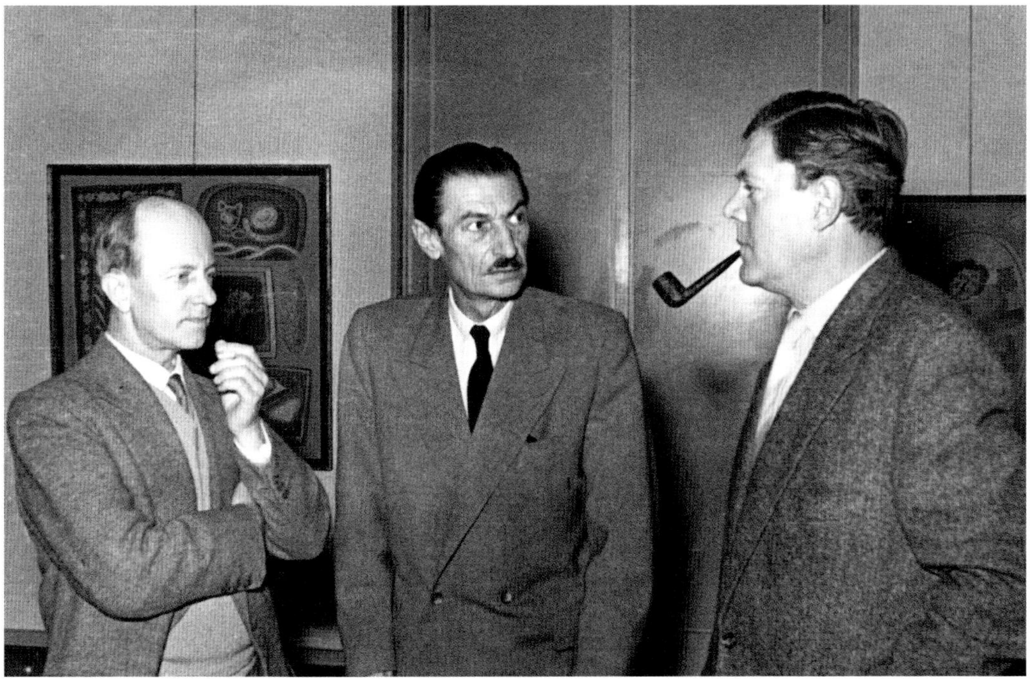

Fig. 6: Bruno Goller, Zoltán Székessy, and Ferdinand Macketanz at a Bruno Goller exhibition, 1954

the strict sense of the term, he did exploit fully the spirit of renewal that energised the Fluxus and Happening artists to advance his own international agenda.

The Fluxus Fest that is now the stuff of legend was put on at the Academy in 1963. However, Günther Uecker, a ZERO Group artist, did not become a professor for sculpture until 1974 – that is, long after the years when ZERO had reigned supreme. During the critical phase of that avant-garde movement, an architect – Hans Schwippert, in fact – was the director of the Academy, so the focus there was on other fields. A department for teaching art at middle schools, for instance, was established in his tenure. Still Beuys was appointed to a chair, a step which would have manifold repercussions, most of them momentous. Beuys had started out teaching as a professor for monumental sculpture. Later the first half of the subject's title, monumental, was dropped as an unwelcome reminder of the Nazi era. Because Beuys had been working at the Academy since 1961, with some judicially enforced interruptions, the impact he made was enormous. Aside from Beuys, there were other tendencies, which were of an Abstract-Conceptual nature. Both Erwin Heerich and Norbert Kricke advocated a concept of sculpture that was entirely different to that represented by Beuys. Indeed it might be more accurate to call them Minimalists, if the term had existed at that time, although there were of course crucial differences between them and the Americans (Figs. 7, 8).

It seems astonishing that both Beuys and Heerich had studied with Mataré since the possibilities provided by their teacher affected them in such entirely different ways. Whereas Beuys took up a holistic approach, which embraced both sculpture and the applied arts and came close to architectonic space, Heerich related to the thoughts on proportion, material economy, and precision, which were also to be found in Mataré. Beuys went beyond all that to seek further possibilities, at first in Dada and MERZ and ultimately in Fluxus. Unlike post-war abstraction, however, Fluxus did not form a school of followers, although that had seemed possible after 1945, when 'abstraction was touted as a world language'. Nor was there a single centre of abstractionism of the kind Paris had for so long represented. Fluxus was able to roam the planet at will: instead of a hub it had many sub-centres, which for some years displayed intense activity. And by the time the Festum Fluxorum Fluxus took place on 2 and 3 February 1963, the movement had also reached Düsseldorf (Figs. 9, 10). The brain behind Fluxus was the Lithuanian-born artist George Maciunas. Beuys became acquainted with him and the Korean artist Nam June Paik, who was living in the Federal Republic, and together they hatched plans for joint projects. The Fluxus movement had in fact grown out of music, dance, and literature rather

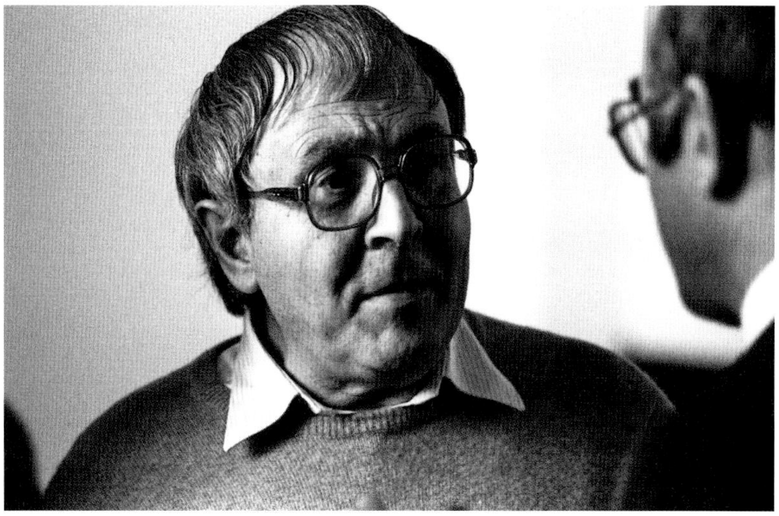

Fig. 7: Erwin Heerich, 1983

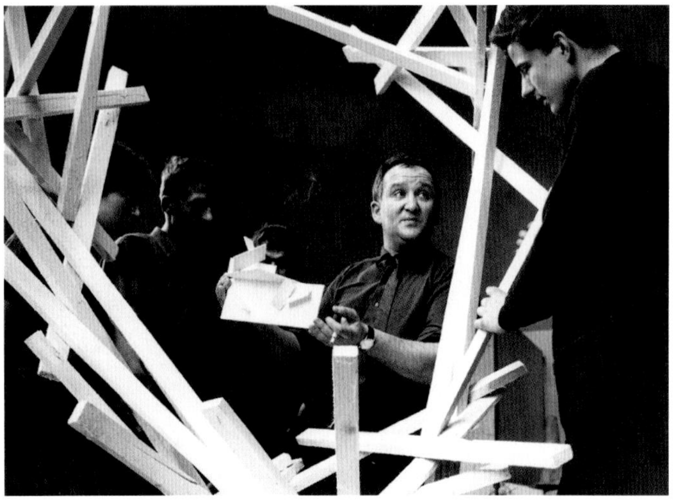

Fig. 8: Norbert Kricke with students, 1960

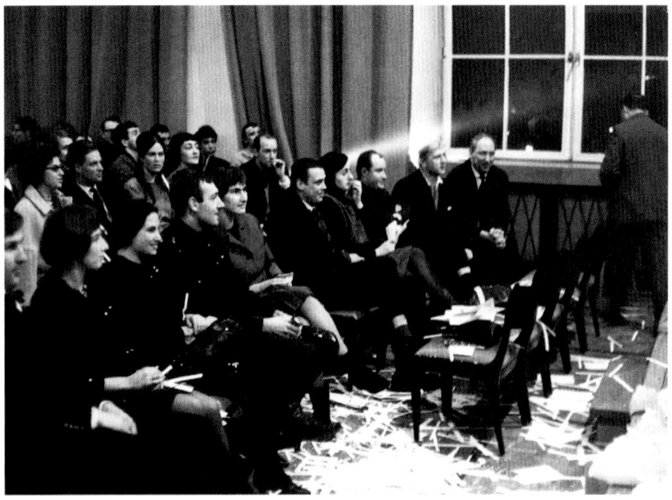

Fig. 9: Festum Fluxorum Fluxus, Düsseldorf Art Academy, 1963, performance of Benjamin Patterson's Paper Piece

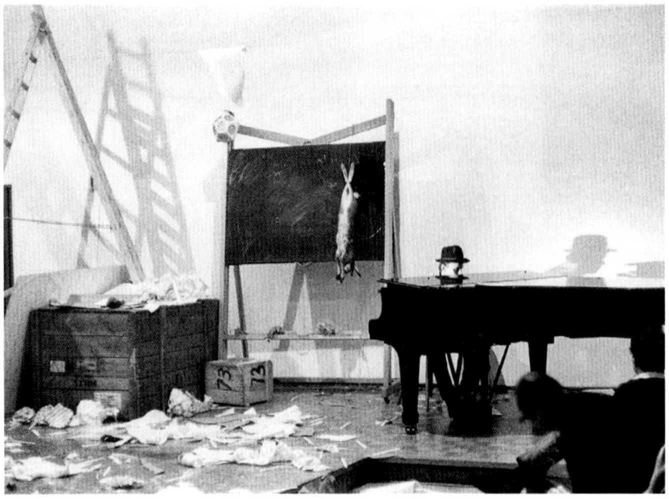

Fig. 10: Festum Fluxorum Fluxus, Düsseldorf Art Academy, 1963, Joseph Beuys's Sibirische Symphonie *[Siberian Symphony], 1st movement*

than fine art. The composer John Cage had been a prime mover and, like Georges Maciunas and Nam June Paik, was actively involved in its early stages in Germany. Beuys participated in the activities but had goals that were tantamount to a different conception of art, hence also his criticism of Duchamp, who, he felt, was stagnating within the art establishment and caught up in the bourgeois mindset. Apart from the contacts Beuys made with the world of Fluxus, many other influences played a role for him, James Joyce and Rudolf Steiner in particular. On the aesthetic plane, however, Beuys also developed complex relationships that offered a wide range of options for his students. Much as things had been under Mataré, studying with Beuys did not entail commitment to a particular style or a fixed principle. When one considers Beuys's best-known pupils, a plurality of actuating principles becomes immediately apparent: Jörg Immendorff, Franz Erhard Walther, Imi Knoebel, Blinky Palermo, Reiner Ruthenbeck, Katharina Sieverding, and many others (Fig. 11). Not all his students started off with Beuys; some brought with them experience gained elsewhere. Immendorff, for instance, had initially studied with Teo Otto. Palermo, on the other hand, had been a pupil of Bruno Goller's, and Knoebel came from the Darmstadt School of Art, to take just a few examples. Possibilities for development in different directions fed by a variety of different sources were the order of the day. It makes just as little sense to speak retrospectively of a 'Beuys School' as it does to speak of a 'Becher School'. In both cases, however, teachers opened up new fields for action in photography and the other visual arts which students could use productively and occupy as their own. Schools as traditionally defined groups of followers sharing ideas and methods have not arisen around Bernd and Hilla Becher and Beuys even though this has often been asserted about photographers. This can be best observed in their earliest independent works. The students were interested in a wide range of phenomena. A similar success story took place in the class taught by Fritz Schwegler. That class has produced artists as wildly diverse as Katharina Fritsch, Martin Honert, and Thomas Schütte. What is discernible here, too, is the effect of stimulation rather than the formation of a school. What once happened in Mataré's class – that is, diversification of his approach to art – can also be attested to the Schwegler students.

The findings outlined above are not meant to belittle the success of other teachers, but still it does occasionally happen that a concentration of that kind crops up in a single generation of students.

There were various reasons, not least artistic ones, for the protests that were voiced against Beuys in 1968. Of course envy played a role because Beuys had gradually risen to be the star of the German art scene; his political activities also annoyed some of his colleagues, not to mention the charismatic aura of the man with a hat who had mustered fifty students, roughly a sixth of the student body, in his class. The opposition to Beuys was led by Karl Bobek (Fig. 12). In November 1968 a manifesto was published that was signed by Bobek, Kurt Arnscheidt, Gerhard Hoehme, Karl Otto Götz, Karl Thomas Robaschik, and Gert Weberg. It took aim at the antics of the student party founded by Beuys in 1967. The paper publicly exposed conflict seething within the Academy, and the press coverage was vast (Fig. 13). The upheavals of the years that followed have often been reported. Eduard Trier, an art historian, was director of the Academy at the time, and he has consistently been described as conducting himself throughout with aplomb and good humour. Nonetheless, he left the Academy in autumn 1972 to take up an appointment at Bonn University. Norbert Kricke was immediately made provisional head of the Academy and was officially elected director on 30 January 1973. By the time he stepped down in 1981, Norbert Kricke had garnered considerable success as the man at the top. Kricke very judiciously rounded off the staff by appointing Gotthard Graubner, Nam June Paik, Günther Uecker, Klaus Rinke, Erich Reusch, Fritz Schwegler, and Werner Spies to teach as well as inviting Anthony Cragg and James Stirling as visiting professors. Kricke was also fortunate in having as his colleague Ruprecht Geiger, who had taken on a chair of painting in 1965 (Fig. 14). Kricke had already collaborated with Geiger in 1957 on work for the theatre built by Werner Ruhnau in Gelsenkirchen; Yves Klein was also in on that project. This was probably the first time after the war that an appointments policy was geared to the top level and encompassed several of the most recent trends informing developments in art. It also marked the post-war opening towards an international bias at the Academy. After Paris had been the goal for Kricke as long ago as the 1950s, by 1960 he had made contacts in the United States, among them Walter Gropius. And similarly, the appointments he made show the tendency at the Academy to be open to international stances. The choice of teaching staff during the years

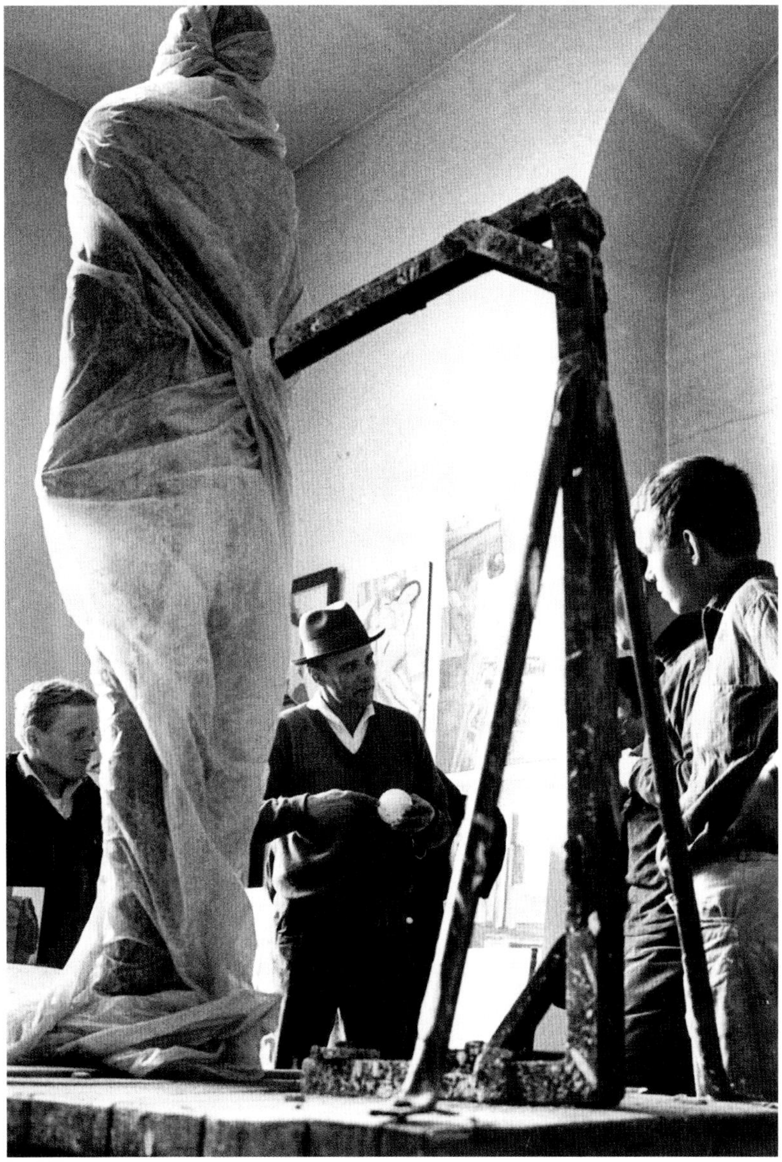

Fig. 11: Reiner Ruthenbeck, Joseph Beuys, and Bernd Lohans, c. 1963

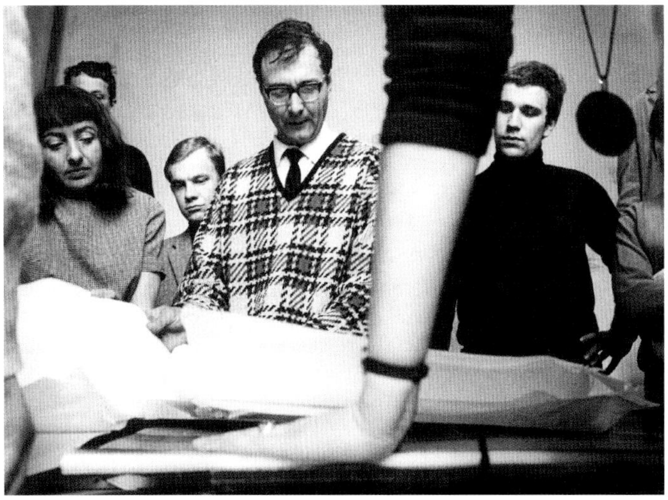

Fig. 12: Karl Bobek (centre) and Beate Schiff (left) with students, 1960

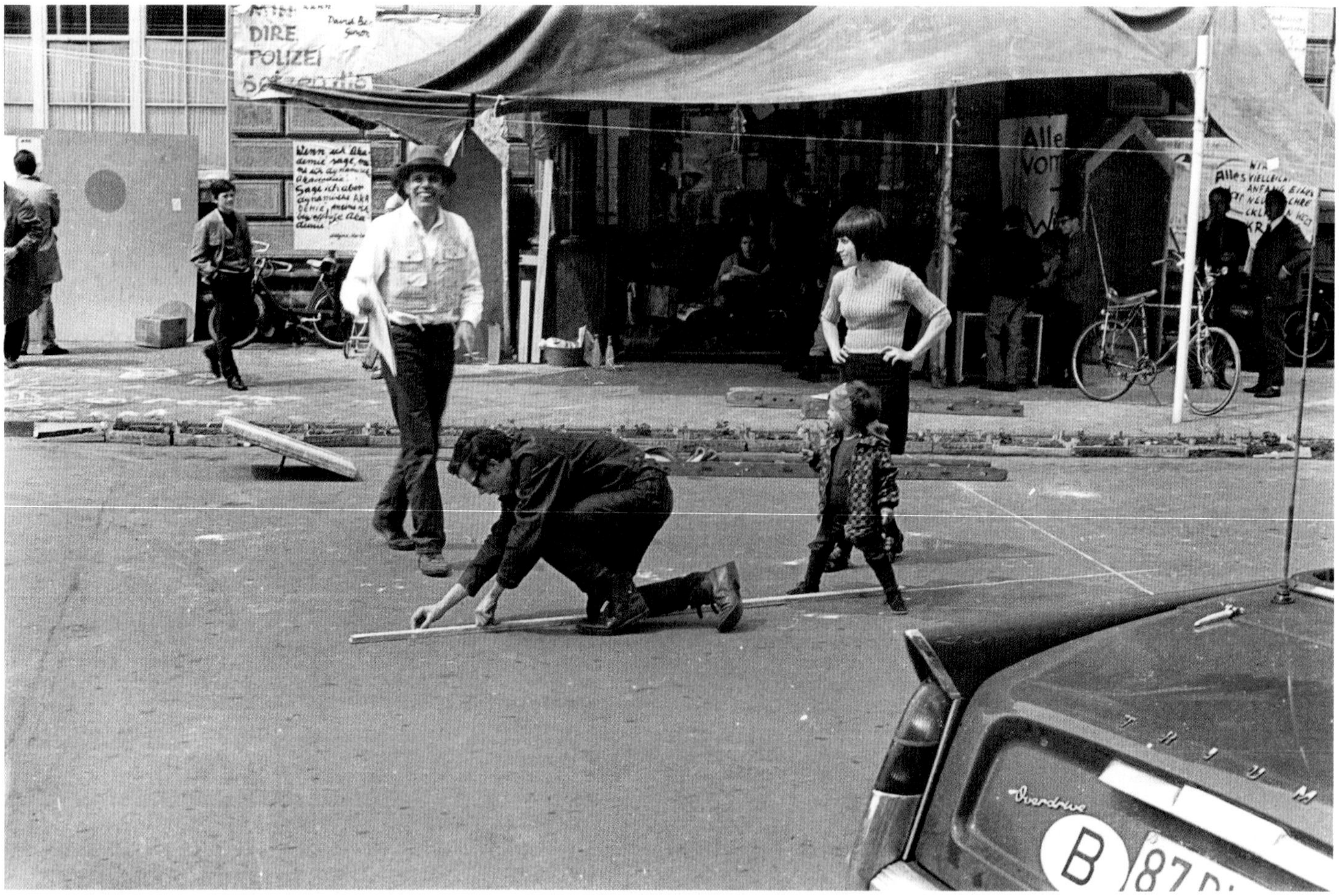

Fig. 13: In front of the entrance to the Düsseldorf Art Academy; from left to right: Joseph Beuys, Johannes Stüttgen (kneeling), and Judith and Ursula Stüttgen, 1969

of Kricke's tenure reflects all that was characteristic of 1970s' art – that is, Conceptualism, the study of figure and space, the resonance of the iconic in painting, and receptiveness to new media. Taken together with the stimulation provided by Beuys, the arts were indeed state of the art at the Academy in that decade. The Academy and the avant-garde were in tandem.

Remarkably, the art movement that had made such an impact since the 1960s, Pop Art in its American, English, and German variants, did not have much of a chance at the Academy. Even though the early activities of Gerhard Richter, Sigmar Polke, and Konrad Lueg are sometimes referred to as German Pop, those artists' inventiveness ran on different lines. They took up a stance opposing Beuys and the Abstractionists to proclaim 'capitalist realism'. However, their concern was not with directly appropriating images from the commodity and media sectors as practised elsewhere; instead they raised fundamental questions about the image as such – that is, Richter and Polke especially were from the outset committed to pictorial criticism in the basic sense of the term and to exploring the issue of what being an artist meant. While the work of those artists targeted social reality and analysed it, the stances of the above-mentioned members of the Academy who had been appointed during the 1970s were grounded in fundamentals, such as image and time, perception and colour, and elements of nature and art.

Gerhard Richter had become a professor at the Academy by 1971, very early in his career. By the time he was appointed, he had long since put his seemingly Pop-affiliated early phase behind him. Hence he was free to concentrate ruminatively and relentlessly on continuing his searching investigation of painting. This ambience was stirred up in the late 1970s when Dieter Krieg and Konrad Klapheck were appointed to chairs for painting. The fields of painting of which the two artists were exponents could not have been more different. Towards the close of the 1970s Krieg's pastose brushwork made simple objects surface aggressively from a flood of colour to startle the viewer. Krieg sometimes linked script and object to defamiliarise both or, alternatively, to showcase them in complementary juxtaposition. Exponents of Informel had already plumbed the potential closeness of brushwork and writing as exemplified in the work of Gerhard Hoehme. Krieg, however, did not take over the idea of organising the entire picture field as a page of writing as Paul Klee, pioneering Modernist that he was, had so brilliantly achieved. Instead Krieg integrated exclamations, neologisms he had coined himself – that is, spoken instructions as perfunctory speech acts that looked fragmentary and were, therefore, ideally suited to accommodating any associations viewers might have and could be further thought out by them.

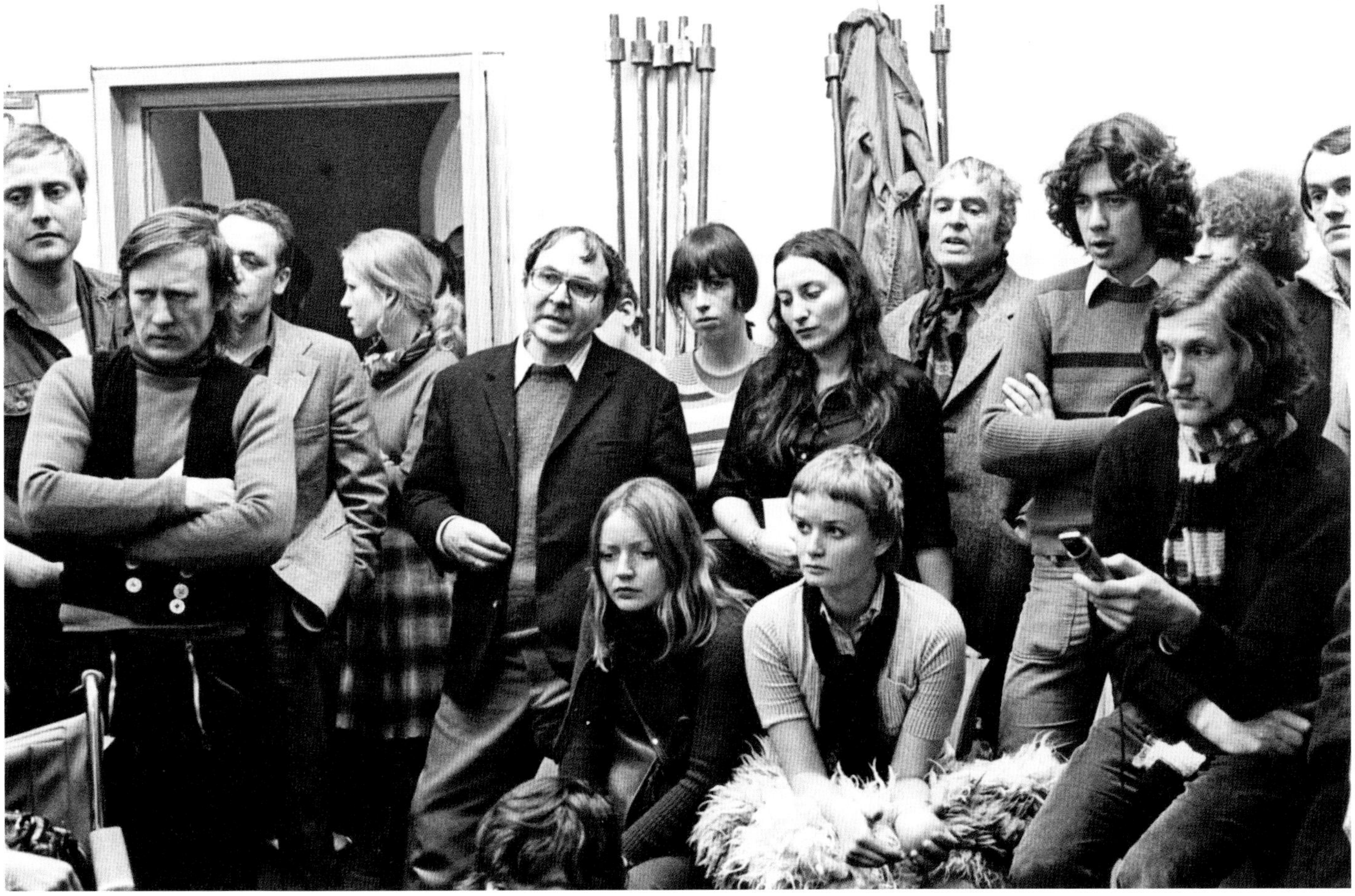

Fig. 14: A discussion on the future of the film class, 1972; among the students: Erwin Heerich (centre), to his left Gerhard Richter, and Rupprecht Geiger (back row, right)

Whereas Krieg had trained at the Karlsruhe Academy, Klapheck had returned in 1979 to the institution at which his career as an artist had begun in the class taught by Bruno Goller (Fig. 15). Since discovering the magic of things produced by modern civilisation, Klapheck found a wide field of fresh pictorial ideas waiting to be used and soon to be appreciated by Surrealists such as André Breton as there were affinities between his ideas and Klapheck's. With engineered precision Klapheck designed a world of objects that managed to look at once mysterious and absurd, comical and non-utilitarian. A first wave of success, activated by the euphoric reception of Pop Art, had carried Klapheck very far indeed in the 1960s' art world before other trends obscured the drive for realism. Hence accepting a post at the Academy seemed like a sensible way of complementing his own work. The appointment of both Krieg and Klapheck heralded the return of representational painting, which had lost ground during the 1970s, a comeback that would become clearly evident in the 1980s. The appointment of Rissa in 1975 can also be viewed as an indication that a turnaround in painting was imminent. While appointments could confirm pre-existing developments, as might be observed in 1960, during Kricke's tenure they mirrored almost synchronously the prevailing artistic situation at the Academy. Towards the close of the 1970s, by contrast, appointments became seismographically attuned to sensing future developments. However, the fact that the stances represented in Berlin by Georg Baselitz or Markus Lüpertz were not represented while downright loners were appointed to Academy posts indicates a certain degree of detachment, particularly since the Berlin interpretation of painting differed markedly from that in Düsseldorf. The subjective-expressive – not to be confused with the Expressionist – aspect and the historical reflections in Baselitz, Lüpertz, Anselm Kiefer, Eugen Schönebeck, and so many others were missing here. The Academy in Karlsruhe, on the other hand, proved a magnet to some of those artists, with the result that the new figurative painting found its first academic home there.

Although representing movements within painting and sculpture had until then been the focus of attention in Düsseldorf, it should be borne in mind that there had always been influential teachers in the field of printmaking at the Academy, among them such luminaries as Otto Coester, Franz Eggenschwiler, Rolf Sackenheim, A. R. Penck, and Dieter Roth. Moreover, Tünn Konerding, Walter Nikkels, Claus Köhler-Achenbach, and Walter Breker also worked as graphic designers, with widely varying fields of specialisation (Figs. 16–19).

Reports from the class taught by Otto Coester indicate that literature also played a role in such classes, since prints are very often associated with texts – for instance, as illustration.

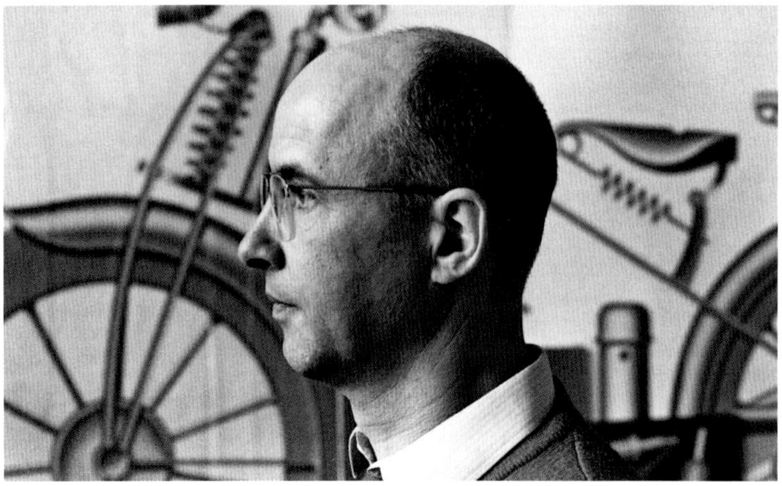

Fig. 15: Konrad Klapheck in front of his painting Der Dämon des Fortschritts *[The Demon of Progress] at the Düsseldorf Art Academy*

Although Joseph Beuys occupied a chair in an entirely different field, the extensive body of graphic work he produced is certain to have been influential, and the same holds for the prints of Sigmar Polke, Gerhard Richter, and Marcel Broodthaers. Broodthaers was not a member of the Academy but he did live in Düsseldorf for several years and maintained contact with Beuys despite the aesthetic distance between them. Another who should be mentioned in this connection is James Lee Byars, who had close links with Beuys and occasionally stayed in Düsseldorf. The graphic arts are usually ranked lower on the scale than fine art, being in fact consigned to the applied arts. This classification is applicable to script and book design and is partly so for graphics in illustration, although Modernism had also enhanced the latter's status since *c.*1880 with the creation of the artist's book in France. However, historical developments since the 1960s had brought about the discovery of the graphic arts as the means for democratising both the promotion and the possession of art. Dieter Roth and Joseph Beuys can be viewed as prime movers in those endeavours. The boundaries between the one-off and the multiple, for three-dimensional, reduplicated work, were fluid. The graphic arts migrated from the domain of classic connoisseurship – although there were notable exceptions – out of museum cabinets to mingle with an expanding art world. That explains why so much of what has been offered for sale since 1967 at the Kölner Kunstmarkt [today called Art Cologne] has consisted of prints in large editions. The organisers of the event published their own portfolios of prints, and numerous new firms sprang up to sell artists' edition portfolios. One of those activists of the early years was Wolfgang Feelisch in Wuppertal, who also dealt in works by Academy artists such as Joseph Beuys. In view of these historical facts, it is simply wrong to write off the graphic arts as being of minor importance. That was where the reaction to experimental movements which used new techniques such as silkscreen printing and photography had to take place. Bold combinations of different processes were tried out, notably by Dieter Roth. The delight in experimentation revealed in art since the 1960s provided the graphic arts with a broad field that was productively exploited. The term 'label edition' has come to be employed more frequently than 'graphic arts'. The techniques traditionally associated with media, such as the woodcut, the linocut, etching, and lithography, have remained in use although they have, of course, undergone changes. Immendorff's linocuts in painting formats are a noteworthy example and so are the ambitious formats of A. R. Penck's woodcuts. However, working with the graphic arts possesses an advantage that cannot be overestimated for the reason that they require craftsmanly processes that are based on knowledge, experience, and curiosity. This observation might seem a commonplace truism yet is all the more important because here everything that belongs to the genesis of an artwork is concentrated as if under a magnifying glass and can, therefore, be deeply and intensively impressed on the memory of the executing artist.

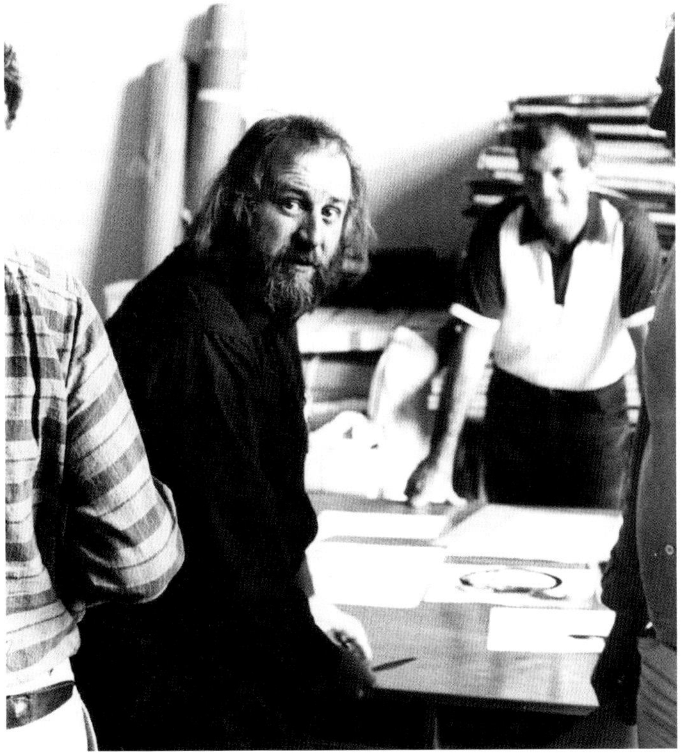

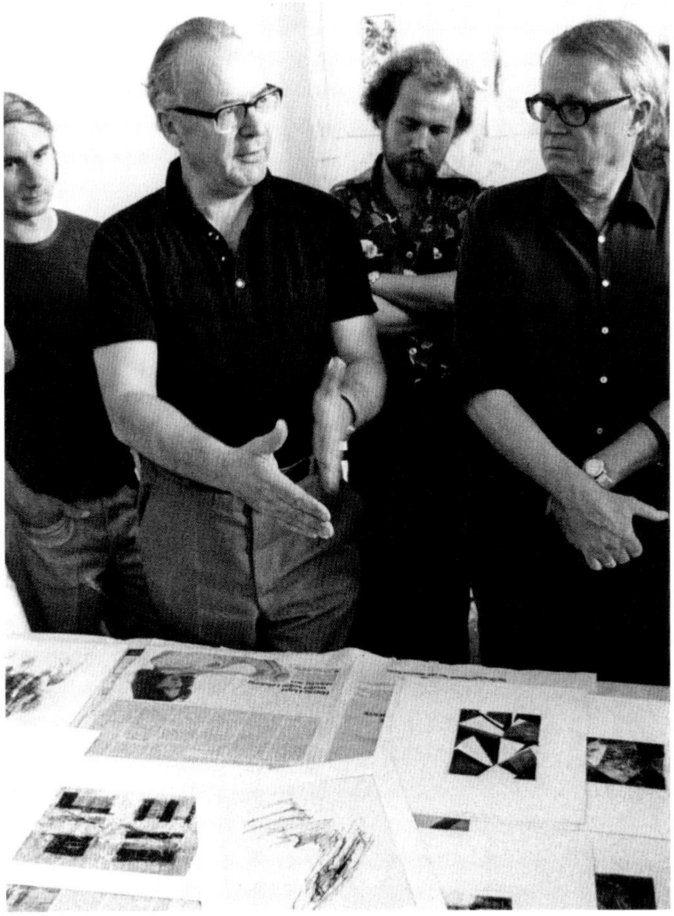

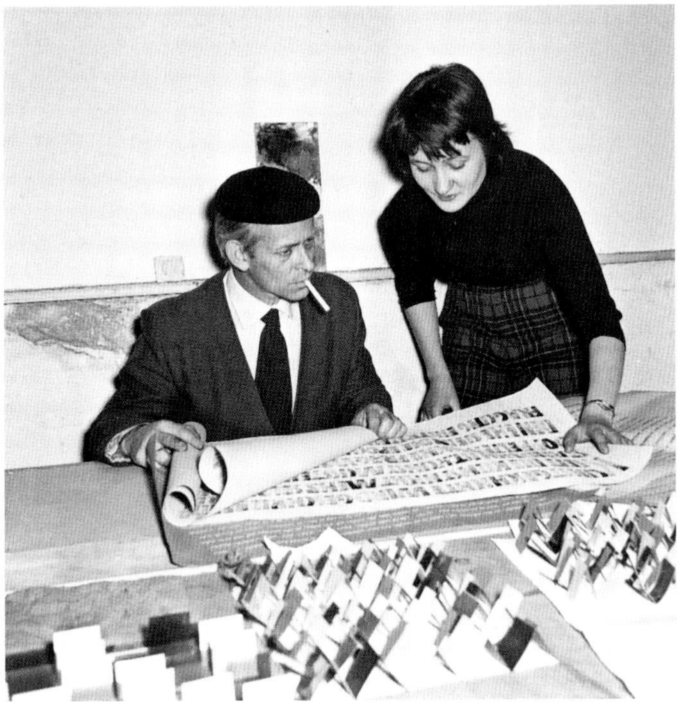

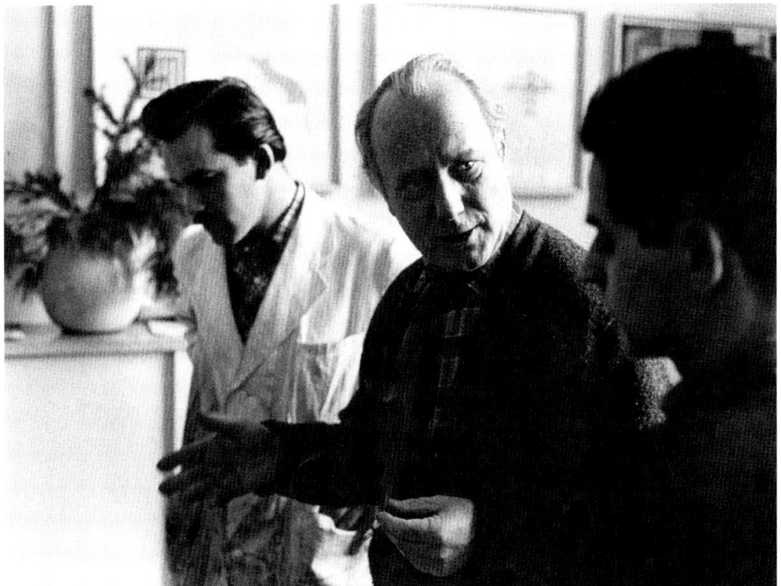

Fig. 16: Franz Eggenschwiler, c.1982

Fig. 17: Claus Köhler-Achenbach with a student, 1960

Fig. 18: Rolf Sackenheim and Karl Wimmenauer with students, c.1970

Fig. 19: Walter Breker conversing with students, 1960

SELECTED WORKS BY ACADEMY PROFESSORS 1960 TO 1985

Joseph Beuys
André Thomkins
Erwin Heerich
David Rabinowitch
Peter Brüning
Erich Reusch
Daniel Buren
Christian Megert
Gerhard Richter
Beate Schiff
Irmin Kamp
Konrad Klapheck
Rissa
Alfonso Hüppi
Joseph Fassbender
Dieter Roth
Jannis Kounellis
Norbert Kricke
Rolf Sackenheim
K. O. Götz
Karl Bobek
Luise Kimme
Nam June Paik
Siegfried Cremer
Fritz Schwegler
Walter Breker
Karl Kneidl
Josef Paul Kleihues
Oswald Mathias Ungers
Manfred Sieler
James Stirling
Hans Hollein
Bernd und Hilla Becher
Klaus Rinke
Jan Dibbets
Gert Weberg
Rupprecht Geiger
Eugen Gomringer

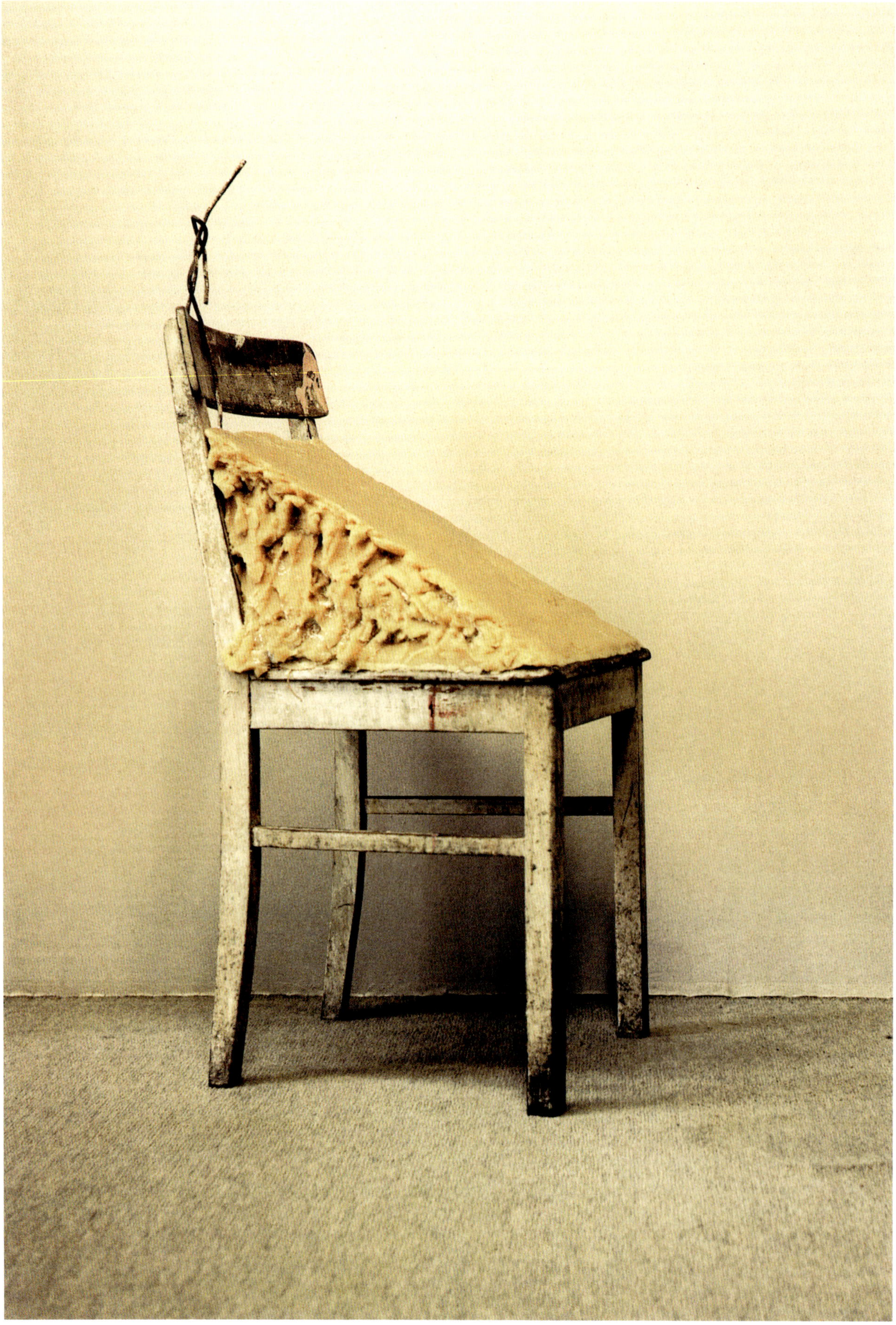

Joseph Beuys, Stuhl mit Fett *[Fat Chair], 1963, wood, wax, metal, 100 × 47 × 42 cm, Hessisches Landesmuseum Darmstadt*

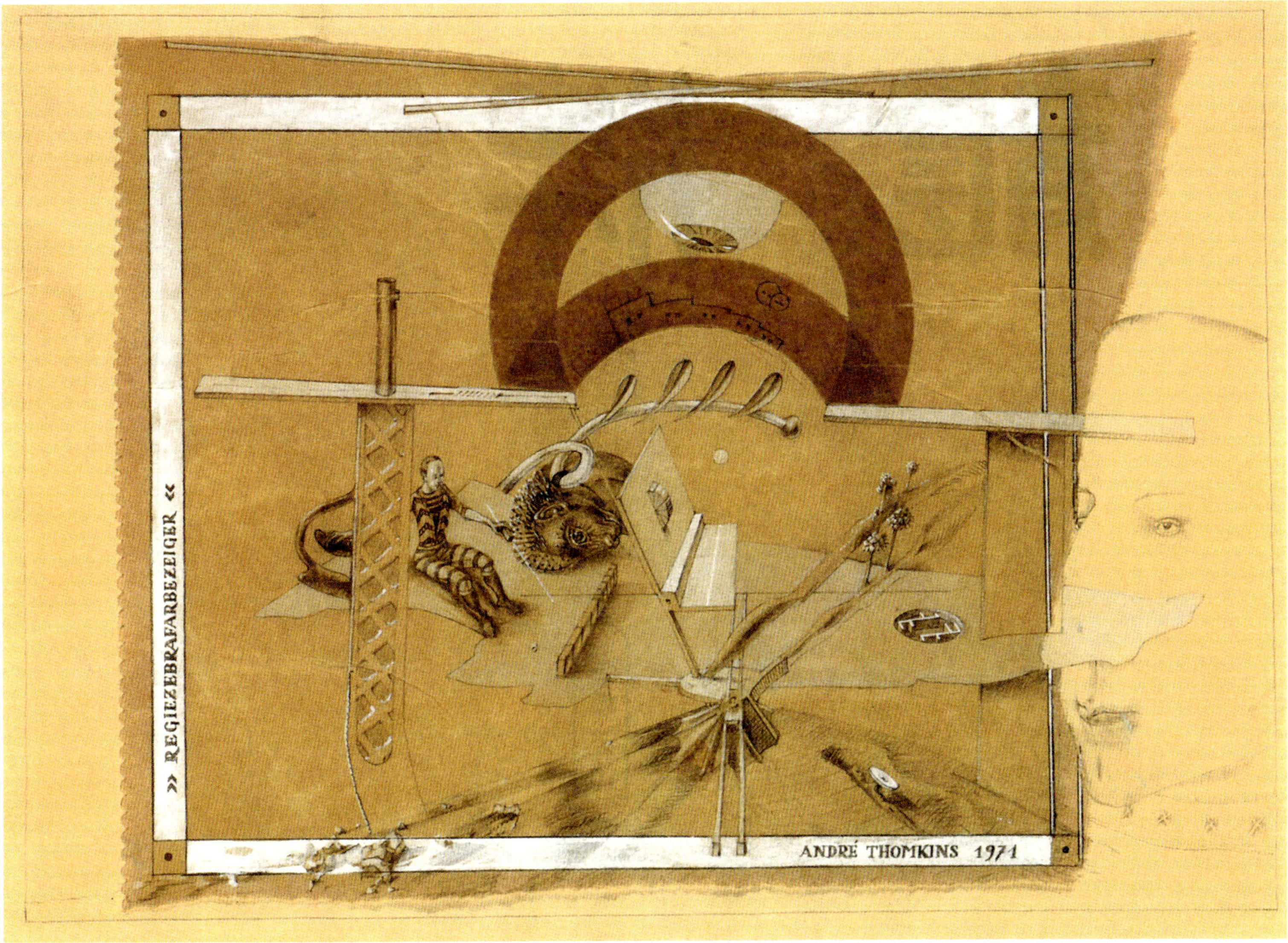

André Thomkins, REGIEZEBRAFARBEZEIGER *[STAGEDIRECTIONZEBRACOLOURINDICATOR], 1971, pencil and opaque white on packing paper, collage, 24 × 33.6 cm, Kunstmuseum Liechtenstein, Vaduz, Thomkins Estate*

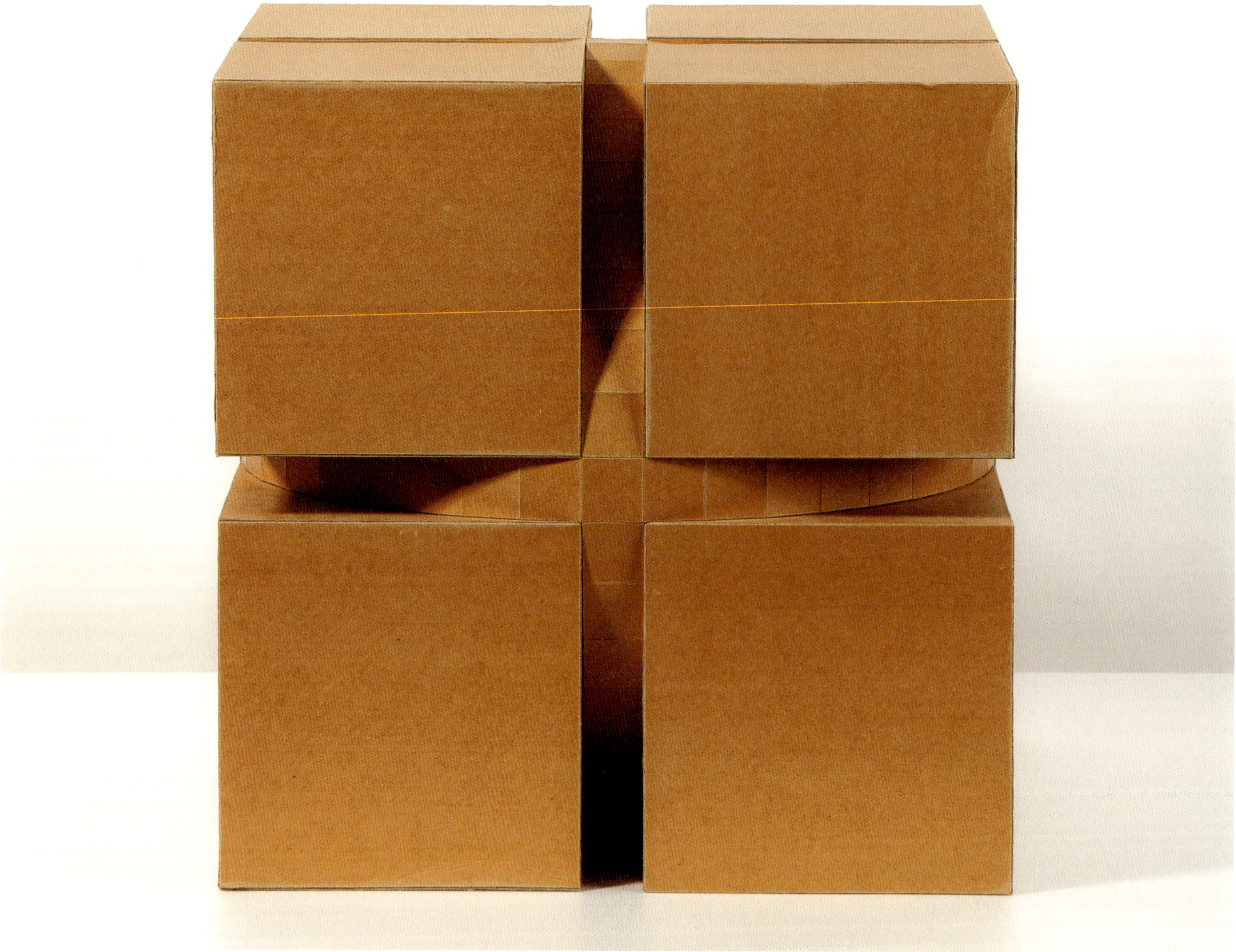

Erwin Heerich, Kartonplastik *[Cardboard Box Sculpture], 1967, cardboard, 44.8 × 44.8 × 44.8 cm, Hessisches Landesmuseum Darmstadt*

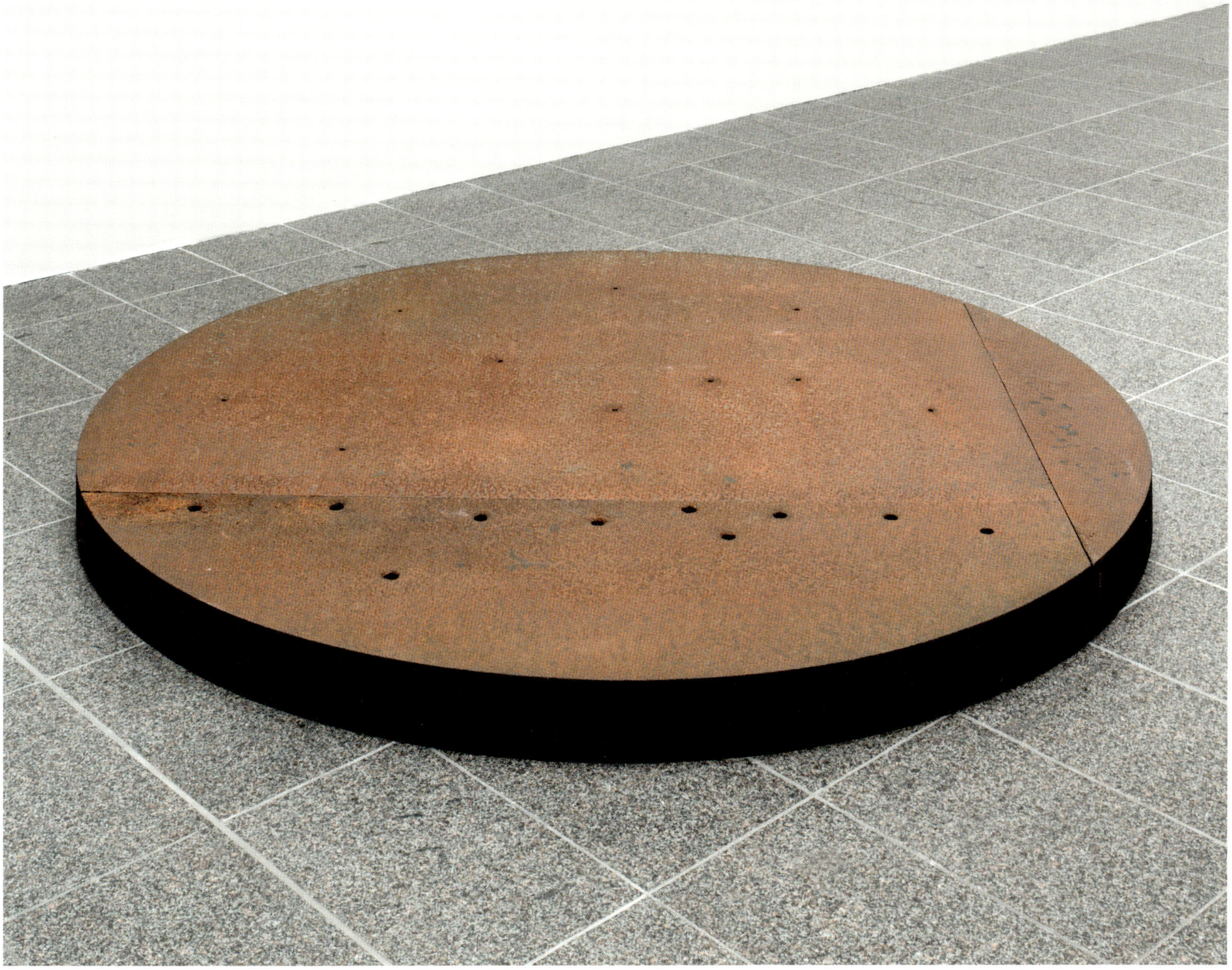

David Rabinowitch, Round Plane in 3 Masses and 2 Scales II, *1977, solid steel, height 12.5 cm, diameter 220 cm, courtesy of Galerie m Bochum*

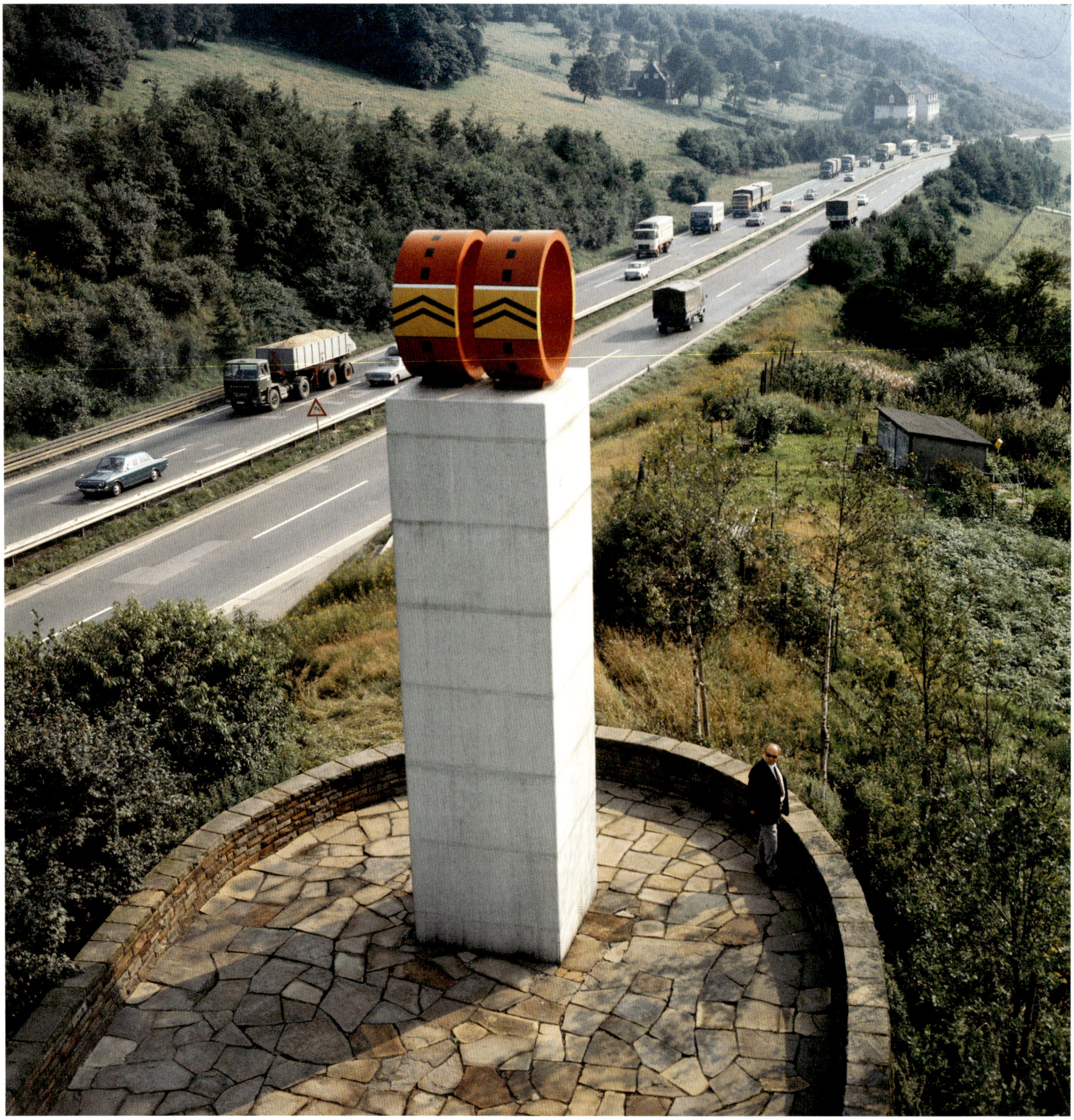

Peter Brüning, Autobahndenkmal *[Motorway Monument], 1968, low-carbon steel and polychrome sheet tin, stone base, 790 × 180 × 180 cm, stands on the Ehrenberg car park between the Wuppertal South and Wuppertal East motorway junctions*

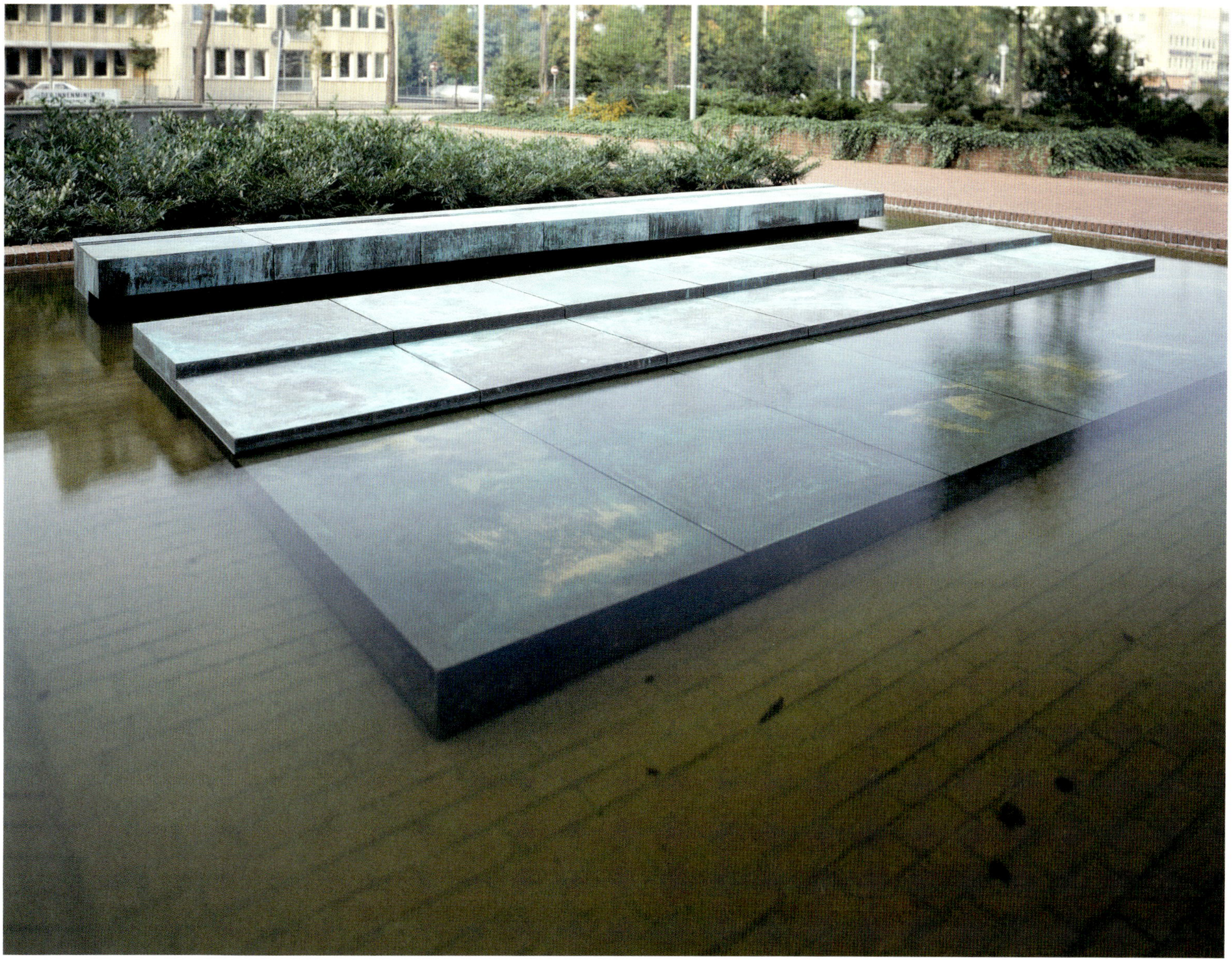

Erich Reusch, sculpture in front of the North Rhine-Westphalia Home Office, Düsseldorf, 1978, bronze, water, 600 × 1,000 cm

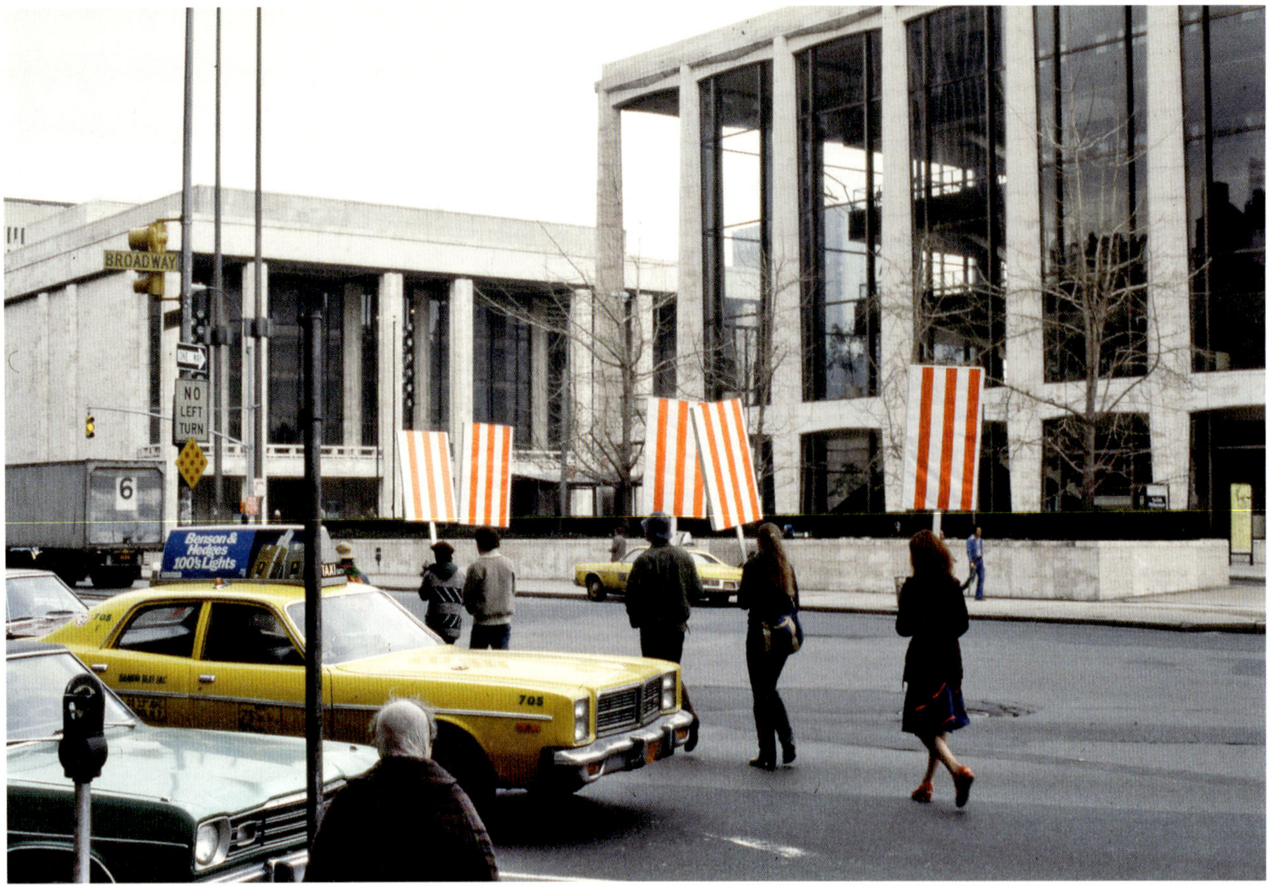

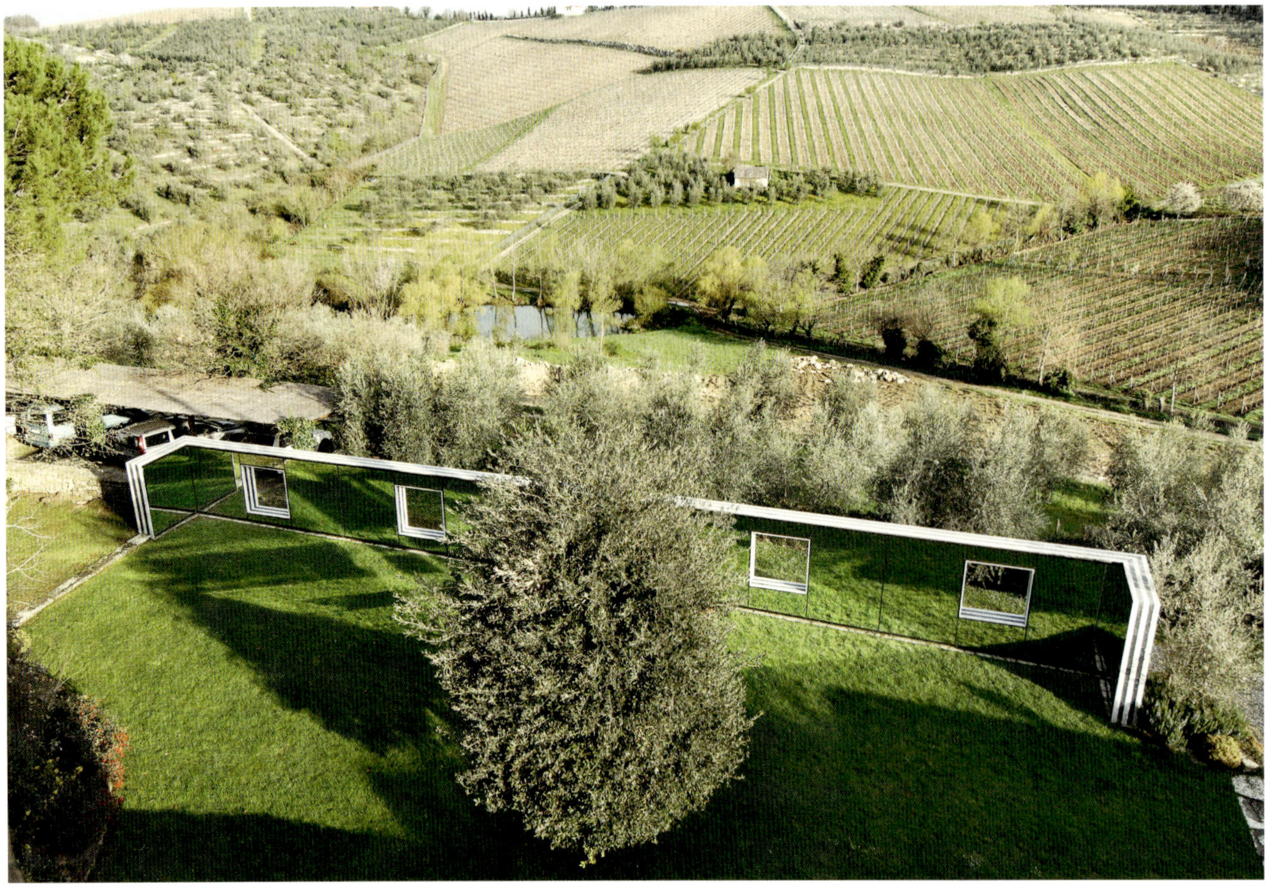

Daniel Buren, Ballets #13, *April 1978, site-specific work (detail), New York*

Daniel Buren, Sulle vigne: punti di vista *[In the Vineyards: Views], 2001, site-specific and permanent work (detail), Castello di Ama, Lecchi in Chianti*

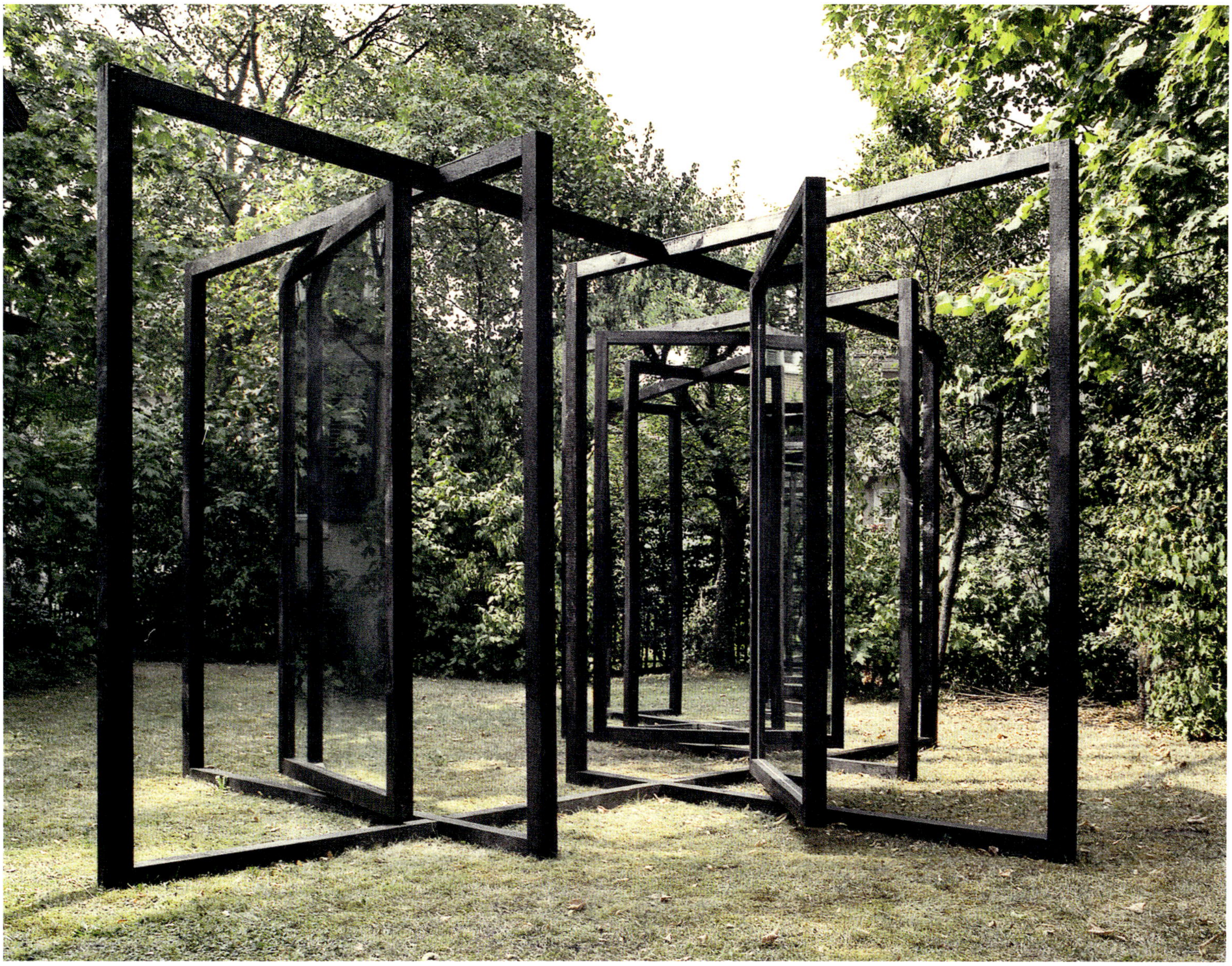

Christian Megert, Drehtüren *[Revolving Doors], 1983, wood, mirror, 400 × 600 × 500 cm, Bern (destroyed)*

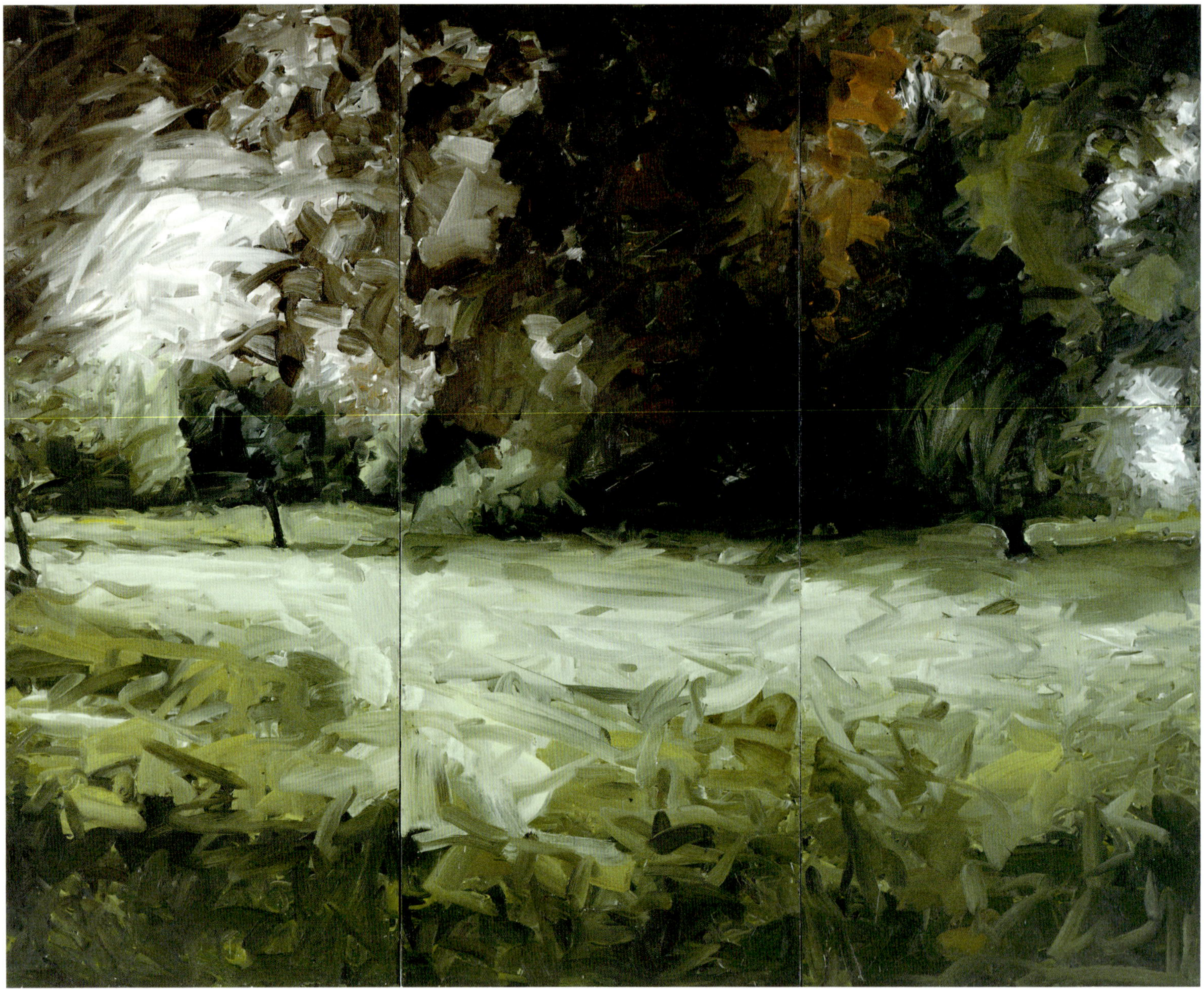

Gerhard Richter, Parkstück *[Park Piece], 1971, oil on canvas, 300 × 375 cm (three panels), private collection*

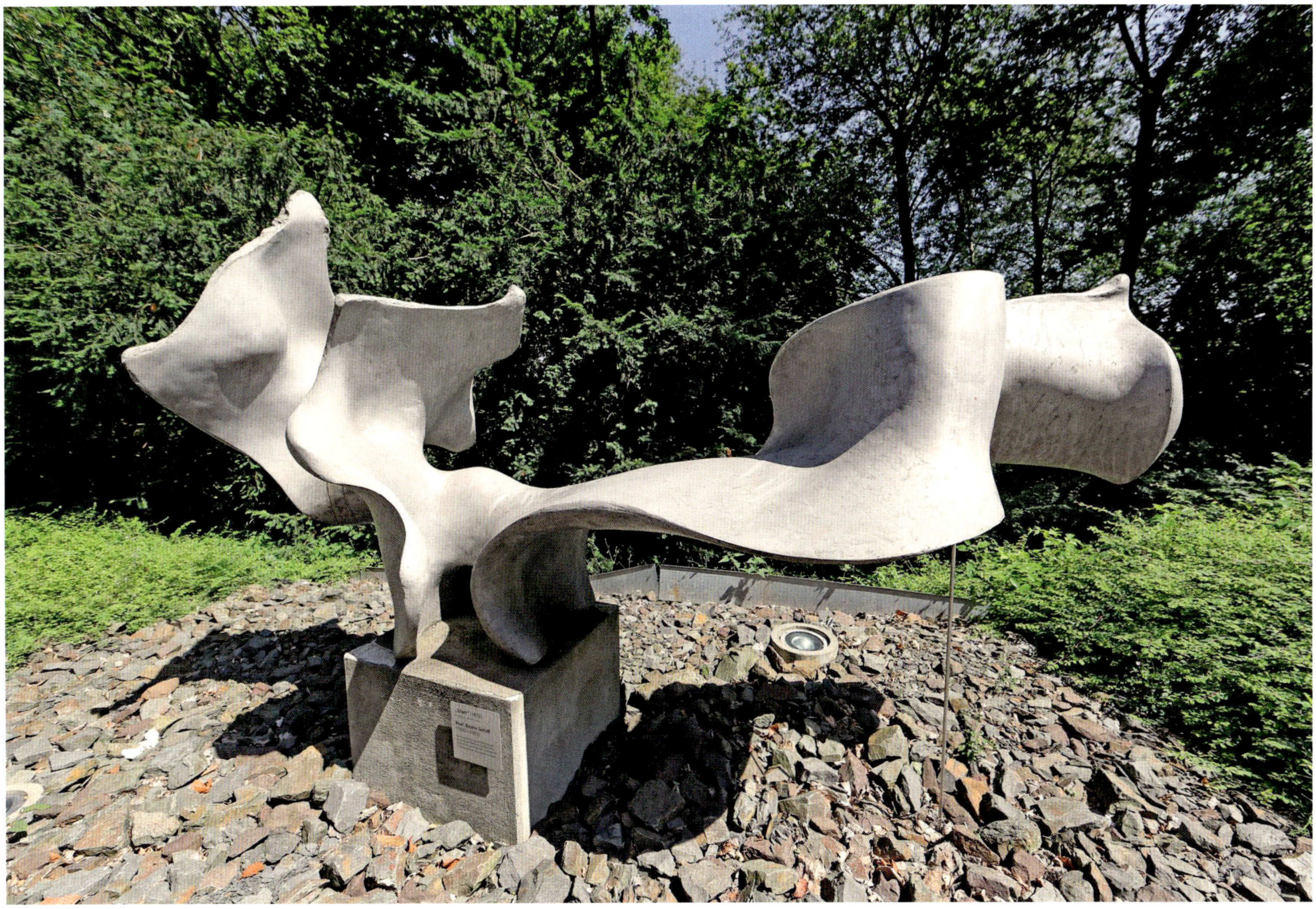

Beate Schiff, Start, *1973, aluminium, acrylic resin, Grifflenberg Campus, Bergische Universität Wuppertal*

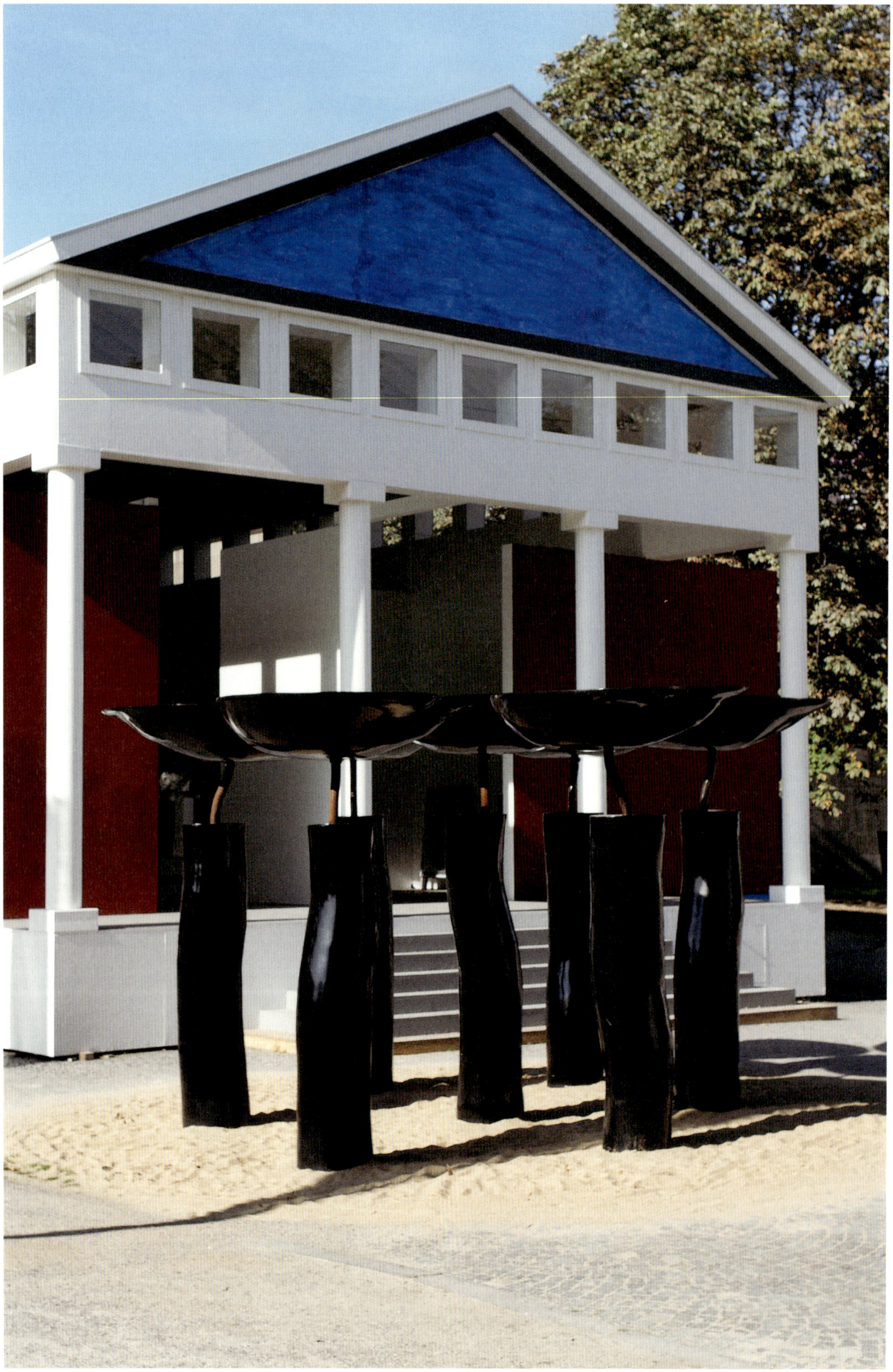

Irmin Kamp, Black Mushrooms, *1974, polyester, steel tubing, high gloss lacquered, 385 × 450 × 420 cm, installation in front of the Markus Lüpertz Sculpture Pavilion, Quadriennale 2006, Düsseldorf*

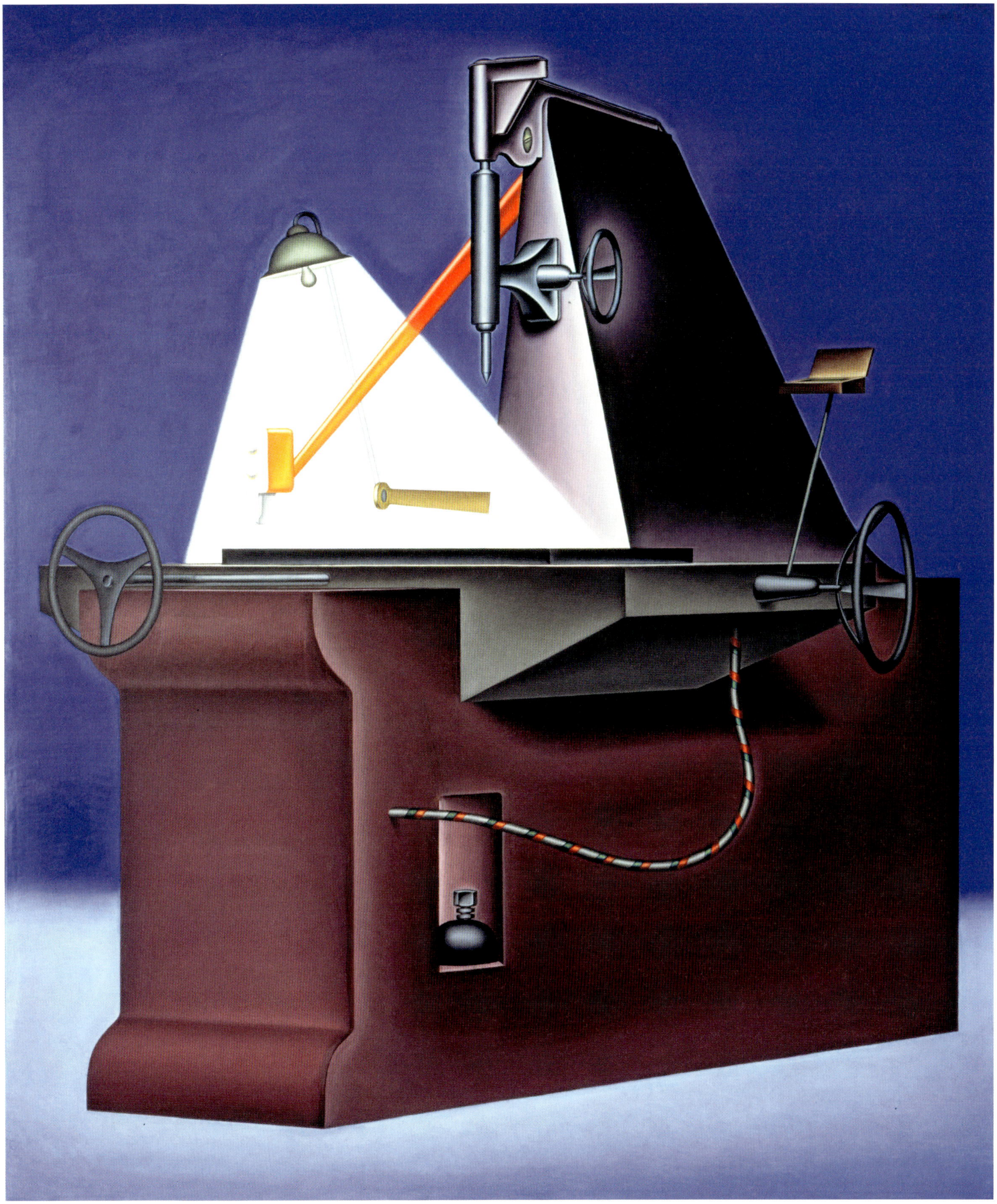

Konrad Klapheck, Die Supermutter *[Super Mother], 1969–94, oil on canvas, 280 × 240 cm, courtesy of Galerie Lelong Paris and Konrad Klapheck*

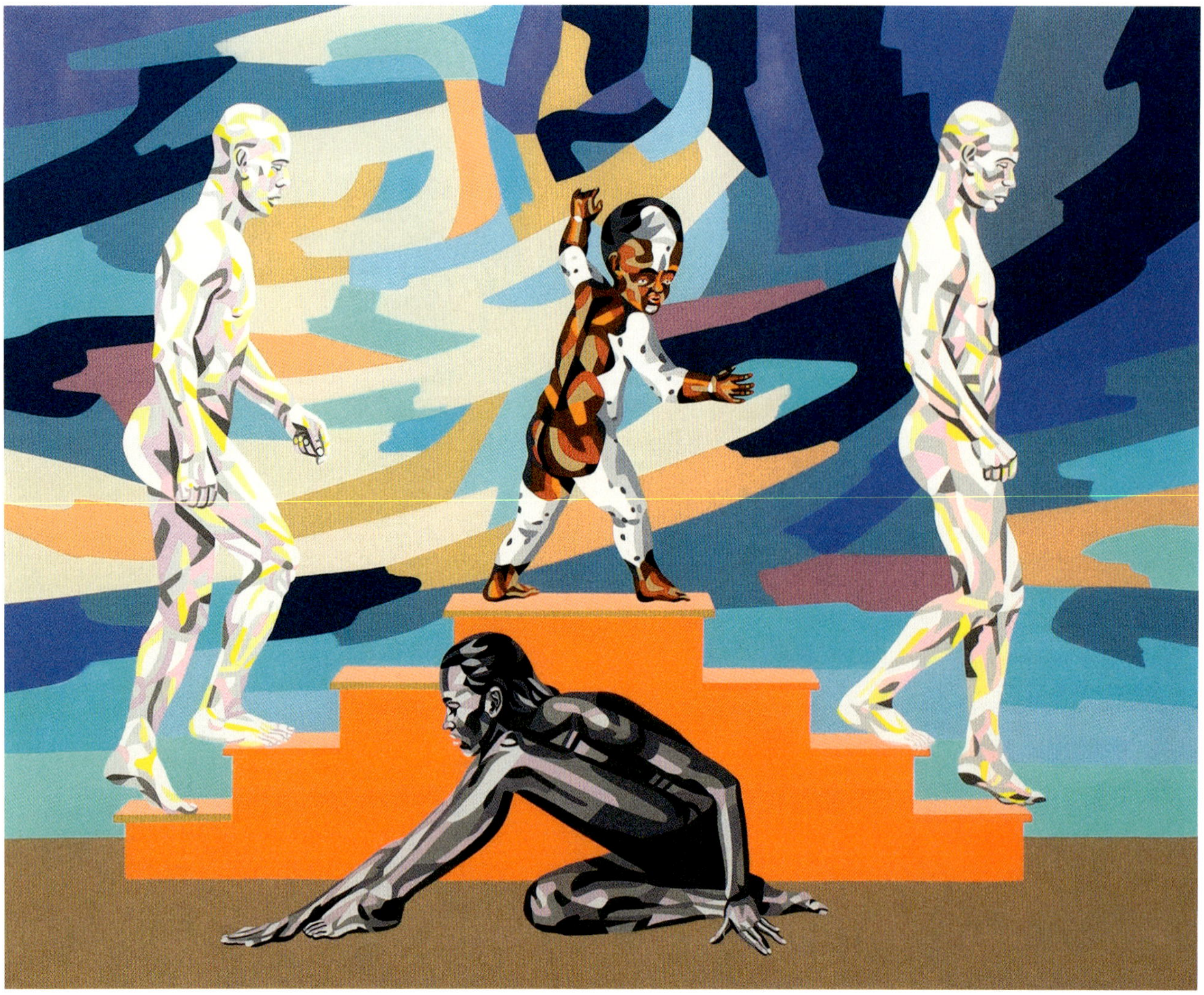

Rissa, Die Familie *[The Family], 1971, oil on canvas, 200 × 260 cm, K. O. Götz- und Rissa-Stiftung, Niederbreitbach-Wolfenacker*

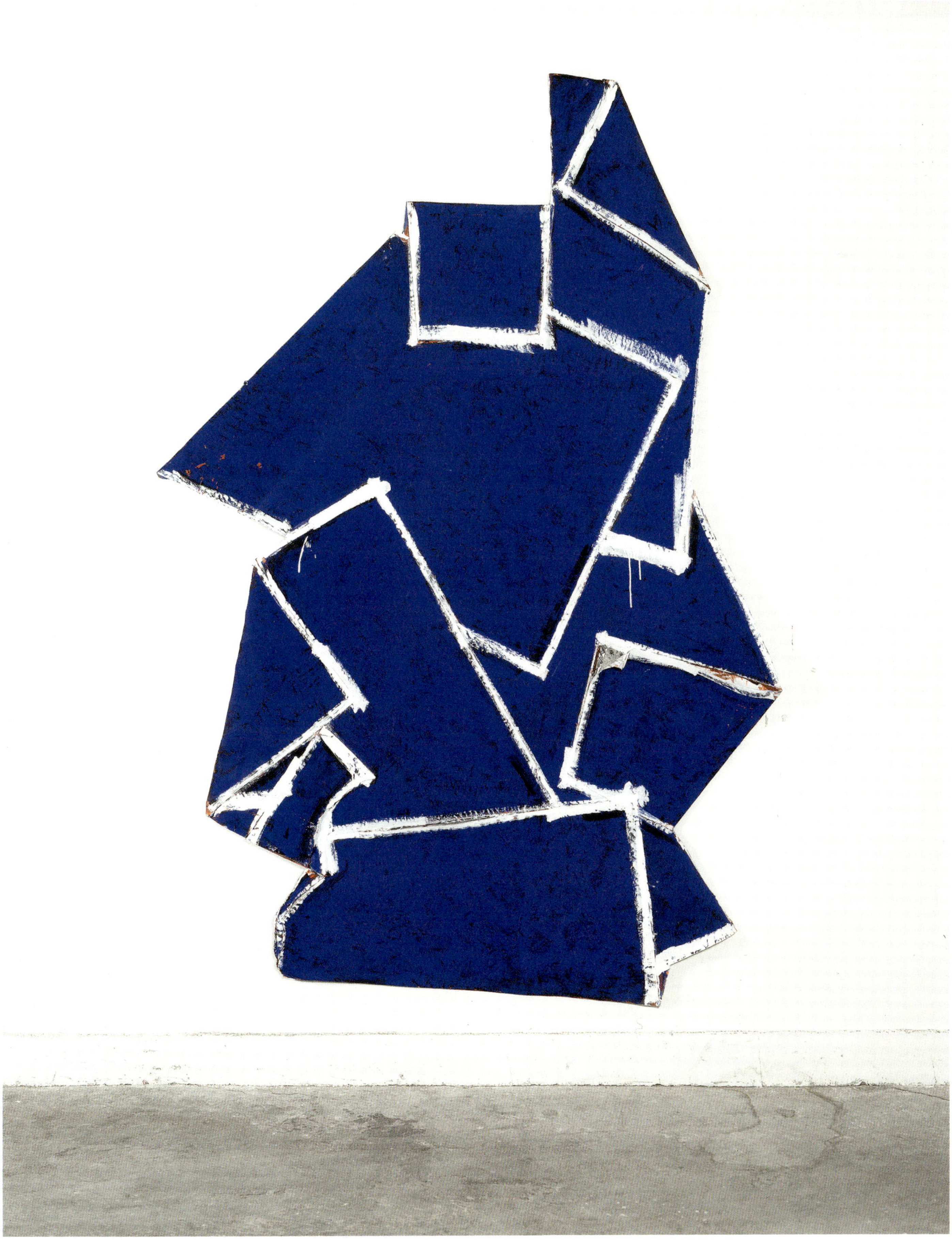

Alfonso Hüppi, Entwürfelung *[Decubisation], 1982, paper collage, casein paint (tempera), 300 × 200 cm, courtesy of Galerie Henze & Ketterer, Wichtrach*

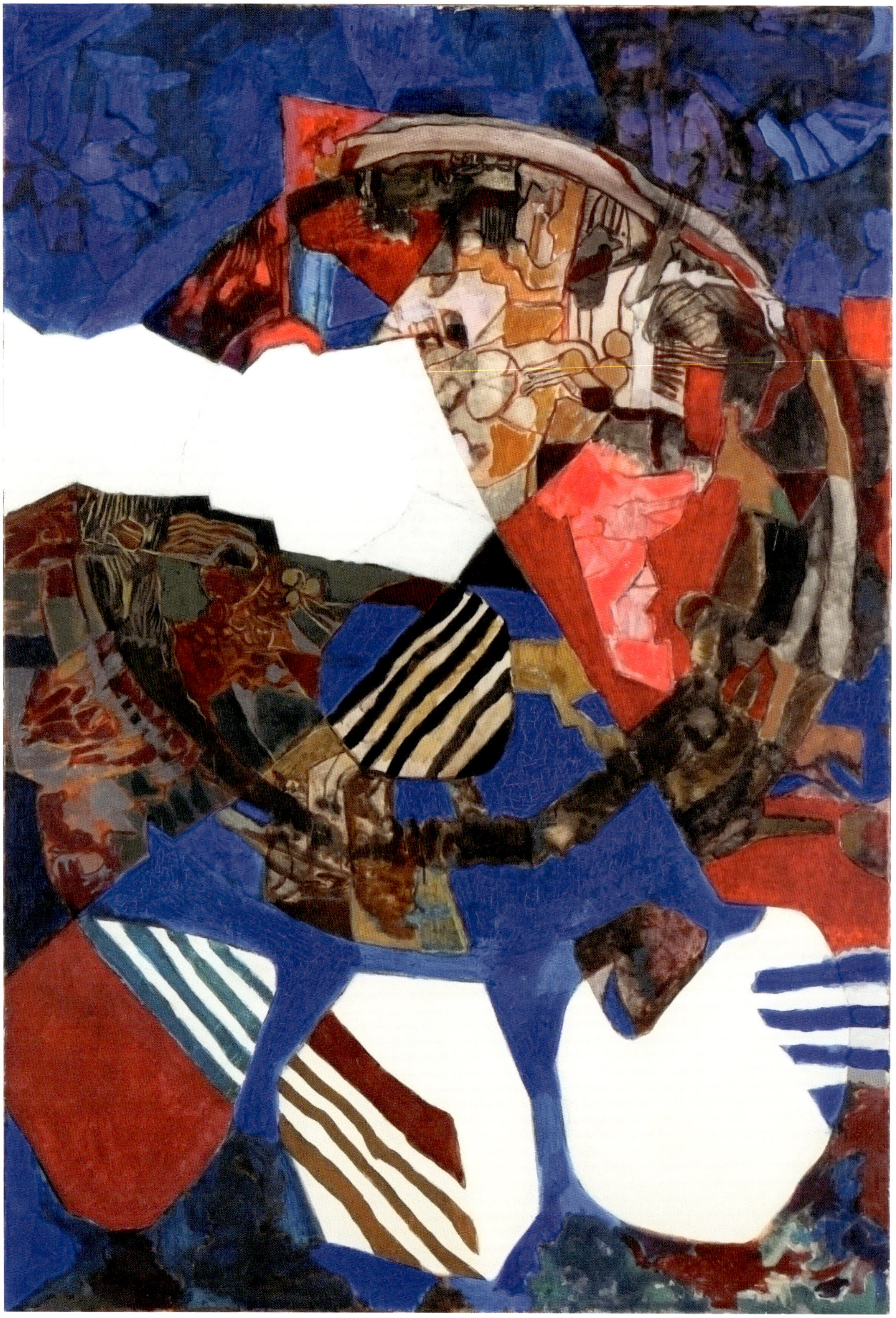

Joseph Fassbender, Ohne Titel [untitled], c.*1965, oil on canvas, 150 × 100.5 cm, Akademie-Galerie – Die Neue Sammlung, Düsseldorf*

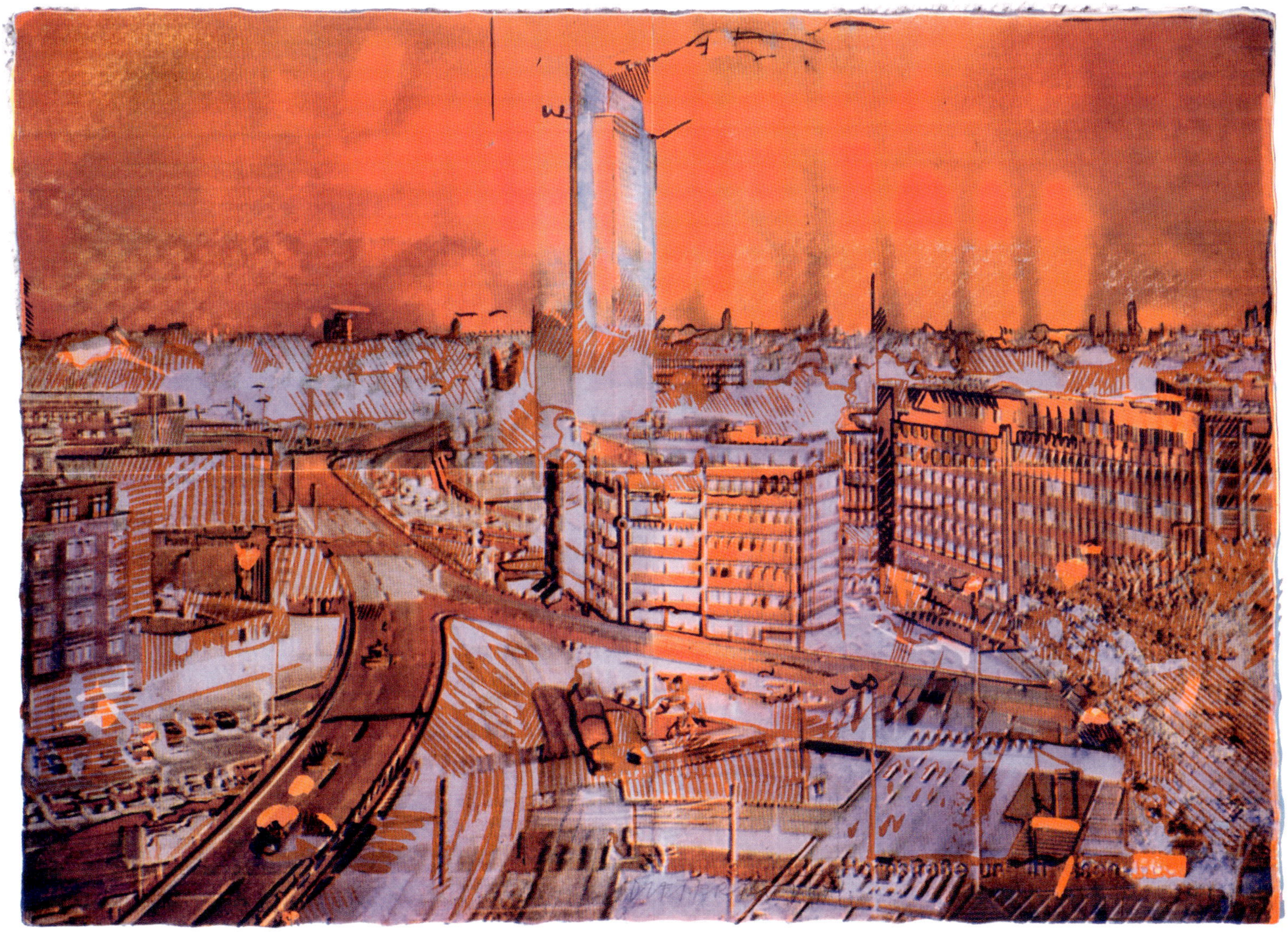

Dieter Roth, Düsseldorf, *1971, silkscreen print, 10–20 colours on white cardboard, positive and negative stencil, worked over, photomechanical reproduction of a picture postcard, 73 × 102 cm, edition of 120 signed one-offs, Dieter Roth Estate/courtesy of Hauser & Wirth*

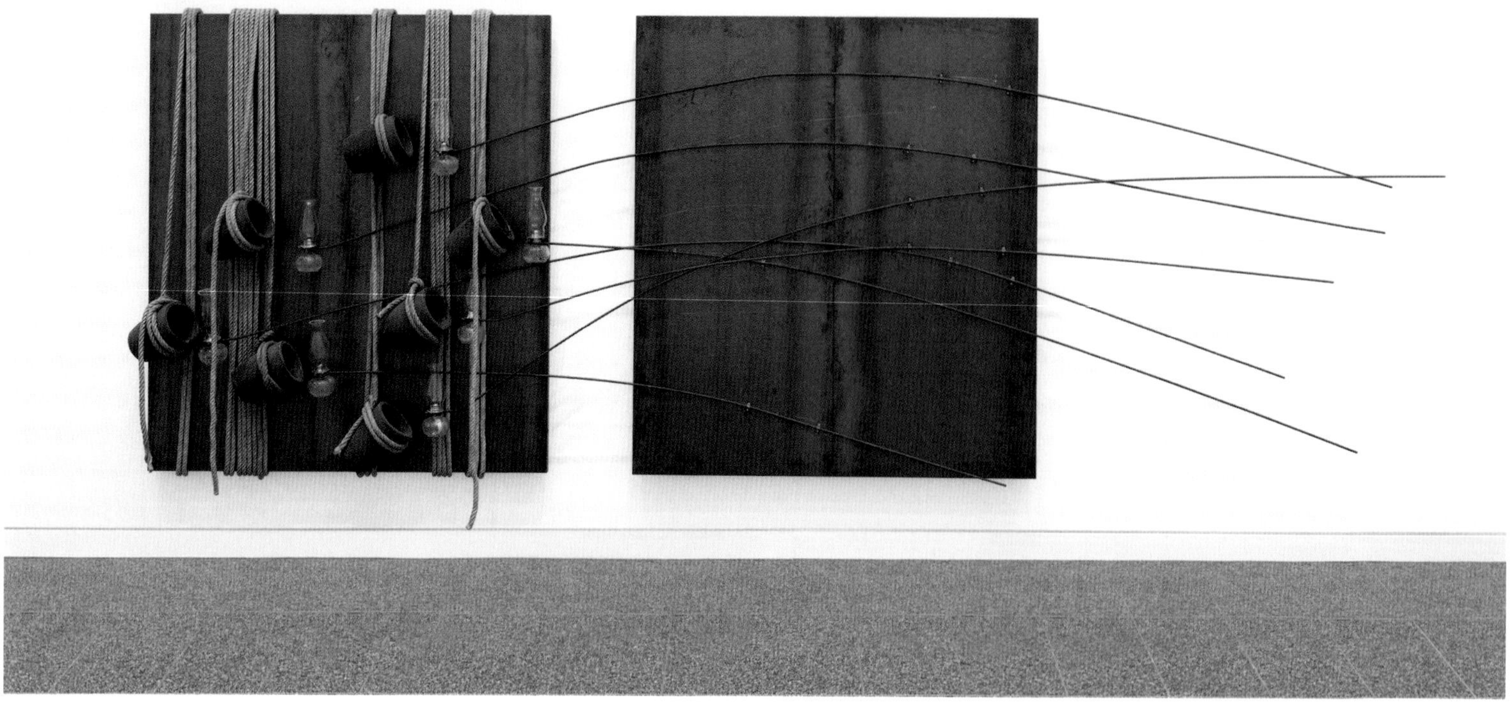

Jannis Kounellis, Ohne Titel [untitled], 1990, steel, rubber, rope, crucible, paraffin lamps, 200 × 570 × 37 cm, Kunstsammlung Nordrhein-Westfalen, Düsseldorf

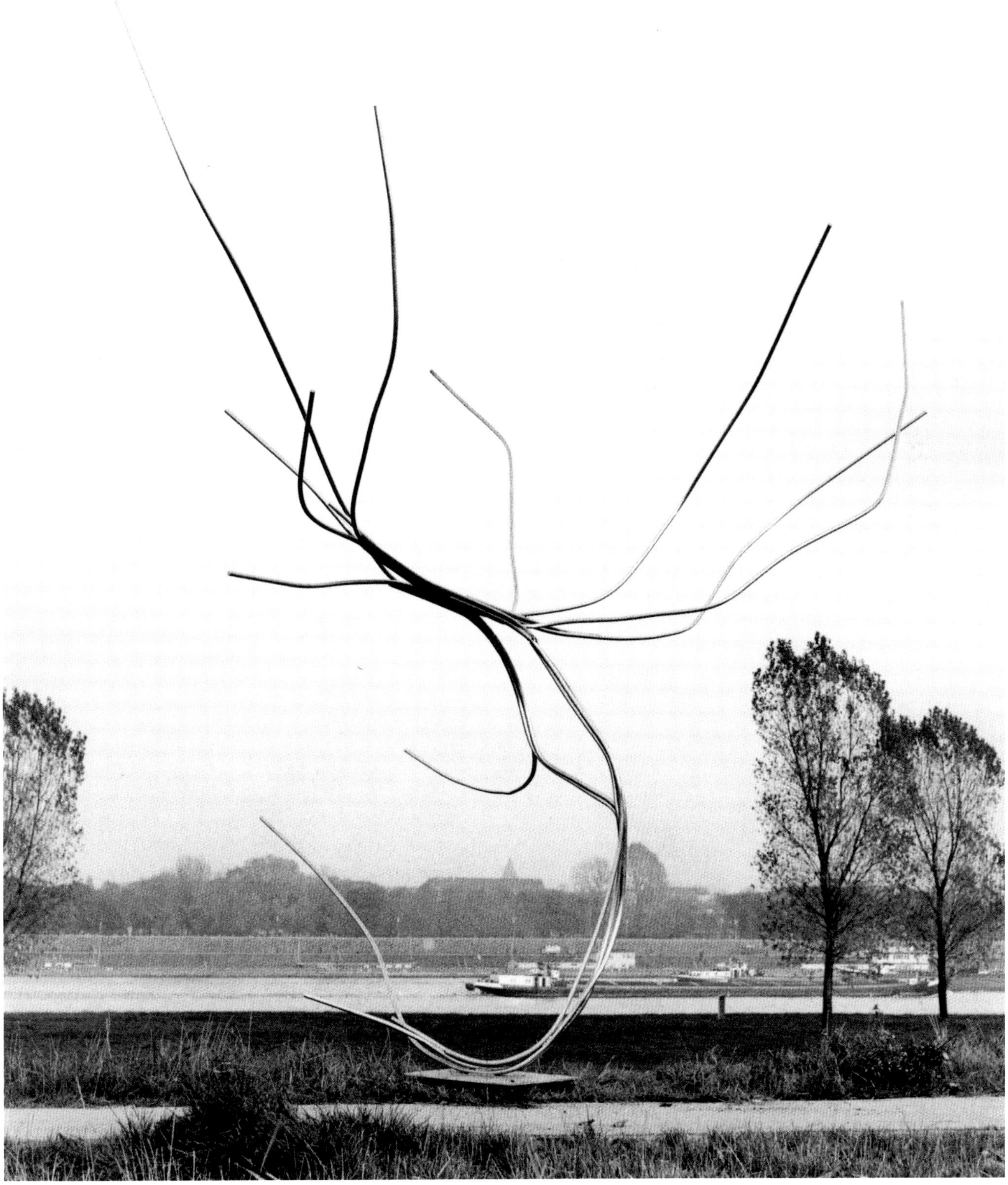

Norbert Kricke, Große Fließende *[The Great Flowing One], 1965/66, stainless steel, 405 × 500 × 315 cm, Fondation Maeght, Saint-Paul-de-Vence*

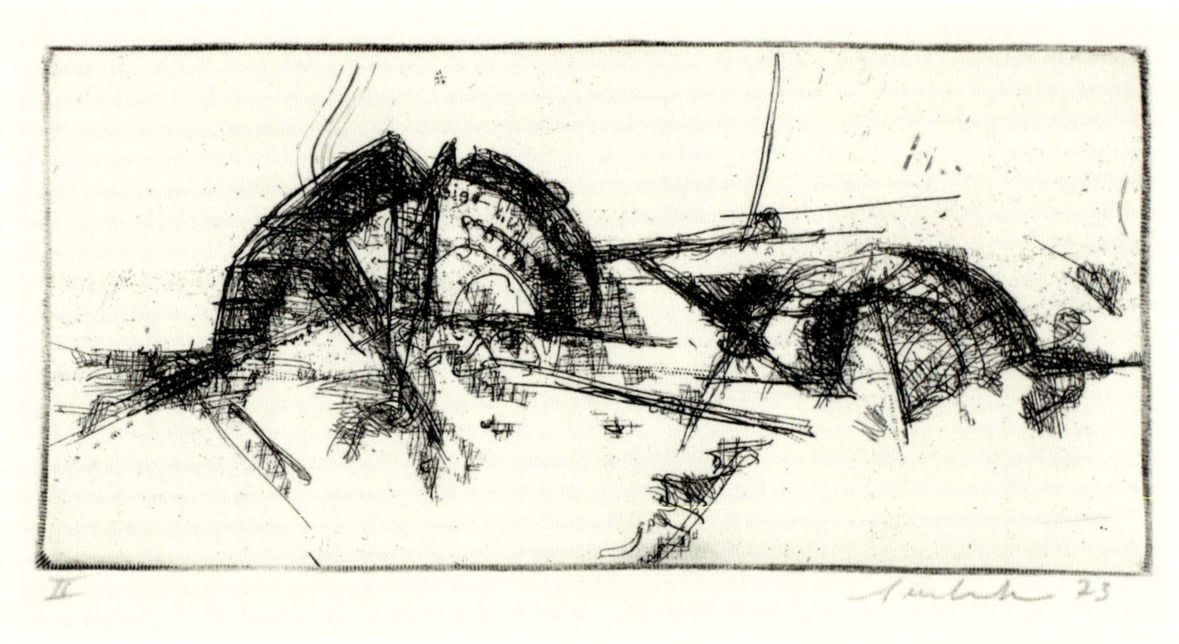

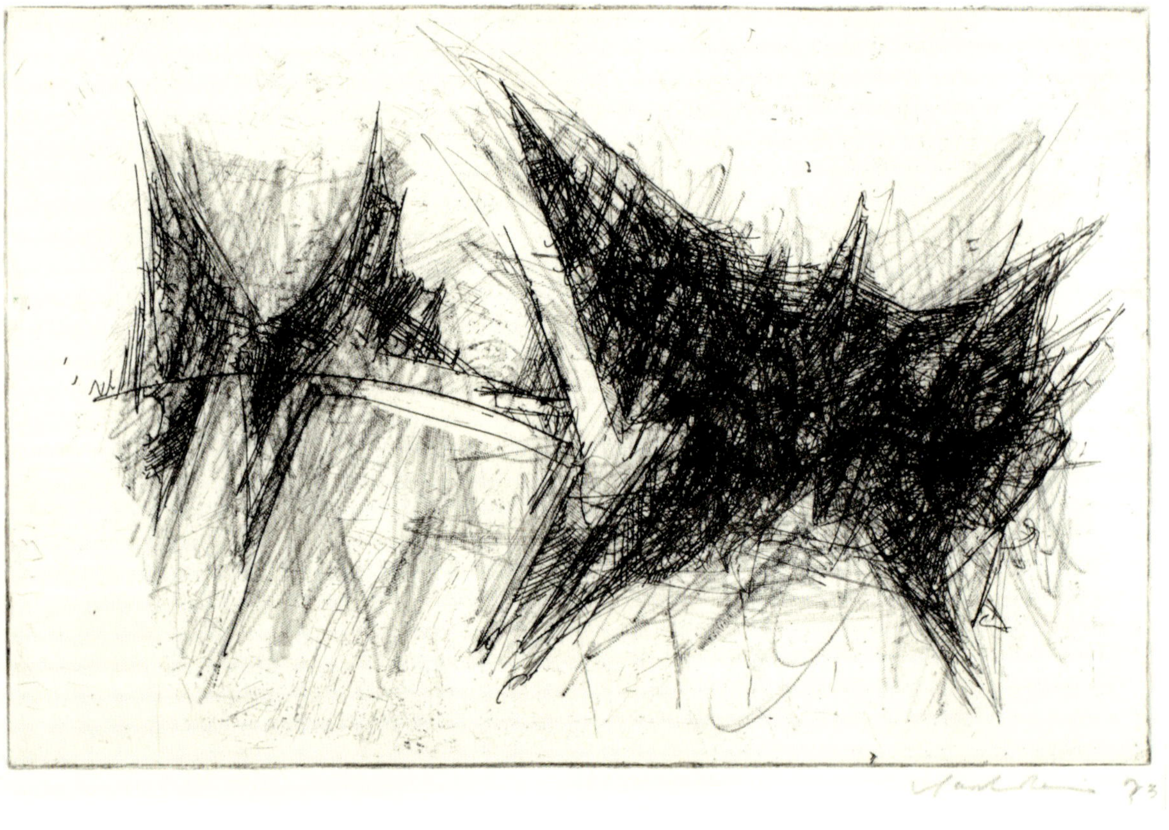

Rolf Sackenheim, *Ohne Titel [untitled]*, 1973, etching, 22.7 × 27.9 cm, Akademie-Galerie – Die Neue Sammlung, Düsseldorf

Rolf Sackenheim, *Ohne Titel [untitled]*, 1973, etching, 26.5 × 39 cm, Akademie-Galerie – Die Neue Sammlung, Düsseldorf

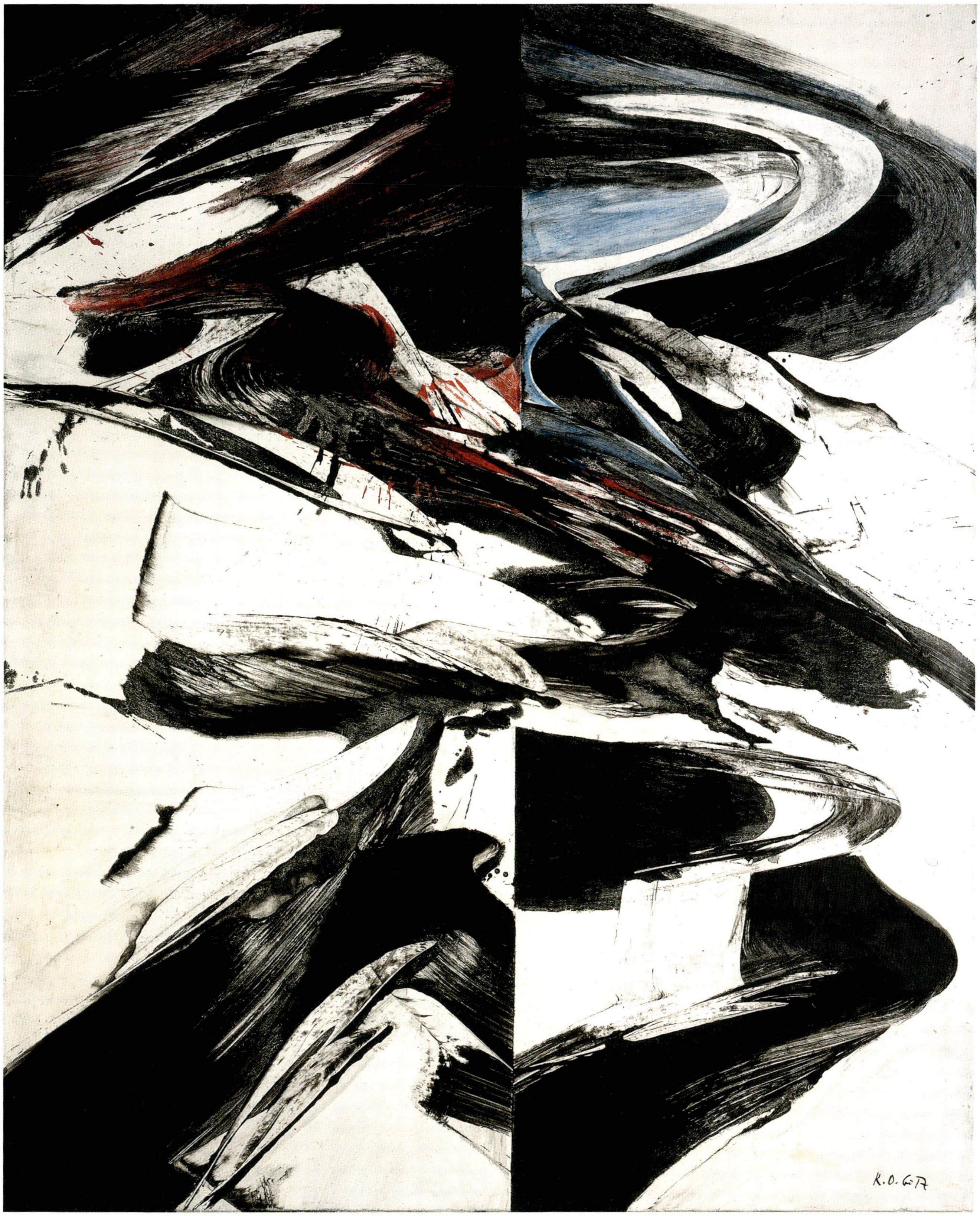

K. O. Götz, Nördli, *1966, mixed media on canvas, 175 × 145 cm, Akademie-Galerie – Die Neue Sammlung, Düsseldorf*

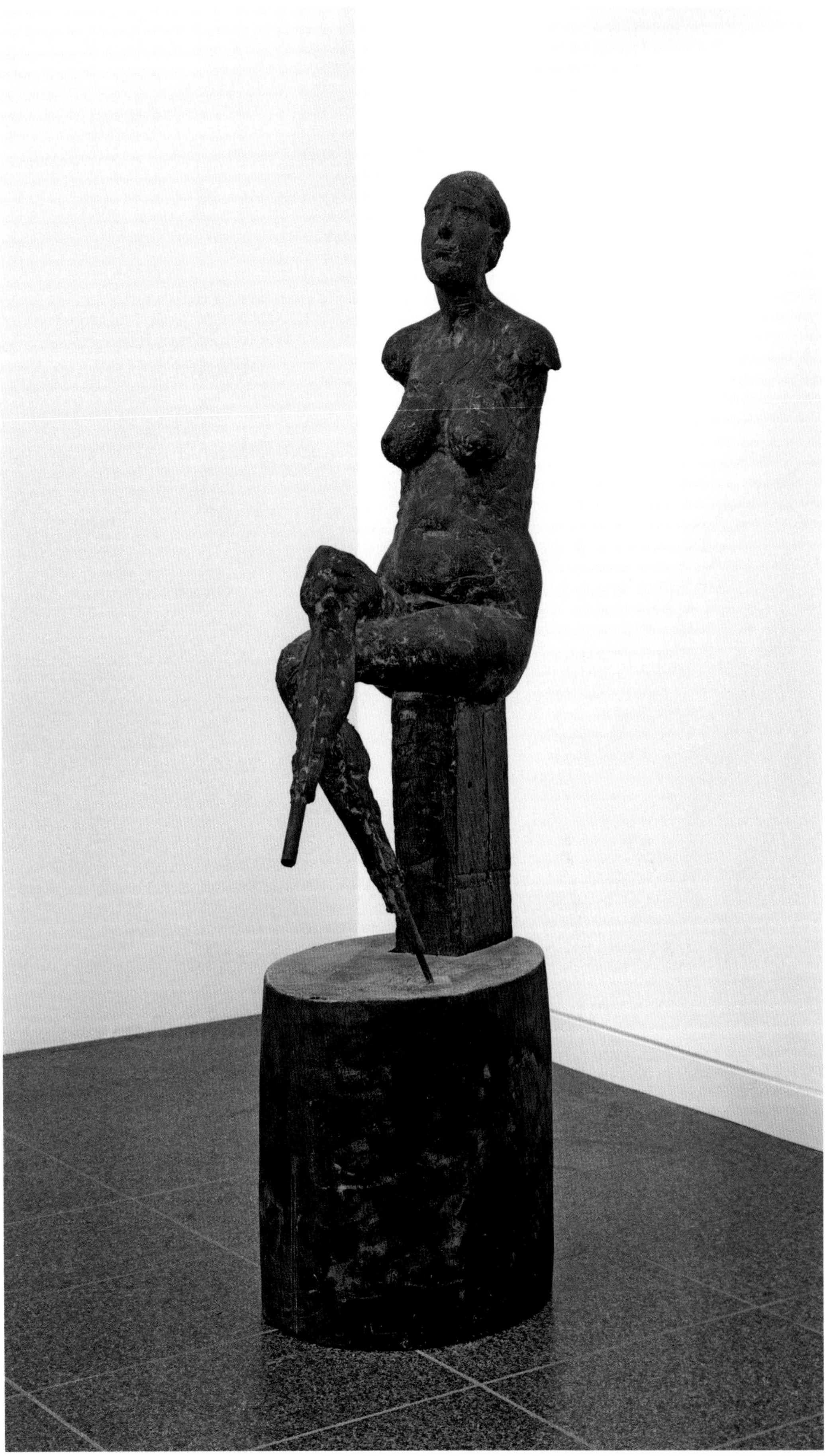

Karl Bobek, Sitzende weibliche Figur auf Hochsockel *[Seated Female Figure on a Pedestal], 1960, bronze, wood, 175 × 41 × 87 cm, Ursula Bobek*

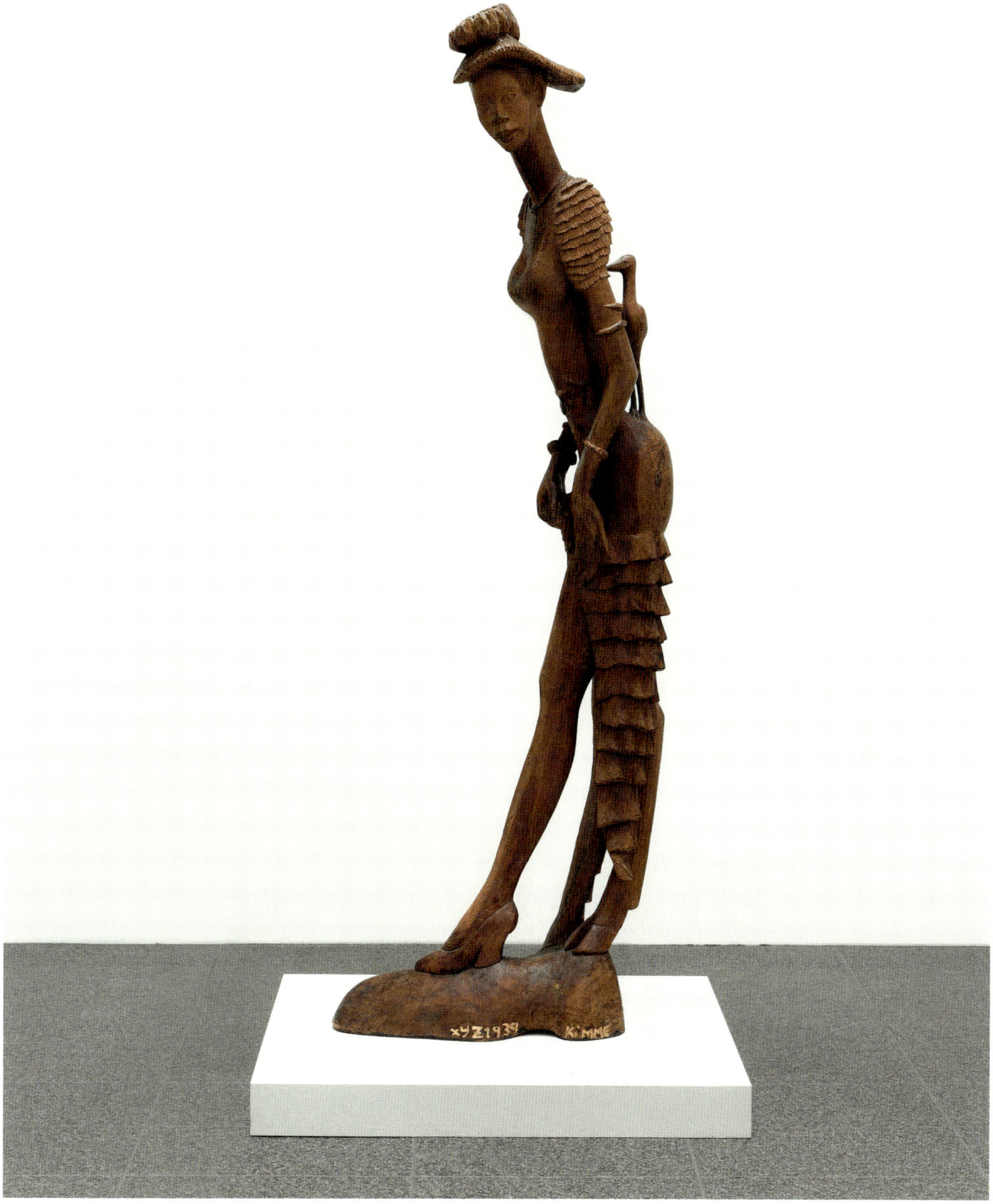

Luise Kimme, Diablesse, *1983, cedar, 214 × 64 cm,* The Castle, *Tobago, the artist's estate*

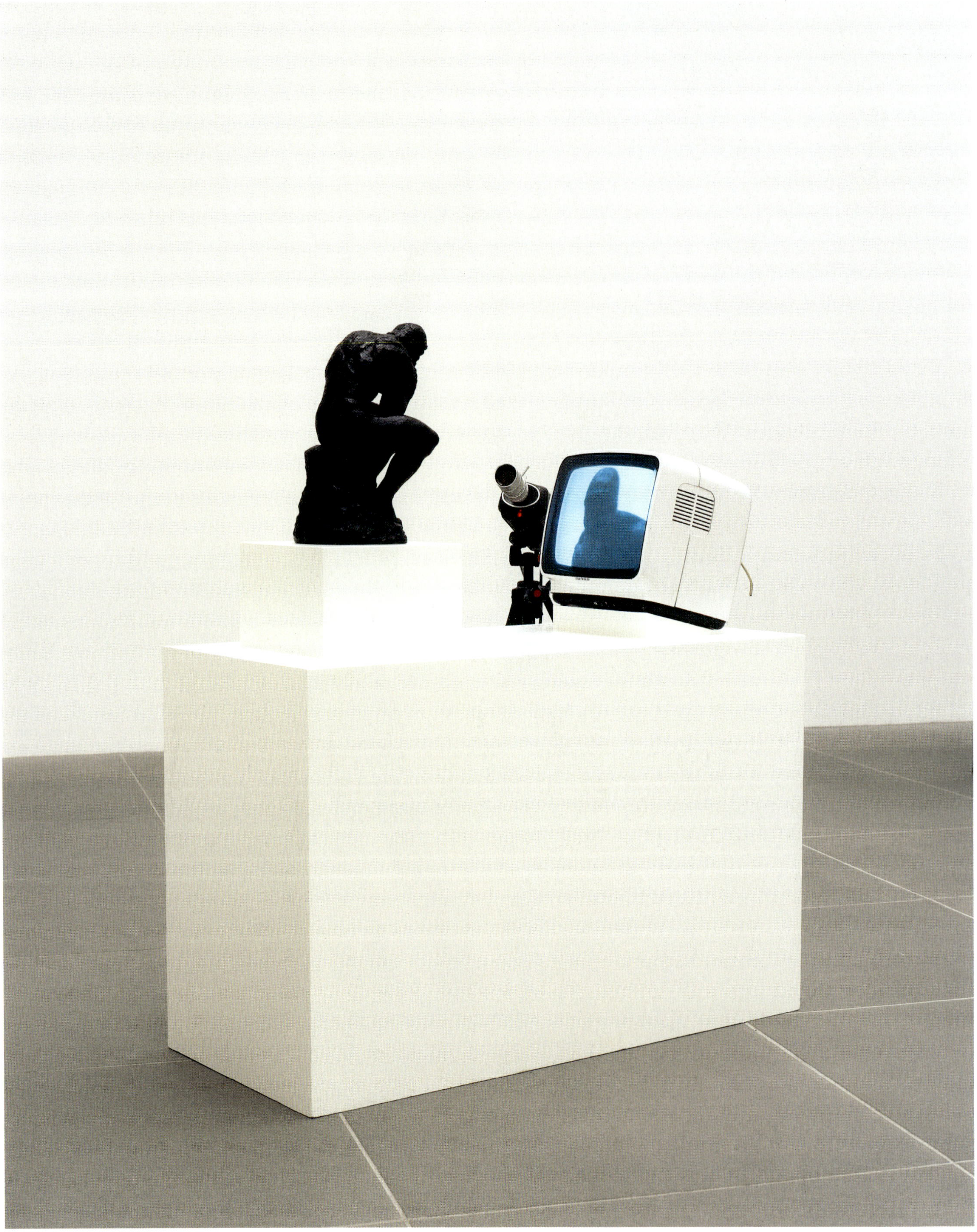

Nam June Paik, Der Denker oder TV Rodin *[The Thinker or TV Rodin], 1976, sculpture after Rodin, video camera, tripod, television set, white lacquered wooden base, 130 × 50 × 110 cm, Block Collection, on loan to the Neues Museum, Nuremberg*

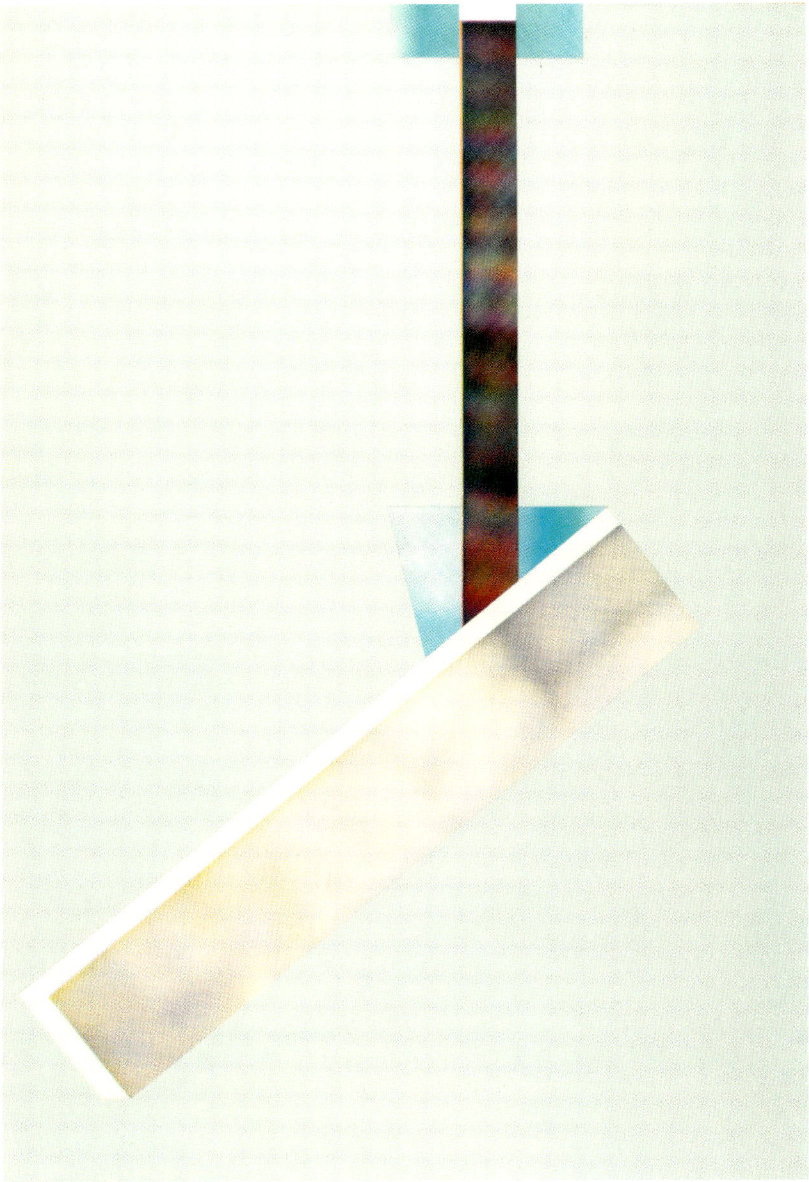

Siegfried Cremer, Hängeskulptur *[Hanging Sculpture],*
18 August 1986, collage (from parts of 'mein täglich Bild von D.' [My Daily Picture of D.]), 62 × 43 cm,
Akademie-Galerie – Die Neue Sammlung, Düsseldorf

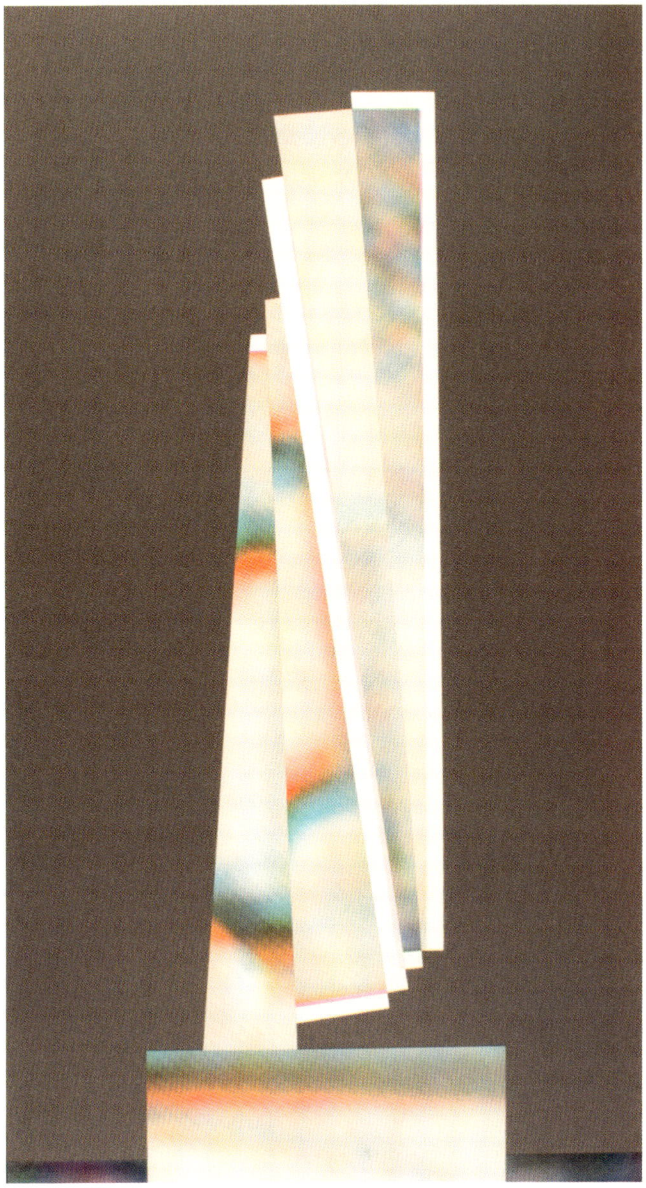

Siegfried Cremer, Turmskulptur *[Tower Sculpture],*
29 November 1986, collage (from parts of 'mein täglich Bild von D.' *[My Daily Picture of D.]), 62 × 43 cm,*
Akademie-Galerie – Die Neue Sammlung, Düsseldorf

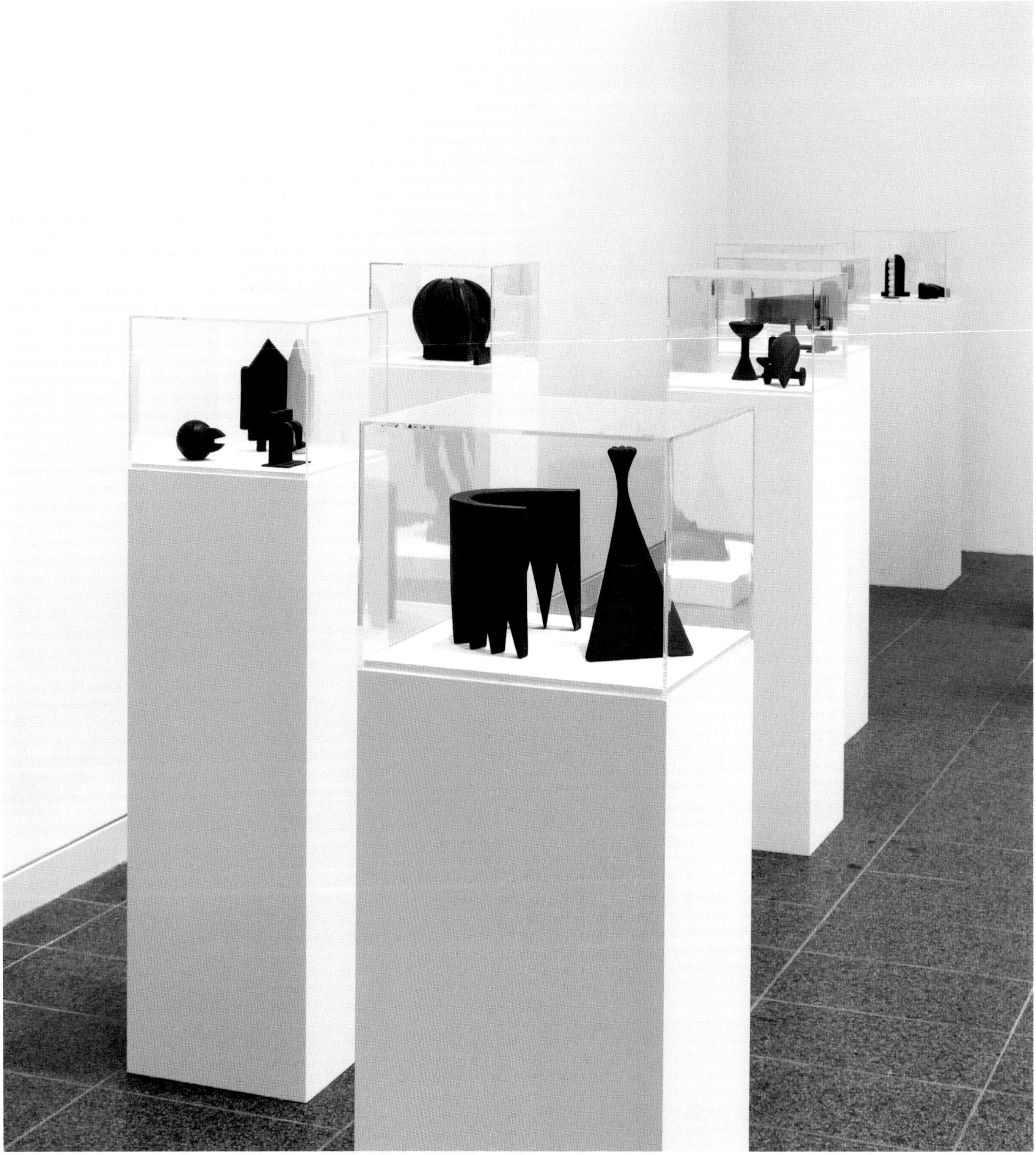

Fritz Schwegler, Frühe Gipse *[Early Works in Plaster of Paris], 1963–67, painted plaster of Paris, size varies, Archiv Fritz Schwegler, Breech*

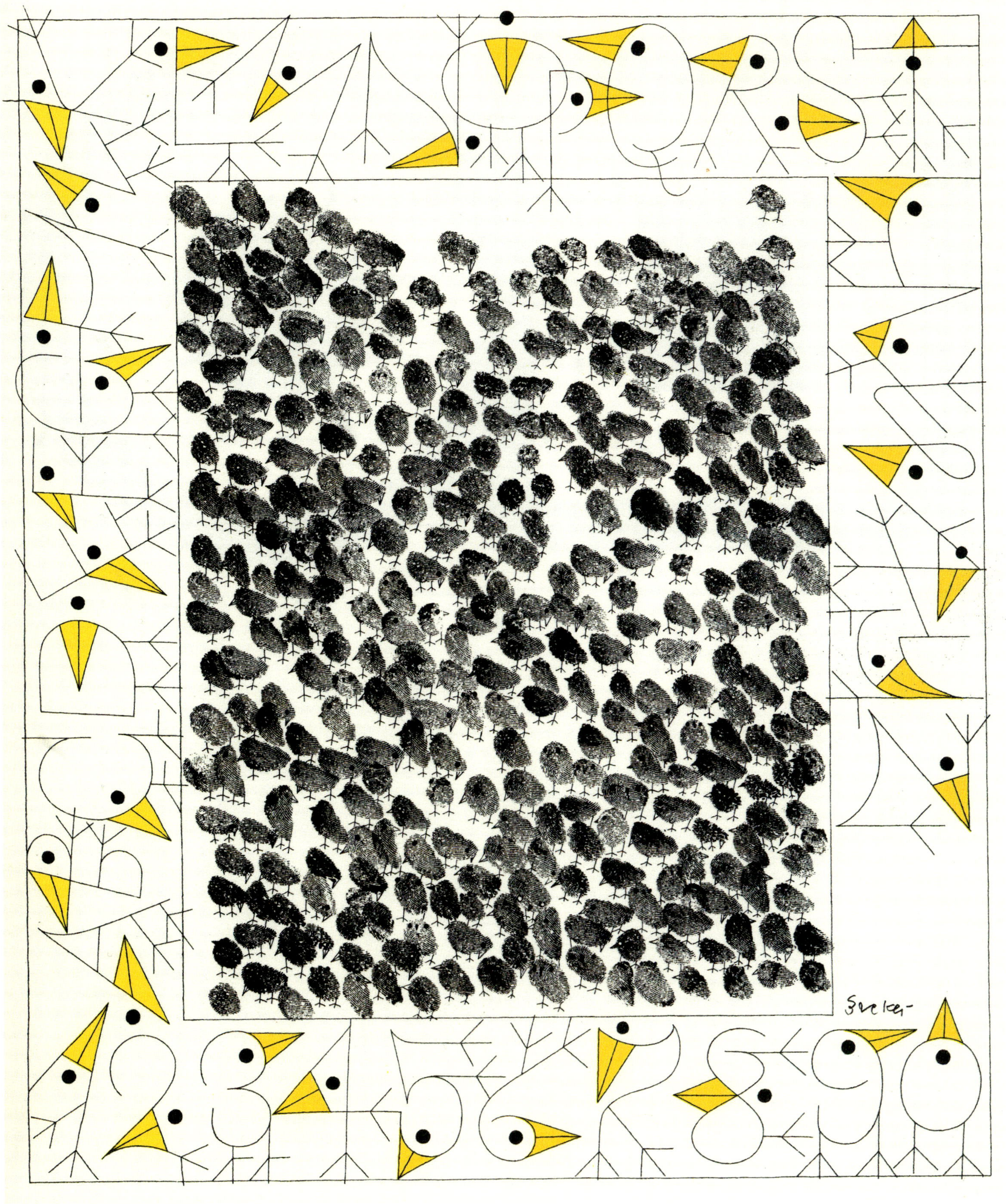

Walter Breker, Fingervögel *[Fingerbirds], n.d., silkscreen print on hand-milled deckle-edged paper, 75 × 63 cm*

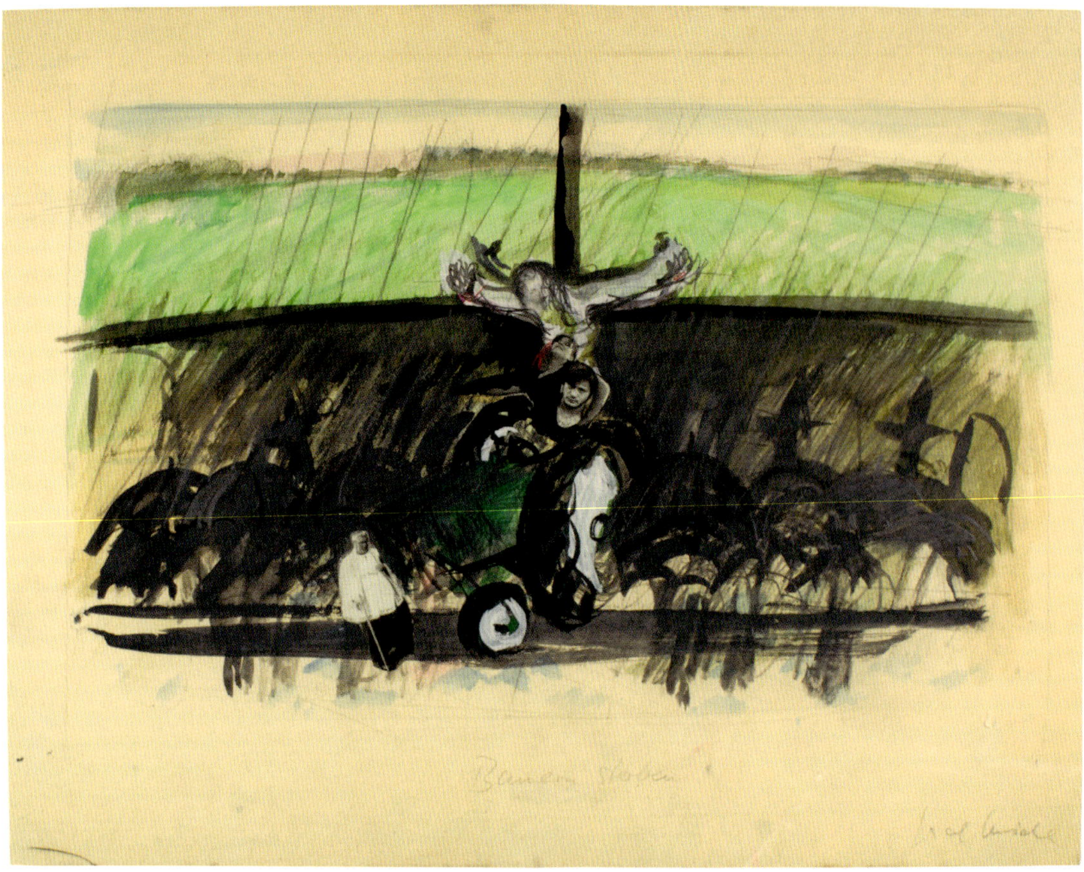

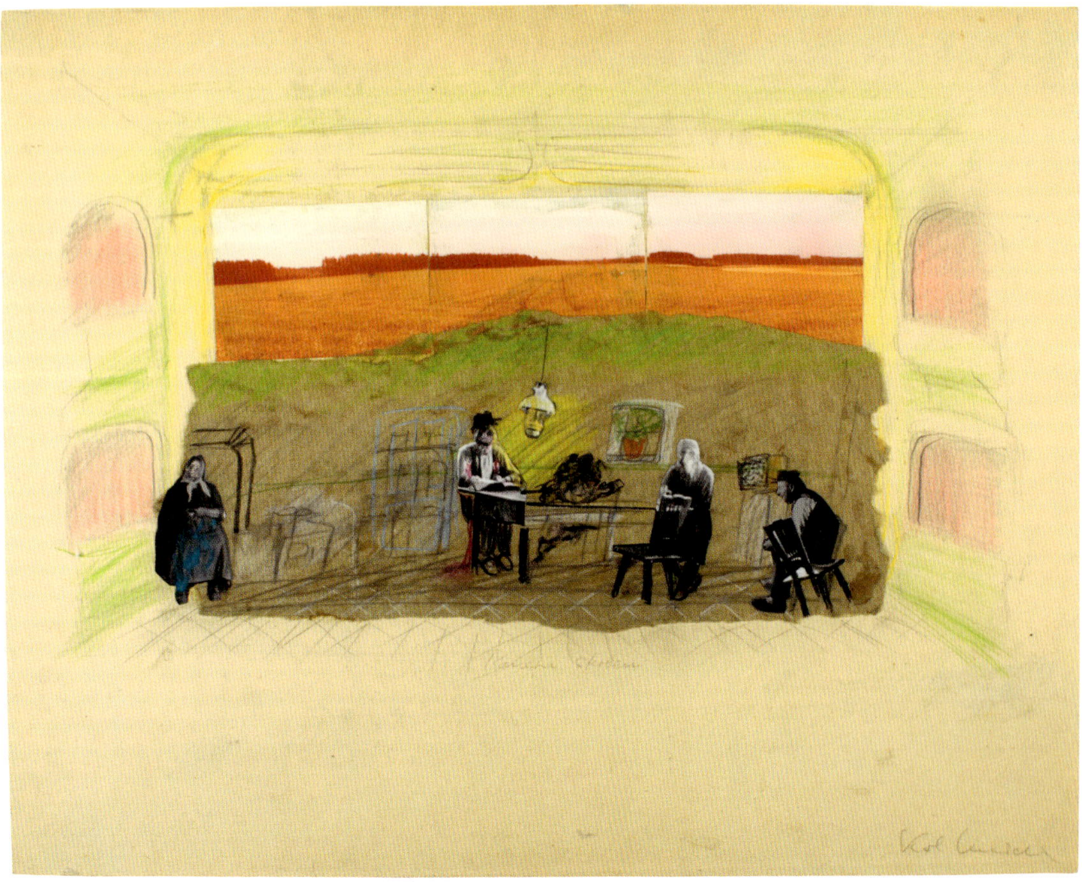

Karl Kneidl, stage designs for Peasants Die *by Franz Xaver Kroetz; director: Franz Xaver Kroetz; stage and costumes: Karl Kneidl, 1984, 2 coloured and collaged sheets, each 51 × 64.6 cm, Akademie-Galerie – Die Neue Sammlung, Düsseldorf*

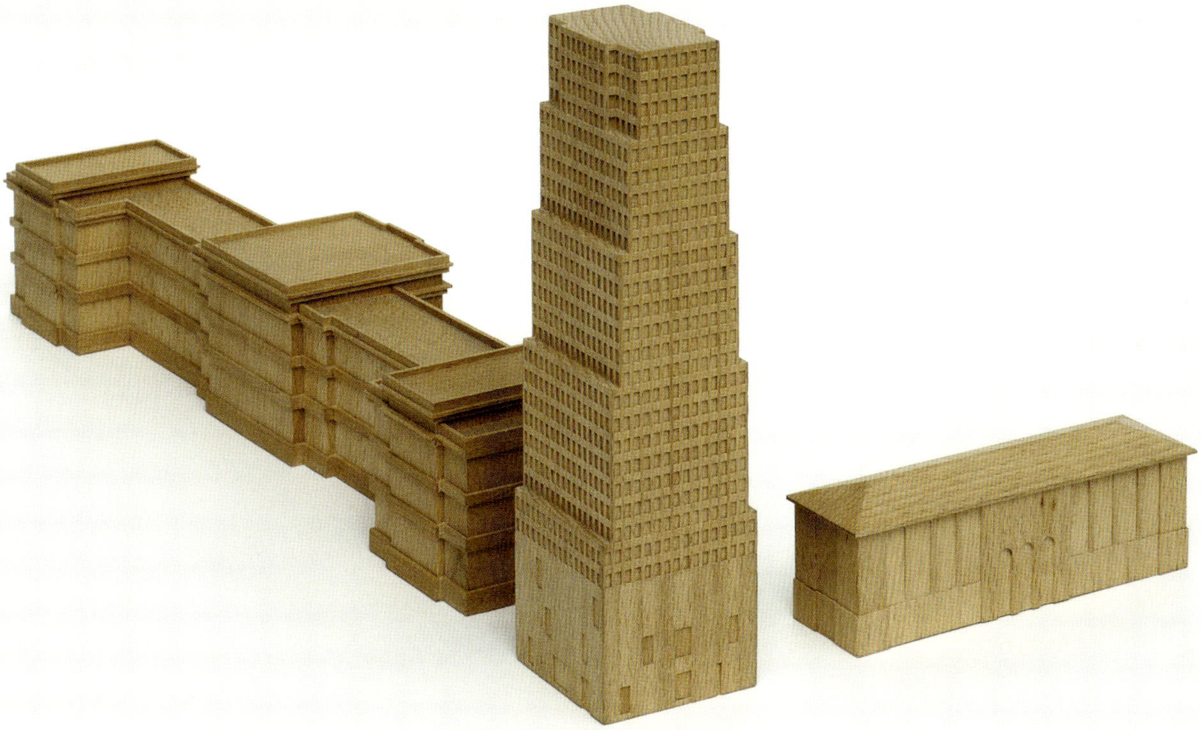

Josef Paul Kleihues, three-part wooden model of the Düsseldorf Art Academy with proposal for enlargement, 1994–98, Akademie-Galerie – Die Neue Sammlung, Düsseldorf

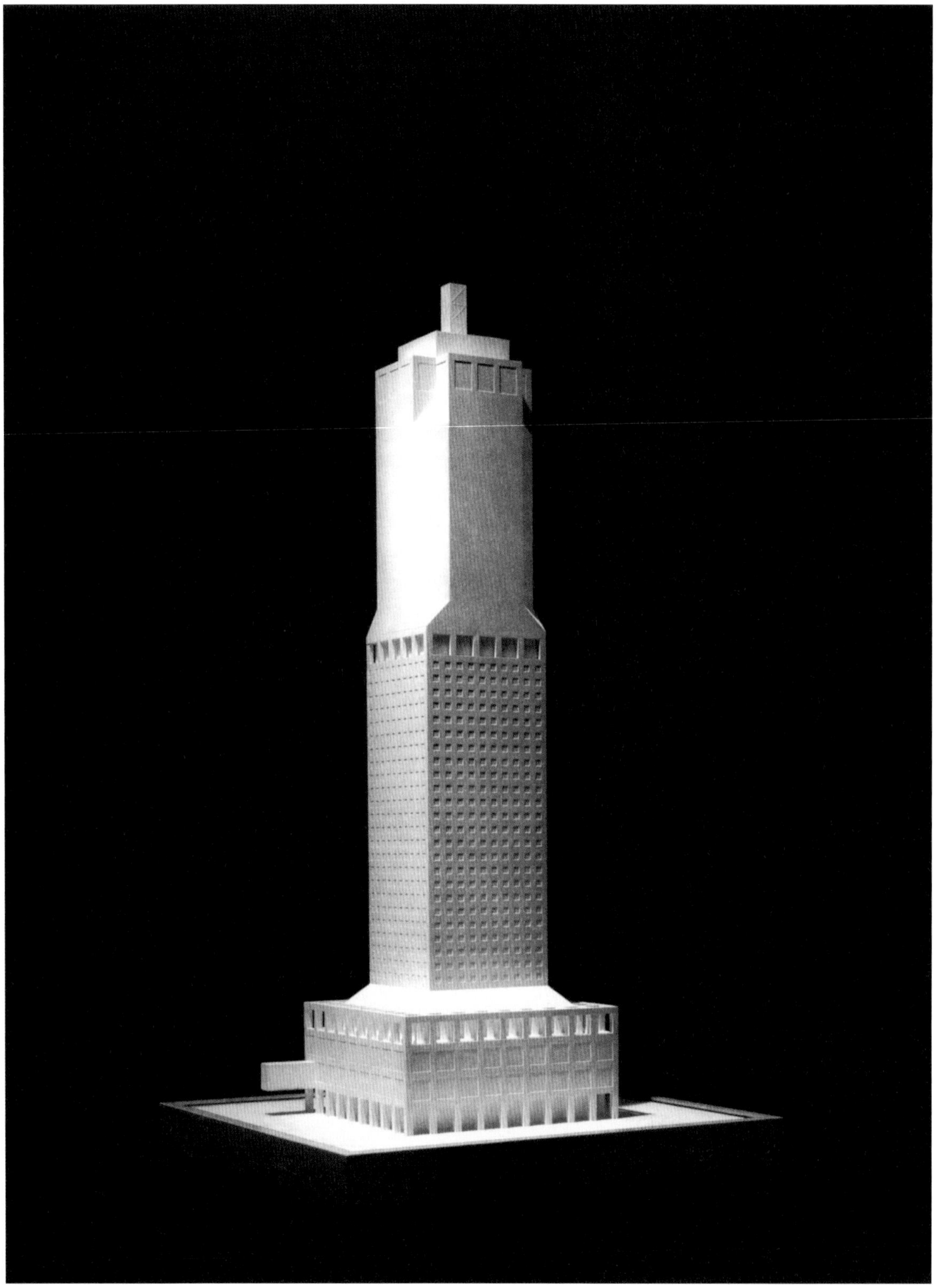

Oswald Mathias Ungers, Architektur *[Architecture], 1994, photogravure, 80 × 60 cm, Akademie-Galerie – Die Neue Sammlung, Düsseldorf*

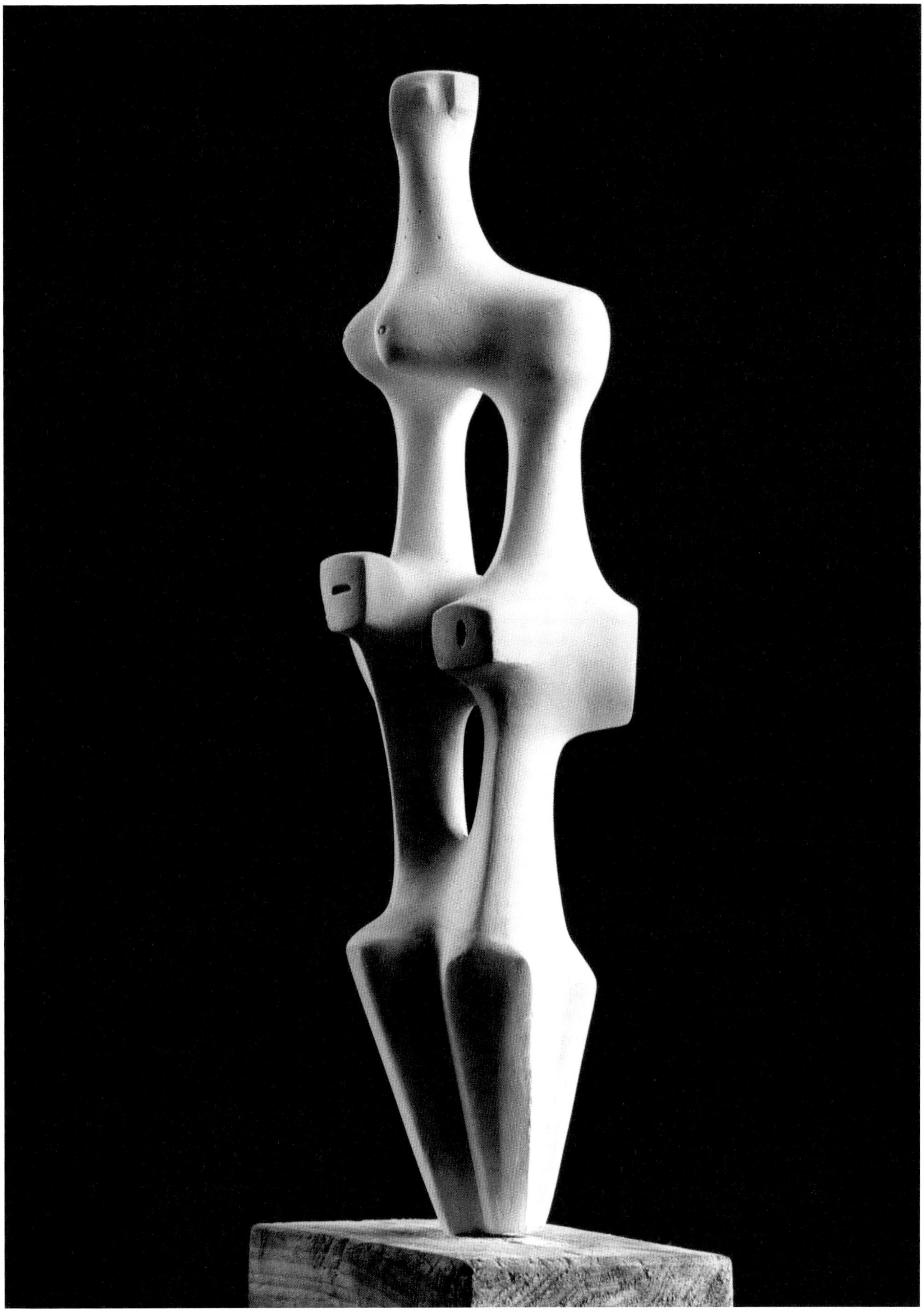

Manfred Sieler, Stehende *[Woman, Standing], c.1955, plaster of Paris, height 29 cm*

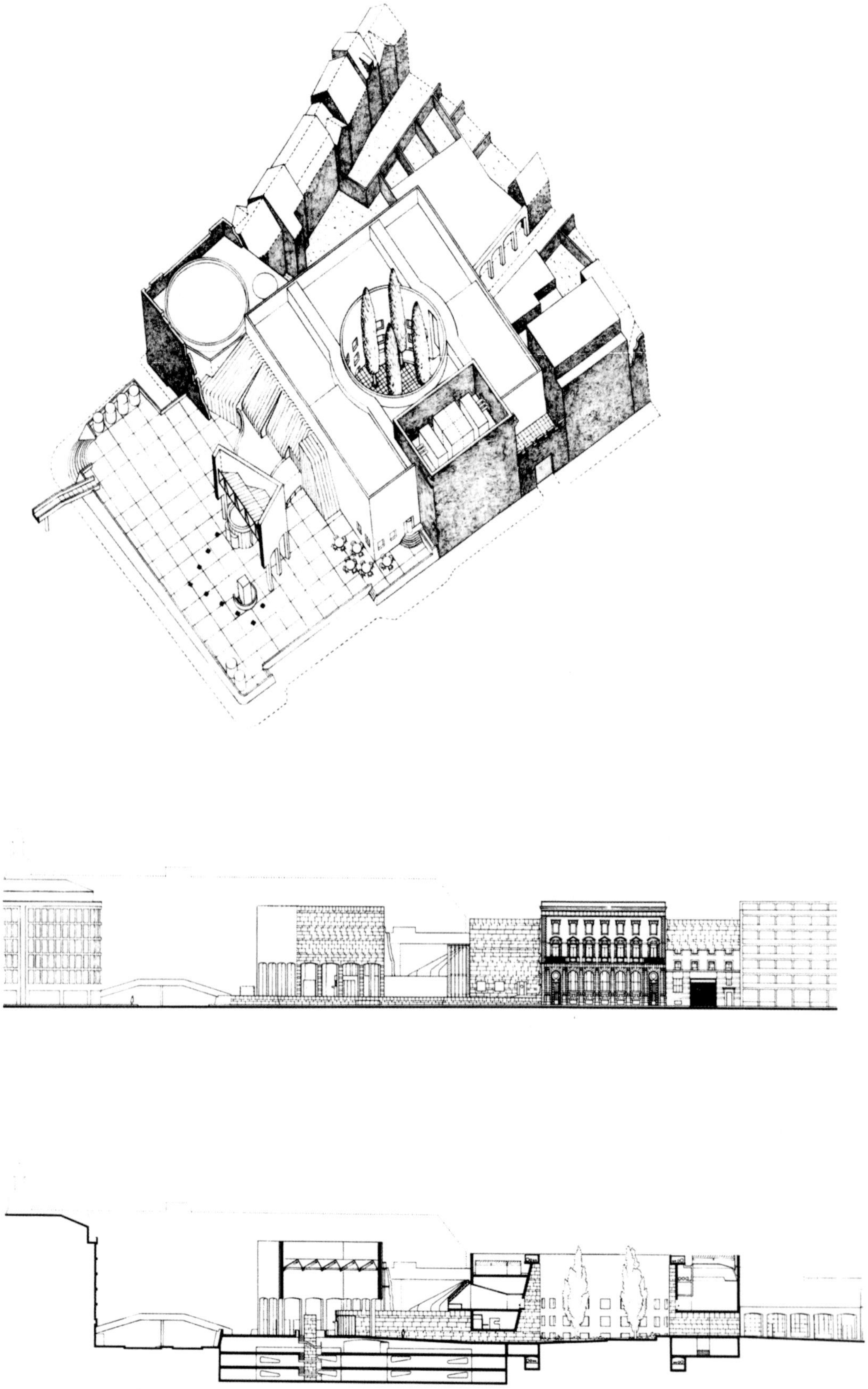

Entwurf zum Wettbewerb der Kunstsammlungen des Landes Nordrhein-Westfalen

James Stirling, plan submitted in competition to design the Kunstsammlungen Nordrhein-Westfalen [North Rhine-Westphalia Art Collections], ground plan and elevation, 1975

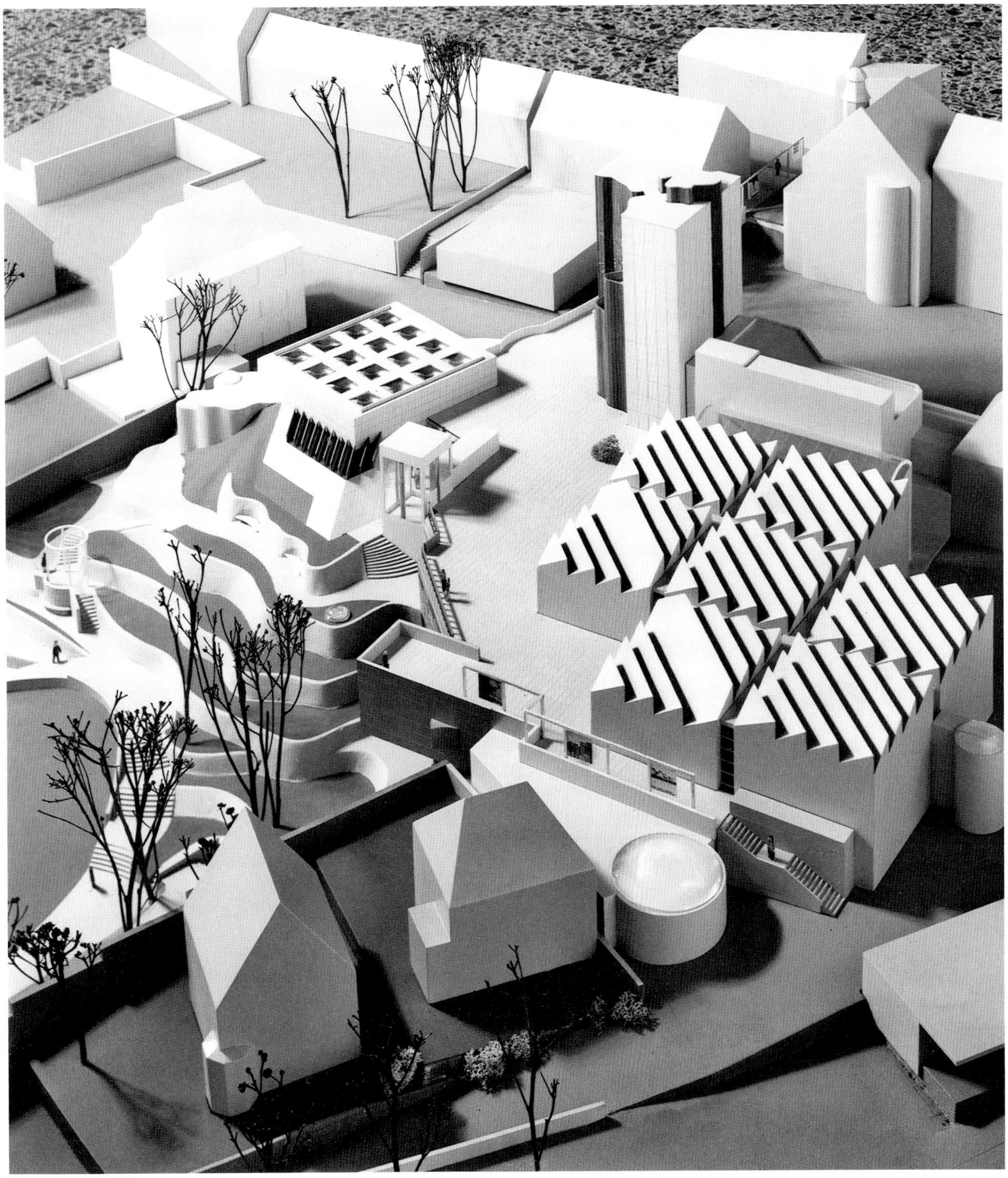

Hans Hollein, model of the Abteiberg Museum in Mönchengladbach, c. 1974, various materials, Museum Abteiberg Mönchengladbach

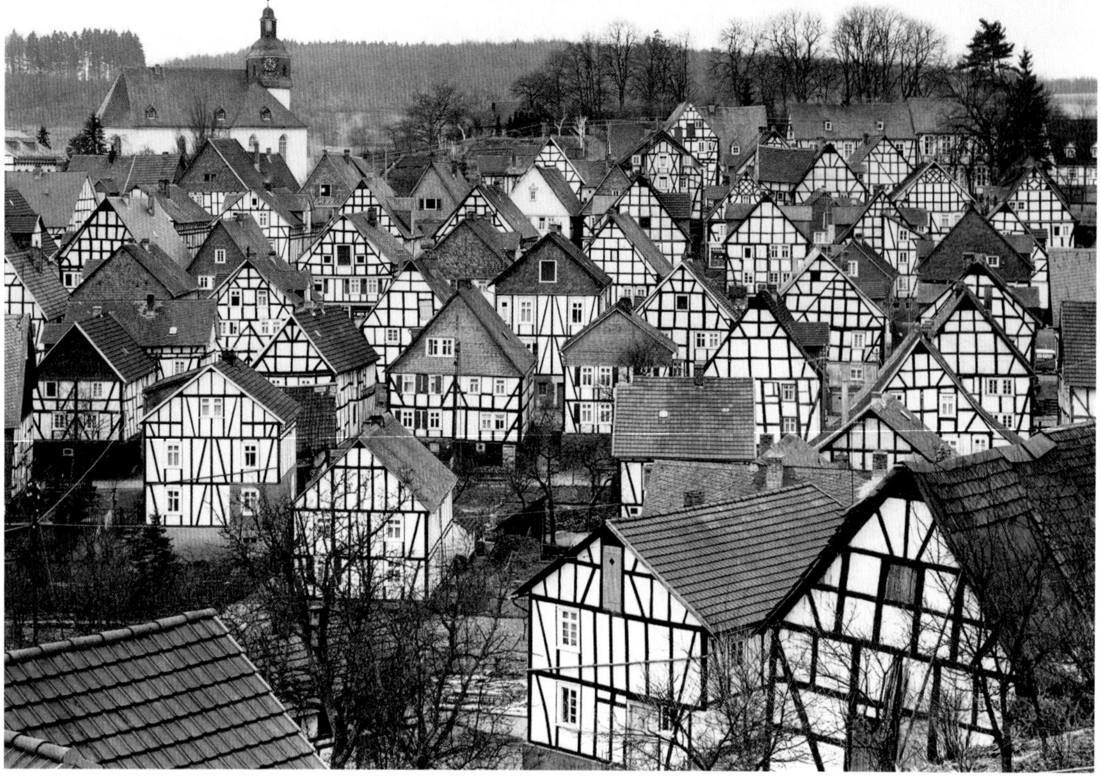

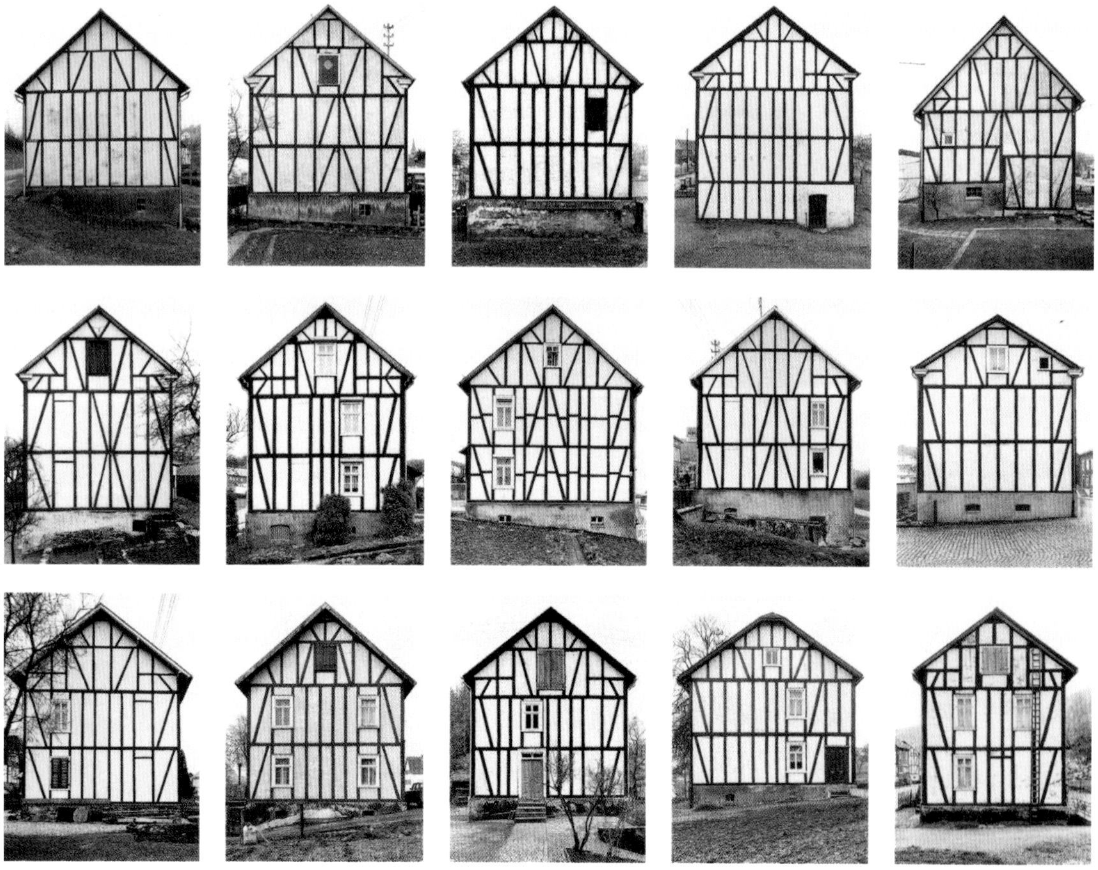

Bernd and Hilla Becher, Freudenberg, *1962, silver gelatin print, 30 × 40 cm, Düsseldorf Art Academy archives*

Bernd and Hilla Becher, Fachwerkhäuser, Siegener Industriegebiet *[Timber-Frame Houses, Siegen Industrial Region], 1959–73, silver gelatin prints, each 40.5 × 31.5 cm, Museum für Gegenwartskunst Siegen*

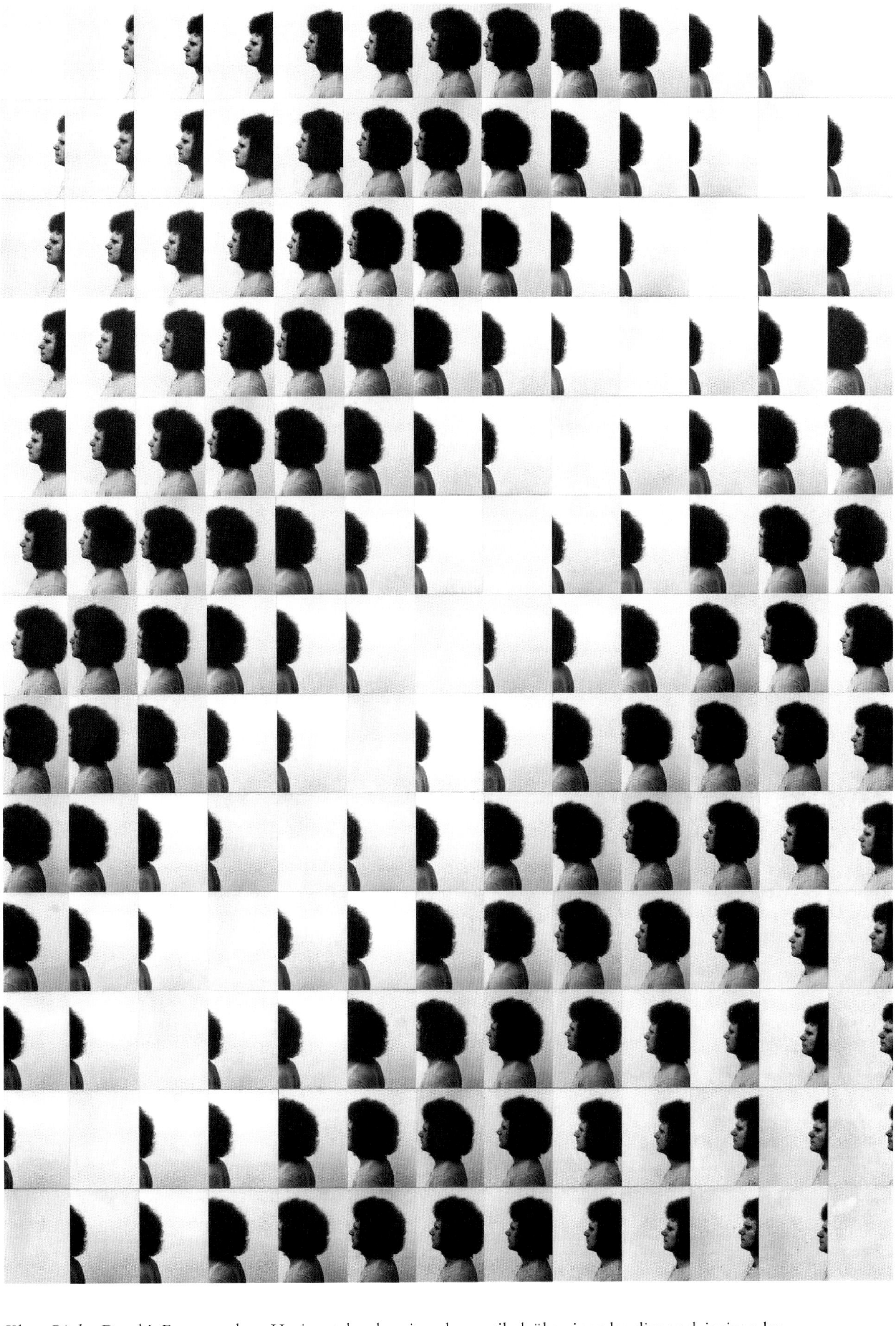

Klaus Rinke, Durch's Format gehen. Horizontal, nebeneinander, vertikal, übereinander, diagonal, ineinander (hin und zurück) *[Going through the Format. Horizontally, In Parallel, Vertically, One above the Other, Diagonally, Meshed (Back and Forth)], 1972, 169-part photo series, silver gelatin prints, each 10 × 7 cm, Von der Heydt-Museum Wuppertal*

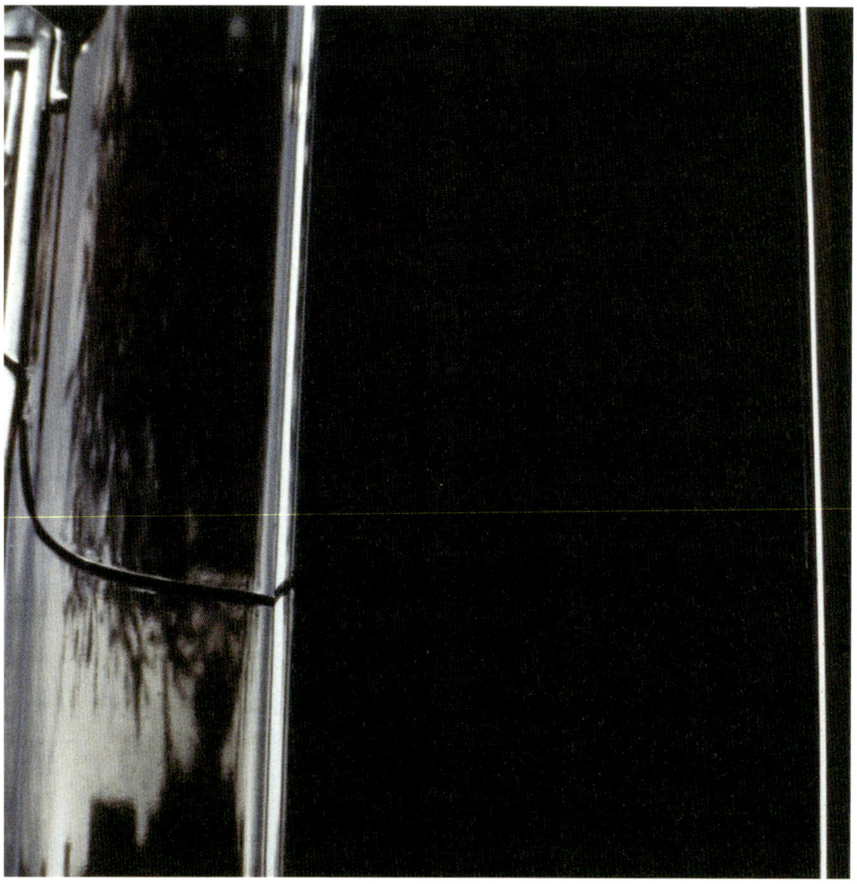

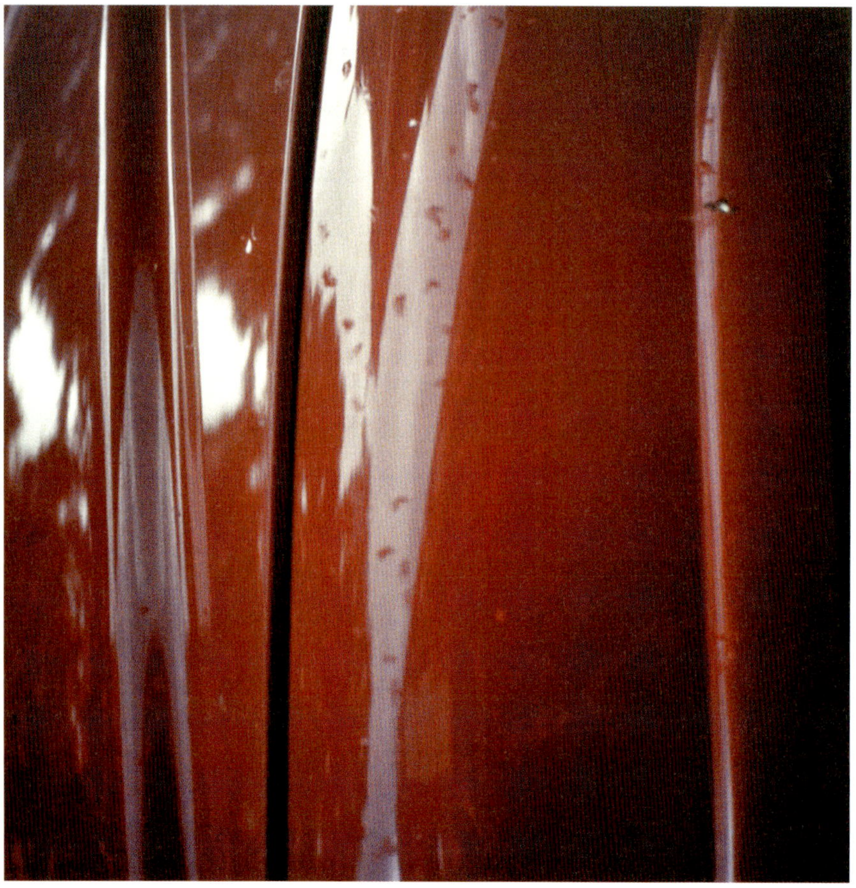

Jan Dibbets, Color Studies H 1 and H 3, *1976, 175 × 175 cm, private collection*

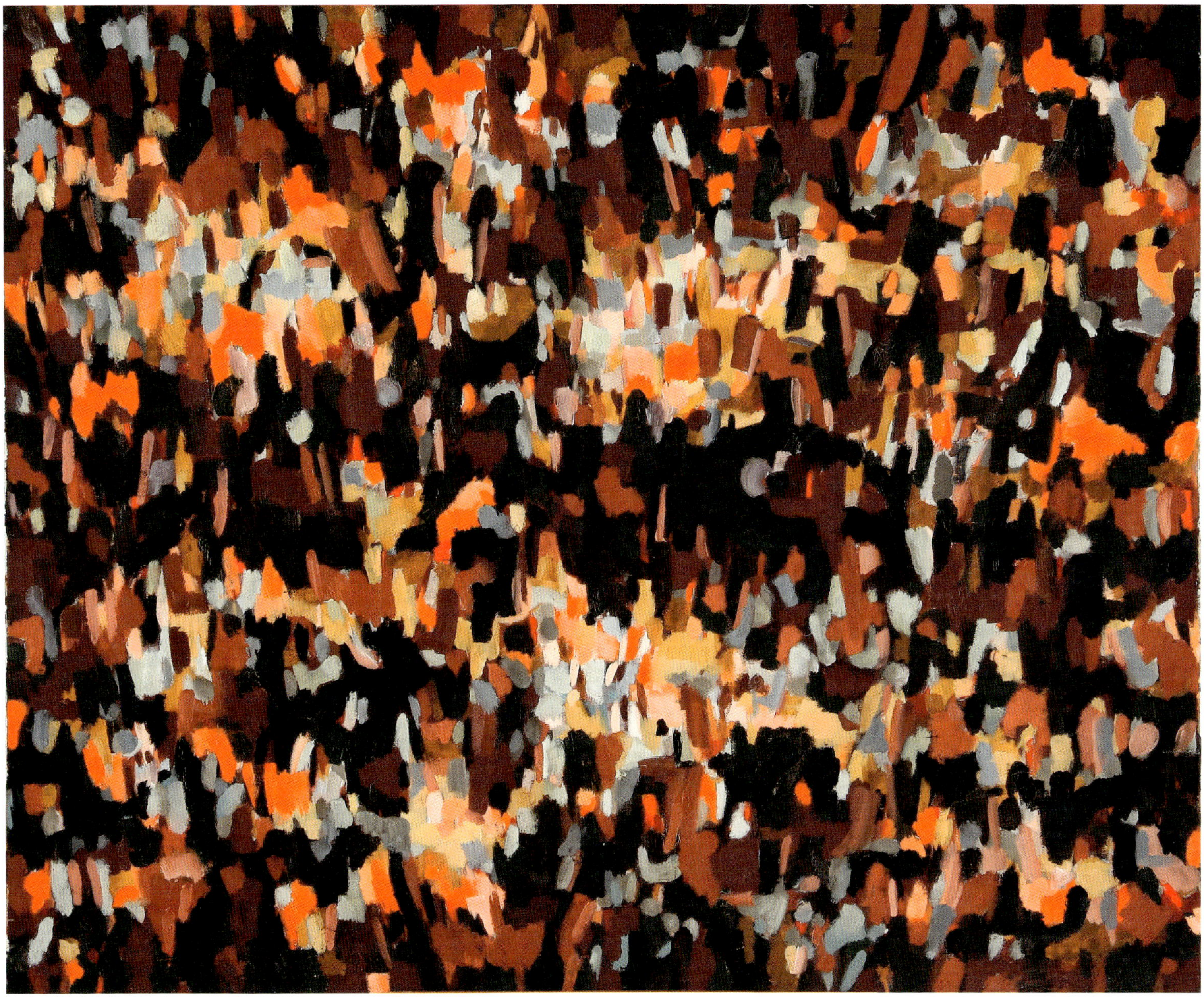

Gert Weberg, Vergessene Wege – verlorene Spuren *[Forgotten Paths – Lost Tracks], 1960, oil on canvas, 110 × 135 cm, Akademie-Galerie – Die Neue Sammlung, Düsseldorf*

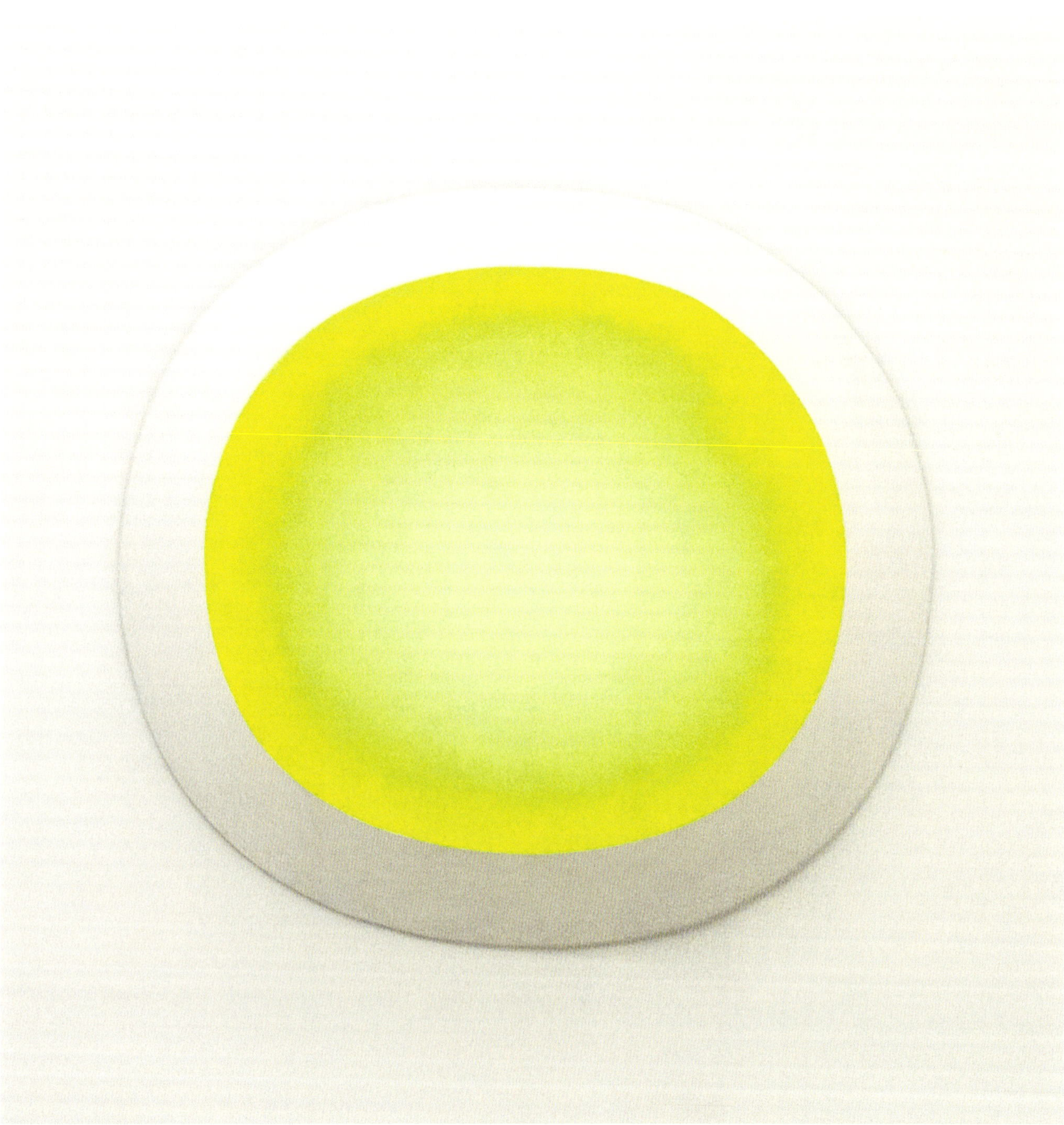

Rupprecht Geiger, 598/70 (Signal Gelb) *[598/70 (Signal Yellow)], 1970, acrylic on wood, 124 × 138 × 25 cm, Geiger archives, Munich*

SHELL and
ESSO

ESSO and
TEXACO

TEXACO and
BP

BP and
TEXACO

TEXACO and
SHELL

SHELL and
BP

BP and
ESSO

ESSO and
SHELL

SHELL and
TEXACO

TEXACO and
ESSO

ESSO and
BP

BP and
SHELL

the common
smell

ping pong
ping pong ping
pong ping pong
ping pong

Eugen Gomringer, Gedichte Shell and Texaco *[Poems Shell and Texaco] and Ping Pong, Concrete Poetry, 15 poems, a cross-section from 1951 to c.1987, Künstleredition ikkp, Akademie-Galerie – Die Neue Sammlung, Düsseldorf*

KONRAD KLAPHECK ON HIS TIME AS A STUDENT AND TEACHER AT THE ACADEMY

In conversation with Siegfried Gohr in Düsseldorf on 8 January 2013

Konrad Klapheck: My father, Richard (*1883), had already taught art history in Düsseldorf before the First World War. His first book was published in 1913. He married Anna Strümpell, who was sixteen years younger than he was. Richard Klapheck was an early high flyer and his first pages were published even before the First World War.

Siegfried Gohr: You grew up in a home steeped in art history.
K. K.: The sound of one or two typewriters being put to use was always with us.

S. G.: When did you decide to go to the Academy?
K. K.: The artistic urge was always there. The only question was which discipline might be the right one: stage design, archaeology with a focus on draughtsmanship for documenting excavations. I had read Heinrich Schliemann's autobiography. Before I sat my exams qualifying for university entrance in 1954, a journalist came into class and asked each of us, one after the other, what we wanted to become. I was too embarrassed to say a painter and said instead a graphic artist. But I already knew that I wanted to go to an art academy in any case and had already expressed the desire to become a painter, meaning an artist, to my teachers. I was good at writing essays and my German teacher disapproved of my career aspirations. He said to my mother, 'Shame about that talented boy.' The idea that a painter had to be dumb and oversexed was still prevalent in the culture-vulture class. And my mother was asked by her women friends, 'Are you going to let that happen?' But she would answer, 'If he wants to become an artist, then he can't be made into a dentist or barrister. If it doesn't work out, he'll be the first to notice.'

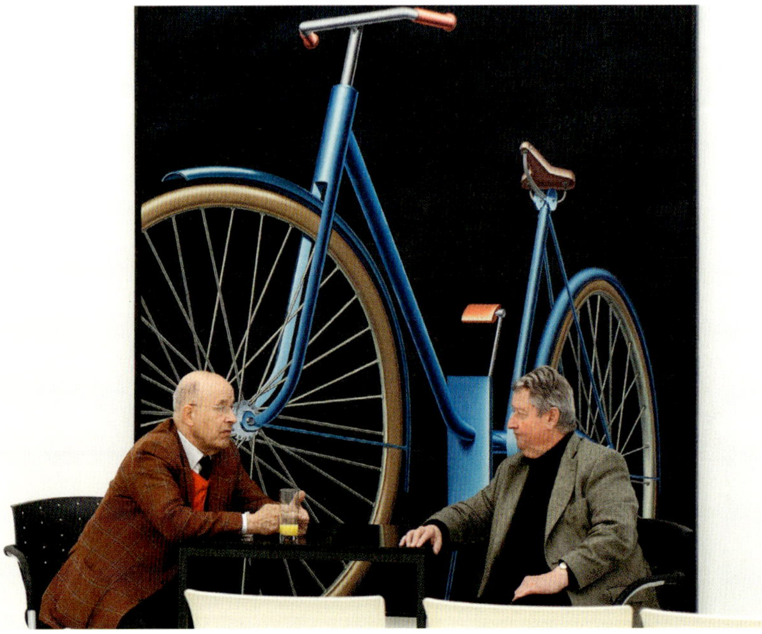

Konrad Klapheck talking with Siegfried Gohr at the vernissage of Rendezvous der Maler I *[Rendezvous of the Painters I] at the Academy Gallery in Düsseldorf on 6 May 2011*

S. G.: What happened to the literary bent?
K. K.: It was strongly nurtured. My mother used to read quite a bit to me, especially after I had just lost my father. To counteract the prevailing Nazi zeitgeist, she would read to me from the Bible, the story of Joseph being sold and the interpretation of Pharaoh's dream, as a feminist, before the term existed, the story of Queen Esther and the story of Ruth. Later she recommended Gottfried Keller's *Green Henry* to me.

S. G.: How did that close link with literature affect you later during your studies and in your own career?
K. K.: The literary component was important. Even just before sitting my school leaving examinations, I could still imagine becoming a writer. My heroes were the great epic writers from Homer to James Joyce. But on the side I had also read Robert Musil, Thomas Mann, and Marcel Proust straight through from beginning to end. Form on a grand scale was what interested me, and I was naive enough to think I could write an epic about the Germans in the post-war era.
I realised, however, that painting came easier to me than writing. And that in painting I would have a chance to 'write' my epic. The work titles also opened up the possibility of adding a piece or a splinter of literature to each picture. 'You'd do better to leave the titles off. They're far-fetched', was Goller's comment. I let him know that *Sewing Machine* was a completely ludicrous title for a painting of a sewing machine; after all, any moron could see what it was.

S. G.: How did you come to be in Bruno Goller's class?
K. K.: I saw my first original Goller at the first post-war Rhenish Secession show, *Mädchen am Fenster* [Girl at the Window].

The subtle shades of grey in that painting did nothing for me, but I noticed that Goller's colleagues, Peter Janssen and Oswald Petersen, always spoke his name with great respect. And I gradually succumbed to the enchantment of the petty bourgeois world of Gummersbach and began to admire the painterly qualities more and more. Goller was quite a frequent guest at my mother's house. I got to know him and said to him two whole years before I was admitted to the Academy, 'I want to become your pupil!'

S. G.: *How did he react to that?*
K. K.: His reaction was, 'There's still plenty of time for that.' But when the time had come, I was put in the preliminary class (drawing class) first. You were assigned by an admissions committee either to Otto Pankok's class or to Bruno Goller's. Fortunately, I was sent to Goller.

S. G.: *That lasted a year?*
K. K.: Yes, two terms. During that time you were expected to draw, daily, from ten o'clock in the morning to one o'clock in the afternoon from male and female nude models. Painting wasn't prohibited but the focus was on drawing.

S. G.: *How did the permanent change to the Goller class come about?*
K. K.: I had said to Goller early on that I wanted to continue studying with him in the painting class. I had really enjoyed drawing live from the model but now I was eager to express myself more. Bruno Goller's pictures showed me the way to do so. Not so much how to do it but what to do. I had nothing but admiration for someone who had remained true to the objects of his childhood even while abstraction was at its height. I believe that finding my way to the object would have taken much longer without Bruno Goller's example.

S. G.: *Have you ever tried to do abstract painting?*
K. K.: Yes, in the Tachiste manner. And I even showed Goller those works. Pictures somewhere between Henri Michaux and Max Ernst, some of them with overtones of Surrealist landscape. Bruno Goller's comment was, 'You're doing that quite cleverly but don't forget there are currently 17,000 painters on earth who are painting like that. Do you want to be number 17,001?' That very evening I destroyed those works (except for perhaps five to ten of them).

S. G.: *Where had you got your information about Michaux and Max Ernst?*
K. K.: I was in Paris regularly from an early age, the first time there still with my mother. You could see anything in the rue de Seine galleries: Max Ernst, Henri Michaux, and Wols.

S. G.: *How did you experience the environment in the Goller class and outside it?*
K. K.: There were various different environments. There were the Informel artists who had banded together to form Group 53: Hoehme, Gaul, Brüning, and so on. And another environment was the Old Town scene that met at Czikosz or in Bobby's Bar. At Czikosz the brilliant Horst Geldmacher ('Flötchen' [Little Flute]) played jazz on the recorder.

S. G.: *Did anyone such as Jean-Pierre Wilhelm play a role?*
K. K.: Yes, the later director of Galerie 22 lived in both Paris and Düsseldorf, and he took charge of my mother and me in Paris. But it was a rather one-sided guided tour, one with a tendency towards Informel painting and nothing else during which Wilhelm used to yawn demonstratively in front of paintings by David and Ingres; those were the pictures I was interested in.

S. G.: *Wasn't it unusual to be interested in the French neo-Classical painters?*
K. K.: Yes, not just in the French classicists. I found the rejection of Raphael that was so prevalent then risible.

S. G.: *What was so fascinating about the despised Raphael?*
K. K.: The beautiful harmony of proportion. Of course I know that there has been an important expressive line stretching from Grünewald, Rembrandt, Goya, and Van Gogh to Bacon, but Raphael has remained my favourite painter to this day. Incidentally, on my first visit to the Rijksmuseum in Amsterdam I impatiently rushed past *The Night Watch* to get to the still life painters of the Dutch Golden Age. Today I'd probably also enjoy lingering for perhaps an hour in front of *The Night Watch*.

S. G.: *Was it the recondite allegorical meaning of the objects depicted in the still lifes that you were so interested in?*
K. K.: For lack of education I didn't grasp the vanitas symbolism; what impressed me was the virtuosic handling of the gleaming metal of standing cups and plates.

S. G.: *When did you sense that the moment had come to stop studying with Goller?*
K. K.: There was a point when I had got enough machine-themed pictures together, and I began to look out for an appropriate gallery, about 1958/59.
Goller would have liked to have me show work at the *Rundgänge* [Academy Tours] but I held back so as not to let the surprise effect of a first public appearance fizzle out. I said, 'No, I'd like to skip this year.' So I refused to take part in the 'Tour', which I now find ungrateful on my part. But Goller forgave me: 'Even my cat won't do what I expect of it!' But he did think it was right that I apologised ten years later.

S. G.: *How did your collaboration with galleries get off to a start?*
K. K.: At that time there were four leading galleries in Düsseldorf: Alex Vömel, who was responsible for classic Modernism; Hella Nebelung, who didn't take me all that seriously because I was an art historian's son; Jean-Pierre Wilhelm's Galerie 22; and Alfred Schmela. How seminal Alfred Schmela's achievement as an avant-garde gallerist was would only become apparent years later. But after his exhibition of Tàpies's work, which I had discovered for myself the previous year in Paris, I knew that was the right gallery for me.

S. G.: *Which phase of Antoni Tàpies?*
K. K.: The sand pictures, small formats, fetched about 800 DM then. On my first attempt at landing in the gallery, I had shown Schmela Tachiste works. Schmela's reaction was, 'You're not there yet.' At an evening reception with canapés in my studio at my mother's house, he said after his last swallow of a Füchsen beer, 'And now?' He was well aware of what I was up to. I had no sooner hung the first typewriter on the only nail in the wall than Schmela came out with, 'Phwoar, let's do a show!' The exhibition didn't happen until a year later and that was just as well. In the meantime dealers, Staempfli and later Castelli, had visited me and bought machine pictures, which did nothing to dampen Schmela's plans for the exhibition. Castelli had seen a group show in New York at the Staempfli Gallery, at which I had shown work: *Paris Obsessions*. Others who showed in it were Yves Klein, Jean Tinguely, and Jesus Raphael Soto. Only two pictures were sold from the Schmela mid-summer 1959 exhibition, to Willy and Fänn Schniewind, a couple from Neviges, and Schmela seemed to me to be somewhat disappointed. In any case, the next exhibition with him was quite a while coming. After a fairly long lean period Rudolf Zwirner turned up and showed me in his Essen and Cologne galleries. Arturo Schwarz in Milan was my first gallerist abroad.

S. G.: *How did you come to be inspired to take up the machine theme?*
K. K.: Tachism was a mere flirtation; it didn't arise in the depths of my soul.

S. G.: *But there would have been other options.*
K. K.: I loved the precision of Hans Holbein's (the Younger's) painting. Besides, I had seen Bronzino in the original in the Uffizi in Florence. And the world of cabarets and night bars in Otto Dix also made a profound impression on me. Stylistically speaking, my inclinations had a goal; what was missing was a subject.

S. G.: *Did Surrealism help in your search?*
K. K.: Yes. On one and the same day I had seen the famous Dalí painting *Six Apparitions of Lenin on a Grand Piano* at the Museé d'Art Moderne in Paris and an old typewriter in the flat of our friend, Jean-Pierre Wilhelm. And I thought to paint that typewriter as Dalí painted the piano keys – that's it. I also painted a label with a representation of the maker's factory on the typewriter I had hired from an office supplies shop for 6 DM per week, and I did that entirely under the sway of Giorgio de Chirico, whom I had also discovered then. Incidentally, I had the 6 DM hire fee reimbursed by the Academy bursar as model fees. The machine theme turned out to be longer-lasting than I had originally assumed it would be. And by the second version of the typewriter, I was even concerned about being repetitive. I had no idea that I would with time manage to produce forty-three versions of the typewriter and an equal number of sewing machines. Those two machines have a leading function, rather like the king and queen in chess. The typewriter is the man and the sewing machine is the woman.

S. G.: How can the machines be imagined as surrogates for human beings?
K. K.: The tools used by human beings are often further developments of biological functions: laying the thumb on top of the index finger led to tongs, the aeroplane represented an imitation of a bird, and so forth.

S. G.: But don't machines also have an indwelling arcane spirit?
K. K.: Yes, but it shouldn't pop out too intrusively at visitors to exhibitions of my pictures. I prefer to leave the secret unsaid so that viewers can discover it for themselves.

S. G.: How did you get back into contact with the Düsseldorf Art Academy?
K. K.: One motive for returning to the Academy, this time as a professor, was entirely mundane, an economic one. After several successful years all at once I was in financial straits; the rise of expressive-figurative painters, such as Baselitz, Immendorff, and Lüpertz, had suddenly made me unmodern. I was getting no more letters from galleries, and the telephone wasn't ringing any more. That would change later, and in fact on the very day in 1979 I was appointed to teach at the Academy, Werner Schmalenbach rang me up and said Federal President Scheel wanted to buy a picture from me and cost was immaterial. Still, I have never regretted joining the Academy.

S. G.: Do you know anything about the backstory behind your appointment?
K. K.: The painter and teacher K. O. Götz had retired and a successor was being sought. I was already friends with Götz, who was close to Surrealism, and he expressed his positive attitude to my candidacy in numerous [senate] sessions. The director, Norbert Kricke, who had known my pictures for some years and had always been very encouraging, also supported me. I was a professor at the Academy from 1979 until 2002.

S. G.: What beneficial effect did you have from working at the Academy?
K. K.: As a teacher you have to give something, especially your experience, both human and professional, but you also get a great deal back from the students.

S. G.: For example?
K. K.: What impressed me about the students was their naive, hands-on way of dealing with colour. Students used to come into my studio at the Academy independently of the courses I taught to hear my opinion of one of their pictures. And sometimes a student's work in vibrant chequered colours would be standing next to a picture I had painted in subtle shades of grey. And I'd wonder whether I too should be a bit bolder about approaching colour.

S. G.: What do you mean by 'courses you taught'?
K. K.: Apart from all the private counselling, we used to meet regularly once a week in the class studio. I called that a class reunion; the students called it a colloquium. The students sat on stools in a semicircle; an armchair was reserved for me at the centre. A student selected at random by the tutor would show their most recent coursework on the wall across from us. Now skill was called for on my part in getting a discussion to start without saying much myself, something that's much more difficult than talking yourself. I doggedly refused to utter. The person who was suffering the most from holding in their pent-up opinions would be the first to say something, and a student would burst out with, 'That still life would be quite nice if it weren't for that ghastly red tomato.' Another would answer at once, 'But the tomato is the only acceptable thing in an otherwise lousy picture.' Then I knew I had won. After a heated discussion I would sometimes say that a vote would now be taken, for instance: 'Who's for the tomato, who's against it? But everyone has to vote, abstention doesn't count.' The outcome was sometimes undecided, and the student would ask me anxiously, 'What am I supposed to do now?' And my answer would be, 'It's up to you. But you'll have to change the picture. The picture can't stay the way it is now. Either you make a grey picture of it – grey can be a colour, too – but then you have to sacrifice the red of the tomato. Or you make a highly coloured picture and then you have to bring colour into the whole context of the tomato.' The student: 'And what should I do?' Whereby the entire class would shout as one voice, 'It's up to you!'
When no one had anything to show, I'd suggest, 'Let's talk about your career prospects and the art market.' The enthusiasm was overwhelming. And some would even ask point-blank, 'What do I have to do to be a successful artist?' My invariable answer to that was, 'Marry a rich woman.' I had taken part

in several group sessions with a psychoanalyst without getting any of the things out of it that he wanted to give me, but I did learn one thing from him: how to manage a group.

S. G.: Can you describe the climate among your colleagues?
K. K.: The climate changed whenever there was a change in rectors. Kricke was very domineering, always trying to get his own way, occasionally with polemics. Intrigues and the unproductive formation of factions also thrived under Irmin Kamp, his successor, all of which vanished into thin air when Markus Lüpertz took the helm. It's well known that Lüpertz is prone to grandstanding, and I was often asked, 'How can you stand it under a director as self-centred as he is?' And I would always reply the man is a blessing for the institution. He's not only a good colleague but he also has a nose for finding the artists we needed as teachers. I hope that this positive spirit will continue to flourish under future rectors, and I believe Tony Cragg is a good guarantor that it will.

During my years at the Academy I had two official functions:

First: I was head of the selection committee (which, if I'm not mistaken, consisted of three to five persons, including me), which screened out the few suitable candidates in a friendly conversation among colleagues and by open (not secret) ballot from the masses of applications for a professorial vacancy as a preliminary to the decisive session of the Department Council. Second: My second job was as chairman of the Department Council. But perhaps I was only the second in command under Siegfried Cremer as chairman, with whom I enjoyed working.

In performing those two tasks I did my best to be objective and fair and endeavoured to put aside personal preferences as far as possible.

AESTHETIC THEORY: EUGEN GOMRINGER AND HIS TEACHING 1976–1991*

Markus Lüpertz

Dear Herr Gomringer, Ladies and Gentlemen,

Don't expect from me what is called an 'appreciation' in German rhetoric. I am not able to deliver such unctuous praise nor would you swallow it from me. Today by felicitous chance the actual encomium will resound in the language of another art form, and you are probably as eager as I am to find out how it will be expressed in music, sister to the word, in a poem by Eugen Gomringer that has been set to music.

I thank the composer, Herr Banasik, and the musicians for their willingness to perform here today, and since this musical event stems from a suggestion made by Eugen Gomringer, I am certain of his consent to it.

I can think of no better or loftier way of honouring a poet than revitalising a poem of his through bringing it to life with music, and it would be indeed welcomed if in future all Academy artists were to be bid farewell in a different art form.

Eugen Gomringer was appointed to teach at the Art Academy in spring 1976. A lectureship established to represent 'the arts and general humanities' was rededicated for him. It was now designated 'Aesthetic Theory', and the intentions pursued by the Academy in making this appointment and Gomringer's teaching agenda are equally recognisable in that designation. Philosophical aesthetics was not to be taught, but rather the aesthetic aspect was to be considered from the perspective of the artistic process and the artwork emerging from it. It is patently obvious that Eugen Gomringer was called to that task. As the initiator of Concrete Poetry and a practitioner of it, he has brought a new aesthetics of his own into the world, and intensively cultivated ties with Josef Albers and Max Bill guaranteed the gap would be bridged between linguistic aesthetics and aesthetics in fine arts. During the search for a successor to Gomringer, the chair he has vacated was advertised only a few months ago under the heading of 'Poetics'. Viewed in retrospect, that designation also describes with telling succinctness Gomringer's activities as a teacher over the past fourteen years.

Before Eugen Gomringer came to the Academy, he had built up an exceptional reputation since the early 1950s. His dazzling years were 1953 and 1954. The year 1953 saw his first volume of poetry published under the programmatic title *konstellationen* [constellations], heralding the foundation of Concrete Poetry. The same year he joined forces with Dieter Rot and Marcel Wyss to launch the art journal *Spirale*, which would become the first forum for Concrete Art. In 1954 readers of the *Neue Züricher Zeitung* could savour Gomringer's first manifesto, *vom vers zur konstellation* [from verse to constellation], which sent the Concrete Art aesthetic out into the world.

The year 1954, however, also marked another start. That year Eugen Gomringer was appointed Max Bill's secretary, as he put it with the understatement he so prizes, at the by then legendary Hochschule für Gestaltung [School of Design] in Ulm, where he stayed until 1958. There he made the acquaintance of leading contemporary artists; there he embarked on his encyclopaedic lecturing activity covering modern art and poetry, through which he has since then become a world ambassador of Modernism, and from Ulm he built his 'Continent of the Concrete', which had probably expanded to its greatest extent and was at its height when Gomringer was appointed to teach at the Düsseldorf Academy. Some series of books on artists and works of Concrete Art were published, of which I should like to single out for mention here only the monographs on Josef Albers and his tribute to Günther Uecker, *wie weiss ist wissen die weisen* [only the wise know what is what with white].

In the meantime Gomringer had charted new experiential territory, which would also be important for his later work at the Art Academy. After stages as head of advertising at a Swiss industrial company and as managing director of the Swiss

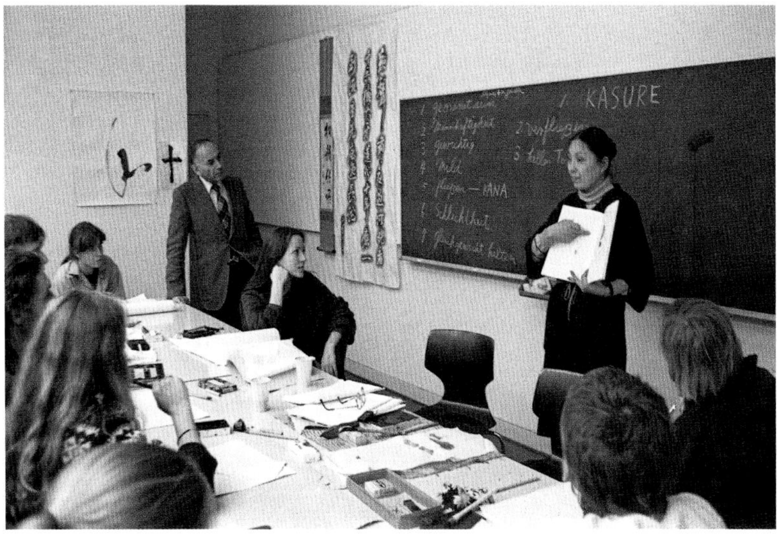

Eugen Gomringer with students, c.1980

Werkbund [Federation of Artists and Architects], he was appointed cultural adviser to the Rosenthal Porcelain Factory in 1967. He acquired the techniques and effective communications skills needed in verbal and visual advertising design and became a specialist in what Germans so awkwardly call public relations work. Gomringer, however, viewed being tasked with culture above all as a commitment to art. He succeeded in arranging many commissions for artists who would not merely design porcelain in the traditional way. From designing retail outlets through constructing new furnishings to creating unusual porcelain objects, Gomringer envisaged a contemporary relationship between art and industry, linking Werkbund with Bauhaus ideas at the highest level. During his time in Düsseldorf, many such commissions also went to artists at the Academy.

At this juncture my brief address turns into acknowledgement, and you will permit me, I am sure, to single out for mention at the end at least one commitment of Eugen Gomringer's. He has always championed the promotion of art students and young artists at the Academy. Many owe to Gomringer the first exhibition of their works, which he often opened himself with one of his celebrated speeches. He arranged first catalogues for many and wrote for them the first interpretive lines about their fledgling oeuvres into those catalogues as if into a pedigree. Through his work on selection committees and other bodies promoting art, Gomringer has contributed substantially to the reputation of the Düsseldorf Art Academy and its endeavours in art.

Sometimes it has seemed to me – and this is my concluding observation – as if Gomringer were the envoy whom the Art Academy sent out into the world. Wherever great exhibitions have been opened, art events have been organised, and artistic encounters have taken place, Gomringer has been there, and, in his person, also the Düsseldorf Art Academy.

He has been a representative, and even if he must now give up his teaching commitments at this institution, I nonetheless wish for both him and for us that he may long continue to represent us.

* Farewell address given in 1991 on the occasion of Eugen Gomringer's 1990 departure. Printed in *Jahreshefte der Kunstakademie Düsseldorf*, Vol. 3, 1990/91, pp. 25–28.

THE ARTS FROM 1985 TO THE PRESENT

Robert Fleck

VIEWED FROM HERE

Autumn 1984 saw the most acclaimed art exhibition worldwide to have taken place on the Düsseldorf Trade Fair grounds in the state capital of North Rhine-Westphalia. Subtitled *Zwei Monate neue deutsche Kunst in Düsseldorf* [Two Months of New German Art in Düsseldorf], *von hier aus* [viewed from here] assembled the works of seventy-one living artists from the Federal Republic of Germany, the United States, France, South Korea, Czechoslovakia, Yugoslavia, Denmark, Switzerland, and the Netherlands.[1]

The title itself, *von hier aus*, underscored the agenda and aspirations of the Düsseldorf art show: the most important generation of German artists since 1960 was working in Düsseldorf/Cologne. Starting from here, reputable galleries operated worldwide, art fairs were mounted, and many artists of international standing were attracted to the region. This made Düsseldorf the sole art hub to counterbalance the influence of New York in the ranking of contemporary art. Forty-three of the seventy-one artists participating in those 'two months of new German art' were living in the Düsseldorf/Cologne conurbation in 1984. Thirty-five artists – responsible for nearly half

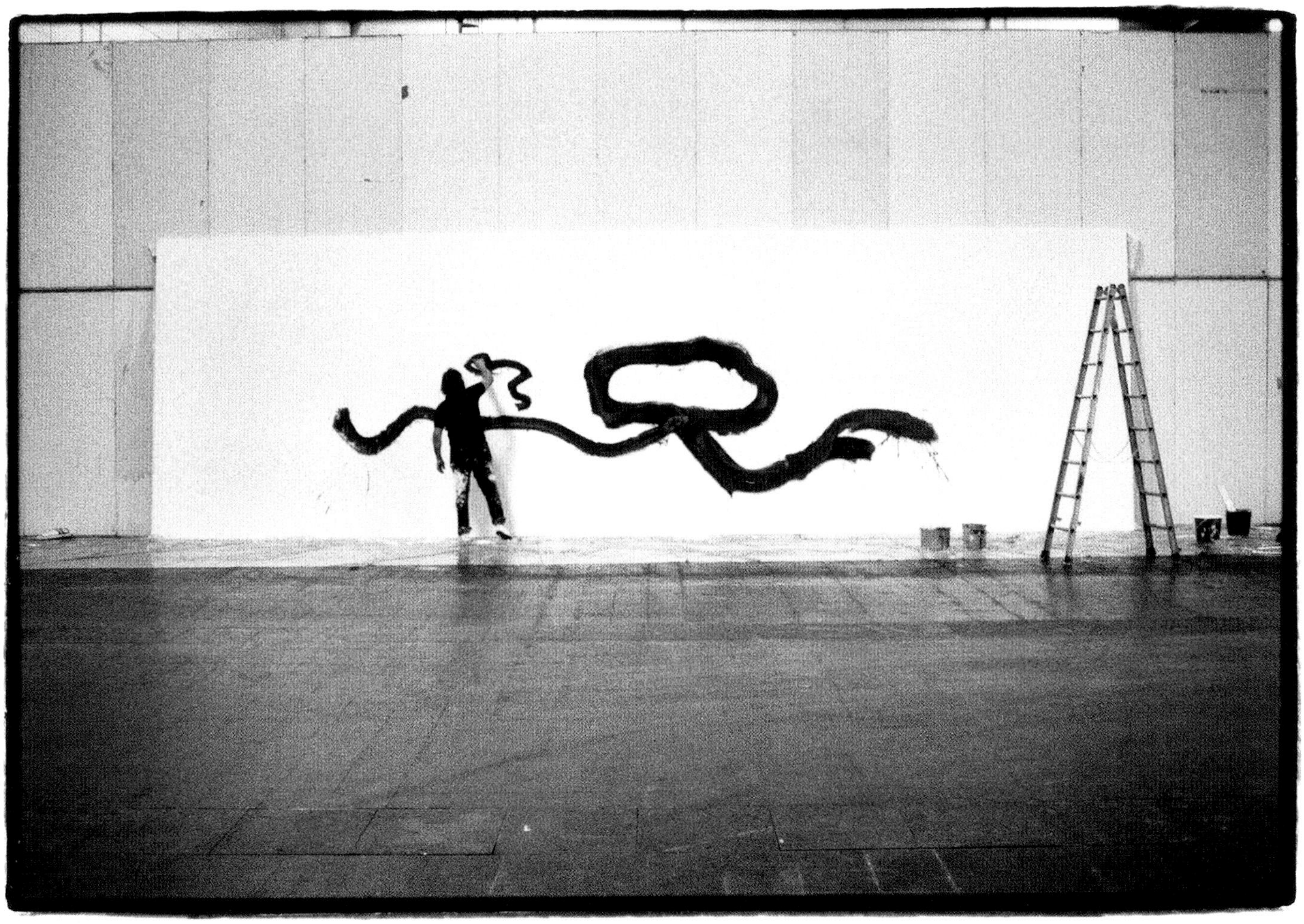

Fig. 1: A. R. Penck painting Quo vadis Germania? *in the Düsseldorf Ausstellungshalle at the exhibition* von hier aus *[viewed from here], 1984*

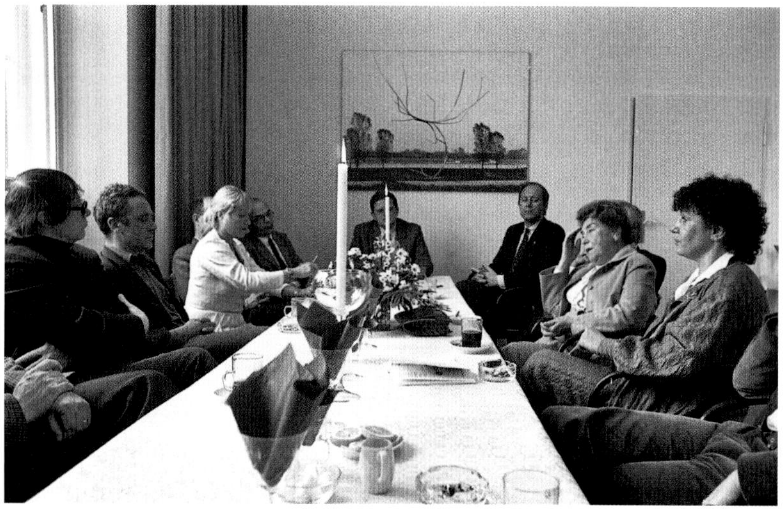

Fig. 2: Austrian Minister of Science Herta Firnberg being received at the Düsseldorf Art Academy rectorate offices; left: Ernst Althoff, Gerhard Richter, Luise Kimme; right: Irmin Kamp next to the Minister, 1982

the exhibition – were, and still are, linked with the Düsseldorf Art Academy by virtue of having studied and/or taught there (Fig. 1).[2] A side effect was that the Düsseldorf Art Academy became an arbiter of contemporary stances in art since 1960.

The international art world was impressed by the exhibition. After a rather dull Venice Biennale that summer, *von hier aus* was viewed as a sequel to the great exhibitions that had been conceived since *Paris – New York* inaugurated the Centre Pompidou in 1977 and that had found a home in the Federal Republic of Germany with *Westkunst* [West Art] (1981) and *Zeitgeist* (1982). The grand gesture of placing Cologne/Düsseldorf exclusively on a par with New York, the dominant art metropolis since 1960, caused a stir and could no longer be countered by Paris despite the spectacular launch of the New Paris Biennale the next year in 1985, which lavish funding could not save from insolvency.[3]

The reputation of the Düsseldorf Art Academy for occupying an exceptional position in the most recent developments in art was consolidated in the international art industry by the late 1960s and early 1970s. *von hier aus* even surpassed that perception of the Academy because, of the twenty-three artists (younger than thirty-five) featured in the exhibition, no fewer than eleven – again almost half their number – were alumni and alumnae of it.[4] The roll would have been even longer had the curators of the exhibition included new approaches to sculpture and photography, which in the years to follow would become a major factor in burnishing the Academy's reputation in later years. Six young participants in the exhibition, Jiří Georg Dokoupil,[5] Katharina Fritsch, Hubert Kiecol, Marcel Odenbach, Albert Oehlen, and Andreas Schulze would later also teach at the Art Academy.

While the much acclaimed large-scale exhibition *von hier aus* was housed in the trade fair halls and confirmed the seminal influence exerted by the Art Academy on contemporary art, the Academy itself was in the throes of preparing for changes to take place within its walls. The position of rector was still held at the time by Irmin Kamp, who had been appointed professor and head of a sculpture class in 1974 under the previous rector Norbert Kricke. Irmin Kamp, who held office from 1982 to 1987, was the first woman to be rector of the Düsseldorf Art Academy in the 208 years since it was founded and at the same time was one of the first women rectors of an art academy worldwide (Fig. 2). The two rectorates before hers (Eduard Trier from 1966 to 1972 and Norbert Kricke from 1972 until 1981) were marred by vehement ideological strife among the professors. Kamp's tenure by contrast was notable for phases of consolidation. Continuity in staff appointments was guaranteed. Unlike other art academies at the time, the Düsseldorf Art Academy under Kamp was not, for instance, tempted to embark on spectacular new beginnings built on a system of workshops and visiting professorships in the teaching sector. Even today a unique feature of the Düsseldorf Art Academy is the comparatively lengthy time span during which teachers are active in the institute, which is in itself a stabilising element.

CONTINUITY IN TEACHING

When one considers those teaching at the Art Academy in the mid-1980s, one encounters several levels of continuity within the teaching sector, which is, first of all, represented by the artists who had been appointed to teach at the Academy as early as the 1960s, some of whom espoused widely varying conceptions of art. The elegant Modernism practised by the figurative sculptor Karl Bobek, who was a professor from 1963 until 1987, contrasts vividly with the radical geometric style of Erwin Heerich's work. From 1945 until 1954 Heerich was, along with Joseph Beuys, one of Ewald Mataré's most outstanding students. As its first head, Heerich built up the Art Teaching Department. The department enabled the institution to retain its independent status as an art academy after the crisis that arose around Beuys in 1972. Heerich had taken part in documenta in 1968 and 1977. One of his last students was the sculptor Meuser.[6]

The painter Gerhard Hoehme – once a student of Otto Coester's from 1952 until 1953 – headed a class of his own in painting from 1960 until 1984 after weighing in to critical

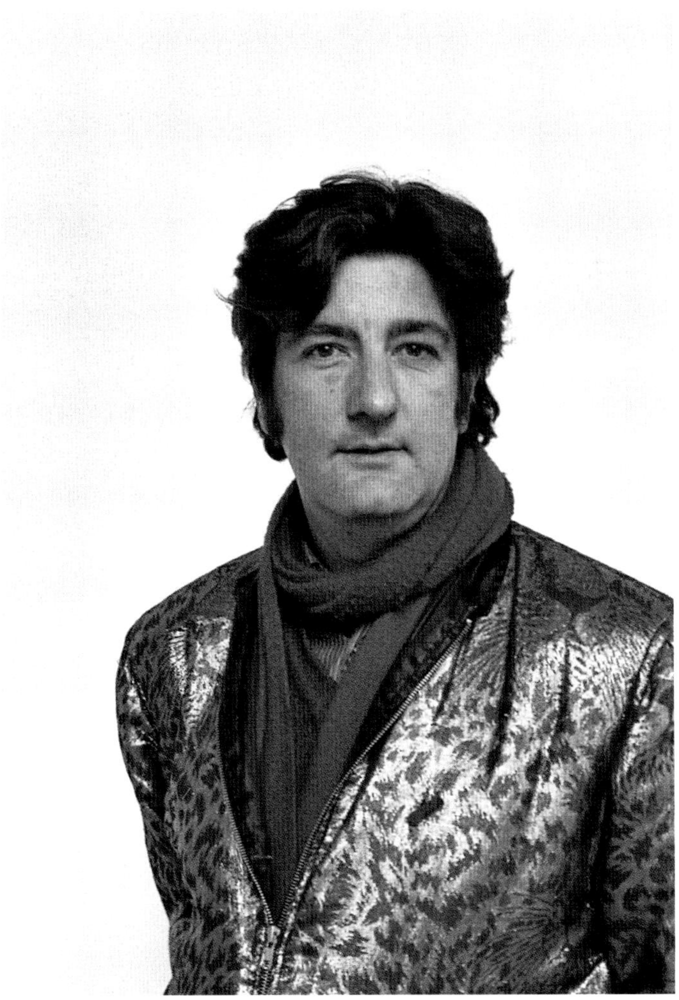

Fig. 3: Michael Buthe, 1982

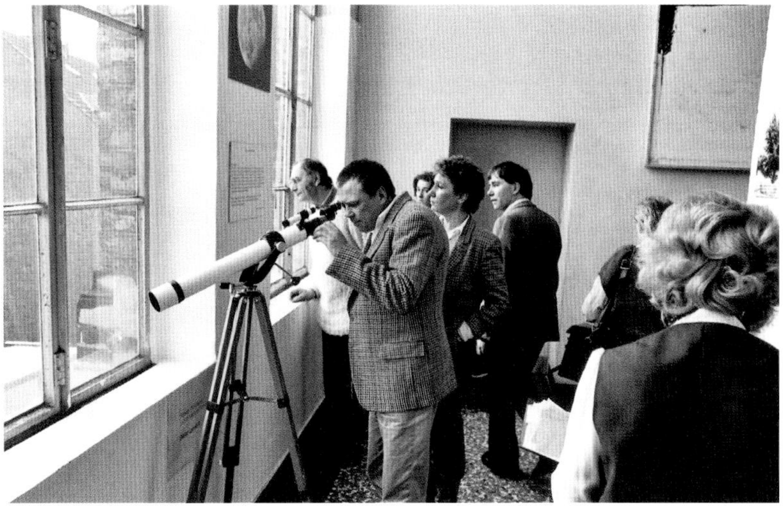

Fig. 4: Academy Tour with professors Günther Uecker, Siegfried Cremer behind him on the left, Beate Schiff on the right, Irmin Kamp, and Fritz Schwegler, 1983

applause with a documenta presence in 1959. An adherent of Informel, Hoehme found manifold reflective ways of addressing form and colour. His works, which intervene in space, often overstep the boundary between the imaginary picture space and reality (shown on p. 277). One of those who studied with Hoehme (and Karl Otto Götz) from 1961 on, Sigmar Polke, would be acclaimed worldwide for his German Pavilion at the 1986 Venice Biennale.

Rolf Sackenheim, who, like Hoehme, had begun his studies at the Art Academy with Otto Coester in 1952 and had been in Coester's master class, was head of a printmaking class from 1965 until 1984. Influenced by Informel, Sackenheim's numerous watercolour wash drawings and etchings are distinguished by dense handling of line rapidly executed with deft precision (shown on p. 208). At the same time, Michael Buthe, one of the most renowned exponents of New Painting, had been working at the Academy since the early 1980s, as a substitute professor from 1981 to 1983, and ultimately as head of a painting class until his premature death in 1994 (Fig. 3). His assemblages often feature motifs and vibrant colours expressive of the oriental feeling for life he had absorbed on numerous trips to southern lands (shown on p. 260).

A second layer of continuity in teaching that can be observed in the mid-1980s concerns the numerous appointments of world-class artists to teach at the Academy that had already taken place during Norbert Kricke's tenure in the 1970s and continued far into Irmin Kamp's rectorate: Günther Uecker, to take one example, was appointed in 1974. He had studied at the Art Academy from 1955 until 1957 with Otto Pankok, later becoming a founding member of ZERO, the first art movement to have originated in the Rhineland after 1945. Until he retired in 1995, he taught sculpture – beginning four years after he had represented the Federal Republic of Germany at the Venice Biennale (Fig. 4). Uecker became famous for his nail pictures and sculptures, which he has been producing with unflagging physical commitment since 1957. The nails and the constantly changing shadows they cast lend the pictures an enhanced sculptural quality and a distinctive vividness (shown on p. 257). The other two founding members of ZERO, Heinz Mack and Otto Piene, tried out new methods of teaching at art academies that sought close links with the basic sciences – Mack in Japan in the early 1970s and Piene at the Massachusetts Institute of Technology in Cambridge, Massachusetts.

Gerhard Richter (along with Sigmar Polke, Manfred Kuttner, and Konrad Lueg, later known as the gallerist Konrad Fischer) had studied with K. O. Götz from 1961 until 1963. He was appointed to teach at the Art Academy in 1973, the year following his solo show in the German Pavilion at the Venice Biennale. Despite the polemics at the time on the importance of photorealism, he was appointed to teach another painting class at the Art Academy that was housed in an annexe in Harkortstraße in the immediate vicinity of the Düsseldorf Central Train Station. Richter taught for more than twenty years before finally leaving the profession in 1994.

An equally legendary appointment was that of Bernd Becher to a chair of photography in 1976. The appointment was synchronous with the recognition given to the works of Bernd and Hilla Becher, which focused on the documenta 6 of 1977. Bernd Becher had studied typography at the Düsseldorf Art Academy from 1959 until 1961. His wife, Hilla, who was closely involved with teaching the class until Bernd Becher retired in 1996, had installed the first photo lab with a darkroom at the Academy in 1958 while she was still a student. By the mid-1980s important artists had come from that class, which was also in Harkortstraße, a group of alumni and alumnae now known as the Düsseldorf School of Photography.[7]

Film as an art medium had been introduced at the Academy in 1971 – a date particularly early for art academies – in the person of the Danish film-maker Ole John (until 1976). The video artist Ursula Wevers succeeded him in this lectureship, which she held until 1986. The appointment that caused a stir internationally, however, was that of the Korean Nam June Paik in 1979 to a chair for film and video.[8] Paik lived in New York but had carried out several important Happenings at the Düsseldorf Art Academy by the 1960s. Since documenta 6 he had been internationally acclaimed as the leading exponent of video art. The sculptor Tony Cragg, who had become a lecturer in the orientation course that same year, recalls the importance of this decades later: '[Paik] was the one who brought video as a medium into art in the first place.'[9] The establishment of a dedicated class in video art in Düsseldorf with Nam June Paik as professor was – until he retired in 1995 – the first magnet to draw students from other countries to the Art Academy since the Beuys years shortly before and after 1968.

Other long-term appointments during Norbert Kricke's tenure included that of the sculptor Erich Reusch (*1925), who worked as an architect on into the 1960s. In 1964 he began to work more in sculpture. He taught a fine art class from 1973 until 1975, then taught in the chair for the integration of fine art and architecture until 1990. He was supported by Christian Megert (*1936), a Swiss artist who was a founding member of the kinetic and environmental art movement in the 1960s. Megert was also appointed to a teaching post at the Academy in 1976 (and stayed there until 2001). Although they were involved with art in public spaces in different ways, both artists focused on it in their own work and teaching.

Born in 1938, the painter Rissa (Karin Götz), who had worked in the Art Academy since 1969 as an assistant in training art teachers and as a lecturer for the Art Teaching Department, became a professor of fine art in 1975 and, after reaching retirement age, continued to teach on the basis of short-term contracts from 2003 until 2007. She attracted attention in 1977 as the author of a manifesto and a founding member of the group of painters known as Axiom. Even 'while studying at the Academy, Rissa invented a distinctive painterly language of forms, which she subsequently described as "Rissa's handling" or "snippet style" [shown on p. 201]. Painterly and representational motifs are combined with small and larger "snippet" forms in confrontation with expressive colours to elicit the painterly charm which, together with thematically unusual motifs, emerges as an unmistakable Rissa tableau.'[10]

During the entire time she was at the Academy, Rissa – together with her husband, K. O. Götz – showed a particularly strong commitment to art teacher training and artistic freedom as Academy policy.

Klaus Rinke was also called to the Academy to teach painting in 1974 during Norbert Kricke's tenure, at first for three years. However, he represented an aesthetic stance that differed in all respects from that of his colleagues. From 1977 until 2004 he taught a sculpture class. For all its sculptural aspects, the work of this frequent documenta exhibitor was closely bound up with Conceptual Art, which at that time was the sole important style of contemporary art to be absent from the Art Academy (shown on p. 223). Nevertheless, the Academy students must have had a good idea of Conceptual Art because the Konrad Fischer Gallery in the immediate vicinity of the Academy specialised in showing it.

IRMIN KAMP'S RECTORATE (1981–1988)

The first artist appointed to teach at the Academy during Irmin Kamp's tenure was the highly regarded Swiss painter Franz Eggenschwiler (1930–2000). In 1967 he had begun to make picture objects from objets trouvés and rubbish. In 1972 he showed work in the legendary Individual Mythologies section at documenta 5 in Kassel. Another Swiss who showed work there was André Thomkins. Influenced by Dada and Surrealism, Thomkins had been appointed to teach at the Academy in 1971, long before Irmin Kamp became rector (Fig. 5).[11] Eggenschwiler was also a member of the Osterath Etching Collective, founded by Holger Runge in Meerbusch-Osterath near Düsseldorf. At the Academy he taught a fine arts graphic class from 1981 until 1996.

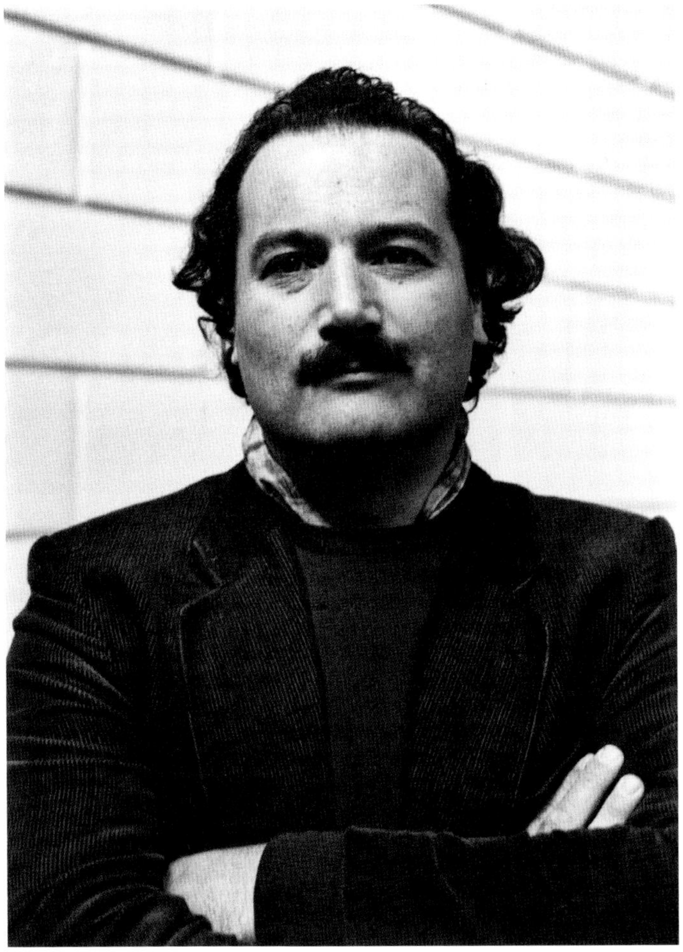

Fig. 5: André Thomkins, 1972

Irmin Kamp also invited Jan Dibbets (*1941), the leading Dutch Conceptual artist, to Düsseldorf as well as Ulrich Rückriem,[12] born in Düsseldorf in 1938, a sculptor who exerted a formative influence on sculpture for decades after also showing work in the Individual Mythologies section of documenta 5. Rückriem (along with Dieter Krieg) represented Germany at the 1978 Venice Biennale and took part in the 1982, 1987, and 1992 documenta exhibitions. The angular shapes of his works are reminiscent of the Minimal Art aesthetic yet are rooted in a European tradition of handling material, in his case the block of stone: divide it, put it together, and respect it.

Although her early work was post-Surrealist, the Canadian media artist Nan Hoover (1931–2008), who had lived in Amsterdam since 1999, became one of the most influential pioneering video and performance artists of the 1970s and 1980s. In 1987 she began to teach alongside Paik in the film and video class and continued to do so until 1996. Several generations of students raved about her teaching in Düsseldorf and later in Berlin. Walter Nikkels (*1940), one of the most important typographers of the latter half of the twentieth century and the present, was a professor of design, book design, and typology at the Düsseldorf Art Academy from 1985 until 2007. He had already made a name for himself both as a graphic artist and as the architect of major exhibitions, such as the 1982 documenta 7 in Kassel. During his time at the Art Academy, Nikkels made his presence felt in daily life there by presenting numerous designs for invitations to the *Rundgang* [Academy Tour] featuring the Art Academy lettering in the letterheads or posters for the Academy Gallery (shown on p. 414, p. 415, and p. 448), thus shaping its public image to the present day.

From 1986 until 1989 the political artist Klaus Staeck was a visiting professor. The Canadian Conceptual and Minimalist artist David Rabinowitch, who represented one of the major stances in sculpture at the time, taught a class in sculpture at the Art Academy from 1984 until 2008 (Fig. 6). Moreover, a new chair in art and public relations was created in 1985, a first at the Art Academy. Kasper König, an exhibition organiser and most recently head of the Museum Ludwig in Cologne, who had conceptualised and curated *von hier aus* in 1984, was appointed to that new chair in 1985. Only three years later, however, he was headhunted by the city of Frankfurt am Main for the Städelschule, where until 1999 he presided as rector over the liveliest German art academy in the 1990s. In 1986 Christoph Schlingensief (1960–2010), who would later become a legendary theatre-maker and Happening artist and posthumously represented Germany at the 2011 Venice Biennale, where he was awarded the Golden Lion, had a teaching contract, a year after the sculptor Jürgen Partenheimer (*1947).

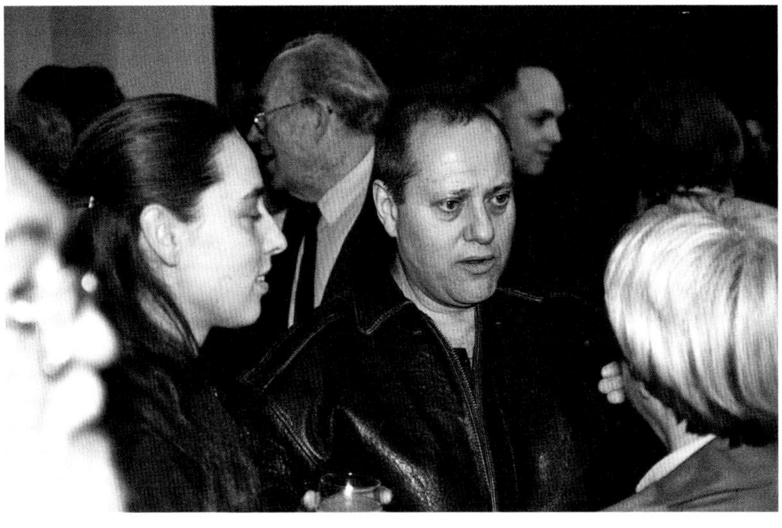

Fig. 6: David Rabinowitch in conversation at the send-off for Gerhard Richter, 1994

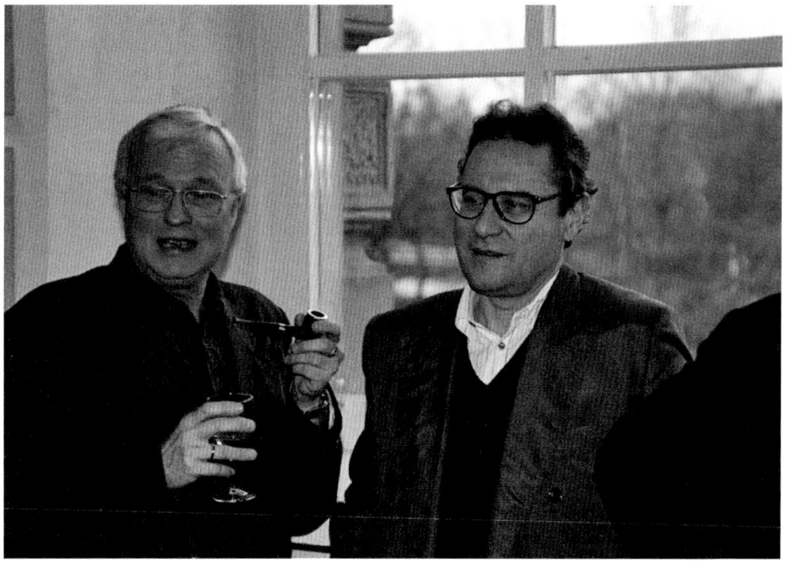

Fig. 7: Heinrich Theissing and Alfonso Hüppi in the Düsseldorf Art Academy Great Hall, 1994

The situation at the Academy during those years was notable for the originality of individual teaching concepts, which derived in diverse ways from the aesthetic experiences of leading practitioners of avant-garde art and the expanded art forms of the 1960s and 1970s. Fritz Schwegler, for one, who began as a lecturer in 1973 and from 1975 until 2001 was a professor of painting then sculpture, had built up an unconventional oeuvre somewhere between script, sculpture, and performance that enabled him to consolidate among his students a new approach to dealing with drawing, colour, and figuration (shown on p. 214). Schwegler was not the only professor to be present on a daily basis during the week in his class, where his students had access to him for discussion at any time in his studio there. He was a particularly 'productive' Academy teacher, who trained many internationally celebrated artists, including Thomas Demand and Katharina Fritsch.

The painting class taught by Alfonso Hüppi between 1974 and 1999 turned out to be a similarly long-term hub of creativity. Like Schwegler and Beuys, Hüppi was an acclaimed leading light of Harald Szeemann's legendary documenta 5 (Fig. 7). Hüppi's class, with which he travelled to Iran and Armenia for study purposes, later produced student initiatives on which several classes would collaborate, including Happenings in the Düsseldorf off scene.

The class taught by Gotthard Graubner represents the outcome of yet another appointment of a leading avant-gardist in the 1960s and 1970s (Figs. 8, 9). Graubner had studied at the Academy with Georg Meistermann from 1954 until 1961, subsequently going his own way to establish what were known as 'cushion pictures', a style of painting devoted solely to the colour space, well beyond the confines of classic panel painting. As the successor to Rupprecht Geiger, the leading early German Colour Field painter, Graubner had represented aesthetic continuity as a professor of painting at the Academy since 1965. From 1976 until he retired in 1998, Graubner taught an influential painting class: one distinguished alumna is the painter Katharina Grosse, who is now a professor at the Düsseldorf Art Academy in her own right.

Konrad Klapheck, scion of an important Düsseldorf dynasty of art critics, studied at the Art Academy from 1954 until 1958. An exponent of the new European figurative painting, Klapheck was a professor of painting at the Academy from 1979 until 2002, where he succeeded K. O. Götz, a pioneering practitioner of post-war Gestural Abstraction. In 1978, the year Krieg and Rückriem represented Germany at the Venice Biennale, Krieg took over a painting class, in which he anticipated the return of figuration with expressive overtones and continued to accompany that 1980s trend in painting. At the same time Siegfried Cremer, an important restorer and a founding father of Kinetic Art, taught painting techniques at the Düsseldorf Art Academy from 1977 until 1994.

THE STUDENT GENERATION SINCE THE 1980S

Yet it was the student generation of the late 1970s and 1980s rather than the encounter with the 1960s avant-garde and the important teaching appointments made in Norbert Kricke's

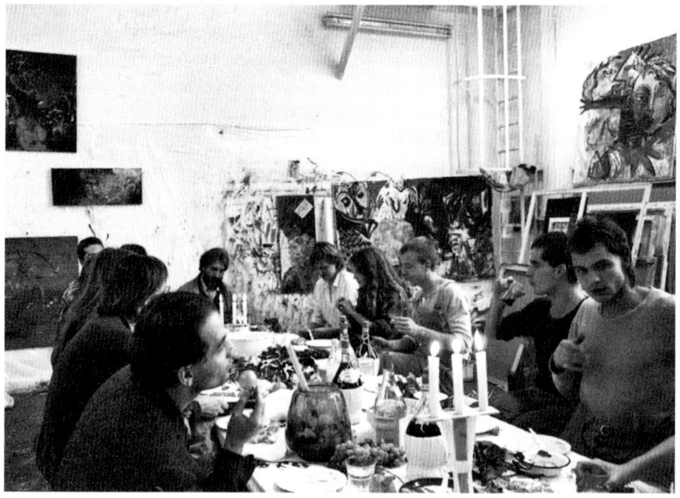

Fig. 8: Gotthard Graubner at the head of the table talking with pupils in his class, November 1983

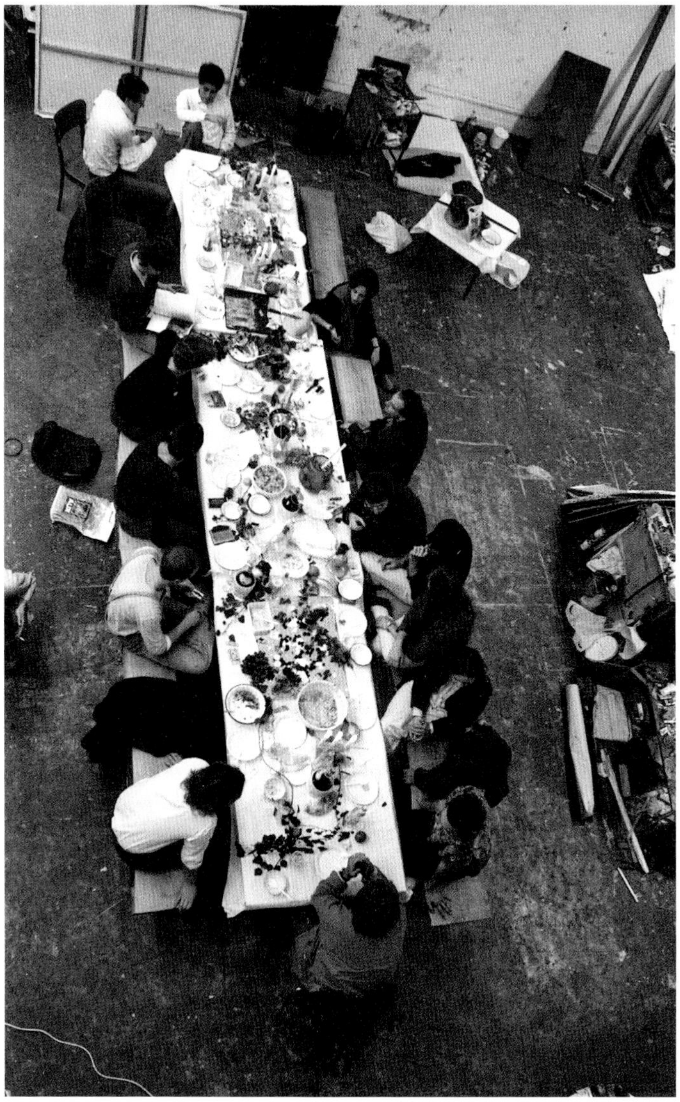

Fig. 9: Gotthard Graubner's class, November 1983

tenure as rector that did the most to place the Düsseldorf Art Academy at the epicentre of the international art world. Benjamin Buchloh, who taught briefly at the Academy in 1978, forced students to form a standpoint of their own and to defend it. An art historian from Cologne who taught in North America before his stint at the Düsseldorf Art Academy and has returned there to teach, Buchloh has been an influential art theorist for the past forty years. He used the incisive arguments and trenchant phrasing of the New York art scene of the day in such hyperbolic form that former students still talk about him today.[13]

By the mid-1980s the Academy had produced dozens of young artists who have forged for the most part international, and in any case very distinguished, careers. The first wave included students from the sculpture class, such luminaries as Peter Josef Abels, Katharina Fritsch, and Martin Honert, who were pupils of Fritz Schwegler's (Thomas Schütte was with Fritz Schwegler in the orientation course but then went to Gerhard Richter's class). Michael Bach, Isa Genzken, and Andreas Schön came from Gerhard Richter's class; Jürgen Drescher (who also taught in the orientation course from 1993 to 1996), Harald Klingelhöller, Reinhard Mucha, and Isolde Wawrin as well as Ulrich Loock (later a museum director as head of the Kunsthalle Bern) were in Klaus Rinke's class. Bogomir Ecker was a graduate of the class taught by Schwegler and Reusch. Pia Stadtbäumer, Thomas Virnich, and Matthias Winzen (later an art historian and museum director in Baden-Baden) were pupils of Alfonso Hüppi's. Paul Schwer was a pupil of Erwin Heerich's and Bernd Kaster a graduate of the Kamp class. In the midst of the euphoria surrounding neo-Expressionism and the Neue Wilden [New Savages] in painting, the Düsseldorf Art Academy stood for an autonomous new line in three-dimensional art, which, at a far remove from the subjective gesture, treats the work of sculpture as a sign and an image. This is also the context of the new linkage of the two-dimensional and the three-dimensional in Ludger Gerdes (Richter class) and Stephan Huber (Schwegler class). The Düsseldorf Art Academy had only an indirect link to the enthusiasm for the return of the gestural, expressive, and subjective manifest in the spectacular young painting of the early 1980s in the person of Walter Dahn (*1954) because he had studied with Joseph Beuys until 1979 and had been in his master class. But even Dahn – who, like Markus Oehlen (*1956), had been in Alfonso Hüppi's master class – and Jiří Georg Dokoupil (*1954), his counterpart in art at that time with whom he shared a lectureship in 1984 at the Art Academy, would soon after a triumph at the 1982 documenta 7 switch to methodological processes that eliminated the solely subjective and the decorative element from expression. The stamping grounds of the Neue Wilden were the Cologne Werkkunstschule, the then Hochschule der Künste in Berlin (now the University of the Arts), and the University of Fine Arts Hamburg, where Martin Kippenberger and Albert Oehlen, two Düsseldorf Art Academy graduates of lasting significance, surfaced around 1980 from the circle of Jörg Immendorff, one of the leading lights of the 1960s Beuys class at the Düsseldorf Art Academy.

The third important art medium in the 1980s and early 1990s along with sculpture and photography was painting. It engaged in an ongoing dialogue with the other media while at the same time keeping content and motif at a distance. From this approach, a line that still exists today developed in the 1980s and is fed by several different classes: Michael Bach, Pia Fries, Karin Kneffel (master class 1987), Michael van Ofen,

Andreas Schön, et al. came from Gerhard Richter's class. Holger Bunk, Claus Föttinger, Berthold Langnickel, Horst Münch, Markus Oehlen, Dirk Skreber, Thomas Virnich, Corinna Wasmuth, and Thomas Rentmeister, who, like Stefan Sehler, had started out in Uecker's class, studied with Alfonso Hüppi.

Even in the 1990s numerous painters whose work has since then become mainstream enrolled in sculpture classes because in sculpture classes there was a tendency at times to do nothing but talk about art, a practice which liberated young students from the constant pressure to produce and compare. The great strengths of the Düsseldorf Art Academy in the 1980s were its interdisciplinary approach to the arts and the permeability of its classes taught by professors – some of whom were famous and all of whom were acclaimed artists – as well as the collective experience of success through immediate recognition in large exhibitions of various kinds.

DIGRESSION: THE PRESENCE OF ART ACADEMY ARTISTS AT THE VENICE BIENNALE SINCE 1945

Although the interdisciplinary approach and permeable classes go some way to explaining the decades-long 'monopoly' the Düsseldorf Art Academy had since 1964 and especially since 1972 on providing the German contingent at the Venice Biennale, they are certainly not the sole reason for it. A unique international exhibition on a grand scale, from the art historical angle, the most significant of its kind in the twentieth century, the Biennale is steeped in a history of scandals, superlatives, and historic events. In 1907 the first countries – Belgium broke the ground – began to erect national pavilions of their own in the immediate vicinity of the main pavilions of the Palazzo delle Esposizioni in the Giardini di Castello because by doing so they could show more of their artists and would no longer be subject to the vagaries of the Italian jury system in selecting and judging participants.[14] The subdivision into national pavilions has been of such lasting importance that it continues to shape this event to the present day. Once the Venice Biennale resumed after a lapse of several years during the Second World War, the twenty-fourth show was inaugurated in 1948 with a dazzling display of Modernist works. Never before had so many works of modern art been assembled in one place: the full range of nineteenth- and twentieth-century modern art was on display for the first time.[15] Once chosen, this path continued to be taken in 1950: only at the Venice Biennale was world-class contemporary art to be seen. Alongside the Blauer Reiter and painters such as Max Beckmann and Emil Nolde, the German Pavilion featured works of a younger generation, including Georg Meistermann, later a professor at the Düsseldorf Art Academy.[16] K. O. Götz and Otto Pankok, also of the Academy, were among a broad selection of artists chosen to represent Germany at the 1958 Biennale. Many of the parameters had changed by the 1964 Biennale: for the first time it was dominated by young American artists, notably Robert Rauschenberg, who was awarded the Grand Prize for Painting. The German Pavilion in turn for the first time concentrated on only two artists: Eduard Trier, the commissioner, showed works by Joseph Fassbender, winner of the Grand Prize for Graphic Art. He had also invited Norbert Kricke to produce his first iron sculptures for the Biennale on site.[17]

The 1968 Biennale, on the other hand, was marred by the student protests of that year. More than half of the pavilions were barricaded by artists and students. Rumours were rife of brutal evictions, arrests, and invitations to exhibit being turned down and were the talk of general assemblies. The Biennale as an international event on a grand scale was turned into a forum for protest.[18] Unlike numerous other pavilions, the German Pavilion and the exhibition it housed were quiet. Alongside a large Richard Oelze retrospective, a Düsseldorf Art Academy professor, K. O. Götz, and Horst Janssen represented the Federal Republic.[19]

Only two years later the Biennale had become a makeshift art venue: it was showing the effect of all too frequent changes of government in Italy. A new Biennale statute had been envisaged but had not yet become law. The upshot was that the opening of the Biennale was only announced a few months before the event.[20] Although this Biennale revealed that art was in crisis, the exhibition nonetheless also had some high points, including the German Pavilion, in which Heinz Mack and Günther Uecker, both of whom had studied at the Düsseldorf Art Academy, joined forces with Kaspar-Thomas Lenk and Georg Karl Pfahler, exponents of Op Art, to put on a show. Uecker had driven nails into a neo-Classical pillar on the pavilion façade to transform it into a temporary artwork.[21]

By 1972 the situation at the Biennale still showed little improvement. Only four pavilions were up to the former standards of the exhibition: the Belgian Pavilion housing a Pierre Alechinsky exhibition, the Dutch Pavilion with Jan Dibbets, the Austrian Pavilion featuring the architect Hans Hollein, and the German Pavilion with Gerhard Richter showing his work in an acclaimed solo show, the first one of its kind in a Biennale pavilion. Richter had conceived a series of Atlas pictures specially for the central room of the pavilion at the Biennale, thus anticipating a later development: creating artworks just for exhibition in the national pavilions.[22]

The Biennale was finally revived from the serious crisis that had stifled it by adopting a thematic presentation under the heading 'Art and Environment' in 1976. The entire range of new pictorial and spatial ideas that had emerged in the 1970s at a far remove from the institutional crisis suffered by the Biennale could now be displayed, a first in Biennale history. Klaus Gallwitz had engaged Joseph Beuys and Reiner Ruthenbeck, a former student of Beuys's, for the German Pavilion. Beuys's contribution was *Straßenbahnhaltestelle* [Tram Stop], one of the most acclaimed sculptures of the century.[23] The Biennale after that saw Dieter Krieg and Ulrich Rückriem sharing the honours in the German Pavilion.

The creation of an international Biennale Committee consisting of Harald Szeemann, Jean-Christophe Ammann, and Tommaso Trini enabled the 1980 Biennale to regain its former reputation as a major international grand-scale exhibition.[24] Once again the German Pavilion attracted visitors' attention with a surprising work, a wooden sculpture, by Georg Baselitz in the main room and an Anselm Kiefer retrospective: Kiefer had been a sort of private student of Joseph Beuys's for years.[25] The two Biennales that followed featured works by Gotthard Graubner, Wolfgang Laib, who was a former pupil of Beuys's, and Hanne Darboven in the German Pavilion. Dieter Roth exhibited in the Swiss Pavilion in 1982. Lothar Baumgarten, another former Beuys pupil, and A. R. Penck, who would become a professor of graphic art at the Düsseldorf Art Academy in 1989, presented their work in Venice in 1984. Sigmar Polke was awarded the Golden Lion in 1986. Daniel Buren, who had been a visiting professor at the Düsseldorf Art Academy in back in 1979, showed work in the French Pavilion. Dierk Stemmler, commissioner for the German Pavilion, and Felix Droese, another Beuys student, exhibited at the next Biennale in 1988. Siegfried Anzinger was engaged by Hans Hollein, the Austrian commissioner, for the exhibition.

Bernd and Hilla Becher, who were art photographers and teachers at the Art Academy, and the sculptor Reinhard Mucha, who had studied with Klaus Rinke, were successfully presented by Klaus Bußmann – the German exhibition presentation was awarded a Grand Prize for the best pavilion.[26] In 1993 there was an exhibition of Nam June Paik's work alongside that of Hans Haacke, who lived in New York and whom Eduard Trier had tried in vain in 1972 to headhunt as a professor for the Düsseldorf Art Academy. Two distinctive features that had already shown up in the early 1970s exhibitions of German artists' work were now becoming established: on the one hand, site-specific interventions – that is, the dialogue between artist and architecture that can only be experienced on site – and, on the other, an investigation of the history of the German Pavilion, which is tainted by association with the National Socialists.[27]

In 1995 Katharina Fritsch, Martin Honert, and Thomas Ruff had to contend with the unpleasantness of renovating the German National Pavilion. The cost of restoring the floor after the 1993 Hans Haacke *Germania* installation had been astronomical.[28] Gerhard Merz and Katharina Sieverding, who had studied with Beuys, showed work in the German exhibition rooms in 1997. The Swiss Pavilion featured Helmut Federle while Austria was represented by artists from the Wiener Gruppe, including Oswald Wiener. A year after being appointed to teach at the Düsseldorf Art Academy, Rosemarie Trockel showed her work in 1999 in the German Pavilion, and Gregor Schneider (awarded the Golden Lion), who had studied with Schwegler, exhibited there in 2001. Candida Höfer, who had studied with the Bechers, was invited to present her work there along with Martin Kippenberger in 2003. The sculptor Isa Genzken (a graduate of the Richter class) exhibited in the German Pavilion while Herbert Brandl represented Austria at the Biennale in 2007. In 2009 the German Pavilion began inviting artists from countries other than Germany to show their work in the German Pavilion. The 2011 Biennale saw the awarding of the Golden Lion for the posthumously realised controversial contribution to Christoph Schlingensief, who had taught at the Düsseldorf Art Academy on a short-term contract in 1986 and died in 2010.

Unparalleled in the history of the Venice Biennale, the weight carried by a single art academy is all the more remarkable because only once, early on, in 1964, was selecting the exhibiting artists in the hands of a German Biennale commissioner, Eduard Trier, who was connected with the Düsseldorf Art Academy.[29] Later commissioners (and since the 1990s, women commissioners) had nothing to do with the Düsseldorf Art Academy although with few exceptions only Art Academy graduates and professors have been selected by them for the German Pavilion in Venice for such a long time. This dense constellation of artists with close links to the Düsseldorf Art Academy shows clearly that teachers and graduates alike have achieved international recognition since 1945 because they have been a major source of inspiration to contemporary art.

MARKUS LÜPERTZ'S TENURE AS RECTOR (1988–2009)

In 1988 the question arose of who would succeed Irmin Kamp as rector, and all eyes were on Gotthard Graubner.[30]

However, he suggested Markus Lüpertz, who after a sensational stint as a professor of painting at the Karlsruhe Art Academy had been headhunted two years previously by the Düsseldorf Art Academy to teach painting.[31]

Markus Lüpertz's tenure as rector was one of the longest – he held the post for more than twenty-one years – in the history of the Düsseldorf Art Academy. This rector's aggressive conduct of his office often gave rise to public discussion, especially his provocative insistence on the artist's exceptional status in society. In fact, however, Markus Lüpertz – despite being constrained to implement the controversial Higher Education Law (Hochschulgesetz) and to restructure the curriculum and the examination regulations, the allocation of space at the Academy, and the departments – turned out to be a champion of the Academy traditions of openness, medial diversity, the appointment of world-class artists as professors, and the free Academy with its system of classes taught by artists as professors in which students of varying cohorts are collected in several rooms and instructed according to the individual standards the artists have developed from working in their own art forms. It was his provocatively bold public persona and self-assured handling of both the public at large and the state authorities who maintained the Academy that enabled Markus Lüpertz to permanently safeguard the autonomy of the Düsseldorf Art Academy during a phase marked by the implementation of far-reaching reorganisation measures affecting all institutions of its kind.

Teaching appointments during this period were made on the basis of including artists who worked in the widest possible variety of art forms and were often of international origin; hence they can be described as continuing the Art Academy tradition of being a bastion of avant-garde art. The first appointment made during Markus Lüpertz's tenure was that of Tony Cragg in 1989: with his amorphous sculpture, he shaped the renewal of the medium and had been teaching newly admitted Academy students as a lecturer in the orientation course since 1979, where Luise Kimme (1939–2013) had also worked until 2002. She had studied in London with Anthony Caro, a grandee of modern sculpture. Since 1979 she had lived mainly in Tobago when she was not teaching in Düsseldorf. Inspired by mythology, folklore, and indigenous art, she produced refreshingly independent, brightly coloured neo-figurative wooden sculptures, for which she built a museum of her own, The Castle (Luise Kimme Sculpture Museum), around her studio in Tobago.

Gerhard Merz taught a painting class from 1990 until 2005. He represents a stringently anti-figurative, neo-Constructivist stance which, in continuing the geometric-abstract formal language of twentieth-century classic Modernism, has developed a distinction between fine art and the contemporary universe of images. In his class, which was radically organised around thinking about arts – with, among others, Florian Baudrexel, Alexander Jasch, Matthias Lahme, and Jens Ullrich – the sculptor Paloma Varga Weisz found a way of again bypassing the prevailing purist mood by opposing it with directly deployed figuration.

Between 1990 and 1993 three vacancies for professors of sculpture were filled. The new professors were Magdalena Jetelová (*1946), whose outsize wooden sculptures, coarsely cut of oak and with unfinished surfaces, usually depict furnishings, which, however, have forfeited their function through the way in which they are presented; Hubert Kiecol (*1950), who in a different way elevates mundane objects such as houses, staircases, or wardrobes to the status of sculpture (shown on p. 282), thus transforming sculpture into architecture and vice versa;[32] and Jannis Kounellis (*1936), not only as internationally acclaimed as the above mentioned colleagues but already a legend in his own lifetime as a founding member of Italian

Arte Povera in the late 1960s and a participant in several documentas, most recently documenta 9 in 1992. These appointments reveal that priority was given to non-figurative trends in sculpture over the numerous figurative approaches of the time. Whereas Gerhard Richter gave up his chair in 1994 to live from art after his work had been given the definitive critical accolades in the international art scene, the appointment of Jannis Kounellis is further confirmation that the Düsseldorf Art Academy is a magnet for international talent.

The situation in which 1990s Academy students found themselves was strongly shaped by independently organised exhibition venues. Closer scrutiny reveals that the exhibition, club, and performance activities at and associated with the Art Academy form another layer of most recent tradition. The free art initiatives that began in 1990 on Worringer Platz and near it still fuel – although with varying intensity – the liveliness of the Düsseldorf art scene. Their roots go back to the studio shows mounted by the early ZERO movement in Gladbacher Straße on the harbour from 1957 on, the 1960s Fluxus Actions in the Art Academy Great Hall, the antics that erupted in the Beuys class in 1968, and the Ratinger Hof, where an ambience conducive to the continual exchange of ideas between the Art Academy and its surroundings was manifest in the 1970s and early 1980s through the presence of Carmen and Imi Knoebel. In 1992 WP8, a combined bar and art room at Worringer Platz 8 run by students from the Hüppi class, played an important role. It was also the venue of the first global computer conference in art with Michael Krome and others associated in some way or other with the new art journal *Texte zur Kunst*. This Düsseldorf hub of arts activity in turn maintained close ties with 'The Thing', the Internet community launched in New York for artists and art projects by the German artist Wolfgang Staehle.[33]

Fritz Schwegler taught Thomas Demand from 1990 until 1992 and Gregor Schneider from 1990 until 1995, both of whom set trends in art in the 2000s. The Austrian Conceptual artist Rainer Ganahl, who was in Nam June Paik's master class until 1991, visited his teacher at his home in New York when Paik did not come to the Düsseldorf Art Academy often enough for his liking, and established a permanent footing in the New York art scene. The painter Cornelius Völker studied with A. R. Penck and Dieter Krieg from 1989 until 1995. Junior Toscanelli studied with Markus Lüpertz from 1987 until 1994 and was in his master class. The photographer Stefan Hostettler was at the Academy from 1988 until 1995, at first studying with Irmin Kamp before switching to the 'free class' in Room 003. The sculptor Felix Schramm came from the Kounellis class while his younger colleague, Andreas Fischer, studied with Klaus Rinke and Georg Herold at the turn of the millennium.

The 1970s saw the emergence of a phenomenal migration: artists of the younger generation from across the Federal Republic – such as Helmut Schweizer, who took part in documenta 9 – moved to Düsseldorf but not to study there. They were lured by the opportunity to participate in the art scene that had sprung up around the Art Academy. Similarly, when the Iron Curtain fell in 1989/90, and especially during the subsequent decade, the migration of great talent from the former Communist bloc countries to the Düsseldorf Art Academy made itself felt there and in the city's art circles. One of the first of those artists to come to Düsseldorf was Danica Dakić from Sarajevo, who studied at the Düsseldorf Art Academy from 1988 until 1990, which enabled her to live safely in exile during the Yugoslav civil war and its aftermath and at the same time, although fully isolated from the upheavals, to plan and realise a work on the war that is among the contributions from Düsseldorf to have attracted the most attention in the art scene of its time. The collapse of the Soviet Union saw a number of students who were very well trained in the applied arts arrive at the Düsseldorf Art Academy from Belarus, among them Alexej Koschkarow, who was in the Schwegler class from 1993 until 1999 and now lives in New York. A somewhat later arrival but equally representative of this development is the Georgian artist Thea Djordjadze, who began to study with Dieter Krieg in 1995 and finished her Art Academy studies in 2001 in the master class taught by Rosemarie Trockel. In 2012 she was granted a solo show at documenta 13. Other examples of the migration from former Eastern bloc countries are the painter Oda Jaune, who came from Sofia in 1998 at the age of eighteen to study at the Düsseldorf Art Academy, subsequently married Jörg Immendorff, and is now successful in Paris, as well as the sculptor Leunora Salihu from Kosovo, who studied with Tony Cragg until 2009. The number of students from Asia has continued to rise since the 1980s: an early arrival was the painter Yong-Chang Chung, who studied with A. R. Penck from 1986 until 1991.

THE GALLERY SCENE EMIGRATION TAKES ITS TOLL IN THE MID-1990s

In around 1995 a massive emigration of Cologne contemporary art galleries to Berlin started. The Cologne gallery scene had been the most diverse in Europe in the 1970s and 1980s, when it provided an important environment in which numerous Art Academy graduates flourished. Cologne in particular was home to a large number of studios occupied by a younger generation of artists from many countries, just as Paris had been in 1945 and New York in the 1970s and 1980s. As late as 1992 Cologne gallerists were still belittling suggestions that the art scene might move to Berlin. Only a few years later almost of all them had decamped to the new capital with its low rents and once again vibrantly cosmopolitan atmosphere. Many graduates of the Düsseldorf Art Academy were also moving to Berlin.

The displacement of the art scene caused the Düsseldorf Art Academy to lose its context temporarily. It became noticeably more difficult for graduates to gain a foothold in the art industry. Two factors essential to Art Academy success since the 1960s had been the large number of important contemporary art galleries in Cologne and the dense clustering of major artists in Düsseldorf and Cologne, which was unique in western Europe, both of which could no longer be drawn on. A further disruptive factor was the weakness of the art market after the crisis in the early 1990s and the temporarily bad prospects for museums and other institutions that functioned as exhibition venues in Düsseldorf. The Kunsthalle shut down and its inventory faced an uncertain future. The Kunstverein was not very active, and dynamic institutions involved with contemporary and young art, such as K21 (an annexe to the Kunstsammlung Nordrhein-Westfalen) and KIT – Kunst im Tunnel [Art in the Tunnel] would not become established until after 2000.

In a situation like that neither students nor graduates of the Academy, let alone their professors, tended to be asked about what talent to look out for or where something new and viable was emerging. Under the impression that something had to be done and done as quickly as possible without waiting to be approached by a potential clientele, artists resorted to creating spaces for working and/or exhibiting work on and near Worringer Platz in the latter half of the 1990s. Their makeshift venues soon represented the cutting edge of art in Düsseldorf. They resembled the artist-run spaces in the United Kingdom, which anticipated and ushered in the London art boom after 2000 rather than today's off scene. Insiders flocked to Düsseldorf from elsewhere in the late 1990s just because of its self-organised art scene, and once again it was the Art Academy with its students and graduates which provided most of the protagonists of the revived scene.

Horten and SITE (as well as *SITE Magazine*), run by Petra Rincke, later a gallerist, and the sculptor Ralf Brög, who had studied with Cragg, Megert, and Merz, were important independent exhibition venues. The Kölnerstrasse Exhibition Space (later Alexanderstrasse Exhibition Space, and also adeline morlon art direction) was run by Alexander Jasch and Jens Ullrich, alumni of the class taught by Gerhard Merz. Other noteworthy artist-run spaces were the Böhlerwerke Studio Collective (*mayday* exhibition in 1998, with Olivia Berckemeyer, Björn Dahlem, Tatjana Doll, Claus Föttinger, Tine Furler, Sophie von Hellermann, Alexej Koschkarow, Svenja Kräh, Dietmar Lutz, Andre Niébur, Thea Djordjadze, et al.) and Parkhaus, an exhibition project launched in 1997 and still very active today. Parkhaus was founded by Karl Heinz Rummeny (an alumnus of the Hoehme class), Jost Wischnewski (who studied with Rinke), and Gregor Russ in the garden of the Malkasten [Paint Box] Association. This particular independent exhibition space, which for a while boasted Katharina Fritsch as its art director, represented an attempt to compensate for the lack of institutions and galleries.[34]

Michaela Odinius and Rupert Huber, who operated the Ego-Club, were the lynchpins of a studio house with very low rents for younger-generation artists which sprang up near the old Parcel Post Office on Worringer Platz next to the Central Train Station (now housing the Municipal Public Order Office and the rehearsal and alternative stage of the Düsseldorf Schauspielhaus [Theatre]. The hobbypopMUSEUM was a group of artists – Sophie von Hellermann, Dietmar Lutz, Christian Jendreiko, Matthias Lahme, André Niebur, Marie- Céline Schäfer, Tine Furler, Markus Vater, Olivia Berckemeyer, Björn Dahlem, and Thea Djordjadze – who banded together around 1997 to create a new, extravagantly multimedia site-specific spatial installation every Friday. With members taught by the likes of Dieter Krieg, Jan Dibbets, Rosemarie Trockel, Laurids Ortner, and Gerhard Merz, the hobbypopMUSEUM became a

Düsseldorf art scene export hit in the early years after the turn of the millennium, putting on brilliant shows in New York and San Francisco, at Tate Britain, and many other venues.[35]

After 2000 these novel groupings of artists who organised their own public appearances made a smooth transition to initiatives such as Konsortium (est. 2004), a combined studio collective and international exhibition space run by Lars Breuer, Sebastian Freytag, Jan Kämmerling, and Guido Münch jointly with Angela Fette, and the scatter-gather exhibition practice of present-day students who show their work in innumerable self-organised spaces in Düsseldorf and its environs while they are still at the Art Academy.

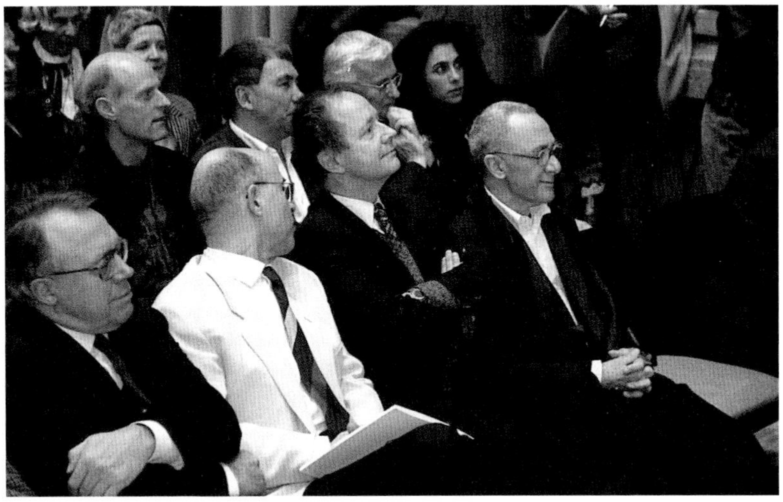

Fig. 10: From left to right: in front Walter Jürgen Hofmann, Konrad Klapheck, Werner Spies, and Gerhard Richter; behind them Tony Cragg, Fritz Schwegler, Heinrich Theissing, at the send-off for Gerhard Richter, 1994

THE TRANSITION TO A NEW GENERATION AT THE ART ACADEMY IN THE MID-1990s

That was the backdrop for a spectacular transition to a new generation of teachers that took place at the turn of the millennium. Gerhard Richter had left the Art Academy in 1994 (Figs. 10, 11). Nam June Paik and Günther Uecker retired in 1995, followed a year later by Bernd Becher, Gotthard Graubner, and Nan Hoover (Fig. 12). In 1998 Josef Paul Kleihues retired, Alphonso Hüppi a year later, and in 2001 Professors Fritz Schwegler, Jannis Kounellis, and Christian Megert. Konrad Klapheck continued to teach on a short-term contract after officially retiring but only until 2002, when he as well as Luise Kimme and Dieter Krieg stopped teaching. In 2004 Jan Dibbets and Klaus Rinke left the Academy whereas Magdalena Jetelová left to teach at the Munich Fine Arts Academy in 2004, followed a year later by Gerhard Merz. After retiring, Rissa had a short-term contract to teach at the Düsseldorf Art Academy until 2007, when she ceased to do so, along with Walter Nikkels. They were followed in 2008 by former rector Irmin Kamp.

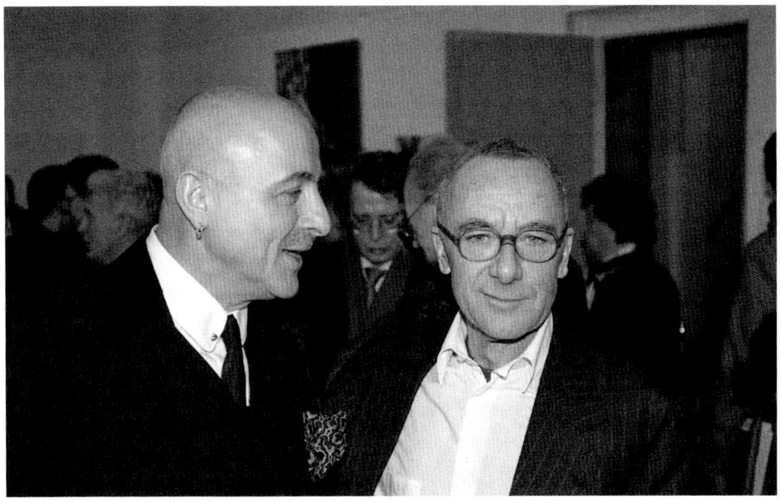

Fig. 11: Markus Lüpertz and Gerhard Richter, send-off for Gerhard Richter, 1994

The change in style embodied by Markus Lüpertz as rector was revealed even more clearly by appointments made thereafter. A. R. Penck, appointed professor of graphic art as early as 1989, was an exponent of neo-Expressionism.

In 1996 Jörg Immendorff, who had studied with Beuys, was appointed professor of painting. Immendorff's work had been distinguished in the late 1970s by a politically motivated, expressive style of figurative painting (Fig. 13). Immendorff,

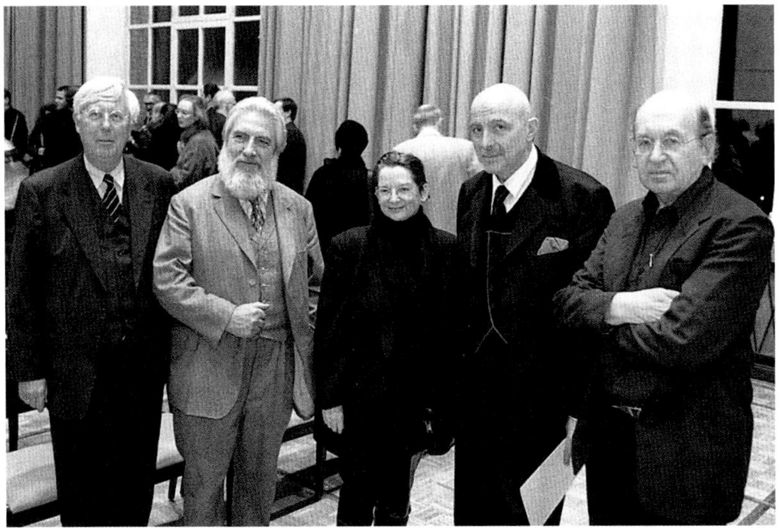

Fig. 12: From left to right: Josef Paul Kleihues, Gotthard Graubner, Nan Hoover, Markus Lüpertz, and Bernd Becher, 1996

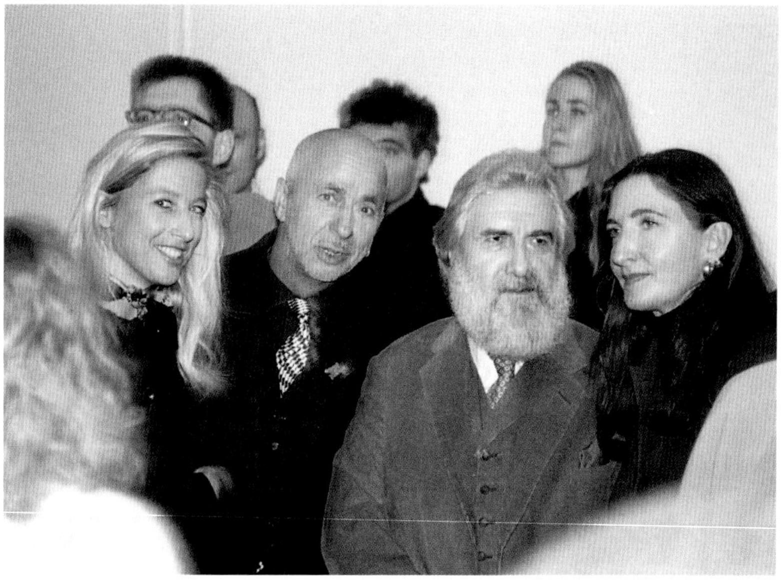

Fig. 13: Jörg Immendorff, Gotthard Graubner, and Kitty Kemr, 1994

Lüpertz, and Penck together made for a new focus on figurative painting at the Art Academy concomitantly with a change in the appearance of the Academy interior. The number of students specialising in painting rose considerably in the years that followed. Although the walls of Art Academy corridors revealed the patina of decades, they had been empty except for a few lockers until the late 1990s. Then they began to fill up with stacked canvases (Fig. 14) and the walls were repainted.

The appointments made to fill vacancies on the teaching staff express the above-mentioned transition to a new generation. The appointment of Rosemarie Trockel to teach in 1998 brought one of the most style-defining contemporary women sculptors to the Academy. Equally distinguished teaching appointments were those of the abstract painter Helmut Federle (*1944) to teach painting, and of Georg Herold (*1947), Siegfried Anzinger (*1953), and Albert Oehlen (*1954), three major talents representative of the artistic awakening around 1980 (Fig. 15). Thomas Ruff (*1958), who succeeded his teacher, Bernd Becher, in the photography class in 1999, was another world-class artist. On Bernd Becher's retirement in 1996, the Canadian photo artist and theorist Jeff Wall was appointed to succeed him, which might have meant international success and been a great enrichment for the Academy. Finding it difficult to teach on a transatlantic basis, however, Wall left after a clash with a student.

The years since the turn of the millennium have been marked by epochal changes in art academies worldwide, with globalisation, digitalisation, and the emergence of new forms of publicity the paramount contributing factors.[36] In the European Union the entire tertiary education sector was restructured on the lines of the Bologna Process to lead to bachelor's and master's degrees. Confronted with this situation, Markus Lüpertz succeeded in preventing the implementation of this system in the fine arts sector, which would have entailed considerable 'schoolification' and bureaucratisation, and in upholding the constitutional freedoms of the Düsseldorf Art Academy; a decline in its influence as an institution would have been otherwise inexorable. Thus he may be said to have re-established the Art Academy in the new millennium. Maintaining the traditional form of the Art Academy with students free to plan their studies as they wish and the system of artists teaching classes was probably his most important act as rector. To the present day, the preservation of the traditional system has ensured the liveliness and unconstrained atmosphere reigning at the Academy. Anthony Cragg described this in his first speech as rector in 2009:

'He took over the Academy as rector in 1988 and at the time was supposed to implement in this institution the new Higher Education Law that had been the subject of controversy for so many years. To do so, he had to restructure the curriculum, the examination regulations, and the departments to match. He had to plan the Academy in its present state in two buildings and the necessary allocation of space, deal with the installation of classrooms, workshops, the library, and the Architecture Department. He placed the financial basis of this institution on a very firm foundation through meaningful cooperation with the then chancellor, renovated the building inside and out, and always ensured that the vacancies for professors and technical assistants at the Academy were filled with highly qualified artists. You can see this in the present staff and that during his entire time in office. He always implemented the amendments to the Higher Education Law with an eye to implementing those legally binding revisions in ways that made sense for this institution. And, finally, he played a key role in ensuring that not only the Düsseldorf Art Academy but all art academies in Germany could avoid having to apply the bachelor and master system to art academies, and in so doing he prevented the demise of a highly successful and universally admired system.'[37]

A symbol of the self-image and awareness of tradition that the Art Academy publicly represents is the Academy Gallery that was inaugurated in 2005 in public rooms on the Rhine Embankment, where the New Collection is exhibited. This collection comprises works by professors who have worked at the

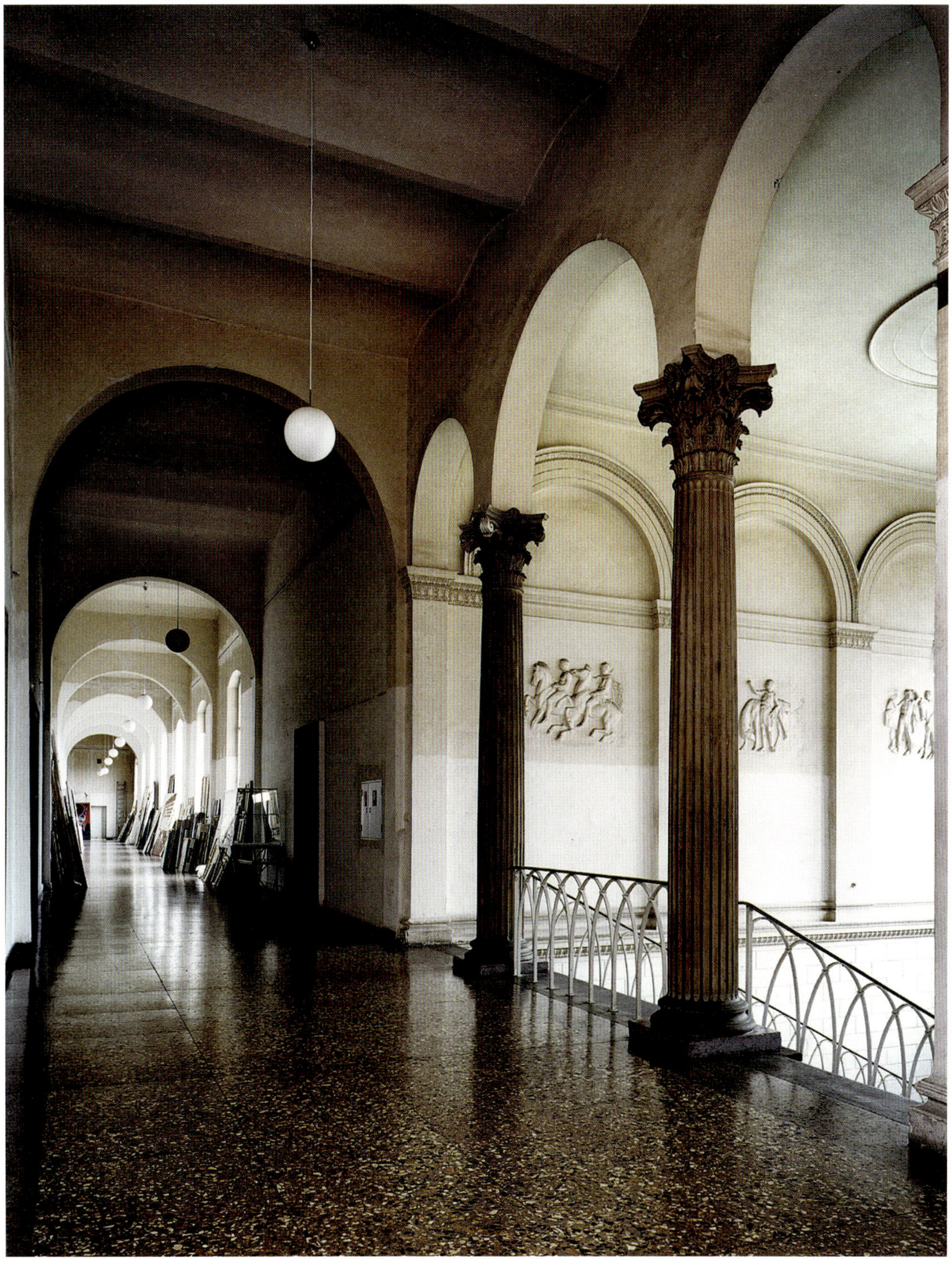

Fig. 14: An interior view of the second floor of the Düsseldorf Art Academy, 2013

Academy in the years since 1945 as well as artworks by important graduates of the Academy.

The teaching appointments made during the first decade of the new millennium completed the transition to a new generation described above. Daniel Buren (*1938), a leading exponent of Conceptual and Minimal Art, had already been a visiting professor at the Academy in 1979/80, which exerted a lasting influence on a number of artists who are well known today. From 2002 until 2006 Daniel Buren substituted as a professor of painting. In 2003 two international exponents of cutting-edge sculpture were brought to the Art Academy: Rita McBride (*1960) from the United States, since the 1990s one of the most highly regarded artists for public spaces whose works deal with sociological and urbanist structures (shown on p. 279), and Didier Vermeiren (*1951) from Belgium, who subverts the concept of sculpture in Postmodernism by making the plinth his subject (Fig. 16). The following year saw the appointment of Martin Gostner (*1957) from Austria, the author of acclaimed culturally critical installations, and Thomas Grünfeld (*1956), an object artist whose diverse oeuvre oscillates in a charged field between painting and sculpture, art and (furniture) design and who became famous for hybrid beings collaged from the bodies of stuffed animals (shown on p. 288). With the addition in 2009 of the important English sculptor Richard Deacon (*1949), whose works in open and curvilinear forms make him, like Tony Cragg, an important representative of the renewal of British sculpture in post-Minimalism, the field of three-dimensional art had been thoroughly reinvigorated in the space of just a few years.

The professors appointed to teach painting at that time are similarly distinguished: Herbert Brandl (*1959), together with Siegfried Anzinger, who had already been called to the Academy in 1997, the most important Austrian painter of his generation and an exponent of abstraction and landscape painting; Peter Doig (*1959), since the 1990s a global superstar of contemporary art with his intensely colourist painting and mythological content; Tal R (*1967), one of the most highly regarded painters of the in-between generation, who works with the inclusion of moments from music, youth, and off culture; and Andreas Schulze (*1955), a leading representative of the group of early 1980s painters known as the Neue Wilden and the author of an essentially figurative stance in contemporary painting. When Thomas Ruff, internationally famous for his large portraits and photographs of stars, particularly at night, left his post as professor of photography in 2006, the class was taught

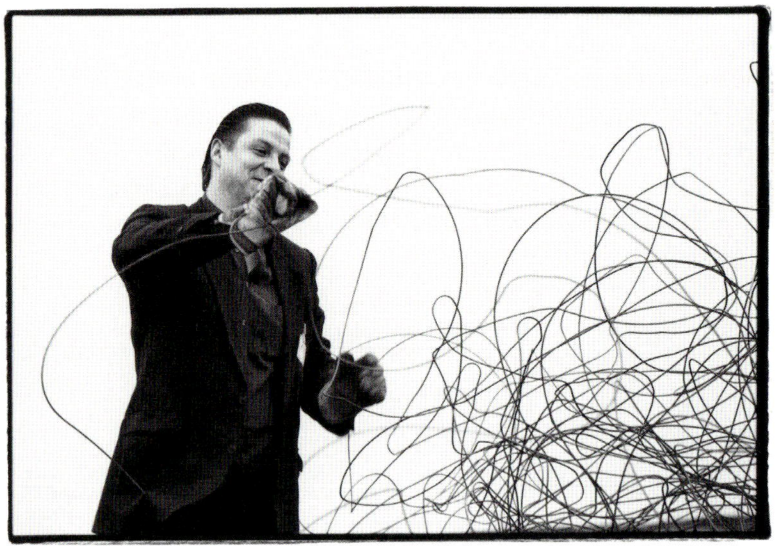

Fig. 15: Georg Herold setting up Orakel *[Oracle] at the exhibition* Bilderstreit *[Iconoclastic Controversy], Cologne, 1989*

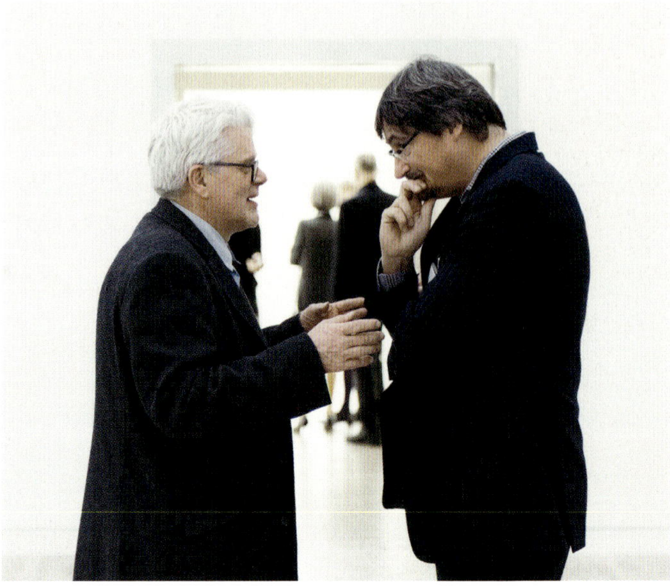

Fig. 16: Didier Vermeiren and Harald Klingelhöller in conversation, sculpture exhibition at K20, 2013

over the short term by Benjamin Katz and Albrecht Fuchs until the American Conceptual artist Christopher Williams (*1956) was appointed in 2008. Williams, a pupil of John Baldessari's, is at present the leading exponent of Conceptual Art based on photography.

Since 2002 Udo Dziersk (*1961) has been a professor in the orientation course for first-year students. Dziersk, who had studied from 1983 until 1991 at the Art Academy with Gerhard Richter and Markus Lüpertz and had finished a master class with distinction, is known for 'pictograms and detailed painterly formulated arrangements [that] form [...] an exciting confrontation.'[38]

ANTHONY CRAGG'S RECTORATE

The appointment of Anthony Cragg as rector in 2009 to succeed Markus Lüpertz on his retirement was admired both at the Academy and outside it in that an internationally influential artist since the 1970s could, along with a spectacular relaunch of his own work on the global exhibition circuit, also manage to revive an institution of this calibre (Fig. 17). Lüpertz had left to his successor several vacant professorships with which the new rector could act immediately. Hence at the very beginning of his rectorate even more world-class artists were appointed to teach, a policy that was perceived by the public at large as a 'boost' for the Art Academy and also showed that the role of women artists had been consolidated at the Academy in recent years. The appointments of women were as follows: Tomma Abts (*1967), the 2006 Turner Prize winner, who represents a quintessential stance in contemporary geometric-abstract art; Katharina Fritsch (*1956), a former student of Fritz Schwegler's and German representative to the 1995 Venice Bi-

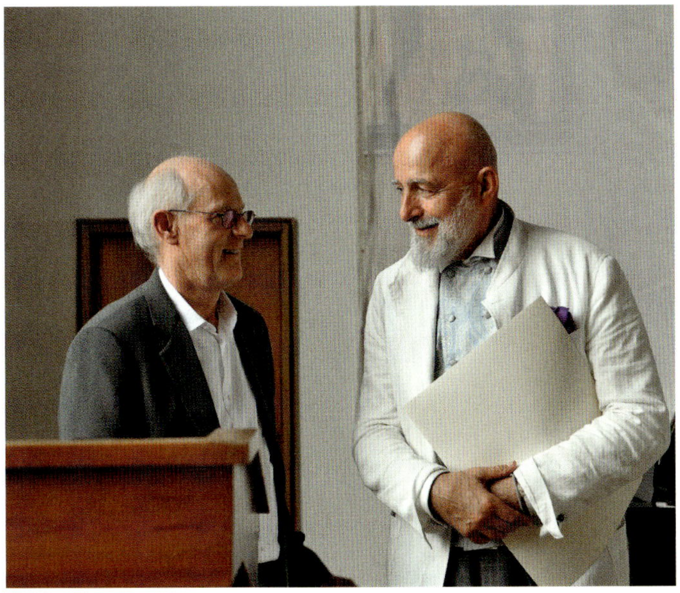

Fig. 17: Anthony Cragg taking over the rectorate from Markus Lüpertz, 2009

ennale, an artist who is present on the international scene and famous for her figurative sculpture, which looks both virtual and realistic; and Katharina Grosse (*1961), a former student of Graubner's and the author of a widely acclaimed oeuvre of abstract painting that extends to installation. Andreas Gursky (*1955), who had studied with Bernd Becher and whose defining photographic images are shown worldwide, was another Cragg appointment. Eberhard Havekost (*1967) also came to the Academy, a German painter of the middle generation who engages in a dialogue with photography, and Marcel Odenbach (*1953), the most important German video artist of his generation. The English painter Lucy McKenzie (*1977) was a professor of painting on a short-term contract from 2011 until 2013. Gereon Krebber (*1973), who had studied with Tony Cragg and Hubert Kiecol and later at the Royal College of Art in London, is another professor appointed during Cragg's tenure. He is the author of boldly invasive sculpture often made from the most rudimentary of mundane materials.[39]

On the whole, a team of artists was created that can beyond all doubt be called one of the most brilliant in the history of the Art Academy as far as the stature and reputation of those artists in the contemporary art scene are concerned.

IN CONCLUSION

Two decisions about art shaped the time span discussed here: on the one hand, the inner identity of the classes which was built up solely on the basis of the experience in art of the artists who taught them was upheld. All classes compete against each other in the annual *Rundgang*, which is open to the public, a policy that forcefully promotes the individual dynamic of each class.[40] On the other hand, the tradition at this Art Academy of teaching as promoting discussion about form in art and thus reaching an understanding has been safeguarded.[41]

In comparison to the late 1990s, the institutional environment surrounding the Art Academy has noticeably recovered lost ground. A new dynamic is palpably present in the opening of K21 as the extension of the Kunstsammlung Nordrhein-Westfalen in the Ständehaus, the Museum Kunstpalast, and KIT – Kunst im Tunnel, dedicated to younger artists, including those at the Art Academy, in the increased number of visitors to the Kunsthalle and the Kunstverein, the inauguration of new galleries, and the opening of private collections to the public. Moreover, an organic infrastructure of artists working internationally, which includes jobs for assistants, and galleries both large and small, has survived since the 1950s so that Academy students and recent graduates can find more art-related work than almost anywhere else in Europe where art academies are located. The current dynamic is also shown in the countless exhibitions organised in the city and environs by students every year, a cultural activity that contributes just as much to the exceptional weight the Art Academy carries in Düsseldorf as it does to the acquisition of early professional experience by the aspiring young artists.

Since August 2013 Rita McBride has been rector of the Art Academy, only the second woman to have held this post since the institution was founded 240 years ago. She is also only the second rector to have non-German nationality, and, finally, only the second to be a native speaker of English. The appointment as rector of an internationally renowned artist, who has taught a sculpture class here for ten years and knows the Art Academy so well, is a clear indication of the continuity of the Academy from within and from knowledge of its structures, which is one of the secrets of the Düsseldorf Art Academy's success.

NOTES

1 Kasper König (ed.), *von hier aus. 2 Monate neue deutsche Kunst in Düsseldorf*, exhib. cat. Düsseldorf, Cologne 1984. Even though the international art scene was impressed, the reaction shown in Federal German newspapers and of critics was reticent. See Annie Pohlen, 'von hier aus. Zwei Monate neue deutsche Kunst in Halle 13 der Düsseldorfer Messe (19 September–2 December 1984)', *Kunstforum International – von hier aus. Dokumentation einer überflüssigen Ausstellung*, Vol. 75, September/October 1984, pp. 37–117; ibid., a valuable photo documentation of the exhibition by Hans Zywicki, pp. 43–115; Axel Hecht, 'von hier aus', *ART. das kunstmagazin*, No. 11/84, pp. 55–61, also with photos of the exhibition.

2 They were Marina Abramović and Ulay, Lothar Baumgarten, Bernd and Hilla Becher, Joseph Beuys, Holger Bunk, Walter Dahn, Jiří Georg Dokoupil, Gerald Domenig, Felix Droese, Katharina Fritsch, Thomas Huber, Jörg Immendorff, Hubert Kiecol, Anselm Kiefer, Imi Knoebel, Silke Leverkühne, Markus Lüpertz, Gerhard Merz, Reinhard Mucha, Gruppe Normal (Peter Angermann, Jan Knap, Milan Kunc), Marcel Odenbach, Albert Oehlen, Markus Oehlen, Nam June Paik, Blinky Palermo, A. R. Penck, Sigmar Polke, Gerhard Richter, Ulrike Rosenbach, Dieter Roth, Reiner Ruthenbeck, Ulrich Rückriem, Andreas Schulze, Thomas Schütte, and Norbert Tadeusz.

3 The ambition of working on a level with the United States again became clear in 1988/89 at the dual exhibition *Binationale*, which showed German and American late 1980s art both in Düsseldorf (Kunsthalle, Kunstsammlung Nordrhein-Westfalen, and the Kunstverein) and in Boston (the Institute of Contemporary Art and the Museum of Fine Art), where the Düsseldorf Art Academy was represented just as much as at the exhibition *von hier aus*.

4 They were Walter Dahn, Gerald Domenig, Felix Droese, Katharina Fritsch, Thomas Huber, Jan Knap, Silke Leverkühne, Reinhard Mucha, Markus Oehlen, Andreas Schulze, and Thomas Schütte.

5 Jiří Georg Dokoupil had a short-term teaching contract at the Düsseldorf Art Academy in 1983/84.

6 Meuser, a sculptor and object artist, studied with Joseph Beuys and Erwin Heerich at the Düsseldorf Art Academy from 1968 to 1976.

7 Bernd Becher 'made photography very important in art. Under his aegis the Becher class became a global concept. From this class a generation of artists emerged that has been acclaimed worldwide.' Anthony Cragg, address given at the Academic Ceremonies on 2 November 2009 in the Great Hall of the Düsseldorf Art Academy. Also see the essay by Maren Polte on photography at the Düsseldorf Art Academy in the present volume, pp. 310–347.

8 On this also Klaus Rinke in the present volume, pp. 65–70.

9 Cragg (see n. 7).

10 Vanessa Sondermann, 'Rissa', in: Siegfried Gohr (ed.), *Akademie-Galerie, Die Neue Sammlung, 2005–2009*, Düsseldorf 2009, p. 168.

11 The painter and poet André Thomkins (1930–1985) was a professor of painting at the Art Academy from 1971 until 1973. He was the only one to deliver on his threat to leave the Academy should Beuys have to go after Beuys was dismissed from the Academy in the midst of all the controversy surrounding him.

12 Ulrich Rückriem was a professor of sculpture from 1984 until 1988 but then left to take up a post at the Städelschule in Frankfurt.

13 Benjamin H. D. Buchloh now teaches at Harvard after many years of teaching at Columbia University in New York.

14 See on this Robert Fleck, *Die Biennale von Venedig. Eine Geschichte des 20. Jahrhunderts*, Hamburg 2009, pp. 42–63.

15 Fleck (see n. 14), pp. 115–135.

16 Ibid., pp. 138–140.

17 Ibid., pp. 156f.

18 Ibid., pp. 164–171.

19 Ibid., p. 172.

20 Ibid., pp. 184f.

21 Ibid., p. 186.

22 Ibid., pp. 186f.

23 Ibid., pp. 189–191.

24 Ibid., pp. 182f.

25 Ibid., p. 180.

26 Ibid., pp. 203f.

27 Ibid., pp. 205–207.

28 Ibid., pp. 207–209.

29 An architect and professor at the Düsseldorf Art Academy, Hans Hollein curated the Austrian Pavilion from 1978 to 1990, followed by Kasper König in 2003 and Robert Fleck in 2007, both professors of art and public relations.

30 See Siegfried Gohr, 'Vorwort' [Foreword], in: Akademie-Galerie (ed.), *Gotthard Graubner*, exhib. cat. Düsseldorf 2013, pp. 5f.; here: p. 5.

31 Born in 1941, professor of painting from 1986 until 2009, rector from 1988 until 2009; on this also see Markus Lüpertz in the present volume, pp. 71–75.

32 See Fritz Neumeyer, 'Der Traum vom eigenen Haus', in: *Hubert Kiecol. Separee public*, exhib. cat. Saarbrücken, Cologne 2009, pp. 71–73; here: p. 71.

33 WP8 still exists. Those participating included at first Tina Assmann, Fenja Braster, Andreas Gursky, Claus Föttinger, Heinz Hausmann, Hendrik Krawen, Michael Krome, and Gertrud Peters. See www.WP8.org (last retrieved 14 September 2015).

34 This forum grew out of the initiative against demolishing the Kunstpalast and for saving the Kunsthalle from a similar threat. Katharina Fritsch ran the Malkasten from 2000 until 2002 with Herbert Koller, who had studied with Günther Uecker in the 1980s, Helmut Schweizer, Bogomir Ecker, the art critic Carl Friedrich Schröer, and Nicola Schrudde, a young, active student.

35 The group is still active. Its members are Sophie von Hellermann, Christian Jendreiko, Matthias Lahme, Dietmar Lutz, André Niebur, and Marie-Céline Schäfer.

36 See Robert Fleck, 'New Forms of Art Schools', in: *Criticism, Legitimacy and Transgression*, Amsterdam 2001, pp. 84–87. Volume III, Issue 2/3 of *European Journal of Arts Education*.

37 Tony Cragg, address given at the Academic Ceremonies on 2 November in the Great Hall of the Düsseldorf Art Academy.

38 Vanessa Sondermann, 'Udo Dziersk', in: Gohr (see n. 10), p. 44.

39 The author holds the professorship for art and public relations, since 2012 reinstated by Tony Cragg; it was held by Kaspar König between 1985 and 1988.

40 In February 2013 the *Rundgang* attracted 44,000 visitors in five days, which matches record numbers of visitors to the most visited museums, such as the Louvre in Paris and the MoMa in New York.

41 The author in conversation with a student who had transferred from Vienna to Düsseldorf in 2012: 'In Vienna we looked for subjects that can be composed in an interesting way. In Düsseldorf one works on form.'

SELECTED WORKS BY PROFESSORS FROM 1985 TO THE PRESENT

Gotthard Graubner
Günther Uecker
Helmut Federle
Markus Lüpertz
Michael Buthe
Peter Doig
Reinhold Braun
Siegfried Anzinger
Franz Eggenschwiler
Udo Dziersk
A. R. Penck
Rosemarie Trockel
Eberhard Havekost
Herbert Brandl
Tomma Abts
Tal R
Jörg Immendorff
Dieter Krieg
Katharina Grosse
Andreas Schulze
Albert Oehlen
Gerhard Hoehme
Didier Vermeiren
Rita McBride
Ulrich Rückriem

Georg Herold
Hubert Kiecol
Gereon Krebber
Magdalena Jetelová
Anthony Cragg
Richard Deacon
Martin Gostner
Thomas Grünfeld
Lucy McKenzie
Katharina Fritsch
Andreas Gursky
Jeff Wall
Marcel Odenbach
Thomas Ruff
Christopher Williams
Gerhard Merz
Odile Decq
Karl-Heinz Petzinka
Elia Zenghelis
Max Dudler
Laurids Ortner
Jórunn Ragnarsdóttir
Nathalie de Vries
Axel Schultes
Nan Hoover

Gotthard Graubner, Ohne Titel (Jadegarten) [untitled (Jade Garden)], 2002, oil on canvas, 162 × 182 × 2 cm, Akademie Galerie – Die Neue Sammlung, Düsseldorf

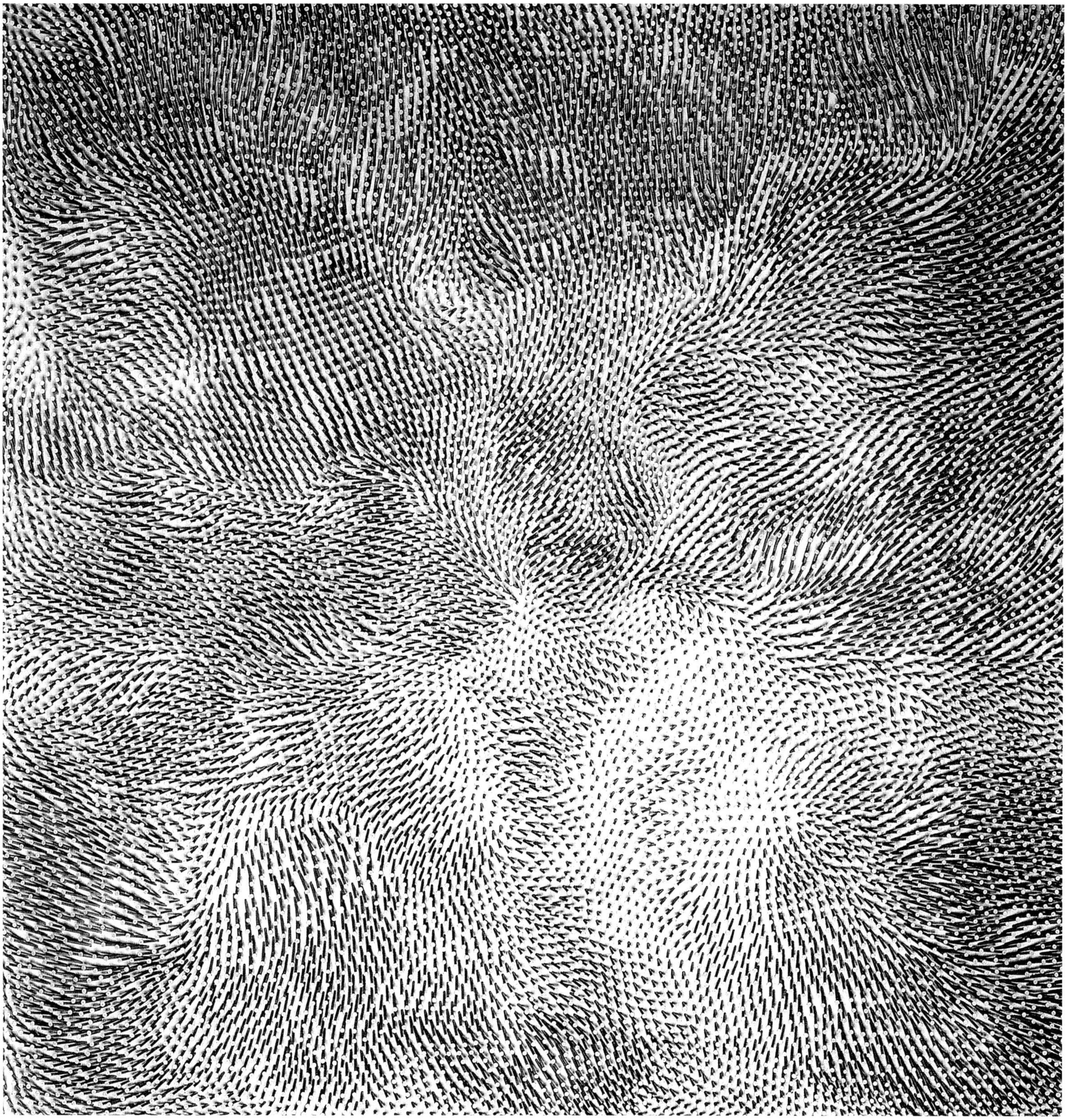

Günther Uecker, Feld *[Field], 1974, nails on canvas, on wood, 160 × 160 × 17 cm, Museum Frieder Burda, Baden-Baden*

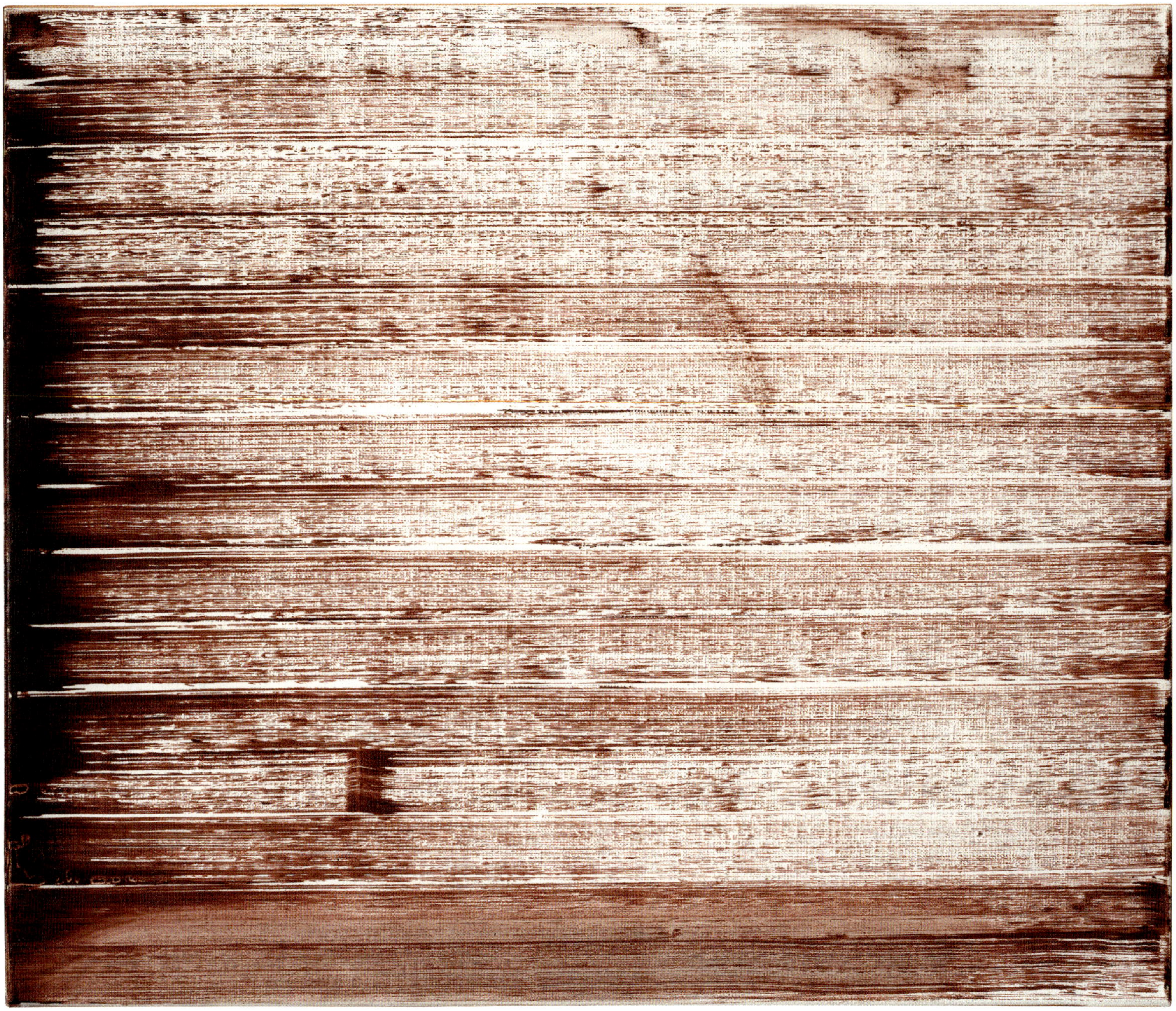

Helmut Federle, Legion XXVI, *1999, acrylic on canvas, 50 × 60 cm, privately owned, courtesy of Galerie nächst St. Stephan Rosemarie Schwarzwälder, Vienna*

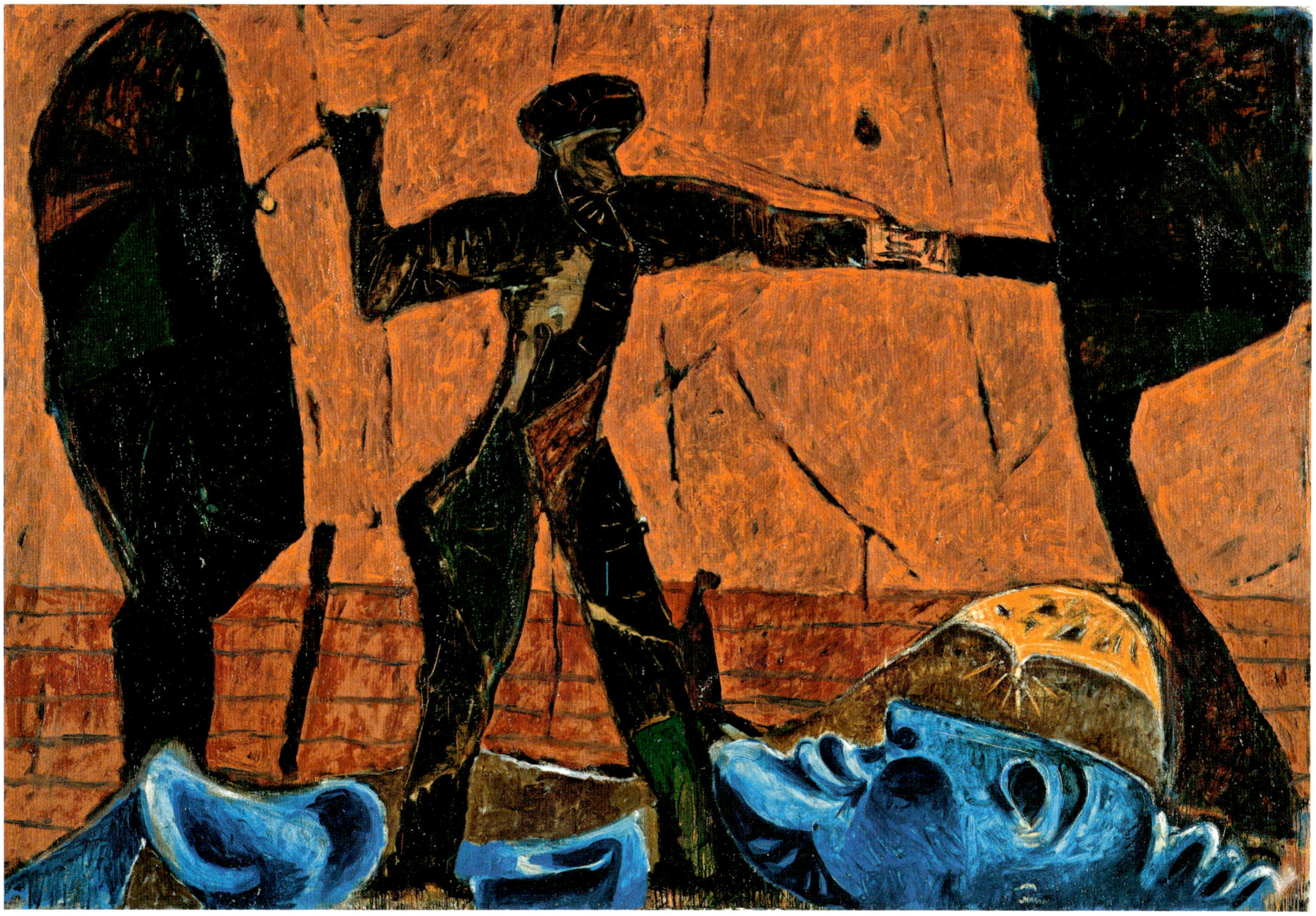

Markus Lüpertz, 5 Bilder über das mykenische Lächeln – Kain und Abel *[5 Pictures on the Mycenean Smile – Cain and Abel], 1985, oil on canvas, 270 × 400 cm, courtesy of Galerie Michael Werner, Cologne, and Märkisch Wilmersdorf*

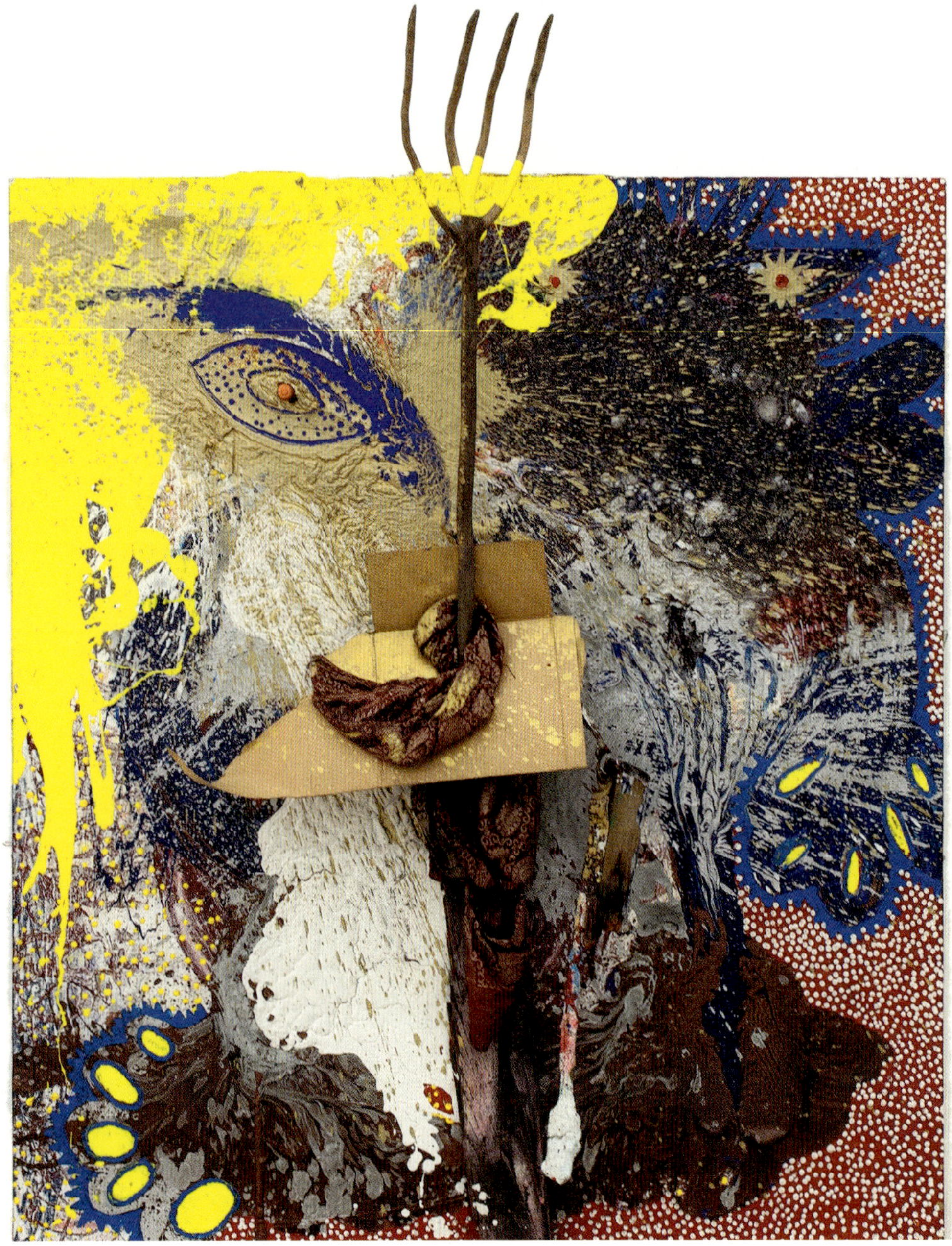

Michael Buthe, Landschaft (spanische Energie) *[Landscape (Spanish Energy)], 1985, mixed media (wood, cardboard, brocade, acrylic) on canvas, 185 × 163 × 38 cm, Michael Buthe Estate, Cologne, courtesy of Galerie Thomas Flor, Düsseldorf*

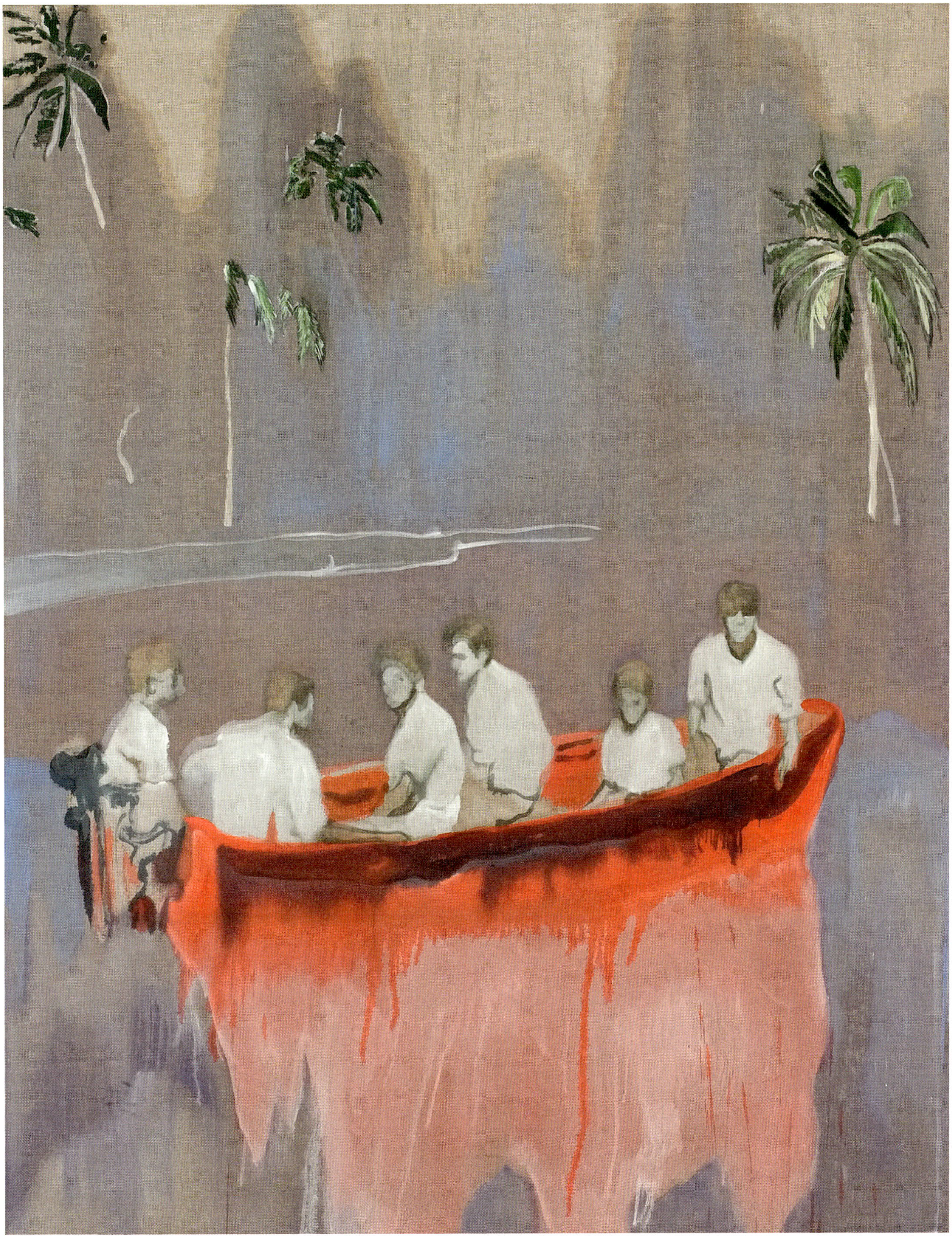

Peter Doig, Figures in Red Boat, *2005–07, oil on canvas, 250 × 200 cm, private collection, courtesy of Michael Werner Gallery, New York/London*

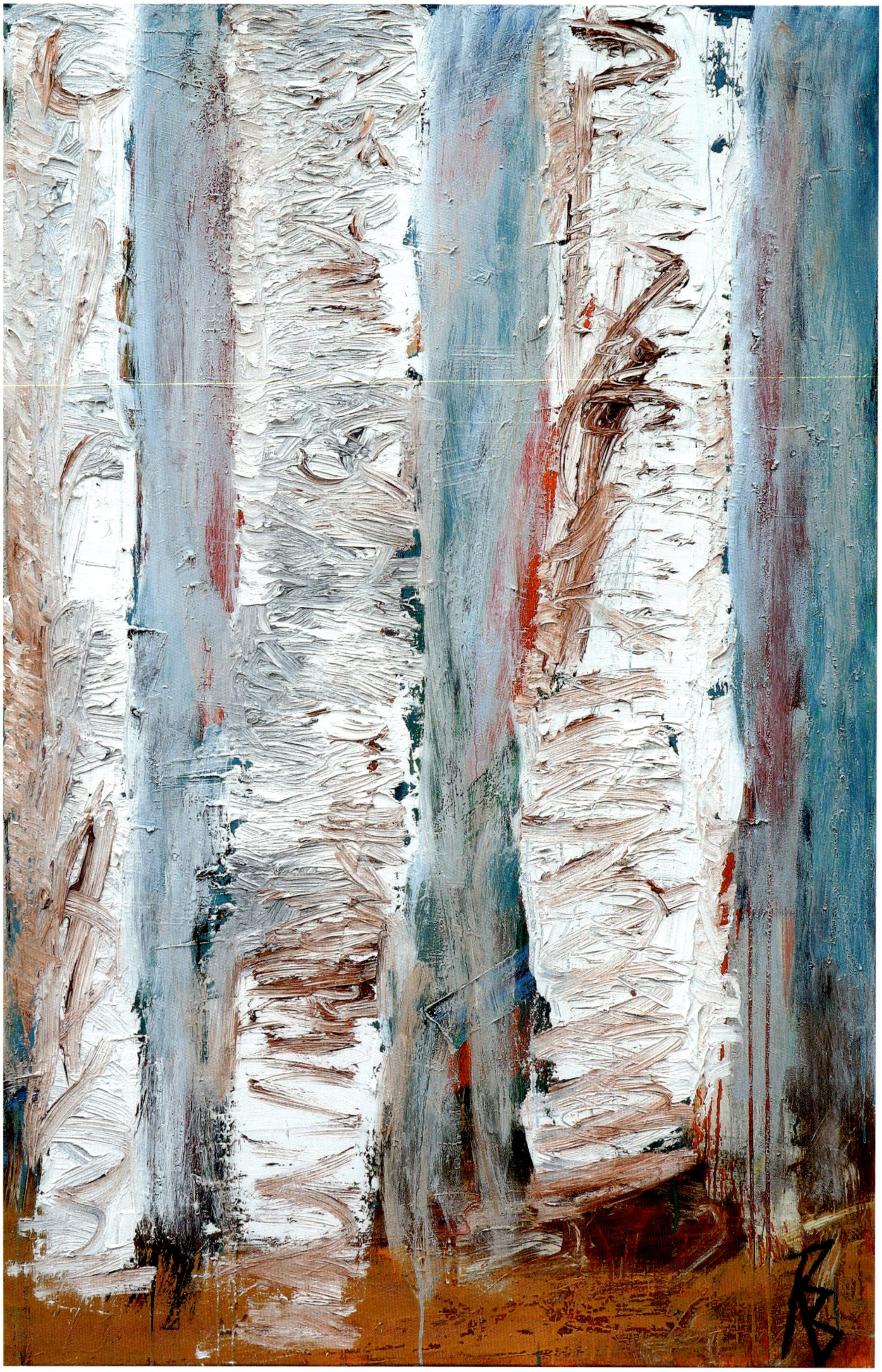

Reinhold Braun, Drei *[Three], 2002/03, oil on canvas, 150 × 100 cm, courtesy of Galerie Supper, Baden-Baden*

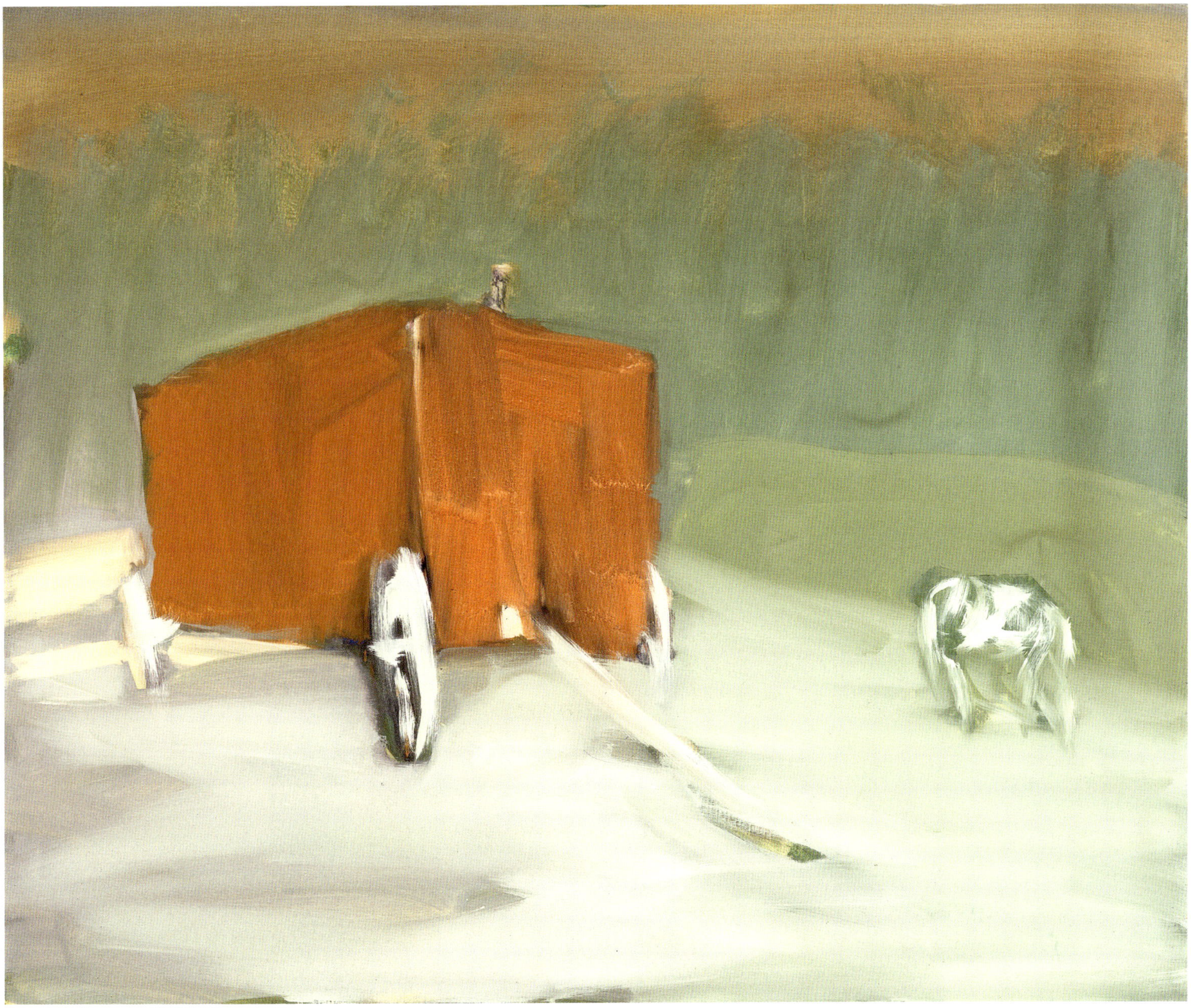

Siegfried Anzinger, Oranger Karren *[Orange Cart], 1996, distemper on canvas, 130 × 160 cm, private collection*

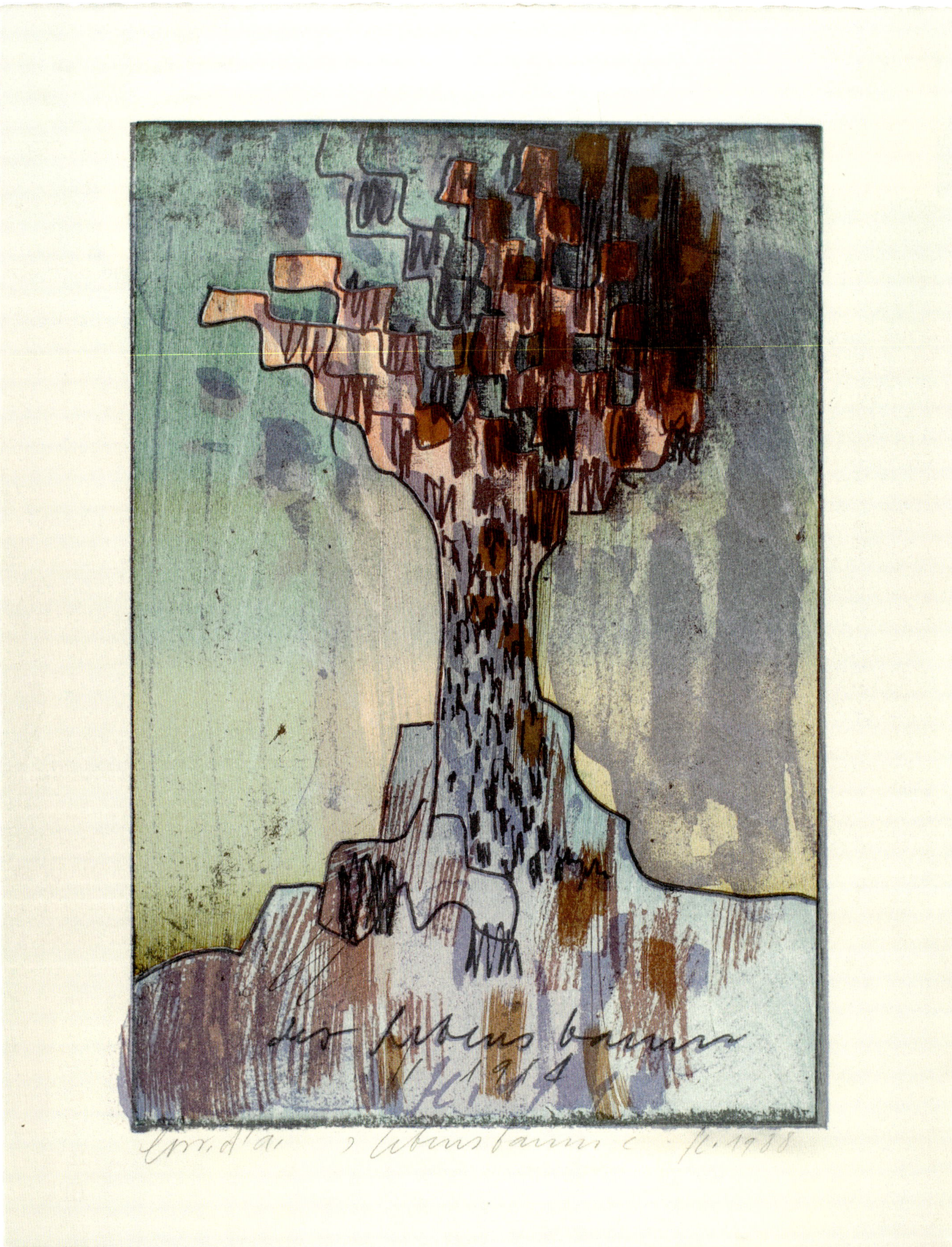

Franz Eggenschwiler, Lebensbaum *[Tree of Life], 1988, lithograph, 57 × 45 cm, Akademie-Galerie – Die Neue Sammlung, Düsseldorf*

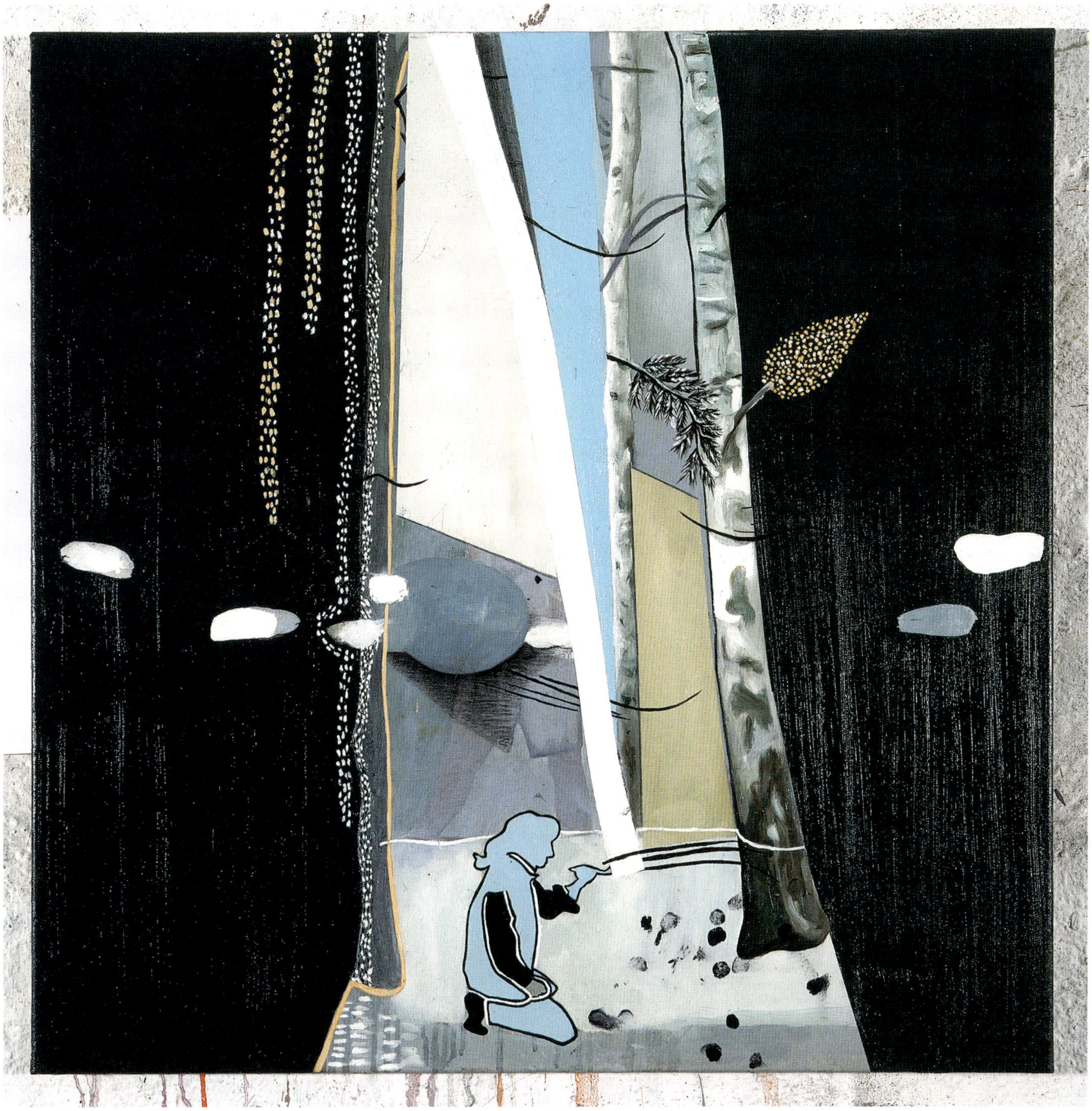

Udo Dziersk, Malerin *[Painter], 2003, oil on canvas, 80 × 80 cm, Akademie-Galerie – Die Neue Sammlung, Düsseldorf*

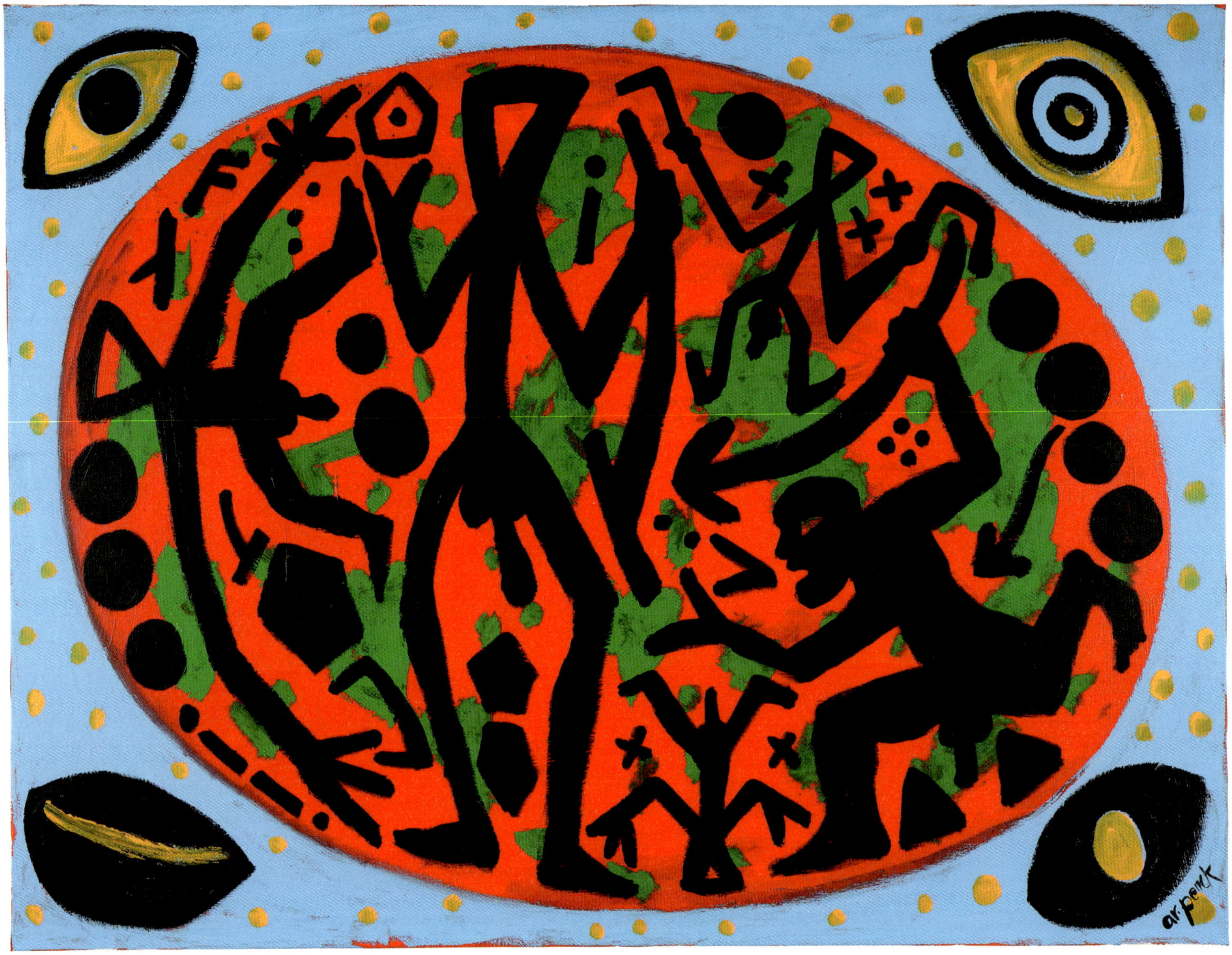

A. R. Penck, Weltbild XXXX *[World View XXXX], 1996, oil on canvas, 150 × 200 cm, Akademie-Galerie – Die Neue Sammlung, Düsseldorf*

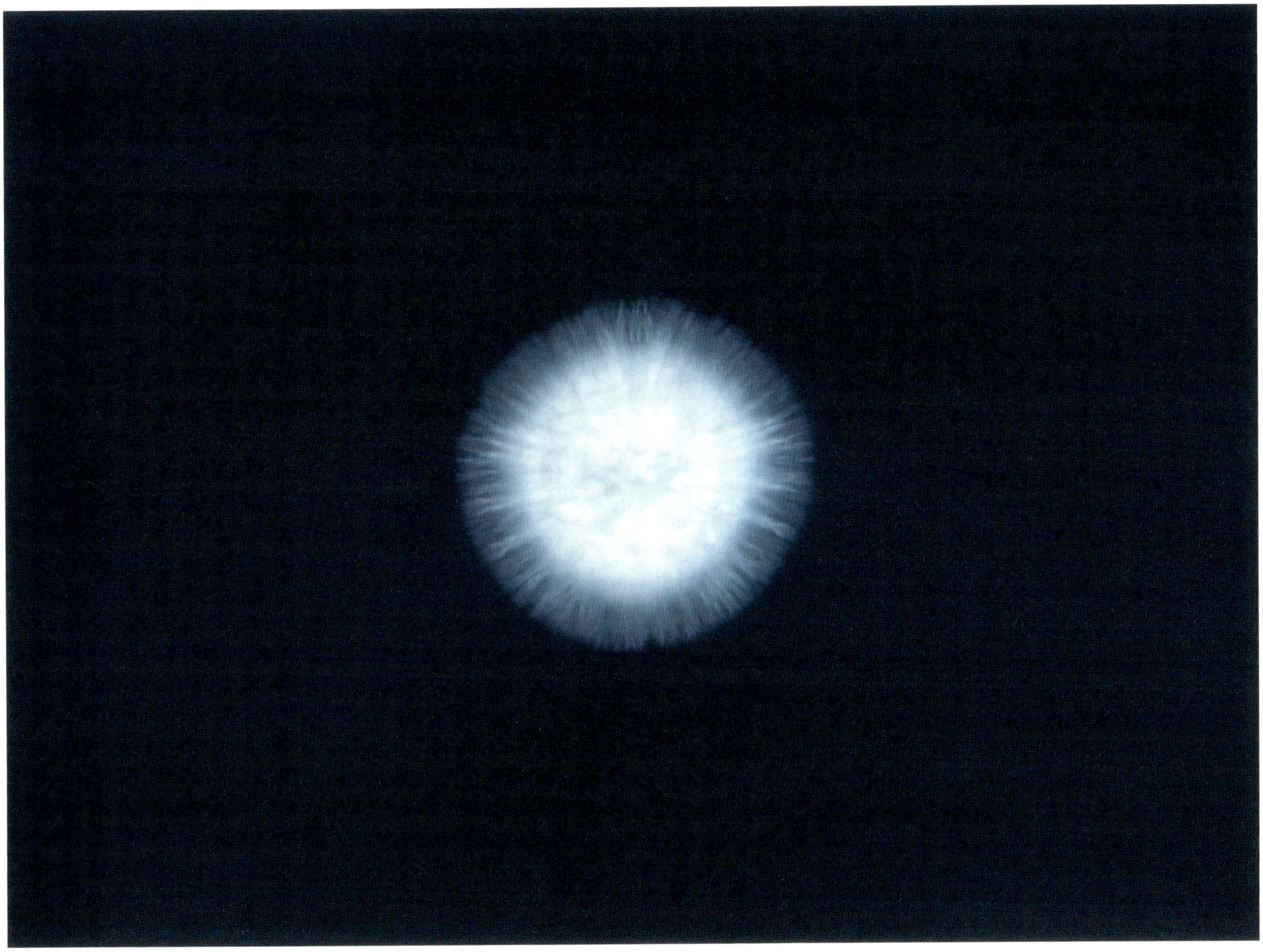

Rosemarie Trockel, Harem Concept, *1988, batik on cotton, 160 × 220 cm, courtesy of Sprüth Magers, Berlin/London*

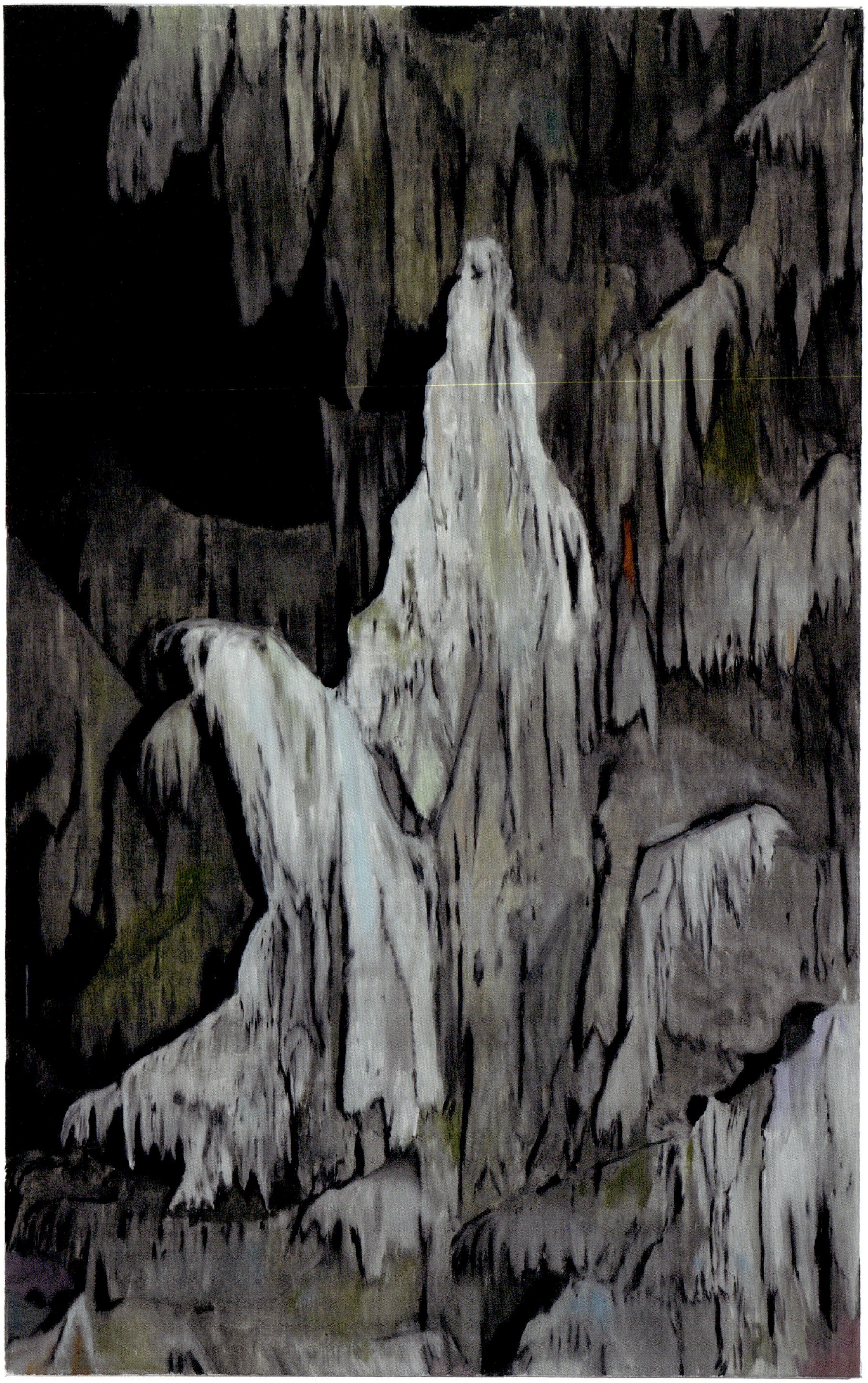

Eberhard Havekost, Gast 1 B10 *[Guest 1 B10], 2010, oil on canvas, 200 × 130 cm, courtesy of White Cube, London, and Galerie Gebr. Lehmann, Berlin/Dresden*

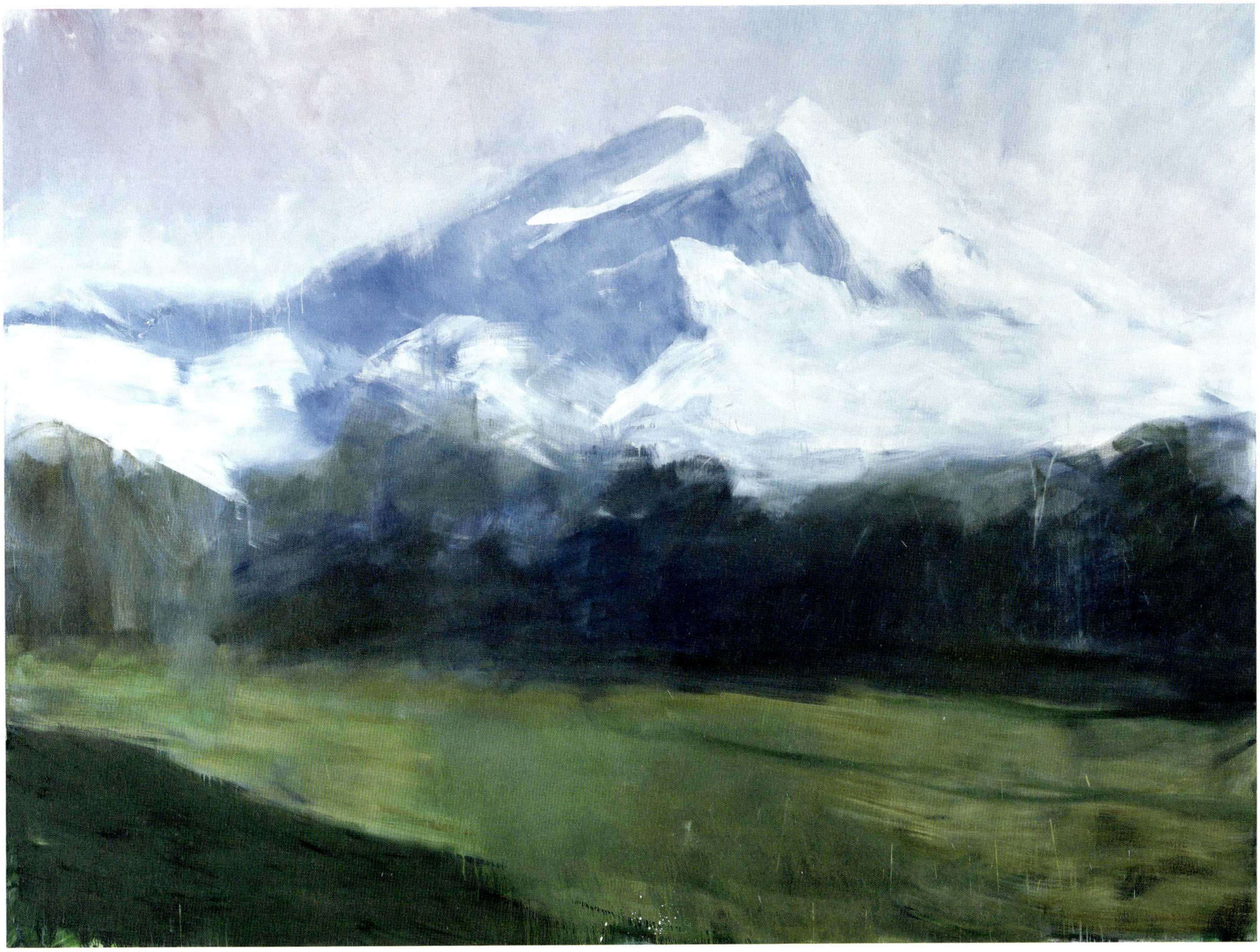

Herbert Brandl, Ohne Titel [untitled], 2004, oil on canvas, 290 × 400 cm, courtesy of Galerie nächst St. Stephan Rosemarie Schwarzwälder, Vienna

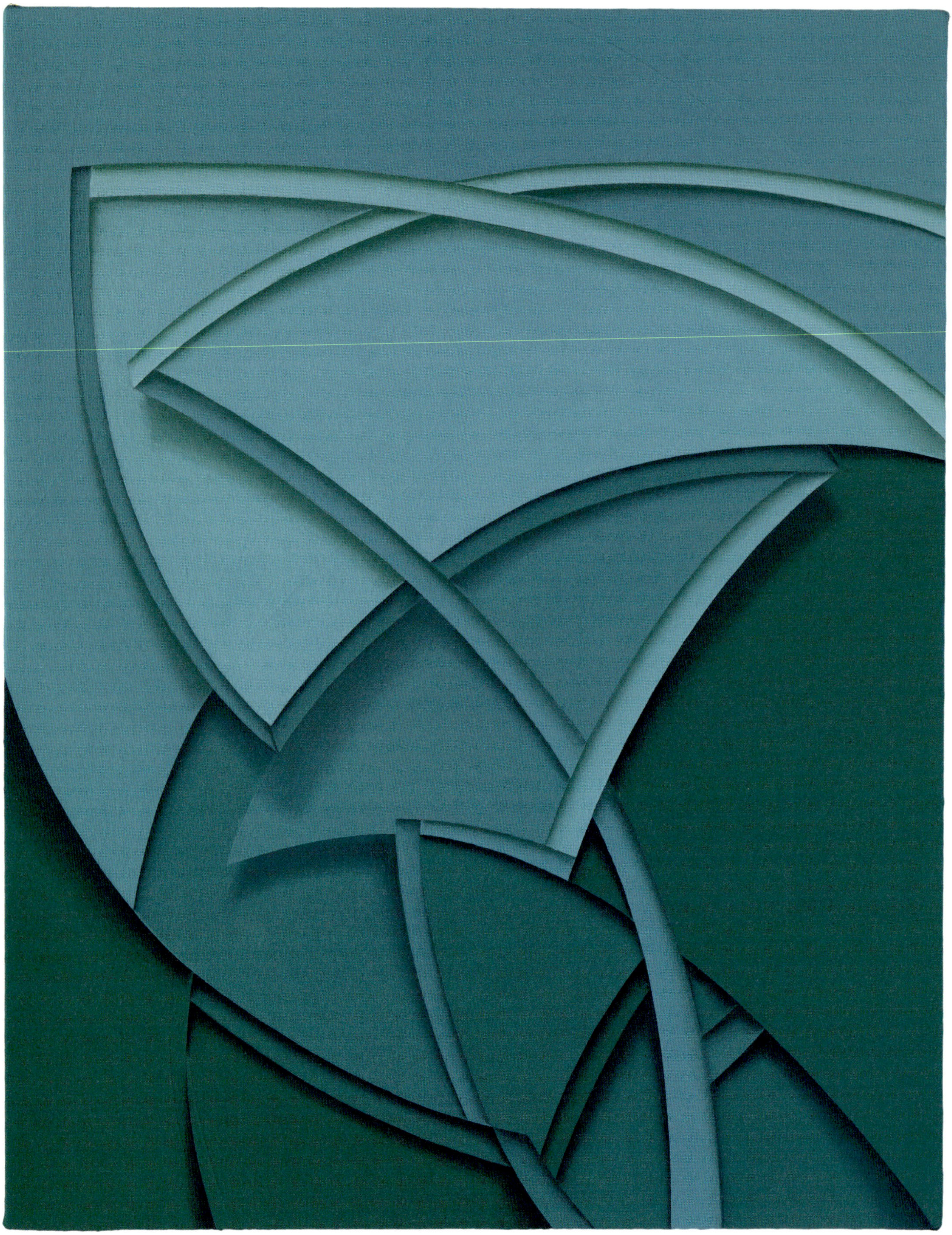

Tomma Abts, Uphe, *2011, acrylic and oil on canvas, 48 × 38 cm, courtesy of Galerie Greengrassi, London, Museum of Modern Art Collection, New York*

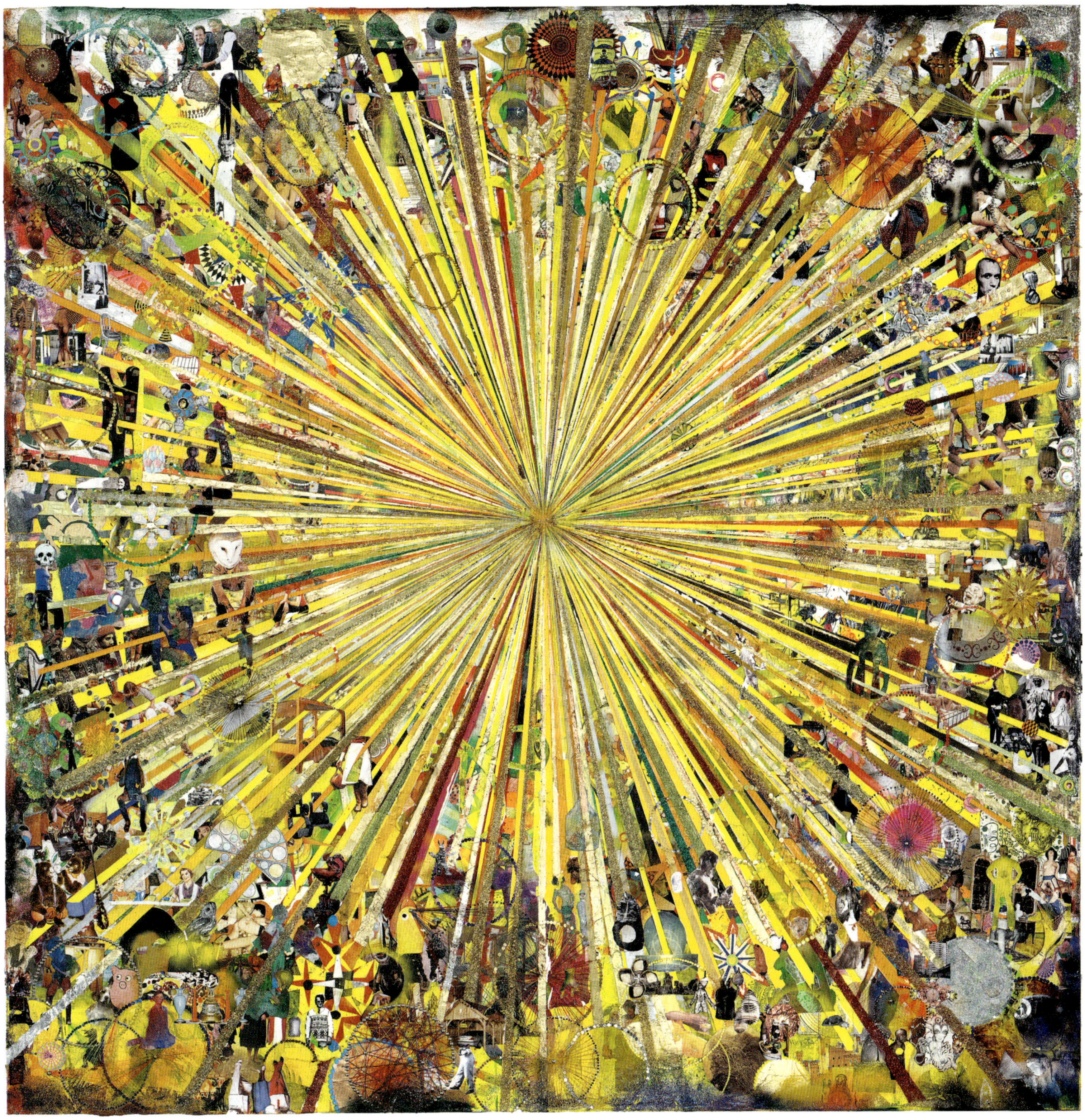

Tal R, Adieu Interessant *[Interesting Farewell], 2005–08, various materials, 250 × 250 cm, courtesy of Contemporary Fine Arts, Berlin*

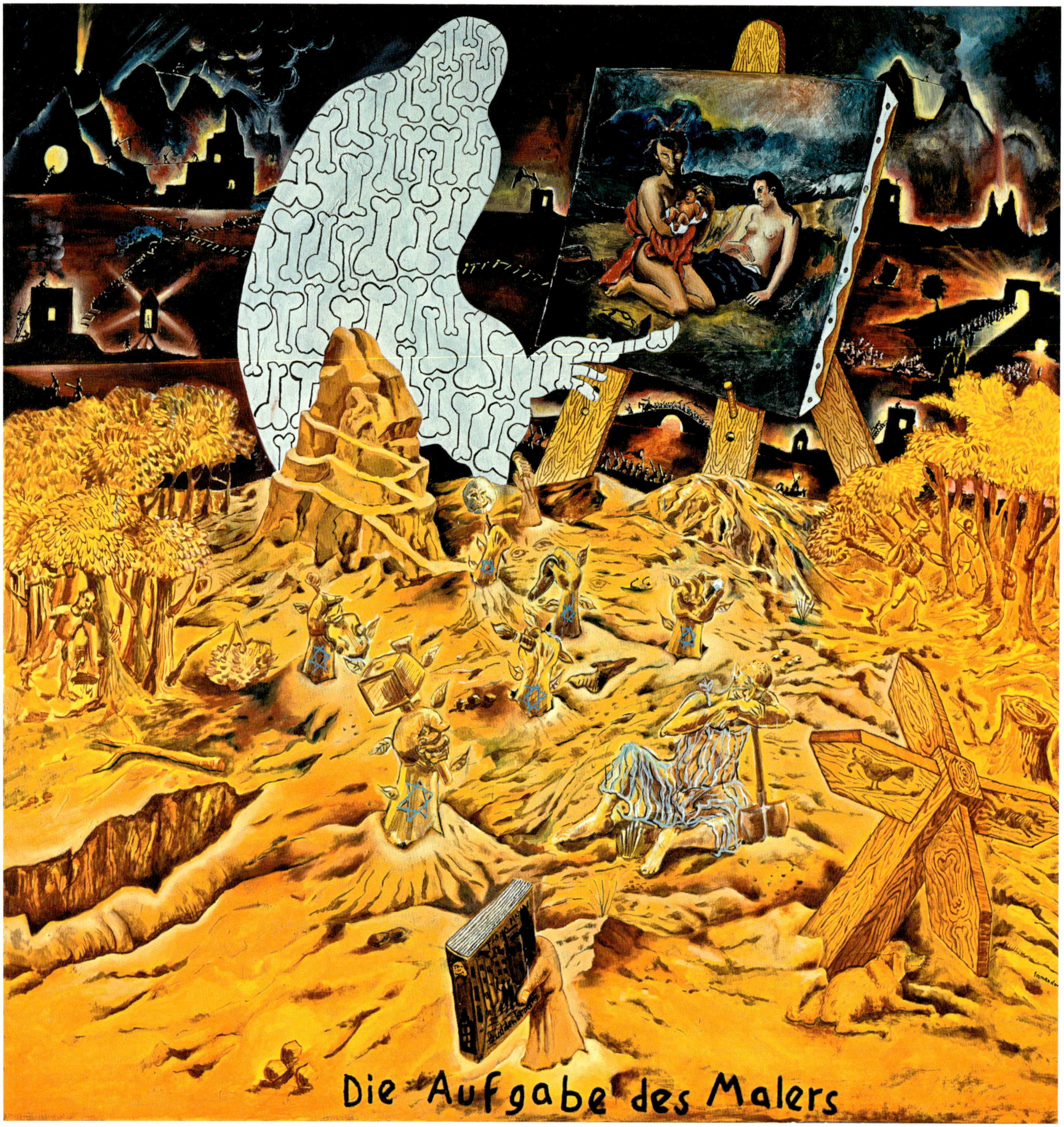

Jörg Immendorff, Die Aufgabe des Malers *[The Painter's Task], 1998, oil on canvas, 250 × 250 cm, courtesy of Galerie Michael Werner, Cologne, and Märkisch Wilmersdorf*

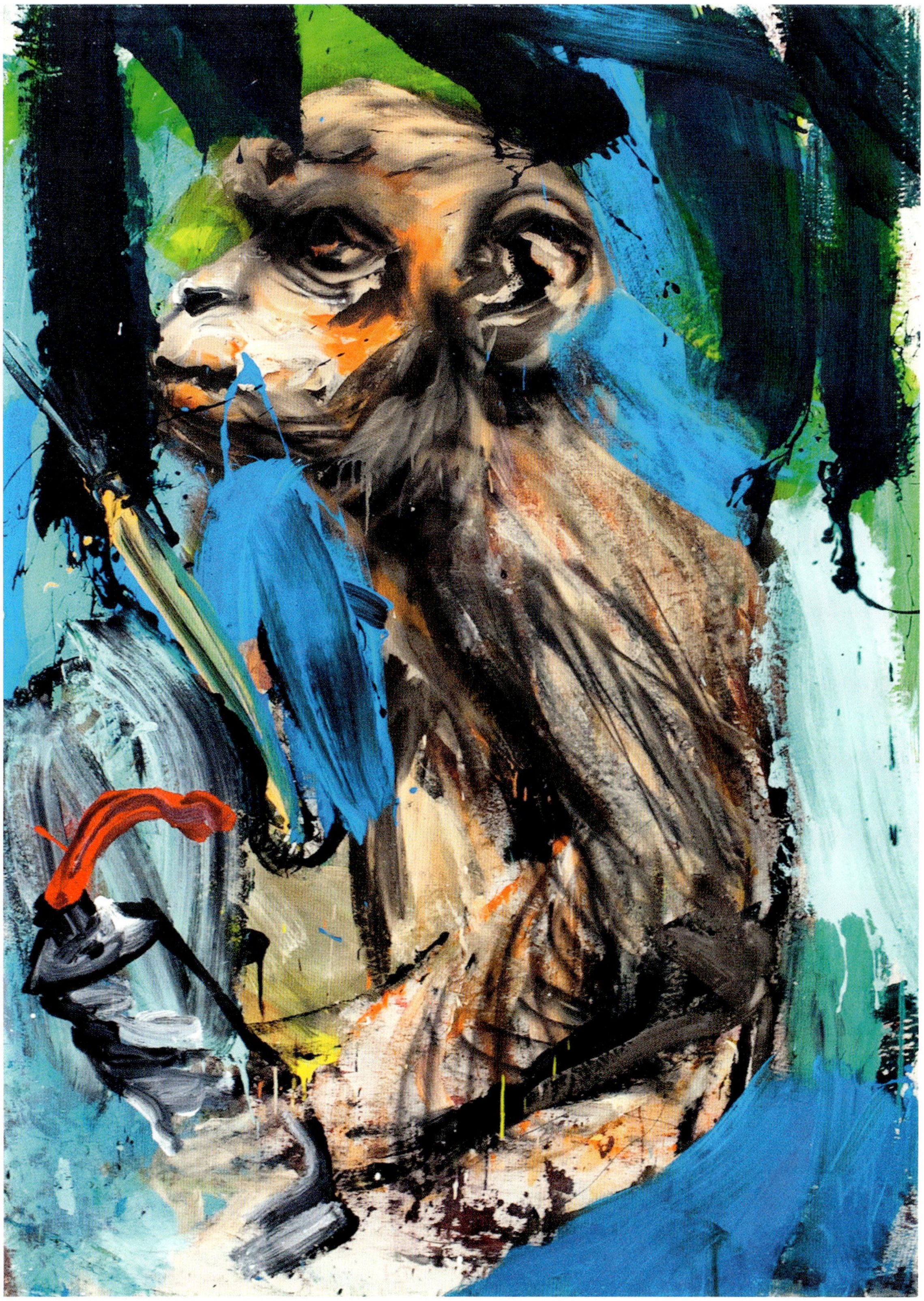

Dieter Krieg, Ohne Titel [untitled], 1979–82, acrylic on canvas, 248 × 180 cm, Kunstmuseum Stuttgart

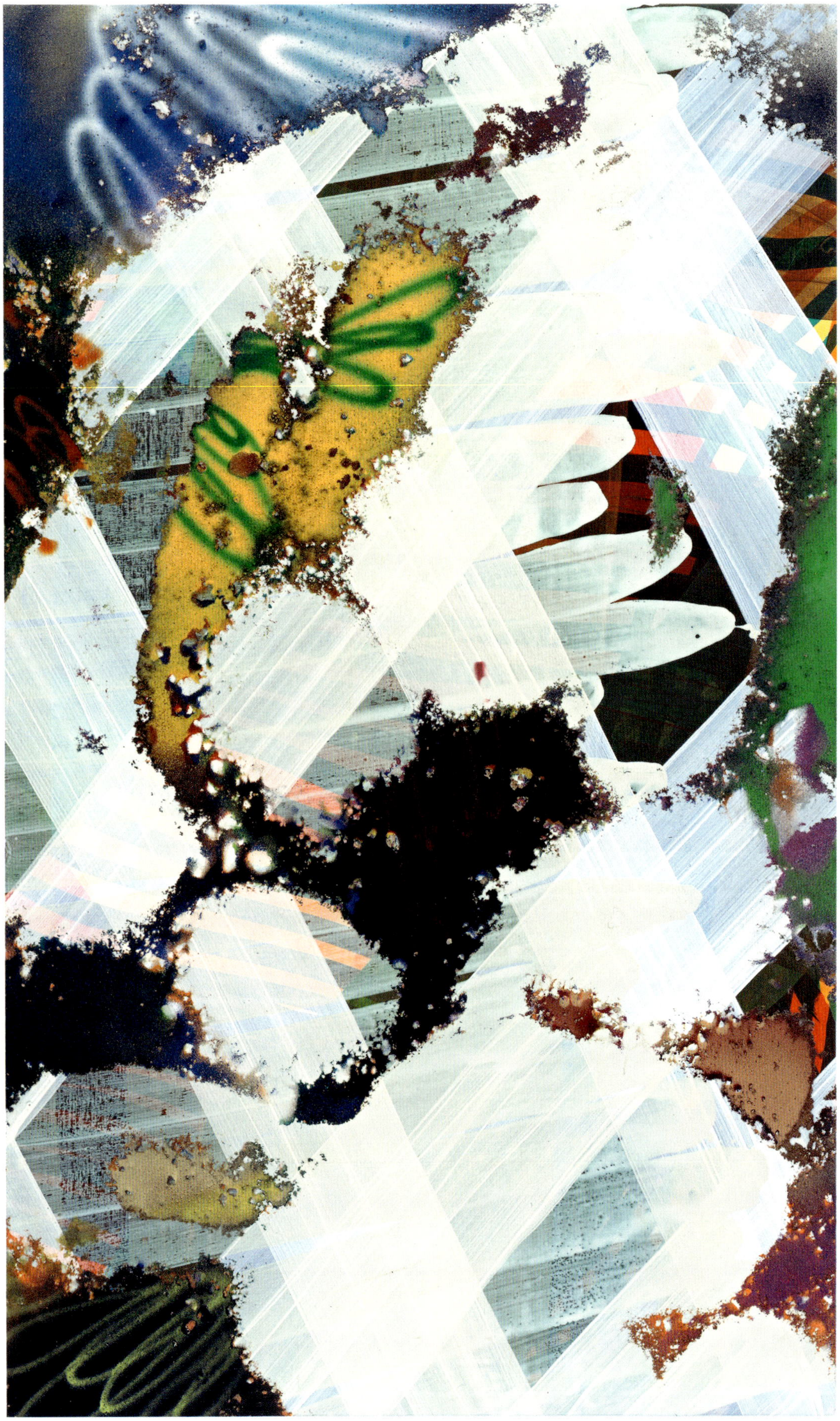

Katharina Grosse, Ohne Titel [untitled], 2009, acrylic, earth on canvas, 219 × 133 cm, owned by the artist

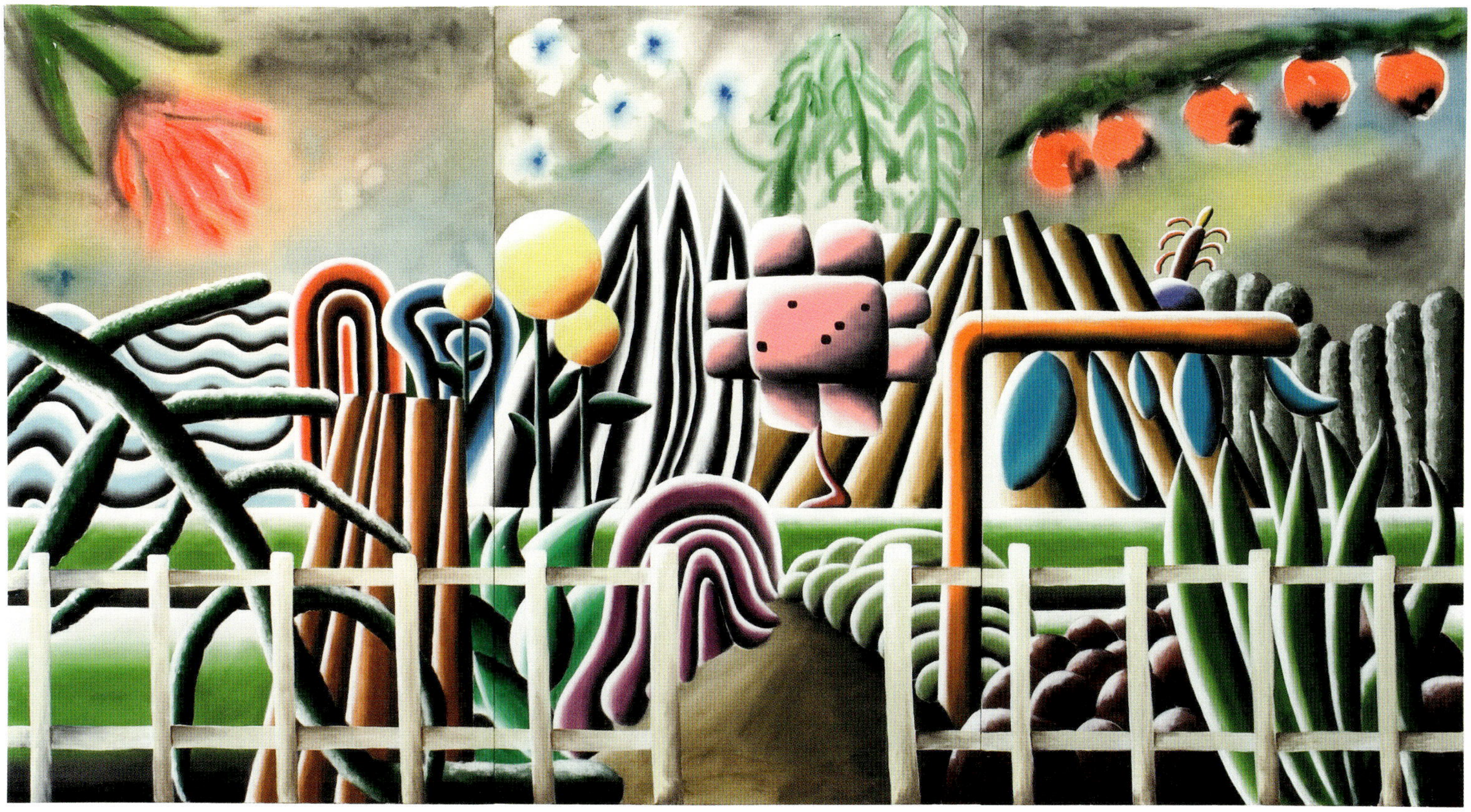

Andreas Schulze, Ohne Titel (Der Garten) [untitled (The Garden)], 2009, acrylic on untreated cotton, 240 × 450 cm (3 parts), courtesy of Sprüth Magers Berlin/London

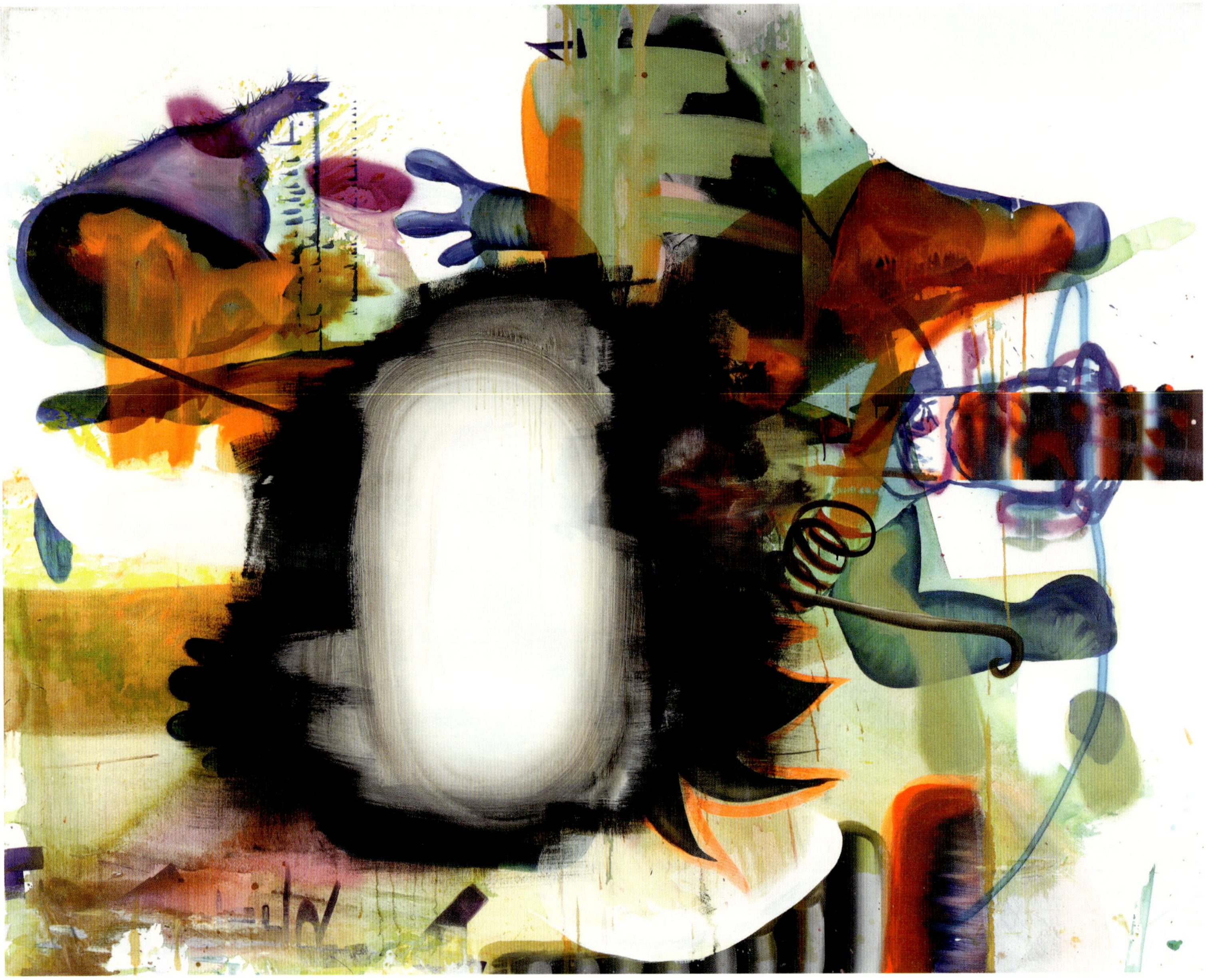

Albert Oehlen, Greifen *[Griffins], 2005, oil on canvas, 180 × 230 cm, Akademie-Galerie – Die Neue Sammlung, Düsseldorf*

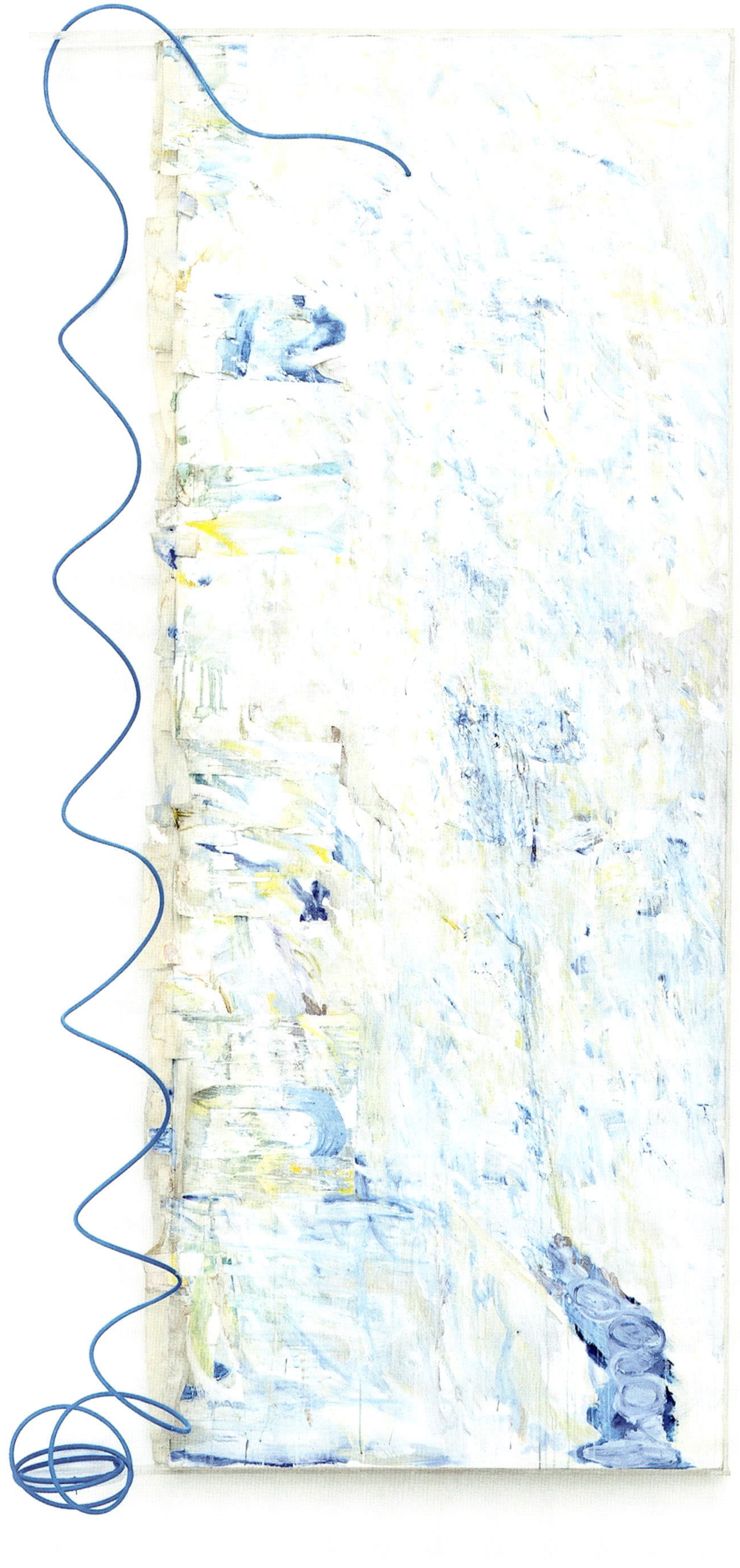

Gerhard Hoehme, Blaustrom *[Blue Stream], 1982, acrylic on paper and canvas, PE cord, acrylic glass, 300 × 127 cm, Akademie-Galerie – Die Neue Sammlung, Düsseldorf*

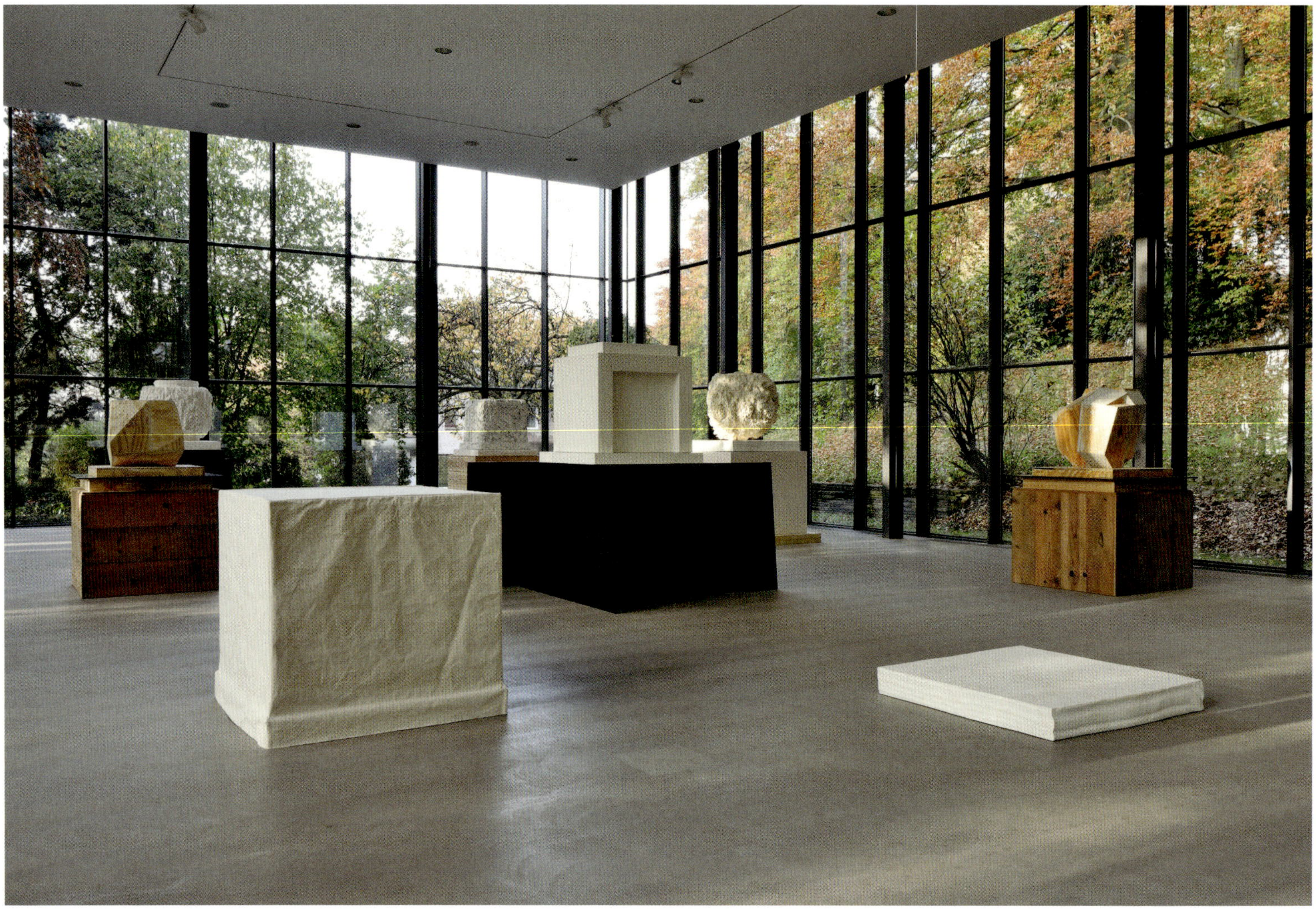

View of the exhibition Didier Vermeiren, *2012/13, in the Waldfrieden Sculpture Park, Cragg Foundation*

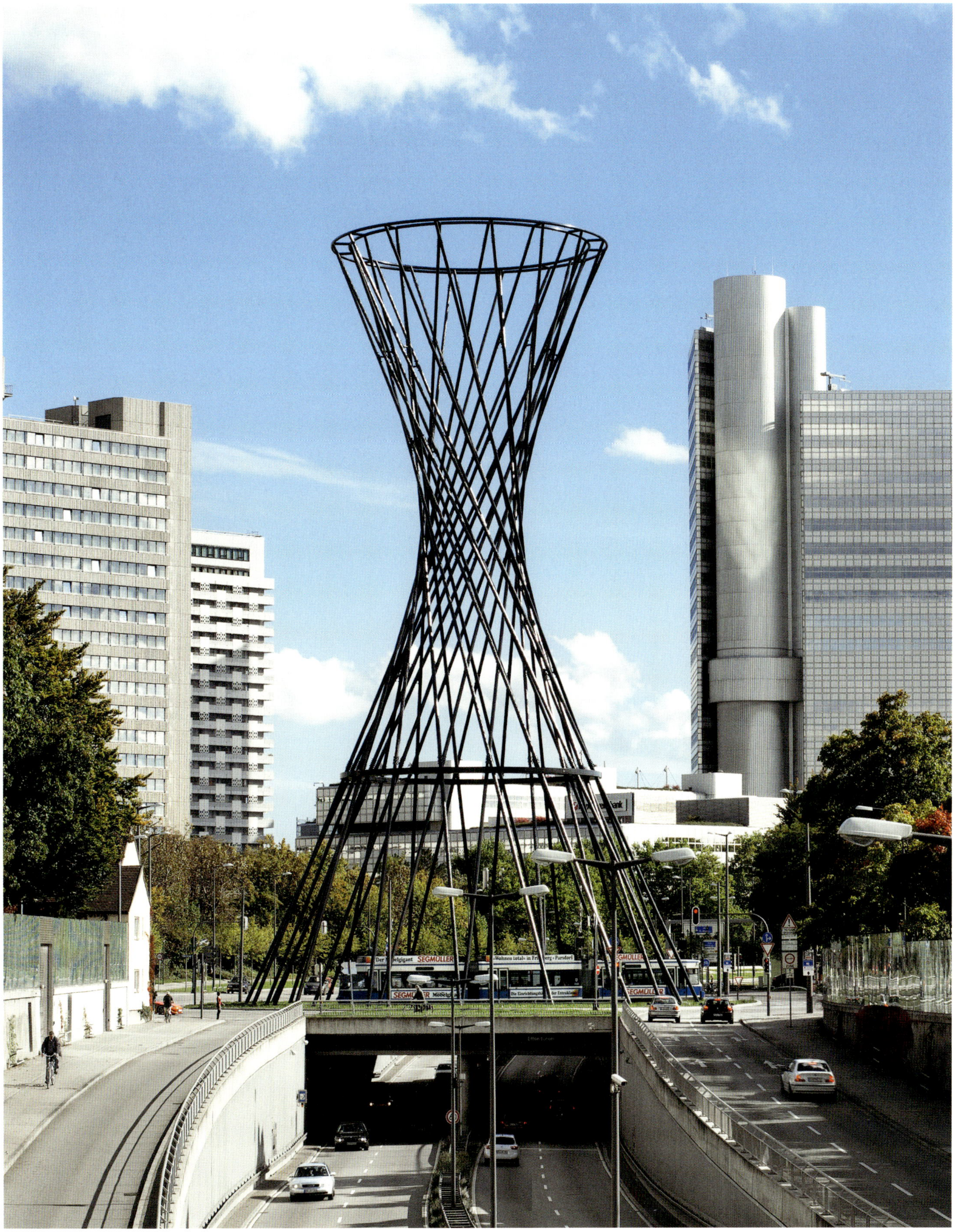

Rita McBride, Mae West, *2011, height 52 m, carbon fibre construction, Effnerplatz, Munich*

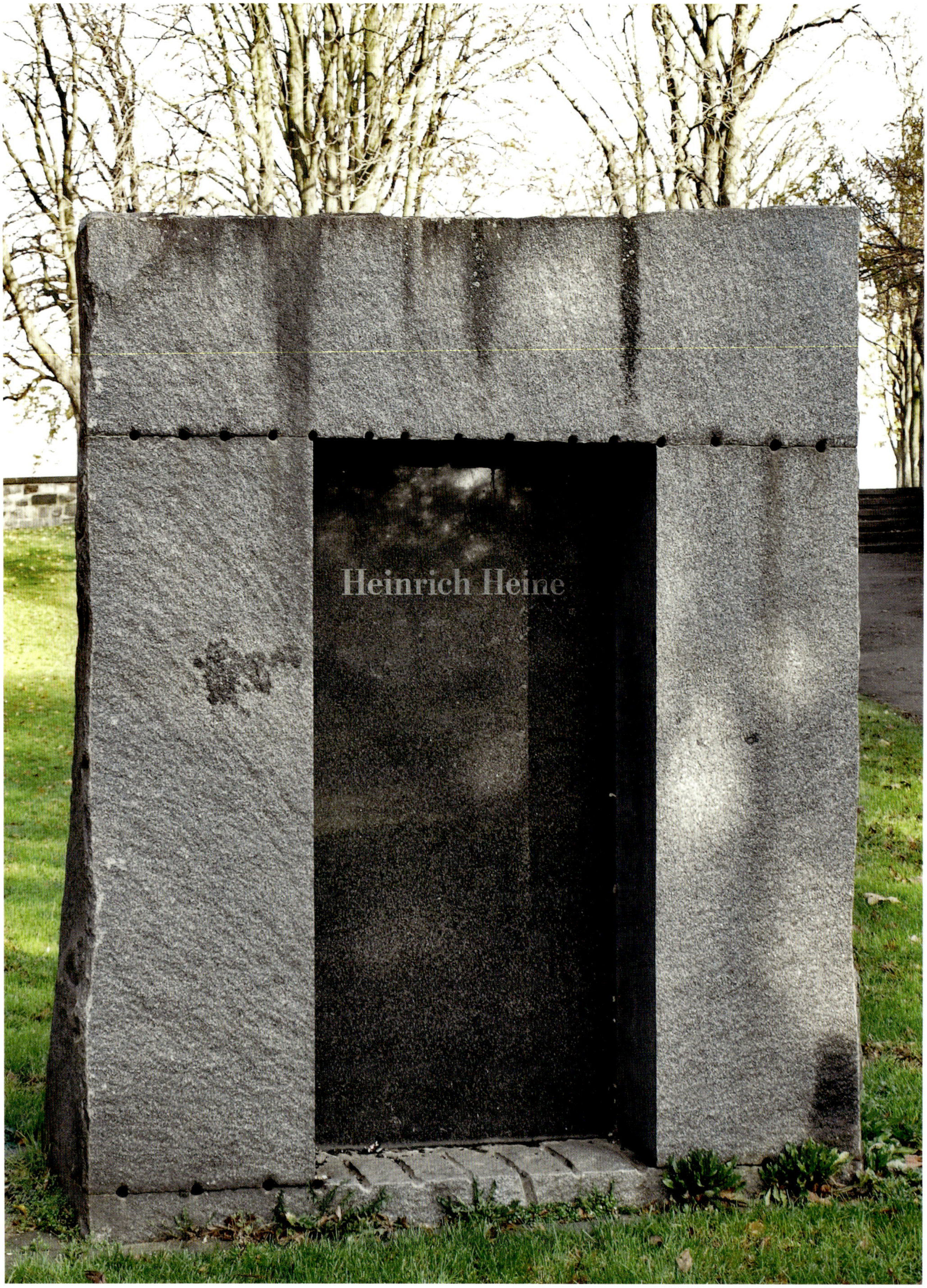

Ulrich Rückriem, Denkmal für Heinrich Heine *[Monument to Heinrich Heine], 1982, split, cut, and polished African granite, 300 × 200 × 100 cm, Stadtgarten, Bonn*

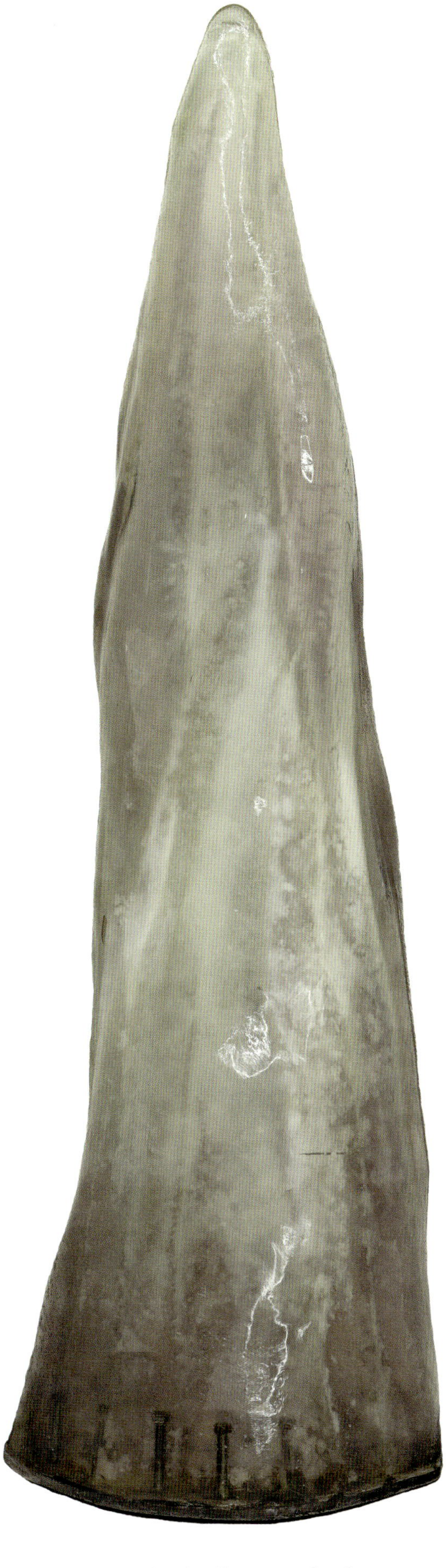

Georg Herold, Mountains of Cocaine V, *1990, cast resin, powdered milk, approx. height 210 cm, Akademie-Galerie – Die Neue Sammlung, Düsseldorf*

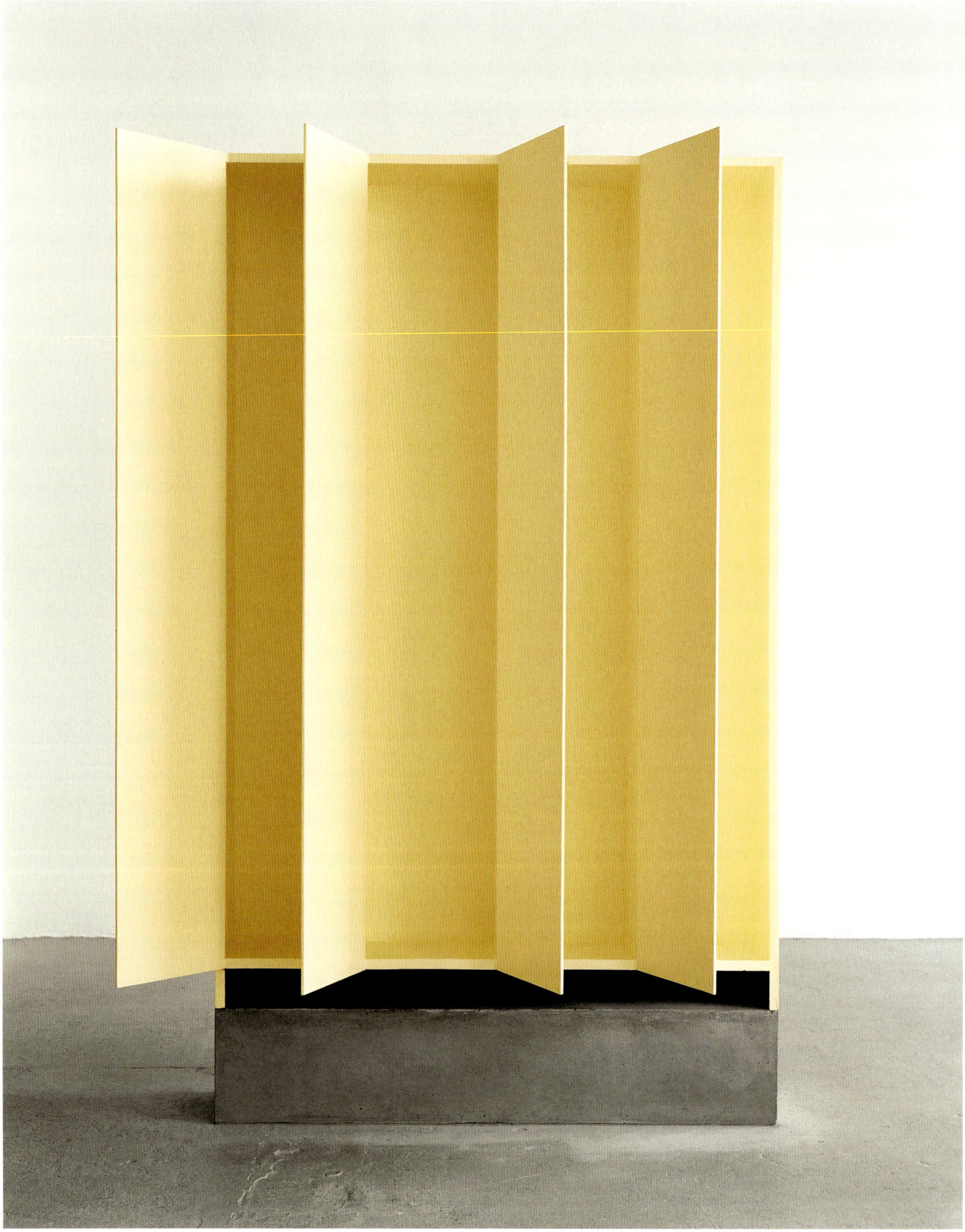

Hubert Kiecol, Schrank *[Cupboard], 1990, concrete, steel, paint, 212 × 129 × 57 cm, courtesy of Hubert Kiecol*

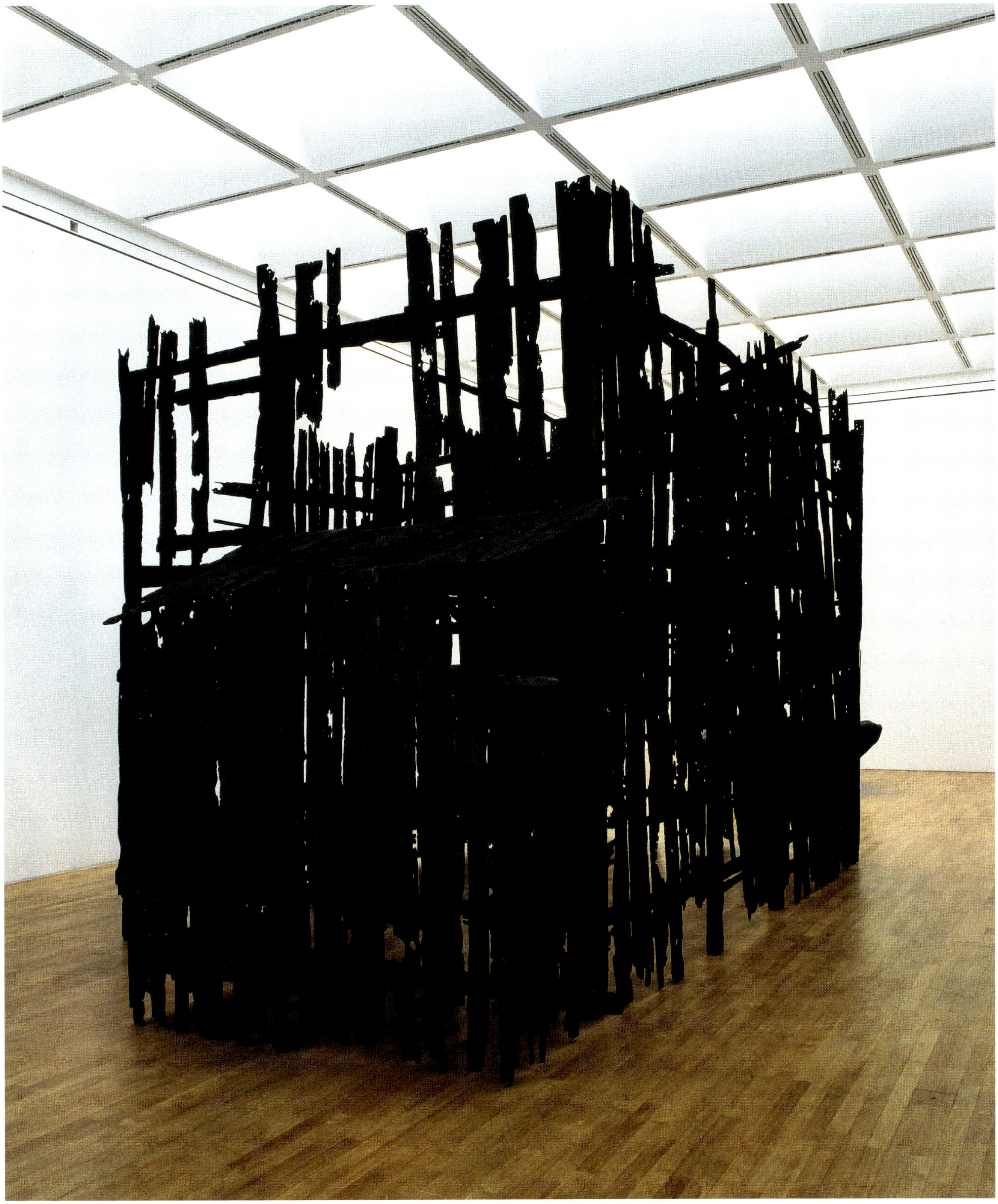

Gereon Krebber, Abgebrannter Stall *[Burnt-Down Stall], 2010, burnt wood, paint, 450 × 400 × 620 cm, courtesy of Gereon Krebber and Galerie Christian Lethert, Cologne*

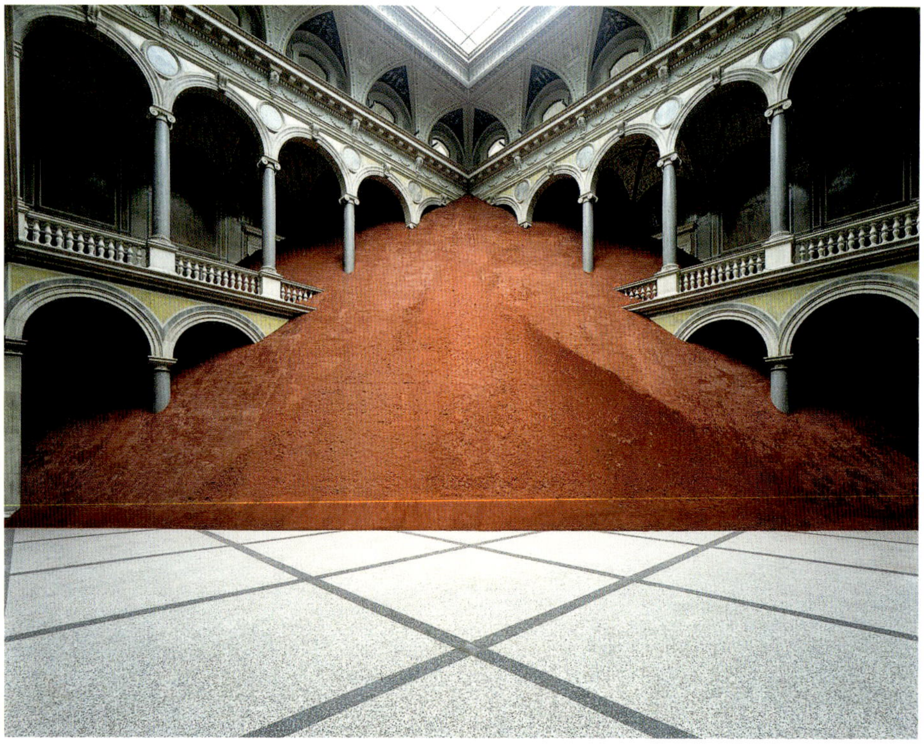

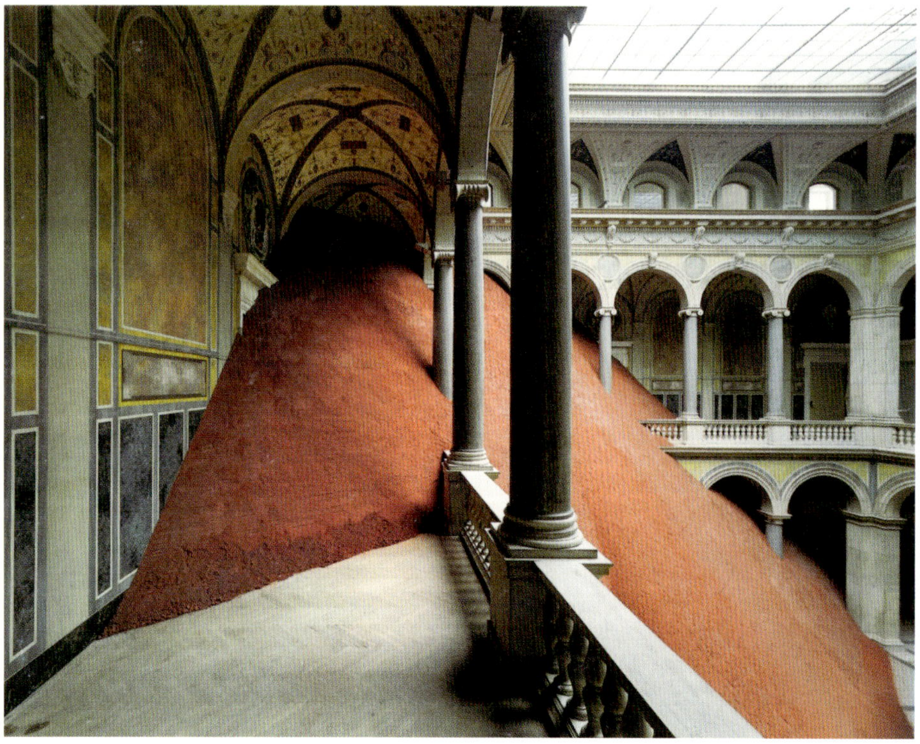

Magdalena Jetelová, Domestizierung einer Pyramide *[Domestication of a Pyramid], 1992, red quartz sand, height 13 m, installation at the Museum für angewandte Kunst, Vienna*

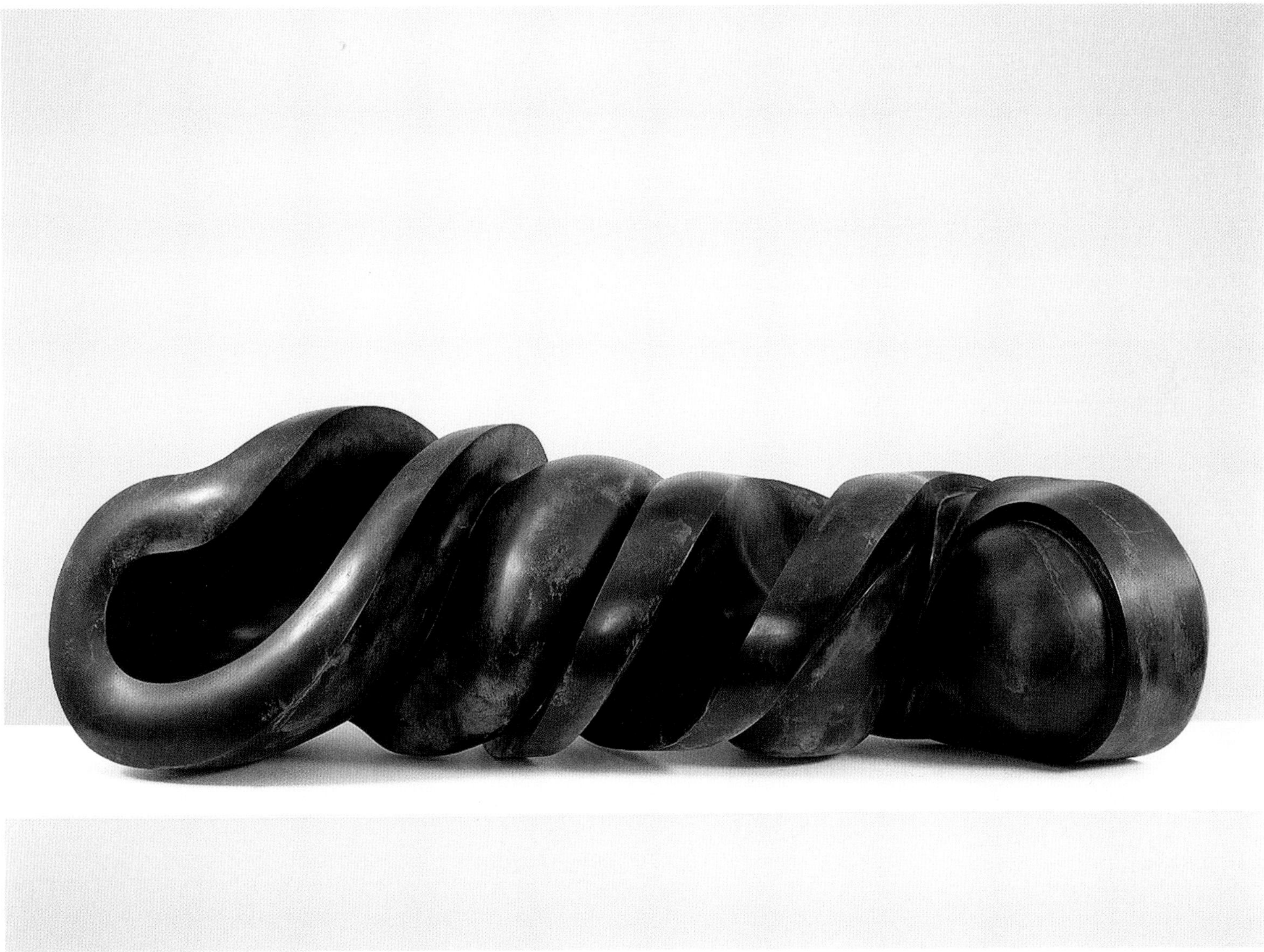

Anthony Cragg, Early Forms St. Gallen, *1997, 85 × 105 × 265 cm, Akademie-Galerie – Die Neue Sammlung, Düsseldorf*

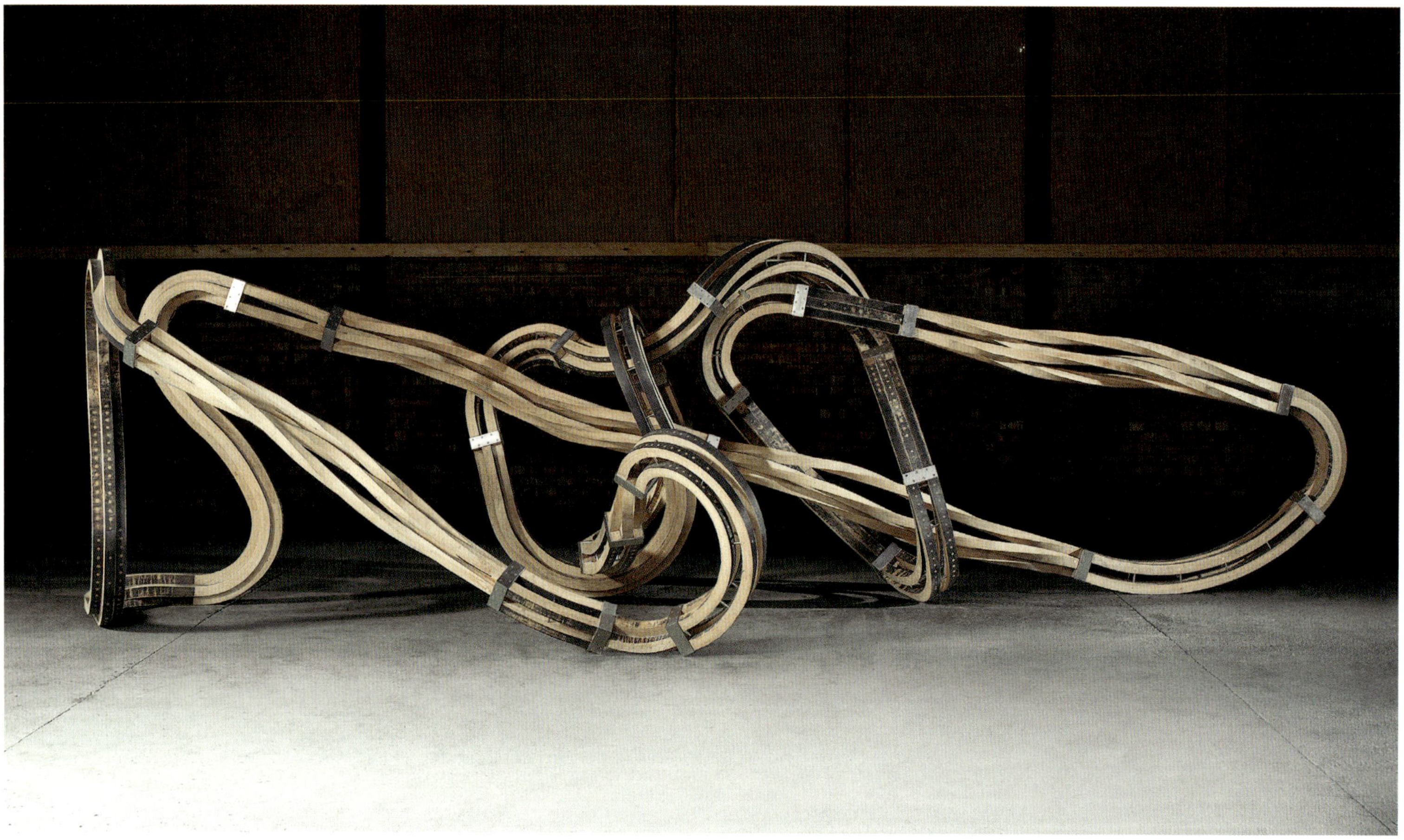

Richard Deacon, Quick, *2009, wood, steel, 180 × 622 × 231 cm, Musée d'Art Moderne et Contemporain de Strasbourg*

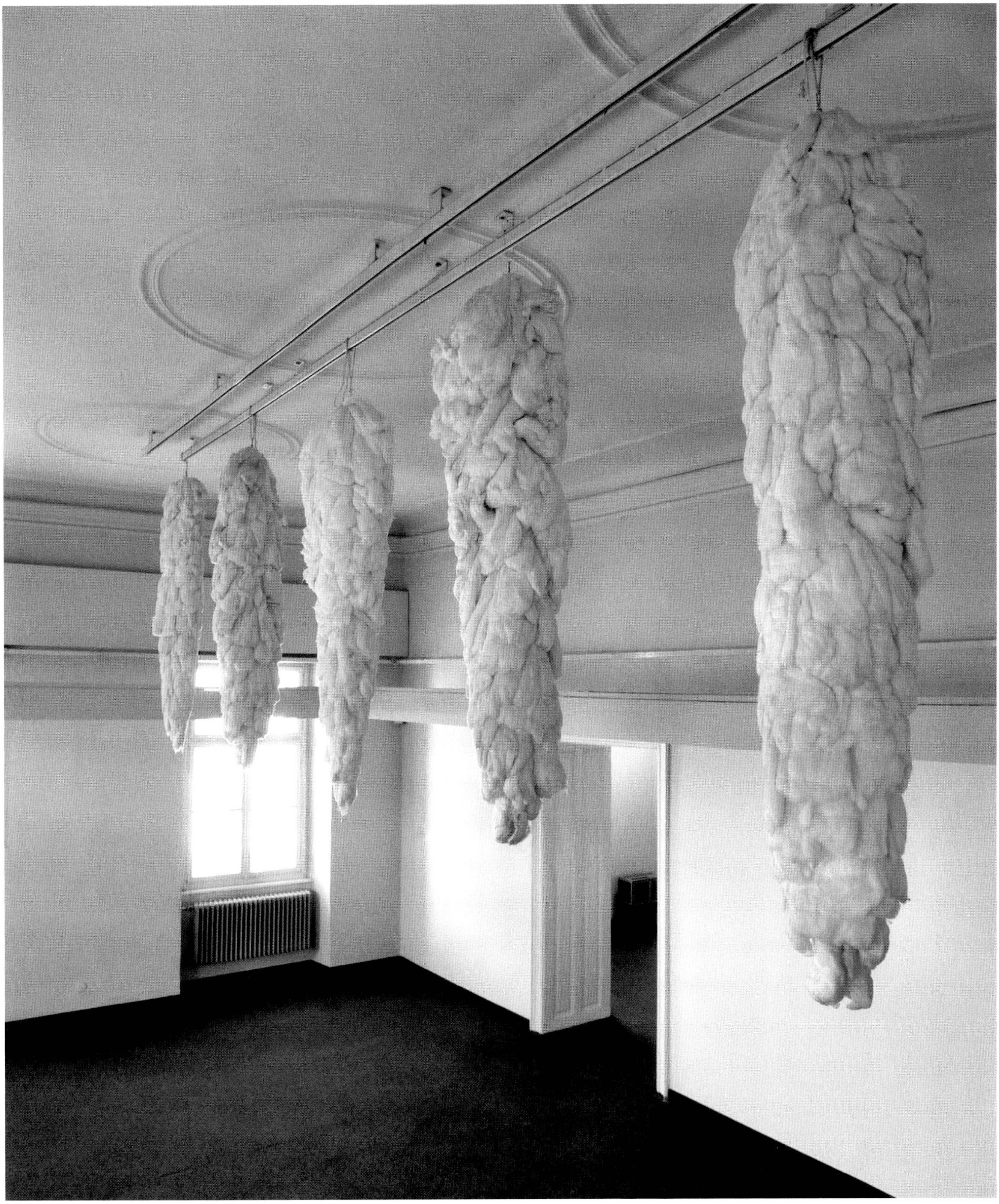

Martin Gostner, Ohne Titel [untitled], 1993, cotton wool, cord, approx. height 270 cm, diameter 65 cm, Akademie-Galerie – Die Neue Sammlung, Düsseldorf

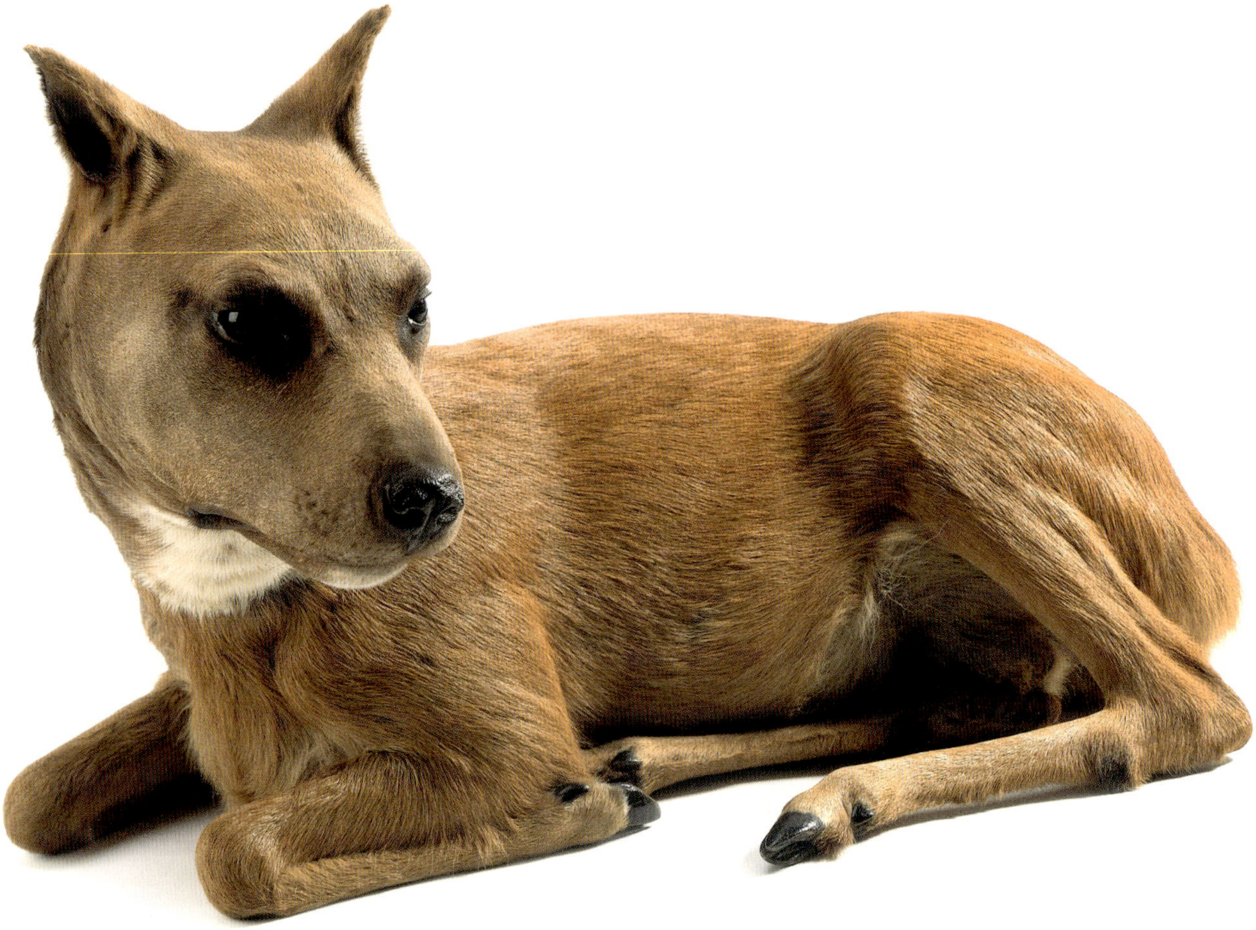

Thomas Grünfeld, Misfit (pitbull/deer), *2005, taxidermy, 41 × 74 × 50 cm, Akademie-Galerie – Die Neue Sammlung, Düsseldorf*

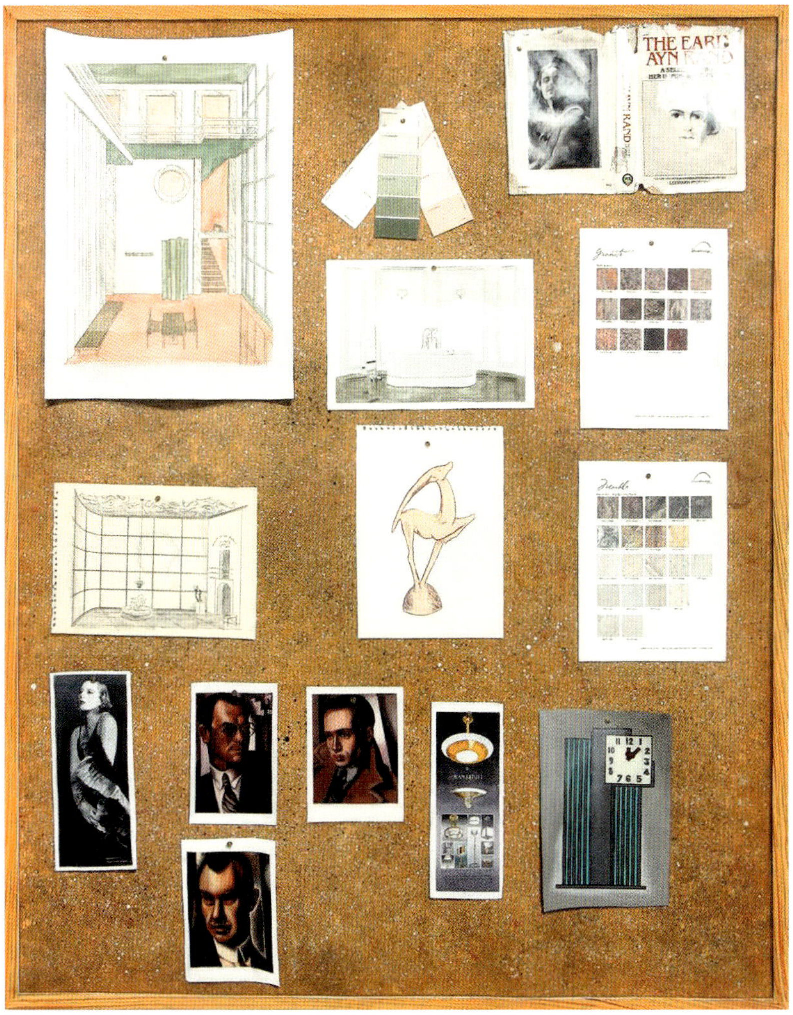

Lucy McKenzie, Quodlibet XXI (Objectivism), *2012, 150 × 120 cm, oil on canvas, Galerie Micheline Szwajcer, Antwerp*

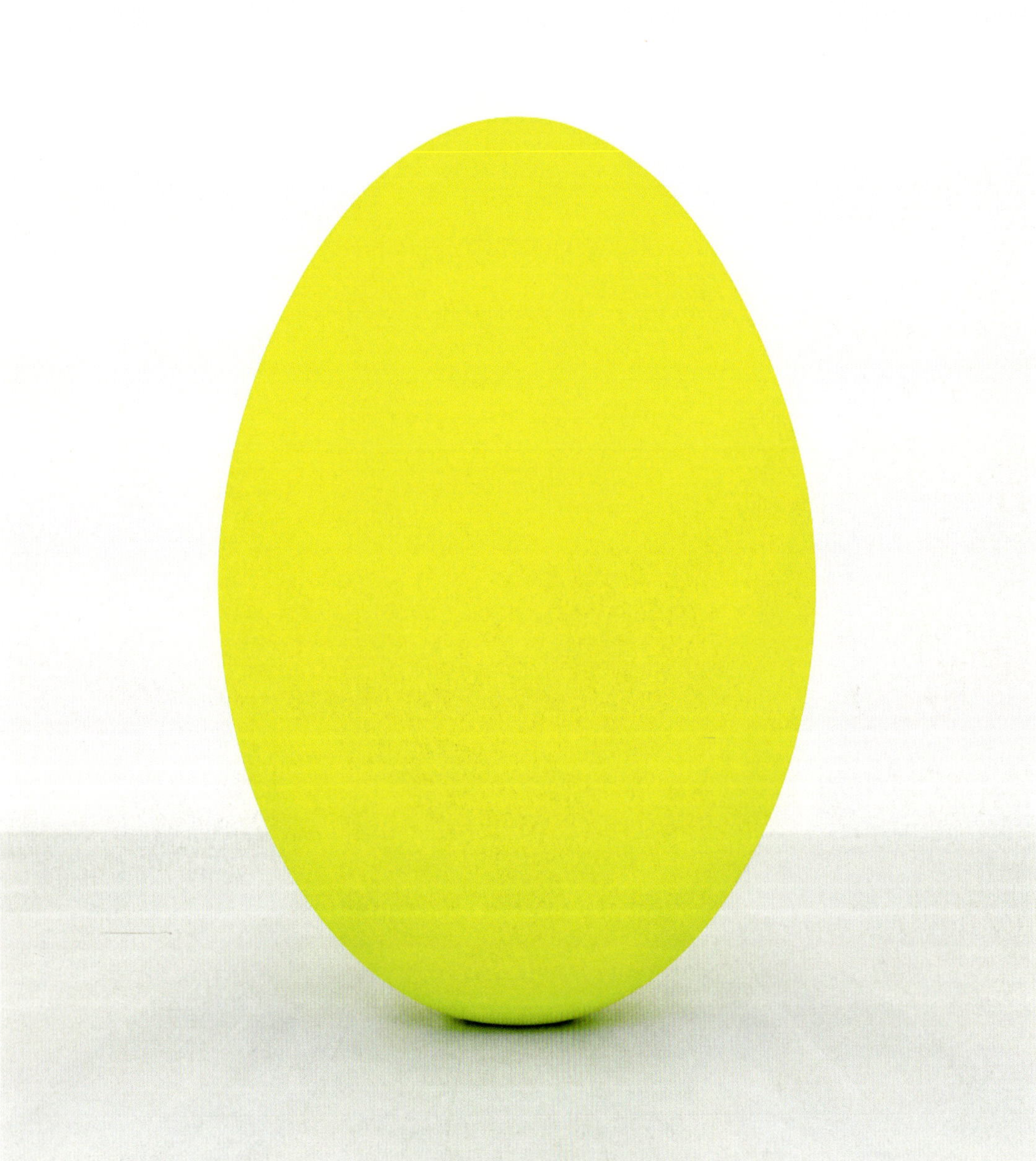

Katharina Fritsch, Ei *[Egg], 2011, plastic, paint, height 124 cm, diameter 84 cm, Akademie-Galerie – Die Neue Sammlung, Düsseldorf*

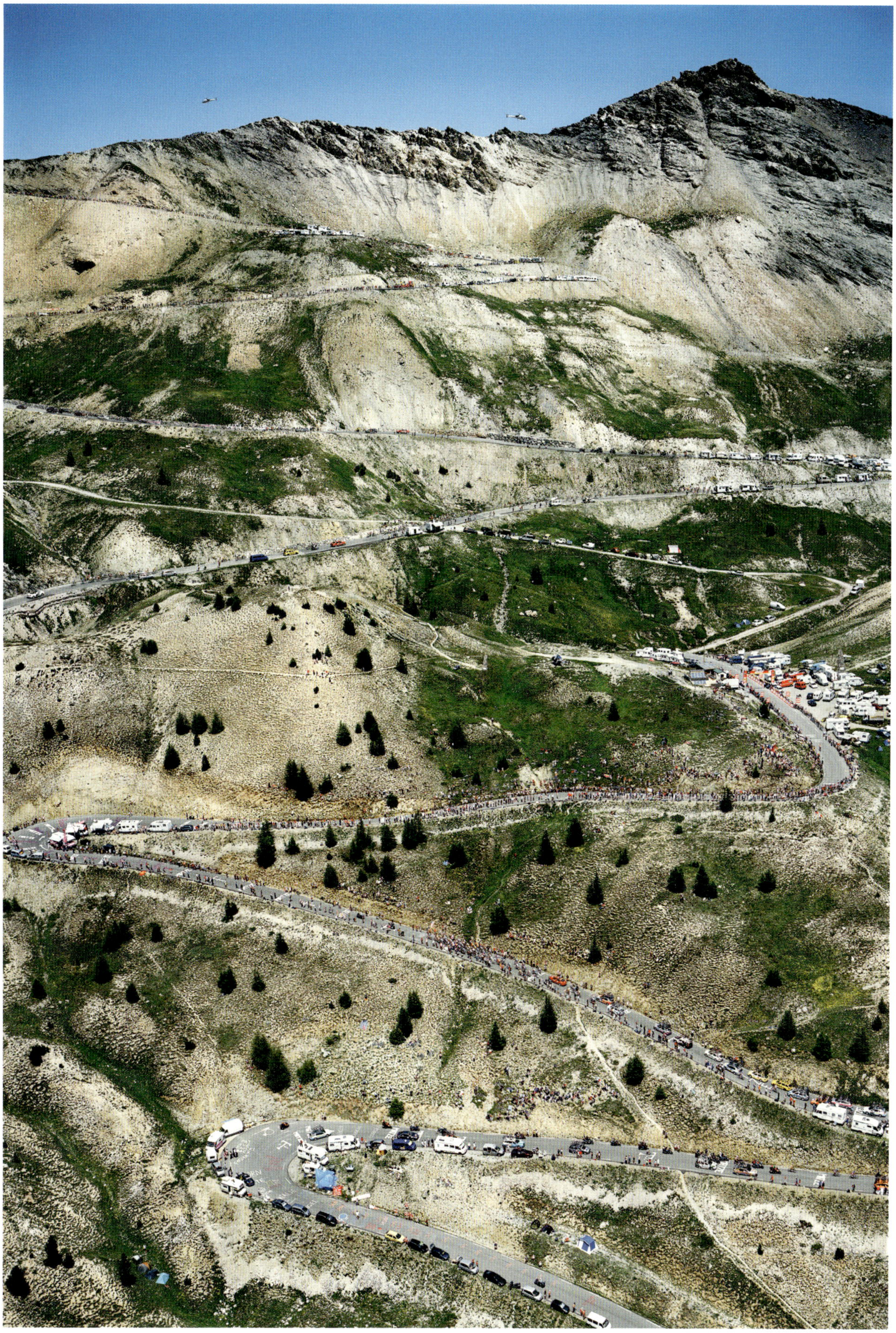

Andreas Gursky, Tour de France I, *2007, C-type print, 307 × 218 × 6.2 cm, courtesy of Sprüth Magers Berlin/London*

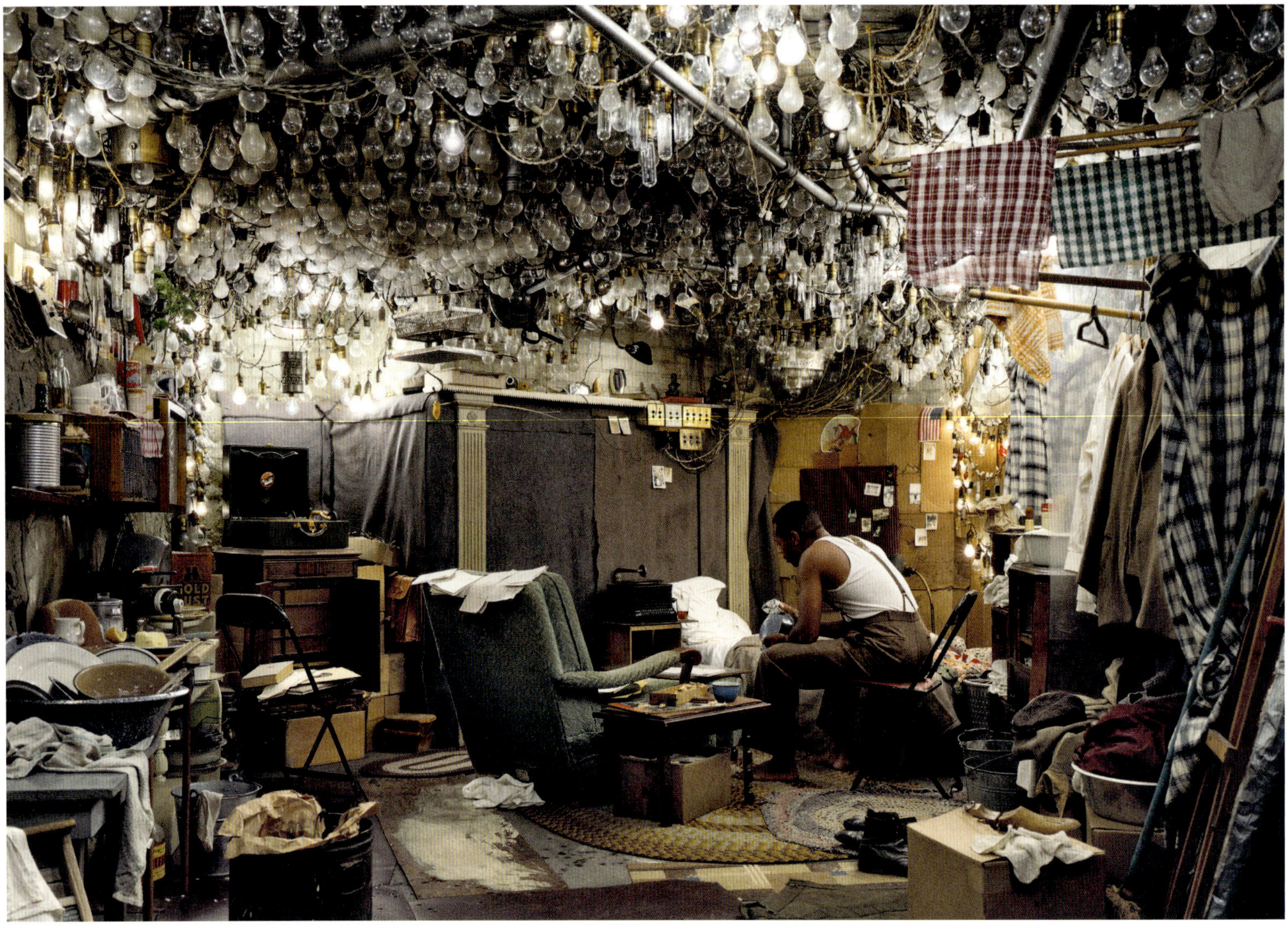

Jeff Wall, After *Invisible Man* by Ralph Ellison, the Prologue, *1999–2001, large-format slide in a light box, 174 × 250.5 cm, Emmanuel Hoffmann-Stiftung, deposited in the Öffentliche Kunstsammlung Basel and the Museum of Modern Art, New York*

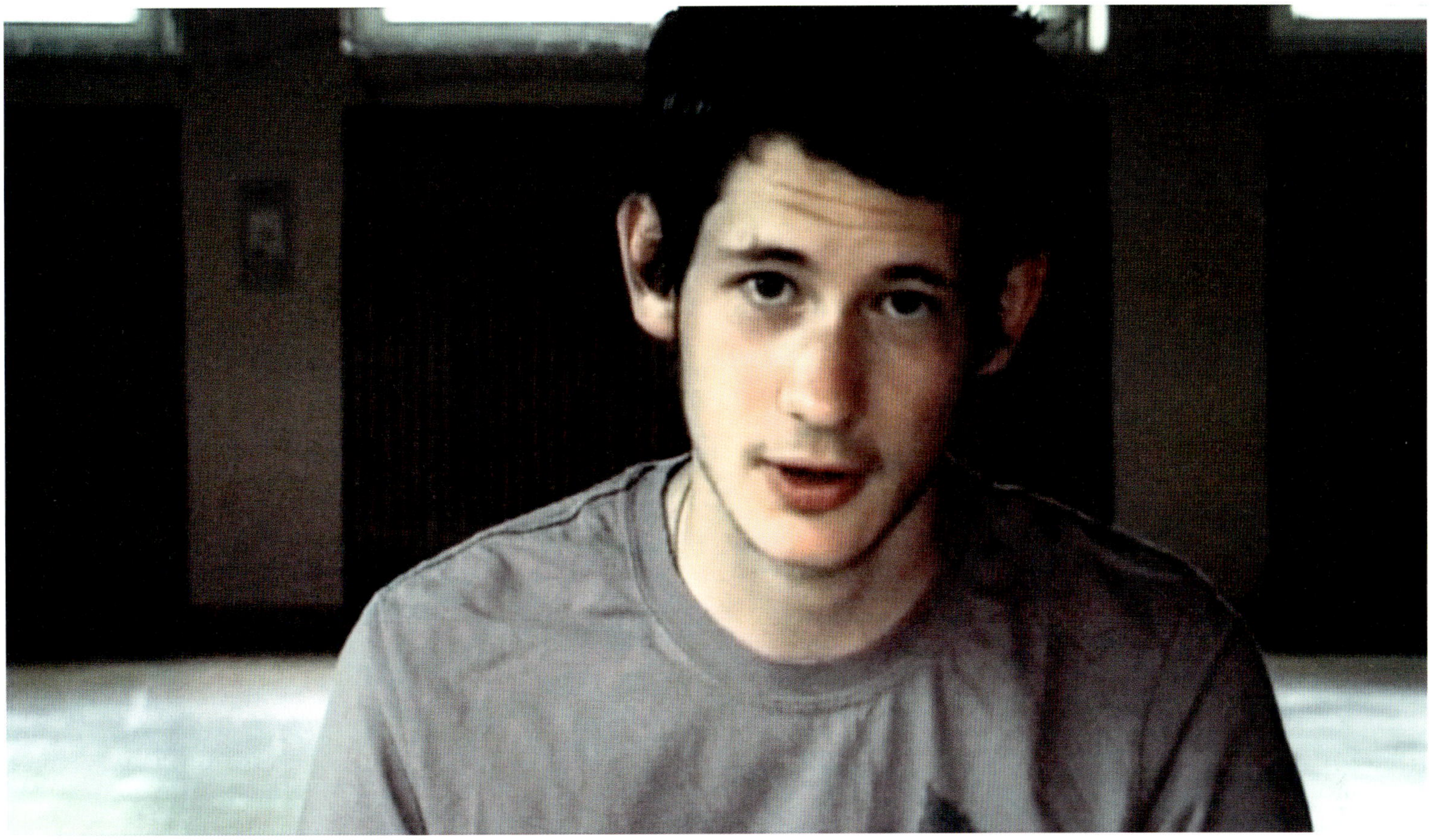

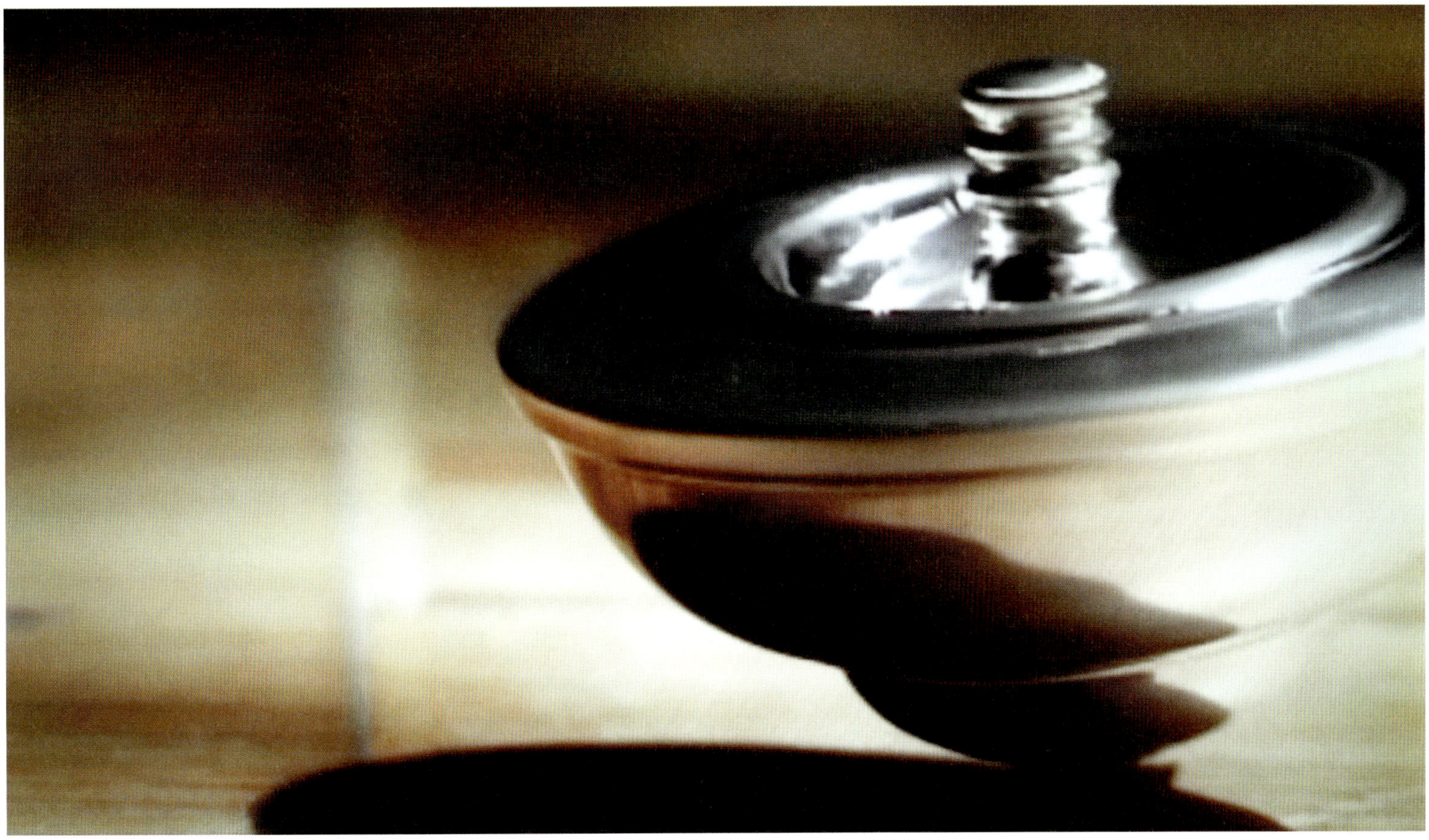

Marcel Odenbach, Deutschstunde *[German Class], 2006, video stills, courtesy of Marcel Odenbach*

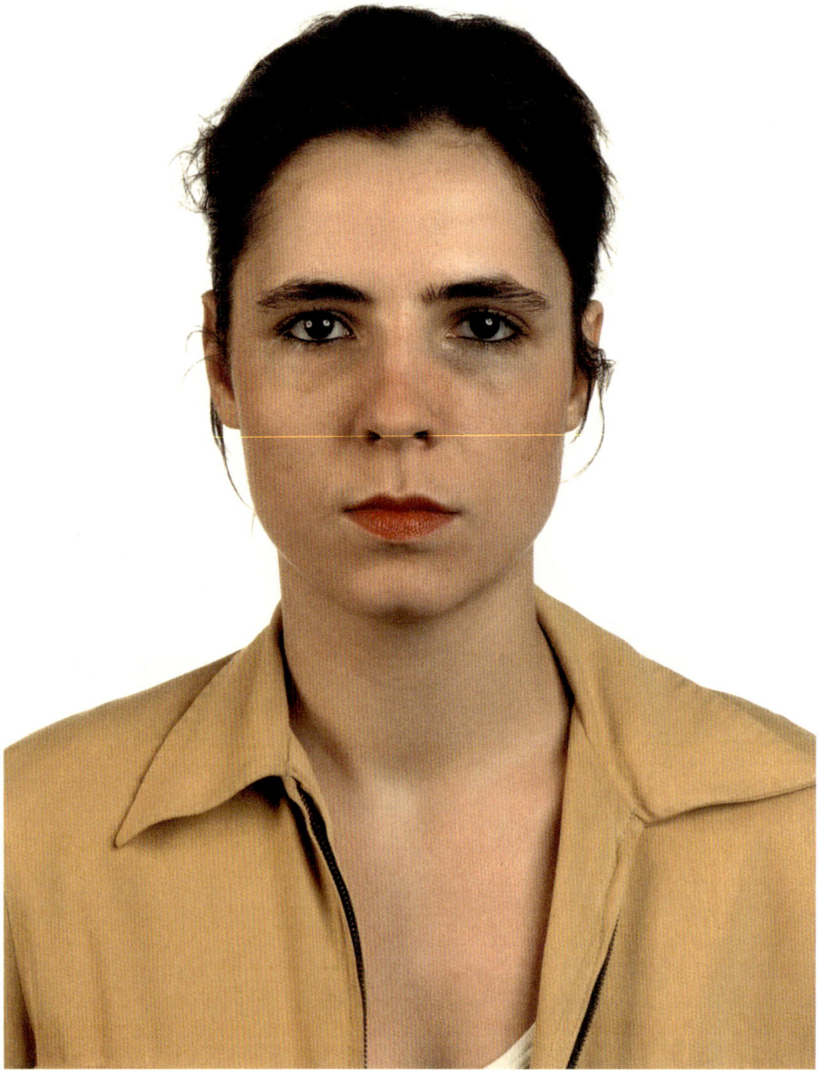

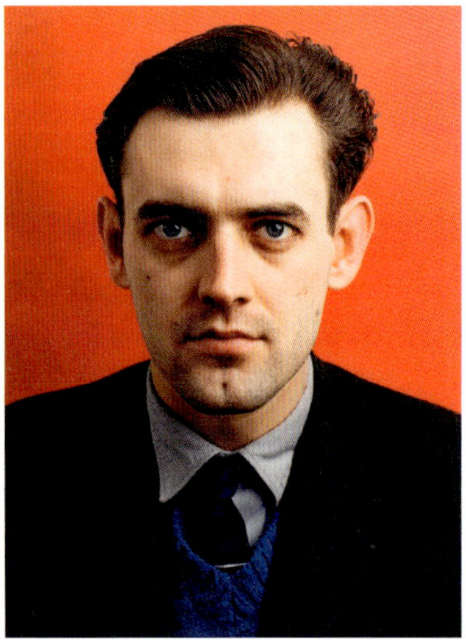

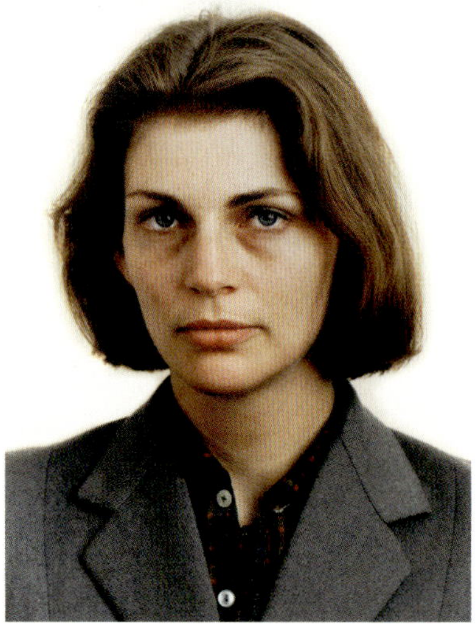

Thomas Ruff, Porträt (Anna Giese) *[Portrait (Anna Giese)], 1989, chromogenic colour print, Diasec face, 210 × 165 cm*

Thomas Ruff, Porträts farbiger Hintergrund (Jörn Stoya) *[Portraits with a Coloured Background (Jörn Stoya)], 1981–85, chromogenic colour print, 24 × 18 cm*

Thomas Ruff, Porträts farbiger Hintergrund (Bettina Elmpt*) [Portraits with a Coloured Background (Bettina Elmpt)], 1981–85, chromogenic colour print, 24 × 18 cm*

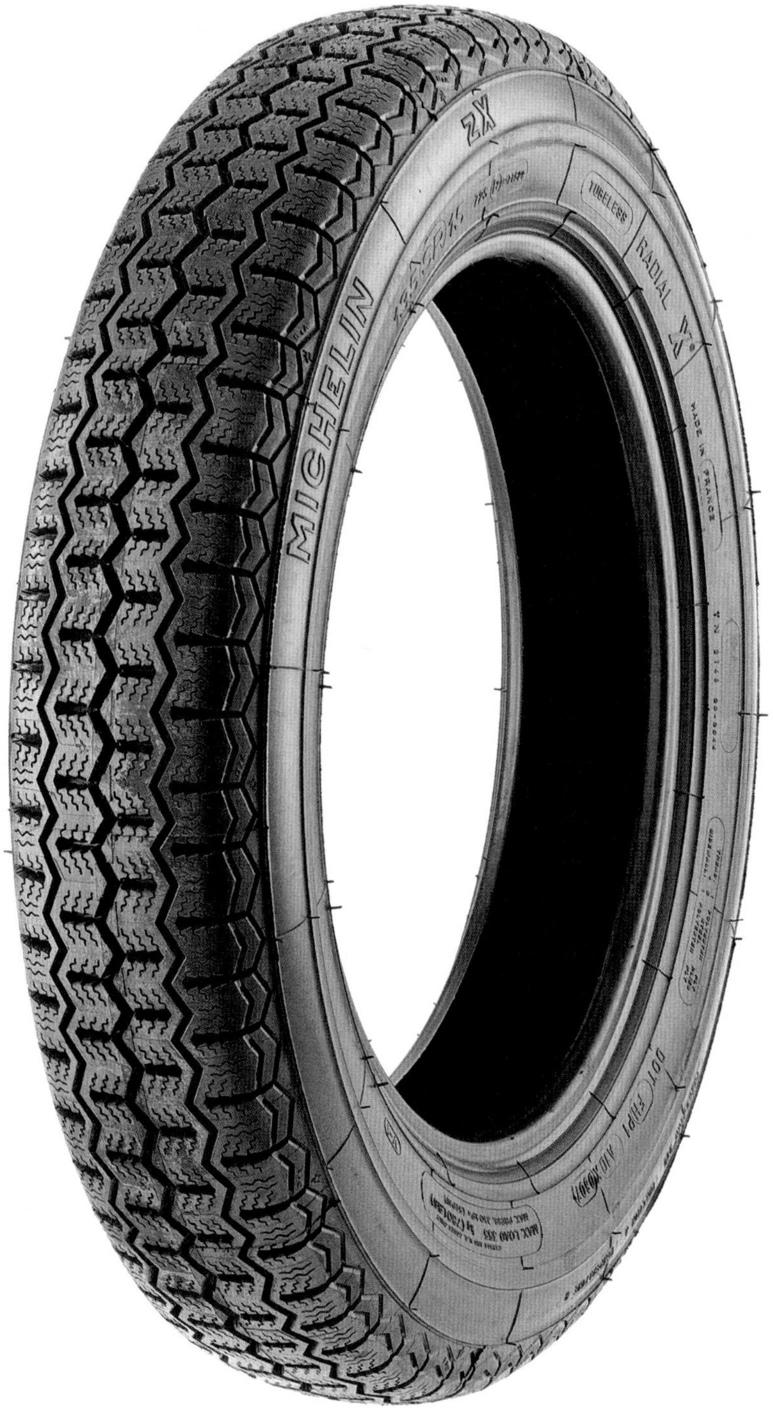

Christopher Williams, Clockwise from Manufacturer Name (Outer Ring) Michelin × M+S 89, × M+S 89, Clockwise from Tire Size (Inner Ring), 135 R 15, 72 Q E2 0281541, M + S Tubeless Radial × TF 852 20-2044 Tread: 1 Polyester Ply + 2 Steel Plies Sidewall: 1 Polyester Ply Canada and U.S. Codes Only Max Load 355 Kg (780 Lbs) Max Press. 350 kPa (51 PSI) V-1 Douglas M. Parker Studio, Glendale, California, January 03, 2008–January 04, 2008, *2008, silver gelatin print, 94.3 × 85.4 × 3.8 cm, framed, courtesy of Christopher Williams, Galerie Gisela Capitain, Cologne, and David Zwirner, New York*

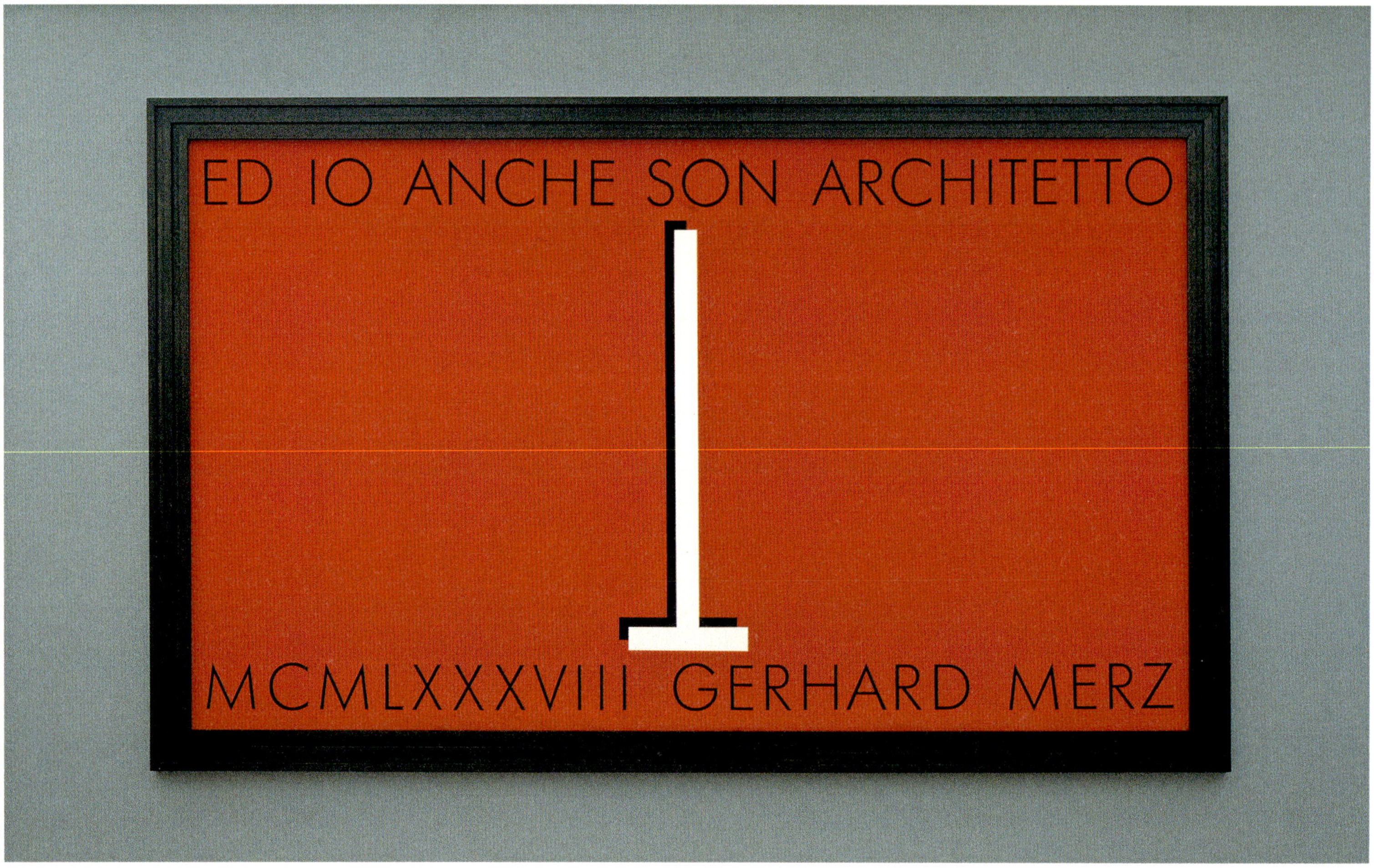

Gerhard Merz, ED IO ANCHE SON ARCHITETTO MCMLXXXVIII *[AND I TOO AM AN ARCHITECT MCMLXXXVIII], 1988, pigment on canvas, 320 × 530 cm, Marx Collection, Hamburger Bahnhof – Museum für Gegenwart, Berlin*

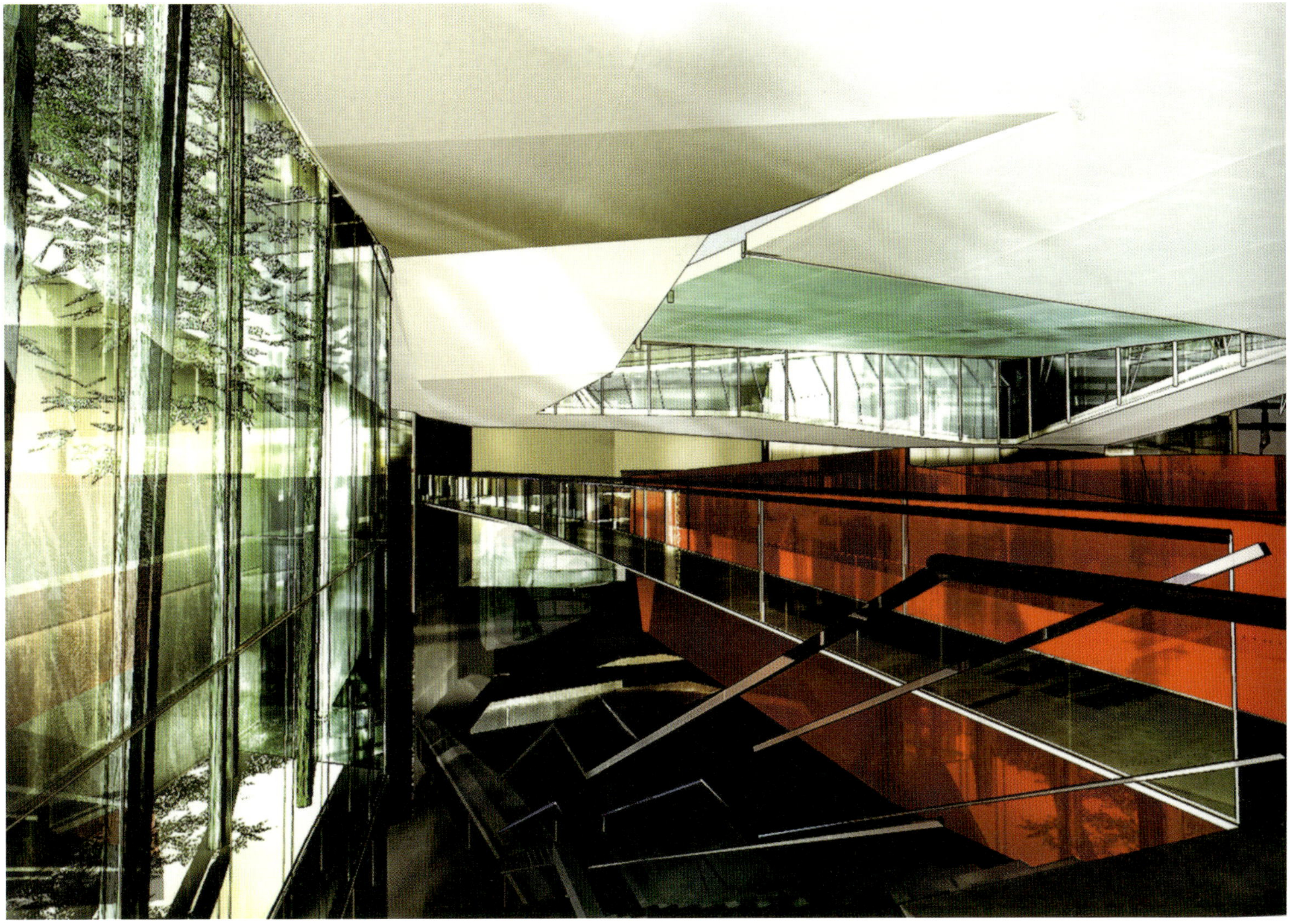

Odile Decq, digital plan for an extension to the Marco Museum of Modern Art in Rome, 2004–10, Studio Odile Decq, Paris

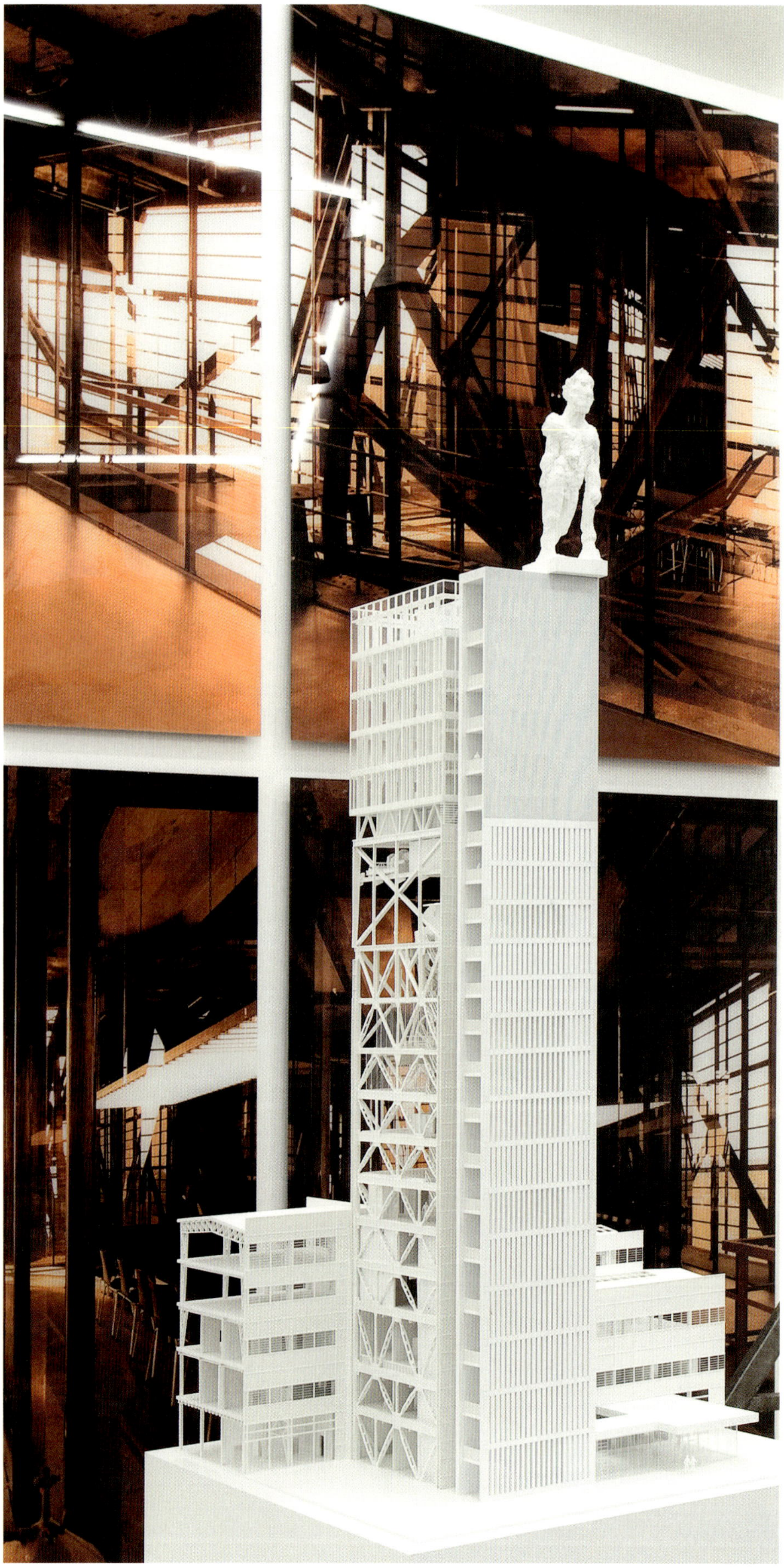

Karl-Heinz Petzinka, model for an extension to the shaft tower, Nordstern Mine, Gelsenkirchen, 2010, Petzinka Pink Architekten, Düsseldorf

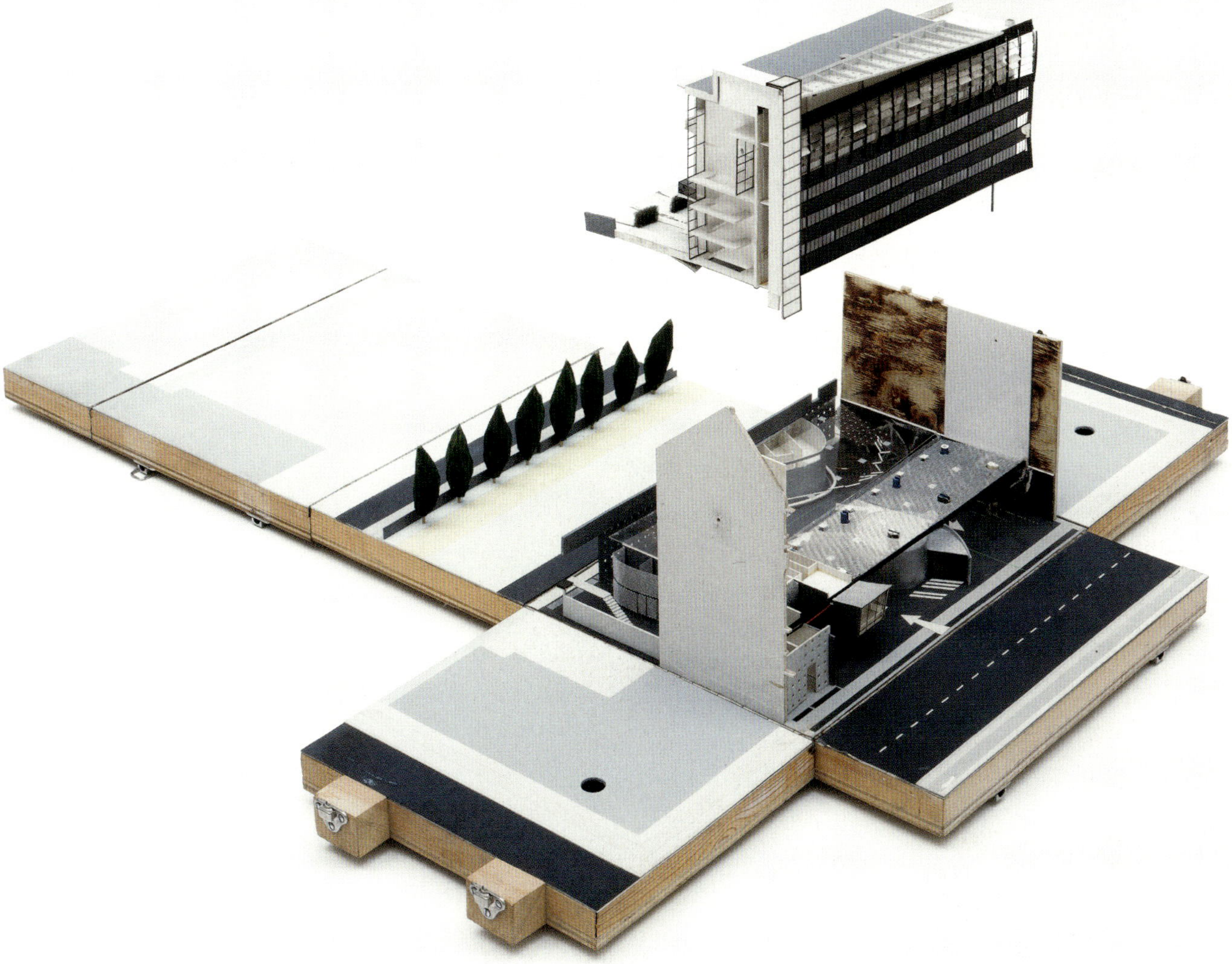

OMA, Office for Metropolitan Architecture (Rem Koolhaas, Matthias Sauerbruch, Elia Zenghelis), presentation and display model of the entire building, House at Checkpoint Charlie, c.1987, 39 × 55 × 43 cm closed; 34.5 × 116 × 130.5 cm opened out, Deutsches Architekturmuseum Collection, Frankfurt am Main

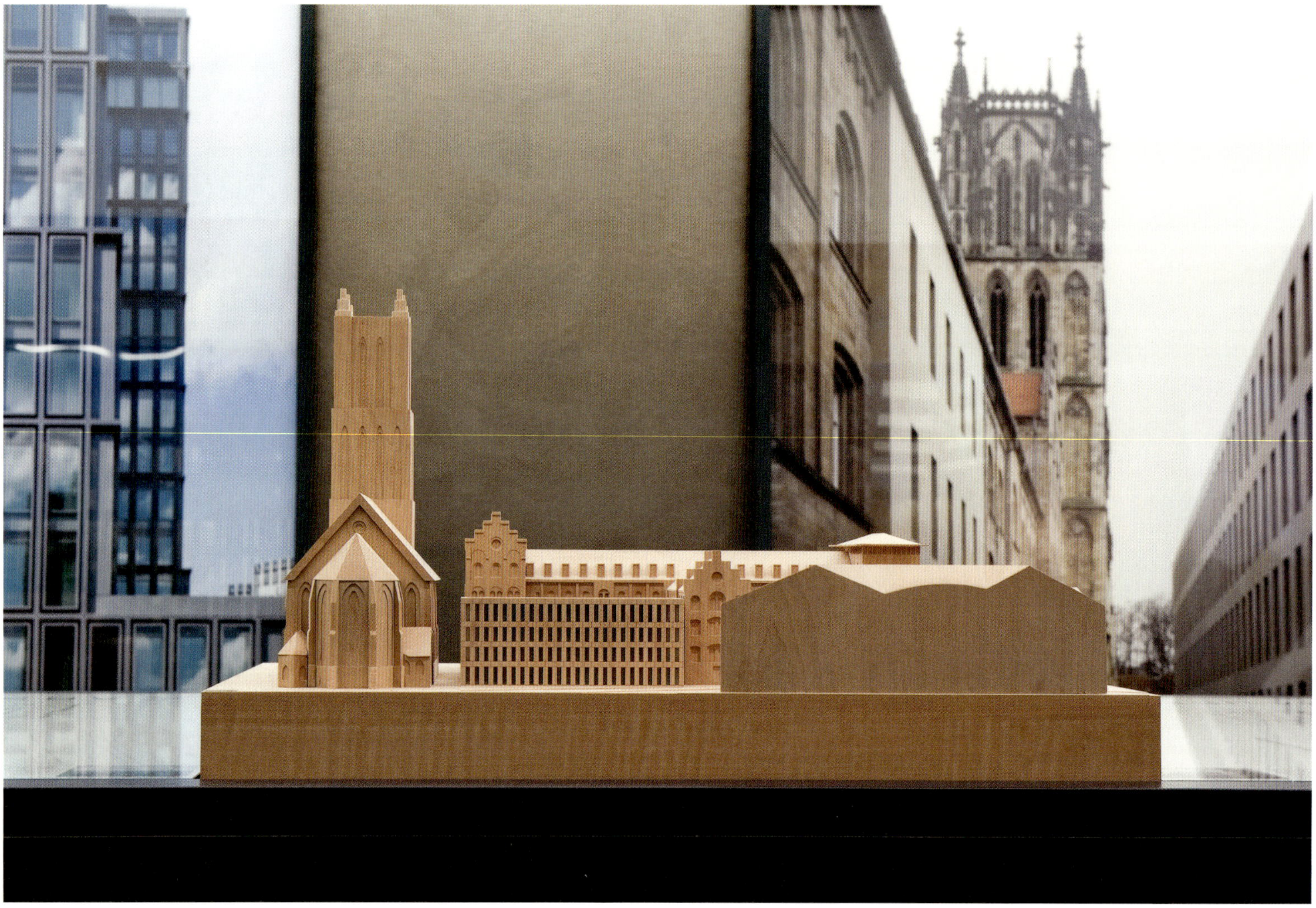

Max Dudler, wooden model for the Diocesan Library in Münster, 2002–05, Max Dudler, Berlin/Zurich/Frankfurt

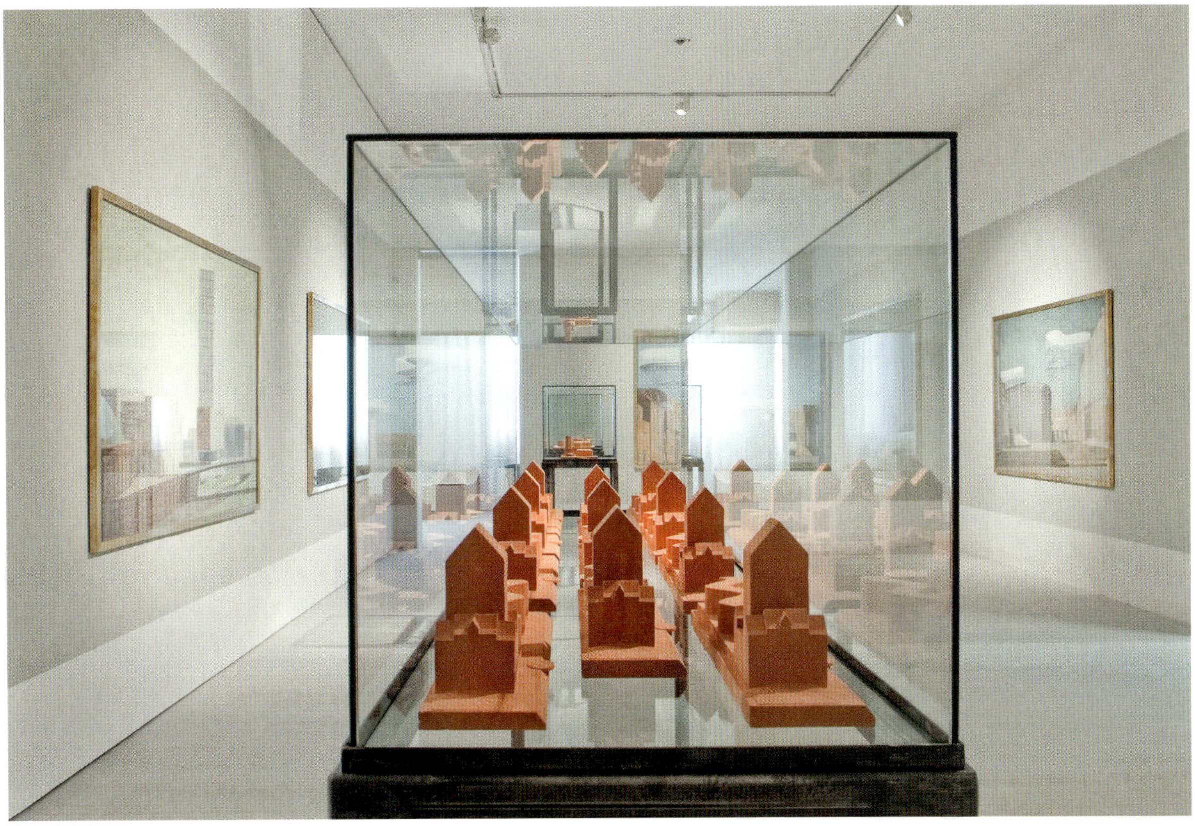

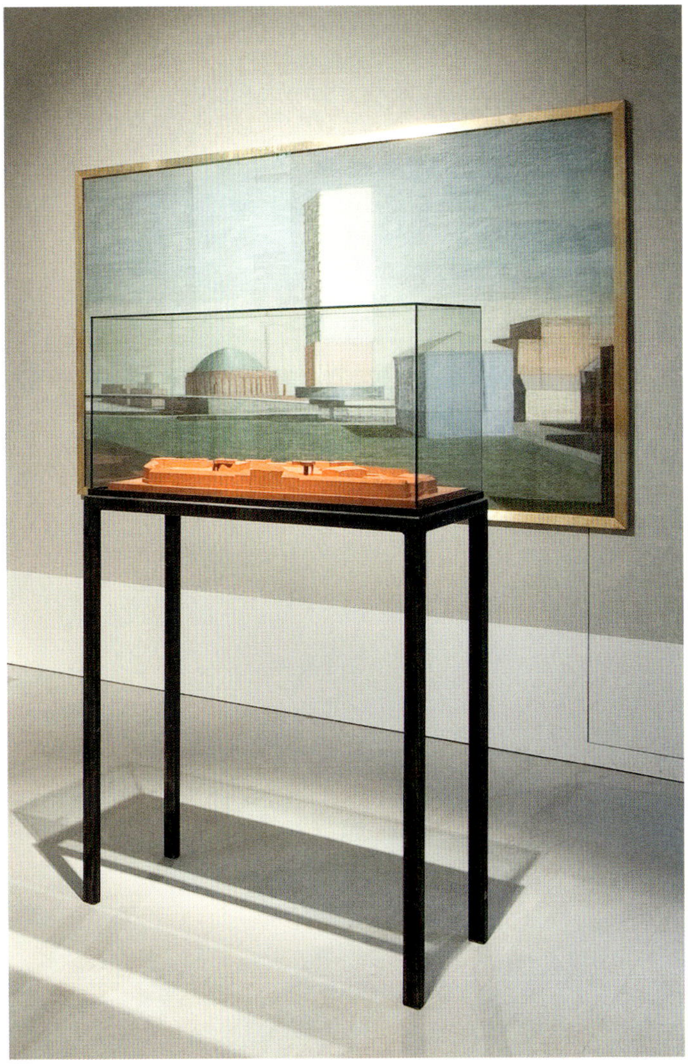

Laurids Ortner, clay models for building the North Rhine-Westphalian State Archives building, Duisburg; installation view in the Academy Gallery, drawings in chalk by Manfred Ortner, 2010

Laurids Ortner, clay model of the Museum Quarter, Vienna, 2010; in the rear: Manfred Ortner, sketch of the Kunstkonsulat Düsseldorf, 2010, chalk on paper, 148 × 222 cm, Ortner & Ortner Baukunst, Vienna/Cologne/Berlin

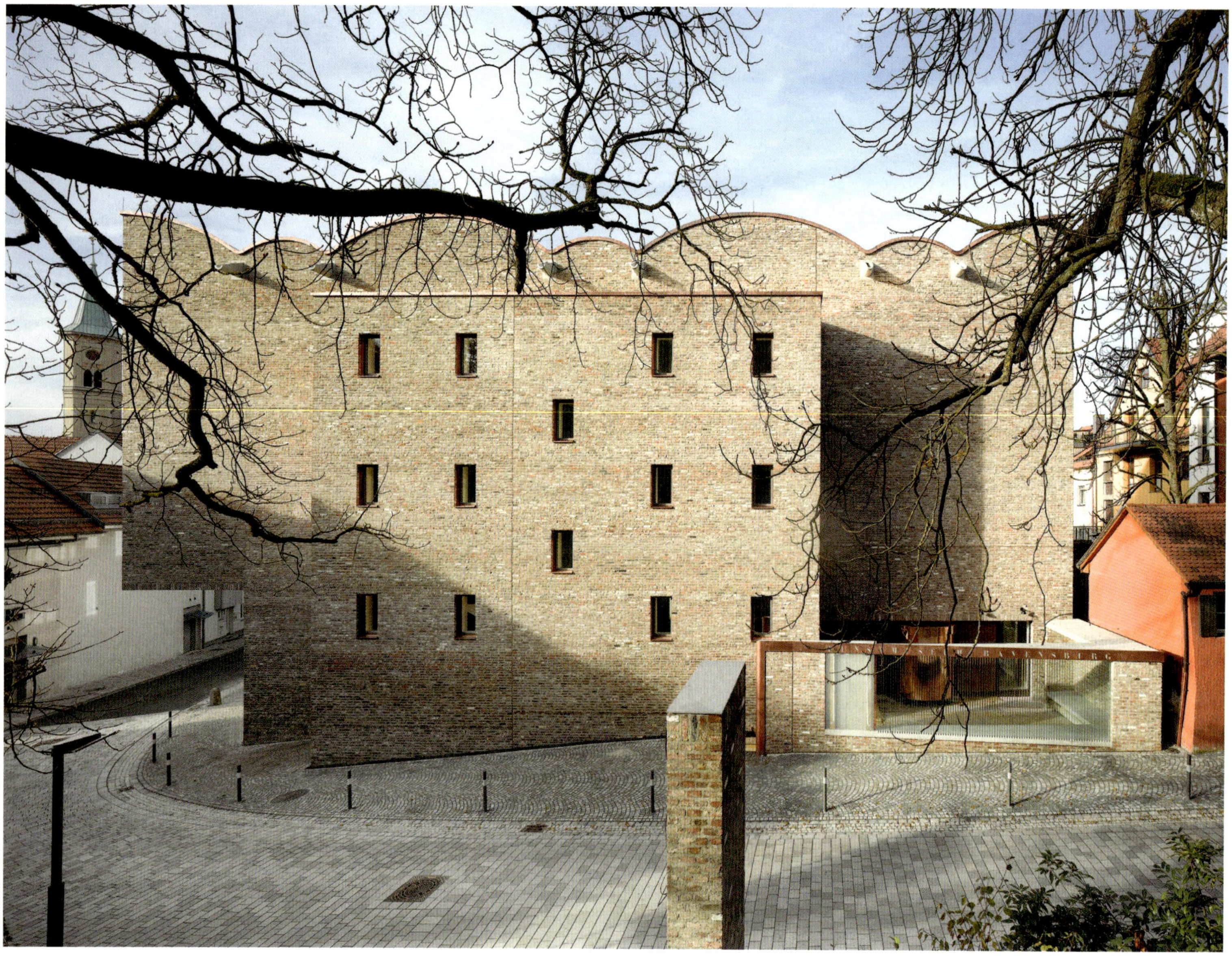

Lederer + Ragnarsdóttir + Oei, Kunstmuseum Ravensburg, 2012

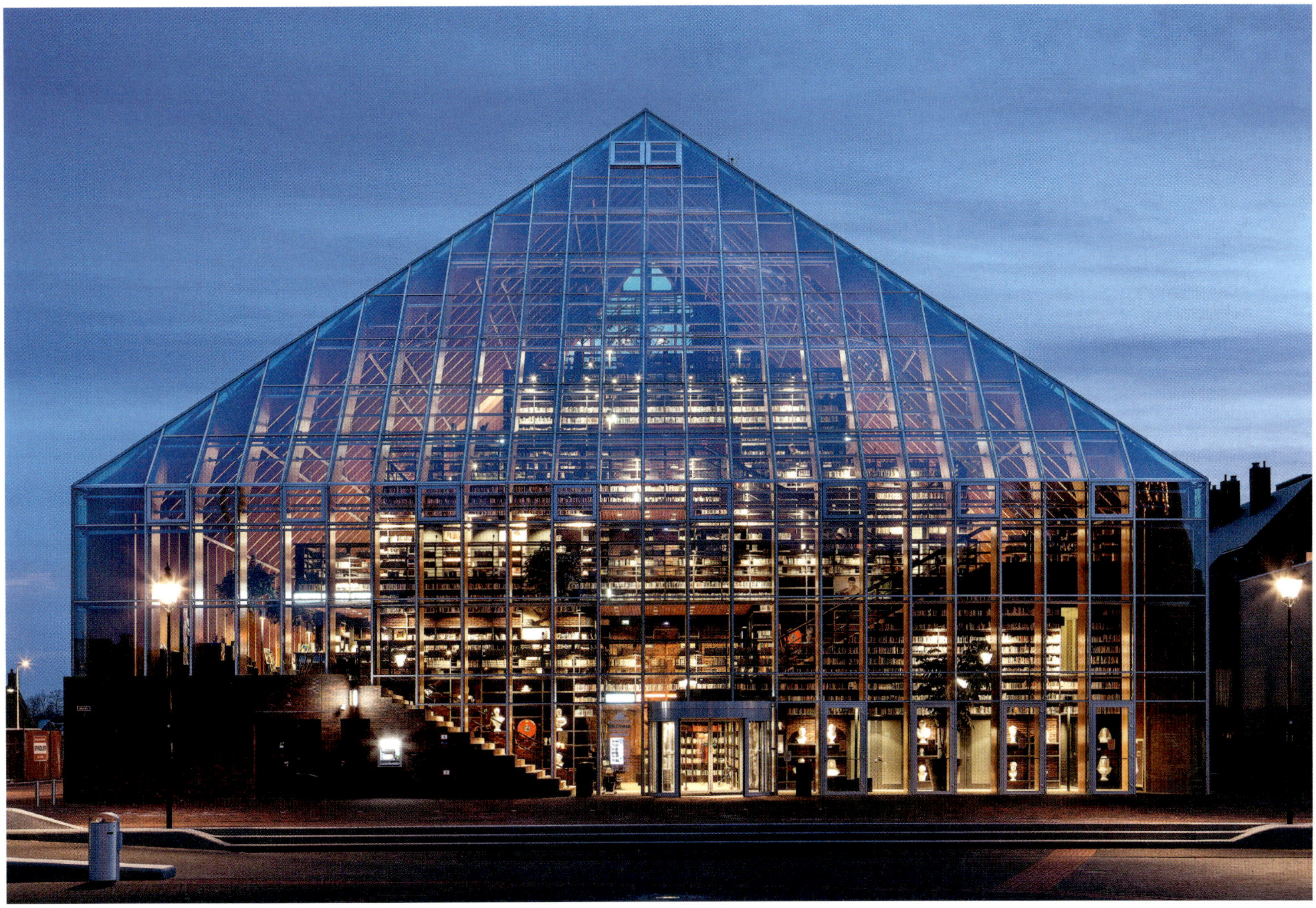

MVRDV (Winy Maas, Jacob van Rijs and Nathalie de Vries), Bibliothek Boekenberg, Spijkenisse, 2012

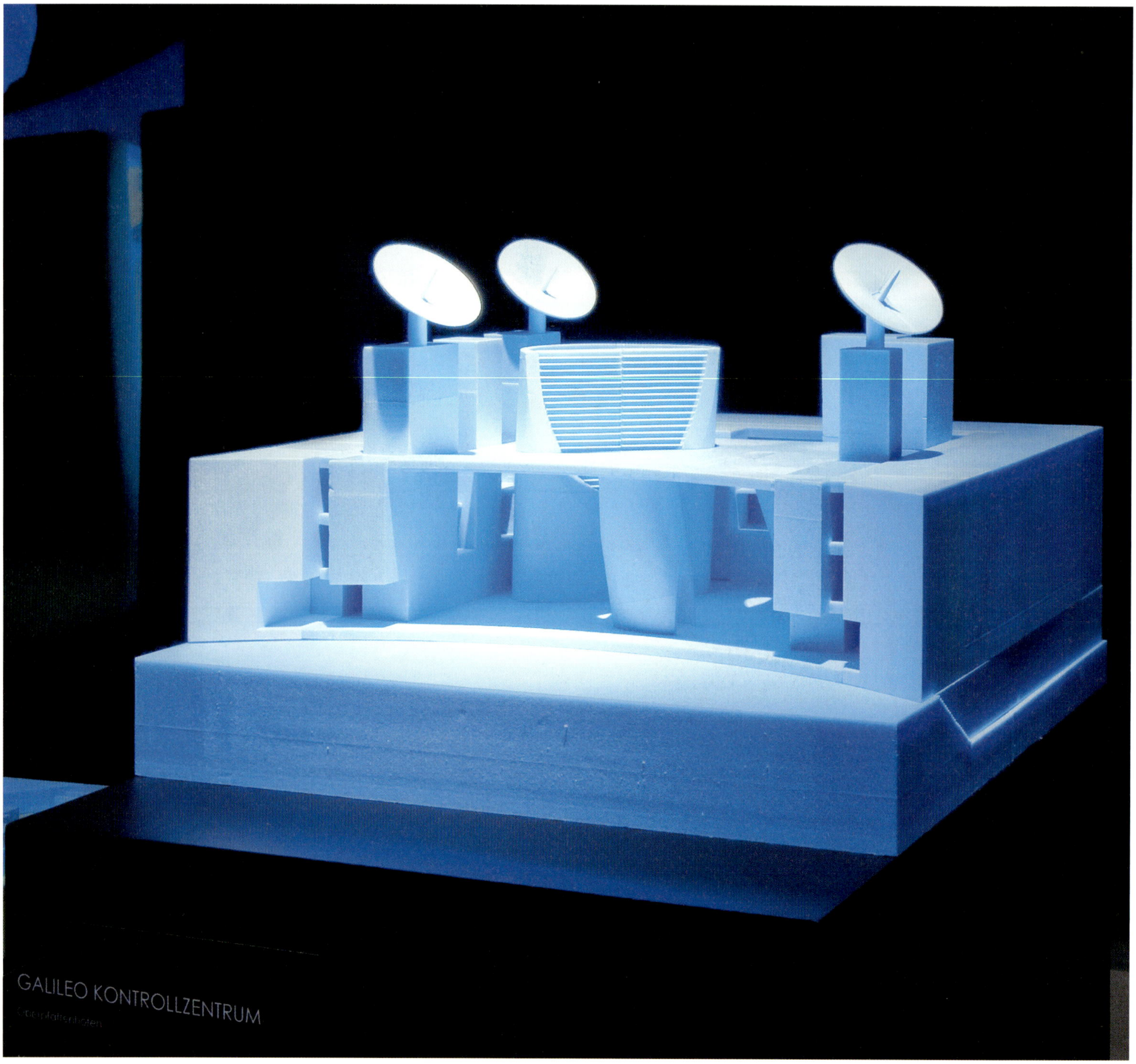

Axel Schultes and Charlotte Frank, model for the Galileo Control Centre in Oberpfaffenhofen, 2005–08, Schultes Frank Architekten, Berlin

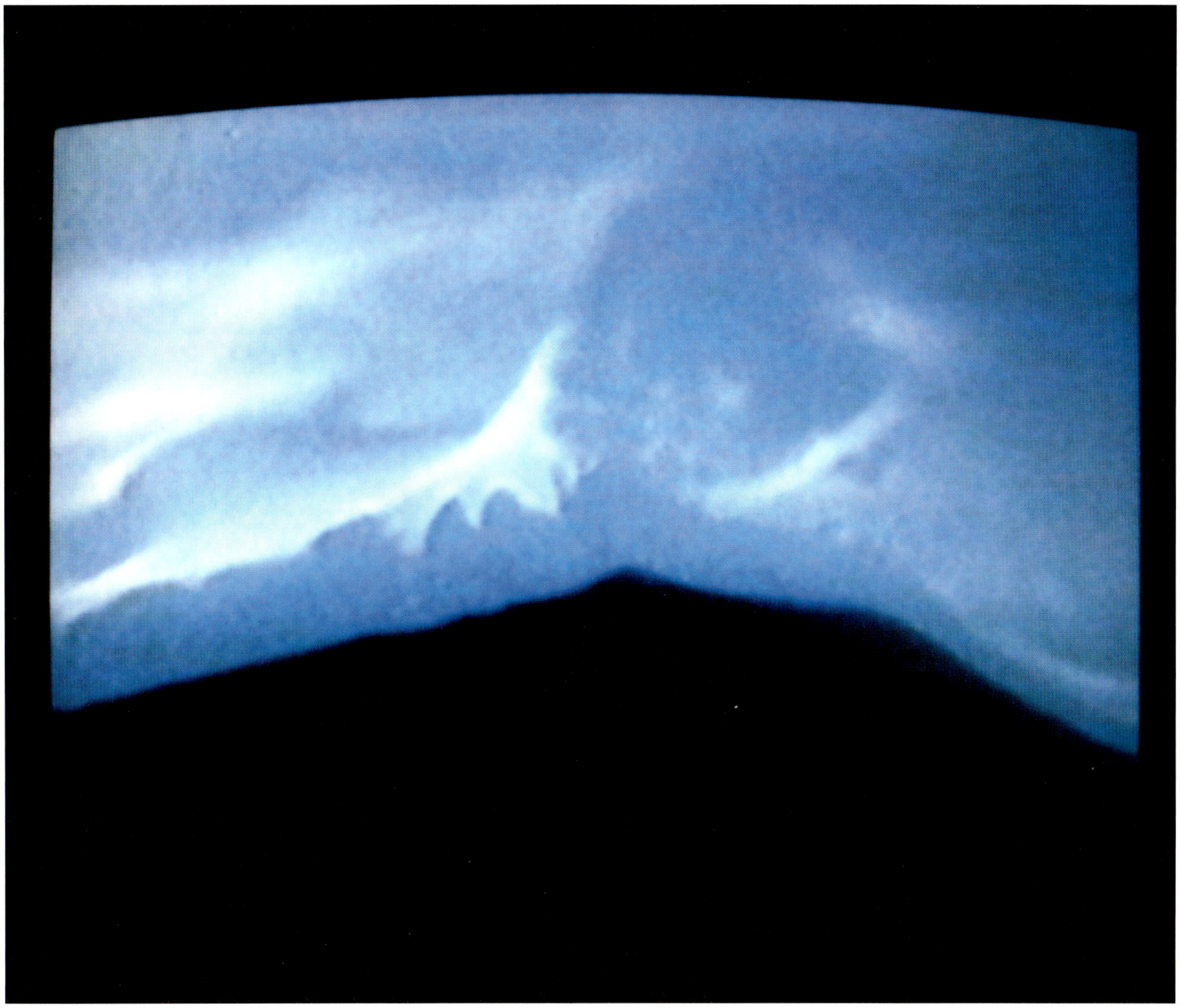

Nan Hoover, Returning to Fuji, *1984, video still, 8-minute loop, Akademie-Galerie – Die Neue Sammlung, Düsseldorf*

MY WORK AT THE DÜSSELDORF ART ACADEMY FROM 1992 UNTIL 2004

Oswald Wiener

My teaching was based on the following considerations:

- Aesthetics cannot masquerade as science. Undoubtedly, the history of aesthetics is important for training artists; however, it is already being taught – more or less explicitly – as part of general art history.

- The contemporary aesthetics discussion remains unproductive if it does not attempt to confront its object with current attempts at scientific psychology and epistemology based on the natural sciences. Contemporary art teaching is not laying the foundations for a confrontation of that kind (C. P. Snow's *The Two Cultures*); the distrust widespread among artists of 'mechanistic' explanations (or of any kind of explanations, for that matter) is – in general – not based on ideas of scientific method that would make possible criticism that can be taken seriously.

- That distrust is, however, definitely justified, particularly where art is concerned, because no one has succeeded to the present day in discovering convincing correlations between physiological facts and the phenomenon of subjective experience. The failure to do so derives in great part from the inability of contemporary psychology to sufficiently describe the phenomena of subjective experience – for instance, what we mean by the word 'consciousness' is entirely unclear. My own work has been defined by the hope that the art of the future would form the avant-garde of research in this field.

- Is it really true that aesthetics has to deal with such issues? A large part of the aesthetics discourse is purely conjectural, but an interest in aesthetics which does not investigate the questions touched on above runs the risk of being overtaken by research in the natural sciences over the longer term – the whole aesthetics issue becomes outdated with reference to art that is limited *ad hoc* to household remedies and brainstorms.

I accordingly brought my teaching and classes into line with these considerations:

- The task remained for me to introduce the aesthetics discussions of the immediate present which had not yet been described by art history, and I concentrated on this particular subject in some seminars.

- Students had to be equipped with a practical idea of the formal way of thinking employed in sciences, especially mathematics and IT. I opted for an elementary introduction to automata theory, which I offered as a two-term integrated course during my entire period of service, and I constantly worked on improving its accessibility.

  It was important to me to establish clearly defined conceptions of 'mechanism' and 'formalism' in order to be able to demonstrate the problems associated with using them as instruments of psychological description and epistemology – in brief, the 'computer metaphor' problem. Automata theory was suitable for what I had in mind because the fundamentals of it can be represented very vividly without loss of stringency, because its so very important limitative findings (which remain easy to understand even up to Kurt Gödel's incompleteness theorems) can accommodate the aspect of paradoxes, which is attractive to the contemporary way of thinking about art, and because automata theory as a 'replica of living thinking' (Jean Piaget) contrasts in a theoretically significant way with that thinking.

- In order to make that contrast obvious, I used a considerable part of my instruction for empirical practice in self-observation as a method of procuring psychological data. Over the course of protracted exercises in imagination and discussions of theory, I plumbed together with the students those broad areas of experience that can be introspectively grasped, which are neglected by contemporary psychology.

- In lectures, seminars, and colloquies, I taught an introduction to the cognitive sciences in so far as they are relevant for discussions of that kind ('artificial intelligence', 'neurophilosophy'). Contemporary dream theories were also subjected to critical observation.

- Other coursework was devoted to sociological and fashionable aspects of aesthetics ideologies: the history of the genius concept, dandyism, metaphysics. One seminar was about the concept of artificiality; another was concerned with a defence of art and its future.

I thank my colleague, Friedrich Wolfram Heubach, for productive collaboration on some of those approaches.

WHY POETICS AT AN ART ACADEMY?

Durs Grünbein

Art is not speechless. It expresses itself where it can do so in conformity with the laws of subjectivity. A tacit consensus among artists goes: it can speak very well for itself and has no need of being interpreted, imparted. And yet there is something that remains unsaid behind all mute observation. The retreat of artworks into the depths of galleries, collectors' private rooms, cannot be delayed with texts. But what would happen to those artworks without the free assistance of literature that buzzes about them and illuminates their recondite backstories like flashes of lightning? They would be condemned to be stifled in a haze of chatter and blithe aesthetic judgements. They would be handed over for interpretation to academic arbiters, to their applications of theory that are only rarely entirely disinterested.

Literature is the long shadow that has accompanied and inspired all great artworks since observing them without constraints became fashionable. It started by anticipating them: the Greek epics and the verses of the first lyric poets gave instructions to the imagination. Mythology was the soil from which the statues and the first panel paintings grew, all of which have been lost.

Under the influence of poetry, which was an exemplary vehicle for myth, art remained for a long time in the shackles of crafts. The roll of directors of the classics who provided visual artists with scenes and motifs ranged from Homer and the ancient Greek tragedians to Vergil and Ovid. It was from their batteries that the electric current flowed, amplified once again in the Renaissance, the Baroque, Classicism, on down to the threshold of Modernism. Its most recent discharges for the time being were registered by Surrealism. After that something different began, the emergence of art from the old magnetic fields, its liberation from the fetters of the representational. In painting, line and colour appeared in confrontational opposition; they became the field for perceptual experimentation, a 'School of Seeing'. In the picture space of a painting, subject and object entered into a relationship liberated from all literalness – only now are we gradually beginning to grasp the consequences of that development. The letters and numerals on the collages of the Synthetic Cubists were its farewell signal.

That prose and poetry, since the old bonds have been rent asunder, can often contribute more to understanding artworks than thousands of studies and articles in the relevant specialist dictionaries is a question of eye level and autonomy. Let us not forget who provided the keywords for art movements such as Cubism or Surrealism – it was the poets. What is needed is the emphatic, independent word that, in a spate of passion, even impatience, reveals more of artworks than the sterile scalpel of theory can ever do. Why do we understand each other all the better the less we treat ourselves as instruments, the more we encounter one another with poise? Since the arts have emancipated themselves from literature and literature can no longer dictate terms to them, the relationship between the two has been open for astonishing insights. Now it is the view from the far side, it is the competitive language that creates moments of rapprochement. Such as when Charles Baudelaire says of the painter who was closest to him in his generation, 'Delacroix, lake of blood haunted by evil angels' – and means by that Supernaturalism, with which the detachment from all previous painting traditions began.

It is the authors (poets, novelists, philosophers), who, from the early Paris Salons to the most recent documentas, have always managed to strike the right note that helps to plumb the novel, as yet unprecedented aspect of works that deviate from the canon. Since time immemorial the word of a writer has belonged to the probes that reliably record leaps in development, which are met with incomprehension by most contemporaries as well as the guild of professional art critics. It is the freely roaming, capricious, nervy judgement distinguished by enhanced alertness given by those versed in the arts and secretly allied with them that forms the hard core to which even art historical writing, which has gradually become mainstream, tends to resort when it is a question of ensuring that justice is meted out to individual works. Since Denis Diderot and Baudelaire, the judicious bon mot has been a reliable counsel in unclarified questions of style. They were the first to set an example of felicitous expression in the bewildering jumble of still life, history paintings, portraits, and works of sculpture. In their hands poetics became an instrument for improvising an oration on the discovery of new continents in art. All at once the earliest human texts could be received unhindered; the most recent artworks could assert themselves in their own right. Literature was dependable. It protected innovation. Now what befell the deviating inventions in the space of infinite variations of expression on the whole was what befell photography, which emerged at the same time and was the first to be sure of its independence because it was protected by the technological innovation it represented. Those deviating inventions were there first, radiant in their own technical innovation, and offered themselves up like the heavenly constellations for pure observation.

In the general hospital of the arts, poetics is the division of internal medicine. The arts will always be a reminder of what literature might have been able to say. Literature has been the long shadow accompanying the arts down through the history of period styles to the open artwork at what is, for the time being, the end of the evolution of those period styles.

The fortune of pictures is tied not to words but more likely to their intelligence. For it, more than the mute eye, is needed; it is only revealed, as exhaled breath is, in clear, frosty air. Words and images are constantly intersecting to form a continuum of overpainting and reciprocal overlayering. The interchange they engage in, driven instinctively by the sensitive, leads to intellectual reactions like those in chemistry when substances meet in a test tube. The word is the acid that dissolves a great deal. Sometimes it triggers off explosions which sharpen our awareness of what is possible in art and change everything. The haughty pictures, all pictures, are little on their own: as independent as they may seem at first glance, the evidence they have to give remains linked to language. 'A picture does not exist if it cannot lead us above and beyond all pictures', was the opinion given by the likes of Francis Picabia. Only to then ask himself, 'Why are you writing? So are you writing, as you say yourself, because literature is painting?'

'I really don't know, and hope I'll never know.'

‘FRAMING REALITY’.*
PHOTOGRAPHY AT THE DÜSSELDORF ART ACADEMY

Maren Polte

Photography has changed our perception of the world more radically than any other medium. It makes it possible to take with you what is immovable, records what is ephemeral, opens up unseen perspectives, and reproduces far more than the naked human eye can grasp. It is a medium which is debated in theory between anecdotal reference and visual construct. From the social angle it is celebrated, challenged by critics, but above all it tends to be uncritically consumed.

Even though artists have always made use of the technology and the impact made by the pictures was recognised early on, photography was not accorded the status of being an art form in its own right. By now, however, it is a force to be reckoned with, not least on the art market, where it fetches record-breaking prices. It has seen a meteoric rise over the past fifty years.

Over that time span the Düsseldorf Art Academy has become established as the alma mater of contemporary German photography. It was here that photography found its first home in a German academic context in the form of the chair for photography founded in 1976 and held by Bernd Becher. Now an institution, it has developed into a powerhouse that has contributed substantially to consolidating the status of photography in the canon of artistic disciplines.

Düsseldorf was the most important theatre of operations in Germany for the emancipation of photography, which has come mainly from Bernd Becher and his students. Nonetheless, this status, while confirmed on the art market, definitely does not imply that Becher and his class were the first to have worked in photography at the Academy or even that they would have remained the sole agency relevant to photography at this institution. The history of photography at the Düsseldorf Art Academy cannot be told from a single historical strand that might be called ‘Becher and the consequences’. The factors that have contributed to make that history are decisive developments, on the one hand in the political and social context, and on the other on the technological plane, including its aesthetic effects on and reception by the media.

The gradual rise in the status of photography was not, even at the Academy, a process confined to a single sector, limited to an explicitly defined part of the curriculum. Long before the photography chair was established, artists in Düsseldorf were working with the medium. It was ultimately due to the political commitment shown by students as well as individual teachers that the traditional painting and sculpture academy opened up to media such as film, video, and also photography. The new technologies had already become art forms even before classes were officially instituted and had done so in a decentralised manner – in the work produced by numerous artists and art students in other disciplines: as resources, as an autonomous form of expression, as the object of artistic reflection. Drawing on individual stances, the present outline will attempt to trace the various parameters of the history of photography at the Düsseldorf Art Academy and to interlink them.

PHOTOGRAPHY AS DOCUMENTATION

That history began with the eruption on the scene of the Happening culture on the artistic side and the political unrest on the social and institutional side. In the late 1950s artists began to rebel against the traditional genre canon by showcasing the fleeting moment instead of the lasting material, experimenting beyond the bounds of genre in music, and making their own bodies the artistic crime scene. Action Art, Happenings, and Fluxus emerged, and with them, as Sophia Stang explains, ‘the status and form of the artwork changed radically’: the works presented did not assume permanent form; they defied both traditional exhibition praxis and the art market.[1] Their ephemeral character fomented a need for visual fixation.

Art production and representation in the media grew to be closely interconnected. Action Art looked for places to perform and found the right artists to document it. One of the first Happenings leading to the Fluxus movement was the John Cage performance at Galerie 22 in October 1958. Like many others of its kind, it was captured on film by the photographer Manfred Leve (Fig. 1).[2] Reiner Ruthenbeck, who would later be a pupil of Beuys’s, was also on the move with a camera and among the events he photographed were Actions mounted by the ZERO group (Fig. 2). Along with those two photographers there were many others – professional photographers, interested laymen, Academy students – who followed the ongoing cultural events and documented the spate of artistic energy. Bernd Jansen, Ute Klophaus, Manfred Tischer, Jörg Boström, and Katharina Sieverding are just a few of the contemporary eyewitnesses who held cameras in their hands at that time to record the disintegration of the traditional notions of what constituted an artwork. This movement administered, as Friedrich Wolfram Heubach writes, 'a radical put-down to the taste in art then prevailing, which was still shaped by the pretentious and fusty spirituality of the 1950s'.[3] Through the new movement Düsseldorf and the Rhineland became a magnet for artists at home and abroad, a development to which avant-garde gallerists, such as Jean-Pierre Wilhelm, Alfred Schmela, and later Konrad Fischer, substantially contributed. The living evolution of the art scene in the midst of official institutions and artist initiatives – such as Capitalist Realism (1963–1966) launched by Gerhard Richter, Konrad Lueg (later Fischer), Manfred Kuttner, and Sigmar Polke; Creamcheese, founded in 1967 as a café with dancing, concert hang-out, and a site for Action Art; and the Lidl Project (1968/69) initiated by Jörg Immendorff and Chris Reinecke – was copiously documented in photographs. Now those photographs often represent the sole evidence preserved from manifold Action events – at once a visual art history and a continuous documentation of the advance of photography into artistic praxis at the Düsseldorf Academy.[4]

Those who wanted to work with photography at the Academy met in cross-class flexible groups. Initiatives of this kind came not from the professors but the students, who viewed photography as a medium in keeping with the time because it was 'democratic' and 'anti-authoritarian'. For them the camera became a handy artistic assistant and companion, an instrument that could be used for both documentary and experimental art purposes.

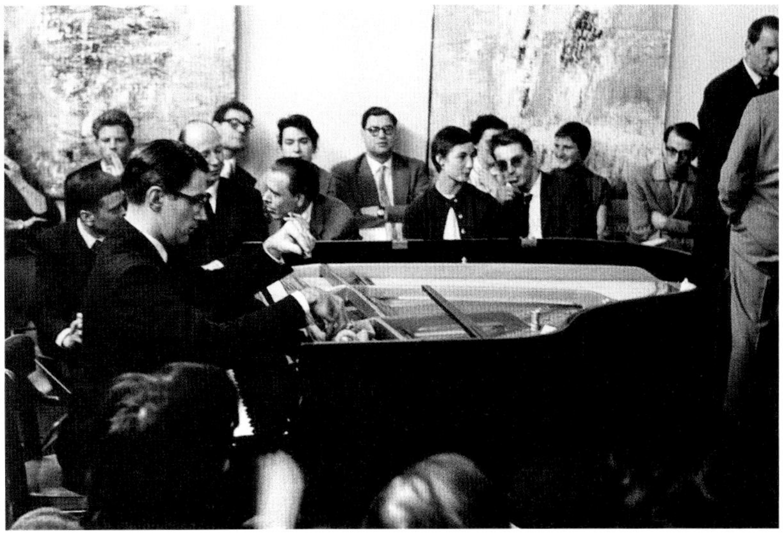

Fig. 1: Manfred Leve, John Cage's Music Walk, *David Tudor at the piano, Galerie 22, Düsseldorf, 14 October 1958, silver gelatin print on baryte paper, 15.7 × 25 cm*

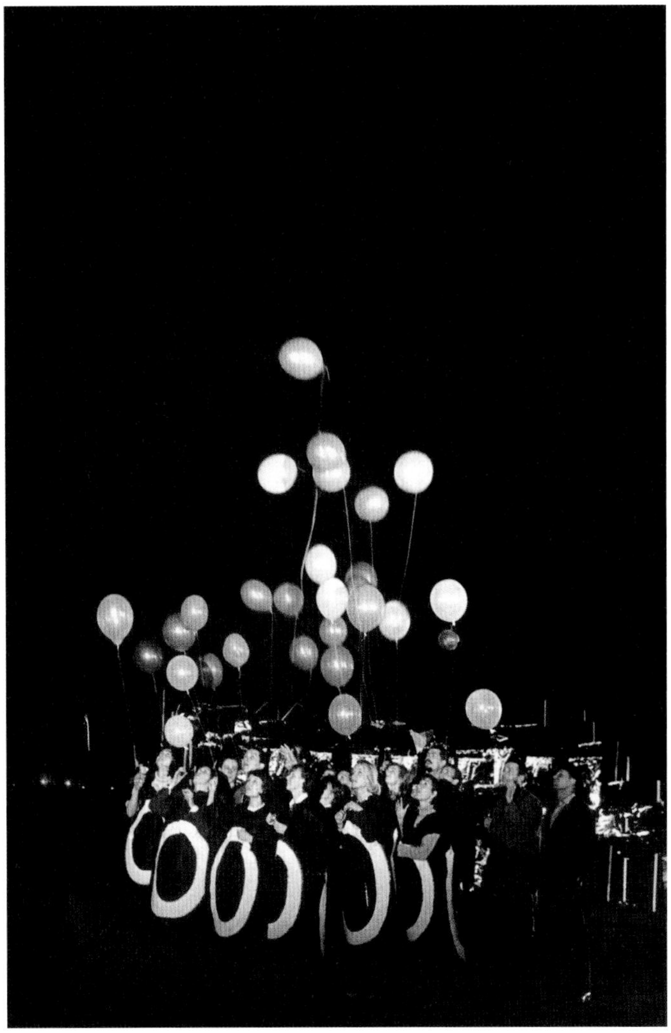

Fig. 2: Reiner Ruthenbeck, ZERO-Fest, *performers with balloons, Rheinwiesen Oberkassel, Düsseldorf, 16 May 1962, black-and-white photograph on chromogenically developed PE paper, 29.7 × 19.9 cm*

Documentation and Grandstanding – Joseph Beuys

The symbolic figure who represented the linkage of artistic and political unrest at the Düsseldorf Art Academy was Joseph Beuys (1921–1986). Called to a professorship for monumental sculpture in 1961, Beuys was one of the great instigators of the 1960s, a man who stood for the radical demolition of the prevailing notions of art, a different cultural policy, and an entirely different approach to teaching. From the late 1960s on, Beuys turned the order which had until then prevailed at the Academy upside down.

For all the trouble the Academy had on his account, it owes its avant-garde ranking among art institutes of the time chiefly

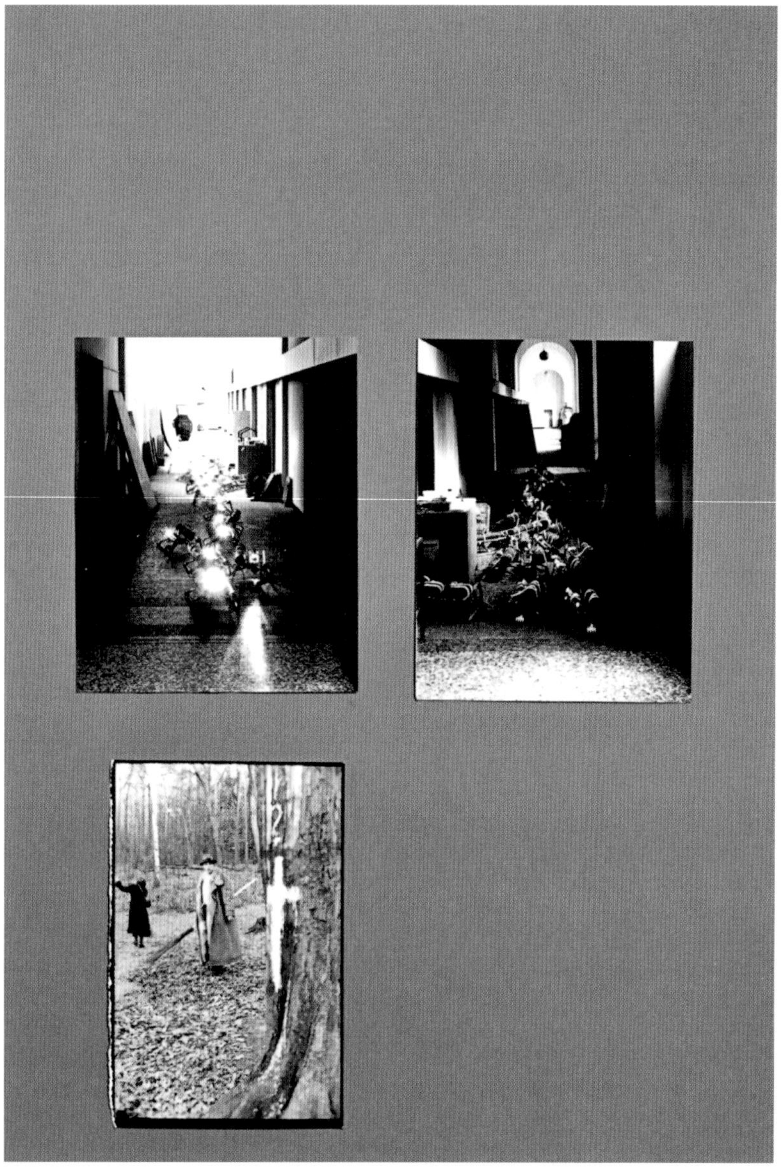

Fig. 3: Joseph Beuys, Arena #16: The pack (das Rudel) 1969, The pack (das Rudel) 1969, Let's come over with the party dictatorship now, *framed photographs, 1971*

to this unflagging gadfly and prime mover and shaker. His energy and open-mindedness were a magnet for many and the engine that drove numerous upheavals. The service he did to the Academy and the Düsseldorf art scene rested in his linkage of the sociopolitical and artistic spheres. Beuys was, as Hannes Böhringer notes in a personal reminiscence, the only professor at a German art institute to have assimilated the 1968 student revolution and the concomitant social crisis in his work. Even though the Art Academy seemed doomed to break down on several occasions due to his pronounced anti-academism, Beuys nonetheless ensured that art production would not be abandoned – as it was at other institutes because it was allegedly superfluous – in order to make room for revolution, discussion, or agitprop.[5]

His own conception of what an artwork was, on the other hand, was based on what was actually a traditional conception of the object, in which the materials he used were not supposed to be regarded as dead matter but rather as sculpturally modulated energy, whose form and state might change even after a work might be finished.[6] Photography is diametrically opposed to this profoundly mystical idea of the unfinished and processual yet is for that very reason of pivotal importance as a means to documenting Joseph Beuys as a person and his work. This dialectic of dependence and rejection runs through his entire career. Christopher Phillips called this dichotomy 'wrestling with paradoxes'.[7]

Although neither film nor photography belonged to Beuys's stock-in-trade, he nonetheless knew how to exploit both to the utmost for grandstanding purposes. His person and his work were captured in photographs from the 1950s on. Twenty years later he produced *Arena*, the sole work based on photography which Beuys himself, as Lynn Cooke writes, assembled and over the years continued to change 'as the autobiographical summation, as an illustrated diary of his public persona' (Fig. 3).[8] *Arena* consisted of '264 photographs worked over with sulphur, acid, wax, and paint, and three hand-made coloured glass plates, which are enclosed in a total of 100 carefully bolted casings reminiscent of crypts. There were also an oil can and twenty-one layers of wax mixed with grease in two stacks as well as sheet copper and wrought iron.'[9] The photographs used were pictures taken by several men and women photographers who captured his actions and works. All shots relate solely to the artistic work although the arbitrary choice of photos, some of whose motifs are scarcely recognisable, the poor quality of the prints, and additional processing make precise classification and attribution impossible. Hence the 'autobiographical summation' is unlikely to have been based on a discernible chronology. It remains open to interpretation, is therefore dependent on individual perception, and thus matches Beuys's ambivalent relationship to the role of photography as a medium.

His use of photos for attracting attention to himself became increasingly sophisticated from the mid-1960s on. They are on posters, in exhibition catalogues, and even in the avant-garde periodical *interfunktionen*, edited from 1968 until 1974 by Friedrich Wolfram Heubach, who would later be an Academy professor. A combination of facsimiles of originals and documents, the periodical provided a forum for the contemporary art movement and its aims, which also included Beuys's

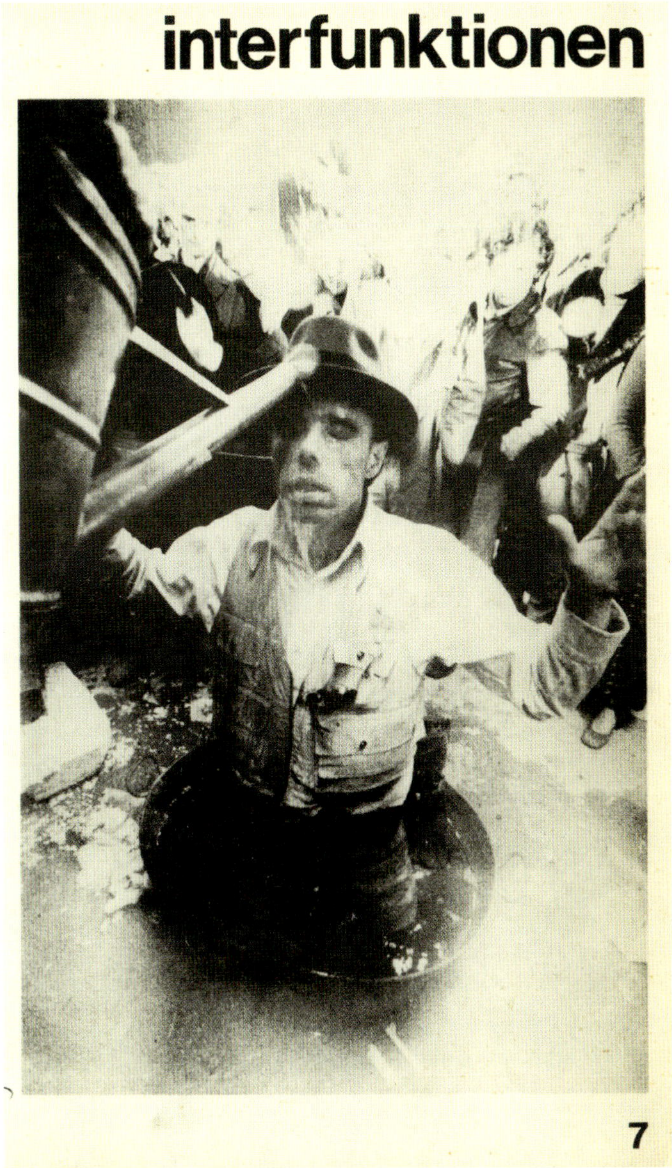

Fig. 4: Ute Klophaus, Joseph Beuys, Fußwaschung *[Washing of Feet],* interfunktionen *7, 1971, cover*

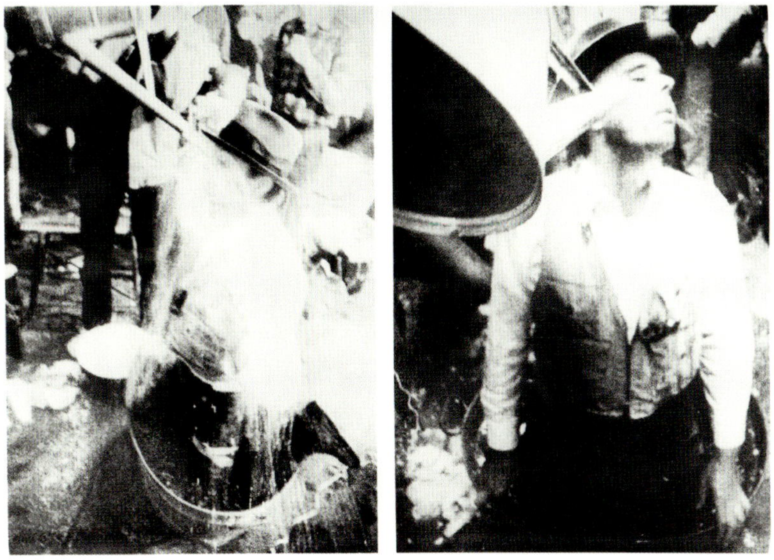

Fig. 5: Ute Klophaus, Joseph Beuys, Fußwaschung *[Washing of Feet],* interfunktionen *7, 1971, pp. 39–40*

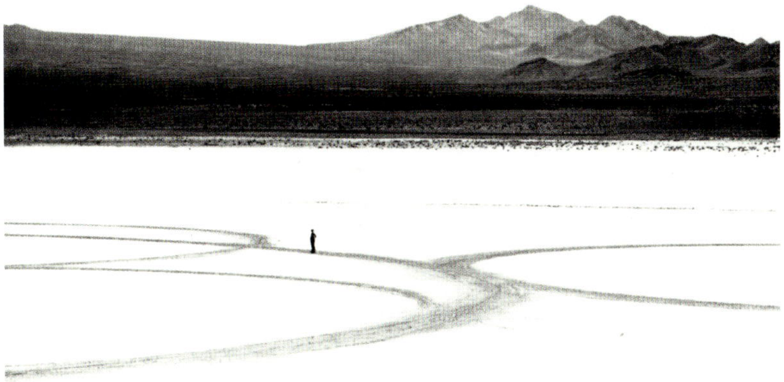

Fig. 6: Michael Heizer, Circular Displacement Drawing, *1970,* interfunktionen *7, 1971, p. 47*

Actions.[10] Some of them, including the Action Day of 5 February 1971 documented by Ute Klophaus, are published there in extensive sequences of photos (Figs. 4, 5).[11] All fifty-nine illustrations are atmospheric, blurred, some of them cropped, others resembling details. They provide an impression of mood and dynamics rather than content. This sets them fundamentally apart from the logically sequenced, clearly structured, and sharply focused shots of the Land Art works produced at the same time by such artists as Denis Oppenheim, Michael Heizer, and Richard Long (Fig. 6). The integration of geometric figurations in landscape can only be physically experienced in sequence. In these photographic documentaries time and form are perceived simultaneously and appear as two-dimensional abstraction. Thus photography serves as an eyewitness account but has already assumed the function of an autonomous visualising medium.

But that was precisely what Beuys did not want. He was not interested in the medium as such and the possibilities for developing it, neither in enlarging the existing hierarchy of genres nor helping what was basically a reproducing medium to advance to the status of an art medium.[12] He was well aware that technical images would shape the historical tradition. Nonetheless, to him they remained purely a crafts resource that was useful for constantly transfixing his person and his work in photos and on film.

Beuys's close collaboration with Ute Klophaus, who accompanied his work for more than twenty years, should also be viewed as a similar balancing act between dependence and distrust. In her quest for a pictorial language of her own, which would reproduce as faithfully as possible the processual aspect of the impact it made, Klophaus, a trained photographer, developed an aesthetic style that incorporated coincidences and errors that occurred in shooting and enlarging. In part Klophaus intervened deliberately, for instance, tearing off the margins of the photo paper to reinforce the impression that everything was unplanned and deficient in order to fittingly express the aspect of the Actions that could not be rationally grasped, the cultic quality. Even though Beuys reserved the right to select the pictures to be used, through them she had a formative influence on the aesthetic of the Beuys works that were documented in photographs.

PHOTOGRAPHY AS A MEDIUM

Despite the sceptical attitude Beuys had towards the technical media where his own work was concerned, he was still always open-minded about his students' interest in those media. In this stance he was virtually alone at the Art Academy in the 1960s. During the two years beginning in 1968, when Dieter Roth taught at the Academy on Beuys's recommendation, his students set up a darkroom in the class in order to experiment with developing, enlarging, and photography in general.[13] There does not seem to have been a photography workshop that was accessible to students at that time. With the support of her professor, Walter Breker, Hilla Becher installed a darkroom as soon as she became a student at the Academy in 1958/59, for which she was responsible and in which she instructed other students in photographic techniques. This facility does not, however, seem to have been seamlessly operative after she finished her studies. There was an officially employed photographer but instruction for students in lab work was not recorded until the winter term of 1972/73, and space and facilities were limited. Some professors set up darkrooms of their own, including Edgar Georg Callahan with his class in interdisciplinary project development and Klaus Rinke, before Bernd Becher took over the chair of photography in 1976 and started with his first students from scratch as far as technical equipment was concerned.

It was very difficult for the new visual medium to gain a foothold at such a traditional academy for painters and sculptors. But the enthusiasm with which students not only leapt at photography but embraced the technical media in general put persistent, and ultimately effective, pressure on the outmoded rejection of such media. Even though the darkroom in the Roth class was only used by a few people, it was nonetheless an important sign of a willingness to experiment and a desire to work on an interdisciplinary basis.

The Film Experiment – Ole John

Interested in integrating the technical media in artistic praxis, the Academy students urged the establishment of a film class and eventually achieved their aim, albeit within limits. Through the Danish composer and Fluxus participant Henning Christiansen contact was made with the experimental film-maker Ole John (*1939), who, at the wish of the students and on an invitation issued by Joseph Beuys, became a lecturer at the Academy in 1971. The year before, Ole John had made a film, *Trans-Siberian Railway*, about the Joseph Beuys Happening of the same title (1961/69), which was shown at the Louisiana Museum of Modern Art in Denmark.[14]

A 16 mm film, it was made with few resources and a limited budget and featured long takes, double exposures, and camera shake and blurring, without panning or zooming and devoid of technical perfection. Although until then film had been viewed as a medium for representing art,[15] this work was based on the experimental idea of making film itself into an art medium. Technology and equipment were expensive and heavy. A lot of equipment and many people were needed – making a mainstream film was an elaborate process. Hence doing without and improvising became artistic methods for introducing film as a medium in the first place and making the use of it as uncomplicated as possible. The experimental artists who worked with Ole John reduced the means to a minimum because the young lecturer only had limited resources at his disposal. 'Much ambition, little money' ran the headline of the *Rheinische Post* article on the new Film Department at the Academy.[16] But there was a lot of interest. Ole John was the reason why film buffs such as Hartmut Kaminski and Rolf Neddermann came to the Academy.

Yet as an offshoot class, film was deliberately left as an underfunded subdivision. Lack of funding made technical

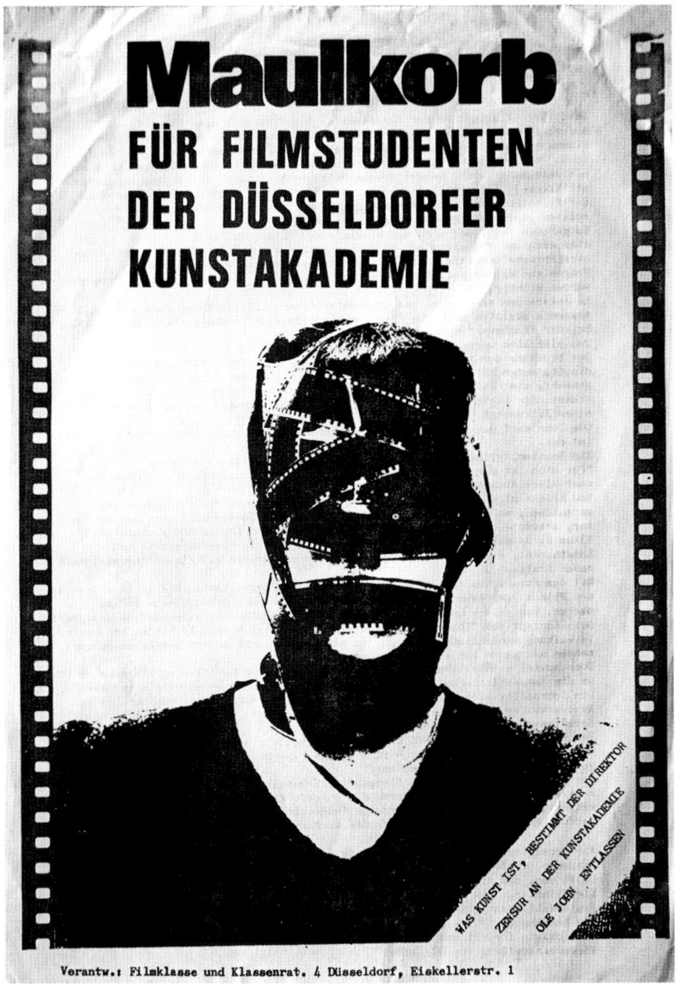

Fig. 7: Maulkorb *[Muzzle], film-class protest poster, 1975*

perfection and professional production impossible. And integration in the experimental art scene was only partly successful because there was no art-film tradition in Düsseldorf and the Rhineland at that time. Ole John joined forces with Lutz Mommartz, Christof Kohlhöfer, and Tony Morgan to found the Düsseldorf Film Group in order to build up a network and arouse interest in the medium.[17] Despite the commitment he showed, his lectureship would remain a five-year intermezzo (1971–1976). During that time John was given more money for equipment, yet without the enormous efforts of the students, which included financial commitments, many projects would not have been realised. For the students, on the other hand, film remained primarily a political instrument. That this was so is the subtext of the dismissal notice sent to John by the Academy: as far as working in art was concerned, there was no discernible rapprochement between film and fine art; further, there was a one-sided bias towards documentary films. Thus a conversion of a lectureship to a chair applied for in 1975 became a summary dismissal, with Ole John unaware of what was coming until five weeks before the end of his stint in Düsseldorf. Klaus Ulrich Reinke and Ursula Wevers were hired on short-term contracts to keep the film class going. With the combination of theoretical and artistic approaches they represented, all experimental leanings were to be channelled into calmer waters in compliance with overarching Academy policy. Only two years later the film subdivision was closed down.

Many students deplored the termination of the film class taught by Ole John as censorship and an assault on artistic freedom (Fig. 7). The local press closely followed the ignominious end of a course that had met with such great interest among the students: 'The film class resolution seems really grotesque considering that the photo class is headed by a senior professor although there are only six students in it,' wrote Sebastian Feldmann in July 1977, when the class taken over by Reinke and Wevers was disbanded.[18]

By then Bernd Becher had taken on the chair of photography that Norbert Kricke, director of the Academy, had offered him some time before. Kricke was determined to put an end to the constant unrest and dissatisfaction at the Academy. In appointing Becher, Kricke accommodated the interest in new media by offering a course that could be kept under control, thus ensuring well-regulated instruction through moderate reforms. He and the appointments committee must surely have been aware that the objective documentary approach developed by Bernd Becher and his wife, Hilla, and strictly observed by them in teaching would not be likely to provide a mouthpiece for the political urges of rebellious students nor would it be suitable for satisfying the interest in experimental and discursive forms that had been awakened by the extended concept of art. Perhaps this limited contemporaneity was the prerequisite for the development of something new that as the 'Becher School' would later become a worldwide success.

Medial and Discursive – Katharina Sieverding

While attempts were being made to provide an established place for the various visual media at the Academy, Katharina Sieverding (*1944) was among the students who actively pursued with a camera the fomentation and turbulence of the years before and after 1968. Starting with an interest in theatre, she first studied in the stage design class before changing over to Beuys in 1967 and then to Ole John. It was a fellow student, Rainer Giese, who lent her the Edixa manhole and pipeline survey camera with which she subsequently captured Actions and goings-on at the Academy. She immediately grasped

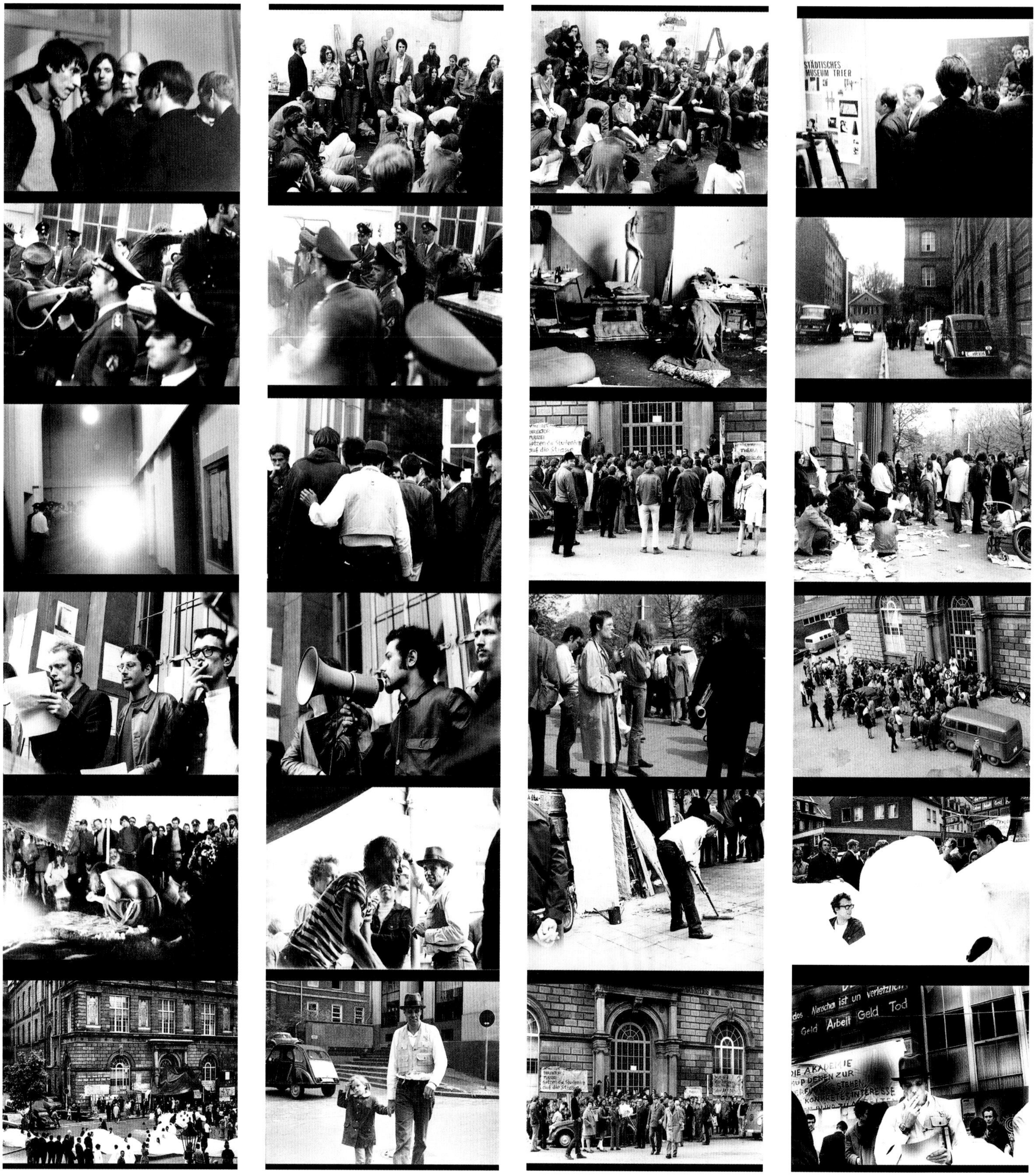

Fig. 8: Photographs by Katharina Sieverding: Eigenbewegung *[Own Movement] 1967–1969 (detail); Academy Tour of the Düsseldorf Art Academy February 1969; 23–26 April 1969,* Beuys Class, *Städtisches Museum Trier; 5–10 May 1969,* Lidl Work Week; *9 May 1969, James Lee Byars's Action* Pink Lane

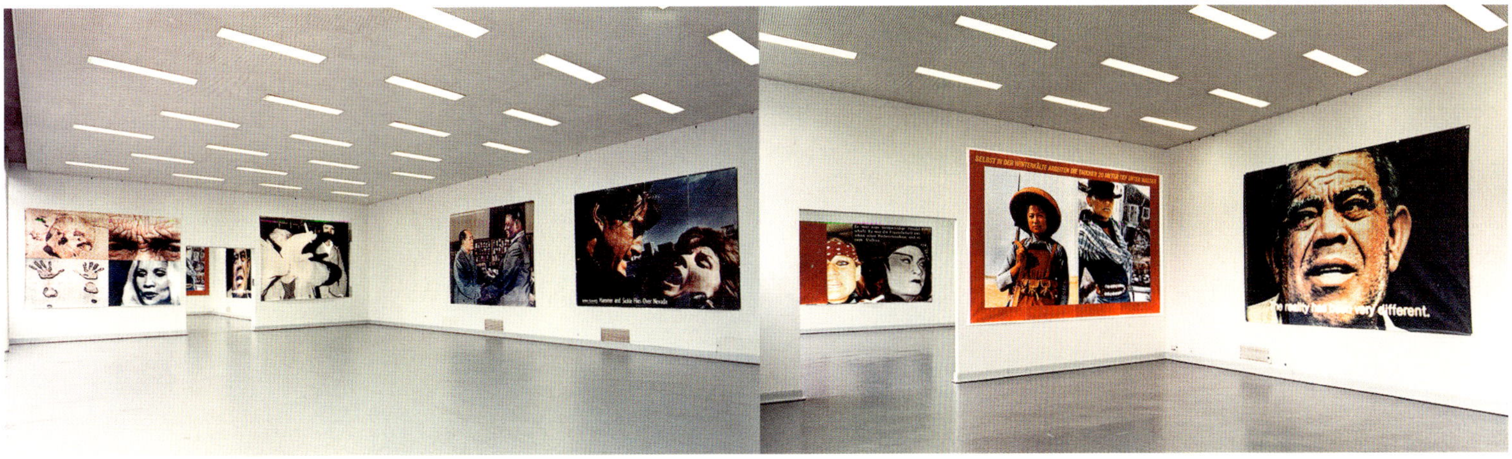

Fig. 9: Katharina Sieverding, Großfotos I–X *[Large Photos I–X], 1975–1977, Museum Folkwang, Essen, 1977*

the possibilities photography offered of participating in those exciting events and developments in a topical yet contemplative way.[19] The photos she took during the day were developed at night and the following day were hung on the Academy façade – an aesthetic statement and photojournalistic diary during the unrest at universities, which culminated in the closure of the Academy in May 1969 as a reaction to the international conference of the Lidl Academy, which had convened there (Fig. 8).[20]

This febrile linkage of art and politics at the time became the object of Katharina Sieverding's aesthetic investigation centring on the artist herself. *Eigenbewegung* [Own Movement] was also the title she gave to the documentation in the form of the collected photos she had taken between 1967 and 1969. In it she captured the impulses originating in herself and the changes they sparked off as well as the general activity and dynamic of the time. Since those beginnings in photography, the artist has been documenting her own life and her surroundings. Systematically archived, the documents form the basis of *Testcuts. Projected Data Images*, an exhibition that ran in 2010, in which Katharina Sieverding interlinked the past forty years of documentation she had experienced and lived through in an eight-channel installation with twenty-four interfaces to make an projection panorama that filled the whole space, and rearranged the constitutive elements by controlled randomisation.[21] Art, politics, and her private life are densely interwoven in her work. They produce a syntax through which communication is to be stimulated and viewers perceive themselves as autonomous subjects in the social fabric. In this process the photographic image serves as a vehicle for recognition, identification, and transformation.

Sieverding has always viewed the world, Düsseldorf, the art scene, and her life as plateaux, which she translates into pictures by means of the camera, thus inscribing both immediacy and distance. Whereas format does not play a major role in purely documentary photos, because what is at stake is the message that must be transported into a wide variety of contexts, it does assume a position of pivotal importance in Katharina Sieverding's work. This is true both of the archive photo works discussed above and of the overall development of her oeuvre, in which she makes herself into a medium by working over existing journalistic, documentary, and scientific pictures and reclaiming them (Fig. 9). She confronts viewers and involves them by surrounding them with picture formats and projections. A relationship is thus created between image, viewer, and space, in which questions arise that reflect Sieverding's sociopolitical and cultural commitment: questions about the reality content of the images, cultural codes and clichés, the ideology thus transported, context. Through aesthetic transformation her works are at a far remove from political agitation yet are informed by the social responsibility we all share as individuals.

In the late 1960s Sieverding met Klaus Mettig, an artist who already had at his disposal large-scale reprographic facilities and the equipment needed for making colour photos in large formats. The partnership in life and work that developed out of the encounter continues to produce the wall-to-wall formats that have been Sieverding's trademark since the early 1970s.[22] While still a student she used works of that kind to confront the prevailing conventional wisdom that photography was a subordinate medium. To her, it was a medium that had not yet acquired art historical connotations, one that allowed her freedom of opportunity to develop independently of male fellow artists. As Armin Zweite noted, she uses photography as an emancipatory medium in three ways: 'emancipating the image from its function of reproducing unmediated reality; emancipating cameras and related equipment from the functions for which they were developed; emancipating representational art from direct evidence'.[23]

How open-ended the possibilities of interpretation are that arise from this approach cannot be attributed to the author's intention alone. She relies on respondents, hence is dependent on spatial and temporal conditions. In the early 1960s the idea of open-ended interpretations began to figure prominently in the theories advanced by, among others, Umberto Eco, Roland

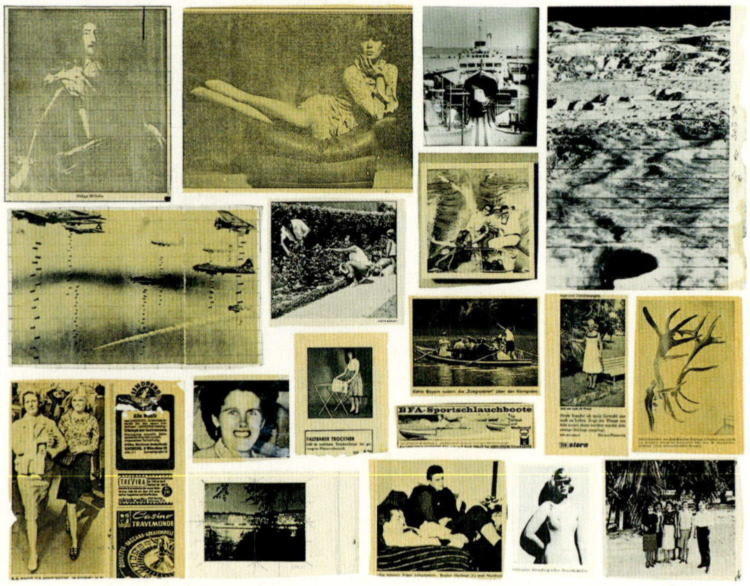

Fig. 10: Gerhard Richter, Atlas, *plate 10, newspaper cuttings, 51.7 × 66.7 cm, Städtische Galerie im Lenbachhaus, Munich*

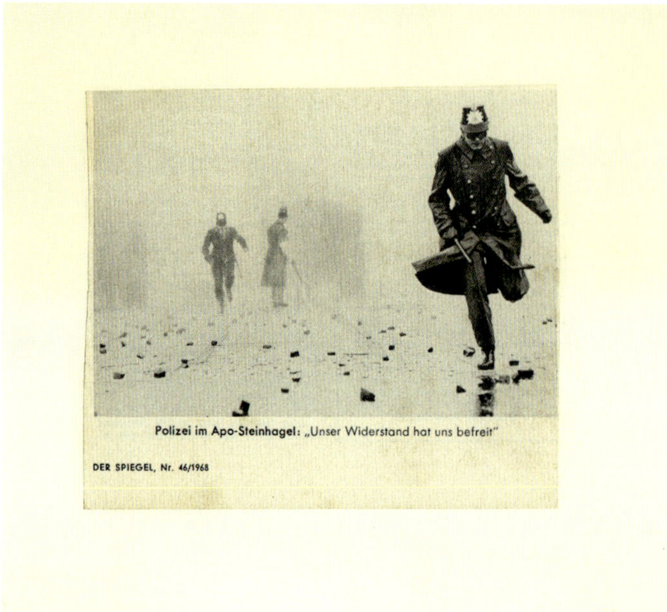

Fig. 11: Erinna König, archive, newspaper cutting from 1968

Barthes, and Michel Foucault and inspired many artists into discursive work in which viewer response to art was part of the overarching conception.[24]

Archiving and Reclaiming – Gerhard Richter, Erinna König, Brigitta Rohrbach

Artists were using pictures from newspapers, magazines, advertising, and photo reportage or filing them in personal archives for future reference as a basis for inspiration and material for the very reason that those pictures were already familiar, that they were in specific connotative contexts. What is surely the best-known archive of this kind is Gerhard Richter's (*1932) *Atlas*, in which he began to file photographs of varying provenance as well as collages and sketches in 1962 (Fig. 10).[25] This archive has long since become an autonomous work of art in its own right and Richter is still adding to it. It began with private photos, cut-out and decontextualised reproductions, and some scraps of text which he has been systematically ordering in groups since the late 1960s.

At that time Erinna König (*1947) also began an archive, an activity which she, too, still keeps up as a system of filing cards for storing newspaper cuttings. 'A convenience operation' is what she calls this collection because 'I no longer need to take all those photos; they were already there. That took a load off me'[26] (Fig. 11). There were enough photos for her to be able to stop producing them herself and proceed to reflecting on reality in the picture and the reality of the picture. König, who had studied with Teo Otto, Dieter Roth, Joseph Beuys, and Ole John, arrived at the Academy already with a knowledge of photography and there she encountered the reservations that her fellow students in particular had about the medium.[27] With Emil Schult and others she belonged to the students who used the photo lab in the Roth class for their work but also experimented with everything imaginable. In 1968 she began to take photographic self-portraits that centred on self-dramatisation. In the early 1970s she made a 16 mm film composed entirely of photographs.[28] As König saw it, photography had too many limitations, which she wanted to avoid in her quest for a new aesthetic. One of its disadvantages was linear perspective, premised on a viewer at a fixed vantage point, a drawback that made it impossible to unite a range of different views in an analogue photograph. Another was the machine-like precision with which photography reproduced everything, even what was not intended to be in the picture. To overcome those problems, the artist began in the mid-1970s to take pictures of surfaces that were as large as possible. At the close of the decade she put an end to her work in photography for the time being with the *Diazentrale Ost* [Slide Headquarters East] project. The project was an imaginary society with headquarters in East Berlin, which she had thought up with Bärbel Freund and Iris Teriet. A spatial utopia, the project was a political reference to the partitioning of a country which was reunified in the real production of *Diazentrale Ost*: within ten weeks the three women photographed 6,000 motifs from Federal German Republic and German Democratic Republic television. Packed in grey boxes representing daily units, the production represents a sort of 'Reunification in medial reality'.[29] Alongside this Conceptually documenting part, the artists developed the *Werbedamen* [Hostesses] project under the same label (Fig. 12). Running through all clichés, the three women staged themselves as

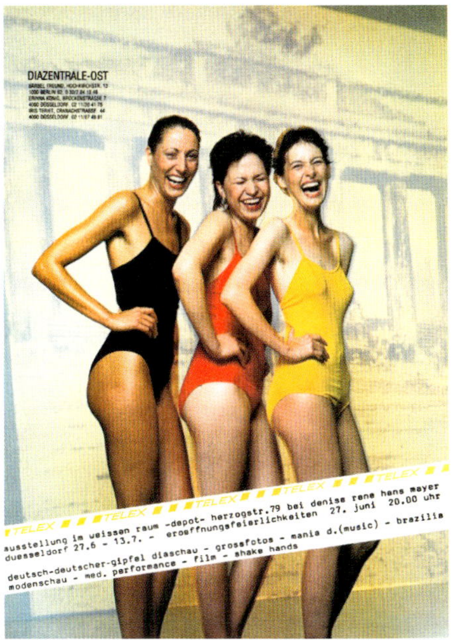

Fig. 12: Erinna König, exhibition poster for Diazentrale Ost *[Slide Headquarters East], Galerie Denise René Hans Meyer, 1980, offset lithographic print, 56.5 × 41.9 cm*

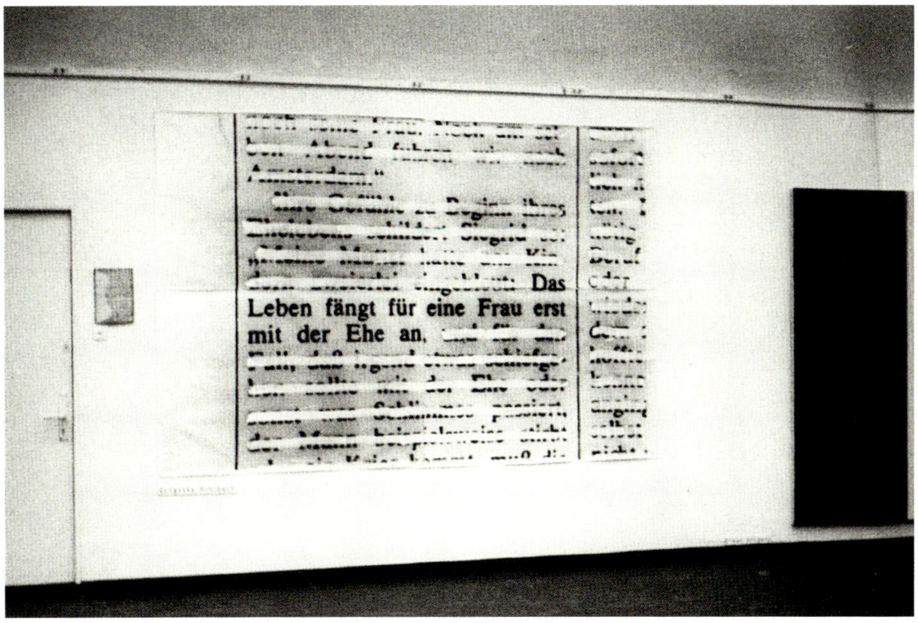

Fig. 13: Brigitta Rohrbach, Das Leben *[Life], 1976*

brides, policewomen, nuns, prostitutes, mothers, and housewives in shots taken by two photographers, the medial unity levelling off the difference between East and West. As with Sieverding, the size of the pictures plays an essential role: with a nod to the billboard aesthetic, motifs produced as 35 mm colour slides are shown in the large formats used for hoardings.

Brigitta Rohrbach's work (*1950) again shows how, despite all the technical difficulties, students interested in the media succeeded in making use of the large formats familiar from advertising and fine arts painting in their productions as early as the 1970s. She, too, uses previously published material, which she copies and from which she enlarges details to concentrate it on gestural and verbal statements. *Das Leben* [Life] (1976) is a work of this kind, in which Brigitta Rohrbach reproduced a text photographically, blew it up to outsized dimensions, and crossed it out except for one sentence that she was focusing on (Fig. 13). On the gigantic surface, reduction opens up space for the imagination that permits diverse conjectures about the patriarchal ideology informing this textual remnant. Here a poster-like appearance and recondite content, convention and rebellion, coincide. In other works she has extrapolated individual gestures or body parts from extant pictorial material. Presented as a sequence, they allow an open-ended narrative to develop. A casual form of suspense is created, not exactly thrilling perhaps but nonetheless inducing psychological tension. Even today the artist continues to pursue visual reduction of extant items of information. All that remains in the most drastic minimisation of visual complexity possible is the abstract element: a number.[30]

Like so many of her generation at the Academy, Brigitta Rohrbach taught herself the technical skills needed for photography through experimentation. Photo labs that produced prints in large formats were few and far between, and the cost of making such prints was enormous. Students working with photography resorted to DIY methods, such as developing films in roof gutters, and helped each other out with advice and hands-on assistance. Even though photography was not yet included in the curriculum, interest in the media spread through the student body.

Photography in the 1960s – Message and Construct

As a contemporary medium, photography became a vehicle for communication along with film, posters, and Happenings. All visual forms which might be inscribed with politicisation played an important role in attempts to escape rigid academicism and open the curriculum up to new trends. In its reproductive function, photography satisfied this demand yet at the same time it was questioned in conformity with the structuralist theories then current as a social and cultural construct: How is the medium used to assert social or political interests? How does it construe gender difference? How is the medium dependent on power structures and institutional, societal, and cultural coding? Photography was neither viewed nor thought of as a picture, let alone a portrayal. It was used to expose extant social, historical, and cultural factors as visual constructs in parallel with theoretical processing. As the British art historian John Tagg sees it, the technological status of photography is dependent on the power relations within which it is used. Practising photography, on the other hand, depends on the institutions and persons who use it. Consequently, according to

Tagg, it entails a constant oscillating within a field of institutional spaces. Should one wish to learn more about the medium, one would have to study that field rather than photography as such.[31]

In summarising the sociological, Marxist, and discourse-analytical approaches that emerged then, Susanne Holschbach goes even further in maintaining that 'there is no such thing as photography. It possesses no identity, no distinctive quality, no specific significance independently of those allocated to it in the cultural, societal, and institutional contexts in which it is used in manifold ways.'[32]

None of the artists using photography had to be theorists in order to come across such thinking, which, in view of the surge in conveying information through images, also resulted from conscious and attentive handling of the medium. Many of them, however, were interested in theory simply due to a commitment to social criticism.

Projections – Imi & Imi

One artist who did not contextualise photography sociopolitically but made it into an experimental stage in his quest for an aesthetic of his own was Imi Knoebel, 'Little Imi' (*1940). He was consistent in his study of the non-representationality of forms. He had come in 1964 from the Darmstadt Werkkunstschule together with Rainer Giese, 'Big Imi' (1942–1974), to study with Beuys at the Düsseldorf Art Academy. The two close friends not only developed their Imi identity over the next few years but also produced parallel oeuvres that assimilated international trends in their Minimalist-Conceptual approach and differed noticeably from their teacher's aesthetic. Both Imis came to the Academy with some photographic skills.[33] Imi Knoebel in particular used the medium to develop an autonomous work complex. Imi Giese also experimented with technical media, as is shown by the two film strips *70/71* (Fig. 14).[34] In them a line running through a spatial part first dissolves by being over exposed until the line seems to vanish and all that is left of the concrete reality that was reproduced is white nothingness. This interest in dissolving the concrete into abstract forms and the transition to white, to light, to amorphic form as the basis for making something appear is what links Big and Little Imi.[35] In his search for the abstract in the concrete, Little Imi worked with light projects between 1968 and 1974. Although minuscule on slides, forms that were reserved or added with retouching colour or Gestural brushstrokes grew into enormous light pictures. In the beginning it was rectangles whose projection surface was painted white and stood still – a refinement of the *Weiße Bilder* [White Pictures] with which Knoebel had already plumbed non-representational nothingness as a sequel to Kazimir Malevich.[36] Out of those rectangles grew the projection of light lines in dark interiors or outdoor spaces (Fig. 15). In the process the projected geometric form encountered an uneven spatial structure that could refract horizontal lines across edges, projections, and objects to the vertical. Changes in the light forms on the wall caused by slightly shifting the projector were documented photographically. Thus the many sequences that captured the curious search, which was as consistent as it was playful, were created. What happens to a simple geometric form surrounded by space? What differences result from merely minimal changes between the initial form and its ultimate appearance? Form was constantly being dissolved, which in the end sealed the fate of the projection work. Without photographic documentation, this work would have remained an immaterial experiment with which Knoebel pursued the intention that also informed his drawings, paintings, installations, and objects: the dissolution of the object into differentiated shapes. Viewed in this light, photography as the artistic final product is a means to an end. At the same time it is far more than that because, in the contrast between projection light and the surrounding darkness, photography eliminates the space-defining givens. The outcome is a two-dimensional black-and-white image in which line, broken at varying depths, is reproduced as surface, thus providing the obvious evidence for abstraction. Only photography makes it possible to negate space and reproduce the various light refractions as a consequence of forms in a surface. Six years' work saw 5,500 photographs taken. Systematically ordered, they are stored in a cupboard made specially for the purpose – a complete work complex that has been consistently shaped into coherent form.

The works analysed here as examples demonstrate that photography, which was still being used mainly for documentation well into the 1960s, subsequently became an independent medium for reflection. In the search for new means of artistic expression, the medium was upgraded from the applied arts to use in fine arts but not without reference to its original

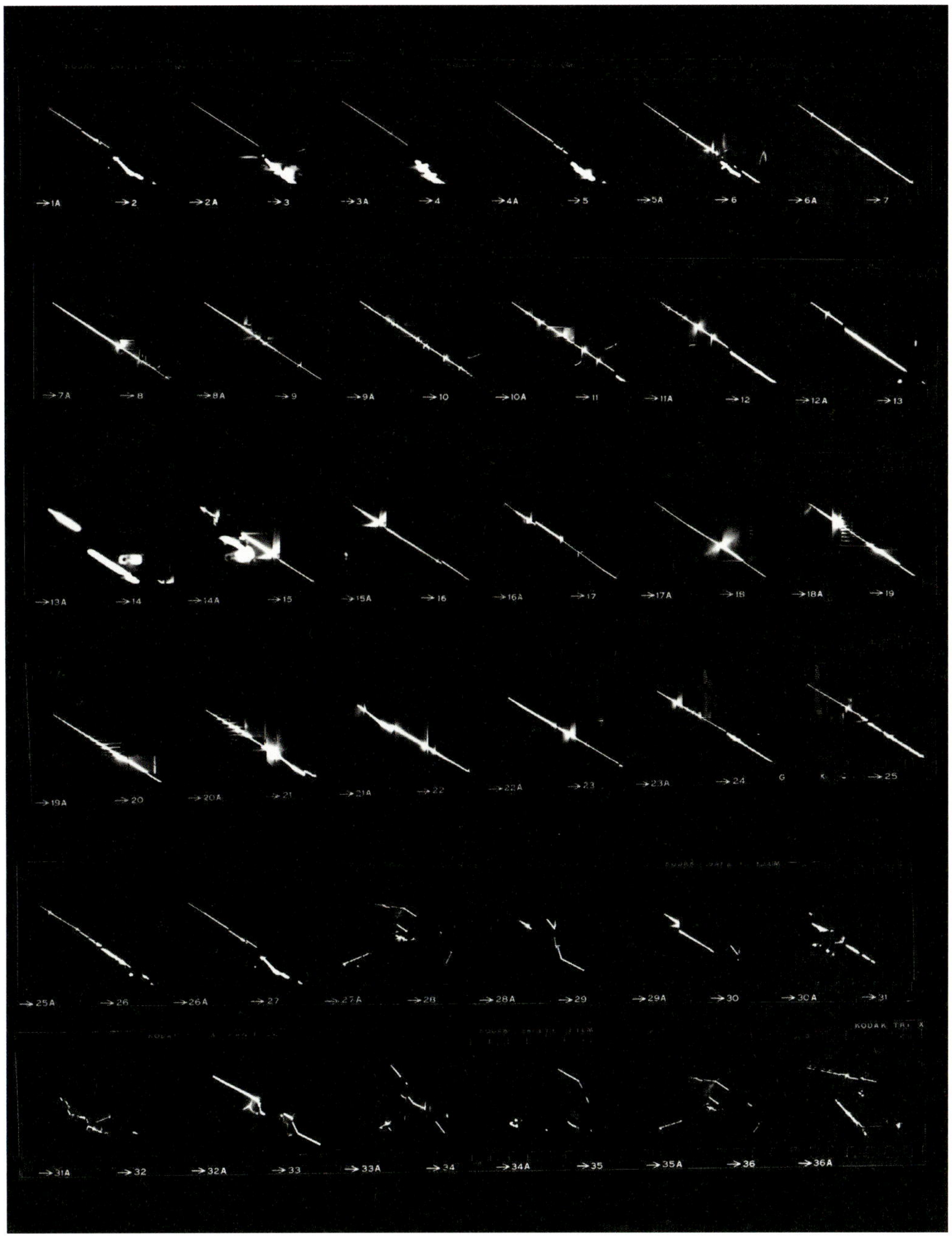

Fig. 15: Imi Knoebel, contact sheet for Projektionen 4/1–11, 5/1–11 *[Projections 4/1–11, 5/1–11], 1972*

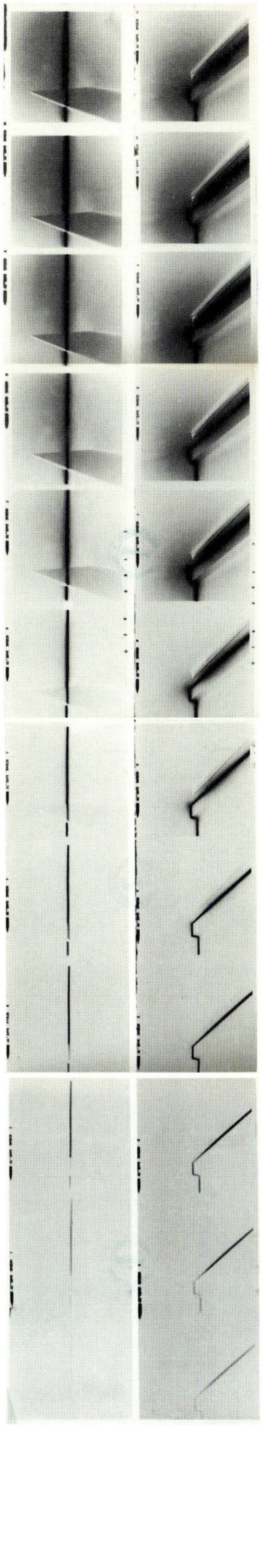

Fig. 14: Imi Giese, 70/71, *fold-out,* interfunktionen *10, 1973*

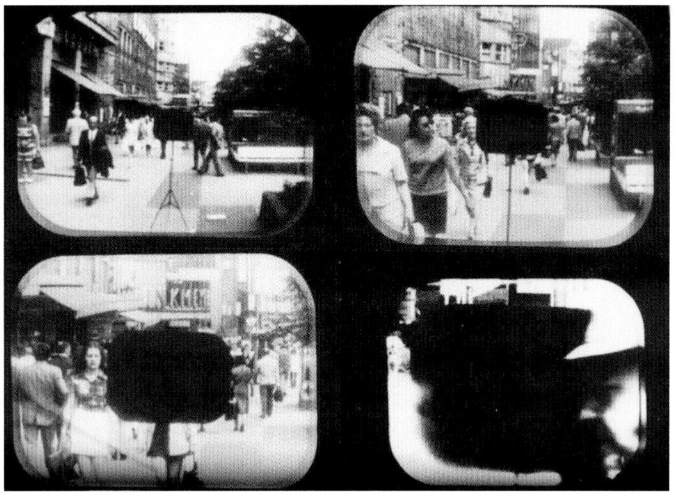

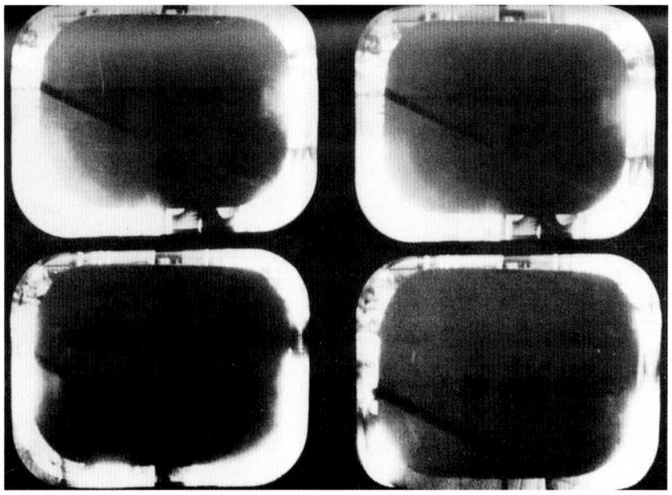

Fig. 16: Reiner Ruthenbeck, Objekt zur teilweisen Verdeckung einer Video-Szene *[Object for Partly Covering a Video Scene], sequence from* Video + Object *in* interfunktionen *10, 1973, pp. 26–27*

connotation. It set about becoming an autonomous visual medium. The visual approach is – apart from exceptions, such as Knoebel's oeuvre – one that reflects on social issues. By means of photography, questions are raised, communications spaces designed, and subjects tabled for discussion. The medium is the means for involving viewers and making reception into a process of reflection. It was still far from being responded to solely as a picture.

PHOTOGRAPHY AS MATERIAL

In parallel with this development artists began to use the media of photography, video, and film, although they had scarcely begun to register art historically, also in a playfully experimental form to push its boundaries and test the aesthetic possibilities of medial art for telling tales, giving mundane phenomena a visual presence, or making the impossible possible in a picture.

Concept and Experiment – Reiner Ruthenbeck, Pidder Auberger, Johannes Brus

Reiner Ruthenbeck (*1937), for instance, mounted a black panel in the form of a TV screen on a stand, which he placed in the middle of a pedestrian zone and filmed (Fig. 16). At first all that can be seen in the video are passers-by thronging the black panel, but the panel itself gradually fills the screen until only a small marginal strip remains in which the movement is perceptible. The take runs for ten minutes, during which the *Objekt zur teilweisen Verdeckung einer Video-Szene* [Object for Partly Covering a Video Scene], thus the title of this 1972 work, virtually masks the picture, making a mockery of the possibilities inherent in the medium and at the same time posing the question of what the media make visible. From the same year is a series of air-raid sirens together with a recording of a one-minute practice alarm. Ruthenbeck called this sequence *Dachskulpturen* [Roof Sculptures] and in these utterly inartistic shots attracts attention to the oddity of the little metal cap on a long stick, which in the midst of the Cold War represented a piece of emergency equipment.

Close to such Conceptual works, photographic works of Pidder Auberger (1946–2012) tend towards touches of Surrealism because he links reality with abstraction.[37] Johannes Brus's (*1942) series – like all his work, most of which is sculpture – are tinged with idiosyncratic humour with overtones of irony. The impossible seems possible: salad cucumbers perform a balancing act next to, with, and on bottles (1972) or in *Endkampf der drei Grazien* [The Three Graces' Fight to the Finish] (1973) dance about a bent stick of wood and a gilded walnut. Coincidence and mystery inform Brus's experimental sequences. The cucumber keeps the balance in these real-unreal scenes, in which mundane objects appear as subjects skilfully performing acrobatic antics (Fig. 17).

For Brus, Ruthenbeck, Auberger, König, and many other Academy students of their time, photography was a medium like any other. What counted was the search for new forms of expression in which experiment and process had become characteristic rather than choosing a particular material or genre. In opting for a single medium to the exclusion of all others, Katharina Sieverding represented the exception rather than the rule. None of those aspiring artists influenced by the Beuys concept of art used photography primarily in its true function as a

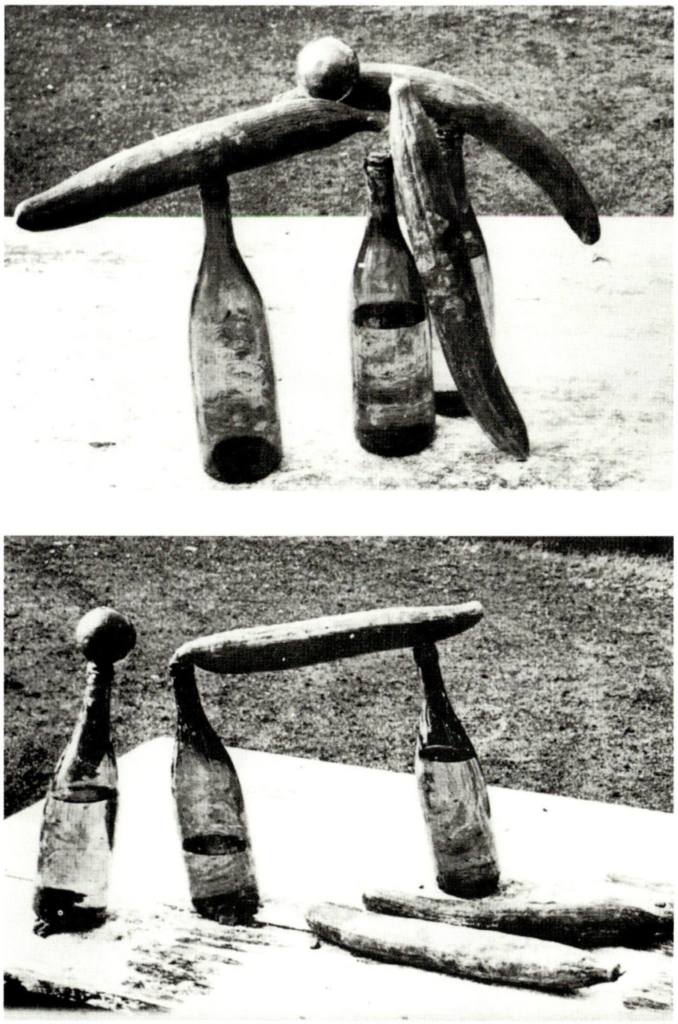

Fig. 17: Johannes Brus, Gurken *[Cucumbers], picture series,* interfunktionen *10, 1973, pp. 115–124*

precise medium for faithfully capturing details. The visual aesthetic of Bernd and Hilla Becher, which was based on just that, by then had been practised for quite some time, and would later be so successful, would not have been an alternative for them. To the contrary, they refused to be satisfied with its boundaries and borders, which they viewed as limitations. Artists such as Johannes Brus and Sigmar Polke as well were among those who therefore experimented with possibilities of overcoming physical and technical contingencies by changing their photographs, blurring them, and subjecting them to chemical processes that left them looking defamiliarised in a painterly way rather than 'technical'. As far as content was concerned, they opened up imaginary worlds oscillating between fiction and reality, which, as the opposite of ultimate explicitness, defy complete comprehension.

Unequivocally ambiguous – Sigmar Polke

Sigmar Polke was already familiar with photography before he came to the Academy in 1961 to study with Karl Otto Götz and Gerhard Hoehme, and once he was there, photography became part of his media repertoire.[38] The camera became a constant companion, his 'alter ego', as Jochen Poetter writes.[39] A snapshot of Bernd Becher, smoking and looking into the camera with a grimace as if conducting a dialogue with either it or Polke, reveals how casually, rapidly, and perceptively Polke photographed scenes (Fig. 18). Even his early photos from the 1960s show Polke was noticeably partial to visual situation comedy.

Like his oeuvre as a whole, his photographs live from ambivalence, the narratives provided, and semantic references that are never resolved and can never be entirely decoded. They are wrapped in a mystery that remains enigmatic. This is true of a diffusely murky 1960s photograph full of streaks and light dots and a white spot at the centre in which the name Beuys can be read in mirror writing (Fig. 19). Darker spots seem to circle about this light centre like planets, leaving ample scope for

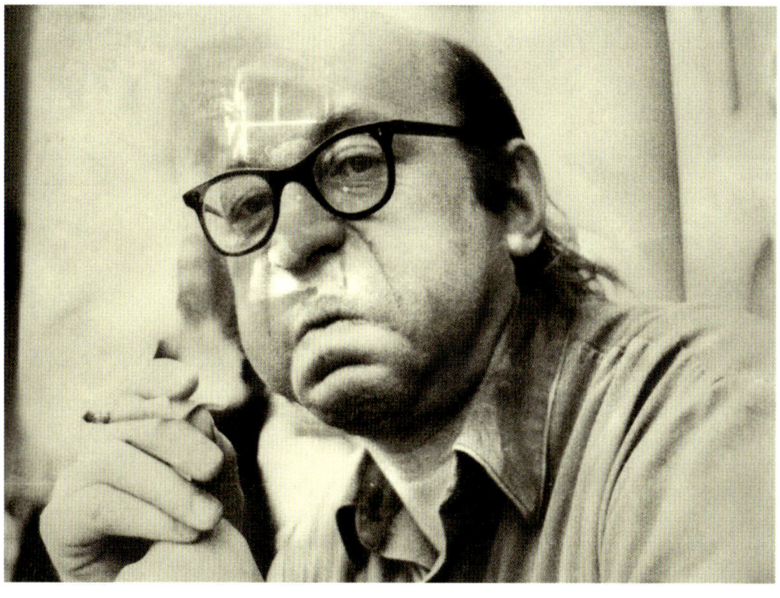

Fig. 18: Sigmar Polke, photograph of Bernd Becher, 1972

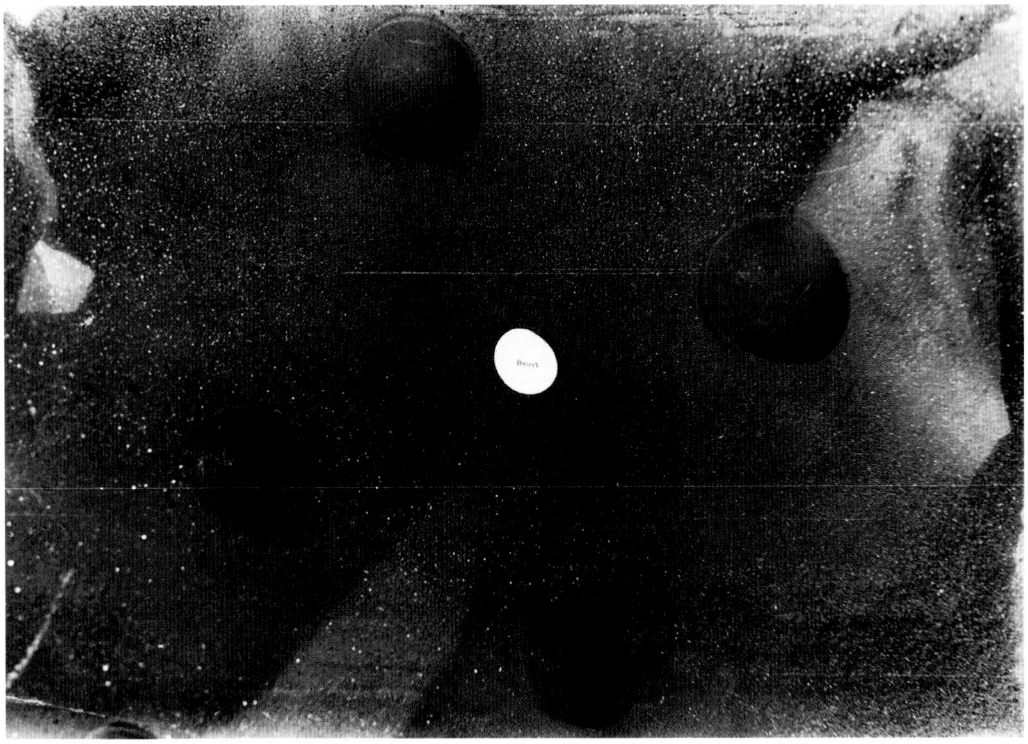

Fig. 19: Sigmar Polke, Ohne Titel [untitled], early 1970s

interpretations, which Siegfried Gohr does not even go into. Preferring merely to hint at their range in the questions, he asks:

'Is the arrangement meant to mean a tribute to Beuys? Is it an allegory of Beuys's thinking and work? Or a criticism by means of which Polke sheds light on the darkness of Beuys's universe? Or does the white spot signify Beuys's self-referentiality, his complete world view, his message that revealed its missionising dimension in his public performances in the early 1970s? Was Polke setting this straight by enclosing its seeming clarity in a dark satellite world, thus putting it into perspective?'[40]

Maren Klinge on the other hand interprets the light centre as a 'radiant blot', through which Polke may even have made the numinous figure Beuys represented at the Düsseldorf Academy into 'spiritistic ectoplasm'.[41]

Polke's visual worlds allow multiple interpretations. They defy unequivocal comprehension. No sooner has one caught them than they elude one's grasp. In painting as in photography, Polke detaches objects from their usual connotations and opens them up to the viewer's imagination. At times the context remains ambivalent; at others the frame of reference is an abstruse construct, or the perspective insinuates psychologically loaded patterns. The emergent world is as imaginative as it is fragile, as Harald Szeemann admiringly points out: 'Polke is universal: revolutionary, sensitive, and merciless, visionary and very human [...]. Typically un-German in his recalcitrance, in his vehemence, he – like all great geniuses – integrates all-encompassing experience.'[42]

Polke's painting, the boundaries of which he widened in a purely mechanical way through studying mechanical reproduction processes, shows that photography was for him more than a medium with which he experimented and pushed to its limits. He took as his starting point the electronic visual overload that shapes our collective idea of reality, in order to confront it, in a sort of reversal processing, with the technical reality of the image, the raster dots. Unlike Andy Warhol, who made use of another endlessly repetitive technical medium, silkscreen printing, in order to print raster dots on canvas, or Roy Lichtenstein, who used stencils to do so, Polke painted every dot painstakingly by hand, dot by dot.[43] 'The imaginary appearance of a figuration, the seemingly discrete singleton, is resolved in the sum of its real parts that turn out to be the actual constitutive elements,' writes Benjamin H. D. Buchloh, adding that the visualisation of its material basis is what indicates the status of the presumed image of reality while at the same time revealing its ideological aspiration.[44] Polke was not interested in capturing conventional pictures of reality. To the contrary, a world opened up to his senses in which the ephemeral aspect, fleeting impressions, shaped a memorably sophisticated aesthetic. Or, as Klaus Honnef notes:

'Not that Polke and Richter, with whom he was linked by close ties of friendship then, would have fallen for the widespread misconception that photography should be regarded as a more authentic report on reality than painting, but in the medium of technical reproduction they tracked down the reflexes of consciousness of a specific collectively effective understanding of reality and at the same time a meaningful indicator of a manifest loss of reality.'[45]

Photography by means of Painting – Gerhard Richter

Like Polke, Gerhard Richter came from East Germany and with the political turnaround, also changed his artistic side. Leaving Socialist Realism behind, his painting, when he began studying at the Academy in 1961, approached the media-saturated visual world of journalism and private amateur photography. If the restorer Christian Scheidemann talks today about everything being possible in the mid-1960s except oil on canvas, Polke and Richter were arguing even then: 'We can't count on good pictures being painted at some time in the future. We'll have to address the matter ourselves!'[46] Whereas Scheidemann got off on the anti-aesthetic drive following Marcel Duchamp, Polke and Richter seemed to have championed continuity. Still, even though both studied with painters from Informel, it is the real world (of images) that forms the starting point of their work rather than the rejection of figurative painting.

Richter did not come to Düsseldorf until three years after the 1958 Dada retrospective mounted in the Düsseldorf Kunsthalle and so he did not see it. Nonetheless, the rediscovery of photomontages and photocollages by George Grosz, Hannah Höch, et al. was one source of inspiration; another was the Pop Art works by Andy Warhol and Robert Rauschenberg, which were based on photographs.[47] Richter and Polke realised that the pictures disseminated by the mass media would make the ideal new material for them.[48] Whereas Polke's work is free of moralistic overtones, a clear socially critical approach can be read in Richter's early choice of motifs but it is toned down by the uniform painterly blurriness. Richter abstains from taking a sociopolitical stance, just as the pupils of Bernd and Hilla Becher would later do on a purely photographic level. One of his motifs is *Tante Marianne* [Aunt Marianne] (1965), who suffered from schizophrenia and did not survive the Nazi regime, having presumably fallen victim to the euthanasia programme (Fig. 20). Another is *Herr Heyde* [Mr Heyde] (1965), a leading euthanasia doctor in the employ of the National Socialist regime. Painted in an identical style, those works avoid the richness of detail provided by the photographic templates and defy contextualisation – 'in painting, he beautifies everything'.[49]

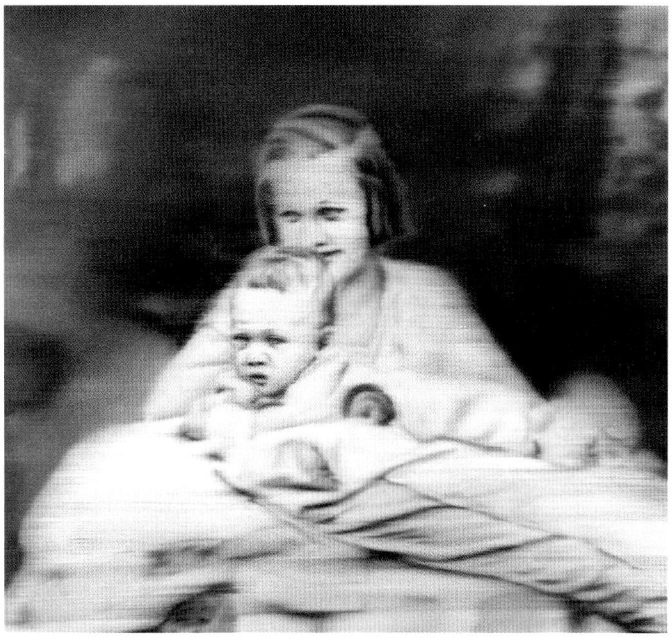

Fig. 20: Gerhard Richter, Tante Marianne *[Aunt Marianne], 1965, oil on canvas, 120 × 130 cm, Yageo Foundation Taiwan*

According to Martin Hentschel, the critical use of mundane clichés, an attitude to consumer goods refracted through irony, and opposition to abstract art can be subsumed under the label of Capitalist Realism, coined in 1963, and applied to both Polke and Richter.[50] Another feature of their work that can be added to the list is clinging to painting. Richter is not a photographer. He collects photographs and uses them as his starting point. The photograph is material, the rest is painting – or, as Richter says himself, he does photography by means of painting.[51] The dialectically Janus-headed approach that can be construed from that statement applies not only to technique but also to content. Richter makes use of photography as a seemingly value-neutral visual pool in order to elevate it to picture status by means of painting. Photography is the basis for thinking about pictures, with which he has enlarged the radius of painting in a contemporary way. By reaching out to another medium to create a different genre, he demonstrates the falsity of objectivism without revealing the extent to which he personally believes in it or is reflecting merely a widespread perception. In 1971 Richter returned to his alma mater as a professor of painting.

Culture, History, Memory – Anselm Kiefer, Reinhard Mucha, Lothar Baumgarten

At that point Anselm Kiefer was still a student of Beuys's. His handling of photography as a cultural storage facility and visual representation of both past and present linked up with developments that had been taking place since the early 1960s. Kiefer (*1945), who after studying art in Freiburg and

Karlsruhe, continued to do so in the late 1960s with Joseph Beuys, used photography as the medium for documenting his 1969 Performance, *Besetzungen* [Occupations/Casts], which he transferred to a cycle of paintings – comparable to Gerhard Richter's photo-painting (Fig. 21). In the examination of German history typical of his work, Kiefer has studied the question of whether he personally would have been a fellow traveller of the fascist system or would have resisted it. Well into the 1990s Kiefer was still working through the problem of individual and collective guilt. He has often used photographs as documents of cultural identity, which, overlaid with many layers of different materials, form an 'objective' basis in the sense of an intersubjective insight.[52]

Several thousand black-and-white and colour photos form the photographic stock drawn on to the present day by Reinhard Mucha (*1950), who is somewhat younger than Kiefer, for his sculptural installations and collages. Mucha, who came to the Academy for the first time just as Kiefer was leaving it, served a blacksmith's apprenticeship before returning in 1975 and ultimately going to Klaus Rinke's class. Since 1966 35 mm photography has accompanied him as a sort of travel diary. He has created a compendious archive, which includes, for instance, the longitudinal documentation of a block of flats being built, which Mucha presented at the close of the winter term of 1976 as his contribution to the *Rundgang* [Academy Tour]. His photographs often become key elements of specific works. Whether as associative montages comprising several detail photos or as single pictures, framed by vitrines or display cases and surrounded by diverse materials, these photos provide the physical concentration point and the semantic crystallisation point of such works. More obviously than any other material, photography belongs to past time. Mucha's entire oeuvre centres on themes such as collective identity and memory. It is about the development of industrial and political landscapes, the historical significance of materials and their transference to the context of art history and the slides used in museum presentation. Photos of station signs, signal boxes, train engines and carriages, railway tracks, switches, and train stations are recurrent motifs, which can be seen as metaphors for movement and stasis – not least with reference to museums as 'the

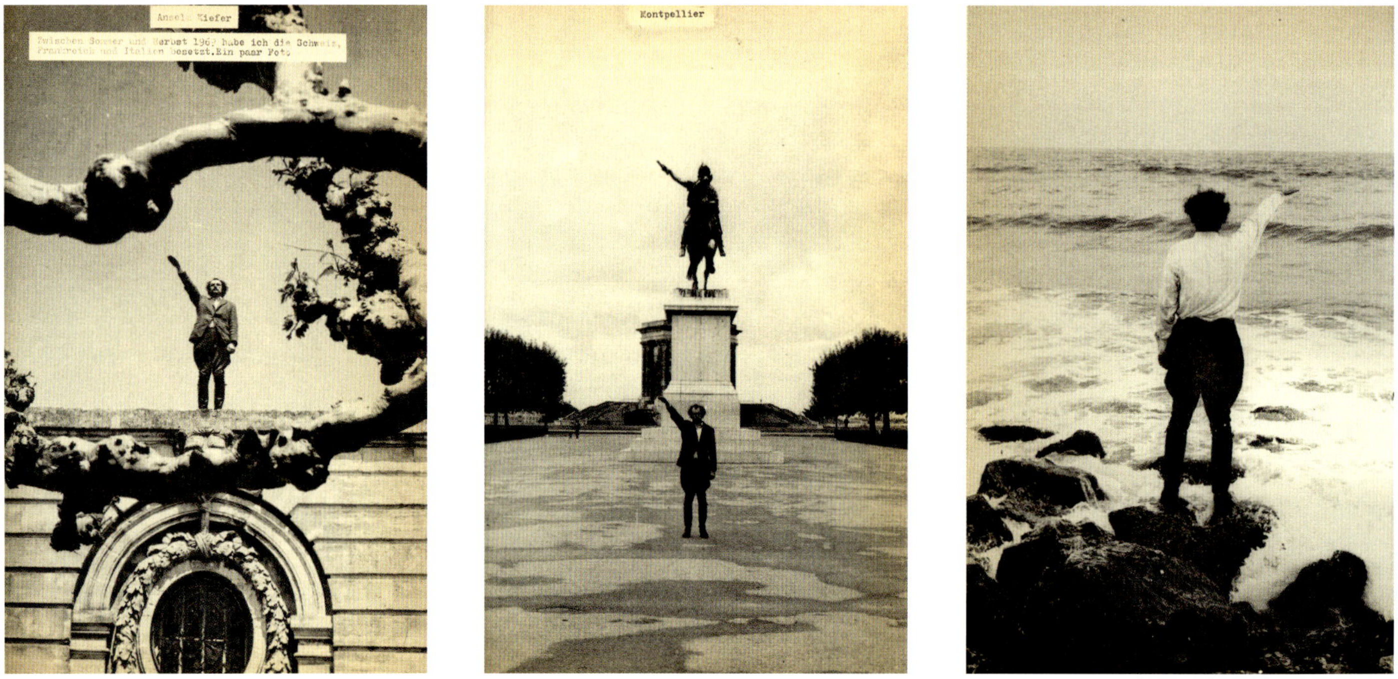

Fig. 21: Anselm Kiefer, Besetzungen *[Occupations/Casts], 1969, photo series,* interfunktionen *12, 1975, pp. 133–144*

explicit sites of sitelessness in art' (Mucha). The basis for investigating the social, historical, and political premises of art and how they are communicated under the conditions of movement and transience grows from his personal everyday life story as an artist. Using found, reclaimed, and recontextualised materials, Mucha makes stage-like constructs to showcase his photographic motifs. Conversely, the attention is directed at the motif rather than the picture because the motif as a trace of history is the vehicle for a narrative that provides an excuse for the material collages, some of which bulk large in space. The artist, whose works are sophisticated magazines for storing knowledge of art and contemporary history, has been dubbed a 'cultural archaeologist'.[53] A photograph serves as a quotation, a visual aid to structuring this compendious cosmos. Thanks to its obvious immediacy, the photograph is the visual anchor for viewers in Mucha's complex installations.

Lothar Baumgarten (*1944), on the other hand, whose preoccupation with ethnology began in the late 1960s, when he started to study art, is regarded as a cultural anthropologist. He left the Academy in Karlsruhe for Düsseldorf, where he continued his studies between 1969 and 1971. During that time he began to take photographs and film primeval forest impressions in the remote region of a tributary of the Rhine very close to where he was studying. Using a quote from Voltaire's *Candide* – 'Da gefällt's mir besser als in Westfalen, Eldorado' [I like it better here than in Westphalia, Eldorado] (1968–1976) – the artist shows in 187 slides a tropical idyll from a thundery night through the following day until darkness sets in again (Fig. 22). Despite a soundtrack of twittering birds and croaking frogs, the idyll is unmasked by traces of civilisation; nature, seemingly pristine, is cultural staging that exposes itself for what it is. Studio pictures crop up between landscape scenes and the water turns out to be a puddle after a rain.

As Friedrich Wolfram Heubach writes on Lothar Baumgarten, culture is dependent on Nature as its polar opposite although it *qua* definition includes its abolition because the aim of culture is to survive in Nature. However, if Nature is no longer hostile, culture need no longer take care of it. What remains is a faded conceptual dialectic whose substrate is scarcely imperceptible to the naked eye in the reality of Western industrial landscapes. In his early work Baumgarten stages it as dissonance. Things are brought together visually that can only be thought of as opposites: ancient forest and kale, crocodile

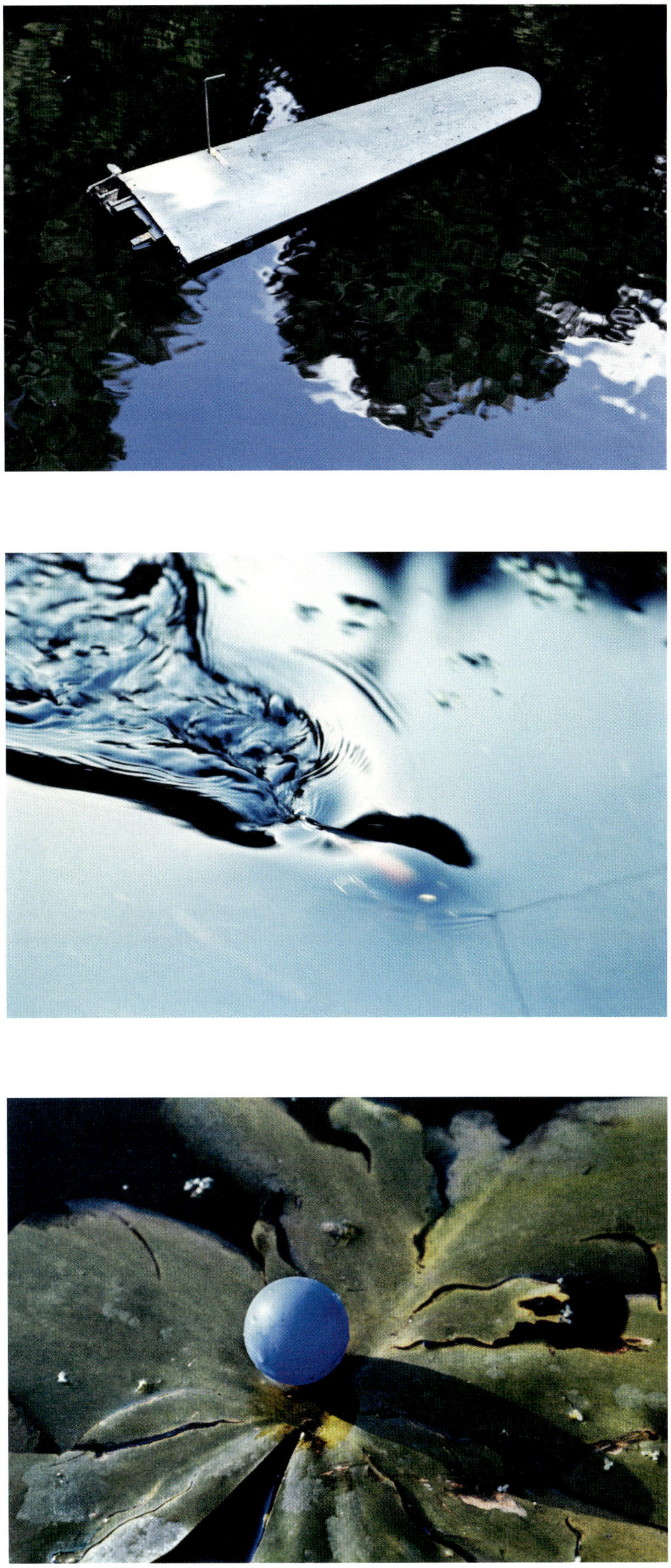

Fig. 22: Lothar Baumgarten, Da gefällt's mir besser als in Westfalen, Eldorado *[I Like it Better Here than in Westphalia, Eldorado], 1968–1976, projection of 187 slides, sound, 35 minutes and 50 seconds*

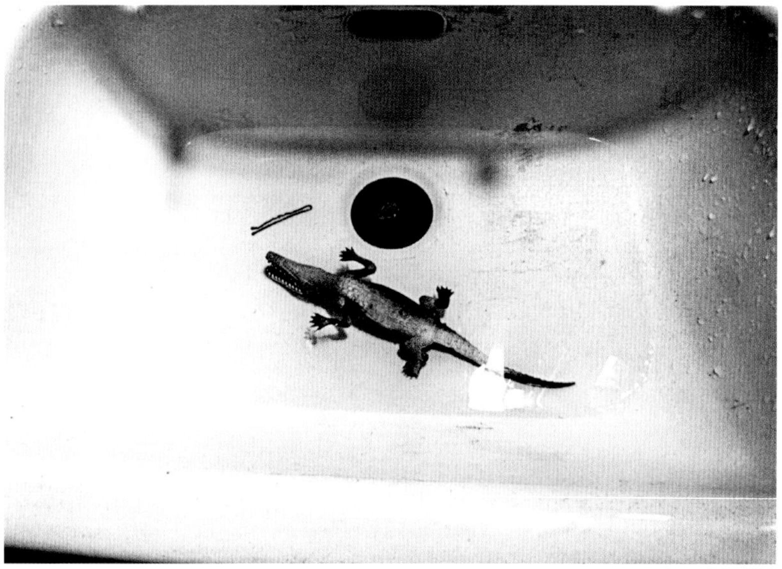

Fig. 23: Lothar Baumgarten, Caiman, *1970, silver gelatin print*

and wash basin, bracket fungus on an arm (Fig. 23).[54] No other medium is better suited to this than photography, the perception of which is still governed by awareness of the fact that it captures visible reality in faithful detail and, on the other hand, that it has always been employed manipulatively. Viewers succumb to the visual conventions, believing they recognise an impenetrable forest in worm's-eye view, which, on closer scrutiny, turns out to be nothing but a vegetable patch. Hence they are doubly duped: the Nature myth is a product of culture, and photographic reality is a construct.

Bringing the interest of a scholar and scientific detachment to bear on the objects he is studying, Baumgarten creates works that are about cultural hubris and the loss of Nature as described above and that challenge the viewer's five senses. For Baumgarten photography is one element of an aesthetic that confronts us with givens by describing historical fact.

Photography in the 1970s – Trace and Index

Although photography was the documentary medium of the 1960s with which the energy of an awakening was recorded, this elan ebbed away in the 1970s. Subsequently stock was taken and the past was reflected upon. Here photography served to construct history and stories. That might be subjective visual iconographies like Christian Boltanski's early works.[55] But it can also mean securing traces that capture a specific historical condition and are part of a local, national, and even international culture of memory, tending to derive from a Conceptual idea of what a work is from Lothar Baumgarten to Bernd and Hilla Becher.[56] In most cases photography was just one medium among many; the use of it was largely self-taught, experimental, and directed by the artists' needs to hone their own aesthetic. Authorship was not mandatory: photographs could also be taken by others or come from other contexts. Many professors and students worked then with photography in this sense, case by case or from time to time. However, only a few integrated the medium in their work. Even fewer made it the starting point of their work, let alone developed a photographic aesthetic of their own.

Action – Klaus Rinke

A step towards doing just that was the development of documentation of Action into Action for documentation as it happened in Klaus Rinke's (*1939) work. Rinke came to teach at the Academy in 1974 and became a professor two years later. His class was housed with that taught by Günther Uecker in an annexe in Karl-Anton-Straße into which Bernd Becher also moved with his first students. The location had the enormous advantage for the students of not being subject to the Academy house rules. There were not all that many students and they could come and go as they pleased.[57] They were more independent, not only in the use of their site but also in the fact that they were not subject to the competition and pressure for success that spread through the corridors of the main building. The colloquies he hosted and the excursions he went on with his class on a regular basis show that Rinke loved teaching.

By the time he became a professor, he had long since arrived with his water sculptures; 'struggling with painting' was behind him.[58] According to his own description of his work, time and change were what always interested him, which speaks both for and against photography since photography captures time yet also transfixes it.[59] From 1970 on photography went from being a documentary medium to a Conceptual constituent of Rinke's Primary Demonstrations and other Actions, in which time and space were shown in the relationship of body to Action. In the 1972 work *Durchs Format gehen* [Going through the Format] Rinke's head is shown sequentially, gradually entering the frame only to disappear from it once again (shown on p. 223). The format is initially entirely empty but gradually the face appears in profile until only part of a curly head is visible in extreme close-up, and zooming out finally results in a return to an empty frame. The sequence of thirteen photographs is staggered by one frame each in thirteen rows, one below the other, resulting in a diagonal movement through space in addition to the movement through the picture.

Rinke's appearance and disappearance is thus visualised in two ways: temporally and spatially. Like so many of the works he produced until 1976, this one was photographed by the photographer and artist Monika Baumgartl. The sequential presentation of the 169 individual pictures is the feature that marks this work as being in transition from the photographic and the photo-Action to the Conceptual-sculptural field.

With the end of the Primary Demonstrations in 1976, Rinke's interest in photography began to wane.[60] The darkroom in his class, however, continued to be much in use. His students were as open in their choice of media as Rinke was in his own career as an artist.

Television, Film, Video – Gerry Schum

That is also shown by his collaboration with Gerry Schum (1938–1973), who was regarded at the Academy as the 'doyen of film'. In the late 1960s and early 1970s Schum figured prominently in the Düsseldorf art scene with his inclusion of the new media in art. A technology freak and unflagging champion of film as art, he advocated the idea of democratising art and opening it up via television, thus converting it from the elitist possession of a few to the aesthetic property of many. This meant making art films rather than screening films about artists. This aim could only be realised with works that were processual in conception, which were staged to be made as films, and could be followed with the camera. The artists who came into question for such films were those whose work consisted in processes such as drawing water and pouring it out for Rinke, or Knoebel with his projections. None of the artists had yet made a film of their own so the necessary division of labour and the concomitant loss of control were not always appreciated.[61] Schum began his talk for the first Television Exhibition in 1969 as follows: 'More and more artists are now proceeding to incorporate the possibilities afforded by incorporating the media of film, television, and photography as well in their works.' Yet only a year later he qualified that assertion by regretting that 'artists have not [succumbed to] the lure of the new medium [...]. "Television art" never happened the way architectural art happened.'[62] Artists were just as unwilling to use television, the mass-communications medium, for their own purposes as editors were interested in films that were art films pure and simple. Film production was extremely labour-intensive and expensive due to the technology and material used. It was only due to the conviction and commitment shown by Gerry Schum and his partner and wife, Ursula Wevers, that film was realised at all at the Academy. Public broadcasting channels did not show much interest. This lack of enthusiasm finally led to the Television Gallery being shelved. In its stead videogalerie schum opened in October 1971, where a Rinke project was shown in November.[63] Both projects were short-lived and linked with Gerry Schum. After he died in spring 1973, hardly any of the artists who had participated in his projects continued to work with film.

Using film, photography, and video as art media to reach a broader public was not, however, merely a sign of the times.[64] This was a time that also saw fresh encouragement given to new uses for those media, ranging from a rapprochement with the mundane through the processual to large-format photography. It was left to the following generation, however, to feel comfortable with using those media, thanks to the technical advances made in them.

Visual analysis – Jan Dibbets

Schum's persuasive powers were considerable and his enthusiasm was contagious. Academy artists enjoyed working with him, as Jan Dibbets (*1941) reports, who realised for the first Television Exhibition with Gerry Schum *12 Hours Tide Object with Correction of Perspective* (Fig. 24).[65] During low tide, early on a frosty winter morning, a wheel loader draws a trapezium in the sand with its bucket. From the raised camera vantage point, the figure looks like a rectangle and gradually disappears with the incoming tide. In this collaborative project, Dibbets explored for the first time in the medium of film the potential of perspective correction, which he was already experimenting with in his photographic work.[66] Two years previously he had taken up photography through documenting his own film work. Perspective became the main theme of his work – and has remained so to the present day. His thematic basis is the analytical view of technical limitation.

That was definitely an innovation for dealing with and understanding photography. Artists had previously often concentrated on an idea or a process but disregarded technical

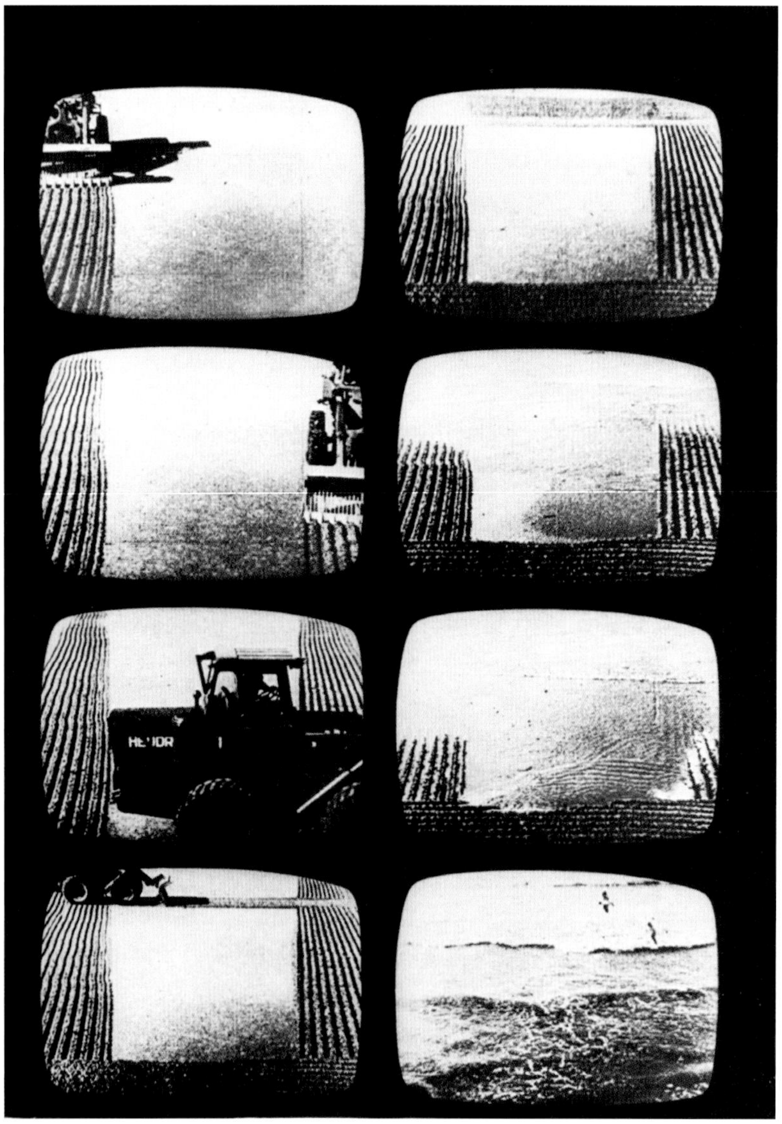

Fig. 24: Jan Dibbets, 12 Hours Tide Object with Correction of Perspective, *1969, 16mm colour and sound film, 7 minutes and 32 seconds*

perfection, finding the technical medium of photography an ideal vehicle. Large formats covered walls like wallpaper; smaller formats were pinned onto walls. Attention was supposed to be directed at the information transported by the medium rather than the medium itself. Content might be social structures, questioning consumerism, the political function of institutions, or the viewers' position in their social context. Jan Dibbets, on the other hand, devoted himself entirely to investigating the medium as such, which, to quote Susan Sontag, reproduces 'fragments of the world' as a legitimate miniature of concrete reality.[67] In his work the artist discloses this illusion by subverting perceptual conventions with perspective corrections and changing space, which is suggested by the alignment of lines, into what it really is: a surface. If the wheel loader had drawn a rectangle in the sand, in the photograph it would have become a trapezium, which viewers would have completed from force of habit as a rectangular form in space. When the trapezium appears as a rectangle, this perceptual habit is overridden and confusion sets in. These are the slight yet significant interventions with which Jan Dibbets explores the artificiality of photographic seeing, decodes the alleged 'miniatures of reality', and reveals the mechanism of the construct.

He takes all his pictures with his first medium-format camera, which he bought in 1967, a Yashica Mat 124-G. He has never been interested in developments in the technology. Nor has he taken any more photos than is absolutely necessary. Dibbets has been working for forty years with the stock he has. After all, what he focuses on in perspective corrections, in horizons, and monochrome pictures (shown on p. 224) is not a constant search for new motifs but rather intense thinking about the few elements that distinguish and limit it. Dibbets's work was Conceptual, in colour, in large formats, and stringently media reflective in approach long before those criteria began to be applied to the pictures of Bernd Becher's first students.[68] Even though Dibbets's photographic work had been shown publicly in Düsseldorf since 1968, thanks to Konrad Fischer, when the artist was appointed to a professorship at the Academy in 1984, it was, typically, for painting rather than photography or film. His focused investigation of photographic techniques – be it in series, individual photographs, or sequences composed like collages – continued to be ignored within the walls of the Academy. The students in his class did work with photography along with other media but his own work was a non-issue. Photography had to become permanently established as a mainstream art form in its own right through growing ever closer to painting before Dibbets's work would be recognised as a photographic reflection authentic in consistency and intensity.

Between Document and Concept – Bernd and Hilla Becher

Bernd (1931–2007) and Hilla (*1934) Becher have contributed substantially to the establishment of photography as a mainstream art form. After serving an apprenticeship as a decoration painter and the beginning of his studies in Stuttgart, Bernd Becher came to the Düsseldorf Art Academy, where he would meet Hilla, later his wife. She, on the other hand, had finished the classic course of training in photography and was working for an advertising agency in Düsseldorf, where she met Walter Breker, who brought her to his class in applied graphic arts at the Academy in 1958 because of her skills in photography.[69] In contrast to the usual Academy career at the time, Hilla Becher (then still née Wobeser) worked entirely in photography in the late 1950s and early 1960s, set up the first Academy darkroom, and shared her interest in the medium with the man who would later be her husband and partner in her work. Bernd Becher's origins in the graphic arts and painting and hers in photography met on common ground in their interest in objectively capturing basic industrial forms. Since beginning to work together in 1959, the two photographers devoted themselves to industrial architecture to the exclusion of other subject matter. Reverting to the pre-war New Objectivity aesthetic, which was no longer appreciated at the time, they developed a definitive photographic pictorial language that could no longer be called into question and be situatively reformulated, and perfected it over the years (shown on p. 222). Creating an encyclopaedia of industrial architecture, which is particularly valuable from today's standpoint as a collective remembrance of industrialisation, called for clear convictions and patience. Because of the typological presentation, it also marks a key position in the history of photographic Conceptual art.

The response to the Bechers' work also oscillated between the two poles of visual heritage conservation and the aesthetic concept. Reception did not set in until the late 1960s and for a long time it was not accompanied by success on the art market. Three factors account for the delayed discovery of the Bechers: their historicising attitude encountered the outliers of the post-war taboo on the German past and at the same time the search for new forms of aesthetic expression; it was a purely photographic oeuvre, hence its artistic value seemed in principle doubtful; finally, the very element that a public interested primarily in the political and social aspects of industry – working conditions – was eliminated as a thematic choice by the Bechers with almost aggressive deliberation. Not until the conventional notion of what constituted art was opened up by the discussion surrounding the expanded concept of art and the provocative delight in experimentation consistently shown by the Bechers was the way smoothed for their photography – in spite of itself, so to speak. The Bechers themselves were unconcerned about whether their work was art or not;[70] Bernd Becher rejected out of hand the idea of parallels in content with Conceptual art.[71] For this artist couple, photographs remained eyewitness accounts of their time, exactly what Susan Sontag meant by 'fragments of reality'. Unlike the thinking on photography through the visualisation of technical conditions that Dibbets engaged in, the Bechers' photography adheres to visual descriptions – that is, to the reproduction of content. In Becher's seeming reticence, in his 'objective' use of technology and his functional neutrality, lies not only respect for the object but also a self-confident artistic stance, which did not attract notice until Bernd Becher was appointed professor of photography at his alma mater.

PHOTOGRAPHY AS PICTURE

The establishment of the first chair of photography at a German art academy in 1976 marked a turnaround in Germany: its pioneering status pinpoints the fact that reservations about recognising the medium as an autonomous art form still existed. On the other hand, it shows that awareness of photography was gradually changing. Bernd Becher's appointment meant that an Academy graduate, who with his wife clung strictly and against all resistance to an aesthetic that did not correspond in any particulars with the prevailing ideas of what a picture was, had now been entrusted with the chair of photography there.[72] Two years before Becher's appointment Norbert Kricke had tried to win him over to take on the task. This shows that the idea of a photography class had already been mooted while the film class still existed. The photography class did not materialise, however, until the death knell had sounded for film; it was a revolving door with Ole John leaving just as Bernd Becher was promoted to tenured status. John and Becher represented entirely different styles of teaching and approaches to it. Whereas John gave priority to his students' work over his own, Becher made it a condition of his taking up the appointment that he could continue working unimpeded. Hence he was rarely in the classroom in person. Students went to him. Colloquies with him and the students of the kind that were the norm in the Rinke class next door took place only rarely. Whereas many students were in the film class, only a handful of kindred spirits started with Becher. Hardly any of them were familiar with their future teacher's work. He was not a public attraction like Beuys nor was he an Actionist like Rinke or an acclaimed painter like Richter. 'Having to deal with photography on a daily basis was at that time for us rather a byway than something to be taken for granted. [...] When there was talk of creating a class just for photography, [...] we basically thought that this was slightly overdoing things,' writes Reinhard Mucha. He had been accepted in Richter's class because of his photographic work for the *Rundgang* but then switched to Rinke.[73] Since the mid-1970s photography had secured a niche for itself in various classes, but as a singular art form it was still far from being established. Hence, although it was not a must, it was far-sighted of the Academy to add photography to the traditional art forms at this time. Beuys's idea of the expanded definition of art and the interest of a generation of students in experimenting with blurring the boundaries between the traditional art forms in the interests of an interdisciplinary opening were left unmentioned on purpose. Instead, as Mucha says, a work method taken for granted was institutionalised as an independent genre. Photography was no longer confined to functioning as a means to, and material for, documentation; it was recognised as autonomous image production. The Conceptual idea of questioning the reproductive character of photography, of tabling social conditions for debate, of decoding power structures was not followed up here. A decision was taken for a concept grounded in the reproductive character of the medium. As Hilla Becher pointed out, the specific strength of photography lay in reproducing the world realistically.[74] Whereas the Bechers were convinced by its capacity for grasping the truth and suitability for visual archiving, for students this facility for immediately capturing information was already overlaid by visually mediated reproduction. 'Photographs are, of course, still reproductions; only the role model for photography is in my generation probably no longer reality but images we know of that reality,' as Thomas Ruff put it.[75] He was among Bernd Becher's first pupils. Together with his fellow students he challenged the artistic uncertainty that studying photography entailed compared to painting, the graphic arts, or sculpture and at the same time benefited from its still undefined scope for unforeseen possibilities. Ruff believes the reason why he and numerous first-generation members of the 'Becher School' became Germany's most successful art photographers is that they were at the right place at the right time.[76]

Staged Photography – Anna and Bernhard Johannes Blume

In fact it has a lot to do with a return in the 1980s to the picture with content. The intellectualisation of Conceptual art was succeeded by an urge for a new sensuality. The Neue Wilden [New Savages] surfaced, and photographic pictorial worlds were created. Daily life was dissected, satirised, and politically loaded. The photo sequences in large formats staged by Anna (*1937) and Bernhard Johannes (1937–2011) Blume since the 1980s exemplified that trend. Former fellow students of the Bechers' who had studied with Karl Otto Götz and Joseph Beuys from 1960 until 1965, the Blumes worked together from that period. They staged themselves in Performances for the camera in which political conventions, familial relationships, and domestic life were subjected to such ironic treatment that they seemed to implode. They subjected everyday life without rules of conduct to critical, comical, and unconventional scrutiny by granting the normal world of things a life of its own. In *Küchenkoller* [Kitchen Rage] (1985) the potato becomes a sign of the soul, expressive of suppressed desires, and unleashes a dynamic under which a housewife is driven to the brink of collapse (Fig. 25).[77] The series are psychoanalytical studies conducted in a laboratory of animate things, trials set up in an experimental and detached spirit of self-reflection.

The 'Becher School'

The aesthetic informing the pointedly objective photographs taken by Bernd and Hilla Becher aims at seriousness and a systematic approach, which precludes any nod to a comparative systematic study. An unshaken positivist basic trust in the reproducibility of the medium was passed on to the students. Bernd Becher expected a consistent investigation of a single subject, if possible, and took on students who were also interested in recording everyday life. That led to Tata Ronkholz's beer hall pictures, the portraits taken by Axel Hütte and Thomas Ruff, and Candida Höfer's interiors. Thomas Struth had already embarked on his street pictures.[78] Documenting real life in photos was the overarching theme in the Becher class even though none of the students, unlike their teachers, had envisaged a clearly defined life project. The rampant

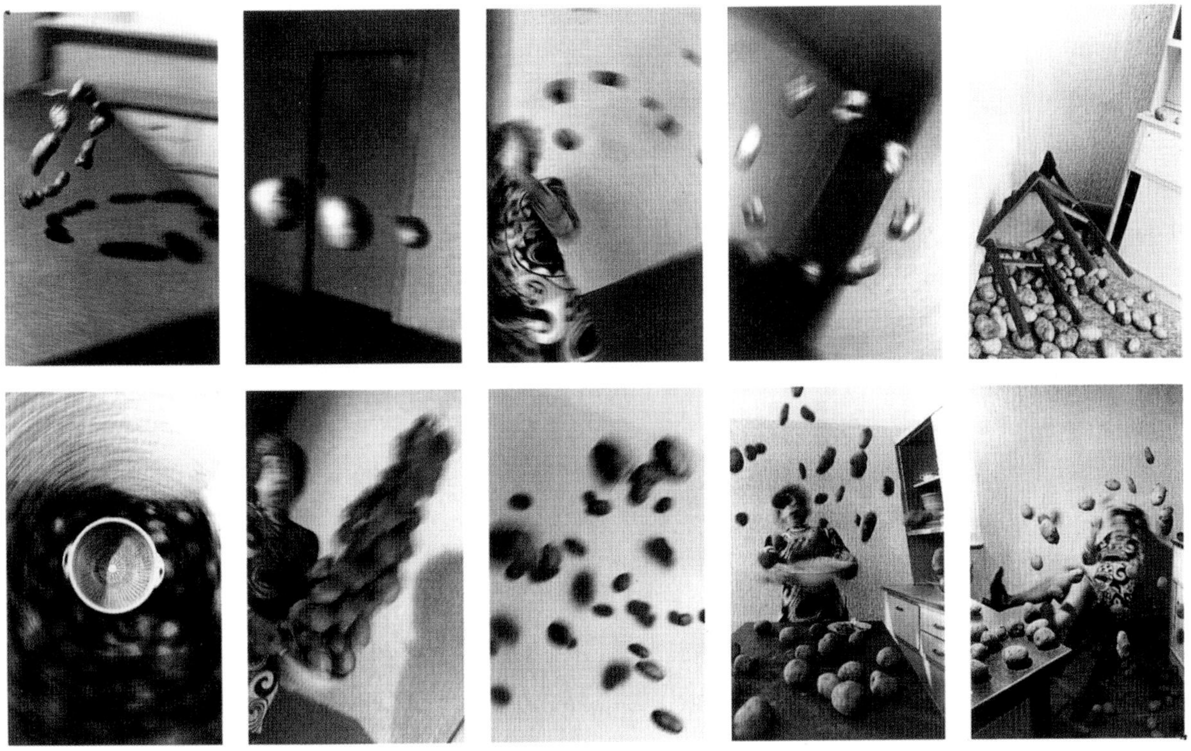

Fig. 25: Anna and Bernhard Johannes Blume, Küchenkoller *[Kitchen Rage], 1985, 10-part photo sequence, each part 200 × 126 cm*

growth of the image overload gave rise to constant reflection in the media, which grew into a swelling chorus of generational opposition. The Bechers, of course, clung undeterred to their conception of photography and photographic technique: they captured industrial buildings frontally, undisguised, and with parallel lines, constructing images in which architecture ideally became free-standing sculpture. Becher's students did not encounter teaching that was open in all directions. Instead, they were confronted with a clear-cut aesthetic of conviction grounded in the history of photography in the person of a teacher who had no qualms as an educator about transmitting undiminished his own experiences and insights to the generation that followed him. Paradoxically, despite the thematic and stylistic consistency that made Becher's work singular and the methodology specific to it, these are the very qualities that seem to have caused a 'school' to have grown out of his tradition-conscious teaching that has been as successful as the following that sprang up from the radically libertarian teaching practised by the likes of Joseph Beuys.

For Bernd Becher's students, the expanded concept of art was already a fact and no longer merely an aim that would have to be fought for. By the late 1970s they were already the beneficiaries of both the revolutionary upheavals and the subsequent gradual calming of the Academy's political climate. Introduced to the Konrad Fischer Gallery by Becher, they absorbed the Conceptual stances shown there as well as developments in the Rhenish art scene. Stimulation, exchange of ideas, and reviews in the media came from all sides while the Becher methodology remained the starting point for developing their own work.

With a total of eighty-seven pupils between 1976 and 1996/98, Bernd Becher had far fewer students in all than Joseph Beuys had on occasion in just one class.[79] However, a higher percentage of Becher's students, notably those of the first generation, have achieved international success. For those former students, being labelled the 'Becher School' or the 'Düsseldorf School (of Photography)' has represented premium brand status. Since the late 1980s Andreas Gursky, Candida Höfer, Axel Hütte, Thomas Ruff, Thomas Struth, and Petra Wunderlich, some ex-pupils of Becher's, have been participating in group shows along with teachers.[80] They are regarded as a group, by the art market, museums, and art critics alike. At least a decade after beginning their studies, the first pupils of Bernd Becher's were profiting from the art boom that set in during the 1980s. Interest in contemporary art had grown, new galleries were being opened, museums were being built, the need for expert commentary from art critics had increased, and by the end of the decade the medium of photography as an independent art form was attracting the interest of a broader public. Being classed as part of a group made it easier for individuals to start climbing the career ladder. No one had to struggle on his or her own. They were fighting together for a common cause. Their first pupils' rise to fame not only made the Bechers bask in reflected glory but came to be linked with their name although the 'Becher School' photographers' work is on the whole

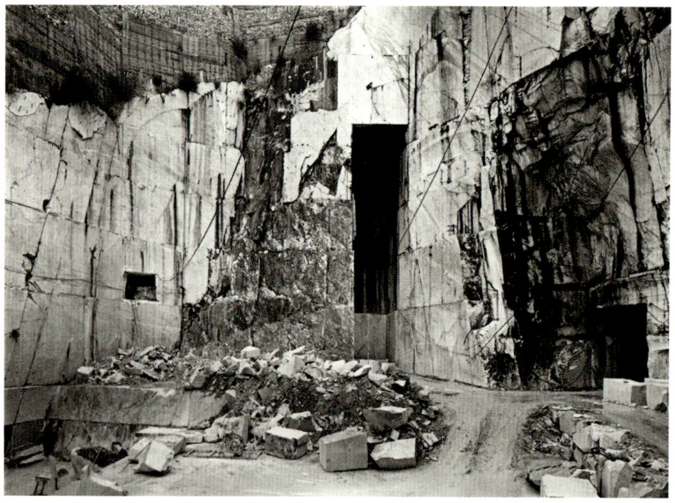

Fig. 26: Petra Wunderlich, Steinbruch I (Italien) *[Stone Quarry I (Italy)], 1989, baryte print, 68 × 82.3 cm*

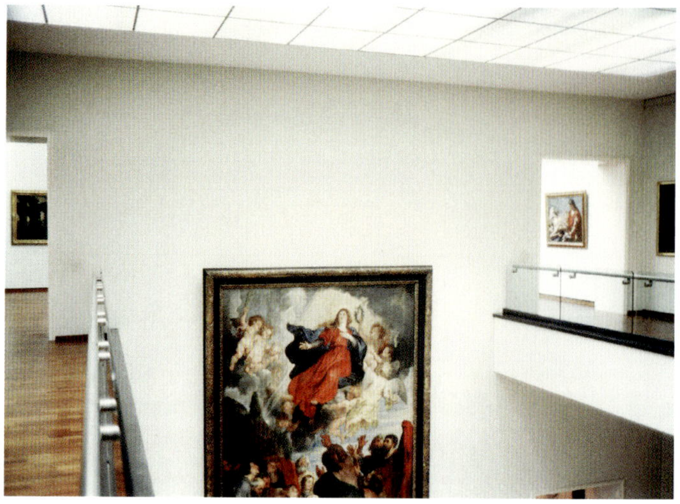

Fig. 27: Candida Höfer, Kunstmuseum Düsseldorf I *[Düsseldorf Art Museum I], 1991, C print, 47 × 61.5 cm*

anything but derivative. As they develop, their oeuvres have become diverse to the extent of negating the Becher's formal and aesthetic paradigms.

The pupil who still owes the most to her teacher's work is Petra Wunderlich (*1954), who photographs stone quarries and architecture with a medium-format camera in soft light (Fig. 26). Black-and-white, frontal, from a raised vantage point – many Becher criteria, even including Becher themes, are encountered in her work. Laurenz Berges, Bernhard Fuchs, Candida Höfer, Matthias Koch, and Simone Nieweg also aim at a consistent thematic focus. Unlike their teachers, however, they have all switched over to colour, which, when the Bechers began to work, was still in the developmental stages. Some of these photographers use the large format so popular on the art market, which borrows its subject matter from painting accordingly. In drawing on the classical genres – landscape, interiors, and portrait – they are not only working through the painterly tradition in photographs but their compositions are also modelled on the extant stock of pictures.

Between Document and Visual Rearrangement – Candida Höfer

Candida Höfer (*1944) trains her sights on institutions of public education, such as museums, libraries, and theatres, from an elevated vantage point, so to speak. *Türken in Deutschland* [Turks in Germany], a socially committed project to which she devoted herself when she left Ole John to switch to Bernd Becher's class, was followed by interiors, which were initially still in small formats and narrative in content. Human beings were no longer focused on but objects assumed a narrative function, communicating a great deal about use and place. The Virgin from the large-scale panel on which Peter Paul Rubens painted his *Assumption of the Virgin* (*c.*1616–1618), which is on permanent loan from the Düsseldorf Art Academy, appears to be about to vanish upwards towards the skylight. That is at least what *Kunstmuseum Düsseldorf I* [Düsseldorf Museum of Art I] (1991) suggests, a photograph taken by Candida Höfer from the gallery, hence looking down from above so that only two thirds of the painting are in the picture (Fig. 27). However, she has captured the symmetrical architecture: remote associations with a face are evoked by the wall and its two passages plus the square raster of the skylight.

This mischievously ironic take on things yielded with the sharp upturn in exhibitions in the 1990s to increasingly centred, formally perfect architectural photographs that grew in scale as the decade progressed. At first Höfer still worked, against her teacher's recommendation but for reasons of practicability, with a 35 mm camera. In 1997 she switched to medium-format (6 × 6 cm) and in 2003 to large-format (4 × 5 in.), in order to ensure the necessary sharpness of detail. The narrative gesture was replaced by a controlled and controlling view, in which interior space appears structurally differentiated through the focus on central perspective. However, the graphics of the picture have rearranged the relationship of things to each other even in the detached photographs without narrative.

With her photographs of interiors Höfer has linked up with a tradition she came to know through Karl Hugo Schmölz, who documented the rebuilding of Cologne after the Second World War as a close associate of the architects. Within the overarching genre of the interior she produced a variety of series, often as projects or on commission. Each photograph remains an individual picture and, even though Höfer seems to be collating material, a comparative viewpoint such as that informing Becher's work is not intended.

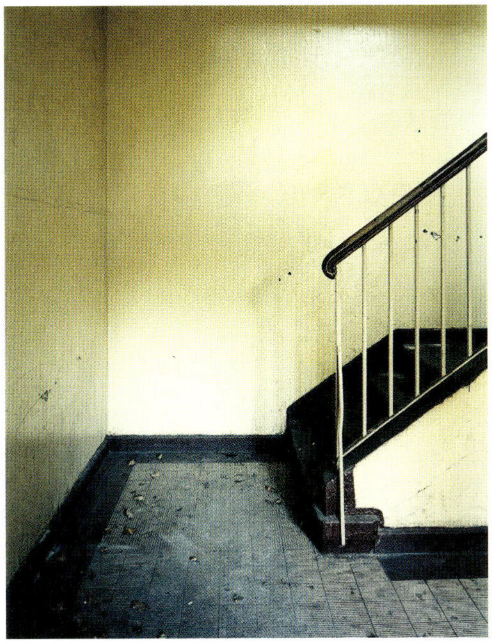

Fig. 28: Laurenz Berges, Potsdam II, *1994, C print, 49.5 × 39.4 cm*

Everyday – 'Becher Pupils' of the Younger Generation

Whereas Höfer mines the cultural sites of high culture, the showy side of our collective memory, for the motifs she chooses, Laurenz Berges (*1966) devotes himself to the dark side of living history, places that have been given up, abandoned rooms. Persistently seeking out places with the life gone out of them, he transfixes anecdotal details of tristesse (Fig. 28). An eye to the mundane yet remote as prescribed by the Bechers before them links the students of the younger generation. Simone Nieweg (*1962) captures the fringe phenomena of cultivation: tilled fields or harvested crops, allotments, scenic borderline areas that are testimonials to usefulness although rarely to beauty (Fig. 29). Matthias Koch focuses on remnants of industrialisation, historic industrial landscapes (Fig. 30). Bernhard Fuchs (*1971) trains his sights on rural life whereas Götz Diergarten (*1972) photographs huts, houses, snack bars in centred, frontal compositions, some of which are arranged in rows for comparison (Fig. 31). In the Bechers' work it is the structure standing out in black and white that makes comparison possible whereas Diergarten does the same with colour forms.

The work of Claus Goedicke (*1966) is discernibly more Conceptual in character. Although he devotes himself to simple everyday utilitarian objects, he detaches things completely from their contexts and defamiliarises them. Be they still lifes composed of plastic bottles or pictures of single objects, these photographs are devoid of narration based on either time or place. Instead they are informed by collective memory – or perhaps merely a dawning awareness of it (Fig. 32).

For Elger Esser (*1967) the environment as it is only gives rise to retro landscapes in soft focus (Fig. 33). Hence he usually directs his attention not to overlooked or neglected aspects but to beautiful scenery and pretty villages, which he stylises into classically composed, clichéd romanticising landscapes.

Analogue recording of the concrete environment, intensive preoccupation with a single theme, and capturing isolated phenomena, at times systematically, are the elements the stances presented in the above examples have in common. None of these artists has moved on to an experimental position. They have all remained true to the foundations of photography taught to them as students; hence, despite divergent pictorial idioms and subject matter, they recognisably form a group.

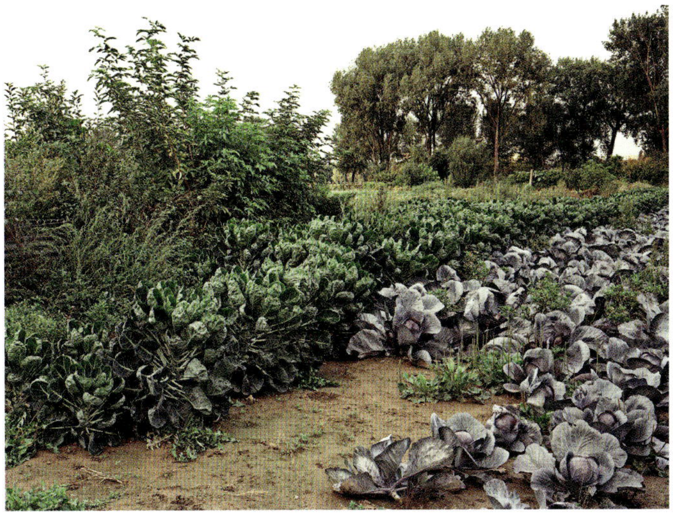

Fig. 29: Simone Nieweg, Kohlfeld *[Cabbage Field],* Düsseldorf Niederkassel II, *chromogenic colour print, 140 × 177 cm*

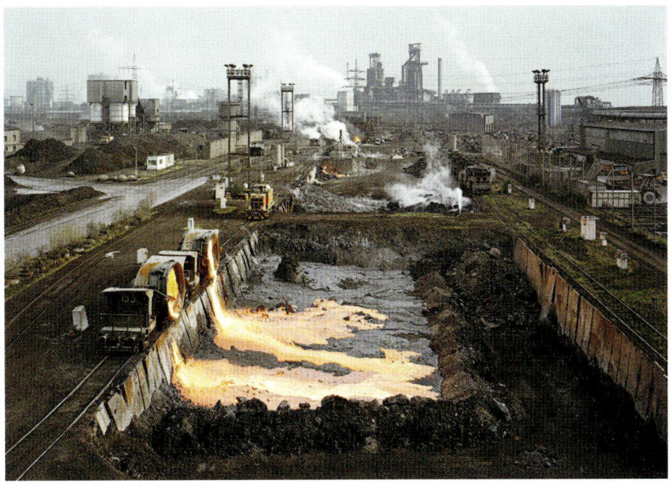

Fig. 30: Matthias Koch, Schlacke-Abschüttung bei Thyssen *[Slag Heap at Thyssen]* in Duisburg, *2010, C print, 125 × 181 cm*

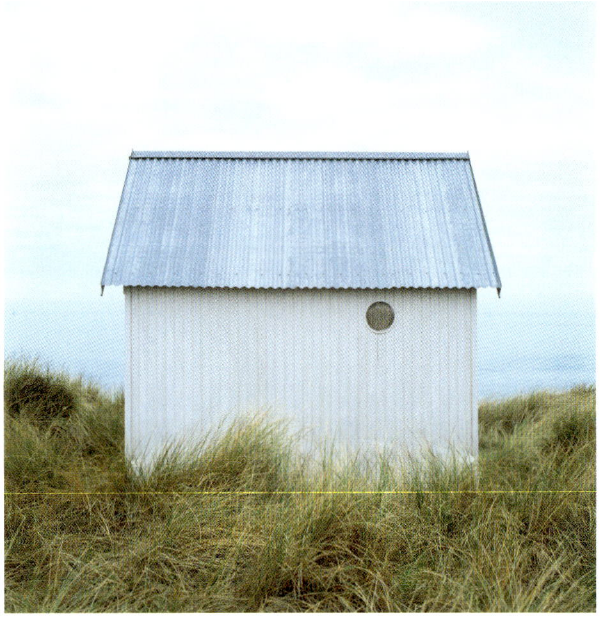

Fig. 31: Götz Diergarten, Ohne Titel [untitled] (Gouville) 5, 2002, colour photograph behind frameless acrylic glass, 100 × 100 cm

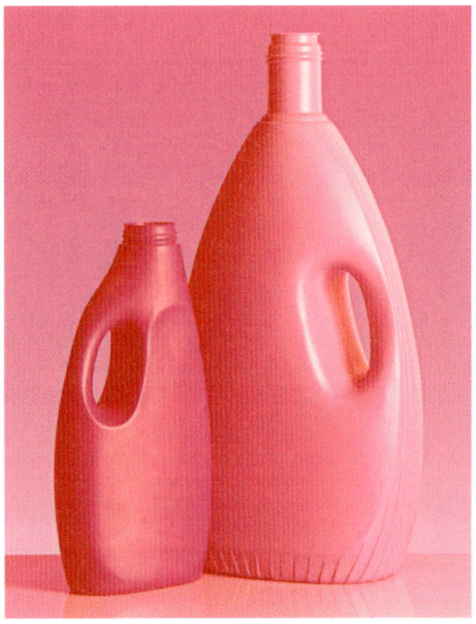

Fig. 32: Claus Goedicke, I–57, *1992, photograph, 36 × 28.5 cm*

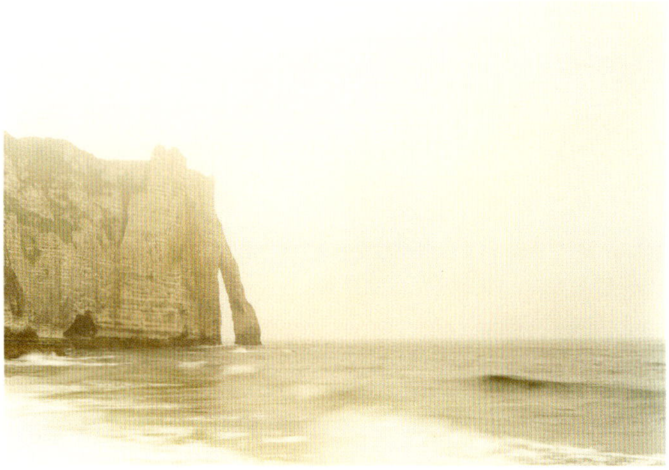

Fig. 33: Elger Esser, Étretat II, *chromogenic colour print, 184 × 246.5 cm*

On the one hand, they can profit from the already established 'Becher School' label, but this does not make it easier to study their work as independent and individual positions.

Technical and Formal Aesthetic Innovation – Thomas Ruff and Photography in the 1980s and 1990s

The surplus in formal aesthetics as compared to their teachers is also grounded in stages of artistic development that took place in Germany from the late 1980s on and are also synonymous with the terms 'Becher School' and 'Düsseldorf School (of Photography)'. What is meant here – apart from the switch to colour – is the orientation in subject matter and composition towards painting, the large formats, covering photos with Perspex – in short, the large, still, detailed pictures of the present.

Colour moves the motif to where it is accessible, returning to it the history which it was deliberately deprived of by the Bechers' emphasis on structure and ahistorical conception in order to transfer it from life to the stasis of archivisation. Advances in technology made it possible and affordable to switch to colour, and aspiring artists were interested in colour because it lent their motifs temporality and liveliness in contrast to the black-and-white graphics perception. Thomas Ruff (*1958), who has a passion for technology, introduced colour into the class repertoire in 1979.[81]

At that time he was still working on his series of interiors, which is the only one of his works to follow the Becher dogma of the authenticity of the medium, according to which objective reproduction of what is there can be attained by means of objectively detached exposure.

In 1986 he was the first of the 'Becher pupils' to switch to large picture formats. He expanded his portraits – which were at first reduced from life-size by one-third – to 210 × 165 cm (shown on p. 294). Portrayed frontally against a light, neutral background, his sitters seem motionless and aloof. Human being and picture surface, or 'face and surface', as Martina Dobbe puts it, have become one.[82] The emphasis has been placed on the construction of the picture rather than authenticity.

These formal aesthetic elements were, however, not in the least new when Ruff began to make use of them. The photographs Katharina Sieverding produced of her face in the early 1970s (*Transformer*, 1973/74, and *Die Sonne um Mitternacht schauen* [Looking at the Sun at Midnight], 1973, each 190 × 125 cm), were in colour, in large formats, frontal, and mask-like. However, although Sieverding was looking for a new form of aesthetic expression, Ruff draws on a pattern familiar from portraiture. With it he has evoked unmediated art historical references that place photography as a matter of course, or so it seems, in the art historical context.

Another element that removes Ruff's portrait photography from the reproducible mass-media status is his adoption of the Diasec® process employed in advertising. It makes it possible to seal a print permanently behind Perspex.[83] This ensures that the paper remains stable in a frame, yet the work as a whole weighs less than it would if it were behind glass, and prevents a motif from being rolled up in an archive or disappearing into a drawer. Use of the Diasec® process would become another formal characteristic of the 'Becher School'. Thus a medium originally classified as belonging to the graphic arts has advanced to the status of space-defining art. Via format and presentation, photography has already become an autonomous pictorial medium and has left its subordinate function as documentary illustration behind. Reproduction has become reality in its own right.

Thomas Ruff was the first Düsseldorf photography student to use digitalisation in what was still an early stage as far as technological advance is concerned. In 1987 he had a company digitally process a façade of terraced houses, a work stage he would later undertake himself until he could resort for entire series to material that was only digitally extant (*JPEG*, 2004, *Nudes*, from 2003 on), and for his part was either reworking analogue material (*Maschinen* [Machines], 2003) or producing purely digital pictures with analogue optics (*Photogramme* [Photograms], since 2012). Paul Virilio describes the difference between analogue photography and digital imaging as the leap from capturing and storing reality to the construction of a reality of one's own – a pictorial reality.[84] Ruff, in fact, tracked down specific themes and also techniques, investigated extant pictures in those areas, and extrapolated image forms of his own from them. This process has just as little to do with storing history as it has with systematically working through a single phenomenon. The focus of attention has clearly switched from reproducing specific extant entities to the production of pictures.

Of course Ruff's works have a great deal to do with social subject matter; after all, the images that feed his own pictorial universe derive thematically from it. His works do not, however, provide information on existing conditions. They have long since become independent pictures rather than photographs in the conventional sense although their content and form are rooted in photographic practice. Ruff stands revealed as a postmodern Conceptualist. Eschewing commentary of any sort, he helps himself from the available stock of material to turn photography against the reproduction of reality with which it was inscribed by producing pictures that constantly confront us with the postulate that a photographic image cannot make any statement about reality.

Thus he at once confirms and negates the much discussed thesis of Jeff Wall according to which 1960s and 1970s Conceptualist photography failed in its attempt to liberate the medium from reproduction because photography must always mediate the experience of an image. That is why, according to Wall, it remains defined by content and has developed as a reaction since the mid-1970s into a medium that is once again used representationally to reproduce experiencing the visible world.[85] Understandably, linguistic Conceptualism has pushed photography to its limits. Most Becher pupils agree that photography has, therefore, experienced a renaissance of its representational function. Thomas Ruff, on the other hand, shows that there is yet another way that defies every standard definition of photography by downgrading the direct reproduction of experience to a second-level experience which is also translated into a colour surface. Sensuous pleasure is possible but recognising or understanding the original event is ruled out. All that can be experienced in Ruff's work is surface, regardless of whether he has reworked pictorial material acquired from NASA, from company archives, or Japanese mangas, regardless of whether he has used a night-vision device, stereo photography, or newspaper cuttings.

In taking up this stance, Ruff has set himself apart from all discussion of media content and has drawn attention to technique and technology, which theory has increasingly focused on since the 1990s concomitantly with the growth in digitalisation. This ensures that Ruff's work is premised on the polar opposite of his teacher's. His taking over Bernd Becher's chair after the brief interlude when it was occupied by the Canadian artist Jeff Wall marked the continuance of a successful school in the institutional sense yet also implies that it had been superseded conceptually.[86]

Digital Constructs – Andreas Gursky, Jörg Sasse

Andreas Gursky (*1955) is another pupil of Becher's who has returned to his alma mater as a professor. Assigned to the Fine Arts Department since 2010, Gursky's class works in a wide range of media and genres. Like Ruff, Gursky has turned his back on the concept of the purely photographic image which still informed his early leisure activity scenes: playing football, enjoying swimming pools, going on walks. Those memorably laconic pictorial narratives have gradually yielded to detached observation and ultimately to a need for seeking the definitive pictorial expression of any particular phenomenon. Art historical pictorial traditions have intervened ever more obviously in composition. They make it possible to transform a profane scene, such as anglers on the Ruhr, taken in 1989, into a classical landscape in the tradition of Claude Lorrain (Fig. 34). Framed by the embankment on both sides, the river flows through the picture in a sinuous diagonal, drawing the viewer's glance into the distance. Anglers are dotted about in this seemingly idyllic rural scenery, lending the picture the look of a pastoral landscape, were it not for the title, which sets the scene in the midst of the urban Ruhr area. A landscape of this kind in an industrial region is not created by reproducing reality but by inventing a picture. Reality is the starting point, not the end product. The decision for larger formats has promoted this development. Concomitantly with the increase in size, everyday reality and its many narrative elements have given way to clearer structuring, which allows a picture to be perceived as form. That in turn has played the paramount role in setting the course for Gursky's further development since it has removed his motifs from their living contexts and made them recognisable as structure. Seven years after the idyll on the Ruhr, a river consists of mere strips in the Gursky aesthetic. Digital processing has turned *Rhein* [Rhine] into a deindividualised waterway or even a picture of an abstract form. Gursky has been using this technique since the early 1990s. Although he finds his motifs in reality, his pictures are created at the computer. By piecing together separately photographed parts, the artist offers viewers overwhelming scenes, some of them spectacular in the journalistic sense, in which physical inaccessibility has been overcome (shown on p. 291). Thus he can make a prison as alluring as the ambience of a party or a high-tech installation. Reality is no longer a factor to be reckoned with.

Like Ruff, Jörg Sasse, et al., Gursky has shed the mechanical constraints of analogue photography. The digitally coded image is not dependent on scenery or photographic equipment. Like every other visual art form, it is produced with intention. Deciding to digitalise therefore means opting for the free production of pictures. Without deliberately renouncing photography, these artists have moved one after another from photography to the picture. 'I try to make pictures that I am amazed at myself,' is how Jörg Sasse (*1962) describes his approach (Fig. 35).[87]

In the analogue photographs Sasse took until 1994, objects were already losing their practical value and forming autonomous shape and colour contexts. Since then he has switched to digitalisation. Photographs of his own or by others are manipulated in such a way that the motifs are discernible but precise recognition has been rendered impossible. Something is confusing – a scene is reminiscent of something that has happened yet never took place as it is now. That interface between a reality that has existed and autonomous pictorial motifs is what Sasse stages, raising the viewer's expectations without fulfilling them. Colourful boats on the shore, a merry-go-round behind a fence, a solitary high-rise vanishing in rising mist – increasingly graphic, sometimes verging on the abstract, the motifs always conceal a secret that attests to Sasse's personal amazement at the picture. His work is a free visual game that reveals his belief in the technical image without any laboured attempts at justification.

Contestation – Thomas Struth, Axel Hütte

One of Bernd Becher's first students, Thomas Struth (*1954) addresses genres familiar from painting: they range from street pictures, portraits, and landscapes to museum pictures. He began as a painter and, taking advantage of the technical possibilities afforded at the Academy, switched from black-and-white photography in small formats to colour and eventually to large formats. As for content, he concentrates on memorable contexts, on making social structures visible in architecture, in relationships between family members or friends, in individual portraits, or in the reception of art. This historically motivated approach differs from that of Axel Hütte (*1951), a former fellow student, even though their motif repertoires partly overlap.

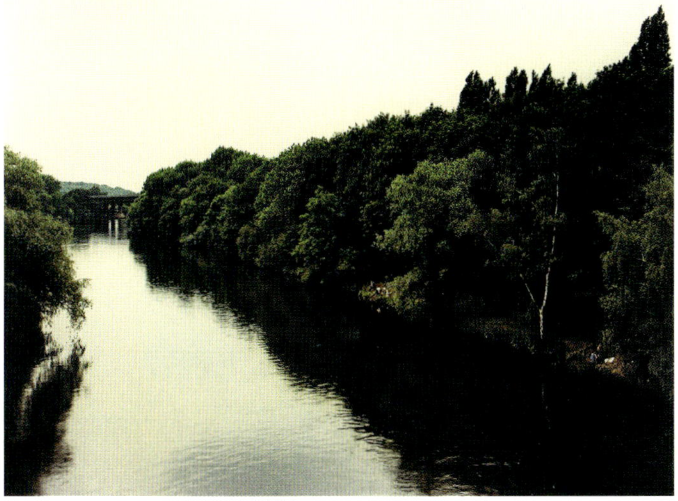

Fig. 34: Andreas Gursky, Mühlheim an der Ruhr, Angler, *1989, colour photograph behind Perspex, 215.5 × 277.5 cm*

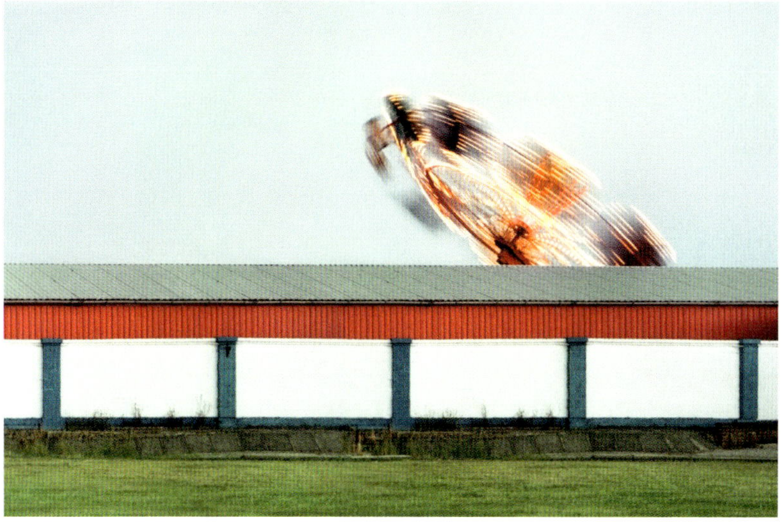

Fig. 35: Jörg Sasse, 8246, *2000, C print, 103 × 160 cm*

Thematic crossover often occurs among Becher pupils as if they wanted to measure themselves against similar performance requirements. Stock exchanges, libraries, or forests – the motifs are similar but the approaches to them vary widely.

Both Axel Hütte and Thomas Struth photographed urban scenes while they were students. Hütte devoted himself to working-class neighbourhoods and social housing. His pictures show places of transition that do not invite one to linger: passages, drives, stairwells, tunnels. With an eye honed on social criticism, he produced technically perfect yet emotionless statements that in this respect resemble Struth's street pictures. Struth focused on streets lined with buildings, which are informative on places and their inhabitants in a blend of interest in social issues and clichéd notions.

Two decades on, approaches that initially looked similar have long since diverged. Yet the primeval forest pictures are once again works that are similar in content, format, and presentation (Figs. 36, 37).[88] Both Struth and Hütte show the forest as an impenetrable wall of vegetation, from which practised visual access bounces off. Hütte, who has advanced from urban spaces to landscape, aims at confusing perception. The devices which constantly seem to subvert viewers' expectations and challenge them to keep trying to find their way in the picture include confrontation with an impossible perspective, the absence of a middle distance, and the lack of a vantage point. Hütte pushes all analogue means to their limits to allow reproduction to become a picture via abstraction.

For Struth, on the other hand, the dense fabric of plants permits meditative immersion in individual forms without, however, being comprehensible as a whole. Viewers are left with a filled void of sorts that forces them back on themselves.

Struth's portraits, which led him to start on his *Museum Photographs* series in 1989, not only reveal his interest in painting but even amount to a personal showdown with it.[89]

The two former photography students have drawn on painting as a store of stylistic devices, as source orientation, and even as motifs. Struth's museum pictures link up with nineteenth-century representations of art cabinets. However, what he photographs is not the place of learning and culture as such but rather formal identities between picture and viewer space, which seem to interlink different planes of reality. That he quite literally sees himself 'as being the equal' of the painters whose works he photographs at eye level is most apparent in the double self-portrait *Thomas Struth – Albrecht Dürer* (2000), hubris on two levels since it is also a deliberate evocation of Dürer's self-stylisation as Christ Pantocrator (Fig. 38).

Volker Kahmen observed as early as 1973 that 'art photography evokes everything that in competitive imitation has tried to measure itself against the qualities of autonomous art'.[90] That was not fair to the technical medium and its social relevance but contestation was needed to liberate photography from the stigma already implicit in the famous advertising slogan launched by Kodak founder George Eastman in 1888: 'You press the button, we do the rest.' Artists working in photography were confronted with the task of freeing the medium from the idea of automatic production and endless reproduction possible for everyone. To accomplish this they developed two paradigmatic strategies in the 1980s: on the one hand, the constructed visual worlds of staged photography and, on the other, the large, still pictures represented by the work of Becher's pupils.

The formal aesthetic characteristics of their work did not represent real innovation in photography on the whole or even in Düsseldorf alone. Sieverding had been working in colour in large formats for a long time. Dibbets's works with integrated passepartout margins were on display at the Konrad Fischer Gallery. Colour photographs of mundane motifs were a commonplace in America, and the spectacular increase in size

Fig. 36: Axel Hütte, Mossman Gorge, Queensland, *1999, C print, 157 × 237 cm*

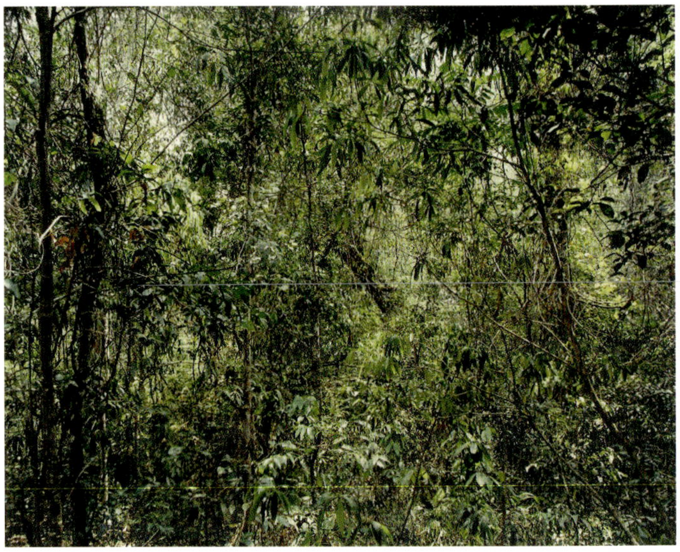

Fig. 37: Thomas Struth, Paradise 9, Xi Shuang Banna, China, *1999, chromogenic colour print, 269.4 × 339.4 cm*

accompanied by borrowing from the tradition of painting was already familiar from Jeff Wall's oeuvre. Nevertheless Bernd Becher's photography class and the reception of his students as a group marked a triumph for the medium that today still burnishes the Academy's reputation.

PARALLEL DEVELOPMENTS – THOMAS DEMAND, GUDRUN KEMSA, ROSEMARIE TROCKEL

One might suppose that the distinction achieved by the photo class was such that it prevented parallel developments and ways of utilising the medium, but this has not been the case.

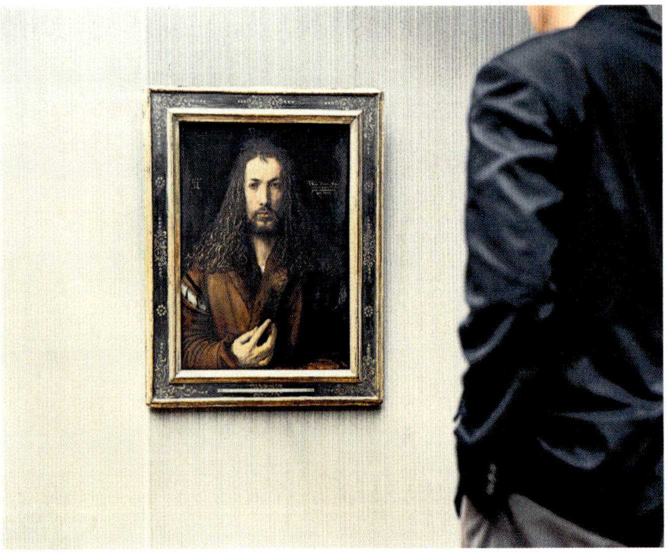

Fig. 38: Thomas Struth, Alte Pinakothek München, Selbstporträt *[Alte Pinakothek Munich, Self-Portrait], 2000, chromogenic colour print, 116.5 × 147 cm*

Photography has been put to use in other art forms in manifold ways. To take one example, Thomas Demand (*1964) is an artist who studied with Fritz Schwegler at the Düsseldorf Art Academy and elsewhere and defies classification as a practitioner of a single art form, including sculpture, installation, media, and photography. His photographs of models of media pictures replicated in paper and cardboard are perceived at once as pictures and not as photographs. This is not a case of reality yielding to construct but rather to reflection in the media via a dual response process: perceiving a picture in the media and translating the motif into a three-dimensional model bereft of all historicising details, such as titles, labels, advertising, and the like. What remains is the architectural scaffolding of a scene that has been perceived by many yet, decontextualised, is remembered by only a few. Demand's material comes from the ubiquitous image overload. He questions those momentarily important images that substantiate arguments, whereby the double transformation of the original context (into a model and then into a picture) parallels the gradual loss of recollection, which in turn calls the original use of the image into question (Fig. 39). The reflection on the media focused on here is already encountered in works by the early Becher pupils. It has dominated the discussion of the media since the Iconic Turn and has become de rigueur for all artists who work on Conceptual lines with technical images.

However, the medium is also used simply to produce images as practised by Gudrun Kemsa (*1961). She does not play the image off against itself. Instead she uses it to investigate the phenomenon of time 'transfixed' in it. Like Demand, Kemsa started in sculpture. She transferred from Karl Bobek to David Rabinowitch, having already discovered photography and sought contact with Bernd Becher but ultimately did not share his documentary approach. Gudrun Kemsa is interested in light, space, and movement (Fig. 40). She experiments with

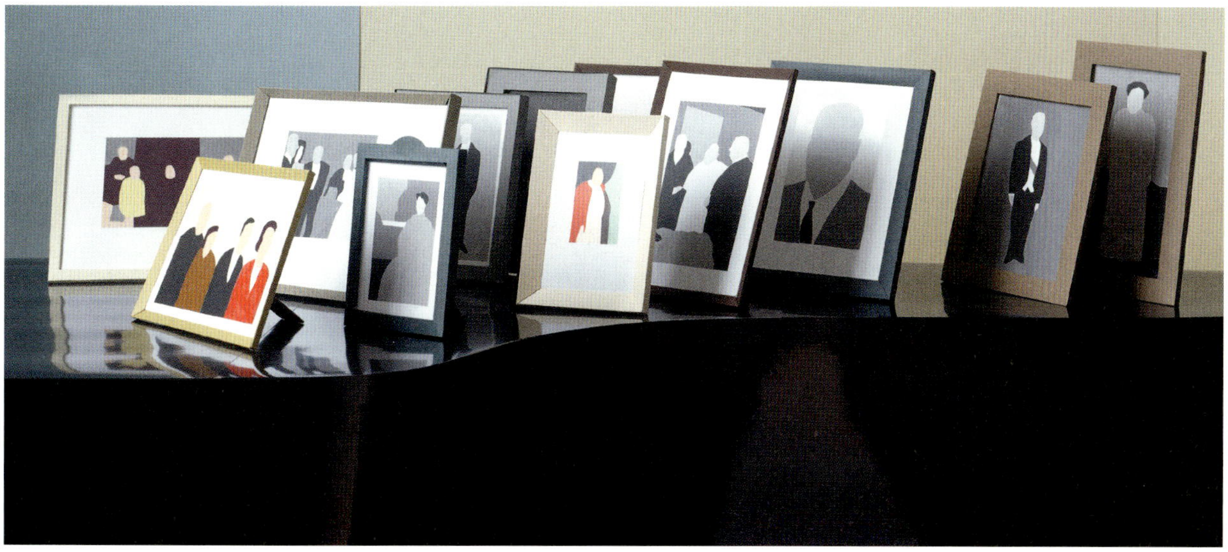

Fig. 39: Thomas Demand, Flügel/Grand Piano, *1993, C print/Diasec®, 62 × 156 cm*

photographic material in order to produce colours that are not the preprogrammed ones, with movement in order to visualise time, with light to reproduce space and atmosphere. In this case, the object of study is not the medial function of photography. Photography furnishes the mechanical technology for producing pictures.

There have been many students outside the photography class who, like Gudrun Kemsa, have made use of the medium, just as in other parts of the Academy painters have used colour and sculptors have worked in stone. Not all of them have been devotees of the high gloss of the postmodern 1980s. The use of contemplative pictures that were also trenchantly critical and revealing continued to evolve – for instance, in the collections of pictures amassed by Hans Peter Feldmann in Düsseldorf as well as in the work of Rosemarie Trockel (*1952), who became a professor at the Academy in 1998. As Christoph Schreier has noted, Trockel is interested neither in self-referential art nor in inaccessible hermetic works.[91] The value of her aesthetic lies in the simplicity of the materials she uses, such as a lined sheet of paper that she knows how to design, and in her playful handling of picture and text and the two combined. She is preoccupied 'with what is heterogeneous and paradoxical, with fractures and "holes" in the system, which provide scope for what has not been thought, is not common, for what is possible'.[92] Published pictures are, like script and drawing, material elements of her work (Fig. 41).

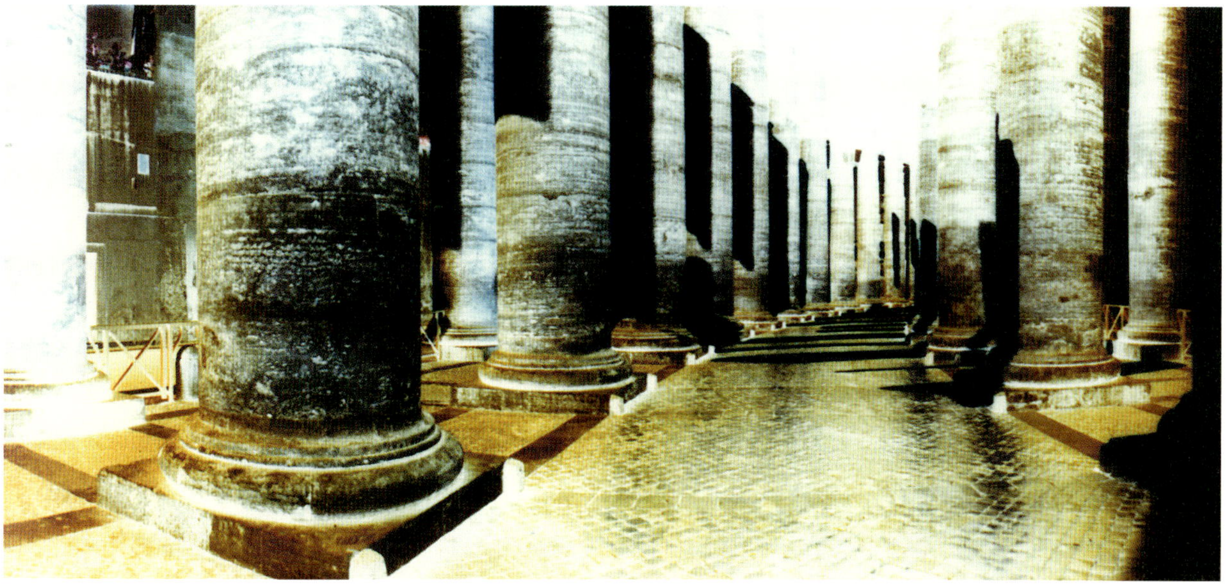

Fig. 40: Gudrun Kemsa, Colonnati, *1996, chromogenic colour print, 80 × 200 cm*

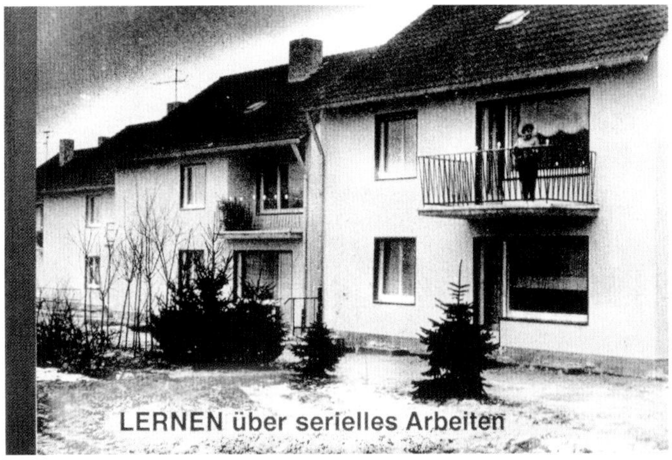

Fig. 41: Rosemarie Trockel, LERNEN über serielles Arbeiten *[LEARNING about Working in Series], 1993, book with photo prints on tracing paper, glossy cover, adhesive binding, 16.8 × 24.1 cm*

The Ruff Class – Photography in the First Decade of the Twenty-First Century

The fact that the uses of photography as art have considerably changed and expanded since it was officially introduced as an art form at the Academy in 1976 can probably also be put down to the appointment of Thomas Ruff to succeed Jeff Wall as professor of photography. Thomas Ruff, who had studied with Bernd Becher, was the perfect choice because he was the candidate who was most interested in the possibilities of generating images. He did not have to abandon the classic analogue photograph to be able to respond to the headlong rush of developments in the medium. With eyes wide open and a keen enjoyment of toying with trial and error, he exploits technological innovation and draws on images made for a wide variety of purposes and gleaned from manifold sources. Hence he made no attempt at forcing on his students the constraints of a specific aesthetic as he had experienced at the Academy. Instead he demanded of students that they experiment with and investigate any approach they might choose and promoted their individual efforts to the utmost.

Thomas Ruff took over all the students from what had been the Becher/Wall class. The explosive upturn in the art market probably goes some way to explaining why there were not only advances in technology; studying with such a successful 'art photographer' also increased the likelihood of market success and hence was viewed as a good strategic move.

The market value of art puts pressure on students early on to be successful and this in turn limits the scope for taking advantage of their time at the Academy as an opportunity for experimenting in looking for an idea and aesthetic of their own.

That means building up a stance that looks promising from the marketing angle is strategically vital. It stood to reason that the photo class should as a group emulate their predecessors' commercially successful strategies. The collective term 'school', problematic in any case, was initially taken on without any further effort on the artists' part – albeit without any objections being raised. Others later subsumed themselves under that heading with definite intent.[93] Ruff students underscore class unity as pupils of a particular professor by presenting themselves with their work and their exhibition activity on a collective website.[94] They are nonetheless far from demonstrating the stylistic coherence that distinguished Becher's pupils. The Ruff students' approaches to their work cover the broadest range imaginable: analogue, digital, mobile phone photography, drawing on extant material.

What can a picture hope to achieve nowadays when everyone photographs, digitally manipulates, and disseminates? What actually constitutes the difference in photography between art and non-art? As Juergen Staack (*1978) sees it, it is the one-off, which is why he works almost exclusively with Polaroids; on the other hand, it is the presentation context which determines the reception of a work as art. In *Left Behind ... Missing Pictures*, a work he produced in 2005/06 while still a student, he has broadened the art framework to include public spaces, presenting Polaroid series and leaving it up to them to tell their story. The materialisation of the individual picture as a one-off is significant in this connection for the reason that the question remains open as to whether, when, and how pictures handed over to the public return. Staack continues to cling to the one-off Polaroid shot even while he may question the significance of what is visible in it to the extent of destroying the content. Oral description then hands down what was once visible in the picture that has in the meantime been overpainted (Fig. 42). Like these two works, others by Staack are based on a single original, which the artist abandons to destruction, either deliberately or fortuitously. The work is manifest in its removal. It causes questions to materialise that an artist working in photography raises when confronted with the visual overload.

Martina Sauter (*1974), a former classmate of Juergen Staack's, is concerned with comparing the essence of the medium with film rather than dealing with photography as such. Her pictures open up dubious worlds that set off an inexhaustible reservoir of pictorial narratives. Taking filmic habits of seeing as her starting point, she composes scenarios each consisting of one photograph and a detail from a film still (Fig. 43). The outcome is a disturbing combination of crisply clear and noticeably blurred detail, coarse and imperceptible pixelation,

Fig. 42: Juergen Staack, Transcription Image, *since 2008, overpainted Polaroid*

front and back, true and untrue. Film and photography form two materially separate picture planes, which the viewer tries to unite. They are also perceived differently. The film picture refers to a before and elicits an after whereas the photograph is a combination of both. The film picture is ephemeral; the photograph is concrete. This difference due to the difference in media creates a tension the artist deploys deliberately because it has associations of something eerily arcane. These are pictures that cannot be deciphered; even their content eludes comprehension. The visible retreats, leaving everything up to the viewer's imagination.

Questioning an image is also the starting point in Anna Vogel's (*1981) work. She mounts her own or found pictorial material to form new compositions in one-off works that are usually in small formats. Glued on or digitally processed, overpainted or slashed with a cutter, the different parts result in new pictorial realities, which are often based on a landscape substrate (Fig. 44). Through inserted forms or graphic structures, mountains, valleys, broad zones of sky, or water surfaces oscillate between depth and shallows, reality and fantasy, content and form. By combining different media and techniques in her work Anna Vogel creates small, autonomous pictures that originated in reflection on photography.

These three most recent graduates exemplify current trends in the ongoing photography discussion. It is not possible to group them under the heading of shared content, aesthetic, or conception of the medium they are using. To the contrary, the medium itself has been tabled for debate. Content, execution, plausibility, presentation, mediacy are just a few of the themes dealt with by the artists of this generation. Technically speaking, the field has been enlarged by intrusion into all forms of imaging. The status of photography as a medium is no longer questioned; the entry of technology into the classic art forms has broken down all barriers to acceptance. Artists are now individually seeking conceptions with which photography can set itself apart from the ubiquitous image overload. Analogue technology and classic themes are just as appropriate as new technology and aesthetic innovation.

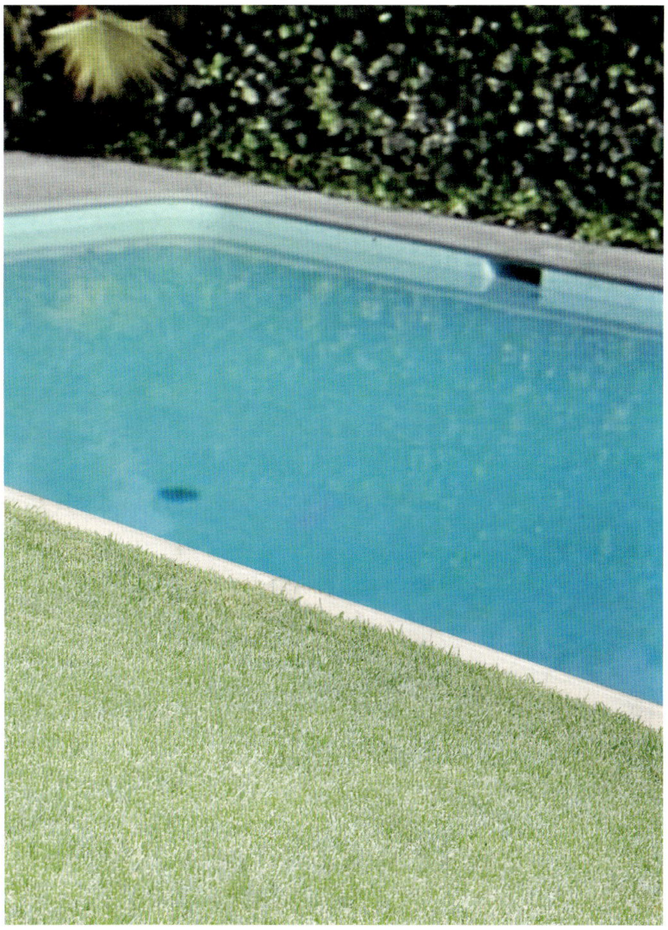

Fig. 43: Martina Sauter, Grün *[Green], 2013, 2-part C print collage behind Diasec®, 140 × 105 cm*

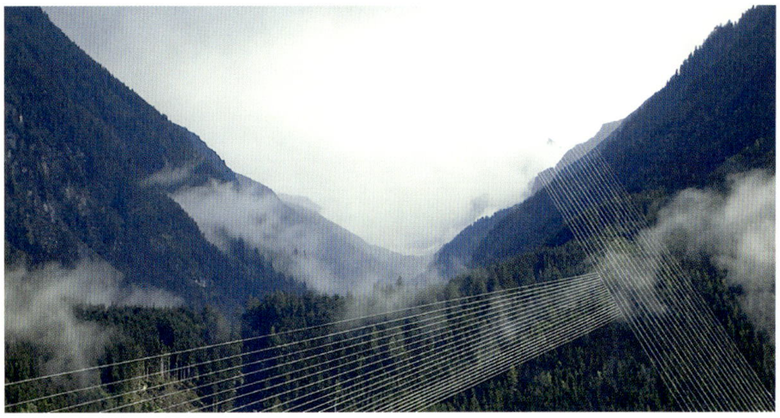

Fig. 44: Anna Vogel, Extended Rays I, *2013, incised inkjet print, 27.9 × 42 cm*

Second-Generation Conceptual Photography – Christopher Williams

Christopher Williams (*1956) is an American Conceptual artist of the second generation who was appointed to the chair of photography as Thomas Ruff's successor in 2008.[95] Karel Schamper calls the first generation 'hardliners' because they focused primarily on abstract ideas whereas they were only interested in material visualisation as an afterthought. Williams, on the other hand, attaches enormous value to the picture itself, its quality, and presentation.[96] Title pictures with the factual and technical information they impart underline the gesture of 'objective' representation. His shots themselves are stunning with their enormous attention to detail and objective coverage of the kind familiar from the documentary tradition. Yet the seeming link to Becher's idea of photography has been broken: the belief in photography as a reproducing medium is for Williams merely the starting point for the critical investigation of what photography can still convey in a society deluged with images or, put differently, what can still be perceived in a photograph. Unlike Thomas Demand, Williams does not appeal to the faculty of recollection nor does he present ways of construction as Ruff does. Williams reverts to ideas of the picture, ways of classification and representation that developed in industrial society to call into question their aesthetic conventions and epistemological form. As photographs of extant documentations or collector's items, his pictures have by now become detached from any historical or institutional source. The subject matter is still aligned with the industrial age, as is indicated by *For Example: Dix-Huit Leçons Sur La Société Industrielle* [Eighteen Lessons on Industrial Society], the title of a work shown for the first time in 2005.[97] Since then seventeen new revised drafts of this work have appeared although the title remains unchanged, a principle that Williams applied between 1993 and 2001 and already to *For Example: Die Welt ist schön* [The World is Beautiful].[98] The title itself implies a universe apart: *Dix-Huit Leçons Sur La Société Industrielle* (Paris 1963) is a work by the French philosopher and sociologist Raymond Aron; *Die Welt ist schön* is a book, published in 1928, by Albert Renger-Patzsch, whose objective documentary style became the basis of a modern aesthetic of photography. The introductory phrase, 'For example', designates the works quoted as examples of Williams's concept. Accordingly the focus is not only on the picture but also on the interplay of picture/title, which is intended to generate a complex context. The objects reproduced can be disarmingly mundane: a camera, a record player, a tyre (shown on p. 295). The title gives information on many underlying data yet the idea still cannot be inferred from them. In the case of the tyre, Christopher Williams was concerned to allude to sociocultural, economic, and political links. A French product, it is supposed to remind viewers of the barricades of car tyres erected in the Paris revolts of 1968 and also that Michelin, the tyre manufacturer, once kept rubber plantations in the former French colony of Vietnam. A broad associative field spanning rebellion, exploitative colonialism, and war opens up to the initiated. Product analysis is needed if one is to understand the context Williams has implied. The research that underpins his work is as accurate as his realisation is meticulous. Since the late 1980s Williams has commissioned professional photo studios to prepare the photographs, which, as beautiful pictures in the classic sense, reveal nothing of what Williams is thinking. Not until one has grasped the overall project of which Williams has been the artistic director does the artist's attempt to insinuate minute cracks into our perceptual conventions become apparent.

OUTLOOK

This Conceptual position has added another facet to the discussion about photography as a medium. It is doubtful whether photography can, therefore, retain its reproduction character in the system of the arts for the purpose of critical questioning alone. What is, of course, obvious is the difficulty of liberating oneself from the prevailing conventions of image and perception. Moreover, the medium remains just as linked to technical production as it has been to the reproduction function. Building up distance between photography and the reproduction function has been the work of the last two generations of photographers. The history of the older art forms teaches us, however, that no medium has hitherto been able to detach itself entirely from its functional fixedness and its conventional use(s) even though those art forms were pushed to the point of dissolution in the past century. The process has ended in freedom to deal with any media as one chooses, a development that renders superfluous further questioning. Painters work figuratively, abstractly, or analytically with their medium of choice without having to determine in advance the most productive approach to the next stage. Similarly, photography is likely to continue to evolve on all levels as an art form. Photographers who are visually more interested in the sumptuous picture are just as likely to find the right instructors, sources of inspiration, and role models as those who tend towards narrative or Conceptual leanings. After all, even though the Düsseldorf Art Academy still sees itself as an academy for painters and sculptors, a crossover culture has long since developed in which students no longer choose a class on the basis of the medium they prefer to work in. Now the work and approach of the professor are what counts. Despite that trend, the social omnipresence of photography ensures that a photography class will continue to be a force to be reckoned with, one that calls for constant re-evaluation. Inevitably, however, the medium has been given an institutional academic home and development platform just because it is so successful. Photography has become – artistically and economically speaking – the premium label of the Düsseldorf Art Academy.

NOTES

* Friedrich Wolfram Heubach in conversation with the author on 25 January 2013.

1 Sophia Stang, 'Aktionskunst im Rheinland. Bewegung im Bild "I welcome whatever happens next" (John Cage)', in: Natalia Gershevskaya and Kai Heymer (eds.), *Faszinierende Dokumente. Künstler in Aktion*, exhib. cat. Moscow/Düsseldorf, Heidelberg 2011, pp. 68–85; here: p. 68.

2 Première of John Cage's *Music Walk* with David Tudor and Cornelius Cardew on three pianos, 14 October 1958. For the activities engaged in by Galerie 22 and the importance of Jean-Pierre Wilhelms for the Düsseldorf art scene at that time, see Susanne Rennert, 'Alles ist im Fluss. Rien n'est figé Jean-Pierre Wilhelm, die Galerie 22 und Düsseldorfs Aufbruch zu einer neuen Kunst', in: Renate Buschmann and Stephan von Wiese (eds.), *Fotos schreiben Kunstgeschichte*, Cologne 2007, pp. 19–27.

3 Friedrich Wolfram Heubach, 'interfunktionen, 1968–1974', in: Stephan von Wiese (ed.), *Brennpunkt Düsseldorf 1962–1987*, exhib. cat. Düsseldorf 1987, pp. 128–130; here: p. 128.

4 As curator of many years' standing at the Museum Kunstpalast and an expert on the Düsseldorf art scene, Stephan von Wiese far-sightedly realised how important these photographic documentaries were as historical evidence. In 2003 he initiated the Archiv künstlerischer Fotografie [Art Photography Archives], a foundation into which went art photographs and documentary photographs from the Rhenish art scene and depicting it. Also see Buschmann and Wiese (see n. 2).

5 Hannes Böhringer in conversation with the author on 21 March 2013.

6 For Beuys's conception of the work, see the informative essay by Benjamin H. D. Buchloh, 'Joseph Beuys. Die Götzendämmerung', in: Buschmann and Wiese (see n. 2), pp. 60–77.

7 Christopher Philipps, 'Arena. Das Chaos des Namenlosen', in: Lynn Cooke and Karen Kelly (eds.), *Joseph Beuys. Arena – wo wäre ich hingekommen, wenn ich intelligent gewesen wäre!*, Ostfildern 1994, pp. 52–62; here: p. 54.

8 Lynn Cooke, 'Arena und ihre Installierung. Eine Einführung', in: Cooke and Kelly (see n. 7), pp. 12–17; here: p. 12. Beuys made *Arena* for *Strategy. Get Arts*, a 1970 exhibition mounted at the College of the Arts in Edinburgh.

9 Pamela Kort, 'Joseph Beuys: Arena. Der Weg nach innen', in: Cooke and Kelly (see n. 7), pp. 18–33; here: p. 18.

10 The protests voiced by Jörg Immendorff and others against documenta were published in 1968 in the first of ten booklets edited by Heubach. They were current works, some of them produced specially for the booklet, and new artists were introduced, theories were discussed, and information given.

11 Invoking Archimedes saying 'Give me a lever long enough and a fulcrum on which to place it, and I shall move the world', Beuys washed his pupils' feet before having himself christened from a watering can. Photographs by Ute Klophaus, *interfunktionen* 7, 1971, cover as well as pp. 2–45.

12 See Philipps (see n. 7), pp. 52–62; here: p. 52.

13 Erinna König in conversation with the author on 18 February 2013.

14 Ole John reports that he had promised Beuys he would make a film about him but he was unable to scrape together enough money for the film material needed. Beuys himself, according to Ole John, gave him material support because he was interested in John's cinematic work. Conversation with Ole John on 8 March 2013.

15 See, for instance, the lecture given by the art historian and art cinematographer Carl Lamb at the Düsseldorf Art Academy in November 1964. Beginning in the mid-1970s John Anthony Thwaites held seminars on this subject at the Academy.

16 Peter Steinhart, 'Viel Ehrgeiz, wenig Geld. Die neue Filmabteilung der Kunstakademie und ihr Dozent Ole John', *Rheinische Post*, 17 November 1971.

17 The Düsseldorf Film Workshop grew out of the Düsseldorf Film Group in 1976 and was integrated in the newly founded City Film Institute in 1980.

18 Sebastian Feldmann, 'Studenten überrascht, Filmklasse wird aufgelöst', *Rheinische Post*, 8 July 1977.

19 See Johannes Stüttgen, *Der ganze Riemen. Der Auftritt von Joseph Beuys als Lehrer. Die Chronologie der Ereignisse an der Staatlichen Kunstakademie Düsseldorf 1966–1972*, Cologne 2008, p. 325.

20 The important events of that year are enumerated in an essay by Stephan von Wiese, 'Brennpunkt Düsseldorf. Eine Chronik', in: Buschmann and Wiese (see n. 2), pp. 10–18. This catalogue and its sequel volume, Stephan von Wiese (ed.), *Brennpunkt Düsseldorf 2. Die Siebziger Jahre. Entwürfe, Joseph Beuys zum 70. Geburtstag, 1970–1991*, exhib. cat. Düsseldorf 1991, give well-grounded insights into the time and provide an outstanding collection of material.

21 Katharina Sieverding, *Testcuts. Projected Data Images*, exhibition at the inter media art institute 2010; Renate Buschmann (ed.), *Katharina Sieverding. Testcuts. Projected Data Images*, exhib. cat. Düsseldorf, Cologne 2010. The previous year there had already been a smaller version at the Thomas Schulte Gallery in Berlin.

22 The aesthetic freedom to push the medium to the limits of the possible is premised on being technically independent of the market and the profit-orientated and temporally limited work of individual firms.

23 Armin Zweite, 'Vergegenwärtigung und Auflösung des Subjekts', in: *Katharina Sieverding 1967–1997*, exhib. cat. Düsseldorf/Amsterdam, Cologne 1997, pp. 240–252; here: p. 245.

24 See Umberto Eco, *Opera aperta* [The Open Work], Milan 1962; Roland Barthes, 'La Mort de l'auteur' [The Death of the Author], 1968; Michel Foucault, 'Qu'est-ce qu'un auteur?' [What Is an Author?], *Bulletin de la société française de philosophie*, 22 February 1969, pp. 75–104.

25 In the mid-1960s Richter began to keep all photographic models and material he used. 'In 1969 he decided to collect in tableaux all photos which were important for his painting or might possibly become important', quoted in Armin Zweite,

'Gerhard Richters "Atlas der Fotos, Collagen und Skizzen"', in: Fred Jahn (ed.), *Gerhard Richter. Atlas*, exhib. cat. Munich/Cologne, Munich 1989, pp. 7–20; here: p. 10.

26 König (see n. 13).

27 'If a photographer is an artist, a baker is an artist, too': Erinna König recalls a statement made by the painter Norbert Tadeusz. König's uncle, Alfred Paulus, was an industrial photographer. Given her first camera at the age of twelve, she was chiefly interested in transfixing permanence rather than capturing the moment.

28 To make the film (running time: 45 minutes), each photo had to be exposed individually on camera film; Ole John helped her by going with her to the company archives in Bremen for the photos that Erinna König had photographed for this film.

29 Erinna König in conversation with the author on 17 April 2013.

30 See Hans Irrek, 'Die Besichtigung einer Passion', in: *Die Erfindung der Wirklichkeit. Photographie an der Kunstakademie Düsseldorf von 1970 bis heute*, exhib. cat. Düsseldorf 2011, pp. 14–31; here: p. 19.

31 John Tagg, *The Burden of Representation. Essays on Photographies and Histories*, Amherst 1988, p. 118.

32 Susanne Holschbach, 'Einleitung' [Introduction], in: Herta Wolf (ed.), *Diskurse der Fotografie, Fotokritik am Ende des fotografischen Zeitalters*, Frankfurt am Main 2003, pp. 7–23; here: p. 7.

33 'There was a basic photography course at the Werkkunstschule in Darmstadt. Kilian Breier had set up a photo lab there while he was a lecturer. That was not a course of study in itself but we learned how to deal with the medium.' Imi Knoebel in conversation with the author on 5 March 2013.

34 See the fold-out in *interfunktionen* 10, 1973.

35 The duo also showed a film, *Imi und Imi*, in 1969 at the Intermedia organised by Klaus Staeck in Heidelberg. It consisted of a live performance in which the two artists did not move more than three of four metres apart from each other for more than a week. The Action was documented by Katharina Sieverding.

36 See Susanne Neubauer, 'Imi Knoebel', in: *Projektion. Chan, Export, Fischli/Weiss, Gander, Gillick, Graham, Knoebel, Parker, Streuli*, exhib. cat. Lucerne, Linz/Frankfurt am Main 2006, pp. 94–95; here: p. 94.

37 See Pidder Auberger, *Fotografien und Holzschnitte*, exhib. cat. Essen, Göttingen 2011.

38 Siegfried Gohr mentions Polke's grandfather and above all his aunt, Else Raschdorf, who instructed him in photography. See Siegfried Gohr, 'Polke. Der Photograph im Als-ob', in: *Sigmar Polke. Photoarbeiten*, Lempertz catalogue, Cologne 2011, n.p.

39 Jochen Poetter, 'Die Augen der Hölle im Himmel, Gedanken zu Sigmar Polkes photographischen Serien', in: *Sigmar Polke. Photographische Arbeiten aus der Sammlung Garnatz*, exhib. cat. Cologne/Karlsruhe, Munich 2008, pp. 13–18; here: p. 13.

40 Gohr (see n. 38), n.p.

41 Maren Klinge, 'Von Gurken und Geistern, Alltagszauber und Bildkritik in der Photographie Sigmar Polkes', in: *Sigmar Polke, Photoarbeiten*, Lempertz catalogue, Cologne 2011, n.p.

42 Harald Szeemann, in: *Sigmar Polke, Werke 1973 bis 1983*, exhib. cat. Zurich 1984, p. 10.

43 Polke began making raster pictures *c.*1963.

44 *Sigmar Polke. Bilder Tücher Objekte*, exhib. cat. Tübingen and elsewhere, Eindhoven 1976, p. 142.

45 Klaus Honnef, 'Malerei als Abenteuer oder Kunst und Leben. Bemerkungen zum künstlerischen Werk von Sigmar Polke im Polke-Jahr', *Kunstforum International*, Vol. 71/72, 1984, pp. 133–151; quoted in: Klaus Honnef, *Nichts als Kunst ..., Schriften zur Kunst und Fotografie*, Cologne 1999, pp. 315–336.

46 See Jörg Häntzschel, 'Eine alte Kartoffel für Matthew Barney, bitte aus Idaho'. Christian Scheidemann specialises in new art. He studies its peculiar, friable materials between home hardware DIY paint, chewing gum, and dung – and tries to prevent its imminent decay. A visit to his New York studio. In *Süddeutsche Zeitung*, 13/14 April 2013, p. 16; Gerhard Richter, Sigmar Polke in a text collage in the Galerie h catalogue, Hannover 1966.

47 DADA, *Dokumente einer Bewegung, Kunstverein für die Rheinlande und Westfalen*, Düsseldorf 1958.

48 A single-day exhibition in honour of Alfred Schmela in December 1966 shows how Richter also investigates technology; there he made Volker Bradke, a student, the subject of the exhibition: in person, in painting, in photos, and in 16 mm film.

49 Laszlo Glozer, 'Die Vor-Bilder der Bilder, Gerhard Richter breitet sein Arbeitsmaterial aus', *Süddeutsche Zeitung*, 26 April 1974.

50 Martin Hentschel, 'Solve et Coagula. Zum Werk Sigmar Polkes', in: *Sigmar Polke. Die drei Lügen der Malerei*, exhib. cat. Bonn, Ostfildern 1997, p. 43.

51 See Peter Sager, 'Ein Pilatus der neuen Malerei?' A conversation with the Venice Biennale exhibitor Gerhard Richter in Düsseldorf. In *Frankfurter Allgemeine Zeitung*, 6 June 1972.

52 See Walter Grasskamp, '"Give up Painting" or the Politics of Art: A West German Abstract', in: John Howell (ed.), *Breakthroughs. Avant-Garde Artists in Europe and America, 1950–1990*, exhib. cat. Ohio, New York 1991, p. 137.

53 See URL: http://www.luhringaugustine.com/artists/reinhard-mucha (last retrieved 14 September 2015).

54 Friedrich Wolfram Heubach, 'Kultur und Natur, oder die Natur ist ziemlich komisch geworden', *interfunktionen* 9, 1972, pp. 53–56, pp. 54f.

55 'Individual mythologies' is the term used by Harald Szeemann for the movement that was showing up then within contemporary art. See documenta 5, Kassel, 1972; Harald Szeemann, *Individuelle Mythologien*, Berlin 1985.

56 Günter Metken introduced the term *Spurensicherung* [securing evidence] in 1974 for that art, which in part draws on scientific methodology.

57 See Thomas Struth in 'Ich glaube ans Warten. Brigitte Kölle im Gespräch mit Thomas Struth', in: Brigitte Kölle (ed.), *Es geht voran. Kunst der 80er. Eine Düsseldorfer Perspektive*, exhib. cat. Düsseldorf, Munich 2010, pp. 172–178; here: p. 174.

58 See Hans-Werner Schmidt, 'Klaus Rinke. Der Versuch, meine Arbeit zu erklären. Ein Versuch, seine Arbeit zu erklären', in: *Klaus Rinke. Retro Aktiv, 1954–1991*, exhib. cat. Düsseldorf 1992, pp. 9–39; here: p. 9.

59 Taken from Klaus Rinke's online autobiography in May 2013 (http://www.klaus-rinke.com/autobiography.htm). The data is unfortunately no longer accessible.

60 See Schmidt (see n. 58), p. 26.

61 See Ursula Wevers, 'Liebe, Arbeit, Fernsehgalerie', in: *Ready to Shoot. Fernsehgalerie Gerry Schum, videogalerie schum*, exhib. cat. Düsseldorf, Cologne 2003, pp. 22–46; here: p. 30.

62 Gerry Schum, 'Zur II. Fernsehausstellung der Video Galerie Gerry Schum/Fernsehgalerie', in: *Ready to Shoot* (see n. 61), p. 169.

63 During the vernissage there was a live broadcast of the artist and the gallerist from the Konrad Fischer Gallery on the Video Gallery so that visitors and performers could be present simultaneously without being in the same place.

64 As the newest technical medium, video would undergo manifold system changes that caused the recording formats to be constantly changed, thus making it difficult to work sequentially.

65 Jan Dibbets in conversation with the author on 28 February 2013.

66 See *Ready to Shoot* (see n. 61), p. 98. *TV as a Fireplace*, 1969, was subsequently made, also for television. With Gerry Schum, Dibbets made *Feuer* [Fire] in 1968/69, *Painting 1+2* in 1970, and *4 Diagonals* in 1971.

67 Susan Sontag, *Über Fotografie*, Frankfurt am Main 1980 [original: *On Photography*, 1977], p. 10.

68 Colour photographs in large formats (220 × 220 cm) were being made as early as 1976.

69 See Susanne Lange, *Was wir tun, ist letztlich Geschichten erzählen ... Bernd und Hilla Becher. Eine Einführung in Leben und Werk*, Munich 2005, pp. 11–15.

70 See Carl Andre, 'A Note on Bernd and Hilla Becher', *Artforum*, December 1972, p. 59.

71 See Bernd Becher in Michael Köhler, 'Interview mit Bernd und Hilla Becher', in: Lothar Romain and Detlef Bluemler (eds.), *Künstler, Kritisches Lexikon der Gegenwartskunst*, 7th edn, Munich 1989, pp. 14f.; here: p. 15.

72 For legal reasons only one person may be entrusted with the task. Nonetheless the students definitely benefited from both.

73 Mucha in a letter to the author dated 4 February 2013.

74 Hilla Becher in Köhler (see n. 71), p. 15.

75 Thomas Ruff in Willi Adam, '"Der Betrachter entscheidet." Im Gespräch: Thomas Ruff', *Kultur Joker*, Issue 4, No. 9/10, 4–17 March 1994, p. 1, p. 46; here: p. 46.

76 Thomas Ruff talking to the author on 6 December 2006.

77 Anna and Bernhard Johannes Blume, 'Statement zu der Sequenz *Küchenkoller*. Ein Interpretationsvorschlag unter vielen', in: Anna and Bernhard Johannes Blume, *Transsubstanz und Küchenkoller. Großphoto-Serien 1985–1994*, Hannover 1996, p. 38.

78 He showed a series of forty-nine streets at the *Rundgang* in the Richter class before transferring to Becher. See Kölle (see n. 57), pp. 173f.

79 See the overview by Werner Lippert and Christoph Schaden, in Werner Lippert and Christoph Schaden (eds.), *Der Rote Bulli. Stephen Shore und die Düsseldorfer Fotografie*, exhib. cat. Düsseldorf 2010, pp. 330–333. Although Bernd Becher officially retired in 1996, he continued to teach his classes until 1998 on the basis of short-term contracts.

80 In 1988 *Klasse Bernd Becher* [The Bernd Becher Class], Johnen and Schöttle Gallery, Cologne; 1991 *Aus der Distanz* [From a Distance], Kunstsammlung Nordrhein-Westfalen, Düsseldorf; and 1992 *Distanz und Nähe* [Far and Near], Institut für Auslandsbeziehungen, Stuttgart.

81 See Kölle (see n. 57), p. 174.

82 Martina Dobbe, *Fotografie als theoretisches Objekt. Bildwissenschaft, Medienästhetik, Kunstgeschichte*, Munich 2007, p. 136.

83 The Grieger Photo Lab made Thomas Ruff aware of the process.

84 See Paul Virilio, *Die Eroberung des Körpers. Vom Übermenschen zum überreizten Menschen*, Munich/Vienna 1994.

85 See Jeff Wall, 'Zeichen der Indifferenz. Aspekte der Photographie in der, oder als, Konzeptkunst', in: Gregor Stemmrich (ed.), *Jeff Wall. Szenarien im Bildraum der Wirklichkeit. Essays und Interviews*, Amsterdam/Dresden 1997, pp. 375–434; here: pp. 432–434.

86 In the winter term of 2000/01 Ruff took over a lectureship that became a professorship. He stopped teaching before the summer term of 2006.

87 Andreas Kreul, 'Arbeiten am Bild', in: Andreas Kreul (ed.), *Jörg Sasse, Arbeiten am Bild*, Munich 2001, pp. 13–19; here: p. 13

88 See Axel Hütte, *Mossman Gorge, Queensland*, 1999, from the *Kontinente* [Continents] series, and Thomas Struth, *Paradise 9*, 1999, from the *Paradise* series.

89 See Maren Polte, *Klasse Bilder*, Berlin 2012, pp. 156–171.

90 Volker Kahmen, *Fotografie als Kunst*, Tübingen 1973, pp. 10f.

91 Christoph Schreier, 'Befragung der Mitte. Menschen, Tiere und Mutanten in Rosemarie Trockels Papierarbeiten', in: *Rosemarie Trockel. Zeichnungen, Collagen und Buchentwürfe*, exhib. cat. Basel/Edinburgh/Bonn, Ostfildern 2010, pp. 39–45; here: p. 39.

92 Schreier (se n. 91), p. 40.

93 Think of the Helsinki School of Photography and also the New Leipzig School.

94 See http://www.ruffklasse.de (last retrieved 14 September 2015).

95 Benjamin Katz and Albrecht Fuchs had short-term contracts to bridge the gap until the vacancy could be filled recently.

96 Karel Schampers, 'Christopher Williams. Observing the World', in: *Christopher Williams. For Example: Die Welt ist schön (Final Draft)*, exhib. cat. Rotterdam/Basel, Basel 1997, pp. 6–9; here: p. 7.

97 The title was taken from a work by the French philosopher Raymond Aron.

98 *For Example: Die Welt ist schön* was in twenty-four different versions between 1993 until 2001.

DEVELOPMENT OF THE STAGE DESIGN CLASS SINCE 1945*

Michael Matzigkeit

A LOVE OF THE TOTAL WORK OF ART – WALTER VON WECUS (1893–1977)

By the end of the war in 1945, the first professor to hold the chair of stage design, Walter von Wecus, could look back on two turbulent decades in his subject (Fig. 1). On 1 May 1925 Professor Walter Kaesbach, then director of the Düsseldorf State Art Academy, had charged von Wecus with building up and heading the class, thus ensuring a first in German-speaking countries.[1]

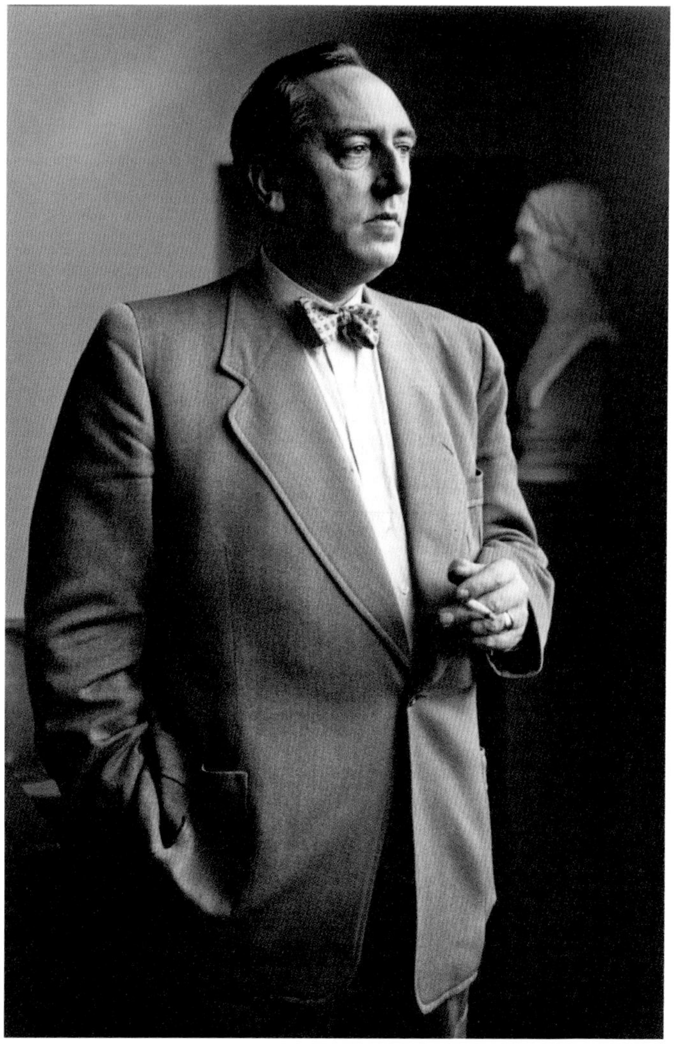

Fig. 1: Walter von Wecus, n.d.

The intervening years saw a brief dynamic phase of new departures during the Weimar Republic, in which the fundamentals of modern stage design could prevail on all counts by drawing on the achievements of the scenographic avant-garde since the turn of the century. With his cubic constructions and stage technology solutions, von Wecus was at times in the vanguard of that movement.

Between 1933 and 1945 there followed, for the stage design class, too, a phase of aesthetic restoration, accompanied by war and far-reaching destruction that in many respects would have a lasting effect on the possibilities – and limitation – for the development of the class. From 1942 until the end of the war, the class consisted of six full-time students;[2] the two men in the class had been exempted from military service for health reasons. In addition, there were some students, who had been given 'study leave'. 'One of those was Ulrich Tramp. [...] Also Kurt Staubitz and Alfons Hartstein, both of whom were able to continue their studies after the war.'[3] Measures were taken to protect the rooms in which the class worked from the ongoing effects of the war. Renate Stendar-Feuerbaum (*1920) had happened to be assigned to the Academy as a fire warden when it sustained severe damage during the bombardment of Düsseldorf in the spring of 1944. She writes, 'Liselotte Bauer and I were standing the obligatory "nightwatch" there, which everyone was required to do in turn, and that night we even managed to achieve something.'[4]

During the night of the fire of 21 March 1945, the Academy had to shut down its teaching facilities. All ceilings had collapsed in the east wing whereas the fire that broke out in the west wing could be kept under control. Nonetheless, the roof was completely destroyed and the building was in ruins, even after the debris and rubble had been removed. 'In September the first students returned and made themselves available for clean-up operations [...]. It was possible by the 1945/46 winter term to renovate enough rooms for students to begin to make themselves ready for working in them.'[5]

Von Wecus, who had refused to the end to join the NSDAP, was asked to become director of the Art Academy because he was politically untainted.[6] 'He refused the offer, however, because he saw himself as an "artist" and did not want to waste time on administrative work.'[7]

Frank-Ulrich Schmidt (*1927) was a pupil of von Wecus's during the period immediately after the war. He is one of the few eyewitnesses still alive. His career is symptomatic of part of that 'lost generation'. Schmidt came to Witten in 1945 as a refugee from East Prussia. During the 1947/48 theatre season, he managed to find work as an intern at a small theatre. There it was not long before he was offered the opportunity of designing some stage sets himself. At first glance, a great opportunity. Schmidt, however, wanted to have a thorough grounding in the profession. He so ardently desired to practise that he accepted the offer made by Peter Emil Noelle, head of the Märkisches Museum in Witten, to arrange contact with Walter von Wecus in Düsseldorf.

The ambitious requirements profile that young aspiring artists had to fulfil was once described as follows by von Wecus:

'To become an art adviser [head stage designer] at a theatre, one needs to prove one's aptitude by submitting creatively free drawings, paintings, and designs for scenery, all in all, therefore, that of a versatile and imaginative artist, a "dedicated artist". That is one crucial requirement for admission to the Stage Art Department; the other condition is being a person who is willing to give his all to the task and is capable of the utmost enthusiasm for his profession – his vocation for the world of the living theatre. The young stage designer grows up under strict discipline, but entirely in his own individual way, in diligent, hard work – knowing that he has been chosen from among many, to find his own personal form of expression under circumspect guidance.'[8]

The samples of his work that Frank-Ulrich Schmidt submitted were convincing. He sums up his recollection of von Wecus as 'an outstanding educator, who transmitted his manifold possibilities for artistic expression to his pupils' (Fig. 2).[9] A fellow student, Ottowerner Meyer (*1927), who is still an active scenographer and costume designer, is more expansive:

'As an experienced and convinced educator, von Wecus adjusted his approach individually to the personality and qualities of each of his pupils. Von Wecus integrated each pupil into what he was teaching at a given time according to that pupil's talent and his degree of maturity. So there was no distinction made between beginners and advanced pupils in the course of studies. As far as internships before or after studying in the stage design class were concerned, von Wecus did not have a blanket opinion: here, too, what mattered was a student's individual personality.'[10]

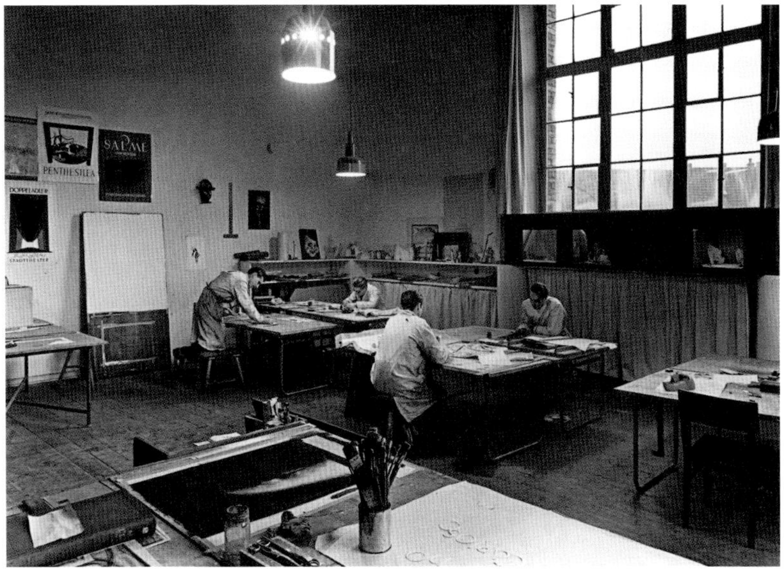

Fig. 2: The stage design class, 1953

Even though every student, male or female, was supposed to find his or her own way to results, von Wecus regarded one principle as unalterable: 'People are on the stage!'[11] Ottowerner Meyer explains: 'No piece of stage equipment was ever allowed [in Walter von Wecus's class] to be designed without reference to the persons acting with it. [...] So designs or models already had to reflect the dramaturgy of the play concerned; the scenic situation, hence what the director would be thinking, had to be readable from them. That is why the characters acting in a particular situation were often also part of the composition and so was the lighting.'[12]

Nevertheless, it was characteristic of von Wecus's thrust as a teacher that he also permitted his pupils to submit designs that were unlikely to be realised, given the technical and financial possibilities available to the average theatre during the post-war era. Even works that were grounded in the illustrative rather than the practical were not rejected out of hand.[13] Meyer goes on to add: 'Von Wecus dealt with each pupil on an individual basis – according to his talent and his disposition – and took what a pupil offered him as a basis for working, which was also discussed. The chief work the course of study entailed for the student consisted in practical work (design, model) and not so much in theory.'[14]

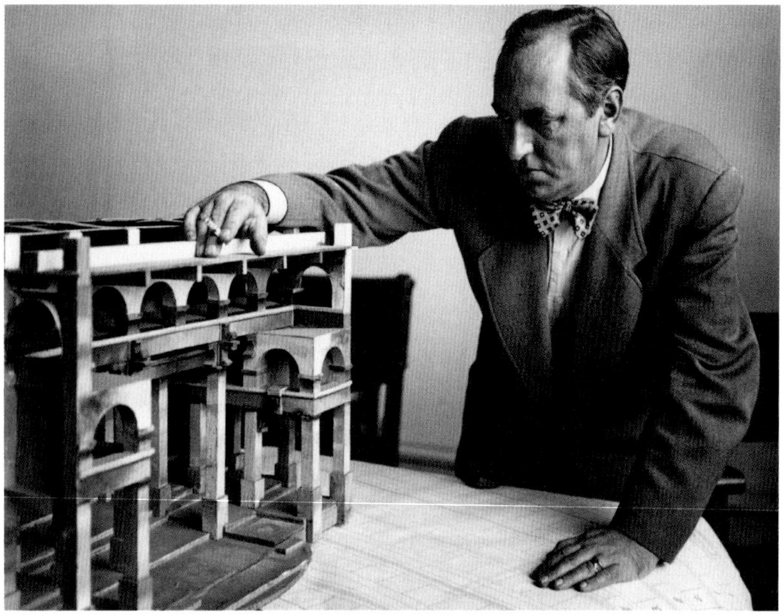

Fig. 3: Walter von Wecus with a stage model, n.d.

In fact, from its inception, the stagecraft class was accompanied by lessons in dramaturgy as part of the conception of an inclusive scenographic education.[15] What was taught was that the event on a stage was ideally a total work of art, in which gestures and facial expressions, costume and masks, the spatial design and lighting, language and music fused into a meaningful unity. To ensure that this happened, the scenographer had to create appropriate sensorily experienceable spatial possibilities as agreed upon with the director (Fig. 3).

Moreover, the students – apart from qualifying through practice for the manifold challenges of what would later be their profession – also had to be sensitised to aesthetic change brought about over the course of history in the medium of theatre and their own, newly acquired freedom in design since National Socialism had been overcome. Up to then, the scenographer had been a theatre painter, whose career possibilities had been in the main restricted to those open to a craftsman.

Strong ideological influence was exerted on the stage design course between 1933 and *c.*1934/35, when the subject-related course content was also supplemented by race study (projected on to the duration of two terms of at first four, then from about 1935/36 a standard period of study comprising six terms), taught by Dr Alexander Schneider, the head dramaturgist at the Düsseldorf Municipal Theatres, who staunchly toed the party line. This ideological indoctrination was evidently regarded as too impracticable to be continued beyond the early years after the 'seizure of power'.[16]

After 1945 the teaching in literature and dramaturgy accompanying the practical part of the course remained an integral constituent of the educational canon of the stagecraft class; it was, however, freed from obvious, regime-supported ideological indoctrination, also because the British occupying power took their re-education in democracy policy seriously. Gerda Bohrer-Borges (*1927), also a Wecus pupil in the early post-war years, who has given an unbiased account of what she experienced and went through at the Art Academy in a memoir of her own,[17] writes: 'Every Tuesday our dramaturge, Herr Dünwald, travels to us from Bonn. Rather short, he pushes a gigantic coat in front of him. I hear softly behind me: "Ship of the Desert". You have to squeeze his hand firmly when greeting him. The lecture is boring. This is the time to be reading the textbook. Our professor sticks to him through thick and thin.'[18]

What might at first glance seem like a form of shirking is deceptive. Bohrer-Borges's memoirs close with a recital of success, which would not have been possible without personal commitment on her part and artistic aptitude: 'I have sent stage designs and figurines to the Munich Kammerspiele, to Wolfgang Znamenacek,[19] who has just [1948] done such good pictures for [Helmut Käutner's controversial film] *Der Apfel ist ab* [The Apple has Fallen]. Horst Schweikart is the chief administrator there.[20] [...] Wolfgang Znamenacek's letter is lying on the table: I can work at the Munich Kammerspiele.'[21]

What remained so remarkable, as the little band of students saw it, was the close collaboration among them, in which von Wecus as an integrative 'father figure' had a considerable share. He let them – according to their individual abilities – take part in his building projects and arranged internships or assistant positions for former pupils of his who had by then made names for themselves,[22] or provided possibilities for enjoyable private parties:

'Professor von Wecus has invited us to his home for his birthday. All the houses in Sternstraße are almost without damage. Everyone is bringing a drawing as a present. From me he's getting a witch from *Faust 2*. We sit at little tables. His beautiful wife in purplish red silk brings in soup along with bright flowers. His garden is surrounded by a high wall. Thus he lives snugly without the bustle of the city next door. And it's also cosy to be just among ourselves (although we see each other constantly at the Academy anyway).'[23]

Von Wecus would have liked to have continued to function as usual at the Art Academy even after reaching retirement age. Civil Service law did not permit him to do so. Nor could the pupils of his whom he had asked to submit a petition to the Ministry to make an exception in his case do anything about it.

'SO THE GATES OF THE IMAGINATION REMAIN OPEN' – TEO OTTO (1904–1968)

By the time Teo Otto was invited on 1 April 1959 to teach at the renowned Düsseldorf Art Academy, he had long since attained the zenith of his career in art as a stage designer – even under the privations he had endured as an exile in Switzerland until 1945 (Fig. 4). His stage sets for the world premiere of *Mutter Courage* [Mother Courage] (19 April 1941) at the Zurich Schauspielhaus [Theatre] and for Gustaf Gründgens's *Faust I* (21 April 1957) at the Deutsches Schauspielhaus in Hamburg were famous worldwide. As the 'man in the background' (Dürrenmatt), however, he did not figure so prominently in the public awareness. Yet consensus reigned among experts: along with Caspar Neher (1897–1962) he was the most important German stage architect of his day.

Understandably, the then director of the Düsseldorf Art Academy, Professor Dr-Ing. Hans Schwippert, who was an architect, did his best to have Teo Otto appointed when the question of a successor to Walter von Wecus (1893–1977) arose, when von Wecus retired after heading for thirty-three years the first class for stagecraft at a German institution of higher learning.[24] Personal sympathies are also sure to have played a role in the appointment of Teo Otto: the stage designer and Schwippert were said to have been friends for years, and occasionally there was talk of a link going back to their school days.[25]

In a three-page paper, 'Betr.: Berufung für die Bühnenklasse. Bemerkungen zu pädagogischen, künstlerischen und organisatorischen Fragen' [Re: Appointment to the Stage Class. Observations on Educational, Artistic, and Organisational Issues],[26] Schwippert laid out the general framework for meaningful collaboration at the Academy. Showing a good grasp of the possibilities of, as well as the limits to, such work, Schwippert wrote very knowledgeably, evidently with only Otto, the candidate of his choice, in mind: 'Masters of this subject do real work. Those who are of the rank that is worthy of our consideration are not only without exception (chiefly) committed to a single theatre but are also to a considerable extent "invited" to work for other theatres. This is true of the best workers in this field at an international level.'[27]

In fact, Schwippert's stance was aimed at the exclusion of von Wecus, the old holder of the chair, who had reached the retirement age of sixty-five. Pointedly, Schwippert worked out the basic difference between stage design and other arts, revealing that his idea of art and its possibilities was definitely still static and shaped by tradition: 'In painting, sculpture, architecture, the focus of work is on the master studio. In stage design, on the other hand, sketches, design, construction documentation represent only a relatively small segment of the work. Here the greatest importance is accorded to fitting in with the dramatic, poetic, musical conception, the constant personal discussion with the interpreting director, the growth of a production in the course of rehearsals, the continual discussion with the workshops for stage and costume.'[28]

Showing astonishing sympathy with the autonomy of stage work, Otto conceded organisational and creative scope, which he, busy and hard-working as he was, would later take full advantage of while teaching at the art academy and could only manage with the hands-on support of his most talented pupils, who were included in his commitments as assistants.

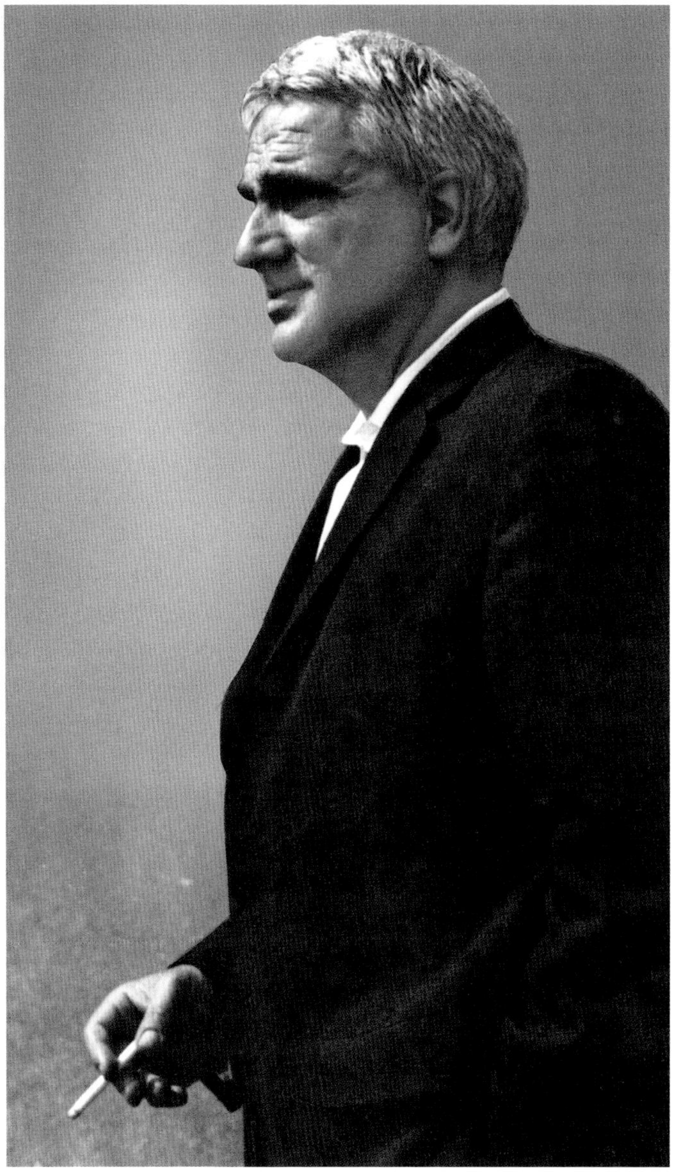

Fig. 4: Teo Otto, n.d.

In his enthusiastic plea for the primacy of extramural praxis of those who taught, which became for him the source of and crucial precondition for his own personal creative activity, Schwippert wrote:

'That means for stage designers of high standing travelling, constant movement, deadlines, and difficult timetables. The laws governing the living creative work in this discipline make it imprudent to commit a master of this subject to regular educational work, which is done in other disciplines without this difficulty, unless the master teacher here neglects his personal work. That would, however, as things stand today, lead to progressive diminution of his own work, ultimately alienation from praxis, deterioration of lively teaching, and with it, a decline of the educational influence to the point of insignificance. [... T]he appointee [must] continue to be granted far-reaching freedoms in the use of his time to maintain his reputation and his artistic powers through constant lively application to his tasks. Accordingly, he will be able to do more than those members of his profession who are more intellectually limited in the more liberated manner of his educational engagement, if he is a distinguished artist and educator.'[29]

In addition, the specific educational needs of teachers and pupils in the stage design sector and the organisatorial requirements at the Academy were clearly outlined. An interdisciplinary curriculum[30] that incorporated painting, fine art graphics, applied graphics, sculpture, and architecture as well as art history, philosophy, the history of literature, and dramaturgy was a quintessential element of this approach to education. However, it also represented both an obligation and a challenge to the rest of the Academy staff.

Finally, the professor to be appointed was to be supported by an 'artistic foreman-like, full-time assistant'[31] to ensure classes were efficiently conducted. Conceivably, this ambitious approach could not always be realised to its fullest extent in view of the lack of all the optimising factors needed.

The above text written by Schwippert was undoubtedly composed with Teo Otto's assent to the content and perhaps even in direct collaboration with him. The intimate knowledge it reveals of the conditions under which a stage designer works would suggest either alternative. As a teacher on a limited contract at the Werkakademie in Kassel,[32] Otto would have been able to contribute from his own experience essential perspectives on and urgently needed aspects of a job description. Even the time frame – June 1958 – in which Schwippert's letter to the Ministry was written speaks for direct contact with the candidate at an early date.

Schwippert had left no stone unturned up to then to create the best possible conditions for ensuring the success of his personnel proposal. Early in May 1958 numerous distinguished representatives of the theatre, both theatre directors and critics, were written to and asked for their opinion confidentially.

Instructive on the tenor of professorial opinions at the Art Academy is the draft of Schwippert's letter to the Minister of Culture of the State of Rhineland-Westphalia of 2 August 1958. Within the space of barely two months the decision-making process had progressed to the point at which he could write:

'The conference of professors has unanimously decided with me on the basis of these considerations [i.e., the Schwippert memorandum entitled "Appointment to the Stage Class. Observations on Educational, Artistic, and Organisational Issues", June 1958] to suggest in the interim sole nomination: the stage designer Teo Otto, Zurich [...]. The professors on the staff have together with me at once according to custom carefully considered further, other nominations. In this connection, the names of Professor [Helmut] Jürgens, Munich, and Gert Richter, Stuttgart, were discussed in particular. The staff are, however, in complete agreement with me on the interim sole petition to appoint Teo Otto.'[33]

In several preliminary conversations Schwippert had worked out with Teo Otto the conditions under which Otto would be willing to limit his numerous commitments in stage design – even to his own disadvantage. Schwippert set out those demands to the Ministry of Culture in the same memorandum of 2 August 1958:

1. The head of the stage design class will be tasked *ex ante* with administering the available H3 post. Otto would like to view the task at first as an experiment, in building on his previous teaching activities of the same kind, which he has been practising for some years now with great success as a lecturer at the Kassel Art Academy.

He would like to view final-phase remuneration for the post available, not as a fee, but rather as compensation, which will help to offset the losses and expenses he will have incurred in taking on this work.

2. The appointment entails heading the class for stage design, reorganising the course of study with increased inclusion of synchronously scheduled studies for pupils in the fine arts disciplines of the institution, the artistic supervision of studies in correction and seminar under the concomitant employment of a full-time artistic assistant to ensure the continuity and order of the studies, in particular also to head practical classes in model building and technical education.

   Otto would be willing to devote 3–4 entire workdays on a regular monthly basis to this work, by comparison, therefore, giving lectures, a seminar, and classes for 8 hours a week. He adds that he regards it as of paramount importance and essential to convey the practical approach to students while they are still studying and to supervise this personally as far as possible outside the institutional framework.

3. The right to use the title of professor is to be linked with the appointment.[34]

Although Schwippert had requested that the matter be dealt with quickly by 1 November 1958, the written reply from the Ministry of Culture was delayed: in it, it is mandated that Teo Otto should at first be appointed to the post of head of the stage design class for the duration of one year only. Conjectures as to the reasons for the delaying tactics of the cultural bureaucracy have already been mooted. It is safe to assume that the conservative state administration in the post-war years, freighted with undetected yet possibly tainted personnel from the era of the NS regime, was in all probability playing out their reservations about the left-wing emigrant Otto via the procedural path.

These difficulties seemed to scarcely touch Otto at all. In any case, he saw himself caught up in a fraught situation, which resulted from the necessities imposed by his freelance everyday job and a self-appointed educationalist approach to a comprehensive, praxis-orientated academic course of training. Hence he viewed his work at the Düsseldorf Art Academy at first as nothing more than a trial phase. Brimming with self-confidence, he placed his work at the Academy's disposal. He wanted to be judged only on his achievements: 'A limited trial phase is supposed to show whether I, with all my extensive praxis in this discipline, can achieve substantial successes in teaching. If the minister, the Academy, and I can ascertain that this has been the case, a permanent appointment with all inherent rights is to follow on the trial phase.'[35]

After Otto's one-year probationary period as a 'non-tenured teacher of stage design' had expired, Schwippert did everything he could to ensure that Otto could stay on at the Academy. However, it was not until 27 July 1961 that the obstacles had been sufficiently removed for Teo Otto to be 'appointed' by the Minister for Culture of the State of North Rhine-Westphalia 'professor at an art institute as a civil servant on probation'.[36] On 31 January 1962 Otto was 'invested with the powers and privileges of a higher civil servant for life'.[37]

Sometime later Teo Otto had an opportunity to reciprocate Schwippert's commitment to him by demonstrating loyalty to Schwippert in return. On 5 September 1963 the head of the Bavarian State Opera in Munich sent the following telegram to Otto: 'Query as to whether in principle interest exists in position of chief stage designer Munich State Opera combined with chair at Academy of Fine Arts STOP Preliminaries discussed with President Henselmann STOP Request expression of interest as promptly as possible Greetings = Rudolf Hartmann+'[38]

Otto answered Professor Rudolf Hartmann promptly: 'Please understand me if I refuse your honourable offer, feel beholden and committed both as an artist and a man to the Düsseldorf Art Academy with its director, Prof. Schwippert.'[39]

Nothing would change in Otto's stance on this for the rest of his life; he died unexpectedly before his time on 9 June 1968. In nine years of working at the Academy, he was able, with the support of his assistants Erwin W. Zimmer (1959–1964), Thomas Richter-Forgách (1964–1966), Heinz Balthes (1966/67), and Wolf-Jürgen Seeßelberg (1967/68) to put over sixty pupils through a thorough, multifaceted, and praxis-orientated course of training. Due to his exceptional abilities as an artist and his great humanity, he succeeded in developing

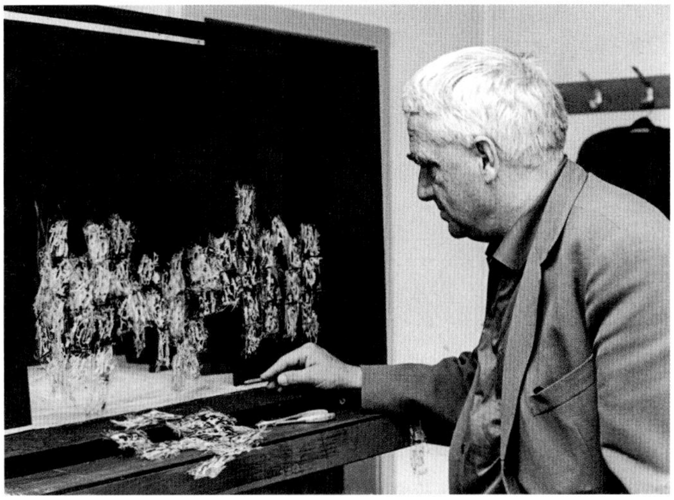

Fig. 5: Teo Otto with model, n.d.

his class into one of the Academy's most creative centres, which lent it an aura and made it attractive far beyond Düsseldorf. At that time, only the class taught by Joseph Beuys could make a similar claim.

A HANDS-ON STAGE PRACTITIONER AS TEACHER

The potential Teo Otto brought to Düsseldorf was without precedent. Otto has already been described as one of the most sought-after and prolific stage designers of his day. For the period up to Otto's death in 1968, Michael Schoemann has verified a total of over 800 production designs.[40] This achievement is all the more remarkable for the challenge represented by each production in relation to the quality of the creative solutions presented. It is not possible to detect a focus on any particular genres: straight theatre is as much in evidence as musical theatre. Otto only rarely permitted himself to copy what had already proved its worth. To the contrary, he constantly tried to find scenic solutions that held up a mirror to play plots that were critical of contemporary issues, to lend those productions his inimitable signature – as agreed on with the directors he worked with, most of whom were kindred spirits (Fig. 5).

He had, however, for quite some time been active in the practical sense in the tertiary education sector, so he could draw on a rich backlog of experience in that field: from 1953 to 1959 he had taught on a short-term contract at the Design Institute of the State Werkakademie Kassel for a friend of long years' standing, Arnold Bode.[41]

What is so astonishing, when one considers how caught up he was in his profession, is that he still continued to freelance as an artist and was represented by international exhibitions. A friend of such giants of German and Swiss-German literature as Bertolt Brecht, Friedrich Dürrenmatt, and Max Frisch, Otto proved that he possessed literary creative powers of his own with lectures and publications in which he discussed theatre-related subjects, particularly the functions and possibilities of stage design. His prose reflects his professional reality, which at the same time reveals his humanist and thoroughly politicised view of the world and its problematic areas.[42]

With his practical bias towards making training in stage design as 'varied and rich' as possible, he called for a consistently interdisciplinary opening towards painting, the graphic arts, sculpture, and architecture, and this made him seem revolutionary compared to his predecessor. Unimpressed by the lack of understanding and the petty jealousies shown by his colleagues, Otto approached that goal in his own way: with time he succeeded in integrating the right students from a wide range of disciplines in his class, thus creating additional sources of artistic stimulation.

By late 1959, he reflected on the brief phase of his work he had just gone through and summed it up positively:

'I believe, for my part, I can say that the approach in the stage design class has been successful, whereby it must be borne in mind that this class began from scratch, as it were, in spring 1959. The attempt to include individual students as assistants in practice has turned out to be very useful and undoubtedly fosters each student's capabilities. I would be delighted to keep on with the work in order to be able to make it productive for the future.'[43]

He was substantially supported by his 'artistic-foreman-like, full-time assistants', without whom Otto would undoubtedly have been unable to pursue two professions simultaneously with such intensity. Erwin W. Zimmer (1931–1998) was by his side as his first assistant, teaching on a limited contract, from April 1959 until April 1964. Zimmer, a pupil of Otto's since his Kassel days,[44] had already been informed by his teacher in summer 1958 of the possibility of being his assistant in the Stage Design Department at the Düsseldorf Art Academy and had evidently shown strong interest in the idea even then.

Fortunately, the letters written by Teo Otto to Erwin W. Zimmer have survived. They provide revealing glimpses of the everyday teaching situation at the Düsseldorf Art Academy. Precise work instructions alternate with appraisals of the strengths and weaknesses of individual pupils. The principle of universal participation and involvement in some stage design projects becomes evident. Two months after being appointed, Otto wrote from Zurich in the upper-case letters typical of his correspondence:

'Dear Herr Zimmer. I have one request. Do not forget to have the detail drawings for *Lady Macbeth* done by Herr Jäger. And it would be a good idea if the deformations are drawn in as far as possible; they are what give the character. Herr Schweitzer and Herr Richter must draw from the nude. I should like to see the works particularly and ensure they are safe. Herr Schweitzer is to complete his *Bohème* model 2 picture, and show me as broad a range of proposals for Don Pasquale. I also would still like to have suggestions for *Diener zweier Herrn* [Servant of Two Masters]. It is extremely important to do easy things after the difficult ones. Pit is to finish the sheets for the *Irre* [La Folle de Chaillot] to be able to show them to a theatre, then *Gespenstersonate* [The Ghost Sonata]. Richter is to take his time over making the model for *Sturm* [The Tempest]. He is not to make a plaster cast of Prospero's cave. It would have to be a transparent, almost glassy material. Dir[ector] Schwippert would like to have all models, also sculptures. See Jäger, Mayer, etc. photographed for the archives. The Breker class has a camera.

Films and contact strips are to be given to the office because [he] needs them for forthcoming publications. Herr Kamel is to finish the [*Madame*] *Butterfly* model, (trees and background) paint in the background. The cellar has not yet been good. Less *Nachtasyl* [The Lower Depths], more concrete and pipe despair. Parties can be given but not too often or too long. [...] I am coming on the 26th [July 1959] for a few days.'[45]

The letter indicates a strong sense of responsibility for the practical development of his pupils. All queries addressed to 'old boys and girls' show that Otto took this particular responsibility very seriously indeed and was regarded by most as at least a person who commanded respect because of his praxis-orientated authority and also because of his empathy; for many he was a father figure. Axel Vater, who was one of Otto's last pupils, did, however, emphasise in an interview that because of Otto's focus on the practical side in a libertarian atmosphere, only the most gifted had a real chance of developing their own potential.[46] This appraisal seems to have been accurate even for Otto's early time at the Art Academy. A colleague, the art historian Anna Klapheck, writes in a series on the 'Teachers at the Art Academy' on the way Otto's teaching was structured:

'Class begins with materials science, free drawing, free playing with forms, then, and only then, are textbooks, worksheets, handed out, models built; painterly designing of the whole only comes at the end. It is not just a matter of training "stage designers", he says; the task of every teacher is to open up buried wellsprings, to wait and listen, and ultimately acknowledge the range of all their possibilities in every young person.'[47]

Otto's love for material, his delight in experimenting, is evident in most of his works. Oleg Kasumovic reports on how he also tried to make that creative sensuous delight useful in the classroom: 'It was mandatory for every student to conduct what was called a "materials experiment" from pure emotion and a wide variety of materials (plastic, glass, wood, metals, cloths, rubbish, etc.) now and then. Imaginary configurations and sculpture of various kinds came out of it.'[48]

The object of study and the admissions requirements are, on the other hand, tersely described as follows in a brochure issued by the Art Academy: 'Stage design, stage area, stage painting, stage model, costume, and mask.'[49] The brochure goes on to add: 'Special artistic talent is decisive for admissions. The course of training is to be supplemented by studies in drawing and is at the same time to include at least one other discipline (painting, the graphic arts, sculpture, architecture). The course of studies also includes dramaturgical practice as well as lectures and classes in perspective, script, art history, and philosophy.'[50]

The will to work, empathy with the unique reality of the stage, and intensive study of the text template in order to find in essential statements a suitable response that was relevant to the stage area were simply taken for granted. The best students also soon had a possibility of acquiring skills that were relevant to professional practice by being interns with production projects which Otto headed. Of course those who had already had some skills from earlier practical training or theatre internships were at an advantage.

The conditions for admission to the Otto class were not at all standardised. The stage designer Heinz Balthes, who turned to Otto after training as a decorator in Hamburg, reported that he had to apply repeatedly over several terms before he was finally accepted. It was only his persistence, burning desire to be admitted, and the development of his artistic capabilities thus provoked by Otto that made admission possible.[51] The admission of Tymian Schneider (Pachl), later a member of Otto's master class, and Katharina Sieverding went off very differently. Both young women were admitted without even having to hand in the portfolios with samples of their work that were usually required.

When Teo Otto first began teaching at the Academy, his class was still manageably small with five pupils. Class sizes were at their peak between the winter terms of 1965/66 and 1966/67 with eighteen pupils, a sizeable majority – twelve and fourteen respectively – of whom were male. Shortly before Otto died, in the summer term of 1968, the class size went back to fourteen. There is still no source material from which inferences on this development might be drawn. Wolf-Jürgen Seeßelberg has this to say about the way Teo Otto handled his students:

'No doubt about it: he loved working with students – but had little time, often came to us only once a month. During those years he was usually working on eight to ten productions at once and spent weeks travelling back and forth by air, overnight sleeper train, or taxi between Zurich – Hamburg – Salzburg – Syracuse – Haifa – New York, and so on. He would telephone the Academy to announce when he would be coming. Truancy or missing or poor work led inevitably to exmatriculation. On the other hand, he would travel all the way from Zurich to settle individual students' problems quickly and without red tape. The intelligent advice he gave, his fatherly concern for his students, his vast knowledge, and his wonderful way of telling stories captivated all who knew him. He soon became a sort of "father figure" to his students. There was no recognisably unique style of teaching; his presence was extremely intensive, his corrections attuned to the individual concerned – evidently aimed at geniuses (even when there weren't any!). I experienced his stage design class as a creative playground: "great freedom". Artistic conceptions from colour and material, "being at home" in all the arts was his objective.'[52]

A characteristic feature of Otto's works was 'lightness of expression', which he succeeded in realising not only in design but also on stage. He became a role model for a whole generation of stage designers through 'the art of omission'.[53] The fragmentary, the physical quote provided the interpretation of a play from the perception of the present.

Understandably, Otto's creative powers and his ability to realise his designs represented to many of his pupils a first alignment and as such was important for the self-discovery process. Wolf-Jürgen Seeßelberg, his last assistant and acting head of his class after Otto's death, on this: 'A lot of Ottoing went on in that class.'[54] However, overt attempts at copying him were reprimanded by Otto.

Things were different when a pupil was being selected as an assistant on a production project of Otto's. In that case, of course, it was necessary to match the author's creative ideas as closely as possible. Günter Walbeck has reported, however, that Otto allowed others' own realisation of details if Otto could see that they were meaningful in the overarching context.[55]

If trust grew out of a working relationship of that kind based on reliability and meticulous execution of a project, Otto was even willing to delegate the power to act and negotiate to his employees, a mandate limited, of course, to the project concerned. Behaviour like this based on partnership,[56] which, generous as it might seem, nonetheless was inexorably premised on fulfilment of the project concerned, shows how magnanimous he could be. Towards the end of his life, Teo Otto increasingly came to depend on such reliable support because there were often ten premieres to be overseen at once. A remark with which the director Fritz Kortner once greeted an assistant of Otto's has often made the rounds: 'So you're the young man who catches the designs Otto throws out of the plane over the theatre?'[57]

Being cast unprotected into such a complex work process as a young person required enormous staying power, organisational skills, and creative powers if one was to keep up with the requirements of daily work and the pace set by the master:

'Organisational, technical, and craftsmanly execution played no role at all. For this area we had been travelling round var[ious] theatres in the Republic as his assistants since the second term: in practice "learning by watching": cold water = asserting oneself at 19 in the workshops against seasoned "theatre hands" – consultations in Otto's absence with the director gods of those days (Gründgens, Kortner, Karajan, etc.) – technical journals for nights on end [...] at 7 o'clock in the morning with Otto on the stage at the Hamburg State Opera – 30 master craftsmen and workmen with drawings and questions. At 8 o'clock through the back door to the theatre: "Where is the till here?" – 9 o'clock consultation with Gründgens – 10 o'clock waiting at the stage door for a taxi to the workshops. Asking after the porter's wife, who is ill. The way through all the trades – minor corrections – in the painting room, he would take up the brush himself, demonstrate how the paint was to be applied – elsewhere with the terse "bark" of a putative old Nazi – and then almost apologetically aside to me: "My boy, that's the only sort of language these people understand." [...] Happy to accept lunch invitation to Michelsen's – talking about Gründgens – during which decorated little scraps of paper, beer mats, and tablecloth with thousands of little biro doodles. Question: "What would the tablecloth cost?" – gather up everything: "Take it to Salzburg to O[scar] F[ritz] Schuh and explain that to him!" 3 p.m. to the airport and to Zurich. I take the precaution of doing a design in Otto's style from all the sketches [...]. He occasionally draws 100 designs in two nights – for *Carmen* with Karajan in Salzburg, for instance.'[58]

The fact that Otto let himself in for such a situation, a division of labour and on a partnership basis, to boot, does prove that it was viable even with those young assistants. Thus protected by the master's name and authority, they gained access to the practical business of staging productions and hands-on experience, which would have been denied them in a purely academic context. It turned out to be beneficial but also burdensome for the young stage design assistants that Otto was commissioned with designing productions at the world's biggest and most important theatres. Of course, the working conditions at such theatres were entirely different to those at smaller, municipal theatres, no comparison. A budget was at their disposal that usually made it possible to realise to the utmost Otto's ideas in consultation with the directors concerned; the stage technology and the personnel at the disposal of such theatres were far superior but they also occupied all one's attention. Seeßelberg:

'Money no longer played a role in Otto stage designs by then. None of us could count. That would become a problem for many of us later on when we were designing our first stage productions of our own.'[59]

A crucial aim of Teo Otto's teaching – apart from all-round artistic development – was certainly to train his pupils to be self-confident, independently acting individuals (Fig. 6). Not only were they supposed to be up to meeting the everyday challenges of theatre life but also to come up with appropriate stage design solutions through intensive study of the text and consultation with the director in a process of 'reciprocal give and take'.[60] To achieve this, he was also willing to put the needs of individuals before those of the class or his projects before his own. When Heinz Balthes, after only a term as his assistant and class teacher on a limited contract, was offered the chance to move to the Freie Volksbühne in Berlin together with the former artistic director of the Düsseldorf Kammerspiele, Hansjörg Utzerath, Otto did not try to keep him but encouraged him to take advantage of the opportunity.[61]

Otto's helpfulness – even outside the confines of the class – has often been described by former pupils. Through his far-flung contacts he was able to arrange jobs for some of them as stage designers, among them Pit Fischer, whom he sent to the Düsseldorf Schauspielhaus, then under Karl Heinz Stroux.[62] To others, including Erwin W. Zimmer, Otto showed his respect by helping them to 'break the apron-strings' while maintaining contact for years. He wrote to Zimmer, who did not feel really comfortable in his job in Freiburg: 'Write specifically what you want. How long do you want to stay in Freiburg? An assistantship with two productions is opening up here. You're beyond that! Can I do something for you?'[63]

To most members of his classes, Teo Otto was a fascinating person, at the very least a person held in respect, even though he would or could not retain all of them for any length of time. Individual success and the intensity of the training experience undoubtedly depended on the teachers with short-term contracts who assisted Otto. Karolus Lodenkämper was unable to spot any helpful teaching structures for the brief period he spent with Otto: 'There was no trace of anything like a teaching plan, style of teaching, practical training, and so on, nor was there of the professorial head of instruction himself.'[64] Yet even he closes what is otherwise a bitter letter with the remark: 'But he was nice somehow, was Teo Otto.'[65]

Oleg Kasumovic was emotionally so stirred by Otto that he made his father enthusiastic about translating Otto's book, *Meine Szene* [My Scene], which was duly published in that version in Zagreb in the early 1970s.

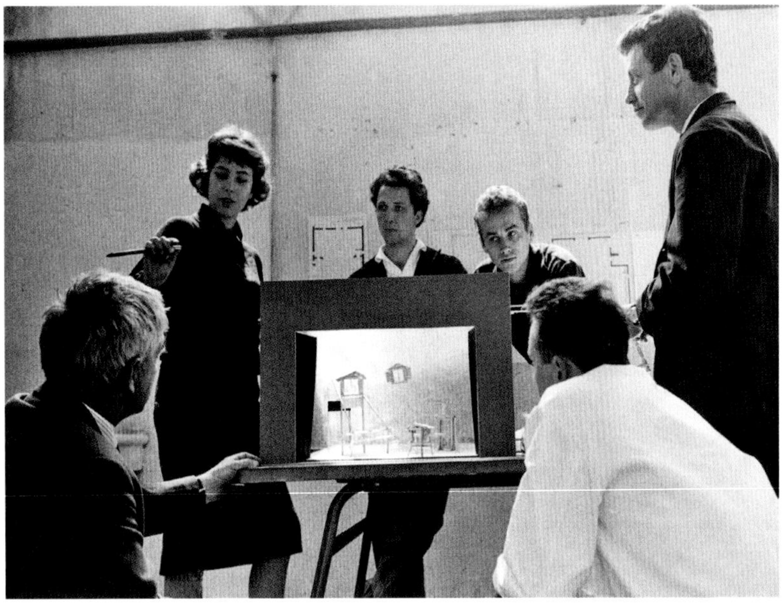

Fig. 6: Teo Otto with his class, 1960

Rolf Doerr, who directed Brecht's *Kleinbürgerhochzeit* [A Respectable Wedding] with his former classmate Talay Toktamis as stage designer as recently as 2000 in Izmir, had little else to talk about in breaks from work besides their time with Teo Otto (Fig. 17).[66] Even decades later, Teo Otto was still an intellectual benchmark for many of his former pupils. He left no one unmoved.

BETWEEN STUDENT PROTEST AND ARTISTIC SELF-DISCOVERY – A TIME OF TRANSITION – WOLF-JÜRGEN SEESSELBERG (*1941)[67]

When Teo Otto suddenly died on 9 June 1968 at the age of sixty-four, he left a gap that found the stage design class[68] unprepared despite the frequent absence of their professor. This feeling of sudden emptiness undoubtedly had its roots in Otto's complex personality. Even from a distance he had conveyed a feeling of support and not just on his brief but intensive teaching stints at the Düsseldorf Academy. His last assistant, Wolf-Jürgen Seeßelberg, once summarised it as follows:

'No matter how burdened with work he was, he would take the time for our most personal affairs [...]. For many of us he became a father figure. He himself hardly wanted that.'[69]

'He was not content with merely giving good advice; there were neither rules nor orders, no dogmas, never any rigid programmes. By letting us take part in his work and his life, he showed the richness of the various possibilities. It was left to everyone as an individual to test them, to use them, or to reject them. I have the reasonable suspicion that he did not think all that much of teaching because he was well aware of how limited the possibilities and effects of teaching were. – He lived by example. – His way of living by example permitted his pupils insight into the existence of their teacher. The distance between teacher and pupil was consciously broken down. We were put in the position of partners, rather – of friends, not of pupils.'[70]

By the beginning of the 1967 summer term, Seeßelberg had been appointed Otto's fourth assistant and teacher on a short-term contract in his class. Teo Otto had made his choice with care: in 1959 Seeßelberg had been one of the first students to be admitted to his class, and he had proved himself as an assistant who had worked on numerous stage productions of Otto's between Hamburg and Salzburg. He writes on the qualifications he brought to bear on his early years in Düsseldorf: 'I was young – very young – when I went to Düsseldorf with a tiny suitcase in May 1959 – had just turned 18: full of expectations – eager to work on my own – yet unsure of myself and totally naive – flat broke but curious and awfully ambitious – that was a mixed bag.'[71]

During his student years and then also as a member of Otto's master class from the winter term of 1963/64 until the winter term of 1964/65, Seeßelberg, by then twenty-four years old, was able to get more of an idea of his teacher's manifold requirements and content objectives. Seeßelberg had also had intense discussions about the future of academic training for scenographers with Teo Otto in the last phase of his life. When the Academy directorate approached Wolf-Jürgen Seeßelberg after Otto's death with the request he should fill in for his former teacher as acting class teacher from the beginning of the 1968/69 winter term, this was not really a surprise.

Seeßelberg was not content with simply working through his sorrow. He was anxious to assert his own ideas and concepts: 'The Otto era was now at an end – we all had to reorientate and reorganise ourselves. Now we had to overcome the master – a painful and distressing process.'[72]

By November 1968 he had contacted Karl-Heinz Stroux (1908–1985), the former artistic director of the Düsseldorf Schauspielhaus. He wrote to Stroux to arrange a date on which he could present his new concept for a stage design class.[73] Behind that move was Seeßelberg's desire not only to present his thoughts for critical review to an expert, an external authority who carried some weight, but undoubtedly also to win over Stroux as a potential ally for his new network, even though Stroux was a member of the theatre establishment.

The position paper has survived. It is so important mainly because it takes into consideration the social dislocations of a post-war society and their effects on the fields of theatre and film and as future work areas for graduates of the stage design class.

'Hence an entirely new form must be found for continuing the stage design class. Here is not the place for proposing the simplest solution in administrative terms: a new appointment. A solution must be found that meets all the requirements of the theatre, no matter what form of theatre is meant (not only the established theatre). One must completely distance oneself from the idea of the stage design specialist [...]. There is scope for stage designers in the cinema and television sector as well as with other artistic and technical problems. Subject-related suggestions for training in these fields must, therefore, be incorporated in a new plan.'[74]

Starting with the specific needs of the theatre and film, Seeßelberg regarded again appointing an 'established stage designer professor' as a not very useful move: 'The new professor would cling too much to the established theatre and would be too committed to it. There would be no possibility for students to develop freely and independently of the establishment and the usual theatre programmes. In my view, limiting the appointment to one teacher would be wrong in the present situation.'[75] Instead he asked that 'teaching and heading the class' should be taken over 'by 2 lecturers working closely together':[76] 'a lecturer for stage design (stage designer, painter) [and] a lecturer for film (cameraman).'[77]

According to Seeßelberg, who had managed to gain some experience of his own in film, the lecturer for film should be 'an experienced cameraman with experience as a cutter. That will provide students, who up to now have usually been self-taught in the work, with the technical foundation needed for realising artistic ideas.'[78]

To meet the manifold new requirements of a society on the brink of becoming multimedia with all the sophisticated needs that entails, in addition up to seven visiting lecturers were to be invited from as wide a range of artistic and academic fields as possible: 'Directors from theatre and film, artistic directors, writers, dramaturges, stage designers, film architects, cameramen, choreographers, actors, critics, architects, painters, sculptors, sociologists, and so forth.'[79]

Entirely in accordance with the aims of the expiring student rebellions, with their aim of the 'democratisation of structures', was also the demand: 'The invitation to the visiting lecturers should be issued on the basis of a collective proposal by the class and the two lecturers via the assembled professors supplemented by the student representatives.'[80] The training facilities offered in this form would (if realised) be open to all interested Academy students.

Moreover, 'all teachers at the Academy [...] should be available to the class for special artistic and visual issues',[81] a position that turned out to be impracticable in the climate prevailing at the time in the Academy, which tended towards keeping the classes separate.

Seeßelberg's contract changed as of the start of the 1969 summer term. The chronicles of the State Art Academy note for May 1969: 'Wolf-Jürgen Seeßelberg has been hired for a year as a lecturer in the stagecraft class and tasked with heading the class.'[82]

The assembled professors had evidently resolved in parallel to establish a 'class for theatre and film' as of the summer term of 1969.[83] However, this decision for technically fitting out a film class was initially not followed up on because no funding was made available for it.

Also the discrepancy between the professionally orientated goals desired by Seeßelberg as a scenographer interested in film and the situation actually prevailing in the 'class for theatre and film' showed up from the start. The group which independently set itself as the film class did take over a room in the Stage Design Department but concentrated mainly on the aesthetics of cinema, hence had a noticeably different focus.

This small band of students had a hard fight on its hands before a film workshop equipped with the relevant facilities was established. How this was managed is described by Erinna König, a leading activist member of the film class:

'As far as the origins of the film class at the Art Academy itself are concerned, the initiative taken by a group of students then at the Academy – Henning Brandis, Peter Holtfreter, Susanne

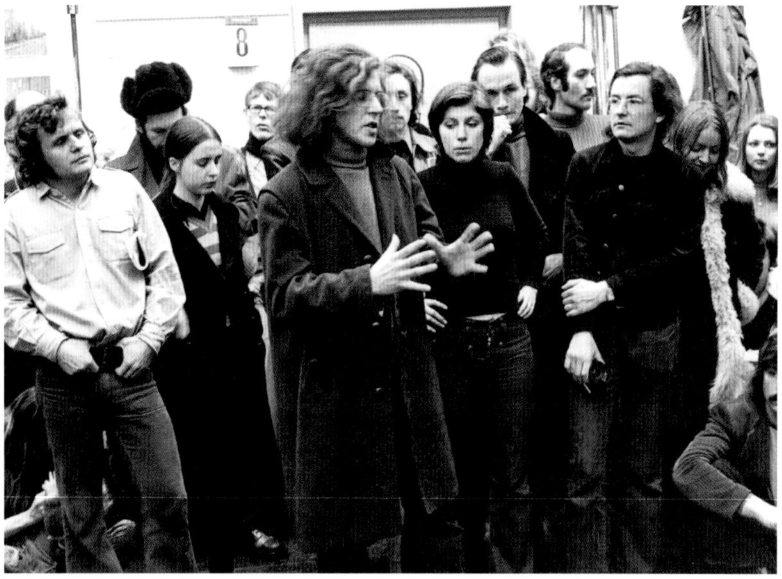

Fig. 7: Discussion on the future of the film class, 1972; left: Wolf-Jürgen Seeßelberg; centre: Ole John Povlsen

Ebert, Peter Bohl, Illona Baltrusch, and Erinna Koenig [*sic*] – was of pivotal importance. Not only did this group of students initiate the setting up and equipping of a room for a film class in the Stage Art Department (with Seeßelberg as lecturer), but it also organised lectures and activities with film-makers such as Hartmut Bitomsky, Harun Farocki, Helma Sanders. The fees for people they invited were paid by the group itself. It was on the basis of this self-organised initiative that it finally became possible to push through the establishment of an official film class via the administrative process (AStA [General Students' Committee], general assembly, appointments).'[84]

The appointment of the Danish cameraman, scriptwriter, and film director Ole John Povlsen (*1939),[85] who linked practical cinematic skills with a considerable interest in art, made it possible to carry out the agenda desired by the film class (Fig. 7).

'The film class started its teaching programme in the 1971/72 winter term as the stage design and film class, initially united under Wolf-Jürgen Seeßelberg. [...] This enlargement of the range of courses offered was above all a demand made by the students. The teaching staff, with the exception of Beuys and a few others, tended to be sceptical about the film experiment. Yet the implantation of the new medium also provided an opportunity: fine art and film could possibly inspire and cross-fertilise each other aesthetically.'[86]

However, the film class headed by Ole John Povlsen would only remain a brief episode. As of the close of the 1975/76 winter term in February 1976, his contract as lecturer was not renewed. The Düsseldorf Employment Tribunal confirmed in July 1976 that Povlsen had been lawfully dismissed. Protests voiced by his pupils in the film class, the General Students' Committee at the Art Academy, and professional organisations throughout the Federal Republic went unheeded.[87]

Seeßelberg's departure from the Düsseldorf Art Academy was, as he has indicated himself, causally connected with the events surrounding Joseph Beuys in autumn 1972: Seeßelberg had dealt with admissions to the 'class for theatre and film' in a manner similar to that practised by Beuys in his class. When Professor Beuys, accompanied by some fifty students who had not been admitted to study at the Academy, occupied the Academy offices on 10 October 1972 to force the Academy to allow them to matriculate, Beuys was summarily dismissed 'for disturbing the peace' by the then Minister for Science, Johannes Rau.[88] Nor was the contract of Wolf-Jürgen Seeßelberg, who sympathised with Joseph Beuys and, like him, was an activist who felt the traditional academic organisation of classes and curriculum was outdated, extended in 1973.[89] In 1974 Seeßelberg became a founding member of the Free International University for Creativity and Interdisciplinary Research, headed by Beuys.[90]

'THE AUSTERITY PRINCIPLE' – KARL KNEIDL (*1940)[91]

The fact that the Academy directorate under director Norbert Kricke (1922–1984) resolved, in close agreement with the North Rhine-Westphalian Administration of Academic Affairs, to fill the chair left vacant since Teo Otto's death (in 1968) by once again appointing a distinguished stage designer (Fig. 8) indicated obvious compliance with a pacification strategy adopted in the aftermath of the upheavals between 1968 and 1973.

The war of ideas fought out with Joseph Beuys and his following for redefining art in society and for conveying this through the appropriate academic agency had left deep wounds on both sides. Kricke skilfully exploited the vacuum created by the dismissal of Beuys in 1972 to push back one by one many of the changes implemented in the face of student protest. Those retrogressive moves also included, after Seeßelberg's dismissal (in 1973), formally returning the stage class to the old ways with the traditional class structure that included a professor at its head. The sole innovation to be preserved in the new class was evidently the incorporation of scenography in the Fine Art Department. This stance distinguished the range of courses on

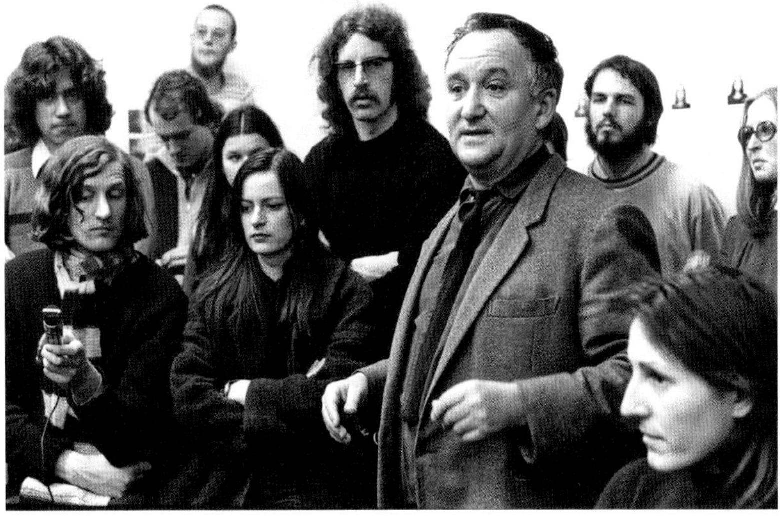

Fig. 8: Norbert Kricke discussing the future of the film class with students, 1972

offer at the Düsseldorf Art Academy from all other institutions of its kind. Retaining the fine art status of scenography would still be a bone of contention tossed about decades later between Kneidl, the Ministry for Science, and the Academy directorate.

By February 1974, the *Rheinische Post*, a leading regional daily, was reporting on the new state of affairs: 'The head of the stage design class at the Art Academy is to be taken over as of 1 April by Karl Kneidl, a distinguished representative of his field. With this appointment, the Minister for Science [Johannes Rau] is following the proposal put forward by the Academy senate.'[92]

The circumstances leading to Kneidl's appointment were quite unusual yet obviously typical of the times. Eberhard Schweigert (1942–2004),[93] who had been named acting director of the class for the winter term of 1973/74 after Seeßelberg left, had evidently contacted Kneidl with Norbert Kricke's assent. At that time Kneidl was busy with rehearsals for the first production for which he was solely responsible for the stage design at the Württembergisches Staatstheater in Stuttgart (Jewgenij Schwarz, *Die Schneekönigin* [The Snow Queen], premiere: 30 November 1973).

An appointment with Kricke came about, at which Kneidl was self-confident enough to present his position so plausibly as a freelance scenographer in an academic context that only a few months later he was chosen for the Academy chair. His appointment also forestalled some problematic thoughts Kricke had at first entertained of subordinating the technical aspect of theatrical production to dramaturgy and content.[94]

Understandably, the new head of the stage design class had no comment to make to the press about the backstory of his appointment. Helga Meister on this: 'Reticent native of Nuremberg that he is, Kneidl is unwilling to say how he came by this distinguished appointment to succeed the former prototypical German stage designer [Teo Otto]. He was simply asked to and "you don't refuse something like that".'[95]

Karl Kneidl, from Nuremberg, had indeed been in the front ranks of Federal German scenographers since the early 1970s, when the choice fell on him. Through his employment at the Bochum Schauspielhaus followed by the essential theatres in the German-speaking countries, he could show an impressive body of work with leading directors such as Hans-Joachim Heyse, Niels-Peter Rudolph, Max Peter Ammann, Franz Xaver Kroetz, Alfred Kirchner, the duo Manfred Karge and Matthias Langhoff, Adolf Dresen, Andrea Breth, Peter Palitzsch, Peter Stein, and, most recently, also Peter Zadek.

In an interview conducted in 1970 by Hans Bertram Bock, who had accompanied Kneidl's career for years in the press, the 'closed-lipped, unconventional' stage designer talked about his open-ended approach to his profession, which he would teach students by example in hands-on practice for decades: '[Director Niels-Peter] Rudolph and I are an ideal team. We have developed a system for working together. Collaborative play-readings, discussions, historical significance of a play, secondary literature. Then I design the first sets, make sketches, discard them. Solutions are ultimately found at rehearsals.'[96]

Kneidl had evidently also developed standards of his own to apply to his aesthetic value system. Invariably claiming the complete absence of artistic role models for his stage solutions, Kneidl said to Bock, 'Every stage set [should] leave actors and audience "scope for the imagination".'[97] And the journalist summed up, 'Kneidl, who in his own words "does not want to push his own style", already has a distinctive signature. To him, aesthetics means "thinking right". He characterises his style as the automatic consequence of this principle.'[98] Kneidl added, 'So I never use any materials in a way that defies common sense. I don't follow fashion there.'[99]

From 1973 on, Kneidl also increasingly took on directorial functions. When asked about his motives for doing so, he answered in an interview, 'I am of the opinion that a set and costume designer should definitely not be just the recipient of a director's commands – because the intention of a play is to be made visible, and content occurrences are to be represented both in stage scenery and costumes.'[100]

In fact his concern was to expand in a complex way the possibilities of theatrical expression and perception, which would also be useful to him in many respects in his capacity as head of the stage design class in Düsseldorf; therefore, unlike his predecessors, who had never taken the step to directing plays, Kneidl was able to open up considerably more employment possibilities for pupils who had assisted him with his productions – an enormous enrichment of the pre-professional store of work experience that the students could draw on. In this, he is also sure to have suited the small band of pupils affiliated with him.

Typical of the times was also Kneidl's first confrontation with the students from the old stage design and film class in spring 1974. They had shown up bearing a full load of grudges against the man whom they presumed to be the representative of the Academy directorate. No sooner had he made a first statement, signalising a willingness to work hard, and a request that portfolios be submitted to him for admission to his class than the group dissolved. Only a handful remained with whom a fresh start could be embarked on.[101]

Anna Viebrock, who was there at that first session, remembers, 'Then I really liked the clear words Karl Kneidl spoke right at the beginning on the subject of "studying": "You have to want it yourself, otherwise leave it alone".'[102] The volatile mood in the class had evaporated by February 1975. Helga Meister wrote with a touch of histrionics:

'Directly under the roof at Eiskellerberg, where rainwater seeps through the walls, hard labour is in progress. Here stage designer Karl Kneidl is exorcising the memory of the interim years after Teo Otto's death, during which deeds were to be replaced by theories. The band huddled about the stage designer in demand is small. Just six to nine students, they are tackling the work as if it were up to them to put the finishing touches on an imminent premiere [...]. In the stage designing work in Stuttgart, Berlin, Munich, the Düsseldorf pupils are not being short-changed; to the contrary, they assist him on site and are learning the craft from the ground up. At home, at Eiskellerberg, they have to model plaster figurines from photos, are made familiar with all sorts of practices in the Academy iron-forging and metalworking workshops, and learn to work together early on. "We never fake it".'[103]

From the perspective of his pupils, Karl Kneidl has come to be viewed as a complex personality. Even though the use of the intimate form of direct address ('Du') might suggest familiarity and closeness between teacher and class, the prevailing tone might be more aptly described as one of 'respect'. Because of his authoritative way of teaching (demand and promote through practice, and discussion and criticism attuned to the individual), he tended to be perceived by many as a master rather than a teacher in the classic sense.

Beginners were at first deliberately kept away 'from the hectic world of the theatre and the politicking that belongs to the theatre'. Timo Dentler quotes Kneidl as saying, 'That'll come soon enough; use the time you have with the freedoms and protection of the Academy.'[104]

Exploring those freedoms and one's personal maturing process also included a commitment to expressing opinions in front of the class, a practice Kneidl evidently often engaged in, as Marius Baumgartner recalls:

'In my eyes, Karl was a person in whom a great deal went through the sensory plane. In that sense, he wasn't an intellectual, which I thought was very good. There were no abstruse philosophical discussions about the significance of the theatre and the like. Society, politics, and art were talked about in a relatively simple way. But all the more passionately. Karl was [...] inwardly seething with rage at such discussions [...]. It was always important to Karl that you had a clear stance on things, from which then art also develops. Working in the theatre is always conflict – he never said that but that is what I sensed from his manner. There was always a lot of debate and discussion. I liked that kind of atmosphere of constructive debate.'[105]

For Dentler in particular, who had studied intensively with Kneidl for years, had often been his assistant, and – like many others in the class – became a member of his master class, placing scenography within the context of fine art was of paramount importance. He writes:

'After finishing school, I travelled to all the art academies in Germany and Austria, looked at stage design classes taught by Wonder, Rose, and Manthey, among others, and talked to the professors. The institutes all seemed to me very school-like: subjects like heraldry, the history of costume and weaponry were taught. The questions I addressed to an artistic understanding of stage design and the theatre seemed to me to be in the background there.

All I had heard about Karl Kneidl was: the stage design course at the Düsseldorf Art Academy was at that time the only place in Germany where the subject of stage design was in the Fine Art Department. That was the reason why I opted for Düsseldorf.'[106]

Chiefly because Ruth Groß, who would become Kneidl's art technician teacher, had been in a position to encounter his novel artistic approach to the stage in her native Nuremberg, she sought him out in person and was admitted to his class: 'I saw he thought on other levels about art; that I could sense even as a beginner that he had very unconventional stage sets built, and that thinking processes were behind it that were entirely different from simply putting up a set that was decorative in relation to the play concerned.'[107]

He did not care for assigning tasks like an educator, and he made no bones about that in public interviews. In 1986 Kneidl spoke about his academic commitments to a journalist named Stoll: 'The education aspects are not in the foreground here, rather working in extreme alternative worlds in which everyone has to pick his way on his own.'[108]

Evidently he – like Teo Otto – was also appealing here to the slumbering geniuses in his class. Ruth Groß is specific about the way the head of the class dealt with his pupils:

'He was demanding and uncompromising, expected, in a very unpedagogical way, only the best solutions to all assignments he set; he would occasionally throw a horrific temper tantrum if you hadn't done your work and hadn't got on – but he was always willing to talk and always reacted in a positive and understanding way if you had finally got started or at least had tried to. That's how I got over my 'cold feet about plunging in' and learned that there's always a solution to be found once you have finally buckled down to the matter at hand.'[109]

Thus Karl Kneidl had in part achieved one of his most important aims in teaching: training his pupils to be emancipated stage and costume designers who would be up to the aesthetic and technical advances in the theatre in a world that was constantly changing because they had faith in their own powers.

A good qualification with less fuss and bother for joining the class, in which advanced pupils worked together with beginners on classroom assignments, was having had previous training in a craft. Training as a carpenter and joiner was sometimes recommended. Karl Kneidl himself had trained as a carpenter and joiner before going to the theatre. The table retained polysemic significance for him. Wolfgang Storch, who was his dramaturge for years, explains:

'As the place where it all happens, the table dominated the stage for Kneidl, it centred it. A table – or whatever replaces it, a bed, a hut – sets the standard for the stage. That overcame the division of stage scenery into space and picture [as it still was with Neher and Otto]. The picture above as atmosphere or as the commentary plane was no longer needed. All that was needed was creating a spatial arrangement that allowed each of the actors to keep the right distance from their opposite numbers.'[110]

Although artistic criteria were essentially the determining factor for admission to the Kneidl class (on the basis of the portfolio applicants had to submit),[111] Martin Kukulies, for one, decided to serve an apprenticeship as a carpenter and joiner before applying, which would ultimately crucially improve his chances of being admitted.[112] Naturally, he had a considerable advantage over those who still had to learn those skills the hard way to be able to deal with the practical side of an artistic assignment.

Over the years various work and thematic priorities emerged. This is also certain to have depended on the particular talents and preferences of the art-technician teachers, who came and went but were the ones who actually guaranteed continuity in the class when Kneidl was absent. They formed a creative unit with the master (Fig. 9). Kneidl recalls, 'My assistant, Christian Göbl, and I used to copy Old Master paintings in the old painting techniques with the students, and that put off some artists at the Academy Tours; Gerhard Richter, however, who had his studio on the floor above us [at Harkortstraße 5–7], told me he should also do that in his class.'[113]

There was often group work on larger projects, for instance, for *Alice in Wonderland* (1977/78) and *Faust* (1978/79), together with Christian Göbl and the dramatist Michael Pehlke, or on key themed tasks such as 'Representing Nature in the Theatre' (1985–1988), supplemented by a practical project with drama students from the Folkwangschule in Essen (1986) together with Vincent Callara.[114]

From the very beginning, model building (on a 1:20 scale) was practised on a high level. A photo of Anna Viebrock (*c.*1975) has survived, in which she is pictured working in the old classroom under the roof of the Art Academy on a proscenium box for the Deutsches Schauspielhaus in Hamburg (Fig. 10).

In the early 1980s, when the contact was so close with the Bochum Schauspielhaus under Claus Peymann that Peymann loaned his chief dramaturge, Hermann Beil, to work with the class, a model was made of the Ruhr region theatre replete with lobby and façade.

The German Academic Exchange Service travel grant for Italy awarded to Ruth Groß was also productive. There she was able to devote herself to intensive on-site study of Renaissance and Baroque theatres. On her return to Düsseldorf in 1991, the students built a model of the Teatro Farnese in Parma.[115] The last models built on a large scale were a model of the Munich Cuvilliés-Theater and one of the Berliner Ensemble (1993–1995). None of these collaborative works has survived, probably simply because they were so large.

For beginners particularly but also for advanced students who were not tied down as assistants somewhere, working on a model provided good practice in perfecting crafts skills and schooling spatial thinking.

The classwork themes changed to be in line with – thus Timo Dentler – the plays Kneidl was staging at a given time: 'Thus there was always direct study of his work.'[116] Karl Kneidl viewed his main sphere of activity as outside the Academy but he still took the tasks he had assumed when he was appointed professor very seriously. The amount of time he spent in his

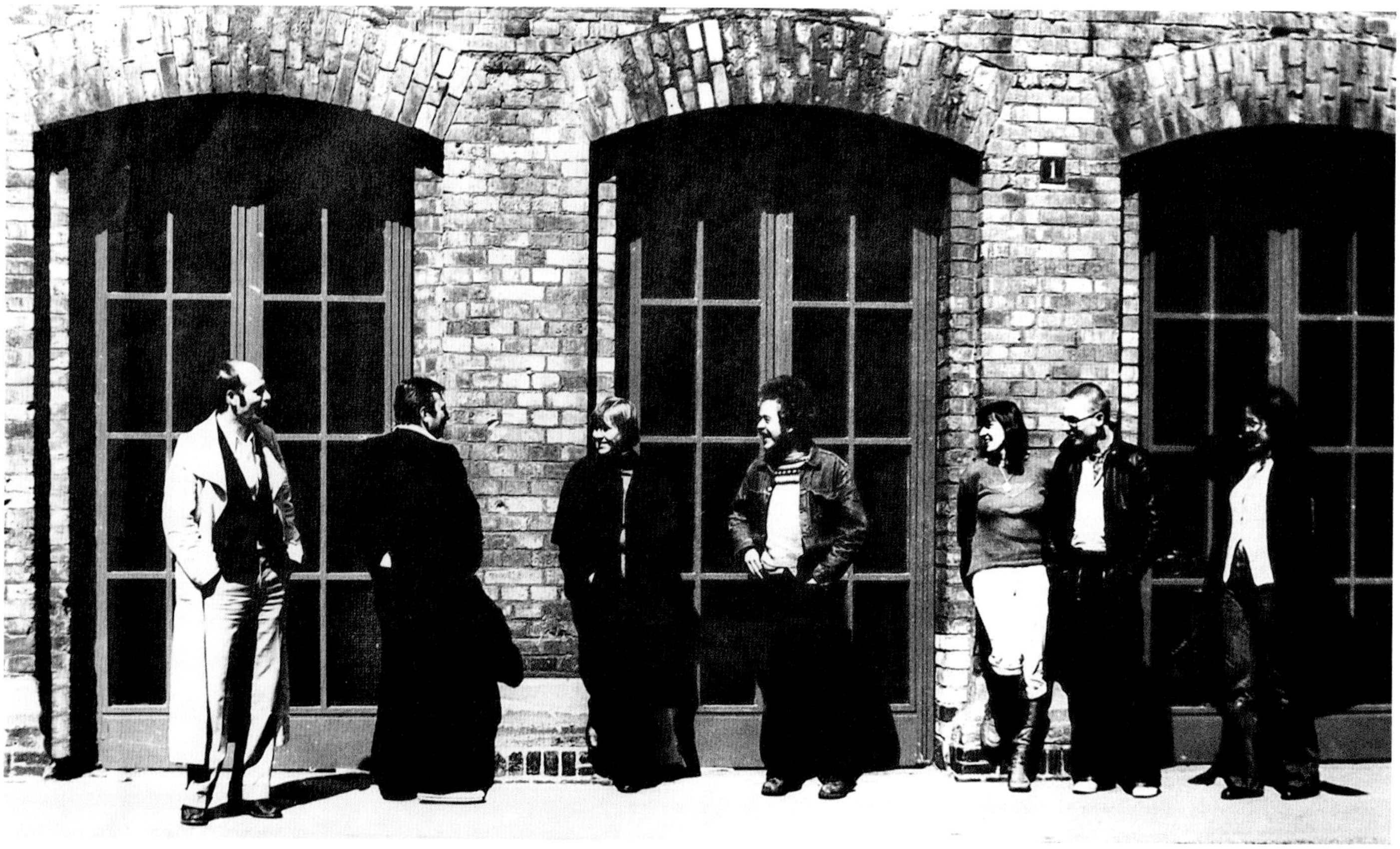

Fig. 9: The Kneidl class in front of the Düsseldorf Art Academy, 1976; from left to right: Christian Göbl (assistant), Karl Kneidl, Tatjana von Stülpnagel, Hartmut Ritzerfeld, Doris Kroner, Claudius Rudek, Anna Viebrock

class varied depending on his commitments to theatres that were not connected with the Academy (Fig. 11). Sometimes he would be at the Academy every day for three weeks, but at others the class would have fourteen days to work on a task.[117] Timo Dentler writes:

'When he came, there was usually a large group in the classroom and we would present what we had been working on. Sometimes there were individual conversations with him. I was always very nervous. He would usually encourage me in my work and urged me to have more courage so as to be free and approach art with a lighter hand. But there could be outspoken criticism, too, which at first would pull the rug out from under my feet but the next minute would get me going in a new direction. [...] The door to KK's studio at the Art Academy was always open to us, and I would often look over his shoulder while he was working or would go and sit down surreptitiously in front of his model in the evening. Usually there would be a complete new design in model form by the next evening. This way of working really impressed me and strongly influenced me in my own work.'[118]

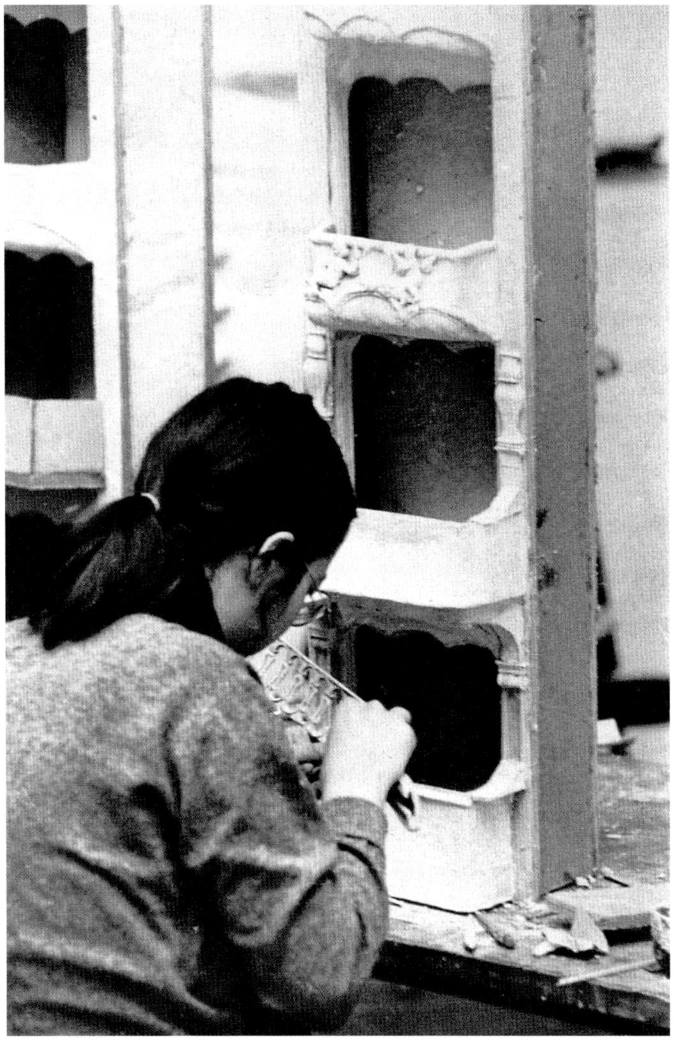

Fig. 10: Anna Viebrock with a model of a proscenium box at the Deutsches Schauspielhaus Hamburg, c. 1975

Ruth Groß adds:

'He assigned work and expected it to be translated into art. The way had to be found individually and that was the most important thing we learnt: asking ourselves questions and finding answers in art to demands made of us. He was against any form of pedagogy although, in retrospect, I realise by doing that he was very clearly carrying out a sort of pedagogy: that of thinking and acting freely and independently as an artistically responsible human being. Some took that in their stride; others couldn't handle it so well.'[119]

Christine Gottschalk, who did not join the Kneidl class until 2007, describes her teacher as essentially cordial and approachable but does not cover up his 'other' side:

'He could also be authoritarian and strict and he would always on principle actually take apart anything you showed him. After a colloquy with him you would be standing there again with nothing at all, would have to start over again, think about it some more. You weren't allowed to finish up an assignment until time was running short, for the *Rundgang* [Academy Tour] or the *Akademiebrief* [Academy certificate], then you had to somehow. Before that the word was always: keep looking, don't be easily satisfied, be even more precise. I found him very supportive, felt upbeat. But I think we were all a bit afraid of him.'[120]

His immense work ethic and his creative energy probably intimidated some. In extreme cases he would suggest a parting of the ways to members of the class who could not take on this attitude and uphold it and who had become mired in artistic stagnation.

Karl Kneidl was dramaturgically supported from the outset by a teaching post that was set up for the purpose. It was held by Dr Axel Bornkessel (*1943), who started out as a specialist in theatre studies and later became a writer and director of TV documentaries.[121] Between 1972 and 1976 he was employed as a dramaturge at the Düsseldorf Schauspielhaus under Ulrich Brecht. Thus a post ensuring crucial further consolidation of content by specialist staff, which had already existed in the stage design class taught by Walter von Wecus, was revived.

Under Teo Otto, on the other hand, the teaching of dramaturgy-related content had been taken over by the various assistants to the class.

Bornkessel was succeeded by Michael Pehlke (*1943), followed by the important Peymann dramaturge Hermann Beil (*1941). With Beil's support, one of the largest class projects was realised at the Bochum Schauspielhaus (Fig. 12). Karl Kneidl proudly stated, 'Each of those performances took up an entire evening simultaneously all over the theatre. They were plays by dramatists ranging from Thomas Bernhard to Dario Fo and Heiner Müller under the collective heading *Unsere Welt* [Our World]. My students could realise their full potential in this project as designers – that is, as stage set and costume designers.'[122]

Klaus-Eduard Zehelein (*1940), who would later become the Stuttgart opera manager and is now president of the German Theatre Asssociation,[123] was even hired from the summer term of 1984 until the summer term of 1986. Highlights of his work with the class included study of Heiner Müller's *Die Schlacht* [The Battle], the Handel opera *Julius Caesar*, and *Karagöz in Alamania*, a play by Emine Sevgi Özdamar.[124] Even though his stint at the Düsseldorf Art Academy is not mentioned in Zehelein's official CV,[125] some former pupils of Kneidl's (Brack, Groß, Kukulies) still clearly recall his excellent teaching.[126] Michael Huthmann, then chief dramaturge under Volker Canaris at the Düsseldorf Schauspielhaus, was Zehelein's successor for a brief while.

Wolfgang Storch (*1943), specialist in theatre studies, art historian, and versed in German language and literature,[127] who taught in the class from 1988 until Kneidl's employment ended officially in 2007, was undoubtedly the dramaturge who accompanied the class most memorably with a wide range of in-depth study areas: inspired by his (exhibition) projects on Heiner Müller and Richard Wagner, 'Greek tragedy' and 'myth' were given new thematic weight. It was only logical that this thematic focus led to the study of more authors from the

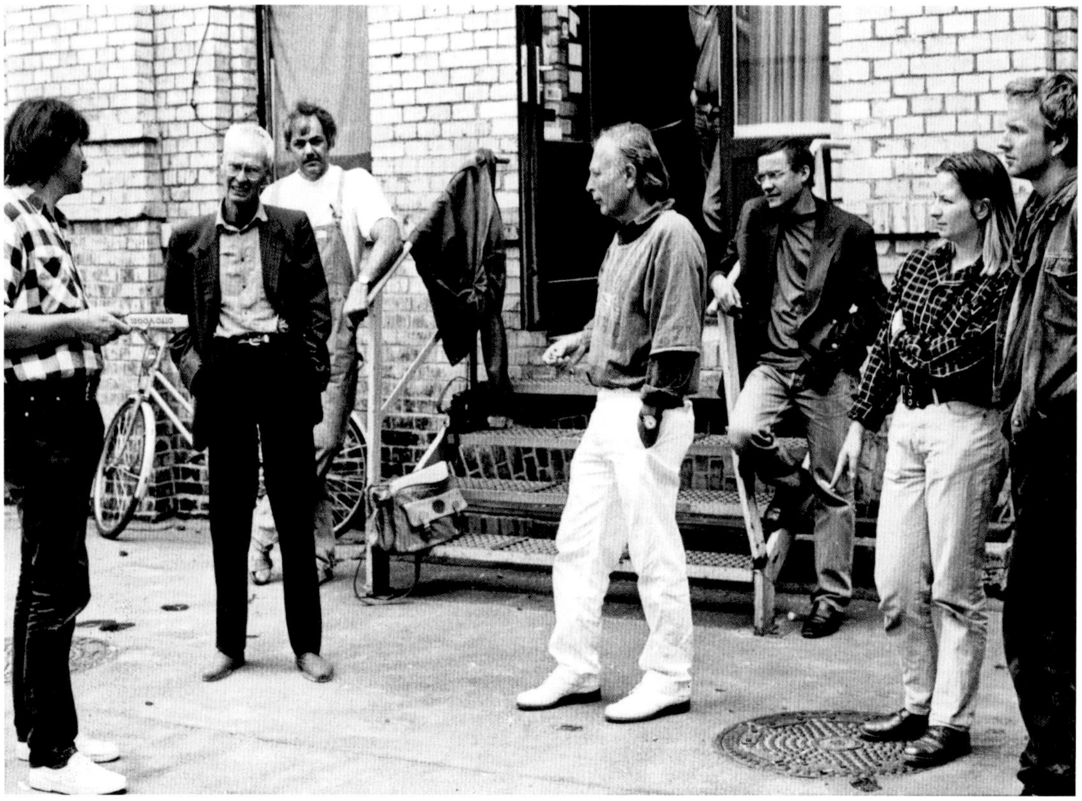

Fig. 11: During a Berliner Ensemble production of Bertolt Brecht's Baal, *1993. Front row from left to right: Uwe Jens Jensen (dramaturge), Peter Palitzsch (director), Karl Kneidl (stage designer), next to them Kneidl assistants Anna Stolze and Timo Dentler*

former GDR, including Einar Schleef, who had also devoted intensive study to the myth of the Nibelungs. For years the Kneidl class convened for a summer academy at Storch's Italian home in Volterra (Fig. 13).

Advanced students from the class were often given the opportunity – each according to his or her ability – of working as assistants at numerous theatres in Germany and abroad. For all of them, having to prove themselves outside the academic cocoon in the real world of the theatre 'put the finishing touches' to their professional training. That was where, under real conditions, the question might first arise of whether their choice of profession was indeed viable. In any case, this live experience would have a formative influence regardless of whether a student continued to work in the theatre after leaving the Academy. Ruth Groß puts it in a nutshell:

'Doing that, students, and I include myself, learned everything they needed. The motivation was there; you wanted to be good, you had to [...] grasp each object first of all, draw it, photograph it, measure it, discover how it was constructed and built [...]; you could experience [...] whether inventions worked, whether they had to be altered [...]; there you learned voluntarily as much and as quickly as possible. Of course, everyone had a different intensity. You might call it an intensive compact course. One person's intensity inspired the others' work and, apart from a modicum of healthy competitiveness, many people learned from each other. And we all had to learn to work with others, to get on with each other, a major precondition for surviving in the theatre (and also in the class).'[128]

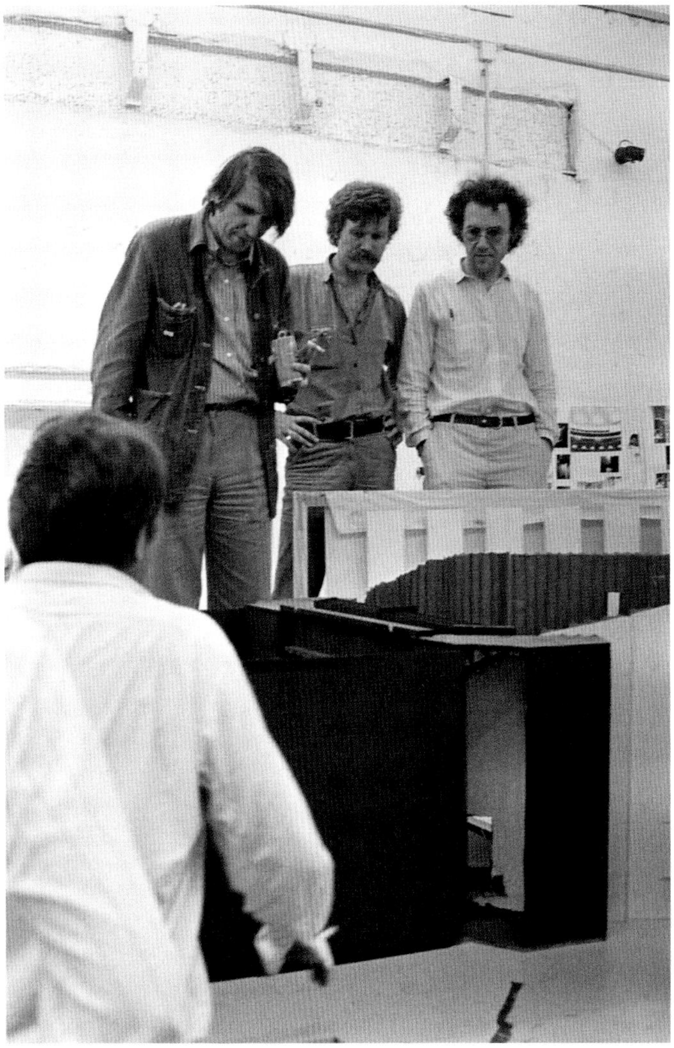

Fig. 12: From left to right: Karl Kneidl, director Matthias Langhoff, and dramaturges Uwe Jens Jensen and Hermann Beil at the model of the Bochum Schauspielhaus in the stage design class, preparing the production Unsere Welt *[Our World], 1981*

Between 1974 and 2009 the way of doing things in the stage design class and its very existence were seriously threatened on two occasions: the first time was during the rectorate of Irmin Kamp, when the Ministry of Science tried to exert an influence on basic working conditions by revising the regulations governing employment (redefining employment/additional occupation). Viewing this attempt as an assault on his autonomy as an artist, Kneidl succeeded, with the aid of compendious legal opinion and the option of going public with the facts of the case, in warding off the Ministry proposal.

Debate engaged in during the rectorate of Markus Lüpertz about detaching the class from the context of fine art at the Academy and affiliating it with the considerably more school-like Folkwangschule in Essen represented an even more serious threat to the existence of the stage design class at the Art Academy. In this case, too, Karl Kneidl succeeded in holding his own. He recalls, in brief, 'There I was, actually very practical, everything in its right place; only for me it would have meant the end of imagination and art.'[129]

The success of Kneidl's combative profession of allegiance to fine art undoubtedly also cleared away considerable hurdles to continuing the stage design class with which his successor, Johannes Schütz, would otherwise have had to deal.

Understandably, since he had over one hundred and twenty pupils over a period of thirty-five years, the image their teacher has left with them varies considerably. After all, generational change shows up here, too, in the generations of pupils Kneidl accompanied. Still, assessments expressed by those pupils tell us just as much about them as they do about the person they are judging. Kneidl as a living role model is still with them decades later, remaining a point of reference even though they

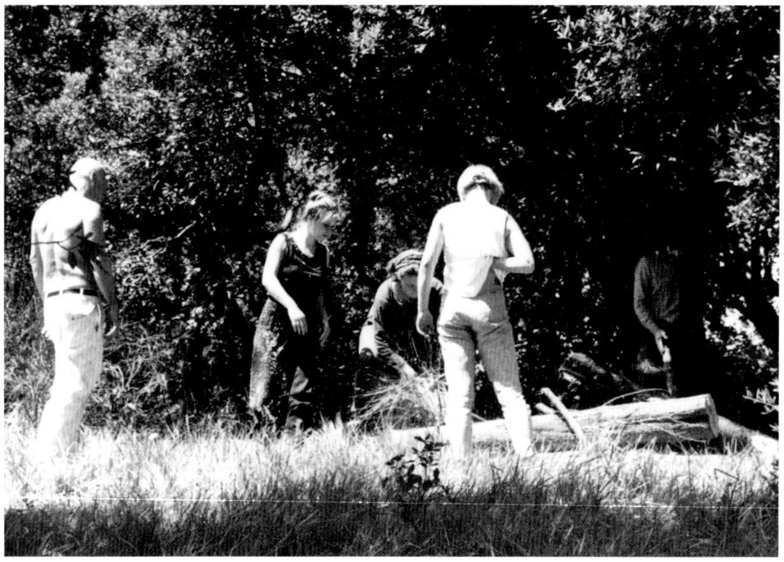

Fig. 13: Stage design students doing hands-on work with Karl Kneidl during a trip for study purposes in Volterra, Italy, 1990; from left to right: Karl Kneidl, Pia Mackert, Monika Frenz, Miriam Möller, N. N.

might think they have overcome their teacher's influence. This is the dialectic of attraction and repulsion exerted by a strong personality to whom one has been in a dependency relationship even while that personality provided the tools for one's personal emancipation. Kneidl's deliberate eschewal of style in favour of method does not simplify matters in the least. A style, a surface, is easier to reject. Thus he has remained a man whose influence lives on, as so many of his former pupils attest (Figs. 14–18):

'Since Karl Kneidl's stage designs had nothing that could be called a style, no student could imitate his stage designs, which ultimately led to an enormous freedom of possible choice.'

Katrin Brack

'I believe that the influence can be seen in all my works, and KK, of course, accompanies me sometimes in the decisions I take [...], but there it has been important that I have separated myself more and more from his "school", and now I sometimes think: KK might have done it in this or that way but here I am doing it just the same way!'

Timo Dentler

'Karl Kneidl exerted a great influence on my work. I was very impressed by his anarchic but also very sensitive and intuitive way of going at things, approaching a play cautiously, his concentrated, chaotic, yet very precise and always self-questioning way of working on the model, and also his tremendous attitude to his work.'

Philipp Fröhlich

'The love for a literary template as the cornerstone of a work in inception, appreciation of a simple sketch to a play, and the courage to follow up on that first, artistic impulse, never thinking about the characters in a play without the space nor the space without the characters. Even today those are three important factors I bear in mind when a new work is beginning and which I, if I trace back their origin, very obviously owe to working with KK.'

Okarina Peter

'I don't regard myself as a Karl Kneidl epigone, and I feel a teacher teaching or accompanying one in such a way that it doesn't come to that is the best thing that can happen.'

Anna Viebrock

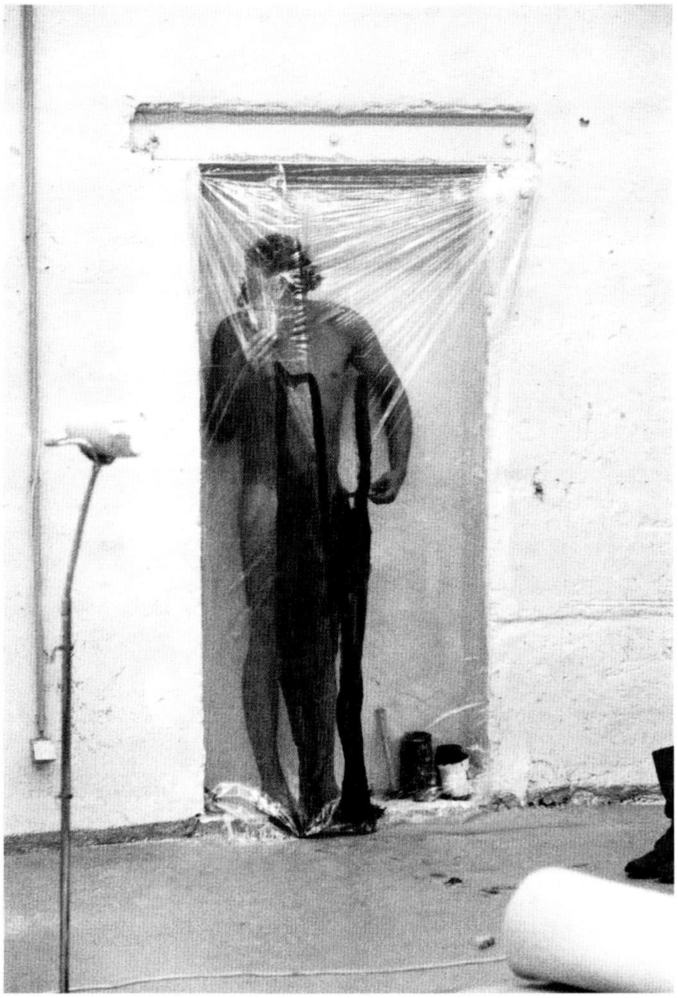

Fig. 14: *Martin Kukulies, Academy Tour, 1981*

Fig. 15: *Katrin Brack, Academy Tour, 1981*

Fig. 16: *Ruth Groß, Academy Tour, 1981*

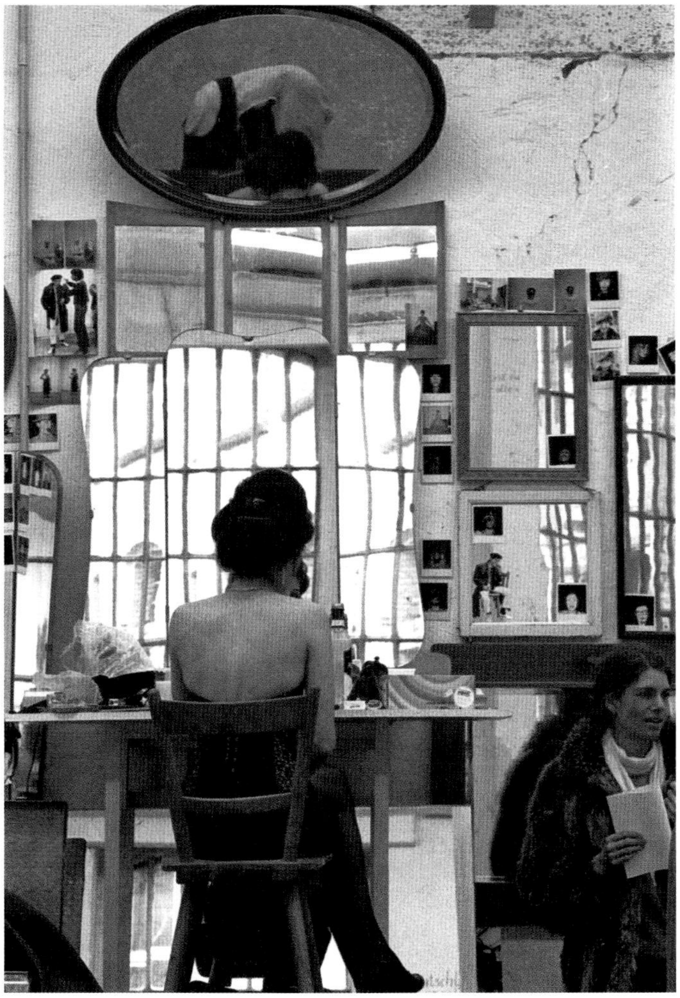

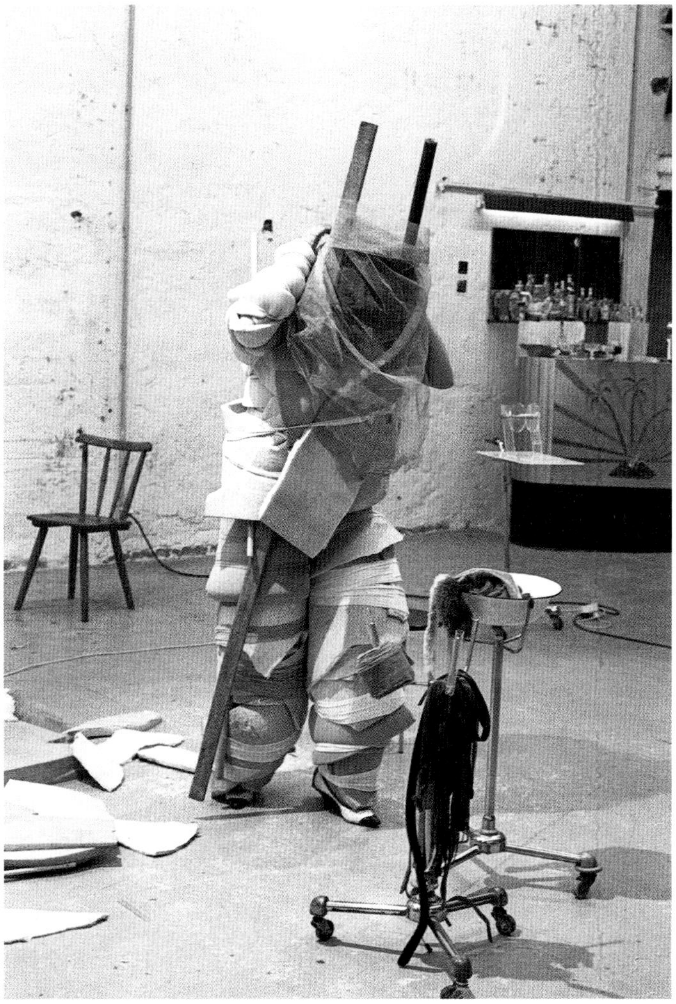

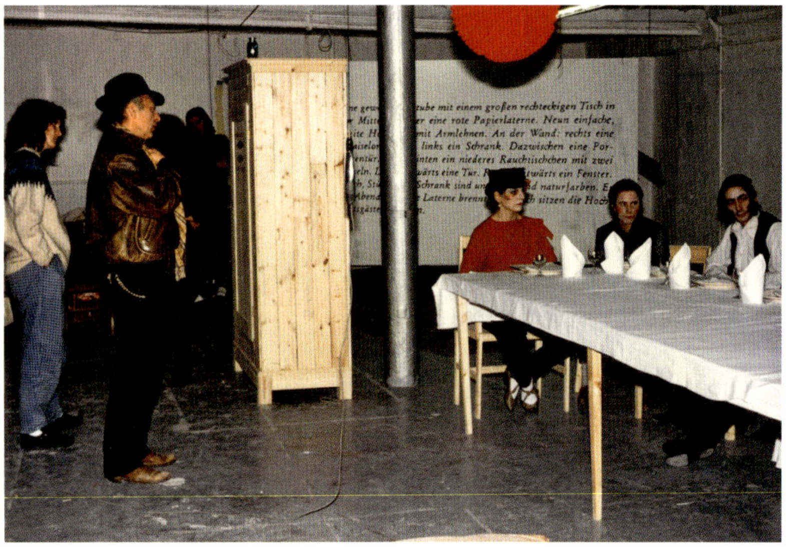

Fig. 17: A scene from Bertolt Brecht's Kleinbürgerhochzeit *[A Respectable Wedding] being read by members of the Kneidl class; from left to right: Monika Frenz, Karl Kneidl, Ruth Groß, Melanie Scheel, Oliver Kostecka, Academy Tour, 1990*

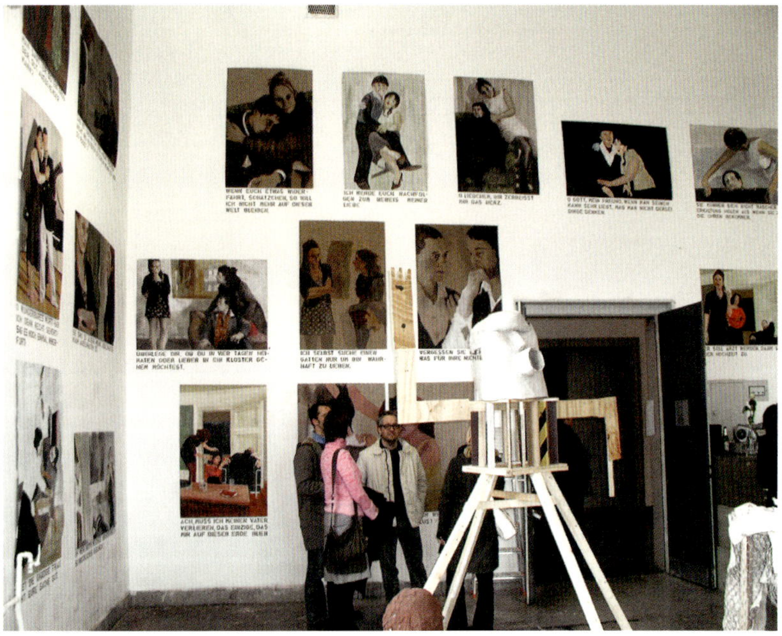

Fig. 18: The stage design class, Academy Tour, 2005

DRAMATURGES IN THE KNEIDL CLASS:[130]

Dr Axel Bornkessel (*1943)
Lectureship: 1 May 1973–15 February 1976

Michael Pehlke (*1943)
Lectureship: 16 May 1977–7 July 1979

Hermann Beil (*1941)
Lectureship: 15 October 1979–15 July 1983

Klaus-Eduard Zehelein (*1940)
Lectureship: 10 October 1983–18 July 1986

Michael Huthmann (*1945)
Lectureship: Winter term 1986/87–summer term 1988

Wolfgang Storch (*1943)
Lectureship: 10 October 1988–13 July 2007

Michael Schmitz-Aufterbeck (*1955)
Lectureship: 13 October 1997–11 February 2000

ART TECHNICIANS:

Eberhard Schweigert (1942–2004)
Summer term 1974–winter term 1974/75

Christian Göbl (*1946)
Assistant: 1 January 1976–31 July 1983

Vincent Callara (1950–1999)
Art technician teacher: 2 April 1984–30 September 1987

Ruth Groß
Teacher for special tasks from 1 July 1988 onwards

NOTES

* I am particularly indebted to Renate Stendar-Feuerbaum, a Wecus pupil, for her support. I should also like to thank the head of the Düsseldorf Art Academy library, Dipl.-Bibliothekarin Brigitte Blockhaus, MA, and Dipl.-Bibliothekarin Miriam Müller, who is responsible for the archives, for making material available, and for reproducing photographs.

1 See Form im Raum, *Walter von Wecus. Das szenische Werk*, exhib. cat. Düsseldorf 1993, p. 150; a comparable education and training institution was not added until 1936 with the Art Academy in Vienna under Emil Pirchan (1884–1957) as head of the master class in stage design.

2 They were Liselotte Bauer, Adelheid Horschik, Karl-Heinz Knoth, Alfred Kuenzer, Edith Szewczuk, and Renate Stendar-Feuerbaum. See letter written by Renate Stendar-Feuerbaum dated 23 August 2012, enclosure: Die 'BÜKUKLA' der Düsseldorfer Kunstakademie in den Jahren 1942 bis Anfang 1947 [The 'BÜKUKLA' at the Düsseldorf Art Academy in the years 1942 until early 1947].

3 Stendar-Feuerbaum (see n. 2).

4 Ibid.

5 *Jahresbericht der Staatlichen Kunstakademie Düsseldorf 1945–1947*, Düsseldorf [1948], p. 21.

6 Hence it was evidently solely Walter von Wecus's outstanding professional skill that recommended him for the 'artistic [...] design of all the lighting and the architectural articulation of the main festival street [...], the great fountain of light on the main festival square' at the 1937 Reich exhibition *Schaffendes Volk* [Creative Folk] in Düsseldorf. Walter von Wecus, 'Die große Leuchtfontäne auf der Reichsausstellung "Schaffendes Volk",' *Siemens-Zeitschrift*, Issue 17, No. 8, pp. 1–3, Berlin and elsewhere 1937; quoted in Form im Raum (see n. 1), p. 113; at the *Große Deutsche Kunstausstellung* [Great German Art Exhibition] in the Haus der Kunst in Munich for the years 1937, 1939, and 1940, he regularly showed sunny landscapes from Dalmatia, his adoptive home, which did not correspond in the slightest to the art motifs desired.

7 Letter from Renate Stendar-Feuerbaum dated 30 September 2012, enclosure: 'Zu einigen Ihrer Fragen' [Re: some of your questions].

8 Walter von Wecus, 'Wir sind ohne Nachwuchssorgen', *Musik und Szene. Theaterzeitschrift der Deutschen Oper am Rhein*, Issue 1, No. 9, Düsseldorf 1956/57, p. 104, pp. 106f.

9 See Form im Raum (see n. 1), p. 100.

10 Ibid., p. 101.

11 Ibid.

12 Ibid.

13 Ibid.

14 Ibid.

15 See *Bühnenkunstklasse der Staatl[ichen] Kunstakademie Düsseldorf* [1927], n.p. [p. 3], quoted in Form im Raum (see n. 1), p. 79. The first dramaturge and lecturer in literature for the stage design class: Dr Heinrich-Wilhelm Keim (1889–1965), verifiable from 1927–1932 on; see Walter Kaesbach (ed.), *Die Kunsthochschule von heute*, Düsseldorf 1932, p. 16; 1933–1945: Dr Alexander Schneider (dramaturgy and stage design [theory/history]; head dramaturge of the Düsseldorf City Theatres); 1933 until presumably 1934/35: outside lecturer Dr med. Fr. Erhard Haag (race study, no longer verifiable from 1940 at the latest), from: [institute brochure] *Staatliche Kunstakademie Düsseldorf*, n.d. [*c.*1933 and 1934/35, 1940, 1956, II-1957] as well as *Jahresberichte der Staatlichen Kunstakademie 1937/38, 1939, 1940, 1941–1944, 1945–1947*; 1 April 1946–ST [summer term] 1958: Willi Dünwald (dramaturgy; head dramaturge at the Bonn City Theatre), non-tenured teacher for dramaturgy. Lectures: WT [winter term] 1945/46–WT 1946/47: dramaturgy and theatre history; ST 1947: Spanish Theatre, Calderon; WT 1947/48: history of English and German theatre, from *Jahresbericht 1945–1947* (see n. 5), p. 98, p. 103; ST 1948: psychological and naturalist drama since Hebbel; WT 1948/49–ST 1949: drama in Russia, China, Japan, and India; WT 1949/50: prehistory of the theatre among Aboriginal peoples. Greek theatre; ST 1950: development of the theatre in France and England, from Heinrich Kamps (ed.), *Jahrbuch der Staatlichen Kunstakademie Düsseldorf 1948–1950*, Düsseldorf 1951, p. 138. Sources: [institute brochure] *Staatliche Kunstakademie Düsseldorf*, n.d. [*c.*1933 and 1934/35, 1940, 1956, II-1957] (unfortunately, the institute brochures are undated; hence the dates can only be cautiously estimated given the present state of the sources). *Jahresbericht der Staatlichen Kunstakademie Düsseldorf 1937/38, 1939, 1940, 1941–1944, 1945–1947*; *Jahrbuch der Staatlichen Kunstakademie 1948–1950*.

16 See the institute brochures cited 1933/34 (see n. 15).

17 See Gerda Bohrer-Borges, *Kunststudenten in Düsseldorf 1946*, Berlin 2005 [print on demand].

18 Ibid., p. 39.

19 The stage designer Wolfgang Znamenacek (1913–1953) was still working at the Düsseldorf City Stages in 1946 before accepting an offer of employment at the Kammerspiele in Munich. For many stage designers, both men and women, in the post-war years, Znamenacek, who died young, was an important point of reference, not only aesthetically but also because of his companionable manner. So the employment of Bohrer-Borges in Munich must be evaluated as particularly important.

20 Bohrer-Borges (see n. 17), p. 81.

21 Ibid., p. 87.

22 They included Max Fritzsche (1906–1999), Walter Gondolf (1912–1989), Helmut Jürgens (1902–1963), Heinz Ludwig (1910–?), Gerd Richter (1903–1979), or Ernst Anton Rufer (1904–1985).

23 Bohrer-Borges (see n. 17), p. 55.

24 That von Wecus was not at all pleased with the way his retirement was handled is shown by the fact that he asked his pupils to make submissions against the appointment of Otto to the district president, who was responsible for supervising the institute at that time. It must remain conjecture whether reservations on his part about the returned emigrant, who was of a left-wing persuasion, might have played a role. Verbal declarations by Thomas Richter-Forgách on 11 April 2000 and Helmut Grosse on 28 April 2000.

25 Interview conducted by the author with Heinz Balthes, stage designer and pupil of Teo Otto, on 24 March 2000. Real friendship on Schwippert's part for Teo Otto probably did not develop until the years during which Otto was active at the Art Academy; this development can be traced through the correspondence the two conducted. See 'Akte Bühnenbildklasse [File Stage Design Class] Teo Otto I', Düsseldorf Art Academy archives.

26 Ibid., pp. 20–22.

27 Ibid., p. 20; von Wecus, whose influence remained largely restricted to the Rhineland region, verifiably received no more commissions for regional theatres in the period after 1939; see Form im Raum (see n. 1), pp. 119–139.

28 Ibid.

29 Ibid., pp. 20f.

30 Ibid., p. 21.

31 Ibid.

32 The data on the activity at the Kassel Werkakademie, in the sources erroneously also called 'Kassel Art Academy', differ in the personnel files at the State Düsseldorf Art Academy: whereas the personal file contains on the back of the first sheet under the heading 'Temporary lecturer' the data for a limited contract for 1955–1958 to teach at the Kassel Art Academy, the CV, probably written in 1957, states: 'Since 1953 limited teaching contract at the Werkakademie in Kassel', in: 'Teo Otto I' (see n. 25), p. 3.

33 Ibid., p. 23.

34 Ibid., p. 24.

35 Letter written by Teo Otto to Hans Schwippert dated 17 March 1959, 'Akte Bühnenbildklasse Teo Otto II', Düsseldorf Art Academy archives, n.p.

36 'Teo Otto I' (see n. 25), p. 74 (copy of the certificate of appointment).

37 Ibid., p. 85 (copy of the certificate of appointment).

38 'Teo Otto II' (see n. 35), p. 59.

39 Ibid., p. 60.

40 See Michael Schoemann, *Der Bühnenbildner Teo Otto* [Univ. Diss. Vienna 1970] Philosophy Faculty, pp. 196–235.

41 See the essay by Heiner Georgsdorf, 'Eine seltsame Stadt. Teo Otto und Kassel', in: *Teo Otto (1904–1968). Der Bühnenbildner, der Maler, der Lehrer*, exhib. cat. Düsseldorf, Bottrop 2000.

42 See Teo Otto, *Nie wieder. Tagebuch in Bildern*, with foreword by Bertolt Brecht, Berlin [1950]; Teo Otto, *An die Neugeborenen, Passgänge. Literarisch-graphische Reihe XIV*, Stierstadt/Taunus 1966.
43 Letter written by Teo Otto to Hans Schwippert dated 31 December 1959, in: 'Teo Otto II' (see n. 35), p. 20.
44 See certificate of study for Zimmer issued by the Staatliche Werkakademie Kassel, Hochschule für Gestaltung, dated 5 March 1959: 'Mr Erwin Zimmer, born 19 July 1931, is herewith certified that he has been a fully matriculated student at the Staatliche Werkakademie Kassel since the summer term of 1954. He has studied specifically [...] from the summer term of 1955 until the winter term of 1958/59 in the stage design studio with the stage designer Teo Otto.' Erwin W. Zimmer estate, Theatermuseum Düsseldorf; Akte [file]: Akademie.
45 Letter written by Teo Otto to Erwin W. Zimmer, dated 5 July 1959; Zimmer estate; Akte [file]: Korrespondenz [Correspondence] Teo Otto – Erwin W. Zimmer 1958–68, Theatermuseum Düsseldorf.
46 Interview conducted by the author with Axel Vater on 14 March 2000.
47 Anna Klapheck, 'Lehrer an der Kunstakademie. Porträts der Professoren (XI: Teo Otto)', *Rheinische Post*, 15 August 1959.
48 Letter from Oleg Kasumovic to the author dated 22 February 2000.
49 [Study brochure] *Staatliche Kunstakademie Düsseldorf. Hochschule für Bildende Künste. Düsseldorf, III-1959*, n.p. (Bühnenkunst [Stage Art] Prof. Teo Otto).
50 Ibid.
51 Interview conducted by the author with Heinz Balthes (see n. 25).
52 Letter from Wolf-Jürgen Seeßelberg to the author dated 8 March 2000.
53 Michael Schoemann, 'Das Porträt. Teo Otto', *Maske und Kothurn*, Issue 14, Nos. 3/4, Vienna and elsewhere 1968, p. 355.
54 Imparted verbally by Wolf-Jürgen Seeßelberg, late February 2000.
55 Interview conducted by the author with Günter Walbeck on 31 March 2000.
56 On dealing with the youth on the basis of partnership, see Teo Otto's written reply to the opinion poll 'Generationswechsel am deutschen Theater? – Jugend und Theater' [A Change of Generation at the German Theatre? – Youth and Theatre], in: *Theater 1967. Chronik und Bilanz des Bühnenjahres* produced by the journal *Theater heute*, p. 43 (I am indebted to O. Kasumovic for pointing this out to me).
57 Interview conducted by the author with Katharina Sieverding on 3 April 2000. The assistant was Herbert Stahl.
58 Seeßelberg (see n. 52).
59 Ibid.
60 Schoemann (see n. 53), p. 355.
61 Heinz Balthes (see n. 25).
62 Note from Pit Fischer to the author dated 18 February 2000.
63 Note from Teo Otto to Erwin W. Zimmer, n.d. [1965/66], from the estate of Erwin W. Zimmer (see n. 45).
64 Letter from Karolus Lodenkämper to the author dated 10 March 2000.
65 Ibid.
66 Interview conducted by the author with Rolf Doerr on 29 March 2000.
67 I should like to thank Erinna König for placing information and material on the film class at my disposal, and Anita Kloten for the kind permission to print two crucial pictorial documents.
68 The stage class had at that time fourteen members. Half of them had begun studying in 1967. See Michael Matzigkeit, '"... damit das Tor der Phantasie geöffnet bleibt ..." Teo Otto als Lehrer an der Kunstakademie Düsseldorf 1959–1968', in: Antje Johanning and Dietmar Lieser (eds.), *StadtLandFluss. Urbanität und Regionalität in der Moderne. Festschrift für Gertrude Cepl-Kaufmann zum sechzigsten Geburtstag*, Neuss 2002, pp. 487f. The stage class would soon swell to some seventy members because Jürgen Seeßelberg – like Joseph Beuys – was against limiting the number admitted to the first term.
69 Wolf-Jürgen Seeßelberg (speech typescript), *Zur Ausstellung 'Teo Otto' im Theatermuseum Düsseldorf*, February 2001, p. 3.
70 Wolf-Jürgen Seeßelberg, 'Erinnerung an Teo Otto', *Nachrichten, Bilder, Berichte. Staatliche Kunstakademie Düsseldorf, Hochschule für Bildende Künste*, ST 1968, n.p.
71 Seeßelberg (see n. 69), p. 1.
72 Ibid., p. 5.
73 Note written by Wolf-Jürgen Seeßelberg to Karl-Heinz Stroux dated 1 December 1968.
74 Wolf-Jürgen Seeßelberg, 'Vorschlag für eine Neufassung der Bühnenbildklasse', n.d. [1968], p. 2.
75 Ibid., p. 2.
76 Ibid., p. 3.
77 Ibid.
78 Ibid.
79 Ibid.
80 Ibid.
81 Ibid.
82 See excerpt from 'Chronik der Staatlichen Kunstakademie Düsseldorf, Mai 1969', *Nachrichten, Bilder, Berichte. Staatliche Kunstakademie Düsseldorf, Hochschule für Bildende Künste*, ST 1970, n.p.
83 'Zeittafel zur Gründung der Kunstakademie seit ihrer Gründung', in: Eduard Trier (ed.), *Zweihundert Jahre Kunstakademie Düsseldorf*, Düsseldorf 1973, pp. 219–221; here: p. 221.
84 Erinna König, quoted in http://www.cultrd.us/Lutz_Mommartz_Film_Duesseldorf_Kunst_Ausstellung_Akademie_Galerie_Kunstakademie.html (last retrieved 14 September 2015).
85 See Ole John, 'Erinnerung an die Filmklasse', in: *Düsseldorf Brennpunkt 2*, exhib. cat. Düsseldorf 1991, pp. 104f.
86 Stephan von Wiese, 'Die Düsseldorfer Filmklasse', in: *Brennpunkt 2* (see n. 85), pp. 105f.
87 'Kündigung von Ole John bestätigt', *Rheinische Post*, 22 July 1976.
88 See Trier (see n. 83), p. 221.
89 Stephan von Wiese, on the other hand, sees Seeßelberg's dismissal in the context of the film class at the Art Academy being given a status of its own with new rooms and a separate budget, which meant that the stage design class was at a disadvantage: see Wiese (see n. 86), pp. 106–108.
90 Seeßelberg (see n. 52), p. 1; since the late 1970s, Seeßelberg has been in evidence mainly as a film architect. Moreover, he was a professor of film architecture, stage scenery, and production design at the Hochschule für Bildende Künste [Fine Arts Institute] in his native Hamburg from 1984 to 2006. He has been responsible for the scenery and costumes of 400 film and television productions, and he has worked, among others, with the following directors: Peter Beauvais, Heinrich Breloer, Egon Monk, Jérôme Savary, and Dieter Wedel.
91 For their support in the last part, I am exceedingly grateful to Karl Kneidl, Ruth Groß, Wolfgang Storch, and the members of the Kneidl class mentioned in the text.
92 'Bühnenbildner der Kunstakademie', *Rheinische Post*, 28 February 1974.
93 See http://de.wikipedia.org/wiki/Eberhard_Schweigert (last retrieved 14 September 2015); erroneous in this entry are above all the times given for Schweigert's stint as acting director of the stage class and the data on Wolf-Jürgen Seeßelberg and Ole John Povlsen, both of whom held lectureships at the Düsseldorf Art Academy for limited terms only.
94 Under consideration at first was a construct, according to which the dramaturge and co-founder of Concrete Poetry, Claus Bremer (*1924), would be given a professorship at the Art Academy while Karl Kneidl would limit himself as an employee to the theatre technology area. The author talked with Karl Kneidl on 21 June 2013.
95 Helga Meister, 'Nach dem Handwerk kam die Kunst. Auf ruhmreichen Posten: der Bühnenbildner Karl Kneidl', *Düsseldorfer Nachrichten*, 15 February 1975.
96 Hans Bertram Bock, 'Ein Nürnberger macht Karriere. Gespräch mit dem Bühnenbildner Karl Kneidl. Die Kargheit als Prinzip. Szenenentwürfe für Aufführungen mit prominenten Regie-Partnern an zahlreichen großen Theatern – Positives Echo', *Nürnberger Nachrichten*, 29/30 August 1970, p. 17.
97 Ibid.
98 Ibid.
99 Ibid.
100 Sibylle Maus, 'Interview zur Premiere. Heiße und kalte Herzen. Der Bühnenbildner Karl Kneidl inszeniert "Die Schneekönigin" von Jewgenij Schwarz', *Stuttgarter Nachrichten*, 29 November 1973, p. 11.
101 Kneidl (see n. 94).

102 Email from Anna Viebrock to the author dated 23 June 2013.
103 Meister (see n. 95).
104 The author presented a questionnaire to a number of members of the Kneidl class; the highly personal answers have become an essential foundation for this essay. Questionnaire, Timo Dentler, June 2013.
105 Questionnaire, Marius Baumgartner, February 2013.
106 Dentler (see n. 104).
107 Questionnaire, Ruth Groß, June 2013.
108 Dieter Stoll, 'Ständige Offenheit in extremen Welten', *Abendzeitung Nürnberg*, 22 November 1986.
109 Groß (see n. 107).
110 Note from Wolfgang Storch, 'In der Bühnenbildklasse von Karl Kneidl' [In Karl Kneidl's stage design class], 25 June 2013.
111 See questionnaire, Jasna Bosnjak, June 2013.
112 See questionnaire, Martin Kukulies, June 2013.
113 Karl Kneidl's written answer to the author's query, 'Did you have a teaching system?' on 25 June 2013.
114 See 'Vorlesungsverzeichnis' [Schedule of Lectures], Vorlesungen, Seminare, Kolloquien, Übungen [Lectures, Seminars, Colloquiums, Classes], Staatliche Kunstakademie Düsseldorf, Hochschule für bildende Künste, WT 1977/78–ST 1986.
115 See ibid., ST 1991.
116 Dentler (see n. 104).
117 Ibid.
118 Ibid.
119 Groß (see n. 107).
120 Questionnaire, Christine Gottschalk, February 2013.
121 Meister (see n. 95); see http://www.dfjp.eu/Plone/preistraeger/preistraeger-2000 (last retrieved 14 September 2015); also see http://d-nb.info/gnd/134301676 (last retrieved 14 September 2015).
122 Kneidl (see n. 113).
123 See http://de.wikipedia.org/wiki/Klaus_Zehelein (last retrieved 14 September 2015).
124 See 'Vorlesungsverzeichnis' (see n. 114), WT 1985/86 and ST1986.
125 See http://www.buehnenverein.de/de/deutscher-buehnenverein/praesidium-und-vorstand/praesidenten/klaus-zehelein_1.html (last retrieved 14 September 2015).
126 Conversation with Oliver Kostecka on 19 June 2013.
127 See also http://de.wikipedia.org/wiki/Wolfgang_Storch_(Dramaturg) (last retrieved 14 September 2015).
128 Groß (see n. 107).
129 Email from Karl Kneidl to the author on the subject of 'Defending artistic freedom' on 25 June 2013.
130 Source: 'Vorlesungsverzeichnis', Vorlesungen, Seminare, Kolloquien, Übungen [Lectures, Seminars, Colloquiums, Classes], Staatliche Kunstakademie Düsseldorf, Hochschule für bildende Künste.

'I AM OF THE OPINION THAT I ALSO MAKE SOMETHING HAPPEN.'*

Johannes Schütz talks to Annette Storr

1:1 MODEL & FAKE

There is a small band of stubbornly sceptical sectarians who assert the moon landing was an event that took place in a studio: a 1:1 model of the moonscape, an unholy alliance between Hollywood and the CIA. When I was at school, I met Neil Armstrong, who would later fly to the moon and was already famous because he had circumnavigated the globe as an astronaut. He was touring all the large European radar stations and thus came to the legendary Wasserkuppe mountain in Hesse, where gliding was born. His request to be flown around there ended up in the hands of Dr Nehrkorn, the physics teacher at my boarding school. The teacher said he would go to the English bookshop in Fulda because he had to give a present, and he bought the English edition of *Peterchens Mondfahrt* [Peter and Anneli's Journey to the Moon]. A year later Neil Armstrong allegedly flew to the moon. It looked pretty authentic on television, but it could just as well have been made in a studio. Beautiful pictures, with the flag and the footprints. A model on a 1:1 scale, like any stage set (Fig. 1).

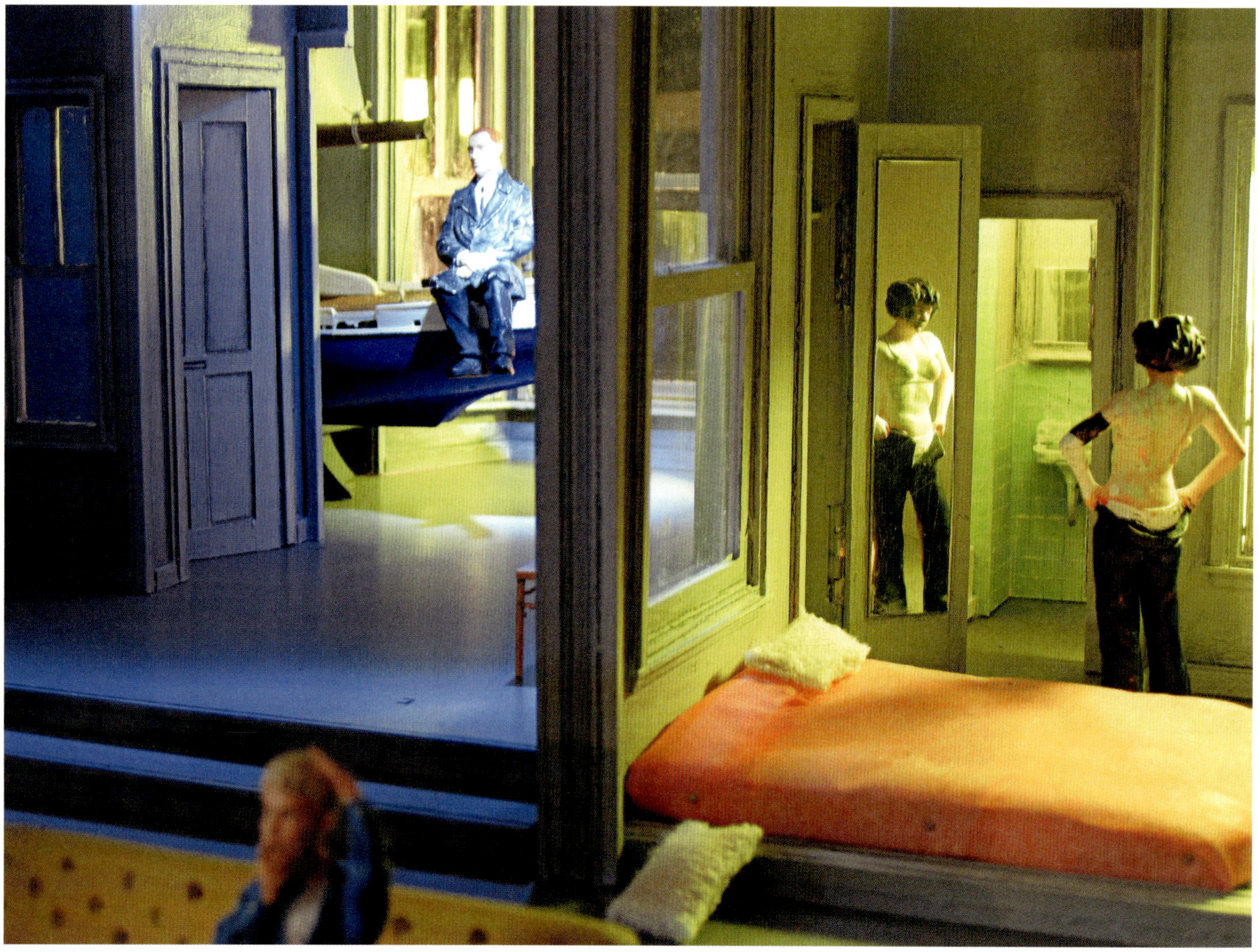

Fig. 1: Johannes Schütz, stage set to the Handel opera Ariodante*; director: Johannes Schütz, Salzburger Landestheater, 2013*

The Acropolis has been replicated by Bernard Tschumi over three floors of the New Acropolis Museum in Athens. You can see the real Acropolis through the upper-floor windows of the museum; in the three-storeyed model, all works of sculpture found have been built around an interior room of the museum: the originals in what is presumably the right place next to plaster copies for the gaps. You read that the originals of those works are displayed in London, Berlin, and Paris. The way this museum is presented is also a polemic against centrifugal archaeological excavation. On one plaster replica it says that the original is in the Würzburg University collection. Great: it's pointed out that it doesn't belong there but is missing here.

MATERIAL ISSUES

There are three materials of choice for models that have to do with antiquity. Plaster relates to the reception of Classical Antiquity but it is also a material for making plaster casts. The Staatliche Gipsformerei [State Plaster Replica Workshop] in Berlin is an interesting place for that. Plaster models were commercially viable as reproductions and the closest to marble. Then there are superb cork models, seventeenth- and eighteenth-century architectural models of Roman Antiquity. Cork cuts very well and is easy to glue. There is a large collection of architectural models made of cork in the Landesmuseum Darmstadt.

A married artist couple, Anne and Patrick Poirier, have built a model of the ruins of the library in Alexandria that burnt to the ground. The majority of ancient manuscripts were lost when the library was gutted. Some six by six metres, puddles of water, Nile water, and black swamp water, the ruins of the burnt repository of the literature of antiquity, emblematically a superlatively beautiful model made of black charcoal. It is in the tradition of those cork models and is naturally a polemic because, when you enter the room in which the model stands, you have an impression of Hiroshima. When you look at black-and-white photos of Hiroshima or black-and-white photos of Dresden after 1945, that model of the Poiriers' is a model by twentieth-century artists who have seen such photos. The decline of the wood-processing industry has been well described by Michael Krüger, as far as books are concerned; replicating the destruction by fire of the ancient library with charcoal as the material is in this sense content-related, and you think of the twentieth century until you go up closer and recognise the ancient urbanisation.

CORK, CHARCOAL, AND PLASTER

are not unrelated materials and are the predecessors of foamed plastic and polystyrene – because they are light materials, inherently stable, and easy to cut. One is the bark of the cork oak, the second is wood that has been carbonised in the absence of oxygen, and the third, nowadays, is also made as a by-product of coke, plaster as a waste product of converting coal into coke.

My models are usually made of cardboard, stiffened with synthetic wood: MDF. They look similar, this cement-grey cardboard and the battens made of wood flour to stabilise it. Dead material, as surface material and as solid material, that has a certain sculptural look about it when you cut it into small volumes; entirely unideologically, it's recycled material, like cardboard. Who knows what that cardboard may have been before it was chopped up. Then varnish, against damp, against greasy fingers; it's oiled, to ensure soundness. Models don't always grow old with dignity. You can tell from a cardboard model whether it was glued ten years ago even if you handle it with care. It's not a material that's planned to age. It's either disposable material or material used as filler or padding. Under carpeting or covered with material in car bodies or for whatever purpose it's used for unseen. But as material that is seen, it isn't meant to age. It's packaging. A model is like a manuscript or a polemic: it's supposed to achieve something. Then it is replaced by the other, the right thing, and the model no longer plays a role. Just as Thomas Demand constructs those model realities that form the basis of his photo works and supposedly destroys them afterwards.

FIREPLACES, AND THEATRE AND STAGE MODELS

Theatre models are models of empty theatres into which model stage sets are built: a model in a model (Fig. 2). Theatre models save trips. You don't have to live in the city where the theatres are in order to keep looking at the empty stage. Theatre

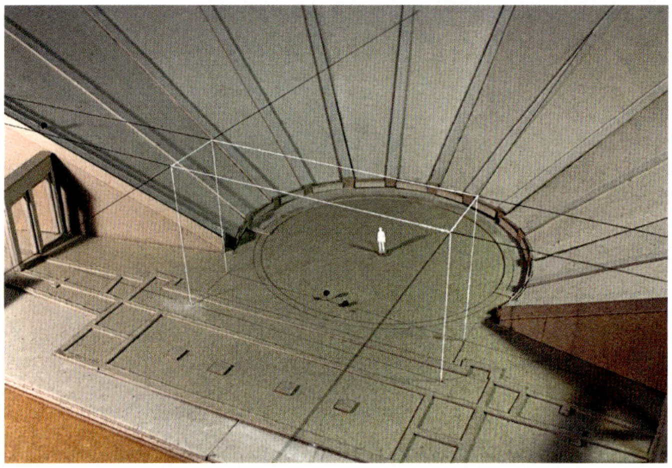

Fig. 2: Johannes Schütz, stage set model for Euripides' Orestes; *director: Yiannis Houvardas, Epidaurus Festival Athens, 2010*

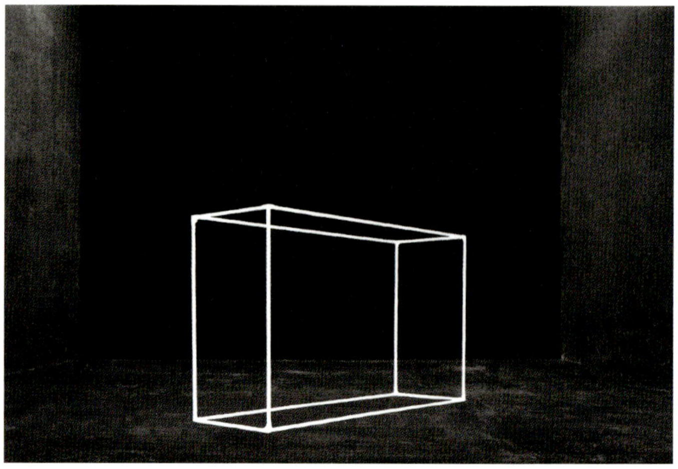

Fig. 3: Johannes Schütz, stage set model for Push Up 1–3 *and* Vor langer Zeit im Mai *[A Long Time Ago in May] by Roland Schimmelpfennig; director: Jürgen Gosch, Deutsches Schauspielhaus Hamburg, 2001*

models have something of a fireplace about them: the opening, the perspective box. Conversely, fireplaces always remind me of opera houses. When you look into that marble surround of a French fireplace, you do tend to think you're sitting in La Monnaie in Brussels. It's funny that these two openings are so very similar in certain respects. This occurred to me when I saw a contemporary print of the fire at the historic Ringtheater in Vienna, which was caused by a gas explosion when the curtain was down. You see people sitting, terrified, in the front stalls and desperate to get out; many died trying. It was an explosion like lightning striking, flames that licked through the curtain into the auditorium. The comparison between a fireplace and a portal in the theatre is obvious. Theatre models, fireplaces, are work boxes. I build most stage set models outside specific theatre models first. The *Vanya* stage set functions on a table; that's where it was developed. Or the *Seagull* model: I don't need the full stage – it's even good not to have it; the result is all the more independent. Later you have a look round where it has to stand in the theatre and sometimes you find out that it's better in front of instead of on the stage. The basic idea is independent of the theatre. It has to work outside, in a free space. That has something to do with the autonomy of a stage set. You create other norms.

THE THEATRE NEEDS CUBATURES

Cubatures are volumes, usually with edges. Cartons from inside when I look into them. From the outside they're cubes. Viewed as concave, they're cartons; seen convex, they're cubes. A room without walls is, admittedly, not a carton but it can still be a cubature, an imagined carton (Fig. 3). The stage set for *Who's Afraid of Virginia Woolf?* is a cubature. A room with eight corners, white threads as edges that are kept taut by black threads. Cubatures as stages were at first a reaction to the awkward proportions of the Düsseldorf Schauspielhaus, where Jürgen Gosch and I realised, after we'd done *Käthchen von Heilbronn* [Katie of Heilbronn] and *Hamlet*, that it's better, considering that auditorium, to play in front of the portal than on stage, and to make very clear use of space to create some sort of effect in this theatre. The stage is much too large and so is the auditorium, with its twenty-eight rows of seats, which gradually but surely slope upwards the way they do in a university lecture theatre. Two overly large rooms facing each other. You can't make the auditorium smaller but you can compress the stage. At that time I began to ask myself questions about what the theatre needs. You can build a stage that can be set up on any square in front of a train station, in any hall, and it works. After a while I made a point of not reaching out to the theatre or play but countering the play with something. Not the way Maxim Gorky imagines what he'll need for his play *Summerfolk*: a drawing-room, veranda in front of the house, a glade. We skipped that, in order to play it in the performance and not anticipate it with a stage set.

OMITTING & MAKING SOMETHING HAPPEN

With *Who's Afraid of Virginia Woolf?* I succeeded for the first time in disrupting a routine: not illustrating this conversation piece in that ghastly pseudo-realism, with the door to the loo and a view of the kitchen, the house door, and cling clang. Not that much put-upon interior that keeps on being flung together in DIY efforts, some of them well done, others less so. After Jürgen Gosch and I had put some thought into the play for a couple of months, the question arose: How far does one have to go and what can be left out? You can't just omit, you also have to make something happen that is more than what you've left out. Anybody can omit who permits himself to entertain the mere thought of it, but I flatter myself – that is why I find the description 'to reduce' wrong, that I do something that goes beyond that. More of nothing is possible. The outcome looks simple. In Roland Schimmelpfennig's *Das Fliegende Kind* [The Flying Child] it's three large bronze bells hanging in a black space – it's quite a long way to get there; you can't leapfrog anything.

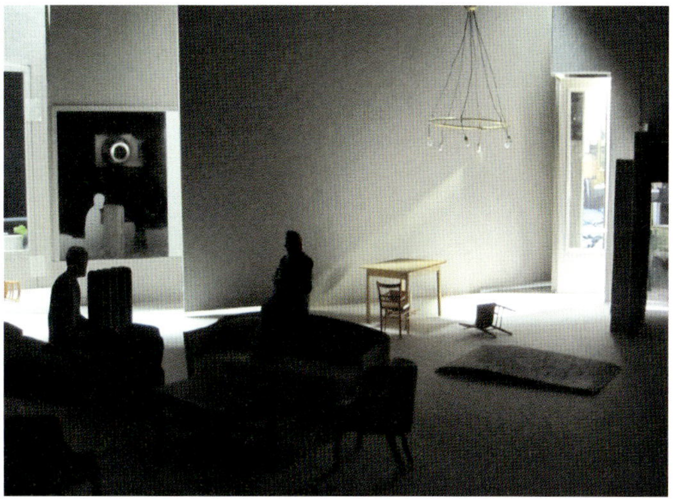

Fig. 4: Johannes Schütz, stage set model for Alkoholikerinnen *[Women Alcoholics] (working title); text and director: Thomas Vinterberg, Burgtheater, Vienna, 2012*

IN THE REAR-VIEW MIRROR: SERIES

In a stage set I rethink what I didn't succeed at in another, earlier one. That's how series come about. Not so much while you're doing it, but two, three years later you notice them. Series never happen under constraint; they always emerge in the rear-view mirror: that's where you see that it was one (Fig. 4). Working with Thomas Vinterberg on *Das Begräbnis* [The Funeral], for example, was extremely important for me. Over the course of the performance, a realistic stage set is completely dismantled. You don't just leave it away to start with and present the public with an informal cubature, but instead you start out realistically and finish abstractly, with the empty stage. This change takes place during the performance. Now this is a play by Thomas Vinterberg, not by Maxim Gorky or even Yasmina Reza, forensic protocols that allow that. I realise that such theatrical narratives are not foreign to me. Just as in the collaboration with Karin Beier, three Elfriede Jelinek plays *Das Werk/Im Bus/Ein Sturz* [The Works/On the Bus/A Fall], all you are practically making happen is a theatrical experimental set-up: how to do a collapse, a flood, on the stage (Figs. 5, 6)?

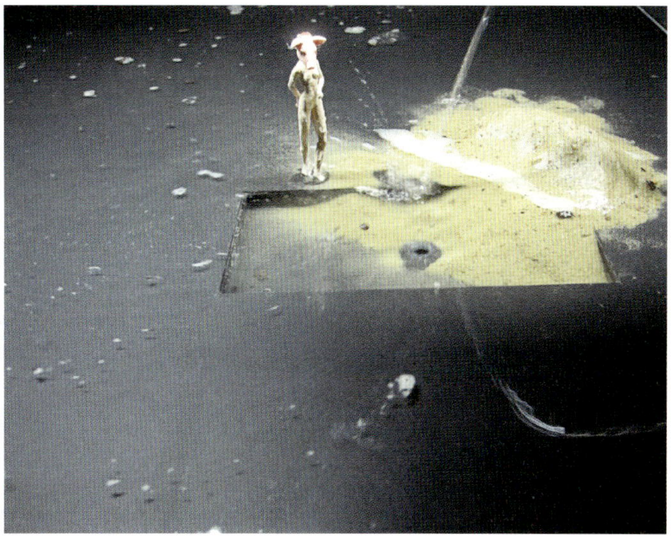

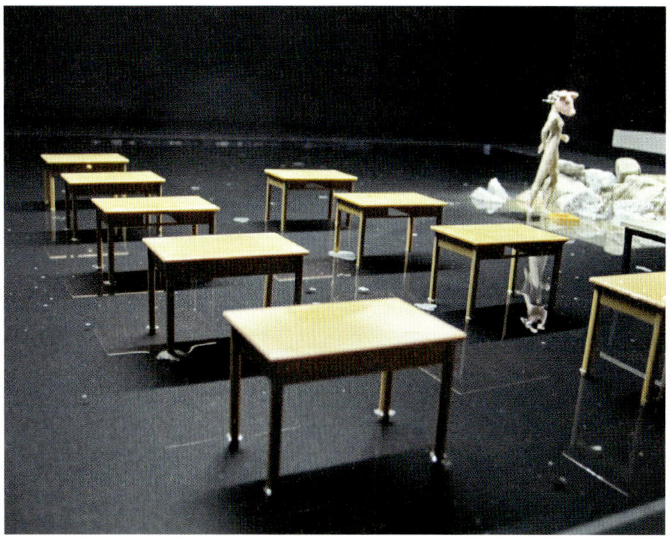

Figs. 5, 6: Johannes Schütz, stage set model for Das Werk/Im Bus/Ein Sturz *[The Works/On the Bus/A Fall] by Elfriede Jelinek; director: Karin Beier, Schauspiel Köln, Cologne, 2010*

SPOKEN IN AN ASIDE

I think quite a bit about earlier works, productions that are over and done with. But only long enough for me to find something about how it's to go on. Anti-nostalgic. I have a great memory for flops but without a therapeutic need for it. Just the question: How must you do it differently, as a craftsman (Fig. 7)?

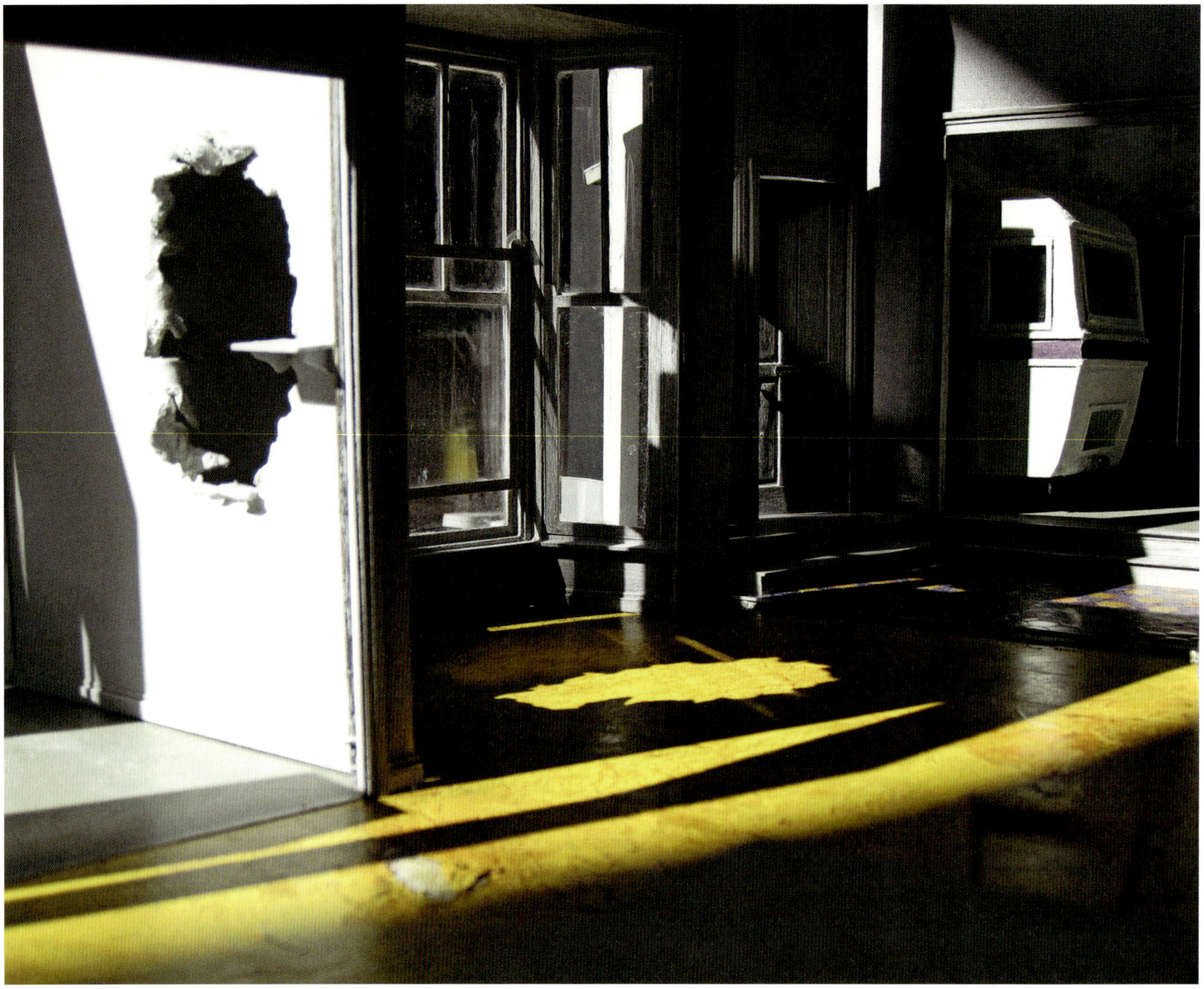

Fig. 7: Johannes Schütz, stage set model for Harold Pinter's Le Retour *[The Homecoming]; director: Luc Bondy, Théâtre de l'Odéon, Paris, 2012*

Annette Storr

Talking with Johannes Schütz, I observed an ability I admire. Jean-Luc Godard heads the phenomenon 'faire une description précise' [doing an accurate description] in his *Histoire(s) du cinéma*. It is illustrated by Johannes Schütz describing, for example, how John Cheever narrates in *The Swimmer*. When Schütz talks this way, you see how scenarios alternate, how details both seem real and mean you only see the detail needed but enhanced. The same thing happens to me sometimes with stage sets. Most recently in Paris with Harold Pinter's *Le Retour* [The Homecoming] (Fig. 7). The stage shows an entire flat, almost as in the stage directions yet differently, at once more formally and more specifically. What is interesting are the places along which the boundaries of plausibility run. For instance, the living-room floor is built far out into the stalls at the Théâtre de l'Odéon. The actors have a huge surface at their disposal on which they are displayed, where they can be subtle about how they handle their positions, and thus do a lot. This surface is glowing yellow and at the same time it's worn linoleum that's modelled like a floor mask, with break lines, dirt, the gap left by a wall that was torn out. The stage set creates – as Schütz says, 'with quality and effrontery' – a relationship of tension in which playing can make an impact.

One summer term, the stage design class was given a syllabus: eighteen points and five rules of the game under the heading 'Sehnsucht nach gekonnter Beobachtung' [Yearning for Skilful Observation]. I think you can really pin down the artist and his art with that.

NOTES

* The text is an excerpt from a discussion about work for the second volume of Johannes Schütz, *Bühnen/Stages 2000–2007*, ed. Siegfried Gohr, Vol. 1, Nuremberg 2008, which is to be published soon as *Models & Interviews 2002–2015*.

ARCHITECTURE AT THE DÜSSELDORF ART ACADEMY SINCE 1945

Agatha Buslei-Wuppermann

Since it was established in 1773, the Architecture Department has figured prominently in the range of studies offered at the Düsseldorf Art Academy. Built up around Friedrich Wilhelm von Schadow, the tradition was realigned by Hans Schwippert after 1945. His idea was to bring as many distinguished architects as possible to the Academy. Their number included Walter Köngeter, Rudolf Schwarz, Thomas Robaschik, Karl Wimmenauer, and Ernst Althoff. After Hans Schwippert's tenure as rector, a long line of eminent architects has continued to accept invitations to teach at the Academy: Hans Hollein, Ernst Kasper, James Stirling, Oswald Mathias Ungers, Laurids Ortner, Elia Zenghelis, Josef Paul Kleihues, Axel Schultes, Jórunn Ragnarsdóttir, Max Dudler, Karl-Heinz Petzinka, and Nathalie de Vries.

Over the past nearly seventy years, architecture at the Art Academy has undergone structural change. Its reorganisation was at first shaped by the traditional crafts apprenticeship, followed by diversification into a 'multilingual' approach during which it has increasingly opened up to global interconnectedness. The reorganisation of the Art Academy after the war derives from a concept advanced by Hans Schwippert, whose comprehensive proposal fell on fertile soil at the Reconstruction Ministry in Düsseldorf and after 1945 exerted the paramount influence on the direction the Art Academy would take.

THE SITUATION IN 1945

Emil Fahrenkamp, an architect who was the incumbent director of the Academy (1919–1945), saw himself as apolitical. By his definition, his teaching was entirely directed at professional practice and the needs of the time. A native of Aachen, Fahrenkamp had started his career in the Düsseldorf architectural practice of Wilhelm Kreis, and in 1911 had become an assistant and assistant teacher at the Düsseldorf Decorative Arts School, which merged with the Art Academy in 1919. Thus Fahrenkamp was a professor of architecture at the Düsseldorf Art Academy from 1919 until 1945. In the 1920s Fahrenkamp's professional successes included the first designs for high-rise buildings with steel skeletons. His best-known project was the Shell-Haus [Shell House] (1930–1932) in Berlin. He also built the Hermann Göring Meisterschule for Painting in Kronenburg/Eifel (1937). He had excellent contacts to industry and important NS leaders. That was why he was no longer acceptable as director of the Art Academy after 1945.

Matters were rather different in the case of Fritz Becker (1919–1947), another architect who had taught at the former Decorative Arts School and risen to professor status at the Düsseldorf Art Academy in 1919. Becker was government buildings overseer in the Hessian civil service until 1908 and was employed by the municipal civil engineering authorities in Darmstadt and Dresden from 1908 until 1912. He was able to stay on as a professor at the Academy until he reached retirement age in 1947 because he had remained inconspicuously in the background during the NS era. After the war Becker joined forces with Hans Schwippert to re-establish the Deutscher Werkbund and the Bund Deutscher Architekten.

RESTRUCTURING BY HANS SCHWIPPERT

Hans Schwippert had been employed by the Reconstruction Ministry in Düsseldorf since 1945. From there he took advantage of the opportunity to return to teaching in the tertiary education sector. After his political integrity had been certified, to which Ludwig Mies van der Rohe, a friend since his Berlin days, had testified,[1] Schwippert was entrusted with work that was only given to persons with the rating of 'sauber' [clean, untainted] and 'beliebig verwendbar' [can be used anywhere]. It was not long before he was being asked to work in personnel recruitment and organisation and proposing suitable teachers for the vacant jobs in architecture: 'Taking into consideration how urgent it is that appointments be made soon to the vacant chairs in the Architecture Department, I charge you additionally with proposing to me distinguished persons suitable for appointment.'[2]

Schwippert's thinking on this, which he had put into practice in drawing up the teaching plans for the Crafts and Applied Arts School in Aachen with Rudolf Schwarz from 1927 until 1934, including the idea of 'relinking artists with building', provided the basic content for the 1946 restructuring proposals. They centred on thoughts about 'upholding the idea of tradition informing the Prussian Academy of Sciences and Arts in its infinitely valuable approach but also extending activity beyond the immediate subject boundaries to the neighbouring arts'.[3]

The idea of a cultural fresh start in the spirit of the 'first' moderns was distilled into this teaching concept. Two months after his comprehensive concept proposal, Schwippert was appointed acting director of the Architecture Department.[4] In 1956 he became director of the State Art Academy, an office he held for roughly ten years.

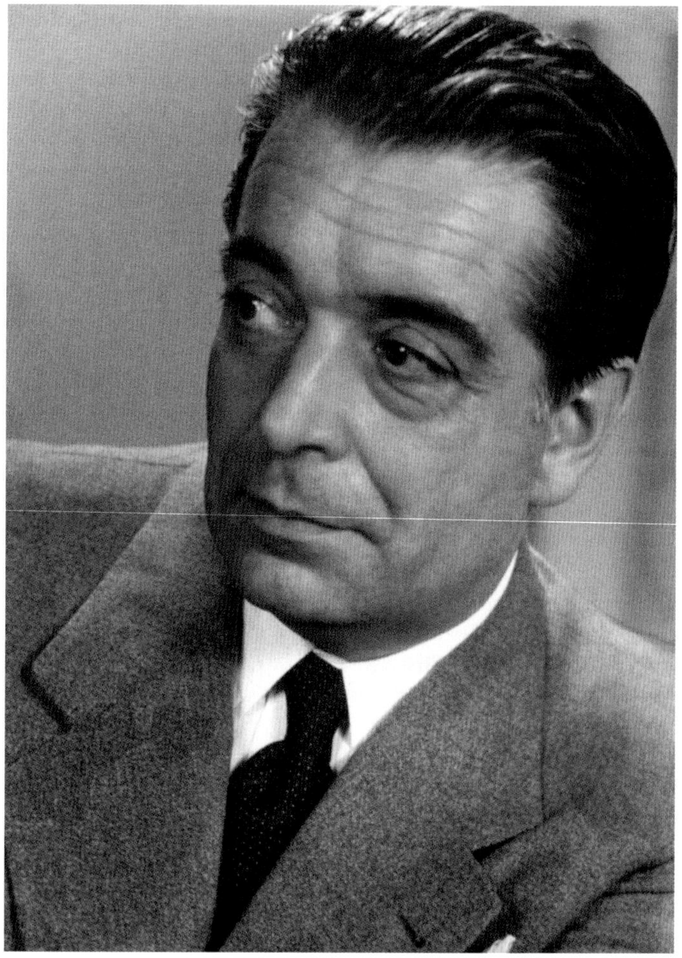

Fig. 1: Hans Schwippert, 1948

THE PROFESSORS OF ARCHITECTURE IN THE RECONSTRUCTION PERIOD

Hans Schwippert (1946–1967)

A teacher's son, Hans[5] Schwippert was himself passionate about being a professor. Students still rave about his enormous pedagogical abilities, which occasionally verged on the histrionic. When he had students design furniture, he would first task them with measuring the furniture in their family homes: how long and how broad is a book, a shoe, a boot, a child's sandal? How much space is taken up by a plate, a knife, a fork?[6]

Hans Schwippert had studied architecture at the polytechnics [today technical universities] in Hannover and Darmstadt. After taking his degree at Stuttgart Polytechnic, where he studied with Paul Schmitthenner, he worked at Erich Mendelssohn's Berlin architectural practice in 1926/27. Then he taught at the Crafts and Applied Arts School in Aachen from 1927 until 1934. There followed a limited teaching contract at what is today the Aachen Technical University, where he took his doctorate in 1943 and wrote his postdoctoral dissertation, 'Von Werklehre und Werkerziehung' [Crafts Apprenticeship and Crafts Training]. In 1945 he became technical mayor of Aachen and, until 1946, was head of architecture in the Rhine Province. That year he also became a professor at Aachen Technical University and at the Düsseldorf Academy. Schwippert was a professor at the Academy from 1946 until 1967 and director of it from 1956 until 1966 (Fig. 1).

A student of his from those days tells of shouts of 'Herr Professor, please, quick, Chicago's on the phone!' suddenly reverberating in the stairwell while a lively correction session would be going on in the Schwippert class on the second floor above the Academy offices. Then Schwippert would dash on his stubby legs down to the floor below and everyone knew that Mies van der Rohe was on the other end of the line, and that the 'Boss', as they all called him, would return to his architecture class after half an hour in the best of moods and continue correcting designs in a state of exhilaration (Fig. 2).

Changes had begun to creep in during Schwippert's last years as director of the State Art Academy. He was subjected to increasing pressure to justify what he was doing in the face of

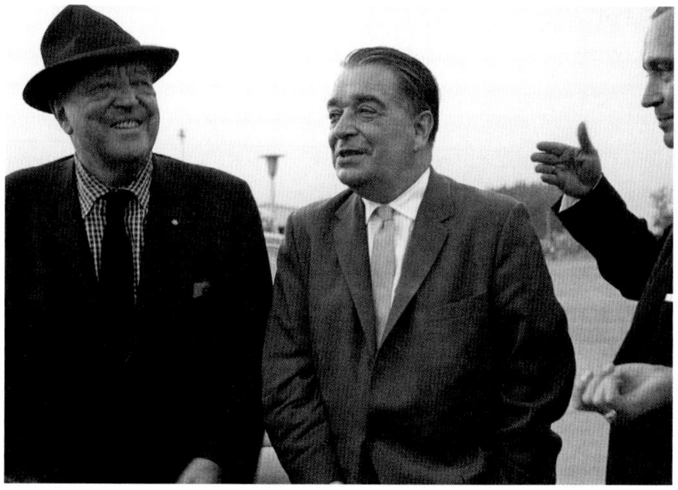

Fig. 2: Ludwig Mies van der Rohe and Hans Schwippert, Düsseldorf 1959

ubiquitous social rationalisation. Worries about left-wing criticism of 'academicism' were also voiced in his addresses, which he published in 1966. He was only too aware that his conception of the Academy as essentially a crafts community could not be reconciled with the guiding principles adhered to by the young generation which since the mid-1960s had been vehemently questioning bourgeois notions of culture and cultural institutions in a generally politicised social environment.[7]

By the time Schwippert's tenure was drawing to a close, a paradigm shift had long since taken place. Beuys and his following ultimately succeeded in pushing through the young Hans Hollein as their candidate for Schwippert's vacant chair, an appointment that shook established perspectives within the Architecture Department.

Walter Köngeter (1954–1969)

Walter Köngeter, a native of Düsseldorf, came to the Academy in 1947 to support the Architecture Department as a non-tenured senior lecturer (Fig. 3). From 1945 until 1947 the architect had been deputy head and then head of the Buildings Department in Düsseldorf. In 1954 he was appointed to the Academy as a tenured professor and was deputy director from 1964 until 1967. Köngeter was an asset to the Academy in building up architecture and ensuring its continuing development for the very reason that he had been deputy head and head of the Düsseldorf Buildings Department.

By the time he was given tenure in 1954, Köngeter had already several practical contributions to his credit to building up the Art Academy and, as a protagonist of the 'Düsseldorf architects' debate', the reconstruction of his native city. Köngeter also belonged to what was known as the Düsseldorf Architects' Association, which had been founded in 1945 to block plans for rebuilding Düsseldorf in the style of NS architecture. Köngeter was unable to prevent the buildings, designed by the architect Julius Schulte-Frohlinde (1894–1968), being built in Düsseldorf by the mid-1950s but he probably did manage to thwart Schulte-Frohlinde's attempts to become a professor at the Art Academy.[8]

Professor Köngeter, known as 'Kön' at the Academy, was a teacher who was extraordinarily popular with his students. The first work project in his architecture class tended to end in a party. He would send a student to the little pharmacy at the corner of Ratinger Straße, which also sold wine, and the bottle would be placed on the table while corrections were being discussed. At one of those correction sessions, the professor lay down on a freshly covered drafting table and asked a student to draw a line around him with a 6B pencil. No sooner was this done than he rolled up the big white sheet of paper with the outline of his body drawn on it and announced, 'I've always wanted to have a coffin made for me in the right size.'[9] He died in 1969 at the age of sixty-three and was sorely missed at the Academy. The impact Köngeter had on the Academy later often tended to be underestimated.[10]

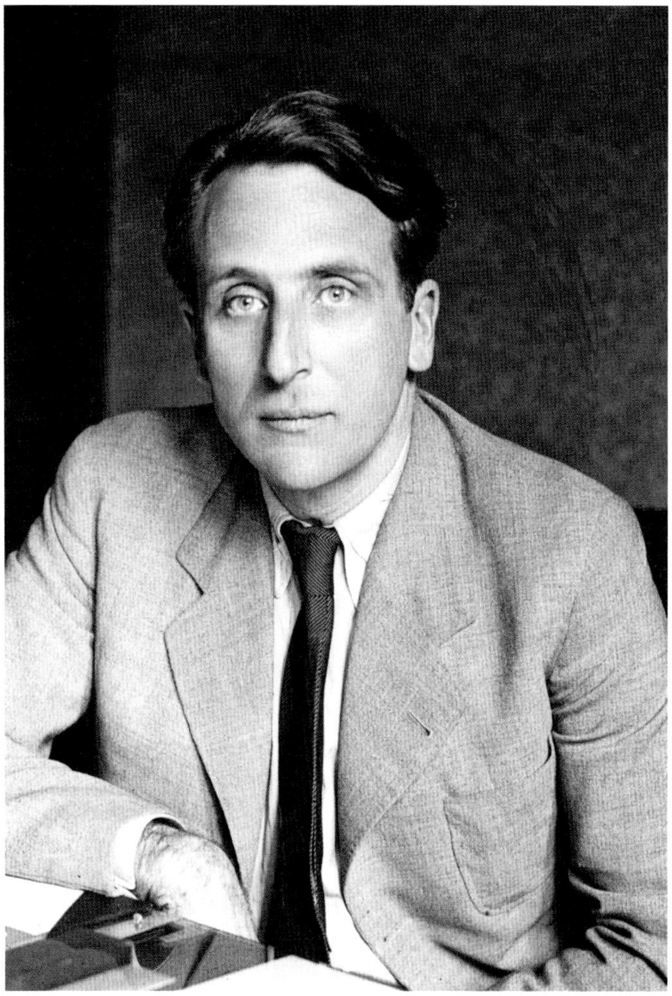

Fig. 3: Walter Köngeter, 1946

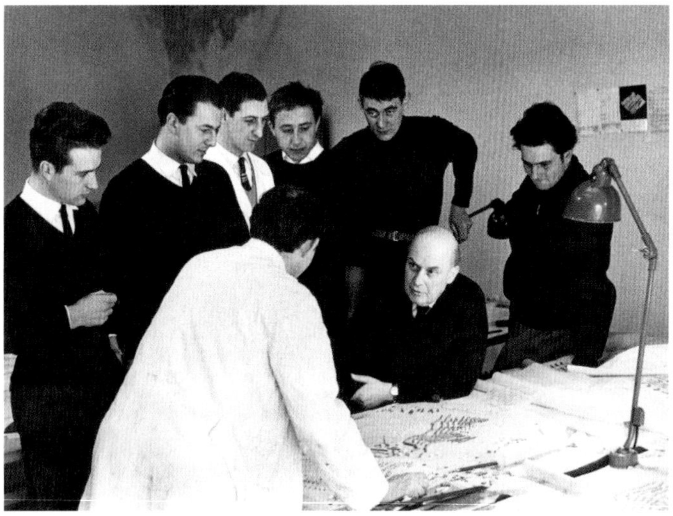

Fig. 4: Rudolf Schwarz with students, 1960

In company with Bernhard Pfau[11] and Hans Schwippert, Köngeter made a name for himself in his day with post-war architecture that was sober, objective, well-crafted, and utterly unshowy.

Rudolf Schwarz had worked closely with Schwippert in Aachen in the early 1930s so Schwippert felt confident that Schwarz was just the man to take over new tasks in architecture at the Art Academy (Fig. 4).

Rudolf Schwarz (1953–1961)

After finishing his studies in Catholic theology and architecture in Berlin and Bonn, Rudolf Schwarz entered Hans Poelzig's master class at the Arts Academy in Berlin. Afterwards he taught structural engineering at the Technische Lehranstalt in Offenbach from 1925 until 1927. Then in 1927 he founded the Crafts and Applied Arts School in Aachen, which the National Socialists closed down in 1934. After the war Rudolf Schwarz was the municipal architect in Cologne from 1946 until 1952 and organised the rebuilding of the city. His professional breakthrough came when he rebuilt the Paulskirche in Frankfurt am Main in 1948. He kept practices in Frankfurt and Cologne.

As early as April 1946, Schwippert was writing to Schwarz to sound him out on an appointment to the Academy on the lines of their successful collaboration in Aachen.[12] Schwarz was finally appointed professor in 1953. From then on he was a keen educator who gave priority to working independently within a collective. He did not want disciples who followed his teachings to the letter; instead he accompanied his students in the process of finding their own individual form of expression. He took great pains with promoting students on an individual basis, using his personal contacts to industry to make travel grants available to his students, under one condition: Schwarz wanted to see a full sketchbook on a student's return from his travels. Those trips were subsequently the subject of lively class discussion so that everyone might benefit from them.[13]

Rudolf Schwarz did not have a driving licence. He went everywhere on foot or took the train. He was so conscientious that he would arrive at the Academy from Cologne Müngersdorf at 8 o'clock in the morning, usually before any students were there.[14] Former students from his class still vividly recall pithy pronouncements of his, such as 'Infantile paralysis has broken out here'. He was able to explain the language of his architecture so lucidly that it is still relevant today.

Schwarz and Schwippert were always on friendly terms as colleagues, yet they retained the formal form of direct address, 'Sie', when talking to one other. Whenever one of them had a problem and was up to his shoulders in work, he could rely on the other. The teamwork Schwarz practised personally with his colleagues distinguishes him as a role model and great teacher (Fig. 5).[15]

His colleagues at the Academy were deeply affected by his untimely death in 1961. It led to the appointment of Karl Thomas Robaschik as his successor at the Academy.

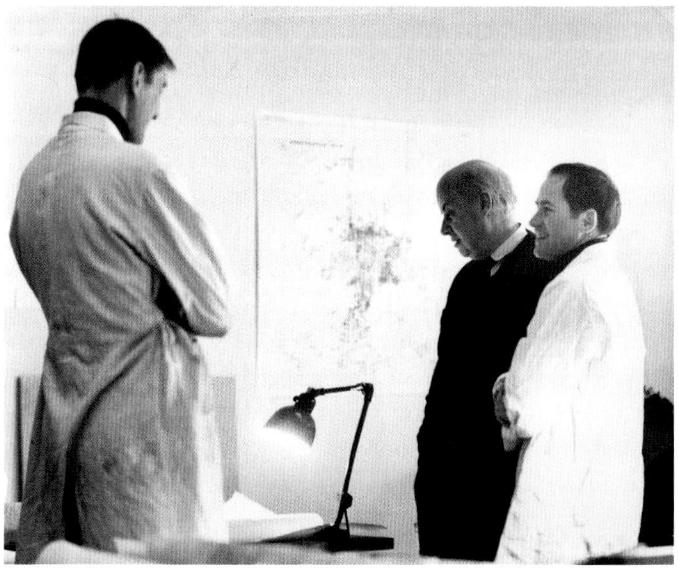

Fig. 5: Rudolf Schwarz, Dieter Georg Baumewerd (left), and Ludwig Tipelmann (right) at the Düsseldorf Art Academy, c. 1960

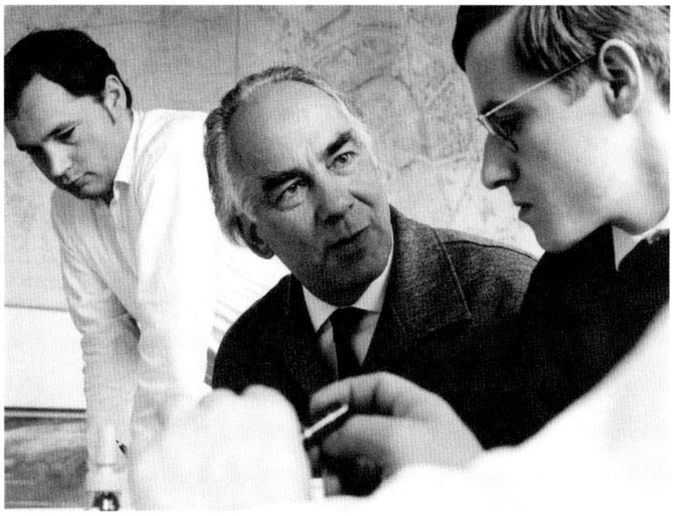

Fig. 6: Karl Thomas Robaschik with students, 1960

Karl Thomas Robaschik (1962–1978)

Robaschik brought with him experience in the fields of urban planning and spatial development that he had acquired after the Second World War as head of the Civil Engineering Authority in Hamburg Altona and director of the Regional Economic Planning Board of the City of Hamburg (Fig. 6).

The student generation of the late 1960s tended to prefer what was known as 'Corbu font' (a special font form developed by Le Corbusier). Robaschik set great store by its use because it was still legible when reduced to A4 format. The professor had come to value its usefulness when he worked in administration.

Thomas Robaschik was skilful at involving his students in his diverse development schemes. They entailed structural studies and the development of entire cities or working hypotheses for future town development. Very typical of his approach were student working groups that collectively studied the topographic situation on site, the site's form, and its significance and documented their findings in book form. The object of their study might well be the place in Switzerland where the professor spent his holidays.[16] When it was a question of local design planning in Düsseldorf, Professor Robaschik might also speak out in the local press with alternative proposals. In one 1970 study he presented a vast development plan for Grabbeplatz, replete with the shopping passages so typical of the time, underground access, escalators, and a high-rise carpark on the site where the K20 Art Museum now stands.[17]

Work was carried out in the manner typical of the times in the Robaschik class on the third floor of the main Academy building (now the photo class taught by Professor Christopher Williams), a long, narrow room with strip fenestration along one side and large drafting tables placed in front of it. Each table was equipped with a T-square and what was known as an architect's lamp. Angles, drawing templates, and drafting stencils belonged to the tools of the trade and so did pencils ranging in hardness and thickness from 4H to 6B as well as a large number of technical drawing pens, 'Rapis' [Rotring Rapidographs], for drawing lines of varying thickness. The opposite wall provided generous surface space for hanging up huge plans. The final version of a plan was drawn with Rapidographs on tracing paper. In one corner of the room there was a deep rectangular porcelain sink[18] that was spotted all over with ink. This was where special mixtures were tried out and experiments were conducted with diluting black drawing ink to create shades of grey. The most difficult thing was cleaning Rapidographs and fitting them with those tiny ink-filled cartridges. That seldom happened without complications and this led in the Academy to the saying, 'Architects are recognised by their inky paws'.

ARCHITECTURE BETWEEN TRADITION AND VISION

Karl Wimmenauer (1963–1979)

After traumatic war experiences and internment as a prisoner of war, Karl Wimmenauer discovered historical plans in the drawings portfolio of his father-in-law, the architect Franz Schneider, which would determine his future career.[19] Wimmenauer had studied architecture at Darmstadt Polytechnic and after the war worked for Rudolf Schwarz's practice for ten years. Then he was Hans Schwippert's assistant from 1957 until 1961. Recognising Wimmenauer's teaching abilities, Schwippert brought him to the Academy as a professor of architectural history. He was given tenure in 1963. Until he retired in 1979, Wimmenauer constantly intervened in what was going on at the Academy with contributions, protests, and also constructive designs (Fig. 7).

Whenever the preservation of historic monuments or conserving historic buildings was concerned, Wimmenauer was always actively and aggressively committed. When a terrace of nineteenth century houses in Berger Allee in Düsseldorf was supposed to be torn down to make way for an extension building at Mannesmann in the early 1970s, Wimmenauer mobilised residents and students alike against the gentlemen from Mannesmann. He organised rallies and demonstrations. And when the houses were demolished after all, he suffered dreadfully.[20]

Karl Wimmenauer was also a gifted draughtsman: his narrative talent was often transferred via his handwriting to

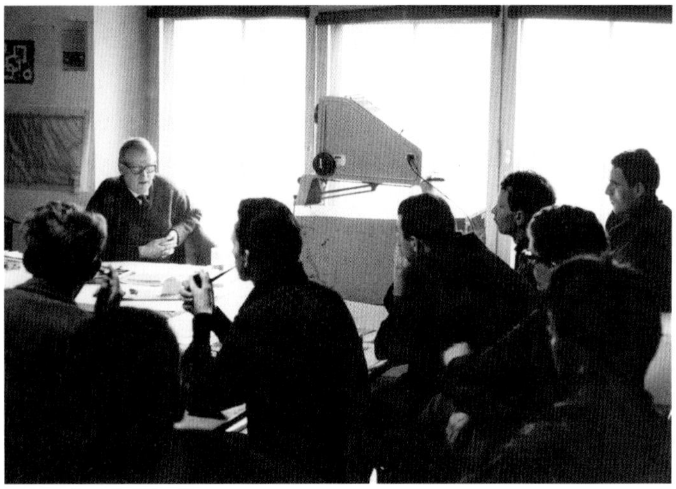

Fig. 7: Karl Wimmenauer with students, 1960

drawings. His great love was nineteenth-century architecture. He was also partial to French Revolutionary architecture as represented by Claude Nicolas Ledoux (1736–1806) and Jean-Nicolas-Louis Durand (1760–1834), and he would rave about Eugène-Emmanuel Viollet-le-Duc (1814–1879). At the same time he succeeded in making the likes of Hendrik Petrus Berlage (1856–1934) and the ground plan of the Amsterdam Commodities Exchange understandable. He could skilfully dissect ad hoc the Postmodernist work of James Stirling, for instance, in its historical context. He could be just as enthusiastic about the 1959 building at the University of Leicester as he was about Stirling's way of dealing with street space. Wimmenauer, shaped as he was by a profound understanding of architectural history, was the one, finally, who proposed James Stirling as a candidate for a professorship in architecture. Stirling was appointed to teach at the Academy in 1979.

The Art Academy is indebted to Karl Wimmenauer for a great many productive ideas. In the great Joseph Beuys controversy, Wimmenauer spontaneously assumed the role of negotiator. When Beuys was finally forbidden to enter the Academy, Wimmenauer stood by him. Meetings with Beuys took place from then on at 'Wimmi's' on Kaiser Wilhelm-Ring 'over the way' on the other side of the Rhine in Düsseldorf-Oberkassel.[21] Wimmenauer always sympathised with his students when they had problems. He would even instruct some of them individually. He also anticipated the coming multilingualism in architecture. He liked to collect exciting people. Beuys himself was often in Wimmenauer's class, where he would contribute to correction sessions with lively discussions.

Ernst Althoff (1973–1993)

Ernst Althoff had – after training as a cabinet-maker in his father's workshop – begun to study architecture in Krefeld in 1944, during the war. While a student at the Düsseldorf Art Academy in 1950, he encountered Hans Schwippert, who discovered Althoff's particular talent for working with wood. After taking his final examinations at the Art Academy in 1957, Althoff was ready to face the enormous challenges that awaited him in Schwippert's practice.

The 'Boss' (Schwippert) was on the planning staff of the young Federal Republic of Germany for the 1958 Brussels World's Fair. Ernst Althoff (Fig. 8) developed and drew furniture and furnishing elements that were then made for the Brussels World's Fair in the workshop run by his father, Johannes Althoff. Ernst Althoff's organisational skills were also in demand at the 1967 Montreal Expo.

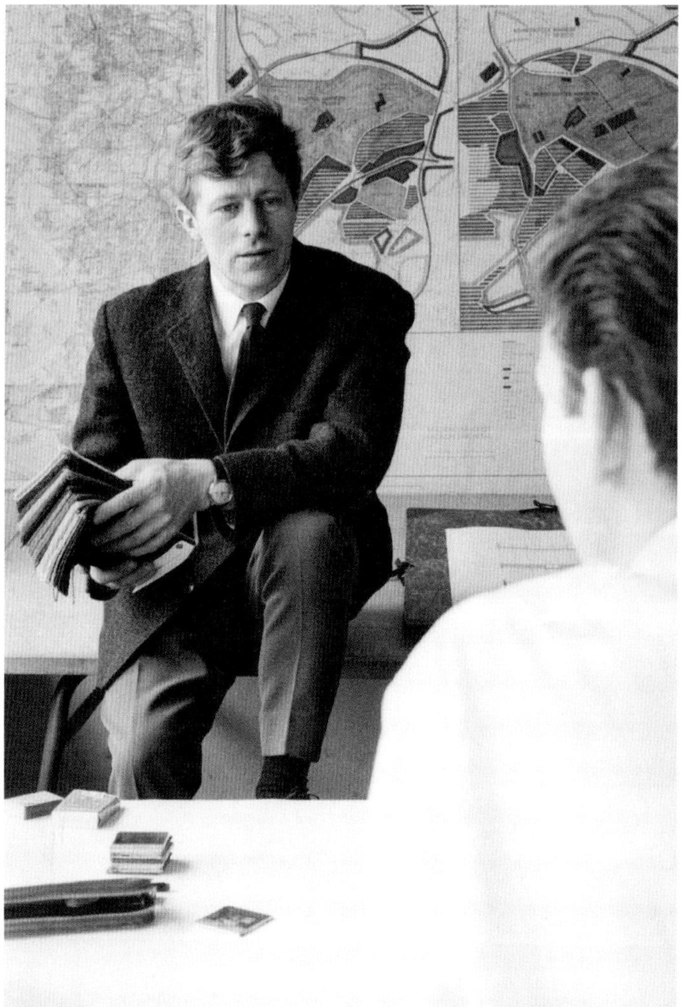

Fig. 8: Ernst Althoff, teaching, 1960s

During the reconstruction era, Althoff was actively involved with the young Deutscher Werkbund, founded in 1950 by Hans Schwippert. In Schwippert's studio he supervised teams working on numerous projects. In 1962 Althoff was awarded the State of North Rhine-Westphalia Promotion Prize for young artists. A year later, in 1963, he began to teach at the Art Academy, at first as a lecturer, then from 1973 until 1986 as professor of interior design and exhibition architecture. From 1986 until 1993 he was a professor of architecture.

In the late 1960s students felt particularly at home in the Althoff class. It was a warm and cosy place particularly conducive to learning. The light was always on and there was always hot tea. The class was in Room 203 on the second floor of the main Academy building: a two-storeyed studio room with a northern exposure and a huge window looking onto the Hofgarten park and the Rhine as well as a narrow steel staircase in the corner leading to the upper floor, where there was occasionally makeshift accommodation for needy students.

The developments of the day were experienced here at close range. For the *Rundgang* [Academy Tour] at the end of the 1967/68 winter term, the Althoff students set up an 'architects' breakfast': empty Coke and beer cans were placed on one of the large studio tables along with paper plates with leftovers and stubbed-out cigarettes on them. The whole thing was covered with plastic film, which didn't keep interested visitors from turning up their noses. Ernst Althoff found himself increasingly attracted to the 1960s zeitgeist. His ideas were listened to by the Art Academy's General Students' Committee. He was the one to urge the necessity of a chair in sociology.

Hans Hollein (1967–1976)

Thirty-six years old at the time, the architect Hans Hollein[22] wasn't really envisaged at the Academy in the mid-1960s. The Academy professors already had their candidate of choice to succeed Schwippert and he was ready and willing. Joseph Beuys, however, who enjoyed being involved with the architecture classes then, had sniffed out what was in the air and spontaneously set off for Vienna in 1965 to headhunt Hans Hollein, still virtually an unknown quantity, to fill the 'Schwippert vacancy'. Hollein would later tell the story of Beuys standing excitedly outside his flat in Vienna, asking him through the door whether he wanted to become a professor at the Düsseldorf Art Academy.[23]

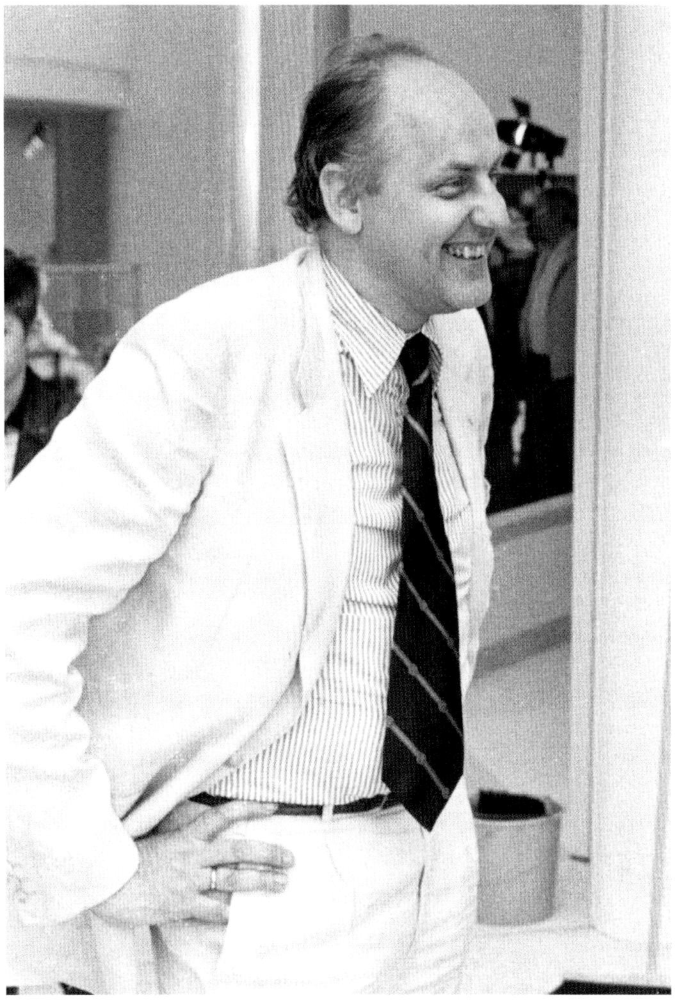

Fig. 9: Hans Hollein, 1982

Yet the idea of employing this rebellious visionary[24] was at first received with extreme scepticism at the Art Academy (Fig. 9). Some professors had never even heard of him as an architect. A member of the appointments committee, to whom the name was unknown, is said to have asked, while leafing through his application papers, whether this Hollein had ever built anything with two storeys.[25] Nor had he, in fact. All that he had to his credit were three little conversions and renovations of Viennese shops, one of which, with only 14m² floor space, was Retty, a shop selling candles at the Kohlmarkt in Vienna. It had conveniently become a magnet for an entire generation of architects in 1965. Hollein's appointment to teach at the Düsseldorf Art Academy was finally approved and he began at the beginning of the winter term of 1967/68.[26]

He taught at the Academy from 1967 until 1976. During that time he designed the Städtisches Museum Abteiberg in Mönchengladbach.[27] While the museum was under construction, a working model filled an entire room used by the Hollein class, which was on the mezzanine above what is now the chancellor's office in the main building. A second classroom was used as a building office. Student design correction, which

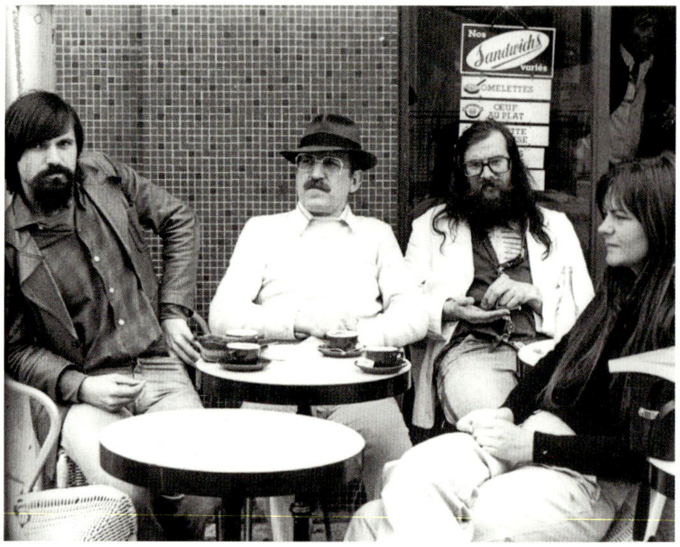

Fig. 10: Trip to Paris; from left to right: Reinhard Scheithauer, Ernst Kasper, Alfons Augustin, and Mechthild Kaiser, 1978

often began late in the evening, took place in the third room. Hollein's enormous success and the award of the Pritzker Prize (1985) came much later.

Strife often escalated among colleagues in the Architecture Department at that time. Hollein enjoyed it when the mood heated up. During a panel discussion in the Great Hall about stances on the postmodern design submitted to the competition to build the Stuttgart Staatsgalerie, which James Stirling had just won, Hollein sat with Stirling, Günter Behnisch, and Werner Oechslin on the podium. The discussion soon lurched out of control. With statements such as, 'We must liberate architecture from building!',[28] Hollein so infuriated Günter Behnisch, who had come from Stuttgart for the discussion, that he jumped up and left the room in a huff. Today Hollein says, 'I particularly appreciated the intense discussions in small groups that didn't become interesting until almost midnight. And there were some students who were particularly important to me, such as Thomas van den Valentyn, who is now a very important architect in Germany.'[29] Hollein was made an honorary member of the Düsseldorf Art Academy in the Great Hall in 2010. After receiving the honour, Hollein insisted on seeing Mönchengladbach again. His time at the Academy was closely bound up with the first museum he built.

Ernst Kasper (1971–2000)

The collaboration between Hans Hollein and Ernst Kasper went well from the start but not without hitches. Kasper was good at boiling architectural phenomena down to their essence. That impressed even Hollein. After studying architecture at RWTH Aachen [Technical University], Ernst Kasper was first employed as a student assistant to the chair held by Professor Mertens there.

In 1963 Kasper was awarded the Promotion Prize of the Federal Association of German Industry, which enabled him to travel extensively in Greece. After that he became an academic assistant to Professor Fritz Eller at the School Architecture institute at RWTH Aachen. In 1964 Kasper founded an architecture practice in Aachen and initially worked in partnership with Karl Wimmenauer. During that time they entered numerous competitions for building schools and wrote essays and gave lectures on the subject. From 1971 until 2000 Ernst Kasper was a professor of architecture at the Düsseldorf Art Academy (Fig. 10). After he retired in 2000, he was a non-tenured professor at the Escuela de Arquitectura, Universidad Austral de Chile in Valdivia. Working there with former students to create simple affordable housing was a task that he found fulfilling.

Whenever Kasper was seen to pull himself up by the stair handrail to reach his studio in the Academy on a Tuesday, that meant, 'He's in pain' and 'watch out' with the corrections. Chronic spinal disease since he was twenty-seven had stiffened his backbone and left him straight as a ramrod. Straightforwardness runs through his work. He liked to assign little design tasks to counter the danger of 'organisation along school lines' to new students. No one was Kasper's equal in making

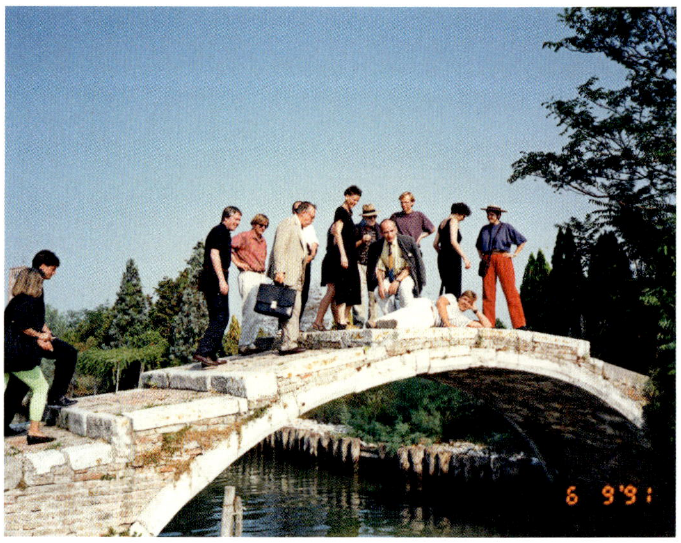

Fig. 11: Trip to the Venice Biennale, excursion to the Ponte del Diavolo on Torcello, 1991

architecture-related phenomena understandable by explaining them simply.

Works were produced in the Kasper class with titles such as Haus am Waldrand [House at the Edge of the Forest] (1982/83), Haus im Haus [House in a House] (1982), Einfaches Haus [Simple House] (1985), Ein Haus an der Steilküste [A House on a Coastal Cliff] (1985), Felsenhaus [Rock House] (1985), and Haus in den Bergen [House in the Mountains] (1986). Those works were selected for the 1991 Venice Architecture Biennale, which provided ample opportunity for an extensive field trip for the entire class (Fig. 11).

As simple as they seemed, such projects became key experiences, especially for students at postgraduate level. The discussion sessions with Kasper were often hard but important if a student was to grow with the challenge. His attitude to architecture made him always open-minded about experimental approaches. He preferred to work with working models, which he would distort during correction sessions or might develop further with a few sketches on tracing paper. Students were given his sketches, which always bore a date, as aids to correction. Students and colleagues alike could always count on Kasper being accessible. Despite a profound dislike of public honours, he did enjoy the big farewell party given for him in the Rheinflügel [Rhine Tract] of the Academy on 6 December 2000, when he retired after twenty-nine years of service. Since his death in 2008, the 'Kasperians' have had a reunion every year in early December.

James Stirling (1979–1989)

James Stirling taught architecture at the Düsseldorf Art Academy for ten years. He had established his first practice in London in 1956. By the time he was appointed to teach at the Academy, he was already extremely successful and had an honorary doctorate from the Royal College of Art in London to show for it. Moreover, he had been a recipient of the Alvar Aalto Medal in 1978 and was awarded the prestigious Pritzker Prize in 1981. Shortly before his death, he was knighted in 1992.

Stirling, fondly dubbed 'Big Jim' by Academy students, exuded a soothing evenness of temperament as a teacher. Completely at ease with himself and his enormous bulk, he was concentrated and curious when he immersed himself in plans

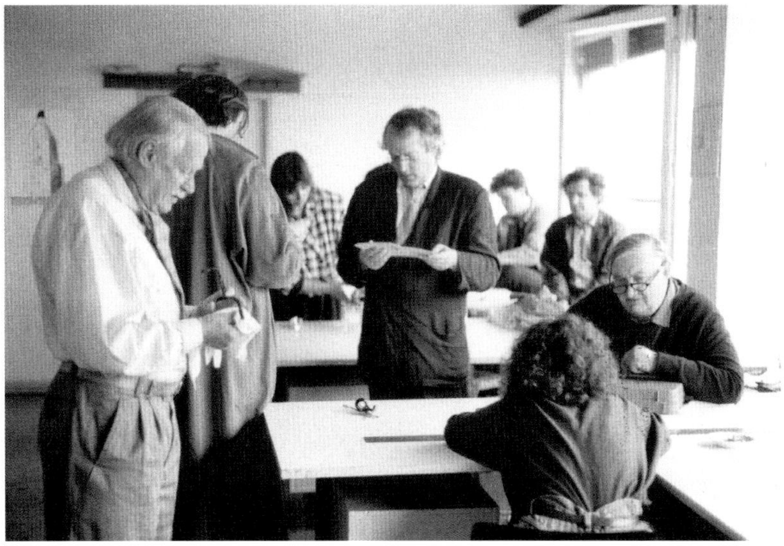

Fig. 12: From left to right: Karl Wimmenauer, Thomas van den Valentyn, and James Stirling in the architecture class, 1985

drawn by students. He obviously enjoyed going through the ground plans. The flock of students whom he collected around him regularly on Tuesdays on the third floor of the main building (formerly the Robaschik, now the Williams class) until his class moved into the Rheinflügel (in 1989) grew larger and larger by the week (Fig. 12). He liked to blend his creed as an educator, 'learning from role models', with a dry English sense of humour. He was always building practical tasks and spontaneous excursions into his classes. He liked taking students with him to consultations on construction sites – for instance, to the new Staatsgalerie in Stuttgart when it was under construction.[30]

His great role model was Karl Friedrich Schinkel. While he was working on a commission for the Tate Gallery[31] from his London practice,[32] he hung his own work up on the long wall – without his name on it – at a pre-presentation among the designs submitted by his students. His work, too, ended up by being vehemently criticised by the students and even panned in part. His delight in such situations and, along with it, his distinctive Anglo-Saxon sense of humour were evident. When 'Big Jim' took up a 6B pencil in his large, fleshy hands to draw his delicate, sophisticated sketches and alternatives to a design at a correction session, a rapt silence would grow up around him. He would generously give his sketches to his students to take home with them (Fig. 13).

As overweight as he was, he liked to sit among his students on one of the small, three-legged stools with seats that were at most 27 cm in diameter. Next to him stood his modest luggage, 'the fuel tank': it was a small, toxic green shell suitcase. He used to rave about the brilliant way the two identical plastic parts fitted together. He was equally fascinated by the design of his transparent plastic wristwatch in a silver-grey watchcase, in which 'the works are constantly working'. On all occasions he wore cobalt-blue shirts – with the sleeves rolled up at correction sessions. His hands and lower arms were chronically

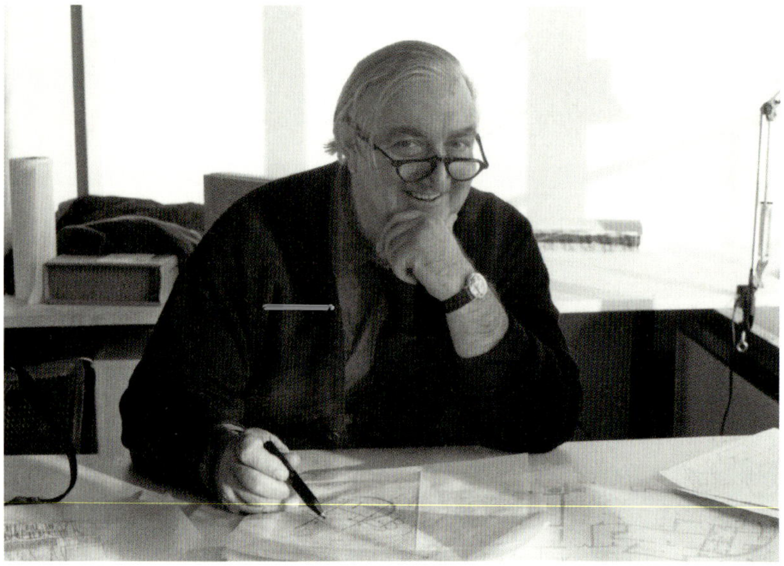

Fig. 13: James Stirling in the Düsseldorf Art Academy, 1987

marked with traces of lead pencil, even on numerous occasions early on Tuesday mornings when he would take the first plane to come to the Art Academy from his London practice. Those correction days usually came to a sudden end in the evening, when he would glance at his plastic watch and notice that it was high time to catch the flight back.

Then some students would quickly pack him into a car. He liked best to be carted around in a 2CV, with the suspension so displaced from the moment he squeezed himself into it that it almost dragged on the ground.[33] The main thing was to have just enough time after checking in at Düsseldorf Airport to top up that little green 'fuel tank' so that it was full to the brim of chocolates for the flight back. The students from his class threw a lavish farewell party for 'Big Jim' in 1989 with a sumptuous repast and fireworks in front of the Rheinflügel.

ARCHITECTURE AT THE ACADEMY SINCE 1986

Oswald Mathias Ungers (1986–1991)

The appointment of Oswald Mathias Ungers in 1986 coincided with a time of structural change (Fig. 14). Long before he was actually appointed to teach at the Art Academy, his name had often cropped up whenever there was a vacancy in architecture. In the 1970s his type of architecture seemed too uncompromising to some Academy professors. Then 'the man with the squares'[34] did make it to the Academy after all in 1986. And he came with a lot of baggage: in specialist publications he had acquired a reputation that was not to be sneezed at as an architect and architecture critic. He had lived for over a decade in the United States, where he had taught at prestigious universities. By the 1950s Ungers had begun to build up an architecture library of his own, which now houses in Cologne such treasures as a first edition of Vitruvius (1495) and early editions from the Weimar Bauhaus era (1919–1923).

The initials 'OMU' symbolise his architecture. Apart from international experience as an architect, he also had the intellectual stature to develop postgraduate studies in architecture at the Academy. Ungers, who preferred to spend his lunch break alone in his studio with a book, was not eager to seek communication with his colleagues. The 'Midday Academy', which usually convened on Tuesdays from 1 p.m. to 4 p.m. at the Italian restaurant in Ratinger Straße, was not his scene. He would react to invitations to join in with lame excuses such as, 'My wife hasn't given me enough money.'[35] It wasn't long before

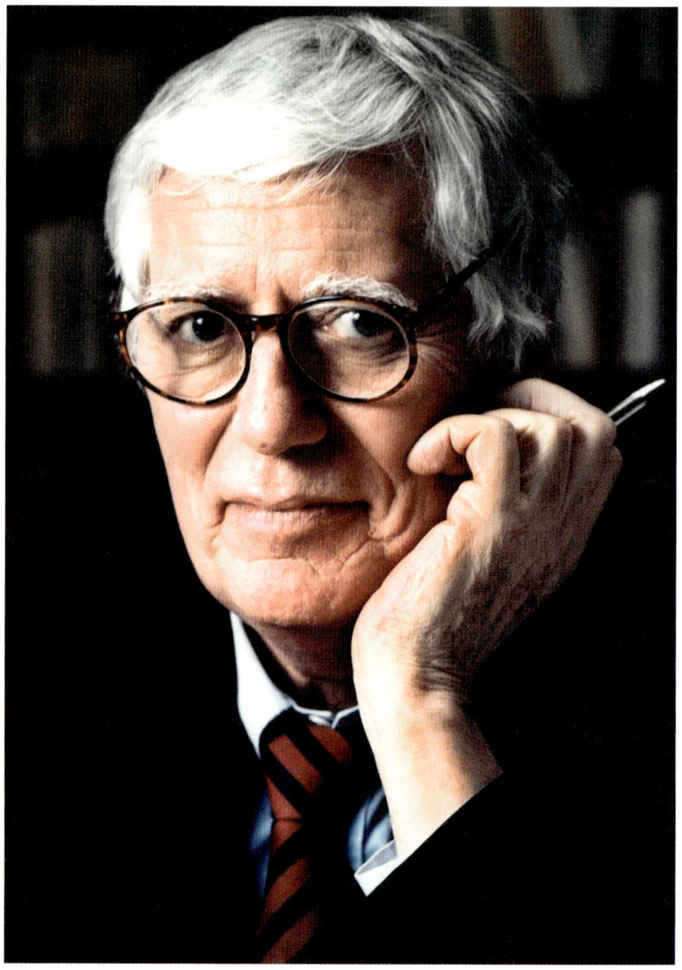

Fig. 14: Oswald Mathias Ungers, 1990

it was clear that social gatherings of that kind or even parties, which had been the norm up to then in the Architecture Department, would take place without Ungers.

However, he impressed the students in his class with his discipline and ascetic modesty. He never said a word about the huge successes he was having at the time.[36] He is always described by former students as being on task and concentrating on the designs. Advanced students especially found in him a teacher of great sophistication and clear orientation. Unsurprisingly, the Ungers era has produced several distinguished architecture professors.

Laurids Ortner (1987–2009)

Laurids Ortner was appointed to teach at the Academy a year after Ungers, in 1987 (Fig. 15). He was one of the Austrian revolutionaries of the 1970s who did their best to liberate architecture from grids and norms. Laurids Ortner taught as a professor at the Art Academy for twenty-two years. After studying architecture at Vienna Technical University, he had his first experience of teaching at the Art Institute in Linz on the Danube from 1976 to 1987. His early work is shot through with provocations and escalations, which gradually gave way to a classical architectural language that is strictly Austrian in its sensuousness. Ortner was a founder member of the collective of architects and artists who called themselves Haus-Rucker-Co. Together with his brother, Manfred Ortner, and Zamp Kelp, he took part in international exhibitions, including documenta in Kassel. In the mid-1980s he became more interested in actually practising architecture. The collective architectural practice Ortner Architects was founded in Düsseldorf in 1987. Later, in 1990, he joined forces with his brother in Vienna to found Ortner & Ortner Baukunst. Since 1994 he has had a practice in Berlin and since 2006 another in Cologne.

In the 1990s at the Art Academy, Laurids Ortner was a founder member of the above-mentioned 'Midday Academy', which used to meet on Tuesdays at the Italian restaurant in Ratinger Straße. In a foreword to an exhibition catalogue for Ernst Kasper written in 2005, he describes the special magic of the place: 'With time this meeting for lunch grew into an Academy institution. Some days rector Markus Lüpertz would issue invitations to lunch, and Pulcinella would be full of art-

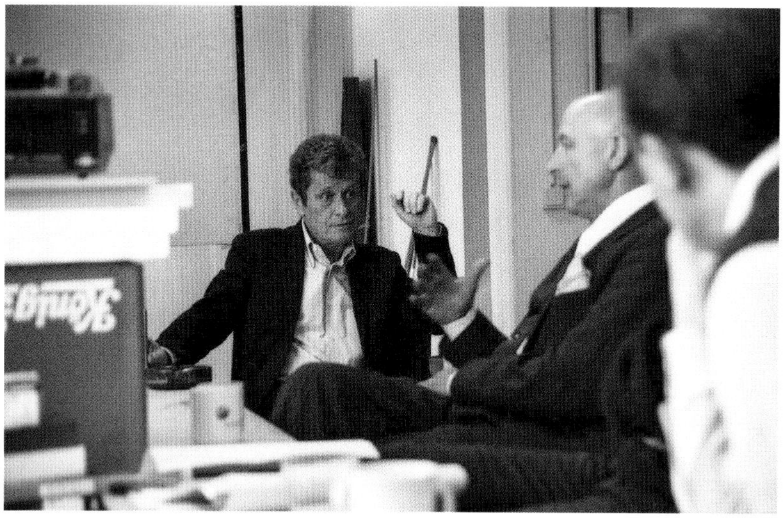

Fig. 15: Table talk with Laurids Ortner (left), Markus Lüpertz, and students, 2002

ists from the Academy. Exhibition organisers would have there in one place what they would have to travel far and wide to assemble for participation in documentas or Biennales.'[37] For professional aesthetes this magical place is still the acid test: yellowing plaster walls, fake beams, and all sorts of kitsch that may be faintly reminiscent of Italy, not to mention a menu that promises more than it delivers. Ultimately, almost everyone went, although at first reluctantly: 'Hollein, Stirling – the benches were a too tight fit for him – and later Kleihues; only Ungers stayed away'.[38] By then it had become a tradition to let the table talk at the Rhine Tract or the lectures in the Great Hall, organised by Christian Heuchel and Björn Severin, to wind down at Ratinger Straße.

As a teacher, Ortner is distinguished by a broad range of experience. Students have confirmed that he was exceptionally calm and relaxed. His global success grew while he was at the Academy, but he always seemed modest and grounded.

Elia Zenghelis (1990–2002)

The Greek architect Elia Zenghelis first taught on a limited contract in 1963 at the Architectural Association School of Architecture in London, where he had finished his studies in 1961. Between 1971 and 1975 he worked with several architects, including Rem Kolhaas and Oswald Mathias Ungers in London, Paris, and New York. Zenghelis was a professor of architecture at the Düsseldorf Art Academy from 1990 to 2002 (Fig. 16).

The number of international teaching contracts he received attest to his popularity as a teacher: from 1993 until 2010 a lectureship at the Berlage Institute in the Netherlands; from 1997 until 1998 visiting professor at the École Polytechnique Fédérale de Lausanne; from 1998 to 2000 visiting professor at ETH Zurich; and from 2000 until 2007 professor at the Accademia di architettura di Mendrisio.

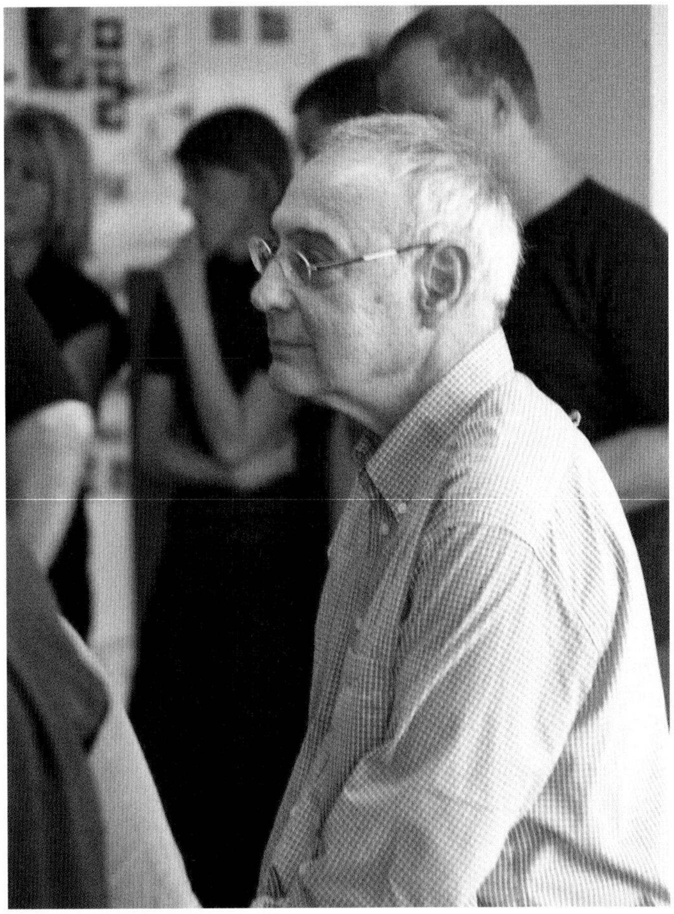

Fig. 16: Elia Zenghelis in the Rhine Tract, 2002

Zengheli's intellectual capacity was particularly appreciated by postgraduate students. A reputation for Anglo-Saxon drill preceded him, but when he worked with students on a solution to a design assignment, he could lose all track of time. He emanated great inner calm while teaching. Disciplined, his eye always on the clock, he wasn't all that enthusiastic about the 'Midday Academy' at first, but this attitude changed over the course of his twelve years at the Academy. Eyewitnesses report, 'As a teacher he was a calm, serious type. But when a party was on, Zenghelis could unwind.'[39]

Josef Paul Kleihues (1994–1998)

Kleihues had studied architecture at Stuttgart University and Berlin Technical University. In 1959 he held a scholarship from the École Nationale Supérieure des Beaux-Arts in Paris and worked as a self-employed architect from 1962 on. From 1973 until 1994 he was a professor at Dortmund University and from 1984 on director of planning at the International Building Exhibition in Berlin. There followed numerous awards, including the Order of Merit of the Federal Republic of Germany in 1988 and the Order of Merit of Berlin in 2000. He founded the architecture practice Kleihues + Kleihues with his son in 1996. A founder of the International Building Academy Berlin, he was its first president from 2001 to 2003.

Kleihues impressed the students at the Art Academy for four years with term projects that were superlatively prepared. Even before the term began, they were available to students in A4 format. He was a professor who managed to 'keep his cool' while juggling the responsibility of managing two architecture practices at once, one in the Münsterland and the other in Berlin, against the demands made by accepting international commissions while also teaching at the Düsseldorf Art Academy. An experienced educator, he felt it was important to involve his students in his architecture commissions worldwide. He took some of them with him to clients in Chicago, where they could introduce designs of their own.[40]

'Josef Paul Kleihues could never really reconcile himself to the environment,'[41] wrote Laurids Ortner in the foreword mentioned above. But then he did come to appreciate the quirks of that 'Midday Academy', which met at the table behind the pizza oven. Witnesses testify to the fact that Kleihues even began to enjoy those Tuesday lunch meetings. He made friends with colleagues and students, and those friendships were sealed at a grand farewell party in 1998 (Fig. 17).[42]

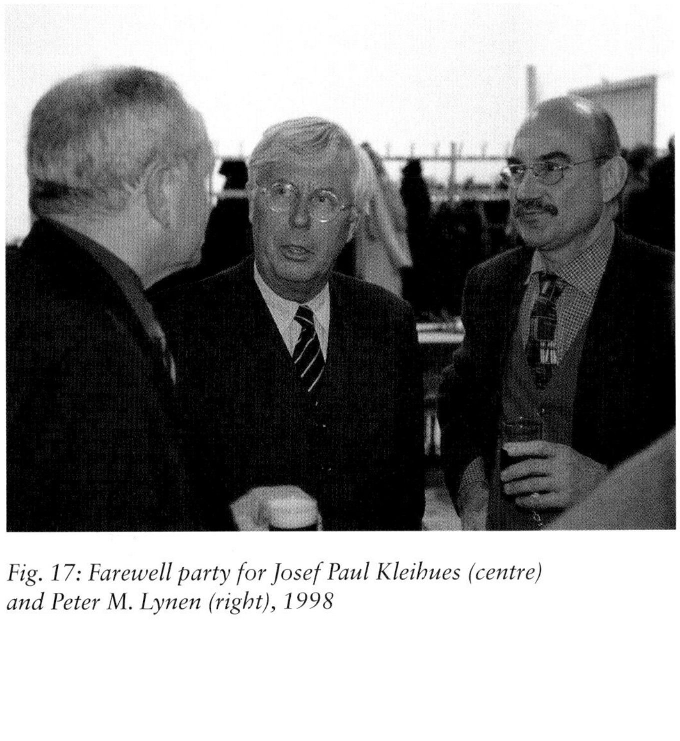

Fig. 17: Farewell party for Josef Paul Kleihues (centre) and Peter M. Lynen (right), 1998

Odile Decq (2004–2005) and Jórunn Ragnarsdóttir (2010–2012)

Odile Decq came to the Düsseldorf Art Academy from France as a deputy professor on the recommendation of Axel Schultes. She had studied architecture, urbanism, and urban planning and taken her diploma at the Institut d'Études Politiques in Paris. In 1985 she founded an architecture practice in Paris. She has been the recipient of numerous awards, including the Golden Lion at the 1996 Venice Biennale. Odile Decq taught in the architecture class for two terms (Fig. 18).

From 1 October 2010 to 31 March 2012 Jórunn Ragnarsdóttir from Iceland took over Laurids Ortner's professorship. After taking her diploma in architecture at Stuttgart University, she worked there from 1982 on with the architect Arno Lederer, who is also her husband. From 1992 to 1993 she worked with Boris Prodecca at Stuttgart University. In 1992 the Lederer + Ragnarsdóttir + Oei architecture practice was founded in Stuttgart, and she has contributed substantially to its success.

There is no mistaking her closeness to Scandinavian architecture. The costumes and stage sets she created for theatres in Reykjavik are exciting. Other remarkable works are the school buildings she has designed for Salem International College in Überlingen, the primary and secondary modern school with a vocational secondary school in Ostfildern, and the Waldorf School in Freiburg im Breisgau. The Art Academy students found her a good listener.

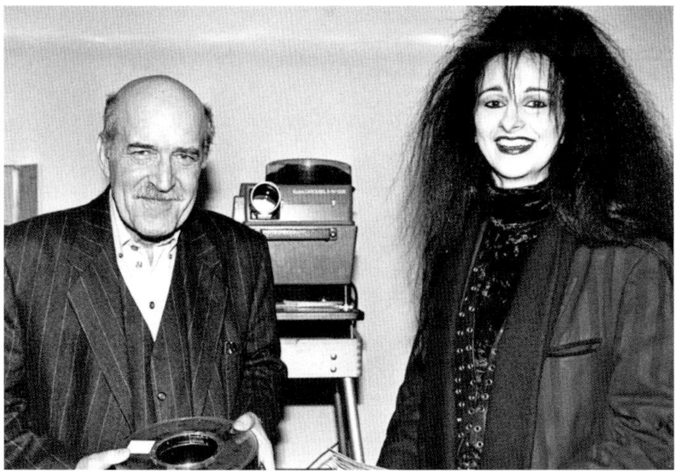

Fig. 18: Ernst Kasper and Odile Decq, 2003

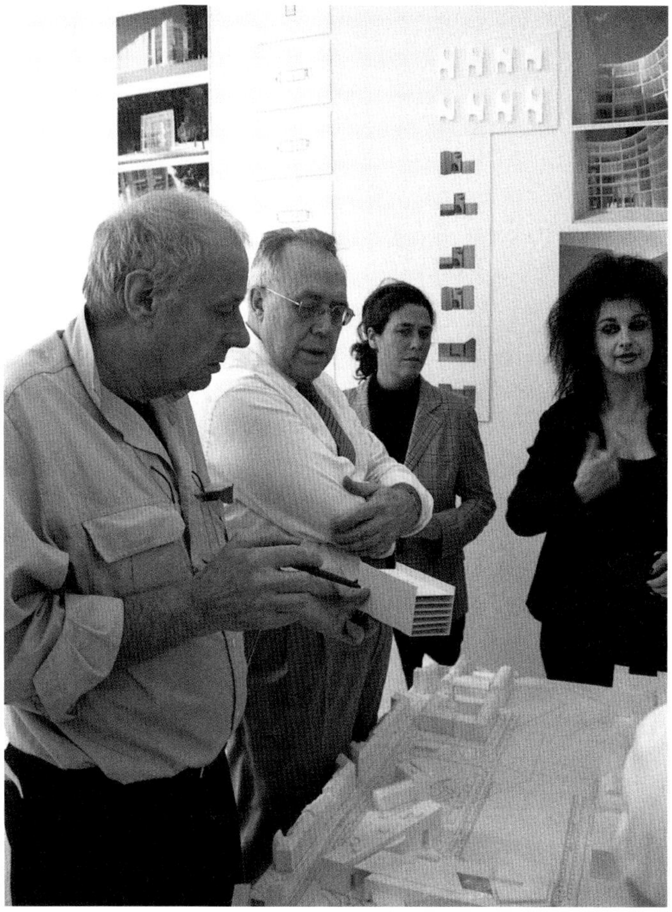

Fig. 19: From left to right: Axel Schultes, Walter Hofmann, Rita McBride, and Odile Decq, 2003

Axel Schultes (2003–2011)

Axel Schultes was already a successful architect when he was appointed to a teaching post at the Academy in 2003 (Fig. 19). He was brought to the Academy that year by Markus Lüpertz, whom he had met while both he and Lüpertz were working in the Berlin Chancellery. Born in Dresden, Schulte had studied at Berlin Technical University, afterwards specialising in architecture competitions. In 1992 he opened a joint practice with Charlotte Frank and Christoph Witt in Berlin. It became famous overnight in 1993 with its brilliant waterside urban-planning design for the Berlin Spreebogen. Known as the *Band des Bundes Ost und West* [East-West Federal Strip], it beat over 850 entries to win the competition. After another competition, Schultes was approved as the architect of the Federal Chancellery, which was inaugurated in 2001.

Schultes was drawn to building projects on a grand scale and to working intensively with students. His capacity for enthusiasm for new tasks spurred his students on. The work rooms in the Rheinflügel were too cramped and too low-ceilinged for him. Nor was Schultes economical with criticism of the Academy. That is how he persuaded rector Markus Lüpertz to include the architecture classes in the Tour exhibitions in the main building.

Max Dudler (2005–The Present)

By the time he received his appointment to teach at the Art Academy in 2005, Dudler was already a successful architect who had received prestigious awards. A Swiss, the son of a stonemason, Dudler was educated at the Städelschule in Frankfurt am Main, where he studied with Günter Bock, and at the Arts Institute in Berlin as a pupil of Ludwig Leo's. From 1981 until 1986 Dudler worked for Oswald Mathias Ungers's practice, and from 1986 to 1992 he collaborated with Peter Welbergen. In parallel Dudler taught at the Architecture Institute in Venice. He gained even more teaching experience between 1996 and 1999 as a visiting professor in the Department of Design and Industrial Architecture at Dortmund University before being appointed professor of architecture at the Düsseldorf Art Academy.

Dudler's architectural language was formatively influenced by Oswald Mathias Ungers. His buildings have been thought through from the large cubic form down to the most minute detail with a subtle feeling for transparency and mass, depth effects, material, and light and shade. They are buildings that attest to his preference for Adolf Loos and Bruno Taut, and occasionally even reveal an indebtedness to Louis Sullivan and the Chicago School. And Ludwig Mies van der Rohe would have been grateful for some of Dudler's corner solutions.

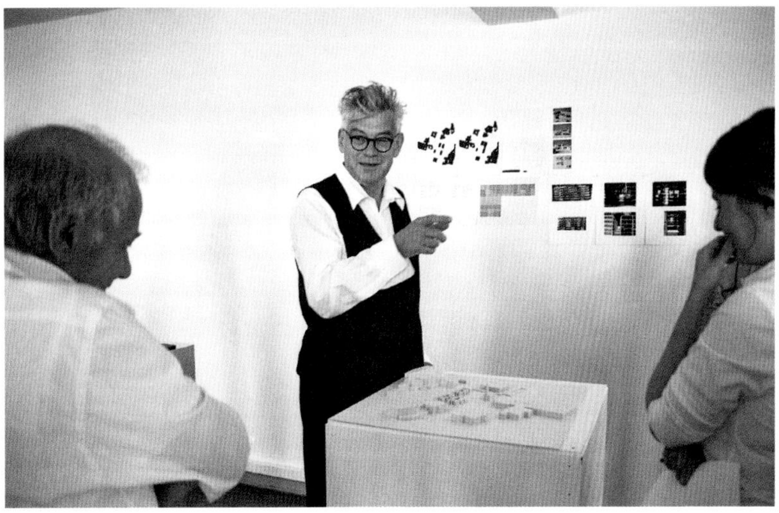

Fig. 20: Axel Schultes and Max Dudler with student Cordula Renner, 2005

Students attest particular skills to Dudler as an educator: he can be enthusiastic even though he tends to be economical with commentary while staring over his Corbusier spectacles during corrections. But when things get really exciting, the Swiss architect – like Le Corbusier on the ten franc note – is known 'to push up his spectacles and look from beneath them on occasion'.[43] This gesture is all more advanced students need to understand him (Fig. 20).

Karl-Heinz Petzinka (2008–The Present)

When Petzinka was appointed to teach architecture at the Art Academy, he looked back on a broad-ranging professional practice, with a number of high-tech buildings to his credit and plenty of teaching experience. Petzinka had finished his studies at RWTH Aachen in 1982 with a diploma in civil engineering. His early professional years in Oswald Mathias Ungers's practice were formative. In 1985 he took over a teaching contract with Professor Döring at RWTH Aachen and subsequently taught at Bergische University in Wuppertal. In 1994 he founded his first practice, jointly with Thomas Pink. That year he also became a professor at Darmstadt Technical University. In 2003 he was a visiting professor of architecture at the Düsseldorf Art Academy. When he was designated art director for the thematic field 'City of Possibilities' by Ruhr.2010 GmbH, European Cultural Capital, Petzinka was able to develop his great organisational talent.

When Professor Petzinka announces the architecture lectures in the Great Hall, which have been organised there for years with great success by Björn Severin, his audience senses his active commitment. He obviously enjoys introducing speakers, appearing to be well prepared, relaxed, and eloquent. At the round of drinks that follows in the stairwell in front of the Great Hall, he'll steal a furtive glance at his watch: anyone who is at all acquainted with him knows that the professor's workday is far from over.

Petzinka takes up subjects that inspire students to identify with the city of Düsseldorf. The design assignments cover multiple areas: the conversion and revitalisation of existing buildings, the tram depot as a studio for Academy artists, and – a perennially popular topic – enlarging the Academy. He knows how to make students enthusiastic and ventures on challenging

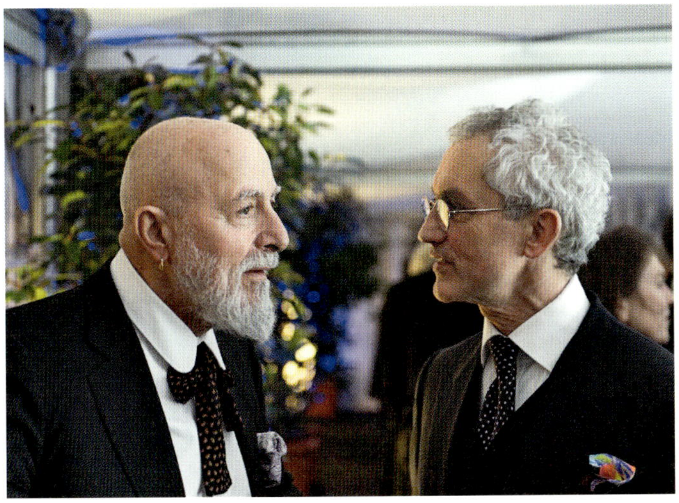

Fig. 21: Markus Lüpertz and Karl-Heinz Petzinka at the unveiling of Herkules *[Hercules], on the Zeche Nordstern Tower, on 17 December 2010*

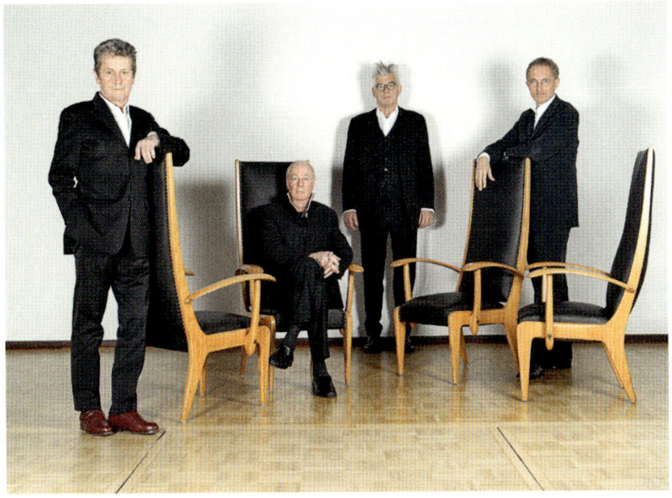

Fig. 22: Architecture professors; from left to right: Laurids Ortner, Axel Schultes, Max Dudler, and Karl-Heinz Petzinka, 2010

projects with them such as the Rudolf Schwarz Steinhaus [Stone House] between the main building and the Rheinflügel. Petzinka sets great store by treating historical buildings with due respect and ensuring that presentations meet the highest aesthetic standards (Fig. 21).

Nathalie De Vries (2013–The Present)

Nathalie de Vries from the Netherlands has been teaching architecture at the Düsseldorf Art Academy since the summer term of 2013. She studied architecture and urban planning from 1984 until 1990 at Delft Technical University. Between 1998 and 2012 she gained teaching experience at such prestigious institutions of higher learning as the Berlage Institute in Rotterdam, Berlin Technical University, and, most recently, the Harvard Graduate School of Design. As co-founder and co-director of the architects' collective MVRDV, she has been working successfully with Winy Maas and Jacob van Rijs. The practice has become internationally renowned for their housing projects in Hilversum and Amsterdam, followed by the Netherlands Pavilion at Expo 2000 in Hannover. Nathalie de Vries has considerable experience in the field of administration and international management.

Concluding Remarks

In the reconstruction era after 1945, the simple wooden pencil was regarded as the architect's most valuable tool. Sketchbooks from that time, full to the brim of sketches, document a way of working that was still crafts orientated. The professional image of the so-called 'barefoot architect', who often had scraped together the economic basis for his first architecture practice by the early 1950s after participating in competitions, must seem utopian to today's young architects. The classic image of the master builder, lord of all he surveys, who is responsible for everything about a building from the foundations up, is by now the exception to the rule. Instead, high-tech and scientifically designed modular systems meet the requirements of changed work forms and sequences. Basic knowledge encounters experiential skills to enter on a symbiosis with nature: a discipline of discovery, invention, technology, and poetry.

The changes wrought in the old courses of study in conformity with the Bologna Process have meant for students a degree that is the equivalent of a master's degree. Ultimately it has been internal reforms and personnel decisions that have shaped for the future the international orientation of architecture as taught at the Düsseldorf Art Academy. Since the new study regulations came into force in 2009, architecture students have finished their studies with an MA, which has brought about a considerable improvement in official recognition.

Once a year at the traditional *Rundgang*, visitors, too, are given some idea of the diversity of the art projects engaged in by the architecture class. At that time student works produced over the course of a year in the Rheinflügel are shown over a few square metres in the main building. They are convincing because they meet the highest quality standards.

It can only be hoped that architecture will in future figure even more prominently in the main building of the Art Academy. It would be fitting indeed for an institution that over the course of a long history has produced not only distinguished teachers but also world-class graduates (Fig. 22). As James Stirling said in 1981, shortly after receiving the Pritzker Prize for Architecture,

'I would be very happy indeed to meet one of my students ahead of me in the history books!'[44]

NOTES

1 Hans Schwippert made the acquaintance of Ludwig Mies van der Rohe (1889–1963) in the Berlin group of architects who called themselves the Zehner Ring, and from then on they were linked by close ties of friendship. Mies van der Rohe received the Honorary Prize of the State of North Rhine-Westphalia in the Great Hall of the Düsseldorf Art Academy in 1959.
2 Hauptstadtarchiv Düsseldorf (HstAD), Ministerialarchiv, NW 60–176.
3 HstAD, Ministerialarchiv, NW 60, Bl. [fols.] 13–29, 'Bericht zum Ausbau der Kunstakademie Düsseldorf im Auftrage des Kultusministeriums des Landes Nordrhein-Westfalen erstattet von Prof. Heuser kommissarischer Direktor der Akademie und Prof. Dr. Hans Schwippert, Abteilungsleiter im Wiederaufbauministerium' [Report on Rebuilding the Düsseldorf Art Academy commissioned by the Ministry of Culture of the State of North Rhine-Westphalia, given by Prof. Heuser, acting director of the Academy, and Prof. Dr. Hans Schwippert, department head in the Reconstruction Ministry], Technische Hochschule Aachen; see Agatha Buslei-Wuppermann, *Hans Schwippert 1899–1973. Von der Werkkunst zum Design*, Munich 2007.
4 HstAD, Ministerialarchiv, NW 60, Bl. [fols.] 26f.
5 Until 1934 he had written his first name, which derives from 'Johannes', with two *ns*; in the NS era; however, he scaled back and from then on wrote it 'Hans'.
6 Maria Schwarz in conversation with the author in April 2013.
7 Schwippert had two addresses to the Academy from 1961 and 1963 bound and privately printed to be sent to friends and colleagues.
8 Werner Durth, 'Der Düsseldorfer Architektenstreit. Vorgeschichte und Folgen', in: *Architektenstreit. Wiederaufbau zwischen Kontinuität und Neubeginn*, exhib. cat. Düsseldorf 2008, pp. 23–42.
9 Bruno Schlagenhauf in conversation with the author in February 2013.
10 He engaged in an intimate dialogue with the fine artists at the Academy. With Ernst Petersen he designed buildings in Düsseldorf for Henkel (1950–1958), the Humboldt-Gymnasium (1955), and the destroyed hall at the Schlösser Brewery (1955).
11 Bernhard Pfau (1902–1989) was the key figure in the Düsseldorf Architects' Association, which was formed in 1949.
12 Agatha Buslei-Wuppermann and Andreas Zeising, *Vom Machen und Brauchen*, Düsseldorf 2008, pp. 28–31.
13 1954 Erfahrungen über Stipendienvergabe für den Kulturkreis im Bundesverband der Deutschen Industrie [Experiences on Granting Scholarships for the Cultural Circle in the Federal Association of German Industry].
14 Friedhelm Debus, a former student, in conversation with the author in January 2009.
15 Maria Schwarz in conversation with the author in April 2013.
16 The *Gries am Seller* project was completed in January 1968.
17 Josef Odenthal, 'Robaschiks Studie wird vorgestellt, Skizzen einer neuen Altstadt, Ausstellung in den Schaufenstern', *Düsseldorfer Stadtpost*, 13 November 1970.
18 It was replaced in the course of overall renovation in 2008.
19 Maria Schwarz in conversation with the author in February 2013.
20 Adelheid Wimmenauer, widow of Karl Wimmenauer, in conversation with the author in March 2013.
21 Former student Thomas van den Valentyn in conversation with the author on 9 March 2013.
22 Born in Vienna in 1934, Hollein was the son of an engineer. He had studied architecture with Clemens Holzmeister at the Fine Arts Academy in Vienna until 1956. In 1958 he was given a grant for study in the United States, which enabled him to study architecture and urban planning at the Illinois Institute of Technology in Chicago.
23 Verbally imparted by Hans Hollein to the author in March 2012.
24 'Architektur ist Bestimmung, Festlegung des Raumes, der Umwelt. Architektur ist Konditionierung eines psychologischen Zustandes.' Quoted in Hans Hollein, 'Alles ist Architektur (1967)', *Bau. Schrift für Architektur und Städtebau*, Issue 23, No. 1/2, Vienna 1968 and http://www.hollein.com/ger/Schriften/Texte/Alles-ist-Architektur (last retrieved 14 September 2015).
25 Verbally imparted by Prof. Rolf Crummenauer, 1998.
26 The appointments committee met in 1967, chaired by Eduard Trier, director of the Academy, and Walter Köngeter, deputy director.
27 The young architect first attracted attention in Mönchengladbach during a 1970 exhibition devoted to the theme of 'Death'.
28 'Wenn wir schon eine Schönheit wollen, dann eine sinnliche Schönheit elementarer Gewalt.' [If we want beauty, then sensuous beauty of elemental power] – 'Wir müssen die Architektur vom Bauen befreien!' [We must liberate architecture from building!] – 'Architekten müssen aufhören, nur in Bauwerken zu denken!' [Architects must stop thinking exclusively in buildings!]
29 Interview with Horst Christoph and Patricia Grzonka, 'Stararchitekt Hollein im großen Interview. Jede Woche das Denkmalamt alarmieren' (2009): http://www.profil.at/home/stararchitekt-hollein-interview-jede-woche-denkmalamt-237070 (last retrieved 14 September 2015).
30 The Neue Staatsgalerie in Stuttgart was inaugurated on 9 March 1984.
31 Tate Britain, London, Clore Gallery annexe, built after plans by James Stirling, inaugurated 1987.
32 Architecture practice James Stirling, Michael Wilford and Associates, which existed until Stirling's death in 1992.
33 Students from the 1982 Stirling class in conversation with the author in February 2013.
34 Karl Wimmenauer on Oswald Mathias Ungers in conversation with students.
35 Laurids Ortner, 'Pulcinella', in: Susanne Gross (ed.), *Ernst Kasper. Bauten und Projekte 1965–2005*, exhib. cat. Frankfurt am Main 2005, pp. 14–17; here: p. 15.
36 In 1987 he became a member of the Academy of Sciences in Berlin, in 1997 he received the Grand Cross of the Order of Merit of the Federal Republic of Germany, and in 1999 he was awarded an honorary doctorate by Berlin Technical University.
37 Ortner (see n. 35); here: p. 17.
38 Ibid., p. 15.
39 Ingrid van Hüllen in conversation with the author on 26 March 2013.
40 Björn Severin in conversation with the author in April 2013.
41 Ortner (see n. 35); here: p. 15.
42 Farewell party in the Rheinflügel in 1998, note from Björn Severin in April 2013.
43 Students from the Dudler class in conversation with the author in February 2013.
44 James Stirling in conversation with students, 1981.

THE ACADEMY AND THE PUBLIC

THE HISTORY OF THE BUILDINGS AND EXPANSION SINCE 1945

Agatha Buslei-Wuppermann

THE MAIN BUILDING

The main building of the Düsseldorf Art Academy on the fringes of the Old Town was designed and built by the architects Wilhelm Lotz and Hermann Riffart between 1875 and 1879. It is a functional building in the style of the Berlin Architecture Academy. A security harbour used to be along the front of the building but it barely existed for more than twenty years, and by the close of the nineteenth century it had been filled in.

With three 'visible sides' (facing east, north, and west) the building faces the Rhine and the Hofgarten park (Fig. 1). Those three façades were magnificently decorated while the south side (the back) was finished in simple brick masonry. The main façade (north side) is symmetrical with a central and side avant-corps. A strip bearing the names of artists runs around the building above the rusticated ground floor. Architecture is represented by Karl Friedrich Schinkel, Iktinos, Erwin von Steinbach, Filippo Brunelleschi, and Donato Bramante. The façades of the two upper floors are enlivened with lavish decoration and coloured mosaics. A balustrade conceals the hipped roof. The plain south side facing Eiskellerstraße is built of yellow brick masonry, a building material with a high limestone content and a low iron content of the kind used on what was once St Ursula's School across the way and also by Rudolf Schwarz for the Steinhaus [Stone House] (1956–1958), the studio building on the abutting plot.

The entrance to the Academy building used to be on the south side – that is, the side facing the Old Town – and was axially aligned. Behind the main entrance was the porter's lodge on the ground floor with a staircase behind it that led to the first floor. From there the stairs divided into two flights, fanning out magnificently on the way to the Great Hall on the second floor.

The Academy building sustained severe damage during the Second World War. After three air raids and a heavy bombardment with incendiary and high-explosive bombs in March 1945, the roof was gutted and the ceiling had collapsed in the east tract (Figs. 2–4, 7).[1] The Great Hall, boasting a vast stuccoed ceiling, ceiling paintings, and murals was also destroyed, with only the outlines of the windows showing. The ceiling paintings were all that could be saved shortly before the bombardment. The side entrance on the east façade could only be reached by scrambling over mountains of rubble. Thanks to the help given by students and volunteers, the Academy was able to reopen on an improvised basis by 31 January 1946.[2]

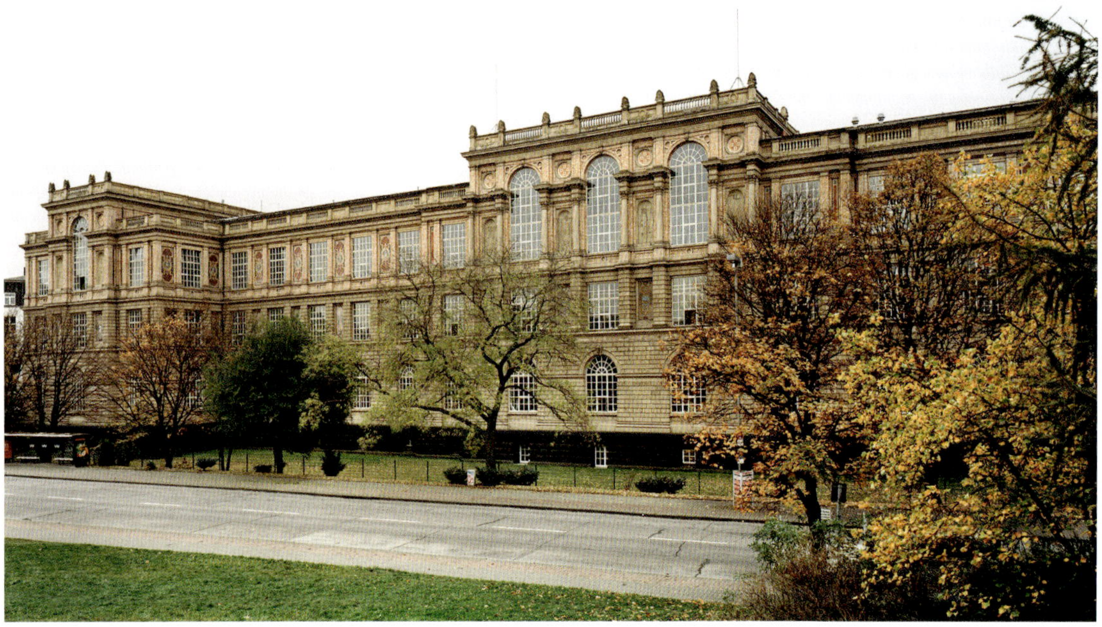

Fig. 1: The north façade of the Düsseldorf Art Academy, 1994

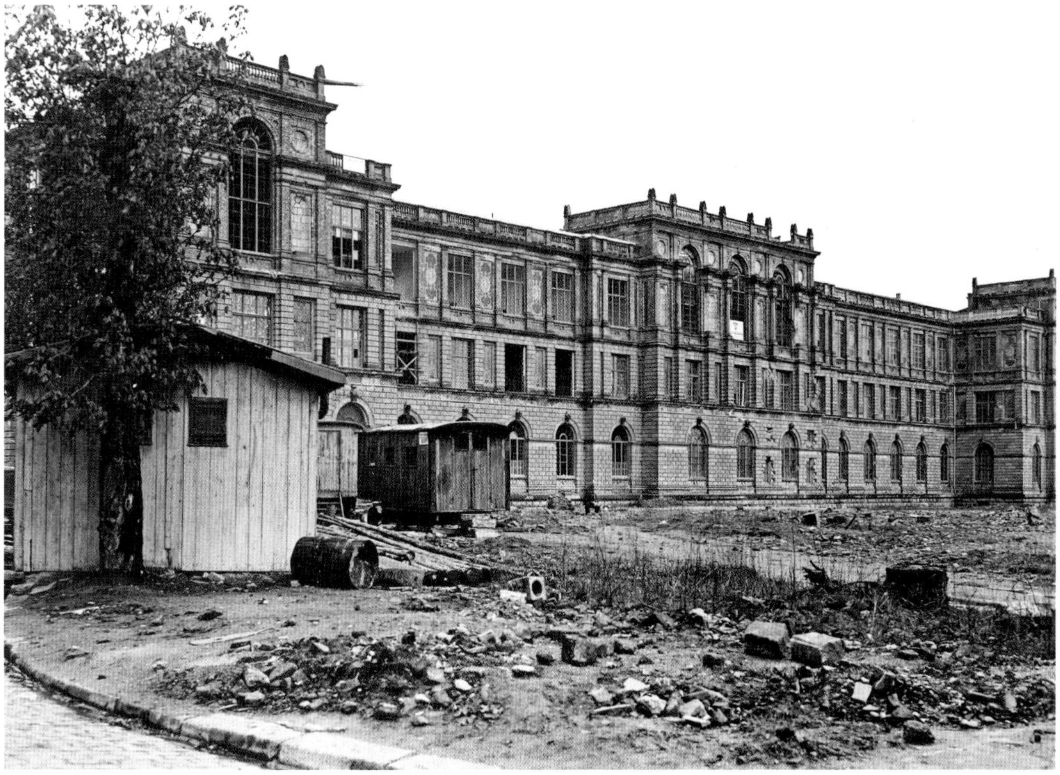

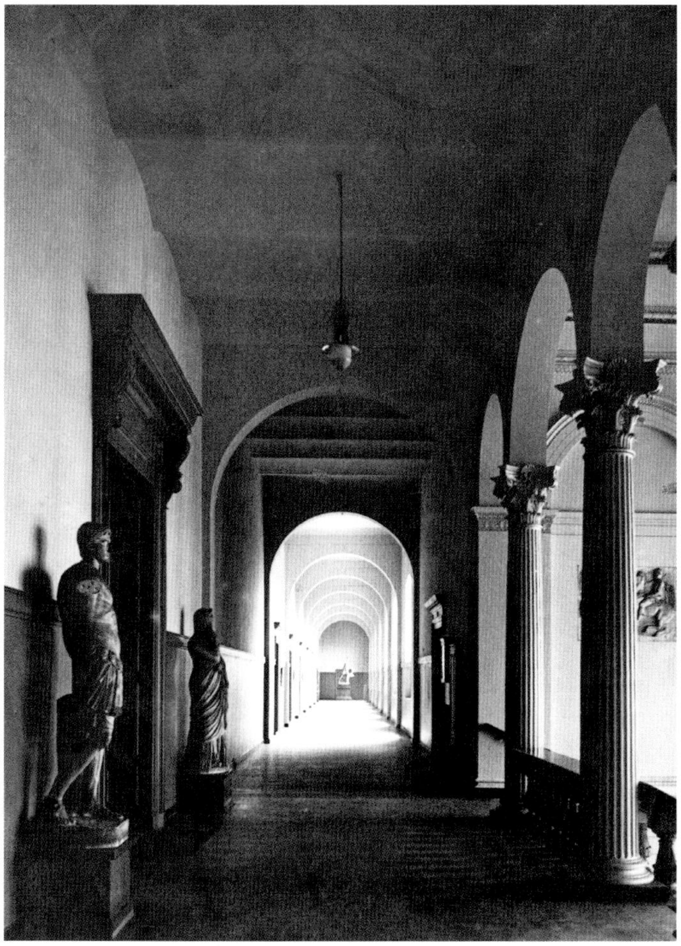

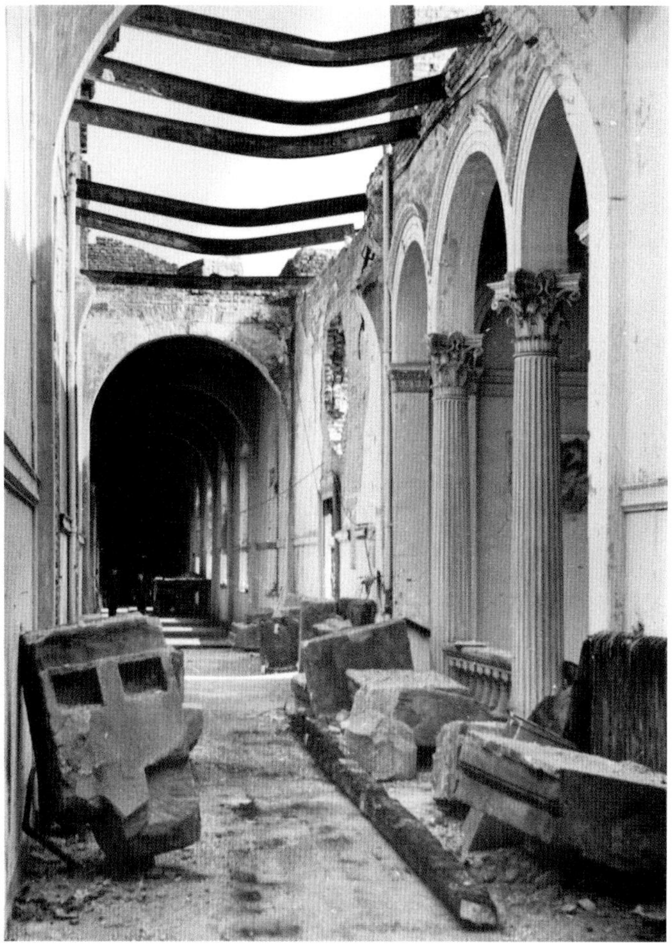

Fig. 2: The destroyed north side of the Düsseldorf Art Academy, c. 1950

Fig. 3: Second floor, corridor and stairwell of the Düsseldorf Art Academy, before 1945

Fig. 4: Second floor, corridor and stairwell of the Düsseldorf Art Academy, 1946

REBUILDING AND DECORATING

Hans Schwippert was charged with rebuilding the destroyed structure at this time. In Walter Köngeter, head of the Düsseldorf Buildings Department and from 1947 on an untenured professor of architecture at the Academy, Schwippert had the ideal partner for carrying out the construction work. They also had the same ideas on how to restore and preserve historic buildings, which were informed by reticence and a lofty sense of social responsibility.[3]

The old main entrance on the south side continued in use only until the early 1950s. After that the spacious staircase became a side entrance since the new entrance, designed by Ewald Mataré, was constructed on the chief façade, or east side (Fig. 5). The ceilings were severely damaged here, too. That led to the architectural solution of building mezzanines. Lower ceiling heights seemed to the architects more suitable for administration, which was to be housed here. Moreover, taking this measure made it easier to carry out the rest of the construction work.

Administration was housed on the first floor above the new entrance. Above it were the director's rooms. Recessed partitions, some of them equipped with built-in cabinets, divided the interior space and formed narrow corridors. The partition on the second floor was made of pine, Hans Schwippert's favourite wood. He used those rooms while he was director of the Academy (1956–1966). Yet traces of destruction remained visible. The holes made by projectiles in the old, hand-set terrazzo floors were only filled in, so the floors still show the wounds of war. In places where the ceilings had fallen in and it was no longer possible to repair the old terrazzo floors, pre-cast terrazzo tiles were laid.

The extensive reconstruction and expansion work was finished by 1953. Once again there was an inauguration ceremony presided over by Heinrich Kamps, the incumbent director. Wend Fischer wrote in 1953:

'The preserved cubic volumes have been used to the full extent so that the entire spatial structure has been restored to its old proportions but in a simpler, clearer form. Halls, workrooms, and studios full of light, simple corridors and stairwells, functional furnishings and decoration provide space and clarity. A prime example has thus emerged of how even when extant cubic volumes are reconstructed, rooms are possible that, rather than being steeped in the spirit of the past, are informed by the spirit of our time.'[4]

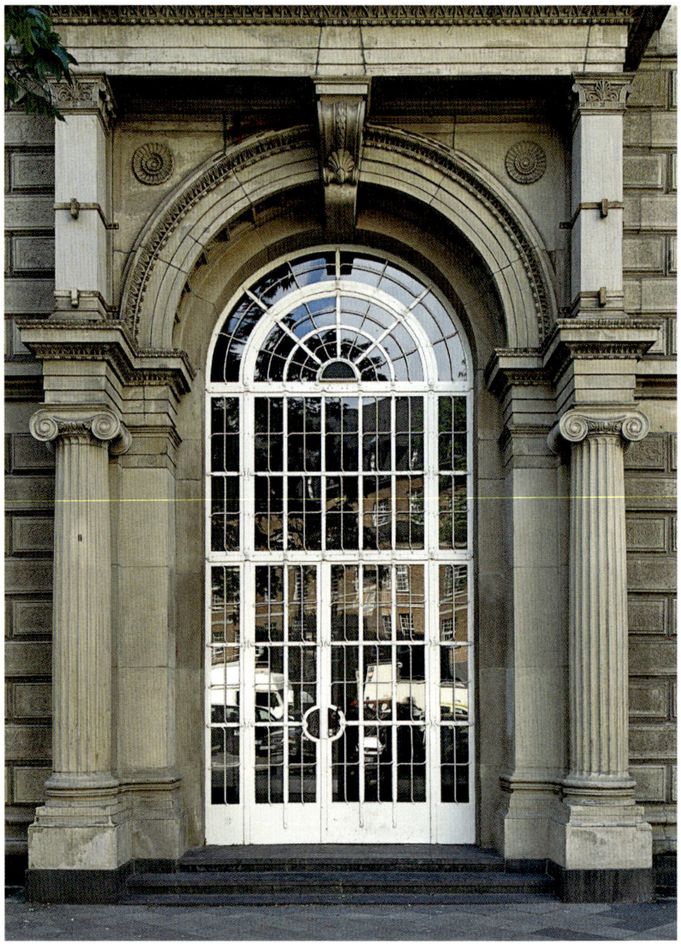

Fig. 5: Ewald Mataré, main entrance to the Düsseldorf Art Academy, 1952/53

The once magnificent Great Hall had already been redesigned by the architect Clemens Holzmeister (who taught at the Academy from 1928 until 1930) before the Second World War, just thirty years after it was built, at the urging of the then director, Walter Kaesbach, who wanted to express a new era. The old, intricate windows were replaced by new ones designed by Heinrich Campendonk[5] (Fig. 6). In the aftermath of war and destruction in 1945, the Great Hall underwent a further spatial reinterpretation: Schwippert, an architect, translated the grid of squares of the once lavish stucco ceiling into a commensurate scale and replaced them with austere elements made of oak. The floor mirrors the double ceiling grid. The choice of flooring materials was in line with a new reticence. It was a commonplace, commercial so-called dwarf parquet flooring consisting of fitted squares in oak, which Schwippert linked with one another to form high-contrast patterns. Gracefully curvilinear light fittings in fine cameo glass[6] underscored the purist elegance of the room (Figs. 8, 9).

Schwippert had the portal to the Great Hall, which is axially aligned with the main stairwell, replaced by three simple double doors of uniform height and fitted with simple door

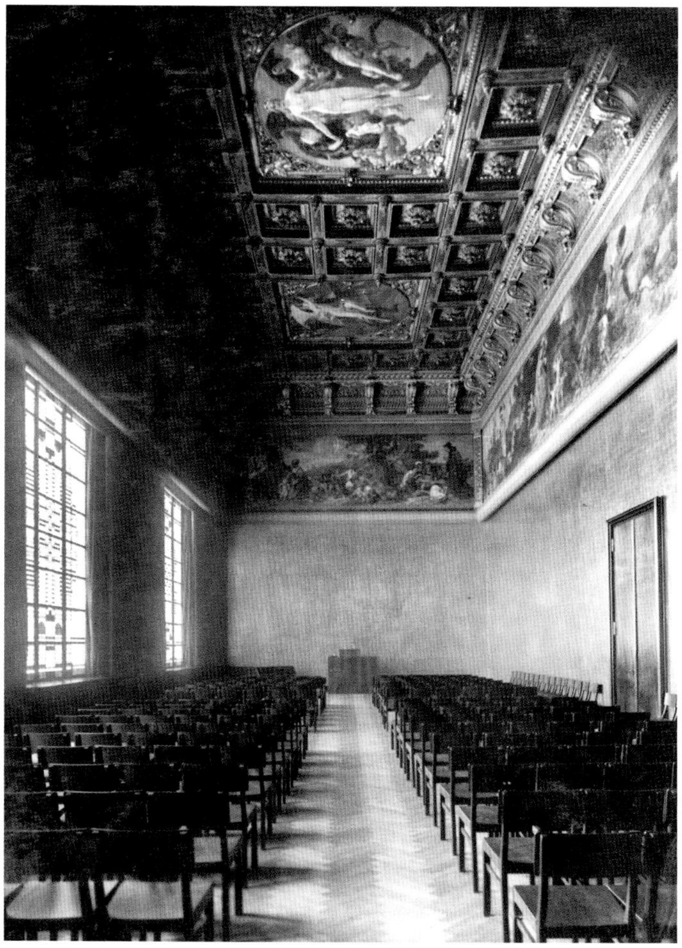

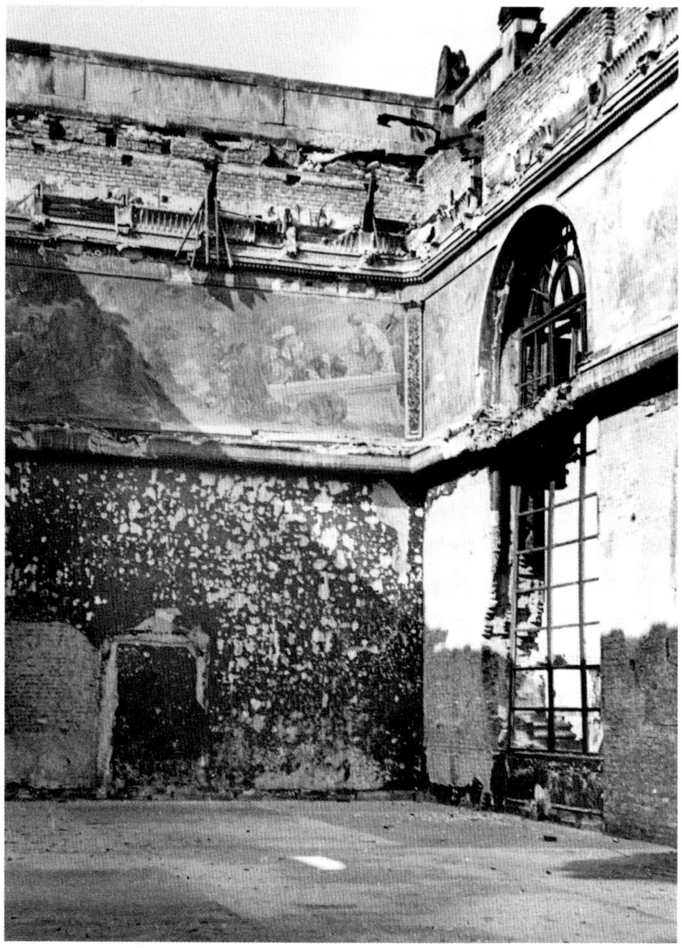

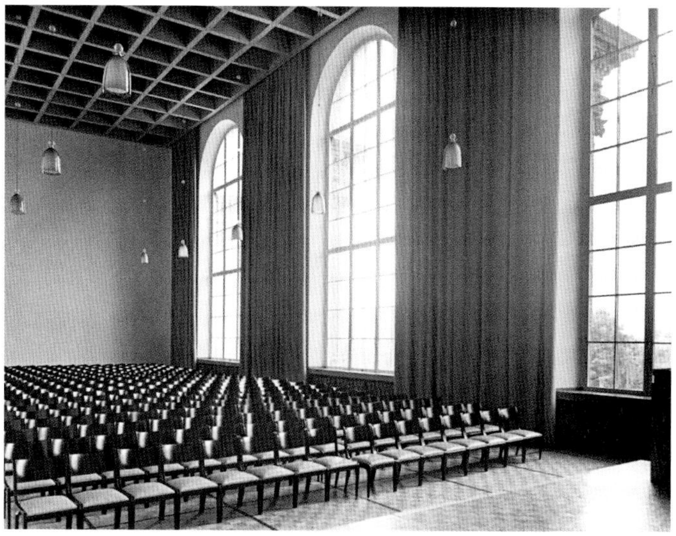

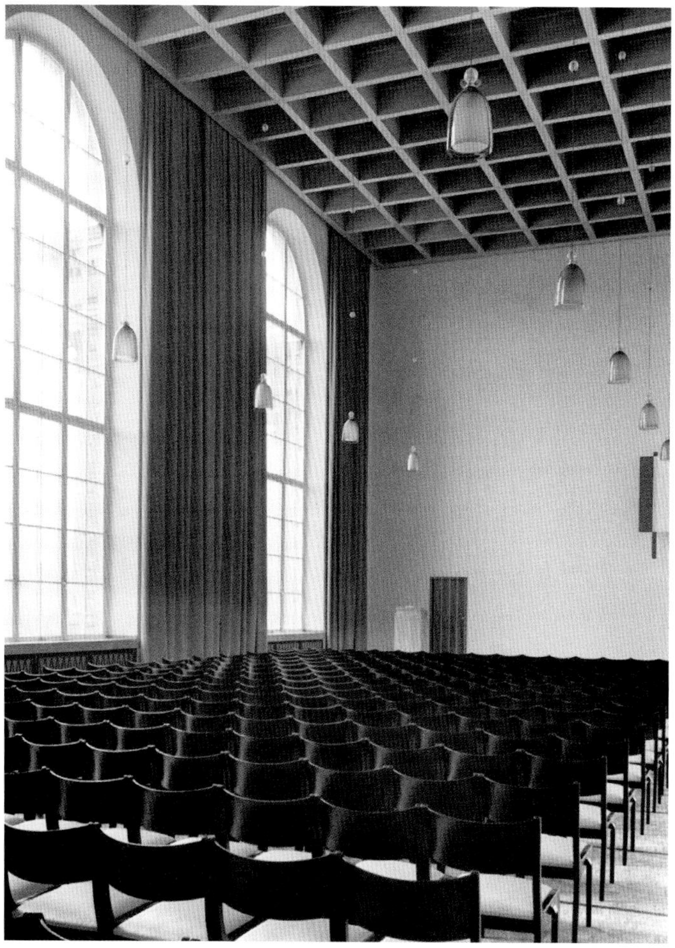

Fig. 6: The 'golden' Great Hall of the Düsseldorf Art Academy, c. 1930

Fig. 7: The Great Hall at the Düsseldorf Art Academy after it was destroyed, 1945

Figs. 8, 9: The Great Hall at the Düsseldorf Art Academy after it was rebuilt, 1953

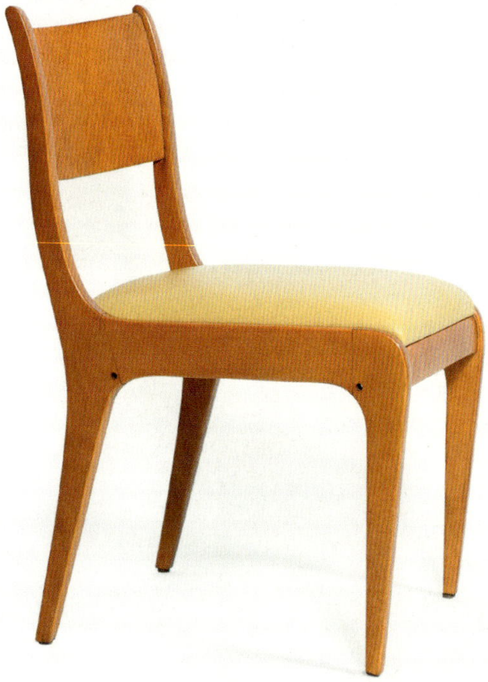

Fig. 10: The Krahn Chair *after a design by Johannes Krahn, 1935*

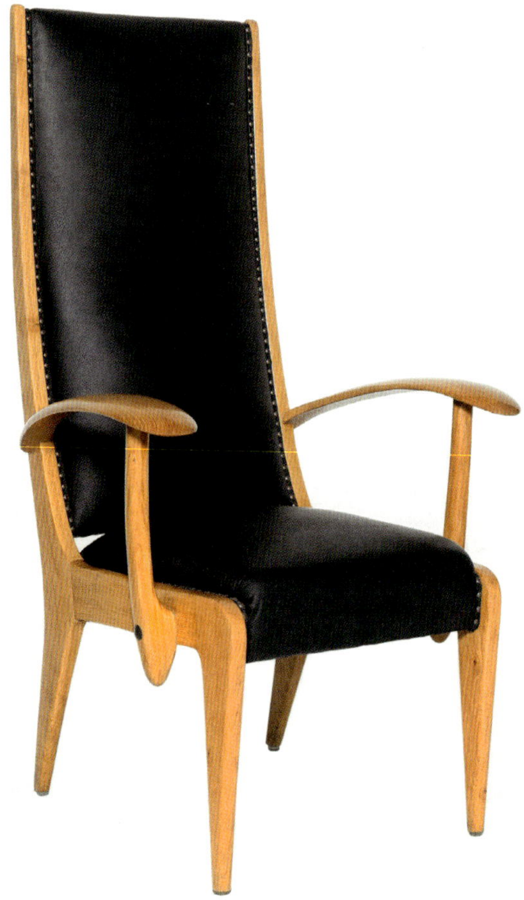

Fig. 11: An armchair after a design by Johannes Krahn, 1935

furniture made of the brass-anodised aluminium typical of the time. For the rows of chairs (seating capacity 320) what was known as the Krahn Chair was used – a model designed back in 1935 by Johannes Krahn (1908–1974) with many form variants.[7] Schwippert selected a variant that was comfortable for sitting on over long periods of time with a back made of bent plywood and simple upholstery, which was replaced by upmarket light leather upholstery in the course of a later renovation and linked with row and seat spacers (Figs. 10, 11).

The original ceiling paintings, which in the course of extensive restoration undergone at the urging of the incumbent rector, Markus Lüpertz, could be returned to their original site, had been rescued before they could be destroyed.

The table plays an exceptional role in Schwippert's oeuvre. Throughout his career as an architect, he designed numerous tables and quite a few smokers' tables,[8] as well as the 'Nation's writing table' for Konrad Adenauer. For the Düsseldorf Art Academy he first designed work tables for the artists' studios and small plywood trolleys with a wheeled metal undercarriage for materials such as paints and brushes. The tables in the conference room[9] were structured along simple lines following a principle that Schwippert also used in the first German Bundestag [Lower House of Parliament] in Bonn in 1949: columnar pedestals with black baked enamel finish and a double worktop veneered in precious elm and mounted with a gap between the table tops to serve as a shelf for documents. It was important to Schwippert that these tables should have multiple functions. The tables were made so they could be slightly shifted for clustering, yet Schwippert also wanted a square arrangement of tables for conferences – 'there is no hierarchy at a square table' (Fig. 12).[10]

The architect found the conference armchair designed by Johannes Krahn particularly suitable for large conferences. These chairs were made of solid elm wood, a European hardwood. The seats were equipped with eight-way hand-tied springs and covered with leather, which was fastened by upholstery nails with low-domed heads in dense rows. This model with its extra-high back, which was supposed to underscore special authority, had until then been reserved for the presiding officer of the parliament of the Federal Republic.[11] For the lighting, Hans Schwippert selected a metal light fixture with a stepped white aluminium shade by the Danish designer Poul Henningsen. The striking plates on the studio doors consisted of semicircular aluminium segments with a cylinder lock and

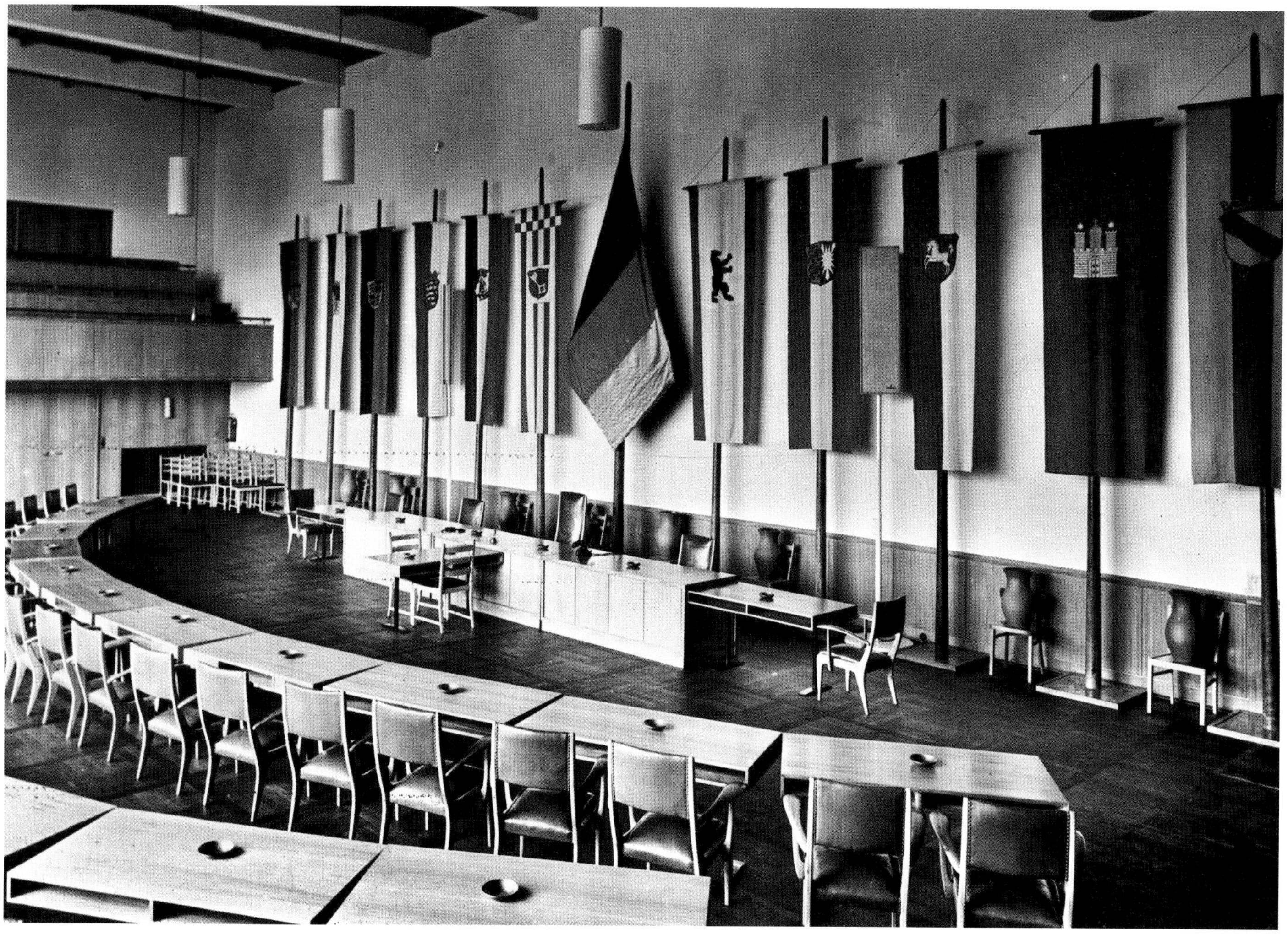

Fig. 12: The first chamber of the Bundesrat [Upper House] of the Federal Republic of Germany, 1949; columnar tables after a design by Hans Schwippert, seat furniture after a design by Johannes Krahn

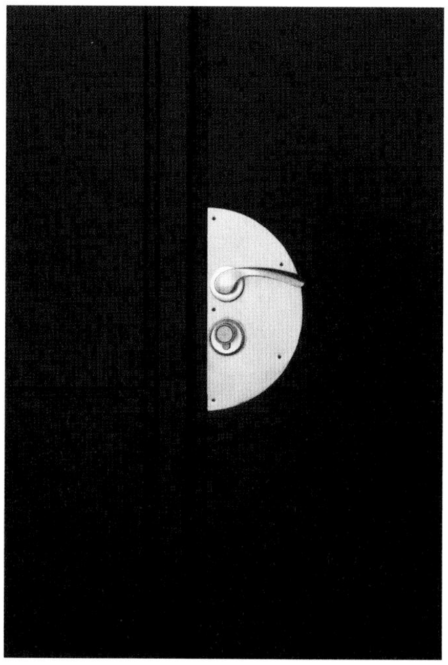

Fig. 13: Door furniture from the classroom doors after a design by Hans Schwippert, c. 1953

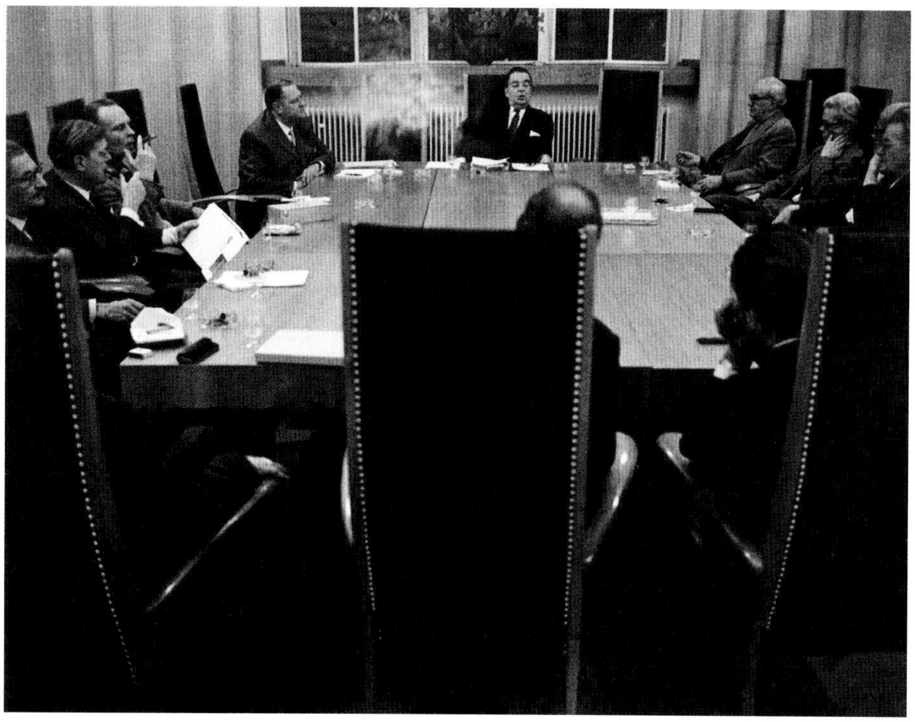

Fig. 14: Hans Schwippert and professors assembled in the Academy conference room, 1960

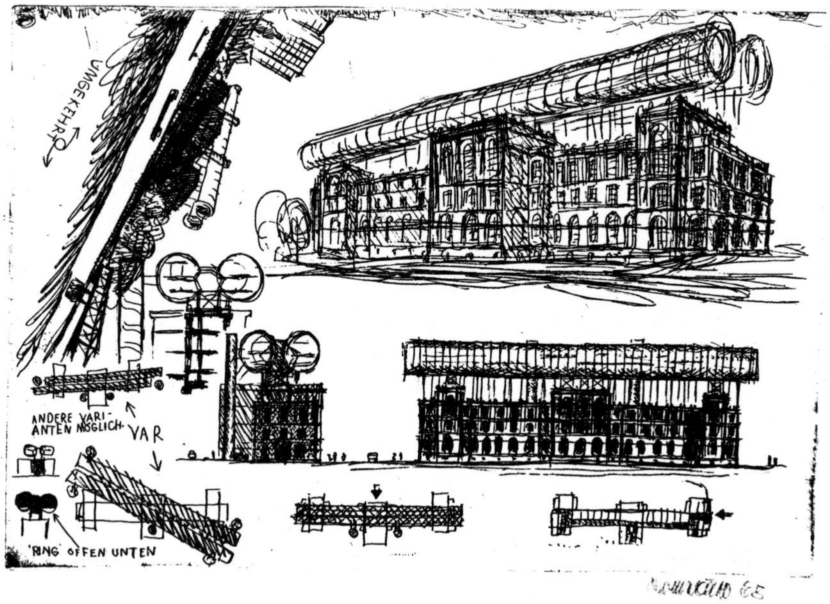

Fig. 15: Design by Karl Wimmenauer for enlarging the Düsseldorf Art Academy, 1968

were hand-made and finished off with latch furniture typical of the time (Fig. 13).

Schwippert belonged to the generation of architects who vividly remembered the history of the Weimar era. For him, refounding the Deutscher Werkbund (1950) was linked with a desire to dare a new beginning in uprightness and humility that would inform all areas of life after the ideological, political, and aesthetic offences committed during the Third Reich. The aesthetic of poverty should not be confused with 'squalor' in Schwippert's thinking. Modesty, simplicity, and reduction were, to him, it went without saying, an affirmation of democracy. In the years that followed he left his stamp on the Art Academy, both on its architecture and what it taught, which is discussed elsewhere. His concern was to reshape the idea of the Academy after 1945 for the future by drawing on its traditions (Fig. 14).

THE STEINHAUS ANNEXE

The subject of enlarging the Academy is nothing new to architecture students. Back in the 1950s the class taught by Professor Rudolf Schwarz was already preoccupied with the issue and how an annexe directly linked to the west side of the Academy building might look.[12]

The studio building planned for master studios – called the Steinhaus by students – was built between 1956 and 1958 on the plot at the corner of Eiskellerstraße and the street Reuterkaserne and was designed by Schwarz. The material used to build it was intended to match the yellow brick in its immediate surroundings. Two sawtooth roofs open to the north side with large glazed areas.[13] But it was not supposed to remain a detached building. Schwarz planned a link with the main building. The place where the link was to be attached was rendered in simple grey that indicates the direct axial link with the west side of the main building. The studio building was fully operational by the summer term of 1959. After Schwarz's death in 1961 the idea of building a link was no longer realised. Today the workshops for plastic and metals are housed in the Steinhaus.

Over the years after 1945 several buildings in the wider vicinity were mooted as extensions for the Art Academy. All those plans were, however, scrapped for organisational reasons or because the buildings were too far away from the main building. Hence the lack of space in the studios and the deferred building enlargement continued to be a pivotal subject for discussion in the Architecture Department. A single suggestion is to be gone into here to stand for the many that were advanced: in 1968 Karl Wimmenauer presented a design for enlarging the Academy by building on top of it. Two pipes resembling an outsized pair of binoculars lie on top of the main building and are at first sight as startling as the utopian designs for which Wimmenauer's favourite architect, Claude Nicolas Ledoux, was notorious. Wimmenauer assigned a supporting function to the existing Academy building as the base of the proposed superstructure (Fig. 15). Multistorey studios were to be housed in the two giant pipes, which were envisaged as a light metal construction. Wimmenauer developed the details with Lyubomir Szabo and Ernst Kasper. Finally, the load-bearing capacity of the design was analysed and certified by structural engineers.[14] Rupprecht Geiger, a painter and fellow academician, was supposed to design the show sides with significant colour surfaces. To document the proposal, photocollages were made in the Academy photo lab by Mladen Lipecki.[15]

ENLARGING THE ACADEMY BUILDING WITH THE RHINE TRACT

Finally the plans made by the state of North Rhine-Westphalia and the city of Düsseldorf to allocate the neighbouring former municipal pawnbrokers building to the Art Academy assumed concrete form between 1982 and 1984. The building had undergone several changes in function over the years: built in 1866 as the warehouse of a shipping company, it was used from 1897 until 1971 as the municipal pawnbrokers, and between 1898 and 1929 it also housed various museum collections. In the NS era the cellar was used as a torture chamber. A bronze memorial plaque attached to the east façade in 1985 recalls the atrocities committed here. Until the building was finally taken over by the Art Academy, the urban planning office used it.[16]

Even today the enlargement of the Art Academy is a pivotal subject in the architecture classes. Although the Rhine plot has provided sufficient space, this assignment is sure to be given in future as well. Professor Ernst Kasper, who had already tested the viability in 1977 with his students (Fig. 16),[17] was commissioned to design the version of the building, and the building was realised in close consultation with the authorities of the city of Düsseldorf.

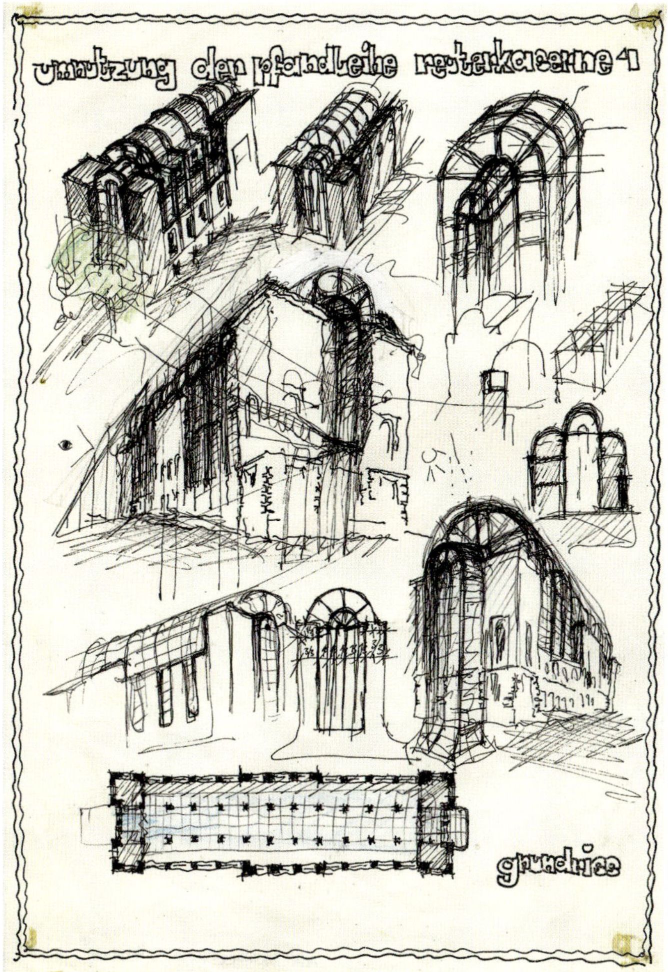

Fig. 16: Design for converting the Reuterkaserne by Agatha Buslei-Wuppermann, Professor Kasper's class, 1977

ACCESS AND SPATIAL PROGRAMME

The extensive conversion work on Reuterkaserne [Reuter Barracks] began in 1987 after plans by Ernst Kasper. The first step was gutting the building. The new approach to the other floors via a stairwell and lift was moved to the centre of the building. The entire project was under enormous deadline pressure: all work on the exterior was supposed to be finished before the 700th anniversary of the founding of the city of Düsseldorf was to be celebrated in 1988. So the once grey Reuterkaserne was resplendent in a sophisticated shade of pinkish grey on the Düsseldorf Rhine embankment and since then has been known as the Rheinflügel [Rhine Tract] (shown on p. 56). The interior of the building was finished over the course of the following year so that it was possible to move into it before the 1989 winter term.[18]

The Orientation Department found their new quarters on the ground floor (half a flight of stairs up) a good replacement for living in former barracks. The library, which had previously been housed in the dark west part of the main building, was given the gift of a lot of light and stunning views of the Rhine on the first floor.

The art history and sociology chairs were settled on the street side facing the Old Town, where there were also rooms for the head librarian and seminar rooms. The stack and archive rooms are on the second floor and the Architecture Department has been given the third floor along with the bursar's office and the funding and financial aid offices. There the architects, who had until then been dispersed about the entire main building, finally occupied contiguous rooms. A very large room facing the Rhine provides the possibility for collective work on building models, conducting round-table discussions in a large group, and throwing parties.

Kasper's design is responsive to the structure of the building, examines spatial phenomena, and forms functional areas: the offices of the four chairs of architecture are housed in the corner avant-corps. The intermediate zone is multifunctional. The offices used by the professors of philosophy, sociology, and education are on the side facing the Old Town.

The Film and Video Department is housed on the fourth floor, where there are spacious possibilities for enlargement and use by adding the attic room with a clear height of four and a half metres.

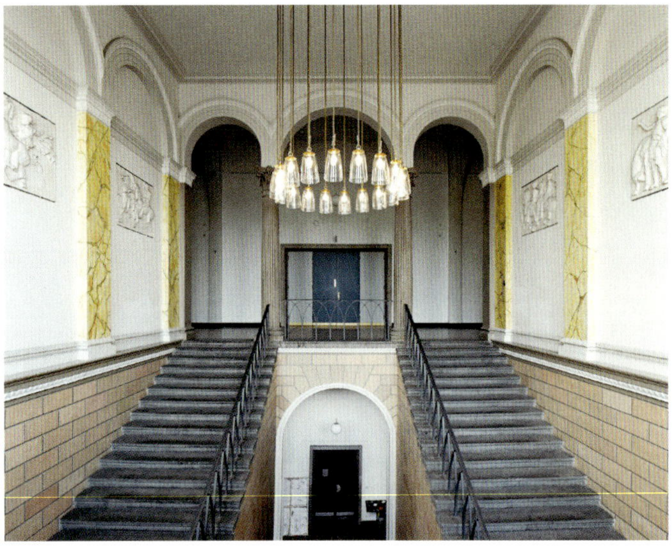

Fig. 17: Staircase leading to the Great Hall at the Düsseldorf Art Academy, 2013

THE MAIN BUILDING RESTORED AND STABILISED

Work on restoring and stabilising the main Academy building began in 1983. The first step was adding new fenestration on the north side. Some fire safety measures had become necessary as well. Finally, the façade was cleaned and the mosaics on the visible sides were restored.

Extensive overall restoration and stabilisation work was carried out from 1997 until 2001 and wrought some changes to the interior: the spacious staircase from the first to the second floor was given a colour makeover. The dado and columns were emphasised, and the pillar strips were given a marbleised finish in luminous yellow with veining in white, orange, and reddish brown that directs the viewer's eye to the Parthenon frieze.[19] In addition, soft light from graceful lighting fixtures lends the stairwell a special atmosphere that invites visitors to linger in front of the Great Hall (Fig. 17).

The Great Hall, too, was given a different colour scheme: a pink strip running around the room alludes to the murals which used to cover the room below the magnificent stucco ceiling. The dusty pink of the curtain was chosen to match it by Professor Markus Lüpertz and decided on with Professor Walter Hofmann.

The three ceiling paintings were waxed and rolled up before the 1945 bombardment so they survived the war. They were restored, put into round segmented frames, and hung from the grid ceiling. The lighting, provided by simple lightbulbs and based on a square basic grid form, is stepped to recede into the coffered ceiling (Figs. 18, 19).

Where to put the large Campendonk window[20] from the old state parliament building, which today is the K21, was the subject of protracted discussion. Finally the decision was taken in 2002 to frame this work in glass by the artist Heinrich Campendonk in wood with backlighting and to fasten it onto the rear wall of the Great Hall. This revitalisation measure taken when Markus Lüpertz was rector was the subject of controversy among the professors of the Art Academy.[21]

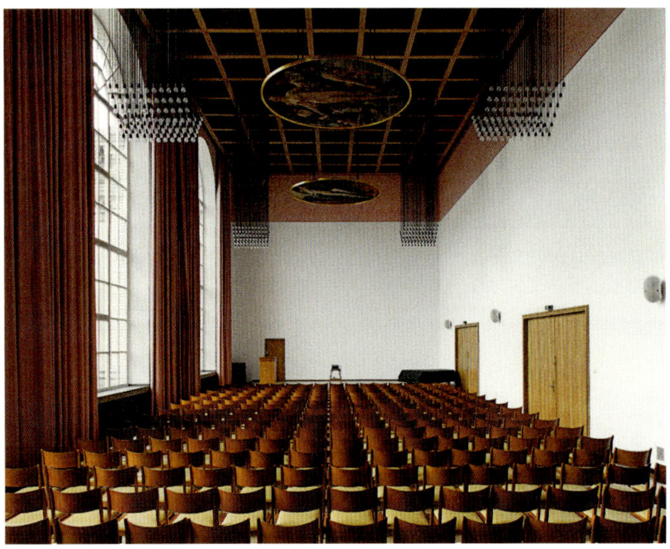

Fig. 18: The Great Hall, Düsseldorf Art Academy, 2013

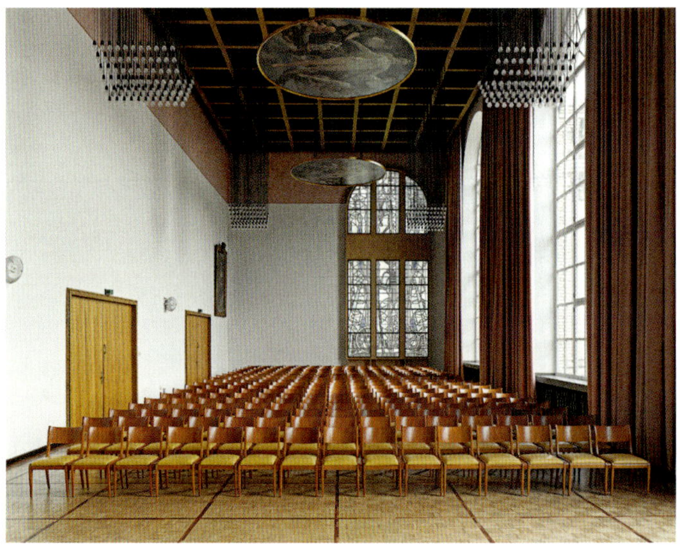

Fig. 19: The Great Hall of the Düsseldorf Art Academy after renovation, with a view of the Campendonk window, 2002

THE ACADEMY GALLERY

Five hundred metres of lovely footpath along the Rhine link the main building with the Akademie-Galerie [Academy Gallery], which was inaugurated in 2005 (Fig. 20). The new Art Academy Collection is devoted chiefly to the work produced by Düsseldorf Academy professors since 1945. The idea of creating a facility for the Art Academy on this historic site originated with Professor Markus Lüpertz, who was head of the Academy for twenty-two years, beginning as director in 1987 and serving from 1988 on as rector. He was supported by the former Lord Mayor of the city, Joachim Erwin, and Michael Vesper, Minister for Construction. In 2005 Professor Lüpertz was succeeded as rector by Professor Dr Siegfried Gohr, who has kept a considerable collection of works from the Art Academy circle here and has successfully organised and documented several exhibitions.

The Gallery is situated behind the ashlar masonry on the ground floor.[22] The building represents the perimeter development linking the Town Hall embankment with Burgplatz. It is on the site of the former Düsseldorf City Palace. Built in 1883 by Eberhard Westhofen, the structure was much simplified after the war. The ground plan is the result of the angular form of the plot (Fig. 21). The façade is first of all aligned with the magnificent architecture on the Rhine embankment, then faces the Rhine and what remains of the palace tower. On the north side it abuts Old Town buildings, which are on a smaller scale, thus clearly defining Burgplatz on this spot.

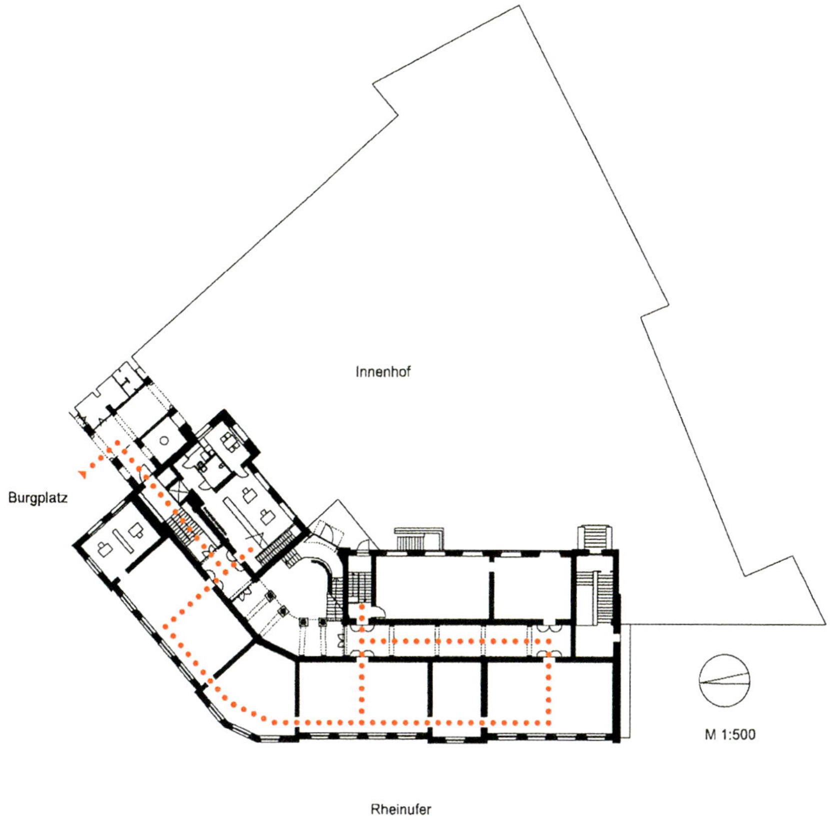

Fig. 21: The Academy Gallery, ground plan and access plan drawn up by Planungsgruppe Ernst Kasper, 2005

The spatial programme and the new concept for the entrance to the Academy Gallery were the work of Professor Ernst Kasper, who was responsible for all detail issues from the beginning of construction until the Gallery was finished on 17 February 2005 (Fig. 22). It was commissioned by the city of Düsseldorf with funding from the State of North Rhine-Westphalia represented by the Office for Property Management. Kasper gave his first instructions in the form of small sketches, which he jotted down spontaneously on paper with the experienced architect's attention to detail[23] and later worked out at his Aachen practice. Thus an access concept was prepared for visitors. The interior rooms are concentrated on a reductive language that gives the art space. The architect's sure eye for detail is revealed here, too, in the handling of the extant terrazzo flooring, which, with its reddish brown, dark brown, and white stone inlays recalls the floors in the main building (Fig. 23).

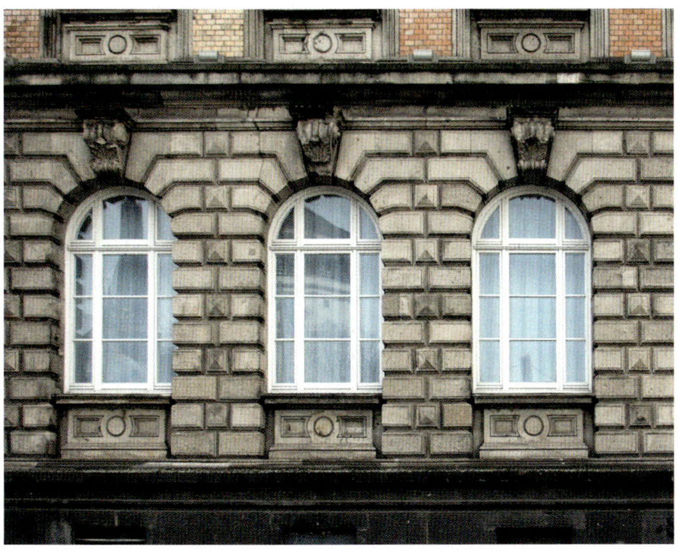

Fig. 20: The façade of the Academy Gallery, Burgplatz 1, 2007

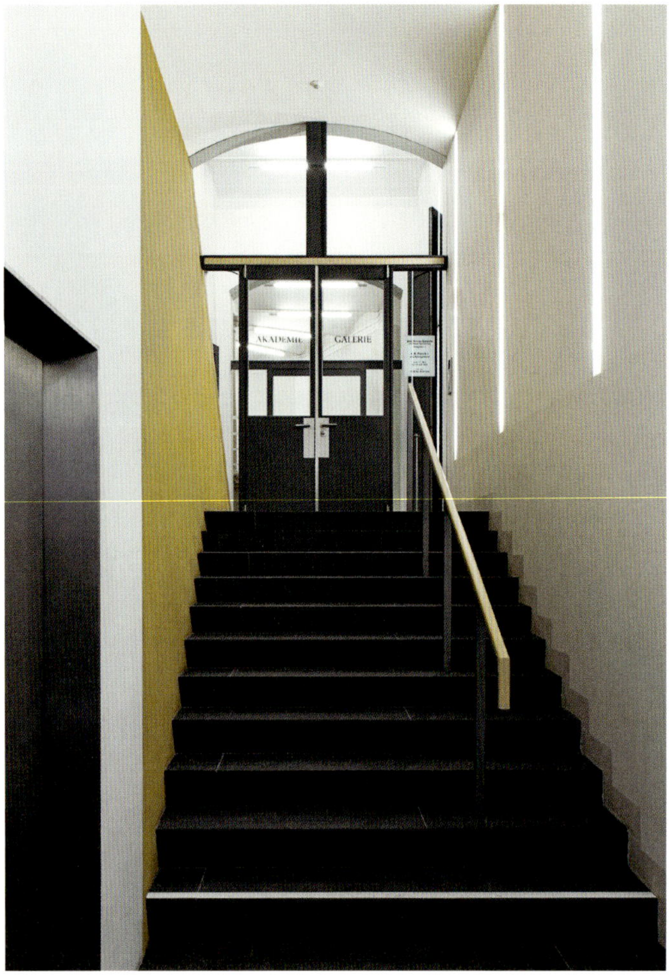

Fig. 22: The Academy Gallery, entrance design by Planungsgruppe Ernst Kasper, 2005

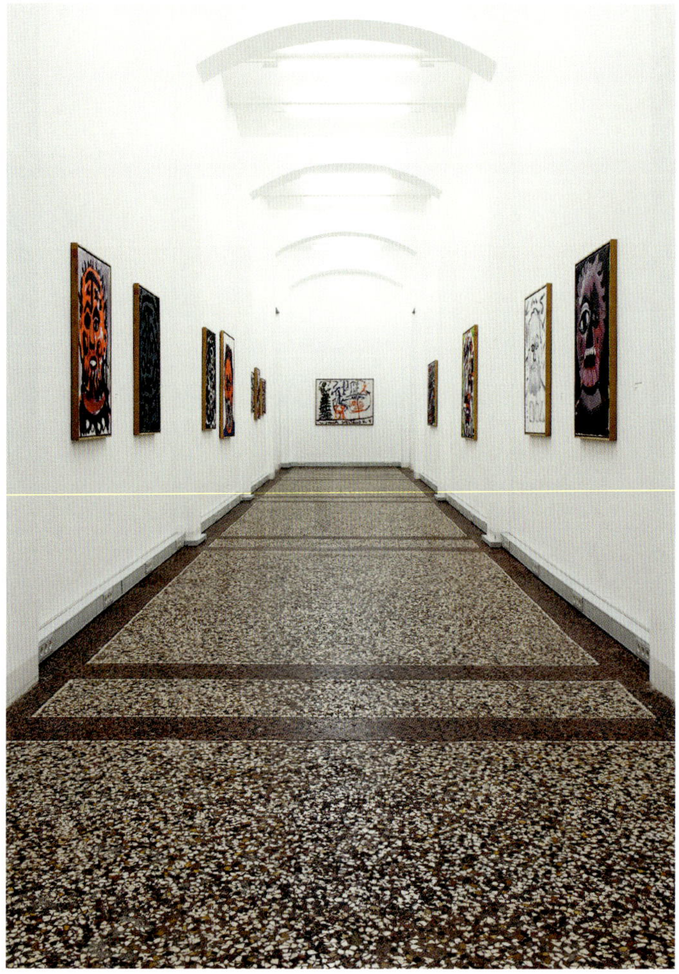

Fig. 23: The hall of the Academy Gallery with terrazzo flooring, 2013

NOTES

1 Eva Brües, 'Das Akademiegebäude', in: Eduard Trier (ed.), *Zweihundert Jahre Kunstakademie Düsseldorf*, Düsseldorf 1973, pp. 127–138; here: p. 134.

2 *Jahresbericht der Staatlichen Kunstakademie Düsseldorf 1945–1947*, Düsseldorf [1948], pp. 7f.; see the essay by Kunibert Bering in the present volume, pp. 20–36.

3 This stance on the restoration and conservation of historic buildings corresponds to that upheld by Otto Bartning, Rudolf Schwarz, and Egon Eiermann.

4 Wend Fischer, in: *Werk und Zeit* 11, January 1953, n.p.

5 Anna Klapheck, 'Die "goldnen" zwanziger Jahre. Die Akademie zwischen den beiden Kriegen', in: Trier (see n. 1), pp. 147–160; here: p. 148.

6 Lighting fixtures were made of fine cameo glass by Peill and Putzler, a firm in Düren.

7 Johannes Krahn worked as a self-employed architect together with Rudolf Schwarz and Hans Schwippert in Aachen in the late 1920s and early 1930s. The basic model of the seat furniture by Johannes Krahn exists in various finishes and form variants and was used by Hans Schwippert in almost all projects after 1958 – for instance, in the First German Bundestag in Bonn. The Krahn Chair, which represented the style of the fledgling Federal Republic of Germany because of where it was used, was awarded a gold medal at the 1951 Milan Triennale.

8 Smokers' tables about 60 to 65 cm high combined with 'ashtrays' were very popular interior design features at that time.

9 He had those tables worked over by Ernst Kasper; see Agatha Buslei-Wuppermann and Andreas Zeising, 'Geleitwort' [Foreword], in: id. (eds.), *Vom Machen und Brauchen. Schriften zu Architektur und Gestaltung*, Düsseldorf 2008, pp. 7f.

10 Markus Lüpertz had the tables replaced by a large, rectangular table.

11 Norbert Helmus, 'Der Krahn-Stuhl', in: Agatha Buslei-Wuppermann and Andreas Zeising (eds.), *Das Bundeshaus von Hans Schwippert in Bonn. Architektonische Moderne und demokratischer Geist*, Düsseldorf 2009, p. 34, pp. 138–141.

12 The Steinhaus replaces the ruins of the studio for monumental sculpture and the former student dormitory; 'Neue Atelierbauten an der Akademie', *Rheinische Post*, 12 September 1957; 'Ein neues Bildhaueratelier', *Mittag*, 8 October 1958.

13 Wolfgang Pehnt and Hilde Strohl, *Rudolf Schwarz 1897–1961. Architekt einer anderen Moderne*, Ostfildern 1997, p. 287.

14 Technical consultants: Integral, Architekten und Ingenieure. Structural engineering certified by Stefan Polónyi, TU Berlin. Professor Dr mult. Stefan Polónyi in conversation with the author in March 2013. Also see the folder with detailed data: 'Projekt zur Erweiterung der Staatlichen Kunstakademie Düsseldorf', Düsseldorf Art Academy archives.

15 Heinrich Klotz (ed.), *Vision der Moderne. Das Prinzip Konstruktion*, exhib. cat. Frankfurt am Main, Munich 1986, pp. 257–263.

16 Ute Rasch, 'Gedenkstätte mitten in der Altstadt?', *Neue Rheinische Zeitung*, 23 February 1985; Marion Hänschen, 'Im Keller folterten die Nazis', *Westdeutsche Zeitung*, 23 February 1985; Gerda Kaltwasser, 'Gedenkstätte in den Folterraum?', *Rheinische Post*, 23 February 1985.

17 Agatha Buslei-Wuppermann, designs for converting the municipal pawnbrokers, Reuterkaserne, into a studio house for students and guests of the Düsseldorf State Art Academy, 1977.

18 The makeshift pavilions put up in 1973 for the Orientation Department, the silkscreen printing class, and the film and video class were demolished after the inauguration.

19 See Brües (see n. 1), pp. 127–138.

20 Heinrich Campendonk (1889–1957) shaped Rhenish Expressionism in a stringently geometric language of forms.

21 The interventions in the reconstruction architecture, which was entirely orientated towards modest reticence, triggered off controversy and heated discussions, especially with the architecture professors.

22 The Decorative Arts School, which was once housed here, was in its heyday from 1903 until 1907, when it was headed by Peter Behrens.

23 Ingrid van Hüllen/Planungsgruppe Kasper, documents for the renovations, Aachen 2005.

THE ACADEMY GALLERY – THE NEW COLLECTION

Siegfried Gohr

When the idea of the ancient academy was revived in the Italian Renaissance, European academicians began to amass collections as teaching aids. In some places the collections grew as large as museum collections because exemplary works by artists outside the academies were also collected. Institutions were founded that are famous today, such as the Galleria dell'Accademia in Venice, and collections along similar lines in Madrid, Vienna, or the Royal Academy of Art Collection in London, to name just a few examples. Lambert Krahe, founder of the Düsseldorf Art Academy, had assembled an extensive collection of drawings and prints, which was finally bought at the behest of the Elector to be made accessible to the public – the 'alte Sammlung' [Old Collection].[1] Astonishingly, collecting did not resume immediately after Krahe died in 1790. On the other hand, works by members of the Academy were acquired fairly systematically from about 1839 on by the neighbouring art museum. Krahe's vast legacy of works on paper ended up being deposited at the art museum, where it was arranged by contract in 1932 that they would be kept and administered for fifty years. The contract was renewed for another thirty years on 8 February 1993.[2]

During his rectorate (1986–2009) Markus Lüpertz revived the idea of founding a proprietary Academy museum where works by members and outstanding graduates could be collected and shown. The city of Düsseldorf had relocated its administration departments during the 1990s so that a building became vacant on Burgplatz, abutting the Town Hall; the local residents' registration office that had been housed there moved into other rooms. Lüpertz succeeded in convincing Joachim Erwin, then Lord Mayor, of the viability of his plans for a gallery. Dating from 1883, the vacant building had once before, not long after it was built, been put to cultural use because from 1893 until 1919 it had housed the Applied Arts School, which for a time was headed by Peter Behrens. Joachim Erwin had at first shown little interest in the project, and it is due to Lüpertz's persistence and powers of persuasion that the Lord Mayor's attitude gradually changed to a positive one. Minister Michael Vesper also lent a helping hand by earmarking state urban development funding for the renovating the interior, which provided 650 m^2 of floor space, and converting it to meet museum standards. A permission-for-use contract was concluded that came into force as of 1 March 2005 for a period of twenty years with the option to renew for a further ten.

When it became possible to begin converting the rooms on the floor halfway up to the first floor, Ernst Kasper, as a professor of architecture at the Academy, took on the task of redesigning them. In close consultation with Markus Lüpertz, he created a flight of cabinets that received natural light from the fenestration facing Burgplatz. The practical side was taken over by Ernst Kasper's architecture practice, specifically by Dieter Willinek, who supervised the work along the lines envisaged by Kasper and Lüpertz. When the gallery was ready for use, the empty rooms were presented to the public on 17 February 2005. On that occasion only two artworks were shown: an early Wilhelm Lehmbruck sculpture owned by the Academy and a work by Paul Klee, who had been a professor in Düsseldorf for a brief while until the National Socialists summarily cut short his teaching career.

The press reportage on the new museum sent out confusing signals to the public right from the start because gallerists maintained that the Academy Gallery was a commercial enterprise for selling art. To the contrary, as in other similar historic institutions that looked back on a long tradition, the aim underpinning the founding of the Gallery was to build up a collection related to the Academy. The fallacious information put about by the media was bad publicity for the Gallery. Still, it is

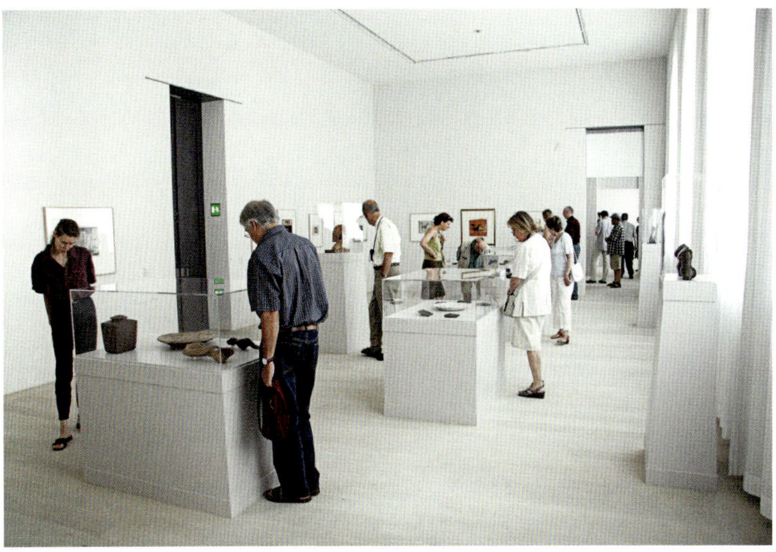

Fig. 1: A view of the Ewald Mataré *exhibition at the Academy Gallery, 2005*

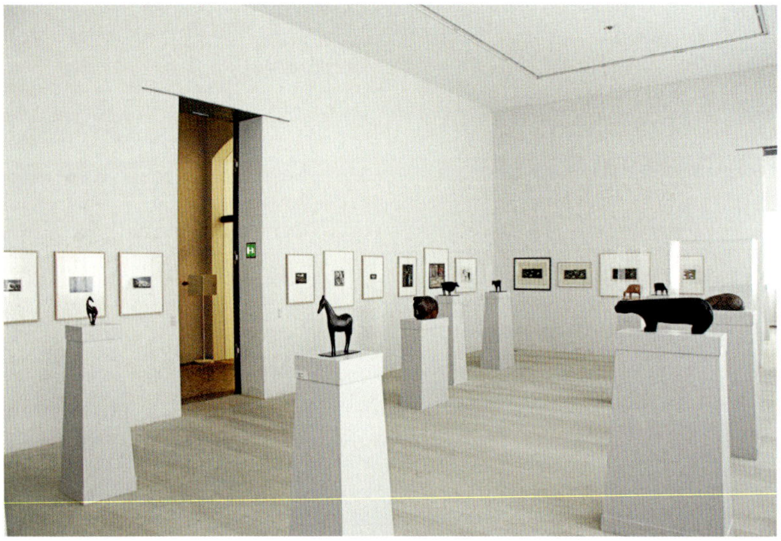

Fig. 2: A view of the first room of the Ewald Mataré *exhibition at the Academy Gallery, 2005*

clear to any thinking person that the Art Academy may neither operate on a commercial basis nor would want to.

The first exhibition opened on 8 June 2005; it was a tribute to Ewald Mataré, who was one of the most influential teachers at the Academy before and after the Second World War (Fig. 1). The calendar of events at the Gallery consists of mounting retrospectives of important professors and presenting the collection that has been growing since 1945. Exhibitions of the work of Bruno Goller, Erwin Heerich, Karl Otto Götz, Markus Lüpertz, and A. R. Penck have been organised. Since the Gallery only has 650 m^2 of floor space that can be used for exhibitions, it does not permit very large presentations. Hence exhibitions are devoted to a particular perspective on each subject chosen; where it has made sense, works on paper have been included – continuing the tradition of the Krahe collection. Photographers, mainly from the Museum Kunstpalast collections, have often been shown documenting artists at work or in the Academy.

Going into the particulars of every exhibition does not seem called for but some notable ones will nonetheless be outlined here. Since Ewald Mataré was the most influential Academy teacher after the war, and since before it he had already left a lasting stamp on the Academy both practically and conceptually, the decision was soon taken to devote the first exhibition to him. Mataré's daughter Sonja still lived where the master had resided so that a whiff of the earlier atmosphere was still perceptible in that environment during preparations for the exhibition. Sonja Mataré did everything she could to help and so did Guido de Werd, director of the Museum Kurhaus Kleve, who had rendered great service in his handling of Mataré's estate, which his museum curates to an exceptional standard. Works to be loaned to the Academy Gallery were assembled from the Museum Kurhaus Kleve, the museum in Moyland Castle, and other public and private collections. Rector Lüpertz was actively involved in the preparations and even did the sketch for the unusual dado, which was made by the Academy carpentry workshop, from an old photograph of a Mataré exhibition (Fig. 2).

The return to Mataré gave the Academy the idea of documenting his work in public spaces in Düsseldorf and the environs. Vanessa Sondermann, an art historian, the photographer Sebastian Riemer, and Sonja Mataré were responsible for the content of the book, which was published by Droste in Düsseldorf in 2009.

Synchronously with the inaugural exhibition at which the rooms of the Academy Gallery were opened to the public on 8 June 2005, soliciting began for donations to the collection that was to be created (Fig. 3). The idea behind this action was to be able to show artists who had taught at the Academy since 1945 with characteristic works. To underscore their personal affiliation with the Academy as an institution, works sought were to have dated preferably from the Academy years of the professors concerned. The number of such works donated soon grew to more than a hundred and by now has risen to nearly a thousand. Since the Art Academy itself has no funding in its budget earmarked for acquisitions, the exhibitions mounted by the Gallery have provided good opportunities for inspiring further donations. Now, with very few exceptions, all Academy artists are represented by works in the collection. What proved quite difficult was including post-war painters with good

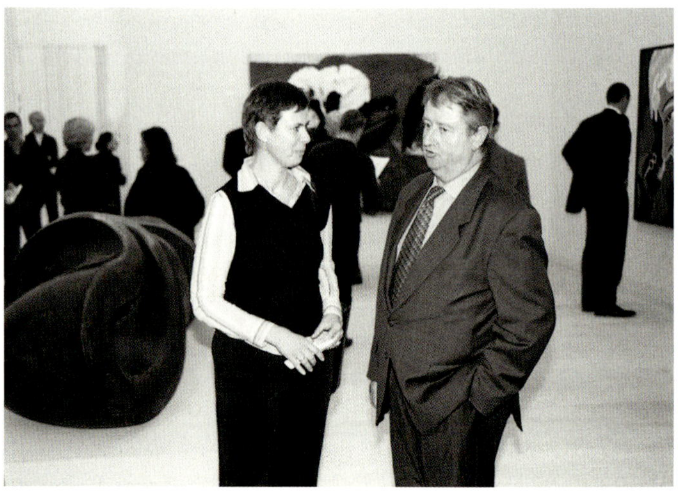

Fig. 3: Siegfried Gohr in conversation, Erste Präsentation *[First Presentation] exhibition at the Academy Gallery, 2005*

examples of their work; last year, however, the panorama was completed thanks to private donations and with the help of the Gesellschaft von Freunden und Förderern der Kunstakademie Düsseldorf e. V. [Society of Friends and Sponsors of the Düsseldorf Art Academy e. V.].

It was not long before the first results of building up the collection could be presented before the series of monographic retrospectives continued in 2006 with Karl Otto Götz. The very elderly painter, who is still actively at work, consulted with his wife, Rissa, and the head of the Gallery on the concept of the exhibition, which comprised several decades of his work up to and including his most recent pictures. Like Mataré, Götz was a charismatic teacher, even though his focus was very different. Whereas Mataré was still rooted in classical Modernism, Götz represented the rise of abstract art as it blazed the way in Düsseldorf or Paris after the Second World War (Fig. 4).

The latter half of 2006 saw the Academy Gallery involved in the first Quadriennale initiated by the city of Düsseldorf with a selection of Bruno Goller's pictures of women. Swimming against the mainstream dominance of abstract art after the Second World War, Goller adhered unwaveringly to painting characterised by the intense, icon-like representation of objects, which were quite often combined with figures, usually of women. These beings seem enigmatic and mysterious, in an austere style that seems to refer back to 1920s' Italian painting, when motifs and stylistic elements from antiquity again found their way into the lexis of painting.

One spectacular event that inflamed passions, the press, and politics and continued to be controversial for quite a while should not be forgotten: the building of a pop-up 'Pavilion for Sculpture' that stood for three months on the grounds of the Ehrenhof in Düsseldorf. Designed by Rector Markus Lüpertz for the 2006 Quadriennale, it was in an antiquising style and housed sixteen works of sculpture. The pavilion represented a playful approach to the situation then prevailing in sculpture (shown on p. 57).

To underscore the links between the historical Academy Collection and its importance for the tradition of the institution and direct renewed attention to it, a representative selection of drawings dating from the sixteenth to the twenty-first centuries was shown at the Gallery in 2007. It was followed by a significant monographic presentation of Erwin Heerich's work. He had begun his studies under Mataré but soon found

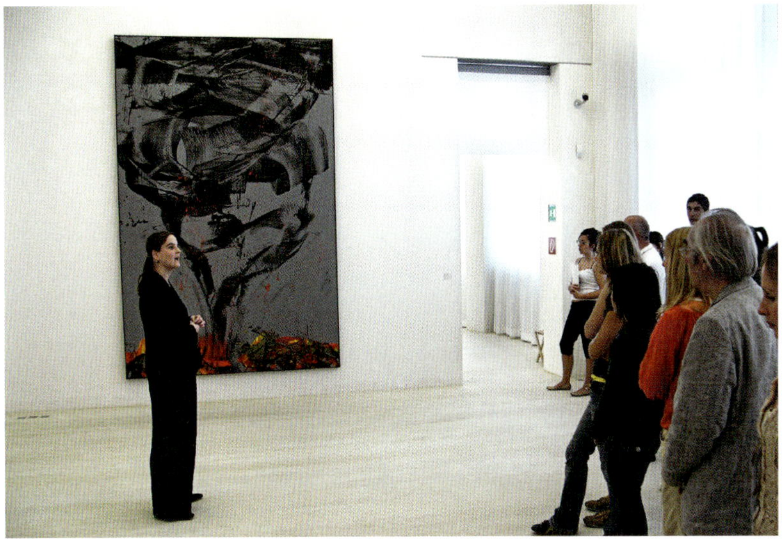

Fig. 4: Vanessa Sondermann guiding through the K. O. Götz *exhibition at the Academy Gallery, 2006*

his way to a concentrated abstract language for his sculpture, architecture, and prints from fine cardboard as the relief surface. His use of wood, metal, stone, or even cardboard may have been a lingering echo of the diversity of materials for which Mataré's work is known but Heerich translated that inspiration into a modern language of his own that revealed parallels with American Minimalism although he was not influenced by it.

It had struck me quite some time before the Academy Gallery opened that Academy artists were constantly invoking Albrecht Dürer, the great German Renaissance artist and theorist. And not just in the nineteenth century, when the 400th anniversary of the Nuremberg master's death sparked off a regular Dürer cult in 1828. Mataré painted landscape watercolours which even down to the design of the signature revealed a closeness to Dürer's revolutionary watercolours. Joseph Beuys, Sigmar Polke, Jörg Immendorff, Markus Lüpertz, Dieter Roth, and many others had produced works that revolved around Dürer. It seemed a good idea, therefore, to select the Dürer prints and drawings from the historic Academy Collection that had inspired the modern masters. Thus links with tradition could again be presented.

Before the Academy bade farewell to Markus Lüpertz as rector and professor with a party in the summer of 2009, the Academy Gallery had exhibited a selection of his works in a themed exhibition devoted to 'Death' as its spring show. Lüpertz had frequently caused the symbol of the skull to appear in his work and the motif also plays a pivotal role in his writing. Hence it was possible to draw on a large number of works and to borrow characteristic and varied examples that were perfectly suited to the rooms of the Academy Gallery. The show had the largest number of visitors of any since the Academy opened in 2005.

The third element of the work done at the Gallery is representing the individual subject areas taught at the Academy: the

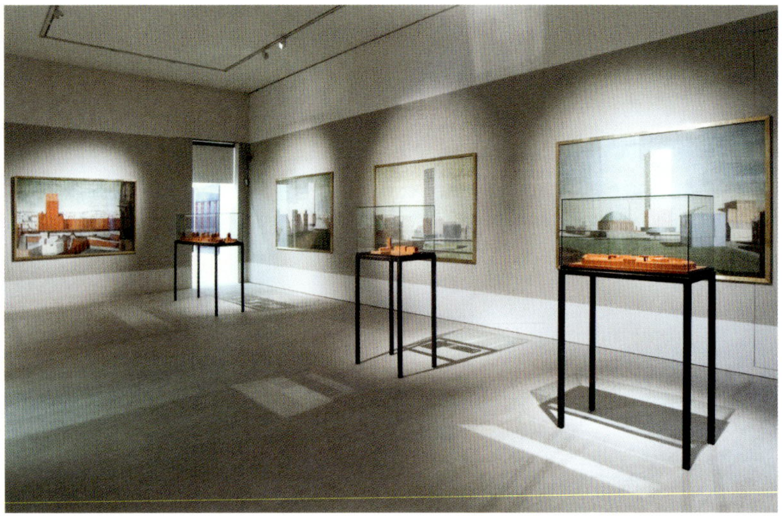

Fig. 5: Installation view of the Ortner room in the Dudler, Ortner, Petzinka, Schultes. Baukunst an der Kunstakademie Düsseldorf *[Architecture at the Düsseldorf Art Academy] exhibition at the Academy Gallery, 2010*

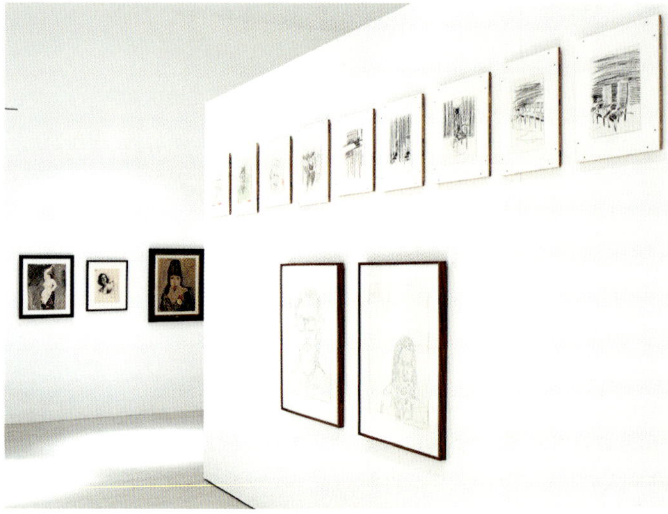

Fig. 6: Installation view of the Kopf und Hand. Variationen zur Zeichnung *[Head and Hand. Variations on Drawing] exhibition; left: three drawings by Francis Picabia, right: drawings by Rosemarie Trockel, at the Academy Gallery, 2010/11*

first discipline to be presented in this framework was architecture, which was very elaborately staged (Fig. 5). Max Dudler, Laurids Ortner, Karl-Heinz (Calle) Petzinka, and Axel Schultes were at that time all teaching the subject, which at the Academy was supposed to be taught in such a manner as to emphasise the special closeness between architecture and art. In a certain sense, the professorship for the integration of fine art and architecture held by Hubert Kiecol represented the linkage of fine art and architecture. A compendious catalogue was published to accompany the exhibition, which not least, like the show itself, was intended to make potential students aware of the possibilities at the Academy.

The series of shows representing courses of study or genres continued at the 2010 Quadriennale 2010 with *Mit Kopf und Hand* [With Head and Hand], an extensive exhibition of drawings. A prologue with drawings by Ernst Ludwig Kirchner, Roy Lichtenstein, Henri Michaux, and Francis Picabia opened the field of the modern possibilities for drawing. A large number of drawings by Academy artists came next. The hanging of them avoided the usual cabinet character of such presentations, and the exhibition was fitted out with installative features (Fig. 6).

How to represent the diversity of painting at the Academy to be represented in a way analogous to the exhibitions drawing on the fields of drawing and architecture that had already taken place? We decided on a two-part presentation entitled *Rendezvous der Maler* [A Painters' Reunion] I and II. The title was an allusion to the celebrated Max Ernst painting *A Friends' Reunion* (1922), which hangs in the Museum Ludwig in Cologne. At the Academy Gallery exhibition, painters from 1945 until 1985 were the first to be shown. In this case it was not all that easy to find representative works from that time span by post-war professors. The second part of the show covered painters from 1985 to the present. Publications associated with it contained information on the artists' lives and Academy years as well as numerous illustrations. The two exhibitions served as preparation for the book on the history of the Academy since 1945 that is now available as the present volume.

The corresponding project devoted to photography at the Düsseldorf Art Academy in 2012 was particularly ambitious. Here basic research was necessary and a great deal of information that could be gleaned from eyewitnesses had to be taken into account. Hans Irrek was engaged as co-curator on the advice of Andreas Gursky. It took numerous visits and conversations for a selection to be made, which would include particularly successful or promising students for the first time – which will remain an exception to the rule – in the representation of contemporary photography.

The exhibition showed the entire panorama of photography since 1960, even including some video pieces; this wide-ranging approach had the effect of relativising any focusing on the so-called 'Becher School' – the term is a journalistic invention and possesses only limited art historical relevance. The catalogue became a rich trove of source materials which further research and representations can draw on.

Whereas the other art museums and exhibition venues in Düsseldorf are part of the national and international events circuit, and naturally also cover historical subject matter, the Academy Gallery concentrates on the past and present of the Academy as an institution for training artists that was founded in 1773, initially on a private basis. That is why the Gallery is integrated in the education offered in the classes, whose members can benefit from Gallery activities through information, discussion, and example. But of course the main concern of the Gallery is to give the public a glimpse into the inner workings of the Academy, which is otherwise only possible at the yearly Academy Tours.

Since the exhibitions mounted at the Academy Gallery were not supposed to – and need not – follow the mainstream and since visitor information and exhibition didactics were to remain in the background behind the artworks, it was possible to shape the experience with, and in front of, art as intensively as it could be. This matches the self-image of an Art Academy like the one in Düsseldorf that has always seen art and artists as being at the centre and source of life.

Catalogues have been issued to accompany all Academy Gallery exhibitions except for the first presentation of the collections. From 2005 until 2010 they were designed by Walter Nikkels, professor of typography. After he reached retirement age and left the Academy, Hans-Georg Kühle, once a visiting student in Nikkels's class, took over this work. In addition to the catalogues, the posters and other printed matter for the Academy Gallery were also designed by Nikkels and Kühle (Figs. 7, 8).

In 2013 two more monographic exhibitions devoted to the work of A. R. Penck and Gotthard Graubner respectively were realised: Penck had held a professorship for the graphic arts from 1989 until 2005. At the Gallery, however, a retrospective of his paintings and sculpture was shown because Penck had never limited his classroom teaching to the graphic arts in the narrowest sense of the term. The early works from the 1960s, which were unknown to most students, were particularly impressive, but so were the diversity and radicalism of the sculpture.

A Gotthard Graubner retrospective featuring a selection of paintings and works on paper was added to the calendar of events on account of the painter's death in Düsseldorf on 24 May 2013. Graubner was not only devoted to the Academy during long years as a professor from 1976 until 1996 and after that as a lecturer on a short-term contract from 1996 until 1998 but later was often seen as a guest on numerous occasions. With what were known as *Kissenbilder* [Cushion Pictures] Graubner had found a method of making colour visible in space as a solid – bypassing gesture and designed form. Many viewers associated the meditative qualities that this sorcerer of colour could conjure up with a spirituality that was not only rooted in the abstraction of Modernism but also derived from profound study of Asian art.

NOTES

1 More extensively covered in the essay by Dawn Leach in the present volume, pp. 416–426.
2 More extensively covered in the essay by Peter M. Lynen in the present volume, pp. 37–64.

Double page overleaf:

Fig. 7: Posters for exhibitions at the Akademie-Galerie – Die Neue Sammlung, 2005 to 2009. Form and typography: Walter Nikkels, assistant Neil Holt.

Fig. 8: Posters for exhibitions at the Akademie-Galerie – Die Neue Sammlung, 2009 to 2013. All posters were designed by Kühle and Mozer in Cologne except the poster for the Fassbender exhibition. Form and typography: Walter Nikkels, assistant Neil Holt.

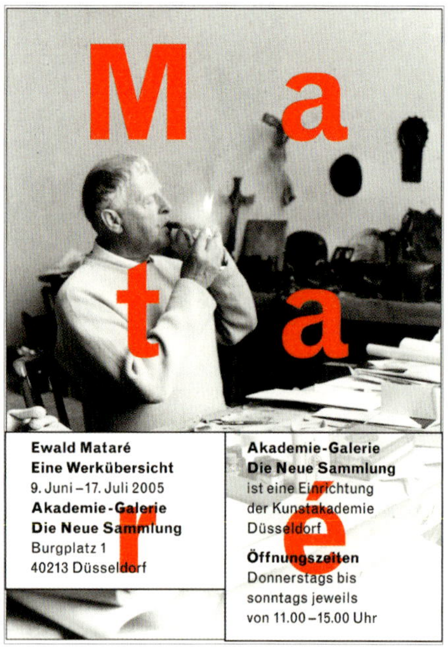
Ma
ta
ré
Ewald Mataré
Eine Werkübersicht
9. Juni – 17. Juli 2005
Akademie-Galerie
Die Neue Sammlung
Burgplatz 1
40213 Düsseldorf
Akademie-Galerie
Die Neue Sammlung
ist eine Einrichtung
der Kunstakademie
Düsseldorf
Öffnungszeiten
Donnerstags bis
sonntags jeweils
von 11.00 – 15.00 Uhr

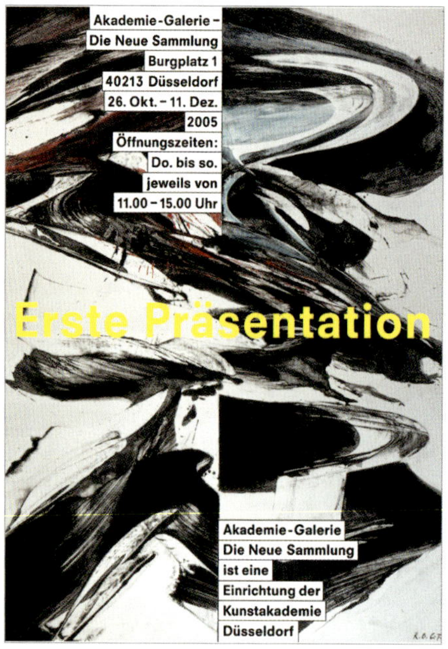
Akademie-Galerie –
Die Neue Sammlung
Burgplatz 1
40213 Düsseldorf
26. Okt. – 11. Dez.
2005
Öffnungszeiten:
Do. bis so.
jeweils von
11.00 – 15.00 Uhr
Erste Präsentation
Akademie-Galerie
Die Neue Sammlung
ist eine
Einrichtung der
Kunstakademie
Düsseldorf

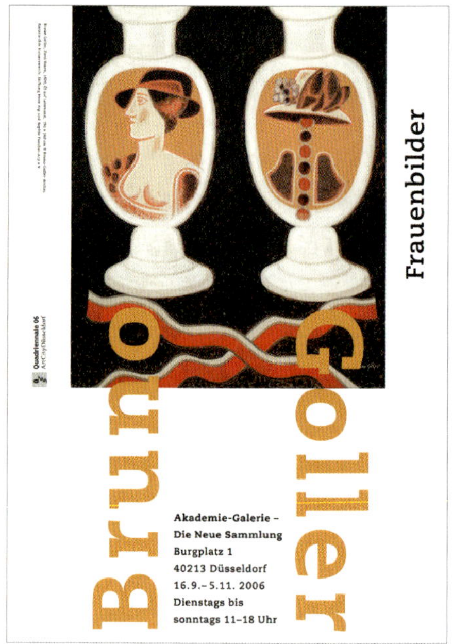
Frauenbilder
Bruno Goller
Akademie-Galerie –
Die Neue Sammlung
Burgplatz 1
40213 Düsseldorf
16.9. – 5.11. 2006
Dienstags bis
sonntags 11–18 Uhr

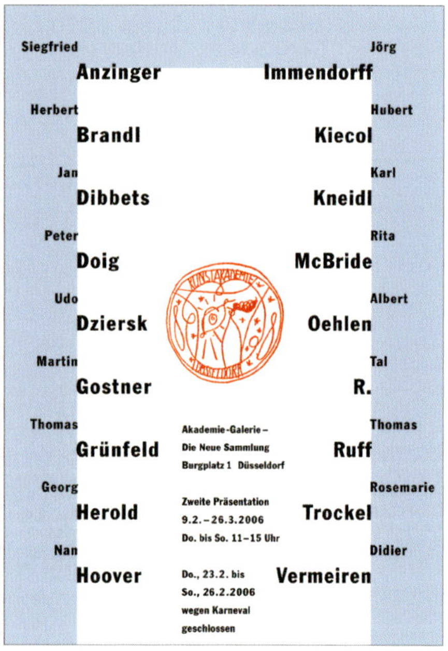
Siegfried Anzinger
Jörg Immendorff
Herbert Brandl
Hubert Kiecol
Jan Dibbets
Karl Kneidl
Peter Doig
Rita McBride
Udo Dziersk
Albert Oehlen
Martin Gostner
Tal R.
Thomas Grünfeld
Thomas Ruff
Georg Herold
Rosemarie Trockel
Nan Hoover
Didier Vermeiren
Akademie-Galerie –
Die Neue Sammlung
Burgplatz 1 Düsseldorf
Zweite Präsentation
9.2. – 26.3.2006
Do. bis So. 11–15 Uhr
Do., 23.2. bis
So., 26.2.2006
wegen Karneval
geschlossen

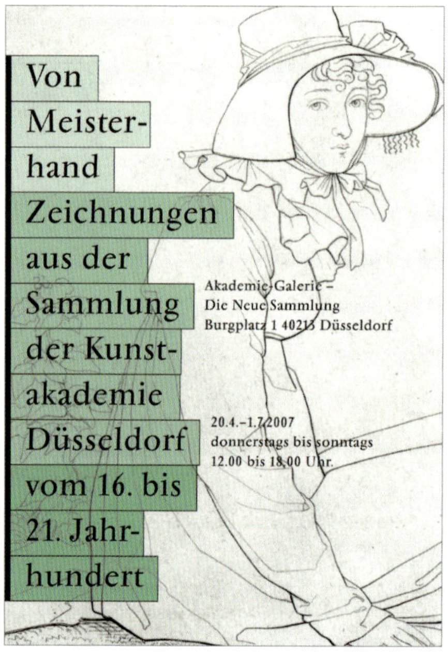
Von
Meister-
hand
Zeichnungen
aus der
Sammlung
der Kunst-
akademie
Düsseldorf
vom 16. bis
21. Jahr-
hundert
Akademie-Galerie –
Die Neue Sammlung
Burgplatz 1 40213 Düsseldorf
20.4. – 1.7.2007
donnerstags bis sonntags
12.00 bis 18.00 Uhr.

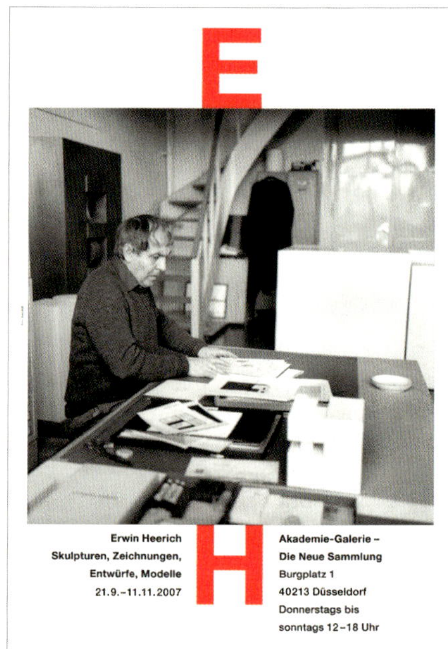
E
H
Erwin Heerich
Skulpturen, Zeichnungen,
Entwürfe, Modelle
21.9. – 11.11.2007
Akademie-Galerie –
Die Neue Sammlung
Burgplatz 1
40213 Düsseldorf
Donnerstags bis
sonntags 12–18 Uhr

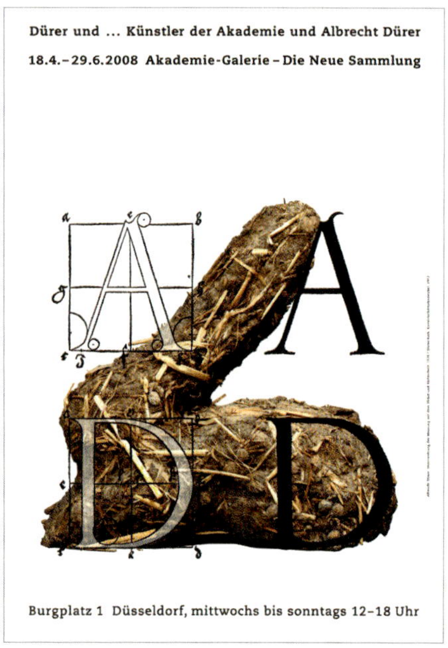
Dürer und ... Künstler der Akademie und Albrecht Dürer
18.4. – 29.6.2008 Akademie-Galerie – Die Neue Sammlung
AA
DD
Burgplatz 1 Düsseldorf, mittwochs bis sonntags 12–18 Uhr

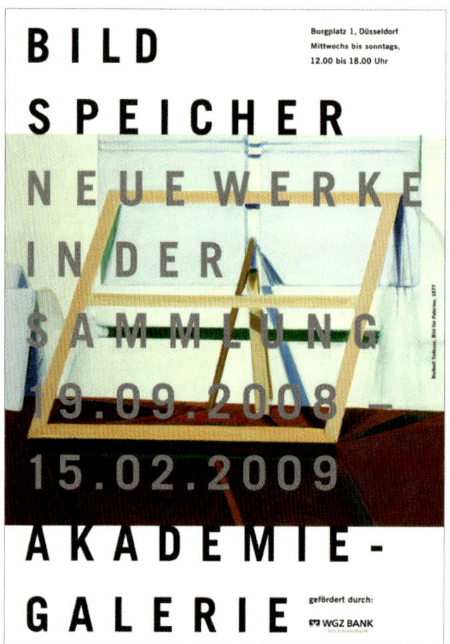
BILD
SPEICHER
NEUE WERKE
IN DER
SAMMLUNG
19.09.2008 –
15.02.2009
AKADEMIE-
GALERIE
Burgplatz 1, Düsseldorf
Mittwochs bis sonntags,
12.00 bis 18.00 Uhr
gefördert durch:
WGZ BANK

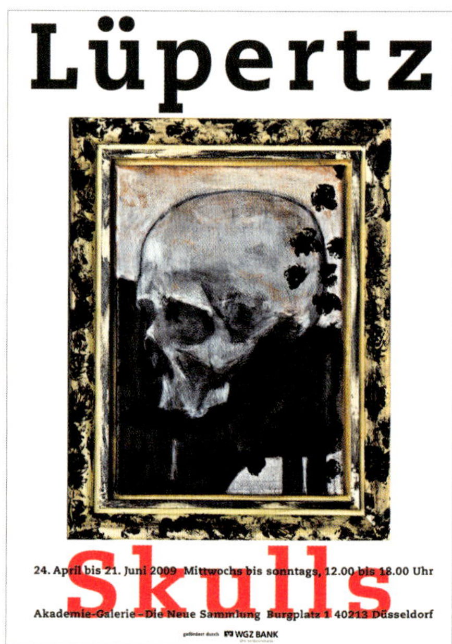
Lüpertz
Skulls
24. April bis 21. Juni 2009 Mittwochs bis sonntags, 12.00 bis 18.00 Uhr
Akademie-Galerie – Die Neue Sammlung Burgplatz 1 40213 Düsseldorf
WGZ BANK

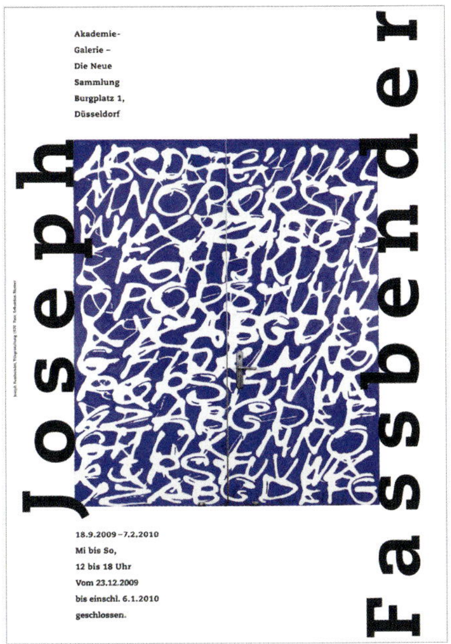
Akademie-
Galerie –
Die Neue
Sammlung
Burgplatz 1,
Düsseldorf
Joseph
Fassbender
18.9.2009–7.2.2010
Mi bis So,
12 bis 18 Uhr
Vom 23.12.2009
bis einschl. 6.1.2010
geschlossen.

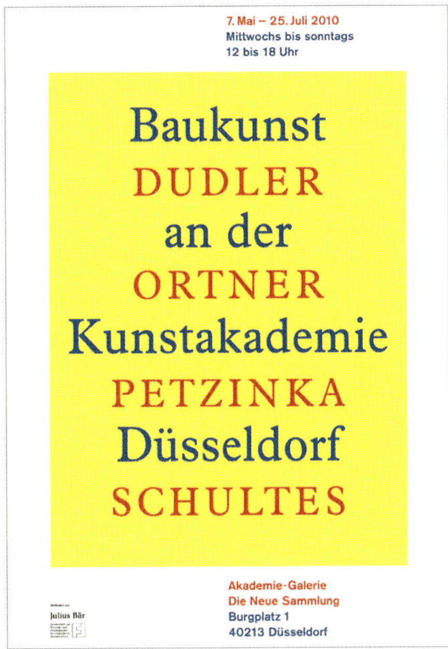
7. Mai – 25. Juli 2010
Mittwochs bis sonntags
12 bis 18 Uhr
Baukunst
DUDLER
an der
ORTNER
Kunstakademie
PETZINKA
Düsseldorf
SCHULTES
Akademie-Galerie
Die Neue Sammlung
Burgplatz 1
40213 Düsseldorf
Julius Bär

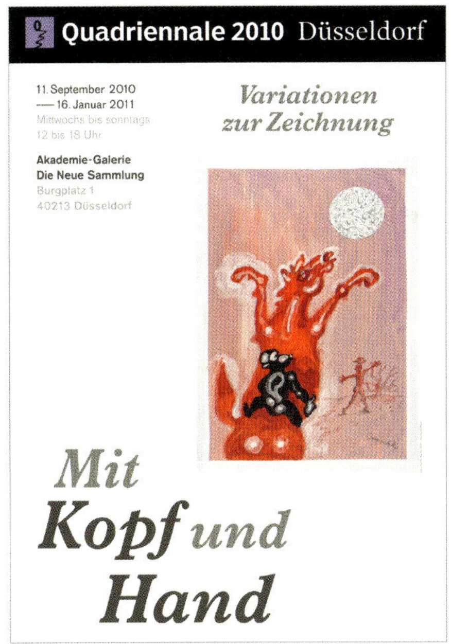
Quadriennale 2010 Düsseldorf
11. September 2010
— 16. Januar 2011
Mittwochs bis sonntags
12 bis 18 Uhr
Akademie-Galerie
Die Neue Sammlung
Burgplatz 1
40213 Düsseldorf
Variationen
zur Zeichnung
Mit
Kopf und
Hand

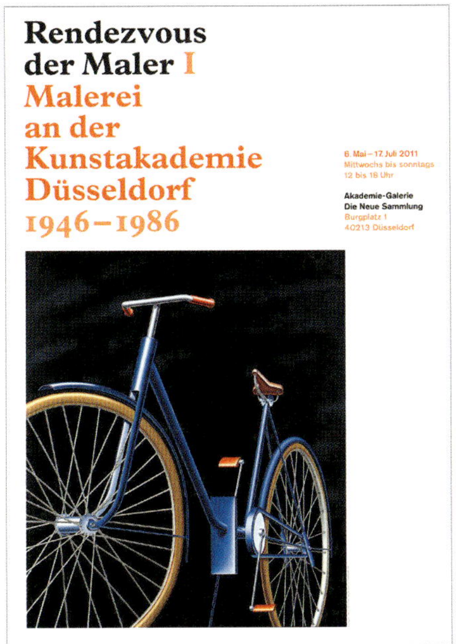
Rendezvous
der Maler I
Malerei
an der
Kunstakademie
Düsseldorf
1946–1986
6. Mai – 17. Juli 2011
Mittwochs bis sonntags
12 bis 18 Uhr
Akademie-Galerie
Die Neue Sammlung
Burgplatz 1
40213 Düsseldorf

DIE ERFINDUNG DER WIRKLICHKEIT
PHOTOGRAPHIE
AN DER KUNSTAKADEMIE DÜSSELDORF
VON 1970 BIS HEUTE
Akademie-Galerie
Die Neue Sammlung
Burgplatz 1
40213 Düsseldorf
16. September 2011
— 5. Februar 2012
Mittwochs bis sonntags
12 bis 18 Uhr
e.on

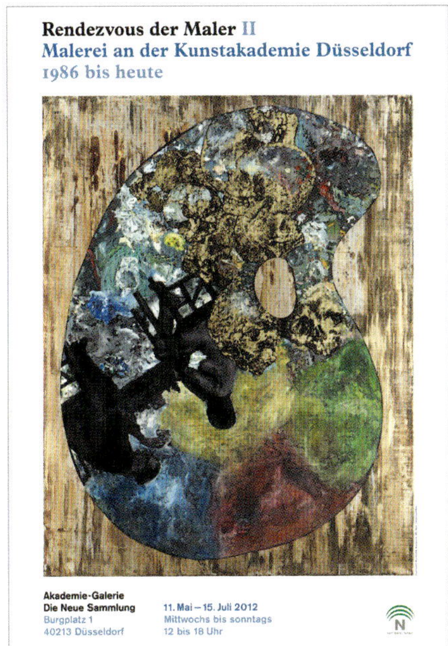
Rendezvous der Maler II
Malerei an der Kunstakademie Düsseldorf
1986 bis heute
Akademie-Galerie
Die Neue Sammlung
Burgplatz 1
40213 Düsseldorf
11. Mai – 15. Juli 2012
Mittwochs bis sonntags
12 bis 18 Uhr

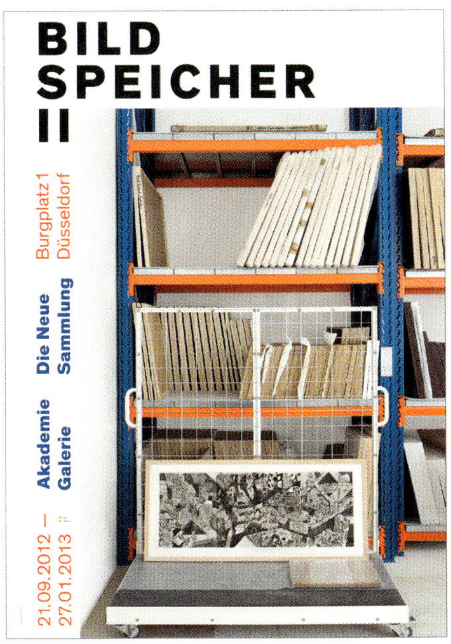
BILD
SPEICHER
II
Burgplatz 1
Düsseldorf
Die Neue
Sammlung
Akademie
Galerie
21.09.2012 –
27.01.2013

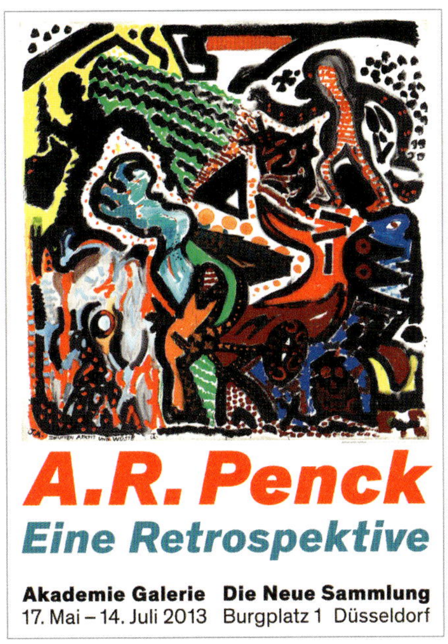
A.R. Penck
Eine Retrospektive
Akademie Galerie Die Neue Sammlung
17. Mai – 14. Juli 2013 Burgplatz 1 Düsseldorf

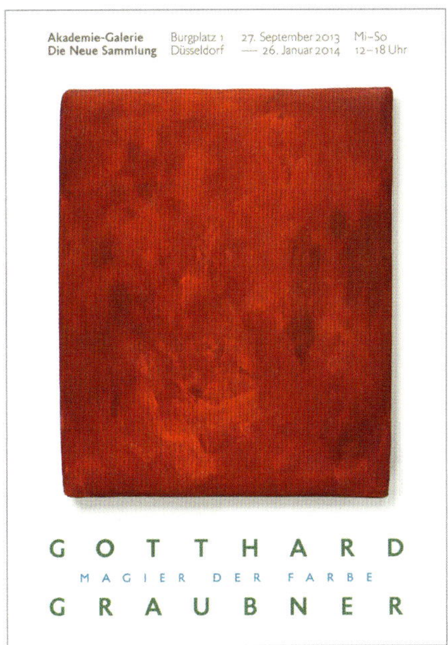
Akademie-Galerie
Die Neue Sammlung
Burgplatz 1
Düsseldorf
27. September 2013
— 26. Januar 2014
Mi–So
12–18 Uhr
GOTTHARD
MAGIER DER FARBE
GRAUBNER

THE ACADEMY ART COLLECTION

Dawn Leach

INTRODUCTION

When one studies the founding and history of the Düsseldorf Art Academy Collection, it very soon becomes apparent that a basic distinction must be drawn between the old and the new collections. This is due to the fact that the bulk of the extensive and important original Art Academy Collection was transferred to the city of Düsseldorf on permanent loan in 1932 and is now in the Museum Kunstpalast. The works remaining at the Academy were mainly a study collection or used as teaching aids.

Nonetheless artworks by former teachers and pupils were made over to the Academy even during the war. In *Jahresbericht der Staatlichen Kunstakademie 1941–1944* [Annual Report of the Düsseldorf Art Academy 1941–1944] it is explained that the focus was to be on 'collecting portraits and pictures that are of particular significance for its [the Academy's] history'.[1]

Still, a deliberate acquisitions policy operating on systematic lines has only been pursued since the Academy was enlarged by the opening of new exhibition rooms and the concomitant founding of the Neue Sammlung [New Collection] in 2005.

THE ORIGINAL COLLECTION IS ESTABLISHED

Like so many academies founded in the eighteenth century, the education of artists in Düsseldorf depended on princely patronage.[2] In the spirit of the Enlightenment and to enhance the fame of the Elector Karl Theodor, who appreciated art, the Electoral paintings gallery and some plaster casts were made accessible to the art students. At that time drawing from casts and other artworks was the tried and tested method of schooling the hand and eye of aspiring artists, craftsmen, and art lovers.

In addition, a study collection was growing that in essentials was built on the considerable collection of drawings, prints, and art books amassed by Lambert Krahe, founding director of the Academy. In his capacity as director of the Electoral galleries, Krahe introduced the first systematic presentation guidelines and, as head of the Art Academy, was responsible for the training of young artists and creating links between renowned artists and art-loving honorary members with the Academy. Krahe ensured that donations rendered to augment the study collection were anchored in the Academy regulations and did his best to have reproduction prints made to a high standard in Düsseldorf.[3] Thus the study collection was supplemented by works from the Academy's own staff and students attesting to the quality of artist training in Düsseldorf. This measure can from today's standpoint be appreciated as extremely foresighted because the transferral of the contents of the paintings gallery to Munich in 1805 due to the succession represented a devastating loss for Düsseldorf and the Academy. It could only be compensated to some extent by the founding of the Royal Prussian Academy and the loan of paintings from the Prussian collection. Only a handful of works that were left behind in Bensberg – including the *Venus and Adonis* (1610) and *The Assumption* (*c.*1620) by Peter Paul Rubens – ever returned to the Academy (Fig. 1).

Apart from mandatory donations made by teachers and pupils, and by patrons, funding began to come from the middle classes over the course of the nineteenth century.[4] The Academy itself also occasionally acquired works to be used by students as study objects.[5] Acquisitions were regulated as follows by the Regulations of 24 November 1831 for the Royal Art Academy at Düsseldorf: 'To increase this Collection funds are earmarked annually, the use of which is intended first of all to meet the needs of this institution. For this purpose the acquisition of classical works of painting that are of importance for study purposes is to be the prime consideration.'[6]

Items from the collection were lost when fire broke out in the buildings of the Old Castle, in which the Academy was then housed, on the night of 19/20 March 1872. These were mainly works that had been in the instructors' studios. The art collection and the library were, fortunately, saved.[7]

After the Art Academy moved into the new building at the Eiskellerberg, some artworks from the Collection were presented in the Great Hall (Fig. p. 16) and in dedicated rooms on the lower floor. Only a small part of the Collection could be shown at a given time in this way so the problem of storing artworks in a manner that ensured their conservation grew more pressing since there was not enough room for the Collection.

The municipal Decorative Arts School in Düsseldorf was disbanded due to reform tendencies in art training in the 1920s and the women's movement after the First World War. For the Art Academy this meant, on the one hand, incorporating subjects from the applied arts course of training and admitting women from the drawing teachers' seminary to train in art. On the other, the closure of the Decorative Arts School led to its study collections and works on paper from the state drawing teachers' seminary, which was affiliated with the Decorative Arts School, being handed over to the Art Academy.

By 1932 the Academy Art Collection had grown to 14,511 drawings, 21,211 graphic works, and 201 paintings,[8] many works of sculpture, 141 death masks, and numerous plaster casts. The need for appropriate storage and conservation grew steadily more pressing. Many works were by then in need of restoration because they had been stored for years under poor conditions, especially during the First World War and its aftermath. A lasting solution to this problem had to be found. The considerable problems linked with conservation and a move to build a central museum in Düsseldorf had by 1916 forced the Academy to cease collecting.[9]

The initiative for founding a central museum started with Fritz Roeber, the then director of the Art Academy, and was associated with the institution being redesigned on Modernist lines and the lack of space which was becoming an ever more pressing problem. In 1912 the Academy director took steps to have a new building erected in Stockum, north Düsseldorf. After the Academy moved there, a central municipal museum would move into the old Academy building at the Eiskellerberg. The project was to be financed by the city, which would receive the old Academy building and the Art Academy Collection in exchange. Only the main building of the new structure was completed because the First World War intervened. The Art Academy could not move. It also owed the city a great deal of money for the new building, and lack of space was still a problem. After Roeber died, protracted negotiations in spring 1932 finally led to the Städtische Kunstsammlungen [City Art Collections] agreeing to house the Art Academy Collection on permanent loan.[10] The terms of this contract discharged all debts incurred by the Academy over the unfinished new building in Stockum.[11]

The copy of the contract confirms that originally 'all paintings, the collection of drawings, and the prints (copperplates, prints of all kinds, woodcuts, lithographs) and works of sculpture, in so far as they should be extant in the original, would be given' to the city of Düsseldorf 'by the close of the twentieth century' (Fig. 2). Also covered by the terms of the contract was the library collection of valuable old books, 'which no longer have any vital significance for the professors and students of the State Art Academy'.[12]

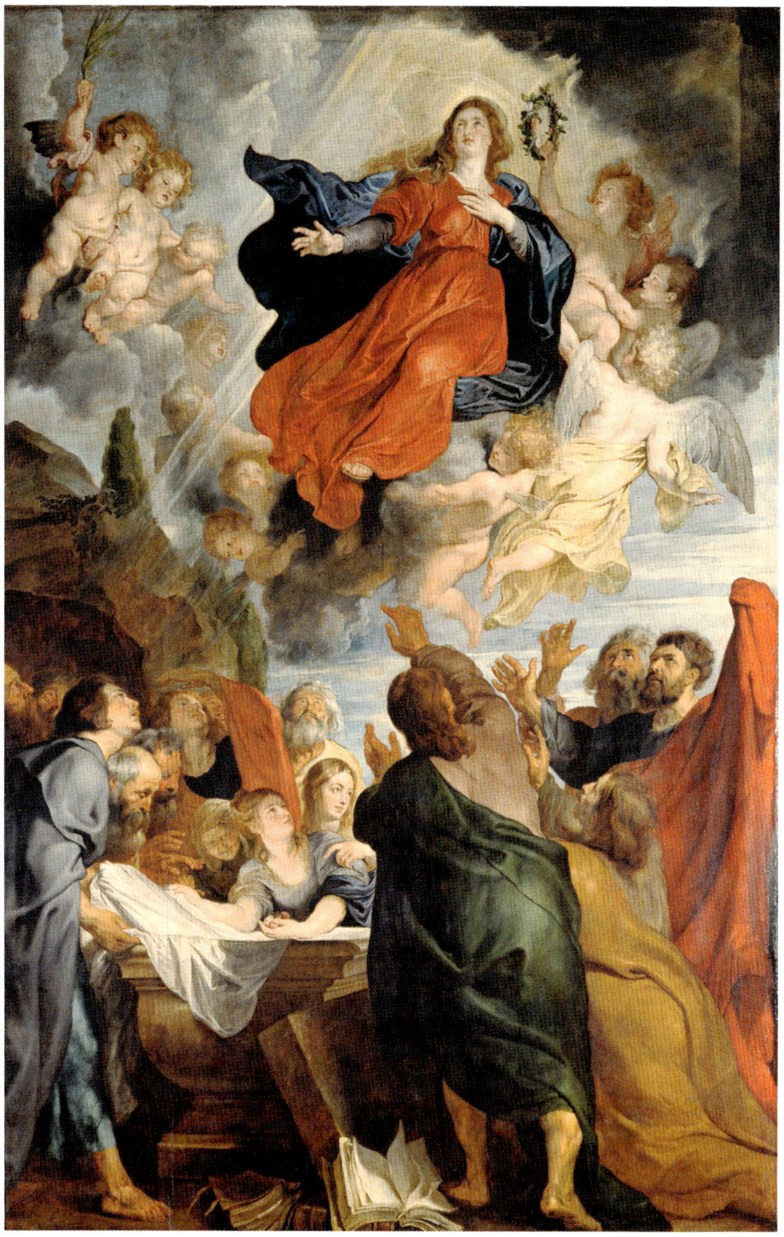

Fig. 1: Peter Paul Rubens and workshop, The Assumption of the Holy Virgin, *oil on wood, 428 × 284 cm, Stiftung Museum Kunstpalast, on permanent loan to the Düsseldorf Art Academy*

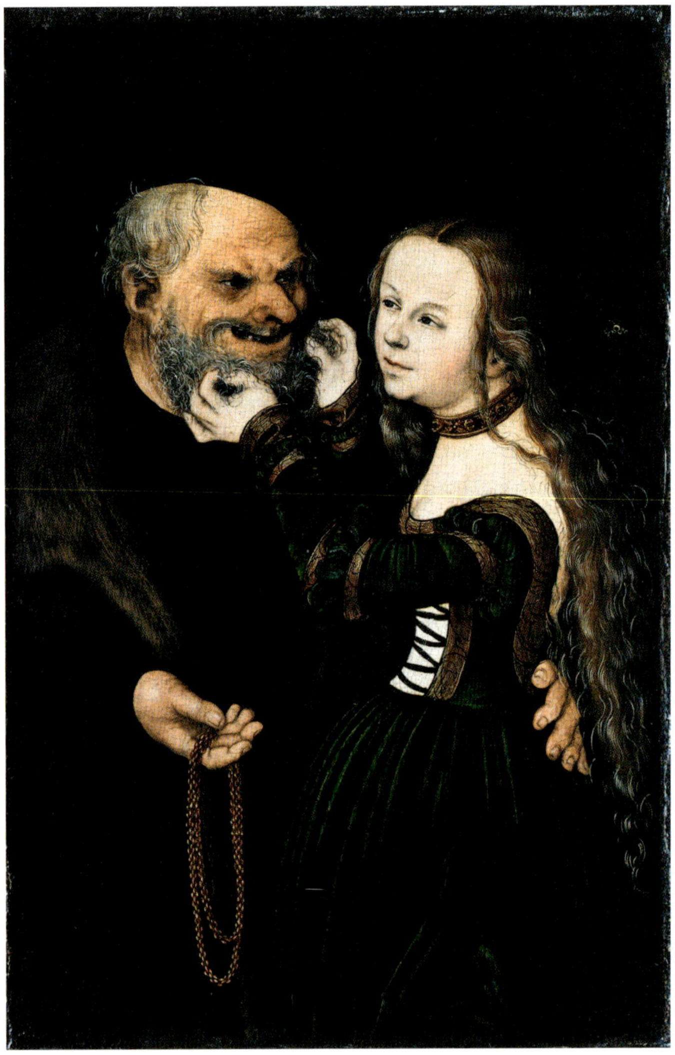

Fig. 2: Lukas Cranach the Elder, Das ungleiche Paar (Der verliebte Alte) *[The Unequal Couple (Old Man in Love)],* c. *1530, oil on wood, 38.8 × 25.7 cm, Stiftung Museum Kunstpalast, on permanent loan to the Düsseldorf Art Academy*

ARTICLES FROM THE COLLECTION THAT SURVIVED THE SECOND WORLD WAR

Historically relevant items that represented highlights in the history of the Academy were ultimately returned to it or had never left it,[13] such as the portraits of former Academy directors (Fig. 3) and part of the Krahe study collection. The latter probably continued in use as teaching aids. Then there were works that had no real value as museum pieces, such as the plaster casts – some of which were set up in the Academy corridors – which, apart from being decorative, provided a survey of major works of sculpture and could be used by students as study objects. A similar function was fulfilled by the collection of death masks – at 141 items one of the world's largest of its kind[14] – whose importance, however, had waned after the twentieth century set in.[15]

The artworks owned by the Academy that were spared the ravages of war included, apart from the above-mentioned portraits of directors,[16] three paintings of Peter Janssen's, *Die Phantasie von einem Greif empor getragen* [The Imagination Borne Aloft by a Gryphon], *Die Mutter Natur* [Mother Nature], and *Die Schönheit die Bildhauerei und die Malerei zur Erde führend* [Beauty Conducting Sculpture and Painting to Earth] (1886–1892, tondi, each 360 cm in diameter), which had been attached to the Great Hall ceiling in around 1896. The rescue of those paintings is owed to a very prudent person who, shortly before the building was subjected to a heavy bombardment in 1944, cut the ceiling paintings from their frames to remove them to a safe place. Waxed and rolled up, they were not rediscovered and restored until over fifty years later while the Academy building was being generally overhauled.[17] In 2002 they were returned to their original location. Anton Hickel's copy of Pompeo Girolamo Batoni's portrait of Karl Theodor, the Elector Palatine and Prince of Bavaria (1724–1799), was also brought into the Great Hall after the building had been renovated. The marble reliefs of Emperor Joseph I and Empress Wilhelmine Amalie by Gabriel Grupello (shortly after 1705) were set up in a place worthy of them in the lobby of the main building.

Photographs of the Academy corridors before the damage sustained during the war show that some plaster casts were set up in them in eye-catching locations or along sight lines (shown on p. 14). It is thanks to Walter Kaesbach that the Academy was no longer freighted with proliferating plaster casts. He was the driving force behind the renovation that took place back in the 1920s.[18] He also saw to it that changes occurred in the Great Hall: all artworks except the Janssen paintings were removed and replaced by golden walls. The windows were redesigned by Heinrich Campendonk (Fig. 6, p. 401).[19] Unfortunately, they were destroyed in the war. The Campendonk ornamental window[20] has been restored and since October 2002 has been in place in the Great Hall, framed in wood with backlighting. It came from the state parliament building (which now houses K21 in the Ständehaus) in Düsseldorf but can be viewed as a replacement for the windows the artist once made for the Great Hall. Moreover, some plaster casts of parts of the west and north friezes of the Parthenon in Athens have remained in the Great Hall stairwell.

In 1940 Emil Fahrenkamp, the then director of the Academy, laid the cornerstone for a new Art Academy Collection by donating a portrait of Friedrich Wilhelm von Schadow, painted

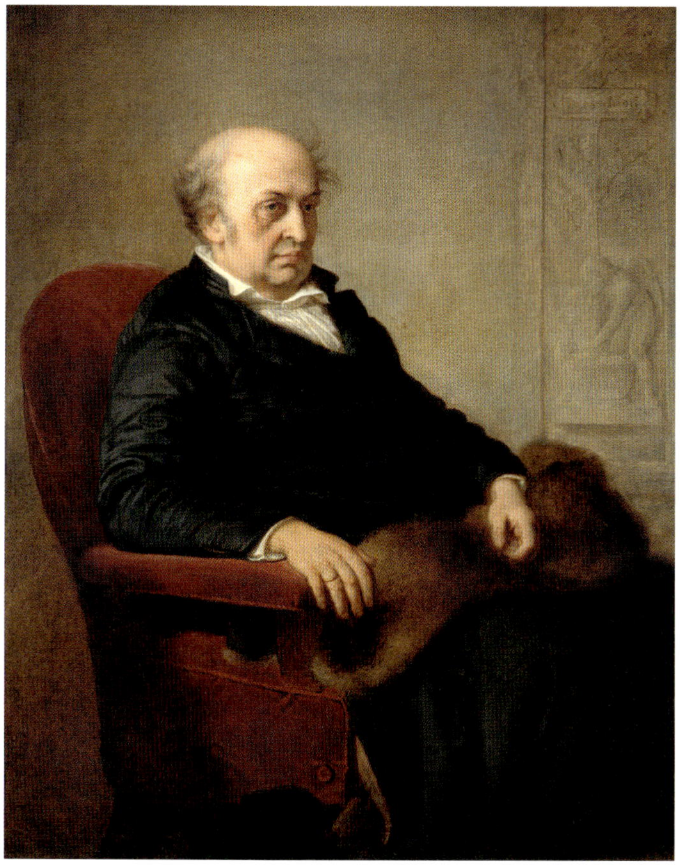

Fig. 3: Eduard Bendemann, portrait of Friedrich Wilhelm von Schadow, oil on canvas, 122 × 100 cm, inscribed 'E. Bendemann 1861', Düsseldorf Art Academy

by a pupil of his, Theodor Hildebrandt (Fig. p. 430).[21] The first self-portrait of an Academy professor – by Oswald Achenbach – was acquired personally in 1944 from the chairman of the Gesellschaft von Freunden und Förderern [Society of Friends and Sponsors] of the Art Academy, Consul-General Dr jur. Hermann Friederich, and donated to the Academy.[22] By 1940 the Academy archives had already been given four sketchbooks of Martha Achenbach's, daughter-in-law of Oswald Achenbach (1840, 1845, 1846, and 31 August 1846), two portfolios of Oswald Achenbach's (1850 and 1857), and a sketchbook of the young Andreas Achenbach's (1833).[23]

Prints which had remained in the Academy after the Collection had been handed over to the city in 1932 also survived the war without damage. As already mentioned, there are still some prints from the collection amassed by the founding director, Lambert Krahe. There are also some copperplates and etching plates of reproductions of paintings from the Düsseldorf paintings gallery. The Academy verifiably possesses copperplates by Heinrich Schmitz, Carl Ernst Christoph Hess, Johann Heinrich Lips, and Heinrich Sintzenich for the 'Gallery Work', which was conceived as a subscription edition but was never completed. Eight other copperplates are by Carl Ernst Forberg and date from between 1878 and 1901.[24]

Moreover, the Art Academy archives still possess numerous prize drawings from the eighteenth century – some of them by pupils of Krahe's – and examples from drawing classes done from plaster casts and from the living model in the nineteenth century as well as over one hundred student works on paper dating from the period between 1932 and 1945 (Figs. 4, 5).

The prints collection that was still at the Academy after the war comprised some 9,000 works executed in a variety of graphic techniques and genres,[25] including 500 portraits dating from the early seventeenth to the mid-twentieth centuries. They range from simple silhouettes to mezzotints in large formats shading into painterly gradations of tone. Variations in style and technique can be studied in one batch of portraits of aristocratic women in small formats. The portraits of famous artists in Giorgio Vasari's *Effigie di celebri Pittori Scultori et Architetti* (1629) function as a genealogy of character heads. The collection also contains artist friendship portraits, such as Carl Ernst Forberg's etching of the two artists Marc Louis Benjamin Vautier and Peter Janssen.

Seven hundred representations dealing with religious, allegorical, and mythological subjects as well as genre pictures in the study collection indicate that role models were supposed to enlarge and form students' appreciation of art. Some series of prints and many individual ones that represent head studies by type, age, gender, and origin also came from systematic teaching in drawing. This group includes many sketches of gestures and hand and foot positions that go beyond mere anatomical study sheets.

The study collection contains a remarkably large number of prints of varying genre by the Berlin copperplate professor Daniel Berger. A batch of coloured Japanese woodcuts can be included in this group, which dates mainly from the nineteenth century, but its presence is presumably due to inspiration from Impressionism and Jugendstil/Art Nouveau.[26] Other prints that are related to this group are coloured Indian autolithographs, brush or pen drawings on a ground stone or plate, which depict twenty-one scenes from the life of Krishna. Objective and painterly architecture editions and vedute round off the study collection of prints used for educational purposes.

Some model pictures executed as lithographs and woodcuts also came – as mentioned at the beginning of this essay – from the state drawing teachers' seminary at the Düsseldorf Decorative Arts School. Several individual leaves from medieval manuscripts probably also came from the same source: these are small treasures such as the sheet richly decorated with

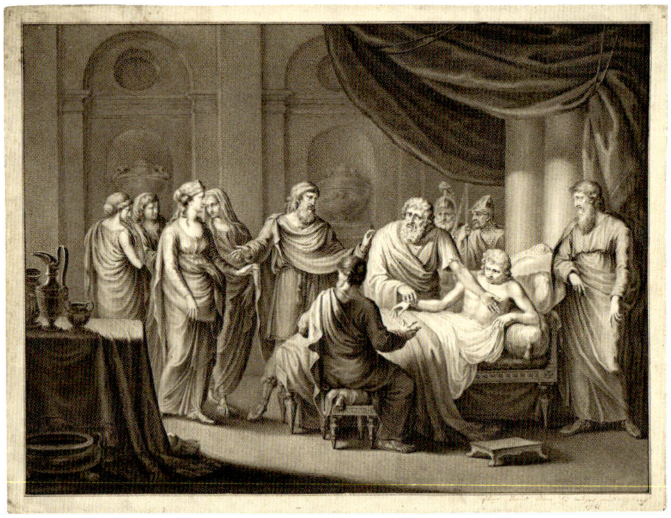

Fig. 4: Johann Heinrich Lips, Antiochus and Stratonice, *1781, pencil in grey on paper, 50 × 67.3 cm (prize drawing, 1st prize), Düsseldorf Art Academy*

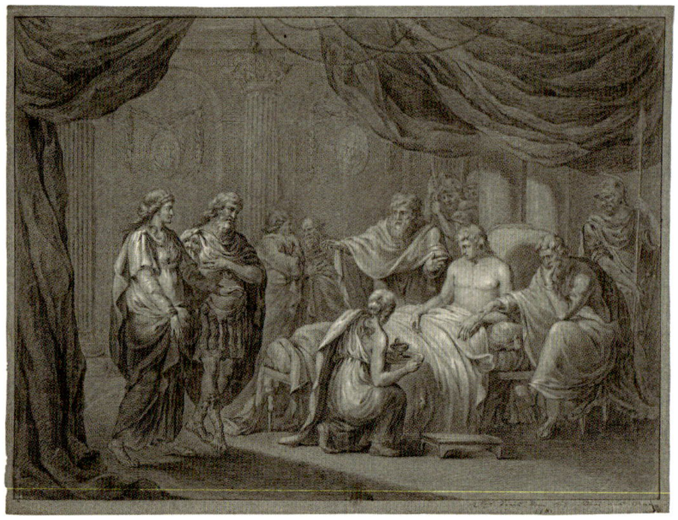

Fig. 5: Friedrich Bury, Antiochus and Stratonice, *1781, carbon pencil heightened with white on blue paper, 48.5 × 65 cm (prize drawing, 2nd prize), Düsseldorf Art Academy*

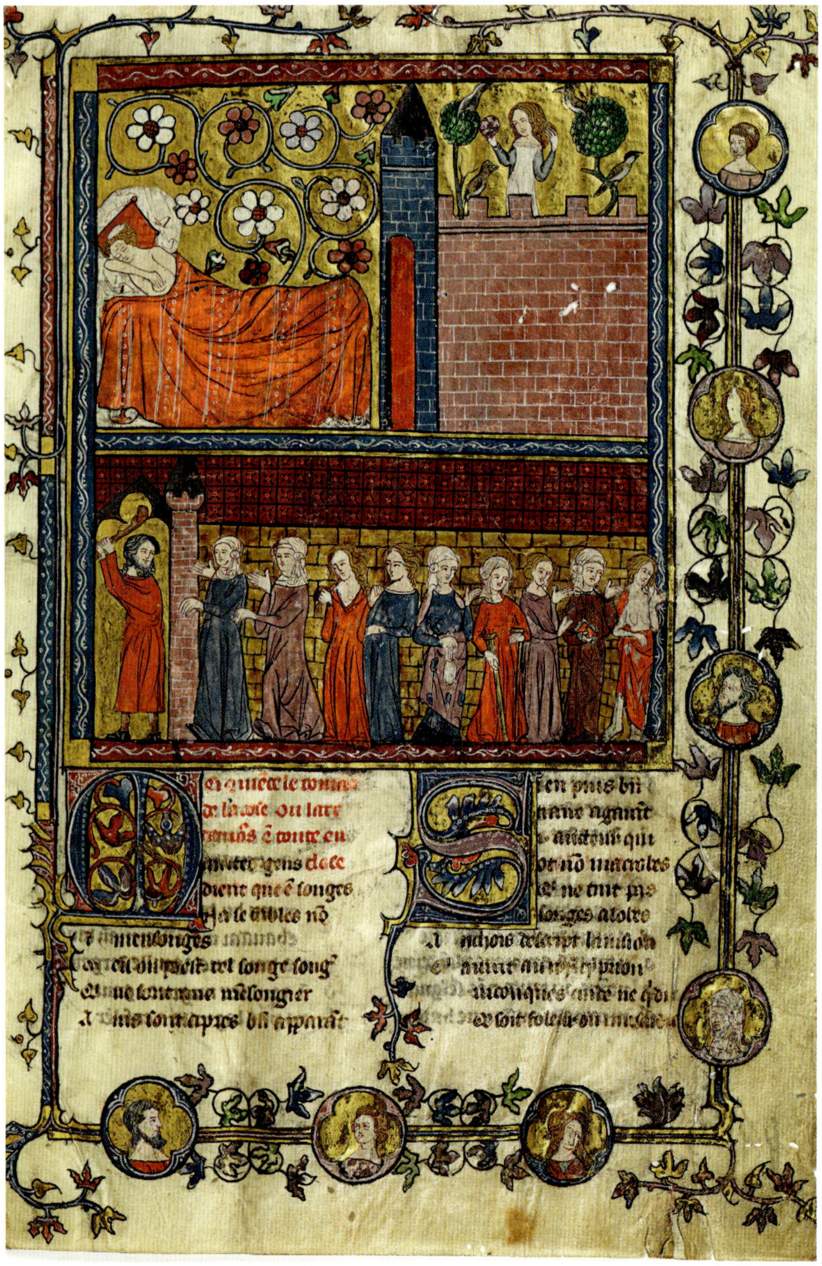

Fig. 6: Roman de la rose, c. *1365, illuminated manuscript, Düsseldorf Art Academy library*

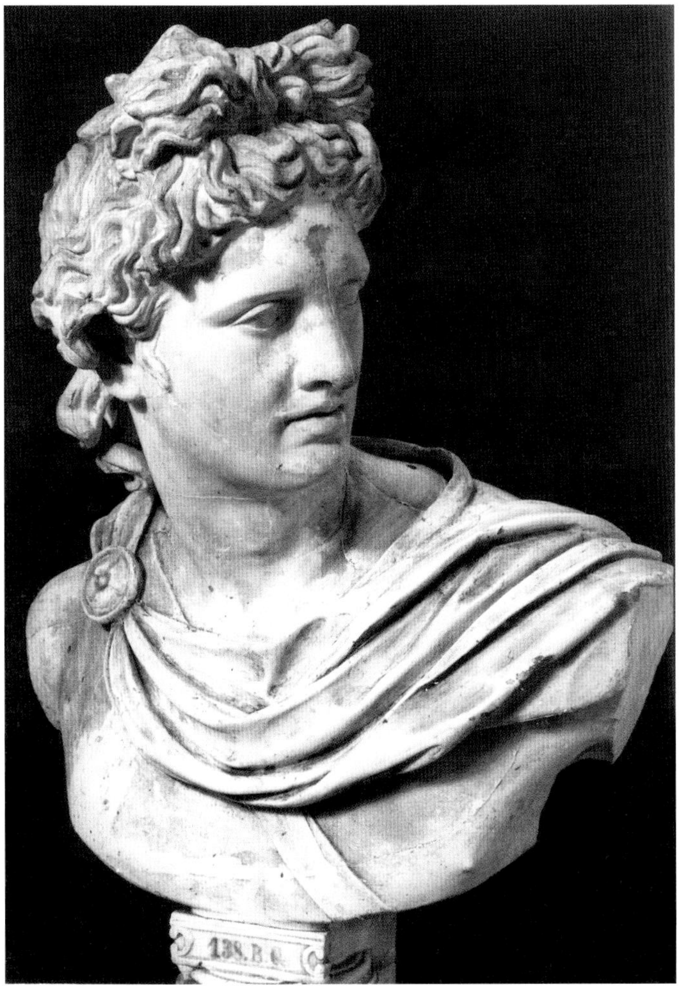

Fig. 7: Plaster cast of the Apollo Belvedere in the Vatican Museums, Düsseldorf Art Academy

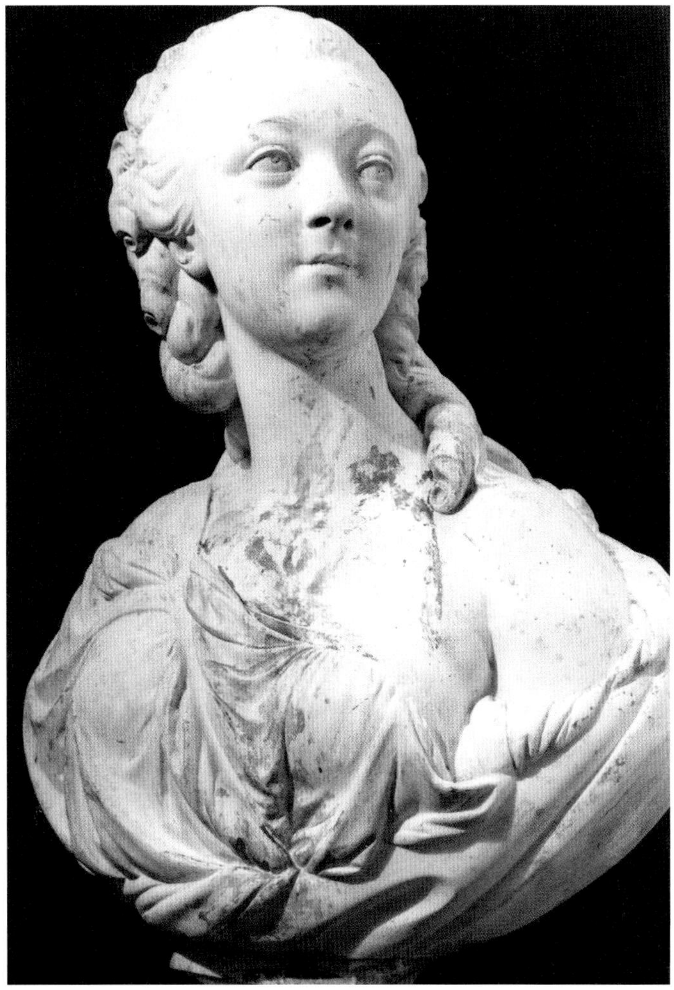

Fig. 8: Plaster cast of the bust of Madame du Barry (1744–1793) by Augustin Pajou in the Musée des Beaux-Arts Rennes, Düsseldorf Art Academy

foliate ornament, initials, and a miniature of St Michael subduing Satan, which was probably part of a book of hours. In this connection, Plate 71 from the *Schedelsche Weltchronik* [Schedel's World Chronicle] (1493) in the German version and five folded sheets of vellum with superb examples of manuscript illumination are also noteworthy. These detached leaves complete the collection of illuminated manuscripts that is in the Art Academy library.[27] The library contains valuable intact books, such as the *Roman de la rose* (fourteenth century; Fig. 6) and a book of hours, the *Très belles heures de Bruges* (fifteenth century) as well as two complete exemplars of the *Schedelsche Weltchronik*.

The plaster casts listed and named in Theodor Levin's *Repertorium*[28] – for instance, in the class devoted to Greco-Roman Antiquity – were probably all destroyed in the war. A handful of plaster casts, not mentioned by name, hence probably not kept in the Antiquities Room, have remained at the Academy. They are highly likely to date from the eighteenth and nineteenth centuries,[29] so that in the latter case the possibility that they were replacements ordered after the war cannot be eliminated (Figs. 7, 8).

In 1955 the value of the plaster casts was estimated at 13,264 DM. Since the 1970s the Academy has occasionally lent plaster casts from its collection for special exhibitions at museums. In 1988 Jochen vom Berg began to identify the remaining 164 plaster casts and to document them in photographs (several hundred plaster casts of architectural ornamentation and separate casts of human limbs that are stored in the Academy attic are not covered by this documentation).[30] At the same time Stanislaw Rosiek began on the scholarly catalogue of the 141 death masks in the Academy Collection.[31]

Among them are masks of numerous distinguished historical persons – Johann Wolfgang von Goethe, Gotthold Ephraim Lessing, Heinrich Heine, Friedrich Nietzsche, Johann Sebastian Bach, Franz Liszt, Nicolas Poussin, Antonio Canova, and Théodore Géricault – as well as masks of Prussian rulers, Henry IV of France, Napoleon, and Peter the Great of Russia. Moreover, the death masks of Academy directors Peter von Cornelius, Friedrich Wilhelm von Schadow, Peter Janssen, Fritz Roeber, and Heinrich Kamps (Figs. 9, 10) are in the collection and so are masks of other persons who have not been identified.[32] This particular art form had its heyday in the nineteenth century among

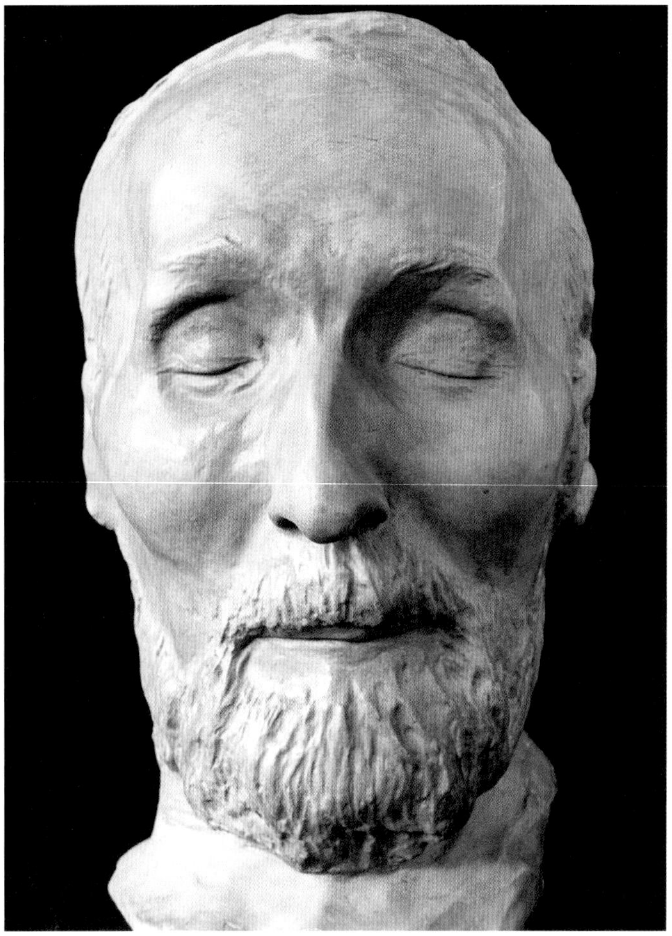

Fig. 9: Heinrich Heine's death mask, 1856, plaster, dimensions not given, Düsseldorf Art Academy

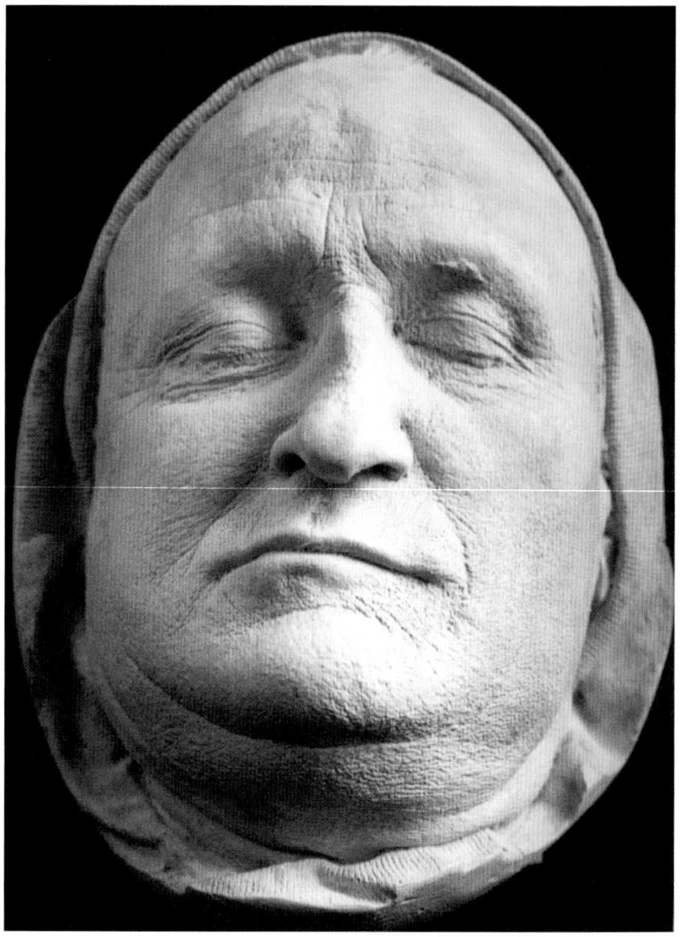

Fig. 10: Heinrich Kamp's death mask, 1954, plaster, dimensions not given, Düsseldorf Art Academy

the Romantics, who venerated the beauty of the dying.[33] 'The intention of survivors is always the same: to save the face of the dead person from decay, to keep it in a material that is more durable than mortal flesh – all for the purpose of enabling encounters with the dead person beyond death.'[34]

As has been noted, this way of commemorating the dead lost its significance in the twentieth century. This extensive collection of death masks,[35] the existence of which is virtually unknown, is unique worldwide.

DEVELOPMENTS IN THE COLLECTION AFTER 1945[36]

Gifts

Whereas the art museum endeavoured in the early years after the war to close painful gaps in their collections that had been caused by the confiscation of works proscribed as 'degenerate', the Academy has had the opportunity, with the support of its Circle of Friends and Sponsors in subsequent years, to document the history of the institution through a number of donated artworks.

In 1947, for instance, the Society of Friends and Sponsors of the Art Academy gave the Art Academy Collection three early drawings by Johann Gottfried Schadow.[37] On 24 February 1949 Helene Plowden – daughter of William Stanley Haseltine – donated the painting *Nächtliche Strandszene* [Nocturnal Beach Scene] (1873) by Andreas Achenbach.[38] It came from her father's estate and was hung at first in the Academy library, then from 1989 in the Art Academy rector's office. In 1991 it was restored by Claudia Harder. Ms Plowden also gave the Academy Collection a painting by her father, a Salomon Corrodi watercolour, and four etchings – two by Carl Friedrich Lessing, one by Oswald Achenbach, and another by Gaspard Dughet.[39]

The 1953 exhibition *Von Gabriel Grupello bis Paul Klee, von Lambert Krahe bis Theo Champion* [From Gabriel Grupello to Paul Klee, from Lambert Krahe to Theo Champion] and the accompanying catalogue of drawings and portraits of former members of the Academy may have awakened a willingness to donate; the following year Dr Hildebrand Gurlitt donated a pencil drawing by Andreas Müller. In 1956 two drawings by Friedrich Wilhelm von Schadow, two by Wilhelm Schirmer, two by Wilhelm Camphausen, and one by Carl Friedrich Lessing were given to the Academy from the

Pettenkofen estate. The following year Anna Maria Gerlach – daughter of Fritz Reusing, who had studied at the Academy – donated a pencil drawing of her father's. In addition, Frau Wagner[40] donated a charcoal drawing each by former Academy pupils Nicola Gilles and Br. Schütz-Briesen, two by Cornelius Wagner, and three unmarked studies to the Academy in 1959. The motifs represented in them – death masks and Greek heads – make clear how important the collection of teaching aids was for studying at the Academy in the late nineteenth century.

Further, in 1969 Professor Dr Dr Friedrich Prager bequeathed to the Academy a watercolour by Adolf Schill: *Palermo, Capella Palatina, 1886*. As the testator had specified, the watercolour was transferred in September 1969 to the Kunstmuseum Düsseldorf, where it is on permanent loan. In 1975 two industrial paintings by Erich Mercker were donated to the Academy by Joseph Theisen of Krefeld.

In 1987 the Academy received seven paintings in quite small formats from the estate of the artist Jean Hendrichs. That year three small Christian Sell paintings from J. Heustuder's estate also entered the Art Academy Collection.

In 1992 the Art Academy also received ten post-Schadow-era sketchbooks of Albert Flamm's from Ruth Flamm's estate as well as three sketchbooks and eighteen loose leaves that presumably belonged to her son, Carl Flamm.

Paralleling those additions to the Academy Collection, the Kunstmuseum Düsseldorf again began to acquire contemporary art – mainly the work of Düsseldorf artists who had also earned international reputations – in order, as Wend von Kalnein put it, 'to avoid the danger of ossifying in the nineteenth-century tradition'.[41] This switch to museum acquisition policies that lean more strongly towards contemporary art has also been mirrored in Art Academy collecting policy since the 1960s.

Donations by Academy Professors

In 1960 Professor Paul Bindel gave the Academy an oil painting in which he had immortalised his colleague, Otto Coester. Here friendship between artists is linked with the valuable eyewitness testimony of artists who shaped teaching at the Academy (shown on p. 167).

Early in 1963 a work by each Academy teacher and two each from their respective pupils were available to be shown at the first exhibition mounted by the small Academy offshoot at Ritterstrasse 2 – by late 1962 it was ready for use and the Society of Friends and Sponsors hosted events there. The exhibits included an ink drawing each by Professors Karl Otto Götz and Manfred Sieler, a lithograph each by Joseph Fassbender and Rupprecht Geiger, and a collage by Gerhard Hoehme. Student works shown included oil paintings by Kuno Gonschior, Norbert Tadeusz, and Reinhart Winterscheidt as well as drawings by Gunda Güttich, Rolf Landen, Hermann Mahlberg, Gisela Mauz, Heinz Scharbert, Udo Jürgen, Detlev Scheel, and Walter Verwoert. Most of those works were given to the Academy in 1967 under the provisions of the Circle of Friends of the Academy charter.

Beginning in 1975, works from the Institut für Drucktechnik [Institute for Print Technology] as well as the classes taught by Willi Sibbel, Walter Breker, and Rolf Sackenheim were contributed to the Academy Collection. The Christian Megert class documented the island trip '25 auf Terschelling' [25 on Terschelling] (1981) as a collection box with mixed works and gave the remaindered stock to the Academy. In the 1990s the Fritz Schwegler class did the same.

In 1992 Walter Huisel, once a pupil of Hans Schwippert's, gave the Academy his carefully collected assignment drawings from the crafts training that had played a pivotal role in his professor's teaching. In 2001 six architecture models were added from the classes taught by Hans Schwippert and Rudolf Schwarz and, moreover, sixteen plans by Karl-Heinz Hohmann.

Hubertus Neuerburg, head of the video and film workshop, gave the Art Academy archives his department's teaching, documentation, and works collection. Its contents include examples of the work of Professors Nam June Paik and Nan Hoover and their students in the form of video presentations for the *Rundgang* [Academy Tour] of the years 1984 to 1986 and 1992 to 1993. Vadim Glowna's film class followed their example in 2001 with its film production.

The collections of children's drawings and works from art classes stored in the archives build on the donation made in 1997 by Günter Blecks, professor of art education. He had amassed 1,744 works by former Düsseldorf Art Academy professors (Kurt Arnscheidt, Gert Weber, Ellen Neumann) and students. Since 1999 more collections have been taken into the archives on the suggestion of Professor Blecks's successor, Professor Dr Kunibert Bering. At present the Collection comprises 3,457 works.[42]

An exception among the artistic legacies left by former Academy professors is that of Gerhard Weber, known as Gert Weberg, which his wife, Ursula Schülke Weberg, bequeathed to the Academy in 2003.[43] Comprising ninety-six paintings, thirty-seven framed works in mixed technique, twelve portfolios of pictures (most of them in oil on canvas or academy board), seven portfolios of drawings and collages, twenty-two 'album leaves' in graphic techniques, fourteen editions of prints, and fifty-three works by artist colleagues and students, it is so extensive that it was transferred to the Neue Sammlung [New Collection], when the Academy Gallery moved into its new rooms.

Acquisitions by the Academy

Most works by Academy students seem to have been donated on into the 1950s – beginning in 1950 occasional entries in the Art Academy inventory ledger note prices. Purchasing student works on the occasion of the *Rundgang* would become an established practice, a custom that persisted until 1995. In this way 1,200 student works – including 133 paintings – were amassed.

In addition, some original 1950s posters were purchased and, in the 1990s some multiples and objects. Book objects, film and video shots, collages, and relatively small pieces of student sculpture were also bought. The Academy also began in 1955 to buy plans by students from the Architecture Department, which are kept with graduate students' final examination works. Moreover, four photographs of Andreas Gursky's from the time he received postgraduate studies funding (1987) and photographs by Bernd and Hilla Becher – a water-tower typology (1963), two photographs of truss work houses (shown on p. 220 top), and a water tower (1963) – should be mentioned in this connection.

It has become obvious that works on paper are a highlight of the 'Old Collection', which is certainly due to the character of the study collection but also to Krahe's focus in collecting. Among the graphics by students, there are also numerous examples of work of this kind by later Academy professors, including drawings by Rolf Crummenauer, Jörg Immendorff, and Gotthard Graubner as well as such artists as Bernhard Blume and Ulrike Rosenbach. In addition there are almost 400 individual graphic works executed in a wide variety of techniques from the classes taught by Otto Pankok, Otto Coester, Rolf Sackenheim, Manfred Sieler, Joseph Fassbender, Dieter Roth, et al., among which there are also graphics by Gerhard Hoehme, who later became an Academy professor.

In 1959 two drawings by Alfred Rethel were added, and in 1960 the Academy acquired a portrait of Heinrich Nauen, painted by Willi Küpper, a pupil of his, as well as a pastel drawing by Fritz Becker, a former professor of architecture.

In 1975 the Ministry for Science and Research of the State of North Rhine-Westphalia made it possible to supplement the graphics collection for the purpose of teaching art history. The works – all from the twentieth century – were handed over to the Kunstmuseum Düsseldorf on permanent loan in October 1975. Dr Wend von Kalnein, the then director of the museum, described the process as follows:

'The individual works were chosen by the museum directorate after thorough examination because they are best suited to supplementing the Collection. The drawings by Piene had already been shown in December 1974 at *Düsseldorf trifft Wien* [Düsseldorf Meets Vienna], an exhibition of drawings in Vienna. Brüning had before then been missing from the Collection. The drawings of his listed came from his estate. The Heerich drawing is one of the few existing drawings of his. It superbly documents Heerich's way of working. The two drawings by Piene are characteristic testimonials to his early years and important illustrations of the principles informing the ZERO Group. The Richter etchings are among the best works in his landscape series. They are aesthetically and technically outstanding. The prices correspond in part to the current market level, some are below it. The latter holds in particular for the Heerich gouache and the gouaches by Piene, which no longer come onto the market in this form.'[44]

THE NEW COLLECTION

The sporadic purchase of works and donations from professors and patrons of the Academy after 1932 cannot be evaluated as a systematic acquisitions policy. Nor do the drawings and plaster casts serve as aids for teaching students as they once did when aspiring artists copied them for the purpose of schooling hand and eye. On the contrary, what the collection of artworks begun after 1932 does document is the history of the Academy and its professors and students. In the past there would not even have been enough space to build up a really new collection. The first important step towards making that possible was enlarging the Academy by adding the Academy Gallery on Burgplatz.[45] Since then numerous important works by incumbent and retired professors and their students have been assembled and presented in an appropriate setting. Thus these works continue to serve as study objects: presented in varying contexts and at a variety of exhibitions, the works in the Academy Art Collection can inspire today's students in their search for ideas, train them to see, and in this way help them to find their individual places in art history.

NOTES

1 *Jahresbericht der Staatlichen Kunstakademie 1941–1944*, Düsseldorf [1945], p. 20.
2 See Max Kunze (ed.), *Kunst und Aufklärung im 18. Jahrhundert. Kunstausbildung der Akademien, Kunstvermittlung der Fürsten, Kunstsammlung der Universität*, exhib. cat. Halle/Stendal/Wörlitz, Rutzen 2005.
3 'The Electoral Academy of the eighteenth century already had a collection of some ninety pictures. Then came an extensive collection of Old Master drawings and a copperplate cabinet.' Richard Klapheck, *Die Kunstsammlungen der Staatlichen Kunstakademie zu Düsseldorf*, Düsseldorf 1928, p. 4.
4 See 'Reglement vom 24. November 1831 für die Königliche Kunst-Akademie zu Düsseldorf', § 17, printed in *Jahresbericht der Staatlichen Kunstakademie Düsseldorf 1945–1947*, Düsseldorf [1948], pp. 87–97; here: p. 93.
5 See Wend von Kalnein, 'Akademiemuseum und Museumstradition in Düsseldorf', in: *Wallraf-Richartz-Jahrbuch*, Vol. 33, Cologne 1971, pp. 329–338; Wend von Kalnein, 'Die Kunstakademie im Spiegel der Städtischen Kunstsammlung', in: Eduard Trier (ed.), *Zweihundert Jahre Kunstakademie Düsseldorf*, Düsseldorf 1973, pp. 167–172.
6 See *Jahresbericht 1945–1947* (see n. 4), p. 93.
7 See Andreas Müller, *Verzeichnis der Gemälde-Sammlung der königl. Kunst-Akademie zu Düsseldorf*, 2nd edn, Düsseldorf 1876.
8 See copy of the 'Übernahmeprotokoll des Besitzes der Staatlichen Kunstakademie in Düsseldorf' of 2 November 1932, Düsseldorf Art Academy archives.
9 See Klapheck (see n. 3), pp. 4f.; see Kalnein 1973 (see n. 5), pp. 167f.
10 For the conditions governing the permanent loan, see the essay by Peter M. Lynen in the present volume, pp. 37–64.
11 Copy of the contract between the Free State of Prussia and the City of Düsseldorf of 17 May 1932, Düsseldorf Art Academy archives.
12 Ibid.
13 *Jahresbericht der Staatlichen Kunstakademie Düsseldorf 1937/38*, Düsseldorf [1939], p. 34.
14 According to the documentation by Stanislav Rosiek, which is in the Düsseldorf Art Academy archives, there are 141 death masks; also see on this, Stanislav Rosiek, 'Archiv toter Gesichter', *Jahreshefte der Kunstakademie Düsseldorf*, Vol. 4, Düsseldorf 1994, pp. 137–158; here: p. 154.
15 Ibid., p. 147.
16 These are the portraits painted by Lambert Krahe of Erich Pauelsen, by Eduard Bendemann of Wilhelm von Schadow, by Hugo Crola of Peter Janssen, and by Franz Josef Kleem of Fritz Roeber.
17 1997–2001.
18 'Der wieder hergestellte Bellini', article of 19 January [1928], with no sources given, Düsseldorf Art Academy archives.
19 See Anna Klapheck, 'Die "goldnen" zwanziger Jahre. Die Akademie zwischen den beiden Kriegen', in: Trier (see n. 5), pp. 147–160; here: pp. 147f.
20 Inv. No. S02.117M, 1948–1950, overall height 8.2 m, overall width 3.79 m, inscribed bottom right 'ENTW: H. Campendonk/Ausf. H. Derix Kevelaer'.
21 *Jahresbericht der Staatlichen Kunstakademie Düsseldorf 1940*, Düsseldorf [1941], p. 60.
22 *Jahresbericht 1941–1944* (see n. 1), p. 20.
23 *Jahresbericht 1940* (see n. 21), p. 60, pp. 70f.
24 These are 104 copperplates engraved between 1777 and 1793. New proofs were pulled in 1988 by Jochen vom Berg.
25 For more on this, Dawn Leach, 'Die Grafiksammlung im Archiv der Kunstakademie Düsseldorf. Funktion und Wandel', in: Benedikt Mauer (ed.), *Das Heute hat Geschichte. Forschungen zur Geschichte Düsseldorfs, des Rheinlands und darüber hinaus. Festschrift für Clemens von Looz-Corswarem zum 65. Geburtstag*, Essen 2012, pp. 319–346.
26 This group grew because the works owned by the Düsseldorf Decorative Arts School were given to the Gallery.
27 At this juncture it must be pointed out that the contents of the Collection and the library are two different entities. Items in the Collection that are not kept in the Academy Gallery are in the Düsseldorf Art Academy archives.
28 Theodor Levin, *Repertorium der königl. Kunst-Akademie zu Düsseldorf aufbewahrten Sammlungen*, Düsseldorf 1883.
29 On the occasion of the ceremony commemorating Lambert Krahe's 300th birthday, a selection of plaster casts was made in several phases, the substance of which will be subjected to analysis.
30 The documentation of the plaster casts in the Düsseldorf Art Academy archives is incomplete. Unfortunately, this work does not seem to have been finished.
31 Unfortunately, this work has never been published; the visual and documentary materials are in the Düsseldorf Art Academy archives.
32 See the documentation of the death masks by Stanislav Rosiek in the Düsseldorf Art Academy archives.
33 See Rosiek 1994 (see n. 14), pp. 137f.
34 Ibid., p. 142.
35 Ibid., p. 154.
36 The data in the records and the inventory ledger of the Collection in the Düsseldorf Art Academy archives are the most important sources here.
37 More on this in the essay by Tanja Wessolowski in the present volume, pp. 427–434.
38 These data are from the Düsseldorf Art Academy inventory ledger.
39 Jakob Heinrich Schmidt, 'William Stanley Haseltine', in: Heinrich Kamps (ed.), *Jahrbuch der Staatlichen Kunstakademie Düsseldorf 1948–1950*, Düsseldorf 1951, pp. 131–133; here: p. 131.
40 Frau Wagner's forename is not mentioned in the inventory ledger in the Düsseldorf Art Academy archives and could no longer be ascertained. This is also true of the forenames missing in the following.
41 Kalnein 1973 (see n. 5), p. 172.
42 See the CD publication by Dawn Leach (ed.), *Kinder zeichnen*, Düsseldorf 2007, and essays on the collections of children's drawings: Dawn Leach, 'Geschichte in Bildern von Kindern', in: Stefan Hölscher et al. (eds.), *BildGeschichte. Facetten*

der Bildkompetenz, Oberhausen 2012, pp. 63–72; Joachim Littke, 'Jungen und Mädchen im Baum. Schülerarbeiten aus den 1950er Jahren und von 2011 im Vergleich', in: ibid., pp. 73–80.

43 The estate of Nan Hoover, which came to the Academy in 2009, consists, on the other hand, chiefly of documents; nevertheless, there are some photo and video works as well as preliminary models for installations, some drawings and work materials for Performances and light installations.

44 Wend von Kalnein, 'Entwurf zu einem Schreiben an das Wissenschaftsministerium über den Ausbau der grafischen Bestände der Sammlung der Kunstakademie Düsseldorf of 16 June 1975', Ordner [File] AZ 2321, Dauerleihverträge [Permanent Loan Contracts], Düsseldorf Art Academy archives.

45 More on this in the essay on the Academy Gallery by Siegfried Gohr in the present volume, pp. 409–415.

THE MISSION AND INFLUENCE OF THE SOCIETY OF FRIENDS AND SPONSORS OF THE DÜSSELDORF ART ACADEMY E. V.

Tanja Wessolowski

FOUNDED IN 1918

When Fritz Roeber became director of the Royal Art Academy in Düsseldorf in 1908, he could not have imagined that his tenure in office would be beset with so many problems and historical upheavals until his death in 1924 (Fig. 1). As it was, he started out managing the Academy as his predecessors had done – that is, still with a marked focus on training in history painting. This meant continuing to align the Academy with the tradition of the successful Düsseldorf School of Painting. Clinging to that tradition, however, led to modern trends in art increasingly showing up outside the Academy, in artist communities such as the Sonderbund or Junges Rheinland [Young Rhineland], promoted by such gallerists as Alfred Flechtheim and Johanna Ey. Roeber realised that reforms to the training system were needed to adjust the Academy curriculum to the trends emerging in the art world.

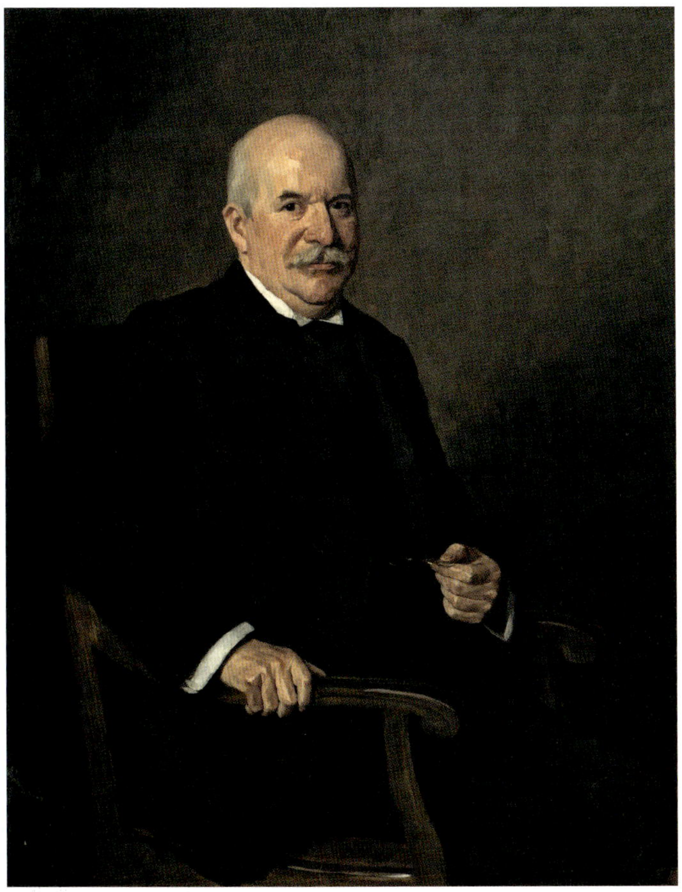

Fig. 1: Franz von Klemm, portrait of Fritz Roeber, c.1921, oil on canvas, 111.5 × 87 cm, Düsseldorf Art Academy

Moreover, he also found himself confronted with political upheavals and the impact made by the First World War, which had particularly severe consequences for the Art Academy: in 1912 Roeber had forged plans with the city of Düsseldorf to move the Art Academy into a new building – the old Academy building was to become a central museum in exchange.[1] The outbreak of war made it impossible to finish the building that was under construction in Stockum so it could not be used for the purpose intended and the Academy was left still having to contend with lack of space and, in addition, a mountain of debt. Under the circumstances, a meagre Academy budget left little scope for promoting a new generation of artists and carrying out reforms in academic training.

Fritz Roeber still managed to make a virtue of necessity: he put his excellent and important connections in politics and commerce to good use[2] and set out to search for potential sponsors for the Academy. He was fortunate in that the centenary of the Academy as the Royal Art Academy would be celebrated the following year. As the correspondence Fritz Roeber conducted with Arthur Hauth, a wine wholesaler, in August 1918 reveals, the director of the Art Academy wanted to take advantage of the occasion to found a friends' association. He suggested the 'endowment capital should be used to finance important functions that would enhance the reputation of Düsseldorf as an art centre and that of the Academy'.[3] His initiative evidently fell on fertile soil because by 16 October 1918 the Gesellschaft von Freunden und Förderern der Königlichen[4] Kunstakademie [Society of Friends and Sponsors of the Royal Art Academy] in Düsseldorf came into being at the Industry Club. The founding of the Society was publicly announced the following day at the Düsseldorf Parkhotel in the presence of thirty-nine gentlemen.[5]

The terms of the first charter of the Society provided for management of affairs by the members' assembly, an administrative council, and a board of directors.[6] Dr Emil Kirdorf was elected as the first chairman of the board; Fritz Roeber was his deputy. The members of the Society's first board of directors were Professor Karl Janssen, Professor August Deusser, Diplom-Ingenieur Karl Wach, an architect and civil engineer, district president Dr Kruse, councillor of commerce Hermann

Schulte, and councillor of commerce Max Trinkaus.[7] Membership dues were established as follows: as a Friend of the Academy, a member could choose between a lump-sum payment of 1,000 marks or an annual donation of fifty marks over a period of at least five years. A member became a sponsor by paying a lump sum of at least 10,000 marks into the Society coffers. In addition, both active and retired Academy teachers and students could become associate members (without voting rights) by paying dues of five marks a year.[8]

The minutes of the board meeting of 2 November 1918 prove that the Society soon had a large membership intake by that time: seventy-one members paying dues that amounted to 721,000 marks.[9] Within a very brief time span the Society's funds increased to about 1,000,000 marks.[10] Distinguished members included Lord Mayor Wilhelm Marx and affluent citizens, art dealers, and professors as well as industrialists from the surrounding region, such as the Krupps von Bohlen und Halbach and even entire businesses such as the Gelsenkirchen Bergwerks-Aktien-Gesellschaft Düsseldorf, the Hanielschen Werke (Oberhausen), and the Rheinisch-Westfälische Kohlen-Syndikat (Essen). The Art Association for the Rhinelands and Westphalia had already joined the Düsseldorf Art Academy Friends' Association in 1918.[11]

Minutes of board meetings and members' assemblies[12] show that membership dues were invested mainly in securities and that a specified annual sum – 5,000 marks in 1933, for example – was available from dividends to the Society to use for its purposes.[13]

Given the new financial possibilities, Fritz Roeber could shift the focus in teaching at the Academy after the First World War: the original function of the Art Academy as a universal educational establishment was to be revived.[14] Roeber accordingly reformed the educational concept while he was still in office with the help of the Society of Friends and Sponsors:

'The founding of the Society is what enabled the then Academy director, Professor Dr Fritz Roeber, to realise his enlargement programme for the newly structured departments of architecture, urban planning, landscape architecture, textiles, the graphic arts, and advertising. The Society's annual interest differential was transferred almost entirely to the Academy or the then Academy director, who used it to pay for new teaching staff and the library assistant, setting up a printing press and looms, procuring materials, and travels for study purposes for students.'[15]

Roeber's successor, Walter Kaesbach, took the incipient reforms further: by appointing distinguished artists, including Heinrich Nauen, Heinrich Campendonk, Paul Klee, and Ewald Mataré, to teach he ensured for a while that a fresh breeze blew through the Academy even though he had much less money than his predecessor at his disposal from the Society of Friends and Sponsors because inflation in 1923 had almost entirely wiped out the Society's funds.[16]

'It was not until 1927 that it became possible to claw back a small part due to currency appreciation. This sum was, however, so small that the decision was taken for the time being to place no larger interest differentials at the disposal of the Academy until the capital had grown again. In 1928 500 Reichsmarks were transferred to the accounts of two students who had to paint the interior of Burg Stahleck near Bacherach as a training assignment. In 1929 5,000 Reichsmarks were paid over to the Art Academy for purely social purposes, such as setting up the student refectory, supporting particularly needy students, and so forth.'[17]

In 1931 and 1932 small sums were still being approved as travel grants for study purposes, and from 1933 until 1935 the annual sums of 2,000 to 5,000 Reichsmarks were used solely for purely social purposes to help the needy. Nor were attempts made at first to woo new members because of the difficult economic situation.[18]

In 1934 and 1935 the support of the workshop divisions (weaving, glass-painting, fonts, and lithography) continued to come under the above-cited heading of 'purely social purposes' along with 'social tasks', travel for study purposes, and the building of a student dormitory for 'the impecunious', but now so did the 'Reich struggle for achievement of the German student body'.[19] In addition, the Academy was granted an interest-free loan of 5,000 Reichsmarks for a planned Land Academy for master pupils in Burg Rindern in Kleve.[20] In 1937 the minutes of the board meeting also mention for the first time[21] that during the previous year 450 Reichsmarks had been used for the purchase of artworks. This seems to be the purchase of student works mentioned in the following annual report; there is no further detailed mention of them anywhere.[22] In 1938 the enlargement of the student refectory in the cellar of the Academy building was partly financed with money from the Society. A look at the sums mentioned and the many purposes for which they were put to use makes clear the extent to which the Academy and its students were dependent on support from the Society of Friends and Sponsors in this difficult economic situation.

THE YEARS 1933–1945

Hitler's rise to power in 1933 had wrought far-reaching changes also to the Academy and its friends' association. Walter Kaesbach, director of the Academy, had been dismissed and the discharge of other professors was to follow. The modern course of study at the Academy was from then on brought into line with teaching prescribed by the National Socialist regime and instrumentalised for the purpose of representing its power. The currency continued to be devalued and this made the funds of the Society of Friends and Sponsors melt away.[23] In 1936 Dr Helmuth Poensgen, Peter Grund, the then Academy director, and most of the professors joined the Society of Friends. In 1937 Professor Dr Richard Klapheck, who had until then been executive secretary of the Society, was allowed to leave the post at his request. His successor, on his suggestion, was Professor Dr Heinrich Schmidt.

In 1939 some changes were made to the Society charter of 1918: quite minor modifications of a formal kind were, for instance, that the attribute 'Königliche' [Royal] was replaced by 'Staatliche' [State] because the Art Academy was now the State Art Academy and the currency was now the Reichsmark instead of the mark. In addition, however, the express purpose of the Society was now widened and it was declared thenceforward: 'The Society has the purpose of promoting the leading position of the Academy as the place where the fine arts are nurtured in the Rhinelands and Westphalia and of spreading and deepening the understanding of art in the broadest classes of folk of the Rhineland, Westphalia, and the neighbouring German regions.'[24]

In addition, more sweeping structural changes were made to the charter. The board[25] was to be replaced by a single Society leader – chosen by the members' assembly – and the administrative council[26] by a council the leader appointed. Members of the council were to be the curator and director of the State Art Academy as well as other persons designated by the leader of the Society. This explicitly meant that the members' assembly could now only elect the leader of the Society and that he in turn appointed his council himself, from which he then appointed a deputy, a secretary, and a treasurer.

THE RECONSTRUCTION PERIOD AFTER 1945

After the Second World War ended, the Society leader was soon replaced by a board of three people chosen by the council. The board elected one of its members as a chairman, another as his deputy, and the third combined the functions of secretary and treasurer.

In the post-war period the Society of Friends and Sponsors focused on supporting quickly and efficiently the construction work going on at the Academy building so that instruction could begin there as soon as possible. In 1946 and 1947 the Society placed 20,000 Reichsmarks annually at the Academy's disposal.[27] After chairman Hermann Friederich died, Dr Josef Wilden was elected as the new chairman in 1945, with Ewald Mataré designated as his deputy. To ensure the tax exempted status continued, the Society charter was altered to accommodate the new provisions. The budget was set for 1946 at 15,000 Reichsmarks.[28] According to the minutes of the council meeting of 22 May 1946, the Society had 133,000 Reichsmarks 'disposable capital'.[29] A drive for new members was to be launched so that the principal of that sum would not have to be touched. One suggested strategy was to make the *Jahresberichte* [Annual Reports] more attractive by including more visual material; another was to make use of the press as an advertising vehicle.[30] There was a change in personnel at the top when Ewald Mataré resigned from his position as deputy chairman to make way for Werner Heuser, the new Academy director. Heuser proposed at the same meeting that the Society should become more involved in organising lectures on modern art and music.

Even after that the Society of Friends and Sponsors had to suffer from being in financial straits because numerous members left due to economic problems of their own.

In 1948 the Society began offering members graphic works by Academy professors (Otto Coester, Ewald Mataré, and

Otto Pankok) as an annual special edition bonus offer at a low price in order to enhance the attractiveness of the Society.[31] The membership aimed at was two hundred regular dues payers in order to make it possible for the Society to promote future projects that it would sponsor with adequate funding. Travels for study purposes were also useful for recruiting new members and were so popular that the Society was concerned to continue supporting them to the same extent.[32] The idea was to be content with just a few lectures but at a high level, which were given from 1949 on in the library reading room as 'symposia'.[33] That year there was an annual bonus edition for Society members (by Paul Bindel, Otto Coester, and Otto Pankok). Records in the archives document that such prints were frequently on offer. The archive material shows that Rolf Sackenheim placed a work at the disposal of the Society in 1966 and that the Friends and Sponsors were able to acquire a bichrome lithograph of Joseph Fassbender's the following year.[34] Moreover, in 1987 the artist Rissa made a graphic work available as an annual Society bonus offer. She was followed in 1988 by Markus Lüpertz and in 1989 by A. R. Penck.[35] Two years later a graphic work by Anthony Cragg could be acquired, followed in 1992 by a Konrad Klapheck and in 1994 by a Gotthard Graubner lithograph.[36]

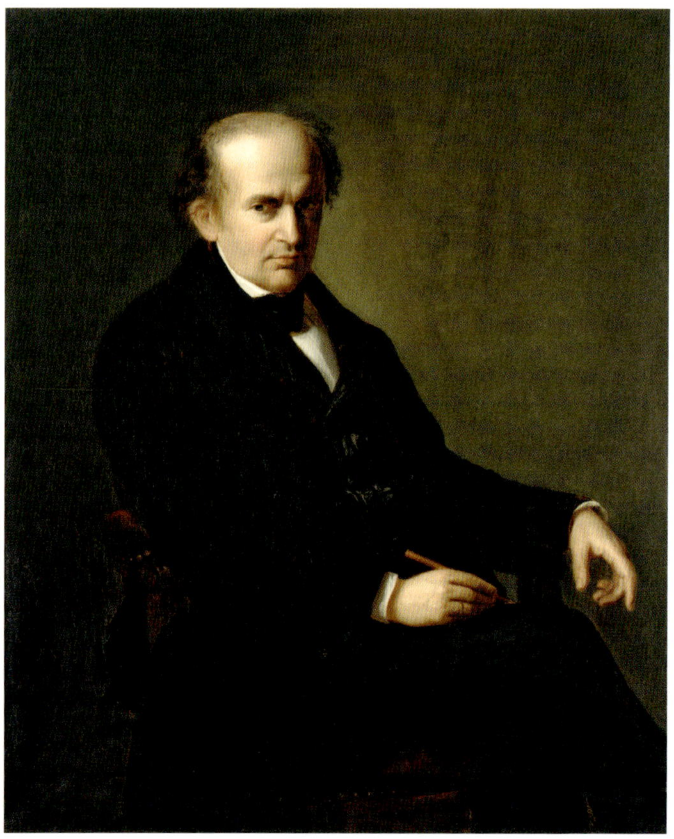

Fig. 2: Theodor Hildebrandt, portrait of Wilhelm Schadow, 1852, oil on canvas, 111 × 91 cm, Düsseldorf Art Academy

In 1949 honorary members of the Society were nominated for the first time: they were Dr Karl Jarres and Arthur Hauth, who were founding members, as well as Professor Franz Kiederich and Dr Eduard Sträter, former district president. Further suggestions for honorary membership were to be made to the chairman in writing.[37] The targeted membership of two hundred was reached when several new Friends and Sponsors joined in 1954. In addition, the Society's finances had stabilised again; by the end of 1954 its capital resources amounted to nearly 14,000 DM.[38] The Society's financial burden was lightened that year because the Academy had got a budget of its own approved for lectures.[39] Hence more extensive student trips could again be sponsored.[40] Personnel changes occurred after Chairman Wilden died. He was succeeded by Dr Ernst Petersen, supported by Dr Franz Schütz as deputy chairman.[41]

ACQUISITIONS FOR THE ART ACADEMY COLLECTION

An appendix to the minutes of meetings in 1954 verifies a special endowment made by Chairman Petersen, by means of which six drawings by Heinrich Nauen, Ernst te Peerdt, Johann Peter Langer, Hubert Netzer, Karl Janssen, and Wilhelm Spatz could be acquired by the Art Academy.[42]

Shortly before much of the original Academy Art Collection was transferred to the city of Düsseldorf in 1932, there had already been individual donations of artworks from the ranks of the Society of Friends and Sponsors which documented the history of the Academy.[43] The first such donation was in 1940, when Emil Fahrenkamp gave the Collection a painting by Theodor Hildebrandt that shows his teacher, Wilhelm von Schadow, as director of the Academy (Fig. 2). It was followed in 1944 by a second donation made by Hermann Friederich, the then chairman of the Circle of Friends: a small self-portrait of Oswald Achenbach, dating from 1845.[44] Not long afterwards, in 1947, the Society decided to acquire three small drawings in pencil by Johann Gottfried Schadow for the Art Academy. They had been offered for sale to the Academy by Schadow's great-granddaughter, Gertrud Helene Kaibel.[45] Measuring 119 × 75 mm each, the drawings dated from around 1780. A brother and two sisters of the artist's are shown, each in a medallion: Rudolf, Charlotte, and Christiane Schadow. Originally portraits of their father and mother belonged to the series, which led the author of the works catalogue to conjecture that this family portrait gallery was probably an assignment given to Schadow by his drawing teacher, Giovanni Battista Selvino.[46]

The portrait of Schadow's sister Christiane (*1768), the whereabouts of which had hitherto been unknown after a catalogue entry dated 1906, is reproduced here for the first time (Fig. 3).[47] The portrait of Charlotte had been published in the *Jahresbericht der Kunstakademie Düsseldorf 1945–1947*;[48] the portraits of her parents, however, have been missing since 1945.

After the purchase of the six drawings in 1954 discussed above, donations – most of them works by students – came sporadically at irregular intervals to the Academy from the Society of Friends and Sponsors. Yet it has only been since the founding of the Neue Sammlung [New Collection] and the opening of the Academy Gallery in 2005 that the Society has stepped up its efforts to concentrate on acquiring artworks specifically to close the gaps in that New Collection. Nowadays the main focus is not so much on documenting the history of the Art Academy as it is on being able to show a body of work representative of as many Academy teachers as possible. In 2009, for instance, the Society bought *Stilleben mit weißer Kerze* [Still Life with White Candle] by Heinrich Kamps (Fig. 4) and in 2012 the Theo Champion painting *Dorfstraße mit Heuschober* [Village Street with Haystack] (shown on p. 160).

SUPPORT FOR STUDENTS THROUGH GRANTS

Alongside the lectures that are given on a regular basis even today and financial support for numerous Academy publications, the training of the younger generation of artists has always been at the centre of the supporting activities engaged in by the Society. Hence grants are given to young artists by the Society for this purpose. The giving of grants on a permanent basis was made possible in 1955 with the endowment of 15,000 DM by the Ernst-Poensgen-Stiftung and the contribution of 10,000 DM annually by the company Henkel.[49] The 1965 *Jahresbericht der Gesellschaft von Freunden und Förderern* reveals that from the above sums 6,200 DM were used to support sixteen students.[50] The sums regularly paid in by the Ernst-Poensgen-Stiftung, by Henkel (both by the firm and individuals), and by the Forberg-Stiftung were used until the mid-1990s to give Art Academy students travel grants amounting to 2,500 DM.

In 1975 the Ministry of Science took out a ninety-year lease on three studios in the Cité Internationale des Arts in

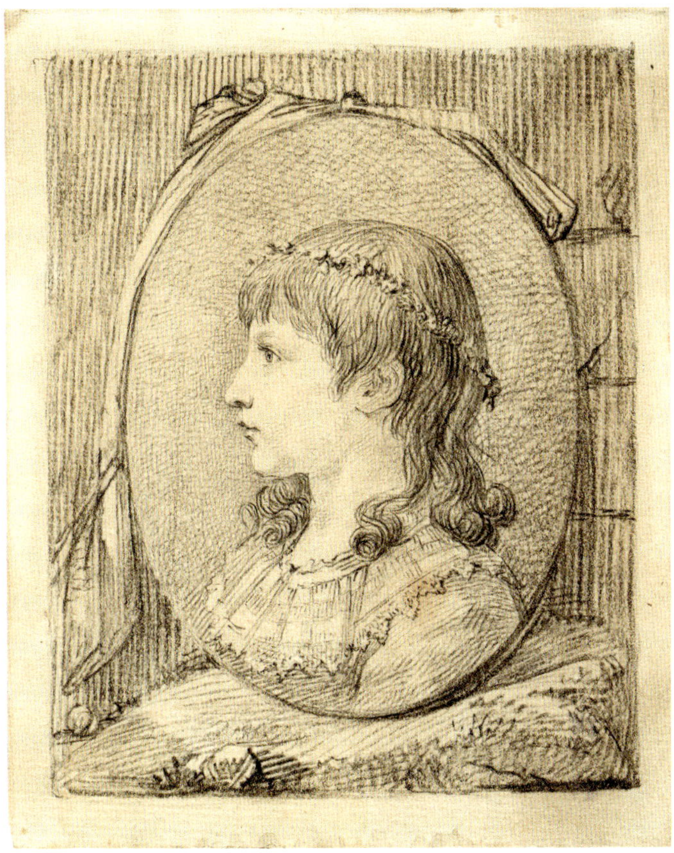

Fig. 3: Johann Gottfried Schadow, portrait of Christiane Schadow, c. 1780, pencil on paper, 119 × 75 mm, Düsseldorf Art Academy

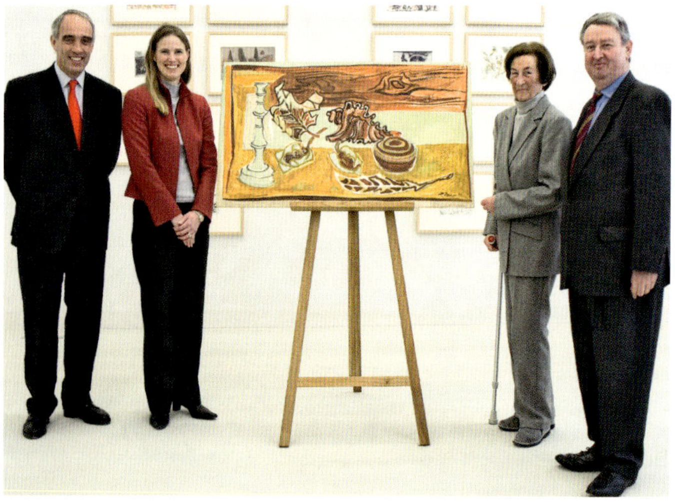

Fig. 4: From left to right: Olaf Huth, Friderike Bagel, Sonja Müller, and Siegfried Gohr when the Heinrich Kamps painting Stillleben mit weißer Kerze *[Still Life with White Candle] was presented on 30 January 2009*

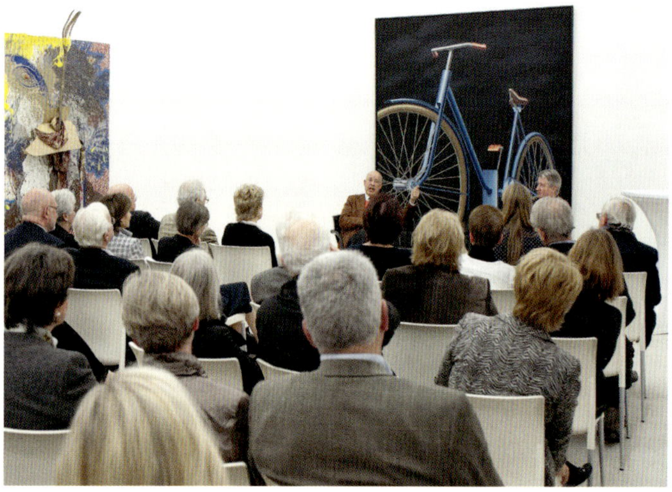

Fig. 5: Konrad Klapheck and Siegfried Gohr in conversation, Academy Gallery, 16 May 2011

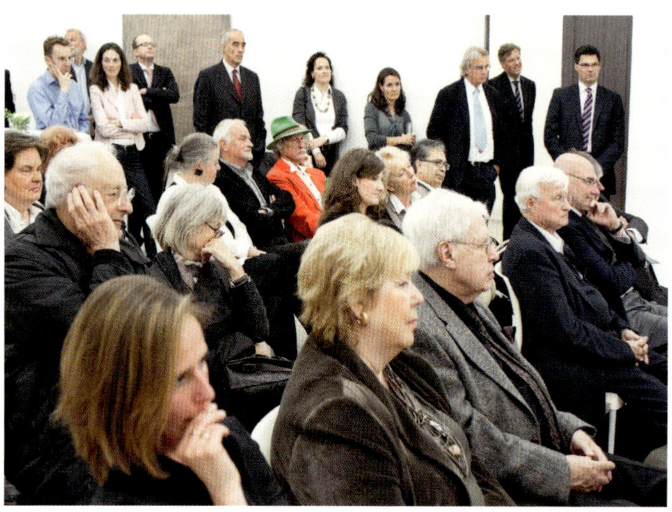

Fig. 6: Friends and Sponsors of the Düsseldorf Art Academy at the Academy Gallery on 16 May 2011

Paris which could be used for six months at a time by Art Academy students and were paid for by the Circle of Friends. From 1 April 1989 on, one of those three studios was allocated to the Münster Art Academy. The two others were finally given up in 2004. Two studios were rented in New York from 1977 until 1986, which were financed by the Society of Friends and Sponsors at a cost of 32,000 DM. Two students at a time could use the New York studios for a period of six months. The students in New York were also given a one-off grant of 4,000 DM each to cover living expenses. In addition, the Society of Friends and Sponsors paid for the cost of insurance for the recipients of the New York grant.

Travel grants of this kind no longer exist. Instead the Society of Friends and Sponsors has been giving graduate grants amounting to 5,000 euros each in the framework of the *Rundgang* [Academy Tour]. In addition, the Society continues to finance excursions undertaken by classes at the Düsseldorf Art Academy.

CRISIS AND RENEWAL

By the late 1970s the Circle of Friends seemed, despite all endeavours to the contrary and a solid financial basis, to be facing ruin. Membership had dropped to about 150, of whom only nineteen members showed up for the March 1977 members' meeting.[51] If that were not bad enough, the Art Academy also seemed to have lost sight of the importance of the Society: it was not even officially represented at said members' meeting, and, in contrast to the usual practice, there was no lecture by a speaker from the professorial staff.[52] That November Anna Klapheck publicly deplored the lack of interest in the Society shown by the Academy: 'Academy director Professor Kricke had sent a surrogate [...] only two members of the large body of teaching staff were present; even professors who were members of the "council" were missing [...]. It is all the more remarkable, therefore, that the board still endeavours to continue its generous patronage.'[53] Yet the Society was fighting for its survival, and by 1988 it had only 130 members and total assets amounting to 190,000 DM.[54] Despite the continuing decline in member numbers – by 1996 there were only 120 – the capital assets had risen to 246,000 DM.[55] With Professor Gabriele Henkel as chairman of the board, the situation gradually stabilised. Since she resigned in 2011, the Society has continued to be successfully headed by her successor, Dr Friderike Bagel. Lectures, special guided tours for the *Rundgang*, and exhibition openings at the Academy Gallery with talks by artists are organised for Society members on a regular basis and are invariably well attended (Figs. 5, 6).

CONCLUSIONS

Throughout the ninety-five years of its existence, the zeal of the members of the Society of Friends and Sponsors of the Düsseldorf Art Academy e. V. has never flagged even in the face of all odds. Without the Society, the departments and workshops initiated at the Academy by Fritz Roeber could not have been financed. Nor would the Academy building have been so rapidly rebuilt and made usable after the Second World War. Through members' active support, Academy students not only had a refectory but also the means for procuring working materials and lodging placed at their disposal. It is probably due to the prudence of the members of the board and council of the Society that, alongside the scholarly commitment to lectures and excursions, students' everyday needs and concerns have not been neglected. Particularly in the early years after the Second World War, when many possessed little more than the clothing on their backs, this support from the Society meant a crucial improvement of their studies.

It is also to the lasting credit of the Society, and should be mentioned here, that it has always supported the Academy library and its contents. The hands-on support offered so readily by the Society once the war was over made it possible to move the books speedily and without complications from the wartime cellar storage facility, where they were threatened by rising damp, to Room 78/79 of the main building. In this connection, the Society had also, among other services, arranged for the manufacture of light metal shelving.[56] Moreover, in the years that followed, acquisitions which the library budget could not have covered were made possible by the Society. Today the Academy library with its important collection of rare books and manuscripts is open to students, teachers, members of the Society, and even, to a limited extent, the public at large.

Considering the diversity of support priorities with which the Society of Friends and Sponsors has been involved, it remains clear that its chief concern has always been to promote the younger generation of artists – by organising lectures, excursions, financial backing for grants, and exhibitions. Due to changing economic and political circumstances, this support has often had to be adjusted accordingly over time, but the Society has always ensured that the core concerns of students and the Academy have not been neglected. It is also due to the Society of Friends and Sponsors that the *Jahresberichte* of the Art Academy and numerous other publications that document the life and activities of the Art Academy are available to us today.

Without the additional financing provided by the Society, the history of the Düsseldorf Art Academy would definitely have been very different. The very fact that the Society was founded in 1918 is so important because it attests to great far-sightedness: after all, the basic situation, in which a good education cannot be financed solely through the available state funding, has not really changed to the present day. Now, as always, at a time when the state is cutting funding for culture, the Art Academy depends on the contributions made by third parties in order to make possible grants, exhibitions, and travel for its students.

NOTES

1 More on this in the essays by Johannes Myssok and Dawn Leach in the present volume, pp. 10–19 and pp. 416–426.

2 Anna Klapheck, 'Die "goldnen" zwanziger Jahre. Die Akademie zwischen den beiden Kriegen', in: Eduard Trier (ed.), *Zweihundert Jahre Kunstakademie Düsseldorf*, Düsseldorf 1973, pp. 147–160; here: p. 148.

3 Letter from Hauth to Roeber of 13 August 1918, Nachlass der Gesellschaft von Freunden und Förderern [Estate of the Society of Friends and Sponsors; in the following: Nachlass GFF], Düsseldorf Art Academy archives.

4 In the founding charter 'Königliche' [Royal] is not yet part of the Society's name; it does not appear until somewhat later (the copy of the charter in the Düsseldorf Art Academy archives does not show a date) and is first officially replaced by 'Staatliche' [State] in 1939. Since the name of the Düsseldorf Art Academy was again changed in 1987, the friends' association has been called the Gesellschaft von Freunden und Förderern der Kunstakademie Düsseldorf e. V. [Society of Friends and Sponsors of the Düsseldorf Art Academy e. V.].

5 Memorandum from Dr Ing. E. H. Kirdorf, privy councillor of commerce, of 5 October 1918, Nachlass GFF, Düsseldorf Art Academy archives.

6 § 4 of the Vereinssatzung der Gesellschaft von Freunden und Förderern der Königlichen Kunstakademie in Düsseldorf e. V. [Charter of the Society of Friends and Sponsors of the Royal Art Academy in Düsseldorf] of 1918, Nachlass GFF, Düsseldorf Art Academy archives.

7 Copies of the minutes of the founding assembly on 18 October 1918 and of the minutes of the first members' general meeting on 17 October 1918 of the Society of Friends and Sponsors of the Royal Art Academy in Düsseldorf, Nachlass GFF, Düsseldorf Art Academy archives.

8 Copy of the minutes of 17 October 1918 (see n. 7); on this also charter of 1918 (see n. 6).
9 Copy of the minutes of the board meeting of 2 November 1918, Nachlass GFF, Düsseldorf Art Academy archives.
10 Report of Chairman Friederich on 1 June 1934, Nachlass GFF, Düsseldorf Art Academy archives.
11 Ibid.
12 Copies of the minutes of the meeting of the Society of Friends and Sponsors since 1918 are in the Düsseldorf Art Academy archives but these records are not complete; some years are missing. From 1937 until 1950 the activities of the Society were also published in the *Jahresberichte* [Annual Reports] or the *Jahrbuch der Kunstakademie Düsseldorf* [Düsseldorf Art Academy Yearbook]. After that there are some minutes up to 1965. That marks the end of this documentation. For subsequent years there are only lists (1980–1994) indicating the bestowal of travel grants as well as individual press reports on the Society in the archives.
13 Copy of the minutes of the board and administrative council meeting in the Düsseldorf Industry Club on 14 December 1932, Nachlass GFF, Düsseldorf Art Academy archives.
14 Jakob Heinrich Schmidt, 'Zur Geschichte der Düsseldorfer Akademie', in: *Jahresbericht der Staatlichen Kunstakademie Düsseldorf 1941–1944*, Düsseldorf [1945], pp. 53–87; here: p. 85.
15 Friederich report (see n. 10).
16 Ibid.
17 Ibid.
18 Ibid.
19 Copy of the minutes of the board and administrative council meeting and the members' meeting of 16 June 1936, Nachlass GFF, Düsseldorf Art Academy archives.
20 Ibid.
21 When minutes have survived.
22 *Jahresbericht der Staatlichen Kunstakademie Düsseldorf 1939*, Düsseldorf [1940], p. 55.
23 In the minutes of the board and administrative council meeting and the members' meeting of 16 June 1936, it is pointed out that the securities had been reduced from eight to four and a half per cent; Nachlass GFF, Düsseldorf Art Academy archives.
24 Copy of the association charter, *c.*1939, Nachlass GFF, Düsseldorf Art Academy archives.
25 According to the association charter of 1918 the board consisted of a chairman, his deputy, and six committee members. It was originally elected from among its members by the administrative council; copy of the charter of 1918 (see n. 6).
26 Under the provisions of the charter of 1918, it consisted of thirty persons; ibid.
27 Copy of the minutes of 20 September 1936, Nachlass GFF, Düsseldorf Art Academy archives. In addition, the running expenses incurred by the Academy for the refectory, the Christmas party, restoring the library, and acquisitions were assumed, financial support for students was provided, and trips for study purposes were organised.
28 Copy of the minutes of the council meeting of 20 December 1945, Nachlass GFF, Düsseldorf Art Academy archives.
29 Copy of the minutes of the council meeting of 22 May 1946, Nachlass GFF, Düsseldorf Art Academy archives
30 Ibid.
31 Copy of the minutes of the council meeting of 1 October 1948, Nachlass GFF, Düsseldorf Art Academy archives.
32 Copy of the minutes of the council meeting of 5 February 1949, Nachlass GFF, Düsseldorf Art Academy archives.
33 Copy of the minutes of the meetings of 1 October 1948 (see n. 31) and 5 February 1949 (see n. 32).
34 Letter from Chairman Dr Knapp to all members, December 1967, Nachlass GFF, Düsseldorf Art Academy archives.
35 *Jahreshefte der Kunstakademie Düsseldorf*, Vol. 2, Düsseldorf 1989, pp. 310–315.
36 *Jahreshefte der Kunstakademie Düsseldorf*, Vol. 4, Düsseldorf 1994, pp. 344–349.
37 Copy of the minutes of the members' meeting of 10 November 1949 and of the council meeting of 15 December 1949, both Nachlass GFF, Düsseldorf Art Academy archives.
38 Copy of the minutes of the members' meeting of 6 July 1955, Nachlass GFF, Düsseldorf Art Academy archives.
39 Anlage [Annex] VII, 'Betr. Arbeitsplan für 1954' [re: Work Plan for 1954], Nachlass GFF, Düsseldorf Art Academy archives.
40 Copy of the minutes of the members' meeting of 19 May 1954, Nachlass GFF, Düsseldorf Art Academy archives.
41 Copy of the minutes of 6 July 1955 (see n. 38). After Wilden died, Academy director Heinrich Kamps took over the deputy position from Petersen but died shortly afterwards in December 1954, when Dr Franz Schütz took over his position.
42 Anlage [Annex] VI, 1954, Nachlass GFF, Düsseldorf Art Academy archives.
43 *Jahresbericht 1941–1944* (see n. 14), p. 20.
44 1845, oil on canvas, 32 × 25.8 cm, signed bottom left: 'O. Achenbach 1845, Kunstakademie Düsseldorf'; reproduced in Jakob Heinrich Schmidt, *Oswald Achenbach*, Düsseldorf 1946, p. 11. Also see Dawn Leach in the present volume, pp. 416–426; *Jahresbericht der Staatlichen Kunstakademie Düsseldorf 1940*, Düsseldorf [1941], p. 60; *Jahresbericht 1941–1944* (see n. 14), p. 20.
45 Confirmation of the purchase of the drawings, approved and undersigned by Werner Heuser and Otto Coester, Nachlass GFF, Düsseldorf Art Academy archives.
46 Sibylle Badstüber-Gröger, Claudia Czok, and Jutta von Simson, *Johann Gottfried Schadow: Die Zeichnungen*, Berlin 2006, Vol. 2, Nos. 3–6, pp. 8–10, and Vol. 3, Anhang [Appendix], No. 1, p. 802.
47 Ibid.
48 *Jahresbericht der Staatlichen Kunstakademie Düsseldorf 1945–1947*, Düsseldorf [1948], p. 89.
49 Copy of the minutes of the members' meeting of 13 April 1956 and of the council meeting of 18 November 1955, both Nachlass GFF, Düsseldorf Art Academy archives.
50 1965 annual report of the Gesellschaft von Freunden und Förderern der Staatlichen Kunstakademie Düsseldorf, Nachlass GFF, Düsseldorf Art Academy archives.
51 'Tagung der "Freunde". Kunstakademie und Bürger', *Rheinische Post*, 23 March 1977.
52 Ibid.
53 Anna Klapheck, 'Förderer der Kunstakademie tagten. Ateliers in New York', *Rheinische Post*, 25 November 1977.
54 Yvonne Friedrichs, 'Freunde und Förderer der Kunstakademie. Pflege der Sammlung', *Rheinische Post*, 20 October 1988.
55 'Akademie-Freunde. Schauraum gesucht', *Rheinische Post*, 5 December 1996.
56 *Jahresbericht 1945–1947* (see n. 48), p. 23, p. 39.

THE ACADEMY TOUR: PAST AND PRESENT

Hans Peter Thurn

THE PAST

'Our painter academy might be [...] one of the first in Germany and will easily become, with Rome and Florence, one of the first schools in the world.'[1] The writer Wilhelm Heinse felt inspired to utter this appraisal after visiting the Düsseldorf Art Academy in 1776. It had only recently been founded at the urging of Lambert Krahe, a painter, who in the years that followed did everything he could to consolidate his establishment aesthetically, intellectually, and economically. Successfully, too, as Heinse found, since all the Academy lacked was 'a teacher in the history of art for the young apprentices' (who would be hired very soon in the person of Heinrich Theodor Bislinger, a librarian, who in turn not long afterwards designated the philosopher Johann Heinrich Jacobi, a resident of nearby Pempelfort, an honorary member of the upwardly mobile institute).[2] Hence, as the writer soon summed it up on balance, 'The rest would soon be as well ordered as possible.'[3] He accurately gave Academy director Krahe the credit for this state of affairs: 'Our director is a German who spent his entire youth in beautiful Italy and a professor at the painting schools in Rome and Florence and is entirely imbued with the sanctity and dignity of fine art and feels in the tips of his fingers every apposite brush stroke.'[4] The artist's cosmopolitan mindset and sensitivity were accompanied by an unflagging drive to collect art, which not least enriched the Academy because the treasures thus amassed served its students as study material and also attracted visitors from near and far (Fig. 1). 'We have a collection of paintings the like of which no place in Germany can boast, not even excepting Dresden', concluded Heinse and praised the city that would thenceforward benefit from Krahe's commitment: 'What would Düsseldorf not be in all of Europe if art were not so appreciated and so honoured?'[5]

As the eyewitness pointed out, the proof of its usefulness was provided, apart from the growing number of students, by the visitors who travelled to the city 'in droves' to regale themselves in the delights of the gallery on the Rhine and to further their education, with some of them not adverse to a walk through the fledgling Academy.[6] Thus art attained the attention and publicity that it deserved. Their number was indeed legion: Düsseldorf became a highly recommended attraction for culture vultures on educational tours, who could now add to the rites of enjoyment a visit to the young school for painters along with a viewing of the gallery once founded by the Elector Jan Wellem and curated jointly with him by Lambert Krahe. They were eager to do so, aristocrats and the middle classes alike, not just the ubiquitous touring *Engelländer* [Englishmen] ('still the first persons regardless of all their unpleasant ways'), whom Heinse viewed with a sceptical eye,[7] but also many a German who wanted to broaden their horizons. Among the latter, Goethe, almost twenty-five years old at the time, sojourned on the Rhine as early as August 1774. 'The good Krah', as Goethe assured his friend Jacobi in retrospect, had made a lasting impression on him,[8] and during a later stay, Goethe reported to his artistic acolyte, Johann Heinrich Meyer, in

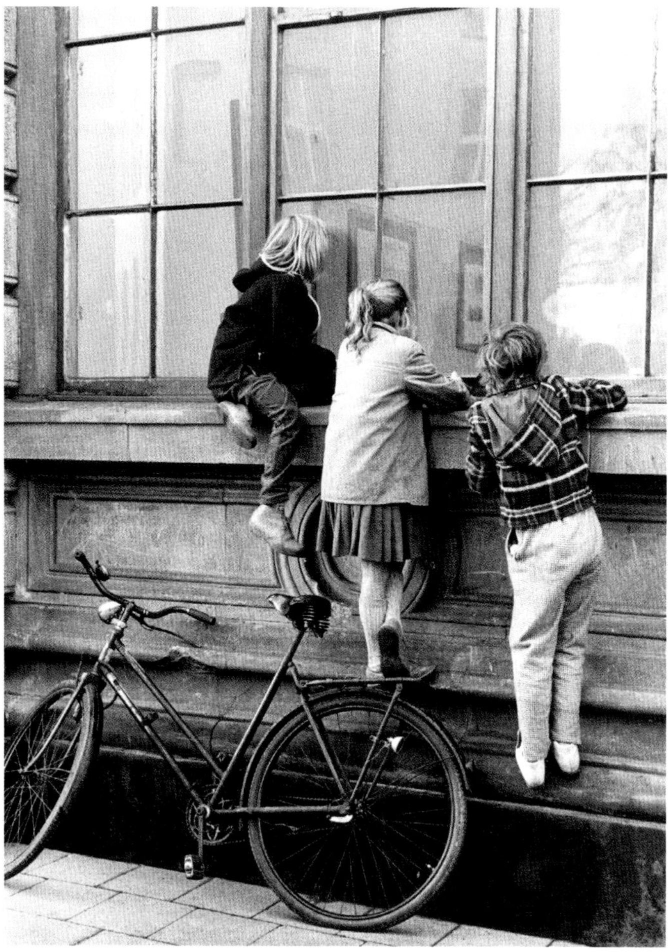

Fig. 1: Children at a window next to the main entrance to the Düsseldorf Art Academy, c. 1960

Weimar, the 'gallery' once again gave him 'great pleasure' because in it he encountered 'an excellent collection of drawings by Italian Masters, which the former director, Krahe, had collected in Rome at a time' (the poet, who was always anxious to add to his own store of collectibles with reasonably priced acquisitions, was forced to concede through gritted teeth) 'when there was still something to be had'.[9] There can be no doubt that Lambert Krahe also belonged to the Pempelfort circle because 'the usual gathering' took place 'at the gallery'. Nor will the Academy have been left out, particularly since Goethe was so interested in pictures and drawings, not only from the theoretical standpoint but also with a view to his own hands-on attempts.[10]

In 1792, of course, the Weimar amateur – in the best sense of the term – who liked to be viewed as a 'solicitous gardener of art',[11] could no longer meet the head of the school and the museum there because Krahe had died two years before. Still he did not forget that Krahe had, like many another, succeeded in providing him with a 'benefit for his entire life'.[12] From the beginning Krahe had viewed (in 1777 in the Academic Regulations, as they were termed in the patent granted by the Elector) the Pflantzschule der Zeichenkunst [Nursery of the Art of Drawing] as an institution that in teaching should devote itself not only to 'youth beginning from its first principles' but, moreover, should grant an interested public access that would be entertaining, possibly even instructive.[13] Artists and not just laymen should profit from this opening, as Article 11 of the Order of the Academic Assembly and its Regulations (Ordnung der Akademischen Versammlung und ihrer Gesetze) promised: 'The Academy is to mount a public exhibition of works by professors and Academy students the following year. The day for this will be established in an Academic assembly and at once announced through the newspapers so that academicians from other cities or abroad can send their works to it.'[14]

Success soon proved Krahe right. Interested visitors came from near and far. It was not long before the 'real director of the Electoral Painter, Sculptor, and Architecture Academy'[15] had to entertain the idea of finding more space. In Hunsrückenstraße nearby, an Academic Art and Bookseller was established, where (as announced in the press) both art and literary products could be appraised and acquired: 'The Fine Arts Academy here has really begun to establish a regular trade in art and books and to that end has acquired a large collection of old and new paintings, drawings, and copperplate prints, as well as good and new books.'[16] Alongside the art on display, it housed a reading library, with an international selection of books that invited browsers to borrow as well as buy them. More information was to be provided at regular intervals in the form of a printed catalogue.[17] Drawn by what was on offer, devotees of pictures and books would make pilgrimages back and forth between the Academy rooms and this annexe at the time designated.

The prevailing circumstances, however, thwarted any consistent continuance of Lambert Krahe's projects. After he died in 1790, many of them ceased to be. Georg Forster, a globetrotting man of letters and connoisseur of the arts, had already visited the 'well-built city' four times in a single year to admire the treasures in Düsseldorf.[18] Once again, he wrote in *Ansichten vom Niederrhein*, published in 1791, 'We browsed for three whole hours in the excellent gallery here.'[19] Yet Forster was in for a bitter disappointment when he visited the Academy afterwards! This time he was not, as he had been in 1778 by Lambert Krahe, guided through the student studios by the 'honest rector' personally (as he recalled to Jacobi) or even his son, Peter Joseph.[20] Remembering the 'very rich collection of copperplates and drawings' at the art school, he inquired 'about the moulds from which the glorious casts of ancient sculpture are made', which he had seen in Mannheim: 'But you couldn't have imagined it – that they have been broken up and used for building roads. Tell me whether we are not still the same old barbarians we always were!'[21] This would not have been possible while Krahe was alive and that 'enthusiast of the arts' was in charge (as Forster had once written enthusiastically to his father).[22]

It was not until the nineteenth century that the Academy was gradually able to liberate itself from the stagnation into which both teaching and public relations had lapsed, which in turn had put an end to the rituals associated with visits to it. After a brief interregnum under Peter Cornelius, the painter Wilhelm von Schadow breathed new life into the Art Academy and made it respected again by implementing reforms instigated by Prussia. They included specific measures aimed at arousing the curiosity of interested people from other places. 'To convey an interest in art', it said in the Regulations for the Royal Art Academy at Düsseldorf (Reglement für die Königliche Kunst-Akademie zu Düsseldorf) issued by the Prussian authorities in 1831, the training institution should do everything it could to promote 'a lively interchange between it and the public'.[23] Not only its pupils but also 'artists from elsewhere and outstanding amateurs, provided the necessary precautions are taken', should be allowed access to the treasure trove of art at the institute. Moreover, 'The collection of paintings is to be open to the public once a week. In addition, the Academy is to ensure that travellers are readily shown the collections at their request.'[24]

Above and beyond such public relations efforts, the new director was also concerned with presenting students' work in a good light. So he ensured that exhibitions of it were duly mentioned in the Academic regulations: 'To give the public an account of the achievements of the Art Academy', it says there, 'a public art exhibition shall be held from time to time, a larger one every two years at least.' The invitation to that event would be extended 'by the Academy through a programme that must contain a brief report on the progress made by the institution and the works of professors and their pupils, further on the art things, specifically paintings, etc. that have in the meantime been acquired'.[25]

The regulations issued by the state deliberately kept open the option of whether the Academy might join forces with an 'already formed association' in organising such exhibitions. After all, the Academy Exhibitions organised in 1828 had been upgraded by the founding of an Art Society for the Rhinelands and Westphalia a year later. It continued to mount its annual exhibitions in the Academy building, offered the works shown at it for sale, even held lotteries, and, with all those attractions, continued to draw the public *en masse* to the Academy until 1872.

When the art school lost its rooms because the castle that housed it was gutted by fire in 1872, another enforced break occurred in the ritualised activities that had worked out so well over the past decades. This time, the impressive new Academy building that had been finished by the late 1870s provided an unprecedented opportunity for cultivating and expanding the established ceremonial links with the city's residents. This was done by invitation, both privately and through the press, to visit the library and the permanent collection. Lectures and discussions were organised, the public was invited to attend parties and encouraged to stroll through Academy studios and rooms, corridors and staircases during the yearly presentation of student work. Success did not fail to materialise: what had been a commoner's Academy, then an Electoral institution, and, finally, the Royal Prussian Art Academy became renowned far beyond the city limits of Düsseldorf, indeed the boundaries of the state, attracting eager students as well as more and more art lovers from all points of the compass. Sometimes the swelling throng of visitors made the magnificently showy building on the Rhine resemble not just a place for learning about art and teaching it but even more a shrine to which aesthetically motivated pilgrims flocked.

Most later Academy heads and their artist colleagues were only too aware that even in the twentieth century with its increasingly democratic public the pressure for paying performative tribute had not lessened. When Walter Kaesbach, who had been designated director of the Academy in 1924, set about opening the institute to current trends in art and the new zeitgeist, he took that development into account, providing two permanently accessible exhibition rooms that were primarily available to students. The need for public representation and debate continued to grow steadily during the 1920s. The upshot was that even as late as 1933, all classroom doors were opened wide to the public at specified times. Still, after the ideological closure enforced by the National Socialists, it would take a long time for the free spirit to return to the Academy and for the Academy to again admit the public to the discussion about art. The radical democratisation so vehemently advocated by Joseph Beuys contributed decisively to the new opening. Nonetheless the idea of 'parading achievement' on a regular basis remained controversial for a long time and was even disapproved of by students. Academy director Norbert Kricke finally managed to re-implement the annual exhibition as an institution in 1972. Now dubbed the *Rundgang* [Academy Tour], it was coupled with the stipulation that every student had to show at least one work. Although this last idea in particular was not popular with everyone, Kricke knew that he would be proved right. And the crowds of curious visitors at the Academy gates, ultimately also the majority of teachers and their pupils inside, have thanked him with their active commitment: confirmed individualists artists may be, but the Academy awakens once a year to a collective buzz of activity.

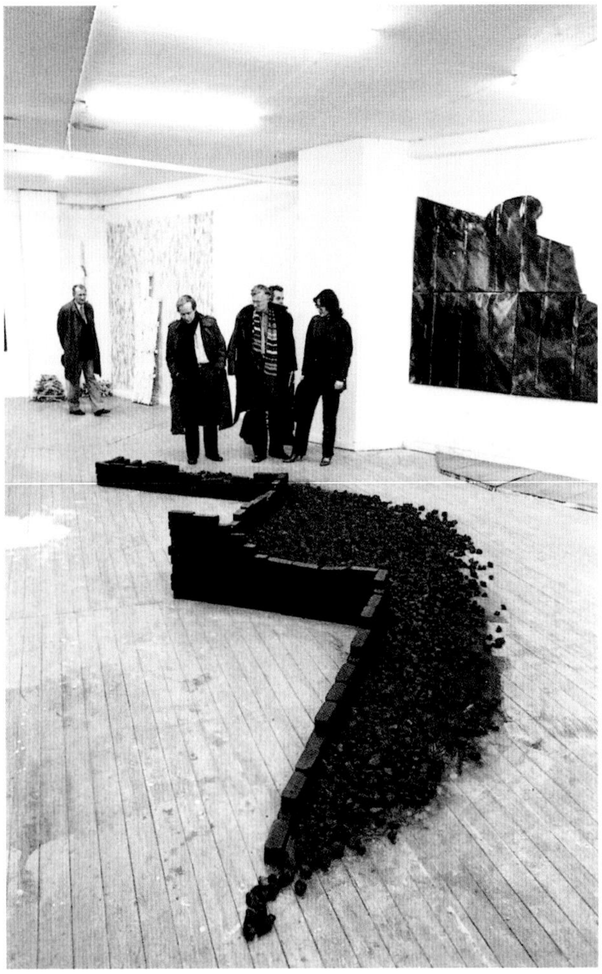

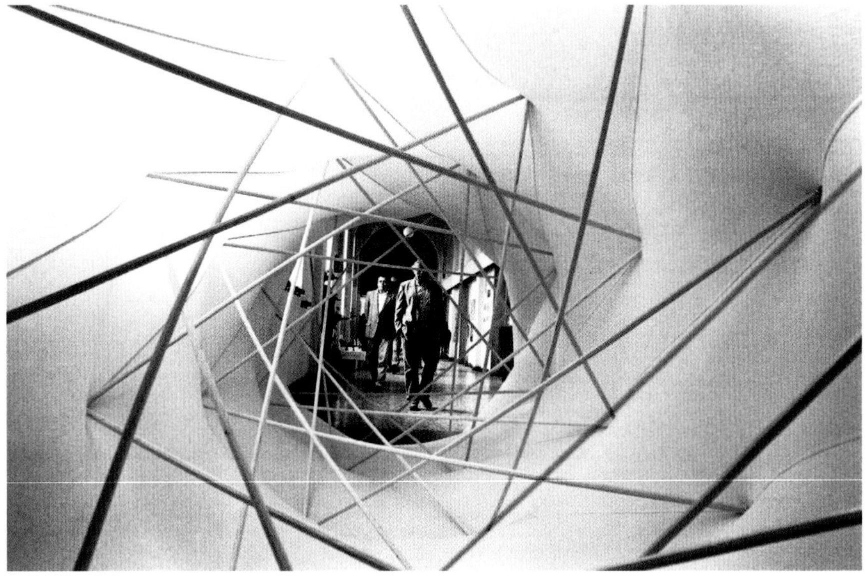

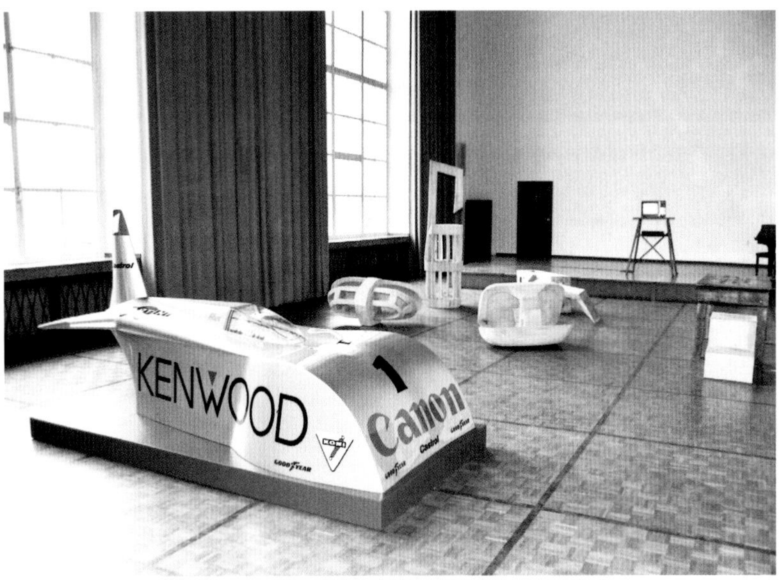

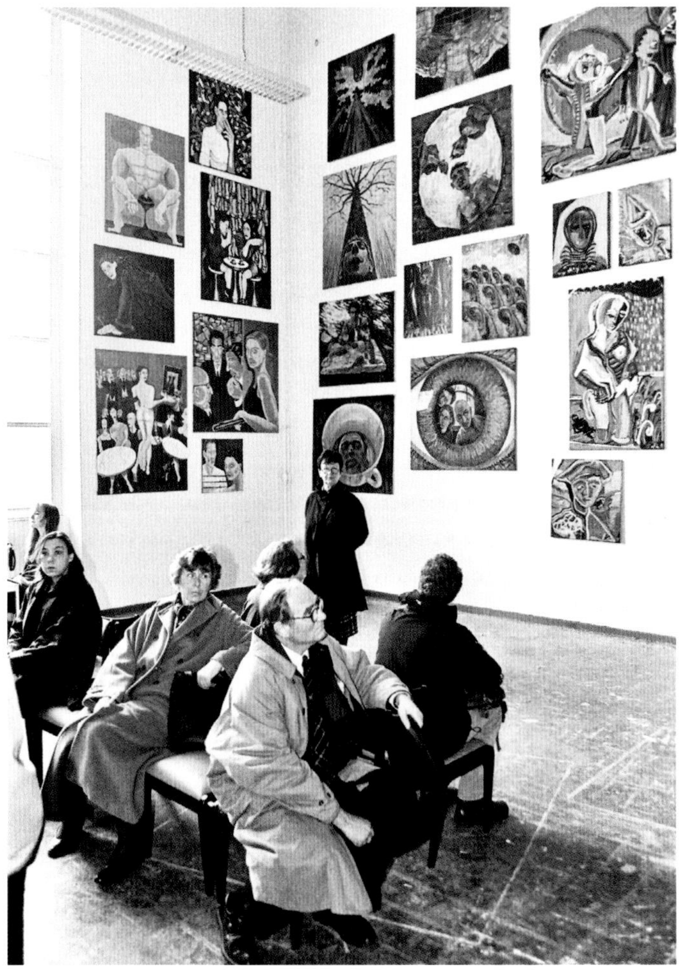

Fig. 2: Werner Spies and Heinrich Theissing, Academy Tour, 1983

Fig. 3: Günther Uecker in a corridor of the Academy, photographed at work by Katsuhito Nishikawa, Academy Tour, 1983

Fig. 4: View of an installation, Great Hall, Düsseldorf Art Academy, Academy Tour, 1992

Fig. 5: Visitors to the Academy Tour, 1998

THE PRESENT

Suddenly all this hustle and bustle. Rushing up and down stairs, the sound of hurried steps in all rooms. Even more of a surge to and fro along the corridors. Carrier bags full of paints and bags with tools, wood, iron, plastic: everything shoved through the portal to accumulate at the side entrance, looked at askance by the porter. Time seems to be fleeting. The workday starts earlier than usual in the classrooms. Anything that is out of place, in the way, seems unsuitable, never seems to be finished, is removed from sight, piled up in broom closets, sheds, cupboards. 'Tidying up' is the watchword everywhere. Space is needed for works that are still emerging, that need to be finished.

Will an idea, a plan that is being urged forwards to execution, be successful? No thought now of seminars, lectures, mandatory programmes. Better off to the workshop, where space is at a premium, its director groaning in agony during those hectic days before the *Rundgang*. Open the doors now, hammering, scraping, chiselling are going on in the corridors, too, while inside the electric saws are screeching ever more shrilly, sparks are brighter and fly further, the printing press squeaks, acridly smoking plastic stings eyes and mouths. Take one more measurement, check, think things over, take a break, decide: has it worked, has all the trouble been worth it, can it keep on going like this? Perhaps some more advice from a materials expert, from an artist teacher, from fellow students (Figs. 2, 3).

Then the way up to the class, by lift, up the stairs. Once there, exposed along with your work to the eyes of the others who all want their work to be seen and accepted, too. Tension mounts, the tone grows ruder, the mood is volatile. Someone shouts more loudly to someone else for help, puts him in his place, shoves away what is in the way. One rejects, another encourages. When time is running short, patience evaporates in strife; energy and attention are directed solely at reaching the goal with the work in progress. Smells of sweat, paint, fruit juices, beer, a chaos of nails, boards, scraps of cloth, pots, and boxes are part and parcel of it, just as much as cursing and beseeching, like praise or censure.

Finally the battle for the place. Everyone wants the best spot, towards the light, at eye level. Territorial rivalry is in the offing. Where to put that sculpture, in the classroom, in the corridor (Figs. 4, 5)? How much surface area are pictures given, how close to each other may they be hung? If a sculpture hides a painting from view, bottled-up annoyance explodes in anger. If anyone claims too much space, perhaps even an entire room, the chance of showing one's own work drops and so does the others' mood. Then the professor has to intervene, put his or her foot down hard. Those who are competing for viewers' favour can now learn cooperation, compromise. It's easier to work together on minor tasks, when drinks have to be procured, guard duty assigned, lists written up. Really venturesome, eternally entrepreneurial students may be planning a pop-up fast-food stall, will later be serving baps, cakes, and cupcakes, perhaps even Asian treats like sushi.

The day the *Rundgang* opens, ritual on a grand scale as a mass spectacle (Figs. 6, 7). The vernissage atmosphere is pervasive. As they have done since antiquity in the days of Roman *pompae*, the masses throng to ceremonial processions, public performances. The Great Hall is not big enough. When the rector appears, he puts the curious onlookers in the right mood, sometimes a lyrical one, sometimes prosaic, either cheery or serious. Visitors, students, colleagues listen with the rapt attention shown otherwise only by concert goers or worshippers in a church. On occasion, choral music, chamber music, even a short opera may follow. Bottled-up irritation used to be soothed at festivities, dancing, rock and jazz, framed by Actions, Performances, Happenings, during which motorbikes, small cars would roar down the corridors, or camels would tramp through the astonished audience.

Nowadays the rector conducts distinguished visitors through well-stocked rooms, pausing here and there to elucidate a work (Fig. 8). Everyone listens to his well-chosen words. Of course no one has to pay to do so, unlike the physician Thomas Cogan in his day.

'Anyone who visits Düsseldorf', wrote the Englishman while sojourning in the Rhineland in the late eighteenth century would 'naturally have to view the large collection of paintings'.[26] To fail to do so would be 'an unforgivable offence against a taste for art and laudable thirst for knowledge'. Another rewarding experience was a walk through the Academy afterwards. Cogan himself undertook to do so and had himself guided through the corridors, classrooms, and exhibition rooms there:

'After Professor Krahe died, the Elector entrusted a Professor W— with being head of the gallery and the Academy, who has apartments within the Academy and is paid a salary. Nonetheless,

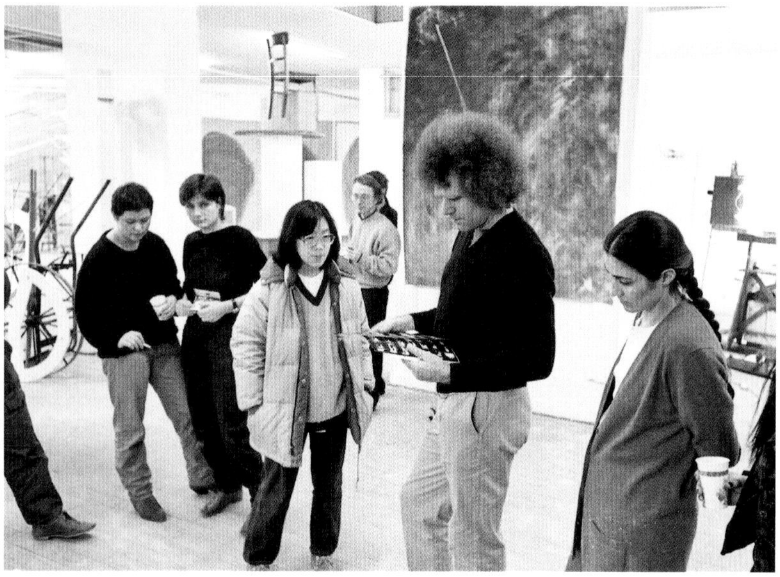

Fig. 6: Klaus Rinke with students, Academy Tour, 1982

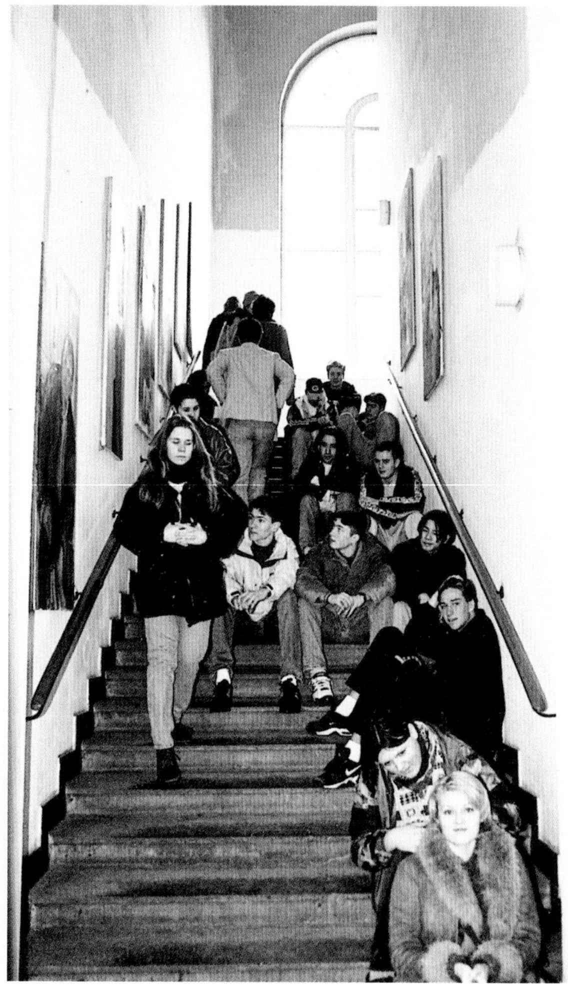

Fig. 7: A crowd jostling in the stairwell during the 1997 Academy Tour

every group of visitors is expected to give him a gratuity for his personal efforts. As instructed by our host, to whom we had addressed queries in the matter, we pressed a Taler (a half-crown) into the professor's hand at parting, with which he seemed most content.'[27]

Curious visitors were only too delighted to pay this sum because the professorial guide 'paid them every imaginable attention', not even failing to point out a 'picture by his own hand', which the English visitors evidently liked, especially since the commentary supplied by its author matched his skill as a painter: 'The manner in which he answered our questions proved that he knew his craft and was able to impart this to others.'[28] After exchanging art viewing for pecuniary remuneration, the professor and the visitors parted amicably. 'The professor's hand' was so familiar with this it would never have occurred to it 'to shrink back from our Taler, perhaps for reasons of delicacy [...]; to the contrary, the hand stretch[ed] out instinctively seeking the coin.'[29] No doubt about it, the British visitor felt, 'this little custom'[30] was beneficial to visitors, art, and the academic *cicerone* alike.

Such practices are frowned upon nowadays. The most that can happen is that self-styled outside experts offer their services in the press or online and take something for being an 'Academy guide'. Still the *Rundgang* does keep surprises for some visitors on hand. It has been known to happen that the Minister responsible has been forced, as one was by Kricke, a sculptor, to mount a high hobbyhorse with the director and have his picture taken by delighted photojournalists. By now no government official or department secretary would refuse an invitation to dance because the underlying idea is that while this show is on, which has been democratised for students and visitors alike, whatever their affiliation, some fun and games are in order to lighten up the rigours of initiation. At times and in some places the *Rundgang* resembles a folk fest even though in most classrooms a hallowed hush that discourages loud utterance prevails in front of the artworks.

All and sundry are invited and they do come in droves. The tide of onlookers continues to swell for a week. Friends and relatives of the aspiring artists showing work stroll about, sometimes concentrating on what they have come to see, at others aimlessly drifting. Some former students recall their hopes (fulfilled or failed) when they were still part of the event. They run into former classmates, linger in each other's company for a brief chat, exchange addresses, promise to see each other soon. Journalists jot down what they think might be worth

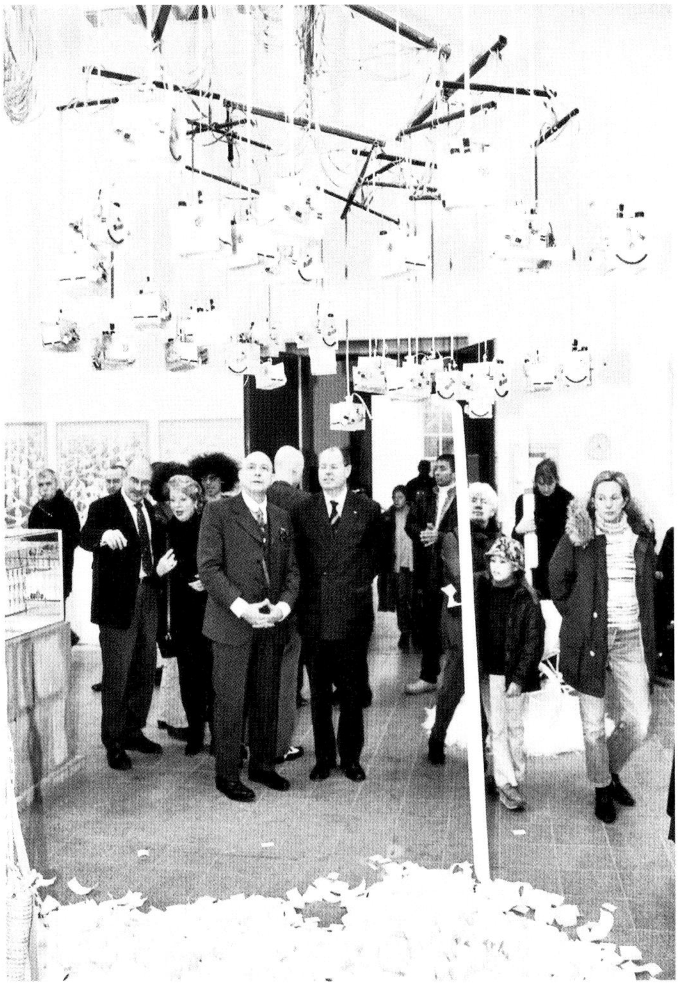

Fig. 8: Markus Lüpertz guiding Peer Steinbrück through the Art Academy rooms, Academy Tour, 2003

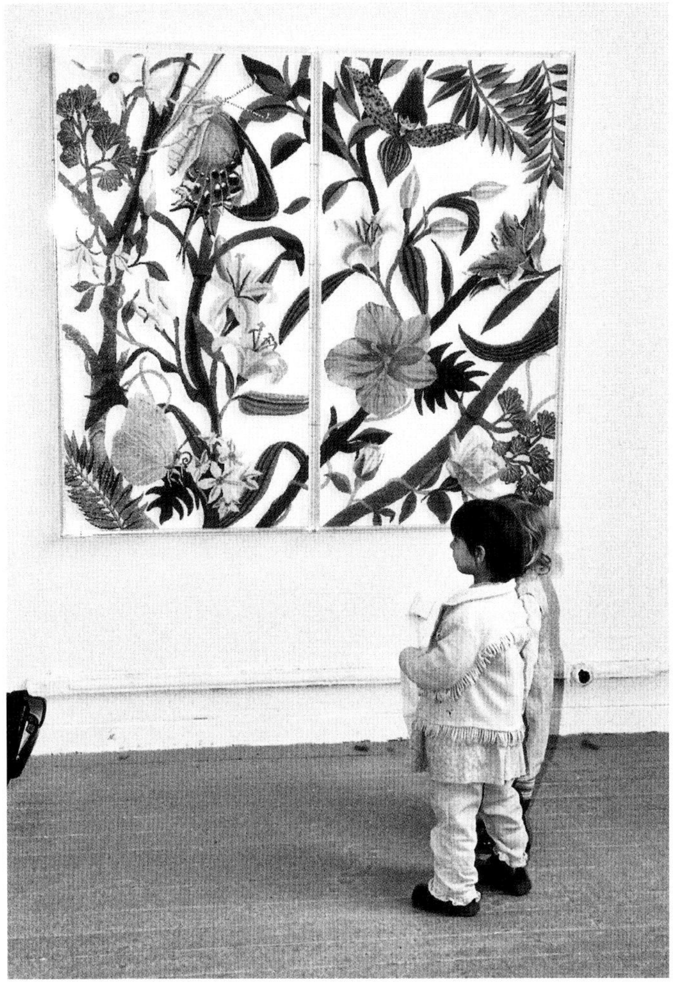

Fig. 9: Children in front of student work, Academy Tour, 2005

mentioning; critics feed the scepticism which they cannot desist from while observing the works. One or two of them might be hoping for a minor sensation to put into the arts section of their paper, as lavishly illustrated as possible. School classes are occasionally at a loss to understand the enthusiasm shown by the teachers who are so desperately trying to explain what it's all about. Hordes of kindergarten children stampede in all directions. The youngest visitors of all, propelled about in pushchairs, doze in the backwash from the crowds and artworks (Fig. 9). Onlookers enhance their gawping capability with cameras or video cameras; eavesdroppers prick up their ears to overhear remarks about weird-looking works. An art dealer might inquire of a companion while viewing paintings, drawings, prints, just as the gallerist Alfred Schmela once asked a friend, the sculptor Erwin Heerich: 'Is that good art, Erwin?' Many here are, admittedly or tacitly, on the lookout: where and who are today's talents, future masters, brand names soon to be reckoned with on the market? In fact everyone showing work is already delighted to receive any encouragement at all, to take constructive comments in the spirit they are meant, to engage in a conversation with a knowledgeable interlocutor, even more so if one of their own works should happen to be spontaneously purchased. In the febrile atmosphere of *Rundgang* week, the cauldron of expectations, rumours, disappointments seethes from morning till night.

During the early days of this spectacle another cult is observed that is partly *rite de séparation*, partly *rite de passage*: examinations leading to the acquisition of the *Akademiebrief* [Academy certificate] are inserted in the viewings of student work. The *Akademiebrief* is supposed to ensure that holders of this diploma with the blessings of the Academy are regarded from the time it is awarded as the artists they already were or have aspired to become. For over half an hour candidates must prove that their work can stand up to the scrutiny of their teachers. To this end an *ad hoc* committee, consisting of two practising artists as future colleagues, so to speak, and a theorist, appears on the scene. Then even academic scholars may have the opportunity of getting a word in edgeways, an art historian, even occasionally a philosopher, psychologists, educationalists. They all talk about the works presented, which mark an ending, a transition, perhaps even a fresh start. The question of what way the creator of these products has gone, whether he or she has learnt anything and, if so, how much has been taught. Since time immemorial the controversy has remained unresolved for some about whether art can be learnt or 'can be taught'.[31] What is certain is that the Academy, as a place of 'encounters', offers the widest range of possibilities for 'discussing' art-related issues.[32] In this aesthetic discourse space an ongoing 'poetic competition' takes place in which everyone must assert themselves, find their way to their own personal expression through their work. Success in this is supposed to be certified by the examination rites as the outcome of the 'good course of study' that Leonardo da Vinci was already convinced was indispensable.[33] Educationalists are not alone in knowing that the *ingenium* of the mature demiurge can be qualified by 'a course of studies' (wherever the individual accent may lie): 'The true artist is a work of his own making.'[34] The exam may reveal for the last time how much ideal, workmanlike, scientific obstetrics they might have needed along the way and whether they made use of it. After all, isn't artistic activity thinking with and in material, isn't art expression via paint, graphite, wood, stone, glass, plastic, and much else besides? Thus in those aspects at least partly learnable and teachable? The examination takes this fraught balancing act between original desire and acceptable achievement into account by seeing to it that it is easy for those participating in it to pass it in what are rather gentle procedures. At best it can be regarded as a residual form of university examination ritual. Be that as it may, the aspiring artists are relieved once everything is over, when the 'pass grade' with the 'temporary certificate' in hand can be announced to the well-wishers waiting outside and a sip of bubbly or beer enjoyed. That evening, at the latest when the *Rundgang* has ground to a close, graduates, classes, and the AStA [the General Students' Committee] all make ready for the big blast to come.

Finally, after the commissions have gone through, purchases have been made, prizes awarded, grants given, all examinations passed, after the mob of visitors has dispersed and the doors have closed, the artworks and their creators are left behind alone. Quiet reigns, meanwhile scraps of paper, rubbish, the detritus of art consumption lies about on floors trampled filthy, beneath tables and chairs, in corners. No sooner than the sigh of relief has been drawn after the stress is over than doubts about whether all the trouble has been worth it begin to creep in. Did one take part of one's own free will, under duress, by force of habit? What was, what is left? One thing is certain: in the time to come there will be peace for more work, for success and failure, for monologues and discussions under the heading of art. Until the next *Rundgang* in a year's time.

NOTES

1 Wilhelm Heinse, *Düsseldorfer Gemäldebriefe*, ed. Helmut Pfotenhauer, Frankfurt am Main/Leipzig 1996, p. 13.
2 Ibid.
3 Ibid.
4 Ibid., p. 12.
5 Ibid.
6 Ibid.
7 Ibid.
8 Johann Wolfgang von Goethe, *Goethes Werke (1887–1912)*, commissioned by and ed. Grand Duchess Sophie of Saxony, Vol. 95, Weimar 1887, p. 188.
9 Ibid., Vol. 103, Weimar 1892, pp. 38f.
10 Ibid., Vol. 37, Weimar 1898, p. 200.
11 Ibid., Vol. 32, Weimar 1890, p. 205: 'sorgfältigen Kunstgärtner'.
12 Ibid., p. 201.
13 Richard Klapheck, *Geschichte der Kunstakademie zu Düsseldorf. Die Vorgeschichte zur Neugründung. Die Kunstsammlungen Johann Wilhelms von der Pfalz. Die Kurfürstliche Maler-, Bildhauerund Bau-Kunst-Akademie 1769–1805*, Düsseldorf 1919, p. 138.
14 Ibid., p. 145.
15 Ibid., p. 74: 'Wirkliche[r] Direktor der Kurfürstlichen Maler-, Bildhauer- und Baukunst-Akademie'.
16 Ibid., p. 146.
17 Ibid.
18 Georg Forster, *Ansichten vom Niederrhein (1791)*, Munich 1985, p. 49.
19 Ibid., p. 52.
20 Georg Forster, *Briefe. Werke in vier Bänden*, ed. Gerhard Steiner, Vol. 4, Frankfurt am Main 1970, p. 78.
21 Forster (see n. 18), p. 101.
22 Forster (see n. 20), p. 73.
23 'Reglement für die Königliche Kunstakademie zu Düsseldorf, Berlin/Düsseldorf 1831', *Jahreshefte der Kunstakademie Düsseldorf*, Vol. 1, Düsseldorf 1988, pp. 317–331; here: p. 326.
24 Ibid., p. 325.
25 Ibid., p. 326.
26 Thomas Cogan, *The Rhine: or, A Journey from Utrecht to Francfort; chiefly by the borders of the Rhine, and the Passage down the River, from Mentz to Bonn: Described in a Series of Letters, Written from Holland, to a Friend in England, in the Years 1791 and 1792* (partly translated from the English by Anja Hegemann, n.d.), Vol. 1, London/Düsseldorf 1794, p. 26.
27 Ibid., p. 32.
28 Ibid., p. 34.
29 Ibid., p. 32.
30 Ibid.
31 Norbert Kricke, in: *Kunstakademie Düsseldorf*, study brochure, Düsseldorf n.d., n.p.; see also Norbert Kricke, 'Die neue Akademie', in: Eduard Trier (ed.), *Zweihundert Jahre Kunstakademie Düsseldorf*, Düsseldorf 1973, p. XIII.
32 Markus Lüpertz, in: *Kunstakademie Düsseldorf*, study brochure, Düsseldorf n.d., n.p.
33 Leonardo da Vinci, *Traktat von der Malerei*, ed. Marie Herzfeld, transl. from Italian Heinrich Ludwig, Jena 1925, pp. 48f.
34 Johannes Bilstein, 'Nichts den Lehrern schulden. Über Künstler als Prototypen der Selbstkonstitution', *Neue Sammlung. Vierteljahres-Zeitschrift für Erziehung und Gesellschaft*, Issue 38, No. 1, Seelze-Velber 1998, pp. 19–39; here: p. 33.

THE ACADEMY TOUR CHANGES FROM AN INTERNAL SHOW OF STUDENT ACHIEVEMENT TO A HIT WITH THE PUBLIC

Vanessa Sondermann

For the year 1932 all press cuttings and documents in the Düsseldorf Art Academy archives record an Academy Exhibition as an event at the end of the winter term. More than 18,000 visitors 'from Düsseldorf and the environs'[1] to the event at the Academy were counted; the Academy doors were opened to admit the public between 17 and 20 January from '10 a.m. to 1 p.m. and from 3 p.m. to 5 p.m.'[2] (Fig. 1). Walter Kaesbach, the young man who had been appointed to succeed Fritz Roeber as director of the Academy in October 1924, issued the invitation. A native of Mönchengladbach, Kaesbach held a doctorate in art history and had been director of the Anger Museum in Erfurt for four years before being appointed director of the Düsseldorf Art Academy. Before the Anger collection of Expressionists and Bauhaus work was disbanded and broken up by the NS regime, it was a groundbreaking one. Erich Heckel's *Lebensstufen* [Life Stages] murals were painted in 1922 and 1923 while Kaesbach was head of the Anger Museum. Kaesbach's proposal to organise an end-of-term exhibition in Düsseldorf sprang from his expressed desire to break with antiquated traditions in the Academy calendar. Moreover, it also reveals the influence of Bauhaus reform ideas: put under pressure by the state government in Thuringia, which wanted to see results since it held the purse strings, the Bauhaus in Weimar – under Walter Gropius, its founding director – in 1923 organised an exhibition with lectures outlining its agenda. The event made art history and may even have been the model for the Düsseldorf end-of-term show; like Gropius in Weimar, who had opened the Bauhaus event with the lecture 'Kunst und Technik – eine neue Einheit' [Art and Technology – a New Unity], Kaesbach inaugurated the Academy Exhibition in Düsseldorf with a lecture entitled 'Deutschlands Siedlungsentwicklung in wirtschaftlicher und menschlicher Hinsicht' [The Development of Housing Estates in Germany in Economic and Human Terms].

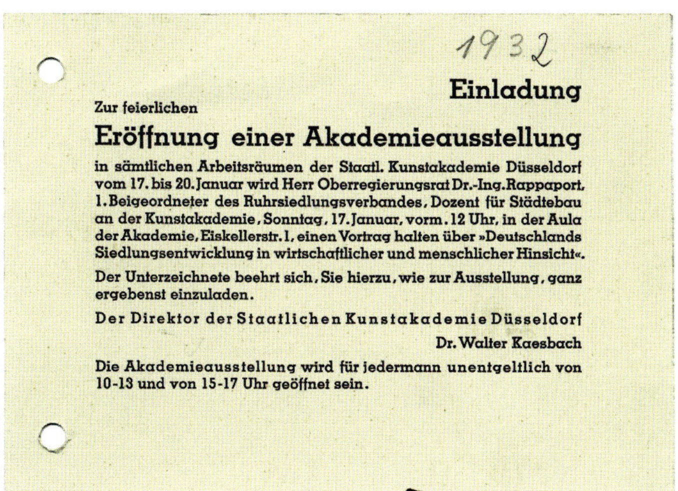
1932

Einladung

Zur feierlichen

Eröffnung einer Akademieausstellung

in sämtlichen Arbeitsräumen der Staatl. Kunstakademie Düsseldorf vom 17. bis 20. Januar wird Herr Oberregierungsrat Dr.-Ing. Rappaport, 1. Beigeordneter des Ruhrsiedlungsverbandes, Dozent für Städtebau an der Kunstakademie, Sonntag, 17. Januar, vorm. 12 Uhr, in der Aula der Akademie, Eiskellerstr. 1, einen Vortrag halten über »Deutschlands Siedlungsentwicklung in wirtschaftlicher und menschlicher Hinsicht«.

Der Unterzeichnete beehrt sich, Sie hierzu, wie zur Ausstellung, ganz ergebenst einzuladen.

Der Direktor der Staatlichen Kunstakademie Düsseldorf

Dr. Walter Kaesbach

Die Akademieausstellung wird für jedermann unentgeltlich von 10-13 und von 15-17 Uhr geöffnet sein.

Fig. 1: Card with an invitation to the Academy Exhibition, 1932

The idea of presenting the Academy's artists to the public at an exhibition was not new: forerunners of the show introduced by Kaesbach, which from then on was to take place annually, had already existed in the Royal Art Academy in Düsseldorf. Under § 20 of the Regulations of 1831, the entry headed 'Kunst-Ausstellungen' [Art Exhibitions] runs:

'To give the public an account of the achievements of the Art Academy, a public art exhibition shall be held from time to time, a larger one every two years at least. An invitation to the larger one, to which artists from outside may also send their works, would be extended by the Academy through a programme that must contain a brief report on the progress made by the institution and the works of professors and their pupils, further on the art things, specifically paintings, etc. that have in the meantime been acquired.'[3]

The basic idea of giving an 'account' of what has been achieved in the year before an exhibition has already been established here and in a form that is identical to that intended by Kaesbach. Essential differences between the two exhibition models are, however, first, that artists from outside the Academy were also invited to participate in the Art Exhibition from 1831 on, and, second, the new acquisitions for the Academy Collection were also presented at it. In these respects the Art Exhibitions more closely resemble the Paris Salon, at which artists who were not just members of the Academy might also show work alongside those who were – although only in an antechamber to the official Salon exhibition. The Paris Salon first took place in 1667 for the purpose of ceremonially commemorating the founding of the Academy each year. A similar concept may be conjectured for the Düsseldorf Art Exhibition as established in 1831.

The year 1933 saw the progressive developments at the Düsseldorf Academy come to an abrupt end: Walter Kaesbach was forced 'to vacate the building [...] within an hour's time; he was forbidden to ever enter it again.'[4] When Kaesbach went, the professors he had appointed not long before, including Heinrich Campendonk, Paul Klee, Alexander Zschokke, and Ewald Mataré, to mention only a few great Modern artists, went with him. As a consequence of a centralised cultural policy with which the National Socialists also controlled the art market, exhibitions supposedly continued to be mounted at the Academy from 1933 on 'at specified times'. Those presentations under the NS regime could not, however, link up with the original reform idea.[5]

After the Second World War the Academy tried to reconnect with the Golden Twenties.[6] The appointment as director of Ewald Mataré, who had had to leave the Academy with Kaesbach in 1933, meant that a step was taken in that direction. While preparing for his future tenure in office, Mataré joined forces with Georg Meistermann, a former student of his, to develop a new curriculum for the Academy. Basically a reform, the Mataré curriculum is reminiscent of the pedagogical and aesthetic principles espoused by the Bauhaus in the way the courses of study are structured with course- and classwork. At the same time the government authorities urged the rapid resumption of teaching. Since that proviso made it impossible for Mataré to realise the concept he had worked out, he resigned as director yet took over a sculpture class that played a groundbreaking role at the Academy as its teacher and as a role model for promoting the younger generation. The painter Werner Heuser, who was also appointed to teach at the Academy by Walter Kaesbach in the 1920s and had had to leave it in 1937 after being dismissed from his post by the NS regime, became director in 1946. The Düsseldorf Art Academy was the 'first German art academy' to resume 'operations'.[7] However, the Academy was at first busy rebuilding after the damage sustained in the war, and students were actively involved in the reconstruction work. So-called 'construction troops'[8] 'worked in groups of fifteen even during term time on rebuilding.'[9]

The end-of-term exhibition was at that time an internal show of what had been achieved by the classes[10] in the form of a *Rundgang* [Academy Tour] undertaken by the professors through all classes at the Academy. The class teachers or students representing the class teacher were responsible for the presentations.[11]

This internal show of what had been accomplished provided for each student showing at least one picture so that the classes could take stock by comparing what had been achieved by each during the year leading up to the exhibition. This practice was continued under directors Werner Heuser and Heinrich Kamps until 1953 because the Academy was still not entirely renovated by then.

The Düsseldorf Art Academy presented its first large exhibition after the war in the freshly renovated rooms on the occasion of its reinauguration in November 1952 at the end of the winter term from mid-January to late February 1953. The catalogue published to accompany the exhibition of drawings shows samples of work by former members of the Academy from Gabriel Grupello to Paul Klee.[12] The catalogue was also used as the annual bonus for members of the Society of Friends and Sponsors of the Academy. After Heinrich Kamps died in 1954, Heinrich Schmidt was temporarily made acting director of the Academy.

Hans Schwippert, who had been appointed to teach at the Academy under Heuser in 1946, was designated director in 1956. During his tenure the professors' internal tour was kept and a press tour was established as an Academy first. Both were as a rule scheduled for the 'last day of [winter] term', with director Schwippert personally guiding through the individual classes. He would constantly reiterate to the press that the event was not an 'art exhibition but a representation of the efforts made to inculcate art education and the level of achievement attained by pupils',[13] thus also pointing out explicitly to the press that 'the exhibition [of students' work] should not be confused with an art exhibition of any kind'.[14] The public was excluded from this internal show of achievement – it was only informed about this event by the press.

Schwippert was sceptical about having a *Rundgang* within the Academy open to the public. Holger Runge, a student of Otto Coester's from 1948 until 1958 and a lecturer in the winter term of 1960/61, reported that the possibility of having an open tour was definitely discussed when Joseph Beuys was appointed to a professorship.[15] In 1962 Hans Schwippert did express some thoughts on presenting an 'Academy in operation' to the press. He would have been complying with the wish for an 'informative' tour open to the public, 'thus intensifying relations between the Academy and the public'.[16]

The expressed desire for improved public relations notwithstanding, Schwippert showed his attitude in 1965 when asked by the press why the end-of-term exhibition shouldn't be open to the public: 'Education doesn't belong in a shop window.'[17]

Larger groups were not guided through the Academy until Eduard Trier became director. Newspapers reported in 1968 that not only Trier but also Joseph Fassbender and Gert Weber had presented the works of their students in the classrooms to a group of invited guests.[18] In the early 1970s the *Rundgang* for the press and the one for the Friends and Sponsors of the Academy were given on two separate days. Trier viewed the end-of-term exhibition as a 'progress report': 'Here teachers can be informed on what is being done in neighbouring classes; here students can measure themselves against their peers.' Moreover, the *Rundgang* served to 'present the work done by students in their two probationary terms, and, finally, to ascertain which students had been conspicuous by their absence during the previous term, so-called "students on paper only"'.[19]

After the Lidl Happenings put on by Jörg Immendorff and Chris Reinecke, which, as they escalated, even led to the Academy being briefly closed, Eduard Trier found it important to make the public aware of the unity and diligence of the student body. So in 1971 he made a statement to journalists: 'Despite all the unrest and problems, this institution is one that works and is highly regarded on the art scene.'[20] As a matter of principle, the public was not given access to the 'progress report' – as the director put it, 'as many persons who are seriously interested in culture as possible in groups' were the only ones to be invited. Trier went on to add, 'And if it is not yet possible to open the Academy to everyone during those days, this is only because there are not enough of the "guards" needed for the artworks shown.'[21] Nonetheless, anyone might inform themselves about student work at many exhibitions 'elsewhere'. 'Trier particularly welcomes this activity because students are thus made familiar early on with the harsh conditions prevailing in the art industry.' The press made a point of emphasising that 'an attitude of this kind [is] new in the institute at Eiskellerberg', 'because under Schwippert's directorate a different opinion was held on this'.[22]

According to a press report, the *Rundgang* must have been open to the public for the first time as long ago as 1972.[23] That heralded a turnaround in the mindset of those at the head of the Academy. Opening the end-of-term exhibition to the public still meant, as director Schwippert saw it, 'renouncing' 'part of' the Academy's 'sovereign rights'. Under Heuser, Kamps, and Schwippert the internal tour had been one of the 'highest authorities of the Academy itself'. It was regarded as an 'agency of control and self-monitoring';[24] should the Academy open its doors to the public in a tour to which everyone had access, it would amount to renouncing this 'sovereign right'. After the sensational Lidl Happenings staged by Immendorff and Reinecke, director Eduard Trier evidently had no other choice but to open the Academy for at least one week a year to all those who were interested and grant a glimpse into the Academy and how it operated.

While Norbert Kricke was director, the *Rundgang* became entirely different in 1973 and 1974. To judge from disappointed reviews, it merely served as an occasion for conducting the professors through the probationary terms or the Orientation Department established in 1973. That visitation would, however, drag on for hours while decisions were taken on which aspirants should be admitted to the main course of study at the Academy after satisfactorily completing the probationary terms.[25]

The exhibition was not opened to the public without reservations until February 1975. That meant the Düsseldorf Academy was one of the first art academies in Germany to again give the public at large access to their tour of student work.[26] Nearly three years after being appointed director, Norbert Kricke declared it open to all and issued an invitation 'to visit the end-of-term exhibition': 'We would be delighted if as many members of the public as possible came who do not always have clear ideas of what goes on here! So that you see work is done here at Eiskellerberg.'[27]

Kricke 'made the rules' by insisting, 'Every student exhibits at least one work.'[28] That was 'not an uncontroversial ruling – there was talk of achievement pressure', as Irmin Kamp summed it up in December 1982 in the introduction to the *Rundgang* publication, *Zeitung 2*, which was supposed 'to inform the public and the Friends of the Art Academy about its activities' but by 1983 had ceased to be printed.[29] The *Rundgang* rapidly became a 'high point' of both the Academy year and the city of Düsseldorf calendar of cultural events. The Academy had also changed structurally since the mid-1970s. Through the addition of the annexe known as the Steinhaus, which was built by Rudolf Schwarz between 1956 and 1958, and the pavilions that were erected in the Academy garden on the left towards the Oberkassel Bridge, the Academy had gained

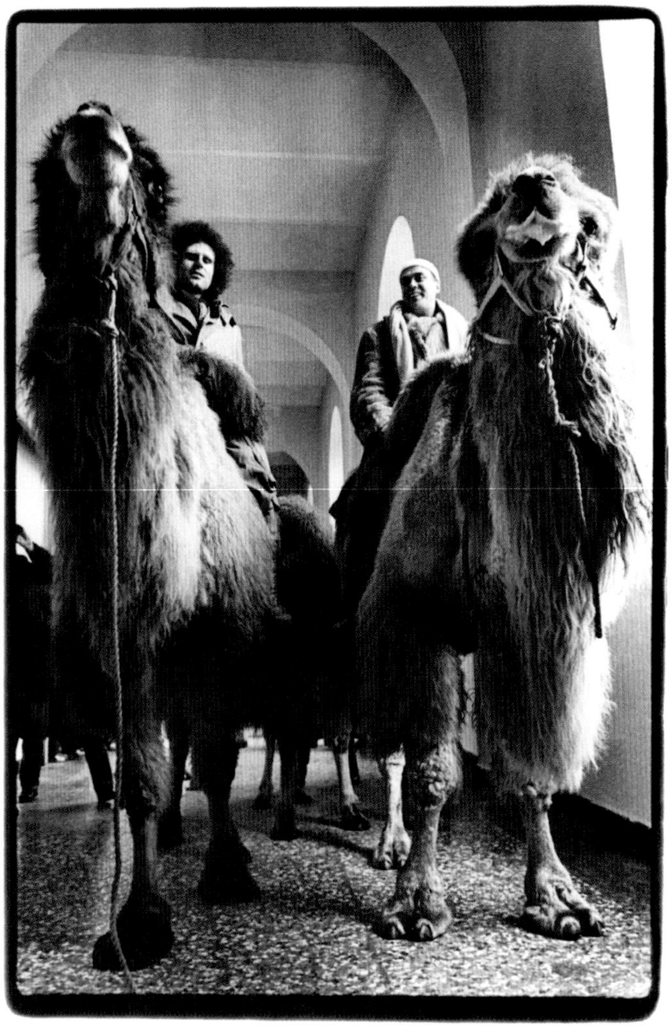

Fig. 2: Klaus Rinke and Günther Uecker riding on camels through the Düsseldorf Art Academy corridors, Academy Tour, 1978

building space, hence exhibition surface as well. Moreover, the classes taught by Professors Günther Uecker and Klaus Rinke, who had been appointed by Kricke, were housed in the 'Academy daughter studios' in the 'rear courtyard at Karl-Anton-Straße 16' so that the *Rundgang* now also took in the annexes and supplementary classrooms.[30] Not long afterwards Gerhard Richter moved with his class into studios in Harkortstraße.

In 1978 Uecker and Rinke organised an Academy fest at the end of the *Rundgang* 'after years of putting the fest on hold', a party to which the public was also invited: 'An Academy fest is to take place [...] tomorrow, on Friday – with a circus, dancing, and food.'[31] Visitors had to pass two 'two elephants swinging their trunks [...] in the lobby. [...] People – chiefly young people – surged through the corridors on three levels – that is, three floors.'[32] The co-organisers, Uecker and Rinke, rode 'stilted high up on stalking camels, smiling and at ease or so it seemed', 'had themselves transported from floor to floor by lift, and strode through the classrooms' (Fig. 2).[33] The animals, from the winter quarters of the Adolfo Circus in Moers, remained 'until about three o'clock in the morning'.

Rinke and Uecker organised another public Academy fest in 1979 to finish off the *Rundgang* – this time, however, without circus animals, just music and festivities. That was the year the Düsseldorf photographer Erika Kiffl began her photographic documentation of the exhibition. Until 1989 she continued to photograph the most spectacular works by students then at the Academy, some of whom are among the most famous contemporary artists.[34] With her photographs of the *Rundgang*, Erika Kiffl became the 'chronicler of the art scene' (Figs. 3–5).[35]

By 1980 the Academy directorate had realised the *Rundgang* had become so popular that internal days would have to be implemented on which examinations could take place undisturbed. The days for the public to attend the event were limited to Wednesday through Saturday, and since 1998 Wednesday through Sunday,[36] every day from morning to eight o'clock in the evening. In 1981 the Academy itself began documenting the *Rundgang* in photographs: Hubertus Neuerburg, who was in charge of public relations and organising the event, presented an illustrated book in 2006 documenting the previous twenty-five years of the *Rundgang*.[37]

In 1981 Wolfgang Robbe, then a student sculptor in the Kamp class, set up an enterable installation of steel, rubber, water, and pigment in the Academy lobby. Measuring four by four metres, the object was only five centimetres high (Fig. 6). A visitor to the exhibition failed to see the low step up, however, and fell and broke her arm. Since then no student works for the *Rundgang* may be set up in the lobby area for insurance-related reasons.[38]

On the occasion of the 1982 *Rundgang*, Norbert Kricke, who had stepped down as director, was made an honorary member of the Düsseldorf Art Academy. Irmin Kamp, a sculptor who had been appointed to teach at the Academy in 1974, became temporary acting director, then director until 1987. From then on the Academy frequently made use of the inauguration of the exhibition to designate honorary members.

Further, in 1984 Gerhard Hoehme spotted a chance to exhibit works from his *Etna* cycle in the Academy's Great Hall while the *Rundgang* was going on. Presentation of works in this context by a professor teaching at the Academy had until then been without precedent, and, indeed, that would remain a one-off event. The Hoehme exhibition was regarded with suspicion by students, not least because it 'blocked' the Great Hall, which was much in demand as a room for putting on student projects.[39]

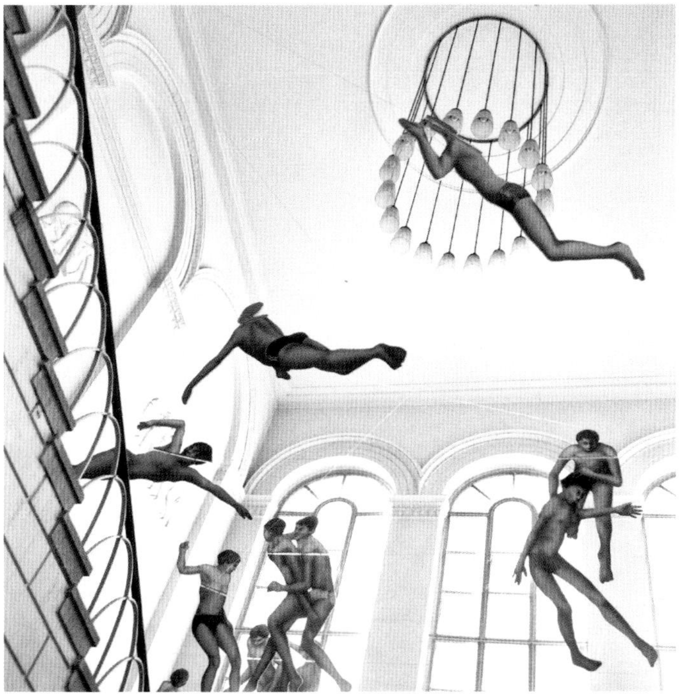

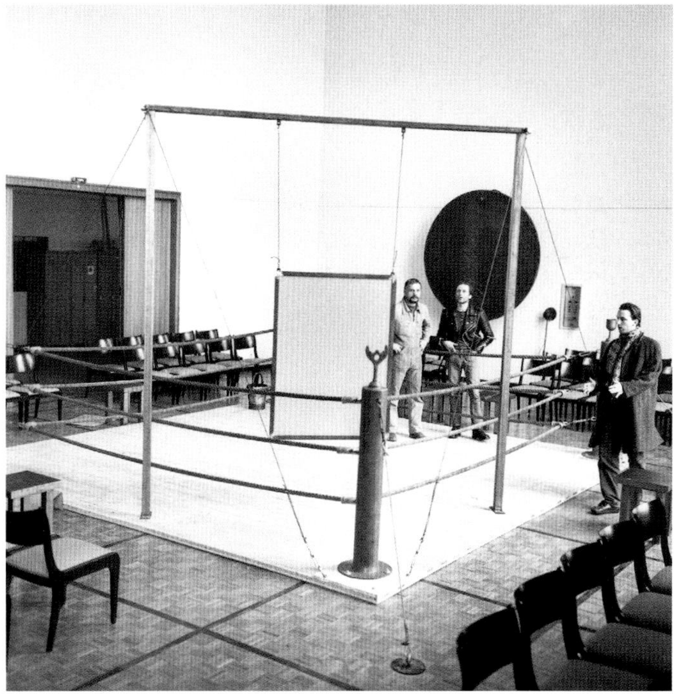

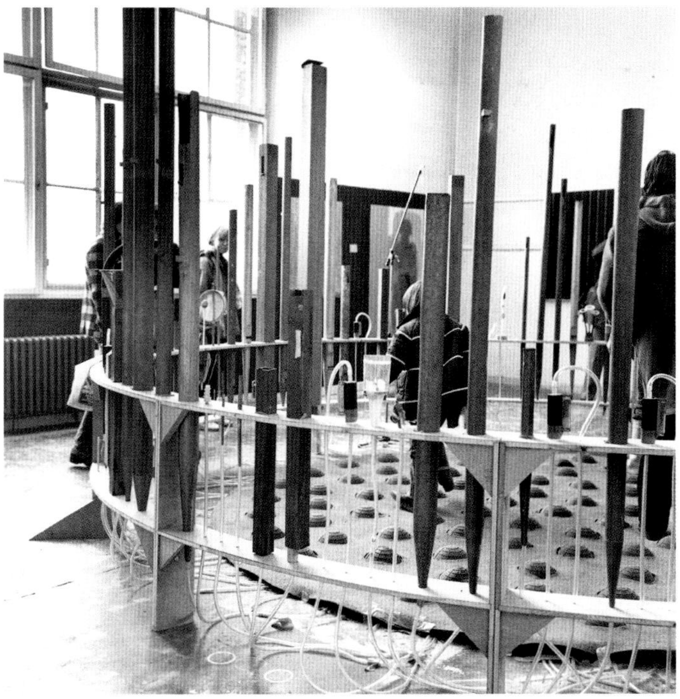

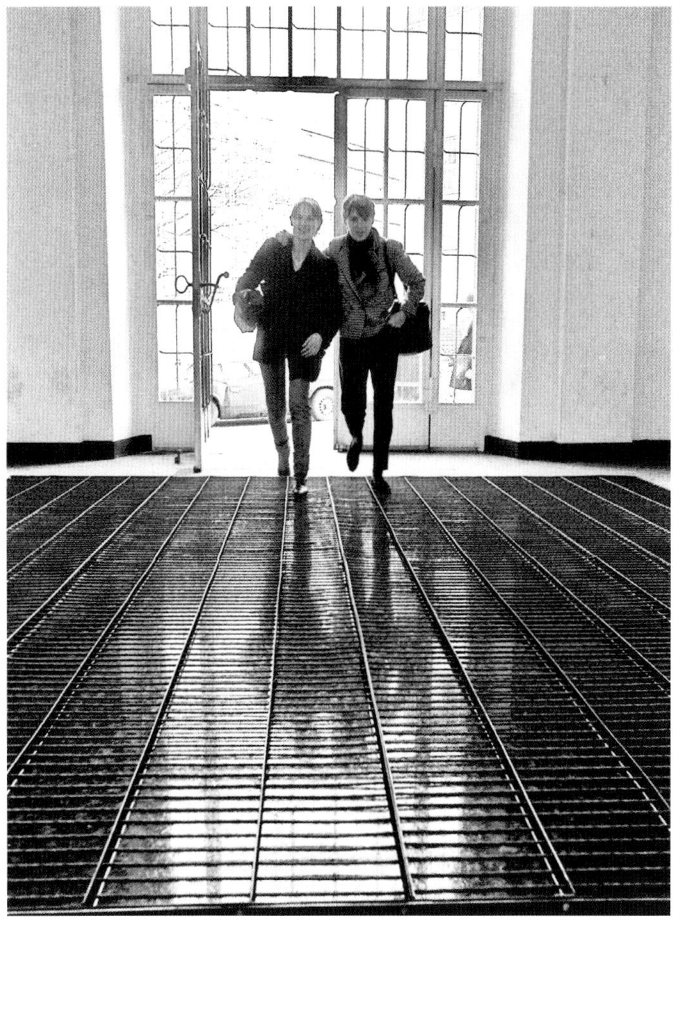

Fig. 3: Mobile Schwimmer *[Mobile Swimmers] by Martin Honert in the stairwell to the Düsseldorf Art Academy Great Hall, Academy Tour, 1985*

Fig. 4: Tretorgel *[Step Organ] by Horst Gläsker, Academy Tour, 1979*

Fig. 5: Boxring *by Sandro Andal in the Great Hall at the Düsseldorf Art Academy, Academy Tour, 1983*

Fig. 6: Begehbar *[Enterable] by Wolfgang Robbe in the lobby of the Düsseldorf Art Academy, Academy Tour, 1981*

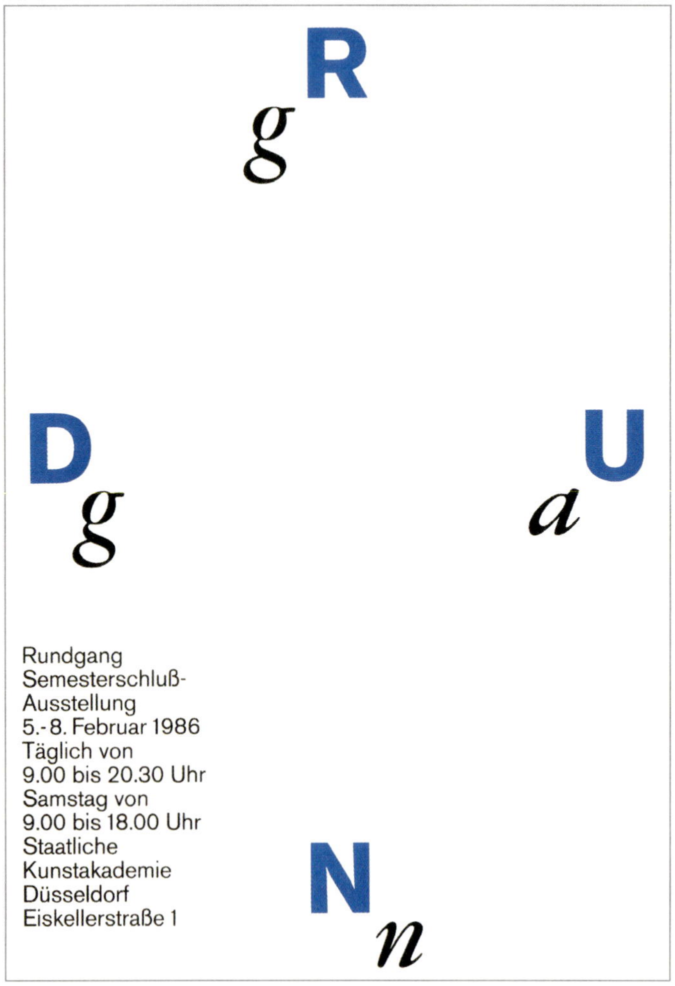

Fig. 7: Poster for the 1986 Academy Tour at the Düsseldorf Art Academy, designed by Walter Nikkels

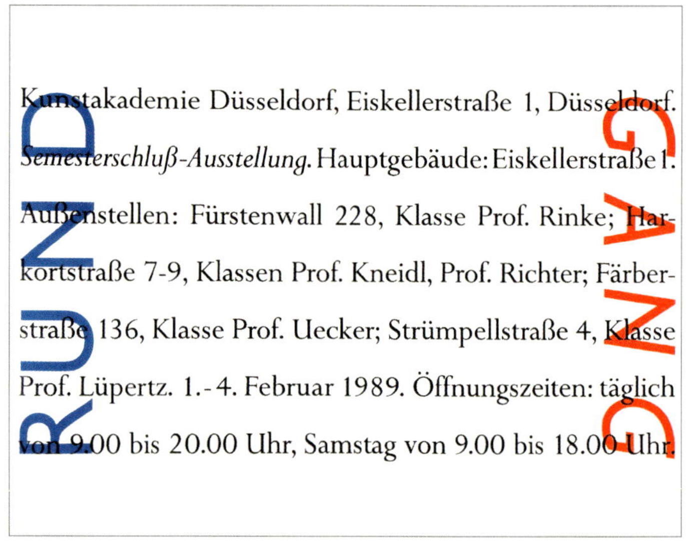

Fig. 8: Poster for the 1989 Academy Tour at the Düsseldorf Art Academy, designed by Walter Nikkels

The year after that, posters were designed to advertise the end-of-term exhibition. Sporting a legend and otherwise blank, they were printed in an edition of 200. Then they were aesthetically upgraded by various professors and students with original drawings, watercolours, and even material pictures so that they could be sold off at an art auction.[40]

Appointed professor at the Academy in 1985, Walter Nikkels shaped the typographic look of publications released by the Academy from 1986 on. From the aesthetic standpoint, the invitation cards and posters he designed for the *Rundgang* were typical of his work and represent the first examples he produced at the Academy revealing his expressive range and skill (Figs. 7, 8). Over the intervening years, posters ceased to be printed for the *Rundgang*; the public has always found its way to the exhibition mounted at the end of the winter term without the need of dedicated advertising campaigns. The only information on the event proffered by the Academy – apart from a press release it dispatches – since the 1980s has been announcing the days of the event and the opening hours of the *Rundgang* by means of a reusable banner mounted above the main entrance.

The *Rundgang* has often been used by Academy students as a 'rear-view mirror' for events and projects of the term just past. In 1986, for instance, students summarily walled up the entrance to their classroom and decked it out with the inscription 'Shall be right back!' as a reaction to the frequent absences of their professor. He in turn showed a sense of humour in his response to the Happening: on his arrival for the *Rundgang*, he kicked down the wall built by his students with his heel.[41]

That year Markus Lüpertz was appointed to teach at the Academy. Not long after taking over Gerhard Hoehme's class, he was appointed rector. From then on the opening of the *Rundgang* was frequently used for imparting information, inspiring suggestions, and decisions relating to cultural policy. For instance, Anke Brunn, then Minister for Science and Research for the state of North Rhine-Westphalia, confirmed at the *Rundgang* that 'negotiations about remaining at the Düsseldorf Academy' were being conducted with Professors Kaspar König, Ulrich Rückriem, and Gerhard Richter, all of whom had been appointed to teach at Frankfurt.[42] The departure of those three professors from the Düsseldorf Academy had become a pressing cultural and political issue yet the negotiations, as history shows, were not crowned with success: König, Rückriem, and Richter[43] went to the Städelschule in Frankfurt, and the *Frankfurter Allgemeine Zeitung* gloated: 'The Städelschule or Sleeping Beauty is awakened by the king's kiss', because '"people such as" the sculptor Rückriem and the painter Richter [...] pulled their "comet tails behind them"'.[44]

Like the directors before him, Markus Lüpertz invited distinguished representatives of cultural and political life to the *Rundgang*. The public relations calendar of events was as follows: the rector personally guided the press starting at 10 a.m. and the Friends and Sponsors of the Academy as well as representatives of the Ministry and the Municipal Cultural Committee from 5 p.m. through the exhibition on Mondays (Fig. 9).

Further, cooperation with other institutions of higher learning was used to organise joint projects opening the event. The Karl Kneidl class at the Academy staged the Rossini opera *La Scala di Seta* to start off the 2000 *Rundgang* jointly with the opera class at the Robert-Schumann-Hochschule class taught by Thomas Gabrisch and Tobias Richter, director of the German Opera on the Rhine.

Markus Lüpertz introduced the Markus Lüpertz Prize, a grant named after him that was awarded by the Academy Tour Committee, at the 1988 *Rundgang*. Other grants awarded since 1974 in Norbert Kricke's directorate[45] were travel grants, New York study grants funded by the Society of Friends and Sponsors, Paris grants for the Cité des Beaux-Arts funded by the state of North Rhine-Westphalia, and – from 1974 every year and from 1980 every two years – a grant for a sculptor, the Bernhard Hoetger Prize. Most of these grants have been discontinued due to cost-cutting.

From 1946 – at that time still at the internal tour – until 1996 the Academy bought in student works, which are now in the Academy archives. The archives inventory ledger shows entries, such as one from 1964 recording the purchase of a Jörg Immendorff watercolour – that is, while Immendorff was still a student in Teo Otto's class – and the purchase of an Immendorff oil painting in 1966.[46] The ledger also contains entries for 1968 on the purchase of *Kopf eines Mannes* [Head of a Man], a picture by Sigmar Polke,[47] and a work in stainless steel by Ansgar Nierhoff.[48]

In recent years, under the rectorate of Anthony Cragg, the Academy has again proceeded to take the initiative on asking Düsseldorf firms to fund grants for a full year. These grants are suggested by the Academy Tour Committee or a jury – composed of Academy representatives and the firm offering to fund the grant – and awarded to students as well as graduates under the auspices of the *Rundgang*. Since 2010 the Society of Friends and Sponsors of the Düsseldorf Art Academy has also funded a grant that the Academy Tour Committee awards each year to an Academy graduate.

In 1998 the *Rundgang* was opened for the first time to the public on Sundays as well as weekdays because the crowds were so huge. The Academy estimates that the event attracted some 30,000 visitors at that time and continues to grow in popularity with each passing year. Against a background of bad experiences with unpredictable mega events in North Rhine-Westphalia in 2010, the Academy has subsequently adopted the policy of counting visitors in order to be able to limit admissions should the need to do so arise. The upshot is that since 2011 queues for admission to the *Rundgang* stretch all the way to Ratinger Straße as the weekend approaches (Fig. 10). In 2013 there were more than 46,000 visitors.

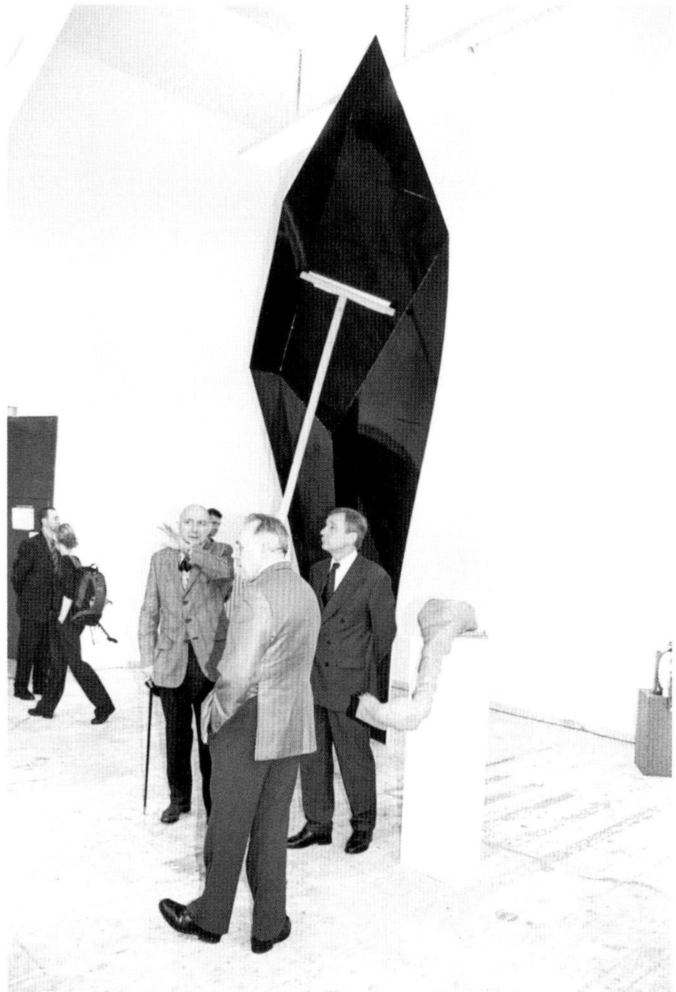

Fig. 9: Markus Lüpertz guiding Wolfgang Clement through the Düsseldorf Art Academy, Academy Tour, 2002

NOTES

1 'Heute beginnt die Arbeit wieder. Die Akademie schließt ihre Ateliers' [Work Begins Again Today. Academy Closes Its Studios], newspaper article, 21 January 1932, no sources given, Düsseldorf Art Academy archives.

2 Card bearing an invitation to the opening of an Academy Exhibition, 1932, Düsseldorf Art Academy archives.

3 'Reglement vom 24. November 1831 für die Königliche Kunst-Akademie zu Düsseldorf, § 20', in: *Jahresbericht der Staatlichen Kunstakademie Düsseldorf 1945–1947*, Düsseldorf [1948], p. 93.

4 Anna Klapheck, *Walter Kaesbach und die zwanziger Jahre an der Düsseldorfer Kunstakademie*, Düsseldorf 1961, p. 14.

5 Hans Peter Thurn, 'Rundgang. Herkunft und Gegenwart eines akademischen Rituals', in: Eckart Liebau (ed.), *Lebensbilder. Streifzüge in Kunst und Pädagogik*, Oberhausen 2009, p. 273.

6 Ibid., p. 6.

7 Stephan von Wiese, 'Kunstszene Düsseldorf', in: Stephan von Wiese and Wulf Herzogenrath (eds.), *Rheingold. 40 Künstler aus Köln und Düsseldorf*, exhib. cat. Turin, Cologne 1985, p. 46.

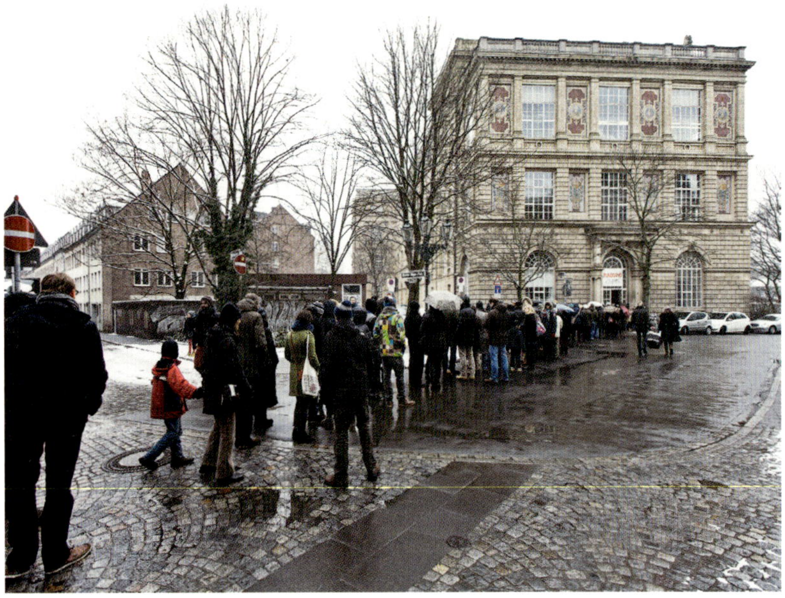

Fig. 10: Visitors queueing in front of the entrance to the Düsseldorf Art Academy, Academy Tour, 2013

8 See conversation with Günter H. Blecks on 16 February 2011 in the present volume, pp. 175–177.
9 *Jahresbericht 1945–1947* (see n. 3), p. 22.
10 Ibid.
11 See letter from Otto Pankok to director Werner Heuser dated 16 March 1949, in which Pankok expresses his indignation that the professorial tour was guided through his class without him, Düsseldorf Art Academy archives, Inv. No. N4.4.2.0.
12 Jakob Heinrich Schmidt (ed.), *Von Gabriel Grupello bis Paul Klee, von Lambert Krahe bis Theo Champion*, exhib. cat. Düsseldorf 1953.
13 'Erst kommt die Zeichnung, dann die Malerei. Studierende der Kunstakademie zeigten Semesterarbeiten – Mangel an handwerklichen Können' [First Comes Drawing, Then Painting. Students at the Art Academy Showed Term Work – Lack of Technical Skill], *Der Mittag*, 7 March 1960, no further source data, Düsseldorf Art Academy archives.
14 'Akademie bereitet auf das Risiko Kunst vor. Prof. Schwippert führte durch die Staatliche Kunstakademie' [Academy Readying for Art Risk. Prof. Schwippert Guided through the State Art Academy], *Neue Rhein Zeitung*, 5 March 1960, no further source data, Düsseldorf Art Academy archives.
15 Holger Runge in his answer of 15 November 2012 to the author in the questionnaire on the *Rundgang*.
16 'Der große Bluff wird nicht geduldet. Prof. Schwippert führte durch die Kunstakademie – Es fehlen Lehrkräfte und Räume' [Big Bluff Not Tolerated. Prof. Schwippert Guided through the Art Academy – Shortage of Teachers and Rooms], *Düsseldorfer Nachrichten*, 16 March 1962, no further source data, Düsseldorf Art Academy archives.
17 'Naturstudium in allen Klassen. Bilanz der Kunstakademie 1964/65' [Nature Study in All Classes. Art Academy Takes Stock 1964/65], *Rheinische Post*, 10 March 1965, no further source data, Düsseldorf Art Academy archives.
18 Anon., 'Im Irrgarten der Stille. Jahresarbeiten der Studenten in der Kunstakademie' [In the Maze of Stillness. Students' Year's Work], *Neue Rhein Zeitung*, 22 February 1968.
19 Dieter Westecker, 'Fleißige Kunstakademie. Studenten zeigten die Arbeiten der letzten Semester' [Industrious Art Academy. Students Show Work of Recent Terms], *Düsseldorfer Nachrichten*, 12 February 1971.
20 'Die Akademie ist ein arbeitendes Haus. Die Semesterarbeiten beweisen es/Neue Professoren erwartet' [The Academy Is a Working Institution. Term Works Prove It/New Professors Expected], *Neue Rhein Zeitung*, 12 February 1971, no further source data, Düsseldorf Art Academy archives.
21 Anna Klapheck, 'Kunstakademie kennt keine Klassen-Doktrin. Ausstellung zum Semesterende/Umfassender Werkstatt-Einblick' [Art Academy Knows No Class Doctrine. End-of-Term Exhibition / Comprehensive Workshop View], *Rheinische Post*, 13 February 1971.
22 Dieter Westecker, 'Ein Haus voller Realisten. In der Kunstakademie sind die Semester-Arbeiten zu sehen' [An Institute Full of Realists. Term Work on View at Art Academy], *Düsseldorfer Nachrichten*, 11 February 1972.
23 Ibid.
24 Ulrich Krempel, 'Rundgang, oder Das Innere nach außen kehren', in: Kunstakademie Düsseldorf (ed.), *Rundgänge 1979–1989. Erika Kiffl – Fotos*, exhib. cat. Düsseldorf 1990, p. 5.
25 Karlheinz Welkens, 'Zum Rundgang gab's Gurken. Akademiestudenten bekommen ihre Chance' [Flops at Tour. Academy Students Get Their Chance], *Rheinische Post*, 19 February 1974.
26 In 1983 the Munich Fine Arts Academy introduced the annual show of students' work only every three years but from 1989 on re-introduced the practice of annual shows. I am indebted to Caroline Steinberg, MA, Munich Fine Arts Academy archives, for this information (email 3 April 2013). The *Rundgang* at Berlin University of the Arts was inaugurated in 1992 and was soon popular with the public. I thank Dr Dietmar Schenk, director of the university archives, Berlin University of the Arts, for imparting this information (email 17 April 2013).
27 'Die Suche nach der Kunst. Akademie lädt zum Besuch der Semesterabschlußausstellung ein' [The Quest for Art. Academy Invites to End-of-Term Exhibition], *Neue Rhein Zeitung*, 5 February 1975.
28 Irmin Kamp, '33 Jahre Klasse Kamp an der Kunstakademie Düsseldorf', in: Kunsthalle Düsseldorf (ed.), *Klasse Kamp 1974–2006*, exhib. cat. Düsseldorf 2006, p. 27.
29 Irmin Kamp, 'Rundgänge', in: Staatliche Kunstakademie Düsseldorf (ed.), *Zeitung 2*, Düsseldorf 1982, p. 3.
30 'Die Suche nach der Kunst' (see n. 27).
31 'Akademie-Fest mit Elefanten' [Academy Fest with Elephants], *Rheinische Post*, 16 February 1978, no further source data, Düsseldorf Art Academy archives.
32 Yvonne Friedrichs, 'Und die Kamele fuhren Fahrstuhl ... Unbeschwerte Fete in der Kunstakademie/Tausende tanzten mit' [And the Camels Took the Lift ... Light-Hearted Party at the Art Academy/Thousands Danced Along], *Rheinische Post*, 20 February 1978.
33 Helga Meister, 'Tiere als animalische Inspiration. Spektakel an der Düsseldorfer Kunstakademie lockte Tausende' [Beasts as Animal Inspiration. Spectacle at Düsseldorf Art Academy Drew Thousands], *Düsseldorfer Nachrichten*, 20 February 1978.
34 Krempel (see n. 24).
35 Regina Goldlücke, 'Chronistin der Kunstszene' [Chronicler of the Art Scene], *Rheinische Post*, 1 March 2012.
36 *Westdeutsche Zeitung*, 11 February 1998, no further source data, Düsseldorf Art Academy Archives.
37 Rektorat der Kunstakademie Düsseldorf (ed.), *Spazierraum Kunstakademie. Fünfundzwanzigmal Rundgang 1982–2006*, with photographs by Hubertus Neuerburg, Düsseldorf 2006.
38 Kamp (see n. 28), p. 41.
39 See 'Studentisches Faltblatt zum Rundgang 1984' [student folder on the Academy Tour 1984], Düsseldorf Art Academy archives.
40 'Kunst von 600 Studenten' [Art of 600 Students], *Neue Rhein Zeitung*, 5 February 1985, no further source data, Düsseldorf Art Academy archives.
41 'Weil Kunst-Professor sich zu selten blicken ließ. Studenten mauerten Klasse zu!' [Because Art Professor Appears Too Seldom. Students Wall Up Classroom!], *Bild*, 4 February 1986, no further source data, Düsseldorf Art Academy archives.
42 *Rheinische Post*, 16 February 1987, no further source data, Düsseldorf Art Academy archives.
43 Gerhard Richter went to Frankfurt only as a visiting lecturer, however. He returned to the Düsseldorf Academy, where he taught painting as a professor of painting until 1993.
44 'Absolut 1 zu 0 für Frankfurt' [Absolutely 1-nil to Frankfurt], *Der Spiegel*, 9 March 1987, no further source data, Düsseldorf Art Academy archives: 'Die Städelschule oder Dornröschen wird vom König wachgeküßt', denn '"solche Leute" wie Bildhauer Rückriem und Maler Richter [...] zögen ihre "Kometen hinter sich her"'.
45 Kamp (see n. 28), p. 3.
46 The picture is regarded as missing.
47 The picture is regarded as missing.
48 Inventory ledger of bought-in student works, Düsseldorf Art Academy archives.

PROFESSORS AT THE DÜSSELDORF ART ACADEMY SINCE 1945

TOMMA ABTS
*1967 Kiel

1989–1995 Studied at the Hochschule der Künste, Berlin
2006 Turner Prize, Tate Gallery, London
Since 2010 professor of painting at the Düsseldorf Art Academy

Gregor Jansen et al. (eds.), *Tomma Abts*, exhib. cat. Düsseldorf, Cologne 2012.
Lisa Phillips and Laura Hoptman, *Tomma Abts*, exhib. cat. New York/Los Angeles, New York/ London 2008.
Bice Curiger (ed.), *Zoe Leonard, Tomma Abts, Mai-Thu Perret. Parkett 84*, Zurich 2008.
Adam Szymczyk (ed.), *Tomma Abts*, exhib. cat. Basel 2005.
Daniel Buchholz et al. (eds.), *Tomma Abts*, with an interview with Peter Doig, Cologne 2004.

ERNST ALTHOFF
*1928 Krefeld

1944–1948 Studied architecture and interior design at the Werkkunstschule in Krefeld
1950–1957 Studied at the Düsseldorf Art Academy
1958–1967 Showed work at the Brussels and Montreal World Expositions
1962 Promotional Prize, State of North Rhine-Westphalia
1963–1973 Lecturer in, and 1973–1986 professor of, interior design and exhibition design at the Düsseldorf Art Academy
1986–1993 Professor of architecture at the Düsseldorf Art Academy
2010 Honorary member of the Düsseldorf Art Academy

Ernst J. Althoff. Spielplatz Kunst, 2 vols., exhib. cat. Viersen 2012.
Ernst Althoff, 'Erziehung und Verhinderung von Erziehung durch Räume', in: *Raum für Bildung und Erziehung*, Düsseldorf 1968, Bl. 15–16.
Ernst Althoff, 'Schulbau für eine demokratische Gesellschaft', in: *Raum für Bildung und Erziehung*, Düsseldorf 1968, Bl. 16–19.

SIEGFRIED ANZINGER
*1953 Weyer

1971–1977 Studied at the Akademie der Bildenden Künste in Vienna, master class with Max Melcher
1982 Showed work at documenta 7 in Kassel
1986 Oskar Kokoschka Prize, Federal Government of Austria
1988 Showed work at the Venice Biennale in the Austrian Pavilion
1990 Prize of the City of Vienna
Since 1997 professor of painting and the graphic arts at the Düsseldorf Art Academy
2003 Grand Austrian State Prize
Since 2008 member of the Austrian Cultural Senate

Siegfried Anzinger. Bilder 2011, exhib. cat. Bregenz/ Heilbronn, Cologne 2011.
Stella Rollig (ed.), *Anzinger*, exhib. cat. Linz, Cologne 2010.
Wilfried Dickhoff (ed.), *Siegfried Anzinger. Backside Angels*, exhib. cat. Innsbruck/Mühlheim an der Ruhr, Innsbruck 2005.
Siegfried Gohr et al. (eds.), *Siegfried Anzinger. Werke auf Papier, 2001–2004*, Grand Austrian State Prize and exhib. cat. Vienna, Cologne 2004.
Wilfried Dickhoff (ed.), *Siegfried Anzinger*, exhib. cat. Duisburg, Bonn 2001.
Wolfgang Dreschler et al. (eds), *Siegfried Anzinger*, exhib. cat. Vienna 1998.

KURT ARNSCHEIDT
*1906 Essen–2001 Düsseldorf

Studied at the Hochschule für Bildende Künste in Berlin and at the Académie Ranson near Bissière as well as with Léger and Ozenfant in Paris
Studied, and took examinations for, teaching art at state schools, Hochschule für Bildende Künste Berlin-Schöneberg
Then as a senior teacher and head supervisor in his subject for trainee teachers at the Studienseminar der Stadt Düsseldorf
1946–1958 Subject consultant for the Schulkollegium Düsseldorf
1947–1958 Teaching assignment for methodology at the Düsseldorf Art Academy
1958–1971 Professor of art teaching at state schools at the Düsseldorf Art Academy

Kurt Arnscheidt, Staatliche Düsseldorf Art Academy, Hochschule für Bildende Künste. *Bericht aus der Arbeit der Abteilung Künstlerisches Lehramt an höheren Schulen*, Düsseldorf 1964.

BERND BECHER
*1931 Siegen–2007 Rostock

1953–1956 Studied with Karl Rössing at the Staatliche Kunstakademie in Stuttgart
1957–1961 Studied typography at the Düsseldorf Art Academy
From 1959 on collaboration with Hilla Wobeser
1972–1982 Showed work at documenta 5, 6, and 7 in Kassel
1976–1996 Professor of photography at the Düsseldorf Art Academy
1996–1999 Teaching assignment for photography at the Düsseldorf Art Academy
Distinctions awarded jointly with Hilla Becher:
1980 Konrad von Soest Prize, Landschaftsverbands Westfalen-Lippe
1990 Golden Lion, Venice Biennale
1994 Kaiserring, City of Goslar
2001 State Prize, State of North Rhine-Westphalia
2002 Erasmus Prize, Amsterdam
2004 Hasselblad Award, Gothenburg, and Award Winners, Kultursalon Düsseldorf e.V.

Bernd and Hilla Becher, *Steinwerke und Kalköfen*, Munich 2012.
Bernd and Hilla Becher, *Zeche Hannover*, exhib. cat. Cologne, Munich 2010.
Bernd and Hilla Becher, *Typologien industrieller Bauten*, exhib. cat. Düsseldorf and elsewhere, Munich 2003.
Bernd and Hilla Becher, *Industrielandschaften*, Munich 2002.
Bernd and Hilla Becher, *Grundformen*, Munich 1999.

FRIEDRICH (Fritz) BECKER
*1882 Worms–1973 Düsseldorf

Studied architecture at the Technische Hochschule Darmstadt
Studied with Friedrich von Thiersch and Carl Hocheder at the Technische Hochschule Munich
1904–1905 Worked for Karl Roth on building the Town Hall in Dresden
1908–1912 Employed by the Communal Civil Engineering Authorities in Darmstadt and Dresden
1912–1919 Taught at the Kunstgewerbeschule Düsseldorf
1919–1947 Professor of architecture at the Düsseldorf Art Academy
Member of the Deutscher Werkbund and the Bund Deutscher Architekten

Erich Georg Kutzner, *Ein neuzeitlicher Grossbau von der Fundierung bis zur Vollendung. Erläutert an dem Beispiel des gemeinsam mit Professor Fritz Becker erbauten Palasthotel Mannheimer Hof*, Stuttgart 1930.
Das neue niederrheinische Dorf. Auf der Deutschen Werkbundausstellung in Köln 1914. Architekten der Einzelausführungen: Friedrich Becker et al., Berlin 1915.

KUNIBERT BERING
*1952 Lüdenscheid

Studied art history, classical archaeology, history, and philosophy in Bochum and Rome
1976 First state examinations for teaching at state schools
1978 Second state examinations for teaching at state schools and doctorate at the Ruhr-Universität Bochum
Until 1998 civil servant status as a higher secondary school teacher and teacher at the Ruhr-Universität Bochum
1987 Habilitation, then non-tenured lecturer without civil-servant status at the Ruhr-Universität Bochum
Since 1998 professor of teaching methodology in the visual arts at the Düsseldorf Art Academy
2008–2011 Visiting professor at Bern University

Kunibert Bering and Rolf Niehoff, *Bildkompetenz. Eine kunstdidaktische Perspektive*, Oberhausen 2013.
Kunibert Bering, *Richard Serra. Skulptur, Zeichnung, Film*, Oberhausen 2009. No. 32, *Artificium* series.
Kunibert Bering and Alarich Rooch, *Raum. Gestaltung, Wahrnehmung, Wirklichkeitskonstruktion*, 2 vols., Oberhausen 2008. Nos. 26 and 27, *Artificium* series.
Kunibert Bering, *Romanik*, Stuttgart 2008. No. 3, *Kunst-Epochen* series.
Kunibert Bering, *Kunst des frühen Mittelalters*, Stuttgart 2002. No. 2, *Kunst-Epochen* series.

JOSEPH BEUYS
*1921 Krefeld–1986 Düsseldorf

1941–1945 Served in the armed forces; internment as a British prisoner of war
1947–1953 Began to study sculpture with Joseph Enseling at the Düsseldorf Art Academy
1949–1951 Switched to Ewald Mataré's sculpture class
1952–1954 In Ewald Mataré's master class
1961–1972 Non-tenured teacher of sculpture at the Düsseldorf Art Academy, contract at first limited to five years, then renewed year by year, last service contract for 1 October 1968–30 September 1973.
1964 First showed work at a documenta III in Kassel; afterwards regularly at documenta
1967 Founded the German Student Party (DSP)
1972 Dismissed by Johannes Rau, Science Minister for the State of North Rhine-Westphalia
1974 Founded the Freien internationalen Hochschule für Kreativität und interdisziplinäre Forschung e. V. with Heinrich Böll; visiting professor at the Hochschule für Bildende Künste in Hamburg
1976 Awarded an honorary doctorate by the Nova Scotia College of Art & Design, Halifax; Lichtwark Prize of the City of Hamburg
1978 Years of civil lawsuits against the State of North Rhine-Westphalia end with an out-of-court settlement, after which Beuys was permitted to use his studio at the Düsseldorf Art Academy until the end of his sixty-fifth year
1979 Kaiserring, City of Goslar; MEP candidate for the German Green Party
1986 Wilhelm Lehmbruck Prize of the City of Duisburg

Sabine Röder (ed.), *Joseph Beuys. Räume 1971–1984, Plastiken und Objekte 1952–1974 im Kaiser Wilhelm Museum Krefeld*, Bielefeld 2010.
Kunstsammlung North Rhine-Westphalia (ed.), *Joseph Beuys. Parallelprozesse*, exhib. cat. Düsseldorf, Munich 2010.
Jörg Schellmann, *Joseph Beuys. Die Multiples 1965–1986. Werkverzeichnis der Auflagenobjekte und Druckgraphik*, Munich and elsewhere 1997 (reprinted 2006).
Lothar Schirmer (ed.), *Joseph Beuys. Eine Werkübersicht, Zeichnungen und Aquarelle, Drucksachen und Multiples, Skulpturen und Objekte, Räume und Aktionen, 1945–1985*, Munich 1996 (reprinted 2006).

WALTER BIEMEL
*1918 Kronstadt

1937–1941 Studied philosophy, psychology, sociology, and art history at Bucharest University
1942–1944 Pupil of Martin Heidegger's in Freiburg im Breisgau
1948 Doctorate from Louvain University
1951–1960 Director of works at the newly founded Husserl Archives at Cologne University
1958 Postdoctorate at Cologne University
1976–1983 Professor of philosophy at the Düsseldorf Art Academy
1980–1981 Deputy director of the Düsseldorf Art Academy
1991 Honorary member of the Düsseldorf Art Academy
Since 2000 honorary president of the Romanian Society for Phenomenology
2003 Honorary doctorate from Bucharest University

Walter Biemel, *Gesammelte Schriften*, 2 vols., Stuttgart-Bad Cannstatt 1996.
Walter Biemel, 'Die Raum-Zeit-Thematik im Werk von Norbert Kricke', *Jahreshefte der Kunstakademie Düsseldorf*, Vol. 4, Düsseldorf 1994, pp. 87–112.
Walter Biemel, 'Philosophische Analysen zur Kunst der Gegenwart,' *Phaenomenologica*, No. 28, The Hague 1968.

JOHANNES BILSTEIN
*1949 Cologne

Studied education, German language and literature, history, philosophy, and psychology at Cologne University
1975 First state examinations in education and German language and literature
1979 Doctorate at Cologne University
1980–2004 Lecturer in education at the Düsseldorf Art Academy
2000 Postdoctorate at the Freie Universität Berlin
2004–2008 Professor at the Folkwang Hochschule Essen
Since 2008 professor of education at the Düsseldorf Art Academy

Johannes Bilstein, 'Homo pictor. Zur Anthropologie der Imagination', in: Doris Schuhmacher-Chilla et al. (eds.), *Image und Imagination*, Oberhausen 2011, pp. 13–29. No. 4, *Kunst und Kulturwissenschaft in der Gegenwart* series.
Johannes Bilstein, 'Mutterauge – Vaterhand. Erziehungsorgane', in: id. et al. (eds.), *Auge und Hand*, Oberhausen 2011, pp. 77–99.
Johannes Bilstein, 'Zur metaphorischen Potenz der Kunst', in: id. (ed.), *Die Künste als Metaphern*, Oberhausen 2011, pp. 13–41. No. 19, *Pädagogik: Perspektiven und Theorie* series.
Johannes Bilstein, 'Die Schule der Kunst', in: Eckart Liebau et al. (eds.), *Die Kunst der Schule. Über die Kultivierung der Schule durch die Künste*, Bielefeld 2009, pp. 69–89. No. 3, *Ästhetik und Bildung* series.
Johannes Bilstein, *Die Kunst der Lehre und die Lehre der Kunst*, Koblenz 2009. No. 2, *Koblenzer Hochschulschriften* series.

PAUL BINDEL
*1894 Magdeburg–1973 Düsseldorf

1914–1918 Served in the armed forces
Member of the artists' association Junges Rheinland
1930–1944 Professor of painting at the Düsseldorf Art Academy
1942–1948 Served in the armed forces; prisoner of war in the Soviet Union
1948–1959 Professor of art teaching at state schools at the Düsseldorf Art Academy
1959–1960 Teaching assignment in art teaching at state schools at the Düsseldorf Art Academy

Paul Bindel, *Jugend sieht Deutschland. Ausgewählte Arbeiten aus einem Jugendwettbewerb des Kuratoriums Unteilbares Deutschland*, Munich 1961.
Paul Bindel and Heinrich Kamps, Klassen für das künstlerische Lehramt, in: Heinrich Kamps (ed.), *Jahrbuch der Staatlichen Kunstakademie Düsseldorf 1948–1950*, Düsseldorf [1950], pp. 11–16.

GÜNTER HEINZ BLECKS
*1930 Rheinhausen

1948–1954 Studied art education for teaching art at state schools at the Düsseldorf Art Academy and history at Cologne and Münster Universities
1956–1964 Taught practical art at state higher secondary schools in Cologne and Düsseldorf while studying art history in parallel at Cologne and Bonn Universities
1964–1968 Taught at the Werkkunstschule in Krefeld
1964–1975 Teaching contract for methodology/teaching art education at the Düsseldorf Art Academy
1975–1995 Professor of art education methodology at the Düsseldorf Art Academy

Günter Heinz Blecks, *Das Problem der aperspektivischen Raum-Zeit-Konzeption im Kunstunterricht an Höheren Schulen, Sonderdruck für Teilnehmer des 26. Kunstpädagogischen Kongresses der INSEA in Hamburg 1987*, Stuttgart 1987.
Günter Heinz Blecks, 'Die mögliche Bedeutung der Lebensarbeit Heinrich Lützelers für eine Neuorientierung der Kunstpädagogik. Werkstattbetrachtungen eines Kunstpädagogen', in: Frank-Lothar Kroll (ed.), *Wege zur Kunst und zum Menschen. Festschrift für Heinrich Lützeler zum 85. Geburtstag*, Bonn 1987, pp. 49–80.
Günter Heinz Blecks, 'Bewusstseinswandel als Thema Kunstdidaktischen Denkens und Kunstpädagogischer Praxis', *Beiträge zur integralen Weltsicht*, No. 2, 1985, pp. 21–37.
Günter Heinz Blecks, 'Kunstpädagogische Literatur der Siebziger Jahre, Fachliteratur zur Kunstpädagogik, Ästhetische Erziehung 1970–1979', *Zeitschrift für Ästhetik und allgemeine Kunstwissenschaft* 26, No. 2, 1981, pp. 153–194.

KARL BOBEK
*1925 Berlin–1992 Maroth

1943–1949 Served in the armed forces; prisoner of war in the Soviet Union
1949–1955 Studied at the Hochschule für Bildende Künste in Berlin, taught by Richard Scheibe and Bernd Heiliger; Renée Sintenis's master class
1955 Georg Kolbe Prize, Beckmann-Gesellschaft grant
1960 Grant for stay at the Villa Massimo, Rome
1961 Young Generation Art Prize, City of Berlin
1963–1987 Professor of sculpture at the Düsseldorf Art Academy
1965 Cornelius Prize, City of Düsseldorf
1987 Member of the Academy of the Arts, Berlin

Lucie Schauer et al., *Karl Bobek, Arbeiten 1952–1980*, exhib. cat. Berlin 1980.
Erwin Heerich, *Karl Bobek. Plastiken und Zeichnungen*, exhib. cat. Nordhorn 1975.

HERBERT BRANDL
*1959 Graz

1978 Studied with Herbert Tasquil and Peter Weibel at the Hochschule für angewandte Kunst in Vienna
1994 Prix Eliette von Karajan (shared with Peter Doig)
1997 Prize of the City of Vienna
Since 2004 professor of painting at the Düsseldorf Art Academy
2007 Showed work in the Austrian Pavilion at the Venice Biennale

Klaus Thoman et al. (eds.), *Herbert Brandl. Katana*, exhib. cat. Innsbruck, Cologne 2013.
Ingried Brugger et al. (eds.), *Herbert Brandl*, exhib. cat. Vienna, Ostfildern 2012.

Antonia Hoerschelmann (ed.), *Herbert Brandl. Berge und Landschaften, Monotypien 2009/2010*, exhib. cat. Vienna 2010.
Robert Fleck (ed.), *Herbert Brandl*, exhib. cat. Hamburg, Cologne 2009.
Robert Fleck (ed.), *Herbert Brandl. La Biennale di Venezia 2007*, exhib. cat. Venice, Ostfildern 2007.
Peter Weibel et al. (eds.), *Herbert Brandl*, exhib. cat. Graz, Ostfildern 2002.

REINHOLD BRAUN
*1961 Karlsruhe

1982–1987 Studied painting at the Karlsruhe and Düsseldorf Art Academies; in Markus Lüpertz's master class
2007–2011 Supply professor of painting at the Düsseldorf Art Academy

Dorothea Eimert et al., *Four-Man-Show Malerei. Dag Seemann, Arnim Tölke, Reinhold Braun, Matthias Köster*, exhib. cat. Düren 1999.
Christa Schübbe, *Rolling surrealis. Ein Panorama für Düsseldorf. Dag Seemann, Arnim Tölke, Reinhold Braun, Matthias Köster*, exhib. cat. Düsseldorf and elsewhere, Düsseldorf 1995.
Christa Schübbe and Joachim Hirschmann, *Reinhold Braun. Bilder*. exhib. cat. Mettmann 1990.

WALTER BREKER
*1904 Bielefeld–1980 Krefeld

1922–1925 Studied at the Kunstgewerbeschule Bielefeld
1930–1934 Assistant to Wilhelm Deffke at the Kunstgewerbeschule Magdeburg, later taught there himself
1934–1954 Head of the Applied Graphics and Book Art Department at the Werkkunstschule Krefeld
1954–1969 Professor of applied graphics at the Düsseldorf Art Academy
Member of the Deutscher Werkbund
Prizes from numerous competitions for posters and typography

Hans Peter Willberg (ed.), *Marken und 'Marken'. Walter Breker und die Gebrauchsgrafik 1904–1980*, Berlin 1984.
Städtische Kunsthalle Düsseldorf (ed.), *Walter Breker*, exhib. cat. Düsseldorf/Bielefeld, Düsseldorf 1973.

PETER BRÜNING
*1929 Düsseldorf–1970 Ratingen

1950–1952 Studied with Willi Baumeister at the Akademie der Bildenden Künste in Stuttgart
From 1953 member of Gruppe 53
1955 Promotional Prize, Cornelius Prize of the City of Düsseldorf
1959–1968 Showed work at documentas II, III, and 4 in Kassel
1961 Villa Romana Prize, Florence
1969–1970 Professor of fine art painting at the Düsseldorf Art Academy

Marie-Luise Otten and Walter Smerling, *Peter Brüning. Retrospektive*, exhib. cat. Duisburg, Cologne 2007.
Marie-Luise Otten, *Peter Brüning. Das zeichnerische Werk. Werkverzeichnis der Zeichnungen*, Cologne 1997.
Marie-Luise Otten and Wolfgang Holler, *Peter Brüning. Arbeiten auf Papier 1952–1970*, exhib. cat. Hannover/ Dresden/ Ratingen, Cologne 1997.
Peter Brüning, *Retrospektive*, exhib. cat. Saarbrücken/ Dortmund, Cologne 1988.

DANIEL BUREN
*1938 Boulogne-Billancourt

1957–1960 Studied sculpture and painting at the École des Métiers d'Art and the École Nationale Supérieure des Beaux-Arts
1972–1982 Showed work at documentas 5, 6, and 7 in Kassel
1979–1980 Visiting professor of painting at the Düsseldorf Art Academy
1986 Golden Lion at the Venice Biennale
2002–2006 Supply professorship for painting
2007 Praemium Imperiale Prize for Painting, Tokyo

Karola Kraus et al. (eds.), *Daniel Buren. Allegro vivace*, exhib. cat. Baden-Baden, Cologne 2011.
Claire Bonnevie (ed.), *Daniel Buren. Travaux in Situ, 2010–2011*, exhib. cat. Luxemburg/Metz, Luxemburg 2011.
Jane Michael (ed.), *Daniel Buren. The Museum that Did Not Exist*, exhib. cat. Paris, Munich 2010.
Bernard Blistène et al. (eds.), *Daniel Buren. Mot à mot*, exhib. cat. Paris 2002.
Daniel Buren 1964–1966, exhib. cat. Villeneuve d'Ascq/Le Bourget 2000. No. 2, *Catalogue raisonné chronologique* series.

MICHAEL BUTHE
*1944 Sonthofen–1994 Bad Godesberg

1964–1968 Studied at the Werkbundschule in Kassel, later with Arnold Bode at the Staatliche Kunstschule in Kassel
1972–1982 Showed work at documentas 5, 6, and 7 in Kassel
1976 Guest at the Villa Romana in Florence
1981–1983 Supply professor at the Düsseldorf Art Academy
1984–1994 Professor of painting at the Düsseldorf Art Academy
1992 Showed work at DOCUMENTA IX in Kassel

Stephan N. Barthelmess (ed.), *Michael Buthe. Den Sternen näher als der Erde. Arbeiten 1968–1994*, exhib. cat. Höxter 2008.
Hans-Michael Herzog (ed.), *Michael Buthe. Frühe Zeichnungen, Collagen und Tagebücher*, exhib. cat. Bielefeld, Ostfildern 1999.
Stephan von Wiese et al. (eds.), *Buthe. Michel de la Sainte Beauté*, exhib. cat. Düsseldorf, Heidelberg 1999.
Michael Buthe, exhib. cat. Gent/Munich, Gent 1984.
Felix Zdenek (ed.), *Michael Buthe. Die endlose Reise der Bilder*, exhib. cat. Essen 1980.

EDGAR GEORG CALLAHAN
*1928 Chandler, OK–1997

Studied mechanical engineering and architecture at the Oklahoma Institute of Technology, Oklahoma State University, also lecturer in applied geometry there
1950 Grant from the Oklahoma Institute of Technology for a two-term stay in the Netherlands
1951–1953 Worked in Milan as a freelance designer
1953 Moved to Düsseldorf
1971–1993 Professor of interdisciplinary project development at the Düsseldorf Art Academy

Edgar Callahan, Gerhard Hoehme and Hans Peter Thurn, 'Modelle', *Mitteilungen des Instituts für Moderne Kunst*, No. 6, Nuremberg 1973.

THEO CHAMPION
*1887 Düsseldorf–1952 Zell

1906–1907 Studied with Eduard von Gebhardt at the Düsseldorf Art Academy
1907–1909 Studied at the Kunstschule in Weimar
1919 Co-founder of the artists' association Junges Rheinland
1924 Member of the Rhine Group
1928 Member of the Rhenish Secession
1932–1933 Taught at the Düsseldorf Art Academy
1947–1952 Professor of painting at the Düsseldorf Art Academy

Inge Zacher (ed.), *Theo Champion. Gemälde und Graphik*, exhib. cat. Düsseldorf/Kleve, Kleve 1987.
Richard E. Tristram, *Theo Champion 1887–1952. Ein Maler der Stille*, exhib. cat. Kleve 1961.
Richard Seiffert-Wattenberg, *Theo Champion*, exhib. cat. Hannover 1934.
'Theo Champion. Ein Interview mit mir selber', *Deutsche Kunst und Dekoration*, No. 70, 1932, pp. 172–175.

OTTO COESTER
*1902 Rödinghausen–1990 Wilhelmsdorf

From about 1920 studied interior design at the Kunstgewerbeschule in Wuppertal-Barmen
From 1922 studied art history at Cologne University
1934–1939 Non-tenured teacher of etching at the Düsseldorf Art Academy
1939–1967 Professor of fine art and applied graphics at the Düsseldorf Art Academy
1940–1941 Served in the armed forces, discharged
1945 Member of the Rhenish Secession
1951 Von der Heydt Prize of the City of Wuppertal, shared with Georg Meistermann
1954–1964 Deputy director of the Düsseldorf Art Academy
1959 Showed work at documenta II in Kassel
1960 Konrad von Soest Prize, Landschaftsverbands Westfalen-Lippe
1967 Cornelius Prize of the City of Düsseldorf

Hans-Ulrich Lehmann (ed.), *Otto Coester. Radierungen, Steindrucke, Siebdrucke*, exhib. cat. Dresden 1992.
Christine Borchers, *Otto Coester. Monographie mit Oeuvreverzeichnis*, Düsseldorf 1991.
Otto Coester. *Druckgraphik der Jahre 1929–1961*, exhib. cat. Neuss 1987.
Otto Coester. Graphik 1930–1960, exhib. cat. Wuppertal 1978.
Otto Coester, *Zweierlei*, Bremen 1948.

ANTHONY CRAGG
*1949 Liverpool

1969–1970 Studied art at the Gloucestershire College of Art and Design, Cheltenham
1970–1973 Continued his studies at the Wimbledon School of Art, London
1973–1977 Studied sculpture at the Royal College of Art, London
1978–1989 Teacher and lecturer in the Orientation Department at the Düsseldorf Art Academy
1988 Turner Prize, Tate Gallery, London
1989–2001 Professor of sculpture at the Düsseldorf Art Academy
1994 Member of the Royal Academy
2001–2006 Professor of sculpture at the Universität der Künste Berlin
2002 Piepenbrock Prize for Sculpture
Since 2006 professor of sculpture at the Düsseldorf Art Academy
2007 Praemium Imperiale Prize for Sculpture, Tokyo
2009–2013 Rector of the Düsseldorf Art Academy
2015 Honorary member of the Düsseldorf Art Academy

Guido Comis and Marco Franciolli (eds.), *Tony Cragg*, exhib. cat. Lugano, Cinisello Balsamo 2012.
Veit Görner and Tony Cragg, *Tony Cragg. Matrix*, exhib. cat. Hannover, Nuremberg 2012.

Walter Smerling (ed.), *Anthony Cragg. Dinge im Kopf. Skulpturen, Zeichnungen, Grafiken*, exhib. cat. Duisburg, Cologne 2011.
Catherine Grenier, *Tony Cragg. Figure Out Figure In*, exhib. cat. Paris 2011.
Staatliche Kunsthalle Karlsruhe (ed.), *Tony Cragg. Second Nature*, exhib. cat. Karlsruhe/Salzburg, Cologne 2009.
Tony Cragg. Signs of Life, exhib. cat. Bonn, Düsseldorf 2003.
Helmut Friedel (ed.), *Anthony Cragg*, exhib. cat. Munich, Ostfildern 1998.

SIEGFRIED CREMER
*1929 Dortmund–2015 Stuttgart

1943–1946 Apprenticeship in sculpture in Dülmen
1947–1952 Studied sculpture and painting at the Werkkunstschule in Münster
1952–1955 Trained as a restorer at the Landesmuseum Münster
1955–1964 Worked as a restorer at the Kaiser Wilhelm Museum in Krefeld
Then head of the restoration studio at the Staatsgalerie Stuttgart
1977–1994 Professor of painting techniques at the Düsseldorf Art Academy

Siegfried Cremer, *Cremer. Arbeiten 1957–1975*, exhib. cat. Ulm/Gelsenkirchen, Stuttgart-Bad Cannstatt 1976.
Siegfried Cremer, *Cremer. Holzreliefs 1959–1975*, exhib. cat. Düsseldorf, Stuttgart 1975.
Siegfried Cremer, *Das Alphabet*, Stuttgart [1970].

ROLF CRUMMENAUER
*1925 Duisburg-Ruhrort–1999 Meerbusch-Osterath

1943–1944 Studied with Paul Bindel and Wilhelm Schmurr at the Düsseldorf Art Academy
1946–1949 Took up his interrupted studies again at the Düsseldorf Art Academy with Heinrich Kamps and Otto Coester
1952–1967 Teaching contract for freehand drawing at the Düsseldorf Art Academy
1967–1989 Professor of freehand drawing for teaching art at state schools at the Düsseldorf Art Academy

Kai Hackemann, 'Dienende Kunst. Das sakrale Werk von Prof. Rolf Crummenauer', *Alte und neue Kunst*, No. 45, 2009, pp. 50–57.
Hans Kisky et al. (eds.), *Hundert Jahre Rheinische Glasmalerei*, part 1, Neuss 1959.

RICHARD DEACON
*1949 Bangor, Wales

1968–1972 Attended the Somerset College of Arts, Taunton, and Saint Martin's School of Art, London
1974–1978 Attended the Royal College of Art, London, and studied art history at the Chelsea School of Art, London
1987 Turner Prize, Tate Gallery, London
Professor at the London Institute, the Viennese Hochschule für Angewandte Kunst, and the École Nationale Supérieure des Beaux-Arts in Paris
1992–1997 Curator, Tate Gallery, London
1996 Made a Chevalier des Arts et Lettres
Since 1998 member of the Royal Academy of the Arts
2004 Will Grohmann Prize, Akademie der Bildenden Künste, Berlin
2005 Honorary doctorate from the University of Leicester
Since 2009 professor of sculpture at the Düsseldorf Art Academy
Member of the Academy of the Arts, Berlin

Fernando Francés and Enrique Juncosa (eds.), *Richard Deacon*, exhib. cat. Málaga 2013.
Ulrich Krempel and Joëlle Pijaudier-Cabot (eds.), *Richard Deacon. The Missing Part*, exhib. cat. Strasbourg/Hannover, Cologne 2010.
Susan Daniel-McElroy, Edmund de Wall, and Clarrie Wallis (eds.), *Richard Deacon. Out of Order*, exhib. cat. St Ives 2005.
Richard Deacon. Recent Sculpture 1985–1987, exhib. cat. Maastricht/Luzern/Madrid/Antwerp, Maastricht 1987.

ODILE DECQ
*1955 Laval

Until 1979 studied architecture; diploma in urbanism and urban planning from the Institut d'Études Politiques de Paris
Since 1992 professor at the École Spéciale d'Architecture in Paris
1996 Golden Lion, Venice Biennale
2003 Made a chevalier of the French Legion of Honour
2004–2005 Supply professor of architecture at the Düsseldorf Art Academy

Enrica Giacobino, *Odile Decq*, Barcelona 2011. No. 21, *Maestros de la arquitectura* series.
Alessandro de Magistris and Michel Vernes, *Odile Decq, Benoît Cornette. Opere e progetti*, Milan 2003. No. 150, *Documenti di Architettura* series.
Andreas Ruby (ed.), *Odile Decq & Benoît Cornette. Hyper-Tension*, exhib. cat. Berlin 1995.

JAN DIBBETS
*1941 Weert

1959–1963 Trained as an art teacher at the Academie voor Beeldende een Bouwende Kunsten in Tilburg
1961–1963 Studied painting with Jan Gregoor in Eindhoven
1964–1967 Art teacher in Enschede
1967 Studied art at Saint Martin's School of Art, London; British Council grant
1972 Showed work in the Dutch Pavilion at the Venice Biennale
1972–1982 Showed work at documentas 5, 6, and 7 in Kassel
1979 Rembrandt Prize, Johann Wolfgang von Goethe Foundation in Basel
1984–2004 Professor of painting at the Düsseldorf Art Academy

Anne Montfort (ed.), *Dibbets. Horizons*, exhib. cat. Paris and elsewhere, Cologne 2010.
Erik Verhagen, *Jan Dibbets. L'Œuvre photographique 1967–2007*, Paris 2007.
Rudi Fuchs and Gloria Moure, *Jan Dibbets. Interior Light. Works on Architecture 1969–1990*, New York 1991.
Rudi Fuchs, *Jan Dibbets*, exhib. cat. Minneapolis/New York, Minneapolis 1987.

PETER DOIG
*1959 Edinburgh

1979–1983 Attended the Wimbledon College of Art and Saint Martin's School of Art, London
1989–1990 Chelsea School of Art, London
1994 Prix Eliette von Karajan; nomination for the Turner Prize
1995–2000 Curator, Tate Gallery, London
Since 2005 professor of painting at the Düsseldorf Art Academy
2008 Wolfgang Hahn Prize for Contemporary Art, awarded by the Modern Art Society, at the Museum Ludwig, Cologne

Catherine Lampert and Richard Shiff, *Peter Doig*, New York 2011.
Judith Nesbitt (ed.), *Peter Doig*, exhib. cat. London/Frankfurt, Cologne 2008.
Alice Koegel (ed.), *Peter Doig. Studiofilmclub*, exhib. cat. Cologne/Zurich, Cologne 2005.
Kadee Robbins (ed.), *Peter Doig. Works on Paper*, exhib. cat. Vero Beach/Toronto, Vero Beach 2005.
Veit Görner and Bernhart Schwenk (eds.), *Peter Doig. Metropolitain*, exhib. cat. Munich/Hannover, Cologne 2004.

MAX DUDLER
*1949 Thal-Altenrhein

Studied at the Städelschule, Frankfurt am Main, with Günter Bock and at the Hochschule der Künste, Berlin, with Ludwig Leo
1981–1986 Architect with Oswald Mathias Ungers
1986–1992 Architecture practice jointly with Karl Dudler and Pete Welbergen
1989–1990 Taught in the Architecture Faculty, Venice
1996–1999 Visiting professor at the chair for design and industrial architecture, Dortmund University
Since 2005 professor of architecture at the Düsseldorf Art Academy

Simone Boldrin and Francesco Saverio Fera (eds.), *Max Dudler. Architectures since 1979*, Milan 2012.
Alexander Bonte (ed.), *Max Dudler*, Heidelberg 2012.
Max Dudler, *Kontinuität*, 7 vols., Sulgen 2011.
Johann Christoph Bürkle (ed.), *Max Dudler. Architektur für die Stadt*, Sulgen 2003.
Max Dudler, *Max Dudler*, 5 vols., Berlin [2002].

UDO DZIERSK
*1961 Gelsenkirchen

1983–1984 Studied painting with Gerhard Richter et al. at the Düsseldorf Art Academy
1985 Worked at the Hochschule der Künste, Berlin, training assignment to the class taught by Georg Baselitz; Advancment Award from the City of Gelsenkirchen
1986–1988 Audited with Per Kirkeby at the Staatliche Akademie der Bildenden Künste Karlsruhe and returned to his studies with Markus Lüpertz at the Düsseldorf Art Academy; in Markus Lüpertz's master class
1989 Promotional Prize, Great Art Exhibition NRW, Düsseldorf
1993 New York grant, Ernst Poensgen Foundation, Düsseldorf
Since 2002 professor in the Orientation Department at the Düsseldorf Art Academy
2003 Prize-winner, Enno and Christa Springmann Foundation, Wuppertal

Udo Dziersk et al., *Just Call It Betty's Bar. Bilder 2005–2012*, Karlsruhe 2013.
Udo Dziersk et al., *Udo Dziersk. Malerei und Zeichnungen*, exhib. cat. Essen, Dortmund 2007.
Leane Schäfer, *Udo Dziersk. Bilder für alle Fälle, Malerei und Zeichnung*, exhib. cat. Gelsenkirchen 2004.
Andreas Steffens, *Udo Dziersk. Unter anderen Vorzeichen, Neue Bilder*, Wuppertal 1996.

FRANZ EGGENSCHWILER
*1930 Solothurn–2000 Bern

1946–1951 Attended Gewerbeschule in Bern; trained as a glass painter
1951–1953 Attended the Max von Mühlenen Malschule in Bern
1963–1964 Swiss Federation Grant for Applied Art
1972 Showed work at documenta 5 in Kassel

1980 Art Prize, Solothurn Canton
1981–1996 Professor of fine art graphics at the Düsseldorf Art Academy

Hans Eggenberger, *Franz Eggenschwiler. Werkverzeichnis der Druckgrafik 1946–2000*, Eriswil 2008.
Hans Eggenberger, *Franz Eggenschwiler. Werke 1950–1985. Objekte, Schmuck, Zeichnungen, Malerei, Druckgraphik*, exhib. cat. Düsseldorf 1985.
Franz Eggenschwiler. Holzdruckzeichnungen und Holzdrucke, exhib. cat. St. Gallen 1976.

JOSEPH ENSELING
*1886 Coesfeld–1957 Düsseldorf

1905–1910 After training as a sculptor, studied with Rudolf Bosselt, Peter Behrens, and Wilhelm Kreis at the Kunstgewerbeschule Düsseldorf
1910–1912 Studied with Aristide Maillol at the Académie Colarossi in Paris
1913 Appointed to teach at the Kunstgewerbeschule (after 1922: Folkwangschule) in Essen
From 1919 resumed teaching at the Folkwangschule in Essen
Member of the artists' association Junges Rheinland
1938–1952 Professor of sculpture at the Düsseldorf Art Academy

Skulpturen von Joseph Enseling, 1886–1957. Ein Bildhauer in Essen, exhib. cat. Essen 1994.
Joseph Enseling. Skulpturen, exhib. cat. Düsseldorf 1986.

EMIL GUSTAV FAHRENKAMP
*1885 Aachen–1966 Breitscheid

1909–1912 Worked in Wilhelm Kreis's architecture practice in Düsseldorf
From 1911 assistant and teaching assistant at the Kunstgewerbeschule Düsseldorf
1919–1945 Professor of architecture at the Düsseldorf Art Academy
1937–1945 Director of the Düsseldorf Art Academy

Brigitte Jacob, *Emil Fahrenkamp. Bauten und Projekte für Berlin*, Berlin 2007.
Christoph Heuter, '"Die harmonischen Formen begeistern uns sehr". Das Spätwerk des Architekten Emil Fahrenkamp in Ratingen', *Die Quecke*, No. 71, 2001, pp. 189–197.
Christoph Heuter, *Emil Fahrenkamp 1885–1966. Architekt im rheinisch-westfälischen Industriegebiet*, Petersberg 2002. No. 59, *Arbeitsheft der rheinischen Denkmalpflege* series.
August Hoff, *Emil Fahrenkamp. Ein Ausschnitt seines Schaffens aus den Jahren 1924–1927*, Stuttgart 1928.
August Hoff, *Architekturen Prof. E. Fahrenkamp, Düsseldorf*, Düsseldorf 1925.

JOSEPH FASSBENDER
*1903 Cologne–1974 Cologne

1926–1928 Studied painting and graphic art at the Cologne Werkschulen with Richard Seewald
1929 Villa Romana Prize, Florence
1941–1946 Served in the armed forces; interment as a prisoner of war
1949 Founder member of the New Rhenish Secession
1954–1955 Visiting lecturer at the Hamburg Landeskunstschule
1955–1958 Head of the Graphics Department at the Werkkunstschule in Krefeld
1957 Grand Art Prize, City of Cologne
1958–1968 Professor of painting and drawing at the Düsseldorf Art Academy
1960 Grand Art Prize, State of North Rhine-Westphalia
1964 Grand Order of Merit; Grand Prize for Graphic Arts at the Venice Biennale
1965 Member of the Academy of the Arts, Berlin

Siegfried Gohr (ed.), *Joseph Fassbender*, exhib. cat. Düsseldorf 2009.
Frank Günter Zehnder (ed.), *Joseph Faßbender 1903–1974. Verwandlungen, Malerei, Zeichnungen und Grafik*, exhib. cat. Cologne 2004.
Wulf Herzogenrath (ed.), *Joseph Fassbender. Malerei zwischen Figuration und Abstraktion*, exhib. cat. Cologne 1988.
Joachim Heusinger von Waldegg (ed.), *Joseph Fassbender. Ausstellung zum 70. Geburtstag*, Bonn 1973. No. 45, *Kunst und Altertum am Rhein* series.
Joseph Fassbender, exhib. cat. Hannover 1961.

HELMUT FEDERLE
*1944 Solothurn

1964–1969 Studied at the Allgemeine Gewerbeschule Basel
1969–1971 Swiss Federation Arts grant
1984 Taught in Reykjavik
1997 Showed work in the Swiss Pavilion at the Venice Biennale
1999–2007 Professor of painting at the Düsseldorf Art Academy
2008 Prix Aurélie-Nemours des Institut de France, Paris

Fanni Fetzer (ed.), *Helmut Federle. American Songline*, exhib. cat. Luzern, Ostfildern 2012.
Helmut Federle, exhib. cat. Nantes/Arles, Nantes 2002.
Helmut Federle, exhib. cat. Bregenz, Cologne 1999.
Bundesamt für Kultur in Bern (ed.), *Helmut Federle*, exhib. cat. Venice, Baden 1997.
Klaus Schrenk, *Helmut Federle*, exhib. cat. Bonn 1995.
Wilfried Dickhoff (ed.), *Helmut Federle. Bilder und Zeichnungen 1975–1988*, exhib. cat. Krefeld/Bielefeld/Hamburg, Bielefeld 1989.

ROBERT FLECK
*1957 Vienna

1976–1981 Studied art history, history, philosophy, and aesthetics at Vienna, Innsbruck, and Paris Universities
1984–1991 Academic employee at the Research Centre for Democratic Movements in Central Europe at Innsbruck University
1987 Doctorate at Innsbruck University
1991–1993 Austrian federal arts curator
1991–1999 France correspondent for art – *Das Kunstmagazin*
1994–1999 Employed at museum in progress, Vienna
2000–2003 Director of the École Régional des Beaux-Arts de Nantes
2004–2008 Director of the Deichtorhallen in Hamburg
2007 Commissioner for the exhibition in the Austrian Pavilion at the Venice Biennale
2009–2012 Director of the Art and Exhibition Hall of the Federal Republic of Germany
Since 2012 professor of art and public relations at the Düsseldorf Art Academy
Since 2013 deputy vice chancellor of the Düsseldorf Art Academy

Robert Fleck, *Das Kunstsystem im 21. Jahrhundert. Museen, Künstler, Sammler, Galerien*, Vienna 2013.
Robert Fleck, *Die Biennale von Venedig. Eine Geschichte des 20. Jahrhunderts*, 2nd edn, Hamburg 2012. No. 177, *Fundus-Bücher* series.
Robert Fleck, *Die Ablösung vom 20. Jahrhundert. Malerei der Gegenwart*, Vienna 2010. No. 190, *Fundus-Bücher* series.
Robert Fleck, *Deleuze schickt mich in die Bibliothek. Über Bücher und Menschen*, Hamburg 2010.
Robert Fleck, *Werner Hofmann. Ein Gespräch*, Hamburg 2012. No. 213, *Fundus-Bücher* series.
Robert Fleck, *Die Mühl-Kommune. Freie Sexualität und Aktionismus. Geschichte eines Experiments*, Cologne 2003.

KATHARINA FRITSCH
*1956 Essen

Studied history and art history at Münster University
1977–1984 Studied with Fritz Schwegler at the Düsseldorf Art Academy; master class
1995 Showed work at the Venice Biennale together with Thomas Ruff and Martin Honert
1996 Aachen Art Prize
2001–2010 Professor of sculpture at Kunstakademie Münster
2002 Konrad von Soest Prize, Landschaftsverband Westfalen-Lippe
2008 Piepenbrock Prize for Sculpture
Since 2010 professor of sculpture at the Düsseldorf Art Academy

Bice Curiger et al., *Katharina Fritsch*, exhib. cat. Zurich/Hamburg, Ostfildern 2009.
Bice Curiger, *Katharina Fritsch*, Cologne 2006.
Iwona Blazwick (ed.), *Katharina Fritsch*, exhib. cat. London/Düsseldorf, Ostfildern 2002.
Theodora Vischer (ed.), *Katharina Fritsch*, exhib. cat. San Francisco/Basel, Basel 1996.
Katharina Fritsch, *Museum*, exhib. cat. Venice, Ostfildern 1995.

PETER GANSEN
*1976 Bad Gandersheim

1998–2001 Studied music, mathematics, and German for teaching at primary schools at Justus-Liebig-Universität Gießen
2002–2004 Second course of university studies in education sciences and music education at Marburg and Gießen Universities
2002–2005 Academic employee at the Institute for School Education Studies and Teaching Methodology at Gießen University
2005–2007 Taught at the Preparatory Service Study Seminary for primary, secondary modern, middle, and special-needs schools in Gießen
2007 Second state examination, temporary academic counsellor
2009 Doctorate at Gießen University
2010–2011 Supply professor for primary school teaching at Koblenz-Landau University
Since 2012 junior professor of education at the Düsseldorf Art Academy

Peter Gansen, 'Leiblichkeit und Sprache. Zur Bedeutung metaphorischen Denkens und Sprechens in der frühen Kindheit', in: Johannes Bilstein et al. (eds.), *Die Bildung des Körpers*, Weinheim 2013, pp. 260–278.
Peter Gansen, 'Kinderphilosophie zwischen Standardisierung und unzensiertem Denken. Erziehung zur "Unverfrorenheit"?', in: Ludwig Duncker et al. (eds.), *Betrachten – Staunen – Denken*, Munich 2012, pp. 13–28i. No. 1, *Philosophieren mit Kindern* series.
Peter Gansen, 'Cultural Turn und Kindheitsforschung. Zur Erforschung von Kindern und Kindheit im Zeichen einer kulturwissenschaftlichen Wende', in: Johannes Bilstein et al. (eds.), *Kulturelle*

Differenzen und Globalisierung, Wiesbaden 2011, pp. 157–174.
Peter Gansen, 'Chancenungleichheit von Anfang an. Heterogenität in der frühen Kindheit als bildungspolitische und pädagogische Herausforderung', in: Carl-Peter Buschkühle et al. (eds.), *Bildung zwischen Standardisierung und Heterogenität*, Wiesbaden 2009, pp. 193–214.

RUPPRECHT GEIGER
*1908 Munich–2009 Munich

1926–1929 Studied architecture at the Munich Kunstgewerbeschule with Eduard Pfeiffer
1933–1935 Studied at the Staatsbauschule Munich
1940–1944 Served in the armed forces
1949 Co-founder of the ZEN 49 group in Munich
1965–1976 Professor of fine arts painting at the Düsseldorf Art Academy
1968 Burda Art Prize for Painting
1970 Member of the Academy of the Arts, Berlin
1979 Honorary member of the Düsseldorf Art Academy
1982–1983 Member of the Baverian Academy of Fine Arts, Munich

Fritz Jacobi and Melanie Wilken (eds.), *100 Jahre Rupprecht Geiger*, exhib. cat. Berlin 2008.
Julia Geiger, *Rupprecht Geiger. Werkverzeichnis der Druckgrafik 1948–2007*, Munich 2007.
Pia Dornacher and Julia Geiger, *Rupprecht Geiger. Werkverzeichnis 1942–2002. Gemälde und Objekte, Architekturbezogene Kunst*, Munich 2003.
Peter-Klaus Schuster (ed.), *Rupprecht Geiger*, exhib. cat. Munich 1988.
Barbara Volkmann and Rose-France Raddatz, *Rupprecht Geiger. Retrospektive*, exhib. cat. Berlin/Ludwigshafen/Düsseldorf, Berlin 1985.

VADIM GLOWNA
*1941 Eutin–2012 Berlin

Since 1962 actor
1980 Founded the production firm Atossa-Film; directed numerous films and written screen plays
1981 Golden Camera, Cannes Film Festival
2000–2009 Supply professor for video and film at the Düsseldorf Art Academy

Vadim Glowna, *Der Geschichtenerzähler. Erinnerungen*, Berlin 2006.
Vadim Glowna, *Desperado City. Wie ein Film entsteht*, Munich/Vienna 1981. No. 5, *Arbeitshefte Film* series.

SIEGFRIED GOHR
*1949 Merkstein near Aachen

Studied archaeology, art history, and philosophy in Cologne and Tübingen
1974 Doctorate and academic assistant at the Wallraf Richartz Museum in Cologne
1978–1985 Director of the Josef Haubrich Kunsthalle, Cologne
1986–1991 Director of Museum Ludwig, Cologne
1993–2004 Professor at the Staatliche Hochschule für Gestaltung in Karlsruhe
Since 2004 professor of art history at the Düsseldorf Art Academy
2008–2013 Vice chancellor of the Düsseldorf Art Academy

Siegfried Gohr, *Magritte. Das Unmögliche versuchen*, Cologne 2009.
Siegfried Gohr, *Pablo Picasso, Leben und Werk: 'Ich suche nicht, ich finde'*, Cologne 2006.
Siegfried Gohr, *Markus Lüpertz*, Cologne 2001.
Siegfried Gohr et al., *Ernst Wilhelm Nay. Werkverzeichnis der Ölgemälde*, 2 vols., Cologne 1990.
Siegfried Gohr, *Museum Ludwig Cologne. Gemälde, Skulpturen, Environments vom Expressionismus bis zur Gegenwart*, 2 vols., Munich 1986.

BRUNO GOLLER
*1901 Gummersbach–1998 Düsseldorf

1919–1921 Taught by landscape painter Julius Jungheim
1927 Member of the artists' association Junges Rheinland; co-founder of the Rhenish Secession
1940–1945 Served in the armed forces
1949–1953 Lecturer in a preliminary class and a drawing class at the Düsseldorf Art Academy
1953–1964 Professor of painting at the Düsseldorf Art Academy
1959 Showed work at documenta II in Kassel
1965 Grand Prize of the State of North Rhine-Westphalia; represented Germany at the 8th São Paulo Biennale
1967 Grand Order of Merit of the Federal Republic of Germany
1967 Member of the Academy of the Arts, Berlin
1984 Honorary member of the Düsseldorf Art Academy

Siegfried Gohr (ed.), *Bruno Goller. Frauenbilder*, exhib. cat. Düsseldorf 2006.
Martin Hentschel (ed.), *Bruno Goller. Retrospektive zum hundertsten Geburtstag*, exhib. cat. Krefeld/Winterthur, Krefeld 2001.
Bruno Goller. Werke aus sechs Jahrzehnten, exhib. cat. Düsseldorf 1986.
Volker Kahmen, *Bruno Goller*, Bonn 1981.

EUGEN GOMRINGER
*1925 Cachuela Esperanza

Studied national economics and art history in Bern and Rome
1954–1958 Max Bill's secretary at the Hochschule für Gestaltung in Ulm
1958 Collaborated on the catalogue of Josef Haydn's works in Ascona
1962–1967 General manager, Schweizerischer Werkbund in Zurich
1976–1979 Lecturer in aesthetic theory at the Düsseldorf Art Academy
1979–1990 Professor of aesthetics at the Düsseldorf Art Academy
1986 Visiting professor of poetics in Bamberg
1988 Director general of the International Forum für Gestaltung in Ulm
2000 Founded the Institut für konstruktive Kunst und konkrete Poesie – Eugen Gomringer Archives in Rehau
2008 Bavarian Order of Merit
2011 Alice Salomon Prize for Poetics of the Hochschule Berlin

Eugen Gomringer, *Admirador*, Berlin 2012.
Eugen Gomringer, *Kommandier(t) die Poesie! Biografische Berichte*, Dozwil 2006.
Eugen Gomringer, *Poesie um den Weißenstädter See. Das Stundenbuch*, Rehau 2006.
Eugen Gomringer, *Gesamtwerk*, 4 vols., Vienna 1995–2006.

PAUL GOOD
*1942 Mels

1962–1965 Novitiate and studied philosophy at the Schöneck Mission Seminary
1965 Studied with Max Müller at Ludwig-Maximilians-Universität Munich
1967–1968 Studied philosophy at the Sorbonne in Paris
1970 Doctorate at Ludwig-Maximilians-Universität Munich
1970–1973 Assistant and postdoctorate at St. Gallen University
1976 Research sojourn at the University of California, Berkeley
1983–2008 Professor of philosophy at the Düsseldorf Art Academy

Paul Good, *Roman Signer. Härtetest des Schönen*, Cologne 2009.
Paul Good, *Zeit-Skulptur. Roman Signers Werk philosophisch betrachtet*, Zurich 2002.
Paul Good, *Minimalia zur Gegenwartskunst*, Düsseldorf 1998.
Paul Good, *Die Unbezüglichkeit der Kunst*, Munich 1998.

MARTIN GOSTNER
*1957 Innsbruck

1978–1979 Studied at Vienna University
1979–1983 Studied with Arnulf Rainer and Max Weiler at the Akademie der Bildenden Künste in Vienna
Since 2004 professor of sculpture at the Düsseldorf Art Academy

Necmi Sönmez (ed.), *Martin Gostner. Of Milk and Honey*, exhib. cat. Essen, Düsseldorf 2004.
Silvia Eiblmayr (ed.), *Martin Gostner. Seitlich aus der Requisite kommend*, exhib. cat. Innsbruck, Ostfildern 2002.
Norbert Brunner and Elisabeth Fiedler, *Martin Gostner. All I See I Cover*, exhib. cat. Graz 2001.
Martin Gostner. *Kupferpfandl und darüber*, exhib. cat. Vienna 2001.
Martin Gostner. *Malerei, Zeichnung, Objekte*, exhib. cat. Vienna 1984.

KARL OTTO GÖTZ
*1914 Aachen

From 1932 studied at the Kunstgewerbeschule Aachen
1935–1945 Forbidden to paint and show work
1936–1938 and 1939–1945 served in the armed forces
1941 Studied at the Akademie der Bildenden Künste in Dresden
1948 Art Prize Junger Westen
1949 Member of CoBrA group
1958 and 1968 Showed work at the Venice Biennale
1959 Showed work at documenta II in Kassel
1959–1979 Professor of fine art painting at the Düsseldorf Art Academy
1989 Order of Merit of the State of North Rhine-Westphalia
1996 State Prize for Painting, State of Rheinland-Pfalz
1997 Honorary member of the Kunstakademie Münster
2004 Honorary member of the Düsseldorf Art Academy

Siegfried Gohr (ed.), *K. O. Götz*, exhib. cat. Düsseldorf 2006.
Joachim Lissmann, *K. O. Götz. Werkverzeichnis. Bilder 2003–2006, Stahlreliefs 2000–2006, Holzvögel 2003–2005*, Alsdorf 2006.
Karl Otto Götz, Erinnerungen, 4 vols., Aachen 1993–1999.
Susanne Anna (ed.), *Karl Otto Götz. Arbeiten auf Papier 1934–1993*, exhib. cat. Chemnitz, Düsseldorf 1993.
Marianne Heinz (ed.), *K. O. Götz. Monotypien, Gemälde, Gouachen, 1935–1983*, exhib. cat. Düsseldorf 1984.
Karl Otto Götz, *Erinnerungen und Werk*, 2 vols., Düsseldorf 1983.

GOTTHARD GRAUBNER
*1930 Erlbach–2013 Neuss

1947–1948 Studied at the Hochschule für Bildende Künste in West Berlin with Arthur Degner
1948–1949 and 1951 Studied at the Kunstakademie Dresden with Wilhelm Rudolph
1954 Left the GDR
1954–1961 Studied with Georg Meistermann and K. O. Götz at the Düsseldorf Art Academy; in Meistermann's master class
1965 Teacher and from 1969 professor at the Hochschule für Bildende Künste Hamburg
1968–1977 Showed work at documentas 4 and 6 in Kassel
1973–1992 Member of the Academy of the Arts, Berlin
1976–1996 Professor of painting at the Düsseldorf Art Academy
1982 Represented Germany at the Venice Biennale and the New Delhi Triennial, Indian State Prize; collaborated on building up the Hombroich Museum Island
1988 North German Art Prize
1992 Order of Merit of the Federal Republic of Germany
2002 Grand Order of Merit of the Federal Republic of Germany
2010 Honorary member of the Düsseldorf Art Academy

Kitty Kemr (ed.), *Gotthard Graubner. Zeichnungen/Drawings*, Düsseldorf 2011.
Heinz Liesbrock (ed.), *Gotthard Graubner. Gespräch mit Josef Albers*, exhib. cat. Bottrop, Düsseldorf 2011.
Dorit Schäfer (ed.), *Gotthard Graubner. Radierungen*, exhib. cat. Karlsruhe, Heidelberg 2008.
Siegmar Holsten (ed.), *Gotthard Graubner. Malerei auf Papier*, exhib. cat. Karlsruhe, Düsseldorf 2001.
Werner Schmidt (ed.), *Gotthard Graubner. Malerei und Zeichnung*, exhib. cat. Dresden/Duisburg, Düsseldorf 2000.

KATHARINA GROSSE
*1961 Freiburg im Breisgau

1982–1986 Studied with Norbert Tadeusz at Kunstakademie Münster
1986–1990 Studied with Gotthard Graubner at the Düsseldorf Art Academy
1992 Villa Romana grant, Florence
1993 Karl Schmidt-Rottluff grant
1995 Grant from the Stiftung Kunstfonds Bonn e. V.
1999 1st Prize of the Deutsche Volks- und Raiffeisenbanken
2000–2010 Professor at the Kunsthochschule Berlin-Weißensee
2003 Fred Thieler Prize, Berlin
Since 2010 professor of painting at the Düsseldorf Art Academy
Member of the Academy of the Arts, Berlin

Ulrich Wilmes, *Katharina Grosse. Eat, Child, Eat!*, Berlin 2011.
Karen Reimer (ed.), *Katharina Grosse. Atoms inside Balloons*, exhib. cat. Chicago 2009.
Katharina Grosse, *Another Man Who Has Dropped His Paintbrush*, exhib. cat. Modena, Cologne 2008.
Ulrich Look et al. (eds.), *Katharina Grosse. Atoms Outside Eggs*, exhib. cat. Porto 2007.
Jonathan Watkins et al. (eds.), *Katharina Grosse. Cool Puppen. Der weisse Saal trifft sich im Wald. Ich wüsste jetzt nichts*, exhib. cat. Munich/St. Gallen/Kiel, Wolfratshausen 2002.

GÜNTER GROTE
*1911 Duisburg–1985 Düsseldorf

1939 Forbidden to paint and show work
1939–1940 Worked as a bookseller
1940–1945 Served in the armed forces; his studio was destroyed by fire
Member of the Rhenish Secession
1960 Cornelius Prize, City of Düsseldorf
1960–1977 Professor of art teaching at state schools at the Düsseldorf Art Academy

Günter Grote et al., *Ludwig Gabriel Schrieber 1907–1975. Gemälde, Skulpturen, Aquarelle, Zeichnungen*, exhib. cat. Düsseldorf, Viersen 1995.
Günter Grote, *Chronometer*, Düsseldorf 1987.

DURS GRÜNBEIN
*1962 Dresden

Until 1987 studied theatre studies in Berlin, then freelanced for magazines and worked as a writer
1992 Bremen Promotional Prize in Literature
1995 Georg Büchner Prize, Deutsche Akademie für Sprache und Dichtung
2006 Berlin Literature Prize
Since 2006 professor of poetics and art aesthetics at the Düsseldorf Art Academy
2007–2008 Visiting professor at the Heinrich-Heine-Universität, Düsseldorf
2008 Pour le mérite Order for Science and the Arts
2009 Grand Order of Merit with Star
2009 Grant for the Villa Massimo in Rome
Memberships: Academy of the Arts, Berlin; Deutsche Akademie für Sprache und Dichtung; Freie Akademie der Künste in Hamburg; Freie Akademie der Künste zu Leipzig; Sächsische Akademie der Künste

Durs Grünbein, *Koloss im Nebel. Gedichte*, Berlin 2012.
Durs Grünbein, *Aroma. Ein römisches Zeichenbuch*, Berlin 2010.
Durs Grünbein, *Vom Stellenwert der Worte. Frankfurter Poetikvorlesung*, Berlin 2010.
Durs Grünbein, *Die Bars von Atlantis. Eine Erkundung in vierzehn Tauchgängen*, Frankfurt am Main 2009.
Durs Grünbein, *Der cartesische Taucher. Drei Meditationen*, Frankfurt am Main 2008.
Durs Grünbein, *Lob des Taifuns. Reisetagebücher in Haikus*, Frankfurt am Main 2008.

THOMAS GRÜNFELD
*1956 Leverkusen

Studied at the Pädagogischen Hochschule in Cologne
1978–1982 Studied with Paul Uwe Deyer at the Staatliche Akademie der Bildenden Künste in Stuttgart
1996–2002 Lecturer at Goldsmiths College, London
Since 2006 professor of sculpture at the Düsseldorf Art Academy

Fritz Emslander (ed.), *Homey. Thomas Grünfeld, Werke von 1981 bis 2013*, exhib. cat. Morsbroich/Leverkusen, Bönen 2013.
Thomas Grünfeld, *Young Steerer (junger Lenker), Erwin, misfit (Bulldog /goat), Colorado, doggy, Augenbilder, gluematic, MCC, misfit (pheasant/ goat), Nottingham, o.T. (shelf) & others by Thomas Grünfeld, Werkauswahl von 1987–2011*, exhib. cat. London 2011.
Hans Irrek, *Thomas Grünfeld. FELT*, exhib. cat. Zurich 2010.
Udo Kittelmann (ed.), *DP. Thomas Grünfeld, Déformation Professionelle: Gummis, misfits & Kleider von Comme des Garçons*, exhib. cat. Cologne, Ostfildern 1999.
Thomas Grünfeld, *Selected Works '86–'95*, Stuttgart 1995.

ANDREAS GURSKY
*1955 Leipzig

1955 Fled the GDR
1978–1981 Studied visual communications with Otto Steinert and Michael Schmidt at the Folkwangschule (GHS) Essen
1981–1987 Studied photography at the Düsseldorf Art Academy with Bernd Becher; in master class
1989 Promotional Prize, State of North Rhine-Westphalia, 1st German Photo Prize, Stuttgart
2008 Kaiserring, City of Goslar
Since 2010 professor of fine art at the Düsseldorf Art Academy
2012 Member of the Nordrhein-Westfälische Akademie der Wissenschaften und der Künste

Beat Wismer (ed.), *Andreas Gursky. Bangkok*, exhib. cat. Düsseldorf, Göttingen 2012.
Werner Spies et al., *Andreas Gursky*, 2 vols., exhib. cat. Beverly Hills, New York 2010.
Martin Hentschel (ed.), *Andreas Gursky. Werke 80–08*, exhib. cat. Krefeld/Stockholm/Vancouver, Ostfildern 2008 (revised new edition 2011).
Thomas Weski (ed.), *Andreas Gursky*, exhib. cat. Munich, Cologne 2007.
Peter Galassi (ed.), *Andreas Gursky*, exhib. cat. New York, Ostfildern 2001.

EBERHARD HAVEKOST
*1967 Dresden

1991–1996 Studied at the Hochschule für Bildende Künste, Dresden
1997 In Ralf Kerbach's master class
1999 Karl Schmidt-Rottluff grant, Studienstiftung des deutschen Volkes
Since 2010 professor of painting at the Düsseldorf Art Academy

Walter Smerling (ed.), *Eberhard Havekost. Titel*, exhib. cat. Duisburg, Cologne 2013.
Dirk Syndram et al., *Eberhard Havekost in India*, exhib. cat. Mumbai, Berlin 2012.
Eberhard Havekost, exhib. cat. Dresden, Berlin 2010.
Heide Häusler and Max Hollein (eds.), *Eberhard Havekost. Retina*, exhib. cat. Frankfurt am Main, Cologne 2010.
Eberhard Havekost, *Graphik 1999–2004*, exhib. cat. Dresden, Cologne 2004.

ERWIN HEERICH
*1922 Kassel–2004 Meerbusch-Osterath

1945–1954 Studied with Ewald Mataré at the Düsseldorf Art Academy
1961 Taught at seminary for working people's education, Düsseldorf
1969–1979 Professor of painting and graphic arts for teachers of art at state schools at the Düsseldorf Art Academy
1974 Member of the Academy of the Arts, Berlin
1978 Will Grohmann Prize, Academy of the Arts, Berlin
1979–1987 Professor of sculpture for teaching at state schools at the Düsseldorf Art Academy
1983 Began planning buildings for the Hombroich Museum Island
1987 Max Beckmann Prize of the City of Frankfurt am Main
1996 Piepenbrock Prize for Sculpture, Berlin

Siegfried Gohr (ed.), *Erwin Heerich. Skulpturen, Zeichnungen, Entwürfe, Modelle*, exhib. cat. Düsseldorf 2007.

Erwin Heerich, *Skulptur und der architektonische Raum*, Cologne 1998.
Ulrich Schumacher (ed.), *Erwin Heerich*, exhib. cat. Bottrop 1993.
Christoph Brockhaus, *Erwin Heerich. Plastische Prozesse*, exhib. cat. Duisburg 1992.
Erwin Heerich, 4 vols., Essen 1979–1984.

WILHELM HERBERHOLZ

*1881 Schwerte–1956 Oberstdorf

Studied at the art academies in Kassel and Düsseldorf
1922–36 Taught an etching class and painting techniques at the Düsseldorf Art Academy
1936–1950 Professor of painting techinques at the Düsseldorf Art Academy

Dirk-Gerd Erpenbeck, 'Bilder aus dem Baltenland. Bilder keiner Ausstellung. Werke von Wilhelm Herberholz und Heinz Becker aus dem 20. Jh.', in: Wolfgang Kessler et al. (eds.), *Westfalen und das Baltikum 1200–2000*, Herne 2007, pp. 121–131.
Hermann Kassebaum, *Bilder und Skizzen aus den baltischen Provinzen. Bilder von Wilhelm Herberholz*, Berlin 1918.

LIESEL-LOTTE HERKENRATH-PÜSCHEL

*1932 Witten/ Ruhr–1996 Düsseldorf

1952–1957 Studied Lutheran theology and German language and literature at Marburg, Tübingen, and Münster Universities
1960–1962 Studied Lutheran theology, sociology, and education at the Westfälische Wilhelms-Universität in Münster
1962–1967 Academic employment at the Education Seminar, Cologne University
1967 Doctorate at Cologne University
1974–1988 Professor of education at the Düsseldorf Art Academy

Liesel-Lotte Herkenrath, 'Aus erinnerter Geschichte das Heute gestalten. Zwischen Kindheit und Zukunft', *Una Sancta*, No. 35, 1980, pp. 96–101.
Liesel-Lotte Herkenrath, 'Vom Kind, das nicht essen wollte oder: Warum guter Rat nicht immer bekömmlich ist', *Wege zum Menschen*, No. 29, 1977, pp. 235–246.
Liesel-Lotte Herkenrath, 'Emanzipation im Verein?', *Wege zum Menschen*, No. 27, 1975, pp. 72–85.

GEORG HEROLD

*1947 Jena

1969–1973 Studied at Burg Giebichenstein in Halle an der Saale
1973 Failed attempt at fleeing the GDR; ransomed by the Federal Republic of Germany after nine months incarceration
1974–1976 Studied at the Fine Arts Academy in Munich
1976–1982 Studied with Sigmar Polke at the Hochschule für Bildende Künste Hamburg
1992–2001 Visiting artist, De Ateliers in Amsterdam
1993–1999 Professor at the Städelschule in Frankfurt am Main
Since 1999 professor of sculpture at the Düsseldorf Art Academy
2008–2013 Vice chancellor of the Düsseldorf Art Academy

Armin Zweite (ed.), *Georg Herold. Multiple Choice*, exhib. cat. Munich, Cologne 2012.
Matthias Winzen (ed.), *What a Life. Georg Herold*, exhib. cat. Baden-Baden/Hannover/Klagenfurt, Cologne 2005.
Anne Schwarz (ed.), *Georg Herold. X. Baracke 1986*, exhib. cat. Berlin 2005.
Georg Herold, *Gekrümmte Poesie*, exhib. cat. Amsterdam 1993.

FRIEDRICH WOLFRAM HEUBACH

*1944 Nordrach

Studied psychology, sociology, and art theory and history at Cologne University
1968–1974 Editor of *interfunktionen* magazine
1969–1971 Taught at the Cologne Werkschulen
1974 Doctorate at Cologne University
1984 Postdoctorate at Cologne University
1985–1989 Professor of psychology at Cologne University and 1998–1992 at the Hochschule für Bildende Künste Hamburg
1992–2008 Professor of education and psychology at the Düsseldorf Art Academy
2008–2010 Taught at the Düsseldorf Art Academy

Friedrich Wolfram Heubach, '"Jeder Mensch ist ein Künstler" (Beuys) und "Kofferpacken – eine Kunst"', in: Johannes Bilstein et al. (eds.), *Curriculum des Unwägbaren 2*, Oberhausen 2009, pp. 119–126.
Friedrich Wolfram Heubach, *Ein Bild und sein Schatten. Zwei randständige Betrachtungen zum Bild der Melancholie und zur Erscheinung der Depression*, Bonn 1997. No. 6, *Schriften zur psychologischen Morphologie* series.
Friedrich Wolfram Heubach, *Das bedingte Leben. Entwurf zu einer Theorie der psychologischen Gegenständlichkeit der Dinge. Ein Beitrag zur psychology des Alltags*, Munich 1987.
Friedrich Wolfram Heubach (ed.), *interfunktionen*, Issues 1–12, Cologne 1968–1975.

WERNER HEUSER

*1880 Gummersbach–1964 Düsseldorf

1900–1901 Studied at the Düsseldorf Art Academy, afterwards in Dresden
Member of the artists' association Junges Rheinland
1926–1937 Professor of drawing at the Düsseldorf Art Academy
1937 Dismissed, his works classified as degenerate and confiscated
1945 Reappointed to teach at the Düsseldorf Art Academy, professor of drawing and painting
1946–1949 Director of the Düsseldorf Art Academy

Werner Heuser, exhib. cat. Düsseldorf, 1965.
Werner Heuser, *Köpfe. 11 Holzschnitte*, Düsseldorf 1921. No. 9, *Ausgaben der Galerie Flechtheim* series.
Werner Heuser, exhib. cat. Düsseldorf 1920.
Maximilien Luce, Otto Sohn-Rethel, Werner Heuser, exhib. cat. Düsseldorf 1914.

GERHARD HOEHME

*1920 Greppin–1989 Neuss

1939–1946 Served in the armed forces; internment as a prisoner of war
1948–1951 His teachers at the Kunsthochschule Burg Giebichenstein in Halle an der Saale included Herbert Post
1952 Moved to West Germany
1952–1953 Studied with Otto Coester at the Düsseldorf Art Academy
1953 Co-founder of Group 53
1954 Cornelius Prize, City of Düsseldorf
1957 2nd Prize, International Biennial of Graphic Arts, New York
1958 1st Promotional Prize, State of North Rhine-Westphalia
1959 Showed work at documenta II in Kassel
1960 Grant for the Villa Massimo in Rome
1960–1984 Professor of painting at the Düsseldorf Art Academy
Member of the Academy of the Arts, Berlin
1984 Paul Klee professorship of fine art, Gießen University

Gottfried Boehm and Susanne Rennert (eds.), *Gerhard Hoehme. Relationen, Texte 1952–1987*, Cologne 2011.
Susanne Rennert (ed.), *Gerhard Hoehme. Die Unruhe wächst. Restlessness Grows, Werke 1955–1989*, Cologne 2009.
Margarete Hoehme et al. (eds.), *Gerhard Hoehme. Catalogue raisonné*, Ostfildern 1998.
Egon Heuer, *Gerhard Hoehme. Die Druckgrafik*, ed. Wolfgang Zemter, Witten 1992.
Giulio Carlo Argan and Hans Peter Thurn, *Gerhard Hoehme. Werk und Zeit 1948–1983*, Stuttgart 1984.
Jürgen Partenheimer (ed.), *Gerhard Hoehme. Bilder. Wenn man nichts sieht, schaut man länger hin*, exhib. cat. Düsseldorf/Heidelberg, Stuttgart 1979.

WALTER JÜRGEN HOFMANN

*1939 Nuremberg

1959 Studied German language and literature, history, art history, literature, and theatre studies at Erlangen and Munich Universities
1966 Doctorate in art history at Erlangen-Nürnberg University
1967 Assistant to Hans Sedlmayr in Salzburg
1969–1970 Grant from the Deutsche Forschungsgemeinschaft
1971 Postdoctorate and non-tenured lecturer in art history at Erlangen-Nürnberg University
1974–2008 Professor of art history at the Düsseldorf Art Academy
1988–2008 Deputy rector of the Düsseldorf Art Academy
2008–2009 Taught at the Düsseldorf Art Academy

Walter Jürgen Hofmann, 'Schriftquelle. Allegorische Lektüre und Schloss Pommersfelden', *Wiener Jahrbuch für Kunstgeschichte*, No. 59, 2010/2011, pp. 127–152.
Walter Jürgen Hofmann, '"In campis pomera-nicis". Ikonologie als Fiktion und Geschichte', *Wiener Jahrbuch für Kunstgeschichte*, No. 43, 1990, pp. 129–155.
Walter Jürgen Hofmann, 'Architektur und Geschichte der Architektur in der Baukunst Balthasar Neumanns', in: Thomas Korth (ed.), *Balthasar Neumann. Kunstgeschichtliche Beiträge zum Jubiläumsjahr 1987*, Munich 1987, pp.143–171.
Walter Jürgen Hofmann, *Über Dürers Farbe*, Nuremberg 1971. No. 42, *Erlanger Beiträge zur Sprachund Kunstwissenschaft* series.
Walter Jürgen Hofmann, *Schloss Pommersfelden. Geschichte seiner Entstehung*, Nuremberg 1968. No. 32, *Erlanger Beiträge zur Sprachund Kunstwissenschaft* series; at the same time Erlangen-Nürnberg, Univ. Diss. 1967.

HANS HOLLEIN

*1934 Vienna–2014 Vienna

Until 1956 Studied architecture with Clemens Holzmeister at the Akademie der Bildenden Künste in Vienna
1960 Master of architecture, University of California, Berkeley
1964–1970 Editor of the magazine *Bau*
1967–1976 Professor of architecture at the Düsseldorf Art Academy
1976–1987 Taught at the Düsseldorf Art Academy
1976–1979 Head of the master class for industrial design and the Institute of Design at the Universität für angewandte Kunst in Vienna

1978–1990 Commissioner for the exhibitions in the Austrian Pavilion at the Venice Biennale
1979–2002 Head of a master class in architecture at the Universität für angewandte Kunst in Vienna
1995–1999 Head of Department I Architecture at the Universität für angewandte Kunst in Vienna
2010 Founded Hollein & Partner ZT-GmbH with Ulf Kotz and Christoph Mondschein; honorary member of the Düsseldorf Art Academy

Peter Weibel (ed.), *Hans Hollein*, exhib. cat. Graz, Ostfildern 2012.
Hans Hollein. Eine Ausstellung, exhib. cat. Vienna 1995.
The Guggenheim Museum Salzburg. A Project by Hans Hollein, exhib. cat. Venice/Salzburg, Salzburg 1990.
Gianni Pettena, *Hans Hollein. Opere 1960–1988*, Milan 1988.
Hans Hollein. Alles ist Architektur, 3 parts, exhib. cat. Mönchengladbach 1970.

NAN HOOVER (NÉE NANCY DODGE BROWNE)
*1931 New York–2008 Berlin

1950–1955 Studied at the Corcoran College of Art and Design in Washington DC
1969 Moved to Amsterdam
1977 Showed work at documenta 6 in Kassel
1980 German Academic Exchange Service grant, Berlin
1984 Showed work at the Venice Biennale
1986 Lecturer at the San Francisco Art Institute; honourable mention, Osnabrück Film and Video Festival
1987–1996 Professor of video and film at the Düsseldorf Art Academy; 1st Prize for Video, Ljubljana Biennial
1987 Showed work at documenta 8 in Kassel
1998–1999 Head of the multimedia class at the Gerrit Rietveld Academie in Amsterdam

Peter Joch (ed.), *'Some times'. Nan Hoover, Bill Viola*, exhib. cat. Darmstadt 2003.
Nan Hoover and Doris Krystof, *Nan Hoover*, exhib. cat. Heilbronn 1996.
Nan Hoover. Photo, Video, Performance 1980–1982, exhib. cat. Montreal 1982.
Toni Stooss (ed.), *Nan Hoover. Photowork, Video, Performance*, exhib. cat. Berlin 1981.
Nan Hoover, exhib. cat. Amsterdam 1979.

ALFONSO HÜPPI
*1935 Freiburg im Breisgau

1958–1959 Studied at the Kunst- und Werkschule in Pforzheim
1960–1961 Studied at the Staatliche Hochschule für Bildende Künste Hamburg
1961–1964 Lecturer for drawing from the nude, calligraphy, and design at the Hochschule für Bildende Künste, Hamburg
1964–1968 Employed at the Staatliche Kunsthalle Baden-Baden
1974–1999 Professor of painting at the Düsseldorf Art Academy
1998 Founder and head of Etaneno, Museum im Busch, Namibia

Hans-Joachim Müller, *Alfonso Hüppi. Holzwege*, exhib. cat. Wichtrach/Düsseldorf, Wichtrach/Bern 2010.
Alfonso Hüppi, exhib. cat. Wichtrach 2002.
Werner Meyer, *Alfonso Hüppi*, 2 vols., exhib. cat. Göppingen/Solothurn, Stuttgart 1990.
Galleria Henze, *Alfonso Hüppi. Zeichnungen, Aquarelle, Bilder, Objekte 1959–1985*, Campione d'Italia 1985.
Hans Albers Peters (ed.), *Alfonso Hüppi. Zeichnungen 1954–1978*, exhib. cat. Baden-Baden 1978.

JÖRG IMMENDORFF
*1945 Bleckede–2007 Düsseldorf

1963–1968 Studied at the Düsseldorf Art Academy with Teo Otto and Joseph Beuys; in Beuys's master class
1968 Founded Lidl Performance Project jointly with Chris Reinecke
1969 Dismissed from the Düsseldorf Art Academy
1972 Showed work at documenta 5 in Kassel
1976 Showed work at the Venice Biennale
1981 Visiting professor at Konsthögskolan in Stockholm
1982 Showed work at documenta 7 in Kassel
1982–1985 Visiting lectureships at the Kunstakademie Hamburg, Klasse F+F in Zurich, Trondheim Art Academy, Werkschule Cologne, and the Munich Academy of Fine Arts
From 1989 professor at the Frankfurter Städelschule
1996–2007 Professor of painting at the Düsseldorf Art Academy
1998 Order of Merit of the Federal Republic of Germany
2000 Cultural Foundation Fine Art Award, Dortmund
2005 Golden Pen media award
2006 Kaiserring, City of Goslar

Karlheinz Essl and Tayfun Belgin, *Jörg Immendorff. Was uns Malerei bedeuten kann*, exhib. cat. Klosterneuburg 2008.
Jörg Immendorff. Zeichne. Arbeiten aus seinem Archiv, exhib. cat. Düsseldorf, Cologne 2008.
Walter Smerling (ed.), *Jörg Immendorff*, exhib. cat. Duisburg, Cologne 2007. No. 6, *Akademos* series.
Beate Reifenscheid and Dirk Geuer, *Jörg Immendorff. Das grafische Werk. Werkverzeichnis*, Düsseldorf 2006.
Anette Hüsch et al. (eds.), *Jörg Immendorff. Male Lago*, exhib. cat. Berlin, Cologne 2005.
Pamela Kort, *Jörg Immendorff. Zeichnungen/Drawings 1964–1993*, Bern 1994.

MAGDALENA JETELOVÁ
*1946 Semily

1965–1971 Studied at the Prague Fine Arts Academy and the Accademia di Brera in Milan
1986 Promotional Prize, City of Munich
1987 Showed work at documenta 8 in Kassel
1988 Visiting professor at the Munich Academy of Fine Arts; Overbeck Fine Art Award, Lübeck
1989 Professor at the Salzburg Summer Academy; Art Prize, City of Darmstadt
1990–2004 Professor at the Düsseldorf Art Academy
Since 2004 professor of sculpture at the Munich Academy of Fine Arts

Ulrike Lorenz (ed.), *Magdalena Jetelová. Landscape of Transformation*, exhib. cat. Mannheim, Cologne 2010.
Ferdinand Ullrich and Hans-Jürgen Schwalm (eds.), *Der neue Raum. Magdalena Jetelová*, exhib. cat. Recklinghausen 2007.
Magdalena Jetelová, *Multipurposes*, artist's book and exhib. cat. Karlsruhe/Kraichtal-Unteröwisheim, Frechen 1997.
Robert Hopper (ed.), *Magdalena Jetelová. Finger-Tips Linking Parallels of Fire's Plane: New Works Made at the Henry Moore Sculpture Trust Studio*, exhib. cat. Halifax/Manchester, Halifax 1991.

IRMIN KAMP
*1940 Delmenhorst

Studied painting with K. F. Dahmen, Winfried Gau, and Johannes Schreiter at the Hochschule der Bildenden Künste in Bremen
Promotional Prize, City of Bremen
Studied sculpture at Saint Martin's School of Art, London, where her teachers included Anthony Caro and Philipp King; British Council grant
1974–2008 Professor of sculpture at the Düsseldorf Art Academy
1981–1982 Deputy head of the Düsseldorf Art Academy
1982–1987 Head of the Düsseldorf Art Academy
Since 2010 honorary member of the Düsseldorf Art Academy

Plastiken am Silbersee. Irmin Kamp, exhib. cat. Moers 2008.
Irmin Kamp, *Umgebungsbeeinflussung mit künstlerischen Mitteln, Forschungsprojekt*, 2 vols., Düsseldorf 1979–1981.
Irmin Kamp, *Polyester-Plastiken*, exhib. cat. Düren 1973.

HEINRICH KAMPS
*1896 Krefeld–1954 Düsseldorf

1916–1917 and 1920 Studied at the Kunstgewerbeschulen in Hamburg and Krefeld as well as at the Düsseldorf Art Academy
1917–1919 Attended Lothar von Kunowski Drawing Seminary in Düsseldorf
1920 Finished studies with examinations for teaching art at state schools
1930–1933 Director of the Staatliche Kunsthochschule in Berlin-Schöneberg
1933–1937 Professor at the Vereinigte Staatsschulen für Freie und Angewandte Kunst in Berlin-Charlottenburg
1937 Forced to retire
1946–1954 Professor of painting, teaching art at state schools, and glass and mosaic art at the Düsseldorf Art Academy
1949–1954 Director of the Düsseldorf Art Academy

Beatrice Thön, *Heinrich Kamps 1896–1954. Monographie mit Werkverzeichnis*, Pfinztal 1992.
Heinrich Kamps. 29. Sept. 1896–21. Dez. 1954, exhib. cat. Düsseldorf 1955.

ERNST KASPER
*1935 Trier–2008 Aachen

1956–1963 Studied at the RWTH Aachen
1963 Promotion Prize of the Federal Association of German Industry
1963–1964 Academic assistant to Fritz Eller at the Schulbauinstitut, RWTH Aachen
From 1964 own architecture practice in Aachen; until 1965 in partnership with Karl Wimmenauer
1971–2000 Professor of architecture at the Düsseldorf Art Academy
1972 Planungsgruppe Kasper
1999–2008 Non-tenured professor at the Escuela de Arquitectura, Universidad Austral de Chile in Valdivia

Martin Hochleitner and Inga Kleinknecht, *Politische Skulptur. Barlach, Kasper, Thorak, Wotruba – Ein Projekt der Landesgalerie Linz*, exhib. cat. Linz, Weitra 2008. Catalogue of the Oberösterreichisches Landesmuseen, No. 77, new series.
Susanne Gross (ed.), *Ernst Kasper. Bauten und Projekte 1965–2005*, Frankfurt am Main 2005.
Ernst Kasper and Klaus Klever, *Das Kaiserbad. Der Neubau und sein historischer Hintergrund*, Aachen 1995.

HUBERT KIECOL
*1950 Bremen-Blumenthal

1971 Began to study at the Werkkunstschule in Hamburg
From 1975 studied at the Hochschule für Bildende Künste Hamburg

1984 Mies van der Rohe grant from the City of Krefeld
1985 Annemarie and Will Grohmann grant from the State of Baden-Württemberg
1991 Will Grohmann Prize, Akademie der Künste, Berlin
Since 1993 professor of integration, fine art, and architecture
2000 Wolfgang Hahn Award for Contemporary Art, Gesellschaft für Moderne Kunst am Museum Ludwig, Cologne

Eva Schmidt (ed.), *Golden. Hubert Kiecol*, exhib. cat. Siegen, Cologne 2010.
Ralph Melcher (ed.), *Hubert Kiecol. Separee public*, exhib. cat. Saarbrücken, Cologne 2009.
Hubert Kiecol and Kay Heymer, *Hubert Kiecol. Glückliche Maße*, exhib. cat. Duisburg, Bonn 2002.
Rudi Fuchs and Dorine Mignot (eds.), *Hubert Kiecol*, exhib. cat. Amsterdam, Cologne 2000.
Johannes Gachnang et al., *Paradies. Hubert Kiecol, Fonds Régional d'Art Contemporain de Picardie*, exhib. cat. Amiens 1997.
Klaus Schrenk and Werner Büttner, *Hubert Kiecol*, exhib. cat. Bonn 1988.

LUISE KIMME
*1939 Bremen–2013 Tobago

1959–1965 Studied sculpture with Paul Dierkes at the Hochschule für Bildende Künste, Berlin
1966–1968 Studied at Saint Martin's School of Art, London
1968–1976 Taught at Wolverhampton Polytechnic, the Rhode Island School of Design, and California State University
1976–2002 Professor in the Orientation Department at the Düsseldorf Art Academy

Luise Kimme, *Sculpture. Kimme's Sculpture Museum, Bethel P. O. Tobago (Trinidad) West*, Düsseldorf 1998.
Herbert Ganslmayer (ed.), *Luise Kimme. Chachalaca, Robinson Crusoe Isle, 11 Grad 15 Minuten Nord – 60 Grad 45 Minuten West*, exhib. cat. Bremen 1985.
Luise Kimme. *Die Tropen 1977–1981*, exhib. cat. Düsseldorf 1981.

ANNA KLAPHECK (NÉE VON STRÜMPELL)
*1899 Erlangen–1986 Düsseldorf

1919–1921 Trained as a bookbinder
1921 Studied philosophy, art history, and archaeology in Leipzig, Berlin, and Marburg
1925 Doctorate, supervised by Heinrich Richard Hamann at Marburg University
1926–1927 Worked at the Museum für bildende Kunst and C. G. Boerner, art publishers in Leipzig
1952–1961 Lecturer in art history at the Düsseldorf Art Academy
1962–1964 Professor of art history at the Düsseldorf Art Academy
1979 Rheinlandtaler award
1983 Mutter Ey posters

Anna Klapheck, *Vom Notbehelf zur Wohlstandskunst. Kunst im Rheinland in der Nachkriegszeit*, Cologne 1979.
Anna Klapheck, 'Die "goldnen" zwanziger Jahre. Die Akademie zwischen den beiden Kriegen', in: Eduard Trier (ed.), *Zweihundert Jahre Kunstakademie Düsseldorf*, Düsseldorf 1973, pp. 147–160.
Anna Klapheck, *Walter Kaesbach und die zwanziger Jahre an der Düsseldorfer Kunstakademie*, Düsseldorf 1961.
Anna Klapheck, *Mutter Ey. Eine Düsseldorfer Künstlerlegende*, Düsseldorf 1958.

KONRAD KLAPHECK
*1935 Düsseldorf

1954–1958 Studied with Bruno Goller at the Düsseldorf Art Academy
1960 Promotional Prize, State of North Rhine-Westphalia for Young Artists
1979–2000 Professor of fine art painting at the Düsseldorf Art Academy
2000–2002 Taught at the Düsseldorf Art Academy
2010 Honorary member of the Düsseldorf Art Academy

Kay Heymer and Beat Wismer (eds.), *Klapheck. Bilder und Texte*, exhib. cat. Düsseldorf, Munich 2013.
Ferdinand Ullrich et al. (eds.), *Menschen und Maschinen. Bilder von Konrad Klapheck*, exhib. cat. Recklinghausen 2006.
Konrad Klapheck, *Porträtzeichnungen 1992–2002. Mit 16 Zeichnungen von Wanda Richter-Forgách*, Munich 2002.
Werner Hofmann (ed.), *Konrad Klapheck. Retrospektive 1955–1985*, exhib. cat. Hamburg/Tübingen/Munich, Munich 1985.
J. C. Ebbinge Wubben, *Konrad Klapheck*, exhib. cat. Rotterdam/Brussels/Düsseldorf, Gent 1974.

JOSEF PAUL KLEIHUES
*1933 Rheine–2004 Berlin

1956–1957 Studied architecture at Stuttgart University and until 1959 at Technische Universität Berlin
1959–1960 Grant from the École Nationale Supérieure des Beaux-Arts, Paris
1973–1994 Professor at Dortmund University
1984 Director of planning at the International Building Exhibition, Berlin
1988 Order of Merit of the Federal Republic of Germany
1994–1998 Professor of architecture at the Düsseldorf Art Academy
1996 Founded architecture practice Kleihues + Kleihues in Berlin
2000 Order of Merit of the State of Berlin
2001–2003 Founding president, Internationale Bauakademie Berlin

Andrea Mesecke and Thorsten Scheer (eds.), *Josef Paul Kleihues. Werke*, 2 vols., Ostfildern 2008–2013.
Paul Kahlfeldt et al. (eds.), *Josef Paul Kleihues. Stadt, Bau, Kunst*, exhib. cat. Berlin 2003.
Kim Shkapich (ed.), *Josef Paul Kleihues. The Museum Projects*, New York 1989.
Dankwart Guratzsch (ed.), *Josef Paul Kleihues. Das neue Berlin. Konzepte der Internationalen Bauausstellung 1987 für einen Städtebau mit Zukunft*, Berlin 1987.

KARL KNEIDL
*1940 Nuremberg

1956 Pupil of the painter and stage designer Ambrosius Hamm
1958 Stage sets for the Erlangen Student Stage
1962 Stage designer and assistant to Max Fritsche at the Schauspielhaus Bochum
1974–2008 Professor of stage design at the Düsseldorf Art Academy
Since 2010 honorary member of the Düsseldorf Art Academy

Karl Kneidl, 'Meine erste Begegnung mit Peter Zadek', in: Elisabeth Plessen (ed.), *Peter Zadek und seine Bühnenbildner: Wilfried Minks, Götz Loepelmann, Daniel Spoerri, Peter Pabst, Horst Sagert, Johannes Grützke, Rouben Ter-Arutunian, Karl Kneidl, André Diot*, Berlin 2012, pp. 150–155.
Peter Zadek, 'Karl Kneidl', in: Elisabeth Plessen (ed.), *Peter Zadek und seine Bühnenbildner. Wilfried Minks, Götz Loepelmann, Daniel Spoerri, Peter Pabst, Horst Sagert, Johannes Grützke, Rouben Ter-Arutunian, Karl Kneidl, André Diot*, Berlin 2012, pp. 145–150.

CLAUS KÖHLER-ACHENBACH
*1912 Frankfurt am Main–1988 Düsseldorf

1946–1972 Lecturer in fonts at the Düsseldorf Art Academy
1972–1977 Professor of drawing and fonts at the Düsseldorf Art Academy

Claus Köhler-Achenbach. Licht-Reflexion, exhib. cat. Düsseldorf 1977.

ANTON (TÜNN) KONERDING
*1928 Vechta–1984 Essen

1950–1954 Studied architecture at the Hochschule für Technik in Stuttgart
1954–1976 Taught at state schools in Stuttgart, Pforzheim, and Essen
1973 Visiting lecturer and from 1975 teaching contract at Duisburg-Essen University
1976–1984 Professor of applied graphic arts (design, fonts, book design) at the Düsseldorf Art Academy

Catalogues designed by Konerding:
Gerhard Hoehme and Erich Franz, *Gerhard Hoehme. Relationen*, exhib. cat. Bielefeld 1980.
Karl Bobek, *Arbeiten 1952–1980*, Berlin 1980.
Die Erweiterung des Wirklichkeitsbegriffs in der Kunst der 60er und 70er Jahre. Wahrnehmungen, Aufzeichnungen, Mitteilungen, exhib. cat. Krefeld 1979.
Reiner Ruthenbeck. *Handzeichnungen 1963–1977*, Krefeld 1978.
László Glózer, *Westkunst. Zeitgenössische Kunst seit 1939*, exhib. cat. Cologne 1981.

WALTER KÖNGETER
*1906 Düsseldorf–1969 Düsseldorf

Until 1930 studied architecture with Paul Bonatz and Paul Schmitthenner at the Technische Hochschule Stuttgart, with a term at the Technische Hochschule Danzig
1931 Doctorate at the Technische Hochschule Stuttgart
Assistant to Paul Bonatz in Stuttgart
From 1935 worked as an architect in Düsseldorf; collaboration with Ernst Petersen
After 1945 councillor in Düsseldorf and head of the Buildings Department
1947–1954 Non-tenured professor at the Düsseldorf Art Academy
1954–1969 Professor of architecture at the Düsseldorf Art Academy
1964–1967 Deputy director of the Düsseldorf Art Academy

Rolf Crummenauer, 'Professor Dr. Ing. Walter Köngeter (1906–1969), Nachruf [obituary]', in: *Nachrichten, Bilder, Berichte 8*, Düsseldorf 1971, pp. 2–8.
Ernst Petersen and Walter Köngeter, *Siedlungen und Wohnhäuser für die Firmen Persil und Henkel 1950–1958*, Lilienhof [c.1958]. No. 3, *Archiv der Arbeitsgemeinschaft* series.
Walter Köngeter and Ernst Petersen, *Bauten für die Firma Henkel, 1950–1958*, Lilienhof [*c.*1958]. No. 4, *Archiv der Arbeitsgemeinschaft* series.
Walter Köngeter and Ernst Petersen, *Bauten und Entwürfe, 1936–1958*, Lilienhof, *c.*1958. No. 3, *Archiv der Arbeitsgemeinschaft* series.

KASPER (RUDOLF HANS) KÖNIG
*1943 Mettingen

1960s Studied in London and New York
1972–1976 Taught at the Nova Scotia College of Art and Design in Halifax
1976 Initiator of the Münster Sculpture Projects jointly with Klaus Bußmann
1985–1988 Professor of art and public relations at the Düsseldorf Art Academy
1988 Professor and 1989 rector of the Frankfurt Städelschule
1998 Binding Cultural Award
2000–2012 Director, Museum Ludwig, Cologne
2003 Commissioner for the exhibition in the Austrian Pavilion at the Venice Biennale
2005 Honorary doctorate, Nova Scotia College of Art and Design in Halifax
2009 Lifetime Achievement Award, Solomon R. Guggenheim Museums, New York

Walter Grasskamp, *Kasper König*, Cologne 2013. No. 13, *Energien – Synergien* series.
Susanne Pfeffer, *Klaus Bußmann im Gespräch mit Kasper König, anlässlich der Gesprächsreihe Alte Hasen im KW Institute for Contemporary Art, KUNST WERKE BERLIN e. V.*, Cologne 2011.
Kasper König (ed.), *Von hier aus. 2 Monate neue deutsche Kunst in Düsseldorf*, exhib. cat. Düsseldorf, Cologne 1984.

JANNIS KOUNELLIS
*1936 Piraeus

Until 1956 studied at the Athens Academy of Fine Arts
1956 Studied at the Accademia di Belle Arti in Rome
1972 Showed work at documenta 5 in Kassel
1972, 1978, 1980, 1984, and 1988 Showed work at the Venice Biennale
1978 V. Premio Pino Pascali Prize
1982 Showed work at documenta 7 in Kassel
1989 Art Award, NORD LB, Hannover
1993–2001 Professor of sculpture at the Düsseldorf Art Academy
1994 Oskar Kokoschka Prize, Vienna

Marc Scheps (ed.), *Jannis Kounellis. XXII Stations on an Odyssey 1969–2010*, Munich 2010.
Angela Schneider and Anke Daemgen (eds.), *Jannis Kounellis in der Neuen Nationalgalerie*, exhib. cat. Berlin, Ostfildern 2008.
Bruno Corà (ed.), *Jannis Kounellis. Atto unico, A cura di Bruno Corà*, Milan 2006.
Gloria Moure (ed.), *Jannis Kounellis. Works, Writings 1958–2000*, Barcelona 2001.

GEREON KREBBER
*1973 Oberhausen

1994–2000 Studied at the Düsseldorf Art Academy with Anthony Cragg and Hubert Kiecol
2000–2002 Royal College of Art, London
2003–2008 Lecturer at the University of East London
2009 Wilhelm Lehmbruck grant, Duisburg; Promotional Prize, State of North Rhine-Westphalia
2010–2011 Visiting professor of sculpture at the Hochschule für Bildende Künste Hamburg
Since 2012 professor in the Orientation Department at the Düsseldorf Art Academy

Gereon Krebber. Here Today, Gone Tomorrow, exhib. cat. Drogheda, Bielefeld 2011.
Marion Ackermann (ed.), *Gereon Krebber*, exhib. cat. Stuttgart 2008.
Stephan Mann, *Gereon Krebber. Sorrysorrysosorry*, exhib. cat. Goch/Essen/Leverkusen, Bielefeld 2009.
Viola Weigel (ed.), *Gereon Krebber. All That Is Solid Melts into Air*, exhib. cat. Wilhelmshaven, Bielefeld 2007.

NORBERT KRICKE
*1922 Düsseldorf–1984 Düsseldorf

1942–1945 Served in the armed forces
1946–1947 Studied at the Hochschule für Bildende Künste, Berlin, with Richard Scheibe
1959, 1964 Showed work at documenta II and III in Kassel
1964 Showed work with Joseph Fassbender in the German Pavilion at the Venice Biennale
1964–1981 Professor of sculpture at the Düsseldorf Art Academy
1971 Wilhelm Lehmbruck Prize, City of Duisburg
1971–1972 Deputy director of the Düsseldorf Art Academy
1972–1981 Director of the Düsseldorf Art Academy
1982 Honorary member of the Düsseldorf Art Academy

Roland Scotti (ed.), *Norbert Kricke. Raum, Linie*, exhib. cat. Appenzell, Göttingen 2012.
Stephan von Wiese and Sabine Kricke-Güse (eds.), *Norbert Kricke. Plastiken und Zeichnungen, eine Retrospektive*, exhib. cat. Düsseldorf 2006.
Volker Adolphs, *Norbert Kricke. Zeichnungen*, exhib. cat. Bonn/Braunschweig, Cologne 1995.
Jürgen Morschel (ed.), *Norbert Kricke*, exhib. cat. Stuttgart/Münster, Stuttgart 1976.
Norbert Kricke, exhib. cat. Duisburg/Düsseldorf, Stuttgart 1975.

DIETER KRIEG
*1937 Lindau am Bodensee–2005 Quadrath-Ichendorf

1958–1962 Studied at the Staatliche Akademie der Bildenden Künste Karlsruhe with HAP Grieshaber and Herbert Kitzel
1966 Deutscher Kunstpreis der Jugend (painting), Baden-Baden
1970 Art Prize, City of Darmstadt
1971–1972 Visiting teacher, Kunstakademie Karlsruhe
1975–1976 Visiting lecturer, Städelschule in Frankfurt am Main
1978 Showed work at the Venice Biennale, together with Ulrich Rückriem
1978–2002 Professor of painting at the Düsseldorf Art Academy
1985 Karl Ströher Prize, Frankfurt
1993 Hans Thoma Prize, State of Baden-Württemberg
2006 Posthumous award: Cologne Fine Arts Prize

Marion Ackermann (ed.), *Dieter Krieg. Fritten und Brillanten*, exhib. cat. Stuttgart, Bielefeld 2007.
Klaus Gerrit Friese (ed.), *Macht nichts. Dieter Krieg, Gezeichnete Bilder 2003–2005*, 2 vols., exhib. cat. Bochum/Rolandseck, Stuttgart 2006.
Margrit Brehm (ed.), *Dieter Krieg*, exhib. cat. Stuttgart 1999.
Johann-Karl Schmidt (ed.), *Dieter Krieg. Kunst ist der Zweck der Kunst*, Stuttgart 1999.
Klaus-Gerrit Friese (ed.), *Dieter Krieg. Arbeiten*, 2 vols., Stuttgart 1993.

MARKUS LÜPERTZ
*1941 Liberec

1948 Refugee in West Germany with his family
1956–1961 Studied with Laurens Goosens at the Werkkunstschule Krefeld
1960 Studied at the Düsseldorf Art Academy for one term
1970–1971 Villa Romana grant, Florence
1971 German Critics' Association Prize
1973 Visiting lecturer and 1974–1986 professor of painting at the Staatliche Akademie der Bildenden Künste Karlsruhe
1982 Showed work at documenta 7 in Kassel
1986–2009 Professor of painting at the Düsseldorf Art Academy
1988–2009 Rector of the Düsseldorf Art Academy
1994 Designed the seal of the Düsseldorf Art Academy
2006 Honorary doctorate, Kunstakademie Breslau
Since 2009 honorary senator, Düsseldorf Art Academy

Franz W. Kaiser, *Markus Lüpertz. In Divine Light/ Markus Lüpertz – in't god'lijk licht*, exhib. cat. The Hague 2011.
Klaus Albrecht Schröder (ed.), *Markus Lüpertz. Metamorphosen der Weltgeschichte*, exhib. cat. Vienna, Ostfildern 2010.
Markus Lüpertz. Hauptwege und Nebenwege. Eine Retrospektive, Bilder und Skulpturen von 1963 bis 2009, exhib. cat. Bonn, Cologne 2009.
Siegfried Gohr (ed.), *Markus Lüpertz*, exhib. cat. Munich 1997.
Armin Zweite (ed.), *Markus Lüpertz. Gemälde, Skulpturen*, exhib. cat. Düsseldorf, Ostfildern 1996.

PETER MICHAEL LYNEN
*1948 Aachen

1969–1973 Studied journalism and law at Mainz and Munich Universities
1973, 1976 First and second state law examinations
1976–1982 Worked at RWTH Aachen, Bonn University, and the Office for the Minister of Cultural Affairs in Bonn
1982–2008 Chancellor of the Düsseldorf Art Academy
1990 Honorary doctorate (Dr phil. h.c.), Robert-Schumann-Hochschule Düsseldorf
2000 Doctorate (Dr iur.) at the Law Faculty of Cologne University
Since 2005 (part-time) and 2008 (full-time) professor at the Hochschule für Musik und Tanz in Cologne and head of the Zentrum für Internationales Kunstmanagement (CIAM) with fellowship as professor of the Düsseldorf Art Academy since 2008
Since 2009 member of the Nordrhein-Westfälische Akademie der Wissenschaften und der Künste, Düsseldorf, and secretary of the class for the arts (vice president of the NRW-Akademie)

Peter M. Lynen, *Kunstrecht 1–3*, 3 vols., Wiesbaden 2013
Peter M. Lynen, 'Kommentar zum Kunsthochschulgesetz NRW', in: Dieter Leuze and Volker Epping (eds.), *HG NRW*, loose-leaf compilation, Bielefeld 2008–2010
Peter M. Lynen, *Rundfunk als Hochschulaufgabe*, Munich 2000
Peter M. Lynen, *Kunst im Recht*, Düsseldorf 1994

FERDINAND MACKETANZ
*1902 Wyganow–1970 Laas

1923–1929 Studied at the Düsseldorf Art Academy; in Heinrich Campendonk's master class
1942 Stayed at Höri on Lake Constance; his Düsseldorf studio was destroyed by bombs
1950–1968 Professor of fine art painting at the Düsseldorf Art Academy
Memberships: Junges Rhineland, Rhenish Secession, later New Rhenish Secesion, and Baden Secession

Vanessa Sondermann, 'Ferdinand Macketanz 1902–1970', in: Siegfried Gohr (ed.), *Bestandskatalog. Akademie-Galerie – Die Neue Sammlung 2005–2009*, Düsseldorf 2009, pp. 138f.
Hans-Dieter Mück, 'Ferdinand Macketanz', in: *Rückkehr der Moderne. Die erste Nachkriegs-Ausstellung verfemter deutscher Kunst, 1945–1995*, exhib. cat. Überlingen am Bodensee and elsewhere, Überlingen 1995, pp. 294f.
Leopold Zahn, *Künstler auf der Höri am Bodensee. Max Ackermann, Curth Georg Becker, Otto Dix, Erich Heckel, Walter Herzger, Hans Kindermann, Helmuth Macke, Ferdinand Macketanz,*

Alexander Rath, Jean Paul Schmitz, R. Schnorrenberg, Konstanz 1956.

JOSEF (SEPP) MAGES
*1895 Kaiserslautern–1977 Kaiserslautern

1913–1920 Studied with Richard Riemerschmid and Joseph Wackerle at the Königliche Kunstgewerbeschule in Munich
1938–1939 Non-tenured teacher of architectural sculpture at the Düsseldorf Art Academy
1939–1961 Professor of sculpture at the Düsseldorf Art Academy

Sepp Mages, *Granitmale*, Munich 1962.
Werner Lindner et al., *Reihengrab und Gräberfeld in ihrer Gestaltung*, Kassel 1955. No. 4, *Friedhof und Denkmal* series.
Sepp Mages, 'Zur Architekturplastik', in: Heinrich Kamps (ed.), *Jahrbuch der Staatlichen Kunstakademie Düsseldorf 1948–1950*, Düsseldorf 1951, pp. 47–50.
Sepp Mages et al., *Grabmale. Steinwerke Rupp und Moeller*, 3 vols., Karlsruhe 1925–1928.

HERMANN JOSEF MAHLBERG
*1938 Cologne

1958 Studied German language and literature, philosophy, and art history at Cologne University
1958–1962 Studied art teaching at state schools at the Düsseldorf Art Academy with Otto Coester, Kurt Arnscheidt, and Günter Grote
1960–1963 Studied German language and literature, geography, and art history at Cologne University
1970–1973 Academic assistant at the Pädagogische Hochschule Rheinland, Wuppertal branch, and doctorate at Cologne University
1973–1974 Professor of art teaching methodology at the Düsseldorf Art Academy
1974–1984 Professor of art teaching methodology at the Pädagogische Hochschule Rheinland, Neuss branch; taught at the Düsseldorf Art Academy until 1976
1984–1985 Professor of art teaching at state schools at the Bergische Universität Gesamthochschule Wuppertal
1986 Founder-director of the Research Centre for the History of Architecture and the Preservation of Historic Monuments at the Bergische Universität Wuppertal

Hermann J. Mahlberg and Hella Nußbaum, *Skulpturenpark Waldfrieden in Wuppertal*, Wuppertal 2011.
Hella Nußbaum (ed.), *Impuls und Begegnung, Zeichnung, Malerei, Skulptur. Hermann J. Mahlberg*, exhib. cat. Solingen-Gräfrath, Wuppertal 2001.
Hermann J. Mahlberg, *Schloß Morsbroich in Leverkusen. Vom Rittersitz zum Avantgarde-Museum*, Wuppertal 1995.
Hermann J. Mahlberg, 'Zur Diskussion einer Curriculum-Revision im Fache Kunst', *Kunstpädagogik*, No. 74: *Konzepte, Aspekte, Marginalien, Festschrift für Reinhard Pfennig*, Ratingen 1974, pp. 169–180.

OLIVER MARCHART
*1968 Vienna

Studied philosophy at Vienna University, as well as political theory and discourse analysis at the University of Essex
1999 Doctorate at Vienna University
2001–2002 Academic adviser and head of the Education Project at documenta 11
2001–2006 Academic assistant at the Institute for Media Studies, Basel University
2003 Doctorate at the University of Essex
2006–2012 Professorship from the Schweizerisches Nationalfonds at the Socological Seminar, Luzern University
Since 2012 professor of sociology at the Düsseldorf Art Academy

Oliver Marchart, *Die politische Differenz. Zum Denken des Politischen bei Nancy, Lefort, Badiou, Laclau und Agamben*, Berlin 2010.
Oliver Marchart, *Cultural Studies*, Konstanz 2008.
Oliver Marchart, *Hegemonie im Kunstfeld. Die documenta-Ausstellungen dX, D11, d12 und die Politik der Biennalisierung*, Cologne 2008. No. 2, *Nbk-Diskurs* series.
Oliver Marchart, *Techno-Kolonialismus. Theorie und imaginäre Kartographie von Kultur und Medien*, Vienna 2004.

EWALD MATARÉ
*1887 Aachen–1965 Meerbusch

1905–1907 Private lessons with the sculptor Karl Kraus and the painter Eugen Klinkenberg in Aachen
1907–1914 Studied at the Hochschule der Bildenden Künste in Berlin
1912 In Arthur Kampf's master class
1914 Pupil of Lovis Corinth's, Silver Medal, Berlin Akademie der Künste
1918 Member of the November Group in Berlin
1932 Professor of sculpture at the Düsseldorf Art Academy
1933 Dismissed by the National Socialists
1937 His art classified as degenerate, forbidden to paint and exhibit
1945–1946 Reappointed professor and acting director of the Düsseldorf Art Academy
1945–1957 Professor of sculpture at the Düsseldorf Art Academy
1953 Grand Art Prize, State of North Rhine-Westphalia
1955 Gold Medal, Milan Triennale
1957 Stephan Lochner Medal, City of Cologne
1958 Grand Order of Merit of the Federal Republic of Germany

Siegfried Gohr and Vanessa Sondermann, *Ewald Mataré in Düsseldorf und Umgebung*, Düsseldorf 2009.
Siegfried Gohr (ed.), *Ewald Mataré. Eine Werkübersicht*, exhib. cat. Düsseldorf 2005.
Sabine Maja Schilling, *Ewald Mataré. Das plastische Werk. Werkverzeichnis*, 2nd edn, Cologne 1994.
Sonja Mataré, *Ewald Mataré. Zeichnungen. Werkverzeichnis*, Kleve 1992.
Sonja Mataré, *Ewald Mataré. Holzschnitte. Werkverzeichnis*, Kleve 1990.
Anna Klapheck (ed.), *Ewald Mataré. Aquarelle 1920–1956, mit einem Werkverzeichnis von Ulrike Köcke*, Munich 1983.

RITA MCBRIDE
*1960 Des Moines, Iowa

1982 Bard College, Annandale-on-Hudson, New York
1987 Californian Institute of the Arts, Valencia
1991 Scholarship American Academy in Rome
1999 Berlin Artists' Programme, German Academic Exchange Service
1999–2000 Visiting professor, Munich Academy of Fine Arts
2002 John Simon Guggenheim Memorial Foundation grant
Since 2003 professor of sculpture at the Düsseldorf Art Academy
Since 2013 rector of the Düsseldorf Art Academy

Dieter Schwarz, *Rita McBride. Previously*, exhib. cat. Winterthur, Düsseldorf 2010.
David Gray (ed.), *Rita McBride. Public Works, A Field Manual by Mark von Schlegell*, exhib. cat. Mönchengladbach, Cologne 2008.
Kunstmuseum Liechtenstein (ed.), *Gina Ashcraft. Nackt kam der Fremde*, exhib. cat. Vaduz 2002.
Dominique van den Boogerd, *Rita McBride. 472 New Positions*, exhib. cat. Tilburg 2001.
Matthias Winzen (ed.), *Werkshow. Rita McBride*, exhib. cat. Baden-Baden/Aachen, Cologne 2000.

LUCY MCKENZIE
*1977 Glasgow

1995–1999 Studied at the Duncan of Jordanstone College of Art and Design in Dundee
1998 Studied at the Staatliche Akademie der Bildenden Künste Karlsruhe
2007–2008 Studied at the Van der Kelen-Logelain Institut Supérieur de Peinture in Brussels
2011–2013 Supply professor of painting at the Düsseldorf Art Academy

Catriona Duffy and Lucy McEachen (eds.), *The Inventors of Tradition. An Independent Project Conceived by Beca Lipccombe. Lucy Mckenzie*, exhib. cat. Glasgow, Cologne 2011.
Julia Friedrich (ed.), *Lucy McKenzie. Editionen*, exhib. cat. Cologne 2010.
Chêne de weekend. Lucy McKenzie, 2006–2009, exhib. cat. Cologne and elsewhere, Cologne 2009.
Brian Eno. Lucy McKenzie, exhib. cat. Aachen, Frankfurt am Main 2004.
Lucy McKenzie. Deathwatch, exhib. cat. Eindhoven 2004.

CHRISTIAN MEGERT
*1936 Bern

1952–1956 Trained at the Kunstgewerbeschule in Bern
Co-founder of the group of artists known as Nouvelle École Européene (N. E. E.) in Lausanne
1961 Wrote the manifesto *Ein neuer Raum*
1968 Showed work at documenta 4 in Kassel
Since 1974 has designed public spaces and realised large works of sculpture in stone
1976–2001 Professor of integration, fine art, and architecture at the Düsseldorf Art Academy

Christian Megert. A New Space, exhib. cat. London 2012.
Tobias Hoffmann (ed.), *Christian Megert. Retrospektive*, exhib. cat. Ingolstadt, Bielefeld 2009.
Christian Megert, *Werke von 1977–1984, Skulpturen, Modelle, Objekte*, Schwäbisch Gmünd 1984.
Christian Megert, *Werke 1956–1978, Bilder, Objekte, Zeichnungen*, exhib. cat. Düsseldorf 1979.
Christian Megert and Claus Bremer, *Warum arbeitet Christian Megert mit nichts als Spiegeln?*, Bern 1973.

GEORG MEISTERMANN
*1911 Solingen–1990 Cologne

1928–1933 Studied with Werner Heuser, Heinrich Nauen, and Ewald Mataré at the Düsseldorf Art Academy
From 1933 forbidden to paint and show work
1949 Karl Ernst Osthaus Prize of the City of Hagen
1950 Showed work at the Venice Biennale
1951 Cultural Award, City of Wuppertal
1952 Stephan Lochner Medal, City of Cologne
1953 Head of the class for fine art graphics at the Frankfurt Städelschule

1955 Grand Art Prize, State of North Rhine-Westphalia
1955–1960 Professor of fine art and monumental painting at the Düsseldorf Art Academy
1959 Grand Order of Merit of the Federal Republic of Germany
1960–1976 Professor at the Staatliche Akademie der Bildenden Künste Karlsruhe
1967–1972 President of the Deutscher Künstlerbund (member since 1950)
1986 Honorary member of the Düsseldorf Art Academy
1989 State Award, State of North Rhine-Westphalia
1990 Order of Merit of the Federal Republic of Germany with Star and Shoulder Sash

Ralph Melcher (ed.), *Georg Meistermann. Die 50er Jahre*, exhib. cat. Saarbrücken 2007.
Justinus Maria Calleen (ed.), *Georg Meistermann. Druckgraphiken, Zeichnungen, Glasfenster-Kartons, Glasbilder, Ölgemälde*, 2nd edn, exhib. cat. Wittlich 1996.
Werner Schäfke (ed.), *Georg Meistermann. Malerei*, exhib. cat. Cologne 1991.
Karl Ruhrberg (ed.), *Georg Meistermann. Monographie und Werkverzeichnis*, Cologne 1991.
Georg Meistermann, *Die Kirchenfenster*, Freiburg 1986.

GERHARD MERZ
*1947 Mammendorf

1969–1973 Studied at the Munich Academy of Fine Arts; in Rudi Tröger's master class
1977–1992 Showed work at documentas 6, 7, 8, and DOCUMENTA IX in Kassel
1983 Arnold Bode Prize of the City of Kassel
1990–2005 Professor of painting at the Düsseldorf Art Academy
1997 Showed work at the Venice Biennale jointly with Katharina Sieverding
2004–2012 Professor of painting and graphic arts at the Munich Academy of Fine Arts

Karlheinz Stierle and Gerhard Merz, *Gerhard Merz.'Château de la pureté'*, exhib. cat. Berlin, Düsseldorf 2011.
Ute Riese (ed.), *Gerhard Merz. '... diese Gipfel haben nichts Lebendiges erzeugt und nichts Lebendiges verschlungen ...' Johann Wolfgang von Goethe 'Über den Granit'*, exhib. cat. Gießen, Düsseldorf 2010.
Gerhard Merz, *Sinopia*, Düsseldorf 2010.
Gerhard Merz, *Menninge. Elfenbeinschwarz, Cobaltgrün, Lichter Ocker*, Düsseldorf 2008.
Gerhard Merz, 2 vols., exhib. cat. Bregenz, Düsseldorf 2007.
Gertrude Stein, *Le chef d'œuvre inconnu. Gerhard Merz*, exhib. cat. Toulouse, Düsseldorf 2005.

ALFRED HERMANN MUNDHENK
*1910 Düsseldorf–1997 Kronenburg (?)

1929–1935 Studied classical languages and German at Cologne, Bonn, and Tübingen Universities
1935–1937 Teacher on probation for higher secondary schools, then probationary schoolmaster, mainly in Rheydt
1940–1946 Served in the armed forces; internment as an American prisoner of war
1946 Academic assistant at the Luther Academy in Göttingen
1947 Tenured state school teacher at Prinz-Georg-Schule, Düsseldorf
1955 Tenured senior teacher, 1962 head of the Latin Department at the Luisenschule, Düsseldorf
1963–1966 Fixed-term teacher and 1966–1974 professor of education at the Düsseldorf Art Academy
1974–1975 Teacher of education at the Düsseldorf Art Academy

Alfred Mundhenk, *Walthers Zuhörer und andere Beiträge zur Dichtung der Stauferzeit*, Würzburg 1993.
Alfred Mundhenk, 'Die Gunst der Natur. Kants Begriff und Deutung des Naturschönen', *Deutsche Vierteljahrsschrift für Literaturwissenschaft und Geistesgeschichte*, No. 57, 1983, pp. 366–398.
Alfred Mundhenk, *Der bildnerische Unterricht und das System unserer Schulbildung*, Düsseldorf 1972.
Alfred Mundhenk, 'Walthers Selbstbewußtsein', *Deutsche Vierteljahrsschrift für Literaturwissenschaft und Geistesgeschichte*, No. 37, 1963, pp. 406–438.

JOHANNES MYSSOK
*1966 Bielefeld

1987 Studied art history, philosophy, and Romance languages and literature at Heinrich-Heine Universität, Düsseldorf
1996 Academic employee in the Phototheque at the German Art Historical Institute in Florence
1996 Doctorate at the Westfälische Wilhelms-Universität, Münster
1998–2004 Academic assistant in the Institute for Art History at the Westfälische Wilhelms-Universität, Münster
2002–2003 Research grant for the German Study Centre in Venice; postdoctorate at the Westfälische Wilhelms-Universität, Münster
2004–2009 Senior academic assistant in the Institut for Art History at the Westfälische Wilhelms-Universität, Münster
Since 2009 professor of modern art at the Düsseldorf Art Academy
Since 2013 vice chancellor of the Düsseldorf Art Academy

Johannes Myssok, *Deutsche Künstler in Rom um August Kestner und Bertel Thorvaldsen. Das Rehberg-Album*, Münster 2012.
Johannes Myssok, 'The Gipsoteca of Possagno. From Artist's Studio to Museum', in: Christopher R. Marshall (ed.), *Sculpture and the Museum*, Farnham 2011, pp. 15–37.
Johannes Myssok, *Antonio Canova. Die Erneuerung der klassischen Mythen in der Kunst um 1800*, Petersberg 2007. No. 48, *Studien zur internationalen Architektur- und Kunstgeschichte* series.
Johannes Myssok, *Bildhauerische Konzeption und plastisches Modell in der Renaissance*, Münster 1999. No. 8, *Beiträge zur Kunstgeschichte des Mittelalters und der Renaissance* series.

NAM JUNE PAIK
*1932 Seoul–2006 Miami Beach

1956 Doctorate in aesthetics, Tokyo University
Studied music, art history, and philosophy at Munich University and music at the conservatories in Freiburg and Cologne
1958–1961 Worked in the Studio for Electronic Music, Westdeutscher Rundfunk (WDR) in Cologne
Member of the Fluxus movement
1979–1995 Professor of film and video at the Düsseldorf Art Academy
1981 Will Grohmann Prize, Akademie der Künste, Berlin
1987 Member of the Academy of the Arts, Berlin
1989 Kurt Schwitters Prize, Hannover
1991 Kaiserring, City of Goslar
1998 Kyoto Prize
2001 Wilhelm Lehmbruck Prize, Duisburg

John G. Hanhardt and Ken Hakuta, *Nam June Paik. Global Visionary*, exhib. cat. Washington, DC, London 2013.
Susanne Rennert (ed.), *Nam June Paik*, exhib. cat. Düsseldorf/Liverpool, Ostfildern 2010.
Dorothea Brunialti (ed.), *Nam June Paik. Exposition of Music, Electronic Television Revisited*, exhib. cat. Vienna, Cologne 2009.
John G. Hanhardt, *The Worlds of Nam June Paik*, exhib. cat. New York 2000.
Nam June Paik, *Niederschriften eines Kulturnomaden. Aphorismen, Briefe, Texte*, Cologne 1992.

ELLEN NEUMANN
*1920 Zorge–1999 Koblenz

Studied at Breslau and Innsbruck Universities
Attended the art academies in Dresden and Düsseldorf
Examinations in teaching art at state schools at the Düsseldorf Art Academy
From 1948 art teacher at several state higher secondary schools
1962–1963 Taught methodology at the Düsseldorf Art Academy
1963–1982 Professor of teaching art at state middle schools at the Düsseldorf Art Academy

Perspektiven. Schüler der Düsseldorfer Kunstakademie stellen ihre Arbeiten vor, aus den Klassen der Professoren Rolf Crummenauer, Ellen Neumann et al., exhib. cat. Düsseldorf 1979.

WALTER NIKKELS
*1940 Lobith-Tolkamer

1956–1960 Studied decorative and applied arts at the Fine Arts Academy in Rotterdam
1961–1962 Studied at the Munich Academy of Fine Arts, Munich
1964 Worked in the production division of the Rotterdam University Press
1966 Grant for a year's study at the Accademia di Belle Arti di Brera, Milan
1975–1987 Worked with Rudi Fuchs for the Van Abbemuseum, Eindhoven
1978 Design for the renovation of the Dordrecht Museum
1979–1984 Lecturer at the Fine Arts Academy in Rotterdam
1981 H. N. Werkman Prize, Amsterdam Fonds voor de Kunst
1982 Architect of documenta 7 in Kassel
1985–2007 Professor of design, book design, and typography at the Düsseldorf Art Academy
1989 Charles Nypels Prize, Maastricht
1989–1997 Designed the renovation and interiors of the Museum Kurhaus Kleve
2006–2012 Extension and new building, Museum Kurhaus Kleve

Walter Nikkels and Wigger Bierma, *Walter Nikkels. Depicted/Afgebeeld/Abgebildet*, Amsterdam/Stuttgart 2013.
Christoph Dohse (ed.), *Walter Nikkels. Ränder/Rahmen, Über das Buch von morgen*, Reutlingen 2008.
Michael Zöllner (ed.), *Walter Nikkels. Der Raum des Buches*, Cologne 1998.
Catalogues designed by Walter Nikkels:
Piet Mondrian 1872–1944, exhib. cat. The Hague/Washington/New York, Bern 1995.
Siegfried Gohr and Johannes Gachnang, *Bilderstreit. Widerspruch, Einheit und Fragment in der Kunst seit 1960*, exhib. cat. Cologne 1989.

MARCEL ODENBACH
*1953 Cologne

1974–1979 Studied architecture, art history, and semiotics at the Technische Hochschule Aachen
1977 Co-founded Alternative Television ATV with Ulrike Rosenbach and Klaus vom Bruch
Since 1992 professor at the Staatliche Hochschule für Gestaltung in Karlsruhe and the Kunsthochschule für Medien in Cologne
Since 2010 professor of video and film at the Düsseldorf Art Academy

Hubert Klocker (ed.), *Marcel Odenbach. Schutzräume*, exhib. cat. Vienna, Cologne 2013.
Marcel Odenbach. Stille Bewegungen, Tranquil Motions, exhib. cat. Danzig and elsewhere, Ostfildern 2013.
Marcel Wulf Herzogenrath (ed.), *Marcel Odenbach. Das im Entwischen Erwischte, Pläne 1975–1983/ Caught While Escaping, Plans 1975–1983*, exhib. cat. Bremen, Cologne 2008.
Vanessa Joan Müller and Nicolaus Schafhausen, *Marcel Odenbach. Blenden/Blinds*, exhib. cat. Frankfurt am Main/Innsbruck, New York 2002.
Udo Kittelmann (ed.), *Marcel Odenbach. Ach, wie gut, daß niemand weiß*, exhib. cat. Cologne 1999.

ALBERT OEHLEN
*1954 Krefeld

1978–1981 Studied with Claus Böhmler and Sigmar Polke at the Hochschule für Bildende Künste in Hamburg
2000–2009 Professor of painting at the Düsseldorf Art Academy

Achim Hochdörfer (ed.), Albert Oehlen. Malerei, artist's book and exhib. cat. Vienna, Cologne 2013.
Stephan Berg (ed.), *Albert Oehlen. Terpentin*, exhib. cat. Bonn, Ostfildern 2012.
Stefan Ratibor (ed.), *Albert Oehlen*, exhib. cat. New York 2012.
Annette Südbeck (ed.), *Albert Oehlen. Secession*, exhib. cat. Vienna, Cologne 2005.
Albert Oehlen, *Peintures 1980–2004/Malerei 1980–2004*, exhib. cat. Lausanne and elsewhere, Zurich 2004.

LAURIDS ORTNER
*1941 Linz

1959–1965 Studied at the Technische Universität in Vienna
1972 Showed work with his brother, Manfred, as the architects' collective Haus-Rucker-Co at documenta 5 in Kassel
1976–1987 Professor at Kunsthochschule Linz
1987 Founded the architecture practice Ortner Architekten in Düsseldorf
1987–2009 Professor of architecture at the Düsseldorf Art Academy
1990 Founded the architecture practice Ortner & Ortner Baukunst in Vienna
1992 Disbanded the collective Haus-Rucker-Co

Laurids Ortner and Manfred Ortner, *O & O. Malerei aus dichtem Staub*, Cologne 2010.
Laurids Ortner and Manfred Ortner, *Ortner & Ortner. Baukunst vom Tag*, Cologne 2009.
Laurids Ortner and Manfred Ortner, *Ortner & Ortner. Bauten für europäische Kultur*, Basel 2008.
Laurids Ortner and Manfred Ortner, *Wörterbuch der Baukunst*, Basel 2001.
Edith Schweiger (ed.), *Ortner & Ortner Baukunst*, exhib. cat. Linz, Cologne 1993.

TEO OTTO
*1904 Remscheid–1968 Frankfurt am Main

1923–1926 Studied at the Kunstakademie Kassel
1924 Stage set designer at the Stadttheater in Kassel
1926–1927 Studied in Paris and at the Bauhochschule Weimar
1927–1931 Stage set desginer at the Staatstheater in Berlin
1931–1933 Head of stage design at the Staatstheater in Berlin
1933 Dismissed and emigrated to Switzerland
From 1934 head stage set designer at the Zurich Schauspielhaus
1947 Gold Medal at the Stage Design Exhibition in Solingen
1952–1957 Taught stage set design at the Staatlichen Werkakademie Kassel
1957 Awarded the Goethe Medal in Kassel; member of the Academy of the Arts, Berlin
1959–1968 Professor of stage set design at the Düsseldorf Art Academy
1963 Austrian Cross of Honour, 1st Class, for Art and Science
1964 Art Prize of the City of Zurich, Grand Order of Merit of the Federal Republic of Germany
1967 Co-director Zurich Schauspielhaus

Rainer Springhorn (ed.), *Teo Otto ... ein Mann der Zauberei (Max Frisch). Bühnenbilder und Malerei aus der Sammlung Höhmann-Müller*, exhib. cat. Detmold 2006.
Teo Otto (1904–1968). Der Bühnenbildner, der Maler, der Lehrer, exhib. cat. Düsseldorf, Bottrop 2000.
Teo Otto, *An die Neugeborenen und andere Texte*, Stierstadt im Taunus 1966. No. 14, *Passgänge* series.
Teo Otto, *Meine Szene. Autobiographie, mit einem Vorwort von Friedrich Dürrenmatt*, Cologne 1965.
Teo Otto, *Nie wieder. Tagebuch in Bildern, mit einem Vorwort von Bertolt Brecht*, Berlin 1949.

OTTO PANKOK
*1893 Mühlheim an der Ruhr–1966 Wesel

1912–1913 Studied at the Düsseldorf Art Academy and the Großherzoglich-Sächsischen Hochschule für bildende Kunst in Weimar
1919 Member of the artists' association Junges Rheinland
1937 Forbidden to paint and show work
1947–1958 Professor of graphic arts at the Düsseldorf Art Academy
1953 Graphics Prize, São Paulo Biennale; member of the German Academy of Arts
1965 Ruhr Prize for Art and Science, Mülheim an der Ruhr

Jutta Moster-Hoos et al. (eds.), *Otto Pankok. Von der Landschaft gezeichnet, frühe Kohlezeichnungen*, exhib. cat. Oldenburg 2013. No. 21, *Veröffentlichungen des Horst-Janssen-Museums Oldenburg* series.
Eva Pankok et al. (eds.), *Otto Pankok. Sinti-Portraits 1931 bis 1949. Kohlebilder, Druckgrafik, Plastik*, exhib. cat. Heidelberg, Berlin 2008.
Otto Pankok, *Werkverzeichnis*, 4 vols., Düsseldorf 1985–2002.
Bernhard Mensch (ed.), *Otto Pankok 1893–1966. Retrospektive zum 100. Geburtstag*, exhib. cat. Mülheim an der Ruhr/Drevenack, Oberhausen 1993.

A. R. PENCK (RALF WINKLER)
*1939 Dresden

1953–1954 Painting and drawing instruction from Jürgen Böttcher in Dresden
1955–1956 Draughtsman's apprenticeship at the Deutsche Werbe- und Anzeigengesellschaft in Dresden; not admitted to the Dresden Hochschule für Bildende Künste
1969 His pictures confiscated by the State Security Police, not admitted to the Society of Fine Artists in the GDR
1971 Founder member of the group of artists known as Lücke
1972–1992 Showed work at documentas 5 and 7 as well as DOCUMENTA IX in Kassel
1975 Will Grohmann Prize, Akademie der Künste, Berlin
1980 Moved to West Germany
1981 Rembrandt Prize, Johann Wolfgang von Goethe Foundation, Basel
1985 Art Prize Aachen
1989–2005 Professor of fine art graphics at the Düsseldorf Art Academy

Siegfried Gohr (ed.), *A. R. Penck. Eine Retrospektive*, exhib. cat. Düsseldorf 2013.
Carsten Ahrens (ed.), *A. R. Penck. Deutschland, Werke aus der Sammlung Böckmann und anderen Sammlungen*, exhib. cat. Bremen 2009.
Gisbert Porstmann and Johannes Schmidt (eds.), *Sein und Wesen. Der unbekannte A. R. Penck, Werke aus der Sammlung Jürgen Schweinebraden*, exhib. cat. Dresden, Munich 2008.
Ingrid Pfeiffer and Max Hollein (eds.), *A. R. Penck Retrospektive*, exhib. cat. Frankfurt am Main and elsewhere, Düsseldorf 2007.
Dieter Brunner et al., *A. R. Penck. Erinnerung, Modell, Denkmal, Memory, Model, Memorial*, exhib. cat. Heilbronn and elsewhere, Heidelberg 1999.

KARL-HEINZ PETZINKA
*1956 Bocholt

Studied architecture at the RWTH Aachen
Since 1988 taught at the Universität Gesamthochschule Wuppertal
1994 Founded architecture practice Petzinka Pink Architekten with Thomas Pink
1994–1998 Professor at the Technischen Universität Darmstadt
2007 Visiting professor at the RWTH Aachen and Columbia University, New York
2007 Art director for the thematic field 'City of Possibilities' of the Ruhr.2010 GmbH, European Cultural Capital
Since 2008 professor of architecture at the Düsseldorf Art Academy

Karl-Heinz Petzinka et al. (eds.), *Ruhrlights. Twilight Zone 2010, Hagen/Dortmund, Witten, Hattingen, Bochum, Essen, Mülheim an der Ruhr, Duisburg*, Ostfildern 2010.
Karl-Heinz Petzinka and Katja Aßmann, 'Kulturhauptstadt Europas Ruhr.2010. Eine Metropole erfindet sich neu', in: *Emscherkunst. Eine Insel für die Kunst*, exhib. cat. Essen, Ostfildern 2010, pp. 23–35.
Georg Giebeler et al. (eds.), *Atlas Sanierung. Instandhaltung, Umbau, Ergänzung*, Basel 2008.
Johannes Busmann (ed.), *Technologische Architektur. Petzinka Pink Architekten*, Basel 2004.

ROBERT PUDLICH
*1905 Dortmund–1962 Düsseldorf

1924–1926 Studied at the Düsseldorf Art Academy
1928 Grand Art Prize, City of Düsseldorf
Member of the Rhenish Secession, the Rheinischer Künstlerbund, and the Deutscher Künstlerbund
1939 Cornelius Prize, City of Düsseldorf
From 1947 stage set and costume designer for Gustaf Gründgens in Hamburg and Düsseldorf
1955–1962 Professor of painting and teaching art at state schools at the Düsseldorf Art Academy

Robert Pudlich. Frühe Werke 1928–1934, with photographs by Ma Pudlich, exhib. cat. Düsseldorf 1991.
Robert Pudlich. Ölbilder, Aquarelle, Graphik und Zeichnungen, exhib. cat. Düsseldorf 1983.
Werner Doede, *Robert Pudlich*, Recklinghausen 1968. No. 35, *Monographien zur rheinisch-westfälischen Kunst der Gegenwart* series.
Miguel de Cervantes Saavedra, *Leben und Taten des scharfsinnigen Edlen Don Quijote von La Mancha*, with images by Robert Pudlich, 2 vols., Bad Salzig 1951.

DAVID RABINOWITCH
*1943 Toronto

1963–1966 Studied English literature and science at the University of Western Ontario
1974–1975 Taught at Yale University
1984–2008 Professor of sculpture at the Düsseldorf Art Academy

Heinz Höfchen, *David Rabinowitch. The Piégros Editions*, exhib. cat. Kaiserslautern 2010.
Klaus Bußmann (ed.), *David Rabinowitch. Metrische (romanische) Konstruktionen*, exhib. cat. Münster/Westfalen, Munich 2000.
David Rabinowitch, *Die Konstruktion des Sehens. Zeichnungen mit farbigen Elementen 1972–1975*, Düsseldorf 1999.
Jochen Poetter (ed.), *David Rabinowitch. Werke 1967–1976*, exhib. cat. Baden-Baden, Stuttgart-Bad Cannstatt 1992.
Catrina Neiman (ed.), *David Rabinowitch. Sculptures 1963–1970*, with selected drawings, plans, and notes, Bielefeld 1987.

JÓRUNN RAGNARSDÓTTIR
*1957 Akureyri

1982 Finished studying architecture at Stuttgart University
Worked with Arno Lederer, founded a joint architecture practice
Since 1992 has worked with Marc Oei in the architecture practice Lederer + Ragnarsdóttir + Oei, Stuttgart
1992–1993 Worked for Boris Podrecca at Stuttgart University
2010–2012 Professor of architecture at the Düsseldorf Art Academy

Jórunn Ragnarsdóttir, 'Funktion und Ästhetik. Funktion und Ökonomie, Gedanken zur Schularchitektur', in: Kunibert Bering and Rolf Niehoff (eds.), *Impulse. Kunstdidaktik 12*, Oberhausen 2012.
Lederer + Ragnarsdóttir + Oie 1, Berlin 2012.
Wolfgang Bachmann (ed.), *Lederer, Ragnarsdóttir, Oei*, Munich 1995.
Jórunn Ragnarsdóttir and Arno Lederer, *Wohnen heute/Housing Today*, Stuttgart 1992.

ERICH REUSCH
*1925 Lutherstadt Wittenberg

1947–1953 Studied sculpture and architecture with Georg Leowald, Richard Scheibe, and Hans Uhlmann at the Hochschule für Bildende Künste, Berlin
From 1953 worked for a Düsseldorf architecture practice
1973–1975 Took over a class in fine art at the Düsseldorf Art Academy
1975–1990 Professor of integration, fine art, and architecture at the Düsseldorf Art Academy
1985–1987 Deputy director of the Düsseldorf Art Academy
2006 Konrad von Soest Prize, Landschaftsverband Westfalen-Lippe
Since 2010 honorary member of the Düsseldorf Art Academy

Alexander von Berswordt-Wallrabe (ed.), *Erich Reusch. Der Raum ist das Ereignis/It Is the Space*, exhib. cat. Bochum, Düsseldorf 2012.
A. S. Wünkhaus (ed.), *Dezentral. Reusch*, Bielefeld 2011.
Erich Franz, *Neue Arbeiten aus der Vergangenheit. Reusch*, Bielefeld 2009.
Erich Reusch and Uwe Obier (eds.), *Erich Reusch. Malerei, Zeichnung, Arbeiten von 1954–2000*, exhib. cat. Lüdenscheid 2000.
Volker Adolphs and Christoph Schreier, *Erich Reusch. Arbeiten 1954–1998*, exhib. cat. Bonn 1998.

GUIDO REUTER
*1968 Mönchengladbach

Studied art history, philosophy, and media sciences at Heinrich-Heine-Universität, Düsseldorf
2000 Doctorate at Heinrich-Heine-Universität Düsseldorf
2000–2008 Academic assistant at the Seminar for Art History and postdoctorate at Heinrich-Heine-Universität, Düsseldorf
Since 2008 professor of recent and more recent art history at the Düsseldorf Art Academy

Guido Reuter, '"Using the Ground Not Just as a Base but as an Important Part of the Sculpture". Anthony Caros Abkehr vom Sockel in den Werken der frühen sechziger Jahre', in: Johannes Myssok and Guido Reuter (eds.), *Der Sockel in der Skulptur des 19. und 20. Jahrhunderts*, Cologne 2013, pp. 121–139. No. 30, *Studien zur Kunst* series.
Guido Reuter, 'Das Atelier im Werk von Matthias Weischer', in: Guido Reuter and Martin Schieder (eds.), *Inside/Outside. Das Atelier in der zeitgenössischen Kunst*, Petersberg 2012, pp. 72–81.
Guido Reuter, *Statue und Zeitlichkeit 1400–1800*, Petersberg 2012.
Guido Reuter, *Am Scheideweg der Hekate. Die Hekate-Bilder Ernst Wilhelm Nays und die Diskussion um die abstrakte Malerei nach 1945 in Deutschland*, Düsseldorf 2002. No. 4, *Düsseldorfer kunsthistorische Schriften* series.

GERHARD RICHTER
*1932 Dresden

1951–1956 Studied painting at the Hochschule der Bildenden Künste in Dresden, then admitted to the three-year Aspiring Artists Programme at the Academy
1961–1963 Studied at the Düsseldorf Art Academy with Ferdinand Macketanz and K. O. Götz et al.
1967 Visiting lecturer at the Hochschule für Bildende Künste Hamburg
1971–1994 Professor of painting at the Düsseldorf Art Academy
1972 Venice Biennale, German Pavilion
1982 Arnold Bode Prize, Kassel
1985 Oskar Kokoschka Prize, Vienna
1988 Kaiserring, City of Goslar; visiting professor at the Frankfurt Städelschule
1997 Venice Biennale, German Pavilion; Praemium Imperiale Prize for Painting, Tokyo
2000 State Prize, State of North Rhine-Westphalia
2001 Honorary doctorate, Louvain University
2010 Honorary member of the Düsseldorf Art Academy

Mark Godfrey et al. (eds.), *Gerhard Richter. Panorama*, exhib. cat. London/Berlin/Paris, Munich 2012.
Uwe M. Schneede (ed.), *Gerhard Richter. Bilder einer Epoche*, exhib. cat. Hamburg, Munich 2011.
Christine Mehring et al. (eds.), *Gerhard Richter. Early Work 1951–1972*, Los Angeles 2010.
Dietmar Elger (ed.), *Gerhard Richter. Text 1961 bis 2007, Schriften, Interviews, Briefe*, Cologne 2008.
Ulrich Wilmes (ed.), *Gerhard Richter. Abstrakte Bilder*, exhib. cat. Cologne/Munich, Ostfildern 2008.

KLAUS RINKE
*1939 Wattenscheid

1957–1960 Studied fine art painting at the Folkwangschule, Essen
1972 Promotional Prize for Fine Art, State of North Rhine-Westphalia
1974 Konrad von Soest Prize, Landschaftsverbands Westfalen-Lippe
1974–1977 Professor of painting at the Düsseldorf Art Academy
1977–2004 Professor of sculpture at the Düsseldorf Art Academy

Ursula Eisenbach (ed.), *Klaus Rinke. Gemacht, gedacht. Texte & Interviews, mit biographischen Daten, Ausstellungsverzeichnis & Bibliographie*, Düsseldorf 2004.
Hans-Werner Schmidt (ed.), *Klaus Rinke. Retro-Aktiv, Werkverzeichnis 1954–1991 der Malerei, Skulptur, Primärdemonstrationen, Fotografie und Zeichnungen ab 1980*, exhib. cat. Düsseldorf 1992.
Klaus Rinke, *Rinke Hand-Zeichner. Die autonomen Werke von 1957–1980*, exhib. cat. Stuttgart 1981.
Klaus Rinke, *Meine Plastik ist Zeichnung*, exhib. cat. Hamburg 1978.
Götz Adriani (ed.), *Klaus Rinke. Zeit, Raum, Körper, Handlungen*, exhib. cat. Tübingen, Cologne 1972.

RISSA (KARIN GÖTZ, NÉE MARTIN)
*1938 Rabenstein

1953 Moved to the Federal Republic of Germany
1959–1965 Studied with K. O. Götz at the Düsseldorf Art Academy
1969–1971 Assistant at the Düsseldorf Art Academy
1971–1975 Lecturer for teaching art at state schools at the Düsseldorf Art Academy
1975–2003 Professor of painting at the Düsseldorf Art Academy
1977 Co-founder of the Axiom group
2003–2007 Taught at the Düsseldorf Art Academy
2009 Order of Merit of the State of Rheinland-Pfalz, shared with K. O. Götz
2012 Honorary member of the Düsseldorf Art Academy

Walter Smerling (ed.), *Rissa. Gemälde und Zeichnungen*, exhib. cat. Duisburg, Bonn 2003.

Rolf Jessewitsch, *Rissa. Bilder 1966–1998*, exhib. cat. Solingen-Gräfrath 1999.
Wolfgang Zemter (ed.), *Rissa. Arbeiten auf Papier 1955–1998*, Bönen 1998.
Susanne Anna (ed.), *Rissa. Gemälde 1964–1994*, exhib. cat. Chemnitz, Düsseldorf 1994.
Rissa. Neue Bilder 1980–1985, exhib. cat. Dortmund 1985.

KARL THOMAS ROBASCHIK
*1914 Hirschberg, Silesia–1992 Staufen

After 1945 head of the Civil Engineering Office in Hamburg Altona District Authority
Appointed to the Central State Planning Office at the Building and Construction Authority
1962–1978 Professor of architecture at the Düsseldorf Art Academy

ARS-Arbeitsgemeinschaft für Raumplanung und Stadtentwicklung, Karl Thomas Robaschik et al., *Inden. Eine Studie über die räumlichen und strukturellen Möglichkeiten der Gemeinde*, Düsseldorf 1971.
Karl Thomas Robaschik et al., *Studie über die Altstadt Düsseldorf. Einkaufszentrum? Vergnügungs- oder Unterhaltungszentrum? Fragen der Altstadtgemeinschaft e. V. Düsseldorf*, Düsseldorf 1970.
Karl Thomas Robaschik, *Voraussetzungen, Möglichkeiten, Probleme der strukturellen und räumlich-funktionalen Ordnung der Raumnutzung im Bereich von Entwicklungsachsen, Landesplanerische Modelluntersuchung am Beispiel der Rheinachse zwischen den Räumen Wesel und Kleve-Emmerich*, Düsseldorf 1968.

DIETER (KARL-DIETRICH) ROTH (ALSO: DITER ROT)
*1930 Hannover–1998 Basel

1947–1951 Apprenticeship in commercial art with Friedrich Wüthrich in Bern
1950 Private lessons in lithography from Eugen Jordi in Kehsatz and an apprenticeship in typography with Jordi at the Gewerbeschule in Bern
1954 Kiefer-Hablitzel Foundation for Painting Prize, Bern
1958 Briefly taught at Yale University
1959 Graphic artist with the Geiry Corporation in New York
1960 William and Norma Copley Foundation Award
1964 Taught in the Architecture Department, Yale University
1965 Taught the graphic arts class at the Rhode Island School of Design for a year
1968 Showed work at documenta 4 in Kassel
1968–1969 Professor of graphic arts for teaching art at state schools at the Düsseldorf Art Academy
1969 Art Prize, City of Iserlohn
1977 Showed work at documenta 6 in Kassel
1979 Taught at the Munich Academy of Fine Arts and briefly at the Reykjavik Art School
1982 Showed work in the Swiss Pavilion at the Venice Biennale
1986 Charles Nypels Prize, Maastricht
1994 Grand Art Prize, Akademie der Künste, Berlin
1998 Multiple Prize, Düsseldorf

Beat Keusch (ed.), *Dieter Roth. Souvenirs*, exhib. cat. Stuttgart, Ostfildern 2011.
Dirk Dobke and Stephan Kunz (eds.), *Dieter Roth. Selbste*, exhib. cat. Aarau/Salzburg, Cologne 2011.
Theodora Vischer and Bernadette Walter (eds.), *Roth-Zeit. Eine Dieter-Roth-Retrospektive*, exhib. cat. Basel and elsewhere, Basel 2003.
Dirk Dobke (ed.), *Dieter Roth. Catalogue raisonné*, 3 vols., Cologne 2002–2004.
Ina Conzen, *Die Haut der Welt. Dieter Roth*, exhib. cat. Stuttgart, Cologne 2000.

ULRICH RÜCKRIEM
*1938 Düsseldorf

1957–1959 Stonemason's apprenticeship in Düren, then worked at the Cathedral workshop in Cologne
Studied at the Cologne Werkschulen with Professor Ludwig Gies
1973 Promotional Prize for Fine Art, State of North Rhine-Westphalia
1974 Professor of sculpture Hochschule für Bildende Künste Hamburg
1972–1992 Showed work at documentas 5, 7, 8, and DOKUMENTA IX in Kassel
1978 Showed work jointly with Dieter Krieg at the Venice Biennale
1984 Konrad von Soest Prize, Landschaftsverband Westfalen-Lippe
1984–1988 Professor of sculpture at the Düsseldorf Art Academy
1988 Professor at the Frankfurt Städelschule
1985 Arnold Bode Prize, Kassel
1998 Piepenbrock Prize for Sculpture, Berlin
2001 Grand Culture Prize, Sparkassen-Kulturstiftung Rheinland

Kunstgeschichtliches Institut, Ruhr-Universität Bochum (ed.), *Ulrich Rückriem. Arbeiten in North Rhine-Westphalia*, Bielefeld 2011.
Ulrich Rückriem. *Zeichnungen/Drawings*, Cologne 2011.
Jürgen Hohmeyer, *Ulrich Rückriem*, with catalogue of works, Munich 1988.
Hannelore Kersting (ed.), *Texte über Ulrich Rückriem 1964–1987*, exhib. cat. Düsseldorf and elsewhere, Düsseldorf 1987.
Klaus Bußmann et al., *Ulrich Rückriem. Skulpturen, Zeichnungen*, exhib. cat. Münster 1985.

THOMAS RUFF
*1958 Zell am Harmersbach

1977–1985 Studied with Bernd Becher at the Düsseldorf Art Academy; in Becher's master class
1985 Promotional Prize for Fine Art, State of North Rhine-Westphalia, and Jürgen Ponto Foundation Award
1990 Dorothea von Stetten Art Prize, Kunstmuseum Bonn
1992 Showed work at DOKUMENTA IX in Kassel
1995 Showed work with Katharina Fritsch and Martin Honert at the Venice Biennale
2000–2006 Professor of photography at the Düsseldorf Art Academy
2003 Hans Thoma Prize, Bern

Enwezor Okwui et al., *Thomas Ruff. Works 1979–2011*, exhib. cat. Munich 2012.
Melanie Bono (ed.), *Thomas Ruff. Stellar Landscapes*, exhib. cat. Münster, Heidelberg/Berlin 2011.
Gerald Matt (ed.), *Thomas Ruff. Oberflächen, Tiefen*, exhib. cat. Vienna 2009.
Thomas Ruff. Schwarzwald, Landschaft, exhib. cat. Freiburg, Nuremberg 2009.
Matthias Winzen (ed.), *Thomas Ruff. Fotografien 1979–heute*, exhib. cat. Baden-Baden, Cologne 2003.

ROLF (RUDOLF JOSEF) SACKENHEIM
*1921 Koblenz–2006 Düsseldorf

1940 Studied at the Meisterschule des deutschen Handwerks in Trier
1943 Began to study at the Staatliche Akademie der Bildenden Künste Karlsruhe
1947 Resumed studies in Karlsruhe with Karl Hubbuch
1952 In Otto Coester's master class at the Düsseldorf Art Academy
1958 Promotional Prize, Cornelius Prize of the City of Düsseldorf
1959 Art Prize Junger Westen
1960–1963 Visiting lecturer at the Werkkunstschule in Krefeld
1962–1965 Lecturer at the Düsseldorf Art Academy
1965–1984 Professor of fine arts graphics at the Düsseldorf Art Academy
1969–1970 and 1972–1977 Deputy director of the Düsseldorf Art Academy
Honorary member of the Kunstakademie Münster

Volker Rattemeyer and Renate Petzinger (eds.), *Rolf Sackenheim. Zeichnungen, Radierungen, Lithographien*, exhib. cat. Wiesbaden 2003.
Marcella van der Grinten (ed.), *Rolf Sackenheim. Zeichnungen 1946–87*, exhib. cat. Kleve 1991.
Irmgard Zepf (ed.), *Rolf Sackenheim. Skizzen, Notizen, Collagen, Druckgraphik. Arbeiten von 1975–1991*, exhib. cat. Düsseldorf 1991.
Patricia Moisan (ed.), *Rolf Sackenheim. Photographien von 1977–1987*, with accompanying texts, Düsseldorf 1988.
Hans Peter Thurn (ed.), *Rolf Sackenheim. Graphische Arbeiten 1950–1985*, with accompanying texts, Düsseldorf 1985.

BEATE SCHIFF
*1932 Berlin–1997 Düsseldorf

1947–1949 Studied at the Meisterschule für Kunsthandwerk in Berlin
1949–1954 Studied with Gustav Sincez and Alexander Gonda at the Hochschule für Bildende Künste in Berlin
1954–1955 Studied at the Düsseldorf Art Academy; in Ewald Mataré's master class
1960s Worked as a scientific draughtsman at the Marine Biological Laboratory in Naples
1965 Assistant to Karl Bobek
1966–1971 Taught a preliminary class for art teaching at state schools
1971–1972 Lecturer for sculpture at the Düsseldorf Art Academy
1972–1997 Professor of sculpture and teaching art at state schools at the Düsseldorf Art Academy

Medium Papier, contains *inter alia* works by Beate Schiff, Bergisch Gladbach 1982. No. 9, *Veröffentlichungen der Städtischen Galerie Zanders* series.
Alice von Richthofen, 'Die Kunst war ihr Lebensinhalt. Gedenkausstellung zu Ehren der Bildhauerin Beate Schiff', *Düsseldorfer Hefte* 43, No. 3, 1998, pp. 18f.

JAKOB HEINRICH SCHMIDT
*1897 Uetersen–1974 Kalkar

Studied art history at Kiel, Hamburg, Halle, and Munich Universities, taking a doctorate in 1924
1928–1935 Academic position at the Staatliche Museen Berlin
1935–1962 Professor of art history and head of the library at the Düsseldorf Art Academy
1935–1954 Deputy director of the Düsseldorf Art Academy
1954–1956 Acting head of the Düsseldorf Art Academy as deputy director

Jakob Heinrich Schmidt and Friedrich Pause, *Pieter Bruegels Dulle Griet. Bildnis einer psychisch Kranken*, Berlin 1967.
Jakob Heinrich Schmidt, 'Italienische Handzeichnungen des Barock der Sammlung Lambert Krahe in Düsseldorf', *Pantheon* 25, 1967, pp. 112–124.

Jakob Heinrich Schmidt, *Alfred Rethel 1816–1859*, Neuss 1959.
Jakob Heinrich Schmidt, *Oswald Achenbach*, Düsseldorf 1944.
Jakob Heinrich Schmidt, 'Zur Farbenlehre Goethes', *Zeitschrift für Kunstgeschichte* 1, 1932, pp. 109–124.

WILHELM SCHMURR
*1878 Hagen–1959 Düsseldorf

1894–1904 Studied at the Düsseldorf Art Academy with Peter Janssen, Arthur Kampf, and Eduard von Gebhardt; in Eduard Claus-Meyer's master class
1909 Founder member of the Sonderbund Westdeutscher Kunstfreunde und Künstler
Other memberships: Kunstverband Düsseldorf, Malkasten, Die Friedfertigen, Rhenish Secession, Westphalian Secession, Westdeutscher Künstlerbund, Düsseldorf Artists' Group
1927–1936 Professor of a drawing class at the Düsseldorf Art Academy
1936–1947 Professor of painting at the Düsseldorf Art Academy
1938 Showed work at the Venice Biennale

Vera Bachmann and Bernd Ernsting, *Alles Große ist still und ernst. Der Maler Wilhelm Schmurr, Biographie und Werkverzeichnis*, Cologne 2009. No. 18, *LETTER Schriften* series.
Uta Husmeier-Schirlitz (ed.), *Wilhelm Schmurr. Die Magie des Augenblicks, Retrospektive zum 50. Todestag*, exhib. cat. Neuss 2009.
Otto Brües, *Wilhelm Schmurr*, Cologne 1957. No. 7, *Monographien zur rheinisch-westfälischen Kunst der Gegenwart* series.

JOHANNES SCHÜTZ
*1950 Frankfurt am Main

1970–1974 Studied in Hamburg and Berlin, assistant to Wilfried Minks
1974 Stage set designer at the Schillertheater in Berlin and the Munich Kammerspiele
Head of stage design at the Schauspielhaus Bochum, from then on regular collaboration with the director Jürgen Gosch in Hamburg, Bochum, Düsseldorf, and Berlin
1992–1998 Professor in scenography at the Zentrum für Kunst und Medientechnologie, Karlsruhe
2007 Gold Medal at the Prague Quadriennial
2009 Berlin Theatre Prize, shared with Jürgen Gosch
2010 Nestroy Theatre Prize, Vienna
Since 2010 professor of stage design at the Düsseldorf Art Academy
2011 German Theatre Prize Der Faust

Johannes Schütz, *Bühnen 2000–2008*, Vol. 1, Nuremberg 2008.
Peter Iden (ed.), 'Johannes Schütz. Welches Theater – Das ist die Frage', in: *Warum wir das Theater brauchen*, Frankfurt am Main 1995, pp. 31–37.
Heinrich Klotz and Ludger Hünnekens (eds.), *Bühnenbild heute. Bühnenbild der Zukunft: Achim Freyer, Dieter Hacker, Johannes Schütz, Erich Wonder*, exhib. cat. Karlsruhe, Stuttgart 1993.

AXEL SCHULTES
*1943 Dresden

1963–1969 Studied at the Technische Universität Berlin
1972 Founded the architecture practice BJSS with Dietrich Bangert, Bernd Jansen, and Stefan Scholz
1992 Founded the architecture practice Axel Schultes Architekten with Charlotte Frank and Christoph Witt
1999 Concrete Architecture Prize
2003–2011 Professor of architecture at the Düsseldorf Art Academy

Axel Schultes and Charlotte Frank, *Bundeskanzleramt Berlin*, Stuttgart 2001.
Axel Schultes, *Kunstmuseum Bonn*, Berlin 1994.
Charlotte Frank (ed.), 'Axel Schultes', in: *Bangert, Jansen, Scholz, Schultes. Projekte 1985–1991*, Berlin 1992.

ANDREAS SCHULZE
*1955 Hannover

1976–1978 Studied at the Gesamthochschule in Kassel
1978–1983 Studied at the Düsseldorf Art Academy; in Dieter Krieg's master class
1997 Sprengel Prize for Fine Art, Hannover
Since 2009 professor of painting at the Düsseldorf Art Academy

Harald Falckenberg (ed.), *Andreas Schulze. Interieur*, exhib. cat. Hamburg/Düren, Cologne 2010.
Barbara Steiner (ed.), *Andreas Schulze*, Ostfildern 1997.
Andreas Schulze, exhib. cat. Meymac 1997.
Andreas Schulze, exhib. cat. Hamburg 1993.
Wilfried Dickhoff (ed.), *Andreas Schulze. Bilder 1980–1988*, exhib. cat. Luzern 1989.

LUDGER SCHWARTE
*1967 Münster

Studied philosophy, literature, and political science in Münster, Berlin, and Paris
1993 Diplôme d'Études Approfondies in philosophy, University of Paris I, Panthéon-Sorbonne
1996 Doctorate at the Freie Universität Berlin
2001 Academic employee at the Special Research Field of Performative Cultures, Freie Universität Berlin
2006–2009 Assistant professor, Basel University
2007 Postdoctorate, Freie Universität Berlin
2009 Lecturer at the Zurich Hochschule der Künste
Since 2009 professor of philosophy at the Düsseldorf Art Academy

Ludger Schwarte, 'Das Auge der Kathedrale. Offenbarung und Theater', in: Andreas Beyer (ed.), *Das Auge der Architektur. Zur Frage der Bildlichkeit in der Baukunst*, Munich 2011, pp. 262–286.
Ludger Schwarte, 'Bilder bezeugen, was nicht ausgesagt werden kann. Überlegungen zur visuellen Performanz', in: Ludger Schwarte (ed.), *Bild-Performanz*, Munich 2011, pp. 137–160.
Ludger Schwarte, *Philosophie der Architektur*, Munich 2009.
Ludger Schwarte (ed.), *Auszug aus dem Lager. Zur Überwindung des modernen Raumparadigmas in der politischen philosophy*, Bielefeld 2007.
Ludger Schwarte, *Die Regeln der Intuition. Kunstphilosophie nach Adorno, Heidegger und Wittgenstein*, Munich 2000.

RUDOLF SCHWARZ
*1897 Strasbourg–1961 Cologne

Until 1918 served in the armed forces and studied architecture at the Technische Universität in Berlin
1923 Doctorate at the Technische Hochschule in Berlin
1924 In Hans Poelzig's master class at the Akademie der Künste in Berlin
1925–1927 Taught structural engineering at the Technische Lehranstalt in Offenbach
1927–1934 Director of, and professor at, the Kunstgewerbeschule in Aachen
1934–1941 Self-employed architect in Offenbach and Frankfurt am Main
1944–1946 Served in the armed forces; internment as a prisoner of war in France
1946–1952 General urban planner, city of Cologne
1953–1961 Professor of architecture at the Düsseldorf Art Academy
1958 Grand Art Prize, State of North Rhine-Westphalia

Wolfgang Pehnt, *Die Plangestalt des Ganzen. Der Architekt und Stadtplaner Rudolf Schwarz (1897–1961) und seine Zeitgenossen*, exhib. cat. Cologne 2011.
Wolfgang Pehnt (ed.), *Bewohnte Bilder. Rudolf Schwarz 1897–1961. Architekt einer anderen Moderne, mit einem Werkverzeichnis von Hilde Strohl*, exhib. cat. Cologne and elsewhere, Ostfildern 1997.
Maria Schwarz (ed.), *Rudolf Schwarz. Kirchenbau, Welt vor der Schwelle*, Heidelberg 1960 (reprint Regensburg 2007).
Rudolf Schwarz, *Von der Bebauung der Erde*, Heidelberg 1949 (new edition Salzburg/Munich 2006).
Rudolf Schwarz, *Wegweisung der Technik, mit Bildern nach Aufnahmen von Albert Renger-Patzsch*, Aachen 1928 (reissued Cologne 2008). No. 1, *Aachener Werkbücher* series.

FRITZ SCHWEGLER
*1935 Breech–2014 Breech

Studied sculpture at the Staatliche Akademie der Bildenden Künste in Stuttgart and in London
1955–1959 Crafts teacher at the academies in Stuttgart and London
1973–1975 Lecturer at the Düsseldorf Art Academy
1975–1985 Professor of painting and 1985–2001 professor of sculpture at the Düsseldorf Art Academy
2010 Honorary member of the Düsseldorf Art Academy

Ulrike Groos (ed.), *Fritz Schwegler. Das unbewegliche Theater*, 2 vols., exhib. cat. Düsseldorf, Ostfildern 2004.
Ferdinand Ullrich (ed.), *Fritz Schwegler. Die tägliche Jubelrolle, 365 Öffnungen nach 25 Jahren ...*, exhib. cat. Recklinghausen 1999.
Fritz Schwegler, *Kunst der Erscheinung konnte so sein – Kleidungen zum Fünfzigsten*, Düsseldorf 1992.
Fritz Schwegler – Lebensmüde? Abulvenz!, exhib. cat. Hagen 1983.
Fritz Schwegler, *Der ganze Winter ist übertrieben – letzte Effeschiade und erste Pheine*, Cologne 1979.

HANS SCHWIPPERT
*1899 Remscheid–1973 Düsseldorf

Studied architecture at the Technische Hochschulen in Hannover and Darmstadt, finished studies with Paul Schmitthenner at the Technischen Hochschule Stuttgart
1926–1927 Employed in Erich Mendelssohn's Berlin architecture practice
1927–1934 Worked as a specialist teacher at the Handwerker- und Kunstgewerbeschule Aachen
1943 Doctorate at RWTH Aachen, followed by postdoctorate
1945 Technical mayor of the city of Aachen and until 1946 head of building and construction in the Rhine Province
1946 Professor at RWTH Aachen
1946–1967 Professor of architecture at the Düsseldorf Art Academy
1956–1966 Director of the Düsseldorf Art Academy

1957 Grand Art Prize in Architecture, State of North Rhine-Westphalia
1959 Grand Order of Merit of the Federal Republic of Germany

Gerda Breuer et al. (eds.), *Hans Schwippert 1899–1973, Moderation des Wiederaufbaus*, Berlin 2010.
Gerda Breuer, *Hans Schwippert. Bonner Bundeshaus 1949*, with letters selected from correspondence with Konrad Adenauer, Tübingen 2009.
Agatha Buslei-Wuppermann and Andreas Zeisig, *Das Bundeshaus von Hans Schwippert in Bonn. Architektonische Moderne und demokratischer Geist*, Düsseldorf 2009.
Agatha Buslei-Wuppermann and Andreas Zeising (eds.), *Hans Schwippert: Vom Machen und Brauchen. Schriften zu Architektur und Gestaltung*, Düsseldorf 2008.
Agatha Buslei-Wuppermann, *Hans Schwippert, 1899–1973*, Munich 2007.
Hans Schwippert, *Denken, Lehren, Bauen*, Düsseldorf 1982.

MANFRED SIELER
*1927 Gelenau–1971 Wuppertal

1950–1956 Studied with Karl Hartung at the Hochschule für Bildende Künste Berlin
1958 Villa Massimo Award, Rome
1958–1971 Professor of sculpture at the Düsseldorf Art Academy

Junge Realisten, German Becerra, Manfred Sieler et al., exhib. cat. Heilbronn and elsewhere, Berlin 1966.
Rainer Maria Rilke, *Sonette an Orpheus. 12 ausgewählte Sonette, mit Lithographien von Manfred Sieler*, Düsseldorf 1963.

WERNER SPIES
*1937 Tübingen

Studied art history, philosophy, and Romance languages and literature in Vienna, Tübingen, and Paris
1960 Moved to Paris; cultural affairs correspondent for the *Frankfurter Allgemeine Zeitung*; numerous projects for the Süddeutscher Rundfunk
1968 Employed at documenta III in Kassel
1974 Doctorate at Bonn University
1975–2002 Professor of twentieth-century art history at the Düsseldorf Art Academy
1997–2000 Director of the Musée national d'art moderne at the Centre Pompidou, Paris
2003 Honorary doctorate, Freie Universität Berlin
2005 Honorary doctorate, Tübingen University
Numerous distinctions, including Commander of the French Legion of Honour and the Grand Order of the Federal Republic of Germany with Star
Since 2010 honorary member of the Düsseldorf Art Academy; Carlo Schmid Prize, Stuttgart

Werner Spies, *Mein Glück. Erinnerungen*, Munich 2012.
Werner Spies, *Zwischen Oberammergau und Guillotine*, Berlin 2011.
Werner Spies, *Der ikonografische Imperativ der Deutschen. Von George Grosz zu Anselm Kiefer*, Berlin 2009.
Thomas W. Gaehtgens and Maria Platte (eds.), *Werner Spies. Auge und Wort, Gesammelte Schriften zu Kunst und Literatur*, 10 vols., Berlin 2008.

URSULA STENGER
*1964 Würzburg

Until 1993 studied for master of arts degree in education, philosophy, and German language and literature at Munich, Freiburg, and Würzburg Universities as well as studying for civil service status as a teacher at state schools in German and in social sciences
1996–2000 Academic employee at the Chair for Education I and doctorate at Würzburg University
2001–2005 Academic assistant to Günther Bittner at the Chair for Education I, Würzburg University
2005–2007 Junior professor of education at the Düsseldorf Art Academy
2008–2011 Professor of education at the Pädagogische Hochschule Ludwigsburg
Since 2011 professor of education at Cologne University

Ursula Stenger et al., *Einführung in die Kindheitsforschung*, Darmstadt 2010.
Ursula Stenger, *Schöpferische Prozesse. Phänomenologisch-anthropologische Analysen zur Konstitution von Ich und Welt*, Weinheim 2002.
Ursula Stenger, *'Die Welt als ein sich selbst gebärendes Kunstwerk'. Nietzsches Phänomen des Schöpferischen*, Freiburg im Breisgau 1997.

JAMES FRAZER STIRLING
*1924 Glasgow–1992 London

1942 Studied at the School of Art, Liverpool University
1945–1950 Studied architecture at the School of Architecture, Liverpool University
1956 Founded architecture practice Stirling and Gowan
1967 Visiting professor at the Yale School of Architecture, New Haven
1977–1979 Visiting professor of architecture at the Düsseldorf Art Academy
1978 Alvar Aalto Medal of the Finish Architecture Museum and Architecture Association, Jyväskylä
1979–1989 Professor of architecture at the Düsseldorf Art Academy
1979 Honorary doctorate, Royal College of Art, London
1981 Pritzker Architecture Prize, Chicago
1990 Praemium Imperiale Prize for Architecture, Tokyo

Amanda Reeser Lawrence, *James Stirling. Revisionary Modernist*, New Haven 2012.
Mark Crinson, *Stirling and Gowan. Architecture from Austerity to Affluence*, New Haven 2012.
Anthony Vidler, *James Frazer Stirling. Modernism in Crisis*, New Haven 2010.
James Stirling, *Michael Wilford and Associates. Buildings & Projects 1975–1992*, Stuttgart 1994.
James Stirling, *Bauten und Projekte 1950–1974*, Stuttgart 1975 (reprint 1996).

ZOLTÁN SZÉKESSY
*1899 Dombiratos–1968 Düsseldorf

1921–1922 Studied at the Free Art School in Budapest
1923–1924 Studied at the Düsseldorf Art Academy
1924–1926 Apprenticeship with journeyman's certificate at a woodcarver's in Budapest
1926–1927 Continued studies with Richard Langer at the Düsseldorf Art Academy
1927 Studied with Gerhard Marcks at the Kunstgewerbeschule Burg Giebichenstein in Halle and Bernhard Bleeker at the Munich Academy of Fine Arts
1938 Cornelius Prize, State Düsseldorf Art Academy
1952–1964 Professor of sculpture at the Düsseldorf Art Academy
1956 Grand Prize for Sculpture, State of North Rhine-Westphalia

Zoltán Székessy. *Skulpturen, Zeichnungen*, exhib. cat. Düsseldorf 1978.
Wend Fischer, *Zoltán Székessy*, Recklinghausen 1965. No. 30, *Monographien zur rheinisch-westfälischen Kunst der Gegenwart* series.
Zoltán Székessy and Franz Josef Kampmann, *Zoltán Székessy als Lehrer*, Düsseldorf 1962.

TAL R (TAL ROSENZWEIG TEKINOKTAY)
*1967 Ramatgan/Israel

1986–1988 Studied at the Billedskolen, Copenhagen, where his teachers included Erik Steffensen
1991–1993 Taught at the Nut Cracker Art School in Copenhagen
1994–2000 Studied at the Royal Danish Art Academy
2005–2009 Supply professor of fine art graphics at the Düsseldorf Art Academy
Since 2009 professor of painting at the Düsseldorf Art Academy
Member of the Kørners Kontor artists' collective

Beate Ermacora (ed.), *Tal R. Mann über Bord*, exhib. cat. Innsbruck/Düsseldorf, Cologne 2012.
Florian Waldvogel (ed.), *Tal R, the Elephant behind the Clown*, exhib. cat. Hamburg, Cologne 2011.
Dirk Luckow (ed.), *Tal R. You Laugh an Ugly Laugh*, exhib. cat. Kiel/Tübingen, Cologne 2009.
Tal R, *Masters and Method*, Ostfildern 2008.
Michael Juul Holm and Anders Kold (eds.), *Tal R. The Sum*, exhib. cat. Humlebæk/Maastricht/London, Humlebæk 2007.

HEINRICH THEISSING
*1940 Breslau

1962 Studied theatre studies, art history, and German language and literature at Cologne University
1966 Doctorate at Cologne University
1967–1969 Academic assistant at the Art Historical Institute, Cologne University
1968–1969 Academic assistant at the Düsseldorf Art Academy
1969–1973 Lecturer in art and cultural history at the Düsseldorf Art Academy
1973–2007 Professor of art history at the Düsseldorf Art Academy
Since 2010 honorary member of the Düsseldorf Art Academy

Heinrich Theissing, 'Die panische Zeit bei Francisco Goya', in: Andrea von Hülsen-Esch et al. (eds.), *Bilderzählungen. Zeitlichkeit im Bild*, Cologne 2003, pp. 127–137. No. 4, *Europäische Geschichtsdarstellungen* series.
Heinrich Theissing, '"THE NOW". Warhols Chronophagie', *Kunstforum International*, Vol. 150, 2000, pp. 268–276.
Heinrich Theissing, 'Wilhelm Busch. Die Romantik und die Renaissance. Die Grotteske und das Groteske', in: Silvio Vietta (ed.), *Romantik und Renaissance. Die Rezeption der italienischen Renaissance in der deutschen Romantik*, Stuttgart 1994, pp. 253–279.
Heinrich Theissing, *Die Zeit im Bild*, Darmstadt 1987.
Heinrich Theissing, *Dürers Ritter. Tod und Teufel, Sinnbild und Bildsinn*, Berlin 1978.

ANDRÉ THOMKINS
*1930 Luzern–1985 Berlin

1947–1949 Trained with Max von Moos at the Kunstgewerbeschule Luzern
1950–1951 Attended the Académie de la Grande Chaumière in Paris
1971–1973 Professor of painting and graphic arts at the Düsseldorf Art Academy
1972–1977 Showed work at documentas 5 and 6 in Kassel
1978 Member of the Academy of the Arts, Berlin
1981 Member of the Gottfried-Keller-Stiftung and the Exhibition Committee, Kunsthaus Zurich
1982 German Academic Exchange Service grant in Berlin and taught at the Salzburg Summer Academy
1984 Taught painting and graphic arts at the Kunstakademie Münster

Dagmar Streckel and Friedemann Malsch (eds.), *André Thomkins. Eternal Network*, exhib. cat. Vaduz/Düsseldorf/Graz, Bielefeld 2013.
Hans-Jörg Heusser et al., *André Thomkins 1930–1985. Umwege, Denkmuster, Leitfäden*, exhib. cat. Bern, Cologne 1999.
Marita Gleiss et al. (eds.), *Labyrinthspiel. André Thomkins, Retrospektive*, 2 vols., exhib. cat. Berlin/Luzern, Berlin 1989.
Ulrich Luckhardt (ed.), *Menschenmöglich. Federzeichnungen 1947–1977, André Thomkins*, exhib. cat. Hamburg, Cologne 1988.
André Thomkins, *Permanentszene. Zeichnungen, Aquarelle, Bilder, Collagen, Objecte und Texte von 1946–1977*, Stuttgart and elsewhere 1978.

HANS PETER THURN
*1943 Krefeld

1963–1965 Studied philosophy, sociology, literature, and art history at Heidelberg and Frankfurt am Main Universities
1966 Studied at Cologne University
1970 Doctorate and taught sociology at the Düsseldorf Art Academy
1970–1972 Assistant in the Architecture Department at the Düsseldorf Art Academy
1972–1973 Teacher of sociology and until 1983 lecturer in sociology at the Düsseldorf Art Academy
1983–2011 Professor of sociology at the Düsseldorf Art Academy
Member of the Deutsche Gesellschaft für Soziologie

Hans Peter Thurn, *Farbwirkungen. Soziologie der Farbe*, Cologne 2007.
Hans Peter Thurn, *Die Vernissage. Vom Künstlertreffen zum Freizeitvergnügen*, Cologne 2002.
Hans Peter Thurn, *Bildmacht und Sozialanspruch. Studien zur Kunstsoziologie*, Opladen 1997.
Hans Peter Thurn, *Der Kunsthändler. Wandlungen eines Berufes*, Munich 1994.
Hans Peter Thurn, *Soziologie der Kunst*, Stuttgart 1973.

EDUARD TRIER
*1920 Cologne–2009 Cologne

After 1945–1952 Studied art history at Bonn and Cologne Universities, doctorate and postdoctorate at Bonn University
1959 Exhibition curator at documenta II in Kassel
1964–1966 Curator at the German Pavilion at the Venice Biennale
1964–1972 Professor of art history at the Düsseldorf Art Academy
1966–1972 Director of the Düsseldorf Art Academy
1970 Order of Merit of the Federal Republic of Germany, 1st Class
1972–1985 Professor and one of two directors of the Art Historical Institute at Bonn University
1979 Honorary member of the Düsseldorf Art Academy

Eduard Trier, *Jetzt ist die Katze aus dem Sack. Kritiken und Kommentare, Eine Auswahl*, Bonn 2000. No. 5, *Sediment* series.
Eduard Trier, *Bildhauertheorien im 20. Jahrhundert*, Berlin 1971 (new, completely revised edition Berlin 1999).
Eduard Trier, *Figur und Raum*, Berlin 1960.
Eduard Trier, *Zeichner des zwanzigsten Jahrhunderts*, Berlin 1956.
Eduard Trier, *Moderne Plastik von Auguste Rodin bis Marino Marini*, Berlin 1954.

ROSEMARIE TROCKEL
*1952 Schwerte

1971 Started studying to be a teacher at state schools in anthropology, sociology, theology, and mathematics at the Pädagogischen Hochschule in Cologne
1974–1978 Studied painting with Werner Schriefers at the Werkschule in Cologne
1992 Konrad von Soest Prize, Landschaftsverband Westfalen-Lippe
1997 Showed work at documenta X in Kassel
1998 State Prize, State of North Rhine-Westphalia
Since 1998 professor of sculpture at the Düsseldorf Art Academy
1999 Showed work in the German Pavilion at the Venice Biennale
2004 Wolfgang Hahn Prize, Gesellschaft für Moderne Kunst at the Museum Ludwig in Cologne
2008 Art Prize, State Capital Düsseldorf
2011 Kaiserring, City of Goslar
Since 2012 member of the Nordrhein-Westfälische Akademie der Wissenschaften und der Künste

Dirk Snauwaert (ed.), *Rosemarie Trockel. Flagrant Delight*, exhib. cat. Zurich and elsewhere, Paris 2013.
Lynne Cooke (ed.), *Rosemarie Trockel. A Cosmos*, exhib. cat. Madrid and elsewhere, New York 2012.
Barbara Engelbach and Rosemarie Trockel (eds.), *Post-Menopause. Rosemarie Trockel*, with catalogue raisonné of her wool works, exhib. cat. Cologne/Rome, Cologne 2005.
Gudrun Inboden (ed.), *Rosemarie Trockel. La Biennale di Venezia, Deutscher Pavillon 1999*, 2 vols., New York 1999.
Birte Frenssen (ed.), *Rosemarie Trockel. Werkgruppen 1986–1998*, exhib. cat. Hamburg and elsewhere, Cologne 1998.

GÜNTHER UECKER
*1930 Wendorf

1949–1953 Studied painting in Wismar and at the Art Academy in Berlin Weißensee
Moved to West Germany
1955–1957 Studied with Otto Pankok at the Düsseldorf Art Academy
1961 Member of the group of artists known as ZERO
1964 Promotional Prize for Fine Art, State of North Rhine-Westphalia für Bildende Kunst
1970 Showed work at the Venice Biennale
1974–1995 Professor of sculpture at the Düsseldorf Art Academy
1983 Kaiserring, City of Goslar
1985 Order of Merit of the Federal Republic of Germany, 1st Class
2000 Pour le mérite Order for Science and Arts
2001 Grand Order of Merit of the Federal Republic of Germany with Star
2010 Honorary member of the Düsseldorf Art Academy

Jürgen Krieger (ed.), *Günther Uecker. Geschriebene Bilder*, exhib. cat. Munich, Berlin 2011.
Neuer Berliner Kunstverein (ed.), *Zwanzig Kapitel. Günther Uecker*, exhib. cat. Berlin, Ostfildern 2005.
Dieter Honisch, *Günther Uecker. Eine Retrospektive*, exhib. cat. Munich 1993.
Günther Uecker and Lóránd Hegyi, *Uecker in Vienna*, exhib. cat. Vienna, Stuttgart 1992.
Dieter Honisch, Günther Uecker, *Werkverzeichnis. Uecker*, Stuttgart 1983.

OSWALD MATHIAS UNGERS
*1926 Kaisersesch–2007 Cologne

1945 Served in the armed forces; internment as a prisoner of war
1947–1950 Studied architecture with Egon Eiermann and Otto Ernst Schweizer at the Technische Hochschule, Karlsruhe
1963–1969 Professor at the Technische Universität Berlin, 1965–1967 dean of the Architecture Faculty there
1967 Professor at Cornell University, Ithaca, New York
1973 Professor at Harvard University, Cambridge, MA
1974–1975 Professor at the University of California, Los Angeles
1979–1980 Professor at the Hochschule für angewandte Kunst in Vienna
1986–1991 Professor of architecture at the Düsseldorf Art Academy, implemented the postgraduate studies programme in architecture
1987 Member of the Academy of Sciences in Berlin
1997 Grand Order of Merit of the Federal Republic of Germany
1999 Honorary doctorate, Technische Universität Berlin
2006 Order of Merit, State of North Rhine-Westphalia

Florian Hertweck and Sébastien Marot (eds.), *Die Stadt in der Stadt. Berlin, Ein grünes Archipel, ein Manifest (1977) von Oswald Mathias Ungers et al., kritische Ausgabe*, Zurich 2013.
Andres Lepik (ed.), *O. M. Ungers. Kosmos der Architektur*, exhib. cat. Berlin, Ostfildern 2006.
Oswald Mathias Ungers and Anja Sieber-Albers, *10 Kapitel über Architektur. Ein visueller Traktat*, exhib. cat. Cologne 1999.
Oswald Mathias Ungers, *Bauten und Projekte 1991–1998*, Stuttgart 1998.
Oswald Mathias Ungers, *Architektur 1951–1990*, Stuttgart 1991.

DIDIER VERMEIREN
*1951 Brussels

Since 1991 lecturer at De Ateliers in Amsterdam
Since 2003 professor of sculpture at the Düsseldorf Art Academy

Juliette Lafond, *Didier Vermeiren. Solides géometriques, Vues d'atelier*, exhib. cat. Paris 2005.
Dominic van den Boogerd and Jean-Pierre Criqui, *Didier Vermeiren. Collection de solides*, exhib. cat. Eindhoven 2003.
Didier Vermeiren, exhib. cat. Zurich, Stuttgart 1995.
Didier Vermeiren and Laurent Busine, *Didier Vermeiren. Sculptures, Photographies. 45. Biennale von Venedig 1995, Belgischer Pavillon*, Brussels 1995.
Didier Vermeiren, exhib. cat. Brussels/Nizza, Brussels 1987.

NATHALIE DE VRIES
*1965 Appingedam

1984–1990 Studied architecture at Delft Technical University
1991 Founded the architecture practice MVRDV with Winy Maas and Jacob van Rijs
1994–2004 Taught at Delft Technical University, Technische Universität Berlin, the Berlage Institute in Rotterdam, and the Architectural Association, London
Since 2013 professor of architecture at the Düsseldorf Art Academy

Nathalie de Vries and Hans van der Heijden, 'Architektur und Ort. Regionalität versus Globalität, Vorträge', in: Wolfgang Sonne (ed.), *Konferenz zur Schönheit und Lebensfähigkeit der Stadt*, Vol. 3, Zurich 2013, pp. 88–91.
Gerald Adler et al. (eds.), 'Nathalie de Vries. Scale in Recent Projects by MVRDV', in: *Scale. Imagination, Perception, and Practice in Architecture*, London 2012, pp. 65–76. No. 7, *Critiques: Critical Studies in Architectural Humanities* series.
MVRDV [Winy Maas, Jacob van Rijs, and Nathalie de Vries], *KM3, Excursions on Capacities*, Barcelona 2005.
Véronique Patteeuw (ed.), *Reading MVRDV*, exhib. cat. Rotterdam 2003.
MVRDV [Winy Maas, Jacob van Rijs, and Nathalie de Vries] (eds.), *FARMAX, Excursions on Density*, Rotterdam 1998.

JEFF WALL
*1946 Vancouver

1968–1973 Studied art and art history at the University of British Columbia
1982, 1987 Showed work at documentas 7 and 8 in Kassel
Since 1987 taught at the University of British Columbia
1996 International Art Prize, Kulturstiftung Stadtsparkasse, Munich
1997, 2002 Showed work at documentas X and 11 in Kassel
1999–2000 Professor of photography at the Düsseldorf Art Academy
2003 Roswitha Haftmann Prize, Zurich

Hans de Wolf (ed.), *Jeff Wall. The Crooked Path*, exhib. cat. Brussels/Santiago de Compostela, Antwerp 2011.
Jeff Wall, *Jeff Wall. Complete Edition. Werkverzeichnis 1978–2009*, London 2009.
Michael Newman, *Jeff Wall. Works and Collected Writings*, Barcelona 2007.
Theodora Vischer et al. (eds.), *Jeff Wall. Catalogue raisonné 1978–2004*, exhib. cat. Basel/London, Göttingen 2005.
Jeff Wall, *Photographs*, exhib. cat. Vienna, Cologne 2003.

WALTER WARNACH
*1910 Metz–2000 Cologne

Studied philosophy, German language and literature, and Romance languages and literature at Bonn, Munich, and Cologne Universities
1935–1936 Reader at Montpellier University
1938 Doctorate at Cologne University
1939–1945 Served in the armed forces
1946–1965 Freelanced at Schwann- und Patmos-Verlag, publishers in Düsseldorf
1961–1964 Lecturer and 1964–1975 professor of philosophy at the Düsseldorf Art Academy

Walter Warnach, *Wege im Labyrinth. Schriften zur Zeit*, with foreword by Heinrich Böll, Pfullingen 1982.
Walter Warnach, *Eugen Senge-Platten*, Recklinghausen 1967. No. 34, *Monographien zur rheinisch-westfälischen Kunst der Gegenwart* series.
Walter Warnach, *Vom Bewusstsein in der Kunst. Vortrag zur Immatrikulationsfeier der Staatlichen Kunstakademie Düsseldorf am 15. November 1961*, Düsseldorf 1962.
Walter Warnach, *Die Welt des Schmerzes*, Pfullingen 1952.

GERT WEBER, CALLED WEBERG
*1910 Düsseldorf–1986

1929–1933 Studied with Oskar Moll, Werner Heuser, Wilhelm Schmurr, and Paul Bindel at the Düsseldorf Art Academy
Until 1956 painter and art teacher
1956–1960 Programme specialist in teaching art at UNESCO in Paris
1960–1975 Professor of painting, teaching art at state schools at the Düsseldorf Art Academy
1967–1969 Deputy director of the Düsseldorf Art Academy

Gert Weberg. Malereien und Zeichnungen der frühen Sechziger, exhib. cat. MeerbuschOsterath, Münsterschwarzach 1994.
Gisela Bisterfeld (ed.), *Gert Weberg. Malereien und Collagen*, exhib. cat. Moers 1980.
Gert Weber, *Kunsterziehung gestern, heute, morgen auch*, Ravensburg 1964.

WALTER VON WECUS
*1893 Düsseldorf–1977 Neuss

1908–1910 and 1912–1914 attended the Kunstgewerbeschule in Düsseldorf
1919 Founded the artists' association Die Form; stage sets at the Düsseldorf Schauspielhaus
Until 1925 varying engagements as a stage set designer at theatres in Bonn, Krefeld, Frankfurt am Main, and Munich
1925–1941 Taught stage design at the Düsseldorf Art Academy; head of the first stage design class
1941–1959 Professor of stage design at the Düsseldorf Art Academy

Ilka Kügler (ed.), *Form im Raum. Walter von Wecus, das szenische Werk*, exhib. cat. Düsseldorf 1993. No. 6, *Dokumente zur Theatergeschichte* series.
August Gotzes, *Walter von Wecus. Der Maler und Zeichner*, Cologne 1947.
Heinrich Appel, *Walter von Wecus. Landschaftszeichnungen*, exhib. cat. Düren 1941.
Graphic layout by Wecus:
Freihochschulbund Düsseldorf (ed.), *Das Schauspielhaus Düsseldorf. Ein Vierteljahrhundert deutscher Baukunst*, Düsseldorf 1930.

OSWALD WIENER
*1935 Vienna

1950s Studied law, musicology, African languages, and mathematics in Vienna; author in the framework of the Wiener Gruppe; jazz musician
1954–1966 Worked in data processing, later in management at Olivetti
1980–1985 Studied mathematics and computer science at the Technische Universität Berlin
1987 Literature Prize of the City of Vienna
1989 Grand Austrian State Literature Prize
1992–2004 Professor of aesthetics at the Düsseldorf Art Academy
1995 Honorary doctorate, Klagenfurt University
2006 Manuscripts Prize, State of Styria

Oswald Wiener, *Literarische Aufsätze*, Vienna 1998.
Oswald Wiener et al., *Eine elementare Einführung in die Theorie der Turing-Maschinen*, Vienna 1998.
Oswald Wiener, *Schriften zur Erkenntnistheorie*, Vienna 1996. No. 10, *Computerkultur* series.
Oswald Wiener, *Probleme der künstlichen Intelligenz*, Berlin 1990.
Oswald Wiener, *Die Verbesserung von Mitteleuropa. Novel*, Reinbek 1969.

CHRISTOPHER WILLIAMS
*1956 Los Angeles

Until 1981 studied with John Baldessari and Douglas Huebler at the California Institute of the Arts in Los Angeles
Since 2008 professor of photography at the Düsseldorf Art Academy

Karola Kraus (ed.), *Christopher Williams. For Example: Dix-huit lecons sur la societé industrielle (revision 11)*, exhib. cat. Baden-Baden, Cologne 2010.
Beatrix Ruf (ed.), *Christopher Williams. 97,5 Mhz**, exhib. cat. Zurich 2007.
Christopher Williams. Couleur européenne, couleur soviétique, couleur chinoise, exhib. cat. Krefeld 2000.
Christopher Williams and Karel Schampers, *Christopher Williams '97. For example: Die Welt ist schön (final draft)*, exhib. cat. Rotterdam/Basel, Rotterdam 1997.
Catherine Gudis et al. (ed.), *Oehlen/Williams '95*, exhib. cat. Ohio 1995.

KARL (JULIUS FRIEDRICH GUSTAV) WIMMENAUER
*1914 Mannheim–1997 Wiesbaden

1933–1939 Studied architecture at the Technische Hochschule Darmstadt
1939–1947 Served in the armed forces; internment as a prisoner of war in the Soviet Union
1947–1957 Worked for Rudolf Schwarz in Frankfurt and Cologne
1957–1962 Worked for Hans Schwippert as an academic assistant at RWTH Aachen
1963–1979 Professor of new architecture and design at the Düsseldorf Art Academy

Karl Wimmenauer, 'Viollet-le-Duc. Restaurateur, Constructeur, Théoricien', Jahreshefte der *Kunstakademie Düsseldorf*, Vol. 2, Düsseldorf 1989, pp. 183–227.
Karl Wimmenauer, *Die Merkmale des Sakralen in der Baukunst. Vortrag, gehalten an der Staatlichen Kunstakademie Düsseldorf, überarbeitete und aktualisierte, mit Handzeichnungen versehene Fassung*, Wiesbaden 1987.
Karl Wimmenauer, 'Bauherr und Architekt im Spannungsverhältnis', in: Hermann Laupsien (ed.), *Wo wohnen – wie bauen? Überlegungen zu unserer zukünftigen Lebensgestaltung*, Düsseldorf 1978, pp. 140–154.

ELIA ZENGHELIS
*1937 Athens

Until 1961 studied architecture at the Architectural Association School, London
1961–1971 Worked for the architecture practice Douglas Stephen and Partners in London
1963 Taught at the Architectural Association School, London
1975 Joined forces with Rem Kolhaas (and both their wives) to found the Office for Metropolitan Architecture OMA in Rotterdam

1990–2002 Professor of architecture at the Düsseldorf Art Academy
1993–2010 Lecturer at the Berlage Institute in the Netherlands
1997–1998 Visiting professor at the École Polytechnique Fédérale de Lausanne
1998–2000 Visiting professor at ETH Zurich
2000–2007 Professor at the Accademia d'Architettura Mendrisio

Elia Zenghelis, 'Die ökologische Stadt. Eine Strategie für die Architektur', in: *Die ökologische Stadt. Entwürfe von Studierenden der Hochschule Liechtenstein*, exhib. cat. Frankfurt am Main, Petersberg 2007, pp. 15–20. No. 1, *Positionen Architektur* series.
Martin van Schaik et al. (eds.), 'Elia Zhengelis. Text and Architecture, Architecture as Text', in: *Exit Utopia. Architectural Provocations 1956–1976*, Munich 2005, pp. 255–262.
Westfälischer Kunstverein Münster (ed.), *Die verstädterte Landschaft. Ein Symposium mit Josef-Paul Kleihues, Elia Zenghelis et al.*, Münster 1995.
Elia Zenghelis, 'Die Ästhetik der Gegenwart', in: Thomas Kesseler (ed.), *Architektur Kunstakademie Düsseldorf 1977–1992*, Düsseldorf 1993, pp. 12–15.
Elia Zenghelis, 'Die Ästhetik der Gegenwart', in: Andreas Papadakis (ed.), *Dekonstruktivismus. Eine Anthologie*, Stuttgart 1989, pp. 239–242.

The biographies were written by Brigitte Blockhaus, Miriam Müller, Klaus Schumann, and Tanja Wessolowski.

INDEX

PHOTO CREDITS

© 2014 for the reproductions of the artists' work and works compared to it:

© Tomma Abts/Courtesy greengrassi London, p. 270
© Ernst Althoff, p. 173
© Siegfried Anzinger, p. 263
© Lothar Baumgarten/VG Bild-Kunst, Bonn 2014, p. 327, Fig. 22; p. 328, Fig. 23
© Bernd and Hilla Becher, p. 222
© Laurenz Berges/VG Bild-Kunst, Bonn 2014, p. 335, Fig 28
© Joseph Beuys/VG Bild-Kunst, Bonn 2014, p. 190
© Paul Bindel, p. 167
© Anna and Bernhard Johannes Blume/VG Bild-Kunst, Bonn 2014, p. 333, Fig. 25
© Karl Bobek/VG Bild-Kunst, Bonn 2014, p. 210
© Herbert Brandl/Courtesy Galerie nächst St. Stephan Rosemarie Schwarzwälder, Vienna, p. 269
© Reinhold Braun/Courtesy Galerie Supper, Baden-Baden, p. 262
© Walter Breker, p. 215
© Peter Brüning/VG Bild-Kunst, Bonn 2014, p. 194
© Johannes Brus/VG Bild-Kunst, Bonn 2014, p. 323, Fig. 17
© Daniel Buren/VG Bild-Kunst, Bonn 2014, p. 196
© Michael Buthe/VG Bild-Kunst, Bonn 2014, p. 260
© Theo Champion, p. 160
© Otto Coester, p. 161
© Anthony Cragg/VG Bild-Kunst, Bonn 2014, p. 285
© Siegfried Cremer, p. 213
© Rolf Crummenauer, p. 171 (left)
© Richard Deacon, p. 286
© Odile Decq/VG Bild-Kunst, Bonn 2014, p. 297
© Thomas Demand/VG Bild-Kunst, Bonn 2014, p. 341, Fig. 39
© Jan Dibbets/VG Bild-Kunst, Bonn 2014, p. 224; p. 330, Fig. 24
© Götz Diergarten/Courtesy Galerie Kicken, Berlin, p. 336, Fig. 31
© Peter Doig/Courtesy Michael Werner Gallery New York London, p. 261
© Max Dudler, p. 300
© Udo Dziersk/VG Bild-Kunst, Bonn 2014, p. 265
© Franz Eggenschwiler, p. 264
© Joseph Enseling, p. 29, Fig. 11; p. 158 (right)
© Elger Esser/VG Bild-Kunst, Bonn 2014, p. 336, Fig. 33
© Emil Gustav Fahrenkamp, p. 28, Figs. 9, 10
© Joseph Fassbender/VG Bild-Kunst, Bonn 2014, p. 204; p. 415
© Helmut Federle/VG Bild-Kunst, Bonn 2014, p. 258
© Katharina Fritsch/VG Bild-Kunst, Bonn 2014, p. 290
© Gotthard Graubner, p. 256
© Rupprecht Geiger/VG Bild-Kunst, Bonn 2014, p. 226
© Imi Giese, p. 321, Fig. 14
© Horst Gläsker/VG Bild-Kunst, Bonn 2014, p. 447, Fig. 4
© Claus Goedicke, p. 336, Fig. 32
© Bruno Goller, p. 169
© Eugen Gomringer, p. 227
© Martin Gostner/VG Bild-Kunst, Bonn 2014, p. 287
© Karl Otto Götz/VG Bild-Kunst, Bonn 2014, p. 209
© Katharina Grosse/VG Bild-Kunst, Bonn 2014, p. 274
© Günter Grote, p. 171 (right)
© Thomas Grünfeld/VG Bild-Kunst, Bonn 2014, p. 288
© Andreas Gursky/VG Bild-Kunst, Bonn 2014, Courtesy Sprüth Magers, Berlin London, p. 291; p. 339, Fig. 34
© Eberhard Havekost/Courtesy White Cube London, Galerie Gebr. Lehmann, Berlin Dresden, p. 268
© Erwin Heerich/VG Bild-Kunst, Bonn 2014, p. 192
© Michael Heizer, p. 313, Fig. 6
© Georg Herold/VG Bild-Kunst, Bonn 2014, p. 281
© Werner Heuser, p. 162
© Gerhard Hoehme/VG Bild-Kunst, Bonn 2014, p. 277
© Candida Höfer/VG Bild-Kunst, Bonn 2014, p. 334, Fig. 27
© Hans Hollein/Courtesy Städtisches Museum Mönchengladbach, p. 221
© Nan Hoover, p. 305
© Leo Sebastian Humer, p. 25, Fig. 5
© Alfonso Hüppi/VG Bild-Kunst, Bonn 2014, p. 203
© Axel Hütte, p. 340, Fig. 36
© Jörg Immendorff/Courtesy Galerie Michael Werner Köln, Märkisch Wilmersdorf, p. 272
© Magdalena Jetelová, p. 284
© Irmin Kamp, p. 200
© Heinrich Kamps, p. 165
© Ernst Kasper/Planungsgruppe Kasper, p. 407, Fig. 21; p. 408, Fig. 22
© Gudrun Kemsa/VG Bild-Kunst, Bonn 2014, p. 341, Fig. 40
© Hubert Kiecol/VG Bild-Kunst, Bonn 2014, p. 282
© Anselm Kiefer, p. 326, Fig. 21
© Luise Kimme, p. 211
© Konrad Klapheck/VG Bild-Kunst, Bonn 2014, p. 201
© Josef Paul Kleihues, p. 217
© Karl Kneidl, p. 216
© Imi Knoebel/VG Bild-Kunst, Bonn 2014, p. 321, Fig. 15
© Matthias Koch, p. 335, Fig. 30
© Walter Köngeter, p. 172
© Erinna König/VG Bild-Kunst, Bonn 2014, p. 318, Fig. 11; p. 319, Fig. 12
© Jannis Kounellis/VG Bild-Kunst, Bonn 2014, p. 206
© Gereon Krebber/Courtesy Galerie Christian Lethert, Cologne, p. 283
© Norbert Kricke, p. 207
© Dieter Krieg/VG Bild-Kunst, Bonn 2014, p. 273
© Lederer + Ragnarsdóttir + Oei, p. 302
© Markus Lüpertz/VG Bild-Kunst, Bonn 2014, p. 259
© Ferdinand Macketanz, p. 166
© Ewald Mataré/VG Bild-Kunst, Bonn 2014, p. 132, Fig. 1; p. 168
© Rita McBride/VG Bild-Kunst, Bonn 2014, p. 279
© Lucy McKenzie/Courtesy Galerie Micheline Szwajcer, Antwerp, p. 289
© Christian Megert/VG Bild-Kunst, Bonn 2014, p. 197
© Georg Meistermann/Georg Meistermann Nachlassverwaltung [estate management], Dr J. N. Callen/VG Bild-Kunst, Bonn 2014, p. 170
© Gerhard Merz/VG Bild-Kunst, Bonn 2014, p. 296
© Klaus Mettig/VG Bild-Kunst, Bonn 2014, p. 317
© MVRDV, p. 303
© Simone Nieweg, p. 335, Fig. 29
© Walter Nikkels, pp. 414–415; p. 448
© Marcel Odenbach/VG Bild-Kunst, Bonn 2014, p. 293
© Albert Oehlen, p. 276
© Laurids and Manfred Ortner, p. 301; p. 412, Fig. 5
© Nam June Paik/Nam June Paik Estate, New York, p. 212
© Otto Pankok, p. 33, Fig. 17; p. 159
© Werner Peiner/VG Bild-Kunst, Bonn 2014, p. 26, Fig. 6
© A. R. Penck/VG Bild-Kunst, Bonn 2014, p. 266
© Karl Heinz Petzinka, p. 298
© Francis Picabia/VG Bild-Kunst, Bonn 2014, p. 412, Fig. 6
© Sigmar Polke/The Estate of Sigmar Polke, Cologne/VG Bild-Kunst, Bonn 2014, p. 323, Fig. 18; p. 324, Fig. 19
© Robert Pudlich, p. 163
© Tal R/Courtesy Contemporary Fine Arts, Berlin, p. 271
© David Rabinowitch/VG Bild-Kunst, Bonn 2014, p. 193
© Erich Reusch/VG Bild-Kunst, Bonn 2014, p. 195
© Gerhard Richter, p. 198; p. 318, Fig. 10; p. 325, Fig. 20
© Klaus Rinke, p. 223
© Rissa/VG Bild-Kunst, Bonn 2014, p. 202
© Brigitta Rohrbach, p. 319, Fig. 13
© Hans Rompel, p. 30, Fig. 13
© Dieter Roth/Dieter Roth Estate/Courtesy Hauser & Wirth, p. 205
© Thomas Ruff/VG Bild-Kunst, Bonn 2014, p. 294
© Ulrich Rückriem, p. 280
© Reiner Ruthenbeck/VG Bild-Kunst, Bonn 2014, p. 322, Fig. 16
© Rolf Sackenheim, p. 208
© Martina Sauter, p. 343, Fig. 43
© Jörg Sasse/VG Bild-Kunst, Bonn 2014, p. 339, Fig. 35
© Beate Schiff, p. 199
© Wilhelm Schmurr, p. 164
© Axel Schultes and Charlotte Frank, p. 304
© Andreas Schulze/VG Bild-Kunst, Bonn 2014, p. 275
© Johannes Schütz, p. 374, Fig. 1; pp. 376–378, Figs. 2–7
© Fritz Schwegler/VG Bild-Kunst, Bonn 2014, p. 214
© Rudolf Schwarz, p. 174

© Manfred Sieler, p. 219
© Katharina Sieverding/VG Bild-Kunst, Bonn 2014, pp. 316–317
© Juergen Staak, p. 343, Fig. 42
© James Stirling, p. 220
© Thomas Struth, p. 340, Figs. 37, 38
© Zoltán Székessy, p. 158 (left)
© André Thomkins/VG Bild-Kunst, Bonn 2014, p. 191
© Rosemarie Trockel/VG Bild-Kunst, Bonn 2014, p. 267; p. 342, Fig. 41
© Günther Uecker/VG Bild-Kunst, Bonn 2014, p. 257
© Oswald Mathias Ungers, p. 218
© Didier Vermeiren/VG Bild-Kunst, Bonn 2014, p. 278
© Anna Vogel, p. 344, Fig. 44
© Manfred Vogel, p. 102, Fig. 8
© Courtesy Jeff Wall, p. 292
© Gert Weber/VG Bild-Kunst, Bonn 2014, p. 225
© Christopher Williams, p. 295
© Petra Wunderlich/VG Bild-Kunst, Bonn 2014, p. 334, Fig. 26
© DAM/OMA, Office for Metropolitan Architecture, Rem Koolhaas/VG Bild-Kunst, Bonn 2014, Elia Zenghelis, Matthias Sauerbruch, p. 299

© 2014 for the photographic documents:

Archiv künstlerischer Fotografie der rheinischen Kunstszene (AFORK) in der Stiftung Museum Kunstpalast Düsseldorf [Art Photography Archives of the Rhenish Art Scene (AFORK) at the Museum Kunstpalast Düsseldorf Foundation]:
© Bernd Jansen/VG Bild-Kunst, Bonn 2014, p. 446
© Benjamin Katz/VG Bild-Kunst, Bonn 2014, p. 235; p. 250, Fig. 15
© Erika Kiffl, p. 447, Figs. 3–5
© Nachlass [estate of] Manfred Leve, p. 67; p. 180; p. 182, Figs. 9, 10; p. 311, Fig. 1
© Inge Mahn/VG Bild-Kunst, Bonn 2014, p. 117, Fig. 5
© Reiner Ruthenbeck/VG Bild-Kunst, Bonn 2014, p. 311, Fig. 2

© Düsseldorf Art Academy:

© Akademie-Galerie [Academy Gallery], p. 26, Fig. 7; p. 411
© Jonas Gerhard/Akademie-Galerie, p. 61; p. 72; p. 95; p. 251
© Anja Meyer Kahlen and Florence Schäfer/Akademie-Galerie, p. 393, Fig. 22
© Bernhard Klaffke, p. 169
© Sebastian Riemer/VG Bild-Kunst, Bonn 2014/Akademie-Galerie, p. 92; p. 159; pp. 165–166; p. 168 (below); p. 204; pp. 208–209; p. 218; p. 213; p. 216; p. 256; pp. 264–266; p. 276; p. 278; p. 285; p. 288; p. 305; p. 400; p. 407, Fig. 20; pp. 409–410
© Archiv Kunstakademie Düsseldorf [Düsseldorf Art Academy archives], p. 10; p. 22; p. 28; p. 29, Fig. 12; p. 30; pp. 30–32; pp. 47–48; p. 50, Fig. 13; p. 81; p. 88; p. 114; pp. 132–135; p. 137; pp. 140–141; p. 143; p. 147; p. 152, Fig. 18; p. 181, Fig. 6; p. 183, Fig. 11; p. 187, Fig. 16; p. 207; p. 349; p. 364; p. 365, Fig. 10; p. 404; pp. 421–422; p. 431, Fig. 2; p. 443
© Rolf Sackenheim/Archiv Kunstakademie Düsseldorf, p. 184
© Julia Gerber and Nadja Nafe/Archiv Kunstakademie Düsseldorf, p. 420, Figs. 4, 5
© Mladen Lipecki/Archiv Kunstakademie Düsseldorf, p. 68; p. 82, Fig. 7; p. 179, Fig. 3; p. 233; p. 240, Fig. 8; p. 241, Fig. 9
© Hubertus Neuerburg/Archiv Kunstakademie Düsseldorf, p. 54; p. 57; p. 86, Fig. 11; p. 87, Figs. 14, 15; p. 90; p. 98; p. 107; p. 115; p. 116, Fig. 3; p. 118, Figs. 8, 9; p. 121; p. 181, Fig. 7; p. 186; pp. 236–237; p. 239, Fig. 6; p. 240, Fig. 7; pp. 247–248; p. 390, Fig. 17; p. 398; p. 438; pp. 440–441; p. 447, Fig. 6; p. 449, Fig. 9
© Carola Abel/Archiv Kunstakademie Düsseldorf, p. 148
© Ruth Lauterbach Baehnisch/Archiv Kunstakademie Düsseldorf, p. 23; p. 27; p. 348; p. 350; p. 401, Figs. 8, 9
© Eckhartz/Archiv Kunstakademie Düsseldorf, p. 40; p. 399, Fig. 2
© Hans Georg Mayer/Archiv Kunstakademie Düsseldorf, p. 187, Fig. 18
© Julius Söhn/Archiv Kunstakademie Düsseldorf, pp. 15–16; p. 399, Fig. 4; p. 401, Fig. 7
© Oskar Söhn/Archiv Kunstakademie Düsseldorf, p. 34; p. 399, Fig. 3
© Siegfried Kühl/Archiv Kunstakademie Düsseldorf, pp. 44–45; pp. 79–80; p. 84; pp. 99–100; p. 136; pp. 138–139; pp. 150–151; p. 152, Fig. 17; p. 153; p. 179, Fig. 4; p. 182, Fig. 8; p. 183, Fig. 12; p. 187, Figs. 17, 19; p. 358; p. 382, Fig. 4; pp. 383–384; p. 403, Fig. 14
© Bibliothek/Kunstakademie Düsseldorf, p. 420
© Babette Bangemann/Kunstakademie Düsseldorf, p. 75; pp. 124–127; p. 200; p. 249; p. 406, Fig. 19; p. 432, Fig. 4
© Hye-Mi Kim/Kunstakademie Düsseldorf, p. 91; pp. 93–94; p. 167; p. 217; p. 228; p. 250, Fig. 16; p. 260; p. 273; p. 277; p. 290; pp. 300–301; p. 304; p. 402; p. 403, Fig. 13; p. 406, Figs. 17, 18; p. 408; p. 412; p. 419; p. 427; p. 431, Fig. 3; p. 432, Figs. 5, 6; p. 450
© Verwaltung [Administration]/Kunstakademie Düsseldorf, p. 49, Fig. 11; pp. 52–53; p. 56, Fig. 18
© Ken Adlard, p. 286
© Bildarchiv Foto Marburg (photo no. 1.214.274), p. 403, Fig. 12
© Agatha Buslei-Wuppermann, p. 405
© Jürgen Cordt, p. 199
© Ute Eichel/Bildarchiv Timo Dentler, p. 267
© Klaus Eschen/SLUB Dresden/Deutsche Fotothek, p. 89
© K. O. Götz und Rissa Stiftung, p. 202
© Archiv Ruth Groß, p. 369
© Roland Halbe, p. 302
© Sabine Haubitz, p. 279
© Robert Häuser, p. 194
© W. J. Hannappel, p. 284
© Marlies Hentrup-Fuhrmann, p. 386, Fig. 10; p. 388, Fig. 13
© Ingrid van Hüllen, p. 386, Fig. 11; p. 391, Fig. 18
© Stefan Johnen, p. 170
© Ruth Kaiser/Städtisches Museum Mönchengladbach, p. 221
© Nachlass [estate of] Luise Kimme, p. 116, Fig. 4; p. 117, Fig. 6; p. 118, Fig. 7
© Ute Klophaus, p. 313, Figs. 4, 5
© Edwin Klose, p. 380, Fig. 2
© Anita Kloten, p. 50, Fig. 14; p. 82, Fig. 6; p. 83; p. 85; p. 108; p. 111; p. 179, Fig. 2; p. 185; p. 239, Fig. 5; pp. 360–361
© Kolbe Museum, Berlin, p. 219
© Oliver Kostecka, p. 368
© Achim Kukulies, pp. 192–193; p. 206; pp. 210–212; p. 214
© Landesarchiv Nordrhein-Westfalen, Abteilung [Dept.] Rheinland, p. 49, Fig. 12
© Markus Leith/greengrassi London, p. 270
© Werner Lieberknecht, p. 268
© Jochen Littkemann/Contemporary Fine Arts Berlin, p. 271
© Franziska Megert, p. 197
© Museum Kulturhaus Kleve, Annegret Gossens, p. 168 (above)
© Veronika Peddinghaus, p. 225
© Petra Petitpierre, Fotoalbum/Paul Klee Zentrum Bern, p. 14
© Kathrin Pongratz, p. 389; p. 390, Fig. 16; p. 391, Fig. 19; p. 392
© Hans Rathschlag, p. 179, Fig. 1
© Dieter Rensing, p. 382, Fig. 5
© Rheinisches Bildarchiv Köln, rba_c012713, p. 12, Fig. 2
© Katja Rid, p. 190
© Thomas Riehle, p. 393, Fig. 21
© Daria Scagliola & Stijn Brakkee, p. 303
© Franz Schachinger, p. 269
© Hugo Schmolz, p. 380, Fig. 1
© Lothar Schnepf, p. 263
© Philipp Schönborn, p. 296
© Stadtarchiv Düsseldorf, p. 17 (Inv. no. 026 640 001 T); p. 25 (Inv. no. 111 413 008 T); p. 29, Fig. 11 (Inv. no. 180 150 045); p. 33, Fig. 16 (Inv. no. 121 300 016 T); p. 43 (Inv. no. 180 240 235 T); p. 381 (Inv. no. 180 330 121); p. 401, Fig. 6 (Inv. no. 026 630 025 T)
© Stadtmuseum Düsseldorf, p. 33
© Städtisches Museum Abteiberg Mönchengladbach, p. 385
© Hagen Stier, p. 299
© Stiftung Museum Kunstpalast/Horst Kolberg/Artothek, p. 12; p. 417; p. 418
© Werner Spies, p. 87, Fig. 13
© Theatermuseum Düsseldorf, p. 351; p. 354
© UAA Ungers Archiv für Architekturwissenschaft, p. 388, Fig. 14
© Archiv Thomas van den Valentyn, p. 387
© Markus Wörgötter, p. 258
© Tanja Wessolowski, p. 56, Fig. 19; p. 119; p. 280

The pictures to be reduced were kindly placed at the general editors' disposal by the artists, galleries, museums, and archives.

The general editors have done their best to locate the copyright holders of all illustrations. Should copyright holders have been overlooked or not found, this has not occurred with intention. In such cases we request that any copyholders affected should contact the general editors as soon as possible.

Compiled and edited by the Düsseldorf Art Academy at the suggestion of Professor Anthony Cragg

Organisation commissioned by the rectorate of the Düsseldorf Art Academy: Siegfried Gohr
Coordination, editing and proofreading, research, and procurement of illustrations: Tanja Wessolowski
Original German version: *Die Geschichte der Kunstakademie Düsseldorf seit 1945*, Berlin/Munich 2014

Working group for preparing this publication since autumn 2010: Professor Dr Kunibert Bering, Professor Dr Johannes Bilstein, Dipl.-Bibl. Brigitte Blockhaus MA, Professor Dr Siegfried Gohr, PD Dr Dawn Leach, Professor Dr Dr h.c. Peter M. Lynen, Professor Dr Johannes Myssok, Professor Dr Guido Reuter, Dr Vanessa Sondermann, Professor Dr Heinrich Theissing, Professor Dr Hans Peter Thurn

We should like to express our heartfelt gratitude for their unflagging commitment to all who have been engaged in this project.

In particular we should like to take this opportunity to thank Professor Anthony Cragg for initiating the project, for being so helpful with his unstinting advice, and, not least, for his very generous support for the present book.
Siegfried Gohr

Gesellschaft von Freunden und Förderern der Kunstakademie Düsseldorf e.V.

NATIONAL-BANK

Readers, German edition: Luzie Diekmann and Maja Stark, Deutscher Kunstverlag
Translation into English: Jane Slominsky Smith
Reader, English edition: Wendy Brouwer, Stuttgart
Editing, English edition: Tanja Wessolowski, Aachen, and Rudolf Winterstein, Deutscher Kunstverlag
Book design: Pina Lewandowsky, Berlin
Layout, English edition: Rüdiger Kern, Berlin
Cover design: Edgar Endl, Deutscher Kunstverlag
Reproductions: Birgit Gric, Deutscher Kunstverlag
Printing and binding: Grafisches Centrum Cuno, Calbe

Bibliographical information: Deutsche Nationalbibliothek
The Deutsche Nationalbibliothek has registered this publication with the Deutsche Nationalbibliografie; detailed bibliographical data can be retrieved online at http://dnb.dnb.de.

Paul-Lincke-Ufer 34
D-10999 Berlin
www.deutscherkunstverlag.de

ISBN 978-3-422-07311-1